BRISTOL RECORD SOCIETY'S PUBLICATIONS

General Editors: Madge Dresser
Peter Fleming
Roger Leech

VOLUME 61

BRISTOL'S TRADE WITH IRELAND AND
THE CONTINENT, 1503–1601

Bristol's trade with Ireland and the Continent 1503–1601

The evidence of the exchequer customs accounts

Susan Flavin & Evan T. Jones

EDITORS

FOUR COURTS PRESS
for the
BRISTOL RECORD SOCIETY

Set in 11pt on 13pt Ehrhardt for
FOUR COURTS PRESS LTD
7 Malpas Street, Dublin 8, Ireland
e-mail: info@fourcourtspress.ie
www.fourcourtspress.ie
and in North America for
FOUR COURTS PRESS
c/o ISBS, 920 N.E. 58th Avenue, Suite 300, Portland, OR 97213.

ISBN 978–1–84682–182–0

This book is printed on a
woodfree and acidfree paper.

Printed in England by
CPI Antony Rowe, Chippenham, Wilts.

Contents

1 Ports in Southwest England and Wales listed in the customs accounts

2 Irish ports and inland towns listed in the customs accounts

3 European ports listed in the custom accounts

Acknowledgments

This volume is an output of an ESRC-financed project undertaken at the University of Bristol on 'Ireland–Bristol trade in the sixteenth century' (2006–8). The volume was funded by the Bristol Record Society and published by Four Courts Press (Dublin) with the assistance of our indexer Sue Vaughan. To all of the above, we offer our thanks.

While many people offered us advice and support on the project, the authors would, above all, like to thank Professor Raymond Gillespie (National University of Ireland, Maynooth) and Dr Brendan Smith (University of Bristol). They were the Co-investigators on the 'Ireland–Bristol' project and the support and advice they gave to Dr Evan Jones (Principal Investigator) and Ms Susan Flavin (Researcher) was vital both to the launching of the project and to ensuring its success.

One of the most encouraging aspects of the project is that it has stimulated the development of new research by a group of doctoral researchers who are also working on customs account material to examine the development of the Bristol Channel region in the late medieval to early modern period. This new work has allowed the authors both to access large amounts of additional data and it has helped them to interpret their own data better. For their contributions to the project's research, we would thus like to thank Duncan Taylor, Tim Bowly and Richard Stone.

Beyond Bristol, we wish to thank Professor Wendy Childs (University of Leeds) and Dr David Ditchburn (Trinity College Dublin), both of whom provided much valuable technical advice on the use and interpretation of the customs accounts. More generally, we have benefited at various times from the expertise of: Professor Bruce Campbell (Queens University, Belfast), Professor Toby Barnard (University of Oxford), Dr David Edwards (University College Cork), Professor Stuart Jenks (Erlangen University), Professor Maryanne Kowaleski (Fordham University) and Professor David Dickson (Trinity College Dublin). In addition, we would like to thank all those who attended the 'Celtic Sea World' conference in September 2008, where we received much stimulating intellectual input.

Lastly, we would like to thank The National Archives (TNA), where the Exchequer Customs Accounts are kept. In particular, we wish to acknowledge both the helpfulness of its staff and the institution's enlightened attitude towards the use of digital cameras in the archive.

Introduction

The English exchequer customs accounts are most thorough, comprehensive and long-running records of foreign trade to exist for any country in the pre-modern period. The most detailed accounts, known as the 'particular' customs accounts until 1565 and the 'port books' thereafter, itemised every item of merchandise entering or leaving the country, alongside details of the owners of the goods, the ships laded and the date of the voyage. Not all of the accounts survive and, of those that do, only a tiny proportion have been analysed in depth. This lack of work is not because historians have thought the source unimportant, however. Rather, it is a reflection of the very size of the repository and the difficulty entailed in processing the millions of pieces of information found in the thousands of surviving accounts kept at the national archives (TNA) in London. Indeed, it is the very quantity of information that has restricted the use of these records, given that, until the advent of cheap computing, it was difficult to collate and analyse the data effectively.

The customs accounts were created to record the payment of the king's duties on overseas trade. These were instituted in 1275 with the levying of a tax on the export of wool and hides, but by the mid-fourteenth century the crown's fiscal net had widened to encompass all forms of merchandise passing in or out of the country.[1] The duties were collected in each port by exchequer-appointed officials known as customers / collectors, who submitted their 'particular' accounts each year to the exchequer in London, where the records were first audited and then stored for future reference.

Historians initially became aware of the customs accounts in the late nineteenth century, with Georg Schantz's work on the 'enrolled' accounts – a set of summary records that were compiled by the crown's clerks when the original 'particular' accounts were submitted to the exchequer.[2] The 'particular' accounts themselves, however, were only rediscovered in 1911 and few historians knew of them until Norman Gras published some extracts in 1918.[3] In the 1920s–1930s work on the exchequer customs accounts began

---

1 N.S.B. Gras, *The Early English customs system* (Harvard, 1918), pp 59–94.　2 G. Schanz, *Englische handelspolitik gegen ende des mittelalters* (Leipzig, 1881).　3 *Royal commission on public records, first report*, appendix I, part I, (Cd 6395/1912) 45 and 47; Gras, *Early English customs system*.

in earnest, especially amongst those working with Eileen Power at the London School of Economics. While much of the early work focussed on the enrolled accounts, attention was also paid to the 'particular' accounts. In part this was because the general reliability of the customs accounts as a record of trade could only be demonstrated by proving, first, that the enrolled accounts were indeed based directly on the 'particular' accounts and, second, that the 'particular' accounts listed real ships, merchants and voyages. Proving the latter was essential because some medieval financial accounts, such as the aulnage accounts, had by this time been shown to be legal fictions.[4] To prove that this was not the case with the customs accounts, it was necessary to show that the ships, merchants and voyages found in the 'particular' accounts could be verified from independent records of the period, such as merchants' ledgers and crown surveys of shipping.

As it became clear that the customs accounts were indeed records of genuine mercantile activity, attempts were made to use the 'particular' accounts to conduct detailed analyses of specific branches of overseas trade. Among such studies, two of the earliest were carried out by Ada Longfield and Eleanor Carus-Wilson, both of whom were protégé's of Eileen Power and both of whom worked on the Bristol accounts. Having completed their respective masters' theses in London, Longfield went on to publish her findings in *Anglo-Irish trade in the sixteenth century*, while Carus-Wilson disseminated her work through a Bristol Record Society volume and a chapter in *Studies in English trade in the fifteenth century*.[5] Since this time, a large number of economic historians have carried out studies based on both the 'particular' accounts and their immediate successors, the port books.[6] On the other hand, the amount of information in these records has meant that such studies have tended to be based only small number of individual accounts.

The significance of the customs accounts lies, as suggested earlier, in their very detail. Even the most limited of the accounts presented in this volume provides the name and home port of each vessel entering or exiting the country, the name of the shipmaster and the date of sailing. In some cases further details are provided – that can include the size of ship, its

4 E.M. Carus-Wilson, 'The Aulnage accounts: a criticism', *Economic History Review*, 2 (1929), 114–23. 5 A.K. Longfield, *Anglo-Irish trade in the sixteenth century* (London, 1929); E.M. Carus-Wilson (ed.), *The overseas trade of Bristol in the later middle ages* (Bristol Record Society publications, 7, 1937); E.M. Carus-Wilson, 'The overseas trade of Bristol' in E.E. Power & M.M. Postan (eds), *Studies in English trade in the fifteenth century* (London, 1933). 6 A.M. Millard, 'The import trade of London, 1600–40' (London University, PhD thesis, 1956); A.P. Hinton, *The port books of Boston, 1601–1640* (Lincoln Record Society, 1956); W.B. Stephens, *Seventeenth-century Exeter* (Exeter, 1958); D. Woodward, *The trade of Elizabethan Chester* (Hull, 1970); W.R. Childs, 'Ireland's trade with England in the later Middle Ages', *Irish Economic & Social History*, 9 (1982); D.H. Sacks, *Trade, society and politics in Bristol, 1500–1640*. 2 vols (New York, 1985); H.S. Cobb (ed.), *The overseas trade of London: exchequer customs accounts: 1480–1* (1990), E.T. Jones, 'The Bristol shipping industry in the sixteenth century' (University of Edinburgh PhD thesis, 1998).

destination and the domicile of the shipmaster. Following these shipping details, the accounts list the names of the merchants who laded goods on the ships, an indication of whether each merchant was a denizen or alien, and, most importantly, a list of all the goods belonging to each merchant. Lastly, the accounts indicate the type of customs levied on the goods and, for those goods subject to duty called 'poundage', their nominal value. Since even goods that were exempt from custom were normally included in the accounts, they should in principal record all of a port's trade for the period they cover.

Like all historical sources, the exchequer customs accounts have their drawbacks. First, they do not survive for every port from every year and, when they do survive, they are sometimes in poor condition. Second, there were some ports, notably those of Wales and the Palatinate of Chester, where the king's custom was not collected until the 1560s. Third, and most seriously, the accuracy of the accounts as a record of trade must depend both on the honesty of the officials who collected the duties and the level of evasion perpetrated by merchants. If smuggling was common, or if the customs officers routinely falsified their records, this would lessen the reliability of any trade statistics derived from the accounts. That problems of this nature do exist has long been known and some have felt that the extent of evasion, particularly after the mid-sixteenth century, might have been sufficient to invalidate any statistical analysis of these records.[7] On the other hand, it seems likely that evasion was only common for those goods that were prohibited, embargoed or subject to high duties.[8] This at least has been shown to be the case for Bristol trade in the 1540s, where a comparison between the 'particular' accounts and private commercial accounts revealed that, while the city's merchants certainly smuggled 'prohibited' wares, they declared the bulk of their trade in full.[9] Given this, it seems likely that most merchandise traded through Bristol was recorded accurately during the first half of the century. Furthermore, while the range and extent of the illicit trade seems to have increased in the second half of the sixteenth century, as the crown imposed new duties and restrictions on overseas trade, the incentive to engage in smuggling was still limited to a narrow range of products. These goods continued to include 'prohibited' wares – especially foodstuffs, leather and, in the later sixteenth century, iron ordnance.[10] To these were

7 N.J. Williams, 'Francis Shaxton and the Elizabethan port books', *EHR*, 66 (1951), 393–4; G.D. Ramsay, 'The Smugglers' trade: a neglected aspect of English commercial development', *Transactions of the Royal Historical Society*, 5:2 (1952), 157, n.1.   8 Prohibited wares were goods that merchants were banned from exporting, the usual justification for this being the crown's desire to hold down domestic prices. Embargoes were typically short-term prohibitions on trade with hostile countries.   9 E.T. Jones, 'Illicit business: accounting for smuggling in mid-sixteenth century Bristol', *Economic History Review*, 54 (2001).   10 D. and G. Mathew, 'Iron furnaces in south-eastern England and English ports and landing places, 1578', *EHR*, 48 (1933); R. Jenkins, 'Early gun founding in England and Wales' *Transactions of the Newcomen Society*, 44 (1974 for 1971–2).

added wine imports and, to a lesser extent, broadcloth exports, following the creation of royal impositions on these goods in 1558.[11] Lastly, during the latter part of the century, some other goods, such as currants, seem to have been either smuggled or falsely declared at the customs house. This was done to avoid paying the licence fees demanded by those who had acquired royal monopolies on the import of such goods.[12] Nevertheless, while all this illicit activity meant that some important trade items were certainly under declared, it must be remembered that most of the wares listed in the customs accounts only paid 'poundage'. This was an *ad valorem* duty, equivalent to one shilling in the pound, based on the nominal value of the product as determined by the customer's 'book of rates'. The duty thus amounted to no more than a five per cent tax and, since the book of rates used by the customer was not updated on a regular basis to take account of inflation, the real burden of poundage was typically much less than this.[13] When duties were this low there was little incentive to smuggle, which explains why even 'dishonest' merchants, who were certainly engaged in the illicit export of prohibited wares, appear to have been willing to declare low-taxed merchandise in full.[14] There is thus little reason for supposing that the Bristol customs accounts would not have continued to provide an accurate record of much of the port's trade during Elizabeth's reign (1558–1603).

Bristol's sixteenth-century overseas trade can be divided into two main branches. The greater part of the city's trade was conducted with western France and Iberia – notably Bordeaux, San Sebastian, Lisbon and Andalusia. At these places merchants sold English cloth, lead, leather and agricultural produce, while importing wine, oil, woad, salt and dried fruit. Trade with these regions, which was dominated by Bristol men and ships, accounted for at least three quarters of the port's overseas commerce. The other branch of Bristol's trade was with southeast Ireland, which accounted for most of the remaining trade.[15] Yet, although the bulk of Bristol's trade was with the Continent, around three quarters of the *individual entries* in the customs accounts relate to the Irish trade. This disparity occurs because,

11 F.C. Dietz, *English public finance, 1558–1641* (New York, 1932, 1964 ed.), pp 306–7, 315–17; T.S. Willan (ed.), *A Tudor book of rates* (1582), (Manchester edition, 1962), pp xii–xviii. For contemporary discussions of the illicit traffic in wine and cloth after 1558, see: PRO SP12/19 fo. 20; E159/350 Hil. 351 r,v,seq.; SP12/111/38 fols. 83–8.   12 M. Epstein, *The early history of the Levant Company* (1908), pp 20–3; O. Dunn, 'The petitions of Thomas Watkins against customer John Dowle 1598–1600' (BA thesis, University of Bristol, 2006), pp 69–70.   13 Willan, *Tudor book of rates*, pp xliii–xlvii. The impact of the failure to update the official valuations of goods paying poundage is readily apparent from the ledger of John Smyth, a Bristol merchant. For instance, in the early 1540s, Smyth was selling his Spanish iron in Bristol for around £6–7 per ton and his olive oil for £12–15 per tun. The customs valuations for these products were, however, just £2 10s. per ton for iron and £4 per tun for oil. The real tax burden on these goods thus amounted to only 2–3 per cent: J. Vanes (ed.), *The ledger of John Smythe, 1538–1550* (Bristol Record Society publications, 28), pp 324–5.   14 Jones, 'Illicit business', 19–26.   15 Using the values adopted by the project for estimating the value of wine, cloth and leather, Irish trade accounted for 21–8 per cent of Bristol's trade in the first half of the century; a typical year being 1541/2 when Irish trade was worth £ 6,386 out of a total of £24,281. In the second half of the century, however, Irish trade only accounted for 5–17 per cent of Bristol's total trade.

while the continental trade was conducted by a fairly small number of merchants trading large consignments of goods in great ships, the Irish trade was carried out by numerous merchants, shifting small consignments in lesser vessels. So, while a large consignment of wine, worth perhaps £400, might be recorded in just a dozen lines of a 'particular' account, the recording of a single shipment to Ireland could take up two or more folios, even though the combined value of the items was lower.[16] All this means that, although the continental trade dwarfed the Irish trade in terms of value, the customs accounts can be a richer source for studying Bristol's trade with Ireland.

While it might be accepted that Bristol's customs accounts are a valuable resource for researching the city's overseas trade, it may not be clear why the eleven individual accounting years covered by this volume were chosen for publication. To understand this requires an appreciation of the aims and objectives of the research project that collected this data. This was a study of 'Ireland-Bristol trade in the sixteenth century', which was carried out at the University of Bristol and was funded by the UK's Economic and Social Research Council (ESRC).[17] The following paragraphs will therefore explain: why the Bristol customs accounts are of particular value to Irish history, how they have been used to study this subject to date and why it was felt that an expanded study of city's customs accounts might allow Irish economic development to be reassessed in this period.

The 'particular' accounts and port books reproduced here were chosen to assist the re-evaluation of the economic development of southern Ireland before and during the Nine Years War (1594–1603); a conflict which was to result in the establishment of English rule over the whole of the island. The Bristol accounts are particularly valuable for the study of the Irish economy because the city accounted for the bulk of trade to southeast Ireland. From Bristol, goods came and went to Cork, Youghal, Dungarvan, Wexford, Kinsale, New Ross and, above all, Waterford. These ports had long been bastions of English rule in Ireland and served as major conduits for trade with the other parts of Ireland that acknowledged English rule, such as Kilkenny, Limerick, Clonmel and Galway. So, even though Bristol rarely traded with Dublin, which was linked to England via Chester, Bristol did account for the bulk of trade between England and those parts of Hibernia that lay under the control of a people who still proudly referred to themselves as the 'English in Ireland'. These people, who were the descendents of the colonists who had come to Ireland following the Anglo-Norman

16 Compare, for example, the entries for *Mary Bride* of Bristol, entered 7 December 1541, with the *Kateryn* of Waterford, exited Bristol 31 July 1542.   17 'Ireland-Bristol trade in the sixteenth century' (RES-000-23-1461), 2006–2008. Principal investigator: Dr Evan Jones (University of Bristol). Co-investigators: Prof. Raymond Gillespie (National University of Ireland, Maynooth) and Dr Brendan Smith (Bristol). Researcher: Ms Susan Flavin (Bristol).

conquests of the twelfth and thirteenth centuries, exploited their lands in ways quite different to the native Irish. The Gaelic Irish, who dominated the northern half of the island and significant parts of the west coast, practiced a form of pastoralism that was focused heavily on cattle raising and, indeed, cattle raiding. By contrast, the colonized parts of southern Ireland were much more settled, urbanised, commercialised and monetized. Given this, it was the 'English in Ireland' who conducted the vast majority of the country's overseas trade. And while they certainly traded to the Continent as well as England, their political and cultural affiliations ensured the primacy of the English link. The Ireland-Bristol trade connection was thus the most important branch of Irish overseas commerce and the Bristol customs accounts provide opportunities for examining this trade in great detail.

The second reason why the Bristol accounts are important for Irish history concerns the sources, or rather lack of sources, that exist for investigating the economic development of Ireland before the seventeenth century. The main reason for this is that many of the materials for studying Irish economic history were destroyed in June 1922 when Dublin's Public Record Office was blown up during the civil war. Since this destroyed most of Ireland's early records, there are few materials available in Ireland itself that can throw light on the economic development of medieval or Tudor Ireland. So, while it is true that overseas trade only ever constituted a fragment of Irish economic activity, the Bristol accounts remain the best quantitative economic record that exists for studying any aspect of Irish economic development in the fifteenth and sixteenth centuries.

Whatever the value of the English customs accounts for Irish economic history, their study has been limited to date. Indeed, other than the aforementioned works of Longfield and Carus-Wilson, the only published works of any moment are those of Wendy Childs and Donald Woodward.[18] Longfield's work remains, however, the key work on Anglo-Irish trade in the sixteenth century, so any further discussion of the subject requires an understanding both of her conclusions and of the evidence on which her findings were based.

Although Longfield employed much valuable qualitative material in her volume, the quantitative basis for her analysis came from just three individual customs accounts – a Bristol 'particular' account of 1503/4, a Bridgwater 'particular' account of 1560/1 and a Chester port book of 1588/9. Of these, the Bristol account was by far the most important for understanding sixteenth-century trade, for the Chester account relates to the end of the century and the Bridgwater account records the trade of what

---

18 Childs, 'Ireland's trade'; W.R. Childs & T. O'Neill, 'Ireland's overseas trade in the later middle ages', in F.X. Martin & T.W. Moody (eds), *A new history of Ireland*, 2 (1993); Woodward, *Trade of Elizabethan Chester*.

was, by comparison to both Bristol and Chester, a very minor port.[19] Having said this, Longfield's work on the Bristol account did produce a striking picture of Ireland's trade with the city at the start of the century. Her analysis revealed a trade that consisted almost entirely of the import of fish and animal skins from Ireland, which were exchanged for English manufactured goods and continental re-exports. Such a pattern of exchange, with raw materials being exchanged for manufactured wares and luxury re-exports, is typical of what might be expected of trade between a relatively backwards economy and a more sophisticated one. This data thus helped to cement the notion that the Irish economy was undeveloped prior to the English interventions of the late sixteenth century. Indeed, for some, such a pattern of trade was enough to suggest that, even before the English conquered the whole of the country, Anglo-Irish trade had 'the classic form of colonial commerce'.[20] Since Childs' work later revealed that the dependence on the export of fish and skins was also a feature of the late fifteenth century Irish trade, it has generally been assumed that the form of trade described by Longfield and Childs was the established pattern of commerce for both the fifteenth and sixteenth centuries. This assumption has had important implications for how the economic development of Ireland in this period has been interpreted, for if this pattern of trade was taken to reflect the level of economic development in the most advanced part of Ireland, it could be assumed that the economy that generated this trade remained undeveloped. From this it might be argued that, while England's seizure of land and resource in Ireland in the late sixteenth and seventeenth centuries might have been brutal, it did at least allow the Irish economy to grow, by creating a political stability and rule of law that encouraged investment in more advanced forms of agricultural production.

That this was not the whole story of Irish economic development in the sixteenth century was something that the author began to question in the 1990s, while conducting an analysis of three Bristol customs accounts from the 1540s.[21] This data revealed a rather different pattern of commerce to that suggested by Longfield. In particular, it was apparent that the import of Irish manufactured goods had grown from about a tenth of total imports in the late fifteenth century to half of Irish imports by the 1540s. The mid-century accounts also revealed that Bristol's exports to Ireland had become more diverse in nature, with a marked increase in the quantity and range of consumer goods – ranging from playing cards and clothing, to spectacles and cutlery. Lastly, the Bristol customs accounts showed that the value of the trade conducted on Irish ships had risen from about half of the trade in

---

19 According to Longfield, Bridgwater's trade in 1560/61 was £843: Longfield, *Anglo-Irish trade*, pp 220–1. By comparison, Bristol's trade with Ireland in 1550/1 was £4998. 20 Sacks, *Widening gate*, p. 39. 21 Jones, 'The Bristol shipping industry', pp 176–82.

1503/4 to three quarters of it by the 1540s. That the 1540s were not anomalous was, moreover, later demonstrated by the co-author of this volume, Susan Flavin, who worked on the Bristol customs account from 1516/17.[22] All this new research indicated that Ireland's trade with Bristol changed radically in the first half of the sixteenth century, with a shift towards the export of manufactured goods, the import of a more sophisticated range of luxury goods and a rising dominance of the trade by Irish merchants. All this looks much less 'colonial' than Longfield's data implied. Moreover, such was the extent of these developments, it seems likely that the underlying Irish economy that was producing these manufactured goods, consuming the luxuries and enjoying the profits of its merchants' trade was undergoing significant change. This in turn would suggest that the economy of southern Ireland was developing economically prior to the English interventions of the late sixteenth century – raising the question of whether political instability prior to this time was really so great as to prevent indigenous economic growth.

Since these new studies revealed that Longfield's findings could not be extrapolated across the sixteenth century, a rationale clearly existed for conducting a much more thorough analysis of the Bristol accounts from this period. This was the justification for undertaking the aforementioned ESRC-financed project. The intent was to input the data from eleven annual accounts from across the century into a database and then analyse this as a way of re-evaluating the development of the southern Irish economy in this period.[23] At the same time the authors were to publish the basic data in both print and electronic form, so that others could both check their findings and perform further analysis of the data. This then was the motivation for publishing the current volume. It should be understood, however, that while this volume reproduces the basic data and provides some useful glossaries, those who wish to carry out their own statistical analyses of the accounts should also consult the electronic versions of the datasets, available on the Bristol Repository for Scholarly E-prints (ROSE).[24] This includes some data that it was impossible to reproduce in this volume for lack of space. So, for instance, if a researcher is interested in information about the packaging of goods, which is often included in the port book entries, they will need to download the electronic version of the data, published in EXCEL format. Similarly, researchers may also want to consult the much more detailed reference guides that can be found on

---

22 S.M. Flavin, 'The development of Anglo-Irish trade in the sixteenth century' (MA thesis, University of Bristol, 2004).   23 The actual accounts chosen depended on source survival and a desire to get a broad spread of dates across the century. The volume includes three accounts from the 1540s (1540/1, 1541/2 and 1545/6) because this data had already been collected and computerised during an earlier study.   24 http://rose.bris.ac.uk/dspace/

ROSE, which include more detailed glossaries of the ports mentioned in the text, the personal names listed and, above all, the commodities carried.

NOTES ON THE SOURCE

To facilitate the collection of customs, the coastline of England had long been divided into sections, each of which lay under the jurisdiction of offi cers residing at the chief port on that section of coast. This chief port, which is generally referred to as the 'head port', might also have 'member ports', where deputies of the chief officers were permitted to collect customs. In the case of Bristol, however, there were no member ports, which meant that all overseas trade passing in or out of Bristol's jurisdiction had to be declared at the customs house in the city.

At the start of the sixteenth century, the wider 'Port of Bristol', which the exchequer defined as the area under the authority of the Bristol officers, consisted of the River Avon and the Gloucestershire reaches of the River Severn up as far as Worcester – fifty miles to the north (Fig. 1).[25] Yet, in 1575, Gloucester began to account separately and in 1580 the queen formally turned Gloucester into an independent head port, with the authority to collect and record all customs upriver of the ferry passage between Aust and Beachley – close to Chepstow.[26] At a stroke this reduced the geographical size of the wider port of Bristol to the six-mile stretch of the River Avon below Bristol and a ten miles stretch of the Severn Estuary running from Aust to the Kingroad – a bay to the west of Avonmouth. Moreover, even within this restricted area, the Bristol officers only had authority over vessels lying on the English side of the Severn Estuary. The division of Bristol into two different head ports is significant for current purposes because it means that the last three years dealt in this volume (1575/6, 1594/5 and 1600/1) are not strictly comparable to the earlier ones. Nevertheless, for practical purposes the division of the port is not that important, given that Gloucester's recorded overseas trade in late sixteenth century was only about one per cent of that of Bristol.[27] The loss of Gloucester can thus have had little impact on the trade recorded in Bristol's customs accounts.

Within the Port of Bristol, as in other ports, there were three main

---

25 TNA E159/350 hil, no. 348. 26 TNA E 190/1129/8, 13, 15; *Calendar of Patent Rolls*, 1578–1580, no. 1338.
27 A precise comparison between Bristol and Gloucester's trade is difficult, given that the gross size of Gloucester's trade varied enormously from year to year and it is possible to reconstruct Gloucester's trade for only three complete years (1581/2, 1597/8 and 1599/1600). Nevertheless, it may be noted that the total value of goods paying poundage at Gloucester in these three years was, respectively, £58, £0 and £109.1 By comparison, the value of goods paying poundage at Bristol in 1594/5 was £25,503: E190 1241/5, 1241/8, 1244/9, 1244/14, 1245/6, 1245/7, 1131/10. We would like to thank Duncan Taylor for the Gloucester data.

customs officers: the customer, the controller and the searcher, all of whom were appointed directly by the crown and all of whom accounted separately to the exchequer. The most important post was the customer, who was sometimes also referred to as the 'collector'. The job of the customer was to record the merchandise entering or leaving the port, determine the dues payable, take the monies from the merchants, and account for the revenues collected to the crown. Eight of the accounts presented in this volume are those of the customer / collector. The controller's function was to sit by the customer in the customs house and take an independent record of all the goods declared there. His sole function was to ensure that the customer did not commit fraud, which he might do either by allowing merchants to pay lower duties on the goods, in return for a bribe, or by collecting the full duty but then recording lower sums and quantities in the 'particular' account / port book than had been received. The controller's accounts, five of which are included in this volume, differ slightly from those of the customer in that they do not record the duties collected. Lastly, the searcher's function was to check that the goods the merchants declared at the customs house corresponded to those laded on their ship. To this end, the searcher or his deputies were expected to supervise the lading and unlading of ships and they had the right to board any vessel lying within the port's jurisdiction to find out if any additional goods had been laded after the ship had cleared customs. From 1565 the searcher's also had to submit accounts to the exchequer, which recorded the goods carried on the ships but not their value or the duties paid. Since the lack of such figures makes it difficult to generate trade figures from the searcher's accounts, none have been reproduced here.[28]

In addition to these three principal officers, there were four crown-appointed 'waiters' at Bristol. They were responsible for accompanying goods sent up or down the River Avon, either in the original ship, or in the lighters that were often employed if the ship itself was too large to make the passage up to Bristol when fully laden.[29] In the 1590s the crown also appointed general surveyors to keep a check on the customs officers in each port.[30] The surveyors too submitted accounts to the exchequer and were technically responsible for collecting the dues during the last years of Elizabeth's reign. Despite this, it seems that in Bristol the surveyors allowed

28 In theory it is possible to assign values to most of the goods in the searcher' accounts by means of the relevant Book of Rates or by assigning the same values applied in customer or controller's accounts of the same period. In practice, however, there are quite a lot of items in the late sixteenth century searcher's books that do not appear in the Book of Rates or in the surviving customer's or controller's account books from the period. Moreover, items are quite often listed using units of measurement not found in other accounts. This makes it difficult to assign values to all the items listed in the surviving searcher's books. For these reasons the project decided not to use any of the searcher's accounts in their study. 29 Bristol was one of only two ports (the other being London) to have crown-appointed waiters: B.Y., *A sure guide to merchants, custom-house officers, &c.* (London, 1730), pp 439–41. 30 Dietz, *English public finance*, pp 322–4.

the port's own customs officers to continue to do the practical work of customs supervision and collection.[31] So while the last two years dealt with in this volume (1594/5 and 1600/1) are surveyors' accounts, these appear to have been based on records generated by the local officers. This is evident, for instance, in the case of the 1594/5 surveyor's account, which is almost identical, bar a few scribal errors, to the two surviving customer's accounts for the same year.[32]

When considering the records presented here, it is important to understand that all of the pre-1565 'particular' accounts would have been compiled from rough workings kept by the customer and controller. For ease of audit, entries for each voyage were nearly always grouped together and recorded under one date, which represents the day that the final entry was declared by a merchant and the ship itself had cleared customs.[33] This recording practice changed with the institution of the port books, since the 'Book of Orders' issued to all customs officers in January 1565 stated that all entries had to be written directly into the 'original' books (i.e. the port books) as they were made by the merchant.[34] By doing this the crown hoped to make it more difficult for corrupt customs officers to collaborate with each other and falsify their records after the fact. In practice, it is unclear whether the customs officers ever complied fully with this particular order, given the practical difficulties of keeping an account book in good order if it were to be left open in a busy customs house for months on end. Nevertheless, the new ruling did mean that, unlike the 'particular' accounts, the port books record the actual day on which each merchant made his individual entry. This means that merchandise on outbound ships was often declared over a period of days or weeks.[35]

The accounts themselves are all written on parchment. All those presented in this volume were selected because individually, or in combination, they allow for the trade for complete accounting years to be reconstructed, thereby making it possible to compare different years in a meaningful way. The accounting year began on Michaelmas (29

31 That the surveyor did not interfere in the collection of customs at Bristol is perhaps most evident from the allegations of fraud made by Thomas Watkyns, a customs clerk in Bristol, against his master, John Dowle, the customer inwards. Watkyns complaints do make reference to the surveyors' returns to the exchequer. After this, however, Watkyns makes no further mention of the surveyor, even though this office had been established to prevent precisely the sort of abuses that Watkyns described: Dunn, 'The Petitions of Thomas Watkins', 56; TNA SP12 267/39, 274/57. 32 TNA E190/1131/11, 13. 33 There are occasional exceptions, in which the same ship is listed twice for the same voyage. For example the departure of the *Mary Conception* of Bristol, Richard Whyte master, is recorded twice (9 August and 28 August 1546), on what can be shown from other sources to be a single voyage to Andalusia: Jones, 'Shipping industry', 216. This presumably happened because the ship cleared customs but was then delayed for some weeks, so that when more goods were added this had to be recorded as a separate entry. 34 'Rules, orders and directions made by queen Elizabeth, and passed under her great seal, to be observed and performed by all her officers, ministers and other persons concerned in and about levying and collecting her customs and subsidies, with all the ports, havens and creeks in England and Wales, and by all the merchants and traders in the said ports', printed in: B.Y., *A sure guide to merchants*, pp 432–3, 35. 35 For example the entries for the *Joseph* of Bristol, master Matthew Honeywell, for a voyage to Livorno and Toulon are recorded on twelve different dates ranging from 25 August–25 September 1601.

September), so all the accounts cover parts of two calendar years. All bar the 1600/1 account are written in medieval Latin, although English words are sometimes used when there was no known Latin equivalent. Most of the individual accounts list the trade of the port, in chronological order, for the entire year. There are some exceptions, however. For the year 1563/4, imports and exports are listed in separate accounts. This was because the post of customer had been split into two by this time, with one officer responsible for inbound traffic and the other for outbound. The 1575/6 accounts, which are the first here to be recorded in official port books according to the recording standards set out in the 1565 book of orders, are again divided between imports and exports. The two surveyor's accounts for 1594/5 and 1600/1 are unitary accounts, because the surveyor had responsibility for both imports and exports and was only required to submit his accounts once a year.

TRANSCRIPTION NOTES

In entering the data, the following general conventions have been followed:

Italics are used to indicate where the transcriber has filled in any word, or part of a word, that is not in the original document. For instance, the ship name 'Jhus' would be transcribed as 'Jhesus' and similarly, dates that appear in the accounts as 'eodem die' (the same day) are transcribed as the actual date and are italicised. Italics have also been used in areas of uncertainty, for example commodities that are as yet unidentified in the manuscript. Such items are typically accompanied by a footnote when they first appear in the account and a more detailed discussion of their possible meaning can be found in the 'Glossary of Commodities' at the back of the volume.

Ship Type: This is only given in the early customs accounts (1503/4, 1516/17 and 1525/6). Most ships in these accounts are described as 'navicula' (small ship) or 'bata' (boat). The term 'navis' was only used for the greatest ships. The Latin terms have been retained because the exact distinction between a 'bata' and a 'navicula' is unclear.

Ship Name: The name of the ship is transcribed as it appears in the manuscript.

Port: The port from which a ship came is transcribed using the modern spellings as they appear in the *Times Atlas*. Foreign versions of port names are generally used. So, for instance, the volume lists Leghorn as Livorno,

Danzig as Gdánsk and Rendry as Errenteria. Exceptions have been made for places that still have a commonly-used English equivalent, such as Seville, Lisbon and Genoa. A full list of the port names, together with their location and the spellings found in the accounts, is given in the 'Glossary of Port Names' at the end of the volume.

In some cases the port is not listed, especially where a ship came from Bristol and had two names (e.g. *Mary Conception* or *Trinitie Smyth*). This was presumably because the customs officer felt that enough information had been given to identify the ship. If the origin of the ship is known from other entries in the account, or other sources, the port name is provided here but italicised. Where a port has not been identified it is transcribed as it appears in the manuscript and is italicised.

In a few cases, the 'port' listed in the account is not on a navigable waterway. For instance, 'Stonehouse' is four miles east of the River Severn and Huntley three miles west of it. It seems likely that, in these cases, the vessel in question was simply so small that it did not have a real port, being kept instead in a boathouse, or on a wharf, on the River Severn. In these instances the 'port' was probably based on the domicile of the boat's owner.

Tonnage: From 1565, the port books list the size of the ship in tuns burden. This indicated the maximum number of tuns of wine the ship could carry. At this time ships were not required, however, to 'register' their tonnage in any formal sense. The size of the ship in these accounts thus appears to be a rough estimate, which could result in the same ship being given a slightly different tonnage in different parts of the same customs account.[36]

Shipmaster's Name: In the manuscript, first names are generally Latinised, (e.g. Johannus for John, Egidius for Giles). These have all been translated into the vernacular. For details, see the 'Glossary of First Names' at the end of the volume. Since the customs officers did not Latinise surnames, they are recorded as they appear in the manuscript.

Destination: All the customs accounts indicate whether the ship was entering or exiting Bristol. Not all of the accounts, however, indicate where exactly the vessel had come from or was going to. When the destination / departure place is stated, the transcription is given using the *Times Atlas* spelling.

---

36 For instance, the *Beniamyne* of London, master William Rickes, is variously described as being of 136 tons (20 December 1600), 135 tons (9 March 1601) and 130 tons (11 May 1601).

Date: The date of almost all the entries is known. However, many entries in the 'particular accounts' are listed as 'eodem die' (the same day). This means the ship sailed, or the goods were entered, on the same day as the previous ship listed in the account. Where this happens the date listed here is based on the last dated entry in the 'particular' account. In such cases the date is italicized to indicate that the actual date is not given in the original manuscript. It should also be noted that, in the 'particular' accounts, the date listed is the date the ship's representative declared an inbound cargo, or the day on which the last item of outbound cargo had been entered and the ship cleared customs. In the port books the outbound entries reflect the actual day on which each individual consignment was declared by its owner. As a result, outbound entries for a single shipment are sometimes found spread across a period of days or weeks in the port books.

Merchant Name: As with the shipmaster's name the first name is transcribed in the vernacular and the surname is transcribed as it appears in the manuscript.

Merchant Domicile: The port books (1565–) include the domicile of the merchant. This is transcribed using the *Times Atlas* spelling.

Merchant Occupation: The port books (1565–) include the occupation of the 'merchant'. While this is often simply '*mercator*' (merchant), other occupations are sometimes given, e.g. draper, glover or fruiterer. Where female merchants occur these are generally listed as 'widow', implying that they were the surviving spouse of an established merchant.

Origin: The customs officers always indicate whether a merchant was considered indigenous, alien or Hansard. Members of the Hanseatic League and other aliens had to be distinguished from indigenous merchants because they paid different duties. Indigenous merchants, which are indicated in the transcription by the letters 'Ind', included merchants from the 'English' communities of Ireland, as well as merchants from England and Wales.

Commodity Quantity and Unit: Where possible this is the same as it appears in the manuscript, albeit with the adoption of modern spellings. However, where a given entry includes more than one unit of measure, the figure is generally converted into a single unit. For instance, if the account reads '2 lasts 3 barrels' white herring, this is rendered as 27 barrels (since 1 last = 12 barrels). Similarly, if an account reads '7 tuns 1 pipe 1 hogshead' wine this is rendered as 7.75 tuns (since 1 pipe = 0.5 tuns and 1 hogshead =

0.25 tuns). Where it has not been possible to determine the conversion ratio, the entry records both measures.

Commodity: In the customs accounts this is generally given in Latin, e.g. 'vini' for wine, 'feri' for iron, 'pan*nus*' for cloth. Sometimes, however, English is used. This was presumably because the customs clerk did not know the Latin name for the particular item of merchandise. In the transcription, the modern English spelling is used. For instance 'cere' and 'wex' are both recorded as wax. Where the meaning of the term used has not been established with certainty (e.g. 'pilus tinctus'), the term used has been left in the original and italicised. Full details of the terms used are given in the 'Glossary of Commodities' at the end of the volume.

Value of Goods: Most goods paid a tax called 'poundage', so called because it was a tax of one shilling in the pound (i.e. 5 percent) on the merchandise. The value of such goods, is given as it appears in the accounts listed in pounds, shillings, pence and farthings ($£$, $s.$ $d.$ $f.$). To determine the tax paid, the customer would first write down the value of the goods. His valuations were based on his 'Book of Rates', which provided the nominal value of most of the goods he might encounter.[37]

Some goods (in particular, wine, broadcloth and tanned hides) did not pay 'poundage'. Instead, they paid 'specific' duties. Wine paid 'tunnage' of 3s. per tun, broadcloth exports paid 1s. 2d. per cloth before 1558 and tanned hides paid duties amounting to 4s. per dicker of ten hides. The payment of such dues are recorded in the customer's accounts and, while the dues paid have not been given here, it is simple to determine the dues that would have been paid. In addition, some good were listed but were not given a value because they were customs exempt – e.g. victuals intended for the army in Ireland, goods intended for the provisioning of the ship and goods that had been spoilt. As in the accounts, values were usually not recorded for such goods.

---

37 Gras, *Early English customs system*, pp 694–706; Willan, *Tudor book of rates*.

PART 1

The 'Particular' Accounts

1503/4

TNA E122/199/1 is an annual 'particular' customs account of John Butteler & William Grene, collectors of customs & subsidies, covering the period Michaelmas 1503 to Michaelmas 1504.

The account records the type of ship, which is described simply as either Bat[ ] or Navicula. Bat[ ] has been transcribed as Bata; this being how it appears in both the 1516/17 and 1525–26 accounts, which are the only other accounts in the E122 series to detail ship types. As the ship's tonnage is not recorded in this series, the exact size of either a *bata* or *navicula* remains uncertain. Based on their comparative cargo sizes, however, it appears that a *bata* was a much smaller vessel than a *navicula*. The later Port Book series, which do record tonnages, indicate that some of the smaller vessels on the Bristol-Ireland route had a tonnage of as little as four tons.[1]

Also recorded are ship names, port of origin, master's name and the destination of the ship, which, in terms of Irish trade, is recorded as either arriving from or going to Hibernia (transcribed as Ireland). The exact port of destination is not recorded in the 'particular accounts'. The account records the date of sailing, merchant's name and details of the cargo, including the quantity, unit of measurement, commodity type, nominal value based on the book of rates and the duty paid.

Types of duty have already been introduced and it has been noted that customs payments have been omitted in these transcriptions. It must be noted however that individual accounts contain certain peculiarities in terms of how nominal values and customs payments are recorded. The 1503/4 account includes, for example, a 'value' for tanned hides, which as has already been explained, did not pay poundage duties. The value of £3 3s. 4d. per dicker noted here is based on a back projection from the subsidy value by the customs officer, and is a meaningless figure. It has however been included where it occurs. Likewise, occasionally, the officers produce similar 'values' for cloth of assize, which again have been included where they occur but would have to be modified for the purpose of comparative statistical analysis.

---

1 TNA E190/1129/12 f18r.

Merchant name	Origin	Qty	Unit	Commodity	£	s.	d.	f.

Bata Mare Bushar, Port Unknown, Peter Hanrekan master, from Ireland, 3rd October 1503

Merchant name	Origin	Qty	Unit	Commodity	£	s.	d.	f.
Peter Hanrekan	Ind	2	C	Skins, Lamb	0	10	0	0
		3	piece	Mantles	0	10	0	0
William Haket	Ind	2	C	Skins, Sheep (no wool)	0	20	0	0
		59	piece	Mantles	9	16	8	0
		4	piece	Skins, Fox	0	0	6	0
		6	lb	Wax	0	2	0	0
		50	yard	Check *Cloth*	0	16	8	0
William Dolie	Ind	40	piece	Mantles	6	13	4	0
		91	yard	Check *Cloth*	0	30	0	0
		1.66	C	Skins, Sheep (no wool)	0	16	8	0
		3	C	Irish Linen *Cloth*	0	30	0	0
		1	quarter	Irish Linen *Cloth*	0	2	6	0
		61	lb	Wax	0	20	4	0
		9	piece	Skins, Fox	0	0	13	2
		12	piece	Skins, Lamb	0	0	6	0
Thomas Axbrigge	Ind	54	piece	Mantles	9	0	0	0
		100	yard	Check *Cloth*	0	33	4	0
		100	lb	Wax	0	33	4	0
		4	C	Irish Linen *Cloth*	0	40	0	0
		3.5	C	Skins, Sheep (no wool)	0	35	0	0
		3	C	Skins, Lamb	0	15	0	0
		9	piece	Skins, Fox	0	0	13	2
Thomas Seis	Ind	4	pipe	Fish, Salmon	6	0	0	0
		1	virken	Fish, Salmon	0	7	6	0
		29.61	C	Skins, Sheep (no wool)	14	16	2	0
		4	C	Irish Linen *Cloth*	0	40	0	0
		240	lb	Wax	4	0	0	0
		29	piece	Mantles	4	16	8	0
		77	yard	Check *Cloth*	0	25	8	0
		7	piece	Hides, Salted	0	9	4	0
		18	lb	Scrofe	0	0	18	0
John Savage	Ind	9	piece	Mantles	0	30	0	0
		40	yard	Check *Cloth*	0	13	4	0
		12	*dozen*	Skins, Sheep (no wool)	0	11	0	0
		1	C	Irish Linen *Cloth*	0	10	0	0
		4	lb	Wax	0	0	16	0
		3	piece	Skins, Fox	0	0	4	2
John Roebuck	Ind	85	yard	Check *Cloth*	0	28	4	0
		28	lb	Wax	0	9	4	0
		3	piece	Mantles	0	10	0	0
John Kassie	Ind	5.25	C	Skins, Sheep (no wool)	0	52	6	0
		6	piece	Mantles	0	20	0	0
		24	yard	Irish Linen *Cloth*	0	2	0	0
		16	lb	Wax	0	5	4	0
		3	piece	Skins, Otter	0	0	15	0
		20	piece	Skins, Lamb	0	0	10	0
Richard White	Ind	2	C	Fish, Hake	0	20	0	0
		10	piece	Mantles	0	33	4	0
Tege Walshe	Ind	4	piece	Mantles	0	13	4	0
		4	stone	Wool, Flocks	0	0	20	0

Merchant name	Origin	Qty	Unit	Commodity	£	s.	d.	f.
Thomas Axbrigge	Ind	2	stone	Wool, Flocks	0	0	10	0
		10	piece	Fish, Hake	0	0	10	0
Edmund Mean	Ind	1	dicker	Hides, Salted	0	13	4	0
		1.75	C	Fish, Hake	0	17	6	0
William Malden	Ind	3	piece	Mantles	0	10	0	0
		194	piece	Fish, Hake	0	17	10	0
John Harries	Ind	4	C	Skins, Sheep (no wool)	0	40	0	0
		12	piece	Mantles	0	40	0	0
		12	lb	Wax	0	4	0	0
		4	stone	Wool, Flocks	0	0	20	0
William Hacket	Ind	2	piece	Whitelles	0	6	8	0
John Fe harry	Ind	10	piece	Mantles	0	33	4	0
		100	piece	Skins, Sheep (no wool)	0	8	4	0
William Hacket	Ind	20	yard	Check *Cloth*	0	6	8	0
Thomas Axbrigge	Ind	11	yard	Check *Cloth*	0	3	8	0
		6	lb	Wax	0	2	0	0

Bata Lenard of Waterford, William Gombon master, from Ireland, 4th October 1503

Merchant name	Origin	Qty	Unit	Commodity	£	s.	d.	f.
William Gombon	Ind	2.125	C	Fish, Hake	0	21	3	0
		1	C	Skins, Sheep (no wool)	0	10	0	0
		14	piece	Mantles	0	46	8	0
Walter Mothell	Ind	130	piece	Mantles	21	13	4	0
		3	M	Skins, Sheep (no wool)	15	0	0	0
		3	C	Wax	6	0	0	0
		100	*yard*	Irish Linen *Cloth*	0	10	0	0
		0.5	C	Skins, Lamb	0	2	6	0
William Gombon	Ind	2	C	Irish Linen *Cloth*	0	20	0	0
Thomas Langton	Ind	40	piece	Mantles	6	13	4	0
		5	C	Skins, Sheep (no wool)	0	50	0	0
		5.25	C	Irish Linen *Cloth*	0	52	6	0
		2.16	C	Check *Cloth*	4	6	8	0
		0.5	C	Wax	0	20	0	0
		0.5	C	Skins, Lamb	0	2	6	0
Philip Powere	Ind	4	pipe	Fish, Salmon	6	0	0	0
		4	C	Fish, Hake	0	40	0	0
		2	dicker	Hides, Salted	0	26	8	0
		6	C	Skins, Sheep (no wool)	0	60	0	0
		4	C	Irish Linen *Cloth*	0	40	0	0
		13	piece	Mantles	0	43	4	0
		30	lb	Wax	0	10	0	0
Walter Mothell	Ind	1	dicker	Hides, Salted	0	13	4	0
Robert Garvie	Ind	2	C	Skins, Sheep (no wool)	0	20	0	0
		4	C	Skins, Lamb	0	20	0	0
		1.75	C	Irish Linen *Cloth*	0	17	6	0
		20	yard	Check *Cloth*	0	6	8	0
		13	lb	Wax	0	4	4	0
		10	piece	Mantles	0	33	4	0
		4	piece	Skins, Fox	0	0	6	0
William White	Ind	8	piece	Mantles	0	26	8	0
		1	piece	Whitelles	0	3	4	0
		20	lb	Wax	0	6	8	0

Merchant name	Origin	Qty	Unit	Commodity	£	s.	d.	f.
Dennis Ffolan	Ind	0.5	pipe	Fish, Salmon	0	15	0	0
		4	piece	Mantles	0	13	4	0
		8	lb	Wax	0	2	8	0
		2	stone	Wool, Flocks	0	0	10	0
Peter Cassie	Ind	14	lb	Wax	0	4	8	0
		2	piece	Mantles	0	6	8	0
		2	stone	Wool, Flocks	0	0	10	0
John Hylle	Ind	3	piece	Mantles	0	10	0	0
Dennis Sherman	Ind	5	piece	Mantles	0	16	8	0
Walter Mothell	Ind	1	C	Check *Cloth*	0	40	0	0
Peter Talbot	Ind	6	piece	Mantles	0	20	0	0
		2	dicker	Hides, Salted	0	26	8	0
Thomas Axbrigge	Ind	140	piece	Skins, Sheep (no wool)	0	11	8	0
Patrick Kente	Ind	6	piece	Mantles	0	20	0	0
Robert Cranesbie	Ind	1	piece	Goshawk	0	60	0	0
		1	unknown	*Taishaill*	0	20	0	0

Bata James of Minehead, John Wrighte master, from Ireland, *4th October 1503*

John Wrighte	Ind	4	C	Fish, Hake	0	40	0	0

Navicula Fraunses of Bristol, Edmund Griffethe master, from Ireland, 6th October 1503

Merchant name	Origin	Qty	Unit	Commodity	£	s.	d.	f.
Edmund Griffethe	Ind	2	pipe	Fish, Salmon	0	60	0	0
		6	barrel	Fish, Herring White	0	30	0	0
		12	piece	Mantles	0	40	0	0
		0.5	C	Skins, Sheep (no wool)	0	5	0	0
William Tirrie, Humphry Brown, William White & Humphry Bosgrove	Ind	15.5	pipe	Fish, Salmon	23	5	0	0
William White	Ind	22.5	barrel	Fish, Herring White	0	112	6	0
		22	piece	Mantles	0	73	4	0
		2	C	Skins, Sheep (no wool)	0	20	0	0
		2.75	C	Fish, Hake	0	27	6	0
Richard Stephins	Ind	5	barrel	Fish, Herring White	0	25	0	0
William Tirrie & Humphry Brown	Ind	63	barrel	Fish, Herring White	15	15	0	0
		1	C	Fish, Hake	0	10	0	0
		5	piece	Mantles	0	16	8	0
Humphrey Bosgrove	Ind	40	barrel	Fish, Herring White	10	0	0	0
		2.25	C	Fish, Hake	0	22	6	0
		22	piece	Mantles	0	73	4	0
		13	stone	Wool, Flocks	0	5	5	0
William Clarke	Ind	6	barrel	Fish, Herring White	0	30	0	0
		95	piece	*Rares/ Raies*[2]	0	2	0	0
		1.25	C	Skins, Sheep (no wool)	0	12	6	0
Thomas Flemynge	Ind	3.5	barrel	Fish, Herring White	0	17	6	0
William Beremake	Ind	5	piece	Mantles	0	16	8	0
		8	yard	Check *Cloth*	0	2	8	0
		3	stone	Wool, Flocks	0	0	15	0

2 Unidentified.

Merchant name	Origin	Qty	Unit	Commodity	£	s.	d.	f.
William Tobyn	Ind	1	barrel	Fish, Herring White	0	5	0	0
John Wase	Ind	21	barrel	Fish, Herring White	0	105	0	0
William White	Ind	80	lb	Wood, Brazil	4	0	0	0
John Stoke	Ind	5	piece	Mantles	0	16	8	0
John Damine	Ind	6	stone	Wool, Flocks	0	2	6	0
William White	Ind	1	piece	Goshawk	0	40	0	0
John Wase	Ind	6	piece	Mantles	0	20	0	0

Bata Trinite of Chepstow, William Heyn master, from Chepstow, *6th October 1503*

Philip Ffoxe	Ind	1	pipe	Oil, Olive	0	40	0	0

Bata Katren of Chepstow, Robert Ffishar master, from Chepstow, *6th October 1503*

Sancho de Fontbie	Alien	0.5	C	Skins, Lamb	0	2	6	0

Katren of Berkeley, Robert Powar master, to Bordeaux, 9th October 1503

William Cogan	Ind	29.5	piece	Cloth of Assize	0	0	0	0
		2	piece	Cloth of Assize, Dozen Strait	0	0	0	0
Thomas Lemon	Ind	2.5	piece	Cloth of Assize	0	0	0	0
		3	piece	Cloth of Assize, Kersey	0	0	0	0
		0.5	piece	Cloth of Assize	0	0	0	0
		2	piece	Welsh *Cloth*, Dozen Strait	0	8	4	0
		70	lb	Silk, Worked	46	13	4	0
		1.75	C	*Pilus Tinctus*	0	70	0	0
Philip Grene	Ind	2	piece	Cloth of Assize	0	0	0	0

Bata Katren of Chepstow, Robert Ffishar master, to Ireland, *9th October 1503*

Thomas Halvard	Ind	1	last	Beer	0	30	0	0

Bata Kerecke of Carmathen, John Thomas master, from *Carmarthen, 9th October 1503*

Richard Reede	Ind	3	ton	Salt	0	25	0	0

Bata Mawdlen of Berkeley, Thomas Swanake master, to Ireland, *9th October 1503*

Thomas Bochier	Ind	20	piece	Cloth of Assize	0	0	0	0
		2.75	ton	Wine, Corrupt	4	2	6	0
		1	tun	Wine, Corrupt	0	30	0	0

Bata Mare Halle of Chepstow, Richard Halle master, from Chepstow, 11th October 1503

William Colston	Ind	8	barrel	Fish, Herring White	0	40	0	0
		2.5	burden	Fish, Salted	0	8	4	0
		1	tun	Oil, Olive	4	0	0	0

Bata Trinite of Chepstow, William Heyn master, from Chepstow, 13th October 1503

William Estbie	Ind	20	C	*Smigmates*	6	13	4	0
Thomas Smythe	Ind	0.5	tun	Oil, Olive	0	40	0	0

Merchant name	Origin	Qty	Unit	Commodity	£	s.	d.	f.
Geroge Book	Ind	0.5	tun	Wine	0	0	0	0

Bata Patricke of Combwich, John Wilkens master, from Ireland, 16th October 1503

Merchant name	Origin	Qty	Unit	Commodity	£	s.	d.	f.
John Wilkens	Ind	4	last	Fish, Herring White	12	0	0	0
		12	barrel	Fish, Herring White	0	60	0	0

Bata George of Chepstow, Thomas Helston master, *to Chepstoow*, 17th October 1503

Merchant name	Origin	Qty	Unit	Commodity	£	s.	d.	f.
William Jeffereis	Ind	34	dozen	Skins, Calf Tanned	4	5	0	0

Bata Peter of Berkeley, Thomas Cockes master, from Ireland, 19th October 1503

Merchant name	Origin	Qty	Unit	Commodity	£	s.	d.	f.
Thomas Cockes	Ind	5	last	Fish, Herring White	15	0	0	0
		1	C	Fish, Hake	0	10	0	0
		8	mease	Fish, Herring Red	0	40	0	0

Bata Nicholas of Berkeley, John Rownyng master, from Ireland, *19th October 1503*

Merchant name	Origin	Qty	Unit	Commodity	£	s.	d.	f.
Richard Partriche	Ind	93	barrel	Fish, Herring White	20	15	0	0

Navicula George of Chepstow, William Webbe master, to Lisbon, *19th October 1503*

Merchant name	Origin	Qty	Unit	Commodity	£	s.	d.	f.
William Estbie	Ind	5	piece	Cloth of Assize	0	0	0	0
John Stalworthe	Ind	2	piece	Cloth of Assize	0	0	0	0
Thomas Smythe	Ind	6	piece	Cloth of Assize	0	0	0	0
Richard Dra*per*	Ind	1	piece	Cloth of Assize	0	0	0	0

Bata Mare Halle of Chepstow, Richard Halle master, from Chepstow, 20th October 1503

Merchant name	Origin	Qty	Unit	Commodity	£	s.	d.	f.
William Colston	Ind	2	barrel	Fish, Herring White	0	10	0	0

Bata Lenard of Waterford, William Gombon master, to Ireland, *20th October 1503*

Merchant name	Origin	Qty	Unit	Commodity	£	s.	d.	f.
Philip Powar	Ind	4	wey	Coal	0	13	4	0
		2	piece	Cloth of Assize	0	0	0	0
		7	lb	Saffron	0	46	8	0
		2	lb	Silk, Worked	0	26	8	0
		40	lb	*Pilus Tinctus*	0	13	4	0
John Pollard	Ind	4	lb	Saffron	0	26	8	0
		1	lb	Silk, Worked	0	13	4	0
William Tirrie	Ind	20	lb	Saffron	6	13	4	0
William Walshe	Ind	3	piece	Cloth of Assize	0	0	0	0
William Gombon	Ind	2	lb	Saffron	0	13	4	0
		24	lb	*Pilus Tinctus*	0	8	0	0
Philip Powar	Ind	5	lb	Saffron	0	33	4	0
David Comyn &								
Henry Scotte	Ind	2	piece	Cloth of Assize	0	0	0	0
		0.5	piece	Cloth of Assize	0	0	0	0
		28	lb	Saffron	9	6	8	0
		5	lb	Silk, Worked	0	66	8	0
John Dowlie	Ind	28	lb	Saffron	9	6	8	0

Merchant name	Origin	Qty	Unit	Commodity	£	s.	d.	f.
		6	lb	Silk, Worked	4	0	0	0
		7	lb	Pepper	0	5	3	0
		6	gross	Points	0	6	0	0
		2	lb	Verdegris	0	0	12	0
		4	dozen	Knives	0	4	2	0
		6	lb	Aniseed	0	0	9	0
		1	piece	Cloth of Assize, Dozen Strait	0	0	0	0
Dennis Lurkan	Ind	2	lb	Saffron	0	13	4	0
William Hacket	Ind	32	lb	*Pilus Tinctus*	0	10	8	0
John Dyneste	Ind	4	piece	Cloth of Assize, Dozen	0	0	0	0
Richard Arthure	Ind	5	piece	Cloth of Assize	0	0	0	0
		12	lb	Saffron	4	0	0	0
		2	lb	Silk, Worked	0	26	8	0
		40	lb	*Pilus Tinctus*	0	13	4	0
		4	dozen	Points	0	4	0	0

Bata James of Cork, Maurice Qwirke master, from Ireland, 21st October 1503

Merchant name	Origin	Qty	Unit	Commodity	£	s.	d.	f.
Maurice Qwirke	Ind	7	last	Fish, Herring White	21	0	0	0
Thomas Braie	Ind	45	barrel	Fish, Herring White	11	5	0	0

Bata Michaell of Tewkesbury, Thomas Pursar master, from Chepstow, *21st October 1503*

Merchant name	Origin	Qty	Unit	Commodity	£	s.	d.	f.
Griffeth Ap Morgan	Ind	4	last	Fish, Herring White	12	0	0	0

Bata Anne of Minehead, Thomas Gregorie master, from Ireland, 24th October 1503

Merchant name	Origin	Qty	Unit	Commodity	£	s.	d.	f.
Thomas Gregorie	Ind	5	last	Fish, Herring White	15	0	0	0
		8	C	Fish, Hake	4	0	0	0
		1	C	Fish, Hake	0	10	0	0
		1	C	Fish, Hake	0	10	0	0

Bata Trinitie of Berkeley, James Atwood master, from Ireland, *24th October 1503*

Merchant name	Origin	Qty	Unit	Commodity	£	s.	d.	f.
James Atwood	Ind	10	last	Fish, Herring White	30	0	0	0

Navicula Franses of Bristol, William Down master, to Ireland, *24th October 1503*

Merchant name	Origin	Qty	Unit	Commodity	£	s.	d.	f.
Humphrey Browne &								
William Tirrie	Ind	3	last	Beer	4	10	0	0
Walter Mothell	Ind	60	lb	Saffron	20	0	0	0
		16	lb	Silk, Worked	10	13	4	0
		3	piece	Cloth of Assize	0	0	0	0
		80	lb	*Pilus Tinctus*	0	26	8	0
		2	dozen	Caps	0	13	4	0
		3	gross	Points	0	3	0	0
William White	Ind	36	lb	Saffron	12	0	0	0
		8	lb	Silk, Worked	0	106	8	0
		1	piece	Cloth of Assize	0	0	0	0
		34	lb	*Pilus Tinctus*	0	11	4	0
Thomas Langton	Ind	24	lb	Saffron	8	13	4	0
		6	lb	Saffron	0	40	0	0

Merchant name	Origin	Qty	Unit	Commodity	£	s.	d.	f.
		1	quarter	Aniseed	0	2	6	0
		2	dozen	Caps	0	13	4	0
		5	gross	Points	0	5	0	0
		0.5	ream	Paper	0	0	12	0
		4	lb	Saffron	0	26	8	0
Thomas Axbrigge	Ind	14	lb	Saffron	4	13	4	0
		2	lb	Silk, Worked	0	26	8	0
		7	gross	Points	0	7	0	0
William Meagh	Ind	12	lb	Saffron	4	0	0	0
		4	lb	Silk, Worked	0	53	4	0
		1.5	piece	Cloth of Assize	0	0	0	0

Navicula George of Gloucester, William Kempe master, from Bordeaux, 26th October 1503

Merchant name	Origin	Qty	Unit	Commodity	£	s.	d.	f.
Walter Rowdon	Ind	5.75	tun	Wine	0	0	0	0
Richard Rowdon	Ind	3.75	tun	Wine	0	0	0	0
Ralph Halsey	Ind	6.75	tun	Wine	0	0	0	0
John Ffarley	Ind	1.25	tun	Wine	0	0	0	0
Gratien de la Plase	Ind	5.25	tun	Wine	0	0	0	0
James Whaley	Ind	3.75	tun	Wine	0	0	0	0
John Harte	Ind	0.5	tun	Wine	0	0	0	0
John Snelle	Ind	0.416	tun	Wine	0	0	0	0
William Goldsmythe	Ind	5.5	tun	Wine	0	0	0	0
John Shipman	Ind	3	tun	Wine	0	0	0	0
Richard Vaghan	Ind	1.75	tun	Wine	0	0	0	0
Robert Rowlowe	Ind	1.5	tun	Wine	0	0	0	0
William Kempe	Ind	1.5	tun	Wine	0	0	0	0
John Powar	Ind	0.25	tun	Wine	0	0	0	0
John Rogers	Ind	1.5	tun	Wine	0	0	0	0
John Grevell	Ind	0.25	tun	Wine	0	0	0	0
Patrick Seere	Ind	0.25	tun	Wine	0	0	0	0
Thomas Dovere	Ind	0.5	tun	Wine	0	0	0	0
John Thomas	Ind	2	tun	Wine	0	0	0	0
James Cooke	Ind	2	tun	Wine	0	0	0	0
Thomas Awsten	Ind	0.5	tun	Wine	0	0	0	0

Bata Sondaie of Minehead, Higon Snarpen master, from Ireland, *26th October 1503*

Merchant name	Origin	Qty	Unit	Commodity	£	s.	d.	f.
Higon Snarpen	Ind	4	last	Fish, Herring White	12	0	0	0
		16.5	barrel	Fish, Herring White	4	2	6	0
		1	C	Fish, Hake	0	10	0	0

Bata Mare of Combwich, John Dodynge master, from Ireland, 31st October 1503

Merchant name	Origin	Qty	Unit	Commodity	£	s.	d.	f.
William Downe	Ind	2	mease	Fish, Herring Red	0	10	0	0

Bata Katren of Minehead, David Tege master, from Ireland, 4th November 1503

Merchant name	Origin	Qty	Unit	Commodity	£	s.	d.	f.
David Tege	Ind	3	last	Fish, Herring White	9	0	0	0
		26	barrel	Fish, Herring White	6	10	0	0
		6	barrel	Fish, Herring White	0	30	0	0

Merchant name	Origin	Qty	Unit	Commodity	£	s.	d.	f.

Bata Mare Bushar, Port Unknown, Peter Hanrekan master, to Ireland, 7th November 1503

Merchant name	Origin	Qty	Unit	Commodity	£	s.	d.	f.
Nicholas Nynes	Ind	6	C	Alum	0	30	0	0
		170	lb	*Pilus Tinctus*	0	56	8	0
		2	piece	Cloth of Assize	0	0	0	0
		12	piece	Porteos	0	38	0	0
Thomas Seis	Ind	120	lb	*Pilus Tinctus*	0	40	0	0
		78	lb	Saffron	26	0	0	0
		3	piece	Cloth of Assize	0	0	0	0
		12	gross	Points	0	12	0	0
		49	lb	Silk, Worked	32	13	4	0
		2	pair	Stock-cards	0	2	4	0
John Fe harry	Ind	16	lb	Saffron	0	106	8	0
		40	lb	*Pilus Tinctus*	0	13	4	0
		2	lb	Silk, Worked	0	26	8	0
William Hacket	Ind	200	lb	*Pilus Tinctus*	0	56	8	0
		1	piece	Cloth of Assize	0	0	0	0
William Clarke	Ind	68	lb	*Pilus Tinctus*	0	22	8	0
Nicholas Nynes	Ind	1	piece	Cloth of Assize	0	0	0	0
		90	lb	*Pilus Tinctus*	0	30	0	0

Navicula Franses of Bristol, William Downe master, to Ireland, *7th November 1503*

Merchant name	Origin	Qty	Unit	Commodity	£	s.	d.	f.
William Braye	Ind	10.5	lb	Saffron	0	70	0	0
		0.5	lb	Silk, Worked	0	6	8	0
		5	gross	Points	0	5	0	0
		2	dozen	Knives	0	0	13	0
Thomas White	Ind	30	lb	*Pilus Tinctus*	0	10	0	0
William Tirrie	Ind	60	lb	*Pilus Tinctus*	0	20	0	0
John Roebuck	Ind	7.5	lb	Saffron	0	50	0	0
		0.5	lb	Silk, Worked	0	6	8	0
		3	quarter	Aniseed	0	7	6	0
		2	gross	Points	0	2	0	0
David Savage	Ind	3	piece	Cloth of Assize	0	0	0	0
		22	lb	Saffron	7	6	8	0
		3	gross	Knives	0	20	0	0
		1.5	dozen	Caps	0	10	0	0
		8	gross	Points	0	8	0	0
		1	quarter	Aniseed	0	2	6	0
		4	lb	Silk, Worked	0	53	4	0
		1	quarter	Alum	0	0	15	0
		20	lb	*Pilus Tinctus*	0	6	8	0
Robert Garvey	Ind	10	lb	Saffron	0	66	8	0
		0.5	lb	Silk, Worked	0	6	8	0
		4	gross	Points	0	4	0	0
		2	lb	Thread	0	0	10	0
William Hacket	Ind	21	lb	*Pilus Tinctus*	0	7	0	0
		2	lb	Saffron	0	13	4	0
		30	lb	Alum	0	0	15	0
Philip Powar	Ind	1	quarter	Alum	0	0	15	0

Merchant name	Origin	Qty	Unit	Commodity	£	s.	d.	f.

Bata Katren of Berkeley, Thomas Nelme master, from Ireland, 8th November 1503

Merchant name	Origin	Qty	Unit	Commodity	£	s.	d.	f.
John Putley	Ind	18	barrel	Fish, Herring White	4	10	0	0

Bata Padorn of Milford Haven, Stephen Barnard master, from Ireland, 9th November 1503

Merchant name	Origin	Qty	Unit	Commodity	£	s.	d.	f.
Thomas Cooke	Ind	21	barrel	Fish, Herring White	0	105	0	0
		1	quarter	Fish, Hake	0	2	6	0
George Monos &								
Thomas Cooke	Ind	7	barrel	Fish, Herring White	0	35	0	0
David Vaghan	Ind	7	barrel	Fish, Herring White	0	35	0	0
William Robyns	Ind	1	barrel	Fish, Herring White	0	5	0	0
John Wade	Ind	0.5	barrel	Fish, Herring White	0	2	6	0
Richard Bulton	Ind	0.5	barrel	Fish, Herring White	0	2	6	0

Bata Katren of Minehead, David Tege master, from Ireland, 13th November 1503

Merchant name	Origin	Qty	Unit	Commodity	£	s.	d.	f.
David Tege	Ind	5	barrel	Fish, Herring White	0	25	0	0
William Haetland	Ind	1	barrel	Fish, Herring White	0	5	0	0

Bata Katren of Chepstow, Robert Ffishar master, from Chepstow, 15th November 1503

Merchant name	Origin	Qty	Unit	Commodity	£	s.	d.	f.
William Colston	Ind	5	ton	Salt	0	41	8	0

Bata Mawdlen of Berkeley, Thomas Senekur master, from Ireland, 16th November 1503

Merchant name	Origin	Qty	Unit	Commodity	£	s.	d.	f.
Thomas Bocher	Ind	50	barrel	Fish, Herring White	12	10	0	0
		3	last	Fish, Herring White	9	0	0	0
Richard Bocher	Ind	37	barrel	Fish, Herring White	9	5	0	0
		4	C	Fish, Hake	0	40	0	0
William Bocher	Ind	6	barrel	Fish, Herring White	0	30	0	0
Thomas Senekur	Ind	14	barrel	Fish, Herring White	0	70	0	0

Bata Anne of Chepstow, John Horsman master, from Chepstow, *16th November 1503*

Merchant name	Origin	Qty	Unit	Commodity	£	s.	d.	f.
Richard Vaghan	Ind	1	tun	Wine	0	0	0	0
William Goldsmyth	Ind	2.25	tun	Wine	0	0	0	0
Thomas Awsten	Ind	0.5	tun	Wine	0	0	0	0

Bata Barbara of Bristol, Philip Nongell master, from Ireland, 17th November 1503

Merchant name	Origin	Qty	Unit	Commodity	£	s.	d.	f.
John Colas	Ind	10	last	Fish, Herring White	30	0	0	0
		0.5	barrel	Fish, Herring White	0	2	6	0
Thomas Flemynge	Ind	4	last	Fish, Herring White	12	0	0	0
William Tobie	Ind	13	barrel	Fish, Herring White	0	65	0	0
William Lawndere	Ind	5	barrel	Fish, Herring White	0	30	0	0
Tege Nele	Ind	8	barrel	Fish, Herring White	0	40	0	0
Matthew Hoper	Ind	3	barrel	Fish, Herring White	0	15	0	0
William Clarke	Ind	1	barrel	Fish, Herring White	0	5	0	0
Matthew Hoper	Ind	1	barrel	Fish, Herring White	0	5	0	0

Merchant name	Origin	Qty	Unit	Commodity	£	s.	d.	f.

Bata Mawdlen of Dingle, John Dowde master, from Ireland, 18th November 1503

Merchant name	Origin	Qty	Unit	Commodity	£	s.	d.	f.
John Dowde, Gerald May, Raymond Graunte, Richard Spiser & Maurice Flemynge	Ind	8	M	Fish, Hake	40	0	0	0
		6	C	Fish, Salted	0	100	0	0
		2.5	C	Fish, Pullock	0	12	6	0
		18	piece	Mantles	0	60	0	0
		1	C	Irish Linen *Cloth*	0	10	0	0
		8	C	Fish, Hake	4	0	0	0
Philip Morgan	Ind	14	C	Fish, Hake	7	0	0	0
		1	quarter	Fish, Hake	0	2	6	0
		4	piece	Mantles	0	13	4	0

Bata John of Newnham, John Brayn master, from Chepstow, *18th November 1503*

Merchant name	Origin	Qty	Unit	Commodity	£	s.	d.	f.
William Goldsmythe	Ind	3.75	tun	Wine	0	0	0	0

Bata Trinitie of Minehead, John Kente master, from Ireland, 20th November 1503

Merchant name	Origin	Qty	Unit	Commodity	£	s.	d.	f.
John Kente	Ind	3	last	Fish, Herring White	9	0	0	0
		13	barrel	Fish, Herring White	0	65	0	0

Navicula Mare Cooke, Port Unknown, Patrick Kelley master, from Ireland, *20th November 1503*

Merchant name	Origin	Qty	Unit	Commodity	£	s.	d.	f.
Patrick Kelley	Ind	4.5	barrel	Fish, Herring White	0	22	6	0
William Gonne	Ind	13	barrel	Fish, Herring White	0	65	0	0
		5	mease	Fish, Herring Red	0	25	0	0
John Kewsack	Ind	2	last	Fish, Herring White	6	0	0	0
Matthew Smythe	Ind	27	barrel	Fish, Herring White	6	15	0	0
William Tirrie	Ind	2	C	Skins, Sheep (no wool)	0	20	0	0
William Jeffereis	Ind	63.5	barrel	Fish, Herring White	15	17	6	0
		12	mease	Fish, Herring Red	0	60	0	0
William Hoper	Ind	6.5	barrel	Fish, Herring White	0	32	6	0
William Jeffereis	Ind	1	C	Fish, Hake	0	10	0	0
William Tirrie	Ind	12	barrel	Fish, Herring White	0	60	0	0
William Crowley	Ind	5	barrel	Fish, Herring White	0	25	0	0
		0.5	barrel	Fish, Herring White	0	2	6	0
William Tirrie	Ind	1	piece	Mantles	0	3	4	0
		0.5	mease	Fish, Herring Red	0	2	6	0

Bata Rose of Tenby, Richard Honter master, from Ireland, *24th November 1503*

Merchant name	Origin	Qty	Unit	Commodity	£	s.	d.	f.
Richard Honter	Ind	12	barrel	Fish, Herring White	0	60	0	0

Bata Katren of *Mometes*, Thomas Hamon, from Ireland, 25th November 1503

Merchant name	Origin	Qty	Unit	Commodity	£	s.	d.	f.
Thomas Hamon	Ind	34	barrel	Fish, Herring White	8	10	0	0
Richard Bochere	Ind	3	last	Fish, Herring White	9	0	0	0

Merchant name	Origin	Qty	Unit	Commodity	£	s.	d.	f.
Bata Gelian of Minehead, John Colen master, from Ireland, 27th November 1503								
John Colen	Ind	30	barrel	Fish, Herring White	7	10	0	0
		11.5	barrel	Fish, Herring White	0	57	6	0
Bata Sondaie of Minehead, William Colren master, from Ireland, 27th November 1503								
William Colren	Ind	9	last	Fish, Herring White	27	0	0	0
		4	C	Fish, Hake	0	40	0	0
Bata Mawdlen of Berkeley, John Horsman master, from Chepstow, 29th November 1503								
William Colston	Ind	1	pipe	Wine	0	0	0	0
Bata Nicolas of Berkeley, John Rogers master, to Ireland, 29th November 1503								
Richard Partriche	Ind	6	wey	Beans	4	0	0	0
		4	wey	Beans	0	53	4	0
Navicula George of Gloucester, William Kempe master, to Bordeaux, 1st December 1503								
Walter Rod[ ]	Ind	4	piece	Cloth of Assize	0	0	0	0
William Goldsmythe	Ind	6	piece	Welsh Cloth	6	0	0	0
		9	piece	Cloth of Assize	0	0	0	0
Thomas Pole	Ind	8	piece	Cloth of Assize	0	0	0	0
Ralph Halsey	Ind	1.5	piece	Cloth of Assize	0	0	0	0
		3	piece	Welsh Cloth	0	60	0	0
Bata Petur of Berkeley, John Roche master, from Ireland, 1st December 1503								
John Roche	Ind	60.5	barrel	Fish, Herring White	15	2	6	0
Bata George of Minehead, Henry Browne master, from Ireland, 1st December 1503								
Henry Browne	Ind	7.5	last	Fish, Herring White	22	10	0	0
Bata Anne of Chepstow, John Horsman master, from Chepstow, 1st December 1503								
Manuel Caldeiro	Alien	32	C	Wood, Brazil, New World	103	6	8	0
		381	lb	Kermes	12	14	0	0
Bata James of Rothe,[3] John Creede master, from Ireland, 2nd December 1503								
Thomas Hatton	Ind	6	last	Fish, Herring White	18	0	0	0
Bata Christofur of Gloucester, John Carter master, from Ireland, 2nd December 1503								
Thomas Hatton	Ind	23	barrel	Fish, Herring White	0	115	0	0

3 Possibly Rothesay harbour in Scotland.

Merchant name	Origin	Qty	Unit	Commodity	£	s.	d.	f.

Bata George of Gatcombe, Walter Nashe master, from Ireland, 5th December 1503

Merchant name	Origin	Qty	Unit	Commodity	£	s.	d.	f.
Walter Nashe	Ind	68.5	barrel	Fish, Herring White	17	2	6	0
		1	C	Fish, Hake	0	10	0	0

Navicula Mare Katren of Bristol, Robert Avyntre master, from Bordeaux, *5th December 1503*

Merchant name	Origin	Qty	Unit	Commodity	£	s.	d.	f.
Robert Avyntre	Ind	1.75	tun	Wine	0	0	0	0
George Monos	Ind	40	tun	Wine	0	0	0	0
		0.75	tun	Rosin	0	20	0	0
John Ware	Ind	11	tun	Wine	0	0	0	0
		6	ton	Iron	15	0	0	0
John Popley	Ind	1.75	tun	Wine	0	0	0	0
Roger Dewes	Ind	2.75	tun	Wine	0	0	0	0
Robert Avyntre	Ind	1	ton	Iron	2	10	0	0
John James	Ind	2	tun	Wine	0	0	0	0
		1	ton	Iron	2	10	0	0
John Tyllynge	Ind	0.25	tun	Wine	0	0	0	0
Thomas Hawkens	Ind	6	tun	Wine	0	0	0	0
William Hurste	Ind	1	tun	Wine	0	0	0	0
Richard Vaghan	Ind	4.5	tun	Wine	0	0	0	0
John Rowland	Ind	7.75	tun	Wine	0	0	0	0
John Wiot	Ind	5.5	tun	Wine	0	0	0	0
Richard Hobie	Ind	5.5	tun	Wine	0	0	0	0
Thomas Smythe	Ind	1	tun	Wine	0	0	0	0
Richard Crosse	Ind	2	tun	Wine	0	0	0	0
John Ram[ ]e	Ind	2	tun	Wine	0	0	0	0
		0.5	pipe	Woad	0	50	0	0
		1	pipe	Rosin	0	13	4	0
John Edee	Ind	11	tun	Wine	0	0	0	0
John Shipman	Ind	9.75	tun	Wine	0	0	0	0
John Lorde	Ind	1	hogshead	Rosin	0	6	8	0

Bata Savioure of Tenby, David Griffeth master, from Tenby, 9th December 1503

Merchant name	Origin	Qty	Unit	Commodity	£	s.	d.	f.
Thomas Marichurche	Ind	1	tun	Oil, Olive	4	0	0	0

Bata James of Gatcombe, John Adams master, from Ireland, 11th December 1503

Merchant name	Origin	Qty	Unit	Commodity	£	s.	d.	f.
John Adams	Ind	2	last	Fish, Herring White	6	0	0	0
John Denys	Ind	21	barrel	Fish, Herring White	0	105	0	0
James Whaley &								
Robert Wiot	Ind	117	barrel	Fish, Herring White	29	5	0	0
		53	mease	Fish, Herring Red	13	5	0	0
		3	pipe	Fish, Salmon	4	10	0	0
		13.5	C	Fish, Hake	6	15	0	0
		2	piece	Mantles	0	6	8	0

Navicula Marget of Bristol, Edward Gibbes master, from Bordeaux, 14th December 1503

Merchant name	Origin	Qty	Unit	Commodity	£	s.	d.	f.
Nicholas Browne	Ind	17	tun	Wine	0	0	0	0
John Stokes	Ind	16.416	tun	Wine	0	0	0	0

Merchant name	Origin	Qty	Unit	Commodity	£	s.	d.	f.
Thomas Smythe	Ind	2	tun	Wine	0	0	0	0
Thomas Barne	Ind	4.5	tun	Wine	0	0	0	0
John Popley	Ind	2.5	tun	Wine	0	0	0	0
William Estbie	Ind	2.75	tun	Wine	0	0	0	0
Henry Dale	Ind	2	tun	Wine	0	0	0	0
Richard Vaghan	Ind	2.75	tun	Wine	0	0	0	0
Richard Hobie	Ind	4.5	tun	Wine	0	0	0	0
William Stephins	Ind	3.25	tun	Wine	0	0	0	0
Stephen Ffostare &								
John Meysam	Ind	2.916	tun	Wine	0	0	0	0
John Vaghan	Ind	3.25	tun	Wine	0	0	0	0
Thomas Smythe	Ind	6	M	Combs	0	60	0	0
Philip Kingston	Ind	14	ton	Iron	35	0	0	0
		4	pipe	Woad	20	0	0	0
John Wiot	Ind	3.75	tun	Wine	0	0	0	0
Robert Barrero	Ind	2.5	tun	Wine	0	0	0	0
John Ware	Ind	2.75	tun	Wine	0	0	0	0
Richard Crosse	Ind	9.666	tun	Wine	0	0	0	0
George Monos	Ind	2	tun	Wine	0	0	0	0
John Edee	Ind	2.5	tun	Wine	0	0	0	0
John Kingston	Ind	1.75	tun	Wine	0	0	0	0
Simon Andrewe	Ind	1.25	tun	Wine	0	0	0	0
John Jones	Ind	1	tun	Wine	0	0	0	0
Robert Carpynter	Ind	0.25	tun	Wine	0	0	0	0
William Hurste	Ind	0.166	tun	Wine	0	0	0	0
John Holkare	Ind	0.5	tun	Wine	0	0	0	0
Thomas Horsman	Ind	9	C	Rosin	0	12	0	0
Thomas Plomley	Ind	0.166	tun	Wine	0	0	0	0
John Garret	Ind	1	tun	Wine	0	0	0	0
Thomas Jones	Ind	2	tun	Wine	0	0	0	0
John Hewes	Ind	0.25	tun	Wine	0	0	0	0
Roger Thomas	Ind	0.5	tun	Wine	0	0	0	0
Philip Kingston	Ind	0.5	ton	Iron	0	25	0	0

Bata Katren of Hanley Castle, John Southall master, from Chepstow, *14th December 1503*

Richard Ffarre	Ind	7	ton	Iron	17	10	0	0

Bata Marget of Cardiff, Thomas Yoma master, from Ireland, 15th December 1503

James Whaley	Ind	100.5	barrel	Fish, Herring White	25	2	6	0

Bata Lenard of Waterford, William Gombon master, from Ireland, 16th December 1503

Dennis Ffolan	Ind	9.5	barrel	Fish, Herring White	0	47	6	0
		1	mease	Fish, Herring Red	0	5	0	0
		2	piece	Mantles	0	6	8	0
William Gombon	Ind	18	barrel	Fish, Herring White	4	10	0	0
		7	mease	Fish, Herring Red	0	35	0	0
		3	quarter	Fish, Hake	0	7	6	0
		2	piece	Whitelles	0	6	8	0
		12	lb	Wax	0	4	0	0

Merchant name	Origin	Qty	Unit	Commodity	£	s.	d.	f.
David Qwirke	Ind	3	C	Skins, Sheep (no wool)	0	30	0	0
		12	piece	Mantles	0	40	0	0
		1	C	Skins, Lamb	0	5	0	0
		10	lb	Wax	0	3	4	0
		1	barrel	Fish, Eels	0	6	8	0
Edmund Doughe	Ind	5	C	Skins, Sheep (no wool)	0	50	0	0
		30	lb	Wax	0	10	0	0
		8	piece	Mantles	0	26	8	0
Richard Harte	Ind	5	C	Skins, Sheep (no wool)	0	50	0	0
		10	barrel	Fish, Herring White	0	50	0	0
		1	dicker	Hides, Salted	0	13	4	0
		1	quarter	Fish, Hake	0	2	6	0
		20	lb	Wax	0	6	8	0
		2	piece	Mantles	0	6	8	0
Richard Arthure	Ind	40	lb	Wax	0	13	4	0
		4	barrel	Fish, Herring White	0	20	0	0
Peter Cassie	Ind	8	barrel	Fish, Herring White	0	40	0	0
		1	quarter	Fish, Hake	0	2	6	0
		2	piece	Mantles	0	6	8	0
Laurence Walshe	Ind	3	barrel	Fish, Herring White	0	15	0	0
		1	mease	Fish, Herring Red	0	5	0	0
John Sewre	Ind	2	piece	Goshawk	4	0	0	0
Arthur Shethe	Ind	1	C	Fish, Hake	0	10	0	0
		1.5	C	Skins, Sheep (no wool)	0	15	0	0
Peter Kalley	Ind	6	barrel	Fish, Herring White	0	30	0	0
		1	mease	Fish, Herring Red	0	5	0	0
		2	piece	Mantles	0	6	8	0
		0.5	quarter	Fish, Hake	0	0	15	0
William Tirrie	Ind	10	pipe	Fish, Salmon	15	0	0	0
		10	dicker	Hides, Salted	6	13	4	0
		17	barrel	Fish, Herring White	4	5	0	0

Bata George of *Nongell*, John Jeffereis master, from Ireland, 18th December 1503

Merchant name	Origin	Qty	Unit	Commodity	£	s.	d.	f.
John Jeffereis	Ind	11	barrel	Fish, Herring White	0	55	0	0
		6	C	Fish, Hake	0	60	0	0
		1	burden	Fish, Salted	0	3	4	0
Cataunis de Gremaldes	Alien	9	pipe	Fish, Salmon	13	10	0	0
Thomas Lombard	Ind	12	barrel	Fish, Herring White	0	60	0	0
		3	quarter	Fish, Hake	0	7	6	0
		0.5	burden	Fish, Salted	0	0	20	0
		1	dicker	Hides, Salted	0	13	4	0
		1.16	C	Skins, Sheep (no wool)	0	11	8	0
		0.5	C	Skins, Lamb	0	2	6	0
		1	piece	Mantles	0	3	4	0
Henry Maye	Ind	5	C	Fish, Hake	0	50	0	0
		12	barrel	Fish, Herring White	0	60	0	0
		63.5	lb	Wax	0	21	2	0
		1	C	Skins, Sheep (no wool)	0	10	0	0
John Jeffereis	Ind	0.5	burden	Fish, Salted	0	0	20	0

Merchant name	Origin	Qty	Unit	Commodity	£	s.	d.	f.

Bata Patrick of *Baldeike,* John Massie master, from Ireland, 19th December 1503

Merchant name	Origin	Qty	Unit	Commodity	£	s.	d.	f.
Martin Brent	Ind	10	pipe	Fish, Salmon	15	0	0	0
		25	C	Fish, Hake	12	10	0	0
		6.5	barrel	Fish, Herring White	0	32	6	0
		19	mease	Fish, Herring Red	4	15	0	0
John Lawles	Ind	4	mease	Fish, Herring Red	0	20	0	0
William Kellie	Ind	0.5	burden	Fish, Salted	0	0	20	0
		1	quarter	Fish, Hake	0	2	6	0
Richard Sutton	Ind	1.25	C	Fish, Hake	0	12	6	0
		0.5	C	Fish, Salted	0	10	0	0

Bata Sampson of Cardiff, John Howell master, from Cardiff, *19th December 1503*

Merchant name	Origin	Qty	Unit	Commodity	£	s.	d.	f.
David Leyson	Ind	1	pipe	Woad	0	100	0	0

Bata Mawdlen of Dingle, John Dowde master, from Ireland, *19th December 1503*

Merchant name	Origin	Qty	Unit	Commodity	£	s.	d.	f.
John Dowde, Gerald Man, Raymond Graunte, Richard Spicer & Maurice Flemynge	Ind	7.5	C	Fish, Hake	0	75	0	0
		0.5	C	Fish, Salted	0	10	0	0

Bata Petur of Combwich, William Cowle master, from Ireland, 20th December 1503

Merchant name	Origin	Qty	Unit	Commodity	£	s.	d.	f.
William Cowle	Ind	12	barrel	Fish, Herring White	0	60	0	0
		12	mease	Fish, Herring Red	0	60	0	0
William Smythe	Ind	3.5	barrel	Fish, Herring White	0	17	6	0
		8	mease	Fish, Herring Red	0	40	0	0
Simon Wynsdan	Ind	4	last	Fish, Herring White	12	0	0	0
		12	mease	Fish, Herring Red	0	60	0	0
		7	mease	Fish, Herring Red	0	35	0	0
		3.25	C	Fish, Hake	0	32	6	0
		2.25	C	Fish, Hake	0	22	6	0
		0.75	pipe	Fish, Salmon	0	22	6	0
		4	C	Skins, Sheep (no wool)	0	40	0	0
		1	piece	Mantles	0	3	4	0
Vincent White	Ind	10	barrel	Fish, Herring White	0	50	0	0
		12	mease	Fish, Herring Red	0	60	0	0
		2	piece	Mantles	0	6	8	0
Philip *St Amiton*	Ind	6	barrel	Fish, Herring White	0	30	0	0
		0.75	pipe	Fish, Salmon	0	22	6	0
		2	piece	Mantles	0	6	8	0
David Cornyshe	Ind	12	barrel	Fish, Herring White	0	60	0	0
		4	mease	Fish, Herring Red	0	20	0	0
		1.25	C	Fish, Hake	0	12	6	0
James White	Ind	1	barrel	Fish, Herring White	0	5	0	0
Simon Wyndsdon	Ind	2	stone	Wool, Flocks	0	0	10	0

Merchant name	Origin	Qty	Unit	Commodity	£	s.	d.	f.
Navicula Mathewe of Bristol, Edmund Griffeth master, to Ireland, *20th December 1503*								
Hugh Eliet	Ind	6	tun	Wine, Corrupt	9	0	0	0
		12	lb	Silk, Worked	8	0	0	0
		3	ton	Salt	0	50	0	0
		4	C	Aniseed	0	40	0	0
		12	stone	Orchil, Worked	0	20	0	0
		2	harrel	Honey	0	23	4	0
		11	piece	Cloth of Assize	0	0	0	0
Edmund Griffeth	Ind	2	piece	Cloth of Assize	0	0	0	0
		20	lb	*Pilus Tinctus*	0	6	8	0
Bata John of Gatcombe, John Male master, from Ireland, *20th December 1503*								
John Male	Ind	3	last	Fish, Herring White	9	0	0	0
		1	C	Fish, Hake	0	10	0	0
John Markes	Ind	6.5	barrel	Fish, Herring White	0	32	6	0
		1	C	Fish, Hake	0	10	0	0
		1	mease	Fish, Herring Red	0	5	0	0
John Snell	Ind	12.5	barrel	Fish, Herring White	0	62	6	0
		1	mease	Fish, Herring Red	0	5	0	0
		4	piece	Mantles	0	13	4	0
Thomas Dryver	Ind	5.5	barrel	Fish, Herring White	0	27	6	0
		1	mease	Fish, Herring Red	0	5	0	0
Richard Hyman	Ind	3	barrel	Fish, Herring White	0	15	0	0
John Burnan	Ind	20	barrel	Fish, Herring White	0	100	0	0
		5	mease	Fish, Herring Red	0	25	0	0
		1.5	pipe	Fish, Salmon	0	45	0	0
		13	piece	Mantles	0	43	4	0
		12	stone	Wool, Flocks	0	3	9	0
		30	piece	Skins, Sheep (no wool)	0	6	8	0
Navicula Mare Towre, Port Unknown,[4] John Graunte master, from Lisbon, 22nd December 1503								
John Graunte	Alien	1	tun	Wine	0	0	0	0
Thomas Smythe	Ind	27.5	tun	Wine	0	0	0	0
		25	C	Wax	0	0	0	0
Nicholas Browne	Ind	2.5	tun	Wine	0	0	0	0
John Shipman	Ind	2	tun	Wine	0	0	0	0
George Monos	Ind	8.75	tun	Wine	0	0	0	0
David Leyson	Ind	2.75	tun	Wine	0	0	0	0
Roger Dawes	Ind	4.5	tun	Wine	0	0	0	0
Richard Hobie	Ind	4.5	tun	Wine	0	0	0	0
John Benet	Ind	3.5	tun	Wine	0	0	0	0
Maurice Leney	Ind	2	tun	Wine	0	0	0	0
John Leye	Ind	0.5	tun	Wine	0	0	0	0
Ralph Aprise	Ind	1	tun	Wine	0	0	0	0
		162	lb	Wax	0	54	0	0
William Bathe	Ind	2	C	Pepper	10	0	0	0

4 This is almost definitely a Bristol ship. A ship of the same name is found in the 1516 account, with Bristol recorded as the port of registration.

Merchant name	Origin	Qty	Unit	Commodity	£	s.	d.	f.
		1	quarter	G [ ]mes, Portugal[5]	0	33	4	0
John Turnor	Ind	5.25	tun	Wine	0	0	0	0
		5	C	Wax	10	0	0	0
John Halle	Ind	13.5	tun	Wine	0	0	0	0
		1.5	tun	Oil, Olive	6	0	0	0
		818	lb	Wax	11	12	8	0
		3	C	Pepper	15	0	0	0
		3	quarter	Kermes	0	6	0	0
		5	dozen	Cork, Black	0	8	4	0
John Stokes	Ind	3.5	tun	Wine	0	0	0	0
William Estbie	Ind	5.75	tun	Wine	0	0	0	0
		194	lb	Wax	0	64	8	0
John Vaghan	Ind	4.5	tun	Wine	0	0	0	0
John Bonware	Ind	2.25	tun	Wine	0	0	0	0
Richard Amerike	Ind	1	tun	Wine	0	0	0	0
		3	C	Wax	6	0	0	0
		1	C	Pepper	0	100	0	0
Robert Barrero	Ind	144	lb	Wax	0	48	0	0
John Rowland	Ind	5	tun	Wine	0	0	0	0
William Jeffereis	Ind	4.5	tun	Wine	0	0	0	0
		6	C	Wax	12	0	0	0
John Popley	Ind	1.75	tun	Wine	0	0	0	0
		3	quarter	Wax	0	30	0	0
John Colas	Ind	6.875	tun	Wine	0	0	0	0
		590	lb	Wax	9	16	8	0
John Ffarre	Ind	1.5	tun	Wine	0	0	0	0
William Bathe	Ind	20	lb	Pepper	0	16	8	0
David Vaghan	Ind	2.5	tun	Wine	0	0	0	0
Humphrey Bradley	Ind	0.5	tun	Wine	0	0	0	0
John Esturfeld	Ind	2.75	tun	Wine	0	0	0	0
		174	lb	Wax	0	58	0	0
William Tirrie	Ind	0.5	tun	Wine	0	0	0	0
		188	lb	Wax	0	62	8	0
John Graunte	Alien	3	M	Oranges	0	30	0	0
		0.25	tun	Wine	0	0	0	0
Thomas Jones	Ind	1	M	Oranges	0	10	0	0
		8	M	Fertes[6]	0	20	0	0
John Bonware	Ind	4	rove	Marmalade	0	10	0	0
		0.5	hogshead	Wine	0	0	0	0
John Lorde & Philip Tewe	Ind	2	C	Marmalade	0	20	0	0
William Tirrie & Humphrey Bosgrove	Ind	1	C	Marmalade	0	10	0	0
John Turnor	Ind	1	M	Oranges	0	10	0	0
Humphrey Grey	Alien	1	rove	Marmalade	0	2	6	0
John Graunte	Alien	0.5	hogshead	Vinegar	0	5	0	0
		1	C	Smigmates	0	6	8	0
		2.5	C	Marmalade	0	25	0	0
William Hofe	Ind	32	dozen	Cork, Black	0	53	4	0
Philip Tewe	Ind	5	dozen	Cork, Black	0	8	4	0

5 Unidentified commodity. 6 Unidentified commodity.

Merchant name	Origin	Qty	Unit	Commodity	£	s.	d.	f.

Navicula Katren of Bristol, Robert Avyntre master, to Andalusia, _22nd December 1503_

Merchant name	Origin	Qty	Unit	Commodity	£	s.	d.	f.
George Monos	Ind	20	piece	Cloth of Assize	0	0	0	0
John James	Ind	66	dozen	Skins, Calf Tanned	7	0	0	0
Roger Dawes	Ind	7	piece	Cloth of Assize	0	0	0	0
Philip Grene	Ind	6	piece	Welsh _Cloth_	6	0	0	0
Humphrey Bosgrove	Ind	16	piece	Cloth of Assize	0	0	0	0
Richard Draper	Ind	2	piece	Welsh _Cloth_	0	40	0	0
Richard Draper	Ind	2	piece	Welsh _Cloth_	0	40	0	0
Thomas Davy	Ind	3	piece	Welsh _Cloth_	0	60	0	0
Thomas Davy	Ind	2	piece	Mantles	0	6	8	0
John Lorde	Ind	4	piece	Welsh _Cloth_	4	0	0	0
John Benet	Ind	14	piece	Cloth of Assize	0	0	0	0
Robert Thorne	Ind	3	piece	Cloth of Assize	0	0	0	0
Robert Thorne	Ind	5	piece	Cloth of Assize, Kersey	0	0	0	0
George Monos	Ind	4	piece	Cloth of Assize	0	0	0	0
Robert Avyntre &								
John James	Ind	15	piece	Cloth of Assize	0	0	0	0
		3	piece	Welsh _Cloth_	3	0	0	0
		4	piece	Welsh _Cloth_, Dozen Strait	0	16	8	0
Thomas Davy	Ind	1	piece	Welsh _Cloth_, Dozen Strait	0	4	2	0
John Burnell	Ind	1	piece	Welsh _Cloth_	0	20	0	0
John Lorde	Ind	1	piece	Cloth of Assize, Kersey	0	0	0	0
John Marchall	Ind	14	piece	Cloth of Assize	0	0	0	0
		8	piece	Welsh _Cloth_	8	0	0	0

Bata Trynite of Cork, Peter Butlare master, from Ireland, 2nd January 1504

Merchant name	Origin	Qty	Unit	Commodity	£	s.	d.	f.
Gerald Goold	Ind	28.5	barrel	Fish, Herring White	7	2	6	0
		11	mease	Fish, Herring Red	0	55	0	0
		3.5	C	Fish, Hake	0	35	0	0
		6	piece	Mantles	0	20	0	0
Richard Mathewe	Ind	23.5	barrel	Fish, Herring White	0	117	6	0
		6	mease	Fish, Herring Red	0	30	0	0
		2	piece	Mantles	0	6	8	0
John Richarde	Ind	19	barrel	Fish, Herring White	4	15	0	0
		8.5	mease	Fish, Herring Red	0	42	6	0
		1	C	Fish, Hake	0	10	0	0
Nicholas Pouche	Ind	4	barrel	Fish, Herring White	0	20	0	0
		6	mease	Fish, Herring Red	0	30	0	0
		1	C	Fish, Hake	0	10	0	0
		8	piece	Mantles	0	26	8	0
William Walshe	Ind	6	barrel	Fish, Herring White	0	30	0	0
		4	mease	Fish, Herring Red	0	20	0	0
		1.5	C	Fish, Hake	0	15	0	0
James Tirrie	Ind	6	piece	Mantles	0	20	0	0
Matthew Hoper &								
John Rowsack	Ind	12	barrel	Fish, Herring White	0	60	0	0
		2	mease	Fish, Herring Red	0	10	0	0
William Clarke	Ind	2	C	Fish, Hake	0	20	0	0
		8.5	mease	Fish, Herring Red	0	42	6	0
		5	barrel	Fish, Herring White	0	25	0	0

Merchant name	Origin	Qty	Unit	Commodity	£	s.	d.	f.
		0.5	pipe	Fish, Salmon	0	15	0	0
		2	piece	Mantles	0	6	8	0
William Jeffereis	Ind	18	barrel	Fish, Herring White	4	10	0	0
William Flemynge	Ind	7	barrel	Fish, Herring White	0	35	0	0
John Rowland	Ind	23.5	barrel	Fish, Herring White	0	117	6	0
William Clarke	Ind	1	barrel	Fish, Eels	0	6	8	0
Katherine Ffosse	Ind	1.5	C	Fish, Hake	0	15	0	0
		1.25	C	Fish, Hake	0	12	6	0
		1	virken	Fish, Salmon	0	7	6	0
William Aphowell	Ind	8	barrel	Fish, Herring White	0	40	0	0
John Colas	Ind	19	barrel	Fish, Herring White	4	15	0	0

Navicula Franses of Bristol, William Downe master, from Ireland, *2nd January 1504*

Merchant name	Origin	Qty	Unit	Commodity	£	s.	d.	f.
William Downe,								
William Tirrie &								
Humphrey Browne	Ind	58	piece	Hides, Salted	0	77	4	0
		5.5	barrel	Fish, Herring White	0	27	6	0
		9	mease	Fish, Herring Red	0	45	0	0
		3	piece	Mantles	0	10	0	0
		100	lb	Wax	0	33	4	0
		0.625	C	Fish, Hake	0	6	3	0
		0.5	burden	Fish, Salted	0	0	20	0
		0.5	C	Fish, Hake	0	5	0	0
John Brown	Ind	10	dicker	Hides, Salted	6	13	4	0
Richard Arthur	Ind	21.5	barrel	Fish, Herring White	0	107	6	0
		13	C	Skins, Sheep (no wool)	6	10	0	0
		8	dicker	Hides, Salted	0	106	8	0
		2.5	barrel	Fish, Eels	0	16	8	0
		1	C	Skins, Lamb	0	5	0	0
		1	C	Wax	0	40	0	0
		2	C	*Rowse*	0	20	0	0
		2	dozen	Skins, Fox	0	3	0	0
		0.5	burden	Fish, Salted	0	0	20	0
Graunte	Alien	?	?	?	0	15	0	0
Richard Arthure	Ind	?	?	?	0	46	8	0
Nicholas Bailie	Ind	54	barrel	Fish, Herring White	13	10	0	0
		5	pipe	Fish, Salmon	7	10	0	0
		1.5	C	Fish, Hake	0	15	0	0
		1.5	burden	Fish, Salted	0	5	0	0
		20	lb	Wax	0	6	8	0
William Rise	Ind	3.5	last	Fish, Herring White	10	10	0	0
		2	pipe	Fish, Salmon	0	60	0	0
		9	C	Fish, Hake	4	10	0	0
		2	burden	Fish, Salted	0	6	8	0
John Lorde	Ind	4	barrel	Fish, Herring White	0	20	0	0
		20	stone	Wool, Flocks	0	8	4	0
William Tirrie	Ind	8.5	barrel	Fish, Herring White	0	42	6	0
Philip Amerike	Ind	2	piece	Mantles	0	6	8	0
		6	lb	Wax	0	2	0	0
		8	stone	Wool, Flocks	0	3	4	0
William Rise	Ind	1.25	burden	Fish, Salted	0	4	2	0

Merchant name	Origin	Qty	Unit	Commodity	£	s.	d.	f.

Bata Mawdolen of Berkeley, Thomas Senekur master, to Ireland, 2nd January 1504

| Richard Bochere | Ind | 8 | wey | Malt | 0 | 106 | 8 | 0 |

Bata Trinite of Chepstow, William Heyn master, from Chepstow, 3rd January 1504

| Manuel Caldere | Alien | 6.5 | C | Wood, Brazil, New World | 10 | 16 | 8 | 0 |
| | | 1 | C | Kermes | 4 | 0 | 0 | 0 |

Bata George of Gatcombe, Walter Nashe master, to Ireland, 3rd January 1504

| *Walter Nashe* | Ind | 10 | wey | Beans & Malt | 6 | 13 | 4 | 0 |

Bata Sundaie of Kinsale, Laurence Tobie master, from Ireland, 5th January 1504

David Shene	Ind	34	C	Fish, Hake	18	0	0	0
		8	burden	Fish, Salted	0	26	8	0
		13	barrel	Fish, Herring White	0	65	0	0
John Denys	Ind	1	M	Fish, Hake	0	100	0	0
		14	barrel	Fish, Herring White	0	70	0	0
		60	yard	Check *Cloth*	0	20	0	0
John Chesan	Ind	10	barrel	Fish, Herring White	0	50	0	0
William Hogan	Ind	3.08	piece	Fish, Hake	0	30	10	0
		7	barrel	Fish, Herring White	0	35	0	0
		1.25	burden	Fish, Salted	0	4	0	0
William Nele	Ind	1.5	C	Fish, Hake	0	15	0	0
		1	quarter	Fish, Salted	0	0	10	0
		4	barrel	Fish, Herring White	0	20	0	0
Edmund Braynok	Ind	5	barrel	Fish, Herring White	0	25	0	0
		1.5	C	Fish, Hake	0	15	0	0
John Downar	Ind	1	C	Fish, Hake	0	10	0	0
		0.5	burden	Fish, Salted	0	0	20	0

Navicula George of Mounts Bay, John Down master, from Bordeaux, 9th January 1504

John Down	Ind	2.5	tun	Wine	0	0	0	0
Roger Dawes	Ind	26	tun	Wine	0	0	0	0
John Popley	Ind	3	tun	Wine	0	0	0	0
William Estbie	Ind	3.5	tun	Wine	0	0	0	0
Robert Rowlowe	Ind	9	tun	Wine	0	0	0	0
John Shipman	Ind	14	tun	Wine	0	0	0	0
		6	ton	Iron	15	0	0	0
John Ware	Ind	4.5	tun	Wine	0	0	0	0
Robert Thorn	Ind	1.75	tun	Wine	0	0	0	0
William Hurste	Ind	2	tun	Wine	0	0	0	0
Thomas Smyth	Ind	2	tun	Wine	0	0	0	0
James Cooke	Ind	0.5	tun	Wine	0	0	0	0
Robert Barrero	Ind	2.5	tun	Wine	0	0	0	0
Henry Goodale	Ind	1.25	tun	Wine	0	0	0	0
John Hickes	Ind	1	tun	Wine	0	0	0	0
John Harries	Ind	0.5	tun	Wine	0	0	0	0
Martin Hoken	Ind	0.5	tun	Wine	0	0	0	0

Merchant name	Origin	Qty	Unit	Commodity	£	s.	d.	f.
John Davy	Alien	0.25	tun	Wine	0	0	0	0
Oliver Marten	Alien	0.75	tun	Wine	0	0	0	0
Laurence John	Ind	0.75	tun	Wine	0	0	0	0

Bata Conell of Kinsale, Richard Walshe master, from Ireland, 9th January 1504

					£	s.	d.	f.
Hugh Prise	Ind	19	C	Fish, Hake	9	10	0	0
		11	barrel	Fish, Herring White	0	55	0	0
		15	burden	Fish, Salted	0	50	0	0
		0.5	pipe	Fish, Salmon	0	15	0	0
James Mores	Ind	16.5	barrel	Fish, Herring White	4	2	6	0
		6	C	Fish, Hake	0	60	0	0
		5	burden	Fish, Salted	0	16	8	0

Bata Michaell of Minehead, Tege Porter master, from Ireland, 9th January 1504

					£	s.	d.	f.
William Scochen	Ind	8.5	C	Fish, Hake	4	5	0	0
		1.25	burden	Fish, Salted	0	4	2	0
		1.25	C	Skins, Sheep (no wool)	0	12	6	0
		9	piece	Mantles	0	30	0	0
		24	yard	Check Cloth	0	8	0	0
John Brewar	Ind	1.5	C	Fish, Salted	0	30	0	0
Tege Porter	Ind	3	last	Fish, Herring White	9	0	0	0
		1	C	Fish, Hake	0	10	0	0
William Veele	Ind	2	C	Fish, Hake	0	20	0	0
		4	barrel	Fish, Herring White	0	20	0	0
		1	C	Fish, Salted	0	20	0	0
David Blake	Ind	1.5	C	Fish, Salted	0	30	0	0
		1	barrel	Fish, Herring White	0	5	0	0
Richard Skynner	Ind	30.5	barrel	Fish, Herring White	7	12	6	0
David Blake	Ind	0.5	C	Fish, Hake	0	5	0	0

Bata Nicolas of Minehead, Henry Veele master, from Ireland, 10th January 1504

					£	s.	d.	f.
Richard Eliet	Ind	44	barrel	Fish, Herring White	11	0	0	0
Richard Dawton	Ind	4.5	C	Fish, Hake	0	45	0	0

Navicula Gelian of Bristol, John Arnold master, from Bordeaux, 10th January 1504

					£	s.	d.	f.
William Stephyns	Ind	10.75	tun	Wine	0	0	0	0
Stephen Ffoster & John Meysam	Ind	4	tun	Wine	0	0	0	0
John Wiot	Ind	1.75	tun	Wine	0	0	0	0
William Plomer	Ind	1	tun	Wine	0	0	0	0
John Keepe	Ind	3.5	tun	Wine	0	0	0	0
Richard Hobie	Ind	1.75	tun	Wine	0	0	0	0
John Pollard	Ind	5.75	tun	Wine	0	0	0	0
Thomas Jones	Ind	0.5	tun	Wine	0	0	0	0
Thomas Hawkens	Ind	1.75	tun	Wine	0	0	0	0
John Shipman	Ind	4.25	tun	Wine	0	0	0	0
		1.5	tun	Rosin	0	26	8	0
Robert Thorn	Ind	1.75	tun	Wine	0	0	0	0

Merchant name	Origin	Qty	Unit	Commodity	£	s.	d.	f.
Thomas Barne	Ind	1	tun	Wine	0	0	0	0
John Shipman	Ind	0.25	tun	Wine	0	0	0	0
Thomas Gryen	Alien	2	C	Rosin	0	2	8	0

Bata Sondaie of Minehead, William Butlare master, from Ireland, 14th January 1504

William Butlare	Ind	3.5	last	Fish, Herring White	10	10	0	0

Bata Trinite of Chepstow, Robert Bocher master, from Ireland, 14th January 1504

John Rowsack	Ind	15.5	barrel	Fish, Herring White	0	77	6	0
William Clarke	Ind	0.5	tun	Wine	0	0	0	0

Bata Trinite of Kinsale, Germain Hole master, from Ireland, 16th January 1504

Cornell Makon	Ind	37.5	C	Fish, Hake	18	15	0	0
		17.5	barrel	Fish, Herring White	4	7	6	0
		15	burden	Fish, Salted	0	50	0	0

Navicula Christofure of Bristol, John Barnard master, from Bordeaux, 16th January 1504

John Barnard	Ind	2.75	tun	Wine	0	0	0	0
George Mones	Ind	28.5	tun	Wine	0	0	0	0
		6	pipe	Fish, Salmon	9	0	0	0
		3	pipe	Woad	15	0	0	0
John Shipman	Ind	0.375	tun	Wine	0	0	0	0
William Jeffereis	Ind	2	tun	Wine	0	0	0	0
Robert Avyntre	Ind	1	tun	Wine	0	0	0	0
John Ware	Ind	3	tun	Wine	0	0	0	0
John Qwirke	Ind	2	tun	Wine	0	0	0	0
		1	hogshead	Rosin	0	6	8	0
William Meriell	Ind	2.25	tun	Wine	0	0	0	0
John Bedford	Ind	1	hogshead	Rosin	0	6	8	0

Navicula Jhesus Bonaventure, Port Unknown,[7] Henry Heurte master, from Bordeaux, 16th January 1504

John Shipman	Ind	3	pipe	Woad	15	0	0	0
Robert Rowlowe	Ind	5	tun	Wine	0	0	0	0
		1	pipe	Woad	0	100	0	0
John Ryngston	Ind	2	tun	Wine	0	0	0	0
Nicholas Brown	Ind	7	tun	Wine	0	0	0	0
John Jansie	Ind	6	pipe	Woad	30	0	0	0
John Esurfeld	Ind	7.5	tun	Wine	0	0	0	0
Richard Draper	Ind	1.5	tun	Wine	0	0	0	0
Edmund Hyman	Ind	4.75	tun	Wine	0	0	0	0
William Estbie	Ind	1.75	tun	Wine	0	0	0	0
Thomas Hawkens	Ind	1.75	tun	Wine	0	0	0	0
William Jeffereis	Ind	21.833	tun	Wine	0	0	0	0
John Vaghan	Ind	9	tun	Wine	0	0	0	0
William Jeffereis	Ind	3	pipe	Woad	15	0	0	0

7 Possibly Bristol.

Merchant name	Origin	Qty	Unit	Commodity	£	s.	d.	f.
		5	mesure	Woad	1	11	3	0
		2	tun	Rosin	0	53	4	0
John Turnor	Ind	1	tun	Wine	0	0	0	0
John Jones	Ind	1	tun	Wine	0	0	0	0
Thomas Baone	Ind	1	tun	Wine	0	0	0	0
William Hurste	Ind	3.75	tun	Wine	0	0	0	0
Richard Hobie	Ind	10.75	tun	Wine	0	0	0	0
William Tirrie	Ind	1.75	tun	Wine	0	0	0	0
William Aphowell	Ind	7	tun	Wine	0	0	0	0
		3	pipe	Woad	15	0	0	0
		1	pipe	Rosin	0	13	4	0
John Rowland	Ind	9	tun	Wine	0	0	0	0
George Monos	Ind	3	pipe	Woad	15	0	0	0
John Lorde	Ind	1	pipe	Wine	0	0	0	0
		1	pipe	Vinegar	0	20	0	0
Thomas Ffenne	Ind	4	tun	Wine	0	0	0	0
Philip Ringston	Ind	6	pipe	Woad	30	0	0	0
Henry Dale	Ind	5.75	tun	Wine	0	0	0	0
Richard Gaie	Ind	1	hogshead	Wine	0	0	0	0
		1	pipe	Rosin	0	13	4	0
Stephen Ffostar &								
John Meysam	Ind	2.75	tun	Wine	0	0	0	0
David Vaghan	Ind	3.5	tun	Wine	0	0	0	0
John Robens	Ind	0.5	tun	Wine	0	0	0	0
Thomas Osney	Ind	2.5	pipe	Woad	12	10	0	0
		2.75	tun	Wine	0	0	0	0
William Jeffereis	Ind	1	hogshead	Pitch	0	6	8	0
Stephen Ffostar	Ind	1	hogshead	Wine	0	0	0	0
Stephen de luse	Alien	1	pipe	Rosin	0	13	4	0
William Aphowell	Ind	1	pipe	Woad	0	100	0	0

Bata Patrike of Kinsale, William Donell master, from Ireland, *16th January 1504*

Merchant name	Origin	Qty	Unit	Commodity	£	s.	d.	f.
Patrick Wente	Ind	2	M	Fish, Hake	10	0	0	0
		8	C	Fish, Hake	4	0	0	0
		17	barrel	Fish, Herring White	4	5	0	0
		9	burden	Fish, Salted	0	30	0	0
William Ley	Ind	21	barrel	Fish, Herring White	0	105	0	0
		15	C	Fish, Hake	7	10	0	0
		1.5	burden	Fish, Salted	0	5	0	0
Thomas Roche	Ind	7	barrel	Fish, Herring White	0	35	0	0
		2	C	Fish, Hake	0	20	0	0
		1	burden	Fish, Salted	0	3	4	0

Navicula Gabriell of Bristol, David Nono master, from Andalusia, *16th January 1504*

Merchant name	Origin	Qty	Unit	Commodity	£	s.	d.	f.
Hugh Eliet	Ind	11.5	tun	Wine	0	0	0	0
		11	ton	Fruit	22	0	0	0
		24	C	Orchil	12	0	0	0
Robert Thorn	Ind	10	tun	Wine	0	0	0	0
		2	ton	Fruit	4	0	0	0
		28.5	C	Orchil	14	5	0	0

Merchant name	Origin	Qty	Unit	Commodity	£	s.	d.	f.
Roger Dreyton	Ind	5	ton	Fruit	10	0	0	0
John Jaie	Ind	4.75	tun	Wine	0	0	0	0
William Tirrie	Ind	1	tun	Wine	0	0	0	0
William Jeffereis	Ind	1.25	tun	Oil, Olive	0	100	0	0
		1	tun	Wine	0	0	0	0
Ralph Aprise	Ind	1	tun	Wine	0	0	0	0
Roger Dawes	Ind	4	tun	Wine	0	0	0	0
Roger Dawes	Ind	1.5	ton	Fruit	0	60	0	0
John Ynon	Ind	3	tun	Wine	0	0	0	0
Thomas Smythe	Ind	1	tun	Wine	0	0	0	0
		6.25	C	Almonds	4	3	4	0
John Knottinge	Ind	1.5	tun	Wine	0	0	0	0
John Edee	Ind	1	tun	Wine	0	0	0	0
John Eliet	Ind	2.75	tun	Wine	0	0	0	0
John Popley	Ind	3	tun	Wine	0	0	0	0
William Estbie	Ind	3	tun	Wine	0	0	0	0
John Colens	Ind	1	tun	Wine	0	0	0	0
Robert Ffortey	Ind	1.5	tun	Wine	0	0	0	0
Henry Collar	Ind	2.5	tun	Wine	0	0	0	0
David Nono	Ind	1.25	tun	Wine	0	0	0	0
John Halle	Ind	1.5	tun	Wine	0	0	0	0
John Thomas	Ind	1	tun	Wine	0	0	0	0
John Lorde	Ind	0.75	tun	Wine	0	0	0	0
Thomas Osney	Ind	2	tun	Wine	0	0	0	0
Henry Ponchard	Ind	4.5	tun	Wine	0	0	0	0
		3	ton	Fruit	6	0	0	0
John Lostes	Ind	2.5	tun	Wine	0	0	0	0
John Edee	Ind	1	pipe	Wine	0	0	0	0
David Wynter	Ind	1	pipe	Wine	0	0	0	0
John Popley	Ind	1	pipe	Wine	0	0	0	0
Thomas Evan	Ind	1	pipe	Wine	0	0	0	0
William Witynge	Ind	1	pipe	Wine	0	0	0	0
John Crabbe	Ind	2	tun	Wine	0	0	0	0
William Dodinge	Ind	1	tun	Wine	0	0	0	0
William Thorn	Ind	1.5	tun	Wine	0	0	0	0
Roger Dawes	Ind	1	tun	Wine	0	0	0	0
Thomas Beck	Ind	1.25	ton	Fruit	0	50	0	0

Navicula Michaell of Bristol, Richard Braie master, from Andalusia, _16th January 1504_

Merchant name	Origin	Qty	Unit	Commodity	£	s.	d.	f.
Hugh Eliet	Ind	5	tun	Wine	0	0	0	0
John Jaie & Hugh Eliet	Ind	6.5	ton	Fruit	13	0	0	0
Hugh Eliet	Ind	5	C	Orchil	0	50	0	0
John Jaie	Ind	5	tun	Wine	0	0	0	0
Robert Thorn	Ind	7.5	tun	Wine	0	0	0	0
		4.25	ton	Fruit	8	10	0	0
		2	ton	Fruit	4	0	0	0
		2.5	C	Orchil	0	25	0	0
William Tirrie	Ind	2.75	tun	Wine	0	0	0	0
		2	C	Dates[8]	0	20	0	0

8 Recorded as 'dactul'. The OED defines dactyl as the fruit of the date palm and the value given here suggests that these are dates.

Merchant name	Origin	Qty	Unit	Commodity	£	s.	d.	f.
Thomas Beck	Ind	4.5	tun	Wine	0	0	0	0
John Andrewe	Ind	4.5	tun	Wine	0	0	0	0
Henry Pouchard	Ind	4.75	tun	Wine	0	0	0	0
Simon Andrewe	Ind	9.5	tun	Wine	0	0	0	0
Richard Bakar	Ind	7.75	tun	Wine	0	0	0	0
John Colens	Ind	1	tun	Wine	0	0	0	0
		0.75	ton	Fruit	0	30	0	0
John Popley	Ind	1.75	tun	Wine	0	0	0	0
John Thomas	Ind	1.75	tun	Wine	0	0	0	0
		1	pipe	Fruit	0	20	0	0
John Halle	Ind	1	pipe	Wine	0	0	0	0
John Colens	Ind	1	tierce	Wine	0	0	0	0
Robert Thorn	Ind	8	C	Hops	0	40	0	0
		2.5	C	Orchil	0	25	0	0
		1	pipe	Fruit	0	20	0	0

Bata Kereck of Milford Haven, John Thomas master, from Milford Haven *16th January 1504*

Merchant name	Origin	Qty	Unit	Commodity	£	s.	d.	f.
Richard Reede	Ind	5	tun	Wine	0	0	0	0

Navicula Gelian Bonaventur, Port Unknown, William Claron master, from Bordeaux, 17th January 1504

Merchant name	Origin	Qty	Unit	Commodity	£	s.	d.	f.
William Jeffereis	Ind	4	measure	Woad	0	25	0	0
John Shipman	Ind	3	pipe	Woad	15	0	0	0
William Aphowell	Ind	3	tun	Wine	0	0	0	0
		73	measure	Woad	12	16	3	0
		1	pipe	Rosin	0	13	4	0
John Taylor	Ind	2	pipe	Woad	10	0	0	0
		1	pipe	Wine	0	0	0	0
John Rowland	Ind	2	tun	Wine	0	0	0	0
Richard Symons	Ind	4.25	tun	Wine	0	0	0	0
Richard Symons	Ind	1	pipe	Rosin	0	13	4	0
Philip Grene	Ind	2.25	tun	Wine	0	0	0	0
Nicholas Browne	Ind	7.5	tun	Wine	0	0	0	0
Richard Hobie	Ind	6	tun	Wine	0	0	0	0
Thomas Smyth	Ind	1	tun	Wine	0	0	0	0
John Jansie	Ind	6.5	tun	Wine	0	0	0	0
John Qwirke	Ind	1.75	tun	Wine	0	0	0	0
Robert Barrero	Ind	1	pipe	Woad	0	100	0	0
Robert Barrero	Ind	1	pipe	Wine	0	0	0	0
Henry Dale	Ind	1	tun	Wine	0	0	0	0
Stephen Ffostar &								
John Meysam	Ind	3	tun	Wine	0	0	0	0
David Vaghan	Ind	1	tun	Wine	0	0	0	0
Thomas Barn	Ind	1.5	tun	Wine	0	0	0	0
William Lane	Ind	1.75	tun	Wine	0	0	0	0
Thomas Aphowell	Ind	2	pipe	Woad	10	0	0	0
		1	hogshead	Wine	0	0	0	0
Richard Vaghan	Ind	8	tun	Wine	0	0	0	0
		3.5	pipe	Woad	17	10	0	0
		1	pipe	Rosin	0	13	4	0

Merchant name	Origin	Qty	Unit	Commodity	£	s.	d.	f.
John Evan	Ind	1	hogshead	Vinegar	0	10	0	0
John Williams	Ind	1	pipe	Rosin	0	13	4	0
Thomas Awsten	Ind	1.75	tun	Wine	0	0	0	0
		3	pipe	Woad	15	0	0	0
William Hurste	Ind	1.166	tun	Wine	0	0	0	0
Richard Gaie	Ind	1	pipe	Woad	0	100	0	0
Robert Ffortey	Ind	2	ton	iron	0	100	0	0
Nicholas Brown	Ind	1	hogshead	Wine	0	0	0	0

Bata Lenard of Waterford, William Gombon master, to Ireland, *17th January 1504*

William Gombon	Ind	1	lb	Silk, Worked	0	13	4	0
		0.5	lb	Saffron	0	3	4	0
Peter Kelley	Ind	30	lb	*Pilus Tinctus*	0	10	0	0
David Qwirke	Ind	3	piece	Cloth of Assize	0	0	0	0
		1	lb	Saffron	0	6	8	0
Thomas Lombard	Ind	4.25	wey	Beans & Malt	0	56	8	0
		10	lb	*Pilus Tinctus*	0	3	4	0
William Gombon &								
Richard Harte	Ind	7.5	wey	Beans & Malt	0	100	0	0
Nicholas Ffox	Ind	3	piece	Cloth of Assize	0	0	0	0
		3	piece	Cloth of Assize, Kersey	0	0	0	0
		3	lb	Silk, Worked	0	40	0	0
		3	lb	Saffron	0	20	0	0
		1	dozen	Caps	0	6	8	0
Ed*mund* Donell	Ind	3	piece	Cloth of Assize	0	0	0	0
		80	lb	*Pilus Tinctus*	0	26	8	0
Thomas Lombard	Ind	14	lb	*Pilus Tinctus*	0	4	8	0

Navicula Mare of Penmarch, Evan Lazar master, from Bordeaux, *17th January 1504*

John Stokes	Ind	1.75	tun	Wine	0	0	0	0
John Jones	Ind	5.5	tun	Wine	0	0	0	0
Thomas Barn	Ind	12.33	tun	Wine	0	0	0	0
Thomas Hawkens	Ind	3	tun	Wine	0	0	0	0
John Jansie	Ind	7.5	tun	Wine	0	0	0	0
Richard Hobie	Ind	1.25	tun	Wine	0	0	0	0
John Shipman	Ind	1	tun	Wine	0	0	0	0
Robert Ffystar	Ind	5.25	tun	Wine	0	0	0	0
William Tirrie	Ind	1	pipe	Wine	0	0	0	0
Thomas Smyth	Ind	7.25	tun	Wine	0	0	0	0
Thomas Awsten	Ind	2.75	tun	Wine	0	0	0	0
William Hurste	Ind	2	tun	Wine	0	0	0	0
John Popley	Ind	2.75	tun	Wine	0	0	0	0
William Stephyns	Ind	4	tun	Wine	0	0	0	0
Evan Danyell	Alien	1	tun	Wine	0	0	0	0
		0.5	C	Britany Linen *Cloth*	0	10	0	0

Bata Mawdlen of Exmouth, Richard Barn master, from Rochell, 18th January 1504

Nicholas Brown	Ind	3.25	tun	Wine	0	0	0	0
Richard Symons	Ind	13.5	tun	Wine	0	0	0	0

Merchant name	Origin	Qty	Unit	Commodity	£	s.	d.	f.
William *Illegible*	Ind	1	tun	Wine	0	0	0	0
Richard Barn	Ind	2	C	*Illegible*	0	2	8	0
William White	Ind	1	hogshead	Wine	0	0	0	0

Bata Andrewe of Youghal, Gerald Powar master, from Ireland, *18th January 1504*

Merchant name	Origin	Qty	Unit	Commodity	£	s.	d.	f.
Gerald Powar	Ind	3.5	C	Fish, Hake	0	35	0	0
		8	barrel	Fish, Herring White	0	40	0	0
		1	burden	Fish, Salted	0	3	4	0
William Donell	Ind	6	C	Fish, Hake	0	60	0	0
		16	barrel	Fish, Herring White	4	0	0	0
		0.5	burden	Fish, Salted	0	0	20	0
Thomas Markes	Ind	14	barrel	Fish, Herring White	0	70	0	0
		1.5	C	Fish, Hake	0	15	0	0
Gerald Powar	Ind	2	C	Fish, Hake	0	20	0	0

Bata Barbara of Minehead, Tege Ffedirsale master, from Ireland, *18th January 1504*

Merchant name	Origin	Qty	Unit	Commodity	£	s.	d.	f.
Tege Fferdisale &								
Edward Powar	Ind	23.5	barrel	Fish, Herring White	0	117	6	0
		1.5	burden	Fish, Salted	0	5	0	0
		3.5	C	Fish, Hake	0	35	0	0
William Ley	Ind	10	barrel	Fish, Herring White	0	50	0	0
John Roche	Ind	6	barrel	Fish, Herring White	0	30	0	0
Thomas Roche	Ind	1	barrel	Fish, Herring White	0	5	0	0
John Dale	Ind	5	barrel	Fish, Herring White	0	25	0	0
Richard Galwey	Ind	1.5	C	Fish, Hake	0	15	0	0
		0.5	burden	Fish, Salted	0	0	20	0

Bata Petur of Berkeley, Thomas Cockes master, to Ireland, 20th January 1504

Merchant name	Origin	Qty	Unit	Commodity	£	s.	d.	f.
Thomas Cockes	Ind	12	wey	Beans & Malt	8	0	0	0

Bata Katren of Hanley Castle, Thomas Butlar master, from Chepstow, 22nd January 1504

Merchant name	Origin	Qty	Unit	Commodity	£	s.	d.	f.
Thomas Smythe	Ind	3.916	tun	Wine	0	0	0	0
John Grene	Ind	1.75	tun	Wine	0	0	0	0
William Hurste	Ind	1	pipe	Woad	0	100	0	0

Navicula Jhesus of Errenteria, Martin de Sesoa master, from Andalusia, *22nd January 1504*

Merchant name	Origin	Qty	Unit	Commodity	£	s.	d.	f.
Martin de Sessoa	Alien	2	tun	Wine	0	0	0	0
George Monos	Ind	11.5	tun	Wine	0	0	0	0
		5	tun	Oil, Olive	20	0	0	0
David Vaghan	Ind	9.5	tun	Wine	0	0	0	0
John Popley	Ind	2.75	tun	Wine	0	0	0	0
John Ringston	Ind	1.75	tun	Wine	0	0	0	0
Robert Barrero	Ind	2.5	tun	Wine	0	0	0	0
Richard Stephens	Ind	1	pipe	Wine	0	0	0	0
John Vaghan	Ind	10.5	tun	Wine	0	0	0	0
William Cogan	Ind	1	tun	Wine	0	0	0	0
David Leyson	Ind	1.75	tun	Wine	0	0	0	0
Matilda Balle	Ind	1	pipe	Wine	0	0	0	0

Merchant name	Origin	Qty	Unit	Commodity	£	s.	d.	f.
William Estbie	Ind	2.25	tun	Wine	o	o	o	o
John Benet	Ind	10	tun	Wine	o	o	o	o
Humphrey Brown	Ind	2.5	tun	Wine	o	o	o	o
Peter Aburden	Alien	11	tun	Wine	o	o	o	o
Humphrey Bosgrove	Ind	2.25	tun	Wine	o	o	o	o
Thomas Smyth	Ind	1	tun	Wine	o	o	o	o
William Jeffereis	Ind	11	tun	Wine	o	o	o	o
John Halle	Ind	1	tun	Wine	o	o	o	o
John Thomas	Ind	1	pipe	Wine	o	o	o	o
Hugh Eliet	Ind	1	pipe	Wine	o	o	o	o
Philip Grene	Ind	2.75	tun	Wine	o	o	o	o
John Smyth	Ind	1.75	ton	Fruit	o	70	o	o
John Colas	Ind	3	tun	Wine	o	o	o	o
Thomas Ffroste	Ind	1.5	tun	Wine	o	o	o	o
John Smythe	Ind	1	hogshead	Fruit	o	10	o	o
John Amomothe	Ind	1	tun	Wine	o	o	o	o
Michael Barbeyro	Alien	3	quarter	Marmalade	o	6	8	o

Navicula Santa Nova, Port Unknown, Evan Cantelet master, from Bordeaux, 23rd January 1504

Merchant name	Origin	Qty	Unit	Commodity	£	s.	d.	f.
Evan Cantelet	Alien	1.5	tun	Rosin	o	40	o	o
		4.5	C	Britany Linen *Cloth*	4	10	o	o
William Cogan	Ind	43	tun	Wine	o	o	o	o
William Aphowell	Ind	2.5	tun	Wine	o	o	o	o
John Williams	Ind	4.75	tun	Wine	o	o	o	o
		1	tun	Rosin	o	26	8	o
James Cooke	Ind	1	tun	Wine	o	o	o	o
Richard Hobie	Ind	11.25	tun	Wine	o	o	o	o
John Popley	Ind	1.75	tun	Wine	o	o	o	o
John Vaghan	Ind	3.5	tun	Wine	o	o	o	o
William Lane	Ind	0.75	tun	Wine	o	o	o	o
Thomas Smyth	Ind	13.166	tun	Wine	o	o	o	o
Roger Dawes	Ind	1.5	tun	Wine	o	o	o	o
David Vaghan	Ind	2.75	tun	Wine	o	o	o	o
Nicholas Browne	Ind	0.33	tun	Wine	o	o	o	o
William Hurste	Ind	0.75	tun	Wine	o	o	o	o
Robert Rowlowe	Ind	4.5	tun	Wine	o	o	o	o
Robert Barrero	Ind	2.5	tun	Wine	o	o	o	o
Robert Avyntre	Ind	0.75	tun	Wine	o	o	o	o
Thomas Hawkens	Ind	1	tun	Wine	o	o	o	o
William Thorn	Ind	0.5	tun	Wine	o	o	o	o
John Jones	Ind	2.5	tun	Wine	o	o	o	o
John Shipman	Ind	3.75	tun	Wine	o	o	o	o
Ambrose de Haies	Alien	2	tun	Wine	o	o	o	o
Thomas Plomley	Ind	0.25	tun	Wine	o	o	o	o
Thomas Maylar	Ind	2	C	Rosin	o	2	8	o

Bata Laurance of Minehead, John Phelipes master, from Ireland, *23rd January 1504*

Merchant name	Origin	Qty	Unit	Commodity	£	s.	d.	f.
John Bolfynche	Ind	116	barrel	Fish, Herring White	29	o	o	o
		20	mease	Fish, Herring Red	o	100	o	o
		1	C	Fish, Hake	o	10	o	o

Merchant name	Origin	Qty	Unit	Commodity	£	s.	d.	f.
Bata Nicolas of Kinsale, Dennis Loden master, from Ireland, _23rd January 1504_								
Dennis Loden	Ind	16.5	barrel	Fish, Herring White	4	2	6	0
		12.5	C	Fish, Hake	6	5	0	0
James Cloke	Ind	15.5	C	Fish, Hake	7	15	0	0
		7	barrel	Fish, Herring White	0	35	0	0
		5	burden	Fish, Salted	0	16	8	0
John Roche	Ind	1	M	Fish, Hake	0	100	0	0
		15	barrel	Fish, Herring White	0	75	0	0
		1.25	burden	Fish, Salted	0	4	2	0
		20	piece	Skins, Sheep (no wool)	0	0	20	0
John Dermyn	Ind	6	barrel	Fish, Herring White	0	30	0	0
Philip Bryne	Ind	5	barrel	Fish, Herring White	0	25	0	0
		2	C	Fish, Hake	0	20	0	0
William Barre	Ind	7	barrel	Fish, Herring White	0	35	0	0
		3	C	Fish, Hake	0	30	0	0
Ed_mund_ Roche	Ind	11	barrel	Fish, Herring White	0	55	0	0
		3	C	Fish, Hake	0	30	0	0
Richard Conell	Ind	5.5	barrel	Fish, Herring White	0	27	6	0
		1	C	Fish, Hake	0	10	0	0
Ed_mund_ Roche	Ind	1	C	Fish, Hake	0	10	0	0
Bata Mawdelen of Berkeley, Thomas Sene_kur_ master, to Ireland, 24th January 1504								
Richard Bocher	Ind	3	piece	Cloth of Assize	0	0	0	0
		4	lb	Saffron	0	26	8	0
		4	gross	Knives	0	26	8	0
Bata Katren of Berkeley, Thomas Kervell master, from Chepsto_w_, _24th January 1504_								
Richard Lepier	Ind	1	tun	Wine	0	0	0	0
Bata Mare of Chepstow, Thomas Smyth master, _from Chepstow, 24th January 1504_								
John Bocher	Ind	1	tun	Wine	0	0	0	0
Thomas Bocher	Ind	1	tun	Wine	0	0	0	0
Navicula Marget of Bristol, Edward Gibbes master, to Bordeaux, 25th January 1504								
Robert Ffortey	Ind	6	piece	Cloth of Assize	0	0	0	0
John Ringston	Ind	2	piece	Cloth of Assize	0	0	0	0
Walter P_a_rkar	Ind	4	piece	Welsh _Cloth_	4	0	0	0
William Tirrie	Ind	6	piece	Cloth of Assize	0	0	0	0
		1	M	Fish, Hake	0	100	0	0
Robert Ffystar	Ind	4	piece	Cloth of Assize	0	0	0	0
Nicholas Brown	Ind	24	piece	Cloth of Assize	0	0	0	0
William Estbie	Ind	6	piece	Cloth of Assize	0	0	0	0
Richard Amerike	Ind	10	piece	Cloth of Assize	0	0	0	0
Ralph Aprise	Ind	1	piece	Cloth of Assize	0	0	0	0
Nicholas Brown	Ind	2	piece	Cloth of Assize	0	0	0	0
David Vaghan	Ind	1.5	piece	Cloth of Assize	0	0	0	0
John Turnor	Ind	1	piece	Cloth of Assize	0	0	0	0
Robert Ffortey	Ind	2	piece	Cloth of Assize	0	0	0	0

Merchant name	Origin	Qty	Unit	Commodity	£	s.	d.	f.
Bata Mare of Chepstow, Owen Gwyn master, from Chepstow, 25th January 1504								
John Wiot	Ind	1	tun	Rosin	0	26	8	0
Owen John	Ind	1	hogshead	Pitch	0	6	8	0
Robert Rowlowe	Ind	0.375	tun	Wine	0	0	0	0
Bata Trynite of Chepstow, Edward Davy master, from Chepstow, 27th January 1504								
William Aphowell	Ind	18	measure	Woad	0	112	6	0
Bata Trynite of Chepstow, Edward Davy master, from Chepstow, 27th January 1504								
William Atwood	Ind	1.25	tun	Wine	0	0	0	0
Edmund Hyman	Ind	0.5	tun	Wine	0	0	0	0
William Hurste	Ind	10	measure	Woad	0	62	6	0
Thomas Aphowell	Ind	6	measure	Woad	0	37	6	0
Navicula Mare of Penmarch, Evan Lazar master, to Brittany, 27th January 1504								
Evan Lazar	Alien	6	wey	Coal	0	23	4	0
		14	tun/ton	Calx	0	35	0	0
James Merike, Evan May & Evan Lazar	Alien	3	piece	Cloth of Assize	6	0	0	0
		5	piece	Mantles	0	16	8	0
Bata Petur of Kinsale, John Roche master, from Ireland, 29th January 1504								
John Roche	Ind	24	barrel	Fish, Herring White	6	0	0	0
		12	C	Fish, Hake	6	0	0	0
		1	virken	Fish, Salmon	0	7	6	0
James Barre	Ind	12	barrel	Fish, Herring White	0	60	0	0
		8	C	Fish, Hake	4	0	0	0
Thomas Donell	Ind	12	barrel	Fish, Herring White	0	60	0	0
		4	C	Fish, Hake	0	40	0	0
		1	burden	Fish, Salted	0	3	4	0
John Roche	Ind	5	barrel	Fish, Herring White	0	25	0	0
		1	burden	Fish, Salted	0	3	4	0
		1.5	C	Fish, Hake	0	15	0	0
Bata Sondaie of Minehead, Thomas Donell master, from Ireland 30th January 1504								
Thomas Donell	Ind	5	last	Fish, Herring White	15	0	0	0
		22.5	C	Fish, Hake	11	5	0	0
		2	burden	Fish, Salted	0	6	8	0
		7	barrel	Fish, Hake	0	35	0	0
		0.5	burden	Fish, Salted	0	0	20	0
Bata Patrike of Minehead, John Goodynowe master, from Ireland, 30th January 1504								
John Goodynowe	Ind	144.5	barrel	Fish, Herring White	36	2	6	0
		1	mease	Fish, Herring Red	0	5	0	0
John Dee	Ind	5	barrel	Fish, Herring White	0	25	0	0

Merchant name	Origin	Qty	Unit	Commodity	£	s.	d.	f.

Bata Katren of New Ross, William Grase master, from Ireland, 31st January 1504

Merchant name	Origin	Qty	Unit	Commodity	£	s.	d.	f.
William Grase	Ind	6	barrel	Fish, Herring White	0	30	0	0
Thomas Benet	Ind	43	barrel	Fish, Herring White	10	15	0	0
		10	piece	Mantles	0	33	4	0
Patrick Kelley	Ind	21.5	barrel	Fish, Herring White	0	107	6	0
		25	piece	Mantles	4	3	4	0
John Clarke	Ind	23	barrel	Fish, Herring White	0	115	0	0
		1	virken	Fish, Salmon	0	7	6	0
		19	piece	Mantles	0	63	4	0
Thomas Shenell	Ind	16	barrel	Fish, Herring White	4	0	0	0
		0.5	pipe	Fish, Salmon	0	15	0	0
		1.5	burden	Fish, Salted	0	5	0	0
		0.5	C	Fish, Hake	0	5	0	0
		6	piece	Mantles	0	20	0	0
Robert Laurens	Ind	3.5	barrel	Fish, Herring White	0	17	6	0
Robert Grase	Ind	5	barrel	Fish, Herring White	0	25	0	0
		3	piece	Mantles	0	10	0	0
John Carpyn*ter*	Ind	4	barrel	Fish, Herring White	0	20	0	0
		3	piece	Mantles	0	10	0	0

Bata Sondaie of Kinsale, Laurence Tobie master, to Ireland, *31st January 1504*

Merchant name	Origin	Qty	Unit	Commodity	£	s.	d.	f.
David Shene	Ind	10	wey	Beans & Malt	6	13	4	0
		2	wey	Beans	0	26	8	0

Bata Sampson of Cardiff, John Howell master, from *Cardiff, 31st January 1504*

Merchant name	Origin	Qty	Unit	Commodity	£	s.	d.	f.
William White	Ind	3.5	tun	Wine	0	0	0	0

Bata James of Minehead, Robert Burke master, from Ireland, *31st January 1504*

Merchant name	Origin	Qty	Unit	Commodity	£	s.	d.	f.
Robert Burke	Ind	6	last	Fish, Herring White	18	0	0	0
		3	C	Fish, Hake	0	30	0	0
John Royle	Ind	6	barrel	Fish, Herring White	0	30	0	0

Bata Mawdlen of Dingle, John Dowde master, to Ireland, *31st January 1504*

Merchant name	Origin	Qty	Unit	Commodity	£	s.	d.	f.
John Dowde	Ind	3	wey	Beans	0	40	0	0
		0.5	wey	Beans	0	6	8	0
		31	piece	Cloth of Assize, Dozen	0	0	0	0
		2	C	*Pilus Tinctus*	4	0	0	0
		0.5	C	Alum	0	2	6	0
		1	piece	Cloth of Assize	0	0	0	0

Bata Conell of Kinsale, Richard Walshe master, to Ireland, 1st February 1504

Merchant name	Origin	Qty	Unit	Commodity	£	s.	d.	f.
Richard Walshe	Ind	2	wey	Beans	0	26	8	0
		2	wey	Barley & Malt	0	26	8	0
Hugh Prise	Ind	2	C	Battery	4	0	0	0
		40	lb	*Pilus Tinctus*	0	13	4	0
		1	wey	Beans	0	13	4	0

Merchant name	Origin	Qty	Unit	Commodity	£	s.	d.	f.
Gerald Goole	Ind	1	piece	Cloth of Assize, Dozen Strait	0	0	0	0
		0.5	C	*Pilus Tinctus*	0	20	0	0
		4	stone	Orchil, Worked	0	6	8	0
Nicholas Pouche	Ind	10	lb	*Pilus Tinctus*	0	3	4	0

Bata Nicolas of Kinsale, Dennis Loden master, to Ireland, *1st February 1504*

Dennis Loden	Ind	2	wey	Beans	0	26	8	0
		1	wey	Beans	0	13	4	0
		6	wey	Beans	4	0	0	0
		2	barrel	Honey	0	23	4	0
John Roche	Ind	1	lb	Silk, Worked	0	13	4	0
		1	lb	Saffron	0	6	8	0
William Barrie	Ind	1	lb	Saffron	0	6	8	0
Raymond Roche	Ind	8	stone	Orchil, Worked	0	13	4	0
John Roche	Ind	15	lb	*Pilus Tinctus*	0	5	0	0

Bata Trinite of Kinsale, Germain Hole master, to Ireland, *1st February 1504*

Germain Hole	Ind	4	wey	Beans	0	53	4	0
		1	piece	Cloth of Assize	0	0	0	0
Cornell Makon	Ind	1	piece	Cloth of Assize	0	0	0	0
		20	lb	*Pilus Tinctus*	0	6	8	0
		4	stone	Orchil, Worked	0	6	8	0
David Shene	Ind	9	stone	Orchil, Worked	0	15	0	0

Bata Mawdlen of Waterford, Nicholas Powar master, from Ireland, *1st February 1504*

Nicholas Powar	Ind	18	barrel	Fish, Herring White	4	10	0	0
		1.5	C	Fish, Hake	0	15	0	0
		1	burden	Fish, Salted	0	3	4	0
		1	piece	Mantles	0	3	4	0
Cornell Hire	Ind	4	last	Fish, Herring White	12	0	0	0
		21	mease	Fish, Herring Red	0	105	0	0
		9	piece	Mantles	0	30	0	0
John Doyle	Ind	32	barrel	Fish, Herring White	8	0	0	0
		8	mease	Fish, Herring Red	0	40	0	0
		5	piece	Mantles	0	16	8	0
		0.5	burden	Fish, Salted	0	0	20	0
James Wise	Ind	4.5	dicker	Hides, Salted	0	60	0	0
Nicholas Powar	Ind	8	barrel	Fish, Herring White	0	40	0	0

Navicula *Christ*pofure *of* Bristol, Richard Saverey master, to Ireland, 3rd February 1504

George Monos	Ind	11	wey	Beans and Peas	7	6	8	0
		2	ton	Lead, Worked	10	0	0	0
John Popley	Ind	8	piece	Cloth of Assize	0	0	0	0
Roger Dawes	Ind	6	piece	Cloth of Assize	0	0	0	0
Roger Dawes	Ind	2	piece	Cloth of Assize, Dozen Welsh	0	8	4	0
Robert Barrero	Ind	14.5	piece	Cloth of Assize	0	0	0	0
George Monos	Ind	8	piece	Cloth of Assize	0	0	0	0
		14	wey	Beans and Peas	9	6	8	0

Merchant name	Origin	Qty	Unit	Commodity	£	s.	d.	f.
John Shipman	Ind	16	piece	Cloth of Assize	0	0	0	0
John Ware	Ind	6	piece	Cloth of Assize	0	0	0	0
John Vaghan	Ind	8	piece	Cloth of Assize	0	0	0	0
John Colas	Ind	16	piece	Cloth of Assize	0	0	0	0

Bata Saviour of Tenby, David Griffeth master, from Tenby, *3rd February 1504*

Merchant name	Origin	Qty	Unit	Commodity	£	s.	d.	f.
Philip Maget	Ind	1	tun	Oil, Olive	4	0	0	0
David Webbe	Ind	0.5	tun	Oil, Olive	0	40	0	0

Bata James of Gatcombe, John Adams master, to La Rochelle, 5th February 1504

Merchant name	Origin	Qty	Unit	Commodity	£	s.	d.	f.
James Whaley	Ind	18	barrel	Fish, Herring White	4	10	0	0
		1	piece	Cloth of Assize	0	0	0	0

Bata Katren of Berkeley, Thomas Smyth master, from Chepstow, *5th February 1504*

Merchant name	Origin	Qty	Unit	Commodity	£	s.	d.	f.
Thomas Bocher	Ind	1	tun	Wine	0	0	0	0
		12	C	Rosin	0	16	0	0
		4	measure	Woad	0	25	0	0

Bata Mare of Chepstow, William Heyn master, from Chepstow, *5th February 1504*

Merchant name	Origin	Qty	Unit	Commodity	£	s.	d.	f.
Humphrey Blount	Ind	2.75	tun	Wine	0	0	0	0

Bata Barbara of Bristol, Dennis Seelie master, to Ireland, *5th February 1504*

Merchant name	Origin	Qty	Unit	Commodity	£	s.	d.	f.
Richard Mathewe	Ind	9	stone	Orchil, Worked	0	15	0	0
		24	lb	*Pilus Tinctus*	0	8	0	0
John Ricarde	Ind	1	piece	Cloth of Assize	0	0	0	0
		9	stone	Orchil, Worked	0	15	0	0
		5	stone	Orchil, Worked	0	8	4	0
		20	lb	*Pilus Tinctus*	0	6	8	0
Nicholas Pouche	Ind	10	stone	Orchil, Worked	0	16	8	0
		1	piece	Cloth of Assize	0	0	0	0
		10	lb	*Pilus Tinctus*	0	3	4	0

Bata Nicolas of Milford Haven, Reginald Jefferey master, from Milford Haven, *5th February 1504*

Merchant name	Origin	Qty	Unit	Commodity	£	s.	d.	f.
Reginald Jefferey	Ind	1.5	last	Fish, Herring White	4	10	0	0
		6	C	Fish, Hake	0	60	0	0
		0.5	C	Fish, Hake	0	5	0	0
		1	burden	Fish, Salted	0	3	4	0
		3	barrel	Fish, Herring White	0	15	0	0

Navicula Elizab*eth* Bonaventur,[9] Port Unknown, John Bullens master, to Ireland, 6th February 1504

Merchant name	Origin	Qty	Unit	Commodity	£	s.	d.	f.
Dominic Darvey	Alien	15	dozen	Skins, Calf Tanned	0	37	6	0
John Colas	Ind	16	piece	Cloth of Assize	0	0	0	0
		4	lb	Silk, Worked	0	53	4	0
		16	lb	Saffron	0	106	8	0

9 Probably Bristol.

Merchant name	Origin	Qty	Unit	Commodity	£	s.	d.	f.
Raphael Morowe	Alien	38	lb	Silk, Worked	25	6	8	0
John Colas	Ind	1	ton	Iron	4	0	0	0
William Vaghan	Ind	5	lb	Silk, Worked	0	66	8	0
		3	lb	Saffron	0	20	0	0

Bata Katren of Chepstow, Robert Ffishar master, from Chepstow, 7th February 1504

William Jefferies	Ind	1.5	hogshead	Wine	0	0	0	0

Bata Kerecke of Milford Haven, William Wade master, from Milford Haven, 8th February 1504

William Wade	Ind	7	barrel	Fish, Herring White	0	35	0	0
		4.5	C	Fish, Hake	0	45	0	0
		1.5	burden	Fish, Salted	0	5	0	0

Bata Mare of Milford Haven, David Smythe master, from Milford Haven, 8th February 1504

David Smythe	Ind	41	barrel	Fish, Herring White	10	5	0	0
		10	C	Fish, Hake	0	100	0	0
		2	burden	Fish, Salted	0	6	8	0
		1	C	Fish, Hake	0	10	0	0
		0.5	burden	Fish, Salted	0	0	20	0

Bata Anne of Chepstow, Nicholas Botman master, from Chepstow, 9th February 1504

John Wiot	Ind	5.75	tun	Wine	23	0	0	0

Bata Trinite of Cork, Peter Butlar master, to Ireland, *9th February 1504*

John Rowland	Ind	1.5	ton	Iron	6	0	0	0
		6	barrel	Honey	0	70	0	0
		2	barrel	Honey	0	23	4	0
		1	tun	Wine, Corrupt	0	30	0	0
William Clarke	Ind	1	pipe	Wine	0	0	0	0
		1	pipe	Wine, Corrupt	0	15	0	0
John Rowland	Ind	1	pipe	Iron	0	40	0	0
William Scochen	Ind	2.5	dozen	Caps	0	16	8	0
		6	lb	Saffron	0	40	0	0
		2	lb	Silk, Worked	0	26	8	0
		0.5	gross	Knives	0	3	4	0
		0.5	C	Combs	0	0	6	0
		1	lb	Cinnamon	0	2	6	0
		1	lb	Pepper	0	0	12	0
		24	lb	*Pilus Tinctus*	0	8	0	0
		3	stone	Orchil, Worked	0	5	0	0
		1	lb	Saffron	0	6	8	0
		1	lb	Thread	0	0	5	0
David White	Ind	0.5	wey	Malt	0	6	8	0
William Clarke	Ind	2	piece	Cloth of Assize	0	0	0	0
		16	stone	Orchil, Worked	0	26	8	0
William Scochen	Ind	2	gross	Points	0	2	0	0

Merchant name	Origin	Qty	Unit	Commodity	£	s.	d.	f.
Navicula Anne of Gibraléon, Gonsalo Daze master from Andalusia, *9th February 1504*								
John Dryvero	Ind	46	tun	Wine	0	0	0	0
		9	ton	Fruit	18	0	0	0
		10.5	C	Almonds	7	0	0	0
		6	C	Orchil	0	60	0	0
Thomas Greynfeld	Ind	11	tun	Wine	0	0	0	0
		21	C	Almonds	14	0	0	0
Simon Ffishar	Ind	2.5	tun	Wine	0	0	0	0
Thomas Hop*er*	Ind	1.5	tun	Wine	0	0	0	0
Richard Smythe	Ind	1.5	tun	Wine	0	0	0	0
John Thomas	Ind	1	tun	Wine	0	0	0	0
Thomas Stile	Ind	1.5	tun	Wine	0	0	0	0
Navicula Edward of Gloucester, John Shipman master, from Andalusia, 10th February 1504								
David Westerbie	Ind	3.5	tun	Wine	0	0	0	0
William Glo[ ]ie	Ind	1	tun	Wine	0	0	0	0
William Estbie	Ind	3.5	tun	Wine	0	0	0	0
		3.75	C	Sugar	7	10	0	0
		3	quarters	Sugar	0	30	0	0
		2.75	C	Fruit	0	5	6	0
		3	quarter	Wax	0	30	0	0
		1.25	C	Pepper	6	5	0	0
John Benet	Ind	16.75	tun	Wine	0	0	0	0
Roger Dawes	Ind	1	tun	Wine	0	0	0	0
Peter Aburden	Alien	8	tun	Wine	0	0	0	0
		19.5	C	*Smigmates*	6	10	0	0
John Rowland	Ind	4.5	tun	Wine	0	0	0	0
John Smythe	Ind	19.5	C	*Smigmates*	6	10	0	0
John Morgan	Ind	0.25	tun	Wine	0	0	0	0
Humphrey Bosgrove	Ind	1	tun	Wine	0	0	0	0
John Vacher	Ind	3	tun	Wine	0	0	0	0
Thomas Smythe	Ind	3	tun	Wine	0	0	0	0
John Domi*n*gus	Alien	2.5	tun	Wine	0	0	0	0
Humphrey Browne	Ind	1	tun	Wine	0	0	0	0
John Grene	Ind	1.25	tun	Wine	0	0	0	0
William Jeffereis	Ind	7.5	tun	Wine	0	0	0	0
		18	C	*Smigmates*	6	0	0	0
David Vaghan	Ind	1.75	tun	Wine	0	0	0	0
John Halle	Ind	1	tun	Wine	0	0	0	0
John Stokes	Ind	2	tun	Wine	0	0	0	0
John Jones	Ind	1	tun	Wine	0	0	0	0
William Estbie	Ind	7	lb	Cinnamon	0	17	6	0
		4	lb	Cloves	0	8	0	0
Richard Stephens	Ind	1	tun	Wine	0	0	0	0
John Popley	Ind	1.75	tun	Wine	0	0	0	0
David Leyson	Ind	1	tun	Wine	0	0	0	0
Thomas Gogh	Ind	2	tun	Wine	0	0	0	0
John Shipman	Ind	2	tun	Wine	0	0	0	0
William Millar	Ind	2.75	tun	Wine	0	0	0	0
Merike Ffloide	Ind	1.5	tun	Wine	0	0	0	0

Merchant name	Origin	Qty	Unit	Commodity	£	s.	d.	f.
William Robnet	Ind	0.75	tun	Wine	0	0	0	0
William Taylor	Ind	0.5	tun	Wine	0	0	0	0
Philip Bocher	Ind	1	tun	Wine	0	0	0	0
Walter Parker	Ind	1	tun	Wine	0	0	0	0
Hugh Eliet	Ind	0.5	tun	Wine	0	0	0	0
Nicholas Prowd	Ind	0.166	tun	Wine	0	0	0	0

Navicula Gelian Bonaventur, Port Unknown, William Clarn master, to Spain, 12th February 1504

Merchant name	Origin	Qty	Unit	Commodity	£	s.	d.	f.
Richard Vaghan	Ind	10	wey	Beans	6	13	4	0
Sebastian de Navegias	Alien	3.5	yard	Cloth of Assize	0	5	10	0
John Otee	Alien	3.5	yard	Cloth of Assize	0	5	10	0
John Darsie	Alien	1	piece	Welsh Cloth, Dozen Strait	0	4	2	0
Richard Hobie	Ind	23	dozen	Skins, Calf Tanned	0	57	6	0
Unknown Mouson	Alien	0.5	piece	Cloth of Assize, Dozen Strait	0	5	0	0
Stephen De Passagen	Alien	3.5	yard	Cloth of Assize	0	5	10	0
Nicholas Browne	Ind	4	wey	Beans	0	53	4	0
		21	dozen	Skins, Calf Tanned	0	52	6	0
Richard Vaghan	Ind	11	piece	Cloth of Assize	0	0	0	0
		6	dozen	Skins, Calf Tanned	0	15	0	0
Peter de Lesso &								
John Dasso	Alien	3	dicker	Hides, Tanned	11	0	0	0
John Shipman	Ind	43	piece	Cloth of Assize	0	0	0	0
George Monos	Ind	20	piece	Cloth of Assize	0	0	0	0
William Hurste	Ind	4	piece	Cloth of Assize	0	0	0	0
Thomas Hawkens	Ind	4	piece	Cloth of Assize	0	0	0	0
Humphrey Brown	Ind	5	piece	Cloth of Assize	0	0	0	0
Thomas Aphowell	Ind	3	piece	Cloth of Assize	0	0	0	0
John Colas	Ind	16	piece	Cloth of Assize	0	0	0	0

Bata Katren of Chepstow, Robert Ffishar master, from Chepstow, 12th February 1504

Merchant name	Origin	Qty	Unit	Commodity	£	s.	d.	f.
Richard Nevell	Ind	3	tun	Wine	0	0	0	0

Bata Mawdlen of Waterford, Nicholas Powar master, to Ireland, 12th February 1504

Merchant name	Origin	Qty	Unit	Commodity	£	s.	d.	f.
Nicholas Powar	Ind	12	wey	Beans, Barley & Malt	8	0	0	0
		30	lb	Pilus Tinctus	0	10	0	0
Nicholas Brown	Ind	8	lb	Pilus Tinctus	0	2	8	0

Bata Katren of New Ross, William Grase master, to Ireland, 13th February 1504

Merchant name	Origin	Qty	Unit	Commodity	£	s.	d.	f.
Patrick Kelley	Ind	1	pipe	Wine, Corrupt	0	15	0	0
John Clarke	Ind	14	lb	Battery	0	5	0	0
John Burnan	Ind	1	pipe	Wine, Corrupt	0	15	0	0
		2.5	lb	Saffron	0	16	8	0
		0.5	lb	Silk, Worked	0	6	8	0
		6	lb	Pilus Tinctus	0	2	0	0
		1	gross	Points	0	0	12	0

Merchant name	Origin	Qty	Unit	Commodity	£	s.	d.	f.

Bata Marget of Chepstow, Robert [ ]er master, from Chepstow, 14th February 1504

Merchant name	Origin	Qty	Unit	Commodity	£	s.	d.	f.
William Hofe	Ind	12	lb	Cork, Black	0	20	0	0

Bata Petur of Kinsale, John Roche master, to Ireland, *14th February 1504*

Merchant name	Origin	Qty	Unit	Commodity	£	s.	d.	f.
John Roche	Ind	4	wey	Beans & Malt	0	53	4	0
Thomas Donell &								
James Barrie	Ind	4	wey	Beans & Malt	0	53	4	0
John Roche	Ind	1	piece	Cloth of Assize, Kersey	0	0	0	0
		4	stone	Orchil, Worked	0	6	8	0
		18	lb	*Pilus Tinctus*	0	6	0	0
James Barrie	Ind	9	stone	Orchil, Worked	0	15	0	0
Thomas Donell	Ind	1	piece	Cloth of Assize, Dozen Strait	0	0	0	0
		0.5	piece	Cloth of Assize, Kersey	0	0	0	0

Bata Trinite of Chepstow, William Heyn master, from Chepstow, *14th February 1504*

Merchant name	Origin	Qty	Unit	Commodity	£	s.	d.	f.
Nicholas Browne	Ind	2	tun	Wine	0	0	0	0
Robert Thorne	Ind	2	tun	Wine	0	0	0	0
John Jaie	Ind	1.75	tun	Wine	0	0	0	0

Bata Elyn of Bristol, Robert Barkar, from Chepstow, 15th February 1504

Merchant name	Origin	Qty	Unit	Commodity	£	s.	d.	f.
Thomas Hanley	Ind	0.75	tun	Wine	0	0	0	0
		6	barrel	Fish, Herring White	0	30	0	0
		1	C	Fish, Hake	0	10	0	0

Bata Patrike of Kinsale, William Donell master, to Ireland, *15th February 1504*

Merchant name	Origin	Qty	Unit	Commodity	£	s.	d.	f.
William Donell,								
William Ley &								
Patrick Went	Ind	13	wey	Beans & Malt	8	13	4	0
William Ley	Ind	1	lb	Silk, Worked	0	13	4	0
Patrick Went	Ind	42	lb	*Pilus Tinctus*	0	14	0	0
William Ley	Ind	14	stone	Orchil, Worked	0	23	4	0
		0.5	wey	Beans & Malt	0	6	8	0

Navicula Santa Nova, Port Unknown, Evan Cantelet master, to Brittany, *15th February 1504*

Merchant name	Origin	Qty	Unit	Commodity	£	s.	d.	f.
Evan Cantelet	Alien	24	tun/ton	Calx	0	60	0	0
Evan Cantelet,								
John Soble &								
William Carlynge	Alien	13	piece	Cloth of Assize	26	0	0	0
		11	piece	Mantles	0	36	8	0
		1.5	piece	Cloth of Assize	0	60	0	0
		9.5	yard	Cloth of Assize	0	15	10	0
		1	piece	Mantles	0	3	4	0

Bata Mare of St Ives, Richard Thomas master, from Ireland, 16th February 1504

Merchant name	Origin	Qty	Unit	Commodity	£	s.	d.	f.
Richard Thomas	Ind	12	C	Fish, Hake	6	0	0	0

Merchant name	Origin	Qty	Unit	Commodity	£	s.	d.	f.

Bata Marget of Chepstow, Roger Bocher master, from Chepstow, *16th February 1504*

| Richard Bucland | Ind | 1 | pipe | Wine | 0 | 0 | 0 | 0 |
| John Halle | Ind | 1 | hogshead | Wine | 0 | 0 | 0 | 0 |

Bata Mare of St Ives, Thomas Sise master, from Ireland, *16th February 1504*

Thomas Sise	Ind	8	C	Fish, Hake	4	0	0	0
Thomas Harrie	Ind	13	C	Fish, Hake	6	10	0	0
Michael Angewe	Ind	2	C	Fish, Hake	0	20	0	0

Bata Sampson of Cardiff, John Davyson master, from Cardiff, 17th February 1504

| John Qwirke | Ind | 1 | tun | Wine | 0 | 0 | 0 | 0 |

Navicula Gelian of Bristol, John Darnald master, to Lisbon, 17th February 1504

William Estbie	Ind	18	piece	Welsh *Cloth*	18	0	0	0
John Halle	Ind	6	piece	Welsh *Cloth*	6	0	0	0
John Jaie	Ind	5	piece	Cloth of Assize	0	0	0	0
William Hofe	Ind	1	piece	Welsh *Cloth*	0	20	0	0
John Grene	Ind	2	piece	Welsh *Cloth*	0	40	0	0
		0.5	piece	Cloth of Assize	0	0	0	0
George Monos	Ind	4	piece	Cloth of Assize	0	0	0	0
		2	piece	Welsh *Cloth*	0	40	0	0
		12	piece	Welsh *Cloth*, Dozen Strait	0	50	0	0

Bata Mare of Berkeley, Thomas Karell master, from Chepstow, *17th February 1504*

| Thomas Bocher | Ind | 1 | pipe | Woad | 0 | 100 | 0 | 0 |
| | | 2 | tun | Wine | 0 | 0 | 0 | 0 |

Bata Katren of Berkeley, William Halle master, from Chepstow, 19th February 1504

| Thomas Tylar | Ind | 1 | tun | Wine | 0 | 0 | 0 | 0 |

Bata Christpofure of St Ives, Nicholas Blake master, from Ireland, *19th February 1504*

Nicholas Blake	Ind	2.5	C	Fish, Hake	0	25	0	0
		4	bolt	Britany Canvas *Cloth*	0	26	8	0
		2	bolt	Britany Canvas *Cloth*	0	13	4	0
		2	C	Britany Linen *Cloth*	0	40	0	0
		4	C	Fish, Hake	0	40	0	0
		1	pipe	Wine	0	0	0	0

Bata Katren of Milford Haven, Richard Jurdan master, from Ireland, *19th February 1504*

Richard Jurdan	Ind	56	barrel	Fish, Herring White	14	0	0	0
		7.5	C	Fish, Hake	0	75	0	0
		2	burden	Fish, Salted	0	6	8	0

Merchant name	Origin	Qty	Unit	Commodity	£	s.	d.	f.

Bata James of Minehead, Richard Wright,master, from Ireland, *19th February 1504*

Merchant name	Origin	Qty	Unit	Commodity	£	s.	d.	f.
Richard Wright	Ind	26.5	barrel	Fish, Herring White	6	12	6	o
Robert Burke	Ind	12	barrel	Fish, Herring White	o	60	o	o

Bata John of Ilfracombe, Walter Yogge master, from Ireland, *19th February 1504*

Merchant name	Origin	Qty	Unit	Commodity	£	s.	d.	f.
Thomas Langall	Ind	12	barrel	Fish, Herring White	o	60	o	o

Bata Mare of Milford Haven, Thomas Jeffereis master, from Ireland, 20th February 1504

Merchant name	Origin	Qty	Unit	Commodity	£	s.	d.	f.
Thomas Jeffereis	Ind	5	last	Fish, Herring White	15	o	o	o
		7	C	Fish, Hake	o	70	o	o
		2	burden	Fish, Salted	o	6	8	o
		3	barrel	Fish, Herring White	o	15	o	o
		2.25	C	Fish, Hake	o	22	6	o

Bata Mare of Milford Haven, Walter Taylor master, from Ireland, *20th February 1504*

Merchant name	Origin	Qty	Unit	Commodity	£	s.	d.	f.
Walter Taylor	Ind	0.5	C	Fish, Hake	o	5	o	o
Thomas Cawlon	Ind	28	barrel	Fish, Herring White	7	o	o	o
		2	pipe	Fish, Salmon	o	60	o	o
		14	piece	Mantles	o	46	8	o
		100	piece	Skins, Sheep (no wool)	o	8	4	o
		22	piece	Fish, Hake	o	o	22	o
Eliott Archer	Ind	40	barrel	Fish, Herring White	10	o	o	o
		0.5	pipe	Fish, Salmon	o	15	o	o
		11	piece	Mantles	o	36	8	o
		1	quarter	Fish, Hake	o	2	6	o
		3	mease	Fish, Herring Red	o	15	o	o
		1	virken	Fish, Salmon	o	7	6	o
		100	piece	Skins, Sheep (no wool)	o	8	4	o
Nicholas Cowle	Ind	34	barrel	Fish, Herring White	8	10	o	o
		3	pipe	Fish, Salmon	4	10	o	o
		0.5	C	Fish, Hake	o	5	o	o
		0.5	burden	Fish, Salted	o	o	20	o
Eliott Archer	Ind	1	piece	Seal	o	6	8	o

Bata Nicholas of Wexford, John Lynge master, from Ireland, 21st February 1504

Merchant name	Origin	Qty	Unit	Commodity	£	s.	d.	f.
Nicholas Kynaie	Ind	3	M	Fish, Hake	15	o	o	o
		3	pipe	Fish, Salmon	4	10	o	o
		20	mease	Fish, Herring Red	o	100	o	o
		1	barrel	Fish, Herring White	o	5	o	o
		0.5	C	Skins, Sheep (no wool)	o	5	o	o
		1	dicker	Skins, Ferret	o	2	6	o
		3	piece	Skins, Fox	o	o	4	2
		20	piece	Skins, Lamb	o	o	10	o
		1	piece	Mantles	o	3	4	o
		2	burden	Fish, Salted	o	6	8	o

Merchant name	Origin	Qty	Unit	Commodity	£	s.	d.	f.

Bata James of Milford Haven, William Vaghan master, from Ireland, 21th February 1504

Merchant name	Origin	Qty	Unit	Commodity	£	s.	d.	f.
William Vaghan	Ind	5	barrel	Fish, Herring White	0	25	0	0
		1	C	Fish, Hake	0	10	0	0

Bata Jhesus of Boscastle, John Tireweneck master, from Ireland, 21th February 1504

Merchant name	Origin	Qty	Unit	Commodity	£	s.	d.	f.
John Tireweneck	Ind	6	C	Fish, Hake	0	60	0	0

Bata Gabriell of Milford Haven, John Bullock master, from Ireland, 21th February 1504

Merchant name	Origin	Qty	Unit	Commodity	£	s.	d.	f.
John Bullock	Ind	20	barrel	Fish, Herring White	0	100	0	0
		7.5	C	Fish, Hake	0	75	0	0
		3.5	burden	Fish, Salted	0	11	8	0

Bata Michael of Bridgwater, John Garret master, from Bridgwater, 21th February 1504

Merchant name	Origin	Qty	Unit	Commodity	£	s.	d.	f.
John Hardinge	Ind	1.5	C	Orchill	0	15	0	0

Navicula Mare Belhouse of _Bristol_,[10] Walter Cooke master, from Algarve, 22th February 1504

Merchant name	Origin	Qty	Unit	Commodity	£	s.	d.	f.
John Rowland	Ind	4.75	ton	Fruit	9	10	0	0
Dominic Carrigero	Alien	7	ton	Fruit	14	0	0	0
		1.5	tun	Wine	0	0	0	0
		2	tun	Oil, Olive	8	0	0	0
		2	burden	Fish, Salted	0	6	8	0
John Rowland	Ind	3	tun	Wine	0	0	0	0
David Vaghan	Ind	4	ton	Fruit	8	0	0	0
John Grene	Ind	5	ton	Fruit	10	0	0	0
Ralph Aprise	Ind	4	ton	Fruit	8	0	0	0
William Estbie	Ind	5	ton	Fruit	10	0	0	0
George Monos	Ind	3	ton	Fruit	6	0	0	0
Robert Barrero	Ind	1	ton	Fruit	0	40	0	0
John Lorde	Ind	1	ton	Fruit	0	40	0	0
Humphrey Brown	Ind	2	ton	Fruit	4	0	0	0
William Hurste	Ind	1	ton	Fruit	0	40	0	0
Roger Dawes	Ind	2.5	ton	Fruit	0	100	0	0
John Shipman	Ind	3	ton	Fruit	6	0	0	0
Thomas Smythe	Ind	4	ton	Fruit	8	0	0	0
Richard Stephins	Ind	2	ton	Fruit	4	0	0	0
William Gonne	Ind	2	ton	Fruit	4	0	0	0
John Halle	Ind	4	ton	Fruit	8	0	0	0
Henry Dale	Ind	5.75	ton	Fruit	11	10	0	0
		1	hogshead	Oil, Olive	0	20	0	0
Nicholas Brown	Ind	1	ton	Fruit	0	40	0	0
William Tirrie	Ind	2	ton	Fruit	4	0	0	0
John Alberton	Ind	1	ton	Fruit	0	40	0	0

10 In some cases the port is not listed, especially where a ship came from Bristol and had two names (e.g. _Mary Conception_ or _Trinitie Smyth_). This was presumably because the customs officer felt that enough information had been given to identify the ship. If the origin of the ship is known from other entries in the account, or other sources, the port is given but put in italics in the worksheet. The Mary Belhouse is found in TNA E122/21/2 f13r, recorded as a Bristol ship.

Merchant name	Origin	Qty	Unit	Commodity	£	s.	d.	f.
William Jones	Ind	2	ton	Fruit	4	0	0	0
John Barnard	Ind	1	ton	Fruit	0	40	0	0
Robert Beysant	Ind	1	hogshead	Fruit	0	10	0	0
Peter Aburden	Alien	2.25	ton	Fruit	4	10	0	0
Johanna Pavie	Ind	2	ton	Fruit	4	0	0	0
John Benet	Ind	8	ton	Fruit	16	0	0	0
Walter Cooke	Ind	1	pipe	Fruit	0	20	0	0
John Harries	Ind	1	ton	Fruit	0	40	0	0
Hugh Eliet	Ind	4	ton	Fruit	8	0	0	0
Thomas Hawkens	Ind	1	ton	Fruit	0	40	0	0
John Ringston	Ind	1	ton	Fruit	0	40	0	0
Robert Avyntre	Ind	1	ton	Fruit	0	40	0	0
William Jeffereis	Ind	2.25	ton	Fruit	4	10	0	0
		0.75	tun	Oil, Olive	0	60	0	0
Dominic Carrigero	Alien	3	burden	Fish, Salted	0	10	0	0
John Harries	Ind	1	ton	Fruit	0	40	0	0
Richard Cooke	Ind	1	hogshead	Oil, Olive	0	20	0	0
William Derick	Ind	1	dicker	Hides, Salted	0	13	4	0
John Canynge	Ind	3	piece	Fruit	0	4	0	0
John Hilsey	Ind	3	piece	Fruit	0	4	0	0
Thomas Palin	Ind	6	piece	Fruit	0	8	0	0

Navicula Mare of Bristol, Philip Nongell master, to Ireland, 23rd February 1504

Merchant name	Origin	Qty	Unit	Commodity	£	s.	d.	f.
William Jeffereis	Ind	1	tun	Wine, Corrupt	0	30	0	0
John Harries	Ind	3	piece	Cloth of Assize	0	0	0	0
William Jeffereis	Ind	1	pipe	Salt	0	8	4	0
		1	hogshead	Salt	0	4	2	0
		6	piece	Cloth of Assize	0	0	0	0
		10	piece	Cloth of Assize, Dozen	0	0	0	0
		120	lb	Pilus Tinctus	0	40	0	0
		1	hogshead	Salt	0	4	2	0
William White	Ind	1.5	tun	Wine, Corrupt	0	45	0	0

Bata Trinite of Milford Haven, Thomas Eliet master, from Ireland, 26th February 1504

Merchant name	Origin	Qty	Unit	Commodity	£	s.	d.	f.
Thomas Eliet	Ind	4	burden	Fish, Salted	0	13	4	0
Philip Powar	Ind	18	barrel	Fish, Herring White	4	10	0	0
		2	pipe	Fish, Salmon	0	60	0	0
		1	virken	Fish, Salmon	0	7	6	0
		6	C	Fish, Hake	0	60	0	0
		4.75	burden	Fish, Salted	0	15	10	0
		30	lb	Wax	0	10	0	0
		14	mease	Fish, Herring Red	0	70	0	0
		8	C	Skins, Sheep (no wool)	4	0	0	0
		3	piece	Mantles	0	10	0	0
		6	piece	Skins, Fox	0	0	9	0
Gerald Vale	Ind	2.25	burden	Fish, Salted	0	7	6	0
William Tirrie	Ind	10.5	dicker	Hides, Salted	7	0	0	0
William Ffemie	Ind	8	piece	Mantles	0	26	8	0
		3	burden	Fish, Salted	0	10	0	0
		6	mease	Fish, Herring Red	0	30	0	0

Merchant name	Origin	Qty	Unit	Commodity	£	s.	d.	f.
John Fforteen	Ind	3	C	Skins, Sheep (no wool)	0	30	0	0
		2	mease	Fish, Herring Red	0	10	0	0

Navicula Trinite of Bristol, John Barnard master, to Bordeaux, 26th February 1504

Merchant name	Origin	Qty	Unit	Commodity	£	s.	d.	f.
George Monos	Ind	40	piece	Cloth of Assize	0	0	0	0
		2	ton	Lead	10	0	0	0
John Ware	Ind	36	piece	Cloth of Assize	0	0	0	0
John Meysan	Ind	5	piece	Cloth of Assize	0	0	0	0
John Vaghan	Ind	16	piece	Cloth of Assize	0	0	0	0
Robert Rowlowe	Ind	5	piece	Cloth of Assize	0	0	0	0
John Ware	Ind	1	piece	Cloth of Assize	0	0	0	0
		2.5	piece	Welsh Cloth	0	50	0	0
John Barnard	Ind	1	ton	Lead, Worked	0	100	0	0

Bata Sondaie of Youghal, Maurice Nogell master, from Ireland, 26th February 1504

Merchant name	Origin	Qty	Unit	Commodity	£	s.	d.	f.
George Monos	Ind	2	last	Fish, Herring White	6	0	0	0
Thomas Flemynge	Ind	1	pipe	Fish, Salmon	0	30	0	0
		1.5	C	Skins, Sheep (no wool)	0	15	0	0
John Lawnder	Ind	2	pipe	Fish, Salmon	0	60	0	0
William Morowe	Ind	2	last	Fish, Herring White	6	0	0	0
		8.5	C	Fish, Hake	4	5	0	0
		3	piece	Mantles	0	10	0	0
		44	lb	Wax	0	14	8	0
		2	pipe	Fish, Salmon	0	60	0	0
		6	burden	Fish, Salted	0	20	0	0
Edmund Fe John	Ind	4	barrel	Fish, Herring White	0	20	0	0
		2	C	Fish, Hake	0	20	0	0
		1	burden	Fish, Salted	0	3	4	0
		3	piece	Mantles	0	10	0	0
William Walshe	Ind	5	barrel	Fish, Herring White	0	25	0	0
		1	C	Fish, Hake	0	10	0	0
William White	Ind	4	mease	Fish, Herring Red	0	20	0	0
		1	burden	Fish, Salted	0	3	4	0
John De Rodes	Alien	58	piece	Mantles	9	13	4	0
Thomas Lefe	Ind	3	piece	Mantles	0	10	0	0
William Moreke	Ind	0.5	C	Skins, Sheep (no wool)	0	5	0	0

Bata Trinite of Waterford, William Browne master, from Ireland, 27th February 1504

Merchant name	Origin	Qty	Unit	Commodity	£	s.	d.	f.
William Browne	Ind	9.5	barrel	Fish, Herring White	0	47	6	0
		4	mease	Fish, Herring Red	0	20	0	0
		1	virken	Fish, Salmon	0	7	6	0
William Arnold	Ind	15.5	barrel	Fish, Herring White	0	77	6	0
		3	mease	Fish, Herring Red	0	15	0	0
		1	quarter	Fish, Hake	0	2	6	0
		2	burden	Fish, Salted	0	6	8	0
		1	C	Irish Linen Cloth	0	10	0	0
		1	quarter	Skins, Sheep (no wool)	0	2	6	0
William Graunte	Ind	9	barrel	Fish, Herring White	0	45	0	0
		4.5	mease	Fish, Herring Red	0	22	6	0

Merchant name	Origin	Qty	Unit	Commodity	£	s.	d.	f.
		5.75	C	Fish, Hake	0	57	6	0
		1.5	burden	Fish, Salted	0	5	0	0
Richard Sutton	Ind	4	barrel	Fish, Herring White	0	20	0	0
John Powar	Ind	11	barrel	Fish, Herring White	0	55	0	0
		2	mease	Fish, Herring Red	0	10	0	0
		3	quarter	Fish, Hake	0	7	6	0
		5	burden	Fish, Salted	0	16	8	0
		2	piece	Mantles	0	6	8	0
John Power junior	Ind	3.5	barrel	Fish, Herring White	0	17	6	0
		2	mease	Fish, Herring Red	0	10	0	0
		1	piece	Mantles	0	3	4	0
William Molen	Ind	3.5	quarter	Fish, Hake	0	8	9	0
		1.5	burden	Fish, Salted	0	5	0	0
Dennis Valen	Ind	4.5	barrel	Fish, Herring White	0	22	6	0
		3	quarter	Fish, Hake	0	7	6	0
		5	piece	Mantles	0	16	8	0
Cornell Bodie	Ind	7	barrel	Fish, Herring White	0	35	0	0
		1	mease	Fish, Herring Red	0	5	0	0
		1.25	C	Fish, Hake	0	12	6	0
		2	burden	Fish, Salted	0	6	8	0
		2	piece	Mantles	0	6	8	0
Philip Powar	Ind	9.5	barrel	Fish, Herring White	0	47	6	0
		4.5	mease	Fish, Herring Red	0	22	6	0
		4.08	C	Fish, Hake	0	40	10	0
		2.25	burden	Fish, Salted	0	7	6	0
		2	dicker	Hides, Salted	0	26	8	0
Edmund Mean	Ind	10	barrel	Fish, Herring White	0	50	0	0
		9.25	C	Fish, Hake	4	12	6	0
		15	burden	Fish, Salted	0	50	0	0
Richard Arthur	Ind	2.5	C	Skins, Sheep (no wool)	0	25	0	0
	-	8	stone	Wool, Flocks	0	3	4	0
Philip Walshe	Ind	2	C	Fish, Hake	0	20	0	0
		1.5	burden	Fish, Salted	0	5	0	0
Philip Nashe	Ind	2.5	C	Skins, Sheep (no wool)	0	25	0	0
		18	piece	Mantles	0	60	0	0
		76	lb	Wax	0	25	4	0
William Molen	Ind	2	barrel	Fish, Herring White	0	10	0	0

Bata Lenard of Waterford, Robert Roche master, from Ireland, 28th February 1504

Merchant name	Origin	Qty	Unit	Commodity	£	s.	d.	f.
Robert Roche	Ind	4	barrel	Fish, Herring White	0	20	0	0
		0.5	pipe	Fish, Salmon	0	15	0	0
		0.5	C	Fish, Hake	0	5	0	0
		3	piece	Mantles	0	10	0	0
John Harold	Ind	17	barrel	Fish, Herring White	4	5	0	0
		1.25	C	Fish, Hake	0	12	6	0
		3	burden	Fish, Salted	0	10	0	0
		3	piece	Mantles	0	10	0	0
		2	stone	Wool, Flocks	0	0	10	0
Peter Nogel	Ind	8.5	barrel	Fish, Herring White	0	42	6	0
		1	C	Fish, Hake	0	10	0	0
		1	burden	Fish, Salted	0	3	4	0

Merchant name	Origin	Qty	Unit	Commodity	£	s.	d.	f.
		4	stone	Wool, Flocks	0	0	20	0
		3	piece	Mantles	0	10	0	0
Maurice Derbie	Ind	7	barrel	Fish, Herring White	0	35	0	0
		3	quarter	Fish, Hake	0	7	6	0
		1	burden	Fish, Salted	0	3	4	0
		2	piece	Mantles	0	6	8	0
		1	mease	Fish, Herring Red	0	5	0	0
Malagur Tailor	Ind	10	barrel	Fish, Herring White	0	50	0	0
		2.25	C	Fish, Hake	0	22	6	0
		0.5	C	Wax	0	20	0	0
		2	piece	Mantles	0	6	8	0
		4	stone	Wool, Flocks	0	0	20	0
		2	C	Fish, Herring Red	0	2	0	0
David Christopofur	Ind	1	virken	Fish, Salmon	0	7	6	0
		1	barrel	Fish, Herring White	0	5	0	0
		3.25	burden	Fish, Salted	0	10	10	0

Bata Clement of Waterford, Walter Barre master, from Ireland, *28th February 1504*

Merchant name	Origin	Qty	Unit	Commodity	£	s.	d.	f.
John Fforlonge	Ind	12	barrel	Fish, Herring White	0	60	0	0
		1	M	Fish, Hake	0	100	0	0
		4	burden	Fish, Salted	0	13	4	0
		8.5	C	Skins, Sheep (no wool)	4	5	0	0
		3	C	Skins, Lamb	0	15	0	0
		6	piece	Mantles	0	20	0	0
		5	stone	Wool, Flocks	0	2	1	0
Walter Maylar	Ind	12	barrel	Fish, Herring White	0	60	0	0
		1	M	Fish, Hake	0	100	0	0
		24	mease	Fish, Herring Red	6	0	0	0

Bata James of Waterford, James Leche master, from Ireland, 1st March 1504

Merchant name	Origin	Qty	Unit	Commodity	£	s.	d.	f.
James Leche	Ind	27	barrel	Fish, Herring White	6	15	0	0
		6.5	C	Fish, Hake	0	65	0	0
		6.5	burden	Fish, Salted	0	21	8	0
		10.5	mease	Fish, Herring Red	0	52	6	0
		8	piece	Mantles	0	26	8	0
		2.5	C	Skins, Sheep (no wool)	0	25	0	0
David Christpofur	Ind	32	barrel	Fish, Herring White	8	0	0	0
		2	pipe	Fish, Salmon	0	60	0	0
		9	C	Fish, Hake	4	10	0	0
		7.5	burden	Fish, Salted	0	25	0	0
		2.5	C	Skins, Sheep (no wool)	0	25	0	0
		60	lb	Wax	0	20	0	0
		12	piece	Mantles	0	40	0	0
William Ffolan	Ind	4	barrel	Fish, Herring White	0	20	0	0
		1	burden	Fish, Salted	0	3	4	0
		8	piece	Mantles	0	26	8	0
		2	C	Fish, Herring Red	0	2	0	0
John Corke	Ind	3	barrel	Fish, Herring White	0	15	0	0
		1	C	Fish, Hake	0	10	0	0
		0.5	mease	Fish, Herring Red	0	2	6	0

Merchant name	Origin	Qty	Unit	Commodity	£	s.	d.	f.
		5	piece	Mantles	0	16	8	0
		1.5	burden	Fish, Salted	5	0	0	0
William Tirrie	Ind	76	lb	Wax	0	25	4	0
David Burnan	Ind	52	lb	Wax	0	17	4	0

Bata John of Cork, Thomas Walshe master, from Ireland, 1st March 1504

Merchant name	Origin	Qty	Unit	Commodity	£	s.	d.	f.
Thomas Walshe	Ind	22	barrel	Fish, Herring White	0	110	0	0
		2.5	C	Fish, Hake	0	25	0	0
		1.5	burden	Fish, Salted	0	5	0	0
		3	piece	Mantles	0	10	0	0
Henry Goold	Ind	26	barrel	Fish, Herring White	6	10	0	0
		7	mease	Fish, Herring Red	0	35	0	0
		1.25	C	Fish, Hake	0	12	6	0
		1	virken	Fish, Salmon	0	7	6	0
		1	C	Fish, Hake	0	10	0	0
		6	piece	Mantles	0	20	0	0
		18	yard	Check *Cloth*	0	6	0	0
		1.5	C	Skins, Sheep (no wool)	0	15	0	0
		1	quarter	Skins, Lamb	0	0	15	0
		1	quarter	Irish Linen *Cloth*	0	2	6	0
Richard Magner	Ind	11	mease	Fish, Herring Red	0	55	0	0
		4	barrel	Fish, Herring White	0	20	0	0
		3.25	C	Fish, Hake	0	32	6	0
		0.5	burden	Fish, Salted	0	0	20	0
Cornell Stoleyn	Ind	11	barrel	Fish, Herring White	0	55	0	0
		6	mease	Fish, Herring Red	0	30	0	0
		3	piece	Mantles	0	10	0	0
David Walshe	Ind	12.5	barrel	Fish, Herring White	0	62	6	0
		1	C	Fish, Hake	0	10	0	0
		1.5	mease	Fish, Herring Red	0	7	6	0
		1	C	Skins, Sheep (no wool)	0	10	0	0
		6	piece	Mantles	0	20	0	0
Thomas Walshe	Ind	9.5	barrel	Fish, Herring White	0	47	6	0
		6	mease	Fish, Herring Red	0	30	0	0
		2	piece	Mantles	0	6	8	0
William Hofe	Ind	8	piece	Mantles	0	26	8	0
Richard Harry	Ind	1	C	Cork, White	0	3	4	0

Bata Mare of Waterford, Peter Fe John master, from Ireland, *1st March 1504*

Merchant name	Origin	Qty	Unit	Commodity	£	s.	d.	f.
Peter Fe John	Ind	4	burden	Fish, Salted	0	13	4	0
		1	C	Fish, Hake	0	10	0	0
		2.5	barrel	Fish, Herring White	0	12	6	0
John Kahan	Ind	5.5	barrel	Fish, Herring White	0	27	6	0
		4.5	C	Fish, Hake	0	45	0	0
		1	piece	Mantles	0	3	4	0
		6.5	burden	Fish, Salted	0	21	8	0
John Doan	Ind	16	barrel	Fish, Herring White	4	0	0	0
		8.5	C	Fish, Hake	4	5	0	0
		3	burden	Fish, Salted	0	10	0	0
Peter Rise	Ind	80	lb	Wax	0	26	8	0

Merchant name	Origin	Qty	Unit	Commodity	£	s.	d.	f.
William Mulgan	Ind	3	barrel	Fish, Herring White	0	15	0	0
		52	yard	Check *Cloth*	0	17	4	0
		6	piece	Mantles	0	20	0	0
David Kirke	Ind	6	piece	Mantles	0	20	0	0
William Dowren	Ind	25	barrel	Fish, Herring White	6	5	0	0
		7.5	burden	Fish, Salted	0	25	0	0
		1	C	Fish, Hake	0	10	0	0
		1	mease	Fish, Herring Red	0	5	0	0
		28	lb	Wax	0	9	4	0
		10	piece	Mantles	0	33	4	0
		3	stone	Wool, Flocks	0	0	15	0
Edmund Bonfeld	Ind	4	C	Fish, Hake	0	40	0	0
		2.5	burden	Fish, Salted	0	8	4	0
		2	last	Fish, Herring White	6	0	0	0
		1	piece	Mantles	0	3	4	0
John Kahan	Ind	0.5	pipe	Fish, Salmon	0	15	0	0
Henry Nele	Ind	1	barrel	Fish, Herring White	0	5	0	0

Navicula Trinitie of Combe Martin, John Berie master, from Algarve, *1st March 150*

Merchant name	Origin	Qty	Unit	Commodity	£	s.	d.	f.
John Berie	Ind	1.25	tun	Wine	0	0	0	0
		2	C	Wax	4	0	0	0
		2.25	ton	Fruit	4	10	0	0
William Crosse	Ind	8.5	ton	Fruit	17	0	0	0
		8.75	tun	Wine	0	0	0	0
		3	dicker	Hides, Salted	0	40	0	0
John Grene	Ind	3.5	tun	Wine	0	0	0	0
Dominic Carrigero	Alien	3	ton	Fruit	6	0	0	0
		1	tun	Oil, Olive	4	0	0	0
		1	tun	Wine	0	0	0	0
John Halle	Ind	2.5	tun	Wine	0	0	0	0
Humphrey Bosgrove	Ind	1	ton	Fruit	0	40	0	0
David Vaghan	Ind	2.5	tun	Wine	0	0	0	0
Thomas Berie	Ind	1.5	tun	Wine	0	0	0	0
		1	ton	Fruit	0	40	0	0
		1	quarter	Wax	0	10	0	0
John Berie	Ind	1	pipe	Wine	0	0	0	0
		1	ton	Fruit	0	40	0	0
		14	lb	Wax	0	4	8	0
John Robens	Ind	1.5	tun	Wine	0	0	0	0
		1	pipe	Fruit	0	20	0	0
John Butlar	Ind	1	tun	Wine	0	0	0	0
		1	pipe	Fruit	0	20	0	0
Owen Walter	Ind	1	pipe	Wine	0	0	0	0
		1	ton	Fruit	0	40	0	0
		1	hogshead	Fruit	0	10	0	0
Richard Goold	Ind	1	pipe	Wine	0	0	0	0
		1	pipe	Fruit	0	20	0	0
John Clarke	Ind	1	pipe	Wine	0	0	0	0
John Nicoll	Ind	1	hogshead	Fruit	0	10	0	0
Richard Walshe	Ind	2	ton	Fruit	4	0	0	0
		1	quarter	Wax	0	10	0	0

Merchant name	Origin	Qty	Unit	Commodity	£	s.	d.	f.
Walter Flemynge	Ind	1.25	ton	Fruit	0	50	0	0
Walter Calicote	Ind	1	hogshead	Fruit	0	10	0	0
Stephen Ffleke	Ind	1	pipe	Fruit	0	20	0	0
Walter Griffen	Ind	0.75	ton	Fruit	0	30	0	0
Adam Griffen	Ind	1	hogshead	Fruit	0	10	0	0
Thomas Flemynge	Ind	1.75	ton	Fruit	0	70	0	0
Geoffrey Williams	Ind	1	ton	Fruit	0	40	0	0
John Harmon	Ind	1	hogshead	Fruit	0	10	0	0
David Gammon	Ind	1	ton	Fruit	0	40	0	0
Henry White	Ind	1	hogshead	Fruit	0	10	0	0
William Carpynter	Ind	1	pipe	Fruit	0	20	0	0
John Harries	Ind	1	hogshead	Fruit	0	10	0	0
Owen Walter	Ind	1.25	burden	Fish, Salted	0	4	2	0
John Goobbe	Ind	1	ton	Fruit	0	40	0	0
William Jenyns	Ind	1	pipe	Fruit	0	20	0	0
John Ynon	Ind	1.75	tun	Wine	0	0	0	0
		0.75	ton	Fruit	0	30	0	0
		1.25	burden	Fish, Salted	0	4	2	0
Robert Ffortey	Ind	1	ton	Fruit	0	40	0	0
John Stokes	Ind	3.25	tun	Wine	0	0	0	0
Richard Crosse	Ind	3	tun	Wine	0	0	0	0
		1	ton	Fruit	0	40	0	0
Richard Draper	Ind	1	tun	Wine	0	0	0	0
		1	ton	Fruit	0	40	0	0
William Tirrie	Ind	1	tun	Wine	0	0	0	0
		1	ton	Fruit	0	40	0	0
John Lorde	Ind	1	ton	Fruit	0	40	0	0
William Symons	Ind	1	pipe	Wine	0	0	0	0
John Shipman	Ind	1.5	tun	Wine	0	0	0	0
		1	ton	Fruit	0	40	0	0
Peter Aburden	Alien	1	ton	Fruit	0	40	0	0
John Goobbe	Ind	3	dozen	Cork, Black	0	5	0	0

Bata Nicolas of Berkeley, William Lawles master, from Ireland, *1st March 1504*

Merchant name	Origin	Qty	Unit	Commodity	£	s.	d.	f.
John Roggers	Ind	20	barrel	Fish, Herring White	0	100	0	0
		7	burden	Fish, Salted	0	23	4	0
		1.25	C	Fish, Hake	0	12	6	0
Richard Partriche	Ind	12	burden	Fish, Salted	0	40	0	0
		1	C	Fish, Hake	0	10	0	0
		11	barrel	Fish, Herring White	0	55	0	0
James Partriche	Ind	8.5	burden	Fish, Salted	0	28	4	0
		1	C	Fish, Hake	0	10	0	0
		2	piece	Mantles	0	6	8	0
		1.16	C	Skins, Sheep (no wool)	0	11	8	0
		80	piece	Skins, Lamb	0	3	4	0
John Adee	Ind	3	burden	Fish, Salted	0	10	0	0
Thomas Bowre	Ind	2.5	burden	Fish, Salted	0	8	4	0
Richard Bocher	Ind	1.5	pipe	Fish, Salmon	0	45	0	0
		0.5	burden	Fish, Salted	0	0	20	0
		0.5	C	Fish, Hake	0	5	0	0
John Adee	Ind	3	C	Fish, Herring Red	0	3	0	0

Merchant name	Origin	Qty	Unit	Commodity	£	s.	d.	f.

Bata Trinite of Cork, David Wyndar master, from Ireland, 2nd March 1504

Merchant name	Origin	Qty	Unit	Commodity	£	s.	d.	f.
David Wyndar	Ind	3	barrel	Fish, Herring White	0	15	0	0
		1.75	C	Fish, Hake	0	17	6	0
William Tirrie	Ind	52.5	barrel	Fish, Herring White	13	2	6	0
		28.5	mease	Fish, Herring Red	7	2	6	0
		1.5	C	Fish, Hake	0	15	0	0
		1.75	quarter	Fish, Salted	0	5	10	0
Patrick Tirrie	Ind	42	barrel	Fish, Herring White	10	10	0	0
		19.5	mease	Fish, Herring Red	4	17	6	0
Owen Atholl	Ind	5.5	barrel	Fish, Herring White	0	27	6	0
		8	mease	Fish, Herring Red	0	40	0	0
		1.5	C	Fish, Hake	0	15	0	0
		6	piece	Mantles	0	20	0	0
Dennis Ffolan	Ind	6	barrel	Fish, Herring White	0	30	0	0
		3	mease	Fish, Herring Red	0	15	0	0
		2	piece	Mantles	0	6	8	0
Germain Cormeck	Ind	2	barrel	Fish, Herring White	0	10	0	0
		2	piece	Mantles	0	6	8	0
Nicholas Longe	Ind	9	mease	Fish, Herring Red	0	45	0	0
Patrick Morow	Ind	7	barrel	Fish, Herring White	0	35	0	0
		1.1	C	Fish, Hake	0	11	0	0
		2	piece	Mantles	0	6	8	0
Dennis Ffynne	Ind	8	barrel	Fish, Herring White	0	40	0	0
		8	mease	Fish, Herring Red	0	40	0	0
		8	piece	Mantles	0	26	8	0
Philip Barret	Ind	6	mease	Fish, Herring Red	0	30	0	0
		0.5	C	Fish, Hake	0	5	0	0
		0.5	C	Skins, Sheep (no wool)	0	5	0	0

Bata Michaell of Minehead, Henry Mongham master, from Ireland, 2nd March 1504

Merchant name	Origin	Qty	Unit	Commodity	£	s.	d.	f.
George Monos	Ind	2	last	Fish, Herring White	6	0	0	0
John Barrie	Ind	1	M	Fish, Hake	0	100	0	0
		3	last	Fish, Herring White	9	0	0	0
		12	mease	Fish, Herring Red	0	60	0	0
		2	pipe	Fish, Salmon	0	60	0	0
John Mongham	Ind	5	burden	Fish, Salted	0	16	8	0
		2	last	Fish, Herring White	6	0	0	0
		1	virken	Fish, Salmon	0	7	6	0
		7	mease	Fish, Herring Red	0	35	0	0
		1	dicker	Hides, Salted	0	13	4	0
Maurice Qwirke	Ind	8	barrel	Fish, Herring White	0	40	0	0
		21	mease	Fish, Herring Red	0	105	0	0
		1	pipe	Fish, Salmon	0	30	0	0
		1	C	Fish, Hake	0	10	0	0
Thomas Awsten	Ind	14	barrel	Fish, Herring White	0	70	0	0
		4.5	mease	Fish, Herring Red	0	22	6	0
		3	piece	Mantles	0	10	0	0
		1	stone	Wool, Flocks	0	0	5	0
		10	piece	Skins, Sheep (no wool)	0	0	10	0
Thomas Hore	Ind	13	barrel	Fish, Herring White	0	65	0	0

Merchant name	Origin	Qty	Unit	Commodity	£	s.	d.	f.
		9	mease	Fish, Herring Red	0	45	0	0
		0.75	pipe	Fish, Salmon	0	22	6	0
Thomas Kerne	Ind	7.5	C	Fish, Hake	0	75	0	0
		5	barrel	Fish, Herring White	0	25	0	0
		2	piece	Mantles	0	6	8	0
Thomas Melon	Ind	4	barrel	Fish, Herring White	0	20	0	0
		12	mease	Fish, Herring Red	0	60	0	0
Patrick Ffroste	Ind	9	mease	Fish, Herring Red	0	45	0	0
		2	barrel	Fish, Herring White	0	10	0	0
		4	piece	Mantles	0	13	4	0
Henry Goold	Ind	17	barrel	Fish, Herring White	4	5	0	0

Bata Mawdlen of Waterford, William Penbroke master, from Ireland, *2nd March 1504*

Merchant name	Origin	Qty	Unit	Commodity	£	s.	d.	f.
William Penbroke	Ind	6	barrel	Fish, Herring White	0	30	0	0
		1	C	Fish, Hake	0	10	0	0
		5	mease	Fish, Herring Red	0	25	0	0
		1	piece	Mantles	0	3	4	0
Philip Digon	Ind	2	last	Fish, Herring White	6	0	0	0
		2	mease	Fish, Herring Red	0	10	0	0
Richard Caden	Ind	6	barrel	Fish, Herring White	0	30	0	0
		1	C	Fish, Hake	0	10	0	0
Richard Walshe	Ind	2	barrel	Fish, Herring White	0	10	0	0
		0.5	C	Fish, Hake	0	5	0	0
John Fforteen	Ind	14	barrel	Fish, Herring White	0	70	0	0
		2	pipe	Fish, Salmon	0	60	0	0
		4	piece	Mantles	0	13	4	0
		46	piece	Fish, Hake	0	3	10	0
		0.5	burden	Fish, Salted	0	0	20	0
Robert White	Ind	27	barrel	Fish, Herring White	6	15	0	0
		2.5	burden	Fish, Salted	0	8	4	0
		1.75	C	Fish, Hake	0	17	6	0
		4	mease	Fish, Herring Red	0	20	0	0
		3	barrel	Fish, Herring White	0	15	0	0
		7	piece	Mantles	0	23	4	0
Gerald Vale	Ind	24.24	C	Fish, Hake	12	2	6	0
		14	burden	Fish, Salted	0	46	8	0
		0.5	burden	Fish, Salted	0	0	20	0
		1	mease	Fish, Herring Red	0	5	0	0
		7	piece	Mantles	0	23	4	0
		7	piece	Hides, Salted	0	9	4	0
		90	piece	Skins, Sheep (no wool)	0	7	6	0
		24	lb	Wax	0	8	0	0
		6	barrel	Fish, Herring White	0	30	0	0
Richard Madan	Ind	11	barrel	Fish, Herring White	0	55	0	0
		6	C	Fish, Hake	0	60	0	0
		140	piece	Skins, Sheep (no wool)	0	11	8	0
		70	lb	Wax	0	23	4	0
Richard Arthur	Ind	5.5	dicker	Hides, Salted	0	73	4	0
		3	piece	Mantles	0	10	0	0
William Brothe	Ind	8	C	Skins, Sheep (no wool)	4	0	0	0
		39	piece	Mantles	6	10	0	0

Merchant name	Origin	Qty	Unit	Commodity	£	s.	d.	f.
		128	lb	Wax	0	42	8	0
		17	piece	Skins, Fox	0	2	1	0
		20	piece	Skins, Lamb	0	0	10	0
Henry Neele	Ind	3.5	C	Skins, Sheep (no wool)	0	35	0	0
		1.08	C	Skins, Lamb	0	5	5	0
		8	barrel	Fish, Herring White	0	40	0	0
John Fe Harrie	Ind	1	C	Fish, Hake	0	10	0	0
		1	pipe	Fish, Salmon	0	30	0	0
		2	piece	Mantles	0	6	8	0
		4	stone	Wool, Flocks	0	0	20	0
Philip Morowe	Ind	8	piece	Mantles	0	26	8	0

Bata Savioure of Waterford, Thomas Meryn master, from Ireland, *2nd March 1504*

Merchant name	Origin	Qty	Unit	Commodity	£	s.	d.	f.
Robert Flemynge	Ind	17	barrel	Fish, Herring White	4	5	0	0
		4	mease	Fish, Herring Red	0	20	0	0
		5	piece	Mantles	0	16	8	0
		0.5	dicker	Hides, Salted	0	6	8	0
Robert Nevell	Ind	9.5	barrel	Fish, Herring White	0	47	6	0
		9	piece	Mantles	0	30	0	0
		2	mease	Fish, Herring Red	0	10	0	0
		20	piece	Skins, Sheep (no wool)	0	0	20	0
		12	piece	Skins, Lamb	0	0	6	0
Robert Reede	Ind	6	barrel	Fish, Herring White	0	30	0	0
		4	piece	Mantles	0	13	4	0
		1	mease	Fish, Herring Red	0	5	0	0
Philip Bowes	Ind	9	barrel	Fish, Herring White	0	45	0	0
		4	piece	Mantles	0	13	4	0
		1	quarter	Fish, Hake	0	2	6	0
		0.5	pipe	Fish, Salmon	0	15	0	0
William Fe Harrie	Ind	7	barrel	Fish, Herring White	0	35	0	0
		6	piece	Mantles	0	20	0	0
Nicholas Morowe	Ind	46	piece	Mantles	7	13	4	0
		168	lb	Wax	0	56	0	0
		9	piece	Skins, Fox	0	0	13	2
		3	piece	Skins, Otter	0	0	15	0
		24	yard	*Irish* Frieze *Cloth*	0	8	0	0
		1	piece	Skins, Marten	0	0	12	0
Francis Dromey	Ind	28	piece	Mantles	4	13	4	0
		5.333	C	Skins, Sheep (no wool)	0	53	4	0
		136	lb	Wax	0	45	4	0
		34	yard	Check, *cloth*	0	11	4	0
		1	dicker	Hides, Salted	0	13	4	0
Laurence Swylwen	Ind	4.4	C	Skins, Sheep (no wool)	0	44	0	0
		38	piece	Mantles	6	6	8	0
		3	quarter	Skins, Lamb	0	3	9	0
		12	yard	Check, *cloth*	0	4	0	0
		10	piece	Skins, Fox	0	0	15	0
		2	piece	Skins, Otter	0	0	10	0
		1	piece	Skins, Marten	0	0	12	0
		1	piece	Mantles	0	3	4	0
		70	lb	Wax	0	23	4	0

Merchant name	Origin	Qty	Unit	Commodity	£	s.	d.	f.
		6	piece	Mantles	0	20	0	0
		4	piece	Whitelles	0	13	4	0
Richard Calley	Ind	10	piece	Mantles	0	33	4	0
		43	yard	Check, *cloth*	0	14	4	0
		9	lb	Wax	0	3	0	0
John Braie	Ind	1.2	C	Skins, Sheep (no wool)	0	12	0	0
		11	lb	Wax	0	3	8	0
James Lye	Ind	2	piece	Mantles	0	6	8	0

Navicula Mawdlen of Pasajes de San Juan, Michael de Nicolalde master, from Andalusia, 2nd March 1504

Merchant name	Origin	Qty	Unit	Commodity	£	s.	d.	f.
John Thomas	Ind	13.5	tun	Wine	0	0	0	0
John Morgan	Ind	3.75	tun	Wine	0	0	0	0
William Draper	Ind	9.5	tun	Wine	0	0	0	0
William Weste	Ind	2	tun	Wine	0	0	0	0
John Howell	Ind	2.75	tun	Wine	0	0	0	0
Thomas Ffroste	Ind	15	tun	Wine	0	0	0	0
		1.5	ton	Fruit	0	60	0	0
Richard Draper	Ind	1	tun	Wine	0	0	0	0
John Benet	Ind	1	tun	Wine	0	0	0	0
Richard Bakar	Ind	2	tun	Wine	0	0	0	0
Thomas Ffroste	Ind	1	pipe	Fruit	0	20	0	0
John Morgan	Ind	1	tun	Wine	0	0	0	0
John Noble	Alien	1	hogshead	Wine	0	0	0	0
		1	pipe	Wine	0	0	0	0

Bata George of Gatcombe, Walter Nashe master, from Ireland, 4th March 1504

Merchant name	Origin	Qty	Unit	Commodity	£	s.	d.	f.
Walter Nashe	Ind	2	burden	Fish, Salted	0	6	8	0
John Bolfenche	Ind	2	tun	Wine	0	0	0	0
		1.25	tun	Rosin	0	33	4	0
John Hawkens	Ind	3	C	Rosin	0	4	0	0
		2	burden	Fish, Salted	0	6	8	0
Thomas Dryver	Ind	1.5	burden	Fish, Salted	0	5	0	0
Thomas Betson	Ind	1.5	burden	Fish, Salted	0	5	0	0

Bata Katren of Berkeley, Thomas Karwell master, from Chepstow, 4th March 1504

Merchant name	Origin	Qty	Unit	Commodity	£	s.	d.	f.
John Bocher	Ind	3	tun	Wine	0	0	0	0
James Atwood	Ind	1	tun	Wine	0	0	0	0

Bata Brithe of Milford Haven, Richard Maylare master, from Ireland, 4th March 1504

Merchant name	Origin	Qty	Unit	Commodity	£	s.	d.	f.
Richard Maylare	Ind	3.5	barrel	Fish, Herring White	0	17	6	0
		1.5	C	Fish, Hake	0	15	0	0

Bata Bestian of St Ives, John Jeffereis master, from Ireland, 7th March 1504

Merchant name	Origin	Qty	Unit	Commodity	£	s.	d.	f.
John Jeffereis	Ind	3	C	Fish, Hake	0	30	0	0
William Tregeyne	Ind	13	C	Fish, Hake	6	10	0	0
John Gilliot	Ind	3.5	C	Fish, Hake	0	35	0	0

Merchant name	Origin	Qty	Unit	Commodity	£	s.	d.	f.
John Jacson	Ind	2	C	Fish, Hake	0	20	0	0
John Stephyn	Ind	2.5	C	Fish, Hake	0	25	0	0
William Tregeyne	Ind	1.5	C	Britany Linen *Cloth*	0	30	0	0

Bata Katren of Chepst*ow*, Robert Ffishar master, from Chepst*ow*, 8th March 1504

William Hurste	Ind	2	tun	Wine	0	0	0	0
John Jaie	Ind	0.75	tun	Wine	0	0	0	0
William Davie	Ind	7.5	C	Pepper	37	10	0	0

Bata James of Minehead, Robert Basher, from Barnstaple, *8th March 1504*

Johanna Salisberie	Ind	2	tun	Oil, Olive	8	0	0	0
Paul Smythe	Ind	1.25	tun	Oil, Olive	0	100	0	0
Thomas Smythe	Ind	0.75	tun	Oil, Olive	0	60	0	0
John Salisberie	Ind	1	hogshead	Oil, Olive	0	20	0	0

Bata of Petur of St Bride's, William Hawkens master, from Ireland, 9th March 1504

William Hawkens	Ind	23	barrel	Fish, Herring White	0	115	0	0
		6	C	Fish, Hake	0	60	0	0
		0.5	burden	Fish, Salted	0	0	20	0

Batu Mare of Milford Haven, Thomas Howell master, from Ireland, *9th March 1504*

Thomas Howell	Ind	21	barrel	Fish, Herring White	0	105	0	0
		5.5	C	Fish, Hake	0	55	0	0
		2	burden	Fish, Salted	0	6	8	0
Richard Hichebon	Ind	6.75	C	Fish, Hake	0	67	6	0
		3	burden	Fish, Salted	0	10	0	0

Bata Mare of *Bloie*[11] John Deymshe master, to Ireland, 11th March 1504

George Monos	Ind	6	tun	Wine, Corrupt	9	0	0	0
		3.5	tun	Wine, Corrupt	0	105	0	0

Bata Gabriell of Milford Haven, John Bullock master, to Ireland, 12th March 1504

Henry Maye	Ind	3	lb	Saffron	0	20	0	0
		40	lb	*Pilus Tinctus*	0	13	4	0

Bata James of Waterford, James Leche master, to Ireland, 13th March 1504

James Leche	Ind	1	wey	Coal	0	3	4	0
David *Christ*pofur &								
James Leche	Ind	3	piece	Cloth of Assize	0	0	0	0
		120	lb	*Pilus Tinctus*	0	40	0	0
		4	gross	Points	0	4	0	0
		71	lb	Battery	0	23	8	0
John Corke	Ind	30	lb	*Pilus Tinctus*	0	10	0	0
David *Christ*pofur	Ind	2.5	lb	Saffron	0	16	8	0

11 Possibly Blavet in France.

Merchant name	Origin	Qty	Unit	Commodity	£	s.	d.	f.
		2	lb	Silk, Worked	0	26	8	0
		50	lb	*Pilus Tinctus*	0	16	8	0
Patrick Rise	Ind	40	lb	*Pilus Tinctus*	0	13	4	0
		8	yard	Cloth of Assize	0	0	0	0

Bata Marten of Milford Haven, William Rynishe master, from Ireland, *13th March 1504*

William Rynishe	Ind	21	barrel	Fish, Herring White	0	105	0	0
		7	C	Fish, Hake	0	70	0	0
		3	burden	Fish, Salted	0	10	0	0
		1	quarter	Fish, Hake	0	2	6	0

Bata Mawdlen of Carmarthen, Maurice Dee master, from Carmarthen, 14th March 1504

Hugh Bromwell	Ind	12	measure	Woad	0	75	0	0
Nicholas Kenaye	Ind	1	piece	Cloth of Assize	0	0	0	0
		40	lb	Battery	0	13	4	0
		26	lb	Battery	0	8	8	0

Bata Sondaie of Youghal, Maurice Nogell master, to Ireland, 14th March 1504

William Morowe	Ind	12	wey	Beans	8	0	0	0

Bata Lenard of Wa*ter*ford, William Gomben master, from Ireland, 15th March 1504

William Gomben	Ind	1.5	C	Fish, Hake	0	15	0	0
		4	burden	Fish, Salted	0	13	4	0
		1	virken	Fish, Salmon	0	7	6	0
		62	lb	wax	0	20	8	0
William Hewe	Ind	2.25	C	Fish, Hake	0	22	6	0
		2.5	burden	Fish, Salted	0	8	4	0
		0.5	barrel	Fish, Herring White	0	2	6	0
		1	piece	Mantles	0	3	4	0
William Brown*er*	Ind	4	pipe	Fish, Salmon	6	0	0	0
		5	piece	Mantles	0	16	8	0
William Kirie	Ind	5.5	barrel	Fish, Herring White	0	27	6	0
		1.5	C	Fish, Hake	0	15	0	0
		1.5	burden	Fish, Salted	0	5	0	0
		5	piece	Mantles	0	16	8	0
		0.5	piece	Seal	0	3	4	0
John Knock	Ind	1	barrel	Fish, Herring White	0	5	0	0
		0.5	quarter	Fish, Hake	0	0	15	0
James Shirlock	Ind	4	piece	Mantles	0	13	4	0
Patrick Rise	Ind	0.5	C	Fish, Hake	0	5	0	0
		7	burden	Fish, Salted	0	23	4	0
Dennis Ffolan	Ind	2	piece	Mantles	0	6	8	0
		0.5	quarter	Fish, Hake	0	0	15	0
William Tirrie	Ind	5.75	pipe	Fish, Salmon	8	12	6	0
		4	C	Fish, Hake	0	40	0	0
		6	barrel	Fish, Herring White	0	30	0	0
		7	piece	Mantles	0	23	4	0
		0.5	dicker	Hides, Salted	0	6	8	0

Merchant name	Origin	Qty	Unit	Commodity	£	s.	d.	f.
		7	lb	Wax	0	2	4	0
		22	burden	Fish, Salted	0	73	4	0
Henry White	Ind	2.25	C	Fish, Hake	0	22	6	0
		12	burden	Fish, Salted	0	40	0	0
		1.5	dicker	Hides, Salted	0	20	0	0
		3.75	C	Skins, Lamb	0	18	9	0
		1	virken	Fish, Salmon	0	7	6	0
		40	piece	Skins, Sheep (no wool)	0	3	4	0
John White	Ind	1.08	C	Skins, Sheep (no wool)	0	10	10	0
		4	piece	Hides, Salted	0	5	4	0
Patrick Rise	Ind	1	barrel	Fish, Herring White	0	5	0	0
Gerald Vale	Ind	3	mease	Fish, Herring Red	0	15	0	0

Bata Nicolas of Chepstow, John Rise master, from Chepstow, *15th March 1504*

William Goldsmythe	Ind	1.5	tun	Wine	0	0	0	0

Bata John of Haverfordwest, Thomas Blanick master, from Haverfordwest, *15th March 1504*

Richard Brokebanck	Ind	1.75	tun	Oil, Olive	7	0	0	0
		1.5	tun	Wine	0	0	0	0

Bata Petur of Berkeley, John Roche master, to Ireland, *15th March 1504*

John Roche	Ind	10	wey	Beans	6	13	4	0

Bata Savioure of Wexford, Thomas Meryn master, to Ireland, *15th March 1504*

Robert Flemynge	Ind	2	piece	Cloth of Assize	0	0	0	0
		28	lb	*Pilus Tinctus*	0	9	4	0
Robert Nevell	Ind	68	lb	*Pilus Tinctus*	0	22	8	0
		3	dozen	Cards, Unspecified	0	15	0	0
William Fe Harrie	Ind	2	yard	Cloth of Assize	0	0	0	0
Thomas Cawlon	Ind	1	piece	Cloth of Assize	0	0	0	0
		46	lb	*Pilus Tinctus*	0	15	0	0
		1	lb	Saffron	0	6	8	0
		1	piece	Cloth of Assize, Kersey	0	0	0	0
		2	gross	Knives	0	13	4	0
		0.5	dozen	Caps	0	3	4	0
Eliott Archer	Ind	4	piece	Cloth of Assize	0	0	0	0
		1	lb	Silk, Worked	0	13	4	0
		1	lb	Saffron	0	6	8	0
		24	lb	*Pilus Tinctus*	0	8	0	0

Bata Lenard of Waterford, Robert Roche master, to Ireland, *15th March 1504*

Robert Roche	Ind	5	wey	Beans	0	66	8	0
Malagur Taylor	Ind	32	lb	*Pilus Tinctus*	0	10	4	0
		1	piece	Cloth of Assize, Kersey	0	0	0	0
		0.5	lb	Saffron	0	3	4	0
		6	gross	Points	0	6	0	0
		2.5	C	Hops	0	12	6	0

Merchant name	Origin	Qty	Unit	Commodity	£	s.	d.	f.
Thomas Karre	Ind	2	piece	Cloth of Assize	0	0	0	0
		1	dozen	Caps	0	6	8	0
		2	C	Fruit	0	4	0	0
John Karvell	Ind	0.5	piece	Cloth of Assize	0	0	0	0

Bata Clement of Wexford, Walter Barrie master, to Ireland, 16th March 1504

Merchant name	Origin	Qty	Unit	Commodity	£	s.	d.	f.
John Fforlonge	Ind	2	wey	Beans	0	26	8	0
		2	piece	Cloth of Assize	0	0	0	0
		1	pipe	Iron	0	40	0	0
Walter Maylar	Ind	3	wey	Beans	0	40	0	0
		60	lb	Pilus Tinctus	0	20	0	0
		1	wey	Beans	0	13	4	0
		2.5	C	Iron	0	10	0	0

Bata John of Cork, Thomas Walshe master, to Ireland, 18th March 1504

Merchant name	Origin	Qty	Unit	Commodity	£	s.	d.	f.
Thomas Walshe	Ind	8.5	stone	Orchil, Worked	0	14	2	0
Richard Magner	Ind	16	stone	Orchil, Worked	0	26	8	0
		9	stone	Orchil, Worked	0	15	0	0
		70	lb	Pilus Tinctus	0	23	4	0
David Walshe	Ind	16	stone	Orchil, Worked	0	26	8	0
		19	stone	Orchil, Worked	0	31	8	0
		42	lb	Pilus Tinctus	0	14	0	0
Cornell Scolen	Ind	18	stone	Orchil, Worked	0	30	0	0
		1	piece	Cloth of Assize, Dozen Strait	0	0	0	0
Thomas Walshe	Ind	8	stone	Orchil, Worked	0	13	4	0
		50	lb	Pilus Tinctus	0	16	8	0
		8	stone	Orchil, Worked	0	13	4	0
		40	lb	Battery	0	13	4	0
Patrick Goold	Ind	3	lb	Silk, Worked	0	40	0	0
		2	lb	Saffron	0	13	4	0
		26	lb	Liquorice	0	5	0	0
		3	lb	Wood, Brazil	0	2	0	0
		1	lb	Pepper	0	0	12	0
		1	dozen	Caps	0	6	8	0
		12	piece	Cushions	0	10	0	0

Bata Mare of Waterford, Peter Fe John master, to Ireland, *18th March 1504*

Merchant name	Origin	Qty	Unit	Commodity	£	s.	d.	f.
Edmund Mean	Ind	0.5	C	Hops	0	2	6	0
David Comyn &								
Richard White	Ind	5	piece	Cloth of Assize	0	0	0	0
		1	piece	Cloth of Assize	0	0	0	0
		1	piece	Cloth of Assize, Kersey	0	0	0	0
		5	dozen	Caps	0	33	4	0
		5	dozen	Red leather	0	15	0	0
		15.5	lb	Saffron	0	103	4	0
John Doan	Ind	1	piece	Cloth of Assize	0	0	0	0
		92	lb	Pilus Tinctus	0	30	8	0
		2	lb	Silk, Worked	0	26	8	0
		0.5	lb	Saffron	0	3	4	0

Merchant name	Origin	Qty	Unit	Commodity	£	s.	d.	f.
William Dowrynge	Ind	1	piece	Cloth of Assize	0	0	0	0
		9	lb	*Pilus Tinctus*	0	3	0	0
Peter Fe John	Ind	12	lb	*Pilus Tinctus*	0	4	0	0
Thomas Karre	Ind	2	piece	Cloth of Assize	0	0	0	0
		12	gross	Points	0	12	0	0
		1.75	C	Fruit	0	3	6	0

Bata Barbara of Bristol, Philip Nongell master, to La Rochelle, 19th March 1504

Merchant name	Origin	Qty	Unit	Commodity	£	s.	d.	f.
John Colas	Ind	8	piece	Cloth of Assize	0	0	0	0

Bata Trinite of Cork, David Wyndar master, to Ireland, *19th March 1504*

Merchant name	Origin	Qty	Unit	Commodity	£	s.	d.	f.
Patrick Morowe	Ind	9	stone	Orchil, Worked	0	15	0	0
		44	lb	Battery	0	14	8	0
		3	stone	Orchil, Worked	0	5	0	0
Dennis Ffynne	Ind	6	stone	Orchil, Worked	0	10	0	0
		44	lb	*Pilus Tinctus*	0	14	8	0
		0.5	piece	Cloth of Assize, Dozen Welsh	0	2	1	0
Dennis Ffolan	Ind	9	stone	Orchil, Worked	0	15	0	0
William Tirrie	Ind	40	lb	*Pilus Tinctus*	0	13	4	0
David Wyndar	Ind	22.5	stone	Orchil, Worked	0	37	6	0
		46	lb	*Pilus Tinctus*	0	15	4	0
		1	piece	Cloth of Assize	2	0	0	0
		20	lb	*Pilus Tinctus*	0	6	8	0
Thomas Awsten	Ind	0.5	C	*Pilus Tinctus*	0	20	0	0
David Wyndar	Ind	40	stone	*Cork*, Red	0	40	0	0

Bata Katren of Chepstow, Robert Ffishar master, from Chepstow, 20th March 1504

Merchant name	Origin	Qty	Unit	Commodity	£	s.	d.	f.
Unknown Harry	Ind	2	C	Orchil	0	20	0	0
William Edwardes	Ind	1	pipe	Wine	2	0	0	0
George Beck	Ind	1.5	ton	Iron	0	75	0	0
		3	C	Rosin	0	4	0	0
John Pollard & Thomas Cooker	Ind	3	ton	Salt	0	50	0	0

Bata Mare Pollard, Port Unknown, Dennis Harte master, to Ireland, *20th March 1504*

Merchant name	Origin	Qty	Unit	Commodity	£	s.	d.	f.
John Pollard & Thomas Cooker	Ind	8	piece	Cloth of Assize	0	0	0	0
		4	tun	Wine, Corrupt	6	0	0	0

Navicula Anne of Gibraléon, Gonsalo Daze, to Andalusia, *20th March 1504*

Merchant name	Origin	Qty	Unit	Commodity	£	s.	d.	f.
Dominic Dortela	Alien	16	dozen	Skins, Calf	0	40	0	0

Bata Trinite of Waterford, William Brown master, to Ireland, *20th March 1504*

Merchant name	Origin	Qty	Unit	Commodity	£	s.	d.	f.
Philip Powar	Ind	1	lb	Silk, Worked	0	13	4	0
		1	lb	Saffron	0	6	8	0
		28	lb	*Pilus Tinctus*	0	9	4	0

Merchant name	Origin	Qty	Unit	Commodity	£	s.	d.	f.
		6	gross	Points	0	6	0	0
Edmund Mean	Ind	11	barrel	Beer	0	13	9	0
		9	stone	Orchil, Worked	0	15	0	0
		1.25	C	*Smigmates*	0	8	4	0
John Powar	Ind	3	piece	Cloth of Assize, Dozen Strait	0	0	0	0
Edmund Mean	Ind	10	lb	Pilus Tinctus	0	3	4	0
		0.5	lb	Saffron	0	3	4	0
		6	gross	Points	0	6	0	0
		2	piece	Cloth of Assize, Dozen	0	0	0	0
		1	lb	Silk, Worked	0	13	4	0
		2	lb	Thread	0	0	10	0
William Graunte &								
Patrick Rise	Ind	4	piece	Cloth of Assize	0	0	0	0
John Powar	Ind	12	bushell	Malt	0	3	4	0
		1	stone	Hemp	0	2	6	0
John Fforlonge	Ind	1	piece	Cloth of Assize, Kersey	0	0	0	0
Dennis Solen	Ind	0.5	lb	Saffron	0	3	4	0
Edmund Mean	Ind	2	wey	Beans &Barley	0	26	8	0

Bata Mawdlen of Waterford, William Penbroke master, to Ireland, 20th March 1504

Merchant name	Origin	Qty	Unit	Commodity	£	s.	d.	f.
William Penbroke	Ind	3	wey	Coal	0	10	0	0
Gerald Vale	Ind	2.5	last	Beer	0	75	0	0
William Penbroke	Ind	8	barrel	Beer	0	10	0	0
		16	lb	*Pilus Tinctus*	0	5	4	0
John Fforteen	Ind	16	stone	Orchil, Worked	0	26	8	0
William Penbroke	Ind	1.25	wey	Beans	0	16	8	0
John Popley	Ind	3	piece	Cloth of Assize	0	0	0	0
		4	C	Rosin	0	5	4	0
William Estbie	Ind	3	piece	Cloth of Assize	0	0	0	0
		2	C	Corde	0	20	0	0
William Downe	Ind	2	piece	Cloth of Assize	0	0	0	0
Philip Digon	Ind	0.5	last	Beer	0	15	0	0
Richard Caden	Ind	4	flege	Bacon	0	5	0	0
William Browgh	Ind	6	piece	Cloth of Assize	0	0	0	0
		60	lb	*Pilus Tinctus*	0	20	0	0
Walter Powar	Ind	3	piece	Cloth of Assize	0	0	0	0
		1	lb	Silk, Worked	0	13	4	0
		1	lb	Saffron	0	6	8	0
		3	gross	Points	0	3	0	0
William Penbroke	Ind	10	lb	*Pilus Tinctus*	0	3	4	0
Dennis Wilkens	Ind	10	lb	Saffron	0	66	8	0
		1.5	lb	Silk, Worked	0	20	0	0
		11	gross	Points	0	11	0	0
		2	gross	Points	0	2	0	0
Richard Maden	Ind	3	piece	Cloth of Assize	0	0	0	0
Richard Kellie	Ind	20	lb	*Pilus Tinctus*	0	6	8	0
		1	lb	Saffron	0	6	8	0
		2	gross	Points	0	2	0	0
Gerald Vale	Ind	66	lb	*Pilus Tinctus*	0	22	0	0
William Brothe	Ind	1	piece	Cloth of Assize	0	0	0	0
Walter Powar	Ind	1	piece	Cloth of Assize	0	0	0	0

Merchant name	Origin	Qty	Unit	Commodity	£	s.	d.	f.
John Fforteen	Ind	20	lb	*Pilus Tinctus*	o	6	8	o
Nicholas Bailie	Ind	11.5	lb	Saffron	o	76	8	o
		16	stone	Orchil, Worked	o	26	8	o
		48	lb	*Pilus Tinctus*	o	16	o	o

Bata Mare of Shirehampton, William White master, from Chepstow, 22nd March 1504

Merchant name	Origin	Qty	Unit	Commodity	£	s.	d.	f.
Thomas Bocher	Ind	34	measure	Woad	10	12	6	o
		2	piece	Cloth of Assize	o	o	o	o
		3	piece	Welsh *Cloth*, Dozen Strait	o	12	6	o

Bata Marget of Milford Haven, David Lloide master, from Ireland, 26th March 1504

Merchant name	Origin	Qty	Unit	Commodity	£	s.	d.	f.
Richard Griffethe	Ind	5.5	tun	Wine	o	o	o	o
David Browne	Ind	1	tun	Wine	o	o	o	o

Bata Savioure of Tenby, David Griffethe master, from Tenby, *26th March 1504*

Merchant name	Origin	Qty	Unit	Commodity	£	s.	d.	f.
Johanna Wiltshire	Ind	1	tun	Oil, Olive	4	o	o	o

Bata Rasin*us* of 'Yealm', Thomas Lover master, from Ireland, 27th March 1504

Merchant name	Origin	Qty	Unit	Commodity	£	s.	d.	f.
Thomas Lover	Ind	16	burden	Fish, Salted	o	53	4	o
		1	dicker	Hides, Salted	o	13	4	o

Bata Lenard of Waterford, William Gombon master, to Ireland, 28th March 1504

Merchant name	Origin	Qty	Unit	Commodity	£	s.	d.	f.
William Brown*er*	Ind	3.5	piece	Cloth of Assize	o	o	o	o
		12	lb	*Pilus Tinctus*	o	4	o	o
Henry White	Ind	1	piece	Cloth of Assize	o	o	o	o
		37	lb	*Pilus Tinctus*	o	12	4	o
		2	lb	Saffron	o	13	4	o
		1	piece	Fustian *Cloth*	o	5	o	o
		1	piece	Cloth of Assize	o	o	o	o
William Tirrie	Ind	60	lb	*Pilus Tinctus*	o	20	o	o
William Gombon	Ind	8	lb	Silk, Worked	o	106	8	o
		1.5	lb	Saffron	o	10	o	o
		40	lb	*Pilus Tinctus*	o	13	4	o
Nicholas Morowe	Ind	11	lb	Saffron	o	73	4	o
		1	piece	Cloth of Assize	o	o	o	o
		1	dozen	Caps	o	6	8	o
		20	lb	*Pilus Tinctus*	o	6	8	o
		0.5	gross	Knives	o	3	4	o
		0.5	gross	Knives	o	3	4	o
		4	dozen	Girdles	o	o	20	o
		1	lb	Ginger	o	2	6	o
		3	gross	Points	o	3	o	o
		3	pair	Stock-cards	o	3	o	o
Patrick Rise	Ind	8	stone	Orchil, Worked	o	13	4	o
		1	barrel	Pitch	o	3	4	o
		30	lb	*Pilus Tinctus*	o	10	o	o
		3	gross	Points	o	3	o	o

Merchant name	Origin	Qty	Unit	Commodity	£	s.	d.	f.
Robert Butlar	Ind	45	lb	Battery	0	15	0	0
William Kirie	Ind	3	lb	*Pilus Tinctus*	0	0	12	0
		1	lb	Pepper	0	0	12	0
		0.5	dozen	Caps	0	3	4	0
John White	Ind	0.5	piece	Cloth of Assize	0	0	0	0
		4	lb	*Pilus Tinctus*	0	0	16	0

Bata Kereck of Milford Haven, William Wade master, from Milford Haven, 29th March 1504

William Wade	Ind	1	barrel	Fish, Herring White	0	5	0	0
Francis Dromey	Ind	2	piece	Cloth of Assize	0	0	0	0
		1	lb	Silk, Worked	0	13	4	0
		16	lb	*Pilus Tinctus*	0	5	4	0
		3	gross	Points	0	3	0	0
Laurence Swylwyn	Ind	12	lb	Saffron	4	0	0	0
		6	gross	Points	0	6	0	0
		6	yard	Cloth of Assize	0	0	0	0

Bata Mare of Berkeley, Thomas Smyth master, from Chepstow, 2nd April 1504

Thomas Bocher	Ind	2.5	tun	Wine	0	0	0	0
		0.75	tun	Wine	0	0	0	0

Bata Mawdlen of Berkeley, Thomas Sene*kur* master, from Ireland, 4th April 1504

Richard Bocher	Ind	47	burden	Fish, Salted	7	16	8	0
		6	barrel	Fish, Herring White	0	30	0	0
		7	piece	Mantles	0	23	4	0
		5	burden	Fish, Salted	0	16	0	0
		2	dicker	Hides, Salted	0	26	8	0
		0.5	C	Check *Cloth*	0	20	0	0
		30	lb	Wax	0	10	0	0
		1	C	Fat, Mutton	0	6	8	0
Maurice Donell	Ind	2	tun	Wine	*8*	*0*	*0*	*0*
		9	burden	Fish, Salted	0	30	0	0
James Atwood	Ind	7	burden	Fish, Salted	0	23	4	0
William Keve	Ind	3	pipe	Fish, Salmon	4	10	0	0
Richard Bocher	Ind	1	quarter	Fish, Hake	0	2	6	0
Maurice Donell	Ind	1	dicker	Hides, Salted	0	13	4	0

Navicula Marget of Bristol, Edward Gibbes master, from Bordeaux, 11th April 1504

Nicholas Browne	Ind	10	tun	Wine	0	0	0	0
		6	pipe	Woad	30	0	0	0
John Stokes	Ind	4.5	tun	Wine	0	0	0	0
Thomas Barne	Ind	6	tun	Wine	0	0	0	0
John Ringston	Ind	3	pipe	Woad	15	0	0	0
		1.25	tun	Wine	0	0	0	0
		1	pipe	Rosin	0	13	4	0
Robert Ffystar	Ind	2	pipe	Woad	10	0	0	0
		2	tun	Wine	0	0	0	0
Ralph Aprise	Ind	1	tun	Wine	0	0	0	0

Merchant name	Origin	Qty	Unit	Commodity	£	s.	d.	f.
John Shipman	Ind	6.5	pipe	Woad	32	10	0	0
		2.25	tun	Wine	0	0	0	0
William Hurste	Ind	6.5	pipe	Woad	32	10	0	0
Stephen Ffostar &								
John Meysam	Ind	1	tun	Wine	0	0	0	0
		4	pipe	Woad	20	0	0	0
Thomas Chapman	Ind	1	tun	Wine	0	0	0	0
William Estbie	Ind	2	tun	Wine	0	0	0	0
Thomas Hawkens	Ind	4.75	pipe	Woad	23	15	0	0
Thomas Plomley	Ind	1.25	tun	Wine	0	0	0	0
William Tirrie	Ind	5	pipe	Woad	25	0	0	0
Walter Parkar	Ind	2	tun	Wine	0	0	0	0
Richard Hobie	Ind	9.5	pipe	Woad	47	10	0	0
John Vaghan	Ind	6	tun	Wine	0	0	0	0
David Vaghan	Ind	3.5	pipe	Woad	17	10	0	0
Robert Ffortey	Ind	3.5	pipe	Woad	17	10	0	0
John Shipman	Ind	1	pipe	Rosin	0	13	4	0
John Ware	Ind	1	tun	Rosin	0	26	8	0
John Popley	Ind	3	pipe	Woad	15	0	0	0
		1.916	tun	Wine	0	0	0	0
John Brooke	Ind	4	pipe	Woad	20	0	0	0
		1	tun	Wine	0	0	0	0
John Colas	Ind	9	pipe	Woad	45	0	0	0
Thomas Veele	Ind	2	tun	Wine	0	0	0	0
Thomas Horsman	Ind	7	C	Rosin	0	9	4	0
John Browne	Ind	0.75	tun	Wine	0	0	0	0
Thomas Turnor	Ind	1.25	tun	Wine	0	0	0	0
Nicholas Bowen &								
Thomas Clarke	Ind	6	tun	Wine	24	0	0	0
Robert Thorn	Ind	3	pipe	Woad	15	0	0	0
Jonn Walshe	Ind	1	hogshead	Wine	0	0	0	0
Thomas Barne	Ind	12	C	Combs	0	12	0	0

Navicula Trinite of Barnstaple, William Bishop master, from Lisbon, *11th April 1504*

Merchant name	Origin	Qty	Unit	Commodity	£	s.	d.	f.
William Bishop	Ind	5.5	tun	Wine	0	0	0	0
		1	hogshead	Oil, Olive	0	20	0	0
		4.5	C	Wax	9	0	0	0
		3.25	C	Pepper	16	5	0	0
		1	C	Sugar	0	40	0	0
		8	dozen	Cork, Black	0	13	4	0
John Smythe	Ind	7.5	tun	Wine	0	0	0	0
		1	hogshead	Oil, Olive	0	20	0	0
		1.75	C	Wax	0	70	0	0
		1	C	Pepper	0	100	0	0
		20	lb	Cloves	0	40	0	0
		20	lb	Nutmeg	0	20	0	0
Thomas Smythe	Ind	8	tun	Wine	0	0	0	0
		1.5	hogshead	Oil, Olive	0	30	0	0
		6	C	Wax	12	0	0	0
		0.5	C	Sugar	0	20	0	0
		1.875	C	Pepper	9	7	6	0

Merchant name	Origin	Qty	Unit	Commodity	£	s.	d.	f.
		28	lb	Cloves	0	56	0	0
Paul Smythe	Ind	7.5	tun	Wine	0	0	0	0
		1	hogshead	Oil, Olive	0	20	0	0
		6.5	C	Wax	13	0	0	0
		4.5	C	Pepper	22	10	0	0
		28	lb	Cloves	0	56	0	0
		2	piece	Mantles, Fox	0	15	0	0
Thomas Smyth	Ind	5	tun	Wine	0	0	0	0
		2	tun	Oil, Olive	8	0	0	0
Robert Symons	Ind	4	tun	Wine	0	0	0	0
		0.5	C	Pepper	0	50	0	0
John Goddisland	Ind	2.75	tun	Wine	0	0	0	0
		2	C	Pepper	10	0	0	0
		1.5	C	Wax	0	60	0	0
Richard Patie	Ind	2	tun	Wine	0	0	0	0
		2.25	C	Pepper	11	5	0	0
		2.875	C	Wax	0	115	0	0
Thomas Becke	Ind	1	pipe	Wine	0	0	0	0
		0.5	C	Pepper	0	50	0	0
Simon Andrewe	Ind	1	tun	Wine	0	0	0	0
John Harton	Ind	1	tun	Wine	0	0	0	0
		0.5	C	Pepper	0	50	0	0
John Thomas	Ind	1	tun	Wine	0	0	0	0
		1	C	Pepper	0	100	0	0
John Scotte	Ind	0.5	hogshead	Oil, Olive	0	10	0	0
		1.625	C	Wax	0	65	0	0
		28	lb	Pepper	0	28	0	0
Richard Broite	Ind	1	tun	Wine	0	0	0	0
		0.5	C	Pepper	0	50	0	0
Richard Cokeran	Ind	1	tun	Wine	0	0	0	0
		1	pipe	Oil, Olive	0	40	0	0
		1	C	Pepper	0	100	0	0
		1	C	Wax	0	40	0	0
John Premet	Ind	1.25	tun	Wine	0	0	0	0
		3	tun	Oil, Olive	12	0	0	0
		4.5	C	Wax	9	0	0	0
		1.125	quarter	Pepper	0	112	6	0
Johanna Salisberie	Ind	2	tun	Wine	0	0	0	0
		3.75	C	Wax	7	10	0	0
		5	C	Pepper	25	0	0	0
		28	lb	Cloves	0	56	0	0
		28	lb	Nutmeg	0	28	0	0
		1.5	quarter	Ginger	0	37	6	0
William Pers	Ind	5	kanters	Oil, Olive	0	7	6	0
James Cockes	Ind	1	pipe	Wine	0	0	0	0
John Halle	Ind	1	pipe	Wine	0	0	0	0
Simon Ffishar	Ind	1.5	tun	Wine	0	0	0	0
John Walter	Ind	3	tun	Wine	0	0	0	0
		1	C	Pepper	0	100	0	0
		2	C	Wax	4	0	0	0
		3	kanters	Oil, Olive	0	4	2	0
Thomas Gomes	Ind	42	lb	Cinnamon	0	105	0	0

Merchant name	Origin	Qty	Unit	Commodity	£	s.	d.	f.
		12	lb	Pepper	0	12	0	0
William Bishop	Ind	8	dozen	Cork, Black	0	13	4	0

Navicula Mare Belhouse of Bristol, Walter Cooke master, to Andalusia, *11th April 1504*

Merchant name	Origin	Qty	Unit	Commodity	£	s.	d.	f.
Roger Dawes	Ind	9.5	piece	Cloth of Assize	0	0	0	0
Robert Thorn	Ind	20	piece	Cloth of Assize	0	0	0	0
David Vaghan	Ind	24	piece	Cloth of Assize	0	0	0	0
		8	C	Britany Linen *Cloth*	8	0	0	0
Thomas Smythe	Ind	22	piece	Cloth of Assize	0	0	0	0
Henry Dale	Ind	6	piece	Cloth of Assize	0	0	0	0
Robert Thorn	Ind	10	piece	Cloth of Assize	0	0	0	0
John Halle	Ind	18	piece	Cloth of Assize, Dozen Strait	0	0	0	0
		8	piece	Welsh *Cloth*	8	0	0	0
John Ringston	Ind	4	piece	Cloth of Assize	0	0	0	0
		1	piece	Welsh *Cloth*	0	20	0	0
John Grene	Ind	7	piece	Cloth of Assize	0	0	0	0
		5	piece	Welsh *Cloth*	0	100	0	0
John Gurdelar	Ind	2	piece	Welsh *Cloth*	0	40	0	0
John Eliet	Ind	16	piece	Cloth of Assize	0	0	0	0
Robert Eliet	Ind	9	piece	Cloth of Assize	0	0	0	0
John Pollard	Ind	10	piece	Welsh *Cloth*	10	0	0	0
John Lorde	Ind	3	piece	Welsh *Cloth*	0	60	0	0
Henry Tollar	Ind	12	piece	*Remmletes*	0	40	0	0
Robert Ffortey	Ind	2	piece	Cloth of Assize	0	0	0	0
John Inon	Ind	1	piece	Welsh *Cloth*	0	20	0	0
		1	piece	Welsh *Cloth*, Dozen Strait	0	4	2	0
Thomas Eliet	Ind	6	piece	Cloth of Assize	0	0	0	0
Thomas Eliet Jun*ior*	Ind	8	piece	Cloth of Assize	0	0	0	0
Philip Tewe	Ind	4	piece	Cloth of Assize, Kersey	0	0	0	0
		1.5	piece	Welsh *Cloth*	0	30	0	0
John Domi*n*gus	Alien	15	piece	Welsh *Cloth*	15	0	0	0
Christopher Payn	Ind	4	piece	Cloth of Assize	0	0	0	0
John Rowland	Ind	9	piece	Cloth of Assize	0	0	0	0
Christopher Godwyn	Ind	2	piece	Welsh *Cloth*	0	40	0	0
		2	piece	Cloth of Assize, Dozen Strait	0	0	0	0
		0.5	piece	Cloth of Assize, Kersey	0	0	0	0

Navicula George of Glouce*ster*, William Kempe master, from Bordeaux, 12th April 1504

Merchant name	Origin	Qty	Unit	Commodity	£	s.	d.	f.
Walter Rowdon	Ind	7.5	tun	Wine	0	0	0	0
William Goldsmythe	Ind	4	tun	Wine	0	0	0	0
Richard Rowdon	Ind	3.5	tun	Wine	0	0	0	0
Thomas Pole	Ind	8.5	tun	Wine	0	0	0	0
Ralph Hasley	Ind	7	tun	Wine	0	0	0	0
Gratien de la Plase	Ind	8	tun	Wine	0	0	0	0
John Ffarley	Ind	4	tun	Wine	0	0	0	0
James Whaley	Ind	1	tun	Wine	0	0	0	0

Bata Sondaie of Youghal, Maurice Nogell master, to Ireland, *12th April 1504*

Merchant name	Origin	Qty	Unit	Commodity	£	s.	d.	f.
William Morowe	Ind	160	lb	*Pilus Tinctus*	0	53	4	0

Merchant name	Origin	Qty	Unit	Commodity	£	s.	d.	f.

Bata Trinite of Kinsale, Dennis Cante master, from Ireland, 15th April 1504

Merchant name	Origin	Qty	Unit	Commodity	£	s.	d.	f.
David Roche	Ind	1.75	pipe	Fish, Salmon	0	52	6	0
		34.5	barrel	Fish, Herring White	8	12	6	0
		5	C	Fish, Hake	0	50	0	0
		2.5	burden	Fish, Salted	0	8	4	0
		3	C	Skins, Sheep (no wool)	0	30	0	0
		1	quarter	Skins, Lamb	0	0	15	0
		4	stone	Wool, Flocks	0	0	20	0

Navicula Marget of Bristol Edward Gibbes master, to Bordeaux, *15th April 1504*

Merchant name	Origin	Qty	Unit	Commodity	£	s.	d.	f.
William Estbie	Ind	12	piece	Cloth of Assize	0	0	0	0
William Jeffereis	Ind	70	piece	Cloth of Assize	0	0	0	0
John Ringston	Ind	5	piece	Cloth of Assize	0	0	0	0
Nicholas Brown	Ind	49	piece	Cloth of Assize	0	0	0	0
Thomas Hochkens	Ind	6	piece	Cloth of Assize	0	0	0	0
John Eliet	Ind	4	piece	Cloth of Assize	0	0	0	0
John Vaghan	Ind	16	piece	Cloth of Assize	0	0	0	0
John Stokes	Ind	10	piece	Cloth of Assize	0	0	0	0
John Turnor	Ind	4	piece	Cloth of Assize	0	0	0	0
John Shipman	Ind	5	piece	Cloth of Assize	0	0	0	0
Robert Ffystar	Ind	2	piece	Cloth of Assize	0	0	0	0
William Jeffereis	Ind	1.5	C	*Smigmates*	0	10	0	0
William Aphowell	Ind	13	piece	Cloth of Assize	0	0	0	0
		6	piece	Cloth of Assize	0	0	0	0
Thomas Awsten	Ind	4	piece	Cloth of Assize	0	0	0	0
John Rowland	Ind	17	piece	Welsh *Cloth*, Dozen Strait	0	70	10	0
John Reepe	Ind	2	piece	Welsh *Cloth*	0	40	0	0
William Wosley	Ind	4	piece	Cloth of Assize	0	0	0	0
Robert Rowlowe	Ind	1	piece	Cloth of Assize	0	0	0	0
John Shipman	Ind	2	piece	Cloth of Assize	0	0	0	0
Thomas Barn	Ind	7	piece	Cloth of Assize	0	0	0	0

Navicula Trinite of Barnstaple, William Bishop master, to Lisbon, *15th April 1504*

Merchant name	Origin	Qty	Unit	Commodity	£	s.	d.	f.
Richard Cokeran	Ind	4	piece	Welsh *Cloth*	4	0	0	0
Thomas Smyth	Ind	3	piece	Welsh *Cloth*	0	60	0	0
Paul Smyth	Ind	1	piece	Cloth of Assize	0	0	0	0

Bata Trynite of Chepstow, John Vicarne master, from Chepstow, 17th April 1504

Merchant name	Origin	Qty	Unit	Commodity	£	s.	d.	f.
William Estbie	Ind	2	tun	Wine	0	0	0	0

Bata Mare of Milford Haven, Thomas Jeffereis master, from Milford Haven, 18th April 1504

Merchant name	Origin	Qty	Unit	Commodity	£	s.	d.	f.
Thomas Bowleis	Ind	1	pipe	Wine	0	0	0	0

Bata Marget of Chepstow, Robert Bocher master, from Chepstow, *18th April 1504*

Merchant name	Origin	Qty	Unit	Commodity	£	s.	d.	f.
William Tirrie	Ind	1	tun	Wine	0	0	0	0
John Eliet	Ind	1	pipe	Wine	0	0	0	0

Merchant name	Origin	Qty	Unit	Commodity	£	s.	d.	f.

Bata Mare of Milford Haven, John Gibons master, from Milford Haven, *18th April 1504*

John Lloid & Robert Hardinge	Ind	11	ton	Salt	4	11	8	o

Bata Katren of Minehead, David Tege master, from Ireland, 20th April 1504

David Tege	Ind	30	burden	Fish, Salted	o	100	o	o
		2	C	Fish, Hake	o	20	o	o
		3	C	Skins, Sheep (no wool)	o	30	o	o
		1	quarter	Skins, Sheep (no wool)	o	2	6	o
		6.5	burden	Fish, Salted	o	21	8	o

Bata Anne Minehead of Thomas Gregorie master, from Ireland, *20th April 1504*

Thomas Gregorie	Ind	30	burden	Fish, Salted	o	100	o	o
		16	burden	Fish, Salted	o	53	4	o

Navicula Mawdlen of Pasajes de San Juan, Michael de Nicolalde master, to Spain, *20th April 1504*

Michael de Nicolade	Alien	183	flege	Bacon	15	5	o	o
		9.5	dicker	Hides, Tanned	34	16	8	o
		4	piece	Welsh Cloth, Dozen Strait	o	16	8	o
John Colas	Ind	10	piece	Cloth of Assize	o	o	o	o
John Shipman	Ind	14	piece	Cloth of Assize	o	o	o	o
Thomas Hawkens & John Shipman	Ind	80	flege	Bacon	6	13	4	o
Thomas Awsten	Ind	6	piece	Cloth of Assize	o	o	o	o
John Edee	Ind	20	piece	Cloth of Assize	o	o	o	o
Michael de Nicolade	Alien	2	dicker	Hides, Tanned	7	6	8	o
John Rowland	Ind	30	piece	Welsh Cloth, Dozen Strait	6	5	o	o
Thomas Badcok	Ind	8	dozen	Skins, Calf Tanned	o	20	o	o

Bata Katren of Chepstow, Robert Ffishar master, from Chepstow, *20th April 1504*

John Colas	Ind	0.5	pipe	Woad	o	50	o	o

Bata Rose of Tenby, Richard Honter master, from Tenby, 24th April 1504

Richard Honter	Ind	11	ton	Salt	4	11	8	o
		3	ton	Salt	o	25	o	o

Bata Mare Halle, Port Unknown, William Halle master, from Chepstow, 24th April 1504

William Colston	Ind	2	tun	Wine	o	o	o	o

Bata Trinite of Kinsale, Dennis Cante master, to Ireland, 26th April 1504

Dennis Cante	Ind	2	last	Beer	o	60	o	o
		9	stone	Orchil, Worked	o	15	o	o
		30	lb	Pilus Tinctus	o	10	o	o

Merchant name	Origin	Qty	Unit	Commodity	£	s.	d.	f.

Bata Katren of Bristol, William Downe master, from Ireland, 26th April 1504

Merchant name	Origin	Qty	Unit	Commodity	£	s.	d.	f.
James Treves	Ind	37	dicker	Hides, Salted	24	13	4	0
		22.5	C	Skins, Sheep (no wool)	11	5	0	0
		25	C	Skins, Lamb	6	5	0	0
		120	lb	Wax	0	40	0	0
		24	piece	Skins, Fox	0	3	0	0
		2	piece	Skins, Otter	0	0	10	0
		1	piece	Skins, Marten	0	0	12	0
Nicholas Brown	Ind	2	C	Skins, Lamb	0	10	0	0
John Pollard	Ind	6	C	Skins, Sheep (no wool)	0	60	0	0
		3	dicker	Hides, Salted	0	40	0	0
		2.25	C	Alum	0	11	3	0
		1	C	Skins, Lamb	0	5	0	0
John Wase	Ind	2.5	dicker	Hides, Salted	0	33	4	0
		20	piece	Skins, Sheep (no wool)	0	0	20	0
		1	piece	Mantles	0	3	4	0
		6	yard	Irish Frieze Cloth	0	2	0	0
James Treves	Ind	1	C	Skins, Lamb	0	5	0	0

Bata Katren of Chepstow, Robert Ffishar master, from Chepstow, 26th April 1504

Merchant name	Origin	Qty	Unit	Commodity	£	s.	d.	f.
Nicholas Sciddie	Ind	3.5	C	Skins, Sheep (no wool)	0	35	0	0
		1	C	Skins, Lamb	0	5	0	0
John Arthur	Ind	1	C	Skins, Lamb	0	5	0	0
Richard Goold	Ind	3	C	Skins, Sheep (no wool)	0	30	0	0
		1.5	C	Skins, Lamb	0	7	6	0
		0.5	pipe	Fish, Salmon	0	15	0	0

Navicula Mare Towre, Port Unknown, John Graunte master, to Lisbon, 26th April 1504

Merchant name	Origin	Qty	Unit	Commodity	£	s.	d.	f.
Alfonso Pars	Alien	28	piece	Cloth of Assize	0	0	0	0
John Jenkens	Ind	2	piece	Welsh Cloth	0	40	0	0
		6.5	dozen	Skins, Calf Tanned	0	16	3	0
Thomas Grey	Ind	3	piece	Cloth of Assize	0	0	0	0
		5	piece	Cloth of Assize, Kersey	0	0	0	0
Alfonso Pars	Alien	5.5	piece	Cloth of Assize	0	0	0	0
John Halle	Ind	70	piece	Welsh Cloth, Dozen Strait	14	11	8	0
		6	piece	Cloth of Assize, Dozen Strait	0	0	0	0
		4	piece	Cloth of Assize, Dozen Strait	0	0	0	0
		1	ton	Lead, Worked	0	100	0	0
John Popley	Ind	12	piece	Cloth of Assize	0	0	0	0
Robert Thorn	Ind	20	piece	Cloth of Assize	0	0	0	0
William Jeffereis	Ind	18	piece	Cloth of Assize	0	0	0	0
Robert Ffortey	Ind	5	piece	Cloth of Assize	0	0	0	0
John Harries	Ind	6	piece	Cloth of Assize	0	0	0	0
John Halle	Ind	3	piece	Welsh Cloth	0	60	0	0
Thomas Smythe	Ind	12	piece	Cloth of Assize	0	0	0	0
Nicholas Browne	Ind	10	piece	Cloth of Assize	0	0	0	0
		4	piece	Welsh Cloth	4	0	0	0
Thomas Aphowell	Ind	5	piece	Cloth of Assize	0	0	0	0
John Jaie	Ind	7	piece	Cloth of Assize	0	0	0	0

Merchant name	Origin	Qty	Unit	Commodity	£	s.	d.	f.
John Turnor	Ind	10	piece	Cloth of Assize	0	0	0	0
		11	piece	Welsh *Cloth*	11	0	0	0
John Marchall	Ind	4	piece	Cloth of Assize	0	0	0	0
John Rowland	Ind	36	piece	Cloth of Assize	0	0	0	0
		20	piece	Welsh *Cloth*, Dozen Strait	4	3	4	0
Alfonso Pars	Alien	5	piece	Cloth of Assize	0	0	0	0
Walter Rise	Ind	2	piece	Welsh *Cloth*	0	40	0	0
Humphrey Brown	Ind	5	piece	Cloth of Assize	0	0	0	0
		2	piece	Welsh *Cloth*	0	40	0	0
John Graunte	Alien	11	piece	Welsh *Cloth*	11	0	0	0
Humphrey Grey	Alien	1.5	piece	Welsh *Cloth*	0	30	0	0
John Ringston	Ind	2	piece	Cloth of Assize	0	0	0	0
John Stokes	Ind	7	piece	Cloth of Assize	0	0	0	0
John Parkar	Ind	3	piece	Welsh *Cloth*	0	60	0	0
John Lorde	Ind	1	piece	Welsh *Cloth*	0	20	0	0
John Ley	Ind	2	piece	Welsh *Cloth*	0	40	0	0
		1	piece	Welsh *Cloth*	0	20	0	0
William Estbie	Ind	10	piece	Cloth of Assize	0	0	0	0
John Rowland	Ind	0.5	C	Cloth of Assize	0	0	0	0
Reginald Sanders	Ind	1	piece	Cloth of Assize	0	0	0	0
John Ffarre	Ind	2	piece	Cloth of Assize	0	0	0	0
William Estbie	Ind	2	C	Tin, Worked	0	60	0	0
John Halle	Ind	1	piece	Cloth of Assize	0	0	0	0
		4	piece	Welsh *Cloth*	4	0	0	0

Bata Laurens of Tewkesbury, John Borefeld master, from Cardiff, 27th April 1504

John Borefeld	Ind	1	pipe	Wine	2	0	0	0

Bata Marget of Tenby, John Rowe master, from Tenby, *27th April 1504*

William Whitinge	Ind	10	ton	Salt	4	3	4	0

Bata Katren of Bristol, William Down master, from Ireland, 30th April 1504

William Tirrie	Ind	1	dicker	Hides, Salted	0	20	0	0
		1.5	C	Skins, Lamb	0	7	6	0
		36	piece	Skins, Sheep (no wool)	0	3	0	0
John Phelip	Ind	5	piece	Mantles	0	16	8	0
		2	stone	Wool, Flocks	0	0	10	0

Bata Mare of Bristol, Philip Kerie master, from Ireland, *30th April 1504*

William Jeffereis	Ind	0.5	C	Skins, Lamb	0	2	6	0
		1	burden	Fish, Salted	0	3	4	0

Batur James of Tenby, David Grigge master, from Tenby, *30th April 1504*

David Grigge	Ind	2	ton	Salt	0	16	8	0
John Lloide	Ind	7	ton	Salt	0	58	4	0
Lewis Grene	Ind	3	ton	Salt	0	25	0	0
William Hurton	Ind	8	ton	Salt	0	66	8	0

Merchant name	Origin	Qty	Unit	Commodity	£	s.	d.	f.
William Speer	Ind	8	ton	Salt	0	66	8	0
William Hurton	Ind	4	ton	Salt	0	33	4	0

Batur Mare of Milford Haven, John Gibbons master, to Ireland, 4th May 1504

Henry Tollar	Ind	4	tun	Wine, Corrupt	6	0	0	0
		1.25	tun	Wine, Corrupt	0	37	6	0
John Ffrebodie	Ind	5	piece	Cloth of Assize	0	0	0	0

Navicula of Mathewe of Bristol, Edmund Griffeth master, from Ireland, *4th May 1504*

Edmund Griffeth	Ind	4.5	dicker	Hides, Salted	0	60	0	0
		11	burden	Fish, Salted	0	36	8	0
Unknown Jonyco	Alien	0.5	C	Wax	0	20	0	0
		1	C	Skins, Lamb	0	5	0	0
		26	piece	Skins, Otter	0	10	10	0
Edmund Griffeth	Ind	2.5	burden	Fish, Salted	0	8	4	0

Navicula Mare of Bristol, Philip Kyrie master, to Ireland, 6th May 1504

John Harries	Ind	2.75	tun	Wine, Corrupt	4	2	6	0
		4	ton	Salt	0	66	8	0
		1	piece	Cloth of Assize	0	0	0	0
John Brewar	Ind	1	pipe	Salt	0	8	4	0
William White	Ind	1	last	*Sine Vicur*[12]	0	30	0	0
William Jeffereis	Ind	32	piece	Cloth of Assize, Dozen	0	0	0	0
		2	piece	Cloth of Assize	0	0	0	0
Nicholas Brown	Ind	4	lb	Saffron	0	26	8	0
Raymond Nashe	Ind	8	stone	Orchil, Worked	0	13	4	0
Nicholas Ffyrter	Ind	9	stone	Orchil, Worked	0	15	0	0
William Jeffereis	Ind	3	piece	Cloth of Assize	0	0	0	0
Bernard Carney	Ind	1	piece	Cloth of Assize	0	0	0	0

Bata Petur of Gatcombe, John Howell master, from Chepstow, *6th May 1504*

Thomas Chapma*n*	Ind	2	tun	Wine	0	0	0	0

Batur Anne of Chepstow, John Horsma*n* master, from Chepstow, 14th May 1504

Nicholas Ffishar	Ind	1	tun	Wine	0	0	0	0

Bata Kemborgh of Glouc*ester*, Philip Ffoxe master, to Ireland, *14th May 1504*

David Westbery & Thomas Ayleworth	Ind	10	wey	Beans & Malt	6	13	4	0
		1	C	Battery	0	40	0	0
		1	piece	Welsh *Cloth*, Dozen Strait	0	4	2	0

Navicula Andrewe of Milford Haven, John Wilke master, to Brittany, 17th May 1504

John Williams	Ind	25	piece	Welsh *Cloth*	25	0	0	0
		2	piece	Cloth of Assize	0	0	0	0

12 Probably beer.

Merchant name	Origin	Qty	Unit	Commodity	£	s.	d.	f.
Batur James of Chepstow, Richard Halle master, from Chepstow, 20th May 1504								
Thomas Harries	Ind	1	tun	Wine	0	0	0	0
Navicula _Christ_pofur of Bristol, Richard Saverey master, from Bordeaux, _20th May 1504_								
Richard Saverey	Ind	1	hogshead	Rosin	0	6	8	0
George Monos	Ind	6	tun	Wine	0	0	0	0
		2	pipe	Woad	10	0	0	0
		1	tun	Rosin	0	26	8	0
William Mewriell	Ind	21	measure	Woad	6	11	3	0
		1	tun	Rosin	0	26	8	0
Roger Dawes	Ind	30	pipe	Woad	150	0	0	0
John Shipman	Ind	4.5	pipe	Woad	22	10	0	0
Thomas Chapma_n_	Ind	1	pipe	Woad	0	100	0	0
John Ware	Ind	1	tun	Wine	0	0	0	0
		5.5	pipe	Woad	27	10	0	0
John Shipman &								
John Ware	Ind	8	M	Combs	4	0	0	0
John Barnard	Ind	1	hogshead	Rosin	0	6	8	0
John Browne	Ind	7	measure	Woad	0	43	9	0
John Edee	Ind	5	pipe	Woad	25	0	0	0
Robert Rowlowe	Ind	2	pipe	Woad	10	0	0	0
Thomas Awsten	Ind	1	pipe	Woad	0	100	0	0
Thomas Barn	Ind	1	tun	Wine	0	0	0	0
Bata Cleme_n_t of Milford Haven, Thomas Blanke master, from Milford Haven, _20th May 1504_								
John Sutton	Ind	1	pipe	Oil, Olive	0	40	0	0
Bata Gabriell of Chepstow of John Brewar master, from Chepstow, 21st May 1504								
John _Brewar_	Ind	1	pipe	Wine	0	0	0	0
Bata Sey_n_t Marke, Port Unknown, Edmund Griffethe master, to Spain, _21st May 1504_								
John Popley	Ind	18	piece	Cloth of Assize	0	0	0	0
		10	piece	Cloth of Assize, Dozen	0	0	0	0
William Estbie	Ind	20	piece	Cloth of Assize	0	0	0	0
		20	piece	Welsh _Cloth_, Dozen Strait	4	3	4	0
John Popley	Ind	3	piece	Cloth of Assize	0	0	0	0
William Estbie	Ind	2	piece	Cloth of Assize	0	0	0	0
		20	piece	Welsh _Cloth_, Dozen Strait	4	3	4	0
		1	C	Tin, Worked	0	30	0	0
Bata Katren of Chepstow, Robert Powar master, from Chepstow, 23rd May 1504								
Michael Lovelade	Ind	1	pipe	Wine	0	0	0	0
James Heny	Ind	1	pipe	Wine	0	0	0	0

Merchant name	Origin	Qty	Unit	Commodity	£	s.	d.	f.
Bata Mare Canynges, Port Unknown, John Maie master, from Chepstow, 24th May 1504								
John Brown	Ind	1.5	tun	Wine	0	0	0	0
John Shipman	Ind	2	pipe	Woad	10	0	0	0
William Hurste	Ind	1	pipe	Woad	0	100	0	0
		1.5	pipe	Rosin	0	20	0	0
John Tyllinge	Ind	1	pipe	Wine	0	0	0	0
Robert Avyntre	Ind	1	tun	Wine	0	0	0	0
Johanna Regent	Ind	1	pipe	Wine	0	0	0	0
Richard Hobie	Ind	1	pipe	Woad	0	100	0	0
Bata Katren of Bristol, Thomas Smythe master, from Ireland, 25th May 1504								
Thomas Smythe	Ind	14	piece	Mantles	0	46	8	0
Navicula *Chris*tpofur of Bristol William Bailie master, to La Rochelle, *25th May 1504*								
George Monos	Ind	12	wey	Coal	0	40	0	0
		8	ton	Lead, Worked	40	0	0	0
		16	C	Madder	0	106	8	0
Navicula Gelian Bonaven*tur*, Port Unknown, William Claron master, from Spain, 30th May 1504								
Nicholas Browne	Ind	30.66	ton	Iron	76	13	4	0
Richard Vaghan	Ind	20	ton	Iron	50	0	0	0
		5	tun	Wine	0	0	0	0
John Keepe	Ind	2	ton	Iron	0	100	0	0
John Shipman	Ind	8	ton	Iron	20	0	0	0
William Estbie	Ind	4.5	ton	Iron	11	5	0	0
Humphrey Brown	Ind	1	ton	Iron	0	50	0	0
William Tirrie	Ind	1	pipe	Iron	0	25	0	0
Thomas Badcok	Ind	5	ton	Iron	12	10	0	0
Thomas Aphowell	Ind	1.5	tun	Wine	0	0	0	0
		1	ton	Iron	0	50	0	0
Thomas Jones	Ind	1	hogshead	Oil, Olive	0	20	0	0
Navicula Mare of St-Jean-de-Luz, Arnold de Baynard master, from Bayonne, *30th May 1504*								
George Monos	Ind	13	tun	Wine	0	0	0	0
		19	dozen	Oars	0	76	0	0
Roger Dawes	Ind	9	tun	Wine	0	0	0	0
John Vaghan	Ind	2	tun	Wine	0	0	0	0
John Ware	Ind	4.5	tun	Wine	0	0	0	0
Robert Barrero	Ind	5.5	tun	Wine	0	0	0	0
		1	ton	Iron	0	50	0	0
John Shipman	Ind	9	tun	Wine	0	0	0	0
Stephen Ffostar	Ind	1	tun	Wine	0	0	0	0
Arnold de Baynard	Alien	1.5	ton	Iron	0	75	0	0
		1.5	pipe	Pitch	0	20	0	0
		1.25	C	Feathers	0	16	8	0
		3	C	Incense (Thures)	0	10	0	0

Merchant name	Origin	Qty	Unit	Commodity	£	s.	d.	f.
		1	dozen	Oars	0	4	0	0
John Ware	Ind	3	dozen	Oars	0	12	0	0
Arnold de Baynard	Alien	1	hogshead	Iron	0	6	3	0
		2	C	Rosin	0	2	8	0
Unknown Moren	Alien	3	rolle	Skins, Bever	0	30	0	0

Navicula Mare Katren of *Bristol*, Robert Avyntre master, from Andalusia, *30th May 1504*

Merchant name	Origin	Qty	Unit	Commodity	£	s.	d.	f.
George Monos	Ind	4	tun	Wine	0	0	0	0
John Shipman	Ind	3.5	tun	Wine	0	0	0	0
Thomas Hawkens	Ind	3	tun	Wine	0	0	0	0
Roger Dawes	Ind	7.5	tun	Wine	0	0	0	0
William Estbie	Ind	1.75	tun	Wine	0	0	0	0
John Popley	Ind	5	tun	Wine	0	0	0	0
Roger Dawes	Ind	1	tun	Wine	0	0	0	0
Thomas Aphowell	Ind	1.25	tun	Wine	0	0	0	0
Thomas Smythe	Ind	2.75	tun	Wine	0	0	0	0
Robert Avyntre	Ind	2	tun	Wine	0	0	0	0
		2	tun	Oil, Olive	8	0	0	0
		1	pipe	Fish, Salmon	0	30	0	0
John James	Ind	1.5	tun	Wine	0	0	0	0
		4	tun	Oil, Olive	16	0	0	0
John Marchall	Ind	8.5	tun	Wine	0	0	0	0
Thomas Barbor	Ind	1	pipe	Wine	0	0	0	0
		1	pipe	Oil, Olive	0	40	0	0
Ralph Aprise	Ind	3.5	tun	Wine	0	0	0	0
David Leyson	Ind	0.666	pipe	Wine	0	0	0	0
		1	hogshead	Oil, Olive	0	20	0	0
Richard Draper	Ind	2.5	tun	Wine	0	0	0	0
Humphrey Bosgrove	Ind	9	tun	Wine	0	0	0	0
		1	tun	Oil, Olive	4	0	0	0
		9	C	*Smigmates*	0	60	0	0
John Smythe	Ind	18	C	*Smigmates*	6	0	0	0
Peter Aburden	Alien	5	tun	Oil, Olive	20	0	0	0
		2	tun	Wine	0	0	0	0
		11	C	*Smigmates*	0	73	4	0
Tege Wigmor	Ind	1	tun	Wine	0	0	0	0
John Grene	Ind	1.5	tun	Oil, Olive	6	0	0	0
		1.5	tun	Wine	0	0	0	0
Robert Thorn	Ind	4	tun	Oil, Olive	16	0	0	0
		1	hogshead	Wine	0	0	0	0
		7.25	C	Wax	14	10	0	0
		34	C	*Smigmates*	11	6	8	0
Philip Ringston	Ind	10.5	C	Wax	21	0	0	0
John Lorde	Ind	1	tun	Oil, Olive	4	0	0	0
Richard Bakar	Ind	5.25	tun	Wine	0	0	0	0
John Benet	Ind	18	tun	Oil, Olive	72	0	0	0
		4.5	C	Wax	9	0	0	0
		43	C	*Smigmates*	14	6	8	0
William Jeffereis	Ind	4.5	tun	Oil, Olive	18	0	0	0
		1	pipe	Wine	0	0	0	0
Humphrey Bosgrove	Ind	1	barrel	Comfits	0	13	4	0

Merchant name	Origin	Qty	Unit	Commodity	£	s.	d.	f.
Lewis Aphowell	Ind	1	hogshead	Wine	0	0	0	0
Robert Avyntre	Ind	1	pipe	Wine	0	0	0	0

Bata Marten of Milford Haven, Richard More master, to Ireland, *30th May 1504*

James Treves	Ind	3	piece	Cloth of Assize	0	0	0	0
		0.5	piece	Cloth of Assize	0	0	0	0
		6	lb	Silk, Worked	4	0	0	0
		4	lb	Saffron	0	26	8	0
		40	lb	*Pilus Tinctus*	0	13	4	0
		12	gross	Points	0	12	0	0
		2	lb	Pepper	0	2	0	0
		1	dozen	Caps	0	6	8	0
		3	dozen	Knives	0	0	20	0
Richard Goold	Ind	1	piece	Cloth of Assize, Dozen Strait	0	0	0	0

Bata Mare of Berkeley, Thomas Smythe master, from Chepstow, 31st May 1504

Richard Hobie	Ind	6	pipe	Woad	30	0	0	0
William Hurste	Ind	3	pipe	Woad	15	0	0	0
John Shipman	Ind	1	pipe	Woad	0	100	0	0
Stephen Ffostar &								
John Meysam	Ind	2	pipe	Woad	10	0	0	0

Bata Miell of Swansea, William Hopkens, from Swansea, 3rd June 1504

John Williams	Ind	8	ton	Salt	0	66	8	0
		1	hogshead	Salt	0	2	1	0

Bata Mare of Berkeley, Thomas Smythe master, from Chepstow, *3rd June 1504*

William Hurste	Ind	2	pipe	Woad	10	0	0	0
Richard Hobie	Ind	3	pipe	Woad	15	0	0	0
John Shipman	Ind	3	pipe	Woad	15	0	0	0
Stephen Ffostar	Ind	1	pipe	Woad	0	100	0	0
Johanna Regent	Ind	1	pipe	Woad	0	100	0	0
William Atwood	Ind	0.75	tun	Wine	0	0	0	0

Navicula George of Bristol, Owen John master, from Spain, *3rd June 1504*

John Colas	Ind	14	C	Boxstaves	9	6	8	0
		15.25	ton	Iron	38	2	6	0
Thomas Smythe &								
Thomas Badcok	Ind	3	ton	Iron	7	10	0	0

Bata Trinite of Chepstow, William Heyn master, from Chepstow, 4th June, 1504

Edmund Secheford	Ind	3	tun	Wine	0	0	0	0
Nicholas Kirie	Ind	5	piece	Mantles	0	16	8	9

Merchant name	Origin	_Qty_	Unit	Commodity	£	s.	d.	f.

Bata Nicolas of Chepstow, Robert Ffishar master, from Chepstow, 8th June 1504

| Thomas Spicer | Ind | 4.25 | C | _Smigmates_ | 0 | 28 | 4 | 0 |

Bata Sampson of Cardiff, John Howell master, from Cardiff, _8th June 1504_

| William Walsall | Ind | 1 | tun | Wine | 0 | 0 | 0 | 0 |
| Thomas Pua[ ]t | Ind | 6 | barrel | Tar | 0 | 20 | 0 | 0 |

Bata Mare of Shirehampton, John Tyllinge master, from Chepstow, _8th June 1504_

| Thomas Bocher | Ind | 1.5 | tun | Wine | 0 | 0 | 0 | 0 |

Bata George of Gatcombe, Walter Nashe master, to Ireland, _8th June 1504_

| _Walter Nashe_ | Ind | 12 | wey | Beans | 8 | 0 | 0 | 0 |
| Thomas Awsten | Ind | 12 | piece | Cloth of Assize | 0 | 0 | 0 | 0 |

Bata Rose of Tenby, Richard Honter master, from Tenby, 11th June 1504

| _Richard Honter_ | Ind | 10 | ton | Salt | 4 | 3 | 4 | 0 |

Bata Mare of Berkeley, Thomas Boller master, from Chepstow, _11th June 1504_

| Thomas Bocher | Ind | 1 | tun | Wine | 0 | 0 | 0 | 0 |
| | | 0.5 | pipe | Woad | 0 | 50 | 0 | 0 |

Bata James of Gatcombe, John Adams master, from Cardiff, 12th June 1504

| James Whaley | Ind | 7 | tun | Wine | 0 | 0 | 0 | 0 |
| | | 2.5 | C | Pitch | 0 | 3 | 4 | 0 |

Bata Mare of Llansteffan, Nicholas Gough master, from Llansteffan, 13th June 1504

| Philip Davy, Thomas Davie & Hugh Bromley | Ind | 16 | ton | Salt | 6 | 13 | 4 | 0 |

Bata Marget of Carmarthen, John Comyn master, from Carmarthen, _13th June 1504_

Hugh Bromley	Ind	2	ton	Salt	0	16	8	0
Richard Draper	Ind	7	ton	Salt	0	58	4	0
		1	pipe	Wine	0	0	0	0
Hugh Bromley	Ind	1	hogshead	Wine	0	0	0	0
		6	C	Rosin	0	8	0	0
		4.5	C	Turpentine	0	60	0	0
John Ynon	Ind	3	ton	Salt	0	25	0	0
Hugh Bromley	Ind	0.5	C	Turpentine	0	6	8	0
John Ynon	Ind	1	pipe	Salt	0	4	2	0
Richard Draper	Ind	1	ton	Salt	0	8	4	0

Merchant name	Origin	Qty	Unit	Commodity	£	s.	d.	f.
Navicula, Mathewe of Bristol, William Claron master, to Bordeaux, *13th June 1504*								
Richard Hobie	Ind	8	piece	Cloth of Assize	0	0	0	0
Robert Barrero	Ind	16	piece	Cloth of Assize	0	0	0	0
Bata Mare of Berkeley, Thomas Smythe master, from Cardiff, 15th June 1504								
John Heydon	Ind	3	ton	Salt	0	25	0	0
Navicula Katren of Berkeley, Robert Powar master, to La Rochelle, *15th June 1504*								
Richard Bocher	Ind	10	dicker	Hides, Tanned	33	6	8	0
		10	dozen	Skins, Calf Tanned	0	25	0	0
		2	piece	Cloth of Assize	0	0	0	0
Bata Clement of Milford Haven, John Kelley master, from Milford Haven, 17th June 1504								
John Sutton	Ind	1	tun	Wine	0	0	0	0
Bata Petur of Milford Haven, John Knock master, to Ireland, *17th June 1504*								
Katherine Powar	Ind	12	lb	*Pilus Tinctus*	0	4	0	0
Bata Kymborgh of Gloucester, Philip Ffoxe master, from Ireland, 19th June 1504								
David Westerbie	Ind	1.5	tun	Wine	0	0	0	0
		1	pipe	Fish, Salmon	0	30	0	0
		2	C	Cork, White	0	6	8	0
		1	C	Rosin	0	0	16	0
		4	piece	Mantles	0	13	4	0
Thomas Ayleworth	Ind	1.5	tun	Wine	0	0	0	0
		1	pipe	Fish, Salmon	0	30	0	0
		2	C	Cork, White	0	6	8	0
		1	C	Rosin	0	0	16	0
Bata Katren of New Ross, William Grase master, from Ireland, 22nd June 1504								
Thomas Mothell	Ind	5.5	M	Skins, Lamb	13	15	0	0
		7	C	Skins, Sheep (no wool)	0	70	0	0
		2	C	Wax	4	0	0	0
		0.5	C	Check *Cloth*	0	20	0	0
		14	piece	Mantles	0	46	8	0
		12	piece	Skins, Otter	0	5	0	0
		0.5	C	Skins, Fox	0	8	4	0
		6	piece	Skins, Marten	0	6	0	0
		20	stone	Wool, Flocks	0	8	4	0
John Archer	Ind	1	M	Skins, Sheep (no wool)	0	100	0	0
		20	piece	Mantles	0	66	8	0
		8	C	Skins, Lamb	0	40	0	0
		37	lb	Wax	0	12	4	0
		13	piece	Skins, Fox	0	0	19	2
		10	yard	Check *Cloth*	0	3	4	0

Merchant name	Origin	Qty	Unit	Commodity	£	s.	d.	f.
Philip Mackey	Ind	14	C	Skins, Lamb	0	70	0	0
		2	C	Skins, Sheep (no wool)	0	20	0	0
		22	piece	Mantles	0	73	4	0
		2	C	Wax	4	0	0	0
		20	piece	Skins, Fox	0	2	6	0
David Savage	Ind	20	C	Skins, Lamb	0	100	0	0
		27	piece	Mantles	4	10	0	0
		4.5	C	Skins, Sheep (no wool)	0	45	0	0
		6	piece	Skins, Fox	0	0	9	0
		4.5	dicker	Hides, Salted	0	60	0	0
		130	lb	Wax	0	43	4	0
Patrick Rothe	Ind	11.5	C	Skins, Lamb	0	57	6	0
		32	piece	Skins, Fox	0	4	0	0
		9	piece	Mantles	0	30	0	0
		70	lb	Wax	0	23	4	0
		2	piece	Skins, Otter	0	0	10	0
Thomas Shenell	Ind	1	C	Skins, Lamb	0	5	0	0

Bata Mare of Chepstow, Richard Halle master, from Chepstow, _23rd June 1504_

Robert Adams	Ind	1	pipe	Wine	2	0	0	0

Bata Mawdlen of Waterford, William Penbroke master, from Ireland, 25th June 1504

Merchant name	Origin	Qty	Unit	Commodity	£	s.	d.	f.
William Penbroke	Ind	3.25	C	Skins, Sheep (no wool)	0	32	6	0
Thomas Nashe	Ind	2.5	C	Skins, Sheep (no wool)	0	25	0	0
		1.5	C	Skins, Lamb	0	7	6	0
		17	piece	Mantles	0	56	8	0
		1	C	Irish Linen _Cloth_	0	10	0	0
		70	lb	Wax	0	23	4	0
Thomas Streche	Ind	93	piece	Mantles	15	10	0	0
		44	lb	Wax	0	14	8	0
		44	yard	Irish Linen _Cloth_	0	3	8	0
		35	yard	Breton Linen _Cloth_	0	5	10	0
		1.5	lb	Bise	0	0	20	0
John Dowlie	Ind	30	piece	Mantles	0	100	0	0
		80	yard	_Irish_ Frieze _Cloth_	0	26	8	0
		14	lb	Wax	0	4	8	0
		1	C	Skins, Lamb	0	5	0	0
Henry Maie	Ind	5.5	C	Skins, Lamb	0	27	6	0
William Archepoll	Ind	25	piece	Mantles	4	3	4	0
		5.16	C	Skins, Lamb	0	25	10	0
		1	C	Skins, Calf	0	25	0	0
		5	C	Skins, Sheep (no wool)	0	50	0	0
		29	lb	Wax	0	9	8	0
		3.75	C	Alum	0	18	9	0
Walter Powar	Ind	8	C	Skins, Sheep (no wool)	4	0	0	0
		2.5	C	Skins, Lamb	0	12	6	0
Thomas Lawnder	Ind	1.5	C	Wax	0	60	0	0
		7	piece	Mantles	0	23	4	0
		1	C	Skins, Lamb	0	5	0	0
		44	piece	Skins, Sheep (no wool)	0	3	8	0

Merchant name	Origin	Qty	Unit	Commodity	£	s.	d.	f.
		2	C	Irish Linen *Cloth*	0	20	0	0
Philip Digon	Ind	6	C	Skins, Sheep (no wool)	0	60	0	0
		4	piece	Mantles	0	13	4	0
		0.5	burden	Fish, Salted	0	0	20	0
John Bailie	Ind	6	piece	Mantles	0	20	0	0
		80	piece	Skins, Sheep (no wool)	0	6	8	0
		0.5	C	Skins, Lamb	0	2	6	0
		0.5	burden	Fish, Salted	0	0	20	0
James Molron	Ind	11.5	C	Skins, Sheep (no wool)	0	115	0	0
		13.5	C	Skins, Lamb	0	67	6	0
		12	piece	Mantles	0	40	0	0
		4	lb	Wax	0	0	16	0
		80	lb	Scrofe	0	6	8	0
Maurice Rowe	Ind	6.3	C	Skins, Sheep (no wool)	0	63	0	0
Germain Bryne	Ind	48	piece	Skins, Lamb	0	2	0	0
		16	lb	Wax	0	5	4	0
		3	stone	Wool, Flocks	0	0	15	0
		2	piece	Mantles	0	6	8	0
		24	lb	Scrofe	0	2	0	0
Peter Nogle	Ind	8	piece	Mantles	0	26	8	0
William Tirrie	Ind	6	C	Skins, Lamb	0	30	0	0
		1	C	Skins, Sheep (no wool)	0	10	0	0
William Stompe	Ind	5.5	dicker	Hides, Salted	0	73	4	0
		4	dicker	Skins, Ferret	0	10	0	0
		1.5	C	Skins, Lamb	0	7	6	0
		1	C	Skins, Rabbit	0	5	0	0
		7	piece	Skins, Marten	0	7	0	0
		35	piece	Skins, Fox	0	4	4	0
		1	C	Check *Cloth*	0	40	0	0
		5	piece	Mantles	0	16	8	0

Bata Katren of Tenby, Richard Williams master, from Tenby, *25th June 1504*

Merchant name	Origin	Qty	Unit	Commodity	£	s.	d.	f.
Richard Williams	Ind	12	ton	Salt	0	100	0	0

Bata Mare of Milford Haven, David Hire master, from Milford Haven, 26th June 1504

Merchant name	Origin	Qty	Unit	Commodity	£	s.	d.	f.
Hugh Bromley	Ind	5.75	tun	Wine	0	0	0	0

Navicula George of Bristol, David Nono master, to Bordeaux, 27th June 1504

Merchant name	Origin	Qty	Unit	Commodity	£	s.	d.	f.
John Colas	Ind	20	piece	Cloth of Assize	0	0	0	0

Navicula Mare St-Jean-de-Luz, Arnold de Baynard master, to La Rochelle, 1st July 1504

Merchant name	Origin	Qty	Unit	Commodity	£	s.	d.	f.
Arnold de Baynard	Alien	30	wey	Coal	0	100	0	0
		140	flege	Bacon	11	13	4	0

Bata Marget of St Ives, John Pars, from St Ives, 2nd July 1504

Merchant name	Origin	Qty	Unit	Commodity	£	s.	d.	f.
John Pars	Ind	1	C	Breton Linen *Cloth*	0	20	0	0

Merchant name	Origin	Qty	Unit	Commodity	£	s.	d.	f.
Navicula Mare of Bristol, Philip Kirie master, from Ireland, *2nd July 1504*								
William Jeffereis	Ind	48.5	burden	Fish, Salted	8	0	20	0
		1	virken	Fish, Salmon	0	7	6	0
		2	C	Skins, Sheep (no wool)	0	20	0	0
		1	C	Skins, Lamb	0	5	0	0
		0.5	dicker	Hides, Salted	0	6	8	0
		10	stone	Wool, Flocks	0	4	2	0
John Harries	Ind	1	pipe	Fish, Salmon	0	30	0	0
James Sciddie	Ind	3	piece	Horses	0	60	0	0
		0.5	C	Skins, Lamb	0	2	6	0
		13	piece	Skins, Otter	0	5	5	0
		12	piece	Skins, Fox	0	0	18	0
		8	piece	Mantles	0	26	8	0
		4	piece	Skins, Marten	0	4	0	0
		0.5	seam	Wood Ashes	0	2	0	0
William White	Ind	7	burden	Fish, Salted	0	23	4	0
William Rise	Ind	0.5	burden	Fish, Salted	0	0	20	0
		2	C	Skins, Lamb	0	10	0	0
		8	piece	Hides, Salted	0	10	8	0
Thomas Fe William	Ind	1	virken	Fish, Salmon	0	7	6	0
William Jeffereis	Ind	2.5	burden	Fish, Salted	0	8	4	0
Navicula Miell of Bristol, William Fforde master, to La Rochelle, *2nd July 1504*								
John Jaie &								
Robert Thorn	Ind	20	wey	Coal	0	66	8	0
		10	wey	Coal	0	33	4	0
John Jansie	Ind	18	piece	Cloth of Assize	0	0	0	0
John Jaie	Ind	2	piece	Cloth of Assize	0	0	0	0
Robert Thorne	Ind	3	piece	Cloth of Assize	0	0	0	0
		2	piece	Cloth of Assize, Kersey	0	0	0	0
John Eliet	Ind	1	piece	Cloth of Assize	0	0	0	0
Bata Mare of Minehead, William Russell, from Ireland, 3rd July 1504								
William Russell	Ind	50	burden	Fish, Salted	8	6	8	0
		3	dicker	Hides, Salted	0	40	0	0
Bata Sampson of Cardiff, John Howell master, from Cardiff, *3rd July 1504*								
John Crowcok	Ind	1	tun	Wine	0	0	0	0
Bata Mare of Berkeley, Thomas Cockes master, from Chepstow, *3rd July 1504*								
Thomas Bocher	Ind	1	pipe	Wine	0	0	0	0
Bata *Christ*pofur of Bristol, Richard Braie master, from Brittany, *3rd July 1504*								
Richard Braie,								
William Jeffereis &								
William Shoile	Ind	30	ton	Salt	12	10	0	0
		2	ton	Salt	0	16	8	0

Merchant name	Origin	Qty	Unit	Commodity	£	s.	d.	f.

Bata Mare of Cardiff, John Kewe master, from Cardiff, 4th July 1504

Merchant name	Origin	Qty	Unit	Commodity	£	s.	d.	f.
Maurice Gurdelar	Ind	6	measure	Woad	o	37	6	o
		1	pipe	Wine	o	o	o	o

Bata Seynt Marke, Port Unknown, Edmund Griffethe master, from Galicia, 4th July 1504

Merchant name	Origin	Qty	Unit	Commodity	£	s.	d.	f.
John Popley	Ind	3.5	tun	Wine	o	o	o	o
		8	ton	Salt	o	66	8	o
William Estbie	Ind	5	tun	Wine	o	o	o	o
		8	ton	Salt	o	66	8	o
Edmund Griffeth &								
William Downe	Ind	32	dozen	Cork, Black	o	53	4	o
		2	ton	Salt	o	16	8	o

Bata Mare of Chepstow, Robert Bocher master, from Chepstow, 5th July 1504

Merchant name	Origin	Qty	Unit	Commodity	£	s.	d.	f.
John Alen	Ind	0.75	tun	Wine	o	o	o	o

Bata Mare of Magor, Andrew Cooke master, from Carmarthen, 6th July 1504

Merchant name	Origin	Qty	Unit	Commodity	£	s.	d.	f.
John Ynon	Ind	1	pipe	Wine	o	o	o	o

Navicula Mare Belhouse of *Bristol*, Walter Cooke master, from Andalusia, 9th July 1504

Merchant name	Origin	Qty	Unit	Commodity	£	s.	d.	f.
Roger Dawes	Ind	9	tun	Oil, Olive	36	o	o	o
		7	ton	Salt	o	58	4	o
John Halle	Ind	1	tun	Wine	o	o	o	o
John Ynon	Ind	0.833	tun	Wine	o	o	o	o
William Jeffereis	Ind	1.5	tun	Oil, Olive	6	o	o	o
		1.75	tun	Wine	o	o	o	o
Robert Ffortey	Ind	1	tun	Wine	o	o	o	o
Walter Snygge	Ind	1	pipe	Wine	o	o	o	o
Henry Dale	Ind	5.75	tun	Wine	o	o	o	o
Robert Thorn	Ind	3.75	tun	Oil, Olive	15	o	o	o
Peter Aburden	Alien	2.25	tun	Wine	o	o	o	o
Richard Bakar	Ind	7.5	tun	Wine	o	o	o	o
Richard Bakar	Ind	2.5	C	*Smigmates*	o	16	8	o
Peter Aburden	Alien	1	hogshead	Wine	o	o	o	o
John Domingus	Alien	1.5	pipe	Oil, Olive	o	60	o	o
		1.5	tun	Wine	o	o	o	o
		1	C	*Smigmates*	o	6	8	o
John Benet	Ind	5.5	tun	Wine	o	o	o	o
Thomas Smythe	Ind	3.75	tun	Wine	o	o	o	o
David Vaghan	Ind	1	pipe	Oil, Olive	o	40	o	o
John Rowland	Ind	5.75	tun	Wine	o	o	o	o
John Ringston	Ind	1	tun	Wine	o	o	o	o
Roger Dawes	Ind	2	tun	Wine	o	o	o	o
John Colyns	Ind	1	pipe	Wine	o	o	o	o
		2	C	*Smigmates*	o	13	4	o
Philip Tewe	Ind	1.75	tun	Wine	7	o	o	o
		1	hogshead	Oil, Olive	o	20	o	o

Merchant name	Origin	Qty	Unit	Commodity	£	s.	d.	f.
John Popley	Ind	1	pipe	Wine	0	0	0	0
John Colas	Ind	2.25	tun	Wine	0	0	0	0
John Gurdelar	Ind	8	C	*Smigmates*	0	53	4	0
Thomas Payne	Ind	1	tun	Wine	0	0	0	0
Margeret Grene	Ind	3.75	tun	Wine	0	0	0	0
John Lorde	Ind	4.75	C	*Smigmates*	0	31	8	0
Richard Vaghan	Ind	3.75	tun	Wine	0	0	0	0

Bata Trynyte of Berkeley, William Lawles master, from La Rochelle, *9th July 1504*

James Atwood	Ind	28	ton	Salt	11	13	4	0

Bata Mare of Berkeley, Robert Barret master, to Ireland, 10th July 1504

Thomas Bocher	Ind	1.5	piece	Cloth of Assize	0	0	0	0

Bata Mawdlen of Waterford, William Penbroke master, to Ireland, 11th July 1504

Merchant name	Origin	Qty	Unit	Commodity	£	s.	d.	f.
William Penbroke	Ind	12	lb	*Pilus Tinctus*	0	4	0	0
Dennis Penbroke	Ind	1	last	Beer	0	30	0	0
John Dowlie	Ind	2	piece	Cloth of Assize	0	0	0	0
		2	lb	Silk, Worked	0	26	8	0
		2.25	lb	Saffron	0	15	0	0
		50	lb	*Pilus Tinctus*	0	16	8	0
		2	dozen	Caps	0	13	4	0
		5.5	gross	Points	0	5	6	0
		0.5	C	Battery	0	20	0	0
		1	dozen	Cards, Unspecified	0	4	0	0
		3	pair	Stock-cards	0	3	0	0
		1	gross	Knives	0	6	8	0
		2	lb	Pepper	0	2	0	0
		1	lb	Cinnamon	0	2	6	0
		1	lb	Ginger	0	0	12	0
		1	lb	Graynes	0	0	10	0
		0.25	lb	Mace	0	0	6	0
		0.25	lb	Boras	0	0	16	0
		3	lb	Verdegris	0	0	16	0
		1	lb	Thread	0	0	5	0
		6	dozen	Thimbles	0	0	12	0
		1.5	clout	Needles	0	0	12	0
		2	dozen	Aniseed	0	3	0	0
William Archepoll	Ind	2	piece	Cloth of Assize	0	0	0	0
		2	lb	Saffron	0	13	4	0
James Molrony	Ind	3.5	piece	Cloth of Assize	0	0	0	0
		1	lb	Saffron	0	6	8	0
		24	lb	*Pilus Tinctus*	0	8	0	0
		1	lb	Silk, Worked	0	13	4	0
		6	gross	Points	0	6	0	0
Thomas Nashe	Ind	2	piece	Cloth of Assize	0	0	0	0
		1	lb	Saffron	0	6	8	0
		60	lb	*Pilus Tinctus*	0	20	0	0
Philip Digon	Ind	2	stone	Orchil, Worked	0	3	4	0

Merchant name	Origin	Qty	Unit	Commodity	£	s.	d.	f.
		8	lb	*Pilus Tinctus*	0	2	8	0
		42	lb	*Pilus Tinctus*	0	14	0	0
		1	lb	Silk, Worked	0	13	4	0
John Dowlie	Ind	4	gross	Points	0	4	0	0
Thomas Nashe	Ind	40	lb	*Pilus Tinctus*	0	13	4	0
		0.5	lb	Saffron	0	3	4	0

Navicula Andrewe of Bristol, John Williams master, from Guernesy, *11th July 1504*

John Williams	Ind	20	wey	Grain	30	0	0	0

Bata Katren of New Ross, William Grase master, to Ireland, *11th July 1504*

Henry Walshe	Ind	0.5	C	*Pilus Tinctus*	0	20	0	0
Thomas Shenell	Ind	0.5	C	*Pilus Tinctus*	0	20	0	0
Thomas Mothell	Ind	7	piece	Cloth of Assize	0	0	0	0
		20	lb	Saffron	6	13	4	0
		7	lb	Silk, Worked	4	13	4	0
		2	C	Aniseed	0	20	0	0
		1	C	*Pilus Tinctus*	0	40	0	0
		3	dozen	Caps	0	20	0	0
		20	gross	Points	0	20	0	0
		2	gross	Knives	0	13	4	0
Philip Mackey	Ind	2	piece	Cloth of Assize	0	0	0	0
		12	lb	Saffron	4	0	0	0
		5	lb	Silk, Worked	0	66	8	0
		0.5	C	Aniseed	0	5	0	0
		12	gross	Points	0	12	0	0
		1	dozen	Caps	0	6	8	0
		0.5	C	*Pilus Tinctus*	0	20	0	0
David Savage	Ind	1	piece	Cloth of Assize	0	0	0	0
		2	lb	Saffron	0	13	4	0
Philip Mackey	Ind	1	gross	Knives	0	6	8	0
Thomas Mothell	Ind	1	piece	Cloth of Assize	0	0	0	0
William Grase	Ind	1	pipe	Wine, Corrupt	0	15	0	0
Patrick Roche	Ind	7	lb	Saffron	0	46	8	0
		1	lb	Silk, Worked	0	13	4	0
		9	gross	Points	0	9	0	0
		14	lb	*Pilus Tinctus*	0	4	8	0

Navicula Gelian of Bristol, John Gasgon master, from Lisbon, 12th July 1504

John Marchall	Ind	8	tun	Oil, Olive	32	0	0	0
John Bolton	Ind	5	C	Pepper	25	0	0	0
Roger Dawes	Ind	1	tun	Wine	0	0	0	0
Richard Hobie	Ind	674	lb	Wax	11	4	8	0
William Hurste	Ind	1.5	tun	Oil, Olive	6	0	0	0
John Grene	Ind	1.75	tun	Wine	0	0	0	0
John Halle	Ind	2	tun	Oil, Olive	8	0	0	0
		2.5	tun	Wine	0	0	0	0
David Leyson	Ind	1	tun	Oil, Olive	4	0	0	0
		1	pipe	Wine	0	0	0	0

Merchant name	Origin	Qty	Unit	Commodity	£	s.	d.	f.
Thomas Smythe	Ind	2.75	tun	Wine	0	0	0	0
		2.5	tun	Oil, Olive	10	0	0	0
Alerno ? Pymento	Alien	16	C	Wood, Brazil, New World	26	13	4	0
William Estbie	Ind	2.75	tun	Oil, Olive	11	0	0	0
William Hofe	Ind	15	dozen	Cork, Black	0	25	0	0
Maurice Leney	Ind	1	tun	Oil, Olive	4	0	0	0
		1.75	tun	Wine	0	0	0	0
David Vaghan	Ind	1	pipe	Oil, Olive	0	40	0	0
John Browne	Ind	1.5	tun	Wine	0	0	0	0
Richard Blewet	Ind	6	dozen	Cork, Black	0	10	0	0
George Monos	Ind	4	tun	Oil, Olive	16	0	0	0

Bata Katren of Chepstow, Robert Ffishar master, from Chepstow, 13th July 1504

Merchant name	Origin	Qty	Unit	Commodity	£	s.	d.	f.
John Davie	Ind	1	hogshead	Wine	0	0	0	0

Bata Mare of Shirehampton, Richard Polen master, from Chepstow, 15th July 1504

Merchant name	Origin	Qty	Unit	Commodity	£	s.	d.	f.
Thomas Mefelyn	Ind	4	pipe	Woad	20	0	0	0
Henry Bonfeld	Ind	12	measure	Woad	0	75	0	0

Bata Mare of Milford Haven, John Bidwyn master, from Milford Haven, 16th July 1504

Merchant name	Origin	Qty	Unit	Commodity	£	s.	d.	f.
Hugh Bromwell	Ind	2	tun	Wine	0	0	0	0
Nicholas Ffishar	Ind	1	tun	Wine	0	0	0	0

Bata Mare Cooke, Port Unknown, Dennis Harte master, from Ireland, 17th July 1504

Merchant name	Origin	Qty	Unit	Commodity	£	s.	d.	f.
John Pollard &								
Thomas Cooke	Ind	32	pipe	Fish, Salmon	48	0	0	0
Dennis Harte	Ind	2	unknown	*Taishaill*	0	20	0	0
Thomas Cooke	Ind	2	unknown	*Taishaill*	0	20	0	0
Dennis Harte	Ind	0.5	pipe	Fish, Salmon	0	15	0	0
Laurence Fflemynge	Ind	0.5	pipe	Fish, Salmon	0	15	0	0
Tege Cathell	Ind	0.5	pipe	Fish, Salmon	0	15	0	0
Nicholas Walshe	Ind	0.5	pipe	Fish, Salmon	0	15	0	0
Dennis Rownam	Ind	1	virken	Fish, Salmon	0	7	6	0
Stephen Barnard	Ind	1	virken	Fish, Salmon	0	7	6	0
Nicholas Nongell	Ind	1	pipe	Fish, Salmon	0	30	0	0

Bata John of Cork, Thomas Walshe master, from Ireland, 18th July 1504

Merchant name	Origin	Qty	Unit	Commodity	£	s.	d.	f.
Thomas Walshe	Ind	2	pipe	Fish, Salmon	0	60	0	0
		80	piece	Skins, Sheep (no wool)	0	6	8	0
		0.5	C	Skins, Lamb	0	2	6	0
		9	piece	Mantles	0	30	0	0
		100	piece	Shipboards	0	16	8	0
William Fe Mores	Ind	2.25	pipe	Fish, Salmon	0	67	6	0
		5	piece	Mantles	0	16	8	0
		1	piece	Whitelles	0	3	4	0
		3.75	C	Skins, Lamb	0	18	9	0
		1	C	Skins, Sheep (no wool)	0	10	0	0

Merchant name	Origin	Qty	Unit	Commodity	£	s.	d.	f.
Patrick Goold	Ind	22	lb	Wax	0	7	4	0
		2.5	C	Skins, Sheep (no wool)	0	25	0	0
		3	C	Skins, Lamb	0	15	0	0
		12	piece	Mantles	0	40	0	0
Richard Mahond	Ind	21	piece	Mantles	0	70	0	0
David Walshe	Ind	2.5	C	Skins, Lamb	0	12	6	0
		0.5	C	Skins, Sheep (no wool)	0	5	0	0
		9	piece	Mantles	0	30	0	0
		0.5	pipe	Fish, Salmon	0	15	0	0
Patrick Fferes	Ind	10	piece	Mantles	0	33	4	0
		80	piece	Skins, Lamb	0	3	4	0
Thomas Midde	Ind	16	piece	Mantles	0	53	4	0
Robert Morowe	Ind	5	piece	Mantles	0	16	8	0
Thomas Rise	Ind	6	piece	Mantles	0	20	0	0
John Adee	Ind	5	piece	Mantles	0	16	8	0
William Tirrie	Ind	1.1	C	Skins, Sheep (no wool)	0	11	0	0
		8	piece	Mantles	0	26	8	0
Richard Hanrekan	Ind	0.5	C	Skins, Sheep (no wool)	0	5	0	0
		3	piece	Mantles	0	10	0	0
John Benet	Ind	2	C	Skins, Lamb	0	10	0	0
		80	piece	Skins, Sheep (no wool)	0	6	8	0

Bata James of Gatcombe, John Adams master, to Ireland, 18th July 1504

Robert Wiet	Ind	12	wey	Beans	8	0	0	0
Nicholas Bowen	Ind	30	ton	Salt	12	10	0	0
Nicholas Harvie	Alien	1	pipe	Salt	0	4	2	0

Bata Mare of Gatcombe, Robert Cooke master, from Chepstow, 19th July 1504

Robert Waxmaker	Ind	1	pipe	Wine	0	0	0	0

Navicula Mare of Penmarch, John Malock master, from Zeeland, *19th July 1504*

John Colas	Ind	78	wey	Grain	117	0	0	0
John Malock	Alien	5	bale	Madder	10	0	0	0

Bata Mare of Tewkesbury, Thomas Colens master, from Chepstow, *19th July 1504*

Thomas Colens	Ind	0.75	ton	Iron	0	37	6	0

Bata Clement of Falmouth, Thomas Pennall master, from Bordeaux, 23rd July 1504

Nicholas Browne	Ind	9	tun	Wine	0	0	0	0
William Jeffereis	Ind	6.75	tun	Wine	0	0	0	0
John Rowland	Ind	4.75	tun	Wine	0	0	0	0
John Vaghan	Ind	6	tun	Wine	0	0	0	0

Navicula Mare of Bristol, John Powar master, to Ireland, *23rd July 1504*

William Jeffereis	Ind	3	ton	Salt	0	50	0	0
Matthew Hoper	Ind	1	pipe	Salt	0	8	4	0

Merchant name	Origin	Qty	Unit	Commodity	£	s.	d.	f.
John Kewsack	Ind	1	pipe	Salt	0	8	4	0
William Tobie	Ind	1	pipe	Salt	0	8	4	0
William Jeffereis	Ind	2.5	tun	Wine, Corrupt	0	75	0	0
John Kewsack &								
Matthew Hoper	Ind	1	pipe	Wine, Corrupt	0	15	0	0
		1	last	Beer	0	30	0	0
William Jeffereis	Ind	1	C	*Pilus Tinctus*	0	40	0	0
Thomas Fflemynge	Ind	1	last	Beer	0	30	0	0
		1	hogshead	Salt	0	4	2	0
William Tobie	Ind	0.5	last	Beer	0	15	0	0
William Jeffereis	Ind	4	piece	Cloth of Assize	0	0	0	0
		14	piece	Cloth of Assize, Dozen	0	0	0	0

Bata Sondaie of Waterford, John Walshe master, from Ireland, 23rd July 1504

Merchant name	Origin	Qty	Unit	Commodity	£	s.	d.	f.
John Walshe	Ind	2	piece	Mantles	0	6	8	0
		0.5	pipe	Fish, Salmon	0	15	0	0
		0.5	C	Skins, Sheep (no wool)	0	5	0	0
		3	lb	Wax	0	0	12	0
John Barn	Ind	20	C	Skins, Sheep (no wool)	10	0	0	0
		23	C	Skins, Lamb	0	115	0	0
		22	piece	Mantles	0	73	4	0
		30	lb	Wax	0	10	0	0
		12	piece	Skins, Fox	0	0	18	0
Malagur Taylour	Ind	23	piece	Mantles	0	76	8	0
		0.5	C	Skins, Sheep (no wool)	0	5	0	0
		40	yard	Check *Cloth*	0	13	4	0
		3	stone	Wool, Flocks	0	0	15	0
Peter Kalley	Ind	3	C	Skins, Sheep (no wool)	0	30	0	0
		1	pipe	Fish, Salmon	0	30	0	0
		4	piece	Mantles	0	13	4	0
Patrick Fe John	Ind	4	piece	Mantles	0	13	4	0
Thomas Axbrigge	Ind	13	piece	Mantles	0	43	4	0
		32	yard	Check *Cloth*	0	10	8	0
		12	lb	Wax	0	4	0	0
William Tirrie	Ind	2	C	Skins, Sheep (no wool)	0	20	0	0
		2.5	C	Skins, Lamb	0	12	6	0
John Walshe	Ind	4	C	Skins, Sheep (no wool)	0	40	0	0

Bata Petur of Berkeley, John Roche master, from Ireland, 23rd July 1504

Merchant name	Origin	Qty	Unit	Commodity	£	s.	d.	f.
John Roche	Ind	0.5	pipe	Fish, Salmon	0	15	0	0

Bata George of Antwerpen, Peter Yanson master, from Antwerpen, *23rd July 1504*

Merchant name	Origin	Qty	Unit	Commodity	£	s.	d.	f.
Dirike Vanquynar	Hansard	58	wey	Grain	87	0	0	0

Bata Miell of New Ross, William Blake master, from Ireland, 24th July 1504

Merchant name	Origin	Qty	Unit	Commodity	£	s.	d.	f.
William Blake	Ind	1.33	C	Skins, Sheep (no wool)	0	13	4	0
		1	C	Skins, Lamb	0	5	0	0
		5	piece	Mantles	0	16	8	0

Merchant name	Origin	Qty	Unit	Commodity	£	s.	d.	f.
Thomas Bryne	Ind	48	piece	Mantles	8	0	0	0
		7.5	C	Skins, Lamb	0	37	6	0
		22	piece	Skins, Fox	0	2	9	0
		2	piece	Skins, Otter	0	0	10	0
		80	lb	Wax	0	26	8	0
		24	piece	Skins, Sheep (no wool)	0	2	0	0
John Donell	Ind	40	piece	Mantles	6	13	4	0
		4	C	Skins, Lamb	0	20	0	0
		3	piece	Whitelles	0	10	0	0
		60	lb	Wax	0	20	0	0
		0.5	C	Skins, Sheep (no wool)	0	5	0	0
		7	piece	Skins, Fox	0	0	10	2
		1	piece	Skins, Marten	0	0	12	0
John Walshe	Ind	29	piece	Mantles	4	16	8	0
		11.25	C	Skins, Lamb	0	56	3	0
		40	lb	Wax	0	13	4	0
		3	piece	Whitelles	0	10	0	0
		3	C	Skins, Sheep (no wool)	0	30	0	0
		9	piece	Skins, Fox	0	0	13	2
		2	piece	Skins, Marten	0	2	0	0
		1	piece	Skins, Otter	0	0	5	0
William Lenard	Ind	24	piece	Mantles	4	0	0	0
		1	piece	Mantles	0	3	4	0
		11	C	Skins, Lamb	0	55	0	0
		3.66	C	Skins, Sheep (no wool)	0	36	8	0
		20	piece	Skins, Fox	0	2	6	0
		1	piece	Skins, Marten	0	0	12	0
		1	piece	Skins, Otter	0	0	5	0
		27	lb	Wax	0	9	0	0
Thomas Bryne	Ind	10	lb	Wax	0	3	4	0
Thomas Shortall	Ind	18	piece	Mantles	0	60	0	0
		4.13	C	Skins, Lamb	0	20	8	0
		24	piece	Skins, Sheep (no wool)	0	2	0	0
		1	piece	Skins, Otter	0	0	5	0
		1.5	lb	Wax	0	0	6	0
Robert Kenaye	Ind	43	piece	Mantles	7	3	4	0
		27	yard	Irish Linen *Cloth*	0	2	3	0
		624	piece	Skins, Sheep (no wool)	0	52	0	0
		3	C	Skins, Lamb	0	15	0	0
		1	quarter	Skins, Fawn	0	0	15	0
		35	lb	Wax	0	11	8	0
		8	piece	Skins, Fox	0	0	12	0
Edward Moyn	Ind	30	piece	Mantles	0	100	0	0
		1.25	C	Skins, Sheep (no wool)	0	12	6	0
		1.75	C	Skins, Lamb	0	8	9	0
		50	lb	Wax	0	16	8	0
Robert Garvey	Ind	7	piece	Mantles	0	23	4	0
John Longe	Ind	4	piece	Mantles	0	13	4	0
		2	C	Skins, Sheep (no wool)	0	20	0	0
		0.5	C	Skins, Lamb	0	2	6	0
Thomas Shartall	Ind	0.5	dicker	Hides, Salted	0	6	8	0

Merchant name	Origin	Qty	Unit	Commodity	£	s.	d.	f.

Bata Marget of Minehead, John White master, from Ireland, *24th July 1504*

Merchant name	Origin	Qty	Unit	Commodity	£	s.	d.	f.
John White	Ind	20	burden	Fish, Salted	o	66	8	o
Walter Marten	Ind	18	piece	Mantles	o	60	o	o
		2	C	Skins, Sheep (no wool)	o	20	o	o
		0.5	C	Skins, Lamb	o	2	6	o
		12	piece	Skins, Fox	o	o	18	o
Patrick Goold	Ind	1	pipe	Wine	o	o	o	o
John White	Ind	10	burden	Fish, Salted	o	33	4	o

Bata Mare of Milford Haven, John Gibons master, from Ireland, *24th July 1504*

Merchant name	Origin	Qty	Unit	Commodity	£	s.	d.	f.
Henry Tollar &								
John Frebodie	Ind	1.5	wey	Grain	o	45	o	o
John Ffrebodie	Ind	36	piece	Mantles	6	o	o	o
		6	C	Irish Linen *Cloth*	o	60	o	o
		1	C	Skins, Sheep (no wool)	o	10	o	o
		2	C	Skins, Lamb	o	10	o	o
		20	yard	Check *Cloth*	o	6	8	o

Bata Trinite of Chepstow, William Heyn master, *to Chepstow, 24th July 1504*

Merchant name	Origin	Qty	Unit	Commodity	£	s.	d.	f.
John Boet	Alien	0.5	piece	Cloth of Assize	o	o	o	o

Bata Marget of Chepstow, Robert Bochere master, from Chepstow, 27th July 1504

Merchant name	Origin	Qty	Unit	Commodity	£	s.	d.	f.
John Shipman	Ind	1	pipe	Woad	o	100	o	o

Bata Mare of Milford Haven, John Owen master, *from Milford Haven, 27th July 1504*

Merchant name	Origin	Qty	Unit	Commodity	£	s.	d.	f.
John Owen	Ind	10	ton	Salt	4	3	4	o
		1	ton	Salt	o	8	4	o

Bata Petur of Milford Haven, Richard Jeffereis master, from Ireland, *27th July 1504*

Merchant name	Origin	Qty	Unit	Commodity	£	s.	d.	f.
Richard Jeffereis	Ind	1.25	pipe	Fish, Salmon	o	37	6	o
		0.5	burden	Fish, Salted	o	o	20	o
		1	virken	Fish, Salmon	o	7	6	o

Bata Katren of Tenby, Richard Williams master, from Tenby, 29th July 1504

Merchant name	Origin	Qty	Unit	Commodity	£	s.	d.	f.
John Walter	Ind	6.25	C	Sugar	12	10	o	o

Bata John of Haverfordwest, Thomas Blanke master, from Haverfordwest, 29th July 1504

Merchant name	Origin	Qty	Unit	Commodity	£	s.	d.	f.
Philip Holwaie	Ind	1	tun	Wine	o	o	o	o
Thomas Aphowell	Ind	1.25	tun	Wine	o	o	o	o
		2	ton	Salt	o	16	8	o

Bata Mare of Berkeley, Thomas Powar master, from Chepstow, 30th July 1504

Merchant name	Origin	Qty	Unit	Commodity	£	s.	d.	f.
Thomas Bocher	Ind	1	pipe	Woad	o	100	o	o

Merchant name	Origin	Qty	Unit	Commodity	£	s.	d.	f.
Bata Mare Cooke, Port Unknown, Stephen Barnard master, to Ireland, *30th July 1504*								
Thomas Cooke	Ind	1	ton	Salt	0	16	8	0
Thomas Woodward &								
Laurence Fflemynge	Ind	1	ton	Salt	0	16	8	0
William Hope*r*	Ind	1.5	pipe	Salt	0	12	6	0
Philip Morgan	Ind	88	lb	*Pilus Tinctus*	0	29	4	0
Bata Marget of Chepstow, Robert Bocher master, from Chepstow, 31st July 1504								
William Webbe	Ind	1	pipe	Wine	0	0	0	0
Bata James of Ushant, Nicholas Harvie master, to Brittany, *31st July 1504*								
Nicholas Harvie	Alien	2.5	piece	Welsh *Cloth*	0	50	0	0
		1.5	wey	Coal	0	5	0	0
		1.5	wey	Coal	0	5	0	0
Bata George of Gatcombe, Walter Nashe master, from Ireland, 2nd August 1504								
Walter Nashe	Ind	2	pipe	Fish, Salmon	0	60	0	0
Richard Arthur	Ind	2.5	pipe	Fish, Salmon	0	75	0	0
		5.75	C	Skins, Sheep (no wool)	0	57	6	0
		6	lb	Wax	0	2	0	0
Walter Nashe	Ind	1	C	Fish, Hake	0	10	0	0
Bata Marke of Bristol, Edmund Griffethe master, to Portugal, *2nd August 1504*								
John Popley	Ind	10	piece	Cloth of Assize	0	0	0	0
William Estbie	Ind	78	piece	Welsh *Cloth*, Dozen Strait	16	5	0	0
William Downe	Ind	0.5	piece	Cloth of Assize	0	0	0	0
Bata George of Chepstow, William Heyn master, from Chepstow, *2nd August 1504*								
William Webbe	Ind	1	tun	Wine	0	0	0	0
		1	hogshead	Vinegar	0	10	0	0
Bata John of Cork, Thomas Walshe master, to Ireland, 3rd August 1504								
Thomas Walshe	Ind	100	lb	*Pilus Tinctus*	0	33	4	0
William Fe Mores	Ind	4.5	stone	Orchil, Worked	0	7	6	0
		1	gross	Knives	0	6	8	0
Richard Mahond	Ind	14	lb	*Pilus Tinctus*	0	4	8	0
		8	stone	Orchil, Worked	0	13	4	0
David Walshe	Ind	8	stone	Orchil, Worked	0	13	4	0
		40	lb	*Pilus Tinctus*	0	13	4	0
Thomas Mirthe	Ind	14	lb	*Pilus Tinctus*	0	4	8	0
		3.5	yard	Cloth of Assize	0	0	0	0
Patrick Fferes	Ind	60	lb	*Pilus Tinctus*	0	20	0	0
John Denys	Ind	9	stone	Orchil, Worked	0	15	0	0
William Tirrie	Ind	12	stone	Orchil, Worked	0	20	0	0
		10	lb	*Pilus Tinctus*	0	3	4	0

Merchant name	Origin	Qty	Unit	Commodity	£	s.	d.	f.
Robert Towkar	Ind	1	piece	Cloth of Assize, Dozen Strait	0	0	0	0
William Hofe	Ind	14	lb	*Pilus Tinctus*	0	4	8	0

Bata Sondaie of Waterford, John Walshe master, to Ireland, 6th August 1504

Merchant name	Origin	Qty	Unit	Commodity	£	s.	d.	f.
John Barne	Ind	8	piece	Cloth of Assize	0	0	0	0
		3	piece	Cloth of Assize, Dozen	0	0	0	0
		6	lb	Saffron	0	40	0	0
		120	lb	*Pilus Tinctus*	0	40	0	0
		1	gross	Knives	0	6	8	0
		1	lb	Silk, Worked	0	13	4	0
Nicholas Morthey	Ind	2	lb	Saffron	0	13	4	0
		1	lb	Silk, Worked	0	13	4	0
		10	gross	Points	0	10	0	0
		1	C	Combs	0	0	12	0
		4	lb	*Pilus Tinctus*	0	0	16	0
Richard Born	Ind	11	lb	Saffron	0	73	4	0
Peter Kalley	Ind	40	lb	*Pilus Tinctus*	0	13	4	0
Malagur Taylor	Ind	1	piece	Cloth of Assize, Dozen Strait	0	0	0	0
		0.5	piece	Cloth of Assize, Kersey	0	0	0	0
		1	lb	Saffron	0	6	8	0
		0.5	dozen	Caps	0	3	4	0
		2	gross	Points	0	2	0	0
		70	lb	*Pilus Tinctus*	0	23	4	0
William Archepoll	Ind	1.5	lb	Silk, Worked	0	20	0	0
		1	lb	Cinnamon	0	2	6	0
		1	lb	Pepper	0	0	12	0
		1	lb	Graynes	0	0	9	0
		2	lb	Verdegris	0	0	12	0
		3	lb	Thread	0	0	15	0
		40	lb	*Pilus Tinctus*	0	13	4	0
		12	pair	Cards, Unspecified	0	4	0	0
		2	dozen	Caps	0	13	4	0
		2	dozen	Aniseed	0	3	0	0
		3	gross	Knives	0	20	0	0
		9	gross	Points	0	9	0	0
John Archer	Ind	4	piece	Cloth of Assize	0	0	0	0
		5	lb	Saffron	0	33	4	0
		1	lb	Silk, Worked	0	13	4	0
		1.5	dozen	Caps	0	10	0	0
Thomas Lawnder	Ind	4	piece	Cloth of Assize	0	0	0	0
John Barne	Ind	20	gross	Points	0	20	0	0
Thomas Streche	Ind	11.5	piece	Cloth of Assize	0	0	0	0
		5	dozen	Caps	0	33	4	0
		6	lb	Saffron	0	40	0	0
		6	lb	Silk, Worked	4	0	0	0
		1	gross	Knives	0	6	8	0
		11	piece	Penners	0	0	11	0
		2	gross	Points	0	2	0	0
Thomas Lawnder	Ind	1	piece	Cloth of Assize	0	0	0	0

Merchant name	Origin	Qty	Unit	Commodity	£	s.	d.	f.
Bata James of Slimbridge, John Rogers master, to Ireland, 6th August 1504								
John Rogers	Ind	3	wey	Malt	0	40	0	0
		1	ton	Salt	0	16	8	0
Bata Miell of New Ross, William Blake master, to Ireland, 6th August 1504								
William Blake	Ind	60	lb	*Pilus Tinctus*	0	20	0	0
John Longe	Ind	15	lb	*Pilus Tinctus*	0	5	0	0
Thomas Bryne	Ind	7	lb	Saffron	0	46	8	0
		1	piece	Cloth of Assize	0	0	0	0
		2	lb	Pepper	0	2	0	0
		1	lb	Cinnamon	0	2	6	0
		1	lb	Ginger	0	0	12	0
		2.5	dozen	Aniseed	0	3	9	0
		40	lb	*Pilus Tinctus*	0	13	4	0
		3	gross	Points	0	3	0	0
		2	lb	Wood, Brazil	0	0	16	0
		1	gross	Knives	0	6	8	0
John Donell	Ind	2	piece	Cloth of Assize	0	0	0	0
		2	lb	Silk, Worked	0	26	8	0
		36	lb	*Pilus Tinctus*	0	12	0	0
		1	lb	Cinnamon	0	2	6	0
		1	lb	Ginger	0	0	12	0
Edward Moyn	Ind	2	piece	Cloth of Assize	0	0	0	0
		2	lb	Saffron	0	13	4	0
		1	lb	Silk, Worked	0	13	4	0
		5	gross	Points	0	5	0	0
		4	lb	*Pilus Tinctus*	0	0	16	0
William Lenard	Ind	5	lb	Silk, Worked	0	66	8	0
		2	lb	Saffron	0	13	4	0
		40	lb	*Pilus Tinctus*	0	13	4	0
		1.5	gross	Knives	0	10	0	0
		6	gross	Points	0	6	0	0
		0.5	ream	Paper	0	0	12	0
		2.5	lb	Wood, Brazil	0	0	20	0
John Walshe	Ind	3.5	lb	Silk, Worked	0	46	8	0
		4	lb	Saffron	0	26	8	0
		0.5	dozen	Caps	0	3	4	0
		1	dozen	Aniseed	0	0	18	0
		4	lb	Verdegris	0	2	0	0
John Walshe	Ind	5	gross	Points	0	5	0	0
		1.5	gross	Knives	0	10	0	0
		2	pair	Stock-cards	0	2	0	0
		2.5	lb	Wood, Brazil	0	0	20	0
		1	lb	Pepper	0	0	12	0
		40	lb	*Pilus Tinctus*	0	13	4	0
Robert Kenaye	Ind	2	piece	Cloth of Assize	0	0	0	0
		3	lb	Saffron	0	20	0	0
		1	dozen	Aniseed	0	0	18	0
		1	lb	Mace	0	2	0	0
		60	lb	*Pilus Tinctus*	0	20	0	0

Merchant name	Origin	Qty	Unit	Commodity	£	s.	d.	f.
		6	gross	Points	0	6	0	0
William Lenard	Ind	20	lb	*Pilus Tinctus*	0	6	8	0

Bata Trinite of Milford Haven, Thomas Eliet master, from Milford Haven, 7th August 1504

Merchant name	Origin	Qty	Unit	Commodity	£	s.	d.	f.
George Monos	Ind	7	ton	Iron	17	10	0	0
		3.5	pipe	Fish, Salmon	0	105	0	0
		1.66	tun	Honey	4	3	4	0
		1	hogshead	Rosin	0	6	8	0
		1	pipe	Pitch	0	13	4	0
		1	pipe	Fish, Salmon	0	30	0	0

Bata Anne of Chepstow, John Horsman master, from Chepstow, *7th August 1504*

Merchant name	Origin	Qty	Unit	Commodity	£	s.	d.	f.
Thomas Smythe	Ind	4.5	tun	Oil, Olive	18	0	0	0

Bata Miell of New Ross, William Blake master, to Ireland, 8th August 1504

Merchant name	Origin	Qty	Unit	Commodity	£	s.	d.	f.
William Sale	Ind	0.5	gross	Knives	0	3	4	0
		4	gross	Points	0	4	0	0

Navicula Fraunses of Bristol, Nicholas Prowde master, to Algarve, 9th August 1504

Merchant name	Origin	Qty	Unit	Commodity	£	s.	d.	f.
William Tirrie	Ind	3	piece	Cloth of Assize	0	0	0	0
Humphrey Bosgrove	Ind	5	piece	Cloth of Assize	0	0	0	0
		12	piece	Welsh *Cloth*	12	0	0	0
John Benet	Ind	6	piece	Welsh *Cloth*	6	0	0	0
		2	piece	Cloth of Assize, Kersey	0	0	0	0
		3	piece	Welsh *Cloth*, Dozen Strait	0	12	6	0
John Ynon	Ind	11	piece	Welsh *Cloth*	11	0	0	0
Edmund Human	Ind	6.5	dozen	Skins, Calf Tanned	0	16	3	0
Humphrey Browne	Ind	10	piece	Welsh *Cloth*	10	0	0	0
Robert Ffortey	Ind	2	piece	Welsh *Cloth*	0	40	0	0

Navicula *Christ*pofur *of* Bristol, William Balie master, from La Rochelle, 12th August 1504

Merchant name	Origin	Qty	Unit	Commodity	£	s.	d.	f.
George Monos	Ind	36	ton	Salt	15	0	0	0
William Mewrell	Ind	4	ton	Salt	0	33	4	0
Thomas Jones	Ind	0.5	*pipe*	Woad	0	50	0	0

Bata George of Shirehampton, Robert Aishurst master, from Chepstow, 12th August 1504

Merchant name	Origin	Qty	Unit	Commodity	£	s.	d.	f.
John Colas	Ind	24	C	Oranges	4	0	0	0
		5	Sack	Hops	10	0	0	0
		1	bale	Madder	0	40	0	0

Navicula Mathewe of Bristol, William Claron master, from Bordeaux, *12th August 1504*

Merchant name	Origin	Qty	Unit	Commodity	£	s.	d.	f.
John Shipman	Ind	99	measure	Woad	40	18	9	0
		1	tun	Vinegar	0	40	0	0
		10	ton	Salt	4	3	4	0
William Jeffereis	Ind	22	pipe	Woad	110	0	0	0

Merchant name	Origin	Qty	Unit	Commodity	£	s.	d.	f.
Richard Hobie	Ind	58	measure	Woad	18	2	6	0
Humphrey Brown	Ind	1.5	pipe	Woad	7	10	0	0
Robert Barrero	Ind	172	measure	Woad	53	15	0	0

Navicula Gelian of Bristol, Walter Snygge master, to Ireland, *12th August 1504*

Merchant name	Origin	Qty	Unit	Commodity	£	s.	d.	f.
John Jaie	Ind	5	tun	Wine, Corrupt	7	10	0	0
		3	ton	Salt	0	50	0	0
William Aphowell	Ind	0.5	last	Beer	0	15	0	0
John Jaie	Ind	1	tun	Wine, Corrupt	0	30	0	0
William Rise	Ind	1	pipe	Wine, Corrupt	0	15	0	0
William Aphowell	Ind	6.5	piece	Cloth of Assize	0	0	0	0
John Jansie	Ind	1	pipe	Wine, Corrupt	0	15	0	0
Tege Wigmor	Ind	1	lb	Silk, Worked	0	13	4	0
Thomas Aishurste	Ind	1	tun	Wine, Corrupt	0	30	0	0
John Jaie	Ind	8	piece	Cloth of Assize	0	0	0	0
		120	lb	*Pilus Tinctus*	0	40	0	0
Thomas Aishurste	Ind	14	piece	Cloth of Assize	0	0	0	0

Navicula Gelian Bonaventur, Port Unknown,[13] Henry Harte master, to Spain, *12th August 1504*

Merchant name	Origin	Qty	Unit	Commodity	£	s.	d.	f.
Nicholas Browne	Ind	25	piece	Cloth of Assize	0	0	0	0
Richard Vaghan	Ind	16	piece	Cloth of Assize	0	0	0	0
		11	dozen	Skins, Calf Tanned	0	27	6	0
Richard Hobie	Ind	35	piece	Cloth of Assize	0	0	0	0
William Hurste	Ind	24	piece	Cloth of Assize	0	0	0	0
Stephen Ffostar	Ind	8	piece	Cloth of Assize	0	0	0	0
		20	dozen	Skins, Calf Tanned	0	50	0	0
Henry Dale	Ind	15	piece	Cloth of Assize	0	0	0	0
John Ringston	Ind	8	piece	Cloth of Assize	0	0	0	0
Stephen Ffostar	Ind	16	piece	Cloth of Assize	0	0	0	0
Thomas Hawkyns	Ind	12	piece	Cloth of Assize	0	0	0	0
		18	piece	Welsh *Cloth*, Dozen Strait	0	75	0	0
John Ware &								
John Shipman	Ind	30	piece	Cloth of Assize	0	0	0	0
Thomas Smythe	Ind	8	piece	Cloth of Assize	0	0	0	0
Richard Vaghan	Ind	7	piece	Cloth of Assize	0	0	0	0
Stephen Ffostar	Ind	3	dozen	Skins, Calf Tanned	0	7	6	0
Robert Barrero	Ind	8	piece	Cloth of Assize	0	0	0	0
Richard Hobie	Ind	1	piece	Cloth of Assize	0	0	0	0
Thomas P[ ]naunt	Ind	2	piece	Cloth of Assize	0	0	0	0
Henry Harte	Ind	1	piece	Cloth of Assize	0	0	0	0
		6	piece	Welsh *Cloth*	6	0	0	0
		4	piece	Welsh *Cloth*, Dozen Strait	0	16	8	0
John Edee	Ind	8	piece	Cloth of Assize	0	0	0	0
Stephen Ffostar	Ind	9	piece	Cloth of Assize	0	0	0	0
John Edee	Ind	1	piece	Cloth of Assize	0	0	0	0
William Aphowell	Ind	7	piece	Cloth of Assize	0	0	0	0
John Grene	Ind	2	dozen	Skins, Calf Tanned	0	5	0	0
John Ware &								
John Shipman	Ind	20	piece	Cloth of Assize	0	0	0	0

13 Probably Bristol.

Merchant name	Origin	Qty	Unit	Commodity	£	s.	d.	f.
Daniel de Caviera	Alien	8	dozen	Skins, Calf Tanned	0	20	0	0
		1	dozen	Welsh *Cloth*, Dozen Strait	0	4	2	0
Richard Gaie	Ind	2	piece	Cloth of Assize	0	0	0	0
John Vaghan	Ind	16	piece	Cloth of Assize	0	0	0	0
John Rowland	Ind	20	piece	Cloth of Assize	0	0	0	0
John Wiot	Ind	10	piece	Cloth of Assize	0	0	0	0
		2	piece	Cloth of Assize	0	0	0	0
Thomas Badcok	Ind	30	dozen	Skins, Calf Tanned	0	75	0	0
David Vaghan	Ind	4	piece	Cloth of Assize	0	0	0	0
John Stokes &								
Richard Crosse	Ind	30	piece	Cloth of Assize	0	0	0	0
Peter Delakeite	Alien	1	piece	Cloth of Assize, Dozen Strait	0	10	0	0

Bata Katren of Bristol, Peter Ffenne master, from Ireland, *12th August 1504*

Merchant name	Origin	Qty	Unit	Commodity	£	s.	d.	f.
Richard Checke	Ind	3	C	Skins, Sheep (no wool)	0	30	0	0
		9	piece	Mantles	0	30	0	0
		0.5	pipe	Fish, Salmon	0	15	0	0
Patrick Prendergras	Ind	3	C	Skins, Sheep (no wool)	0	30	0	0
		4	stone	Wool, Flocks	0	0	20	0
William Tirrie	Ind	2	pipe	Fish, Salmon	0	60	0	0
		1	C	Skins, Sheep (no wool)	0	10	0	0
William Clarke	Ind	1.5	C	Skins, Sheep (no wool)	0	15	0	0
		1.5	C	Skins, Lamb	0	7	6	0
John Doryn	Ind	1	pipe	Fish, Salmon	0	30	0	0

Navicula Marget of Bristol, Edward Gibbes master, from Bordeaux, 13th August 1504

Merchant name	Origin	Qty	Unit	Commodity	£	s.	d.	f.
Robert Barrero	Ind	5	pipe	Woad	25	0	0	0
John Ringston	Ind	2	pipe	Woad	10	0	0	0
Roger Dawes	Ind	3	pipe	Woad	15	0	0	0
John Benet	Ind	4	pipe	Woad	20	0	0	0
Ralph Aprise	Ind	10	measure	Woad	0	62	6	0
William Hurste	Ind	9	measure	Woad	0	56	3	0
Richard Stephins	Ind	1.5	pipe	Woad	7	10	0	0
William Estbie	Ind	115	measure	Woad	35	18	9	0
William Wosley	Ind	52	measure	Woad	16	5	0	0
John Vaghan	Ind	339	measure	Woad	105	18	9	0
Thomas Hochens	Ind	1.5	pipe	Woad	7	10	0	0
John Popley	Ind	9	pipe	Woad	45	0	0	0
John Domingus	Alien	3	pipe	Woad	15	0	0	0
William Aphowell	Ind	4	pipe	Woad	20	0	0	0
Thomas Aphowell	Ind	1	pipe	Woad	0	100	0	0
John Stokes	Ind	4	pipe	Woad	20	0	0	0
Robert Ffystar	Ind	12	measure	Woad	0	75	0	0
Robert Rowlowe	Ind	2	pipe	Woad	10	0	0	0
David Vaghan	Ind	9	measure	Woad	0	56	3	0
William Jeffereis	Ind	285	measure	Woad	89	15	0	0
		3	tun	Wine	12	0	0	0
Robert Thorn	Ind	5	pipe	Woad	25	0	0	0
Thomas Horsman	Ind	1	pipe	Rosin	0	13	4	0
Humphry Brown	Ind	4	pipe	Woad	20	0	0	0

Merchant name	Origin	Qty	Unit	Commodity	£	s.	d.	f.
Nicholas Brown	Ind	9	pipe	Woad	45	0	0	0
Thomas Awsten	Ind	1.5	pipe	Woad	7	10	0	0
Edward Gibbes	Ind	6	measure	Woad	0	37	6	0
Thomas Clarke	Ind	33	measure	Woad	10	6	3	0
		1	hogshead	Lye Ashes	0	6	8	0
Peter Aburden	Ind	1	pipe	Woad	0	100	0	0
John Turnor	Ind	28	measure	Woad	8	15	0	0
Richard Gaie	Ind	1.5	pipe	Woad	7	10	0	0
		1	pipe	Rosin	0	13	4	0
John Eliet	Ind	35	measure	Woad	10	18	9	0
John Jones	Ind	0.5	pipe	Woad	0	50	0	0
Henry Harte	Ind	1	tun	Vinegar	0	40	0	0
Thomas Smythe	Ind	4.5	pipe	Woad	22	10	0	0
John Shipman	Ind	11	pipe	Woad	55	0	0	0
John Ware &								
John Shipman	Ind	117	measure	Woad	36	11	3	0
John Ware	Ind	1	barrel	Fish, Sturgeon	0	6	8	0

Bata Katren of Gloucester, Thomas Cockes master, from Chepstow, 14th August 1504

Merchant name	Origin	Qty	Unit	Commodity	£	s.	d.	f.
David Westberie	Ind	10	ton	Salt	4	3	4	0

Bata Kymborgh of Gloucester, John Blisse master, from Chepstow, *14th August 1504*

Merchant name	Origin	Qty	Unit	Commodity	£	s.	d.	f.
David Westberie	Ind	10	ton	Salt	4	3	4	0

Bata Mare Cooke, Port Unknown, Stephen Barnard master, to Ireland, *14th August 1504*

Merchant name	Origin	Qty	Unit	Commodity	£	s.	d.	f.
Thomas Woodward	Ind	1	hogshead	Wine, Corrupt	0	7	6	0
		1	pipe	Salt	0	8	4	0

Navicula Gelian of Le Croisic, Bernard Lucas master, from Brittany, 16th August 1504

Merchant name	Origin	Qty	Unit	Commodity	£	s.	d.	f.
Bernard Lucas	Alien	60	ton	Salt	25	0	0	0
John Keepe	Ind	1	pipe	Rosin	0	13	4	0
Rewe Osam	Alien	4	bolt	Canvas *Cloth*	0	26	8	0
Bernard Lucas	Alien	12	ton	Salt	0	100	0	0
		8	ton	Salt	0	66	8	0
		3.5	ton	Salt	0	29	2	0
		1.5	ton	Salt	0	12	6	0
		2	ton	Salt	0	16	8	0

Navicula Mare Belhous*e* of *Bristol*, Walter Cooke master, to Algarve, *16th August 1504*

Merchant name	Origin	Qty	Unit	Commodity	£	s.	d.	f.
Roger Dawes	Ind	14	piece	Cloth of Assize, Dozen	0	0	0	0
		10	piece	Welsh *Cloth*	10	0	0	0
Philip Ringston	Ind	20	piece	Cloth of Assize	0	0	0	0
John Thomas	Ind	18	piece	Cloth of Assize	0	0	0	0
Ralph Aprise	Ind	2	piece	Cloth of Assize	0	0	0	0
		0.5	piece	Cloth of Assize	0	0	0	0
		1.5	piece	Welsh *Cloth*	0	30	0	0
Richard Crosse	Ind	6	piece	Cloth of Assize	0	0	0	0

Merchant name	Origin	Qty	Unit	Commodity	£	s.	d.	f.
William Jeffereis	Ind	14	piece	Cloth of Assize	0	0	0	0
Thomas Pernaunt	Ind	2	piece	Cloth of Assize	0	0	0	0
John Domingus	Alien	9	piece	Welsh *Cloth*	9	0	0	0
John Lorde	Ind	3	piece	Cloth of Assize	0	0	0	0
Nicholas Browne	Ind	40	piece	Welsh *Cloth*, Dozen Strait	8	6	8	0
John Brewar	Ind	4	piece	Mantles	0	13	4	0
Roger Dawes	Ind	18	piece	Cloth of Assize	0	0	0	0
		8	piece	Cloth of Assize, Dozen	0	0	0	0
William Jeffereis	Ind	8	piece	Cloth of Assize	0	0	0	0
Henry Dale	Ind	8	piece	Cloth of Assize	0	0	0	0
John Gurdelar	Ind	2	piece	Welsh *Cloth*	0	40	0	0
Richard Vaghan	Ind	22	piece	Welsh *Cloth*, Dozen Strait	4	11	8	0
		6	piece	Cloth of Assize	0	0	0	0
John Eliet	Ind	8	piece	Cloth of Assize	0	0	0	0
John Shipman	Ind	6	piece	Cloth of Assize	0	0	0	0
Roger Dawes	Ind	1	piece	Cloth of Assize	0	0	0	0
		3	piece	Welsh *Cloth*	0	60	0	0
William Estbie	Ind	1	piece	Cloth of Assize	0	0	0	0
		1	piece	Welsh *Cloth*	0	20	0	0
Margery Grene	Ind	12	piece	Welsh *Cloth*, Dozen Strait	0	50	0	0
John Benet	Ind	60	piece	Cloth of Assize	0	0	0	0
Humphrey Brown	Ind	4	piece	Cloth of Assize	0	0	0	0
John Thomas	Ind	1	piece	Cloth of Assize	0	0	0	0
John Benet	Ind	20	piece	Cloth of Assize	0	0	0	0
Peter Aburden	Ind	10	piece	Welsh *Cloth*	10	0	0	0
John Colens	Ind	1	piece	Cloth of Assize	0	0	0	0
John Rowland	Ind	8	piece	Cloth of Assize	0	0	0	0
Richard Bakar	Ind	2.5	dicker	Hides, Tanned	8	6	8	0
		2.5	dozen	Skins, Calf Tanned	0	6	3	0
Robert Barrero	Ind	3	piece	Welsh *Cloth*	0	60	0	0
Robert Ffortey	Ind	2	piece	Cloth of Assize	0	0	0	0
Thomas Smythe	Ind	7	piece	Cloth of Assize	0	0	0	0
George Monos	Ind	16	piece	Cloth of Assize	0	0	0	0
John Jaie	Ind	5	piece	Cloth of Assize	0	0	0	0

Bata *Christ*pofur of Bristol, Richard Braie master, to Ireland, *16th August 1504*

Merchant name	Origin	Qty	Unit	Commodity	£	s.	d.	f.
John Brewar	Ind	1	wey	Malt	0	13	4	0
William Jeffereis	Ind	16	piece	Cloth of Assize, Dozen	0	0	0	0
		4	piece	Cloth of Assize	0	0	0	0
		1	pipe	Wine, Corrupt	0	15	0	0
Nicholas Browne	Ind	3	tun	Wine, Corrupt	4	10	0	0
Richard Braie	Ind	1.5	ton	Salt	0	25	0	0
Matthew Smythe	Ind	1	pipe	Wine, Corrupt	0	15	0	0
John Browne	Ind	1	pipe	Wine, Corrupt	0	15	0	0
John Harries	Ind	100	lb	*Pilus Tinctus*	0	33	4	0
		0.5	last	Beer	0	15	0	0
Richard Braie	Ind	1	piece	Cloth of Assize	0	0	0	0
		20	lb	*Pilus Tinctus*	0	6	8	0
		4	barrel	Beer	0	5	0	0
Richard Arthure	Ind	80	lb	*Pilus Tinctus*	0	26	8	0
		2	lb	Silk, Worked	0	26	8	0

Merchant name	Origin	Qty	Unit	Commodity	£	s.	d.	f.
Nicholas Ffishar	Ind	1	hogshead	Wine, Corrupt	0	7	6	0
John Wase	Ind	1	tun	Wine, Corrupt	0	30	0	0
Robert Barrero	Ind	80	lb	*Pilus Tinctus*	0	26	8	0

Navicula Awsten of Bristol, Richard Russel master, to Ireland, *16th August 1504*

Merchant name	Origin	Qty	Unit	Commodity	£	s.	d.	f.
Hugh Eliet	Ind	4	ton	Salt	0	56	8	0
Ralph Aprise	Ind	1	pipe	Wine, Corrupt	0	15	0	0
Hugh Eliet	Ind	1	pipe	Wine, Corrupt	0	15	0	0

Bata Petur of Newport, Walter Willia*m* to Combe Martin, *16th August 1504*

Merchant name	Origin	Qty	Unit	Commodity	£	s.	d.	f.
John James	Ind	5	piece	Welsh *Cloth*	0	100	0	0
William Crosse	Ind	12	piece	Cloth of Assize	0	0	0	0
John Edee	Ind	7	piece	Cloth of Assize	0	0	0	0
Richard Symons	Ind	17	piece	Welsh *Cloth*	17	0	0	0
		3	piece	Cloth of Assize	0	0	0	0
		9	dozen	Skins, Calf Tanned	0	22	6	0
John Grene	Ind	3	piece	Welsh *Cloth*	0	60	0	0
John Thomas	Ind	5	piece	Cloth of Assize	0	0	0	0
		6	piece	Welsh *Cloth*	6	0	0	0
Richard Cooke	Ind	4	piece	Cloth of Assize	0	0	0	0
William Jeffereis	Ind	28	piece	Cloth of Assize	0	0	0	0
John Lorde	Ind	4	piece	Welsh *Cloth*	4	0	0	0
Richard Drap*er*	Ind	5	piece	Welsh *Cloth*	0	100	0	0
		1	piece	Cloth of Assize	0	0	0	0
Richard Cooke	Ind	4	piece	Welsh *Cloth*	4	0	0	0

Navicula Mare of Penmarch, John Malock master, to Brittany, 16th August 1504

Merchant name	Origin	Qty	Unit	Commodity	£	s.	d.	f.
John Malock	Alien	13	tun/ton	Calx	0	32	6	0
George Monos	Ind	5	ton	Lead, Worked	25	0	0	0

Navicula Mare Katren of *Bristol*, Robert Avyntre master, to Lisbon, 20th August 1504

Merchant name	Origin	Qty	Unit	Commodity	£	s.	d.	f.
David Vaghan	Ind	10	piece	Cloth of Assize	0	0	0	0
John Dryver	Ind	22	piece	Welsh *Cloth*	22	0	0	0
		2	ton	Lead, Worked	10	0	0	0
Roger Dawes	Ind	4	piece	Cloth of Assize	0	0	0	0
		4	piece	Cloth of Assize, Dozen	0	0	0	0
George Monos	Ind	8	piece	Cloth of Assize	0	0	0	0
Richard Hobie	Ind	16	piece	Cloth of Assize	0	0	0	0
William Estbie	Ind	9	piece	Welsh *Cloth*	9	0	0	0
Thomas Smythe	Ind	42	piece	Cloth of Assize	0	0	0	0
Nicholas Brown	Ind	2	piece	Cloth of Assize	0	0	0	0
		4	piece	Welsh *Cloth*	4	0	0	0
Richard Vaghan	Ind	8	piece	Cloth of Assize	0	0	0	0
Thomas Hawkens	Ind	5	piece	Cloth of Assize	0	0	0	0
John Shipma*n*	Ind	11	piece	Cloth of Assize	0	0	0	0
John Halle	Ind	17	piece	Cloth of Assize	0	0	0	0
		13	piece	Cloth of Assize, Dozen	0	0	0	0
		100	piece	Welsh *Cloth*, Dozen Strait	20	16	8	0

Merchant name	Origin	Qty	Unit	Commodity	£	s.	d.	f.
		1	piece	Welsh *Cloth*	0	20	0	0
John Vaghan	Ind	8	piece	Cloth of Assize	0	0	0	0
John Halle	Ind	6	piece	Cloth of Assize	0	0	0	0
		3	piece	Cloth of Assize, Dozen	0	0	0	0
		50	piece	Welsh *Cloth*, Dozen Strait	10	8	4	0
John Rowland	Ind	9	piece	Cloth of Assize	0	0	0	0
John Benet	Ind	3	piece	Welsh *Cloth*	0	60	0	0
		0.5	piece	Cloth of Assize	0	0	0	0
John James	Ind	10	piece	Welsh *Cloth*	10	0	0	0
		4	piece	Cloth of Assize	0	0	0	0
Thomas Smythe	Ind	1	dozen	Skins, Calf Tanned	0	2	6	0
		4	piece	Welsh *Cloth*, Dozen Strait	0	16	8	0
		1	piece	Cloth of Assize, Kersey	0	0	0	0
Humphrey Bosgrove	Ind	2	piece	Welsh *Cloth*	0	40	0	0
Robert Avyntre	Ind	3	piece	Cloth of Assize	0	0	0	0
		3	piece	Welsh *Cloth*	0	60	0	0
		14	piece	Welsh *Cloth*, Dozen Strait	0	58	4	0
		1	piece	Cloth of Assize, Kersey	0	0	0	0
		10	dozen	Skins, Calf Tanned	0	25	0	0
John Stokes	Ind	8	piece	Cloth of Assize	0	0	0	0
Thomas Smythe	Ind	4	piece	Cloth of Assize	0	0	0	0
David Leyson	Ind	1	piece	Cloth of Assize	0	0	0	0
		4	piece	Welsh *Cloth*, Dozen Strait	0	16	8	0
John Jaie	Ind	5	piece	Cloth of Assize	0	0	0	0
John Bonwaie	Ind	16	piece	Welsh *Cloth*	16	0	0	0
		1	piece	Cloth of Assize	0	0	0	0
John Colas	Ind	6	piece	Cloth of Assize	0	0	0	0
Thomas Osney	Ind	8	piece	Cloth of Assize	0	0	0	0
John James	Ind	6	dozen	Skins, Calf Tanned	0	15	0	0
		1	piece	Cloth of Assize, Kersey	0	0	0	0
John Laurens	Ind	35	piece	Welsh *Cloth*	35	0	0	0
John Halle	Ind	3	piece	Welsh *Cloth*	3	0	0	0
		10	piece	Welsh *Cloth*, Dozen Strait	0	41	8	0
		1	piece	Cloth of Assize, Dozen	0	0	0	0
John Dryver	Ind	8	piece	Cloth of Assize	0	0	0	0
		2	piece	Cloth of Assize, Dozen Strait	0	0	0	0
Thomas Smythe	Ind	4	piece	Cloth of Assize	0	0	0	0

Bata Mare Shirehampton, William White master, from Chepstow, 21st August 1504

Merchant name	Origin	Qty	Unit	Commodity	£	s.	d.	f.
Thomas Bocher	Ind	0.5	pipe	Woad	0	50	0	0

Navicula Katren Bocher, Port Unknown,[14] Robert Powar master, to Ireland, 22nd August 1504

Merchant name	Origin	Qty	Unit	Commodity	£	s.	d.	f.
Thomas Bocher	Ind	4	piece	Cloth of Assize	0	0	0	0
		6	piece	Cloth of Assize	0	0	0	0
John Tillinge	Ind	4	piece	Welsh *Cloth*, Dozen Strait	0	16	8	0
Thomas Bocher	Ind	1	piece	Cloth of Assize	0	0	0	0

14 Possibly Bristol.

Merchant name	Origin	Qty	Unit	Commodity	£	s.	d.	f.
Bata Phelip of Bristol, Thomas Jones master, from La Rochelle, 23rd August 1504								
Thomas Jones	Ind	22	ton	Salt	9	3	4	0
Bata Katren of Bristol, Peter Ffenne master, to Ireland, *23rd August 1504*								
Patrick Prendergras	Ind	108	lb	*Pilus Tinctus*	0	42	8	0
Nicholas Barn	Ind	12	lb	*Pilus Tinctus*	0	4	0	0
William Tirrie	Ind	30	lb	*Pilus Tinctus*	0	10	0	0
Bata Miell of Gloucester, David Walshe master, from Chepstow, *23rd August 1504*								
David Westberie	Ind	10	ton	Salt	4	3	4	0
Bata Mare of Cork, Laurence Tobyn master, from Ireland, 28th August 1504								
Edmund Roche	Ind	34.5	barrel	Fish, Herring White	8	12	6	0
		3	quarter	Fish, Hake	0	7	6	0
		0.5	C	Skins, Sheep (no wool)	0	5	0	0
		2	piece	Mantles	0	6	8	0
		3	barrel	Fish, Herring White	0	15	0	0
Bata Trinite of Milford Haven, Thomas Alen master, from Ireland, *28th August 1504*								
Thomas Alen	Ind	16	burden	Fish, Salted	0	53	4	0
		11	C	Fish, Hake	0	110	0	0
		5	burden	Fish, Salted	0	16	8	0
		4	C	Fish, Hake	0	40	0	0
Bata Marget of Chepstow, Robert Bocher master, from Chepstow, *28th August 1504*								
Richard Crane	Ind	3	tun	Wine	0	0	0	0
Navicula *Christ*pofur *of* Bristol, William Bailie master, to Lisbon, *28th August 1504*								
John Colas	Ind	24	wey	Grain	36	0	0	0
John Stone	Ind	1	piece	Welsh *Cloth*	0	20	0	0
John Bedford	Ind	2	piece	Welsh *Cloth*	0	40	0	0
Navicula Mathewe of Bristol, William Claron master, to Spain, 28th August 1504								
Roger Dawes	Ind	1	piece	Cloth of Assize	0	0	0	0
		14	piece	Cloth of Assize, Dozen	0	0	0	0
William Hurste	Ind	13.5	piece	Cloth of Assize	0	0	0	0
John Grene	Ind	1.5	piece	Cloth of Assize	0	0	0	0
		2	dozen	Skins, Calf Tanned	0	5	0	0
John Shipman &								
John Ware	Ind	36	piece	Cloth of Assize	0	0	0	0
John Shipman	Ind	8	C	Tin, Worked	12	0	0	0
Richard Hobie	Ind	43	C	Lead, Worked	10	15	0	0
		9	piece	Cloth of Assize	0	0	0	0
John Meysam	Ind	8	piece	Cloth of Assize	0	0	0	0

Merchant name	Origin	Qty	Unit	Commodity	£	s.	d.	f.
Thomas Hawkens	Ind	8	piece	Cloth of Assize	0	0	0	0
Robert Barrero	Ind	10	piece	Cloth of Assize	0	0	0	0
William Thorn	Ind	5	piece	Cloth of Assize	0	0	0	0
John Edee	Ind	20	piece	Cloth of Assize	0	0	0	0
William Aphowell	Ind	7	piece	Cloth of Assize	0	0	0	0
John Shipman &								
John Ware	Ind	6	piece	Cloth of Assize	12	0	0	0
John Jansie	Ind	8	piece	Cloth of Assize	0	0	0	0
Richard Hobie	Ind	7	piece	Cloth of Assize	0	0	0	0
Robert Rowlowe	Ind	8	piece	Cloth of Assize	0	0	0	0
John Qwirke	Ind	1	piece	Cloth of Assize	0	0	0	0
John Rowland	Ind	17	piece	Welsh Cloth, Dozen Strait	0	70	10	0
Thomas Badcok	Ind	8	piece	Cloth of Assize	0	0	0	0
Robert Rowlowe	Ind	2	piece	Cloth of Assize	0	0	0	0
Thomas Aphowell	Ind	2	piece	Cloth of Assize	0	0	0	0
William Estbie	Ind	5	piece	Cloth of Assize	0	0	0	0
Robert Rowlowe	Ind	7	piece	Cloth of Assize	0	0	0	0

Navicula Mare Bonaventur, Port Unknown, Humphrey Braie, to Brittany, 29th August 1504

Humphrey Braie	Alien	10	wey	Coal	0	33	4	0
		7.5	tun/ton	Calx	0	18	9	0

Bata Trinite of Berkeley, Thomas Reve master, to Ireland, 29th August 1504

Ralph Halsey	Ind	9	piece	Cloth of Assize	0	0	0	0
		8	piece	Welsh Cloth	8	0	0	0
		10	dozen	Skins, Calf Tanned	0	25	0	0
		6	C	Mutton Fat	0	40	0	0
		3	wey	Malt	0	40	0	0
		2	ton	Salt	0	33	4	0

Bata Mare of Berkeley, Thomas Hickes master, to Ireland, 29th August 1504

Thomas Hickes	Ind	0.75	ton	Salt	0	12	6	0

Bata Sondaie of Waterford, John Walshe master, from Ireland, 30th August 1504

John Walshe	Ind	0.5	C	Fish, Hake	0	5	0	0
		0.5	C	Britany Linen Cloth	0	10	0	0
		2	piece	Mantles	0	6	8	0

Bata George of Gatcombe, Walter Nashe master, to Ireland, 31st August 1504

Walter Nashe	Ind	2.5	wey	Beans	0	33	4	0
		2	piece	Cloth of Assize, Dozen Strait	0	0	0	0

Bata John of Gatcombe, John Markes master, to Ireland, 31st August 1504

Walter Nashe	Ind	2.5	wey	Beans	0	33	4	0

Merchant name	Origin	Qty	Unit	Commodity	£	s.	d.	f.

Bata Sondaie of Waterford, John Walshe master, to Ireland, 2nd September 1504

Merchant name	Origin	Qty	Unit	Commodity	£	s.	d.	f.
Walter Clarke	Ind	2.5	tun	Wine	0	0	0	0
		3	lb	Saffron	0	20	0	0
		80	lb	*Pilus Tinctus*	0	26	8	0
		3	piece	Cloth of Assize	0	0	0	0
		20	lb	*Pilus Tinctus*	0	6	8	0
		1	piece	Cloth of Assize	0	0	0	0
		1	lb	Silk, Worked	0	13	4	0
		40	lb	*Pilus Tinctus*	0	13	4	0
John Walshe	Ind	21	lb	*Pilus Tinctus*	0	7	0	0
John Dokerell	Ind	2	dozen	Aniseed	0	3	0	0

Navicula Marget of Bristol, Edward Gibbes, to Bordeaux, 5th September 1504

Merchant name	Origin	Qty	Unit	Commodity	£	s.	d.	f.
Edmund Bodie	Ind	30	dozen	Skins, Calf Tanned	0	75	0	0
Henry Dale	Ind	10	piece	Cloth of Assize	0	0	0	0
Nicholas Brown	Ind	21	piece	Cloth of Assize	0	0	0	0
		19	piece	Cloth of Assize, Kersey	0	0	0	0
William Tirrie	Ind	4	piece	Cloth of Assize	0	0	0	0
Thomas Awsten	Ind	8	piece	Cloth of Assize	0	0	0	0
Thomas Smythe &								
Thomas Badcok	Ind	28	piece	Cloth of Assize	56	0	0	0
John Vaghan	Ind	25	piece	Cloth of Assize	0	0	0	0
Philip Ringston	Ind	9	piece	Cloth of Assize	0	0	0	0
William Jeffereis	Ind	66	piece	Cloth of Assize	0	0	0	0
John Taylour	Ind	4.5	piece	Cloth of Assize	0	0	0	0
Edmund Bodie	Ind	4	dozen	Skins, Calf Tanned	0	7	6	0
John Stokes	Ind	18	piece	Cloth of Assize	0	0	0	0
John Wiot	Ind	8	piece	Cloth of Assize	0	0	0	0
William Goune &								
Edmund Bodie	Ind	3	piece	Welsh *Cloth*	0	60	0	0
William Goune	Ind	1	C	Fish, Hake	0	10	0	0
John Meysam	Ind	8	piece	Cloth of Assize	0	0	0	0
Richard Vaghan	Ind	2	ton	Lead, Worked	10	0	0	0
John Stokes	Ind	13	piece	Cloth of Assize	0	0	0	0
William Stephins	Ind	16	piece	Cloth of Assize	0	0	0	0
William Jeffereis	Ind	14	piece	Cloth of Assize	0	0	0	0
Thomas Barn	Ind	8	piece	Cloth of Assize	0	0	0	0
David Vaghan	Ind	5	piece	Cloth of Assize	0	0	0	0
John Jaie	Ind	2	piece	Cloth of Assize	0	0	0	0
Richard Symons	Ind	24	piece	Cloth of Assize	0	0	0	0
		24	piece	Welsh *Cloth*, Dozen Strait	0	100	0	0
John Williams	Ind	1	piece	Cloth of Assize	0	0	0	0
		1	piece	Welsh *Cloth*	1	0	0	0
William Estbie	Ind	5	piece	Cloth of Assize	0	0	0	0
John Dame	Ind	1.5	piece	Cloth of Assize	0	0	0	0
John Dame	Ind	1.5	piece	Cloth of Assize, Dozen Strait	0	0	0	0
Thomas Hochkens	Ind	2	piece	Cloth of Assize	0	0	0	0
Thomas Veell	Ind	3	piece	Cloth of Assize	0	0	0	0
John Rowland	Ind	3	piece	Cloth of Assize	0	0	0	0
Edmund Hyman	Ind	4	piece	Cloth of Assize	0	0	0	0

Merchant name	Origin	Qty	Unit	Commodity	£	s.	d.	f.
Henry Tollar	Ind	2	piece	Cloth of Assize	0	0	0	0
Robert Barrero	Ind	7	piece	Cloth of Assize	0	0	0	0
William Goldsmyth	Ind	6	piece	Cloth of Assize	0	0	0	0
Thomas Aphowell	Ind	6	piece	Cloth of Assize	0	0	0	0
James Cooke	Ind	17	dozen	Skins, Calf Tanned	0	42	6	0
Merike Lloid	Ind	1	piece	Welsh Cloth	0	20	0	0
Thomas Aphowell	Ind	5	piece	Cloth of Assize	0	0	0	0
		1	piece	Cloth of Assize	0	0	0	0
William Jefferels	Ind	10	piece	Cloth of Assize	0	0	0	0
William Cogan	Ind	32	piece	Cloth of Assize	0	0	0	0
		14	piece	Cloth of Assize	0	0	0	0
William Estbie	Ind	5	piece	Cloth of Assize	0	0	0	0
William White	Ind	16	barrel	Fish, Herring White	4	0	0	0
William Cogan	Ind	1	piece	Cloth of Assize	0	0	0	0
Roger Dawes	Ind	0.5	piece	Cloth of Assize	0	0	0	0
Richard Vaghan	Ind	5.5	piece	Cloth of Assize	0	0	0	0

Navicula Mare of Errenteria, John de Sasty master, from Spain, 6th September 1504

Merchant name	Origin	Qty	Unit	Commodity	£	s.	d.	f.
Roger Dawes	Ind	32	ton	Iron	80	0	0	0
Ralph Aprise	Ind	7.166	ton	Iron	17	18	4	0
William Wosley	Ind	19	ton	Iron	47	10	0	0
William Estbie	Ind	14	ton	Iron	35	0	0	0
Robert Thorn	Ind	7.5	ton	Iron	18	15	0	0
William Hurste	Ind	1	ton	Iron	0	50	0	0
Thomas Hawkens	Ind	1	ton	Iron	0	50	0	0
John Shipman	Ind	2	ton	Iron	0	100	0	0
Matilda Balle	Ind	1.66	ton	Iron	4	3	4	0
Henry Dale	Ind	18.66	ton	Iron	46	13	4	0
Robert Burnan	Ind	9.66	ton	Iron	24	3	4	0
William Jeffereis	Ind	1.66	ton	Iron	4	3	4	0
John Popley	Ind	12.5	ton	Iron	31	5	0	0

Bata Marget of Minehead, John White master, from Ireland, 7th September 1504

Merchant name	Origin	Qty	Unit	Commodity	£	s.	d.	f.
Richard Eliet	Ind	1	C	Fish, Hake	0	10	0	0

Navicula George of Bristol, David Nono master, from Bordeaux, 7th September 1504

Merchant name	Origin	Qty	Unit	Commodity	£	s.	d.	f.
John Colas	Ind	45	pipe	Woad	225	0	0	0
		3.75	tun	Wine	15	0	0	0
Ffernandus Dassa	Alien	6	pipe	Woad	30	0	0	0
David Nono	Ind	12	measure	Woad	0	75	0	0
John Marcsay	Ind	18	measure	Woad	0	112	6	0
John Colas	Ind	1.5	pipe	Woad	7	10	0	0

Bata Barbara of Bristol, William Kempe master, to Bordeaux, 9th September 1504

Merchant name	Origin	Qty	Unit	Commodity	£	s.	d.	f.
John Colas	Ind	3	wey	Grain	4	10	0	0

Merchant name	Origin	Qty	Unit	Commodity	£	s.	d.	f.

Bata Mare of Cork, Laurence Tobyn master, to Ireland, 10th September 1504

Merchant name	Origin	Qty	Unit	Commodity	£	s.	d.	f.
Edmund Roche	Ind	2	last	Beer	0	60	0	0
		1.5	pipe	Wine, Corrupt	0	22	6	0
		0.5	last	Beer	0	15	0	0
William Clarke	Ind	1	tun	Wine, Corrupt	0	30	0	0
Edmund Roche	Ind	1	pipe	Wine, Corrupt	0	15	0	0

Bata Mare of Gloucester, John Brownynge master, to Ireland, 11th September 1504

Merchant name	Origin	Qty	Unit	Commodity	£	s.	d.	f.
John Brownyng &								
Laurence Mede	Ind	2	wey	Beans	0	26	8	0

Bata Nicolas of Chepstow, Richard Halle master, to Chepstow, *11th September 1504*

Merchant name	Origin	Qty	Unit	Commodity	£	s.	d.	f.
John Halle	Ind	15	piece	Welsh *Cloth*, Dozen Strait	0	52	6	0
		1	piece	Cloth of Assize, Dozen	0	0	0	0

Navicula Gelian of Le Croisic, Bernard de Lucas master, to Bordeaux, *11th September 1504*

Merchant name	Origin	Qty	Unit	Commodity	£	s.	d.	f.
Bernard de Lucas	Alien	6	piece	Cloth of Assize	12	0	0	0

Bata Katren of Minehead, John Goodynowe master, from Ireland, 12th September 1504

Merchant name	Origin	Qty	Unit	Commodity	£	s.	d.	f.
John Goodynowe	Ind	16	burden	Fish, Salted	0	53	4	0
		6	C	Fish, Hake	0	60	0	0

Navicula Mare of Errenteria, John de Sasty master, to Andalusia, 16th September 1504

Merchant name	Origin	Qty	Unit	Commodity	£	s.	d.	f.
Martin Derasty	Alien	17	dozen	Skins, Calf Tanned	0	42	6	0
Sebastian Navegias	Alien	21.5	dozen	Skins, Calf Tanned	0	53	9	0
John de Sasty	Alien	21	dozen	Skins, Calf Tanned	0	52	6	0
Richard Drap*er*	Ind	3	piece	Cloth of Assize	0	0	0	0
		4	piece	Cloth of Assize, Kersey	0	0	0	0
John Popley	Ind	16	piece	Cloth of Assize	0	0	0	0
Ralph Aprise	Ind	4	piece	Cloth of Assize	0	0	0	0
John Eliet	Ind	4	piece	Cloth of Assize	0	0	0	0
		10	dozen	Skins, Calf Tanned	0	25	0	0
John Vaghan	Ind	12	piece	Cloth of Assize	0	0	0	0
John Benet	Ind	7	piece	Cloth of Assize	0	0	0	0
John de Sasty	Alien	4	dozen	Skins, Calf Tanned	0	10	0	0
Robert Barrero	Ind	34	piece	Welsh *Cloth*, Dozen Strait	7	0	20	0
		4	piece	Welsh *Cloth*	4	0	0	0
Philip Ringston	Ind	5	piece	Cloth of Assize	0	0	0	0
Maurice Leney	Ind	4	piece	Cloth of Assize	0	0	0	0
Matilda Balle	Ind	1	piece	Cloth of Assize	0	0	0	0
John de Sasty	Alien	3.5	dozen	Skins, Calf Tanned	0	8	9	0
John Thomas	Ind	4	piece	Cloth of Assize	0	0	0	0
Thomas Vaghan	Ind	9	piece	Welsh *Cloth*	9	0	0	0
Robert Thorn	Ind	17	piece	Cloth of Assize	0	0	0	0
David Vaghan	Ind	8	piece	Welsh *Cloth*, Dozen Strait	0	33	4	0
Thomas Awsten	Ind	4	piece	Cloth of Assize	0	0	0	0

Merchant name	Origin	Qty	Unit	Commodity	£	s.	d.	f.

Bata Mare of St Davids, Walter Weye master, from Ireland, 17th September 1504

Merchant name	Origin	Qty	Unit	Commodity	£	s.	d.	f.
William Tirrie	Ind	10.5	pipe	Fish, Salmon	15	15	0	0
		17.75	C	Skins, Sheep (no wool)	8	17	6	0
		30	lb	Wax	0	10	0	0
Walter Weie	Ind	3	barrel	Fish, Herring White	0	15	0	0

Bata Mare of Shirehampton, John Hobbes master, to Tenby, 19th September 1504

Merchant name	Origin	Qty	Unit	Commodity	£	s.	d.	f.
Henry Tollar	Ind	10	piece	Cloth of Assize	0	0	0	0

Bata Phelip of Bristol, Thomas Jones master, to Ireland, 22nd September 1504

Merchant name	Origin	Qty	Unit	Commodity	£	s.	d.	f.
Richard Vaghan	Ind	1.5	ton	Salt	0	25	0	0
William Mewrell	Ind	3	piece	Cloth of Assize	0	0	0	0
		1.5	tun	Wine, Corrupt	0	45	0	0
		1	pipe	Salt	0	8	4	0
		2.5	tun	Wine, Corrupt	0	75	0	0
William Clarke	Ind	1.5	tun	Wine, Corrupt	0	45	0	0
Thomas Jones &								
John Parkar	Ind	1	ton	Salt	0	16	8	0
Thomas Jones	Ind	1	pipe	Wine, Corrupt	0	15	0	0
John Parkar	Ind	140	lb	*Pilus Tinctus*	0	46	8	0
William Clarke	Ind	2	C	*Pilus Tinctus*	4	0	0	0
		1	piece	Cloth of Assize	0	0	0	0
		3	piece	Cloth of Assize, Dozen	0	0	0	0
		1	pipe	Wine, Corrupt	0	15	0	0
Richard Vaghan	Ind	46	lb	*Pilus Tinctus*	0	15	4	0

Bata Lenard of Waterford, Patrick Prendigras master, from Ireland, *22nd September 1504*

Merchant name	Origin	Qty	Unit	Commodity	£	s.	d.	f.
Patrick Prendigras	Ind	2	barrel	Fish, Herring White	0	10	0	0
		2	piece	Mantles	0	6	8	0
Walter Clarke	Ind	4.75	pipe	Fish, Salmon	7	2	6	0
		20	barrel	Fish, Herring White	0	100	0	0
		2	piece	Mantles	0	6	8	0
		20	lb	Wax	0	6	8	0
		24	stone	Wool, Flocks	0	10	0	0
		2	barrel	Purpes (porpoises)	0	10	0	0
Thomas Langton	Ind	20	C	Skins, Sheep (no wool)	10	0	0	0
		90	piece	Mantles	15	0	0	0
		1.5	C	Wax	0	60	0	0
		1.25	C	Check *Cloth*	0	50	0	0
		3	quarter	Skins, Lamb	0	3	9	0
		12	piece	Skins, Fox	0	0	18	0
William Tirrie	Ind	8	pipe	Fish, Salmon	12	0	0	0
		10	barrel	Fish, Herring White	0	50	0	0
Robert Kenne	Ind	2	barrel	Fish, Herring White	0	10	0	0
Walter Clarke	Ind	3	mease	Fish, Herring Red	0	15	0	0
Patrick Prendergras	Ind	1	C	Skins, Lamb	0	5	0	0
Thomas Walshe	Ind	2	barrel	Fish, Herring White	0	10	0	0
William Griffen	Ind	3	piece	Mantles	0	10	0	0

Merchant name	Origin	Qty	Unit	Commodity	£	s.	d.	f.
		8	lb	Wax	0	2	8	0
John Barnard	Ind	2	piece	Mantles	0	6	8	0
		20	lb	Wax	0	6	8	0
Robert Kenne	Ind	4	piece	Mantles	0	13	4	0
Thomas Walshe	Ind	2	piece	Mantles	0	6	8	0
		8	lb	Wax	0	2	8	0
Thomas Bathe	Ind	2	barrel	Fish, Herring White	0	10	0	0
William Tirrie	Ind	5	barrel	Fish, Herring White	0	25	0	0
Thomas Langton	Ind	24	piece	Mantles	4	0	0	0
		2	piece	Mantles	0	6	8	0
		4.5	C	Skins, Sheep (no wool)	0	45	0	0
		1.25	C	Wax	0	50	0	0
		0.5	C	Check Cloth	0	20	0	0

TNA E122/21/2 is an annual 'particular' customs account of John Lloyd, controller of customs & subsidies, covering the period Michaelmas 1516 to Michaelmas 1517. The controller of customs was required to supervise the two collectors and submit an equally full account to the exchequer. The 1516/17 account contains the same details as the 1503/4 account, but differs in that it contains no subsidy values, just the nominal values for commodities, based on the book of rates. As in the 1503/4 account, it contains 'values' for tanned hides.

Merchant name	Origin	Qty	Unit	Commodity	£	s.	d.	f.

Bata Mare of Paimpol, Gillam Tote master, from La Rochelle, 30th September 1516

Merchant name	Origin	Qty	Unit	Commodity	£	s.	d.	f.
John Drewis	Ind	8.75	tun	Wine	0	0	0	0

Bata Mare of Carmarthen, Thomas Walter master, *from Carmarthen, 30th September 1516*

Merchant name	Origin	Qty	Unit	Commodity	£	s.	d.	f.
Thomas Walter	Ind	10	ton	Salt	5	0	0	0
		16	C	Fish, Hake	8	0	0	0
		1	C	Fish, Salted	0	20	0	0
		60	piece	Skins, Sheep (no wool)	0	5	0	0

Bata Mare of Tewkesbury, Roger Horne master, from Ireland, *30th September 1516*

Merchant name	Origin	Qty	Unit	Commodity	£	s.	d.	f.
Roger *Horne*	Ind	30	barrel	Fish, Herring White	117	10	0	0
		2	hogshead	Fish, Hake	0	20	0	0
		9	piece	Mantles	0	30	0	0

Bata Kateryn of Minehead, David Blake master, from Ireland, 1st October 1516

Merchant name	Origin	Qty	Unit	Commodity	£	s.	d.	f.
David Blake	Ind	27	barrel	Fish, Herring White	6	15	0	0
		80	piece	Fish, Salted	0	13	4	0
		0.25	C	Fish, Hake	0	2	6	0

Navicula Frances of St Brieuc, Peter Galter master, from the New World, *1st October 1516*

Merchant name	Origin	Qty	Unit	Commodity	£	s.	d.	f.
Peter *Galter*	Alien	14	M	Fish, Salted	93	13	4	0
Richard Avynell	Alien	1	tun	Oil, Train	0	46	8	0

Bata Mare of Bristol Thomas *Nongull* master, to Ireland, 2nd October 1516

Merchant name	Origin	Qty	Unit	Commodity	£	s.	d.	f.
Thomas *Nogull*	Ind	4	wey	Beans	3	6	8	0
		1	piece	Cloth of Assize	0	0	0	0
Leonard Creaghe	Ind	8.5	piece	Cloth of Assize	0	0	0	0

Merchant name	Origin	Qty	Unit	Commodity	£	s.	d.	f.
		0.5	piece	Cloth of Assize, Kersey	0	0	0	0
		1	piece	Welsh *Cloth*, Dozen Strait	0	4	2	0
		4.5	gross	Cutts	0	15	0	0
William Creaghe	Ind	4	piece	Cloth of Assize	0	0	0	0
		1.5	piece	Cloth of Assize, Kersey	0	0	0	0
		3	dozen	Red–Lash	0	8	0	0
		2.5	gross	Cutts	0	8	4	0
		29	lb	Saffron	14	10	0	0
		6	lb	Silk, Worked	4	0	0	0
Tibald Bluet	Ind	2	lb	Saffron	0	20	0	0
Edmund Nashe	Ind	1	piece	Cloth of Assize	0	0	0	0
		1	lb	Silk, Worked	0	13	4	0
		0.5	lb	Saffron	0	5	0	0
		0.5	gross	Cutts	0	0	20	0
		2	gross	Points	0	2	0	0

Bata Anne of Chepstow, Robert Ffisher master, from Chepstow, 10th October 1516

John Poper	Ind	2	tun	Wine	0	0	0	0

Bata John of Tewkesbury, John Laughton master, from Chepstow, 15th October 1516

Maurice Bocher	Ind	85	measure	Woad	26	11	3	0

Bata Marget of Milford Haven, Philip Webbe master, from Ireland, 20th October

Philip Webbe	Ind	4.5	C	Fish, Hake	0	45	0	0

Bata Markyr of Tenby, Germaine Griffith master, from Ireland, 21st October 1516

Germain Griffith	Ind	27	barrel	Fish, Herring White	6	15	0	0
		18.25	C	Fish, Hake	9	2	6	0
Mathew Sinyth	Ind	1	barrel	Fish, Herring White	0	5	0	0
John Tailor	Ind	3	C	Tallow	0	15	0	0

Bata Trynyte of Chepstow, William Heyne, from Chepstow, 24th October 1516

Thomas Dale	Ind	4	pipe	Woad	20	0	0	0
John Shipman	Ind	1	pipe	Woad	5	0	0	0
John Ware	Ind	29	measure	Woad	9	15	0	0
William Woseley	Ind	1	pipe	Woad	5	0	0	0

Bata Frances of St Pol de Léon, Thomas Dero master, from Bordeaux, 27th October 1516

John Greneway	Ind	29.5	tun	Wine	0	0	0	0
John Dero	Alien	0.25	ton	Rosin	0	6	8	0

Navicula Seint John of Pasajes de San Juan, John Samual master, from Spain, *27th October 1516*

William Woseley	Ind	57	ton	Iron	142	10	0	0
John Samual	Alien	3.75	ton	Iron	9	7	6	0

Merchant name	Origin	Qty	Unit	Commodity	£	s.	d.	f.
Martin de Care*fe*	Alien	8	dozen	Serches	0	32	0	0

Bata Mare of Carmarthen, Martin Davy master, *from Carmarthen, 27th October 1516*

John Banks	Ind	12	ton	Salt	6	0	0	0

Navicula *Christ*pofur of Dartmouth, William Bere master, from Bordeaux, 28th October 1516

Roger Dawes	Ind	5.5	tun	Wine	0	0	0	0
John Shipman	Ind	3	tun	Wine	0	0	0	0
John Ware	Ind	3.75	tun	Wine	0	0	0	0
William Shipman	Ind	3.5	tun	Wine	0	0	0	0
Thomas Dale	Ind	6.5	tun	Wine	0	0	0	0
John Drewis	Ind	1	tun	Wine	0	0	0	0
Robert Pophin	Ind	7.75	tun	Wine	0	0	0	0
John Wyot	Ind	2.75	tun	Wine	0	0	0	0
John Sparcheford	Ind	2.75	tun	Wine	0	0	0	0
Thomas Hawkyns	Ind	5.25	tun	Wine	0	0	0	0
John Thomas	Ind	5.25	tun	Wine	0	0	0	0
John Brampton	Ind	6.25	tun	Wine	0	0	0	0
Auger De Noga	Alien	2.5	tun	Wine	0	0	0	0
William Bere	Ind	3.5	tun	Wine	0	0	0	0
Katerine Wale	Ind	2	tun	Wine	0	0	0	0

Navicula Peter of Dartmouth, Thomas Colle master, from Bordeaux, *28th October 1516*

John Grenwey of London	Ind	33.5	tun	Wine	0	0	0	0

Bata Kynborow of Gatcombe, John Marks master, from Wales, 31st October 1516

John *Mark*	Ind	4.5	tun	Wine	0	0	0	0

Navicula Frances *St Brieuc* Peter Gawter, from Brittany, *31st October 1516*

Peter *Gawter*	Alien	24	wey	Coal	4	0	0	0
		3	piece	Wes*tern* White *Cloth*	6	0	0	0
		1	piece	Welsh *Cloth*	0	20	0	0

Bata Kateryn of Milford Haven, Howell Smyth master, from Ireland, *31st October 1516*

Howell Smyth	Ind	4.25	C	Fish, Hake	0	42	6	0

Navicula Mawdelen of Hondarribia, Master Unknown, from Sanlúcar de Barrameda, 3rd November 1516

John Shipman	Ind	4	tun	Wine	0	0	0	0
William Shipman	Ind	4.25	tun	Wine	0	0	0	0
Robert D. Coke	Ind	18.5	tun	Wine	0	0	0	0
Robtus Elyot	Ind	13.75	tun	Wine	0	0	0	0
Richard Hoby	Ind	1.5	tun	Wine	0	0	0	0

Merchant name	Origin	Qty	Unit	Commodity	£	s.	d.	f.
John Thomas	Ind	1.5	tun	Wine	0	0	0	0
John Cook	Ind	18.75	tun	Wine	0	0	0	0
John Jay	Ind	1	tun	Wine	0	0	0	0
Martisaime ?	Alien	2	tun	Wine	0	0	0	0
Thomas Maileyeard	Ind	1.75	tun	Wine	0	0	0	0
		4.05	M	Orchil	27	0	0	0
John de Casanova	Alien	1	tun	Wine	0	0	0	0
		3.5	piece	Fruit	0	5	0	0
John De Medina	Alien	13.75	tun	Wine	0	0	0	0

Navicula Saint John of Cadiz John Camache, from Sanlúcar de Barrameda, 4th November 1516

Leonard Osburn	Ind	12.25	tun	Wine	0	0	0	0
		2	ton	Fruit	4	0	0	0
		1	C	Pepper	5	0	0	0
		1	cashe	Sugar	0	40	0	0
Walter Petwyne	Ind	11.5	tun	Wine	0	0	0	0
		2	ton	Fruit	4	0	0	0
James Fitzjamyes	Ind	10.25	tun	Wine	0	0	0	0
Thomas Tyson	Ind	2.5	tun	Wine	0	0	0	0

Bata Trinite of Chepstow, William Heyne master, *from Chepstow, 4th November 1516*

Evan Le Mullet	Alien	8	modul?	Chestone	0	3	4	0

Bata George of Bristol, William Apprice master, from Ireland, 5th November 1516

William Edwards	Ind	8	barrel	Fish, Herring White	0	40	0	0
		1	C	Fish, Hake	0	10	0	0
William Flemyng	Ind	12.5	barrel	Fish, Herring White	3	2	6	0
Mathew Hop	Ind	1	barrel	Fish, Herring White	0	5	0	0
John Morecok	Ind	4	barrel	Fish, Herring White	0	20	0	0
Howell Baker	Ind	2	last	Fish, Herring White	6	0	0	0
Thomas Stamford	Ind	7.5	barrel	Fish, Herring White	0	37	6	0
		1	mease	Fish, Herring Red	0	5	0	0
David Vaghan	Ind	1.5	tun	Wine	0	0	0	0

Bata Mighell of Tenby, Richard More master, from Ireland, *5th November 1516*

Richard *More*	Ind	15	barrel	Fish, Herring White	3	15	0	0
Mathew Hop	Ind	25.5	barrel	Fish, Herring White	6	7	6	0

Bata Mighell of Tenby, Walter Taillor master, from Ireland, 6th November 1516

Richard Mathew	Ind	27	barrel	Fish, Herring White	6	15	0	0
		1.75	C	Fish, Hake	0	17	6	0
Roger Dawes	Ind	12	barrel	Fish, Herring White	3	0	0	0
Walter Tailor	Ind	12.5	barrel	Fish, Herring White	3	2	6	0
		0.5	C	Fish, Hake	0	5	0	0
Richard Howell	Ind	2	barrel	Fish, Herring White	0	10	0	0

Merchant name	Origin	Qty	Unit	Commodity	£	s.	d.	f.

Bata Robert of Tewkesbury, Richard Serle master, from Chepstow, 6th November 1516

| John Bullyughin? | Ind | 6 | tun | Wine | o | o | o | o |

Bata Mare of Milford Haven, Thomas Wathen master, from Ireland, 6th November 1516

Thomas *Wathen*	Ind	6	barrel	Fish, Herring White	o	30	o	o
		1	C	Fish, Hake	o	10	o	o
William Spcclicky	Ind	22	barrel	Fish, Herring White	5	10	o	o
Mathew Hop	Ind	26.5	barrel	Fish, Herring White	6	12	6	o
		4	C	Fish, Hake	o	40	o	o
Richard Hopkyns	Ind	2	last	Fish, Herring White	6	o	o	o
		2	C	Fish, Hake	o	20	o	o
John Watson	Ind	6	barrel	Fish, Herring White	o	30	o	o
William Marks	Ind	43.5	barrel	Fish, Herring White	10	17	6	o
Thomas Woodward	Ind	7	barrel	Fish, Herring White	o	35	o	o

Bata Trynyte of Chepstow, William Heyne master, *from Chepstow*, 7th November 1516

| John Alen | Ind | 1 | pipe | Wine | o | o | o | o |

Bata Sonday of Milford Haven, Philip Vaghan master, from Ireland, 9th November 1516

Philip Vaghan	Ind	16	barrel	Fish, Herring White	4	o	o	o
		16	C	Fish, Hake	8	o	o	o
William Edwards	Ind	1	C	Fish, Hake	o	10	o	o

Navicula Jhesus of Bristol, Robert Power master, from Bordeaux, 9th November 1516

Richard Hoby	Ind	6.75	tun	Wine	o	o	o	o
John Vaghan	Ind	6	tun	Wine	o	o	o	o
William Rowley	Ind	7	tun	Wine	o	o	o	o
John Rowland	Ind	3.5	tun	Wine	o	o	o	o
John Brampton	Ind	8.75	tun	Wine	o	o	o	o
John Thomas	Ind	5.25	tun	Wine	o	o	o	o
Thomas Yeate	Ind	9	tun	Wine	o	o	o	o
James Brynne	Ind	1	tun	Wine	o	o	o	o
		1	hogshead	Pitch	o	6	8	o
Thomas Hawkyns	Ind	5.25	tun	Wine	o	o	o	o
Robert Pophin	Ind	2	tun	Wine	o	o	o	o
Thomas Ashehurst	Ind	2.75	tun	Wine	o	o	o	o
Richard Wilde	Ind	2.875	tun	Wine	o	o	o	o
Awger de Noga	Alien	4	tun	Wine	o	o	o	o
Thomas Bilford	Ind	9	tun	Wine	o	o	o	o
John Drewis	Ind	9.75	tun	Wine	o	o	o	o
John Jay	Ind	1.75	tun	Wine	o	o	o	o
Walter Comrowe	Ind	2.75	tun	Wine	o	o	o	o
John Shipman	Ind	10	tun	Wine	o	o	o	o
William Shipman	Ind	6	tun	Wine	o	o	o	o
Humphrey Browne	Ind	1.75	tun	Wine	o	o	o	o
John Sparchford	Ind	5.5	tun	Wine	o	o	o	o
John Staunton	Ind	1.25	tun	Wine	o	o	o	o
John Gravell	Ind	0.75	tun	Wine	o	o	o	o

Merchant name	Origin	Qty	Unit	Commodity	£	s.	d.	f.
		0.25	ton	Rosin	0	6	8	0
Richard Bocher	Ind	9	tun	Wine	0	0	0	0
Thomas Clarke	Ind	1	pipe	Wine	0	0	0	0
		0.25	ton	Rosin	0	6	8	0
		0.5	C	Boxstaves	0	20	0	0
William Yold	Ind	1	pipe	Wine	0	0	0	0
John Bullyughin	Ind	3.75	tun	Wine	0	0	0	0
John Crome	Ind	1	pipe	Wine	0	0	0	0
		0.25	ton	Rosin	0	6	8	0
John Davis	Ind	0.41	tun	Wine	0	0	0	0

Bata Mare Bosher of Waterford, Nicholas Power master, from Ireland, *9th November 1516*

Merchant name	Origin	Qty	Unit	Commodity	£	s.	d.	f.
William Everard	Ind	11	dicker	Skins, Salted	7	6	8	0
		20	C	Skins, Sheep (no wool)	10	0	0	0
		0.5	pipe	Fish, Salmon	0	15	0	0
		2	C	Fish, Hake	0	20	0	0
		32	piece	Mantles	5	6	8	0
		2	stone	Wool, Flocks	0	0	10	0
Philip Nele	Ind	4.5	C	Skins, Sheep	0	45	0	0
		3	C	Skins, Lamb	0	20	0	0
		14	piece	Mantles	0	46	8	0
James Barret	Ind	6.5	C	Skins, Sheep	3	5	0	0
		14	piece	Mantles	0	46	8	0
		24	yard	Irish Linen *Cloth*	0	2	0	0
		4	lb	Wax	0	0	16	0
		0.25	C	Skins, Lamb	0	0	20	0
Raymond Galshe	Ind	3	C	Skins, Sheep	0	30	0	0
		16	piece	Mantles	0	53	4	0
		8	lb	Wax	0	2	4	0
		0.25	C	Skins, Lamb	0	0	20	0
Gerald Wale	Ind	10	C	Skins, Sheep	5	0	0	0
		0.5	pipe	Fish, Salmon	0	15	0	0
		50	piece	Mantles	8	6	8	0
		2	stone	Wool, Flocks	0	0	10	0
John Lye	Ind	3	C	Skins, Sheep (no wool)	0	30	0	0
		0.5	pipe	Fish, Salmon	0	15	0	0
		0.5	C	Fish, Hake	0	5	0	0
		8	piece	Mantles	0	26	8	0
John Doan	Ind	3	C	Skins, Sheep	0	30	0	0
		3	C	Fish, Hake	0	30	0	0
		0.5	pipe	Fish, Salmon	0	15	0	0
		12	piece	Mantles	0	40	0	0
William Arlond	Ind	10	C	Skins, Sheep	5	0	0	0
		2	pipe	Fish, Salmon	3	0	0	0
		16	stone	Wool, Irish	0	42	8	0
		30	stone	Wool, Flocks	0	12	6	0
		16	piece	Mantles	0	53	4	0
		0.25	C	Skins, Lamb	0	0	20	0
		0.5	dicker	Skins, Salted	0	6	8	0
		0.25	C	Fish, Hake	0	2	6	0
Thomas Nongull	Ind	4.75	C	Skins, Sheep	0	47	6	0

Merchant name	Origin	Qty	Unit	Commodity	£	s.	d.	f.

Bata Konylagh of Kinsale, Richard Donell master, from Ireland, 9th November 1516

Merchant name	Origin	Qty	Unit	Commodity	£	s.	d.	f.
Richard *Donell*	Ind	7	C	Fish, Hake	3	10	0	0
William Co[ ]sy	Ind	8	C	Skins, Sheep	4	0	0	0
		10	C	Skins, Lamb	3	6	8	0
		1	C	Fish, Hake	0	10	0	0
Edmund Denys	Ind	4	C	Fish, Hake	0	40	0	0
Nicholas Rothe	Ind	2.5	C	Fish, Hake	0	25	0	0
		0.5	burden	Fish, Salted	0	2	1	0
		1	C	Skins, Sheep	0	10	0	0
Thomas Donell	Ind	26	pipe	Fish, Salmon	39	0	0	0

Bata Trynyte of Kinsale, Germaine Fforan master, from Ireland, 9th November 1516

Merchant name	Origin	Qty	Unit	Commodity	£	s.	d.	f.
Germain Foran	Ind	26	C	Fish, Hake	13	0	0	0
		0.5	pipe	Fish, Salmon	0	15	0	0
		1	C	Skins, Sheep	0	10	0	0
Richard Arthur	Ind	5	C	Fish, Hake	0	50	0	0
David Doan	Ind	3	C	Skins, Sheep	0	30	0	0
		1.5	pipe	Fish, Salmon	0	45	0	0
		4.5	C	Fish, Hake	0	45	0	0

Bata Kateryn of Shirehampton, John Jenkyn master, from Ireland, 10th November 1516

Merchant name	Origin	Qty	Unit	Commodity	£	s.	d.	f.
Thomas Donell	Ind	6	pipe	Fish, Salmon	9	0	0	0
		2	last	Fish, Herring White	6	0	0	0
		4	piece	Mantles	0	13	4	0
		1	C	Skins, Sheep	0	10	0	0
		0.75	tun	Wine	0	0	0	0
Robert Avyntre	Ind	6	pipe	Fish, Salmon	9	0	0	0
		23	barrel	Fish, Herring White	5	15	0	0

Bata Sonday of Cardiff, William Deane master, *from Cardiff*, 10th November 1516

Merchant name	Origin	Qty	Unit	Commodity	£	s.	d.	f.
John Towke	Ind	2	ton	Salt	0	20	0	0

Navicula Jhesus of Bristol, John Barnard master, from Bordeaux, 10th November 1516

Merchant name	Origin	Qty	Unit	Commodity	£	s.	d.	f.
Thomas Donell	Ind	14.5	tun	Wine	0	0	0	0
Robert Avyntre	Ind	14.5	tun	Wine	0	0	0	0
John Kyng	Ind	4.5	tun	Wine	0	0	0	0
		0.5	ton	Rosin	0	13	4	0
Roger Monouse	Ind	2.5	tun	Wine	0	0	0	0
John Balle	Ind	1	pipe	Wine	0	0	0	0

Bata Nicholas of Tidenham, John Taillor master, from Ireland, 10th November 1516

Merchant name	Origin	Qty	Unit	Commodity	£	s.	d.	f.
Oliver Tirry	Ind	33	piece	Mantles	5	10	0	0
		3	C	Skins, Sheep	0	30	0	0
William Mirry	Ind	20	piece	Mantles	3	6	8	0
		1.5	C	Skins, Sheep	0	15	0	0
		12	stone	Wool, Flocks	0	5	0	0

Merchant name	Origin	Qty	Unit	Commodity	£	s.	d.	f.
		0.5	barrel	Fish, Herring White	0	2	6	0
James Galwan	Ind	28	piece	Mantles	4	13	4	0

Bata George of Bristol, William Donell master, from Ireland, *10th November 1516*

Merchant name	Origin	Qty	Unit	Commodity	£	s.	d.	f.
Robert Avyntre	Ind	5	last	*Fish, Herring White*	15	0	0	0
		4.5	C	Fish, Hake	0	45	0	0
Thomas Donell	Ind	4.5	last	Fish, Herring White	13	10	0	0
		4.5	C	Fish, Hake	0	45	0	0

Navicula Matthew of Bristol, Richard Savere master, from Bordeaux, *10th November 1516*

Merchant name	Origin	Qty	Unit	Commodity	£	s.	d.	f.
John Rowland	Ind	7	tun	Wine	0	0	0	0
John Drewis	Ind	7	tun	Wine	0	0	0	0
Robert Pophin	Ind	2.75	tun	Wine	0	0	0	0
John Shipman	Ind	15.5	tun	Wine	0	0	0	0
		8	ton	Iron	20	0	0	0
		0.5	ton	Pitch and Rosin	0	13	4	0
William Shipman	Ind	9	tun	Wine	0	0	0	0
Richard Hoby	Ind	5.25	tun	Wine	0	0	0	0
Auger de Noga	Alien	1	tun	Wine	0	0	0	0
Thomas Bilford	Ind	3.5	tun	Wine	0	0	0	0
John Sparcheford	Ind	4	tun	Wine	0	0	0	0
William Rowley	Ind	3.75	tun	Wine	0	0	0	0
John Wyot	Ind	4.25	tun	Wine	0	0	0	0
John Ware	Ind	8.75	tun	Wine	0	0	0	0
Robert Coke	Ind	3.5	tun	Wine	0	0	0	0
John Thomas	Ind	3.5	tun	Wine	0	0	0	0
Edward Jonys	Ind	1.25	tun	Wine	0	0	0	0
Robert Avyntre	Ind	2.75	tun	Wine	0	0	0	0
Thomas Pasheley	Ind	1	hogshead	Wine	0	0	0	0
Thomas Dale	Ind	8.5	tun	Wine	0	0	0	0
Gilbert Cogan	Ind	3.75	tun	Wine	0	0	0	0
Richard Savery	Ind	0.5	ton	Rosin	0	13	4	0
George Harte	Ind	1	hogshead	Wine	0	0	0	0

Navicula Edward of Bristol, John Gorwey master, from Bordeaux, *10th November 1516*

Merchant name	Origin	Qty	Unit	Commodity	£	s.	d.	f.
John Rowland	Ind	3.75	tun	Wine	0	0	0	0
Nicholas Gay	Ind	13	tun	Wine	0	0	0	0
		11	bale	Woad	13	15	0	0
		2	ton	Rosin	0	53	4	0
Roger Dawes	Ind	7.5	tun	Wine	0	0	0	0
David Vaghan	Ind	7	tun	Wine	0	0	0	0
John Shipman	Ind	4	tun	Wine	0	0	0	0
Auger de Noga	Alien	1.5	tun	Wine	0	0	0	0
William Rowley	Ind	4.5	tun	Wine	0	0	0	0
William Tirry	Ind	4.5	tun	Wine	0	0	0	0
Richard Hoby	Ind	4.25	tun	Wine	0	0	0	0
Thomas Yeate	Ind	4.5	tun	Wine	0	0	0	0
John Brampton	Ind	1.75	tun	Wine	0	0	0	0
John Halle	Ind	6.25	tun	Wine	0	0	0	0

Merchant name	Origin	Qty	Unit	Commodity	£	s.	d.	f.
George Halle	Ind	5.75	tun	Wine	0	0	0	0
John Williams	Ind	1	pipe	Wine	0	0	0	0
John Vaghan	Ind	1	hogshead	Wine	0	0	0	0
		0.25	ton	Rosin	0	6	8	0
William Hurst	Ind	0.33	pipe	Wine	0	0	0	0
Robert Coke	Ind	2.75	tun	Wine	0	0	0	0
John Gefferes	Ind	1.75	tun	Wine	0	0	0	0
John Pasheley	Ind	1	tun	Wine	0	0	0	0
Thomas Cogan	Ind	1	hogshead	Wine	0	0	0	0
Peter Sonne?	Ind	1	hogshead	Wine	0	0	0	0

Navicula Frances of Granville, Kator Pigyon master, from Bordeaux, 12th November 1516

Thomas Dikkynson	Ind	45.25	tun	Wine	0	0	0	0

Bata Katryn of New Ross, William Blake master, from Ireland, *12th November 1516*

Merchant name	Origin	Qty	Unit	Commodity	£	s.	d.	f.
Thomas Laugton	Ind	100	piece	Mantles	16	13	4	0
		27	C	Skins, Sheep (no wool)	13	10	0	0
		1	C	Check *Cloth*	0	40	0	0
		1.5	C	Irish Linen *Cloth*	0	15	0	0
		0.5	pipe	Fish, Salmon	0	15	0	0
Alexander Chaplend	Ind	52	piece	Mantles	8	13	4	0
		7	C	Skins, Sheep (no wool)	3	10	0	0
		80	yard	Check *Cloth*	0	26	8	0
		8	stone	Wool, Irish	0	21	0	0
		10	lb	Wax	0	3	4	0
		8	stone	Wool, Flocks	0	3	4	0
David Penbroke	Ind	10	C	Skins, Sheep (no wool)	5	0	0	0
		0.25	C	Skins, Lamb	0	0	20	0
		45	piece	Mantles	9	3	4	0
		31	yard	Check *Cloth*	0	10	4	0
		100	yard	Irish Linen *Cloth*	0	8	4	0
		2	piece	Skins, Fox	0	0	4	0
Philip Morhoo	Ind	16	C	Skins, Sheep	8	0	0	0
		67	piece	Mantles	11	3	4	0
		14	stone	Wool, Irish	0	37	4	0
		30	yard	Check *Cloth*	0	10	0	0
		10	piece	Skins, Fox	0	0	20	0
Cornell Walshe	Ind	8	C	Skins, Sheep	4	0	0	0
		48	piece	Mantles	8	0	0	0
		0.25	pipe	Fish, Salmon	0	7	6	0
Patrick Brian	Ind	1	C	Skins, Sheep	0	10	0	0
John Conrowe	Ind	6	C	Skins, Sheep	3	0	0	0
		3	pipe	Fish, Salmon	4	10	0	0
Richard Barkeley	Ind	0.5	pipe	Fish, Salmon	0	15	0	0
		0.5	C	Skins, Sheep	0	5	0	0
		4	piece	Mantles	0	13	4	0
		9	stone	Wool	0	24	0	0
William Co[ ]sy	Ind	112	piece	Mantles	18	13	4	0
		20	C	Skins, Sheep	10	0	0	0
		2	C	Irish Linen *Cloth*	0	20	0	0

Merchant name	Origin	Qty	Unit	Commodity	£	s.	d.	f.
		1	C	Skins, Lamb	0	6	8	0
		26	yard	Check *Cloth*	0	8	8	0
		21	stone	Wool	0	56	0	0
William Blake	Ind	5	barrel	Fish, Herring White	0	25	0	0
Robert Morhoo	Ind	87	piece	Mantles	14	10	0	0
		11	C	Skins, Sheep	5	10	0	0
		8	piece	Skins, Fox	0	0	16	0
		2	C	Check *Cloth*	4	0	0	0
		1	dicker	Skins, Salted	0	13	4	0
Walter Digon	Ind	43	piece	Mantles	7	3	4	0
		280	yard	Check *Cloth*	4	13	4	0
		2.5	C	Irish Linen *Cloth*	0	25	0	0
John Brother	Ind	60	yard	Check *Cloth*	0	20	0	0
		9	piece	Mantles	0	30	0	0
Thomas Nongull	Ind	3	pipe	Fish, Salmon	4	10	0	0
Philip Ffurbor	Ind	9	piece	Mantles	0	30	0	0

Bata Kateryn of Tewkesbury, Thomas White master, from Wales, 13th November 1516

Richard Pulton	Ind	3.75	tun	Wine	0	0	0	0
		3	ton	Salt	0	30	0	0

Bata Jamys of Carmarthen, William Cradok master, from Carmarthen, *13th November 1516*

William *Cradok*	Ind	2	tun	Wine	0	0	0	0
		5	ton	Salt	0	50	0	0

Bata Mighell of Gatcombe, John Symonds master, from Ireland, *13th November 1516*

John *Symonds*	Ind	4.5	dicker	Skins, Salted	3	0	0	0
		14	piece	Mantles	0	46	8	0
		4	stone	Wool, Flocks	0	0	20	0

Bata John of St Ives, William Godeale master, from Bordeaux, 14th November 1516

William *Godeale*	Ind	16	tun	Wine	0	0	0	0
		1	C	Rosin	0	0	20	0

Bata Nicholas of Milford Haven, David Philips master, from Ireland, 17th November 1516

David *Philips*	Ind	13	barrel	Fish, Herring White	3	5	0	0
		2.25	C	Fish, Hake	0	22	6	0
		39	piece	Fish	0	6	6	0

Navicula Marget of *Morles*,[1] Evan Gentill master, from Seville, *17th November 1516*

Francis de la Porte	Alien	31.5	tun	Wine	0	0	0	0
		4.25	ton	Fruit	8	10	0	0

1 Possibly relates to the Morales river in southern Spain. Alternatively, it may be Morlaix in Brittany, although the nature of the cargo makes the former more likely.

Merchant name	Origin	Qty	Unit	Commodity	£	s.	d.	f.

Navicula John of Errenteria, Anthony de la Sola master, from Spain, *17th November 1516*

Merchant name	Origin	Qty	Unit	Commodity	£	s.	d.	f.
John Shipman	Ind	26	ton	Iron	65	0	0	0
John Ware	Ind	10	ton	Iron	25	0	0	0
William Shipman	Ind	22.5	ton	Iron	56	5	0	0
Thomas Bilford	Ind	11.33	ton	Iron	28	6	8	0
William Rowley	Ind	13	ton	Iron	32	10	0	0
Walter Nashe	Ind	1.66	ton	Iron	4	3	4	0
Richard Savery	Ind	0.25	ton	Iron	0	12	6	0

Bata Bonaventure of Cork, Richard Colle master, from Ireland, 18th November 1516

Merchant name	Origin	Qty	Unit	Commodity	£	s.	d.	f.
Richard *Colle*	Ind	8	barrel	Fish, Herring White	0	40	0	0
James Vuchedon	Ind	12	barrel	Fish, Herring White	3	0	0	0
		1	C	Skins, Sheep	0	10	0	0
		3	piece	Mantles	0	10	0	0
Robert Mirre	Ind	12	barrel	Fish, Herring White	3	0	0	0
		0.5	pipe	Fish, Salmon	0	15	0	0
		2	piece	Mantles	0	6	8	0
Jordan Roche	Ind	31	barrel	Fish, Herring White	7	15	0	0
		4.5	C	Skins, Sheep	0	45	0	0
		80	piece	Fish, Hake	0	6	8	0
		9	piece	Mantles	0	30	0	0
James Creagh	Ind	16	barrel	Fish, Herring White	4	0	0	0
		6	piece	Mantles	0	20	0	0
Edmund Copner	Ind	12	barrel	Fish, Herring White	3	0	0	0
		12	piece	Mantles	0	40	0	0
		2	C	Skins, Sheep (no wool)	0	20	0	0
Thomas Donell	Ind	4	barrel	Fish, Herring White	0	20	0	0
		0.75	pipe	Fish, Salmon	0	22	6	0
William Tirry	Ind	1.75	pipe	Fish, Salmon	0	52	6	0
		16	barrel	Fish, Herring White	4	0	0	0
		5	piece	Mantles	0	16	8	0
Dennis Diar	Ind	6	barrel	Fish, Herring White	0	30	0	0
		8	stone	Wool, Flocks	0	3	4	0
William Power	Ind	3	piece	Mantles	0	10	0	0
Robert Barrett	Ind	10	barrel	Fish, Herring White	0	50	0	0

Navicula Nunny of Penmarch, John le Payne master, from Bordeaux, 20th November 1516

Merchant name	Origin	Qty	Unit	Commodity	£	s.	d.	f.
Richard Hoby	Ind	2.25	tun	Wine	0	0	0	0
John Shipman	Ind	8	tun	Wine	0	0	0	0
John Ware	Ind	10.08	tun	Wine	0	0	0	0
William Shipman	Ind	8.25	tun	Wine	0	0	0	0
Gilbert Cogan	Ind	17.5	tun	Wine	0	0	0	0
John Sparchford	Ind	12	tun	Wine	0	0	0	0
Robert Pophin	Ind	7.75	tun	Wine	0	0	0	0
John Brampton	Ind	2.75	tun	Wine	0	0	0	0
Thomas Bilford	Ind	7	tun	Wine	0	0	0	0
Katerina Wale	Ind	1.5	tun	Wine	0	0	0	0
David Vaghan	Ind	1.75	tun	Wine	0	0	0	0
Robert Rowlow	Ind	1	tun	Wine	0	0	0	0

Merchant name	Origin	Qty	Unit	Commodity	£	s.	d.	f.
John Pasheley	Ind	2.25	tun	Wine	0	0	0	0
John Thomas	Ind	2.5	tun	Wine	0	0	0	0
Auger de Noga	Ind	1	tun	Wine	0	0	0	0
John le Payne	Alien	1.5	ton	Pitch and Rosin	2	0	0	0
		1	barel	Turpentine	0	26	8	0
Thomas Yeate	Ind	3.5	tun	Wine	0	0	0	0
Thomas Palmer	Ind	0.375	ton	Rosin	0	10	0	0
Nicholas Box	Ind	0.375	ton	Pitch and Rosin	0	10	0	0
Nicholas Alwyne	Ind	1	pipe	Pitch and Rosin	0	13	4	0
John Hathewey	Ind	0.25	ton	Rosin	0	6	8	0
Edward Jonys	Ind	1	hogshead	Wine	0	0	0	0

Navicula Jenet of *Kynprollantyne*,[2] James Morvan master, from La Rochelle, *20th November 1516*

James Morvan	Ind	8	tun	Wine	0	0	0	0
		92	ton	Salt	46	0	0	0

Bata *Christ*ofur of Longney, John Carter master, from Cardiff, 21st November 1516

John Brother	Ind	2.5	tun	Wine	0	0	0	0

Navicula John of Errenteria, Anthony de la Sola master, to Spain, 22st November 1516

John Shipman	Ind	40	wey	Beans	33	6	8	0

Bata George of Gloucester, Peter Knethell master, from Wales, 24th November 1516

Peter Knethell	Ind	1	barrel	Fish, Herring White	0	5	0	0
		0.5	C	Fish, Hake	0	5	0	0

Bata Kateryn of Tenby, Richard Hunter master, from Ireland, 26th November 1516

Richard *Hunter*	Ind	14	barrel	Fish, Herring White	3	10	0	0

Bata *Christ*ofur of Tewkesbury, Laurence Mede master, from Ireland, *26th November 1516*

William Tailor	Ind	20	C	Fish, Hake	10	0	0	0
		6	barrel	Fish, Herring White	0	30	0	0

Navicula Mare Walsyngham,[3] Port Unknown, John Whitford master, from Sanlúcar de Barrameda, *26th November 1516*

Paul Smyth	Ind	25.5	tun	Wine	0	0	0	0
		18.5	ton	Fruit	37	0	0	0
		11	C	*Smigmates*	5	10	0	0
		0.33	tun	Oil, for lamps	0	13	4	0
Richard Pole	Ind	7.5	tun	Wine	0	0	0	0
		1.25	ton	Fruit	0	50	0	0
		3	C	*Smigmates*	0	30	0	0
John Rayment	Ind	6.25	tun	Wine	0	0	0	0

2 Possibly Quimper in France.   3 Probably Bristol.

Merchant name	Origin	Qty	Unit	Commodity	£	s.	d.	f.
		0.5	ton	Fruit	0	20	0	0
		4	C	*Smigmates*	0	40	0	0
Thomas Smyth	Ind	1.75	tun	Wine	0	0	0	0
		1	ton	Fruit	0	40	0	0
John Whitford	Ind	2	tun	Wine	0	0	0	0
		2.5	ton	Fruit	5	0	0	0
		10	C	*Smigmates*	5	0	0	0
Thomas Westcote	Ind	1	tun	Wine	0	0	0	0
Robert Whitson	Ind	1	C̃	Marmalade	0	13	4	0

Bata Trynyte of Chepstow, William Heyne master, from Chepstow, 27th November 1516

Merchant name	Origin	Qty	Unit	Commodity	£	s.	d.	f.
Arthur Kyng	Ind	5.75	tun	Wine	0	0	0	0
Edmund Richard	Ind	5.5	tun	Wine	0	0	0	0
		25	C	Alum	12	10	0	0
		0.75	ton	Fruit	0	30	0	0
		2	C	*Smigmates*	0	20	0	0

Bata Trynyte of Kinsale, Germaine Fforan master, to Ireland, 28th November 1516

Merchant name	Origin	Qty	Unit	Commodity	£	s.	d.	f.
Germain Foran	Ind	6	wey	Beans	5	0	0	0
		2	stone	Hops	0	0	15	0
		1	lb	Saffron	0	10	0	0
David Doan	Ind	2	lb	Silk, Worked	0	26	8	0
		3	lb	Saffron	0	30	0	0
Edmund Deane	Ind	2	lb	Saffron	0	20	0	0
Oliver Tirry	Ind	20	lb	Saffron	10	0	0	0
		5	lb	Silk, Worked	3	6	8	0
		5	piece	Cloth of Assize, Dozen Strait	0	0	0	0
William Mirry	Ind	18	lb	Saffron	9	0	0	0
		2	lb	Silk, Worked	0	26	8	0
		1.5	piece	Cloth of Assize	0	0	0	0

Bata Kateryn of New Ross, Walter Blake master, to Ireland, *28th November 1516*

Merchant name	Origin	Qty	Unit	Commodity	£	s.	d.	f.
Walter Blake	Ind	6	wey	Beans	5	0	0	0
Philip Marow	Ind	6	wey	Beans	5	0	0	0
		8	lb	Silk, Worked	5	6	8	0
		5	lb	Saffron	0	50	0	0
		1	dozen	Skins, Golden	0	5	0	0
		1	gross	Knives	0	6	8	0
		1	gross	Cutts	0	3	4	0
		40	lb	*Pilus Tinctus*	0	16	8	0
		0.5	piece	Fustian *Cloth*	0	5	0	0
		5	gross	Points	0	5	0	0
		1	dozen	Caps	0	10	0	0
		2	piece	Cloth of Assize	0	0	0	0
Alexander Cappell	Ind	8.5	lb	Saffron	4	5	0	0
		1.5	lb	Silk, Worked	0	20	0	0
		4	gross	Points	0	4	0	0
		12	lb	*Pilus Tinctus*	0	4	0	0
		2	pair	Stock-Cards	0	2	0	0

Merchant name	Origin	Qty	Unit	Commodity	£	s.	d.	f.
Thomas Laugton	Ind	5	lb	Silk, Worked	3	6	8	0
		10	lb	Saffron	5	0	0	0
		30	lb	*Pilus Tinctus*	0	10	0	0
		3	gross	Points	0	3	0	0
		1	dozen	Caps	0	10	0	0
		0.5	gross	Knives	0	3	4	0
		2	dozen	Aniseed	0	3	4	0
		3	dozen	Penners	0	3	4	0
		3	piece	Cloth of Assize	0	0	0	0
William Co[ ]sy	Ind	5	lb	Silk, Worked	3	6	8	0
		5	lb	Saffron	0	50	0	0
		30	lb	*Pilus Tinctus*	0	10	0	0
		2	gross	Cutts	0	6	8	0
		3	dozen	Aniseed	0	4	6	0
		6	gross	Points	0	6	0	0
		0.5	dozen	Caps	0	5	0	0
		1	lb	Mace	0	2	6	0
		1	lb	Cinnamon	0	2	6	0
		4	piece	Cloth of Assize	0	0	0	0
David Pembroke	Ind	2	piece	Cloth of Assize	0	0	0	0
		5	lb	Saffron	0	50	0	0
		2	lb	Silk, Worked	0	26	8	0
		1	gross	Cutts	0	3	4	0
		7	gross	Points	0	7	0	0
		9	piece	Caps	0	7	6	0
		1	dozen	Penners	0	0	20	0
		40	lb	*Pilus Tinctus*	0	13	4	0
		1	dozen	Aniseed	0	0	18	0
		1	lb	Ginger	0	2	6	0
		1	lb	Verdigris	0	0	10	0
		1	lb	Pepper	0	0	12	0
		1.5	dozen	*Unknown*	0	0	20	0
		1	dozen	Penners	0	0	20	0

Bata Mare of Carmarthen, John Laurens master, from Carmarthen, *28th November 1516*

John Hyes?	Ind	8	ton	Salt	4	0	0	0

Bata Konylagh of Kinsale, Richard Donell master, to Ireland, *28th November 1516*

Richard *Donnell*	Ind	8	wey	Beans	6	13	4	0
Jordan Roche	Ind	2	piece	Cloth of Assize, Dozen Strait	0	0	0	0
		2	piece	Cloth of Assize	0	0	0	0
		5	lb	Saffron	0	50	0	0
		1	lb	Silk, Worked	0	13	4	0
		1	dozen	Red-Lash	0	4	0	0
		0.5	dozen	Skins, Golden	0	2	6	0
		1	gross	Cutts	0	3	4	0
		4	gross	Points	0	4	0	0
James Creagh	Ind	6.5	piece	Cloth of Assize, Dozen Strait	0	0	0	0
		1	piece	Cloth of Assize	0	0	0	0
		4	lb	Saffron	0	40	0	0

Merchant name	Origin	Qty	Unit	Commodity	£	s.	d.	f.
		2	lb	Silk, Worked	0	26	8	0
		2	gross	Cutts	0	6	8	0
		4	gross	Points	0	4	0	0
Thomas Donnell	Ind	7	piece	Cloth of Assize	0	0	0	0
		10	lb	Saffron	5	0	0	0
Robert Avyntre	Ind	7	piece	Cloth of Assize	0	0	0	0
		10	lb	Saffron	5	0	0	0

Bata Mare Bosher of Bristol Nicholas Power master, to Ireland, *28th November 1516*

Merchant name	Origin	Qty	Unit	Commodity	£	s.	d.	f.
Gerald Wale	Ind	7	wey	Beans	5	16	8	0
		2	lb	Silk, Worked	0	26	8	0
		2	lb	Saffron	0	20	0	0
		40	lb	*Pilus Tinctus*	0	13	4	0
		0.5	piece	Cloth of Assize	0	0	0	0
William Arlond	Ind	9	wey	Beans	7	10	0	0
		2	lb	Saffron	0	20	0	0
		20	lb	*Pilus Tinctus*	0	6	8	0
		2	piece	Cloth of Assize	0	0	0	0
William Everard	Ind	2	piece	Cloth of Assize	0	0	0	0
		4	lb	Silk, Worked	0	53	4	0
		6	lb	Saffron	3	0	0	0
		1	gross	Cutts	0	3	4	0
		30	lb	*Pilus Tinctus*	0	10	0	0
		4	gross	Points	0	4	0	0
James Barret	Ind	1	piece	Cloth of Assize	0	0	0	0
		6	lb	Saffron	3	0	0	0
		1.5	gross	Cutts	0	5	0	0
		2	stone	Orchil	0	3	4	0
		20	lb	*Pilus Tinctus*	0	6	8	0
		3	gross	Points	0	3	0	0
Thomas Yonge	Ind	7	lb	Saffron	3	10	0	0
		3	lb	Silk, Worked	0	40	0	0

Bata Marget of Gloucester, Thomas Nongull, from Cardiff, 1st December 1516

Merchant name	Origin	Qty	Unit	Commodity	£	s.	d.	f.
Thomas Hop	Ind	3.75	tun	Wine	0	0	0	0
Thomas Olyver	Ind	2	tun	Wine	0	0	0	0

Bata Nicholas of Tenby, John Philips master, from Ireland, *1st December 1516*

Merchant name	Origin	Qty	Unit	Commodity	£	s.	d.	f.
John Philips	Ind	10	C	Fish, Hake	5	0	0	0

Navicula *Christofur* of Shirehampton, Robert Walsh master, from Ireland, *1st December 1516*

Merchant name	Origin	Qty	Unit	Commodity	£	s.	d.	f.
John Hase	Ind	151	barrel	Fish, Herring White	37	15	0	0
		12	C	Fish, Hake	6	0	0	0
		2	C	Irish Linen *Cloth*	0	20	0	0

Merchant name	Origin	Qty	Unit	Commodity	£	s.	d.	f.

Navicula Andrew of Milford Haven, Richard Sawtre master, from Ireland, 4th December 1516

Merchant name	Origin	Qty	Unit	Commodity	£	s.	d.	f.
John Newton	Ind	1.5	C	Fish, Hake	0	15	0	0
		1	barrel	Fish, Herring White	0	5	0	0

Bata Mare of Milford Haven, John Keraugh master, from Wales, 4th December 1516

Merchant name	Origin	Qty	Unit	Commodity	£	s.	d.	f.
John Keraugh	Ind	1	barrel	Fish, Herring White	0	5	0	0

Bata Mare of Carmarthen, Robert Doyow? Master, from Ireland, 5th December 1516

Merchant name	Origin	Qty	Unit	Commodity	£	s.	d.	f.
Thomas Walter	Ind	18	barrel	Fish, Herring White	4	10	0	0
		1	virkin	Fish, Salmon	0	7	6	0
		1	tun	Wine	0	0	0	0
William Tirry	Ind	31	barrel	Fish, Herring White	7	15	0	0
		2.75	pipe	Fish, Salmon	4	2	6	0
		12	piece	Skins, Fox	0	2	0	0
		40	piece	Skins, Sheep	0	3	4	0
James Gowls	Ind	5.25	pipe	Fish, Salmon	7	17	6	0
		11	C	Fish, Hake	5	10	0	0
		6	barrel	Fish, Herring White	0	30	0	0
		4	C	Skins, Sheep (no wool)	0	40	0	0

Bata Andrew of Milford Haven, John Knethell master, from Ireland, 9th December 1516

Merchant name	Origin	Qty	Unit	Commodity	£	s.	d.	f.
John White	Ind	2	barrel	Fish, Herring White	0	10	0	0
		0.75	C	Fish, Hake	0	7	6	0

Bata George of Wicklow Patrick Albury master, from Ireland, 9th December 1516

Merchant name	Origin	Qty	Unit	Commodity	£	s.	d.	f.
Edward a Bek	Ind	15.5	pipe	Fish, Salmon	23	5	0	0
		1	pipe	Wine	0	0	0	0
Walter Archepolle	Ind	12	barrel	Fish, Herring White	3	0	0	0
		1	C	Fish, Hake	0	10	0	0
Richard Mathew	Ind	21.5	barrel	Fish, Herring White	5	7	6	0
		2	mease	Fish, Herring Red	0	10	0	0
Patrick Fitzsymonds	Ind	58	barrel	Fish, Herring White	14	10	0	0
John Candell	Ind	2	last	Fish, Herring White	6	0	0	0
John Watson	Ind	26	barrel	Fish, Herring White	6	10	0	0

Bata Jamys of Tewkesbury, John Mekyns master, from Chepstow, 9th December 1516

Merchant name	Origin	Qty	Unit	Commodity	£	s.	d.	f.
Edward Richards	Ind	6	tun	Wine	0	0	0	0
		0.75	ton	Rosin	0	20	0	0
		15	C	Smigmates	7	10	0	0
William Berde	Ind	6.5	tun	Wine	0	0	0	0
		2	ton	Fruit	4	0	0	0

Bata Anthony of Tewkesbury, John Lawton master, from Chepstow, 9th December 1516

Merchant name	Origin	Qty	Unit	Commodity	£	s.	d.	f.
William Berde	Ind	2.5	ton	Fruit	5	0	0	0

Merchant name	Origin	Qty	Unit	Commodity	£	s.	d.	f.

Bata Mighell of Tenby, Thomas Evan master, from Tenby, 10th December 1516

Merchant name	Origin	Qty	Unit	Commodity	£	s.	d.	f.
Richard Draper	Ind	19	ton	Salt	9	10	0	0

Bata Christofur of Mathern, John Packer master, from Chepstow, 11th December 1516

Merchant name	Origin	Qty	Unit	Commodity	£	s.	d.	f.
Thomas Tilar	Ind	1.25	tun	Wine	0	0	0	0
Robert Lane	Ind	1	tun	Wine	0	0	0	0

Bata Bonaventure of Cork, Richard Cole master, to Ireland, 12th December 1516

Merchant name	Origin	Qty	Unit	Commodity	£	s.	d.	f.
Edmund Copner	Ind	3	piece	Cloth of Assize, Dozen Strait	0	0	0	0
		12	lb	Silk, Worked	8	0	0	0
		13	lb	Saffron	6	10	0	0
		1	gross	Cutts	0	6	8	0
		8	gross	Points	0	8	0	0
		16	lb	Pilus Tinctus	0	5	4	0
		1	dozen	Red-Lash	0	4	0	0
		1	dozen	Skins, Golden	0	5	0	0
James Wynehedon	Ind	16	stone	Orchil	0	26	8	0
		4	lb	Saffron	0	40	0	0
		2	gross	Cutts	0	6	8	0
		1	lb	Silk, Worked	0	13	4	0
Maurice Drady	Ind	13	lb	Saffron	6	10	0	0
		3	lb	Silk, Worked	0	40	0	0
		3	stone	Orchil	0	5	0	0
		14	lb	Pilus Tinctus	0	4	8	0

Bata Nicholas of Tewkesbury, John Boyfild master, from Cardiff, *12th December 1516*

Merchant name	Origin	Qty	Unit	Commodity	£	s.	d.	f.
John Mey	Ind	2	tun	Wine	0	0	0	0

Navicula Marget of Bristol, John Stevyns master, from Algarve, 17th December 1516

Merchant name	Origin	Qty	Unit	Commodity	£	s.	d.	f.
Nicholas Browne	Ind	28.5	ton	Fruit	57	0	0	0
John Walshe	Ind	2.5	ton	Fruit	5	0	0	0
Robert Rowlow	Ind	3.625	ton	Fruit	7	5	0	0
Roger Dawes	Ind	3.125	ton	Fruit	6	5	0	0
John Rowland	Ind	3.625	ton	Fruit	7	5	0	0
William Tirry	Ind	1.875	ton	Fruit	3	15	0	0
William Shipman	Ind	1	ton	Fruit	0	40	0	0
John Shipman	Ind	2	ton	Fruit	4	0	0	0
Walter Comrowe	Ind	0.75	ton	Fruit	0	30	0	0
Walter Petwyn	Ind	2.25	ton	Fruit	4	10	0	0
John Cappis	Ind	2.875	ton	Fruit	5	15	0	0
John Stevyns	Ind	0.5	ton	Fruit	0	20	0	0
William Crosse	Ind	0.75	ton	Fruit	0	30	0	0
		1	C	Marmalade	0	13	4	0
		30	lb	Comfits	0	10	0	0
William Sewell	Ind	4	ton	Fruit	8	0	0	0

Merchant name	Origin	Qty	Unit	Commodity	£	s.	d.	f.

Navicula Nonny of Penmarch, John le Payne master, to Brittany, 19th December 1516

John Le Payne	Ind	16	tun	Lime	0	40	0	0

Bata Jhesus of Cardiff, William a Deane master, from Cardiff, 13th December 1516[4]

Richard Leynam	Ind	1	tun	Wine	0	0	0	0
Elizabeth Hockyns	Ind	1	pipe	Wine	0	0	0	0

Bata Mighell of Gatcombe, John Symonds master, to Ireland, 20th December 1516

John *Symonds*	Ind	4.5	wey	Beans	3	15	0	0

Navicula Jenet of *Kynprollantyne*,[5] James Morvan master, to Brittany, *20th December 1516*

James Morvan	Alien	12	tun	Lime	0	30	0	0

Bata George of Newport, Walter Williams master, from Wales, *20th December 1516*

Tibald Bluet	Ind	13	piece	Mantles	0	43	4	0

Bata Nicholas of Drogheda, Nicholas Johnys master, from Ireland, *20th December 1516*

Prior de Lantony	Ind	9.02	C	Fish, Salted	9	4	0	0
		10	C	Fish, Hake	5	0	0	0
		3	pipe	Fish, Salmon	4	10	0	0
		4	last	Fish, Herring White	12	0	0	0
		6.5	C	Irish Linen *Cloth*	3	5	0	0
		1	hogshead	Wine	0	0	0	0
Richard Coksall	Ind	2	C	Skins, Sheep	0	20	0	0
		6	barrel	Fish, Herring White	0	30	0	0

Navicula Matthew of Bristol, Richard Savere master, to Spain, 23rd December 1516

John Shipman	Ind	45	wey	Beans	37	10	0	0
		24	piece	Cloth of Assize	0	0	0	0
John Ware	Ind	11	piece	Cloth of Assize	0	0	0	0
William Shipman	Ind	24	piece	Cloth of Assize	0	0	0	0
William Woseley	Ind	30	piece	Cloth of Assize	0	0	0	0
		58	dozen	Hides, Tanned Calf	9	13	4	0
Edward Jonys	Ind	1	piece	Cloth of Assize	0	0	0	0

Bata George of Berkeley, Philip Nogull master, from Ireland, 23rd December 1516

John Rownan	Ind	10	C	Fish, Hake	5	0	0	0
James Browne	Ind	15	C	Fish, Hake	7	10	0	0
		1	burden	Fish, Salted	0	4	2	0
James *Browne*	Ind	8	wey	Beans	6	13	4	0
Patrick Alley	Ind	10	piece	Milstones	5	0	0	0
Mathew Hop	Ind	3	piece	Milstones	0	30	0	0
John Morecok	Ind	1	pipe	Wine, Corrupt	0	15	0	0

4 This is most likely a recording error.   5 Perhaps Quimper in France.

Merchant name	Origin	Qty	Unit	Commodity	£	s.	d.	f.

Navicula Jhesus of Bristol, Robert Power master, to Spain, 2nd January 1517

Merchant name	Origin	Qty	Unit	Commodity	£	s.	d.	f.
John Drewis	Ind	50	wey	Beans	41	13	4	0
		4	piece	Cloth of Assize	0	0	0	0
Maurice Bocher	Ind	25	wey	Beans	20	16	8	0
		5	dicker	Hides, Tanned	16	13	4	0
		20	dozen	Skins, Calf	3	6	8	0
		10	piece	Cloth of Assize	0	0	0	0
Thomas Clarke	Ind	1	piece	Cloth of Assize	0	0	0	0
Thomas Hawkyns	Ind	26	piece	Welsh *Cloth*, Dozen Strait	5	8	4	0
John Shipman	Ind	22	piece	Cloth of Assize	0	0	0	0
		15	piece	Welsh *Cloth*, Dozen Strait	3	2	6	0
		6.5	wey	Beans	5	8	4	0
John Ware	Ind	20	piece	Cloth of Assize	0	0	0	0
William Shipman	Ind	19	piece	Cloth of Assize	0	0	0	0
		15	piece	Welsh *Cloth*, Dozen Strait	3	2	6	0
Thomas Yeate	Ind	6	piece	Cloth of Assize	0	0	0	0
John Vaghan	Ind	8	piece	Cloth of Assize	0	0	0	0

Bata George of Bristol, William Donell master, to Ireland, 2nd January 1517

Merchant name	Origin	Qty	Unit	Commodity	£	s.	d.	f.
Thomas Donnell	Ind	6	wey	Beans	5	0	0	0
Robert Avyntre	Ind	6	wey	Beans	5	0	0	0
Tibald Blewet	Ind	1	piece	Cloth of Assize	0	0	0	0
		1	piece	Welsh *Cloth*	0	20	0	0
		8	lb	Saffron	4	0	0	0
		36	lb	*Pilus Tinctus*	0	12	0	0

Navicula Mawdelen of Hondarribia, Stephen de Casa Nova master, to Spain, 2nd January 1517

Merchant name	Origin	Qty	Unit	Commodity	£	s.	d.	f.
John de Seint Stevyn	Alien	1.6	dicker	Hides, Tanned	5	17	4	0
		28	dozen	Skins, Calf Tanned	4	13	4	0

Navicula Mare *Christ*ofur of Bristol, Robert Avyntre master, from Sanlúcar de Barrameda, 3rd January 1517

Merchant name	Origin	Qty	Unit	Commodity	£	s.	d.	f.
John Rowland	Ind	7	tun	Wine	0	0	0	0
		1	tun	Oil, *Olive*	4	0	0	0
Humphrey Browne	Ind	1	tun	Wine	0	0	0	0
John Shipman	Ind	4.25	tun	Wine	0	0	0	0
		1.25	tun	Oil, *Olive*	6	0	0	0
William Shipman	Ind	2.5	tun	Wine	0	0	0	0
		1	tun	Oil, *Olive*	4	0	0	0
John Ware	Ind	4.5	tun	Wine	0	0	0	0
		1	pipe	Oil, *Olive*	0	40	0	0
David Vaghan	Ind	3.5	tun	Wine	0	0	0	0
		18	lb	Pepper	0	18	0	0
George Halle	Ind	2	tun	Wine	0	0	0	0
Thomas Dale	Ind	3	tun	Wine	0	0	0	0
		1	tun	Oil, *Olive*	4	0	0	0
Robert Avyntre	Ind	6	tun	Wine	0	0	0	0

Merchant name	Origin	Qty	Unit	Commodity	£	s.	d.	f.
		4.25	tun	Oil, *Olive*	17	0	0	0
		2	C	Pepper	10	0	0	0
		3	C	Marmalade	0	40	0	0
		1	C	Comfits	0	33	4	0
		10	dozen	Cork, Black	0	16	8	0
John Kyng	Ind	4.75	tun	Wine	0	0	0	0
		3	tun	Oil, *Olive*	12	0	0	0
		1.5	C	Pepper	7	10	0	0
		1	C	Marmalade	0	13	4	0
William Avyntre	Ind	1.75	tun	Wine	0	0	0	0
		2	C	Marmalade	0	26	8	0
Thomas Donnell	Ind	1.25	tun	Wine	0	0	0	0
		1	pipe	Oil, *Olive*	0	40	0	0
Richard Arthur	Ind	1.75	tun	Wine	0	0	0	0
		1	tun	Oil, *Olive*	4	0	0	0
		1	C	Pepper	5	0	0	0
Thomas Bilford	Ind	1.5	tun	Wine	0	0	0	0
		1	pipe	Oil, *Olive*	0	40	0	0
Robert Rowland	Ind	2.75	tun	Wine	0	0	0	0
			illegible	illegible	4	0	0	0
Henry Woswold	Ind	1.75	tun	Wine	0	0	0	0
		5	C	Pepper	25	0	0	0
		1	pipe	Oil, *Olive*	0	40	0	0
Robert Peers	Ind	0.75	tun	Oil, *Olive*	3	0	0	0
Roger Monouse	Ind	0.75	tun	Wine	0	0	0	0
Thomas Sparchford	Ind	2	tun	Wine	0	0	0	0
		1	quart	Pepper	0	25	0	0
John Wyot	Ind	2.75	tun	Wine	0	0	0	0
		1	pipe	Oil, *Olive*	0	40	0	0
William Tirry	Ind	2	tun	Wine	0	0	0	0
John Drewis	Ind	7	tun	Wine	0	0	0	0
William Woseley	Ind	2	tun	Wine	0	0	0	0
		2	tun	Oil, *Olive*	8	0	0	0
Roger James	Ind	2.5	tun	Wine	0	0	0	0
Robert Coke	Ind	1.75	tun	Wine	0	0	0	0
		1.75	tun	Oil, *Olive*	7	0	0	0
Richard Donnell	Ind	1	hogshead	Oil, *Olive*	0	20	0	0
John Hall	Ind	4	tun	Wine	0	0	0	0
Richard Bocher	Ind	2	tun	Wine	0	0	0	0
		0.5	C	Pepper	0	50	0	0
Thomas illegible	Ind	1	tun	Wine	0	0	0	0
John Clot	Ind	1	pipe	Wine	0	0	0	0
Walter Conrowe	Ind	2	C	Marmalade	0	26	8	0
Philip Morgan	Ind	3.5	C	Marmalade	0	46	8	0
		3	quart	Comfits	0	30	0	0
William Woseley	Ind	0.5	C	Marmalade	0	6	8	0
Unknown Plomley	Ind	0.5	hogshead	Oil, *Olive*	0	10	0	0
Unknown Porter	Ind	1	C	Marmalade	0	13	4	0
Unknown Payne	Ind	0.25	C	Marmalade	0	3	4	0
Unknown Halle	Ind	1	C	Marmalade	0	13	4	0
Unknown Dale	Ind	0.5	C	Marmalade	0	6	8	0
Unknown Nashe	Ind	2	C	Marmalade	0	26	8	0

Merchant name	Origin	Qty	Unit	Commodity	£	s.	d.	f.

Navicula Mare Redcliffe of Bristol, Richard Boughton master, from Ireland, 7th January 1517

Merchant name	Origin	Qty	Unit	Commodity	£	s.	d.	f.
Nicholas Browne	Ind	52.5	C	Fish, Hake	26	5	0	0
		43	barrel	Fish, Herring White	10	15	0	0
		1	dicker	Skins, Salted	0	13	4	0
		6	burden	Fish, Salted	0	25	0	0
Richard Bonghton	Ind	2	C	Fish, Hake	0	20	0	0
Richard Diar	Ind	6	C	Fish, Hake	3	0	0	0

Bata Christofur of Tewkesbury, Laurence Mede master, to Ireland, 7th January 1517

Merchant name	Origin	Qty	Unit	Commodity	£	s.	d.	f.
William Tailor	Ind	11	wey	Beans	9	3	4	0

Bata Trynyte of Chepstow, William Heyne master, from Chepstow, 7th January 1517

Merchant name	Origin	Qty	Unit	Commodity	£	s.	d.	f.
Thomas Browne	Ind	8	C	Cork, White	0	26	8	0

Bata Savior of Milford Haven, Thomas Harry master, from Ireland, 9th January 1517

Merchant name	Origin	Qty	Unit	Commodity	£	s.	d.	f.
Thomas Harry	Ind	12	barrel	Fish, Herring White	3	0	0	0
		14	C	Fish, Hake	7	0	0	0
		1	C	Fish, Salted	0	20	0	0

Bata Mare of Youghal, David Walshe master, from Ireland, 20th January 1517

Merchant name	Origin	Qty	Unit	Commodity	£	s.	d.	f.
David Walshe	Ind	24	C	Fish, Hake	12	0	0	0
		1.5	burden	Fish, Salted	0	6	3	0
John Savy	Ind	31.5	C	Fish, Hake	15	15	0	0
		0.5	pipe	Fish, Salmon	0	15	0	0
		1.5	burden	Fish, Salted	0	6	3	0

Navicula Philip of Bristol, Robert Avyntre master, to Ireland, 21st January 1517

Merchant name	Origin	Qty	Unit	Commodity	£	s.	d.	f.
Illegible Avyntre	Ind	12.5	wey	Beans	10	8	4	0
		1	wey	Grain	0	20	0	0
		12.5	lb	Silk, Worked	8	6	8	0
		12.5	lb	Saffron	6	5	0	0
		14	piece	Cloth of Assize	0	0	0	0
Thomas Donnell	Ind	12.5	wey	Beans	10	8	4	0
		12.5	lb	Silk, Worked	8	6	8	0
		12.5	lb	Saffron	6	5	0	0
		11	piece	Cloth of Assize	0	0	0	0
John White	Ind	2	lb	Saffron	0	20	0	0
John Kyng	Ind	5	lb	Silk, Worked	3	6	8	0
		5	lb	Saffron	0	50	0	0

Navicula Christofur of Cabo de San Adriàn, Robert Willetto master, to Spain, 22nd January 1517

Merchant name	Origin	Qty	Unit	Commodity	£	s.	d.	f.
John Hase	Ind	50	wey	Grain	50	0	0	0
			illegible		0	0	0	0

Merchant name	Origin	Qty	Unit	Commodity	£	s.	d.	f.
			illegible		0	0	0	0
			illegible		0	0	0	0

Bata Mighell of Gatcombe, John Marks master, from Chepstow, *22nd January 1517*

| Thomas Hoper | Ind | 3.75 | tun | Wine | 0 | 0 | 0 | 0 |

Bata Trynyte of Chepstow, William Heyne master, to Chepstow, *22nd January 1517*

| John Welshote | Ind | 40 | piece | Cloth of Assize | 0 | 0 | 0 | 0 |

Bata Mare of Tewkesbury, John Andrew master, from Chepstow, *22nd January 1517*

Robert Elyot	Ind	3	C	Woad, Azores	0	20	0	0
William Halford	Ind	50	C	Woad, Azores	16	13	4	0
Francis Pernuf	Alien	3	C	Woad, Azores	0	20	0	0
John Ballyaghin	Ind	8	tun	Wine	0	0	0	0
John Mathew	Ind	9	C	Woad, Azores	3	0	0	0

Bata Trynyte of Chepstow, William Heyne master, from Chepstow, *22nd January 1517*

| William Shipman | Ind | 1 | hogshead | Wine | 0 | 0 | 0 | 0 |

Navicula John of Cadiz, John de Camache master, to Chepstow, 26th January 1517

James Fitzjamys	Ind	21	piece	Cloth of Assize	0	0	0	0
		22	piece	Welsh *Cloth*	22	0	0	0
William Tirry	Ind	5	piece	Welsh *Cloth*	5	0	0	0

Bata Trynyte of Milford Haven, William Philipe master, *from Ireland*, 29th January 1517

William Philipe	Ind	7	barrel	Fish, Herring White	0	35	0	0
		3	C	Fish, Hake	0	30	0	0
		1	burden	Fish, Salted	0	4	2	0

Navicula Fyaker of Penmarch, Michael de Wyke master, from Bordeaux, *29th January 1517*

Michael de Wyke	Alien	1.25	tun	Wine	0	0	0	0
		0.375	ton	Rosin	0	10	0	0
Robert Coke	Ind	19	tun	Wine	0	0	0	0
		0.5	ton	Rosin	0	13	4	0
Robert Pers	Ind	16.5	tun	Wine	0	0	0	0
		0.5	ton	Rosin	0	13	4	0
William Rowley	Ind	10	tun	Wine	0	0	0	0
		0.5	ton	Rosin	0	13	4	0
John Bocher	Ind	4.5	tun	Wine	0	0	0	0
Robert Paphin	Ind	1	hogshead	Wine	0	0	0	0
John Thomas	Ind	6.5	tun	Wine	0	0	0	0
John Coke	Ind	7	tun	Wine	0	0	0	0
John Shipman	Ind	5.25	tun	Wine	0	0	0	0
William Shipman	Ind	3	tun	Wine	0	0	0	0
Edward Jonys	Ind	1	tun	Wine	0	0	0	0

Merchant name	Origin	Qty	Unit	Commodity	£	s.	d.	f.
John Ware	Ind	1	tun	Wine	0	0	0	0
Roger Monouse	Ind	1	tun	Wine	0	0	0	0
Robert Dane	Ind	5.25	tun	Wine	0	0	0	0
John Brampton	Ind	1.25	tun	Wine	0	0	0	0
Robert Rowlow	Ind	10.75	tun	Wine	0	0	0	0
John a Bek	Ind	1.25	tun	Wine	0	0	0	0

Navicula Mare Tower of Bristol, William Robynet master, from Sanlúcar de Barrameda, 29th January 1517

Merchant name	Origin	Qty	Unit	Commodity	£	s.	d.	f.
John Collas	Ind	35	tun	Wine	0	0	0	0
Adam Skelton	Ind	8	tun	Wine	0	0	0	0
David Vaghan	Ind	10	tun	Wine	0	0	0	0
Thomas Hikke	Ind	6.5	tun	Wine	0	0	0	0
		1	tun	Oil, *Olive*	4	0	0	0
Katerina Wale	Ind	13	tun	Wine	0	0	0	0
John Ware	Ind	3.5	tun	Wine	0	0	0	0
		2	C	*Smigmates*	1	0	0	0
George Hall	Ind	4.25	tun	Wine	0	0	0	0
Roger Dawes	Ind	1	tun	Wine	0	0	0	0
Robert Home	Ind	16	tun	Wine	0	0	0	0
		2	ton	Fruit	3	0	0	0
John Pill	Ind	4	tun	Wine	0	0	0	0
		1	tun	Oil, *Olive*	4	0	0	0
William Tirry	Ind	2	tun	Wine	0	0	0	0
Thomas Palmer	Ind	1	tun	Wine	0	0	0	0
John Thorne	Ind	6.5	tun	Wine	0	0	0	0
		3	tun	Oil, *Olive*	12	0	0	0
		0.5	C	Marmalade	0	6	8	0
Richard Bonnes	Ind	2	tun	Wine	0	0	0	0
		0.5	C	Marmalade	0	6	8	0
Robert Hawke	Ind	1.5	tun	Wine	0	0	0	0
William Robynet	Ind	5.25	tun	Wine	0	0	0	0
John Grene	Ind	1	tun	Wine	0	0	0	0
Nicholas Ward	Ind	1	hogshead	Wine	0	0	0	0
		1.25	C	*Smigmates*	0	12	6	0
William Hederstall	Ind	1	hogshead	Wine	0	0	0	0
John Pollard	Ind	1	C	*Smigmates*	0	10	0	0
John Gifford	Ind	0.5	hogshead	Wine	0	0	0	0

Bata Kateryn of Tenby, Richard Hunter master, from Ireland, 31st January 1517

Merchant name	Origin	Qty	Unit	Commodity	£	s.	d.	f.
Richard Hunter	Ind	24.5	barrel	Fish, Herring White	6	2	6	0
		1.5	C	Fish, Hake	0	15	0	0

Navicula Mare Kateryn of Bristol, William a Deane master, from Sanlúcar de Barrameda, 3rd February 1517

Merchant name	Origin	Qty	Unit	Commodity	£	s.	d.	f.
George Halle	Ind	5.5	tun	Wine	0	0	0	0
		1	hogshead	Fruit	0	10	0	0
Nicholas Gay	Ind	3.5	tun	Wine	0	0	0	0
John Halle	Ind	8.5	tun	Wine	0	0	0	0

Merchant name	Origin	Qty	Unit	Commodity	£	s.	d.	f.
		5	ton	Fruit	10	0	0	0
William Tirry	Ind	1.5	tun	Wine	0	0	0	0
Richard Bonrine(?)	Ind	1	ton	Fruit	0	40	0	0
Clement Yonge	Ind	2	tun	Wine	0	0	0	0
Richard Hoby	Ind	4	tun	Wine	0	0	0	0
John Jay	Ind	3.5	tun	Wine	0	0	0	0
John Kynon	Ind	7	tun	Wine	0	0	0	0
		3.75	tun	Oil, Olive	15	0	0	0
		1.5	ton	Fruit	3	0	0	0
		1.75	C	Smigmates	0	17	6	0
Robert Avyntre	Ind	2	tun	Oil, Olive	8	0	0	0
John Kyng	Ind	1	tun	Oil, Olive	4	0	0	0
John Wyot	Ind	3.5	tun	Wine	0	0	0	0
Thomas Yeate	Ind	8.5	tun	Wine	0	0	0	0
Thomas Hop	Ind	5	tun	Wine	0	0	0	0
John Thorne	Ind	22	C	Smigmates	11	0	0	0
Robert Thorne	Ind	10	tun	Wine	0	0	0	0
Philip Ffox	Ind	1	tun	Wine	0	0	0	0
John Greene	Ind	1	tun	Wine	0	0	0	0
Walter Comrowe	Ind	7.25	tun	Wine	0	0	0	0
David Vaghan	Ind	7.25	tun	Wine	0	0	0	0
William Deane	Ind	2.75	tun	Wine	0	0	0	0
John Ward	Ind	2.75	tun	Wine	0	0	0	0
Robert Elyot	Ind	4.5	tun	Wine	0	0	0	0
John Cappis	Ind	1	tun	Oil, Olive	4	0	0	0
		10	C	Smigmates	5	0	0	0
William Woseley	Ind	8	C	Alum	4	0	0	0
Thomas Nongull	Ind	0.5	tun	Wine	0	0	0	0
John Clarke	Ind	0.5	hogshead	Fruit	0	5	0	0
George de Coste	Alien	4.5	tun	Wine	0	0	0	0
Walter Coke	Ind	1	hogshead	Wine	0	0	0	0
William Stevyns	Ind	0.75	tun	Wine	0	0	0	0
John Gefferes	Ind	0.5	hogshead	Wine	0	0	0	0
Humphrey Bradley	Ind	1.5	tun	Wine	0	0	0	0

Navicula Trynyte of Bristol, Evan Danyell master, from Sanlúcar de Barrameda, *3rd February 1517*

Merchant name	Origin	Qty	Unit	Commodity	£	s.	d.	f.
John Jay	Ind	1.25	tun	Wine	0	0	0	0
John Thorne	Ind	3.25	tun	Wine	0	0	0	0
Walter Comrowe	Ind	5.5	tun	Wine	0	0	0	0
John Ravyn	Ind	7.25	tun	Wine	0	0	0	0
Robert Hille	Ind	11.38	tun	Wine	0	0	0	0
		22.5	C	Smigmates	11	5	0	0
		1.75	C	Marmalade	0	23	4	0
Nicholas Browne	Ind	3.25	tun	Wine	0	0	0	0
John Cappis	Ind	14.25	tun	Wine	0	0	0	0
		2.75	ton	Fruit	5	10	0	0
		1	quart	Comfits	0	10	0	0
		1.75	C	Marmalade	0	23	4	0
John Brampton	Ind	3.5	tun	Wine	0	0	0	0
Evan Danyell	Ind	2	tun	Wine	0	0	0	0

Merchant name	Origin	Qty	Unit	Commodity	£	s.	d.	f.
		1	pipe	Fruit	0	20	0	0
		1	hogshead	Vinegar	0	10	0	0
John Sumpter	Ind	2.875	tun	Wine	0	0	0	0
		1	ton	Fruit	0	40	0	0
John Walshe	Ind	3.5	tun	Wine	0	0	0	0
Thomas Hart	Ind	3.5	tun	Wine	0	0	0	0
Thomas Jonys	Ind	3	C	*Smigmates*	0	30	0	0

Bata Mare of Milford Haven, David Smyth master, from Ireland, 4th February 1517

David *Smyth*	Ind	3.5	last	Fish, Herring White	10	10	0	0
		3	M	Fish, Hake	15	0	0	0

Bata John of Milford Haven, David Smyth master, from Ireland, *4th February 1517*

David *Smyth*	Ind	1	burden	Fish, Salted	0	4	2	0
William Tasker	Ind	16	barrel	Fish, Herring White	4	0	0	0
		13	C	Fish, Hake	6	10	0	0
		2	burden	Fish, Salted	0	8	4	0

Bata Anthony of Tenby, John Tege master, from Ireland, 5th February 1517

John Tege	Ind	62	barrel	Fish, Herring White	15	10	0	0
Thomas Howell	Ind	13	barrel	Fish, Herring White	3	10	0	0

Bata St Mary of Milford Haven, Richard Rustan master, from Ireland, 5th February 1517

Richard *Rustan*	Ind	34	barrel	Fish, Herring White	8	10	0	0
		24	C	Fish, Hake	12	0	0	0
William Trannter	Ind	1	barrel	Fish, Herring White	0	5	0	0

Bata Martyn of Milford Haven, Richard Gryndam master, from Ireland, 5th February 1517

Richard *Gryndam*	Ind	12	barrel	Fish, Herring White	3	0	0	0
		10	C	Fish, Hake	5	0	0	0
		1	burden	Fish, Salted	0	4	2	0

Bata Mare of Youghal, David Walshe master, to Ireland, 6th February 1517

David Walshe	Ind	2	wey	Beans	0	33	4	0
		20	lb	*Pilus Tinctus*	0	6	8	0
John Davys	Ind	40	lb	*Pilus Tinctus*	0	13	4	0
		2	C	Iron	0	8	0	0

Bata Katheryn of Tenby, Richard Hunter master, to Ireland, *6th February 1517*

James Gofe	Ind	12	wey	Beans	10	0	0	0

Bata Trynyte of Chepstow, William Heyne master, from Chepstow, 7th February 1517

Gilbert Cogan	Ind	3	pipe	Woad	15	0	0	0
Hugh Elyot	Ind	9	piece	Cloth of Assize	0	0	0	0

Merchant name	Origin	Qty	Unit	Commodity	£	s.	d.	f.
		6	piece	Welsh *Cloth*	6	o	o	o

Bata Jamys of Milford Haven, Stephen Oriell master, from Ireland, *7th February 1517*

Merchant name	Origin	Qty	Unit	Commodity	£	s.	d.	f.
Stephen Oriell	Ind	16	barrel	Fish, Herring White	4	o	o	o
		12.5	C	Fish, Hake	6	5	o	o

Bata Mare of Minehead, Richard Dawton master, to Ireland, *7th February 1517*

Merchant name	Origin	Qty	Unit	Commodity	£	s.	d.	f.
Richard Dawton	Ind	18	wey	Beans	15	o	o	o

Bata George of Milford Haven, Philip Webbe master, from Ireland, 9th February 1517

Merchant name	Origin	Qty	Unit	Commodity	£	s.	d.	f.
Philip Webbe	Ind	40	barrel	Fish, Herring White	10	o	o	o
		13	C	Fish, Hake	6	10	o	o

Bata Anthony of Bristol, John Pygot master, from Ireland, 10th February 1517

Merchant name	Origin	Qty	Unit	Commodity	£	s.	d.	f.
Richard Fagan	Ind	91	barrel	Fish, Herring White	22	15	o	o
		12.5	pipe	Fish, Salmon	18	15	o	o
		1	piece	Mantles	o	3	4	o
John Halle	Ind	14	barrel	Fish, Herring White	3	10	o	o

Bata Mare of Tenby, John Harrye master, from Bordeaux, 11th February 1517

Merchant name	Origin	Qty	Unit	Commodity	£	s.	d.	f.
Griffith Towker	Ind	4.75	tun	Wine	o	o	o	o

Bata Trinite of Chepstow, William Heyn*e master,* from Chepstow, *11th February 1517*

Merchant name	Origin	Qty	Unit	Commodity	£	s.	d.	f.
Robert Ellyot	Ind	24	C	Woad, Azores	8	o	o	o
William Edwards	Ind	12	C	Woad, Azores	4	o	o	o

Navicula Edward of Bristol, John Gorwey master, to Bordeaux, *11th February 1517*

Merchant name	Origin	Qty	Unit	Commodity	£	s.	d.	f.
Nicholas Gay	Ind	11	piece	Cloth of Assize	o	o	o	o
		3	ton	Lead, Worked	15	o	o	o
Thomas Yeate	Ind	13	piece	Cloth of Assize	o	o	o	o
George Hall	Ind	13	piece	Cloth of Assize	o	o	o	o
David Vaghan	Ind	17	piece	Cloth of Assize	o	o	o	o
John Hall	Ind	11	piece	Cloth of Assize	o	o	o	o

Bata Sonday of St Ives, John Richards master, from Ireland, *11th February 1517*

Merchant name	Origin	Qty	Unit	Commodity	£	s.	d.	f.
John Richards	Ind	3	C	Fish, Hake	o	30	o	o

Navicula Mare*Christ*ofur of Bristol, John Barnard master, to Bordeaux, *11th February 1517*

Merchant name	Origin	Qty	Unit	Commodity	£	s.	d.	f.
Roger Dawes	Ind	4	piece	Cloth of Assize	o	o	o	o
Edward Body	Ind	8	piece	Cloth of Assize	o	o	o	o
Thomas Bilford	Ind	4	piece	Cloth of Assize	o	o	o	o
Thomas Dale	Ind	15	piece	Cloth of Assize	o	o	o	o
Nicholas Gay	Ind	8	piece	Cloth of Assize	o	o	o	o

Merchant name	Origin	Qty	Unit	Commodity	£	s.	d.	f.
Robert Rowlow	Ind	6	piece	Cloth of Assize	0	0	0	0
John Shipman	Ind	2.5	piece	Cloth of Assize	0	0	0	0
John Ware	Ind	1	piece	Cloth of Assize	0	0	0	0
William Shipman	Ind	2.5	piece	Cloth of Assize	0	0	0	0

Bata Mighell of Gatcombe, John Symonds master, from Ireland, 12th February 1517

John *Symonds*	Ind	4	dicker	Skins, Salted	0	53	4	0
		2	C	Skins, Sheep	0	20	0	0
		2	burden	Fish, Salted	0	8	4	0
		1	barrel	Fish, Herring White	0	5	0	0
		2	ton	Salt	0	20	0	0
		6	piece	Mantles	0	20	0	0

Bata Dellyn of Padstow, John Thomas master, from Ireland, *12th February 1517*

John Thomas	Ind	30	C	Fish, Hake	15	0	0	0

Bata Mare of Milford Haven, WilliamHawkyns master, from Ireland, 16th February 1517

William Hawkyns	Ind	10	C	Fish, Hake	5	0	0	0
		7	barrel	Fish, Herring White	0	35	0	0
		1	burden	Fish, Salted	0	4	2	0

Navicula Mawdlen of Errenteria, John Surre master, from Sanlúcar de Barrameda, 17th February 1517

Roger Dawes	Ind	8	tun	Wine	0	0	0	0
William Woseley	Ind	8.5	tun	Wine	0	0	0	0
John Surre	Alien	8	tun	Wine	0	0	0	0
		0.75	ton	Fruit	0	30	0	0
Robert Thorne	Ind	7	tun	Wine	0	0	0	0
		12	M	Orchil	80	0	0	0
Francis Bawdwyn (of London)	Ind	12.75	tun	Wine	0	0	0	0
Thomas Maileyeard (of London)	Ind	5	tun	Wine	0	0	0	0
Robert Rowlow	Ind	3.75	tun	Wine	0	0	0	0
Ralph Apprice	Ind	5	tun	Wine	0	0	0	0
David Vaghan	Ind	3.5	tun	Wine	0	0	0	0
Walter Comrowe	Ind	13.5	tun	Wine	0	0	0	0
		13.75	C	*Smigmates*	6	17	6	0
		1	hogshead	Fruit	0	10	0	0
John Thorne	Ind	5.25	tun	Wine	0	0	0	0
John Greene	Ind	1.75	tun	Wine	0	0	0	0
Leonard Osburn	Ind	8.5	tun	Wine	0	0	0	0
John Ware	Ind	2.25	tun	Wine	0	0	0	0
Paul Smyth	Ind	5.25	tun	Wine	0	0	0	0

Bata Trinite of Milford Haven, Thomas Tewe master, from Ireland, *17th February 1517*

Thomas Tewe	Ind	14	C	Fish, Hake	7	0	0	0

Merchant name	Origin	Qty	Unit	Commodity	£	s.	d.	f.
		4	barrel	Fish, Herring White	0	20	0	0
		1	burden	Fish, Salted	0	4	2	0

Navicula John Baptist of Pasajes de San Juan, Michael de Lumaly master, from Sanlúcar de Barrameda, *17th February 1517*

Merchant name	Origin	Qty	Unit	Commodity	£	s.	d.	f.
John Shipman	Ind	9	tun	Wine	0	0	0	0
Roger Dawes	Ind	17.5	tun	Wine	0	0	0	0
John Ware	Ind	8.5	tun	Wine	0	0	0	0
William Shipman	Ind	8.5	tun	Wine	0	0	0	0
Thomas Dale	Ind	8	tun	Wine	0	0	0	0
Robert Avyntre	Ind	2.5	tun	Wine	0	0	0	0
Thomas Donell	Ind	1	tun	Wine	0	0	0	0
John Kyng	Ind	2.75	tun	Wine	0	0	0	0
Richard Arthur	Ind	1	tun	Wine	0	0	0	0
William Avyntre	Ind	2	tun	Wine	0	0	0	0
Thomas Bilford	Ind	2.5	tun	Wine	0	0	0	0
John Thomas	Ind	1.5	tun	Wine	0	0	0	0
John Rowlond	Ind	7	tun	Wine	0	0	0	0
Robert Rowlow	Ind	3.75	tun	Wine	0	0	0	0
David Vaghan	Ind	3	tun	Wine	0	0	0	0
		1.5	ton	Fruit	3	0	0	0
William Woseley	Ind	2.75	tun	Wine	0	0	0	0
Robert Thorne	Ind	32	C	Orchil	21	6	8	0
Thomas Lawden	Ind	2	ton	Fruit	4	0	0	0
Walter Comrowe	Ind	1	ton	Fruit	0	40	0	0
		3	ton	Iron	7	10	0	0
John Sumpter	Ind	1	ton	Fruit	0	40	0	0
Thomas Penson	Ind	2.5	tun	Wine	0	0	0	0
Humphrey Bradley	Ind	1	pipe	Wine	0	0	0	0
Martin Spencer	Alien	2	C	Marmalade	0	26	8	0
Anthony de Pickardia	Alien	18	piece	Skins, Civit *Cat*	0	24	0	0

Bata George of Bristol, William Donell master, to Ireland, *17th February 1517*

Merchant name	Origin	Qty	Unit	Commodity	£	s.	d.	f.
Robert Avyntre & Thomas Donnel	Ind	16	wey	Beans	13	6	8	0

Bata Trynyte of Chepstow, William Heyne master, *from Chepstow, 17th February 1517*

Merchant name	Origin	Qty	Unit	Commodity	£	s.	d.	f.
John Mathewe	Ind	40	C	Woad, Azores	13	6	8	0
		3	pipe	Woad	15	0	0	0
Thomas Hop	Ind	3	tun	Wine	0	0	0	0

Navicula Jamys of Arnemuiden, Libard Harmans master, from Zeeland, *17th February 1517*

Merchant name	Origin	Qty	Unit	Commodity	£	s.	d.	f.
William Dale	Ind	28	last	Fish, Herring White	84	0	0	0
		6	bale	Madder	15	0	0	0
		13	pocket	Hops	19	10	0	0
		2	cashe	Sugar	4	0	0	0
		12.5	lb	*Sernis*	0	2	6	0
		3	lb	Mastic	0	8	2	0

Merchant name	Origin	Qty	Unit	Commodity	£	s.	d.	f.
		1	lb	Spikenard	0	0	10	0
		1	lb	Camphor	0	3	4	0
		12.5	lb	Copperas, White	0	2	6	0
		3	lb	Oil, Petrolium	0	2	6	0
Henry Edwards	Ind	35	dozen	Brushes	3	10	0	0
		3	C	Frying pan (3 clb)	0	30	0	0
		30	bundle	Paper, Black	0	10	0	0
Christopher Gomer	Ind	2	barrel	Tar	0	6	8	0

Bata Jamys of Milford Haven, John Webbe master, to Ireland, *17th February 1517*

Merchant name	Origin	Qty	Unit	Commodity	£	s.	d.	f.
Richard Bonnce	Ind	10	wey	Beans	8	6	8	0

Bata Mare of St Ives, John Davys master, from Ireland, 18th February 1517

Merchant name	Origin	Qty	Unit	Commodity	£	s.	d.	f.
John Savior	Ind	5	M	Fish, Hake	25	0	0	0

Bata Kateryn of Chepstow, Robert Ffisher master, from Chepstow, *18th February 1517*

Merchant name	Origin	Qty	Unit	Commodity	£	s.	d.	f.
John Rowland	Ind	8	tun	Wine	0	0	0	0
John Mathewe	Ind	1	pipe	Wine	0	0	0	0
Humphrey Browne	Ind	0.66	pipe	Wine	0	0	0	0

Bata Mare of St Ives, Thomas Edmonds master, from Ireland, *19th February 1517*

Merchant name	Origin	Qty	Unit	Commodity	£	s.	d.	f.
Thomas *Edmonds*	Ind	3	M	Fish, Hake	15	0	0	0

Bata Kateryn of Milford Haven, Richard Webbe master, from Ireland, 20th February 1517

Merchant name	Origin	Qty	Unit	Commodity	£	s.	d.	f.
Richard *Webbe*	Ind	67	barrel	Fish, Herring White	16	15	0	0
		22	C	Fish, Hake	11	0	0	0
		3	burden	Fish, Salted	0	12	6	0

Bata Mare of St Ives, John Pascall master, from Ireland, *20th February 1517*

Merchant name	Origin	Qty	Unit	Commodity	£	s.	d.	f.
John Pascall	Ind	4	M	Fish, Hake	20	0	0	0

Bata Keryk of Milford Haven, William Wade master, from Ireland, *20th February 1517*

Merchant name	Origin	Qty	Unit	Commodity	£	s.	d.	f.
William Wade	Ind	35	C	Fish, Hake	17	10	0	0
		2.5	last	Fish, Herring White	7	10	0	0
		1	C	Fish, Salted	0	20	0	0

Bata Bastian of St Ives, William Sampler master, from Ireland, *20th February 1517*

Merchant name	Origin	Qty	Unit	Commodity	£	s.	d.	f.
William Sampler	Ind	3	M	Fish, Hake	15	0	0	0
		2	bolt	Poldavis *Cloth*	0	20	0	0

Navicula Mare Kateryn of Bristol, William a Deane master, to Lisbon, 21st February 1517

Merchant name	Origin	Qty	Unit	Commodity	£	s.	d.	f.
Robert Avyntre	Ind	50	wey	Grain	50	0	0	0
Roger Dawes	Ind	33	piece	Welsh *Cloth*	33	0	0	0

Merchant name	Origin	Qty	Unit	Commodity	£	s.	d.	f.
Oliver Pynto	Alien	16	piece	Welsh *Cloth*	16	0	0	0
David Vaghan	Ind	9	piece	Cloth of Assize	0	0	0	0
		5	piece	Welsh *Cloth*	5	0	0	0
Thomas Yeate	Ind	6	piece	Welsh *Cloth*	6	0	0	0
John Hall	Ind	24	piece	Cloth of Assize	0	0	0	0
John Hall	Ind	20	piece	Welsh *Cloth*, Dozen Strait	4	4	2	0
John Shipman	Ind	9	piece	Cloth of Assize	0	0	0	0
		7.33	piece	Welsh *Cloth*	7	6	8	0
John Ware	Ind	5	piece	Cloth of Assize	0	0	0	0
		7.33	piece	Welsh *Cloth*	7	6	8	0
Robert Avyntre	Ind	15	piece	Cloth of Assize	0	0	0	0
John Kyng	Ind	25	piece	Cloth of Assize	0	0	0	0
		12	piece	Cloth of Assize, Kersey	0	0	0	0
Thomas Donell	Ind	9	piece	Cloth of Assize	0	0	0	0
William Avyntre	Ind	12	piece	Cloth of Assize	0	0	0	0
Thomas Dale	Ind	14	piece	Cloth of Assize	0	0	0	0
George Hall	Ind	12	piece	Cloth of Assize	0	0	0	0
		5	piece	Welsh *Cloth*	5	0	0	0
Andrew Palmer	Ind	1	piece	Welsh *Cloth*	0	20	0	0

Bata Mare of Bristol, Thomas Nongull master, to Ireland, *21st February 1517*

Thomas Nongull	Ind	7	wey	Beans	5	16	8	0

Navicula Mawdelen of Errenteria, John Surre master, to Spain, *21st February 1517*

Roger Dawes	Ind	3	wey	Beans	0	50	0	0
John Shipman, Roger Dawes & William Woseley	Ind	50	wey	Beans	41	13	4	0
William Rowley	Ind	8	C	Fish, Hake	4	0	0	0
		38	piece	Cloth of Assize	0	0	0	0
John Martinus	Alien	10	C	Fish, Hake	5	0	0	0
Thomas Hawkyne	Ind	10	piece	Cloth of Assize	0	0	0	0
Thomas Dale	Ind	42	piece	Cloth of Assize	0	0	0	0
William Woseley	Ind	28	piece	Cloth of Assize	0	0	0	0
John Shipman	Ind	16	piece	Cloth of Assize	0	0	0	0
John Ward	Ind	12	piece	Cloth of Assize	0	0	0	0
William Shipman	Ind	11	piece	Cloth of Assize	0	0	0	0

Navicula Marget of Bristol, John Stevyns master, to Lisbon, *21st February 1517*

Nicholas Browne	Ind	38	piece	Cloth of Assize	0	0	0	0
Thomas Maileyeard	Ind	20	piece	Welsh *Cloth*	20	0	0	0
William Sewell	Ind	3	piece	Cloth of Assize	0	0	0	0

Bata John Baptist of Newnham, Richard File master, from Cardiff, 23rd February 1517

Leonard Osburne	Ind	1	tun	Wine	0	0	0	0

Merchant name	Origin	Qty	Unit	Commodity	£	s.	d.	f.

Bata Mighell of Milford Haven, Thomas Hioches master, from Ireland, 23rd February 1517

Merchant name	Origin	Qty	Unit	Commodity	£	s.	d.	f.
Thomas *Hioches*	Ind	16.5	barrel	Fish, Herring White	4	2	6	0
		3	stone	Wool, Irish	0	8	0	0

Bata Trynyte of Chepstow, William Heyne master, *from Chepstow*, 25rd February 1517

Merchant name	Origin	Qty	Unit	Commodity	£	s.	d.	f.
Nicholas Browne	Ind	5	tun	Wine	0	0	0	0
John Palmer	Ind	1	hogshead	Wine	0	0	0	0
John Welshof	Ind	24	C	Woad, Azores	8	0	0	0

Bata Jamys of Milford Haven, John Webbe master, from Ireland, 26th February 1517

Merchant name	Origin	Qty	Unit	Commodity	£	s.	d.	f.
John Webbe	Ind	9	barrel	Fish, Herring White	0	45	0	0
		6.5	C	Fish, Hake	3	5	0	0

Navicula Fyaker of Penmarch, Michael de Wyke master, to Brittany, *26th February 1517*

Merchant name	Origin	Qty	Unit	Commodity	£	s.	d.	f.
Michael *de Wyke*	Alien	3.75	tun	Lime	0	9	4	0

Bata Mare of Milford Haven, Thomas Howell master, from Ireland, 2nd March 1517

Merchant name	Origin	Qty	Unit	Commodity	£	s.	d.	f.
Thomas *Hawell*	Ind	20	barrel	Fish, Herring White	5	0	0	0
		17	C	Fish, Hake	8	10	0	0
		4	burden	Fish, Salted	0	16	8	0
Mathew Hop	Ind	4	barrel	Fish, Herring White	0	20	0	0

Navicula Veronica of Hondarribia, Stephen Primat master, from Sanlúcar de Barrameda, *2nd March 1517*

Merchant name	Origin	Qty	Unit	Commodity	£	s.	d.	f.
Thomas Maileyeard (of London)	Ind	74.5	tun	Wine	0	0	0	0
		25	C	Alum	12	10	0	0
		10.5	ton	Fruit	21	0	0	0
		34	C	Almonds	23	0	0	0
William Woseley	Ind	2	ton	Fruit	4	0	0	0
Thomas Lawden	Ind	5.5	C	Fish, Hake	0	55	0	0
		3	dicker	Skins, Salted	0	40	0	0

Bata Marget of Milford Haven, Henry Willis master, from Ireland, 2nd March 1517

Merchant name	Origin	Qty	Unit	Commodity	£	s.	d.	f.
Henry Willis	Ind	24	barrel	Fish, Herring White	6	0	0	0
		15	C	Fish, Hake	7	10	0	0

Bata Kerik of Milford Haven, William Wade master, to Ireland, *2nd March 1517*

Merchant name	Origin	Qty	Unit	Commodity	£	s.	d.	f.
Richard Arthur	Ind	8	wey	Beans	6	13	4	0
John Walshe	Ind	8	wey	Beans	6	13	4	0
		2	lb	Silk, Worked	0	26	8	0
		1	C	Battery	0	40	0	0
		6	dozen	*Precars*	0	2	0	0
Nicholas Harrys	Ind	0.5	piece	Cloth of Assize	0	0	0	0

Merchant name	Origin	Qty	Unit	Commodity	£	s.	d.	f.
		30.5	lb	Silk, Worked	20	3	4	0
		12	lb	Saffron	6	0	0	0
		8	gross	Points	0	8	0	0
		12	lb	*Pilus Tinctus*	0	4	0	0
Robert Morow	Ind	2	piece	Cloth of Assize	0	0	0	0
		14	lb	Silk, Worked	9	6	8	0
		14	lb	Saffron	7	0	0	0
		30	lb	*Pilus Tinctus*	0	10	0	0
		6	gross	Points	0	6	0	0
		1	gross	Knives	0	6	8	0
		0.5	gross	Cutts	0	0	20	0
John Keny	Ind	3	lb	Silk, Worked	0	40	0	0
		4	lb	Saffron	0	40	0	0

Bata St Mare of Milford Haven, Richard Rustan master, to Ireland, *2nd March 1517*

Richard Arthur	Ind	9	wey	Beans	7	10	0	0
John Walshe	Ind	9	wey	Beans	7	10	0	0

Navicula Santa Maria of Errenteria, John Marting master, from Sanlúcar de Barrameda, 5th March 1517

John Shipman	Ind	1.5	tun	Wine	0	0	0	0
		1.5	tun	Oil, *Olive*	6	0	0	0
		2.5	C	*Smigmates*	0	25	0	0
Robert Avyntre	Ind	7	tun	Wine	0	0	0	0
		2	cashe	Sugar	4	0	0	0
William Bowe	Ind	12	tun	Wine	0	0	0	0
John Kyng	Ind	5.5	tun	Wine	0	0	0	0
John Mathew	Ind	1	pipe	Oil, *Olive*	0	40	0	0
Humphrey Browne	Ind	1.75	tun	Wine	0	0	0	0
Nicholas Gay	Ind	2.25	tun	Wine	0	0	0	0
Clement Yonge	Ind	2.25	tun	Wine	0	0	0	0
Robert Dane	Ind	3.25	tun	Wine	0	0	0	0
Thomas Donell	Ind	3	tun	Wine	0	0	0	0
Alice Davis	Ind	1.5	tun	Wine	0	0	0	0
Robert Pers	Ind	3.25	tun	Wine	0	0	0	0
Thomas Bilford	Ind	1	tun	Oil, *Olive*	4	0	0	0
		1.75	tun	Wine	0	0	0	0
John Rowland	Ind	7	tun	Wine	0	0	0	0
Nicholas Browne	Ind	2.25	tun	Wine	0	0	0	0
William Shipman	Ind	1	pipe	Wine	0	0	0	0
		1	pipe	Oil, *Olive*	0	40	0	0
Henry Wasewole	Ind	1	pipe	Wine	0	0	0	0
		4.25	tun	Oil, *Olive*	17	0	0	0
Richard Arthur	Ind	3	tun	Wine	0	0	0	0
Robert Thorne	Ind	30	C	Orchil	20	0	0	0
John Wyot	Ind	1	tun	Wine	0	0	0	0
John Hall	Ind	1	tun	Wine	0	0	0	0
John Griffand	Ind	1	tun	Wine	0	0	0	0
John Vaghan	Ind	8	tun	Wine	0	0	0	0
Thomas Palmer	Ind	1	pipe	Wine	0	0	0	0

Merchant name	Origin	Qty	Unit	Commodity	£	s.	d.	f.
Illegible Illegible	Ind	6.5	tun	Wine	0	0	0	0

Bata Mare of Tewkesbury, John Whitney master, from Chepstow, 5th March 1517

John Bullyughin	Ind	8	C	Woad, Azores	0	53	4	0
		2	tun	Wine	0	0	0	0

Bata Mare of Milford Haven, Thomas Gefferes master, from Ireland, 5th March 1517

Thomas Gefferes	Ind	16.5	barrel	Fish, Herring White	4	2	6	0
		18	C	Fish, Hake	9	0	0	0
		3.5	C	Fish, Salted	3	10	0	0

Bata Andrew of Bewdley, Peter Nethaway from Chepstow, 5th March 1517

Gratien de la Place	Alien	9.5	tun	Wine	0	0	0	0

Bata Jamys of Tewkesbury, John Andrew master, from Chepstow, 5th March 1517

John Bullyughin	Ind	7.5	tun	Wine	0	0	0	0

Bata Nicholas of Tewkesbury, William Bradford master, from Chepstow, 5th March 1517

Richard Bocher	Ind	9.5	tun	Wine	0	0	0	0

Bata George of Bristol, John Harrys master, from Carmarthen, 5th March 1517

Howell Baker	Ind	1	tun	Wine	0	0	0	0

Navicula Laurence of Penmarch, James Monyk master, from Bordeaux, 7th March 1517

John Sparchford	Ind	23.25	tun	Wine	0	0	0	0
		20	bale	Woad	25	0	0	0
Robert Paphin	Ind	12.9	tun	Wine	0	0	0	0
Roger Monouse	Ind	2.25	tun	Wine	0	0	0	0
Auger de Noga	Alien	2.75	tun	Wine	0	0	0	0
Gilbert Cogan	Ind	3.75	tun	Wine	0	0	0	0
James Monyke	Alien	1	hogshead	Wine	0	0	0	0
		0.875	ton	Pitch and Rosin	0	23	4	0
		4	piece	Breton Linen *Cloth*	0	20	0	0
Richard Hoby	Ind	2	tun	Wine	0	0	0	0

Bata Nicholas of Wexford, John Roche master, from Ireland, 7th March 1517

Nicholas Turnor	Ind	6	pipe	Fish, Salmon	9	0	0	0
		8	barrel	Fish, Herring White	0	40	0	0
		30	mease	Fish, Herring Red	7	10	0	0
		8	C	Fish, Hake	4	0	0	0
		0.5	barell	Fish, Eels	0	6	8	0
		4	C	Skins, Sheep	0	40	0	0
		6	piece	Mantles	0	20	0	0

Merchant name	Origin	Qty	Unit	Commodity	£	s.	d.	f.

Bata Mare Redcliffe of Bristol, Richard Bonghton master, to Ireland, 7th March 1517

Merchant name	Origin	Qty	Unit	Commodity	£	s.	d.	f.
Nicholas Browne	Ind	3	piece	Cloth of Assize	0	0	0	0
		6	wey	Beans	5	0	0	0
		7	tun	Wine, Corrupt	10	10	0	0

Bata Jhesus of Wexford, Nicholas Stafford master, from Ireland, 7th March 1517

Merchant name	Origin	Qty	Unit	Commodity	£	s.	d.	f.
Nicholas Stafford	Ind	10	mease	Fish, Herring Red	0	50	0	0
		3	C	Fish, Hake	0	30	0	0
		20	mease	Fish, Herring Red	5	0	0	0
		12	barrel	Fish, Herring White	3	0	0	0
		3	C	Fish, Hake	0	30	0	0
		2	barell	Fish, Eels	0	26	8	0
		3	piece	Mantles	0	10	0	0
		0.5	C	Skins, Sheep	0	5	0	0
Thomas Stafford	Ind	1.5	C	Fish, Hake	0	15	0	0
		10	mease	Fish, Herring Red	0	50	0	0
		4	C	Skins, Sheep (no wool)	0	40	0	0

Bata Trinite of Kinsale, John Roche master, from Ireland, 7th March 1517

Merchant name	Origin	Qty	Unit	Commodity	£	s.	d.	f.
John Roche	Ind	3	M	Fish, Hake	15	0	0	0
		4	C	Fish, Salted	4	0	0	0

Bata Sonday of Wexford, Nicholas Vele master, from Ireland, 7th March 1517

Merchant name	Origin	Qty	Unit	Commodity	£	s.	d.	f.
Patrick Turnor	Ind	20	mease	Fish, Herring Red	5	0	0	0
		8	barrel	Fish, Herring White	0	40	0	0
		2	pipe	Fish, Salmon	3	0	0	0
		4	C	Fish, Hake	0	40	0	0
		12	piece	Mantles	0	40	0	0
		1	burden	Fish, Salted	0	4	2	0

Bata Jhesus of Kinsale, Jordan Roche master, from Ireland, 7th March 1517

Merchant name	Origin	Qty	Unit	Commodity	£	s.	d.	f.
Jordan Roche	Ind	8	C	Fish, Hake	4	0	0	0
		5	burden	Fish, Salted	0	20	10	0
William Nangull	Ind	23	C	Fish, Hake	11	10	0	0
		1	pipe	Fish, Salmon	0	30	0	0
		1	barrel	Fish, Herring White	0	5	0	0
		1	hogshead	Fish, Sardines	0	5	0	0
		2	burden	Fish, Salted	0	8	4	0
Peter Roche	Ind	7.5	C	Fish, Hake	3	15	0	0
		2	burden	Fish, Salted	0	8	4	0
Adam Roche	Ind	10	C	Fish, Hake	5	0	0	0
		1.5	burden	Fish, Salted	0	6	3	0
Edward Roche	Ind	10	C	Fish, Hake	5	0	0	0
		0.5	C	Wool, Flocks	0	2	6	0
		1.5	barell	Fish, Sardines	0	3	4	0
		24	piece	Skins, Sheep	0	2	0	0
		1	burden	Fish, Salted	0	4	2	0

Merchant name	Origin	Qty	Unit	Commodity	£	s.	d.	f.
Tege Skynn	Ind	9.5	C	Fish, Hake	4	15	0	0
		1	quart	Fish, Salted	0	5	0	0
William Fleming	Ind	4.5	C	Fish, Hake	0	45	0	0
		0.5	burden	Fish, Salted	0	2	1	0

Bata Mare of Milford Haven, William Rynyshe master, from Ireland, 9th March 1517

William Rynyshe	Ind	4	barrel	Fish, Herring White	0	20	0	0
		1	C	Fish, Hake	0	10	0	0

Bata Jamys of Berkeley, Thomas Sonoger master, from Ireland, 9th March 1517

John Rogers	Ind	7	C	Fish, Hake	6	0	0	0
		4	burden	Fish, Salted	0	16	8	0
		2	piece	Mantles	0	6	8	0
		3	C	Rosin	0	4	0	0
John Amidas?	Ind	5.5	pipe	Fish, Salmon	8	5	0	0
		8.5	C	Fish, Hake	4	5	0	0
		1.5	C	Skins, Sheep	0	15	0	0
Oliver Arthur	Ind	1	pipe	Fish, Salmon	0	30	0	0
Thomas Ley	Ind	4	C	Skins, Sheep	0	40	0	0
		2	C	Fish, Hake	0	20	0	0

Navicula Santa Maria of Punto Candalaria, Rodrigo de Arezate master, from Lisbon, 9th March 1517

John Shipman	Ind	1	tun	Wine	0	0	0	0
Robert Avyntre	Ind	1	tun	Wine	0	0	0	0
		1	pipe	Oil, Olive	0	40	0	0
William Avyntre	Ind	1	tun	Wine	0	0	0	0
John Kyng	Ind	1	pipe	Oil, Olive	0	40	0	0
Robert Pers	Ind	1.75	tun	Wine	0	0	0	0
William Bowe	Ind	3.25	tun	Wine	0	0	0	0
Thomas Jonys	Ind	3	tun	Oil, Olive	12	0	0	0
Thomas Jonys	Ind	9.25	tun	Wine	0	0	0	0
John Rayment	Ind	4.5	tun	Wine	0	0	0	0
		1	pipe	Oil, Olive	0	40	0	0
		2.25	C	Wax	4	10	0	0
		3.125	C	Pepper	15	14	0	0
Simon Andrews	Ind	10.75	tun	Wine	0	0	0	0
		114	lb	Pepper	5	14	0	0
		1	quart	Ginger	0	42	0	0
		1.375	C	Kermes	4	3	4	0
John Hollewey	Ind	1	tun	Wine	0	0	0	0
John Thomas	Ind	1	pipe	Wine	0	0	0	0
David Philip	Ind	96	lb	Pepper	4	16	0	0
John Auger	Alien	0.5	C	Pepper	0	50	0	0
Domingus Deverrus	Alien	4.5	ton	Fruit	9	0	0	0
Francis Marting	Alien	11	tun	Wine	0	0	0	0
John Coke	Alien	1.75	tun	Wine	0	0	0	0
Gonsalo Torroka	Alien	5.5	tun	Wine	0	0	0	0
		6	M	Orchil	40	0	0	0

Merchant name	Origin	Qty	Unit	Commodity	£	s.	d.	f.
John Palmer	Ind	1	tun	Wine	0	0	0	0
		2	C	Marmalade	0	26	8	0
Francis Marting	Alien	1.5	C	Comfits	0	56	0	0
		201	lb	Marmalade (in box)	0	57	0	0
Thomas Penson	Ind	1	hogshead	Wine	0	0	0	0
William Cardmaker	Ind	0.5	C	Marmalade	0	6	8	0

Bata Mare of Wexford, Nicholas Ffrenshe master, from Ireland, _9th March 1517_

Merchant name	Origin	Qty	Unit	Commodity	£	s.	d.	f.
John Mason	Ind	35	mease	Fish, Herring Red	8	15	0	0
		8	barrel	Fish, Herring White	0	40	0	0
		1	pipe	Fish, Salmon	0	30	0	0
		6	C	Fish, Hake	3	0	0	0
		7	C	Skins, Sheep	3	10	0	0
		0.5	C	Skins, Lamb	0	3	4	0
		12	piece	Mantles	0	40	0	0

Bata Kateryn of Youghal, Dennis Griffith master, from Ireland, _9th March 1517_

Merchant name	Origin	Qty	Unit	Commodity	£	s.	d.	f.
Dennis Griffith	Ind	11.5	C	Fish, Hake	5	15	0	0
		1.5	burden	Fish, Salted	0	6	3	0
		5	stone	Wool, Flocks	0	2	1	0
		2	C	Skins, Sheep	0	20	0	0
		1	C	Skins, Lamb	0	6	8	0
Nicholas _Christ_ofur	Ind	2.5	C	Fish, Hake	0	25	0	0
		1.75	pipe	Fish, Salmon	0	52	6	0
		4	C	Skins, Sheep	0	40	0	0
		20	piece	Skins, Lamb	0	0	20	0
		3	piece	Mantles	0	10	0	0
		1	piece	Skins, Otter	0	0	5	0
Robert Fforest	Ind	4	C	Fish, Hake	0	40	0	0
		9.5	C	Skins, Sheep	4	15	0	0
		1.25	burden	Fish, Salted	0	5	2	0
		4	piece	Mantles	0	13	4	0
Maurice Colen	Ind	17.5	C	Fish, Hake	8	15	0	0
		5	burden	Fish, Salted	0	20	10	0
		12	C	Skins, Sheep	6	0	0	0
		1.75	C	Skins, Lamb	0	11	8	0
		7	piece	Mantles	0	23	4	0
John Dye	Ind	4	pipe	Fish, Salmon	6	0	0	0
		2	C	Skins, Sheep	0	20	0	0
		4	C	Fish, Hake	0	40	0	0
Thomas Ley	Ind	2	C	Fish, Hake	0	20	0	0
		1.5	C	Skins, Sheep	0	15	0	0

Bata George of Wexford, Robert Roche master, from Ireland, _9th March 1517_

Merchant name	Origin	Qty	Unit	Commodity	£	s.	d.	f.
John Waden	Ind	11	barrel	Fish, Herring White	0	55	0	0
		20	mease	Fish, Herring Red	5	0	0	0
		4	C	Fish, Hake	0	40	0	0
		20	piece	Mantles	3	6	8	0

Merchant name	Origin	Qty	Unit	Commodity	£	s.	d.	f.
Bata Patrike of Youghal, Maurice Heron master, from Ireland, *9th March 1517*								
Maurice Heron	Ind	16	C	Fish, Hake	8	0	0	0
		1	burden	Fish, Salted	0	4	2	0
Oliver Arthur	Ind	13	pipe	Fish, Salmon	19	10	0	0
		0.75	C	Fish, Hake	0	7	6	0
		36	piece	Fish, Salted	0	6	0	0
		8	C	Skins, Sheep	4	0	0	0
John Bluet	Ind	3	pipe	Fish, Salmon	4	10	0	0
		3	C	Skins, Sheep	0	30	0	0
		5	C	Fish, Hake	0	50	0	0
		40	piece	Fish, Salted	0	6	8	0
John Davy	Ind	16	C	Fish, Hake	8	0	0	0
		1	pipe	Fish, Salmon	0	30	0	0
		2	burden	Fish, Salted	0	8	4	0
Robert Forest	Ind	2.25	pipe	Fish, Salmon	3	7	6	0
		7.5	C	Fish, Hake	3	15	0	0
		3.5	C	Skins, Sheep	0	35	0	0
Thomas Ley	Ind	4	C	Fish, Hake	0	40	0	0
Robert Avyntre	Ind	3	pipe	Fish, Salmon	4	10	0	0
Thomas Donell	Ind	3	pipe	Fish, Salmon	4	10	0	0
Bata Makerell of Wexford, John Code master, from Ireland, *9th March 1517*								
Robert Canton	Ind	10	mease	Fish, Herring Red	0	50	0	0
		7	barrel	Fish, Herring White	0	35	0	0
		7	C	Fish, Hake	3	10	0	0
		0.5	C	Fish, Salted	0	10	0	0
		8	piece	Mantles	0	26	8	0
		3	C	Skins, Sheep	0	30	0	0
Bata Anne of Paimpol, Nicholas Jake master, from Brittany, *9th March 1517*								
John Boborry	Alien	13	tun	Wine, of Anngew	0	0	0	0
		4	C	Breton Linen *Cloth*	0	40	0	0
Bata Patryk of Youghal, Maurice Fynne master, from Ireland, *9th March 1517*								
Maurice Fynne	Ind	10	C	Fish, Hake	5	0	0	0
		1	burden	Fish, Salted	0	4	2	0
William Barry	Ind	20	C	Fish, Hake	10	0	0	0
		2	burden	Fish, Salted	0	8	4	0
William Austyn	Ind	21	C	Fish, Hake	10	10	0	0
		3	burden	Fish, Salted	0	12	6	0
		18	piece	Mantles	3	0	0	0
		2	C	Skins, Sheep	0	20	0	0
		0.5	pipe	Fish, Salmon	0	15	0	0
Thomas Ley	Ind	6	C	Skins, Sheep	3	0	0	0
Robert Avyntre	Ind	5.5	pipe	Fish, Salmon	8	5	0	0
Thomas Donell	Ind	5.5	pipe	Fish, Salmon	8	5	0	0

Merchant name	Origin	Qty	Unit	Commodity	£	s.	d.	f.

Bata Fawken of Waterford, William Rothe master, from Ireland, 9th March 1517

Merchant name	Origin	Qty	Unit	Commodity	£	s.	d.	f.
William Rothe	Ind	30	piece	Fish, Salted	0	5	0	0
Thomas Shirlok	Ind	9.5	C	Fish, Hake	4	15	0	0
		6.75	pipe	Fish, Salmon	10	2	6	0
		7.5	C	Skins, Sheep	3	15	0	0
		7	barrel	Fish, Herring White	0	35	0	0
		1.33	C	Fish, Salted	0	26	8	0
		4	dicker	Skins, Salted	0	53	4	0
Walter Wodlok	Ind	4	piece	Mantles	0	13	4	0
Robert Clere	Ind	3.5	C	Fish, Hake	0	35	0	0
		6.5	C	Skins, Sheep	3	5	0	0
		50	piece	Fish, Salted	0	8	4	0
		0.5	pipe	Fish, Salmon	0	15	0	0
		16	piece	Mantles	0	53	4	0
		4	stone	Wool, Flocks	0	0	20	0
		2	piece	Skins, Fox	0	0	4	0
		18	piece	Skins, Lamb	0	0	20	0
Thomas Awnell	Ind	9	C	Skins, Sheep	4	10	0	0
		5	piece	Mantles	0	16	8	0
		2	C	Fish, Hake	0	20	0	0
		30	piece	Fish, Salted	0	5	0	0
Edmund Maydoll	Ind	30	piece	Fish, Salted	0	5	0	0
		0.5	C	Fish, Hake	0	5	0	0
		4	piece	Mantles	0	13	4	0

Bata Mawdlen of Cork, John White master, from Ireland, 9th March 1517

Merchant name	Origin	Qty	Unit	Commodity	£	s.	d.	f.
John Drady	Ind	12	barrel	Fish, Herring White	3	0	0	0
		7	C	Fish, Hake	3	10	0	0
		3	C	Skins, Sheep	0	30	0	0
		0.75	pipe	Fish, Salmon	0	22	6	0
		1	C	Mutton Fat	0	6	8	0
John White	Ind	3	C	Fish, Hake	0	30	0	0
		2	barrel	Fish, Herring White	0	10	0	0
		0.5	pipe	Fish, Salmon	0	15	0	0
		5	piece	Mantles	0	16	8	0
Robert Barrett	Ind	9	barrel	Fish, Herring White	0	45	0	0
		1	barrel	Mutton Fat	0	13	4	0
		4	C	Skins, Sheep	0	40	0	0
		4	pipe	Fish, Salmon	6	0	0	0
		2	C	Fish, Hake	0	20	0	0
James Roche	Ind	16	C	Skins, Sheep	8	0	0	0
		1.5	pipe	Fish, Salmon	0	45	0	0
		1	C	Fish, Hake	0	10	0	0
		7	barrel	Fish, Herring White	0	35	0	0
		5	piece	Mantles	0	16	8	0
		1	kilderkin	*Eels*, Conger	0	3	4	0
William Mirry	Ind	12	barrel	Fish, Herring White	3	0	0	0
		1.5	pipe	Fish, Salmon	0	45	0	0
		7	C	Fish, Hake	3	10	0	0
		2	burden	Fish, Salted	0	8	4	0

Merchant name	Origin	Qty	Unit	Commodity	£	s.	d.	f.
		1	barrel	Mutton Fat	0	13	4	0
		4	C	Skins, Sheep	0	40	0	0
		40	stone	Wool, Flocks	0	16	8	0
		2	piece	Mantles	0	6	8	0

Bata Kateryn of Kinsale, William Dale master, from Ireland, *9th March 1517*

Merchant name	Origin	Qty	Unit	Commodity	£	s.	d.	f.
Philip Leman	Ind	10	C	Fish, Hake	5	0	0	0
Philip Brynne	Ind	10	C	Fish, Hake	5	0	0	0
Leonard Roche	Ind	12.5	C	Fish, Hake	6	5	0	0
		1	C	Fish, Salted	0	20	0	0
Maurice Keryn	Ind	2	pipe	Fish, Salmon	3	0	0	0
		3	C	Fish, Hake	0	30	0	0
		1	burden	Fish, Salted	0	4	2	0
Edmund Roche	Ind	5	C	Fish, Hake	0	50	0	0
William Yonge	Ind	8	C	Fish, Hake	4	0	0	0
		80	piece	Fish, Salted	0	13	4	0
		2.5	barrel	Fish, Herring White	0	12	6	0
Edmund Denys	Ind	6	C	Fish, Hake	3	0	0	0
		80	piece	Fish, Salted	0	13	4	0
Edward Roche	Ind	3	C	Fish, Hake	0	30	0	0
		30	piece	Fish, Salted	0	5	0	0

Bata Kateryn of Youghal, Patrick Browne master, from Ireland, *9th March 1517*

Merchant name	Origin	Qty	Unit	Commodity	£	s.	d.	f.
William Compton	Ind	36	C	Fish, Hake	18	0	0	0
		80	piece	Fish, Salted	0	13	4	0
		1	barrel	Fish, Herring White	0	5	0	0
		0.5	pipe	Fish, Salmon	0	15	0	0
		4	piece	Mantles	0	13	4	0
		0.75	tun	Wine	0	0	0	0

Bata George of Waterford, Thomas Marys master, from Ireland, *9th March 1517*

Merchant name	Origin	Qty	Unit	Commodity	£	s.	d.	f.
Thomas *Marys*	Ind	2.5	C	Fish, Hake	0	25	0	0
		40	piece	Fish, Salted	0	6	8	0
		6	piece	Mantles	0	20	0	0
Patrick Fitzjohn	Ind	6	barrel	Fish, Herring White	0	30	0	0
		3.5	C	Fish, Hake	0	35	0	0
		40	piece	Fish, Salted	0	6	8	0
		6	piece	Mantles	0	20	0	0
Richard Denys	Ind	3	C	Fish, Hake	0	30	0	0
		24	piece	Fish, Salted	0	4	2	0
		5	piece	Mantles	0	16	8	0
		0.5	C	Skins, Sheep	0	5	0	0
Richard Malrony	Ind	2.5	C	Fish, Hake	0	25	0	0
		1.5	C	Skins, Sheep	0	15	0	0
		10	piece	Mantles	0	33	4	0
		0.5	pipe	Fish, Salmon	0	15	0	0
Thomas Shirlok	Ind	13	pipe	Fish, Salmon	19	10	0	0
		13	barrel	Fish, Herring White	3	10	0	0
	1 barell &1 virkin			Fish, Eels	0	16	8	0

Merchant name	Origin	Qty	Unit	Commodity	£	s.	d.	f.
		7	C	Skins, Sheep	3	10	0	0
		3.5	C	Fish, Hake	0	35	0	0
		13	piece	Mantles	0	43	4	0
		30	piece	Fish, Salted	0	5	0	0
Philip Tallow	Ind	4	piece	Mantles	0	13	4	0
Thomas Yonge	Ind	10	piece	Mantles	0	33	4	0
		3	C	Skins, Sheep	0	30	0	0
		1	virkin	Fish, Salmon	0	7	6	0
Patrick Combford	Ind	9	pipe	Fish, Salmon	13	10	0	0
		11.5	C	Fish, Hake	5	15	0	0
		7.5	C	Skins, Sheep	3	15	0	0
		5	barrel	Fish, Herring White	0	25	0	0
		40	piece	Fish, Salted	0	6	8	0
		20	piece	Mantles	3	6	8	0
		80	piece	Skins, Lamb	0	5	0	0

Bata Patrik of Youghal, Maurice Russell master, from Ireland, *9th March 1517*

Merchant name	Origin	Qty	Unit	Commodity	£	s.	d.	f.
Maurice Russell	Ind	56	C	Fish, Hake	28	0	0	0
		2	burden	Fish, Salted	0	8	4	0
		5	piece	Mantles	0	16	8	0
Patrick Arthur	Ind	7	C	Fish, Hake	3	10	0	0
		1	pipe	Fish, Salmon	0	30	0	0
		7	C	Skins, Sheep	3	10	0	0
		6	piece	Skins, Fox	0	0	12	0
		1	pipe	Wine	0	0	0	0
John Amidas?	Ind	7.5	C	Skins, Sheep	3	15	0	0
Nicholas Bennett	Ind	1	virkin	Fish, Salmon	0	7	6	0
Nicholas Rowland	Ind	2.5	pipe	Fish, Salmon	3	15	0	0
		6	C	Fish, Hake	3	0	0	0

Navicula Seint Sebastian, Port Unknown, Sebastian de Dawen master, from Andalusia, *9th March 1517*

Merchant name	Origin	Qty	Unit	Commodity	£	s.	d.	f.
Thomas Lawden of London	Ind	70.5	tun	Wine	0	0	0	0
		150	piece	Skins, Salted	10	0	0	0
		0.25	ton	Fruit	0	10	0	0
		10	barrel	Pitch and Tar	0	33	4	0
Thomas Maileyeard of London	Ind	28	tun	Wine	0	0	0	0
		8	M	Orchil	53	6	8	0
John Hall	Ind	66	piece	Camlet *Cloth*	44	0	0	0
Jonof? de la Sersa	Alien	1	pipe	Wine	0	0	0	0

Bata Mare of Bristol, Thomas Nongull master, from Ireland, *9th March 1517*

Merchant name	Origin	Qty	Unit	Commodity	£	s.	d.	f.
Thomas *Nongull*	Ind	10	pipe	Fish, Salmon	15	0	0	0
		16	C	Fish, Hake	8	0	0	0
		3	burden	Fish, Salted	0	12	6	0
		3	M	Skins, Sheep	15	0	0	0
		3	barrel	Fish, Herring White	0	15	0	0

Merchant name	Origin	Qty	Unit	Commodity	£	s.	d.	f.
		8	stone	Wool, Flocks	0	3	4	0
		8	piece	Mantles	0	26	8	0
James Leche	Ind	5	C	Fish, Hake	0	50	0	0
		80	piece	Fish, Salted	0	13	4	0
		0.5	C	Skins, Sheep	0	5	0	0
		8	piece	Mantles	0	26	8	0
Edmund Mehan	Ind	50	piece	Mantles	8	6	8	0
		3	quart	Skins, Sheep	0	7	6	0

Bata Nicholas of Youghal, John Grant master, from Ireland, *9th March 1517*

Merchant name	Origin	Qty	Unit	Commodity	£	s.	d.	f.
John Grant	Ind	13.5	C	Fish, Hake	6	15	0	0
		0.5	burden	Fish, Salted	0	2	1	0
John Clowan	Ind	20	C	Fish, Hake	10	0	0	0
		1	barrel	Fish, Herring White	0	5	0	0
		2	burden	Fish, Salted	0	8	4	0
Robert Sarset	Ind	12	C	Fish, Hake	6	0	0	0
John Yuak	Ind	5.5	C	Skins, Sheep	0	55	0	0
		1.25	pipe	Fish, Salmon	0	37	6	0
		0.5	burden	Fish, Salted	0	2	1	0
Nicholas Rowley	Ind	9.5	C	Fish, Hake	4	15	0	0
		1	burden	Fish, Salted	0	4	2	0
		2	pipe	Fish, Salmon	3	0	0	0
		2	C	Skins, Sheep	0	20	0	0
Richard Malroney	Ind	9	C	Skins, Sheep	4	10	0	0
		2	pipe	Fish, Salmon	3	0	0	0
		4	C	Fish, Hake	0	40	0	0
Nicholas Benet	Ind	20	C	Fish, Hake	10	0	0	0
		4	pipe	Fish, Salmon	6	0	0	0
		8.5	C	Skins, Sheep	4	5	0	0
		50	piece	Fish, Salted	0	8	4	0
		2	piece	Mantles	0	6	8	0
Thomas Ley	Ind	2.5	pipe	Fish, Salmon	3	15	0	0

Bata Savior of New Ross, Thomas Shenill master, from Ireland, *9th March 1517*

Merchant name	Origin	Qty	Unit	Commodity	£	s.	d.	f.
Thomas *Shenill*	Ind	40	piece	Fish, Salted	0	6	8	0
		2	piece	Mantles	0	6	8	0
Patrick Burna	Ind	14.5	C	Fish, Hake	7	5	0	0
		70	stone	Wool, Irish	9	6	8	0
		7	stone	Wool, Flocks	0	2	11	0
		2	piece	Mantles	0	6	8	0
Philip Bowes	Ind	2.5	pipe	Fish, Salmon	3	15	0	0
		1	C	Fish, Hake	0	10	0	0
		20	piece	Fish, Salted	0	3	4	0
		1.25	C	Skins, Sheep	0	12	6	0
		8	piece	Mantles	0	26	8	0
Richard Browne	Ind	1	C	Skins, Sheep	0	10	0	0
		1	piece	Mantles	0	3	4	0
William Mathewe	Ind	1.5	C	Skins, Sheep	0	15	0	0
		6	stone	Wool, Irish	0	16	0	0
		4	stone	Wool, Flocks	0	0	20	0

Merchant name	Origin	Qty	Unit	Commodity	£	s.	d.	f.
Nicholas Gregory	Ind	7.5	C	Skins, Sheep	3	15	0	0
Thomas *Nongull*	Ind	2.5	C	Skins, Sheep	0	25	0	0

Bata Sonday of Cork, William Barry master, from Ireland, *9th March 1517*

Merchant name	Origin	Qty	Unit	Commodity	£	s.	d.	f.
William *Barry*	Ind	3	last	Fish, Herring White	9	0	0	0
		7	C	Fish, Hake	3	10	0	0
Robert Verdon	Ind	39	barrel	Fish, Herring White	9	15	0	0
		8	C	Fish, Hake	4	0	0	0
		0.5	C	Ship-Boards	0	10	0	0
		4	piece	Mantles	0	13	4	0
		1	barrel	Fish, Eels	0	13	4	0
		1	virkin	Fish, Salmon	0	7	6	0

Bata Patrik of Cork, Robert Broder master, from Ireland, *9th March 1517*

Merchant name	Origin	Qty	Unit	Commodity	£	s.	d.	f.
William Millan	Ind	10	C	Fish, Hake	5	0	0	0
		1	C	Ship-Boards	0	20	0	0
		6	barrel	Fish, Herring White	0	30	0	0
		6	piece	Mantles	0	20	0	0
		1	pipe	Wine	0	0	0	0
Dennis Mortill	Ind	5	C	Fish, Hake	0	50	0	0
		5.5	barrel	Fish, Herring White	0	27	6	0
		2	pipe	Fish, Salmon	3	0	0	0

Bata Nicholas of Waterford, Robert Keny master, from Ireland, *9th March 1517*

Merchant name	Origin	Qty	Unit	Commodity	£	s.	d.	f.
Robert Beary	Ind	0.5	pipe	Fish, Salmon	0	15	0	0
		2	barrel	Fish, Herring White	0	10	0	0
		3	piece	Mantles	0	10	0	0
		1	C	Fish, Hake	0	10	0	0
Robert Strange	Ind	7	pipe	Fish, Salmon	10	10	0	0
		6	C	Fish, Hake	3	0	0	0
		16	stone	Wool, Flocks	0	6	8	0
		7	C	Skins, Sheep	3	10	0	0
		30	piece	Mantles	5	0	0	0
		7	dicker	Skins, Salted	4	13	4	0
Nicholas Lambard	Ind	5	pipe	Fish, Salmon	7	10	0	0
		2	barrel	Fish, Herring White	0	10	0	0
		7.5	C	Skins, Sheep	3	15	0	0
		13	piece	Mantles	0	43	4	0
Henry Leman	Ind	10	C	Fish, Hake	5	0	0	0
		1	C	Fish, Salted	0	20	0	0
		1.25	pipe	Fish, Salmon	0	37	6	0
		3	barrel	Fish, Herring White	0	15	0	0
		8	C	Skins, Sheep	4	0	0	0
		0.5	C	Skins, Lamb	0	3	4	0
		11	piece	Mantles	0	36	8	0
James Gough	Ind	3.5	C	Skins, Sheep	0	35	0	0
		2.25	C	Fish, Hake	0	22	6	0
		25	piece	Mantles	4	3	4	0
Robert Denys	Ind	3.5	pipe	Fish, Salmon	5	5	0	0

Merchant name	Origin	Qty	Unit	Commodity	£	s.	d.	f.
		18	barrel	Fish, Herring White	4	10	0	0
		11	C	Fish, Hake	5	10	0	0
		1	C	Fish, Salted	0	20	0	0
		2.5	C	Skins, Sheep	0	25	0	0
		3	piece	Mantles	0	10	0	0
Robert Bosher	Ind	7.5	C	Fish, Hake	3	15	0	0
		2	barrel	Fish, Herring White	0	10	0	0
		4	piece	Mantles	0	13	4	0
		0.5	C	Fish, Salted	0	10	0	0
Edmund Lumbard	Ind	2.5	C	Fish, Hake	0	25	0	0
		0.5	C	Fish, Salted	0	10	0	0
		2.25	C	Skins, Sheep	0	22	6	0
		8	piece	Mantles	0	26	8	0
Richard Grant	Ind	13	barrel	Fish, Herring White	3	5	0	0
		0.5	pipe	Fish, Salmon	0	15	0	0
		0.5	barrel	Fish, Eels	0	6	8	0
		17	C	Fish, Hake	8	10	0	0
		3.25	C	Skins, Sheep	0	32	6	0
		17	piece	Mantles	0	56	8	0
William Hakket	Ind	11	C	Skins, Sheep	5	10	0	0
		18	piece	Mantles	3	0	0	0
James Lambard	Ind	2	pipe	Fish, Salmon	3	0	0	0
		80	piece	Fish, Salted	0	13	4	0
		11	C	Fish, Hake	5	10	0	0
		20	piece	Mantles	3	6	8	0
		15	C	Skins, Sheep	7	10	0	0
		9	piece	Skins, Fox	0	0	18	0
		10	C	Fish, Hake	5	0	0	0
		1	burden	Fish, Salted	0	4	2	0

Bata Trynyte of Milford Haven, Thomas Alen master, from Ireland, *9th March 1517*

Merchant name	Origin	Qty	Unit	Commodity	£	s.	d.	f.
Thomas *Alen*	Ind	6	barrel	Fish, Herring White	0	30	0	0
		1.5	C	Fish, Salted	0	30	0	0
		5	C	Fish, Hake	0	50	0	0
John Jay	Ind	1	pipe	Vinegar	0	20	0	0
John Mayne	Ind	1	pipe	Wine	0	0	0	0
Walter *Alen*	Ind	12	barrel	Fish, Herring White	3	0	0	0
		5	C	Fish, Hake	0	50	0	0
		4	burden	Fish, Salted	0	16	8	0

Bata Conylagg of Kinsale, James White master, from Ireland, *9th March 1517*

Merchant name	Origin	Qty	Unit	Commodity	£	s.	d.	f.
Walter *Alen*	Ind	16	C	Fish, Hake	8	0	0	0
		2	burden	Fish, Salted	0	8	4	0
William Co[ ]sy	Ind	10	C	Fish, Hake	5	0	0	0
		2	pipe	Fish, Salmon	3	0	0	0
		20	burden	Fish, Salted	4	3	4	0
William Barry	Ind	18	C	Fish, Hake	9	0	0	0
		1	burden	Fish, Salted	0	4	2	0
William Hey	Ind	18	C	Fish, Hake	9	0	0	0
		0.5	C	Fish, Salted	0	10	0	0

Merchant name	Origin	Qty	Unit	Commodity	£	s.	d.	f.
Richard Walshe	Ind	10	C	Fish, Hake	5	0	0	0
		2	burden	Fish, Salted	0	8	4	0

Bata Patrik of New Ross, Nicholas Gregorie master, from Ireland, *9th March 1517*

Nicholas Gregorie	Ind	5.5	pipe	Fish, Salmon	8	5	0	0
		8	C	Skins, Sheep	4	0	0	0
		6	barrel	Fish, Herring White	0	30	0	0
John Cotrell	Ind	16	barrel	Fish, Herring White	4	0	0	0
		1.5	pipe	Fish, Salmon	0	45	0	0
		10.5	C	Skins, Sheep	5	5	0	0
		12	piece	Mantles	0	40	0	0
		1	burden	Fish, Salted	0	4	2	0
John Caulan	Ind	2.5	pipe	Fish, Salmon	3	15	0	0
		6.5	C	Skins, Sheep	3	5	0	0
James Garrat	Ind	35	C	Skins, Sheep	17	10	0	0
		2	dicker	Skins, Salted	0	26	8	0
		38	stone	Wool, Flocks	0	15	10	0
		10	piece	Mantles	0	33	4	0

Bata Savior of Milford Haven, Thomas Harrys master, from Ireland, *9th March 1517*

Thomas Harrys	Ind	1.5	barrel	Fish, Herring White	0	7	6	0

Navicula Salvado*r* of *Susare*, John P*e*ers master, from Lisbon, *9th March 1517*

Alvero Pynto	Alien	35.5	tun	Wine	0	0	0	0
		50	dozen	Cork, Black	4	3	4	0
		2	dozen	Skins, Fish	0	2	8	0
		13	dozen	*Seroticaros*[6]	0	80	0	0
		0.5	C	Marmalade	0	6	8	0
George Ffurnandus	Alien	17.5	tun	Wine	0	0	0	0
John Pers	Alien	6	ton	Salt	3	0	0	0
John Ffrancista	Alien	314	lb	Cloves	32	16	3	0
Peter de Lyon	Alien	0.25	ton	Fruit	0	10	0	0

Bata John of Milford Haven, John Nutte master, from Ireland, 10th March 1517

John *Nutte*	Ind	4	barrel	Fish, Herring White	0	20	0	0
		2	C	Fish, Hake	0	20	0	0

Navicula Veronica of Hondarribia, Stephen Prymat master, to Spain, *10th March 1517*

Robert Avyntre	Ind	30	wey	Grain	30	0	0	0
		5	piece	Cloth of Assize	0	0	0	0
Rodrigo de Alkayte	Alien	38	piece	Welsh *Cloth*, Dozen Strait	7	18	4	0
John Shipman	Ind	16	piece	Cloth of Assize	0	0	0	0
John Ware	Ind	11	piece	Cloth of Assize	0	0	0	0
William Shipman	Ind	10	piece	Cloth of Assize	0	0	0	0

6 Unidentified.

Merchant name	Origin	Qty	Unit	Commodity	£	s.	d.	f.

Navicula St James (?) of Portugal, Martin Afonso master, from Portugal, 10th March 1517

Merchant name	Origin	Qty	Unit	Commodity	£	s.	d.	f.
Lopo Garsia	Alien	19	tun	Wine	0	0	0	0
		33	C	Cork, White	5	10	0	0
Gravell Forinosa	Alien	11	cashe	Sugar	22	0	0	0
		3	quart	Comfits	0	27	6	0
		0.5	C	Marmalade	0	6	8	0
Martin Gunsalius	Alien	30	M	Oranges	5	0	0	0
		40	dozen	Cork, Black	3	6	8	0
John Vincent	Alien	4	dozen	Skins, Fish	0	5	0	0

Bata Mare Bosher of Waterford, John Ley master, from Ireland, 10th March 1517

Merchant name	Origin	Qty	Unit	Commodity	£	s.	d.	f.
John Ley	Ind	0.75	pipe	Fish, Salmon	0	22	6	0
		4	piece	Mantles	0	13	4	0
James White	Ind	32	C	Skins, Sheep	16	0	0	0
		13	piece	Mantles	0	43	4	0
		3.5	dicker	Skins, Salted	0	46	8	0
		0.5	pipe	Fish, Salmon	0	15	0	0
Thomas Cahill	Ind	12	C	Skins, Sheep	6	0	0	0
		24	piece	Mantles	4	0	0	0
		1	C	Skins, Lamb	0	6	8	0
		12	stone	Wool, Flocks	0	5	0	0
Geoffrey Malroney	Ind	7	C	Skins, Sheep	3	10	0	0
		0.5	C	Skins, Lamb	0	3	4	0
		6	piece	Mantles	0	20	0	0
Gerald Wale	Ind	8	C	Skins, Sheep	4	0	0	0
		1	virkin	Fish, Salmon	0	7	6	0
		12	piece	Mantles	0	40	0	0
John Doaine	Ind	8	barrel	Fish, Herring White	0	40	0	0
		3	C	Fish, Hake	0	30	0	0
		40	piece	Fish, Salted	0	6	8	0
		1.75	pipe	Fish, Salmon	0	52	6	0
		4	piece	Mantles	0	13	4	0
		1.25	C	Skins, Sheep	0	12	6	0
Peter Felow	Ind	4	piece	Mantles	0	13	4	0
Peter Nogull	Ind	2	piece	Mantles	0	6	8	0
Richard Arthur	Ind	2	barrel	Fish, Eels	0	26	8	0
		3	C	Skins, Sheep	0	30	0	0
Walter Rothe	Ind	5	C	Skins, Sheep	0	50	0	0

Bata Christofur of Kinsale, Richard Donell master, from Ireland, 10th March 1517

Merchant name	Origin	Qty	Unit	Commodity	£	s.	d.	f.
Richard Donell	Ind	12.5	C	Fish, Hake	6	5	0	0
		2	burden	Fish, Salted	0	8	4	0
William Lylie	Ind	7	C	Fish, Hake	3	10	0	0
		1	burden	Fish, Salted	0	4	2	0
Peter Copner	Ind	3	C	Fish, Hake	0	30	0	0
		0.5	burden	Fish, Salted	0	2	1	0
James Nogull	Ind	1.5	pipe	Fish, Salmon	0	45	0	0
		14	C	Fish, Hake	7	0	0	0
		2	burden	Fish, Salted	0	8	4	0

Merchant name	Origin	Qty	Unit	Commodity	£	s.	d.	f.
John Monohan	Ind	4	C	Fish, Hake	0	40	0	0
		1	burden	Fish, Salted	0	4	2	0
Maurice Kerne	Ind	1	pipe	Fish, Salmon	0	30	0	0
		4	C	Fish, Hake	0	40	0	0

Navicula Antony of Bristol, John a Mayne master, from Sanlúcar de Barrameda, *10th March 1517*

Merchant name	Origin	Qty	Unit	Commodity	£	s.	d.	f.
Robert Elyot	Ind	32	tun	Wine	0	0	0	0
Thomas Ashehurst	Ind	15	tun	Wine	0	0	0	0
Robert Rowland	Ind	7.25	tun	Wine	0	0	0	0
George de Costa	Alien	7	tun	Wine	0	0	0	0
John a Mayne	Ind	4.5	tun	Wine	0	0	0	0
Walter Comrowe	Ind	1.5	tun	Wine	0	0	0	0
		4	C	*Smigmates*	0	40	0	0
John Ware	Ind	1	tun	Wine	0	0	0	0
Peter Gonnez	Alien	1	pipe	Wine	0	0	0	0
Haus Gonnez	Alien	1	pipe	Wine	0	0	0	0
John Revyn	Ind	1	pipe	Wine	0	0	0	0
John Dappes	Ind	1	pipe	Wine	0	0	0	0
Thomas Palmer	Ind	1	pipe	Wine	0	0	0	0
George Hall	Ind	1	tun	Wine	0	0	0	0

Bata Trinite of Chepstow, William Heyne master, from Chepstow, 11th March 1517

Merchant name	Origin	Qty	Unit	Commodity	£	s.	d.	f.
John Balle	Ind	1	tun	Wine	0	0	0	0

Bata Sonday of Waterford, Edmund Malrony master, from Ireland, *11th March 1517*

Merchant name	Origin	Qty	Unit	Commodity	£	s.	d.	f.
Edmund Malroney	Ind	4	C	Fish, Hake	0	40	0	0
		0.5	pipe	Fish, Salmon	0	15	0	0
		2	barrel	Fish, Herring White	0	10	0	0
		12	piece	Mantles	0	40	0	0
		11	piece	Fish, Salted	0	6	8	0
		1	hogshead	Wine	0	0	0	0
Walter Gough	Ind	4.5	C	Fish, Hake	0	45	0	0
		2	barrel	Fish, Herring White	0	10	0	0
		1	C	Fish, Salted	0	20	0	0
		10	piece	Mantles	0	33	4	0
Thomas Whaley	Ind	6	barrel	Fish, Herring White	0	30	0	0
		1.5	pipe	Fish, Salmon	0	45	0	0
		1	dicker	Skins, Salted	0	13	4	0
		1.5	tun	Wine	0	0	0	0
Robert Clery	Ind	2.66	C	Skins, Sheep	0	26	8	0
Walter Com*rowe*	Ind	2.25	C	Skins, Sheep	0	22	6	0

Bata Mare of Bewdley, John Glover master, from Chepstow, *11th March 1517*

Merchant name	Origin	Qty	Unit	Commodity	£	s.	d.	f.
Humphrey Wodnall	Ind	9	tun	Wine	0	0	0	0

Merchant name	Origin	Qty	Unit	Commodity	£	s.	d.	f.

Bata Mighell of Bewdley, Thomas White master, from Chepstow, *11th March 1517*

| Humphrey Wodnall | Ind | 3 | tun | Wine | 0 | 0 | 0 | 0 |

Bata Kateryn of Kinsale, Cornell Mason master, from Ireland, 12th March 1517

Merchant name	Origin	Qty	Unit	Commodity	£	s.	d.	f.
James Meaghe	Ind	24	C	Fish, Hake	12	0	0	0
		3	burden	Fish, Salted	0	12	6	0
		6	barrel	Fish, Herring White	0	30	0	0
William Yonge	Ind	6	C	Fish, Hake	3	0	0	0
		0.5	C	Fish, Salted	0	10	0	0
		1	barrel	Fish, Herring White	0	5	0	0
William Hogan	Ind	13	C	Fish, Hake	6	10	0	0
		30	piece	Fish, Salted	0	5	0	0
		12	C	Fish, Hake	6	0	0	0
		1.5	burden	Fish, Salted	0	6	3	0

Bata Seint Mark of Lisbon, John Aldus master, from Lisbon, *12th March 1517*

Francis Lapus	Alien	71.5	tun	Wine	0	0	0	0
		10.5	C	Pepper	52	10	0	0

Bata Elizabethe of Milford Haven, Watkyn Jon master, from Ireland, 13th March 1517

Watkyn? Jon	Ind	3	C	Fish, Salted	3	0	0	0
		3	barrel	Fish, Herring White	0	15	0	0
William Robynet	Ind	1	hogshead	Wine	0	0	0	0

Navicula Saint John of Vila do Conde, George Furnandus master, from Algarve, *13th March 1517*

John Hewes	Ind	40	ton	Fruit	80	0	0	0
		6	dozen	Cork, Black	0	10	0	0
Peter Jang	Alien	3.75	ton	Fruit	7	10	0	0

Bata Nicholas of Milford Haven, David Philip master, from Ireland, 16th March 1517

David Philip	Ind	7.5	barrel	Fish, Herring White	0	37	6	0
		1.66	C	Fish, Salted	0	33	4	0
John Mayne	Ind	1	pipe	Wine	0	0	0	0

Bata Mare Belhouse *of Bristol*, John Harrys master, from Ireland, *16th March 1517*

John Candell	Ind	21.5	C	Skins, Sheep	10	15	0	0
		0.5	C	Skins, Ouprars?	0	8	4	0
		50	stone	Wool, Irish	6	13	4	0
		18	stone	Wool, Flocks	0	7	6	0
		45	yard	Check *Cloth*	0	15	0	0
		10	piece	Skins, Fox	0	0	20	0
		4	piece	Skins, Otter	0	0	20	0
		1	barrel	Fish, Herring White	0	5	0	0
		2	dicker	Skins, Salted	0	26	8	0

Merchant name	Origin	Qty	Unit	Commodity	£	s.	d.	f.
Thomas Springan	Ind	19	barrel	Fish, Herring White	4	15	0	0
		1	C	Fish, Hake	0	10	0	0
		0.5	C	Fish, Salted	0	10	0	0
Nicholas Pepart	Ind	9	C	Skins, Sheep	4	10	0	0
		1	stone	Wool, Flocks	0	0	5	0
		18	barrel	Fish, Herring White	4	10	0	0
		30	mease	Fish, Herring Red	7	10	0	0
		2.5	dicker	Skins, Salted	0	33	4	0
Patrick Fitzsymonds	Ind	6	barrel	Fish, Herring White	0	30	0	0

Bata Trynyte of Chepstow, William Heyne master, *from Chepstow*, 17th March 1517

Merchant name	Origin	Qty	Unit	Commodity	£	s.	d.	f.
John Laurence	Alien	1	C	Frankincense	0	5	0	0
		1	C	Turpentine	0	5	0	0

Bata Mare of Malahide, Maurice Dirhin master, from Ireland, 19th March 1517

Merchant name	Origin	Qty	Unit	Commodity	£	s.	d.	f.
Mark Cadell	Ind	41	mease	Fish, Herring Red	10	5	0	0
		3	last	Fish, Herring White	9	0	0	0
		5	piece	Mantles	0	16	8	0
		15	piece	Skins, Fox	0	2	6	0
		4	piece	Skins, Otter	0	0	20	0
		11	piece	Skins, Lamb	0	0	8	0
		20	yard	Check *Cloth*	0	6	8	0
		13	yard	Irish Linen *Cloth*	0	0	15	0
		1.1	C	Skins, Sheep	0	11	0	0
		0.5	C	Fish, Hake	0	5	0	0
Christopher Bidford	Ind	49	barrel	Fish, Herring White	12	5	0	0
		1	C	Fish, Hake	0	10	0	0
		1	hogshead	Fish, Salmon	0	30	0	0
		2	barrel	Fish, Herring White	0	10	8	0
		0.5	dicker	Skins, Salted	0	6	8	0
		4.2	C	Skins, Sheep	0	42	8	0
Walter Kelly	Ind	2	last	Fish, Herring White	6	0	0	0
		5	mease	Fish, Herring Red	0	25	0	0
Thomas Rowland	Ind	4	barrel	Fish, Herring White	0	20	0	0
		1.5	C	Skins, Sheep	0	15	0	0
		3	mease	Fish, Herring Red	0	15	0	0
		30	stone	Wool, Flocks	0	12	6	0
		40	yard	Irish Linen *Cloth*	0	3	4	0
		3	yard	Check *Cloth*	0	4	4	0
John Mongan	Ind	6	mease	Fish, Herring Red	0	30	0	0
		1	barrel	Fish, Herring White	0	5	0	0
		30	piece	Skins, Sheep	0	2	6	0
John Kolche	Ind	6	C	Fish, Hake	3	0	0	0
		9.5	mease	Fish, Herring Red	0	47	6	0
		3	quart	Skins, Sheep	0	7	6	0

Bata Mare Bosher of Waterford, John Ley master, to Ireland, *19th March 1517*

Merchant name	Origin	Qty	Unit	Commodity	£	s.	d.	f.
James White	Ind	5.5	piece	Cloth of Assize	0	0	0	0
		12	wey	Beans	10	0	0	0

Merchant name	Origin	Qty	Unit	Commodity	£	s.	d.	f.
		2	lb	Saffron	0	20	0	0
		1	gross	Cutts	0	3	4	0
		4	gross	Points	0	4	0	0
Thomas Cahill	Ind	3	piece	Cloth of Assize	0	0	0	0
		2	lb	Silk, Worked	0	26	8	0
		3	lb	Saffron	0	30	0	0
		6	gross	Points	0	6	0	0
		3	dozen	Cutts	0	0	10	0
		40	lb	*Pilus Tinctus*	0	13	4	0
Geoffrey Malroney	Ind	0.5	lb	Saffron	0	5	0	0
		0.5	gross	Cutts	0	0	20	0
		4	gross	Points	0	4	0	0
		1	lb	Thread	0	0	5	0
Walter Rothe	Ind	1	piece	Cloth of Assize	0	0	0	0
		28	lb	*Pilus Tinctus*	0	9	4	0
		8	gross	Points	0	8	0	0
		1	dozen	Aniseed	0	0	20	0

Bata Sonday of *Glomene* (?) , Hugh Brother master, from Ireland, *19th March 1517*

Nicholas Stafford	Ind	8	C	Fish, Hake	4	0	0	0
		1.5	pipe	Fish, Salmon	0	45	0	0
Walter Raymond	Ind	4	C	Fish, Hake	0	40	0	0
		5	burden	Fish, Salted	0	20	10	0
		6	barrel	Fish, Herring White	0	30	0	0
		20	mease	Fish, Herring Red	5	0	0	0

Bata Savior of New Ross, Thomas Shenill master, to Ireland, 20th March 1517

Thomas Shenill	Ind	2	wey	Beans	0	33	4	0
Patrick Burna	Ind	1.25	piece	Cloth of Assize, Dozen Strait	0	0	0	0
		2	lb	Silk, Worked	0	26	8	0
		1	lb	Saffron	0	10	0	0
		1	gross	Cutts	0	3	4	0
		3	gross	Points	0	3	0	0
		1	barrel	Honey	0	16	8	0
		0.5	dozen	Caps	0	5	0	0

Navicula Trinite of Bristol, Evan Danyell master, to Sanlúcar de Barrameda, *20th March 1517*

Robert Avyntre	Ind	15	wey	Grain	15	0	0	0
John Kyng	Ind	10	piece	Cloth of Assize	0	0	0	0
Richard Arthur	Ind	4	piece	Cloth of Assize	0	0	0	0
Robert Hille	Ind	10	piece	Cloth of Assize	0	0	0	0
John Cappes	Ind	16	piece	Cloth of Assize	0	0	0	0
		40	piece	Welsh *Cloth*, Dozen Strait	12	10	0	0
		10	piece	Welsh *Cloth*	10	0	0	0
Evan Danyell	Alien	17	piece	Welsh *Cloth*	17	0	0	0
Thomas Maileyeard	Ind	2	piece	Cloth of Assize	0	0	0	0
William Ostrich	Ind	6	piece	Cloth of Assize	0	0	0	0
Robert Ellyot	Ind	5	piece	Cloth of Assize	0	0	0	0

Merchant name	Origin	Qty	Unit	Commodity	£	s.	d.	f.
		2.5	M	Pipe-Boards	0	41	8	0
		24	C	Hoperods[7]	0	12	0	0
Walter Comrowe	Ind	7	piece	Welsh *Cloth*	7	0	0	0
		4	piece	Welsh *Cloth*	4	0	0	0
Thomas Hart	Ind	1	piece	Cloth of Assize	0	0	0	0
		5	piece	Welsh *Cloth*	5	0	0	0
Thomas Evan	Ind	2	piece	Cloth of Assize	0	0	0	0
George Ffurnandes	Alien	7	piece	Welsh *Cloth*	7	0	0	0

Bata *Christo*fur of Cardiff, William Deane master, from Cardiff, *20th March 1517*

Merchant name	Origin	Qty	Unit	Commodity	£	s.	d.	f.
John Ledon	Ind	1.75	tun	Wine	0	0	0	0

Bata John of Tewkesbury, John Bayfild master, from Cardiff, *20th March 1517*

Merchant name	Origin	Qty	Unit	Commodity	£	s.	d.	f.
Thomas Harteley	Ind	4.5	tun	Wine	0	0	0	0

Bata George of Waterford, Thomas Marris master, to Ireland, *20th March 1517*

Merchant name	Origin	Qty	Unit	Commodity	£	s.	d.	f.
Patrick Comb*er*ford	Ind	8	wey	Beans	6	13	4	0
		3	wey	Malt	0	50	0	0
		1	wey	Grain	0	20	0	0
		100	lb	*Pilus Tinctus*	0	33	4	0
Thomas Shirlock	Ind	2	piece	Cloth of Assize	0	0	0	0
		1	C	*Pilus Tinctus*	0	40	0	0
		4	lb	Silk, Worked	0	53	4	0
		2	lb	Saffron	0	20	0	0
William Hakket	Ind	4	lb	Silk, Worked	0	53	4	0
		3	lb	Saffron	0	30	0	0
		1	dozen	Red-Lash	0	3	4	0
		0.5	dozen	Skins, Golden	0	3	4	0
		16	gross	Points	0	16	0	0
		1	dozen	Aniseed	0	0	20	0
		3	gross	Cutts	0	10	0	0

Bata Mathew of Milford Haven, Richard Sawter master, from Ireland, 21st March 1517

Merchant name	Origin	Qty	Unit	Commodity	£	s.	d.	f.
Richard Sawter	Ind	4.5	barrel	Fish, Herring White	0	22	6	0
		1	burden	Fish, Salted	0	4	2	0

Bata Fawcon of Waterford, Nicholas Rothe master, to Ireland, *21st March 1517*

Merchant name	Origin	Qty	Unit	Commodity	£	s.	d.	f.
Thomas Shirlock	Ind	6	wey	Beans	5	0	0	0
Robert Clere	Ind	50	lb	*Pilus Tinctus*	0	16	8	0
		0.5	lb	Saffron	0	5	0	0
		4	gross	Points	0	4	0	0
Thomas Awnell	Ind	1	piece	Cloth of Assize	0	0	0	0
		1	lb	Silk, Worked	0	13	4	0
		1	lb	Saffron	0	10	0	0
		6	gross	Points	0	6	0	0
Robert Strange	Ind	4	lb	Silk, Worked	0	53	4	0

7 Perhaps a staff used to remove hops from the poles on which they grow.

Merchant name	Origin	Qty	Unit	Commodity	£	s.	d.	f.
		2	lb	Saffron	0	20	0	0
		1	C	*Pilus Tinctus*	0	40	0	0

Navicula Laurence of Penmarch, James le Monyk master, to La Rochelle, 23rd March 1517

Merchant name	Origin	Qty	Unit	Commodity	£	s.	d.	f.
John Sparcheford	Ind	4	ton	Lead, Worked	20	0	0	0
James Langinyk?	Alien	15.75	tun	Lime	0	39	4	0

Bata Patrike of Youghal, Maurice Russell master, to Ireland, *23rd March 1517*

Merchant name	Origin	Qty	Unit	Commodity	£	s.	d.	f.
Maurice Russell	Ind	40	lb	*Pilus Tinctus*	0	13	4	0
		1	C	Hops	0	5	0	0
		2	stone	Orchil, Worked	0	3	4	0
Nicholas Rowley	Ind	2	lb	Silk, Worked	0	26	8	0
		2	lb	Saffron	0	20	0	0
		0.5	C	Hops	0	2	6	0
		0.5	C	Alum	0	6	8	0
		5	dozen	Aniseed	0	7	6	0
		2	gross	Cutts	0	6	8	0
		3	gross	Points	0	3	0	0
		6	lb	Liquorice	0	0	10	0
		3	stone	Orchil, Worked	0	5	0	0

Bata Kateryn of Kinsale, William Dale master, to Ireland, 24th March 1517

Merchant name	Origin	Qty	Unit	Commodity	£	s.	d.	f.
William Dale	Ind	7	wey	Beans & Malt	5	16	8	0
Philip Leynam	Ind	1.5	C	Hops	0	12	6	0

Bata Konylagh of Kinsale, James White master, to Ireland, *24th March 1517*

Merchant name	Origin	Qty	Unit	Commodity	£	s.	d.	f.
James *White*	Ind	5	wey	Beans	4	3	4	0
		4	stone	Orchil, Worked	0	6	8	0
		3	stone	Hops	0	0	20	0
		0.75	C	Alum	0	9	12	0
		2	piece	Cloth of Assize, Dozen Strait	0	0	0	0
William Barry	Ind	6	stone	Orchil, Worked	0	10	0	0
		2	stone	Hops	0	0	15	0
		0.125	C	Alum	0	0	20	0
William Hey	Ind	6	stone	Orchil, Worked	0	10	0	0
		2	stone	Hops	0	0	15	0
William Co[ ]sy	Ind	2	piece	Welsh *Cloth*	0	40	0	0
		1	dozen	Aniseed	0	0	20	0
		1	dozen	Liquorice	0	0	20	0

Bata *Christ*ofur of Kinsale, Richard Donell master, to Ireland, *24th March 1517*

Merchant name	Origin	Qty	Unit	Commodity	£	s.	d.	f.
James Nongull	Ind	4	wey	Beans	3	6	8	0
		0.5	C	Aniseed	0	5	0	0
		1	piece	Cloth of Assize	0	0	0	0

Merchant name	Origin	Qty	Unit	Commodity	£	s.	d.	f.
Bata Sonday of Wexford, Nicholas Vele master, to Ireland, 26th March 1517								
Nicholas *Vele*	Ind	3	wey	Beans	0	50	0	0
Navicula John Baptist of Pasajes de San Juan, Michael de Lana master, to Spain, *26th March 1517*								
Maurice Bocher &								
Gilbert Cogan	Ind	70	wey	Grain	70	0	0	0
		8	piece	Cloth of Assize	0	0	0	0
John Carry	Alien	16	dozen	Hides, Tanned Calf	0	53	4	0
John Shipman	Ind	16	piece	Cloth of Assize	0	0	0	0
John Ware	Ind	11	piece	Cloth of Assize	0	0	0	0
William Shipman	Ind	9	piece	Cloth of Assize	0	0	0	0
Bata Jhesus of Kinsale, Jordan Roche master, to Ireland, *26th March 1517*								
William Nogull	Ind	4	wey	Beans	3	6	8	0
		4	wey	Malt	3	6	8	0
		0.5	wey	Grain	0	10	0	0
		7	stone	Hops	0	5	0	0
		10	stone	Orchil, Worked	0	16	8	0
		0.5	stone	Wool, Welsh	0	2	6	0
Bata George of Wexford, Robert Roche master, to Ireland, *26th March 1517*								
John Waden	Ind	1	tun	Wine, Corrupt	0	30	0	0
		1.5	wey	Malt	0	25	0	0
		0.5	wey	Beans	0	8	4	0
Bata Nicholas of Waterford, Robert Keny master, to Ireland, *26th March 1517*								
Robert Keny	Ind	16	wey	Beans	13	6	8	0
		2	wey	Malt	0	33	4	0
		1	wey	Grain	0	20	0	0
Robert Strange	Ind	2	piece	Cloth of Assize	0	0	0	0
		0.5	C	Aniseed	0	5	0	0
		2	lb	Saffron	0	20	0	0
		0.5	gross	Cutts	0	0	20	0
		6	gross	Points	0	6	0	0
Henry Leman	Ind	3	piece	Cloth of Assize	0	0	0	0
		1	lb	Silk, Worked	0	13	4	0
		12	lb	*Pilus Tinctus*	0	4	0	0
		3	gross	Points	0	3	0	0
Robert Denys	Ind	5	piece	Cloth of Assize	0	0	0	0
		50	lb	*Pilus Tinctus*	0	16	8	0
Nicholas Lumbard	Ind	1	lb	Saffron	0	10	0	0
		4	gross	Points	0	4	0	0
		0.5	piece	Cloth of Assize	0	0	0	0

Merchant name	Origin	Qty	Unit	Commodity	£	s.	d.	f.

Bata George of Bristol, William Donell master, from Ireland, 26th March 1517

Merchant name	Origin	Qty	Unit	Commodity	£	s.	d.	f.
Robert Avyntre	Ind	6	C	Fish, Salted	6	o	o	o
		0.5	dicker	Skins, Salted	o	6	8	o
Thomas Donell	Ind	6	C	Fish, Salted	6	o	o	o
		0.5	dicker	Skins, Salted	o	6	8	o

Bata Mawdelen of Cork, John White master, to Ireland, 26th March 1517

Merchant name	Origin	Qty	Unit	Commodity	£	s.	d.	f.
John *White*	Ind	1	pipe	Wine, Corrupt	o	15	o	o

Bata Mare of Wexford, Nicholas Ffrenshe master, to Ireland, 26th March 1517

Merchant name	Origin	Qty	Unit	Commodity	£	s.	d.	f.
John Mason	Ind	3	tun	Wine, Corrupt	4	10	o	o
		2	C	Iron	o	8	o	o
		1.25	wey	Malt	o	20	10	o
		1	wey	Beans	o	16	8	o
		1	lb	Silk, Worked	o	13	4	o
		1	lb	Saffron	o	10	o	o
		0.5	C	Hops	o	2	6	o

Bata Jhesus of Wexford, Nicholas Stafford master, to Ireland, 26th March 1517

Merchant name	Origin	Qty	Unit	Commodity	£	s.	d.	f.
Nicholas *Stafford*	Ind	2	tun	Wine, Corrupt	3	o	o	o
		2	wey	Beans	o	33	4	o
		1	wey	Malt	o	16	8	o

Bata Sonday of Waterford, Edmund Malrony master, to Ireland, 26th March 1517

Merchant name	Origin	Qty	Unit	Commodity	£	s.	d.	f.
Edmund *Malroney*	Ind	4.5	wey	Beans	3	15	o	o
		1.5	wey	Malt	o	25	o	o
		1	wey	Grain	o	20	o	o

Bata Makerell of Wexford, John Codde master, to Ireland, 26th March 1517

Merchant name	Origin	Qty	Unit	Commodity	£	s.	d.	f.
Robert Canton	Ind	1	tun	Wine, Corrupt	o	30	o	o
		1.75	wey	Malt	o	29	2	o

Bata Patrik of Cork, Robert Barrett master, to Ireland, 28th March 1517

Merchant name	Origin	Qty	Unit	Commodity	£	s.	d.	f.
Robert Barrett	Ind	4	wey	Beans	3	6	8	o
		2	wey	Malt	o	33	4	o
		1	wey	Grain	o	20	o	o

Bata Patrik of Youghal, Maurice Herne Master, to Ireland, 28th March 1517

Merchant name	Origin	Qty	Unit	Commodity	£	s.	d.	f.
Maurice Herne	Ind	2	stone	Orchil, Worked	o	3	4	o
		1	quart	Hops	o	o	15	o
		0.25	C	Alum	o	3	4	o
John Blewet	Ind	2	piece	Cloth of Assize	o	o	o	o
		0.5	C	Hops	o	2	6	o
		0.5	C	Alum	o	6	8	o

Merchant name	Origin	Qty	Unit	Commodity	£	s.	d.	f.
		6	dozen	Aniseed	o	9	o	o
		6	stone	Orchil	o	10	o	o
Robert Forest	Ind	2.5	piece	Cloth of Assize	o	o	o	o
		4	lb	Silk, Worked	o	53	4	o
		2	lb	Saffron	o	20	o	o
		2	gross	Cutts	o	6	8	o
		1	stone	Hops	o	o	12	o
Oliver Arthur	Ind	1.33	piece	Cloth of Assize	o	o	o	o
		5	piece	Cloth of Assize, Dozen Strait	o	o	o	o
		1	piece	Welsh Cloth, Dozen Strait	o	4	2	o
		5	gross	Cutts	o	16	8	o

Bata Trynyte of Chepstow, William Heyne master, *from Chepstow, 28th March 1517*

Katerina Wale	Ind	2	tun	Wine	o	o	o	o

Bata Kateryne of Kinsale, Cornell Mason master, to Ireland, 30th March 1517

James Mehan	Ind	3.5	wey	Beans	o	58	4	o
		3.5	wey	Malt	o	58	4	o
Robert Canton	Ind	0.5	C	Hops	o	2	6	o
		4	stone	Orchil, Worked	o	6	8	o
		0.25	wey	Grain	o	5	o	o

Bata Patrik of Youghal, Maurice Fynne master, to Ireland, 31st March 1517

Maurice Fynne	Ind	2	wey	Beans	o	33	4	o
		1	wey	Malt	o	16	8	o
William Barry	Ind	2	wey	Beans	o	33	4	o
		1	wey	Malt	o	16	8	o
		0.25	wey	Grain	o	5	o	o
William Austen	Ind	2	wey	Beans	o	33	4	o
		2	wey	Malt	o	33	4	o

Bata Nicholas of Wexford, John Roche master, to Ireland, *31st March 1517*

Nicholas Turner	Ind	1	tun	Wine, Corrupt	o	30	o	o
		1	C	Hops	o	5	o	o
		1	C	Alum	o	13	4	o
		1.5	wey	Beans	o	25	o	o

Bata Trinite of Chepstow, William Heyne master, *from Chepstow, 31st March 1517*

Peter Deargant	Alien	1	bale	Woad	o	25	o	o
William Appowell	Ind	1.25	tun	Wine	o	o	o	o

Bata Mare Towre of Bristol, William Robynet master, to Ireland, 1st April 1517

John Collas	Ind	20	tun	Wine, Corrupt	30	o	o	o

Merchant name	Origin	Qty	Unit	Commodity	£	s.	d.	f.

Bata Nicholas of Youghal, John Grant master, to Ireland, *1st April 1517*

Merchant name	Origin	Qty	Unit	Commodity	£	s.	d.	f.
John Grante	Ind	3	wey	Beans	0	50	0	0
John Sloan	Ind	1	piece	Welsh *Cloth*	0	20	0	0
Nicholas Benet	Ind	4	lb	Saffron	0	40	0	0
		2	gross	Cutts	0	6	8	0
		40	lb	*Pilus Tinctus*	0	13	4	0
		1	lb	Silk, Worked	0	13	4	0
		2	piece	Cloth of Assize, Dozen Strait	0	0	0	0

Bata Sonday of Cork, William Barry master, to Ireland, 2nd April 1517

Merchant name	Origin	Qty	Unit	Commodity	£	s.	d.	f.
William Barry	Ind	2	wey	Malt	0	33	4	0

Navicula Matthew of Bristol, Richard Savery master, from Spain, 2nd April 1517

Merchant name	Origin	Qty	Unit	Commodity	£	s.	d.	f.
John Rowland	Ind	10	ton	Iron	25	0	0	0
John Ware	Ind	20	ton	Iron	50	0	0	0
William Woseley	Ind	12	ton	Iron	30	0	0	0
William Shipman	Ind	20	ton	Iron	50	0	0	0
John Shipman	Ind	58	ton	Iron	145	0	0	0
Edward Jonys	Ind	1	hogshead	Iron	0	12	6	0

Navicula John of Errenteria, Anthony de la Sola master, from Spain, *2nd April 1517*

Merchant name	Origin	Qty	Unit	Commodity	£	s.	d.	f.
John Shipman	Ind	35	ton	Iron	87	10	0	0
John Ware	Ind	20	ton	Iron	50	0	0	0
William Shipman	Ind	21	ton	Iron	52	10	0	0
William Woseley	Ind	12	ton	Iron	30	0	0	0
Thomas Dale	Ind	5	ton	Iron	12	10	0	0
Edward Jonys	Ind	1	ton	Iron	0	50	0	0
Mathew Hopes	Ind	0.66	ton	Iron	1	13	4	0

Bata Trynyte of Chepstow, William Heyne master, *from Chepstow*, 3rd April 1517

Merchant name	Origin	Qty	Unit	Commodity	£	s.	d.	f.
John Gabull	Ind	1	bale	Woad	0	25	0	0
Richard Kewe	Ind	1	tun	Wine	0	0	0	0
William Heyne	Ind	1.5	tun	Wine	0	0	0	0

Bata Mare White of Malahide, Maurice Dirhin master, to Ireland, *3rd April 1517*

Merchant name	Origin	Qty	Unit	Commodity	£	s.	d.	f.
John Shipman	Ind	0.75	ton	Iron	3	0	0	0
Thomas Bowland	Ind	12	gross	Points	0	12	0	0
		1	dozen	Liquorice	0	0	20	0
		1	lb	Pepper	0	0	12	0
		1	lb	Ginger	0	2	6	0
Nicholas Fagan	Ind	2	piece	Cloth of Assize	0	0	0	0
		6	piece	Cloth of Assize, Dozen Strait	0	0	0	0

Bata Sonday of *Glomene*, Hugh Brother master, to Ireland, 4th April 1517

Merchant name	Origin	Qty	Unit	Commodity	£	s.	d.	f.
Nicholas Stafford	Ind	5	wey	Beans	4	3	4	0

Merchant name	Origin	Qty	Unit	Commodity	£	s.	d.	f.

Bata Anthony of Bristol, John Harrys master, to Ireland, 6th April 1517

Merchant name	Origin	Qty	Unit	Commodity	£	s.	d.	f.
John Halle	Ind	1.25	tun	Wine, Corrupt	0	37	6	0
Mathew Hop	Ind	5	wey	Beans	4	3	4	0

Navicula Mare of Errenteria, John Marting master, to Spain, 7th April 1517

Merchant name	Origin	Qty	Unit	Commodity	£	s.	d.	f.
John *Marting*	Alien	10	C	Fish, Hake	5	0	0	0
John Kyng	Ind	10	wey	Grain	10	0	0	0
John Marting	Alien	10	wey	Grain	10	0	0	0
Roger Dawes	Ind	20	wey	Grain	20	0	0	0
John Rowland	Ind	10	piece	Welsh *Cloth*, Dozen Strait	0	41	8	0
		10	wey	Grain	10	0	0	0
		23	piece	Cloth of Assize	0	0	0	0
William Woseley	Ind	6	piece	Cloth of Assize	0	0	0	0
John Shipman	Ind	15	piece	Cloth of Assize	0	0	0	0
John Ware	Ind	8	piece	Cloth of Assize	0	0	0	0
William Shipman	Ind	10	piece	Cloth of Assize	0	0	0	0
John Sparchford	Ind	24	piece	Cloth of Assize	0	0	0	0
John Brampton	Ind	10	piece	Cloth of Assize	0	0	0	0
Thomas Dale	Ind	4	piece	Cloth of Assize	0	0	0	0

Navicula John of Errenteria, Anthony de la Sola master, to Spain, *7th April 1517*

Merchant name	Origin	Qty	Unit	Commodity	£	s.	d.	f.
John Shipman	Ind	10	wey	Grain	10	0	0	0
		5	wey	Beans	4	3	4	0
Edward Jonys	Ind	12	C	Fish, Hake	6	0	0	0

Navicula John of Pasajes de San Juan, John de Burgong master, to Spain, *7th April 1517*

Merchant name	Origin	Qty	Unit	Commodity	£	s.	d.	f.
Richard Bocher	Ind	30	wey	Grain	30	0	0	0

Bata *Christ*ofur of Tewkesbury, Laurence Mede master, from Ireland, 16th April 1517

Merchant name	Origin	Qty	Unit	Commodity	£	s.	d.	f.
Laurence Mede	Ind	12	burden	Fish, Salted	0	50	0	0
		6	piece	Mantles	0	20	0	0
Thomas Roche	Ind	320	lb	Pepper	16	0	0	0

Bata Trinite of Huntley, John Browning master, from Ireland, *16th April 1517*

Merchant name	Origin	Qty	Unit	Commodity	£	s.	d.	f.
Robert Avyntre	Ind	3.5	burden	Fish, Salted	0	14	7	0
Thomas Donell	Ind	3.5	burden	Fish, Salted	0	14	7	0
John Kyng	Ind	3.5	burden	Fish, Salted	0	14	7	0
		1	C	Pepper	5	0	0	0
Nicholas Cokk	Ind	1	tun	Wine	0	0	0	0
		80	lb	Pepper	4	0	0	0
		2	piece	Mantles	0	6	8	0
		1	burden	Fish, Salted	0	4	2	0

Bata Mare Belhouse *of Bristol*, Richard Boughton master, to Ireland, *17th April 1517*

Merchant name	Origin	Qty	Unit	Commodity	£	s.	d.	f.
William Edwards	Ind	12	wey	Beans	10	0	0	0

Merchant name	Origin	Qty	Unit	Commodity	£	s.	d.	f.
		3	wey	Malt	0	50	0	0
Owen Cole	Ind	1	piece	Welsh *Cloth*	0	20	0	0

Navicula Seint James of Portugal, Martin Afonso master, to Portugal, 18th April 1517

Merchant name	Origin	Qty	Unit	Commodity	£	s.	d.	f.
George Vase	Alien	1	quart	Grain	0	3	4	0
Lepo Garsea	Alien	9	piece	Cloth of Assize, Northern	18	0	0	0
		1	piece	Cloth of Assize, Dozen Strait	0	0	0	0
		1	piece	Welsh *Cloth*	0	20	0	0

Navicula Matthew of Bristol, Richard Savere master, to Spain, *18th April 1517*

Merchant name	Origin	Qty	Unit	Commodity	£	s.	d.	f.
John Shipman	Ind	15.5	piece	Cloth of Assize	0	0	0	0
John Ware	Ind	2.5	piece	Cloth of Assize	0	0	0	0
William Shipman	Ind	8	piece	Cloth of Assize	0	0	0	0
Thomas Bilford	Ind	27	piece	Cloth of Assize	0	0	0	0
John Drewes	Ind	9	piece	Cloth of Assize	0	0	0	0

Navicula Anthony of Bristol, John Crok master, to Sanlúcar de Barrameda, *18th April 1517*

Merchant name	Origin	Qty	Unit	Commodity	£	s.	d.	f.
John Drewes	Ind	19	piece	Cloth of Assize	0	0	0	0
William Woseley	Ind	24	piece	Cloth of Assize	0	0	0	0
Robert Thorne	Ind	10	piece	Cloth of Assize	0	0	0	0
William Cardmaker	Ind	1	piece	Welsh *Cloth*	0	20	0	0
Robert Ellyot	Ind	8	piece	Cloth of Assize	0	0	0	0
John Hall	Ind	22	piece	Welsh *Cloth*, Dozen Strait	4	11	8	0
Thomas Ashehurst	Ind	9	piece	Cloth of Assize	0	0	0	0

Navicula Santa Maria of Candelária,[8] Ochoa de la Sona master, to Ireland, 20th April 1517

Merchant name	Origin	Qty	Unit	Commodity	£	s.	d.	f.
Robert Ellyot	Ind	20	tun	Wine, Corrupt	30	0	0	0
		4	ton	Salt	3	6	8	0
		2	C	Battery	4	0	0	0
		8	piece	Cloth of Assize	0	0	0	0
John Drewes	Ind	15	tun	Wine, Corrupt	22	10	0	0
		2.25	ton	Salt	0	37	6	0
		10	piece	Cloth of Assize	0	0	0	0
		2	piece	Cloth of Assize, Dozen Strait	0	0	0	0
John Hop	Ind	3	tun	Wine, Corrupt	4	10	0	0
John Coke	Ind	2	tun	Wine, Corrupt	3	0	0	0

Bata Trynyte of Chepstow, William Heyne master, from Chepstow, 21st April 1517

Merchant name	Origin	Qty	Unit	Commodity	£	s.	d.	f.
William Bruar	Ind	40	C	Woad, Azores	13	6	8	0

Bata George of Berkeley, James Browne master, from Ireland, 22nd April 1517

Merchant name	Origin	Qty	Unit	Commodity	£	s.	d.	f.
James *Browne*	Ind	4	burden	Fish, Salted	0	16	8	0

8 This may be Candelária in São Miguel (Azores) or in Spain.

Merchant name	Origin	Qty	Unit	Commodity	£	s.	d.	f.

Navicula St John of Vila do Conde, George Furnandus master, to Portugal, 24th April 1517

Merchant name	Origin	Qty	Unit	Commodity	£	s.	d.	f.
Furnandus Martin	Alien	17	piece	Frieze *Cloth*	17	0	0	0
		4	wey	Grain	4	0	0	0
John Hewes	Ind	40	wey	Grain	40	0	0	0
		6	piece	Welsh *Cloth*	6	0	0	0
		3	piece	Welsh *Cloth*, Dozen Strait	0	12	6	0
Gonsalo Terroka	Alien	2	piece	Cloth of Assize	0	0	0	0
Francis Marting	Alien	1	piece	Cloth of Assize	0	0	0	0
		1	piece	Welsh *Cloth*	0	20	0	0

Bata Jamys of Gatcombe, John Symonds master, to Ireland, *24th April 1517*

Merchant name	Origin	Qty	Unit	Commodity	£	s.	d.	f.
John *Symonds*	Ind	14	wey	Beans	11	13	4	0
		2	wey	Malt	0	33	4	0

Navicula Mare*Christ*ofur of Bristol, John Barnard master, from Bordeaux, 27th April 1517

Merchant name	Origin	Qty	Unit	Commodity	£	s.	d.	f.
John Shipman	Ind	7	tun	Wine	0	0	0	0
		11.5	pipe	Woad	57	10	0	0
John Ware	Ind	11	tun	Wine	0	0	0	0
		19.5	bale	Woad	24	7	6	0
William Woseley	Ind	1	tun	Wine	0	0	0	0
William Shipman	Ind	3	tun	Wine	0	0	0	0
		6	pipe	Woad	30	0	0	0
John Pasheley	Ind	2.75	tun	Wine	0	0	0	0
Auger de Noga	Alien	4.5	tun	Wine	0	0	0	0
John Clotte	Ind	0.75	tun	Wine	0	0	0	0
Thomas Dale	Ind	13.5	tun	Wine	0	0	0	0
Thomas Bilford	Ind	2.75	tun	Wine	0	0	0	0
		3	pipe	Woad	15	0	0	0
Robert Rowlow	Ind	7	tun	Wine	0	0	0	0
		21.5	bale	Woad	26	17	6	0
Henry Green	Ind	1	hogshead	Wine	0	0	0	0
David Vaghan	Ind	6	pipe	Woad	30	0	0	0
Robert Avyntre	Ind	4.5	tun	Wine	0	0	0	0
		3	pipe	Woad	15	0	0	0
		1.5	ton	Rosin and Pitch	0	40	0	0
Robert Coke	Ind	17.13	pipe	*Woad*	85	12	6	0
Edmund Body	Ind	3	pipe	Woad	15	0	0	0
Robert Hillesey	Ind	1	hogshead	Wine	0	0	0	0
Robert Shipman	Ind	2.5	tun	Wine	0	0	0	0
		3	bale	Woad	3	15	0	0
John Jeynye	Ind	1	pipe	Wine	0	0	0	0
Thomas Hawykns	Ind	1	tun	Wine	0	0	0	0
William Kisson	Ind	1	pipe	Wine	0	0	0	0
Walter Wynseley	Ind	0.5	ton	Rosin	0	13	4	0
Thomas Pleinley	Ind	1	hogshead	Wine	0	0	0	0

Bata Jamys of Carmarthen, William Cradok master, *from Carmarthen, 27th April 1517*

Merchant name	Origin	Qty	Unit	Commodity	£	s.	d.	f.
William Cradok	Ind	2.5	tun	Wine	0	0	0	0

Merchant name	Origin	Qty	Unit	Commodity	£	s.	d.	f.
		15	C	Rosin and Pitch	1	0	0	0

Navicula Edward of Bristol, John Gorwey master, from Bordeaux, *27th April 1517*

Merchant name	Origin	Qty	Unit	Commodity	£	s.	d.	f.
George Hall	Ind	7.25	tun	Wine	0	0	0	0
		2	pipe	Woad	10	0	0	0
		1	pipe	Rosin and Pitch	0	13	4	0
David Vaghan	Ind	7.5	tun	Wine	0	0	0	0
Nicholas Gay	Ind	20	tun	Wine	0	0	0	0
		31	bale	Woad	38	15	0	0
Roger Dawes	Ind	4	tun	Wine	0	0	0	0
		3	pipe	Woad	15	0	0	0
Thomas Yeate	Ind	3.916	tun	Wine	0	0	0	0
		9	bale	Woad	11	5	0	0
Thomas Dale	Ind	5.5	tun	Wine	0	0	0	0
Edmund Body	Ind	5	pipe	Woad	25	0	0	0
John Hall	Ind	10	tun	Wine	0	0	0	0
		2	pipe	Woad	10	0	0	0
Robert Pophin	Ind	1	hogshead	Wine	0	0	0	0
Robert Galle	Ind	1	hogshead	Wine	0	0	0	0
Thomas Stogan	Ind	1	hogshead	Wine	0	0	0	0
William Mannyng	Ind	1	hogshead	Wine	0	0	0	0
Peter Randal	Ind	1	hogshead	Wine	0	0	0	0
John Vaghan	Ind	1	hogshead	Rosin	0	6	8	0

Bata *Christ*ofur of Cardiff, William a Deane master, *from Cardiff*, 28th April 1517

Merchant name	Origin	Qty	Unit	Commodity	£	s.	d.	f.
Richard Bonnae ?	Ind	1	C	Pepper	5	0	0	0
		4	stone	Wool, Flocks	0	0	20	0
		1	bolt	Poldavis *Cloth*	0	10	13	0
		1	piece	Mantles	0	3	4	0

Bata Trinite of Chepstow, William Heyne master, *from Chepstow*, 29th April 1517

Merchant name	Origin	Qty	Unit	Commodity	£	s.	d.	f.
Peter de Argulf	Alien	1	bale	Woad	0	25	0	0
John Thomas	Ind	3.75	tun	Wine	0	0	0	0
John Laurence	Ind	2.75	tun	Wine	0	0	0	0

Bata Leonard of Magor, John Broke master, *from Magor, 29th April 1517*

Merchant name	Origin	Qty	Unit	Commodity	£	s.	d.	f.
Walter Ap Roser	Ind	5	ton	Salt	0	50	0	0

Bata Mare of Bristol, Thomas Nongull master, from Ireland, 5th May 1517

Merchant name	Origin	Qty	Unit	Commodity	£	s.	d.	f.
Thomas *Nongull*	Ind	0.5	pipe	Fish, Salmon	0	15	0	0
		1	C	Skins, Sheep	0	10	0	0

Bata Mare of Bristol, Thomas Nongull master, to Ireland, 5th May 1517

Merchant name	Origin	Qty	Unit	Commodity	£	s.	d.	f.
Thomas *Nongull*	Ind	11	wey	Beans	9	3	4	0
		2	wey	Malt	0	33	4	0

Merchant name	Origin	Qty	Unit	Commodity	£	s.	d.	f.

Bata Anthony of Bristol, Robert Baker master, Destination Unknown, *5th May 1517*

| John Griffith | Ind | ? | ? | ? | 0 | 23 | 4 | 0 |

Navicula Fy*aker* of Penmarch, Michael de *W*yk master, from Brittany, 6th May 1517

| Michael de *W*yk | Alien | 138 | ton | Salt | 69 | 0 | 0 | 0 |

Navicula Salvador of *Susare*, John Peris master, to Portugal, 9th May 1517

| John Peris | Alien | 12 | wey | Grain | 12 | 0 | 0 | 0 |

Navicula Mare Tower of Bristol, John Halfey master, to Ireland, *9th May 1517*

John Collas	Ind	20	tun	Wine, Corrupt	30	0	0	0
		10	wey	Grain	10	0	0	0
		10	wey	Beans	8	6	8	0
		30	piece	Cloth of Assize	0	0	0	0
Adam Skelton	Ind	2	piece	Welsh *Cloth*	0	40	0	0

Bata Trinite of Chepstow, William Hey*n*e master, *from Chepstow, 9th May 1517*

| Prior de Bathe | Ind | 1 | tun | Wine | 0 | 0 | 0 | 0 |

Bata Mighill of Tenby, David Thomas master, to Ireland, 10th May 1517

| John Heyn | Ind | 11 | wey | Beans & Malt | 9 | 3 | 4 | 0 |
| | | 1 | wey | Grain | 0 | 20 | 0 | 0 |

Bata Mark of Tenby, Gerald Griffith master, *from Tenby*, 11th May 1517

| Gerald Griffith | Ind | 6 | ton | Salt | 3 | 0 | 0 | 0 |

Bata Trynyte of Longney, John Brether master, to Ireland, *11th May 1517*

| John Brother | Ind | 8 | wey | Beans | 6 | 13 | 4 | 0 |

Bata Mighell of Gatcombe, John Marks master, from Ireland, *11th May 1517*

John *Marks*	Ind	3	tun	Wine	0	0	0	0
		1	tun	Oil, *Olive*	4	0	0	0
		6	C	Skins, Sheep	3	0	0	0
		4	C	Skins, Lamb	0	26	8	0
		4	piece	Mantles	0	13	4	0
Nicholas Harrys	Ind	22	C	Skins, Lamb	7	6	8	0
		18	C	Skins, Sheep	9	0	0	0
		15	piece	Mantles	0	50	0	0
		40	yard	Check *Cloth*	0	13	4	0
		12	piece	Skins, Fox	0	2	0	0
		3	piece	Skins, Otter	0	0	15	0
		2	piece	Skins, Marten	0	2	0	0
Alexander Capell	Ind	8.5	C	Skins, Lamb	0	56	8	0

Merchant name	Origin	Qty	Unit	Commodity	£	s.	d.	f.
		1	C	Skins, Sheep	0	10	0	0
		18	piece	Skins, Fox	0	3	0	0

Navicula Marget of Bristol, John Stevyns master, from Lisbon, 12th May 1517

Merchant name	Origin	Qty	Unit	Commodity	£	s.	d.	f.
Nicholas Browne	Ind	6.25	tun	Oil, *Olive*	25	0	0	0
		49.5	ton	Salt	24	15	0	0
		20	dozen	Cork, Black	0	33	4	0
John Stevyns	Ind	1	ton	Salt	0	10	0	0

Bata Marget of Oldbury-on-Severn, Philip Bocher master, to Ireland, *12th May 1517*

Merchant name	Origin	Qty	Unit	Commodity	£	s.	d.	f.
Robert Adams & John Hake	Ind	16	wey	Beans & Malt	13	6	7	0
		2	wey	Grain	0	40	0	0

Bata Marget of Carmarthen, Martin Davids master, *from Carmarthen, 12th May 151*

Merchant name	Origin	Qty	Unit	Commodity	£	s.	d.	f.
Gerome Grene	Ind	4	C	Prunes	0	26	8	0
Clement Pun[ ]t	Ind	1	tun	Wine	0	0	0	0
		1	pipe	Salt	0	5	0	0
David Vaghan	Ind	1	tun	Wine	0	0	0	0

Navicula Jhesus of Bristol, Robert Avyntre master, from Ireland, 15th May 1517

Merchant name	Origin	Qty	Unit	Commodity	£	s.	d.	f.
Robert *Avyntre*	Ind	147	dicker	Skins, Salted	98	0	0	0
		6	piece	Mantles	0	20	0	0
		24	piece	Skins, Fox	0	4	0	0
		1	C	Skins, Lamb	0	6	8	0
		1	quart	Skins, Sheep	0	2	6	0
Thomas Donell	Ind	154	dicker	Hides, Salted	102	13	4	0
		6	piece	Mantles	0	20	0	0
		24	piece	Skins, Fox	0	4	0	0
		1	C	Skins, Lamb	0	6	8	0
		1	quart	Skins, Sheep	0	2	6	0
John Kyng	Ind	21	dicker	Hides, Salted	14	0	0	0
		7	dicker	Hides, Salted	4	13	4	0
Nicholas Yeo?	Ind	4.5	C	Pepper	22	10	0	0
		152	lb	Cloves	17	2	6	0
		1	quart	Nutmeg	0	25	0	0
Nicholas Ffox	Ind	2	C	Irish Linen *Cloth*	0	20	0	0
Richard Arthur	Ind	5	C	Irish Linen *Cloth*	0	50	0	0
		12	piece	Skins, Fox	0	2	0	0
		15	piece	Mantles	0	50	0	0

Bata Katerin of Youghal, Dennis Griffith master, from Ireland, *15th May 1517*

Merchant name	Origin	Qty	Unit	Commodity	£	s.	d.	f.
Dennis Griffith	Ind	1.5	C	Skins, Sheep	0	15	0	0
Robert Avyntre	Ind	12.5	dicker	Skins, Salted	8	6	8	0
Thomas Donell	Ind	12.5	dicker	Skins, Salted	8	6	8	0
William Meagh	Ind	4	dicker	Hides, Salted	0	53	4	0
Henry Meagh	Ind	2	C	Skins, Sheep	0	20	0	0
Philip Furbur	Ind	2.5	C	Skins, Sheep	0	25	0	0

Merchant name	Origin	Qty	Unit	Commodity	£	s.	d.	f.
		1.5	C	Skins, Lamb	0	10	0	0
		4	dicker	Skins, Wild	0	10	0	0
		2	stone	Wool, Flocks	0	0 · 10	0	

Bata Patrik of Waterford, John Fitzharry master, from Ireland, 16th May 1517

Merchant name	Origin	Qty	Unit	Commodity	£	s.	d.	f.
John *FitzHarry*	Ind	2	piece	Mantles	0	6	8	0
William Everard	Ind	8	dicker	Skins, Salted	5	6	8	0
		20	C	Skins, Sheep	10	0	0	0
		9	piece	Mantles	0	30	0	0
		2	burden	Fish, Salted	0	8	4	0
		2	C	Skins, Lamb	0	13	4	0
James Sutton	Ind	2	dicker	Skins, Salted	0	26	8	0
		2.5	C	Skins, Sheep	0	25	0	0
		8	piece	Mantles	0	26	8	0
		1	quart	Skins, Lamb	0	0	20	0
John Walsh	Ind	8	tun	Wine	0	0	0	0
Richard Arthur	Ind	6	C	Skins, Lamb	0	40	0	0
		2	dicker	Hides, Salted	0	26	8	0
Maurice Walsh	Ind	2	C	Skins, Sheep	0	20	0	0
		40	piece	Fish, Salted	0	6	8	0
		9	piece	Mantles	0	30	0	0
Robert Long	Ind	1.75	C	Skins, Sheep	0	17	6	0
		1	C	Skins, Lamb	0	6	8	0
		6	piece	Mantles	0	20	0	0

Bata Kateryn of Youghal, Dennis Griffith master, to Ireland, 18th May 1517

Merchant name	Origin	Qty	Unit	Commodity	£	s.	d.	f.
Thomas Donell	Ind	5	wey	Beans	4	3	4	0
Robert Avyntre	Ind	5	wey	Malt	4	3	4	0
Henry Meagh	Ind	1.5	piece	Cloth of Assize	0	0	0	0
		7	piece	Cloth of Assize, Dozen Strait	0	0	0	0
		2	piece	Welsh *Cloth*	0	40	0	0
		8	gross	Points	0	8	0	0

Bata Anthony of Bristol, John Harrys master, from Ireland, *18th May 1517*

Merchant name	Origin	Qty	Unit	Commodity	£	s.	d.	f.
John Hall	Ind	2.5	C	Pepper	12	10	0	0
John Watson	Ind	0.5	C	Pepper	0	50	0	0

Navicula Jhesus of Bristol, Robert Power master, from Bordeaux, 22nd May 1517

Merchant name	Origin	Qty	Unit	Commodity	£	s.	d.	f.
John Vaghan	Ind	2.75	tun	Wine	0	0	0	0
		30	bale	Woad	37	10	0	0
John Shipman	Ind	3	pipe	Woad	15	0	0	0
John Drewes	Ind	27	tun	Wine	0	0	0	0
		32	bale	Woad	40	0	0	0
		4	ton	Iron	10	0	0	0
Maurice Bocher	Ind	50	bale	Woad	62	10	0	0
		10	ton	Iron	25	0	0	0
		1.5	tun	Wine	0	0	0	0
Thomas Yeate	Ind	4.5	tun	Wine	0	0	0	0

Merchant name	Origin	Qty	Unit	Commodity	£	s.	d.	f.
		3.5	pipe	Woad	15	0	0	0
Thomas Batcok	Ind	20	bale	Woad	25	0	0	0
John Brampton	Ind	5	pipe	Woad	25	0	0	0
Thomas Bilford	Ind	2.75	tun	Wine	0	0	0	0
		3	pipe	Woad	15	0	0	0
Thomas Hawykns	Ind	2	tun	Wine	0	0	0	0
Edmund Body	Ind	3	pipe	Woad	15	0	0	0
Auger de Noga	Alien	4	tun	Wine	0	0	0	0
David Vaghan	Ind	2	bale	Woad	2	10	0	0
Walter Comrowe	Ind	1.25	tun	Wine	0	0	0	0
Richard Wilde	Ind	3.75	tun	Wine	0	0	0	0
		6	bale	Woad	7	10	0	0
William Yeate	Ind	1	pipe	Wine	0	0	0	0
Henry Chamber	Ind	1	hogshead	Wine	0	0	0	0
John Willis	Ind	2	tun	Wine	0	0	0	0
John Crome	Ind	1	pipe	Wine	0	0	0	0
		0.5	ton	Rosin	0	13	4	0
John Gravell	Ind	1	pipe	Wine	0	0	0	0
John Godwyne	Ind	1	hogshead	Wine	0	0	0	0
James Brynne	Ind	1.25	tun	Wine	0	0	0	0
		2	C	Iron	0	6	8	0
Nicholas Alwyn	Ind	1	hogshead	Pitch	0	6	8	0
John Williams	Ind	1	hogshead	Pitch	0	6	8	0
John Davis	Ind	1	pipe	Wine	0	0	0	0
Edward Geavell	Ind	1	pipe	Wine	0	0	0	0
William Hetherstall	Ind	1	hogshead	Wine	0	0	0	0
John Ware	Ind	1	pipe	Woad	5	0	0	0
William Yeole	Ind	18	piece	Boxstaves	0	5	0	0

Navicula Tremer*d* of Penmarch, John Gurreo master, from Brittany, 22nd May 1517

John *Gurreo*	Alien	46.5	ton	Salt	23	5	0	0

Bata Sonday of Waterford, Edmund Malrony master, from Ireland, *22nd May 1517*

William Brothe*r*	Ind	10	C	Skins, Sheep	5	0	0	0
		4	C	Skins, Lamb	0	26	8	0
		24	piece	Mantles	4	0	0	0
		16	piece	Skins, Fox	0	2	8	0
James Nashe	Ind	5	C	Skins, Sheep	0	50	0	0
		9	piece	Mantles	0	30	0	0
Richard Barkeley	Ind	9	C	Skins, Sheep	4	10	0	0
		9	piece	Mantles	0	30	0	0
John Blake	Ind	10	C	Skins, Sheep	5	0	0	0
		8	piece	Mantles	0	26	8	0
		2	C	Fish, Salted	0	40	0	0
		4	stone	Wool, Flocks	0	0	20	0
Edmund Rothe	Ind	1.5	C	Skins, Sheep	0	15	0	0
		6.5	C	Skins, Lamb	0	43	4	0
		19	piece	Mantles	3	3	4	0
		10	piece	Skins, Fox	0	0	20	0
John Walshe	Ind	1	hogshead	Wine	0	0	0	0

Merchant name	Origin	Qty	Unit	Commodity	£	s.	d.	f.

Bata Sonday of Waterford, Edmund Malrony master, to Ireland, *22nd May 1517*

Merchant name	Origin	Qty	Unit	Commodity	£	s.	d.	f.
Edmund *Malroney*	Ind	0.5	wey	Grain	0	10	0	0
		2.5	wey	Malt	0	41	8	0
James Nashe	Ind	4	piece	Cloth of Assize	0	0	0	0
		1	lb	Saffron	0	10	0	0
		4	gross	Points	0	4	0	0
		0.5	dozen	Red-Lash	0	2	0	0
		7	lb	*Pilus Tinctus*	0	4	0	0
Richard Barkeley	Ind	3.25	piece	Cloth of Assize	0	0	0	0
		3	lb	Saffron	0	30	0	0
		1	lb	Silk, Worked	0	13	4	0
		0.5	gross	Cutts	0	0	20	0
		1	lb	Verdigris	0	0	10	0
		6	gross	Points	0	6	0	0
		0.5	dozen	Aniseed	0	0	9	0
William Brother	Ind	3.5	piece	Cloth of Assize	0	0	0	0
		2	lb	Silk, Worked	0	26	8	0
		3	lb	Saffron	0	30	0	0
		20	lb	*Pilus Tinctus*	0	6	8	0
		1	dozen	Aniseed	0	0	18	0
		6	lb	Cumin	0	0	10	0
William Tirry	Ind	2	piece	Cloth of Assize	0	0	0	0

Navicula Laurence of Penmarch, James le Mony*k* master, from Brittany, 23rd May 1517

Merchant name	Origin	Qty	Unit	Commodity	£	s.	d.	f.
John Shipman	Ind	17.25	ton	Salt	8	12	6	0
John Ware	Ind	17.25	ton	Salt	8	12	6	0
William Shipman	Ind	17.25	ton	Salt	8	12	6	0
John Sparchford	Ind	17.25	ton	Salt	8	12	6	0
James le Mony*k*	Alien	1.25	ton	Rosin and Pitch	1	13	4	0
		1	C	Breton Linen *Cloth*	0	20	0	0
		1	hogshead	Wine	0	0	0	0

Navicula Fiaker of Penmarch, Michael le Wik master, to Brittany, *23rd May 1517*

Merchant name	Origin	Qty	Unit	Commodity	£	s.	d.	f.
Michael *le Wik*	Alien	2.25	tun	Lime	0	5	7	2

Navicula Kateryn of Tenby, Richard Hunter master, *from Tenby*, 28th May 1517

Merchant name	Origin	Qty	Unit	Commodity	£	s.	d.	f.
Richard *Hunter*	Ind	17	ton	Salt	8	10	0	0

Bata Lewer of Blavet, John Clark master, from Brittany, *28th May 1517*

Merchant name	Origin	Qty	Unit	Commodity	£	s.	d.	f.
John *Clark*	Ind	12	ton	Salt	6	0	0	0
		20	yard	Breton Linen *Cloth*	0	0	20	0

Navicula Laurence of Penmarch, James le Mony*k* master, to Brittany, 4th June 1517

Merchant name	Origin	Qty	Unit	Commodity	£	s.	d.	f.
James *le Monyk*	Alien	8.25	tun	Lime	0	20	0	0
		8	piece	Mantles	0	53	4	0

Merchant name	Origin	Qty	Unit	Commodity	£	s.	d.	f.
Bata Patrike of Youghal, Maurice Russell master, from Ireland, *4th June 1517*								
Maurice Russell	Ind	1	hogshead	Wine	0	0	0	0
		2	piece	Mantles	0	6	8	0
Richard Nongull	Ind	30	lb	Pepper	0	30	0	0
		2	lb	Cloves	0	5	0	0
		2	lb	Nutmeg	0	2	0	0
		2	lb	Cinnamon	0	5	0	0
		0.5	C	Skins, Lamb	0	3	4	0
		3	piece	Skins, Fox	0	0	6	0
		4.75	tun	Wine	0	0	0	0
Tibald Blewet	Ind	1	C	Pepper	5	0	0	0
James Gallewey	Ind	160	lb	Pepper	8	0	0	0
		6	C	Skins, Lamb	0	40	0	0
		14	piece	Skins, Fox	0	2	4	0
William Walshe	Ind	1.5	C	Kermes	7	0	0	0
Bata Mare of Tenby, John Kenny master, *from Tenby, 4th June 1517*								
John *Kenny*	Ind	10	C	Pitch and Rosin	0	13	4	0
Bata George of Waterford, Thomas Marrys master, from Ireland, *4th June 1517*								
William *Cranysborow*	Ind	24	C	Skins, Sheep	12	0	0	0
		25	C	Skins, Lamb	8	6	0	0
		4	dicker	Skins, Salted	0	53	4	0
		20	piece	Mantles	3	6	8	0
		48	stone	Wool, Flocks	0	20	0	0
		12	stone	Wool, Irish	0	30	0	0
		18	piece	Skins, Fox	0	3	0	0
Robert Murho[ ]	Ind	20	C	Skins, Sheep	10	0	0	0
		40	C	Skins, Lamb	13	6	8	0
		1	dicker	Skins, Salted	0	13	4	0
		80	yard	Check *Cloth*	0	26	8	0
Robert Dowly	Ind	4	C	Skins, Sheep	0	40	0	0
		3	C	Skins, Lamb	0	20	0	0
Philip Cranysborow	Ind	60	yard	Check *Cloth*	0	20	0	0
		4	C	Skins, Sheep	0	40	0	0
		2	C	Skins, Lamb	0	13	4	0
		4	piece	Mantles	0	13	4	0
John Kenny	Ind	7	C	Skins, Sheep	3	10	0	0
		4	C	Skins, Lamb	0	26	8	0
		12	piece	Skins, Fox	0	2	0	0
		9	piece	Mantles	0	30	0	0
Bata Patrick of Waterford, John Fitzharry master, to Ireland, *4th June 1517*								
Edmund Mean	Ind	2	piece	Cloth of Assize	0	0	0	0
		1	C	*Smigmates*, Black	0	6	8	0
		1	gross	Cutts	0	3	4	0
William Everard	Ind	2	piece	Cloth of Assize	0	0	0	0
		1	lb	Silk, Worked	0	13	4	0

Merchant name	Origin	Qty	Unit	Commodity	£	s.	d.	f.
		1	lb	Saffron	0	10	0	0
		1	gross	Cutts	0	3	4	0
		8	gross	Points	0	8	0	0
John White	Ind	1	piece	Cloth of Assize	0	0	0	0
		54	lb	*Pilus Tinctus*	0	18	0	0
		8	gross	Points	0	8	0	0
Richard Lewes	Ind	1.5	piece	Cloth of Assize	0	0	0	0
		4.5	piece	Cloth of Assize, Kersey	0	0	0	0
		2	dozen	Red-Lash	0	6	0	0
		18	lb	Saffron	9	0	0	0
		8	lb	Silk, Worked	5	6	8	0
		4	gross	Cutts	0	13	4	0
		20	gross	Points	0	20	0	0
Nicholas Creagh	Ind	3	piece	Cloth of Assize	0	0	0	0
		4.5	piece	Cloth of Assize, Kersey	0	0	0	0
		1.5	gross	Cutts	0	5	0	0
		12	gross	Points	0	12	0	0
		10	lb	Silk, Worked	6	13	4	0
		14	lb	Saffron	7	0	0	0
William Verdon	Ind	40	lb	Saffron	20	0	0	0
		10	lb	Silk, Worked	6	13	4	0
		16	gross	Points	0	16	0	0
		7	gross	Cutts	0	20	0	0
		3	dozen	Red-Lash	0	6	0	0
		1	dozen	Skins, Golden	0	5	0	0

Bata Mare of Minehead, Stephen Cole master, *from Minehead, 4th June 1517*

Stephen *Cole*	Ind	2.5	burden	Fish, Salted	0	10	6	0

Bata Mare of Cardiff, William a Deane master, *from Cardiff, 6th June 1517*

Francis Cordone	Alien	2.5	piece	Camlet *Cloth*	0	30	0	0
		8.5	piece	Pany Brittishe Fox?	0	20	0	0
		6.5	piece	Pany Catt?	0	6	8	0
		8.5	piece	Pany Corse Fichew?	0	20	0	0

Bata Mare of Carmarthen, Martin Davy master, *from Carmarthen, 8th June 1517*

John Griffith	Ind	3	C	illegible	0	23	4	0

Bata Patrick of Youghal, Maurice Russell master, to Ireland, 9th June 1517

Richard Nogull	Ind	2	last	Beer	3	0	0	0
William Meagh	Ind	1	piece	Cloth of Assize	0	0	0	0
		5	piece	Welsh *Cloth*	5	0	0	0
		2	lb	Silk, Worked	0	26	8	0
		2	lb	Saffron	0	20	0	0
		4	gross	Cutts	0	13	4	0
Tibald Blewet	Ind	3.5	piece	Cloth of Assize	0	0	0	0
		3	piece	Welsh *Cloth*	3	0	0	0
		1.5	C	Hops	0	12	6	0

Merchant name	Origin	Qty	Unit	Commodity	£	s.	d.	f.
		2	gross	Cutts	0	6	8	0
		4	gross	Points	0	4	0	0
		0.5	C	Alum	0	6	8	0
William Heyn	Ind	3	lb	Silk, Worked	0	40	0	0
		3	lb	Saffron	0	30	0	0
		1	gross	Cutts	0	3	4	0
		2	gross	Points	0	2	0	0

Bata Mawdelen of Combwich, John Kent master, from Ireland, 12th June 1517

Richard Arthur	Ind	9	C	Skins, Lamb	3	0	0	0
		8	C	Skins, Sheep	4	0	0	0
		8	stone	Wool, Flocks	0	3	4	0
		12	piece	Mantles	0	40	0	0
		10	yard	Irish Frieze *Cloth*	0	3	4	0
		1	pipe	Wine	0	0	0	0
John Kent	Ind	2	tun	Wine	0	0	0	0
		1	tun	Vinegar	0	40	0	0

Bata Konylagh of Kinsale, Richard Dale master, to Ireland, 15th June 1517

William Dale	Ind	3	last	Beer	4	10	0	0

Navicula Matthew of Bristol, Richard Savery master, from Spain, 16th June 1517

John Ware	Ind	15	ton	Iron	37	10	0	0
Thomas Dale	Ind	6	ton	Iron	15	0	0	0
William Woseley	Ind	43	measure	Woad	13	8	8	0
William Shipman	Ind	22	ton	Iron	55	0	0	0
		4	pipe	Woad	20	0	0	0
		2	bale	Pect	0	40	0	0
Gilbert Cogan	Ind	4	ton	Iron	10	0	0	0
Thomas Bilford	Ind	13	ton	Iron	32	10	0	0
		8	pipe	Woad	40	0	0	0
William Rowley	Ind	4	ton	Iron	10	0	0	0
John Shipman	Ind	43	ton	Iron	107	10	0	0
		53	measure	Woad	16	11	3	0
		2	bale	Pect	0	40	0	0
Edward Jonys	Ind	1	bale	Pect	0	20	0	0
		1	pipe	Wine	0	0	0	0

Bata Kateryn of Kinsale, Thomas Donell master, from Ireland, *16th June 1517*

Thomas *Donell*	Ind	3	dicker	Skins, Salted	0	40	0	0
		100	piece	Skins, Sheep	0	8	4	0
		5	C	Skins, Lamb	0	33	4	0

Navicula Jhesus of Pasajes de San Juan, John de Burgomy master, from Spain, 19th June 1517

John *Burgomy*	Alien	1.5	ton	Iron	3	15	0	0
Thomas Hawkyn	Ind	8	ton	Iron	20	0	0	0
		4.5	pipe	Woad	22	10	0	0

Merchant name	Origin	Qty	Unit	Commodity	£	s.	d.	f.
Richard Bocher	Ind	20	ton	Iron	50	0	0	0
John Burgomy	Alien	6	dozen	Serches	0	24	0	0

Bata Kateryn of Youghal, Maurice Heron master, from Ireland, *19th June 1517*

Maurice Herne	Ind	1	virkin	Fish, Salmon	0	7	6	0
		5	piece	Mantles	0	16	8	0
		1	quart	Skins, Sheep	0	2	6	0

Bata George of Waterford, Thomas Marrys master, to Ireland, 25th June 1517

William Cranysborow	Ind	2	lb	Silk, Worked	0	26	8	0
		1	lb	Saffron	0	10	0	0
		1	C	Aniseed	0	10	0	0
		8	gross	Points	0	8	0	0
		5	lb	Thread	0	2	1	0
		8	lb	Liquorice	0	0	12	0

Bata Sonday of Cardiff, William a Deane master, *from Cardiff, 25th June 1517*

Peter Coselyn	Alien	3	tun	Wine, of Anngew	12	0	0	0
		4	piece	Ticks	0	13	4	0

Navicula Anne of Berrow, Geoffrey Rise master, from Flanders, *25th June 1517*

William Dale	Ind	9	bale	Madder	18	0	0	0
		2.5	ton	Fruit	5	0	0	0
		50	bundle	Paper, Brown	0	16	8	0
		4.5	cashe	Sugar	9	0	0	0
		12	C	Aniseed	6	0	0	0
		37	C	Alum	18	10	0	0
		1	barrel	Plate, Laten	6	0	0	0
		9	pocket	Hops	13	10	0	0
		1	C	Liquorice	0	3	4	0
Thomas Yonge	Ind	50	bundle	Paper, Brown	0	16	8	0
		3	C	Copperas	0	10	0	0
		2	bale	Madder	4	0	0	0
		2	C	*Woad*	1	6	8	0
		2	C	Aniseed	0	20	0	0
		6	barell	Plates, Latten	6	0	0	0
		20	C	Alum	10	0	0	0
		3	pocket	Hops	4	10	0	0
		1	barell	Oil, *Olive*	0	13	4	0
		1	tun	Wine	0	0	0	0
		8	dozen	Ribbons	0	33	4	0
		4	dozen	Thread, Outnall	0	20	0	0
		2	dozen	Thread, Brigges	0	13	4	0
		1	quart	Verdigris	0	10	0	0
		3	dozen	Thread Inkle	0	13	4	0
		8	dozen	Pins, Flanders	0	16	0	0
		1	M	Tennis Balls	0	10	0	0
John Snygg	Ind	6	balette	Canvas *Cloth*	9	0	0	0

Merchant name	Origin	Qty	Unit	Commodity	£	s.	d.	f.
Henry Edwards	Ind	8	balette	Canvas *Cloth*	12	0	0	0
		13	piece	Kettle (full?)	0	42	0	0
Michael Andrews	Alien	1	ton	Iron	0	50	0	0
		8	piece	Coverlet, Coarse	0	40	0	0
		6.5	piece	Fustian *Cloth*	0	15	0	0
		2.5	gross	Ribbons de fiba?	0	10	0	0
		4	gross	Points (Lasis)	0	4	2	0
		10	piece	Pin Coffers	0	0	20	0
		1	gross	Combs	0	2	6	0
		6	dozen	Combs	0	2	0	0
		1	gross	Comb Cases	0	2	6	0

Bata Kateryn of Youghal, Maurice Herne master, to Ireland, 26th June 1517

Maurice Herne	Ind	3	last	Beer	4	10	0	0
Robert Avyntre	Ind	2	piece	Cloth of Assize	0	0	0	0

Bata Kateryn of Kinsale, Thomas Donell master, to Ireland, 26th June 1517

Thomas *Donell*	Ind	2	last	Beer	3	0	0	0

Bata *Christ*ofur of Kinsale, James Cloke master, from Ireland, 26th June 1517

Richard Rownam	Ind	2.8	C	Ship-Boards	0	53	4	0
		12	stone	Wool, Flocks	0	5	0	0
		7	C	Skins, Lamb	0	46	8	0
		2.5	C	Skins, Sheep	0	25	0	0

Bata Mare of Penmarch, Thomas Dowlas master, from Brittany, 26th June 1517

Thomas *Dowlas*	Alien	20	ton	Salt	10	0	0	0
		0.5	C	Breton Linen *Cloth*	0	10	0	0

Bata Mare of Penmarch, John le Vallant master, from Brittany, 26th June 1517

John le Vallant	Alien	17	ton	Salt	8	10	0	0
		9	unknown	Poldavis *Cloth*	9	10	0	0
		1	quart	Breton Linen *Cloth*	0	5	0	0

Navicula Mare Kateryn of Bristol, William a Deane master, from Lisbon, 31st June 1517

John Shipman	Ind	10.75	tun	Oil, *Olive*	43	0	0	0
		8	ton	Salt	4	0	0	0
John Ware	Ind	5.75	tun	Oil, *Olive*	23	0	0	0
		4	ton	Salt	2	0	0	0
William Shipman	Ind	8	tun	Oil, *Olive*	32	0	0	0
		1	ton	Salt	0	10	0	0
George Hall	Ind	4.75	tun	Oil, *Olive*	19	0	0	0
		3	ton	Salt	0	30	0	0
John Thomas	Ind	3.5	tun	Oil, *Olive*	14	0	0	0
		1	ton	Salt	0	10	0	0
Robert Avyntre	Ind	10.5	tun	Oil, *Olive*	42	0	0	0

Merchant name	Origin	Qty	Unit	Commodity	£	s.	d.	f.
William Avyntre	Ind	7.5	tun	Oil, *Olive*	30	0	0	0
		2.375	C	Pepper	11	17	6	0
		1	pipe	Wine	0	0	0	0
John Kyng	Ind	10	tun	Oil, *Olive*	40	0	0	0
Roger Dawes	Ind	3.75	tun	Oil, *Olive*	15	0	0	0
Richard Bocher	Ind	1.25	tun	Oil, *Olive*	5	0	0	0
David Vaghan	Ind	3	tun	Oil, *Olive*	12	0	0	0
Thomas Dale	Ind	4.5	tun	Oil, *Olive*	18	0	0	0
William Ostrioche	Ind	1.5	tun	Oil, *Olive*	6	0	0	0
Nicholas Gay	Ind	*damaged*	tun	Oil, *Olive*	1	13	4	0
Richard Arthur	Ind	3.25	tun	Oil, *Olive*	13	0	0	0
Margareta Browne	Ind	7.5	tun	Oil, *Olive*	30	0	0	0
John Halle	Ind	5.75	tun	Oil, *Olive*	23	0	0	0
Thomas Donell	Ind	5	tun	Oil, *Olive*	20	0	0	0
David *Vaghan*	Ind	0.375	tun	Oil, *Olive*	0	30	0	0
John de Flanders	Alien	0.5	hogshead	Oil, *Olive*	0	10	0	0
Hugh Gomer	Alien	0.5	hogshead	Oil, *Olive*	0	10	0	0
Alvero Pynto	Alien	1.625	C	Pepper	8	4	0	0
		1.5	C	Comfits	0	50	0	0
Thomas Penson	Ind	1	hogshead	Oil, *Olive*	0	20	0	0
Clement Yonge	Ind	1	hogshead	Oil, *Olive*	0	20	0	0
John Porte	Ind	1	hogshead	Oil, *Olive*	0	20	0	0
Thomas Yeate	Ind	1.5	tun	Oil, *Olive*	6	0	0	0

Bata Mare Belhouse of Bristol, Richard Boughton master, from Ireland, 1st July 1517

William Edwards	Ind	10	dicker	Skins, Salted	6	13	8	0
		3	C	Ship–Boards	3	0	0	0
		3	C	Pepper	15	0	0	0
Robert Compton	Ind	1	C	Unknown	0	20	0	0

Bata Mare of Quimperlé, Henry Russell master, from Brittany, 4th July 1517

Henry *Russell*	Alien	22	ton	Salt	11	0	0	0
		5.25	C	Breton Linen *Cloth*	0	52	6	0
		2	dozen	Serches	0	6	0	0

Navicula Anne of Bergen-op-Zoom, Geoffrey Rise master, to Flanders, *4th July 1517*

William Jonys	Ind	8	piece	Welsh *Cloth*	8	0	0	0
John de Brittanyy	Alien	1	piece	Welsh *Cloth*, Dozen Strait	0	4	2	0

Bata Mare Redcliffe of Bristol, John Evans master, from Ireland, *4th July 1517*

Nicholas Browne	Ind	21.5	burden	Fish, Salted	4	10	7	0
		3	barell	Eels, Con*ger*	0	20	0	0
		6	dicker	Skins, Salted	4	13	4	0

Bata Mare of Waterford, Thomas Hewe, from Ireland, 6th July 1517

Thomas Con*r*owe	Ind	15	C	Skins, Sheep	7	10	0	0
		15	C	Skins, Lamb	5	0	0	0

Merchant name	Origin	Qty	Unit	Commodity	£	s.	d.	f.
		5	piece	Mantles	0	16	8	0
		24	stone	Wool, Flocks	0	10	0	0
		50	yard	Irish Linen *Cloth*	0	4	2	0
		36	piece	Skins, Fox	0	6	0	0
James Barrett	Ind	6	C	Skins, Sheep	3	0	0	0
		5	C	Skins, Lamb	0	33	4	0
		6	piece	Mantles	0	20	0	0
		30	yard	Check *Cloth*	0	10	0	0
		4	piece	Skins, Fox	0	0	8	0
James Fenne	Ind	3	C	Skins, Sheep	0	30	0	0
		1.3	C	Skins, Lamb	0	8	4	0
		18	piece	Mantles	3	0	0	0
		5	piece	Skins, Fox	0	0	10	0
Nicholas Walshe	Ind	4	C	Skins, Sheep	0	40	0	0
		80	piece	Skins, Lamb	0	5	0	0
		3	piece	Mantles	0	10	0	0
		2	lb	Wax	0	0	8	0
		2	piece	Skins, Fox	0	0	4	0
Walter Gough	Ind	32	piece	Skins, Salted	0	42	8	0
		24	piece	Skins, Sheep	0	2	0	0
		1	piece	Mantles	0	3	4	0
Maurice Power	Ind	0.25	C	Skins, Sheep	0	2	6	0
		0.5	C	Skins, Lamb	0	3	4	0
		2	piece	Mantles	0	6	8	0
John Hibbard	Ind	2	piece	Mantles	0	6	8	0

Navicula Jamys of Morbihan, Geoffrey Kargre master, from Brittany, *6th July 1517*

Merchant name	Origin	Qty	Unit	Commodity	£	s.	d.	f.
Geoffrey Kargres	Alien	32	ton	Salt	16	0	0	0
		4	C	Breton Linen *Cloth*	0	40	0	0
		2	piece	Oleron *Cloth*	0	13	4	0
		1	C	Breton White *Cloth*	1	0	0	0

Bata *Christo*fur of Kinsale, James Cloke master, to Ireland, 8th July 1517

Merchant name	Origin	Qty	Unit	Commodity	£	s.	d.	f.
Richard Ronan	Ind	2	last	Beer	3	0	0	0

Bata Kateryn of Cork, William Walshe master, to Ireland, 9th July 1517

Merchant name	Origin	Qty	Unit	Commodity	£	s.	d.	f.
William Walshe	Ind	1.5	last	Beer	0	45	0	0

Bata Patrik of Youghal, Richard Staunton master, from Ireland, 13th July 1517

Merchant name	Origin	Qty	Unit	Commodity	£	s.	d.	f.
Patrick Walshe	Ind	3	pipe	Fish, Salmon	4	10	0	0
		12	burden	Fish, Salted	0	50	0	0
		12	piece	Mantles	0	40	0	0
		2	C	Ship–Boards	0	40	0	0
		1	tun	Wine	0	0	0	0
Richard Bluet	Ind	5.5	C	Skins, Sheep	0	55	0	0
		2	C	Skins, Lamb	0	13	4	0
		205	lb	Pepper	10	5	0	0
Dennis P*hilips*	Ind	5.5	pipe	Fish, Salmon	8	5	0	0

Merchant name	Origin	Qty	Unit	Commodity	£	s.	d.	f.
Robert White	Ind	1.5	C	Skins, Sheep	0	15	0	0
		2	C	Skins, Lamb	0	13	4	0
		6	piece	Mantles	0	20	0	0
		30	lb	Pepper	0	30	0	0
William Ffox	Ind	2	pipe	Fish, Salmon	3	0	0	0
		4	piece	Mantles	0	13	4	0
		2	C	Pepper	10	0	0	0
		4	C	Skins, Sheep	0	40	0	0
Richard Avyntre	Ind	1.5	pipe	Fish, Salmon	0	45	0	0
		1	C	Skins, Sheep	0	10	0	0
Tibald Bluet	Ind	23	piece	Mantles	4	0	0	0
James Grene	Ind	16	piece	Mantles	0	53	4	0
Patrick Flanygan	Ind	12	lb	Pepper	0	12	0	0

Bata Fawcon of Waterford, Nicholas Rothe master, from Ireland, 15th July 1517

Merchant name	Origin	Qty	Unit	Commodity	£	s.	d.	f.
Richard Bluet	Ind	10	lb	Cloves	0	23	0	0
Nicholas Rothe	Ind	2	piece	Mantles	0	6	8	0
Thomas Sherlok	Ind	10	C	Skins, Lamb	3	6	8	0
		10	piece	Mantles	0	33	4	0
		2.5	C	Skins, Sheep	0	25	0	0
Nicholas Mealy	Ind	8	C	Skins, Sheep	4	0	0	0
		4.5	C	Skins, Lamb	0	30	0	0
		24	piece	Skins, Fox	0	4	0	0
		16	piece	Mantles	0	53	4	0
Edward White	Ind	7	C	Skins, Sheep	3	10	0	0
		8	C	Skins, Lamb	0	53	4	0
		10	piece	Mantles	0	33	4	0
		20	piece	Skins, Fox	0	3	4	0
James Baron	Ind	8	C	Skins, Sheep	4	0	0	0
		5	C	Skins, Lamb	0	33	4	0
		2	piece	Skins, Fox	0	0	4	0
		20	piece	Mantles	3	6	8	0
		2	piece	Skins, Marten	0	2	0	0
		1	piece	Skins, Otter	0	0	5	0
Nicholas Gower	Ind	7	C	Skins, Sheep	3	10	0	0
		2	C	Skins, Lamb	0	13	4	0
		4	piece	Skins, Fox	0	0	8	0
		19	piece	Mantles	3	3	4	0
William Rowirk?	Ind	7	C	Skins, Sheep	3	10	0	0
Thomas Awnell	Ind	2	piece	Mantles	0	6	8	0
		3	stone	Wool, Flocks	0	0	15	0
		1	C	Skins, Lamb	0	6	8	0
Edmund Maydoft	Ind	3	piece	Mantles	0	10	0	0
Walter Wodlok	Ind	150	piece	Skins, Sheep	0	12	6	0
Robert Clere	Ind	3	C	Skins, Lamb	0	20	0	0
		6	piece	Mantles	0	20	0	0
		7	piece	Skins, Salted	0	9	4	0
John Dawny	Ind	5	C	Skins, Sheep	0	50	0	0
		28	piece	Mantles	4	13	4	0
		24	yard	Check Cloth	0	8	0	0
Dennis Donell	Ind	2.5	C	Skins, Sheep	0	25	0	0

Merchant name	Origin	Qty	Unit	Commodity	£	s.	d.	f.
		1.5	C	Skins, Lamb	0	10	0	0

Bata Anne of Cardiff, Robert Marshall master, from Ireland, *15th July 1517*

Merchant name	Origin	Qty	Unit	Commodity	£	s.	d.	f.
William Rowirk?	Ind	5	C	Skins, Lamb	0	33	4	0
Thomas Shirlok	Ind	1	C	Skins, Sheep	0	10	0	0
		5	piece	Mantles	0	16	8	0

Bata Sonday of Waterford, Edmund Malroney master, from Ireland, 17th July 1517

Merchant name	Origin	Qty	Unit	Commodity	£	s.	d.	f.
Edward Malrony	Ind	2	C	Skins, Lamb	0	13	4	0
		1.5	C	Skins, Sheep	0	15	0	0
		3	stone	Wool, Flocks	0	0	15	0
Thomas Hedyn	Ind	10	C	Skins, Sheep	5	0	0	0
		3	C	Skins, Lamb	0	9	0	0
		12	piece	Skins, Fox	0	2	0	0
James Quirke	Ind	57	piece	Mantles	9	10	0	0
		14	piece	Skins, Fox	0	2	4	0
John Walshe	Ind	2	C	Skins, Sheep	0	20	0	0
		1.5	dicker	Skins, Salted	0	20	0	0
		7	piece	Mantles	0	23	4	0
John Blake	Ind	0.75	tun	Wine	0	0	0	0
		3	dicker	Skins, Salted	0	40	0	0
		1.5	C	Skins, Sheep	0	15	0	0
		3.5	C	Skins, Lamb	0	23	4	0
		6	piece	Mantles	0	20	0	0
		4	stone	Wool, Flocks	0	0	20	0
Nicholas *illegible*	Ind	0.5	C	Pepper	0	50	0	0
Peter Dobyn	Ind	1	C	Skins, Sheep	0	30	0	0
		2	C	Skins, Lamb	0	13	4	0
		12	stone	Wool, Flocks	0	5	0	0
		0.5	pipe	Fish, Salmon	0	15	0	0
		12	piece	Mantles	0	40	0	0
		10	lb	Wax	0	3	4	0
		12	piece	Skins, Fox	0	2	0	0
Dennis Donell	Ind	18	piece	Mantles	3	0	0	0
		0.5	C	Skins, Sheep	0	5	0	0
Thomas Sherlock	Ind	8	piece	Skins, Salted	0	10	8	0
		0.75	C	Skins, Sheep	0	7	6	0
		0.5	C	Skins, Lamb	0	3	4	0

Bata Mare Bosher of Waterford, Nicholas Power master, from Ireland, *17th July 1517*

Merchant name	Origin	Qty	Unit	Commodity	£	s.	d.	f.
Gerald Wale	Ind	5	C	Skins, Sheep	0	50	0	0
		3	C	Skins, Lamb	0	20	0	0
		16	piece	Mantles	0	53	4	0
		0.5	dicker	Skins, Salted	0	6	8	0
	damaged		?	Canvas *Cloth*	0	33	4	0
Philip Doan	Ind	80	piece	Skins, Sheep	0	6	8	0
		10	piece	Mantles	0	33	0	0
		1	dicker	Skins, Salted	0	13	4	0
		4	stone	Wool, Flocks	0	0	20	0

Merchant name	Origin	Qty	Unit	Commodity	£	s.	d.	f.
John Ley	Ind	4	piece	Mantles	0	13	4	0
Nicholas Power	Ind	2.75	tun	Wine	0	0	0	0
		2	dicker	Skins, Salted	0	26	8	0
		2	piece	Mantles	0	6	8	0
Peter Follows	Ind	80	piece	Skins, Sheep	0	6	8	0
		2	piece	Mantles	0	6	8	0
Peter Walshe	Ind	10	piece	Mantles	0	33	4	0
		30	yard	Check *Cloth*	0	10	0	0
		10	C	Skins, Lamb	3	6	8	0
		9	C	Skins, Sheep	4	10	0	0
		30	piece	Skins, Fox	0	5	0	0
John Dawes	Ind	40	piece	Mantles	6	13	4	0
Isaac Malony	Ind	40	piece	Mantles	6	13	4	0
		2	C	Irish Linen *Cloth*	0	20	0	0
		3.25	C	Skins, Sheep	0	32	6	0
		1.5	C	Skins, Lamb	0	10	0	0
		5	piece	Skins, Fox	0	0	10	0
David Rothe	Ind	70	piece	Mantles	11	13	4	0
		30	yard	Check *Cloth*	0	10	0	0
		4.5	C	Skins, Sheep	0	35	0	0
		1	C	Skins, Lamb	0	6	8	0
		6	piece	Skins, Fox	0	0	12	0
		8	stone	Wool, Irish	0	20	0	0
		5	stone	Wool, Flocks	0	2	1	0
James Savage	Ind	74	piece	Mantles	12	6	8	0
		1.5	C	Skins, Lamb	0	10	0	0
		3	C	Skins, Sheep	0	30	0	0
		10	stone	Wool, Flocks	0	4	2	0
Thomas Rafter	Ind	4.5	C	Skins, Sheep	0	45	0	0
		7	C	Skins, Lamb	0	46	8	0
		72	piece	Skins, Fox	0	12	0	0
		26	piece	Mantles	4	6	8	0
Thomas Gibbs	Ind	4	C	Skins, Sheep	0	40	0	0
		9	piece	Mantles	0	30	0	0
Thomas Ragget	Ind	4	C	Skins, Sheep	0	40	0	0
		2	C	Skins, Lamb	0	13	4	0
		18	piece	Mantles	3	0	0	0
Peter Nogull	Ind	8	piece	Mantles	0	26	8	0
		12	stone	Wool, Flocks	0	5	0	0
John Cashyn	Ind	1.5	C	Skins, Sheep	0	15	0	0
		1	C	Skins, Lamb	0	6	8	0
		11	piece	Mantles	0	36	8	0

Bata Patrik of New Ross, Nicholas Gregorie master, from Ireland, 18th July 1517

Merchant name	Origin	Qty	Unit	Commodity	£	s.	d.	f.
Nicholas *Gregorie*	Ind	0.5	pipe	Fish, Salmon	0	15	0	0
		2	C	Skins, Sheep	0	20	4	0
		2	C	Skins, Lamb	0	13	4	0
		3	piece	Mantles	0	10	0	0
James Edwards	Ind	50	piece	Mantles	8	6	8	0
		80	yard	Check *Cloth*	0	26	8	0
		4	C	Skins, Sheep	0	40	0	0

Merchant name	Origin	Qty	Unit	Commodity	£	s.	d.	f.
		3.5	C	Skins, Lamb	0	30	0	0
		24	piece	Skins, Fox	0	4	8	0
		2	dicker	Skins, Salted	0	26	8	0
Philip Furbur	Ind	14	piece	Mantles	0	46	8	0
Edmund Seise?	Ind	68	piece	Mantles	11	6	0	0
		5	C	Skins, Sheep	0	50	0	0
		4	C	Skins, Lamb	0	26	8	0
Thomas Axbrigg	Ind	28	piece	Mantles	4	13	4	0
		6.5	C	Skins, Lamb	0	43	4	0
		30	piece	Skins, Fox	0	5	0	0
		80	yard	Check Cloth	0	26	8	0
Patrick Axbrigg	Ind	47	piece	Mantles	7	16	7	0
		3	C	Skins, Sheep	0	30	0	0
		4	piece	Skins, Fox	0	0	8	0
		1	piece	Skins, Marten	0	0	12	0
		20	yard	Irish Linen Cloth	0	0	20	0
		2	C	Skins, Lamb	0	13	4	0
Dennis Taillor	Ind	1	C	Skins, Sheep	0	10	0	0
		2.25	C	Skins, Lamb	0	15	0	0
		6	piece	Skins, Fox	0	0	12	0
Thomas Baron	Ind	2.25	C	Skins, Lamb	0	15	0	0
		1.5	C	Skins, Sheep	0	15	0	0
		13	piece	Skins, Fox	0	2	2	0
		2	piece	Skins, Otter	0	0	10	0
		47	piece	Mantles	8	0	0	0
		2	pipe	Fish, Salmon	3	0	0	0
Robert Garrat	Ind	55	piece	Mantles	9	3	4	0
		60	yard	Check Cloth	0	20	0	0
		8	C	Skins, Lamb	0	53	4	0
		1	C	Skins, Sheep	0	10	0	0
		1	C	Skins, Kid	0	5	0	0
		10	piece	Skins, Fox	0	0	20	0
		75	yard	Irish Linen Cloth	0	6	3	0
		50	stone	Wool, Flocks	0	20	10	0
Edward Leonard	Ind	6	C	Skins, Sheep	3	0	0	0
		2	C	Skins, Lamb	0	13	4	0
		2	C	Skins, Kid	0	10	0	0
		30	piece	Mantles	5	10	0	0
		20	piece	Skins, Fox	0	4	0	0
		12	stone	Wool, Flocks	0	5	0	0
John Cotrell	Ind	8	C	Skins, Lamb	0	53	4	0
		2	C	Skins, Sheep	0	20	0	0
		20	piece	Mantles	3	6	8	0
		1.75	pipe	Fish, Salmon	0	52	6	0

Bata Mare of Cork, Philip Walsh master, from Ireland, 20th July 1517

Merchant name	Origin	Qty	Unit	Commodity	£	s.	d.	f.
Philip Walshe	Ind	8	piece	Mantles	0	26	8	0
Robert Tirry	Ind	5	C	Ship-Boards	5	0	0	0
		2.75	pipe	Fish, Salmon	4	2	6	0
		13	piece	Skins, Salted	0	30	8	0
		6	piece	Mantles	0	20	0	0

Merchant name	Origin	Qty	Unit	Commodity	£	s.	d.	f.
		3	C	Skins, Sheep	0	30	0	0
		16	piece	Skins, Lamb	0	0	10	0
		3	piece	Skins, Fox	0	0	6	0
		5	stone	Wool, Flocks	0	2	1	0
James Vurhedon	Ind	12	piece	Mantles	0	40	0	0
		0.5	C	Skins, Sheep	0	5	0	0
		0.75	pipe	Fish, Salmon	0	22	6	0
		6	stone	Wool, Flocks	0	2	6	0
		0.3	C	Skins, Lamb	0	0	20	0
Edmund Serchsile	Ind	17	piece	Mantles	0	56	8	0
		21	piece	Skins, Lamb	0	0	16	0
		6	piece	Skins, Fox	0	0	12	0
		0.5	pipe	Fish, Salmon	0	15	0	0
Oliver Tirry	Ind	1	pipe	Fish, Salmon	0	30	0	0
		16	piece	Mantles	0	53	4	0
		2	C	Skins, Sheep	0	20	0	0
		6	stone	Wool, Flocks	0	2	6	0
James Mathew	Ind	19	piece	Mantles	3	3	4	0
		2.5	C	Skins, Sheep	0	25	0	0
		1.2	C	Skins, Lamb	0	7	9	0
		24	piece	Skins, Fox	0	4	0	0
		3	stone	Wool, Flocks	0	0	15	0
Clement Skid[ ]	Ind	8	piece	Mantles	0	26	8	0
		0.5	C	Skins, Sheep	0	5	0	0
James Creagh	Ind	1	pipe	Fish, Salmon	0	30	0	0
		18	piece	Mantles	3	0	0	0
		30	piece	Skins, Sheep	0	2	6	0
Gerald Mather	Ind	14	piece	Mantles	0	46	8	0
		1.5	pipe	Fish, Salmon	0	45	0	0
John Meagh	Ind	16	piece	Mantles	0	53	4	0
		1.75	pipe	Fish, Salmon	0	22	6	0
Robert Meryk	Ind	8	piece	Mantles	0	26	8	0
		0.25	pipe	Fish, Salmon	0	7	6	0
		1	C	Skins, Sheep	0	10	0	0
		12	stone	Wool, Flocks	0	5	0	0
		2	piece	Skins, Salted	0	2	8	0
James Power	Ind	6	piece	Mantles	0	20	0	0
Edmund Copner	Ind	2.25	pipe	Fish, Salmon	3	7	6	0
		4	C	Skins, Sheep	0	40	0	0
		1	dicker	Skins, Salted	0	13	4	0
		1.5	C	Skins, Lamb	0	10	0	0
		40	piece	Skins, Fox	0	6	8	0
		3	piece	Skins, Otter	0	0	15	0
		24	piece	Mantles	4	0	0	0
Thomas Morow	Ind	4	piece	Mantles	0	13	4	0
		0.5	C	Skins, Lamb	0	3	4	0
Edmund Tirry	Ind	2	pipe	Fish, Salmon	3	0	0	0
		2	C	Skins, Sheep	0	20	0	0
		2	C	Skins, Lamb	0	13	4	0
		6	piece	Skins, Fox	0	0	12	0
		3	piece	Mantles	0	10	0	0
Nicholas Tirry	Ind	3	dicker	Skins, Salted	0	40	0	0

Merchant name	Origin	Qty	Unit	Commodity	£	s.	d.	f.
		1.5	C	Skins, Sheep	0	15	0	0
		16	piece	Skins, Wild	0	0	8	0
		2	piece	Mantles	0	6	8	0
		0.8	C	Skins, Lamb	0	4	5	0
		1	burden	Fish, Salmon	0	7	6	0
		8	piece	Skins, Fox	0	0	16	0

Navicula Laurence of Penmarch, James le Monyk master, from La Rochelle, *20th July 1517*

Merchant name	Origin	Qty	Unit	Commodity	£	s.	d.	f.
Nicholas Tirry	Ind	2	piece	Skins, Otter	0	0	10	0
John Shipman	Ind	28	ton	Salt	14	0	0	0
John Ware	Ind	16	ton	Salt	8	0	0	0
William Shipman	Ind	22	ton	Salt	11	0	0	0
James le Monyk	Alien	1.5	C	Breton Linen *Cloth*	0	15	0	0

Bata Clement of Wexford, Thomas Caron master, from Ireland, *20th July 1517*

Merchant name	Origin	Qty	Unit	Commodity	£	s.	d.	f.
John Synot	Ind	5	C	Skins, Lamb	0	33	4	0
		1	C	Skins, Sheep	0	10	0	0
		2	piece	Mantles	0	6	8	0
		2	dicker	Skins, Salted	0	26	8	0
Thomas Butlar	Ind	6	pipe	Fish, Salmon	9	0	0	0
		2.5	dicker	Skins, Salted	0	33	4	0
Nicholas Stafford	Ind	3	C	Skins, Lamb	0	20	0	0
		3	C	Skins, Sheep	0	30	0	0
		2	C	Skins, Kid	0	10	0	0
		9	piece	Mantles	0	30	0	0
		3	dicker	Skins, Salted	0	40	0	0
Thomas Stafford	Ind	12	piece	Mantles	0	40	0	0
		1.5	C	Skins, Sheep	0	15	0	0
		2	C	Skins, Lamb	0	13	4	0
		2	dicker	Skins, Salted	0	26	8	0
Francis Tornor	Alien	6	C	Skins, Sheep	3	0	0	0
		6	C	Skins, Lamb	0	40	0	0
		12	piece	Mantles	0	40	0	0
		4	C	Skins, Kid	0	20	0	0

Bata Mare of Bristol, Thomas Nongull master, from Ireland, 21st July 1517

Merchant name	Origin	Qty	Unit	Commodity	£	s.	d.	f.
Thomas *Nongull*	Ind	8	C	Fish, Hake	4	0	0	0
		8	burden	Fish, Salted	0	33	4	0
Thomas Fyan	Ind	8	piece	Mantles	0	26	8	0
George Hall	Ind	0.75	tun	Oil, *Olive*	3	0	0	0
William Avyntre	Ind	1	pipe	Wine	0	0	0	0
Robert Morow	Ind	150	piece	Skins, Sheep	0	12	6	0
Thomas Nongull	Ind	1	tun	Wine	0	0	0	0
John Jay	Ind	1	tun	Vinegar	0	40	0	0
Edmund Pers	Ind	1	tun	Wine	0	0	0	0
Alice Poplay	Ind	1	pipe	Wine	0	0	0	0

Merchant name	Origin	Qty	Unit	Commodity	£	s.	d.	f.

Bata Marget of Oldbury-on-Severn, Philip Bocher master, from Ireland, 22nd July 1517

Merchant name	Origin	Qty	Unit	Commodity	£	s.	d.	f.
John Lynke	Ind	4.5	pipe	Fish, Salmon	6	15	0	0
		6	piece	Mantles	0	20	0	0

Navicula John of Pasajes de San Juan, Michael de Lana master, from Spain, 24th July 1517

Merchant name	Origin	Qty	Unit	Commodity	£	s.	d.	f.
Gilbert Cogan	Ind	25	ton	Iron	62	10	0	0
		86	measure	Woad	26	17	6	0
Thomas Batcok	Ind	16	ton	Iron	40	0	0	0
John Drewes	Ind	7	ton	Iron	17	10	0	0
		121	measure	Woad	37	16	3	0
John Coke	Ind	5	ton	Iron	12	10	0	0
John Hunter	Ind	7.5	ton	Iron	18	15	0	0
John Brampton	Ind	2	ton	Iron	5	0	0	0
Lucas Bordway	Alien	1	ton	Rosin and Pitch	0	26	8	0
Michael Calker	Alien	4	dozen	Serches	0	16	0	0
Robert Pers	Ind	4.5	ton	Iron	11	5	0	0
		15.5	bale	Woad	19	7	6	0
Richard Hoby	Ind	1	bale	Woad	0	25	0	0
Maurice Bocher	Ind	21.25	ton	Iron	53	2	6	0
		4	bale	Paper, Writing	4	0	0	0
Richard Bocher	Ind	13.5	ton	Iron	33	15	0	0

Navicula John of Errenteria, Anthony de la Sola master, from Spain, 27th July 1517

Merchant name	Origin	Qty	Unit	Commodity	£	s.	d.	f.
John Shipman	Ind	18	ton	Iron	45	0	0	0
John Ware	Ind	19	ton	Iron	47	10	0	0
William Shipman	Ind	18	ton	Iron	45	0	0	0
John Wyot	Ind	3	ton	Iron	7	10	0	0
Thomas Bilford	Ind	2	ton	Iron	5	0	0	0
		4.5	pipe	Woad	22	10	0	0
John Rowland	Ind	3	ton	Iron	7	10	0	0
John de la Sola	Alien	2	ton	Iron	5	0	0	0
Robert Rowlow	Ind	4.5	pipe	Woad	22	10	0	0
		5	pipe	Woad	25	0	0	0
John Vaghan	Ind	1	ton	Iron	0	50	0	0
		2.25	pipe	Woad	11	5	0	0
Edward Jonys	Ind	1.25	ton	Iron	3	2	6	0
John Kyng	Ind	45	measure	Woad	14	15	0	0
Michael de Claregin	Alien	4	dozen	Serches	0	16	0	0
Thomas Dale	Ind	4.5	pipe	Woad	22	10	0	0
John Sparcheford	Ind	13	ton	Iron	32	10	0	0

Bata Trynyte of Chepstow, William Heyne master, *from Chepstow*, 27th July 1517

Merchant name	Origin	Qty	Unit	Commodity	£	s.	d.	f.
Richard Kew	Ind	5	C	Cork, White	0	16	8	0
		2	C	Fish, Hake	1	0	0	0

Bata Trynyte of Carmarthen, John Raynold master, *from Carmarthen, 27th July 1517*

Merchant name	Origin	Qty	Unit	Commodity	£	s.	d.	f.
Philip Davy	Ind	2.25	pipe	Fish, Salmon	3	7	6	0

Merchant name	Origin	Qty	Unit	Commodity	£	s.	d.	f.

Bata Jhesus of Cardiff, Thomas Raynold master, *from Cardiff, 27th July 1517*

| Philip Jonys | Ind | 2 | tun | Wine | 0 | 0 | 0 | 0 |

Bata, Name Unknown, of Milford Haven, Thomas Gefferies master, *from Milford Haven, 27th July 1517*

| Thomas Gefferies | Ind | 0.5 | C | Fish, Salted | 0 | 10 | 0 | 0 |

Bata Trinite of Cardiff, John Browne master, *from Cardiff, 27th July 1517*

John Amidas?	Ind	2	pipe	Fish, Salmon	3	0	0	0
Thomas Donell	Ind	1	C	Pepper	5	0	0	0
Thomas Yonge	Ind	514	lb	Pepper	25	14	0	0
Richard Blewet	Ind	0.25	pipe	Fish, Salmon	0	7	6	0

Navicula Mawdelen of Errenteria, John Surre master, from Spain, *27th July 1517*

Humphrey Bosgrove	Ind	3.33	ton	Iron	8	6	8	0
Roger Dawes	Ind	4	ton	Iron	10	0	0	0
		10	bale	Woad	12	10	0	0
Thomas Dale	Ind	6.25	ton	Iron	16	17	6	0
		70.5	bale	Woad	88	2	6	0
John Shipman	Ind	10	ton	Iron	25	0	0	0
William Shipman	Ind	10	ton	Iron	25	0	0	0
John Rowland	Ind	4	pipe	Woad	20	0	0	0
William Rowley	Ind	20	ton	Iron	50	0	0	0
		5.9	pipe	Woad	29	15	0	0
Thomas Batcok	Ind	4	ton	Iron	10	0	0	0
		19	bale	Woad	23	15	0	0
John Kyng	Ind	2	ton	Iron	5	0	0	0
William Woseley	Ind	40	ton	Iron	100	0	0	0
		63	bale	Woad	78	15	0	0
		3	measure	Woad	0	19	0	0
Johanna Bromwell	Ind	2	dozen	Serches	0	8	0	0
William White	Ind	1	hogshead	Wine	0	0	0	0

Bata Jamys of Hanley Castle, Richard Nethawey master, from Chepstow, 28th July 1517

| John Bullyughin | Ind | 4 | ton | Salt | 2 | 0 | 0 | 0 |
| | | 17 | dozen | Cork, Black | 0 | 28 | 4 | 0 |

Navicula Trynyte of Bristol, Evan Danyell master, from Sanlúcar de Barrameda, 29th July 1517

Thomas Harte	Ind	2.5	tun	Wine	0	0	0	0
		1	pipe	Oil, *Olive*	0	40	0	0
		0.25	tun	Vinegar	0	10	2	0
		2.25	C	Soap	0	22	6	0
Thomas Evan	Ind	2.5	tun	Wine	0	0	0	0
		3.25	C	*Smigmates*	1	12	6	0
Robert Avyntre	Ind	2.25	tun	Oil, *Olive*	9	0	0	0

Merchant name	Origin	Qty	Unit	Commodity	£	s.	d.	f.
		7.5	C	*Smigmates*	3	15	0	0
Thomas Donell	Ind	2	tun	Oil, *Olive*	8	0	0	0
William a Dean	Ind	1	pipe	Wine	0	0	0	0
John Kyng	Ind	4	tun	Oil, *Olive*	16	0	0	0
		14	C	*Smigmates*	6	10	0	0
William Avyntre	Ind	2	tun	Oil, *Olive*	8	0	0	0
Evan Danyell	Ind	1.75	tun	Oil, *Olive*	7	0	0	0
		20	C	Alum	10	0	0	0
		3	C	*Smigmates*	1	10	0	0
		0.375	tun	Vinegar	0	15	0	0
John Cappes	Ind	17.25	C	*Smigmates*	8	12	6	0
		10	tun	Wine	0	0	0	0
		3.75	tun	Oil, *Olive*	15	0	0	0
Walter Comrowe	Ind	10.5	tun	Wine	0	0	0	0
Richard Arthur	Ind	2	tun	Oil, *Olive*	8	0	0	0
William Ostriche	Ind	2	tun	Oil, *Olive*	8	0	0	0
Leonard Osburn	Ind	4.75	tun	Wine	0	0	0	0
Robert Elyot	Ind	4.75	tun	Wine	0	0	0	0
Robert Hille	Ind	4	tun	Oil, *Olive*	16	0	0	0
William Shipman	Ind	1.5	tun	Wine	0	0	0	0

Bata Patrik of Youghal, Richard Staunton master, to Ireland, *29th July 1517*

Merchant name	Origin	Qty	Unit	Commodity	£	s.	d.	f.
John Dee	Ind	5	piece	Cloth of Assize	0	0	0	0
		1	piece	Welsh *Cloth*	0	20	0	0
		2	gross	Cutts	0	6	8	0
		3	gross	Points	0	3	0	0
		2	lb	Saffron	0	20	0	0
George Meaghe	Ind	7	piece	Cloth of Assize, Dozen Strait	0	0	0	0
		5	piece	Cloth of Assize	0	0	0	0
		1	gross	Cutts	0	6	8	0
Patrick Walshe	Ind	4.5	piece	Cloth of Assize	0	0	0	0
		1	C	Hops	0	6	8	0
		0.5	C	Alum	0	6	8	0
		50	lb	*Pilus Tinctus*	0	16	8	0
		0.5	C	Aniseed	0	5	0	0
		1	gross	Cutts	0	3	4	0
		1	lb	Silk, Worked	0	13	4	0
		1	lb	Saffron	0	10	0	0
		4	lb	Thread	0	0	20	0
		0.5	dozen	Red-Lash	0	2	6	0
		0.5	dozen	Skins, Golden	0	3	4	0
William Ffox	Ind	7	piece	Cloth of Assize, Dozen Strait	0	0	0	0
		3.5	piece	Cloth of Assize	0	0	0	0
		1	piece	Welsh *Cloth*	0	20	0	0
		2	gross	Cutts	0	6	8	0
		8	gross	Points	0	8	0	0
Tibald Bluet	Ind	3	piece	Cloth of Assize, Dozen Strait	0	0	0	0
		1	gross	Cutts	0	3	4	0
		6	lb	Saffron	3	0	0	0
John Amidas?	Ind	4	piece	Cloth of Assize	0	0	0	0
		1	piece	Welsh *Cloth*	0	20	0	0

Merchant name	Origin	Qty	Unit	Commodity	£	s.	d.	f.

Bata Mare of Waterford, Thomas Hewe master, to Ireland, 30th July 1517

Merchant name	Origin	Qty	Unit	Commodity	£	s.	d.	f.
Thomas Conrowe	Ind	5	piece	Cloth of Assize	0	0	0	0
		5	lb	Saffron	0	50	0	0
		3	lb	Silk, Worked	0	40	0	0
		4	gross	Cutts	0	13	4	0
		3	quart	Aniseed	0	7	6	0
		18	gross	Points	0	18	0	0
		3	lb	Cumin	0	0	4	0
James Barrett	Ind	1	piece	Cloth of Assize	0	0	0	0
		3	lb	Silk, Worked	0	40	0	0
		3.5	lb	Saffron	0	35	0	0
		2	dozen	Aniseed	0	3	4	0
		12	lb	Alum	0	0	20	0
		13	gross	Points	0	13	0	0
		2	gross	Cutts	0	6	8	0
James Finine	Ind	1	lb	Saffron	0	10	0	0
		0.5	lb	Silk, Worked	0	6	8	0
		1	dozen	Aniseed	0	0	20	0
		1	gross	Cutts	0	3	4	0
		4.5	gross	Points	0	4	6	0
Nicholas Walshe	Ind	0.5	lb	Saffron	0	5	0	0
		0.5	lb	Silk, Worked	0	6	8	0
		4	gross	Points	0	4	0	0
		0.5	gross	Cutts	0	0	20	0
		12	lb	Alum	0	0	20	0
		0.5	dozen	Aniseed	0	0	9	0

Navicula Grabriell of Palma, Evan de Guan master, from La Rochelle, 31st July 1517

Merchant name	Origin	Qty	Unit	Commodity	£	s.	d.	f.
Robert Barbew	Alien	57	ton	Salt	28	10	0	0
		4	piece	Oleron Cloth	0	26	8	0
		3	bolt	Poldavis Cloth	0	30	0	0

Bata Mare Bosher of Bristol, Nicholas Power master, to Ireland, 31st July 1517

Merchant name	Origin	Qty	Unit	Commodity	£	s.	d.	f.
Thomas Rafter	Ind	2.5	piece	Cloth of Assize	0	0	0	0
		3	lb	Saffron	0	30	0	0
		5	lb	Silk, Worked	3	6	8	0
		6	lb	Thread	0	2	6	0
		4	pair	Stock-Cards	0	4	0	0
		3	gross	Cutts	0	10	0	0
		2	dozen	Caps, for Children	0	13	4	0
		1	dozen	Aniseed	0	0	18	0
		16	gross	Points	0	16	0	0
		6	lb	Cumin	0	0	10	0
James Savage	Ind	3	lb	Saffron	0	30	0	0
		2	lb	Silk, Worked	0	26	8	0
		3	gross	Cutts	0	10	0	0
		4	dozen	Aniseed	0	6	0	0
		6	gross	Points	0	6	0	0
		2	dozen	?	0	0	8	0

Merchant name	Origin	Qty	Unit	Commodity	£	s.	d.	f.
Thomas Rugges	Ind	1	piece	Cloth of Assize	0	0	0	0
		2	lb	Silk, Worked	0	26	8	0
		2	lb	Saffron	0	20	0	0
		1	gross	Cutts	0	3	4	0
		6	gross	Points	0	6	0	0
		3	dozen	Aniseed	0	4	6	0
		12	lb	*Pilus Tinctus*	0	4	0	0
		0.5	dozen	Caps	0	5	0	0
Peter Walshe	Ind	2.5	piece	Cloth of Assize	0	0	0	0
		1	piece	Cloth of Assize, Dozen Strait	0	0	0	0
		5	lb	Silk, Worked	3	6	8	0
		2	lb	Saffron	0	20	0	0
		13	gross	Points	0	13	0	0
		3	gross	Cutts	0	10	0	0
		2.5	dozen	Caps, for Children	0	20	0	0
		6	pair	Stock-Cards	0	6	0	0
John Danyell	Ind	5	piece	Cloth of Assize	0	0	0	0
		1	lb	Silk, Worked	0	13	4	0
		1	lb	Saffron	0	10	0	0
		1	gross	Cutts	0	3	4	0
		7	gross	Points	0	7	0	0
illegible Hall	Ind	2	lb	Silk, Worked	0	26	8	0
		3	dozen	Aniseed	0	4	6	0
		6	lb	*Pilus Tinctus*	0	2	0	0
		1	dozen	Skins, Golden	0	5	0	0

Navicula Mare of Bayonne, Nicholas Richard master, from Brittany, 1st August 1517

Merchant name	Origin	Qty	Unit	Commodity	£	s.	d.	f.
Nicholas Richard	Alien	38	ton	Salt	19	0	0	0

Navicula Tremurd of Penmarch, John Gurreo master, from Brittany, *1st August 1517*

Merchant name	Origin	Qty	Unit	Commodity	£	s.	d.	f.
Richard Bocher	Ind	49.25	ton	Salt	24	12	6	0

Bata Savior of Milford Haven, Thomas Harry master, from Ireland, *1st August 1517*

Merchant name	Origin	Qty	Unit	Commodity	£	s.	d.	f.
Thomas Harry	Ind	1.5	C	Fish, Hake	0	15	0	0
		2	burden	Fish, Salted	0	8	4	0

Bata Fawcon of Waterford, Nicholas Rothe master, to Ireland, *1st August 1517*

Merchant name	Origin	Qty	Unit	Commodity	£	s.	d.	f.
Nicholas Morty	Ind	1	piece	Cloth of Assize	0	0	0	0
		2	lb	Saffron	0	20	0	0
		1.5	lb	Silk, Worked	0	20	0	0
		3	dozen	Aniseed	0	4	6	0
		1	gross	Points	0	0	12	0
		0.5	gross	Cutts	0	0	20	0
Richard Gwere	Ind	3	lb	Silk, Worked	0	40	0	0
		2	lb	Saffron	0	20	0	0
		1	dozen	Aniseed	0	0	18	0
		4	gross	Points	0	4	0	0
Robert Clere	Ind	1	piece	Cloth of Assize	0	0	0	0

Merchant name	Origin	Qty	Unit	Commodity	£	s.	d.	f.
		1	dozen	Aniseed	0	0	18	0
		1.5	gross	Cutts	0	5	0	0
		12	lb	*Pilus Tinctus*	0	4	0	0
John Dawny	Ind	5	piece	Cloth of Assize	0	0	0	0
		3	lb	Saffron	0	30	0	0
		1	lb	Silk, Worked	0	13	4	0
		2	dozen	Aniseed	0	3	4	0
		10	gross	Points	0	10	0	0
		1	gross	Cutts	0	3	4	0
James Baron	Ind	1.5	piece	Cloth of Assize	0	0	0	0
		2	lb	Saffron	0	20	0	0
		2	lb	Silk, Worked	0	26	8	0
		2	gross	Cutts	0	6	8	0
		5	gross	Points	0	5	0	0
Thomas Sherlock	Ind	3	piece	Cloth of Assize	0	0	0	0
		2	lb	Silk, Worked	0	26	8	0
		2	lb	Saffron	0	20	0	0
		20	lb	*Pilus Tinctus*	0	6	8	0
		1	C	Battery	0	40	0	0
		0.5	gross	Cutts	0	0	20	0
Bernard White	Ind	1	piece	Cloth of Assize	0	0	0	0
		3	lb	Silk, Worked	0	40	0	0
		3	lb	Saffron	0	30	0	0
		0.5	C	Battery	0	20	0	0
		60	lb	*Pilus Tinctus*	0	20	0	0
		1	gross	Cutts	0	3	4	0
		28	lb	Aniseed	0	2	2	0
		2	gross	Points	0	2	0	0
Dennis Donell	Ind	1.5	lb	Saffron	0	15	0	0
		1	lb	Silk, Worked	0	13	4	0
		1	gross	Cutts	0	3	4	0
		0.5	gross	Knives	0	3	4	0
		1	dozen	Aniseed	0	0	18	0
		4	gross	Points	0	4	0	0

Bata Mare of Cork, Philip Walsh master, to Ireland, *1st August 1517*

Merchant name	Origin	Qty	Unit	Commodity	£	s.	d.	f.
Edmund Serchefild	Ind	5	piece	Cloth of Assize	0	0	0	0
		1	C	Alum	0	13	4	0
		1	lb	Silk, Worked	0	13	4	0
		4	gross	Points	0	4	0	0
James Creaghe	Ind	5.5	piece	Cloth of Assize	0	0	0	0
		3	lb	Silk, Worked	0	40	0	0
		2	lb	Saffron	0	20	0	0
		2	C	Alum	0	26	8	0
		1	dozen	Skins, Golden	0	5	0	0
		0.5	dozen	Red-Lash	0	0	20	0
		2	dozen	Aniseed	0	3	0	0
		2	gross	Cutts	0	6	8	0
		6	gross	Points	0	6	0	0
		0.5	C	Hops	0	4	2	0
		3	stone	Orchil	0	5	0	0

Merchant name	Origin	Qty	Unit	Commodity	£	s.	d.	f.
John Meaghe	Ind	14	piece	Cloth of Assize, Dozen Strait	0	0	0	0
		8	stone	Orchil, Worked	0	13	4	0
Patrick Mathow	Ind	5	lb	Saffron	0	50	0	0
		1	lb	Silk, Worked	0	13	4	0
		1	gross	Cutts	0	3	4	0
Oliver Tirry	Ind	17	piece	Cloth of Assize, Dozen Strait	0	0	0	0
		2	stone	Orchil, Worked	0	3	4	0
		20	lb	Alum	0	2	6	0
		0.5	gross	Cutts	0	0	20	0
		2	gross	Points	0	2	0	0
		0.5	dozen	Aniseed	0	0	9	0
James Mathow	Ind	2	lb	Silk, Worked	0	26	8	0
		4	lb	Saffron	0	40	0	0
		2.5	gross	Cutts	0	8	4	0
		6	gross	Points	0	6	0	0
		1	dozen	Skins, Golden	0	6	0	0
		1	dozen	Red-Lash	0	4	0	0
		1	dozen	Aniseed	0	0	18	0
		0.5	C	Alum	0	6	8	0
		0.5	C	Hops	0	5	0	0
		4	stone	Orchil, Worked	0	6	8	0
Edmund Copner	Ind	11	piece	Cloth of Assize, Dozen Strait	0	0	0	0
		4	lb	Silk, Worked	0	53	4	0
		4	lb	Saffron	0	40	0	0
		5	gross	Cutts	0	16	8	0
		1.5	dozen	Caps	0	15	0	0
		1	dozen	Skins, Golden	0	6	0	0
		1	dozen	Red-Lash	0	4	0	0
		16	lb	*Pilus Tinctus*	0	5	4	0
		0.5	C	Hops	0	5	0	0
		0.5	C	Alum	0	6	8	0
		1	dozen	Aniseed	0	0	18	0
		8	gross	Points	0	8	0	0
Robert Tirry	Ind	5	piece	Cloth of Assize	0	0	0	0
		5	lb	Silk, Worked	3	5	8	0
		6	lb	Saffron	3	0	0	0
		6	gross	Cutts	0	20	0	0
		3	C	Alum	0	40	0	0
		5	dozen	Aniseed	0	7	6	0
		8	gross	Points	0	8	0	0
		1.5	C	Hops	0	15	0	0
		1	gross	Cutts	0	3	4	0
		6	gross	Points	0	6	0	0

Bata Patrik of New Ross, Nicholas Gregory master, to Ireland, *1st August 1517*

Merchant name	Origin	Qty	Unit	Commodity	£	s.	d.	f.
James Dee	Ind	2.5	piece	Cloth of Assize	0	0	0	0
		4	lb	Silk, Worked	0	53	4	0
		5	lb	Saffron	0	50	0	0
		40	lb	*Pilus Tinctus*	0	20	0	0
		12	stone	Orchil, Worked	0	20	0	0
		2	C	Aniseed	0	20	0	0

Merchant name	Origin	Qty	Unit	Commodity	£	s.	d.	f.
		13	gross	Points	0	13	0	0
		6.5	gross	Cutts	0	21	8	0
		4	lb	Thread	0	0	20	0
		0.5	dozen	Red-Lash	0	0	20	0
John Cotrell	Ind	2	piece	Cloth of Assize	0	0	0	0
		2	lb	Silk, Worked	0	26	8	0
		1	lb	Saffron	0	10	0	0
		1	gross	Cutts	0	3	4	0
		0.5	C	Aniseed	0	5	0	0
		6	gross	Points	0	6	0	0
Edmund Caise	Ind	2	piece	Cloth of Assize, Dozen Strait	0	0	0	0
		3	lb	Silk, Worked	0	40	0	0
		2	lb	Saffron	0	20	0	0
		3	dozen	Aniseed	0	4	6	0
		2	gross	Cutts	0	6	8	0
		4	gross	Points	0	4	0	0
		0.5	dozen	Skins, Golden	0	3	4	0
		4	stone	Orchil, Worked	0	6	8	0
Richard Fitzharry	Ind	2	piece	Cloth of Assize	0	0	0	0
		4.5	lb	Silk, Worked	3	0	0	0
		5.5	lb	Saffron	0	55	0	0
		0.5	C	Aniseed	0	5	0	0
		1.5	gross	Cutts	0	5	0	0
		11	gross	Points	0	11	0	0
		30	lb	*Pilus Tinctus*	0	10	0	0
Edward Leonard	Ind	1.5	piece	Cloth of Assize	0	0	0	0
		2	lb	Silk, Worked	0	26	8	0
		1	lb	Saffron	0	10	0	0
		1	dozen	Caps	0	10	0	0
		1	gross	Cutts	0	3	4	0
		1	piece	Fustian *Cloth* Coarse	0	5	0	0
		6	gross	Points	0	6	0	0
Thomas Baron	Ind	2	lb	Silk, Worked	0	26	8	0
		2	gross	Points	0	2	0	0
		0.5	gross	Cutts	0	0	20	0
		2	dozen	Aniseed	0	3	0	0
Robert Garret	Ind	1	piece	Cloth of Assize, Dozen Strait	0	0	0	0
		5	lb	Silk, Worked	3	6	8	0
		2.5	lb	Saffron	0	20	0	0
		5	stone	Orchil, Worked	0	8	4	0
		30	lb	*Pilus Tinctus*	0	10	0	0
		4	dozen	Aniseed	0	6	0	0
		8	gross	Points	0	8	0	0
		1.5	gross	Knives	0	10	0	0
		0.5	dozen	Caps	0	5	0	0

Bata Clement of Wexford, Thomas Caron master, to Ireland, *1st August 1517*

Nicholas Sparchford	Ind	1	tun	Wine, Corrupt	0	30	0	0
Francis Tower	Ind	1	tun	Wine, Corrupt	0	30	0	0
John Symonds	Ind	2	tun	Wine, Corrupt	3	0	0	0
Thomas Stafford	Ind	1.5	piece	Cloth of Assize	0	0	0	0

Merchant name	Origin	Qty	Unit	Commodity	£	s.	d.	f.
Bata Sonday of Waterford, Edmund Malrony master, to Ireland, 4th August 1517								
Thomas Hedy	Ind	2	piece	Cloth of Assize	0	0	0	0
		3.33	dozen	Aniseed	0	5	0	0
		1	gross	Cutts	0	3	4	0
Peter Dowen	Ind	3	lb	Silk, Worked	0	40	0	0
		1	lb	Saffron	0	10	0	0
		0.5	dozen	Caps	0	5	0	0
		0.5	dozen	Skins, Golden	0	2	6	0
		9	pack	Cards, Hand	0	3	4	0
		8	gross	Points	0	8	0	0
		13	lb	*Pilus Tinctus*	0	6	0	0
		0.5	gross	Cutts	0	0	20	0
James Duyrk?	Ind	3.5	piece	Cloth of Assize	0	0	0	0
		1	lb	Silk, Worked	0	13	4	0
		1	lb	Saffron	0	10	0	0
		7	gross	Points	0	7	0	0
		6	dozen	Aniseed	0	9	0	0
		0.5	dozen	Caps	0	5	0	0
		2	lb	Verdigris	0	0	20	0
		2	gross	Cutts	0	6	6	0
Bata Blanche of Morbihan, Peter Badot master, from Brittany, 7th August 1517								
Peter Badot	Alien	16	ton	Salt	8	0	0	0
Bata George of Bristol, John Harrys master, from Ireland, *7th August 1517*								
George Jerlond	Ind	1.5	C	Skins, Sheep	0	15	0	0
		0.5	C	Skins, Lamb	0	3	4	0
		4	piece	Skins, Otter	0	0	20	0
		4	piece	Skins, Fox	0	0	8	0
		10	piece	Mantles	0	33	4	0
Richard Sholhe	Ind	5	piece	Mantles	0	16	8	0
Bata *Christo*fur of Cardiff, William Deane master, from Cardiff, *7th August 1517*								
Philip Jonye	Ind	3	tun	Wine	0	0	0	0
Bata Mare Bronne,[9] Port Unknown, John David master, from Ireland, 12th August 1517								
Richard Polton	Ind	2	C	Ship-Boards	0	40	0	0
		1	pipe	Fish, Salmon	0	30	0	0
		2	C	Fish, Hake	0	20	0	0
		2	burden	Fish, Salted	0	8	4	0
		6	piece	Mantles	0	20	0	0
Walter Lane	Ind	1	C	Irish Linen *Cloth*	0	10	0	0
Bata Mare of Bayonne, Nicholas Dichard master, to Ireland, 13th August 1517								
William Woseley	Ind	3	tun	Wine, Corrupt	4	10	0	0

9 Possibly Bristol.

Merchant name	Origin	Qty	Unit	Commodity	£	s.	d.	f.
Roger Dawes	Ind	5	piece	Cloth of Assize	0	0	0	0
Richard Mathew	Ind	1.5	tun	Wine, Corrupt	0	45	0	0
		3	piece	Cloth of Assize	0	0	0	0

Bata Mare Belhouse of *Bristol*, Richard Boughton master, to Ireland, *13th August 1517*

William Edwards	Ind	1	piece	Cloth of Assize	0	0	0	0

Bata Barbara of Penmarch, Gilo Gtobo (?), from Brittany, 17th August 1517

John Brittanyy	Alien	14	ton	Salt	7	0	0	0
		3	piece	Oleron *Cloth*	0	20	0	0
		1	bale	Paper	1	0	0	0
		3	C	Pitch	0	4	2	0
		3	dozen	Playing Cards	0	2	6	0
		1	C	Combs	1	0	0	0

Navicula Tremurd of Penmarch, John Gurreo master, to Bordeaux, 18th August 1517

Roger Dawes	Ind	12	piece	Cloth of Assize	0	0	0	0
David Vaghan	Ind	10	piece	Cloth of Assize	0	0	0	0
Richard Hoby	Ind	4	piece	Cloth of Assize	0	0	0	0
William Tirry	Ind	3	piece	Welsh *Cloth*	3	0	0	0

Navicula Mare of Errenteria, Peter de Ricvalo master, from La Rochelle, *18th August 1517*

Peter de Ricvalo	Alien	103	ton	Salt	51	10	0	0

Bata Mare of Bristol, Thomas Nongull master, to Ireland, *18th August 1517*

Thomas Nogull	Ind	2.5	tun	Wine, Corrupt	3	15	0	0
John Watson	Ind	1	piece	Cloth of Assize	0	0	0	0
John Amidas?	Ind	2	piece	Cloth of Assize	0	0	0	0
		2	piece	Welsh *Cloth*	0	40	0	0
		20	lb	*Pilus Tinctus*	0	6	8	0
Nicholas Tirry	Ind	2.5	piece	Welsh *Cloth*	0	50	0	0

Navicula Antony of Bristol, John Crok master, from Sanlúcar de Barrameda, 19th August 1517

Robert Thomas	Ind	4.75	tun	Oil, *Olive*	19	0	0	0
		37.5	C	*Smigmates*	18	15	0	0
Richard Hoby	Ind	4.75	tun	Wine	0	0	0	0
John Drewis	Ind	15	tun	Wine	0	0	0	0
		30	ton	Salt	15	0	0	0
Leonard Osburn	Ind	13.25	tun	Wine	0	0	0	0
William Woseley	Ind	3	tun	Oil, *Olive*	12	0	0	0
Robert Avyntre	Ind	5.5	C	*Smigmates*	2	15	0	0
John Crok	Ind	1	pipe	Wine	0	0	0	0
William Cardmaker	Ind	1	tun	Vinegar	2	0	0	0
John Robynet	Ind	1	pipe	Wine	0	0	0	0
John Jay	Ind	2.875	tun	Wine	0	0	0	0

Merchant name	Origin	Qty	Unit	Commodity	£	s.	d.	f.
Roger Barlow	Ind	13.5	C	*Smigmates*	6	15	0	0
		3	C	Aniseed	0	30	0	0

Navicula Marget of Bristol, John Stevyns master, to Faro, *19th August 1517*

Merchant name	Origin	Qty	Unit	Commodity	£	s.	d.	f.
Roger Dawes	Ind	6	piece	Welsh *Cloth*	6	0	0	0
David Vaghan	Ind	4	piece	Cloth of Assize	0	0	0	0
		4	piece	Welsh *Cloth*	4	0	0	0
Robert Avyntre	Ind	12.5	piece	Cloth of Assize	0	0	0	0
John Kyng	Ind	12.5	piece	Cloth of Assize	0	0	0	0
		8	piece	Cloth of Assize, Dozen	0	0	0	0
		14	piece	Cloth of Assize, Dozen Strait	0	0	0	0
John Sumpter	Ind	6	piece	Welsh *Cloth*	6	0	0	0
Thomas Palmer	Ind	4	piece	Welsh *Cloth*	4	0	0	0
Margareta Browne	Ind	32	piece	Cloth of Assize	0	0	0	0
		12	piece	Welsh *Cloth*	12	0	0	0
William Sewell	Ind	1	piece	Cloth of Assize	0	0	0	0
		2	piece	Welsh *Cloth*	0	40	0	0
William Woseley	Ind	17	piece	Welsh *Cloth*	17	0	0	0
Philip Shipman	Ind	4	piece	Welsh *Cloth*	4	0	0	0
Thomas Yonge	Ind	0.33	piece	Cloth of Assize	0	0	0	0
Nicholas Gay	Ind	2	piece	Cloth of Assize	0	0	0	0

Bata Anne of Palma, John Rolls master, from Brittany, *19th August 1517*

Merchant name	Origin	Qty	Unit	Commodity	£	s.	d.	f.
Robert Illegible	Alien	?		Salt	0	0	0	0

Bata Marget of Milford Haven, Henry Willis master, from Ireland, *19th August 1517*

Merchant name	Origin	Qty	Unit	Commodity	£	s.	d.	f.
Henry Willis	Ind	19	C	Fish, Hake	9	10	0	0

Navicula Laurence of Penmarch, James le Monyk master, to Bordeaux, *19th August 1517*

Merchant name	Origin	Qty	Unit	Commodity	£	s.	d.	f.
William Shipman	Ind	1.25	ton	Lead, Worked	6	5	0	0
John Sparchford	Ind	15	piece	Cloth of Assize	0	0	0	0
John Shipman	Ind	2.25	ton	Lead, Worked	11	5	0	0

Bata George of Bristol, John Harrys master, to Ireland, *19th August 1517*

Merchant name	Origin	Qty	Unit	Commodity	£	s.	d.	f.
Henry Pers	Ind	1	pipe	Wine, Corrupt	0	15	0	0

Bata John of Milford Haven, John Nutte master, from Ireland, 25th August 1517

Merchant name	Origin	Qty	Unit	Commodity	£	s.	d.	f.
John Nuttte	Ind	1	C	Fish, Salted	0	20	0	0
		1.5	C	Fish, Hake	0	15	0	0
Thomas Jurdan	Ind	12	dicker	Skins, Salted	8	0	0	0
		8.5	C	Skins, Sheep	4	5	0	0
		80	yard	Check *Cloth*	0	26	8	0
		4	piece	Mantles	0	13	4	0
Robert Avyntre	Ind	107	lb	Pepper	5	7	0	0

Merchant name	Origin	Qty	Unit	Commodity	£	s.	d.	f.

Bata John of Milford Haven, John Nutte master, to Ireland, 28th August 1517

Merchant name	Origin	Qty	Unit	Commodity	£	s.	d.	f.
Thomas Jurdan	Ind	2	ton	Iron	8	0	0	0
		12	gross	Points	0	12	0	0
		1	C	Smigmates, Black	0	6	8	0

Navicula Mare Kateryn of Bristol, William a Deane master, to Sanlúcar de Barrameda, 28th August 1517

Merchant name	Origin	Qty	Unit	Commodity	£	s.	d.	f.
Nicholas Gay	Ind	5	piece	Cloth of Assize	0	0	0	0
John Thomas	Ind	22	piece	Cloth of Assize	0	0	0	0
		7	piece	Welsh Cloth	7	0	0	0
John Cappis	Ind	10	piece	Welsh Cloth	10	0	0	0
		16	piece	Welsh Cloth, Dozen Strait	3	6	8	0
John Bynon	Ind	4	piece	Cloth of Assize, Dozen Strait	0	0	0	0
		1.5	piece	Cloth of Assize, Kersey	0	0	0	0
		6.5	piece	Welsh Cloth	6	10	0	0
George Hall	Ind	11	piece	Cloth of Assize	0	0	0	0
John Hall	Ind	7	piece	Cloth of Assize	0	0	0	0
		20	piece	Welsh Cloth	20	0	0	0
		8	piece	Welsh Cloth, Dozen Strait	0	33	4	0
John Kyng	Ind	10	piece	Welsh Cloth	10	0	0	0
David Vaghan	Ind	1	piece	Welsh Cloth	0	20	0	0
		1	piece	Mantles	0	5	0	0
John Hall	Ind	12	piece	Cloth of Assize, Dozen Strait	0	0	0	0
John Davys	Ind	25	piece	Welsh Cloth	25	0	0	0
Thomas Hicks	Ind	7	piece	Cloth of Assize	0	0	0	0
Robert Ellyot	Ind	15	piece	Cloth of Assize	0	0	0	0
John Hop	Ind	3	piece	Cloth of Assize	0	0	0	0

Navicula Jhesus of Bristol, Robert Avyntre master, to Ireland, 28th August 1517

Merchant name	Origin	Qty	Unit	Commodity	£	s.	d.	f.
Robert Avyntre	Ind	95.33	piece	Cloth of Assize	0	0	0	0
		10	seam	Wood Ashes	0	50	0	0
		32	stone	Orchil, Worked	0	53	4	0
		8	piece	Welsh Cloth	8	0	0	0
		5	lb	Silk, Worked	3	6	8	0
		5	lb	Saffron	0	50	0	0
		0.5	C	Aniseed	0	5	0	0
		1	gross	Cutts	0	3	4	0
		4	dozen	Red-Lash	0	24	0	0
Thomas Donell	Ind	47	piece	Cloth of Assize	0	0	0	0
		10	seam	Wood Ashes	0	50	0	0
		32	stone	Orchil	0	53	4	0
		8	piece	Welsh Cloth	8	0	0	0
		5	lb	Silk, Worked	3	6	8	0
		5	lb	Saffron	0	50	0	0
		0.5	C	Aniseed	0	5	0	0
		1	gross	Cutts	0	3	4	0
		20	gross	Points	0	20	0	0
		20	lb	Liquorice	0	2	6	0
Nicholas Ward	Ind	1.5	tun	Wine, Corrupt	0	45	0	0

Merchant name	Origin	Qty	Unit	Commodity	£	s.	d.	f.
		24	stone	Orchil, Worked	0	40	0	0
Thomas Arthur	Ind	17	piece	Cloth of Assize	0	0	0	0
		2	piece	Welsh *Cloth*	0	40	0	0
		8	lb	Saffron	4	0	0	0
		1	gross	Cutts	0	3	4	0
Nicholas Ffox	Ind	7	piece	Cloth of Assize	0	0	0	0
		8	lb	Saffron	4	0	0	0
		1	gross	Cutts	0	3	4	0

Navicula Trynyte of Bristol, Evan Danyell master, to Lisbon, 29h August 1517

Merchant name	Origin	Qty	Unit	Commodity	£	s.	d.	f.
Robert Avyntre	Ind	23	piece	Cloth of Assize	0	0	0	0
		3000/pipe		*Burdes*[10]	2	10	0	0
Thomas Bilford	Ind	3	piece	Cloth of Assize	0	0	0	0
		4	piece	Welsh *Cloth*	4	0	0	0
Richard Bocher	Ind	20	piece	Cloth of Assize, Dozen	0	0	0	0
		7	piece	Cloth of Assize	0	0	0	0
Thomas Donell	Ind	11	piece	Cloth of Assize	0	0	0	0
John Kyng	Ind	33	piece	Cloth of Assize	0	0	0	0
		10	piece	Cloth of Assize, Dozen Strait	0	0	0	0
		2	piece	Welsh *Cloth*	0	40	0	0
John Shipman	Ind	1.5	piece	Cloth of Assize	0	0	0	0
		7	piece	Welsh *Cloth*	7	0	0	0
William Shipman	Ind	4.5	piece	Cloth of Assize	0	0	0	0
		7	piece	Welsh *Cloth*	7	0	0	0
John Rowlond	Ind	5	piece	Cloth of Assize	0	0	0	0
David Vaghan	Ind	5	piece	Welsh *Cloth*	5	0	0	0
		1	piece	Mantles	0	5	0	0
John Cappis	Ind	14	piece	Welsh *Cloth*, Dozen Strait	2	18	4	0
Ralph Apprece	Ind	1.5	piece	Cloth of Assize	0	0	0	0
William Pastriche	Ind	4.5	piece	Welsh *Cloth*	4	10	0	0
Robert Hille	Ind	11	piece	Cloth of Assize	0	0	0	0
John Vaghan	Ind	8	piece	Cloth of Assize	0	0	0	0
Evan Danyell	Alien	18	piece	Welsh *Cloth*	18	0	0	0
Thomas Hart	Ind	2	piece	Cloth of Assize	0	0	0	0
		10	piece	Welsh *Cloth*	10	0	0	0
Robert Box	Ind	2	piece	Cloth of Assize	0	0	0	0

Bata Mare of Bristol, Robert Baker master, from Cardiff, 29th August 1517

Merchant name	Origin	Qty	Unit	Commodity	£	s.	d.	f.
Philip Jonyes	Ind	4	tun	Wine	0	0	0	0

Navicula Mare of Errenteria, Peter de Kesavale master, to Sanlúcar de Barrameda, *29th August 1517*

Merchant name	Origin	Qty	Unit	Commodity	£	s.	d.	f.
Roger Dawes	Ind	27	piece	Cloth of Assize	0	0	0	0
		8	piece	Welsh *Cloth*	8	0	0	0
John Kyng	Ind	9	piece	Cloth of Assize	0	0	0	0
		10	piece	Cloth of Assize, Dozen Strait	0	0	0	0
William Avyntre	Ind	30	piece	Cloth of Assize	0	0	0	0
		10	piece	Cloth of Assize, Dozen Strait	0	0	0	0

10 Unidentified.

Merchant name	Origin	Qty	Unit	Commodity	£	s.	d.	f.
		2	piece	Welsh *Cloth*	0	40	0	0
Walter Comrowe	Ind	17	piece	Cloth of Assize	0	0	0	0
		5	piece	Mantles	0	16	8	0
John Rowland	Ind	16	piece	Welsh *Cloth*	16	0	0	0
Thomas Dale	Ind	4	piece	Cloth of Assize	0	0	0	0
David Vaghan	Ind	16.5	piece	Cloth of Assize	0	0	0	0

Navicula Veronica of Hondarribia, Stephen Primat master, from Spain, 1st September 1517

Merchant name	Origin	Qty	Unit	Commodity	£	s.	d.	f.
Hugh *Unknown*	Ind	25.5	ton	Iron	63	15	0	0
		6	dozen	Serches	0	24	0	0
Robert Hamont	Ind	15	ton	Iron	37	10	0	0
William Rowley	Ind	15	ton	Iron	37	10	0	0
John Shipman	Ind	9	ton	Iron	22	10	0	0
William Shipman	Ind	9	ton	Iron	22	10	0	0
John Ward	Ind	5	ton	Iron	12	10	0	0
Gilbert Cogan	Ind	4	ton	Iron	10	0	0	0
John Mathew	Ind	1	ton	Iron	0	50	0	0
		2.25	ton	Rosin and Pitch	3	0	0	0
		0.25	tun	Turpentine	0	20	0	0
Robert Hamont	Ind	2	dozen	Serches	0	8	0	0

Navicula John of Pasajes de San Juan, Michael de Lana master, to Sanlúcar de Barrameda, *1st September 1517*

Merchant name	Origin	Qty	Unit	Commodity	£	s.	d.	f.
Martysannie								
Unknown	Alien	17.5	dozen	Hides, Tanned Calf	2	18	4	0
Robert Avyntre	Ind	26	dozen	Hides, Tanned Calf	4	6	8	0
Lucas Bowdewey	Alien	9	piece	Mantles	0	36	0	0
Robert Rowlow	Ind	11	piece	Cloth of Assize	0	0	0	0
		50	piece	Welsh *Cloth*	50	0	0	0
Richard Hoby	Ind	4	piece	Cloth of Assize	0	0	0	0
Thomas Bilford	Ind	5	piece	Welsh *Cloth*	5	0	0	0
Thomas Gefferes	Alien	6	dozen	Hides, Tanned Calf	1	0	0	0
Michael Calker	Alien	8	dozen	Hides, Tanned Calf	1	6	8	0
George de Coste	Alien	10	piece	Welsh *Cloth*	10	0	0	0
		1.5	piece	Cloth of Assize	0	0	0	0

Navicula John of Errenteria, Anthony de la Sola master, to Bordeaux, *1st September 1517*

Merchant name	Origin	Qty	Unit	Commodity	£	s.	d.	f.
Nicholas Gay	Ind	2	piece	Cloth of Assize, Dozen Strait	0	0	0	0
John Shipman	Ind	59.66	piece	Cloth of Assize	0	0	0	0
		28	dozen	Hides, Tanned Calf	4	13	4	0
John Ware	Ind	59.66	piece	Cloth of Assize	0	0	0	0
William Shipman	Ind	63.66	piece	Cloth of Assize	0	0	0	0
Thomas Bilford	Ind	39	piece	Cloth of Assize	0	0	0	0
John Brampton	Ind	14	piece	Cloth of Assize	0	0	0	0
Richard Hoby	Ind	27	piece	Cloth of Assize	0	0	0	0
Martin de Tolosa	Alien	8	dicker	Hides, Tanned	29	6	8	0
		8	dozen	Hides, Tanned Calf	1	6	8	0
Martin de Leso	Alien	1	dicker	Hides, Tanned	3	13	4	0
		6	dozen	Hides, Tanned Calf	1	0	0	0

Merchant name	Origin	Qty	Unit	Commodity	£	s.	d.	f.
John Sparchford	Ind	27	piece	Cloth of Assize	0	0	0	0
William Woseley	Ind	14	piece	Cloth of Assize	0	0	0	0
William Rowley	Ind	18	piece	Cloth of Assize	0	0	0	0
John Kyng	Ind	8	piece	Cloth of Assize, Dozen	0	0	0	0
		14	piece	Welsh *Cloth*, Dozen Strait	2	18	4	0
Martysannie	Alien	10	dozen	Hides, Tanned Calf	1	13	4	0
Maurice Bocher	Ind	49	dozen	Hides, Tanned Calf	8	3	4	0
Gilbert Cogan	Ind	27	piece	Cloth of Assize	0	0	0	0
Robert Coke	Ind	51	piece	Cloth of Assize	0	0	0	0
		3	piece	Welsh *Cloth*	3	0	0	0
John Rowland	Ind	10	piece	Cloth of Assize	0	0	0	0
Thomas Dale	Ind	19	dozen	Skins, Calf	3	3	4	0
John Drewis	Ind	13	piece	Cloth of Assize	0	0	0	0
Thomas Batcok	Ind	29	dozen	Hides, Tanned Calf	4	16	8	0

Bata George of Blavet, John Newton master, from Cardiff, *1st September 1517*

Merchant name	Origin	Qty	Unit	Commodity	£	s.	d.	f.
Thomas Oliver	Ind	1	pipe	Wine	0	0	0	0

Navicula Mawdelen of Errenteria, John Surre master, to Sanlúcar de Barrameda, 4th September 1517

Merchant name	Origin	Qty	Unit	Commodity	£	s.	d.	f.
William Shipman	Ind	3	M	Pipe-Staves	2	10	0	0
Nicholas Thorne	Ind	8	ton	Lead, Worked	40	0	0	0
		22	piece	Welsh *Cloth*	22	0	0	0
		14	piece	Cloth of Assize, Dozen Strait	0	0	0	0
Thomas Bilford	Ind	4	piece	Cloth of Assize	0	0	0	0
		4	piece	Welsh *Cloth*	4	0	0	0
William Woseley	Ind	6	piece	Cloth of Assize	0	0	0	0
		1	piece	Welsh *Cloth*	0	20	0	0
Robert Thorne	Ind	20	piece	Cloth of Assize	0	0	0	0
		16	piece	Welsh *Cloth*	16	0	0	0
John Rowland	Ind	5	piece	Cloth of Assize	0	0	0	0

Navicula Matthew of Bristol, Richard Savere master, to Bordeaux, *4th September 1517*

Merchant name	Origin	Qty	Unit	Commodity	£	s.	d.	f.
Richard Hoby	Ind	4.5	piece	Cloth of Assize	0	0	0	0
Thomas Bilford	Ind	5	piece	Cloth of Assize	0	0	0	0
Thomas Hawkyne	Ind	2	ton	Lead, Worked	10	0	0	0
John Thomas	Ind	2	ton	Lead, Worked	10	0	0	0
John Shipman	Ind	2.5	piece	Cloth of Assize	0	0	0	0
William Shipman	Ind	2.5	piece	Cloth of Assize	0	0	0	0

Bata Trynyte of Longney, John Gelle master, from Chepstow, 9th September 1517

Merchant name	Origin	Qty	Unit	Commodity	£	s.	d.	f.
William Brother	Ind	0.75	tun	Oil, *Olive*	3	0	0	0

Bata Trynyte of Longney, John Gelle master, from Chepstow, 9th September 1517

Merchant name	Origin	Qty	Unit	Commodity	£	s.	d.	f.
William Brother	Ind	720	lb	Wax	*12*	0	0	0

Merchant name	Origin	Qty	Unit	Commodity	£	s.	d.	f.

Navicula Edward of Bristol, John Gorwey master, to Bordeaux, *9th September 1517*

Merchant name	Origin	Qty	Unit	Commodity	£	s.	d.	f.
Nicholas Gay	Ind	25.5	piece	Cloth of Assize	0	0	0	0
George Hall	Ind	7	piece	Cloth of Assize	0	0	0	0
		2	piece	Cloth of Assize	0	0	0	0
		50	piece	Welsh *Cloth*, Dozen Strait	10	8	4	0
William Tirry	Ind	1	piece	Cloth of Assize	0	0	0	0
		3	piece	Welsh *Cloth*	3	0	0	0
		2.75	C	Fish, Hake	1	7	6	0
Thomas Yeate	Ind	10	piece	Cloth of Assize	0	0	0	0
John Grene	Ind	7	piece	Cloth of Assize	0	0	0	0
		1	piece	Welsh *Cloth*	0	20	0	0

Navicula Mare *Christ*ofur of Bristol, John Barnard master, to Bordeaux, *9th September 1517*

Merchant name	Origin	Qty	Unit	Commodity	£	s.	d.	f.
John Pasheley	Ind	3	piece	Cloth of Assize	0	0	0	0
		10	piece	Welsh *Cloth*, Dozen Strait	0	41	8	0
		4	piece	Welsh *Cloth*	4	0	0	0
Thomas Plinley	Ind	2	piece	Cloth of Assize	0	0	0	0
John Hop	Ind	2	piece	Cloth of Assize	0	0	0	0

Navicula Kateryn of Honfleur, Peter Bowenfise master, from New World, 10th September 1517

Merchant name	Origin	Qty	Unit	Commodity	£	s.	d.	f.
Peter Bowenfise	Alien	13	M	Fish, Salted (New World)	86	13	4	0
		1	tun	Oil, Train	2	6	8	0

Navicula Jh*es*us of Bristol, Robert Power master, to Bordeaux, 10th September 1517

Merchant name	Origin	Qty	Unit	Commodity	£	s.	d.	f.
Thomas Dale	Ind	10	piece	Cloth of Assize	0	0	0	0
John Vaghan	Ind	8	piece	Cloth of Assize	0	0	0	0
John Drewis	Ind	2 pipe & 1	hogshead	Cheese	1	13	4	0
John Sparcheford	Ind	4	ton	Lead, Worked	20	0	0	0
Thomas Yeate	Ind	6	piece	Cloth of Assize	0	0	0	0
John Coke	Ind	2	ton	Lead, Worked	10	0	0	0
Thomas Hawkyne	Ind	12	piece	Cloth of Assize	0	0	0	0
		5	piece	Welsh *Cloth*	5	0	0	0
Robert Hille	Ind	1	ton	Lead, Worked	5	0	0	0
David Vaghan	Ind	5.5	piece	Cloth of Assize	0	0	0	0
William Bocher	Ind	6	piece	Cloth of Assize, Dozen	0	0	0	0
		4	dozen	Hides, Tanned Calf	0	13	4	0

Bata Trynyte of Chepstow, William Heyn*e* master, *from Chepstow*, 11h September 1517

Merchant name	Origin	Qty	Unit	Commodity	£	s.	d.	f.
William Broth*er*	Ind	4.75	tun	Oil, *Olive*	19	0	0	0

Bata Trynyte of Carmarthen, John Ragnele, *from Carmarthen, 11h September 1517*

Merchant name	Origin	Qty	Unit	Commodity	£	s.	d.	f.
Thomas Wale	Ind	6	ton	Salt	3	0	0	0

Merchant name	Origin	Qty	Unit	Commodity	£	s.	d.	f.

Navicula Antony of Bristol, William Robynet master, to Lisbon, 17th September 1517

Merchant name	Origin	Qty	Unit	Commodity	£	s.	d.	f.
Henry Wosewole	Ind	11	piece	Cloth of Assize	0	0	0	0
John Drewis	Ind	7	piece	Welsh *Cloth*	7	0	0	0
Richard Arthur	Ind	7	piece	Cloth of Assize	0	0	0	0
Thomas Yeate	Ind	2	piece	Cloth of Assize	0	0	0	0
John Cole	Ind	10	piece	Cloth of Assize	0	0	0	0
		27	piece	Welsh *Cloth*	27	0	0	0
Thomas Evans	Ind	1	piece	Welsh *Cloth*	0	20	0	0
Richard Hoby	Ind	1	piece	Welsh *Cloth*	0	20	0	0
Richard Tonell	Ind	2	piece	Cloth of Assize	0	0	0	0

Bata Kateryn of Chepstow, Robert Ffisher master, *from Chepstow*, 18th September 1517

Merchant name	Origin	Qty	Unit	Commodity	£	s.	d.	f.
George Maynard	Ind	2.25	tun	Oil, *Olive*	9	0	0	0

Bata Mighell of Tenby, John More master, *from Tenby*, 26th September 1517

Merchant name	Origin	Qty	Unit	Commodity	£	s.	d.	f.
Richard Shipman	Ind	1	C	Fish, Hake	0	10	0	0

Bata Mark of Tenby, William Philips master, from Ireland, *26th September 1517*

Merchant name	Origin	Qty	Unit	Commodity	£	s.	d.	f.
William Philips	Ind	2.5	last	Fish, Herring White	7	10	0	0

Bata Mare of Penmarch, Thomas Dolas master, from La Rochelle, *26th September 1517*

Merchant name	Origin	Qty	Unit	Commodity	£	s.	d.	f.
Thomas Dolas	Alien	24.25	tun	Wine	0	0	0	0

1525/26

TNA E122/21/5 is an annual 'particular' customs account of John Bartholomew & William Goodwyn, collectors of customs and subsidies, covering the period Michaelmas 1525 to Michaelmas 1526. This account contains the same information as the earlier two accounts with the important exception that it does not record the port of destination of the ships, indicating only whether the ship is entering or exiting the port. It has been transcribed here as it appears in the document, but it is important to note that despite this omission, it is nevertheless possible to distinguish between Irish and Continental trade. Bristol's international trade focused almost exclusively on three areas during this period; Biscay, south-west Iberia and Ireland. While there is a considerable overlap in the shipping, commodities and personnel involved in the Iberian and Biscay trade, the Irish trade involved a very different set of commodities, smaller ships and, in general, different merchants, making it possible, in terms of trade analysis, to determine which ships were involved in Irish or Continental trade.

Unlike the 1516/17 account, the 1525–6 account records the custom and subsidy paid by the merchant's. It does not record any 'values' for tanned hides or cloth of assize.

Merchant name	Origin	Qty	Unit	Commodity	£	s.	d.	f.
Navicula Anne of Bristol, George Hart master, Exiting, 30th September 1525								
Thomas Hykke	Ind	16	piece	Cloth of Assize	0	0	0	0
		8	C	Alum	5	6	8	0
Robert Chapman	Ind	10	piece	Cloth of Assize	0	0	0	0
Edward Altham	Ind	18	piece	Cloth of Assize	0	0	0	0
Alvero de Castro	Alien	15	piece	Cloth of Assize	0	0	0	0
John Thorn	Ind	2	piece	Cloth of Assize	0	0	0	0
		2	dicker	Hides, Tanned	0	0	0	0
Robert Ellyot	Ind	8	wey	Beans	6	13	4	0
		16	C	Alum	10	13	4	0
		6	piece	Welsh *Cloth*, Dozen Strait	0	25	0	0
		6	piece	Cloth of Assize, Dozen Strait	0	0	0	0
William Yate	Ind	24	piece	Cloth of Assize	0	0	0	0
George Hall	Ind	4	piece	Cloth of Assize	0	0	0	0
		13	dozen	Skins, Calf	2	3	4	0
Bata Mighell of Tewkesbury Richard Puston master, Entering, *30th September 1525*								
Richard Hyggyns	Ind	1	tun	Wine	0	0	0	0

Merchant name	Origin	Qty	Unit	Commodity	£	s.	d.	f.

Navicula Kateryn of Bridgwater, John Barnarde master, Exiting, *30th September 1525*

Merchant name	Origin	Qty	Unit	Commodity	£	s.	d.	f.
John Gorney	Ind	2	ton	Lead worked	10	0	0	0
		21	piece	Cloth of Assize	0	0	0	0
Richard Arthur	Ind	5	dicker	Hides, Tanned	0	0	0	0
John Coke	Ind	26	piece	Cloth of Assize	0	0	0	0
		6	piece	Welsh *Cloth*	6	0	0	0
		3	ton	Lead worked	15	0	0	0
		10	lb	An... (?)	3	6	8	0
		6	dozen	Skins, Calf	1	0	0	0
David Ford	Ind	4	piece	Cloth of Assize, Dozen Strait	0	0	0	0

Bata Nicholas of Bristol, Thomas Baylle master, Exiting, *30th September 1525*

Merchant name	Origin	Qty	Unit	Commodity	£	s.	d.	f.
Thomas Sompter	Ind	1	barrel	Aqua vitae	0	20	0	0
		3.5	tun	Wine, Corrupt	5	5	0	0

Navicula Trinite of Mutricu, Francis de Franks master, Exiting, 2nd October 1525

Merchant name	Origin	Qty	Unit	Commodity	£	s.	d.	f.
Nicholas Thorn	Ind	12	dozen	Skins, Calf	0	40	0	0
		4.5	ton	Lead worked	22	10	0	0
		4	piece	Tin	10	0	0	0
		44	dozen	Skins, Calf	7	6	8	0
		13	dicker	Hides, Tanned	0	0	0	0

Navicula Santa *Marya* of Rome, Christopher Capacheo master, Exiting, *2nd October 1525*

Merchant name	Origin	Qty	Unit	Commodity	£	s.	d.	f.
Christopher Capacheo	Alien	1	piece	Cloth of Assize, Dozen Strait	0	0	0	0
		36	ell	Flannel *Cloth*	0	12	0	0
Domingo de Arasubra	Alien	25	lb	Tin, Worked	0	8	4	0

Bata Mary of Gatcombe, Christopher Taillor master, Exiting, 5th October 1525

Merchant name	Origin	Qty	Unit	Commodity	£	s.	d.	f.
John Marks	Ind	3	ton	Salt	0	30	0	0

Bata Mary of Tenby, John More master, Entering, 9th October 1525

Merchant name	Origin	Qty	Unit	Commodity	£	s.	d.	f.
William Baynam	Ind	1	tun	Wine	0	0	0	0

Bata Mary of Milford Haven, Richard Salvat master, Entering, *9th October 1525*

Merchant name	Origin	Qty	Unit	Commodity	£	s.	d.	f.
Walter Kelly	Ind	58	barrel	Fish, Herring White	13	10	0	0
		21	barrel	Fish, Herring White	5	5	0	0
		0.75	C	Fish, Hake	0	7	6	0
		48	piece	Fish, Hake	0	3	8	0
		2	C	Tallow, Rough	0	6	8	0
		3	piece	Mantles	0	10	0	0
Mathew Hoper	Ind	1	barrel	Fish, Herring White	0	5	0	0
Richard Ellyot	Ind	3	mease	Fish, Herring White	0	15	0	0

Merchant name	Origin	Qty	Unit	Commodity	£	s.	d.	f.
Bata Sonday of Caerleon, John Tydder master, Entering, *9th October 1525*								
John Craddock	Ind	0.5	ton	Salt	0	5	0	0
Bata George of Bristol, Thomas Lee master, Entering, 14th October 1525								
Richard Artur	Ind	1.8	C	Skins, Sheep	9	0	0	0
		10	burden	Fish, Salted	0	41	8	0
		1	pipe	Iron	0	25	0	0
		0.5	pipe	Fish, Salmon	0	15	0	0
		12	piece	Mantles	0	40	0	0
Patrick Meagh	Ind	15	C	Fish, Hake	7	10	0	0
		15.5	stone	Wool, Flocks	0	6	3	0
		4	C	Skins, Lamb	0	26	8	0
		8	piece	Mantles	0	26	8	0
		3	C	Iron	0	3	9	0
Robert Donnell	Ind	5	C	Fish, Hake	0	50	0	0
Bata Mary of Milford Haven, Richard Salvat master, Exiting, 27th October 1525								
Nicholas Hakett	Ind	12	lb	Saffron	6	0	0	0
		8	lb	Silk Worked	5	6	8	0
		8	gross	Points	0	8	0	0
		1	gross	Cutts	0	3	4	0
		1	C	Aniseed	0	13	4	0
		2	piece	Cloth of Assize, Dozen Strait	0	0	0	0
Michael Boyd	Ind	12	lb	Saffron	6	0	0	0
		5	lb	Silk Worked	3	6	8	0
		1.5	gross	Cutts	0	5	0	0
		1	C	Aniseed	0	13	4	0
		1	gross	Points	0	0	12	0
		1	C	Hops	0	10	0	0
		3	piece	Cloth of Assize, Dozen Strait	0	0	0	0
Patrick Ragett	Ind	4	piece	Cloth of Assize, Dozen Strait	0	0	0	0
		6	lb	Silk Worked	4	0	0	0
		7	lb	Saffron	3	10	0	0
		1	C	Aniseed	0	13	4	0
		12	gross	Points	0	12	0	0
		1	dozen	Caps	0	10	0	0
		1.5	gross	Cutts	0	5	0	0
		4	lb	Liquorice	0	0	6	0
Oliver Cranysboro	Ind	3	lb	Saffron	0	30	0	0
		1	dozen	Caps	0	10	0	0
		1	C	Aniseed	0	13	4	0
		1	lb	Silk Worked	0	13	4	0
Patrick Flanynghin	Ind	3	lb	Silk Worked	0	40	0	0
		5	lb	Saffron	0	50	0	0
		8	gross	Points	0	8	0	0
		0.5	gross	Cutts	0	0	20	0
		0.5	piece	Cloth of Assize	0	0	0	0

Merchant name	Origin	Qty	Unit	Commodity	£	s.	d.	f.
Bata Mary Rose of Bristol, Thomas Buttler master, Entering, 8th November 1525								
Thomas Jonys	Ind	4	tun	Wine	0	0	0	0
Navicula Santa Marya of Rome, Christopher Capacheo master, Entering, 11th November 1525								
Richard Babyngton	Ind	0.875	tun	Wine	0	0	0	0
Bata George of Bristol, Thomas Lee master, Exiting, 13th November 1525								
George Creagh	Ind	39.75	lb	Saffron	19	17	6	0
		3	lb	Silk Worked	0	40	0	0
		4	dozen	Skins, Red	0	8	4	0
		2	C	Aniseed	0	26	8	0
		2	lb	Thread	0	0	10	0
		8	lb	Cumin	0	0	15	0
		1.5	gross	Cutts	0	5	0	0
		1	lb	Mercury	0	0	5	0
		4	lb	Liquorice	0	0	5	0
James Lofte	Ind	14	piece	Cloth of Assize, Dozen Strait	0	0	0	0
		4	dozen	Skins, Red	0	8	4	0
		0.75	C	Aniseed	0	10	0	0
		2	lb	Oil, Bay	0	0	15	0
		1	lb	Pepper	0	0	12	0
		1	lb	Ginger	0	0	16	0
		2	lb	Thread	0	0	10	0
		3	lb	Liquorice	0	0	4	0
		8	lb	Cumin	0	0	15	0
		4	lb	Silk, *Worked*	0	53	4	0
		8	gross	Points	0	8	0	0
		29	lb	Saffron	14	10	0	0
Roland Artur	Ind	3	dozen	Skins, Red	0	6	3	0
		1	C	Aniseed	0	13	4	0
		0.5	C	Alum	0	6	8	0
		4	gross	Cutts	0	13	4	0
		2	lb	Thread	0	0	10	0
		1	lb	Silk Worked	0	13	4	0
		8.5	lb	Saffron	0	4	5	0
		2	lb	Sulpher	0	0	3	0
		1	lb	Mercury	0	0	5	0
		8	lb	Cumin	0	0	15	0
		12	gross	Points	0	12	0	0
		1	gross	Combs	0	0	15	0
		1	dozen	Balances	0	0	15	0
		2	lb	Liquorice	0	0	2	0
Dennis Whyte	Ind	3	gross	Cutts	0	10	0	0
		5	dozen	Skins, Red	0	10	5	0
		2	lb	Silk Worked	0	26	8	0
		0.75	C	Aniseed	0	10	0	0
		8	lb	Cumin	0	0	15	0
		2	lb	Mercury	0	0	10	0

Merchant name	Origin	Qty	Unit	Commodity	£	s.	d.	f.
		3	oz	Tin	0	0	15	0
		2	oz	Sugar, of Roses	0	0	4	0
		2	lb	Oil, Bay	0	0	15	0
		4	lb	Thread	0	0	20	0
		1	dozen	Knives, in Pairs	0	0	20	0
		1	dozen	Balances	0	0	15	0
		3	lb	Liquorice	0	0	4	0
		24	gross	Points	0	24	0	0
		14	lb	Saffron	7	0	0	0
		4	piece	Cloth of Assize, Dozen Strait	0	0	0	0
William Meagh	Ind	4	piece	Cloth of Assize	0	0	0	0
		7	lb	Saffron	3	10	0	0
		2	lb	Silk Worked	0	26	8	0
		1.5	gross	Cutts	0	5	0	0
		1	dozen	Skins, Red	0	2	1	0
		1	gross	Points	0	0	12	0
		2	lb	Thread	0	0	10	0
Nicholas Harres	Ind	14	dozen	Skins, Red	0	29	2	0
		3	C	Combs	0	3	4	0
		16	lb	Saffron	8	0	0	0

Bata Clement of Worcester, John Aworcest master, Exiting, 14th November 1525

Merchant name	Origin	Qty	Unit	Commodity	£	s.	d.	f.
Walter Kelly	Ind	6	lb	Silk Worked	4	0	0	0
		10	lb	Saffron	5	0	0	0
		2	gross	Points	0	2	0	0

Bata Christofer of Mumbles, John Robyns master, Entering, 29th November 1525

Merchant name	Origin	Qty	Unit	Commodity	£	s.	d.	f.
Thomas Jonys	Ind	7	ton	Salt	3	10	0	0
		2	C	Vetery Canvas *Cloth*	2	0	0	0

Bata Trinite of Chepstow, William Haynes master, Entering, *29th November 1525*

Merchant name	Origin	Qty	Unit	Commodity	£	s.	d.	f.
Edmund Mighell	Ind	30	piece	Mantles	5	0	0	0
		1.75	C	Skins, Sheep	0	17	6	0
		2	C	Skins, Lamb	0	13	4	0
		5	piece	Skins, Fox	0	0	10	0
John Denys	Ind	1.5	C	Skins, Sheep	0	15	0	0
		4	piece	Mantles	0	13	4	0

Bata Walsynghin of Tenby, John More, Entering, *29th November 1525*

Merchant name	Origin	Qty	Unit	Commodity	£	s.	d.	f.
John Cole	Ind	1	tun	Wine	0	0	0	0

Bata George of Tewkesbury, William Roche master, Entering, *29th November 1525*

Merchant name	Origin	Qty	Unit	Commodity	£	s.	d.	f.
Thomas Hoggs	Ind	8	pipe	Fish, Salmon	12	0	0	0
	Ind	10	burden	Fish, Salted	0	41	8	0
	Ind	1	C	Fish, Hake	0	10	0	0

Merchant name	Origin	Qty	Unit	Commodity	£	s.	d.	f.

Bata Clement of Worcester, John Brytton master, Entering, 2nd December 1525

Merchant name	Origin	Qty	Unit	Commodity	£	s.	d.	f.
Richard Hyggons	Ind	4.5	tun	Wine	0	0	0	0

Bata Trinite of Chepstow, William Haynys master, Entering, *2nd December 1525*

Merchant name	Origin	Qty	Unit	Commodity	£	s.	d.	f.
John Hopar	Ind	3	tun	Wine	0	0	0	0

Bata Anne Bonaventure, *Port Unknown*,[1] George Hart master, Entering, 4th December 1525

Merchant name	Origin	Qty	Unit	Commodity	£	s.	d.	f.
Robert Ellyot	Ind	13.75	tun	Wine	0	0	0	0
		3	ton	Iron	7	10	0	0
		1	pipe	Woad	5	0	0	0
		5.5	balette	Woad	3	3	2	0
		4	C	Rosin	0	5	4	0
Robert Chapman	Ind	10	tun	Wine	0	0	0	0
		3	ton	Iron	7	10	0	0
		4	C	Rosin	0	5	4	0
Thomas Hykke	Ind	12.75	tun	Wine	0	0	0	0
		3	ton	Iron	7	10	0	0
		4	C	Rosin	0	5	0	0
William Yate	Ind	8.5	tun	Wine	0	0	0	0
George Hart	Ind	1	hogshead	Wine	0	0	0	0
		12	piece	Boxstaves	0	0	15	0
Howell Codmor	Ind	1	pipe	Wine	0	0	0	0
		11	*lb*	Serches	0	3	4	0
Henry Fryse	Alien	1	kilderkin	Vinegar	0	2	6	0

Navicula Mathew of Bristol, Thomas Dowdyng master, Entering, 7th December 1525

Merchant name	Origin	Qty	Unit	Commodity	£	s.	d.	f.
John Shipman	Ind	31.75	tun	Wine	0	0	0	0
		8	ton	Iron	20	0	0	0
John Ware	Ind	8.5	tun	Wine	0	0	0	0
William Dale	Ind	5	tun	Wine	0	0	0	0
William Shipman	Ind	18.25	tun	Wine	0	0	0	0
Gilbert Cogan	Ind	2	tierce	Wine	0	0	0	0
John Thomas	Ind	5	tun	Wine	0	0	0	0
William Appowell	Ind	3.75	tun	Wine	0	0	0	0
John Brampton	Ind	9	tun	Wine	0	0	0	0
William Rowley	Ind	14.08	tun	Wine	0	0	0	0
		10	C	Rosin	0	13	4	0
		15	unknown	Pitch, Hearth	0	12	6	0
Thomas Nongull	Ind	1	tun	Wine	0	0	0	0
Nicholas Dukket	Ind	6.75	tun	Wine	0	0	0	0
Thomas Roland	Ind	2.75	tun	Wine	0	0	0	0
Mathew Smyth	Ind	1	pipe	Wine	0	0	0	0
John Smyth	Ind	4	tun	Wine	0	0	0	0
Thomas Dowdy	Ind	1.75	tun	Wine	0	0	0	0
		0.66	ton	Iron	0	33	4	0
William Deane	Ind	1	pipe	Wine	0	0	0	0

1 Probably a Bristol ship.

Merchant name	Origin	Qty	Unit	Commodity	£	s.	d.	f.
Navicula Kattryn of Lyme Regis, John Yonge master, Entering, 7th December 1525								
John Welshe	Ind	16.5	tun	Wine	o	o	o	o
Awger de Noga	Alien	16.5	tun	Wine	o	o	o	o
Thomas Rowland	Ind	0.33	ton	Iron	o	16	8	o
John Baylly	Ind	1	pipe	Woad	5	o	o	o
		3.5	balette	Woad	1	17	6	o
		3	ton	Iron	7	10	o	o
		2	ton	Rosin	o	53	4	o
John Yonge	Ind	1	ton	Iron	o	50	o	o
Navicula Mary Spert of Bristol, Robert Spert master, Entering, 7th December 1525								
John Blakalle	Ind	9	tun	Wine	o	o	o	o
		20	piece	Raisins, *Great*	o	32	6	o
		2	C	Ginger	5	o	o	o
		21	lb	Cloves	o	52	6	o
		1	chest	Sugar	o	40	o	o
		2.5	C	Pepper	o	12	10	o
		0.75	C	Ginger	3	7	6	o
		13	lb	Mace	o	32	6	o
Gilbert Kyrke	Ind	25	tun	Wine	o	o	o	o
William Bode	Ind	13	tun	Wine	o	o	o	o
John Michell	Ind	13.25	tun	Wine	o	o	o	o
		2	chest	Sugar	4	o	o	o
		3.75	C	Pepper	19	7	6	o
		0.5	C	Graines	o	25	o	o
		0.75	C	Ginger	3	7	6	o
John Mores	Ind	12.25	tun	Wine	o	o	o	o
		4	chest	Sugar	8	o	o	o
		16.25	C	Fruit	o	32	6	o
		271	lb	Pepper	13	10	6	o
		10	lb	Ginger	o	10	o	o
		20	lb	Mace	o	50	o	o
		5	lb	Cloves	o	12	6	o
		1	C	Graines	o	50	o	o
John Phillyppys	Ind	12.5	tun	Wine	o	o	o	o
		2	chest	Sugar	4	o	o	o
		1.5	C	Pepper	7	10	o	o
		0.75	C	Ginger	o	37	6	o
		0.75	C	Ginger	3	7	6	o
		30	lb	Cloves and mace	3	15	o	o
		7	lb	Nutmeg	o	7	o	o
		7	lb	Cinnamon	o	13	o	o
John Sellar	Ind	16	tun	Wine	o	o	o	o
Roger Pery	Ind	5.5	tun	Wine	o	o	o	o
John Holand	Ind	4	tun	Wine	o	o	o	o
Robert Spert	Ind	1.75	tun	Wine	o	o	o	o
John Clement	Ind	1	pipe	Wine	o	o	o	o
Gilbert Kyrke	Ind	0.75	C	Marmalade	o	10	o	o
		0.5	C	**Gsua?**	o	10	o	o
Walter Bosome	Ind	2	C	Raisins, *Great*	o	4	o	o

Merchant name	Origin	Qty	Unit	Commodity	£	s.	d.	f.
Roger Pery	Ind	95	lb	Pepper	4	15	0	0
		0.5	C	Ginger	0	25	0	0
		2	lb	Cinnamon	0	4	0	0
		13	lb	Ginger	0	13	0	0
		4	lb	Mace	0	10	0	0
		10	lb	Cloves	0	25	0	0
John Way	Ind	1	C	Pepper	5	0	0	0
		1	C	Graines	0	50	0	0
		4	lb	Mace	0	10	0	0
John Way	Ind	6	lb	Cloves	0	15	0	0
Elliott Berry	Ind	3.75	C	Pepper	19	7	6	0
John Mayn[ ]de	Ind	4	C	Pepper	20	0	0	0
		1.25	C	Ginger	3	2	6	0
		105	lb	Cloves	13	2	6	0
		5	lb	Nutmeg	0	5	0	0
		8	lb	Mace	0	20	0	0
		1	chest	Sugar	0	40	0	0

Bata Jamys of Milford Haven, Thomas Adams master, *Entering,* 11th December 1525

Merchant name	Origin	Qty	Unit	Commodity	£	s.	d.	f.
Thomas *Adams*	Ind	8.5	barrel	Fish, Herring White	0	42	6	0
		6	C	Fish, Hake	0	60	0	0
		8	mease	Fish, Herring White	0	40	0	0
Prior de Lantony	Ind	3	last	Fish, Herring White	9	0	0	0
		2	pipe	Fish, Salmon	0	60	0	0
		1	C	Irish Linen *Cloth*	0	10	0	0
		1	C	Irish Woollen *Cloth*	0	40	0	0
		1	piece	Mantles	0	3	4	0
		8	C	Fish, Salted	8	0	0	0
John Cokks	Ind	1	barrel	Fish, Herring White	0	5	0	0

Navicula Jesus of Barnstaple, John Tyddle master, Entering, 12th December 1525

Merchant name	Origin	Qty	Unit	Commodity	£	s.	d.	f.
Paul Smyth	Ind	7.25	tun	Wine	0	0	0	0
		4.5	C	Wood, Brazil	7	10	0	0
		1	hogshead	Oil, *Olive*	0	20	0	0
		2.375	C	Pepper	11	17	6	0
		0.875	C	Graines	0	43	9	0
		1	chest	Sugar	0	40	0	0
		20	lb	Cloves	0	50	0	0
Nicholas Thorn	Ind	5	tun	Wine	0	0	0	0
John Thorn	Ind	2.75	tun	Wine	0	0	0	0
John Cappys	Ind	1.75	tun	Wine	0	0	0	0
John Ayllworth	Ind	1.75	tun	Wine	0	0	0	0
Richard Pryn	Ind	2.75	tun	Wine	0	0	0	0
Thomas Smyth	Ind	2.5	tun	Wine	0	0	0	0
		4.5	C	Wood, Brazil	7	10	0	0
		4.375	C	Raisins, *Great*	0	8	9	0
		214	lb	Pepper	10	12	6	0
		0.5	C	Graines	0	25	0	0
Richard Pole	Ind	3	tun	Wine	0	0	0	0
		4.5	C	Wood, Brazil	7	10	0	0

Merchant name	Origin	Qty	Unit	Commodity	£	s.	d.	f.
		4.375	C	Raisins, *Great*	o	8	9	o
		0.25	C	Graines	o	12	6	o
		19.5	lb	Pepper	o	19	6	o
Thomas Raffe	Ind	3.75	tun	Wine	o	o	o	o
		1	pipe	Oil, *Olive*	2	o	o	o
		1	C	Pepper	5	o	o	o
Thomas Westcote	Ind	6.5	tun	Wine	o	o	o	o
		4.375	C	Raisins, *Great*	o	8	9	o
		0.5	C	Marmalade	o	6	8	o
John Holloway	Ind	2.5	tun	Wine	o	o	o	o
John Andrew	Ind	2	tun	Wine	o	o	o	o
		0.375	C	Graines	o	18	9	o
Bawdewyn Pert	Ind	1.75	tun	Wine	o	o	o	o
		44.5	lb	Pepper	2	3	6	o
Richard Skynn	Ind	1.5	tun	Wine	o	o	o	o
John Tyddorley	Ind	1.5	tun	Wine	o	o	o	o
John Wyllet	Ind	1	tun	Wine	o	o	o	o
		1.125	C	Wood, Brazil	o	37	6	o
		1	piece	Raisins, *Great*	o	o	20	o
James Mortem	Ind	0.375	tun	Wine	o	o	o	o
William Deane	Ind	1	pipe	Wine	o	o	o	o
Thomas Roo	Ind	1	hogshead	Fruit	o	10	o	o
Thomas Palmer	Ind	1.375	tun	Marmalade	o	18	4	o
Thomas Blake	Ind	0.5	chest	Sugar	o	20	o	o
		30	lb	Unknown Commodity	o	10	o	o

Bata *Christ*pofer of Errenteria, Gregory de Corde master, Entering, 12th December 1525

John Wyot	Ind	4.5	balette	Woad	o	50	o	o
John Sannche	Alien	10	M	Oranges	o	33	4	o

Bata Trinite of Chepstow, William Hayne master, Entering, 12th December 1525

Roger Dawys	Ind	7.5	tun	Wine	o	o	o	o
		1	tun	Wine	o	o	o	o
William Woseley	Ind	7	C	Rosin	o	9	4	o

Bata Sonday of Coombe, Henry Wyse master, *Entering,* 13th December 1525

John Lowar	Ind	3	ton	Salt	o	30	o	o

Bata Mary Smyth of Bristol, David Smyth master, Entering, 14th December 1525

David *Smyth*	Ind	4	C	Fish, Hake	o	40	o	o
		11	barrel	Fish, Herring White	o	55	o	o
Thomas Long	Ind	12	barrel	Fish, Herring White	3	o	o	o
		1	C	Fish, Hake	o	10	o	o
Richard Hopkyns	Ind	29	barrel	Fish, Herring White	7	5	o	o
		6	mease	Fish, Herring White	o	30	o	o
		7	C	Fish, Hake	3	10	o	o
Patrick Stevyns	Ind	12	barrel	Fish, Herring White	3	o	o	o
		2.5	C	Fish, Hake	o	25	o	o

Merchant name	Origin	Qty	Unit	Commodity	£	s.	d.	f.
Richard Cokksall	Ind	6	barrel	Fish, Herring White	0	30	0	0
William Jaksen	Ind	4	C	Fish, Hake	0	40	0	0
		1	C	Check *Cloth*	0	40	0	0
		1.5	C	Tallow	0	5	0	0
Philip Elyot	Ind	4.5	barrel	Fish, Herring White	0	22	6	0

Bata Mary John, *Port Unknown,* [2] **John Benys master, Entering,** *14th December 1525*

Richard Bright	Ind	168	barrel	Fish, Herring White	42	0	0	0

Bata *Christ***pofer of Padstow, Robert Phillypp master, Entering,** *15th December 1525*

John Shipman	Ind	1	last	Fish, Herring White	3	0	0	0
Richard William	Ind	7	last	Fish, Herring White	21	0	0	0
Nicholas Allwyn	Ind	3	last	Fish, Herring White	9	0	0	0
Thomas Sumpter	Ind	34	barrel	Fish, Herring White	8	10	0	0
Nicholas Fox	Ind	1	last	Fish, Herring White	3	0	0	0
John More	Ind	1	last	Fish, Herring White	3	0	0	0
Richard Borne	Ind	38	barrel	Fish, Herring White	9	10	0	0
Edward Jonys	Ind	6	barrel	Fish, Herring White	0	30	0	0
Walter Smyth	Ind	1	last	Fish, Herring White	3	0	0	0
Robert Phillypp	Ind	30	barrel	Fish, Herring White	7	10	0	0

Bata Trinite of Chepstow, William Hayne master, Entering, *15th December 1525*

Roger Dawys	Ind	1	ton	Iron	2	10	0	0
Thomas Roland	Ind	4	ton	Iron	10	0	0	0

Bata John of Milford Haven, William Taskar master, Entering, *16th December 1525*

William *Taskar*	Ind	5	barrel	Fish, Herring White	0	25	0	0

Navicula Mawdelyn of Berkeley, John Rogers master, Entering, *18th December 1525*

Maurice Bocher	Ind	6	ton	Iron	15	0	0	0
		1	C	Raisins, *Great*	0	2	0	0
		5	C	Oranges	0	0	20	0
		1	pipe	Wine	0	0	0	0

Navicula Mary Grace of *Bristol,* **William Benet master, Entering,** *18th December 1525*

John Shipman	Ind	2	last	Fish, Herring White	6	0	0	0
William Horton	Ind	88	barrel	Fish, Herring White	22	0	0	0
Thomas Smyth	Ind	45	barrel	Fish, Herring White	11	5	0	0
Nicholas Fox	Ind	5	last	Fish, Herring White	15	0	0	0
Robert Avyntre	Ind	1	last	Fish, Herring White	3	0	0	0
William Benet	Ind	17	barrel	Fish, Herring White	4	5	0	0
William Dukkar	Ind	1	last	Fish, Herring White	3	0	0	0
Richard Hopkyns	Ind	13.5	barrel	Fish, Herring White	3	7	6	0
Nicholas Orton	Ind	3	barrel	Fish, Herring White	0	15	0	0

2 This may be the same Mary John which is found registered as a Bristol ship on 26th April 1526, although the route and master are different.

Merchant name	Origin	Qty	Unit	Commodity	£	s.	d.	f.
John Borwen and assoc.	Ind	16.5	barrel	Fish, Herring White	4	2	6	0

Navicula John Baptyst, Port Unknown, William Walter master, Entering, 18th December 1525

Merchant name	Origin	Qty	Unit	Commodity	£	s.	d.	f.
Robert Avyntre	Ind	2	last	Fish, Herring White	6	0	0	0
Hugh Ellyot	Ind	6	barrel	Fish, Herring White	0	30	0	0
Richard Hope	Ind	5	last	Fish, Herring White	15	0	0	0
John Warner	Ind	2.5	last	Fish, Herring White	7	10	0	0
Dennis Dyar	Ind	13	barrel	Fish, Herring White	3	5	0	0
Walter Feld	Ind	1	last	Fish, Herring White	3	0	0	0
John Bek	Ind	10	barrel	Fish, Herring White	2	10	0	0
Richard Fleming	Ind	18	barrel	Fish, Herring White	4	10	0	0
William Loid	Ind	7	barrel	Fish, Herring White	0	35	0	0
Francis Jay	Ind	6	barrel	Fish, Herring White	0	30	0	0
John Aylworth	Ind	4	barrel	Fish, Herring White	0	20	0	0
William Tyrn	Ind	2	last	Fish, Herring White	6	0	0	0
Richard White	Ind	3.5	barrel	Fish, Herring White	0	17	6	0
William Walter and assoc.	Ind	5	barrel	Fish, Herring White	0	25	0	0

Navicula Mary Christpofer of Bristol, John Welshe master, Entering, 18th December 1525

Merchant name	Origin	Qty	Unit	Commodity	£	s.	d.	f.
Robert Avyntre	Ind	192	barrel	Fish, Herring White	48	0	0	0
		3.5	C	Fish, Salted	3	10	0	0
		13	C	Fish, Hake	6	10	0	0
		1	dicker	Skins, Salted	0	13	4	0
		3	hogshead	Fish, Eels	4	0	0	0
William Shipman	Ind	1	last	Fish, Herring White	3	0	0	0
William Lorde	Ind	6	barrel	Fish, Herring White	0	30	0	0
Walter Feld	Ind	1	hogshead	Fish, Herring White	0	10	0	0
Richard Fleming	Ind	7	barrel	Fish, Herring White	0	35	0	0
Jerome Grene	Ind	1	kilderkin	Fish, Herring White	0	2	6	0
John Ysgard	Ind	1	last	Fish, Herring White	3	0	0	0
John Welshe and assoc.	Ind	17	barrel	Fish, Herring White	4	5	0	0
Peter Spaynde	Alien	2.5	hogshead	Fish, Salmon	4	2	6	0
		1	barrel	Fish, Salmon	1	2	0	0
		5	barrel	Fish, Herring White	0	25	0	0

Bata Margaret of Newnham, Thomas Symonds, Entering, 19th December 1525

Merchant name	Origin	Qty	Unit	Commodity	£	s.	d.	f.
Thomas Lowthar	Ind	10	ton	Salt	5	0	0	0

Bata Trinite of Chepstow, William Hayn master, Entering, 20th December 1525

Merchant name	Origin	Qty	Unit	Commodity	£	s.	d.	f.
Roger Dawys	Ind	2.66	ton	Iron	6	13	4	0
John de la Sard	Alien	1	pipe	Wine	0	0	0	0
		4.5	balette	Woad	0	50	0	0
		3	C	Rosin	0	4	0	0
John Sannche	Alien	1	M	Oranges	0	3	4	0
William Woseley	Ind	2	ton	Iron	5	0	0	0

Merchant name	Origin	Qty	Unit	Commodity	£	s.	d.	f.
Bata Antony of Chepstow, Henry Roche master, Entering, *20th December 1525*								
Michael de Arysinendy	Alien	5	C	Rosin	0	6	8	0
Bata Nicholas of Kidwelly, Olven Williams master, Entering, 23rd December 1525								
John Yerward	Ind	1.25	tun	Wine	0	0	0	0
Bata Mary Walsynghin,[3] Walter Bryt master, Entering, *23rd December 1525*								
Walter Bryt	Ind	9	ton	Salt	4	10	0	0
Bata George of Tewkesbury, John Roche master, Exiting, *23rd December 1525*								
Thomas Hoggs	Ind	12	wey	Grain	12	0	0	0
Bata Trynyte of Chepstow, William Hayens master, Entering, 31st December 1525								
William Woyseley	Ind	8	ton	Iron	20	0	0	0
Bata John Baptyst, *Port Unknown*, Evan Bryttan master, Exiting, *31st December 1525*								
Thomas Sumpter	Ind	3	last	Fish, Herring White	9	0	0	0
		8	wey	Coal	0	26	8	0
		10	piece	Welsh *Cloth*	10	0	0	0
Navicula Mary Chrystofer of Bristol, John Welshe master, Exiting, *31st December 1525*								
Robert Avyntre	Ind	29	wey	Coal	4	16	8	0
		45	yard	Check *Cloth*	0	15	0	0
Navicula Mary Penrycy, *Port Unknown*, John Wylkyns master, Entering, *31st December 1525*								
Hugh Elyott	Ind	7	last	Fish, Herring White	21	0	0	0
Navicula Mary Grace of Bristol, Richard Miller master, Entering, *31st December 1525*								
John Savage	Ind	6	last	Fish, Herring White	18	0	0	0
Nicholas Roper	Ind	25.5	barrel	Fish, Herring White	6	7	6	0
John Warn	Ind	40	barrel	Fish, Herring White	10	0	0	0
Griffith Caker	Ind	10	barrel	Fish, Herring White	0	50	0	0
Richard Hops	Ind	6	barrel	Fish, Herring White	0	30	0	0
Thomas & William Mower	Ind	23	barrel	Fish, Herring White	5	15	0	0
John Mansell	Ind	16	barrel	Fish, Herring White	4	0	0	0
John Reys	Ind	1.5	barrel	Fish, Herring White	0	7	6	0

3 This could be from either Bristol or Tenby, as ships of this name are found registered at both ports in this account. The master's name does not help to clarify, but the fact that the port name is omitted suggests that it is probably a Bristol ship.

Merchant name	Origin	Qty	Unit	Commodity	£	s.	d.	f.

Navicula Mary Bonaventure of Bristol, Thomas Nungull master, Entering, *31st December 1525*

Merchant name	Origin	Qty	Unit	Commodity	£	s.	d.	f.
Thomas *Nungull*	Ind	24.5	tun	Wine	0	0	0	0
William Appowell	Ind	4.5	tun	Wine	0	0	0	0
		1	hogshead	Rosin	0	6	8	0
John Thomas	Ind	1.75	tun	Wine	0	0	0	0
		1	pipe	Rosin	0	13	4	0
William Rowley	Ind	1.75	tun	Wine	0	0	0	0
Thomas Ashehurst	Ind	1	tun	Wine	0	0	0	0

Navicula Mawdelyn de Bonaventura, *Port Unknown*, Anthony Pykarde master, Entering, *31st December 1525*

Merchant name	Origin	Qty	Unit	Commodity	£	s.	d.	f.
Nicholas Gay	Ind	128	barrel	Fish, Herring White	32	0	0	0
		8	C	Fish, Salted	8	0	0	0
		7	C	Fish, Hake	0	70	0	0
		2	ton	Salt	0	20	0	0
John Shipman	Ind	9	last	Fish, Herring White	27	0	0	0
William Shipman	Ind	27	barrel	Fish, Herring White	6	15	0	0
William Rowley	Ind	13.5	barrel	Fish, Herring White	0	67	7	0
Anthony Pygotte and assoc.	Ind	34.5	barrel	Fish, Herring White	8	12	6	0

Bata Tawdere of Gatcombe, John Drew*is* master, Entering, 2nd January 1526

Merchant name	Origin	Qty	Unit	Commodity	£	s.	d.	f.
John Marks	Ind	12.5	last	Fish, Herring White	37	10	0	0

Navicula Bonaventure of Quimperlé, William Pedron master, Entering, *2nd January 1526*

Merchant name	Origin	Qty	Unit	Commodity	£	s.	d.	f.
Roland Kyng	Alien	48.5	tun	Wine	0	0	0	0
		1	pipe	Iron	0	25	0	0
		1	pipe	Rosin	0	13	4	0
		170	yard	Irish Linen *Cloth*	0	56	8	0

Navicula Mary Kateryn, *Port Unknown*,[4] John Gorway master, Entering, *2nd January 1526*

Merchant name	Origin	Qty	Unit	Commodity	£	s.	d.	f.
Andrew Palmer	Ind	159	barrel	Fish, Herring White	39	15	0	0
		2	C	Fish, Salted	0	40	0	0
Roger Dawys	Ind	7	last	Fish, Herring White	21	0	0	0
John Hall	Ind	5	last	Fish, Herring White	15	0	0	0
		1	C	Fish, Salted	0	20	0	0
Robert Shipman	Ind	32	barrel	Fish, Herring White	8	0	0	0
William Cockys	Ind	103	barrel	Fish, Herring White	25	0	0	0
John Bannkys	Ind	8	last	Fish, Herring White	24	0	0	0
		1	hogshead	Fish, Salmon	0	30	0	0
Robert Avyntre	Ind	1	last	Fish, Herring White	0	60	0	0
Nicholas Warde	Ind	59	barrel	Fish, Herring White	14	15	0	0
		4	hogshead	Fish, Salmon	6	0	0	0
		1	kilderkin	Fish, Eels	0	6	8	0
Thomas Stannforde	Ind	62	barrel	Fish, Herring White	15	10	0	0

4 Probably Bristol.

Merchant name	Origin	Qty	Unit	Commodity	£	s.	d.	f.
		0.5	C	Fish, Salted	0	10	0	0
Humphrey Cosgrove	Ind	9	barrel	Fish, Herring White	0	45	0	0
John Cappys	Ind	3	barrel	Fish, Herring White	0	15	0	0
Thomas Harte	Ind	1.5	last	Fish, Herring White	4	10	0	0
Thomas Aporttysmowth	Ind	27	barrel	Fish, Herring White	6	15	0	0
Thomas Willmottys	Ind	29.5	barrel	Fish, Herring White	7	7	6	0
Griffith Caker	Ind	1	last	Fish, Herring White	0	60	0	0
Nicholas Roper	Ind	2	last	Fish, Herring White	6	0	0	0
Nicholas Turner	Ind	33	barrel	Fish, Herring White	8	5	0	0
John Ysgard	Ind	6	barrel	Fish, Herring White	0	30	0	0
John Pylle	Ind	1	last	Fish, Herring White	0	60	0	0
Philip Furbor	Ind	8.5	barrel	Fish, Herring White	0	42	6	0
John Coke	Ind	1	last	Fish, Herring White	0	60	0	0
William Kyssam	Ind	6	barrel	Fish, Herring White	0	30	0	0

Navicula Mawdelyn of Berkeley, John Crocke master, Entering, 3rd January 1526

Merchant name	Origin	Qty	Unit	Commodity	£	s.	d.	f.
Maurice Bocher	Ind	15	last	Fish, Herring White	45	0	0	0
Richard Williams	Ind	5	last	Fish, Herring White	15	0	0	0
John Bristoll and assoc.	Ind	1	last	Fish, Herring White	0	60	0	0

Navicula Vyncent of Bristol, John Amayn master, Entering, 3rd January 1526

Merchant name	Origin	Qty	Unit	Commodity	£	s.	d.	f.
William Woseley	Ind	12	last	Fish, Herring White	36	0	0	0
John Amayne	Ind	45	barrel	Fish, Herring White	11	5	0	0
Thomas Smyth	Ind	80	barrel	Fish, Herring White	20	0	0	0
Thomas George	Ind	16.5	barrel	Fish, Herring White	4	0	15	0
Thomas Pynn	Ind	2	last	Fish, Herring White	6	0	0	0
William Popley	Ind	11	barrel	Fish, Herring White	0	55	0	0
Dennis Flemyng	Ind	10.5	barrel	Fish, Herring White	0	52	6	0
Dennis Mullen and assoc.	Ind	14	barrel	Fish, Herring White	0	70	0	0
John Averke	Ind	1	piece	Knives	0	3	4	0

Navicula Mary of Crozon, Peter Harvy master, Entering, 3rd January 1526

Merchant name	Origin	Qty	Unit	Commodity	£	s.	d.	f.
William Dale	Ind	18	tun	Wine	0	0	0	0
		8	C	Rosin	0	10	8	0
John Ware	Ind	1.75	tun	Wine	0	0	0	0
William Shipman	Ind	4.5	tun	Wine	0	0	0	0
Gilbert Cogan	Ind	4.5	tun	Wine	0	0	0	0
John Thomas	Ind	8.75	tun	Wine	0	0	0	0
William Rowley	Ind	2	tun	Wine	0	0	0	0
John Brampton	Ind	4.5	tun	Wine	0	0	0	0
Thomas Ashehurst	Ind	4.25	tun	Wine	0	0	0	0
John Roland	Ind	1.75	tun	Wine	0	0	0	0
Thomas Roland	Ind	1.75	tun	Wine	0	0	0	0
Nicholas Dokett	Ind	1.75	tun	Wine	0	0	0	0
Peter Harvy	Alien	1	tun	Wine	0	0	0	0
		30	C	Rosin	0	40	0	0

Merchant name	Origin	Qty	Unit	Commodity	£	s.	d.	f.
		21	piece	Poldavis *Cloth*	10	10	0	0
		120	yard	*Lemagois Cloth*	0	40	0	0
		1	C	Incense	0	6	8	0
John Smyth &								
Edward Jonys	Ind	1.33	tun	Wine	0	0	0	0

Bata Margaret of Elmore, William Fox master, Entering, 4th January 1526

Merchant name	Origin	Qty	Unit	Commodity	£	s.	d.	f.
William Fox	Ind	7.5	last	Fish, Herring White	22	10	0	0
William Towker	Ind	1	last	Fish, Herring White	0	60	0	0

Navicula Mary John of Bristol, Thomas Harte master, Entering, 11th January 1525

Merchant name	Origin	Qty	Unit	Commodity	£	s.	d.	f.
John Shipman	Ind	3.5	tun	Wine	0	0	0	0
William Shipman	Ind	2.75	tun	Wine	0	0	0	0
Robert Shipman	Ind	1.75	tun	Wine	0	0	0	0
George Hall	Ind	5.75	tun	Wine	0	0	0	0
		6.5	tun	Oil, *Olive*	26	0	0	0
		2	ton	Fruit	4	0	0	0
		1	chest	Sugar	0	40	0	0
John Cappys	Ind	5.25	tun	Wine	0	0	0	0
		4.5	tun	Oil, *Olive*	18	0	0	0
Humphrey Cosgrove	Ind	3.75	tun	Wine	0	0	0	0
Nicholas Thomas	Ind	6	tun	Wine	0	0	0	0
John Thorn	Ind	5.25	tun	Wine	0	0	0	0
William Ostrege	Ind	3.5	tun	Wine	0	0	0	0
Richard Pryn	Ind	2.75	tun	Wine	0	0	0	0
John Coke	Ind	1.75	tun	Wine	0	0	0	0
		2	tun	Oil, *Olive*	8	0	0	0
Nicholas Gay	Ind	1.75	tun	Wine	0	0	0	0
John Thomas	Ind	1.25	tun	Wine	0	0	0	0
Thomas Roland	Ind	2.5	tun	Wine	0	0	0	0
		1	hogshead	Oil, *Olive*	1	0	0	0
William Spratt	Ind	1.625	tun	Wine	0	0	0	0
		1	pipe	Oil, *Olive*	2	0	0	0
James Jarndyn	Ind	4.5	tun	Wine	0	0	0	0
William Water	Ind	3	tun	Wine	0	0	0	0
Thomas Barry	Ind	1	tun	Wine	0	0	0	0
John Wodwall	Ind	2.625	tun	Wine	0	0	0	0
Thomas Harte	Ind	4	tun	Wine	0	0	0	0
		2	tun	Oil, *Olive*	8	0	0	0
John Pylle	Ind	3.5	tun	Wine	0	0	0	0
		1	hogshead	Oil, *Olive*	1	0	0	0
John Adevynshere	Ind	3.5	tun	Wine	0	0	0	0
		1	pipe	Fruit	1	0	0	0
		1	pipe	Prunes	0	53	4	0
William Deyn	Ind	1	tun	Wine	0	0	0	0
John Welshe	Ind	1	tun	Wine	0	0	0	0
Thomas Palmer	Ind	1.125	tun	Wine	0	0	0	0
		1	tun	Oil, *Olive*	4	0	0	0
		0.75	C	Marmalade	0	10	0	0
Humphrey Bradley	Ind	1.5	tun	Wine	0	0	0	0

Merchant name	Origin	Qty	Unit	Commodity	£	s.	d.	f.
William Cagenney & William Jaccobbe	Ind	1	tun	Wine	0	0	0	0
Edmund Pope and assoc.	Ind	1.5625	tun	Wine	0	0	0	0
Richard Symons	Ind	0.5	C	*Sokatt*	0	10	0	0

Navicula Denys of Penmarch, John Brayrro, Entering, 12th January 1526

Merchant name	Origin	Qty	Unit	Commodity	£	s.	d.	f.
John Shipman	Ind	8	tun	Wine	0	0	0	0
William Shipman	Ind	2.75	tun	Wine	0	0	0	0
Gilbert Cogan	Ind	9	tun	Wine	0	0	0	0
Thomas Hickys	Ind	5	tun	Wine	0	0	0	0
George Hall	Ind	1.5	tun	Wine	0	0	0	0
John Roland	Ind	7	tun	Wine	0	0	0	0
William Rowley	Ind	3.75	tun	Wine	0	0	0	0
Thomas Roland	Ind	1	pipe	Wine	0	0	0	0
John Thomas	Ind	7.75	tun	Wine	0	0	0	0
Thomas Ashehurst	Ind	4.25	tun	Wine	0	0	0	0
Nicholas Dokett	Ind	0.16	tun	Wine	0	0	0	0
		3.5	C	Rosin	0	4	8	0
John Ware	Ind	4.25	tun	Wine	0	0	0	0
Jerome Greyn	Ind	2.125	tun	Wine	0	0	0	0
John Brerow	Alien	1	ton	Rosin	0	26	8	0
		1	C	Spanish Linen *Cloth*	0	40	0	0
		3	C	Frankincense	0	20	0	0
John Smith	Ind	1	tun	Wine	0	0	0	0

Bata Antony of Chepstow, John David master, Entering, *12th January 1526*

Merchant name	Origin	Qty	Unit	Commodity	£	s.	d.	f.
Thomas Alondon	Ind	4	tun	Wine	0	0	0	0

Bata Dragon of Milford Haven, Henry Webbe master, Entering, *12th January 1526*

Merchant name	Origin	Qty	Unit	Commodity	£	s.	d.	f.
Henry Webbe	Ind	6	barrel	Fish, Herring White	0	30	0	0
		1	C	Fish, Salted	0	20	0	0

Navicula Mary of Crozon, Harvy Trevysyon master, Entering, 13th January 1526

Merchant name	Origin	Qty	Unit	Commodity	£	s.	d.	f.
John Shipman	Ind	7.75	tun	Wine	0	0	0	0
John Ware	Ind	1.75	tun	Wine	0	0	0	0
William Dale	Ind	23.5	tun	Wine	0	0	0	0
		6.5	C	Rosin	0	8	6	0
William Shipman	Ind	4.75	tun	Wine	0	0	0	0
Gilbert Cogan	Ind	3.75	tun	Wine	0	0	0	0
John Thomas	Ind	9	tun	Wine	0	0	0	0
Thomas Ashehurst	Ind	3.5	tun	Wine	0	0	0	0
William Rowley	Ind	2.5	tun	Wine	0	0	0	0
John Brampton	Ind	4.75	tun	Wine	0	0	0	0
John Rolande	Ind	1.75	tun	Wine	0	0	0	0
Thomas Rolande	Ind	1.75	tun	Wine	0	0	0	0
Nicholas Dowker	Ind	6.41	tun	Wine	0	0	0	0
Edward Jonys	Ind	0.25	tun	Wine	0	0	0	0

Merchant name	Origin	Qty	Unit	Commodity	£	s.	d.	f.
Harvy Trevysyon	Alien	25	C	Rosin	0	33	4	0

Bata Antony of Bristol, Thomas Howell master, Entering, 15th January 1526

Thomas *Howell*	Ind	7	last	Fish, Herring White	21	0	0	0

Bata Antony of Chepstow, Lewis Hayens master, Entering, 17th January 1526

Maurice Appowell	Ind	8	C	Fruit	0	16	0	0

Navicula Mathew of Bristol, Nicholas Dowdyng master, Exiting, *17th January 1526*

John Shipman	Ind	37	wey	Grain	37	0	0	0
		52	piece	Cloth of Assize	0	0	0	0
		20	dozen	Skins, Calf	0	66	8	0
William Shipman	Ind	28	dozen	Skins, Calf	4	13	4	0
		37	piece	Cloth of Assize	0	0	0	0
John Wynter	Ind	26	wey	Grain	26	0	0	0
		22	piece	Cloth of Assize	0	0	0	0
John de Lesarde	Alien	3	dicker	Hides, Tanned	0	0	0	0
William Appowell	Ind	4	piece	Cloth of Assize	0	0	0	0
		9	dicker	Hides, Tanned	0	0	0	0
		26	dozen	Skins, Calf	4	6	8	0
Nicholas Thorne	Ind	10	piece	Cloth of Assize	0	0	0	0
William Spratt	Ind	17	piece	Cloth of Assize	0	0	0	0
William Woseley	Ind	13	piece	Cloth of Assize	0	0	0	0
John Ware	Ind	14	piece	Cloth of Assize	0	0	0	0

Bata Antony of Chepstow, William Hayens master, Exiting, *17th January 1526*

William Appowell	Ind	3	piece	Cloth of Assize	0	0	0	0

Bata Mawdelyn of Bristol, Anthony Pykarde master, Exiting, 19th January 1526

Roger Dawys	Ind	4.8	dicker	Hides, Tanned	0	0	0	0
		11	dozen	Skins, Calf	0	36	8	0

Bata Margaret of Mumbles, John Braggge, Entering, 20th January 1526

Richard Evans	Ind	85	barrel	Fish, Herring White	21	5	0	0
		0.5	C	Pullock	0	2	6	0
Richard Draper	Ind	2.5	C	Soap	0	25	0	0

Bata Mary of Carmarthen, Richard Davys master, Entering, *20th January 1526*

Richard Mower	Ind	10	ton	Salt	0	100	0	0

Bata Jamys of Tewkesbury, Walter Webbe master, Entering, 22nd January 1526

Robert Fyseylde	Ind	2	tun	Wine	0	0	0	0
Richard Ogan	Ind	2.5	tun	Wine	0	0	0	0
Griffith Hygon	Ind	2	C	Woad	0	20	0	0

Merchant name	Origin	Qty	Unit	Commodity	£	s.	d.	f.

Bata Mary Barkett of Tewkesbury, Robert Tawundy master, Entering, 22nd January 1526

Merchant name	Origin	Qty	Unit	Commodity	£	s.	d.	f.
Robert Tawundy	Ind	2	tun	Wine	0	0	0	0

Bata Mary of Tenby, James Kethyn master, Entering, 22nd January 1526

Merchant name	Origin	Qty	Unit	Commodity	£	s.	d.	f.
Richard Tanner	Ind	7	tun	Wine	0	0	0	0
		1	ton	Fruit	0	40	0	0
		3	C	Rosin	0	4	0	0
		3	ton	Salt	0	30	0	0
		17	barrel	Fish, Herring White	4	5	0	0
		15	C	Soap	7	10	0	0
		0.5	C	Pepper	0	50	0	0
		25	lb	Ginger	0	37	6	0
John Mower	Ind	15	barrel	Fish, Herring White	0	75	0	0

Bata Peter of Bristol, Thomas Barett master, Entering, 23rd January 1526

Merchant name	Origin	Qty	Unit	Commodity	£	s.	d.	f.
Thomas Barett	Ind	2.5	tun	Wine	0	0	0	0
		4	last	Fish, Herring White	12	0	0	0
		2	C	Fish, Hake	0	20	0	0
Silvia Tucker	Ind	9	last	Fish, Herring White	27	0	0	0
		5	C	Fish, Hake	0	50	0	0

Bata Mary of Wexford, Robert Roche master, Entering, 24th January 1526

Merchant name	Origin	Qty	Unit	Commodity	£	s.	d.	f.
John Denyshe	Ind	6	C	Fish, Hake	0	60	0	0
		2	barrel	Fish, Herring White	0	10	0	0
		3	C	Skins, Sheep	0	30	0	0
		22	mease	Fish, Herring Red	0	110	0	0

Bata Kateryn of Tenby, Thomas Longe master, Entering, 24th January 1526

Merchant name	Origin	Qty	Unit	Commodity	£	s.	d.	f.
Thomas Longe	Ind	6	last	Fish, Herring White	18	0	0	0

Bata John of Bristol, John Whyte master, Entering, 24th January 1526

Merchant name	Origin	Qty	Unit	Commodity	£	s.	d.	f.
Howell Baker	Ind	9	last	Fish, Herring White	27	0	0	0
William Fleming	Ind	2	barrel	Fish, Herring White	0	10	0	0
John Whyte	Ind	2	barrel	Fish, Herring White	0	10	0	0

Bata Mary of Tenby, John Evans master, Entering, 24th January 1526

Merchant name	Origin	Qty	Unit	Commodity	£	s.	d.	f.
Roland Hynstocke	Ind	1.5	tun	Wine	0	0	0	0

Navicula Crystofer of Errenteria, Gregory de Corde master, Exiting, 25th January 1526

Merchant name	Origin	Qty	Unit	Commodity	£	s.	d.	f.
Stephan de Shaler	Alien	82	dozen	Skins, Calf	13	13	4	0
		5	dicker	Hides, Tanned	0	0	0	0
William Woseley	Ind	9	piece	Cloth of Assize	0	0	0	0
Richard Thorne	Ind	14	dozen	Skins, Calf	0	46	8	0
William Foyley	Ind	10	piece	Cloth of Assize	0	0	0	0

Merchant name	Origin	Qty	Unit	Commodity	£	s.	d.	f.
		16	dozen	Skins, Calf	0	53	4	0

Navicula Kateryn of San Sebastián, John Yonge master, Exiting, 25th January 1526

Merchant name	Origin	Qty	Unit	Commodity	£	s.	d.	f.
William Foyley	Ind	17.5	wey	Grain	17	10	0	0
William Spratt	Ind	10	wey	Grain	10	0	0	0

Bata Trinite of Chepstow, William Hayens master, Entering, 25th January 1526

Merchant name	Origin	Qty	Unit	Commodity	£	s.	d.	f.
William Appowell	Ind	5.5	tun	Wine	0	0	0	0

Bata George of *Bawdenolle*, William Benett master, Entering, 26th January 1526

Merchant name	Origin	Qty	Unit	Commodity	£	s.	d.	f.
Thomas Whyte	Ind	3.5	tun	Wine	0	0	0	0

Bata Fawkyn of Waterford, Nicholas Rowth master, Entering, 26th January 1526

Merchant name	Origin	Qty	Unit	Commodity	£	s.	d.	f.
Nicholas *Rowth*	Ind	1.5	pipe	Fish, Salmon	0	45	0	0
		5	C	Skins, Sheep	0	50	0	0
James Whyte	Ind	9.25	pipe	Fish, Salmon	13	17	4	0
		1	kilderkin	Fish, Eels	0	6	8	0
		6.25	C	Fish, Hake	0	62	6	0
		11	C	Skins, Sheep	0	110	0	0
		0.5	C	Fish, Salted	0	10	0	0
		15	piece	Mantles	0	50	0	0
Richard Arthur	Ind	2	C	Skins, Sheep	0	20	0	0
Maurice Welshe	Ind	2.5	pipe	Fish, Salmon	0	75	0	0
		3	C	Skins, Sheep	0	30	0	0
		0.5	C	Fish, Salted	0	10	0	0
		12	piece	Mantles	0	40	0	0
John Glassam	Ind	1	butt	Fish, Salmon	0	15	0	0
		1.5	C	Skins, Sheep	0	15	0	0
		40	piece	Fish, Salted	0	6	8	0
		14	piece	Mantles	0	46	8	0
		1	barrel	Fish, Herring White	0	5	0	0
James Stryche	Ind	4	pipe	Fish, Salmon	6	0	0	0
		12	C	Skins, Sheep	6	0	0	0
		2	piece	Mantles	0	6	8	0
Peter Donell	Ind	3	C	Skins, Sheep	0	30	0	0
		9	piece	Mantles	0	30	0	0
		15	piece	Fish, Salted	0	2	6	0
Nicholas Caroll	Ind	4	barrel	Fish, Herring White	0	20	0	0
		1	C	Fish, Salted	0	20	0	0
		1	C	Fish, Hake	0	10	0	0
		4	piece	Mantles	0	13	4	0
David Deverus	Ind	3	barrel	Fish, Herring White	0	15	0	0
		0.5	C	Fish, Hake	0	5	0	0
		20	piece	Fish, Salted	0	3	4	0
Richard Ball	Ind	3	C	Skins, Sheep	0	30	0	0

Merchant name	Origin	Qty	Unit	Commodity	£	s.	d.	f.

Bata Mathew of Milford Haven, William Philippis master, Entering, *26th January 1526*

Merchant name	Origin	Qty	Unit	Commodity	£	s.	d.	f.
Robert Granger	Ind	44	barrel	Fish, Herring White	11	0	0	0
William Philippis	Ind	43	barrel	Fish, Herring White	4	15	0	0
James Bath	Ind	55	yard	Check *Cloth*	0	18	4	0
		30	yard	Irish Linen *Cloth*	0	2	6	0
		0.5	C	Linen yarn	0	10	0	0

Bata John of Milford Haven, Simon Watts master, Entering, *26th January 1526*

Merchant name	Origin	Qty	Unit	Commodity	£	s.	d.	f.
Nicholas Pypart	Ind	39	barrel	Fish, Herring White	9	15	0	0
		1	pipe	Fish, Salmon	0	30	0	0
		1	hogshead	Fish, Eels	0	26	7	0
		2	C	Check *Cloth*	4	0	0	0
		14	C	Skins, Sheep	7	0	0	0
		30	stone	Wool, Flocks	0	12	6	0
		1	burden	Fish, Salted	0	4	2	0
		8	piece	Skins, Fox	0	0	16	0
		2	piece	Skins, Otter	0	0	10	0
James Cordy	Ind	1	pipe	Fish, Salmon	0	30	0	0
Walter Pypart	Ind	1.5	last	Fish, Herring White	4	10	0	0
		3	C	Skins, Sheep	0	30	0	0
		26	stone	Wool	0	69	4	0
		11	stone	Wool, Flocks	0	4	7	0
		26	yard	Check *Cloth*	0	8	8	0
		3	C	Fish, Hake	0	30	0	0
Thomas Barby	Ind	6	barrel	Fish, Herring White	0	30	0	0

Bata Fran*ncis* of Dublin, John Kylege master, Entering, *26th January 1526*

Merchant name	Origin	Qty	Unit	Commodity	£	s.	d.	f.
Thomas Barby	Ind	118	barrel	Fish, Herring White	32	10	0	0
		4	mease	Fish, Herring Red	0	20	0	0
Walter Fyan	Ind	28	barrel	Fish, Herring White	7	0	0	0
		3	balette	Woad	0	37	6	0
		0.5	C	Skins, Sheep	0	5	0	0
James Cordy	Ind	2	last	Fish, Herring White	6	0	0	0
		3	C	Skins, Sheep	0	30	0	0
		1	C	Skins, Lamb	0	6	8	0
		3	C	Check *Cloth*	6	0	0	0
		2	piece	Mantles	0	6	8	0
		0.5	C	Skins, Kid	0	2	6	0
Richard Welshe	Ind	35	barrel	Fish, Herring White	8	15	0	0
		2.5	C	Skins, Sheep	0	25	0	0
		1	barrel	Meat	0	6	8	0
Walter Pyparte	Ind	280	yard	Irish Linen *Cloth*	0	26	8	0
		60	yard	Irish Frieze *Cloth*	0	20	0	0
		1	barrel	Tallow, Rendered	0	0	10	0

Bata Kateryn of Waterford, Maurice Power master, Entering, *26th January 1526*

Merchant name	Origin	Qty	Unit	Commodity	£	s.	d.	f.
Maurice Power	Ind	80	piece	Fish, Salted	0	13	4	0
		0.5	C	Fish, Hake	0	5	0	0

Merchant name	Origin	Qty	Unit	Commodity	£	s.	d.	f.
		5	piece	Mantles	0	16	8	0
Peter Baron	Ind	13	C	Skins, Sheep	6	10	0	0
		6	piece	Mantles	0	20	0	0
Robert Bocher	Ind	1.5	C	Fish, Hake	0	15	0	0
		0.5	C	Fish, Salted	0	10	0	0
		1	kilderkin	Fish, Herring White	0	2	6	0
		6	piece	Mantles	0	20	0	0
John Power	Ind	1	C	Fish, Hake	0	10	0	0
		4	piece	Mantles	0	13	4	0
		1	kilderkin	Fish, Herring White	0	2	6	0
		40	piece	Fish, Salted	0	6	8	0
Richard Arthur	Ind	3.5	C	Skins, Sheep	0	35	0	0
		80	piece	Fish, Salted	0	13	4	0
		1	C	Fish, Hake	0	10	0	0

Bata Jhesus of Wexford, John Stafford master, Entering, 26th January 1526

Merchant name	Origin	Qty	Unit	Commodity	£	s.	d.	f.
John Stafford	Ind	3	C	Fish, Hake	0	30	0	0
		9	barrel	Fish, Herring White	0	45	0	0
		3	piece	Mantles	0	10	0	0
		6	mease	Fish, Herring Red	0	30	0	0
		1	C	Skins, Sheep	0	10	0	0
Laurence Syer	Ind	4	C	Fish, Hake	0	40	0	0
		9	barrel	Fish, Herring White	0	45	0	0
		6	piece	Mantles	0	20	0	0
		0.5	C	Skins, Sheep	0	5	0	0
		0.5	C	Skins, Lamb	0	3	4	0
		2.5	pipe	Fish, Salmon	0	75	0	0

Bata Antony of Milford Haven, John Gryndam master, Entering, 26th January 1526

Merchant name	Origin	Qty	Unit	Commodity	£	s.	d.	f.
Edmund Peers	Ind	8	last	Fish, Herring White	24	0	0	0

Bata John of Elmore master, John Nashe master, Entering, 27th January 1526

Merchant name	Origin	Qty	Unit	Commodity	£	s.	d.	f.
John Nashe	Ind	5	ton	Salt	0	50	0	0

Bata Peter of Waterford, Robert Fetzjohn master, Entering, 28th January 1526

Merchant name	Origin	Qty	Unit	Commodity	£	s.	d.	f.
Robert Fetzjohn	Ind	2	C	Fish, Hake	0	20	0	0
		1	C	Fish, Salted	0	20	0	0
Henry Dowryng	Ind	1.5	C	Fish, Hake	0	15	0	0
		1	C	Fish, Salted	0	20	0	0
Robert Clere	Ind	8	C	Fish, Hake	4	0	0	0
Patrick Stoke	Ind	3	C	Fish, Hake	0	30	0	0
		1.5	C	Skins, Sheep	0	15	0	0
		30	piece	Fish, Salted	0	5	0	0
		1.5	pipe	Fish, Salmon	0	45	0	0
Robert Leye	Ind	16	piece	Mantles	0	53	4	0
		1	C	Skins, Sheep	0	10	0	0
Geoffrey Foster	Ind	2	pipe	Fish, Salmon	0	60	0	0
		80	piece	Skins, Salted	0	13	4	0

Merchant name	Origin	Qty	Unit	Commodity	£	s.	d.	f.
		0.5	C	Liquorice	0	0	20	0
		1	C	Skins, Sheep	0	10	0	0
		3	piece	Mantles	0	10	0	0
Patrick Flanyngan	Ind	6	C	Skins, Sheep	0	60	0	0
Thomas Whyte	Ind	3.5	C	Skins, Sheep	0	35	0	0
		14	barrel	Fish, Herring White	0	70	0	0
		4	barrel	Fish, Eels	0	53	4	0
		16	piece	Mantles	0	53	4	0
		80	yard	Check Cloth	0	26	8	0
James Ffox	Ind	25	piece	Mantles	4	3	4	0
		7	C	Skins, Lamb	0	46	8	0
		24	piece	Skins, Sheep	0	2	0	0
		5	piece	Skins, Marten	0	5	0	0
		3	piece	Skins, Calf	0	0	7	2

Bata Patryke of New Ross, William Blake master, Entering, *28th January 1526*

Merchant name	Origin	Qty	Unit	Commodity	£	s.	d.	f.
James Barode	Ind	30	piece	Mantles	0	100	0	0
		5	C	Skins, Lamb	0	33	4	0
		3	C	Skins, Sheep	0	30	0	0
		40	yard	Check Cloth	0	13	4	0
John Savage	Ind	7.5	C	Skins, Sheep	0	75	0	0
		55	piece	Mantles	9	3	4	0
		50	yard	Check Cloth	0	16	8	0
William Blake	Ind	2	C	Skins, Sheep	0	20	0	0
		1.5	C	Fish, Hake	0	15	0	0
		1	burden	Fish, Salted	0	4	0	0
John Coterell	Ind	2	pipe	Fish, Salmon	0	60	0	0
		16	piece	Mantles	0	53	4	0
		3	C	Skins, Sheep	0	30	0	0

Bata George of Waterford, Robert Keyn master, Entering, *28th January 1526*

Merchant name	Origin	Qty	Unit	Commodity	£	s.	d.	f.
Robert *Keyn*	Ind	2	burden	Fish, Salted	0	8	4	0
		12	piece	Mantles	0	40	0	0
Robert Clere	Ind	12	pipe	Fish, Salmon	18	0	0	0
		13	C	Fish, Hake	6	10	0	0
		12	C	Skins, Sheep	6	0	0	0
		4	C	Fish, Salted	4	0	0	0
		2	barrel	Fish, Herring White	0	10	0	0
		12	piece	Mantles	0	40	0	0
		1.5	barrel	Fish, Eels	0	20	0	0
Patrick Stoke	Ind	13	pipe	Fish, Salmon	19	10	0	0
		1.5	C	Skins, Sheep	0	15	0	0
		18	piece	Mantles	0	60	0	0
Thomas Sherlock	Ind	2	pipe	Fish, Salmon	0	60	0	0
		2	piece	Mantles	0	6	8	0
		1	burden	Fish, Salted	0	4	2	0
John Mower	Ind	3	C	Fish, Hake	0	30	0	0
		0.5	burden	Fish, Salted	0	2	1	0
		3	piece	Mantles	0	10	0	0
Thomas Crystofer	Ind	2	C	Fish, Hake	0	20	0	0

Merchant name	Origin	Qty	Unit	Commodity	£	s.	d.	f.
		1	virken	Fish, Salmon	0	7	6	0
		60	piece	Fish, Salted	0	10	0	0
		4	piece	Mantles	0	13	4	0
Nicholas Comyn	Ind	40	piece	Fish, Salted	0	6	8	0
		5	piece	Mantles	0	16	8	0
Richard Artur	Ind	12	C	Skins, Sheep	6	0	0	0
Richard Galle	Ind	2	piece	Mantles	0	6	8	0
		1	C	Fish, Hake	0	10	0	0

Bata Nicholas of Bristol, Thomas Bayle master, Entering, *28th January 1526*

Merchant name	Origin	Qty	Unit	Commodity	£	s.	d.	f.
John Mower	Ind	2	last	Fish, Herring White	6	0	0	0
Thomas Sumpter	Ind	23	barrel	Fish, Herring White	0	115	0	0
John Bannoks	Ind	1	last	Fish, Herring White	0	60	0	0
Thomas Apportsinowth?	Ind	6	barrel	Fish, Herring White	0	30	0	0
John Warner	Ind	2	barrel	Fish, Herring White	0	10	0	0
Walter Feylde	Ind	7	barrel	Fish, Herring White	0	35	0	0
		1	C	Fish, Hake	0	10	0	0
		14	piece	Skins, Otter	0	5	10	0

Bata Sonday of Waterford, Walter Wodlocke master, Entering, *28th January 1526*

Merchant name	Origin	Qty	Unit	Commodity	£	s.	d.	f.
Walter *Wodlocke*	Ind	1	butt	Fish, Salmon	0	15	0	0
		46	piece	Fish, Salted	0	7	8	0
		82	piece	Fish, Salted	0	13	8	0
		16	piece	Mantles	0	53	4	0
		0.5	C	Skins, Sheep	0	5	0	0
Henry Com*er*forde	Ind	2.25	pipe	Fish, Salmon	0	67	6	0
		6	C	Skins, Sheep	0	60	0	0
		6	piece	Mantles	0	20	0	0
		6	piece	Skins, Fox	0	0	12	0
Robert Lewys	Ind	40	piece	Mantles	6	13	4	0
		9	burden	Fish, Salted	0	36	0	0
		23.5	C	Skins, Sheep	11	15	0	0
		8	C	Skins, Lamb	0	53	4	0
		7.5	pipe	Fish, Salmon	11	5	0	0
		7	barrel	Fish, Herring White	0	35	0	0
		1	barrel	Fish, Eels	0	13	4	0
		2	C	Irish Linen *Cloth*	0	20	0	0
Laurence Bruer	Ind	1.5	pipe	Fish, Salmon	0	45	0	0
		36	C	Skins, Sheep	18	0	0	0
		70	piece	Mantles	11	13	4	0
		40	yard	Check *Cloth*	0	13	4	0
		1	burden	Fish, Salted	0	4	2	0
Richard Maldony	Ind	4	barrel	Fish, Herring White	0	20	0	0
		0.25	C	Skins, Sheep	0	2	6	0

Bata Sonday of Wexford, Thomas Skolyke master, Entering, *28th January 1526*

Merchant name	Origin	Qty	Unit	Commodity	£	s.	d.	f.
Thomas *Skolyke?*	Ind	8	barrel	Fish, Herring White	0	40	0	0
		2	C	Fish, Hake	0	20	0	0

Merchant name	Origin	Qty	Unit	Commodity	£	s.	d.	f.
		2	piece	Mantles	0	6	8	0
		2	burden	Fish, Salted	0	8	4	0
Patrick Coan	Ind	10	barrel	Fish, Herring White	0	50	0	0
		1	C	Fish, Hake	0	10	0	0
		1	C	Skins, Sheep	0	10	0	0

Bata Mary of Milford Haven, Thomas Evanns master, Entering, *28th January 1526*

Merchant name	Origin	Qty	Unit	Commodity	£	s.	d.	f.
Richard Higons	Ind	6	tun	Wine	0	0	0	0

Bata John of Milford Haven, John Hobys master, Entering, *28th January 1526*

Merchant name	Origin	Qty	Unit	Commodity	£	s.	d.	f.
John Hobys	Ind	9	barrel	Fish, Herring White	0	45	0	0

Bata Trynyte of Cork, Edmund Barry master, Entering, 29th January 1526

Merchant name	Origin	Qty	Unit	Commodity	£	s.	d.	f.
Edmund Barry &								
Edmund Feylde	Ind	10	pipe	Fish, Salmon	15	0	0	0
		3.5	C	Skins, Sheep	0	35	0	0
Robert Barett	Ind	6	C	Fish, Hake	0	60	0	0
		5.5	C	Skins, Sheep	0	55	0	0
		0.5	pipe	Fish, Salmon	0	15	0	0
		24	piece	Skins, Fox	0	4	0	0
		1	barrel	Fish, Herring White	0	5	0	0
		20	lb	Wax	0	6	8	0
		1	dicker	Skins, Deer	0	2	6	0
		1.5	C	Gac[ ]oll Molie?	0	2	6	0
		2.5	C	Wool, Flocks	0	7	4	0
		2	piece	Fish, Salted	0	6	8	0
		2	piece	Mantles	0	6	8	0
Edmund Barry	Ind	3.25	pipe	Fish, Salmon	4	17	6	0
		3	C	Fish, Hake	0	30	0	0
		1	C	Skins, Sheep	0	10	0	0
		2	C	Wool, Flocks	0	5	10	0
		1	piece	Mantles	0	3	4	0
William Artur	Ind	1.25	pipe	Fish, Salmon	0	37	6	0
		1.5	C	Skins, Sheep	0	15	0	0
		1.5	C	Wool, Flocks	0	5	0	0
William Mangner	Ind	4	C	Fish, Hake	0	40	0	0
		2	C	Skins, Sheep	0	20	0	0
		1	dicker	Skins, Deer	0	2	6	0
		1.5	C	Wool, Flocks	0	5	0	0
		0.5	burden	Fish, Salted	0	2	1	0

Bata Mary of Carmarthen, Thomas Hankocke master, Entering, *29th January 1526*

Merchant name	Origin	Qty	Unit	Commodity	£	s.	d.	f.
John Davys	Ind	2.75	tun	Wine	0	0	0	0
		1	C	Fruit	0	2	0	0

Bata Patrycke of New Ross, Thomas Shenell master, Entering, *29th January 1526*

Merchant name	Origin	Qty	Unit	Commodity	£	s.	d.	f.
Thomas *Shenell*	*Ind*	6	piece	Mantles	0	20	0	0

Merchant name	Origin	Qty	Unit	Commodity	£	s.	d.	f.
David Archerde	Ind	30	piece	Mantles	0	100	0	0
		8	C	Skins, Sheep	4	0	0	0
		1	C	Check *Cloth*	0	40	0	0
Thomas Gybbonds	Ind	7	C	Skins, Sheep	0	70	0	0
		20	piece	Mantles	0	66	8	0
		30	yard	Check *Cloth*	0	10	0	0
		8	stone	Wool, Flocks	0	3	4	0
John Barrett	Ind	30	piece	Mantles	0	100	0	0
		1	C	Check *Cloth*	0	40	0	0
		1	pipe	Fish, Salmon	0	30	0	0
		1.5	C	Skins, Sheep	0	15	0	0
Thomas Baron	Ind	4	pipe	Fish, Salmon	6	0	0	0
		8	C	Skins, Sheep	4	0	0	0
		24	piece	Mantles	4	0	0	0
Robert Mortge	Ind	58	piece	Mantles	9	13	4	0
		1.25	C	Check *Cloth*	0	50	0	0
		1	C	Irish Linen *Cloth*	0	10	0	0
		11	C	Skins, Sheep	0	110	0	0
Philip Savage	Ind	5	pipe	Fish, Salmon	7	10	0	0
		5	C	Skins, Sheep	0	50	0	0
		2	piece	Mantles	0	6	8	0
		8	stone	Wool, Flocks	0	3	4	0
		0.5	C	Fish, Hake	0	5	0	0
		2	stone	Tallow, Rendered	0	0	20	0
Richard Doffe	Ind	4	piece	Mantles	0	13	4	0

Bata Nicholas of Cork, James Welshe master, Entering, *29th January 1526*

James *Welshe*	Ind	2	last	Fish, Herring White	6	0	0	0
		2	stone	Wool, Irish	0	5	4	0
		2	dozen	Oars	0	8	0	0
		2	piece	Mantles	0	6	8	0
James Creaghe	Ind	1.5	pipe	Fish, Salmon	0	45	0	0
		2.5	C	Skins, Sheep	0	25	0	0
David Welshe	Ind	3	last	Fish, Herring White	9	0	0	0
		3.75	pipe	Fish, Salmon	0	112	6	0
		2	piece	Mantles	0	6	8	0
		4	C	Skins, Sheep	0	40	0	0
		1	hogshead	Wine	0	0	0	0
William Smoche	Ind	5	barrel	Fish, Herring White	0	25	0	0
		1	C	Wool, Flocks	0	3	11	0
		1	piece	Mantles	0	3	4	0

Bata Trynyte of Kinsale, John Roche master, Entering, 30th January 1526

John *Roche*	Ind	15	C	Fish, Hake	7	10	0	0
		2	burden	Fish, Salted	0	8	4	0
Jordan Roche	Ind	14	C	Fish, Hake	7	0	0	0
		3	burden	Fish, Salted	0	12	6	0
		1	ton	Iron	0	50	0	0
Philip Bryon	Ind	6	C	Fish, Hake	0	60	0	0
		1	burden	Fish, Salted	0	4	2	0

Merchant name	Origin	Qty	Unit	Commodity	£	s.	d.	f.
Adam Roche	Ind	12	C	Fish, Hake	6	0	0	0
		2	burden	Fish, Salted	0	8	4	0
		3	stone	Wool, Flocks	0	0	15	0

Navicula Vynsent of Bristol, John Amayn master, Exiting, 30th January 1526

William Woseley &								
John Amayn	Ind	41	wey	Grain	41	0	0	0
		9	piece	Cloth of Assize	0	0	0	0
Edmund Pryn	Ind	8	piece	Cloth of Assize	0	0	0	0
William Ffoxley	Ind	11	piece	Cloth of Assize	0	0	0	0
Robert Elyott	Ind	8	piece	Cloth of Assize	0	0	0	0
John Welshe	Ind	6.5	piece	Cloth of Assize	0	0	0	0

Bata Trynyte of Chepstow, William Hayens master, Entering, 31st January 1526

William Appowell	Ind	12	unknown	Pitch, Hearth	0	10	0	0
		1	hogshead	Wine	0	0	0	0

Bata Patrycke of Kinsale, Jerome Foran master, Entering, *31st January 1526*

Jerome Foran	Ind	1	M	Fish, Hake	0	100	0	0
		2	barrel	Fish, Herring White	0	10	0	0
		6	stone	Wool, Flocks	0	2	6	0
		2	burden	Fish, Salted	0	8	4	0
Peter Roche	Ind	1	M	Fish, Hake	0	100	0	0
		1	burden	Fish, Salted	0	4	2	0
		1	virken	Fish, Salmon	0	7	6	0

Bata Conelagh of Kinsale, Nicholas Rothe master, Entering, *31st January 1526*

Nicholas *Rothe*	Ind	18	C	Fish, Hake	9	0	0	0
		2	virken	Fish, Salmon	0	15	0	0
		2	barrel	Fish, Herring White	0	10	0	0
		8	piece	Fish, Salted	0	0	16	0
		2	stone	Wool, Flocks	0	0	10	0
William Hay	Ind	13	C	Fish, Hake	6	10	0	0
		40	piece	Fish, Salted	0	6	8	0
William Monohan	Ind	11	C	Fish, Hake	0	110	0	0
		1	barrel	Fish, Herring White	0	5	0	0
		40	piece	Fish, Salted	0	6	8	0
Maurice Dale	Ind	6	C	Fish, Hake	0	60	0	0
		2	barrel	Fish, Herring White	0	10	0	0
		1	butt	Fish, Salmon	0	15	0	0
		30	piece	Fish, Salted	0	5	0	0
Philip Furbur	Ind	1	pipe	Iron	0	25	0	0

Navicula Mawdelyn of Berkeley, John Croke master, Exiting, *31st January 1526*

Maurice Bocher &								
John Mody	Ind	43	wey	Grain	43	0	0	0
		2	wey	Peas	0	33	4	0

Merchant name	Origin	Qty	Unit	Commodity	£	s.	d.	f.
		43	dozen	Skins, Calf	7	6	8	0
		21	dicker	Hides, Tanned	0	0	0	0
		3.33	piece	Cloth of Assize	0	0	0	0

Bata Mary of Wexford, Robert Rowth master, Exiting, 3rd February 1526

John Denyshe	Ind	4	wey	Grain	4	0	0	0
		2	wey	Malt	0	33	4	0

Bata Anne of Milford Haven, Nicholas Whyte master, Entering, 3rd February 1526

John Elyott	Ind	30	piece	Fish, Hake	0	2	0	0
		0.5	burden	Fish, Salted	0	2	1	0

Bata George of Waterford, Robert Keyn master, Exiting, 5th February 1526

Robert Clere	Ind	6	wey	Grain	6	0	0	0
		6	wey	Rye	0	100	0	0
		6	wey	Malt	0	100	0	0
		5	stone	Orchil	0	8	4	0
		1	C	Aniseed	0	13	4	0
		3	gross	Points	0	3	0	0
		0.5	gross	Cutts	0	0	20	0
		2	piece	Cloth of Assize, Dozen Strait	0	0	0	0

Bata Nicholas of Bristol, Thomas Bayle master, Exiting, *5th February 1526*

Robert Clere	Ind	8	wey	Grain	8	0	0	0
		8	wey	Rye	6	13	4	0
		4	wey	Malt	0	66	8	0
James Striche	Ind	4	piece	Cloth of Assize, Dozen Strait	0	0	0	0
		4	lb	Silk Worked	0	4	4	0
		4	lb	Saffron	0	40	0	0
		14	gross	Points	0	14	0	0
		4	gross	Cutts	0	13	4	0
David Neyll	Ind	2	lb	Saffron	0	20	0	0
John Harrolde	Ind	4	piece	Cloth of Assize	0	0	0	0
		2	dozen	Skins, Red	0	4	2	0
		24	gross	Points	0	24	0	0
		2	gross	Cutts	0	6	8	0
		8	lb	Saffron	4	0	0	0
		8	lb	Silk, *Worked*	5	6	8	0
		9	piece	Caps	0	7	6	0
		6	lb	Wood, Brazil	0	2	0	0
		4	lb	Thread	0	0	20	0
		1	lb	Mercury	0	0	15	0
James Ffox	Ind	2.5	piece	Cloth of Assize	0	0	0	0
		8	lb	Saffron	4	0	0	0
		2	lb	Silk, *Worked*	0	26	8	0
		3	gross	Cutts	0	10	0	0
		2	dozen	Skins, Red	0	4	2	0
		3	gross	Points	0	3	0	0

Merchant name	Origin	Qty	Unit	Commodity	£	s.	d.	f.
		4	lb	Thread	0	0	20	0
		0.5	lb	Mercury	0	0	7	0
		1	lb	Wood, Brazil	0	0	4	0
		1	dozen	Glasses, Looking	0	0	2	0
		6	pair	Playing Cards	0	0	6	0
		1	dozen	Books, Primers	0	0	15	0

Bata Mary Walsynghin of Tenby, William Walter master, Exiting, *5th February 1526*

Merchant name	Origin	Qty	Unit	Commodity	£	s.	d.	f.
Patrick Stoke	Ind	9	wey	Grain	9	0	0	0
		6	wey	Beans	0	100	0	0
		6	wey	Malt	0	100	0	0
		1	lb	Silk, *Worked*	0	13	4	0
		2	lb	Saffron	0	20	0	0
		3	gross	Points	0	3	0	0
		1	gross	Cutts	0	3	4	0
		0.25	C	Hops	0	2	6	0
		0.5	dozen	Caps	0	5	0	0

Bata J*he*sus of Bristol, Gerald Hubberte master, Exiting, *5th February 1526*

Merchant name	Origin	Qty	Unit	Commodity	£	s.	d.	f.
Robert Leey	Ind	6	wey	Malt	0	100	0	0
		11	wey	Beans	9	3	4	0
		3	wey	Grain	0	60	0	0

Bata Fawkyn of Waterford, Nicholas Rowthe master, Exiting, *5th February 1526*

Merchant name	Origin	Qty	Unit	Commodity	£	s.	d.	f.
Maurice Welshe	Ind	4	wey	Grain	4	0	0	0
		8	wey	Rye	6	13	4	0
		4	wey	Malt	0	66	8	0
James Whyte	Ind	1	pipe	Wine	0	0	0	0
		0.5	piece	Cloth of Assize	0	0	0	0

Bata Kateryn of Milford Haven, Philip Webb master, Exiting, *5th February 1526*

Merchant name	Origin	Qty	Unit	Commodity	£	s.	d.	f.
James Whyte	Ind	7	wey	Grain	7	0	0	0
		7	wey	Rye	0	116	8	0
		4	wey	Malt	0	66	8	0
		1	lb	Silk, *Worked*	0	13	4	0
		1.5	lb	Saffron	0	15	0	0
		1	gross	Cutts	0	3	4	0
		0.5	dozen	Caps	0	5	0	0
		6	gross	Points	0	6	0	0
		0.5	piece	Cloth of Assize	0	0	0	0

Bata Antony of Milford Haven, John Gryndam master, Exiting, *5th February 1526*

Merchant name	Origin	Qty	Unit	Commodity	£	s.	d.	f.
John Denyshe	Ind	10	wey	Beans	8	6	8	0
		5	wey	Malt	4	3	4	0
		1	wey	Grain	0	20	0	0

Merchant name	Origin	Qty	Unit	Commodity	£	s.	d.	f.
Bata Kateryn of Tenby, Thomas Reynolde master, Entering, *5th February 1526*								
Hugh Davys	Ind	35.5	barrel	Fish, Herring White	8	17	6	0
Bata Kateryn of Milford Haven, Philip Webbe master, Entering, *5th February 1526*								
Philip *Webbe*	*Ind*	68	barrel	Fish, Herring White	17	0	0	0
Bata Margaret of Milford Haven, Henry Willys master, Entering, *5th February 1526*								
Henry *Willys*	Ind	99	barrel	Fish, Herring White	24	15	0	0
Bata Peter of Waterford, Robert Ffetzjohn master, Exiting, *5th February 1526*								
Robert *Ffetzjohn*	Ind	6	wey	Grain	6	0	0	0
		2	wey	Malt	0	33	4	0
Geoffrey Forstall	Ind	1	piece	Cloth of Assize, Dozen Strait	0	0	0	0
		1	gross	Cutts	0	3	4	0
Bata Patricke of New Ross, William Blake master, Exiting, *5th February 1526*								
William *Blake*	Ind	3	wey	Grain	0	60	0	0
		3	wey	Malt	0	50	0	0
		0.25	C	Hops	0	2	6	0
James Garode	Ind	4	lb	Saffron	0	40	0	0
		3	lb	Silk, *Worked*	0	40	0	0
		1	C	Aniseed	0	13	4	0
		1	gross	Cutts	0	3	4	0
		0.5	dozen	Caps	0	5	0	0
		6	gross	Points	0	6	0	0
		0.25	C	Alum	0	3	4	0
		0.25	C	Hops	0	2	6	0
Bata Sonday of Wexford, Thomas Skolycke master, Exiting, *5th February 1526*								
Thomas *Skolyke*	Ind	2.5	wey	Grain	0	50	0	0
		1.5	wey	Rye	0	25	0	0
		1.5	wey	Malt	0	25	0	0
Navicula Denysh of Penmarch, John Brerow master, Exiting, 6th February 1526								
John *Brerow*	Alien	15	pipe	Lime	0	18	9	0
Bata Jamys of Gatcombe, Richard Hyatt master, Entering, *6th February 1526*								
John Thoma	Ind	5	tun	Wine	0	0	0	0
Navicula Mary of Crozon, Peter Harvy master, Exiting, *6th February 1526*								
Mathew Chapalyn	Alien	5	piece	Mantles	0	16	8	0
Henry Garlonde	Ind	6	barrel	Fish, Herring White	0	30	0	0

Merchant name	Origin	Qty	Unit	Commodity	£	s.	d.	f.

Bata Trynyte of of Kinsale, John Roche master, Exiting, *7th February 1526*

Merchant name	Origin	Qty	Unit	Commodity	£	s.	d.	f.
John *Roche*	Ind	4	wey	Malt	0	66	8	0
		2	wey	Grain	0	40	0	0
		1	lb	Saffron	0	10	0	0
		1	C	Hops	0	10	0	0
		6	stone	Orchil	0	10	0	0
Jordan Roche	Ind	0.5	piece	Cloth of Assize	0	0	0	0
		1	lb	Saffron	0	10	0	0
		1	gross	Cutts	0	3	4	0
		0.25	C	Hops	0	2	6	0
		6	stone	Orchil	0	10	0	0

Bata George of Milford Haven, Thomas Wade master, Entering, *7th February 1526*

Merchant name	Origin	Qty	Unit	Commodity	£	s.	d.	f.
Thomas Wade	Ind	4	last	Fish, Herring White	12	0	0	0

Navicula Mary John of *Bristol*, Thomas Harte master, Exiting, *7th February 1526*

Merchant name	Origin	Qty	Unit	Commodity	£	s.	d.	f.
George Hall	Ind	5	ton	Lead worked	25	0	0	0
		15	piece	Cloth of Assize	0	0	0	0
William Appowell	Ind	3	dicker	Hides, Tanned	0	0	0	0
Thomas Harte	Ind	8	piece	Cloth of Assize	0	0	0	0
		1	pipe	Lead worked	0	50	0	0
William Yate	Ind	7	piece	Cloth of Assize	0	0	0	0
		1	piece	Welsh *Cloth*	0	20	0	0

Bata Patryke of Kinsale, Jerome Foran master, Exiting, *7th February 1526*

Merchant name	Origin	Qty	Unit	Commodity	£	s.	d.	f.
Jerome Foran	Ind	2	wey	Grain	0	40	0	0
		2	wey	Malt	0	33	4	0
		0.5	C	Hops	0	5	0	0

Bata Konelowgth of Kinsale, Nicholas Rothe master, Exiting, *7th February 1526*

Merchant name	Origin	Qty	Unit	Commodity	£	s.	d.	f.
Nicholas *Rothe*	Ind	4	wey	Grain	4	0	0	0
		4	wey	Malt	0	66	8	0
		1	lb	Silk, *Worked*	0	13	4	0
		1	lb	Saffron	0	10	0	0
William Haye	Ind	1	lb	Silk, *Worked*	0	13	4	0
		1	lb	Saffron	0	10	0	0
		3	stone	Orchil	0	5	0	0
Maurice Dale	Ind	4	stone	Orchil	0	6	8	0

Bata Clement of Wexford, Nicholas Brown master, Entering, 8th February 1526

Merchant name	Origin	Qty	Unit	Commodity	£	s.	d.	f.
Patrick Furlong	Ind	12	C	Fish, Hake	6	0	0	0
		1	last	Fish, Herring White	0	60	0	0
		8	mease	Fish, Herring Red	0	40	0	0
		1	pipe	Fish, Salmon	0	30	0	0
		3	C	Skins, Sheep	0	30	0	0
		2	C	Skins, Kid	0	10	0	0

Merchant name	Origin	Qty	Unit	Commodity	£	s.	d.	f.
Bata Sonday of Wexford, Thomas Harper master, Entering, *8th February 1526*								
Thomas *Harper*	Ind	12	mease	Fish, Herring Red	0	60	0	0
		2	C	Fish, Hake	0	20	0	0
		2	piece	Mantles	0	6	8	0
William Vele	Ind	2	pipe	Fish, Salmon	0	60	0	0
		5	barrel	Fish, Herring White	0	25	0	0
		10	mease	Fish, Herring Red	0	50	0	0
		1	C	Fish, Hake	0	10	0	0
Bata Mary of Youghal, Robert Payn master, Entering, *8th February 1526*								
Richard Stewytt	Ind	3	M	Fish, Hake	15	0	0	0
		1	pipe	Fish, Salmon	0	30	0	0
		1	barrel	Fish, Herring White	0	5	0	0
		10	burden	Fish, Salted	0	40	0	0
		1	C	Skins, Sheep	0	10	0	0
Bata Patrycke of New Ross, Thomas Shenell master, Exiting, *8th February 1526*								
Philip Savage	Ind	6	wey	Grain	6	0	0	0
		6	wey	Malt	0	100	0	0
		1	wey	Beans	0	16	8	0
		0.75	tun	Wine, Corrupt	0	22	6	0
Thomas Baron	Ind	4	lb	Silk, *Worked*	0	53	4	0
		1	dozen	Aniseed	0	0	18	0
		2	lb	Saffron	0	20	0	0
		1	dozen	Caps	0	10	0	0
		1	gross	Cutts	0	3	4	0
		1	dozen	Knives, Brazil	0	0	20	0
		12	gross	Points	0	12	0	0
		1	piece	Cloth of Assize, Dozen Strait	0	0	0	0
Robert Murro	Ind	1	piece	Cloth of Assize, Dozen Strait	0	0	0	0
		3	lb	Silk, *Worked*	0	40	0	0
		2	lb	Saffron	0	20	0	0
		1	dozen	Caps	0	10	0	0
		1	gross	Cutts	0	3	4	0
		6	gross	Points	0	6	0	0
		2	dozen	Aniseed	0	3	0	0
		6	lb	Wood, Brazil	0	2	0	0
David Archer	Ind	2.25	piece	Cloth of Assize	0	0	0	0
		4	lb	Silk, *Worked*	0	53	4	0
		3	lb	Saffron	0	30	0	0
		2	gross	Cutts	0	6	8	0
		1.5	gross	Lacquer	0	2	6	0
		6	dozen	Aniseed	0	9	0	0
		10	gross	Points	0	10	0	0
		1	dozen	Caps	0	10	0	0
		3	dozen	Knives	0	3	9	0
		1	dozen	Books, Primers	0	0	15	0
John Savage	Ind	0.5	piece	Cloth of Assize, Kersey	0	0	0	0
		0.5	gross	Cutts	0	0	20	0

Merchant name	Origin	Qty	Unit	Commodity	£	s.	d.	f.
		1	dozen	Caps	0	10	0	0
		6	stone	Orchil	0	10	0	0
		1	lb	Pepper	0	0	12	0
		2	dozen	Alum	0	3	0	0
		6	dozen	Aniseed	0	9	0	0
		30	lb	*Pilus Tinctus*	0	10	0	0
		1	barrel	Honey	0	16	8	0
		4	stone	Hops	0	5	0	0
		2	lb	Silk, *Worked*	0	26	8	0
		2	lb	Saffron	0	20	0	0
		10	gross	Points	0	10	0	0
Thomas Gybbys	Ind	2	lb	Silk, *Worked*	0	26	8	0
		2	lb	Saffron	0	20	0	0
		2	dozen	Aniseed	0	3	0	0
		1	dozen	Skins, Red	0	2	1	0
		1	gross	Cutts	0	3	4	0
		2	gross	Points	0	2	0	0
		1	piece	Cloth of Assize, Dozen Strait	0	0	0	0

Bata Kateryn of Youghal, Dennis Gryfyth master, Entering, *8th February 1526*

Merchant name	Origin	Qty	Unit	Commodity	£	s.	d.	f.
William Hore	Ind	25	C	Fish, Hake	12	10	0	0
		10	burden	Fish, Salted	0	40	0	0
		4.5	C	Skins, Sheep	0	45	0	0
Dennis Gryfyth	Ind	15	C	Fish, Hake	7	10	0	0
		6	burden	Fish, Salted	0	24	0	0
		1	C	Skins, Sheep	0	10	0	0
Thomas Smyth	Ind	2	pipe	Fish, Salmon	0	60	0	0
		2	C	Fish, Hake	0	20	0	0
		3	C	Skins, Sheep	0	30	0	0

Bata Sonday of Wexford, Nicholas Rothe master, Entering, *8th February 1526*

Merchant name	Origin	Qty	Unit	Commodity	£	s.	d.	f.
Robert Canton	Ind	20	barrel	Fish, Herring White	0	100	0	0
		9	mease	Fish, Herring Red	0	45	0	0
		1	burden	Fish, Salted	0	4	2	0
		6	C	Fish, Hake	0	60	0	0
		2	C	Skins, Sheep	0	20	0	0
		3	C	Skins, Lamb	0	20	0	0

Bata Mary of Milford Haven, Hugh Alyn master, Entering, 9th February 1526

Merchant name	Origin	Qty	Unit	Commodity	£	s.	d.	f.
Nicholas Hamlyn	Ind	53	barrel	Fish, Herring White	13	5	0	0
		109	piece	Fish, Hake	0	9	1	0
		3	mease	Fish, Herring Red	0	15	0	0

Bata Kateryn of Waterford, Maurice Power master, Exiting, *9th February 1526*

Merchant name	Origin	Qty	Unit	Commodity	£	s.	d.	f.
Maurice Power	Ind	4	wey	Grain	4	0	0	0
		2	wey	Malt	0	33	4	0
Peter Baron	Ind	2	wey	Rye	0	33	4	0

Merchant name	Origin	Qty	Unit	Commodity	£	s.	d.	f.
Bata Mary of Milford Haven, John Bolocke master, Entering, *9th February 1526*								
Thomas Howell	Ind	8	last	Fish, Herring White	24	0	0	0
		2	C	Fish, Hake	0	20	0	0
Bata Antony of Bristol, Thomas Howell master, Exiting, 10th February 1526								
Thomas *Howell*	Ind	8	wey	Grain	8	0	0	0
		7	wey	Malt	0	116	8	0
Bata Jhesus of Wexford, John Staford master, Exiting, *10th February 1526*								
John *Staford*	Ind	2	wey	Grain	0	40	0	0
		1	wey	Malt	0	16	8	0
		1	wey	Rye	0	16	8	0
Laurence Seyre	Ind	1	wey	Grain	0	20	0	0
		1	wey	Rye	0	16	8	0
		1	wey	Beans	0	16	8	0
Bata Myghell of Milford Haven, Philip Stevyn master, Entering, 12th February 1526								
Philip *Stevyn*	Ind	80	barrel	Fish, Herring White	20	0	0	0
Bata Mary of Milford Haven, John Kerawgh master, Entering, *12th February 1526*								
John *Kerawgh*	Ind	6	barrel	Fish, Herring White	0	30	0	0
		4	C	Fish, Hake	0	40	0	0
		5	burden	Fish, Salted	0	20	0	0
Thomas Adams	Ind	2.5	barrel	Fish, Herring White	0	12	6	0
Prior de Lanngetony	Ind	2	pipe	Fish, Salmon	0	60	0	0
Bata Mary of Milford Haven, Robert Patricke master, Entering, *12th February 1526*								
Henry Doff	Ind	12	last	Fish, Herring White	36	0	0	0
		4	C	Skins, Sheep	0	40	0	0
		2.5	dicker	Skins, Salted	0	33	4	0
David Smyth	Ind	5	wey	Tallow, Rough	0	25	0	0
		0.5	last	Fish, Herring White	0	30	0	0
Navicula Anne of Bristol, George Harte master, Exiting, 13th February 1526								
Robert Elyott	Ind	16	C	Alum	10	13	4	0
Thomas Harte	Ind	1	pipe	Lead worked	0	50	0	0
John Robe	Alien	3.25	piece	Cloth of Assize	0	0	0	0
		1	piece	Welsh *Cloth*	0	20	0	0
Navicula Mawdelyn of Bristol, Antony Pykett master, Exiting, 13th February 1526								
Nicholas Gay	Ind	8.5	dicker	Hides, Tanned	0	0	0	0
		26	dozen	Skins, Calf	4	6	8	0
		17.5	wey	Grain	17	10	0	0
		20	piece	Cloth of Assize	0	0	0	0

Merchant name	Origin	Qty	Unit	Commodity	£	s.	d.	f.
John Welshe	Ind	6	piece	Cloth of Assize	o	o	o	o
		17.5	wey	Grain	17	10	o	o
		105.5	pipe	Fish, Herring White	158	5	o	o
		7	dozen	Skins, Calf	o	23	4	o
		3.5	dicker	Hides, Tanned	o	o	o	o
Richard Palmer	Ind	5	dozen	Skins, Calf	o	16	8	o
John Cappys	Ind	5	piece	Cloth of Assize	o	o	o	o
		14	piece	Welsh Cloth, Dozen Strait	o	58	4	o
William Appowell	Ind	5	piece	Cloth of Assize, Dozen Northern	o	o	o	o
		3	dicker	Hides, Tanned	o	o	o	o

Bata Mary of Milford Haven, David Smyth master, Entering, 14th February 1526

Merchant name	Origin	Qty	Unit	Commodity	£	s.	d.	f.
David Smyth	Ind	41.5	barrel	Fish, Herring White	10	7	6	o
		3.5	C	Fish, Hake	o	35	o	o
		2	burden	Fish, Salted	o	8	4	o

Bata Nicholas of Cork, James Welshe master, Exiting, 15th February 1526

Merchant name	Origin	Qty	Unit	Commodity	£	s.	d.	f.
David Welshe	Ind	2	piece	Cloth of Assize	o	o	o	o
		1	dozen	Skins, Red	o	2	1	o
		2	lb	Saffron	o	20	o	o
		2	gross	Cutts	o	6	8	o
		7	gross	Points	o	7	o	o
		1	dozen	Aniseed	o	o	18	o
		2	C	Hops	o	20	o	o
		3	stone	Orchil	o	5	o	o

Navicula Bonaventewre of Quimperle, William Pedron master, Exiting, *15th February 1526*

Merchant name	Origin	Qty	Unit	Commodity	£	s.	d.	f.
William Myrrell	Ind	18	wey	Coal	o	60	o	o
		1	piece	Cloth of Assize	o	o	o	o
Alan Ryante	Alien	10	wey	Coal	o	33	4	o
		4.5	piece	Cloth of Assize	o	o	o	o
		0.75	piece	Cloth of Assize, Northern	o	20	o	o

Bata Trynyte of Cork, Edmund Barry master, Exiting, *15th February 1526*

Merchant name	Origin	Qty	Unit	Commodity	£	s.	d.	f.
Edmund Serchefylde	Ind	10	lb	Saffron	o	100	o	o
		8	lb	Silk, Worked	o	106	8	o
		1	gross	Cutts	o	3	4	o
		1	dozen	Caps	o	10	o	o
		4	gross	Points	o	4	o	o
		1	piece	Cloth of Assize	o	o	o	o
Robert Barett	Ind	4	gross	Cutts	o	13	4	o
		2	dozen	Caps	o	20	o	o
		4	gross	Points	o	4	o	o
John Strange	Ind	4	lb	Saffron	o	40	o	o
		3	lb	Silk Worked	o	40	o	o
		2	gross	Cutts	o	6	8	o
		4	stone	Orchil	o	6	8	o
		0.5	dozen	Caps	o	5	o	o

Merchant name	Origin	Qty	Unit	Commodity	£	s.	d.	f.
		4	gross	Points	o	4	o	o
Dominic Martyn	Ind	6	lb	Saffron	o	60	o	o
		1	lb	Silk, *Worked*	o	13	4	o
		1	gross	Cutts	o	3	4	o
		1	dozen	Skins, Red	o	2	1	o
		4	gross	Points	o	4	o	o
		1	dozen	Aniseed	o	o	18	o
		3	piece	Cloth of Assize, Dozen Strait	o	o	o	o
Thomas Fagan	Ind	28	lb	Saffron	14	o	o	o
		3	lb	Silk, *Worked*	o	40	o	o
		3	quarter	Aniseed	o	10	o	o
Thomas Sylke	Ind	2	stone	Orchil	o	3	4	o

Bata Mighell of Minehead, Robert Magkeynglyag master, Exiting, *15th February 1526*

Merchant name	Origin	Qty	Unit	Commodity	£	s.	d.	f.
William Lombard	Ind	5.25	piece	Cloth of Assize	o	o	o	o
		10	lb	Saffron	o	100	o	o
		6	lb	Silk, *Worked*	4	o	o	o
		4	gross	Points	o	4	o	o
		0.5	C	Aniseed	o	6	8	o
		3	gross	Cutts	o	10	o	o
		1.5	dozen	Caps	o	15	o	o
		14	lb	*Pilus Tinctus*	o	4	8	o
Robert Mackeynglyng	Ind	10	wey	Grain	10	o	o	o
William Artur	Ind	5	lb	Saffron	o	50	o	o
		5	lb	Silk, *Worked*	o	66	8	o
		4	gross	Cutts	o	13	4	o
		6	gross	Points	o	6	o	o
		2	dozen	Aniseed	o	3	o	o
		1	gross	Lacquer	o	o	20	o
		2	dozen	Caps	o	20	o	o
		1	piece	Cloth of Assize	o	o	o	o

Bata Kateryn of Minehead, Robert Karett master, Exiting, *15th February 1526*

Merchant name	Origin	Qty	Unit	Commodity	£	s.	d.	f.
Robert *Karett*	Ind	10	wey	Grain	10	o	o	o

Bata Antony of Waterford, Walter Power master, Exiting, *15th February 1526*

Merchant name	Origin	Qty	Unit	Commodity	£	s.	d.	f.
Henry Gall	Ind	8	wey	Grain	8	o	o	o
		4	wey	Rye	o	66	8	o
		6	wey	Malt	o	100	o	o
		1	gross	Cutts	o	3	4	o
		1	piece	Cloth of Assize, Dozen Strait	o	o	o	o

Bata Francis of Dublin, John Kyl[ ]cge master, Exiting, *15th February 1526*

Merchant name	Origin	Qty	Unit	Commodity	£	s.	d.	f.
Walter Fyan	Ind	1	dozen	Caps	o	10	o	o
		3	gross	Points	o	3	o	o
		1	lb	Saffron	o	10	o	o
		3	dozen	Knives	o	5	o	o

Merchant name	Origin	Qty	Unit	Commodity	£	s.	d.	f.
		1	C	Hops	0	10	0	0
		24	lb	*Pilus Tinctus*	0	8	0	0
		2.33	C	Hops	0	23	4	0
		4	dozen	Skins, Red	0	8	4	0
		4	piece	Pots, Brass (60lb)	0	40	0	0
James Smith	Ind	2	wey	Grain	0	40	0	0
		2	wey	Peas	0	33	4	0
		0.5	wey	Malt	0	8	4	0
		1	barrel	Meal	0	16	8	0
		2	gross	Points	0	2	0	0
		3	C	Hops	0	30	0	0
Nicholas Pyperte	Ind	2	piece	Cloth of Assize, Dozen Strait	0	0	0	0
Nicholas Whyte	Ind	6	gross	Points	0	6	0	0
Richard Welshe	Ind	6	piece	Caps	0	5	0	0
		8	gross	Points	0	8	0	0

Bata Kateryn of Youghal, Dennis Gryfyth master, Exiting, 17th February 1526

Merchant name	Origin	Qty	Unit	Commodity	£	s.	d.	f.
Dennis Gryfyth	Ind	6	wey	Grain	6	0	0	0
		4	wey	Malt	0	66	8	0
		3	lb	Saffron	0	30	0	0
		0.5	C	Hops	0	5	0	0
		2	stone	Orchil	0	3	4	0
William Hore	Ind	2	lb	Saffron	0	20	0	0
		2	lb	Silk, *Worked*	0	26	3	0
		2	gross	Points	0	2	0	0
		0.5	gross	Cutts	0	0	20	0
		1	C	Hops	0	10	0	0
		5	stone	Orchil	0	8	4	0
		2	dozen	Aniseed	0	3	4	0

Bata Mary of Youghal, Robert Payne master, Exiting, 19th February 1526

Merchant name	Origin	Qty	Unit	Commodity	£	s.	d.	f.
Richard Blewett	Ind	3.5	wey	Grain	0	70	0	0
		4	wey	Malt	0	66	8	0
		0.5	wey	Rye	0	8	4	0
		1.5	C	Hops	0	15	0	0
		2	lb	Saffron	0	20	0	0
		1	lb	Silk, *Worked*	0	13	4	0
		12	stone	Orchil	0	20	0	0
		1	dozen	Skins, Red	0	2	1	0
		1	dozen	Skins, Golden	0	4	2	0
		1	quarter	Alum	0	3	4	0
		1	quarter	Aniseed	0	3	4	0
		3	piece	Cloth of Assize, Dozen Strait	0	0	0	0

Bata Sonday of Waterford, Walter Wodeloke master, Exiting, *19th February 1526*

Merchant name	Origin	Qty	Unit	Commodity	£	s.	d.	f.
Henry Bryan	Ind	11	wey	Grain	11	0	0	0
		1	wey	Malt	0	16	8	0
Laurence Brewer	Ind	4	gross	Points	0	4	0	0
		1.5	gross	Cutts	0	5	0	0

Merchant name	Origin	Qty	Unit	Commodity	£	s.	d.	f.
		2	piece	Cloth of Assize	0	0	0	0
Robert Ley	Ind	3	lb	Silk, *Worked*	0	40	0	0
		3	lb	Saffron	0	30	0	0
		2	gross	Cutts	0	6	8	0
		8	gross	Points	0	8	0	0
		0.5	C	Aniseed	0	6	8	0
		1	dozen	Caps	0	10	0	0
		1	piece	Cloth of Assize	0	0	0	0
Walter Wodeloke	Ind	2	gross	Cutts	0	6	8	0

Bata Keryke of Milford Haven, Thomas Symond master, Entering, *19th February 1526*

John Riys	Ind	25	barrel	Fish, Herring White	6	5	0	0
		4	C	Fish, Hake	0	40	0	0

Bata Kateryn of Milford Haven, William Wade master, Entering, *19th February 1526*

William *Wade*	Ind	7	last	Fish, Herring White	21	0	0	0
		4	C	Fish, Hake	0	40	0	0
		72	piece	Fish, Salted	0	12	0	0

Bata Mary of Milford Haven, David Smyth master, Exiting, *19th February 1526*

Nicholas Harrys	Ind	10	wey	Grain	10	0	0	0
		8	wey	Malt	6	13	4	0

Bata Jamys of Milford Haven, John Gryndam master, Entering, *19th February 1526*

John Gryndam	Ind	5.5	C	Fish, Hake	0	55	0	0
		1.5	burden	Fish, Salted	0	6	3	0
		5	barrel	Fish, Herring White	0	25	0	0

Bata Trynyte of Carmarthen, Robert Dyer master, Entering, 20th February 1526

Thomas Walter	Ind	2.5	last	Fish, Herring White	7	10	0	0

Bata Sonday of Wexford, Nicholas Rowth master, Exiting, *20th February 1526*

Robert Taunton	Ind	4	wey	Grain	4	0	0	0
		3	wey	Malt	0	50	0	0
		2	dozen	Wool-Cards	0	8	4	0

Bata Antony of Chepstow, John Willis master, Entering, 21st February 1526

John Haws?	Ind	1.5	tun	Wine	0	0	0	0

Bata Sonday of Wexford, Thomas Harper master, Exiting, 21th February 1526

Thomas Harper	Ind	2	wey	Grain	0	40	0	0
		2	wey	Malt	0	33	4	0
William Vele	Ind	2	wey	Grain	0	40	0	0
		2	wey	Malt	0	33	4	0

Merchant name	Origin	Qty	Unit	Commodity	£	s.	d.	f.

Bata Trynyte of Chepstow, William Hayens master, Entering, 22nd February 1526

Richard Stoke	Ind	1	pipe	Wine	0	0	0	0

Bata Nicholas of Carmarthen, Owyn Thomas, Entering, 22nd February 1526

Owyn Thomas	Ind	1	pipe	Wine	0	0	0	0

Bata Trynyte of Chepstow, William Hayens master, Entering, 23rd February 1526

Thomas Dyer	Ind	3	tun	Wine	0	0	0	0

Bata George of Youghal, Nicholas Vele master, Entering, 26ᵈ February 1526

Merchant name	Origin	Qty	Unit	Commodity	£	s.	d.	f.
Nicholas *Vele*	Ind	5	burden	Fish, Salted	0	20	0	0
		1	pipe	Fish, Salmon	0	30	0	0
		1	C	Skins, Sheep	0	10	0	0
Patrick Rowley	Ind	8	C	Fish, Hake	4	0	0	0
		8	burden	Fish, Salted	0	32	0	0
		1.5	pipe	Fish, Salmon	0	45	0	0
		2	piece	Mantles	0	6	8	0
Philip Catchepole	Ind	2	pipe	Fish, Salmon	0	60	0	0
		6.5	C	Fish, Hake	0	65	0	0
		3	burden	Fish, Salted	0	12	0	0
		10	C	Skins, Sheep	0	100	0	0
		1	C	Skins, Lamb	0	6	8	0
		3	piece	Mantles	0	10	0	0
John Cusshyn	Ind	15	burden	Fish, Salted	0	60	0	0
		6.25	C	Fish, Hake	0	62	6	0
		1	virken	Fish, Salmon	0	7	8	0
		2	piece	Mantles	0	6	8	0
William Morths	Ind	8	C	Fish, Hake	4	0	0	0
		2	burden	Fish, Salted	0	8	0	0

Bata Clement of Wexford, Nicholas Browne master, Exiting, *26th February 1526*

Patrick Furlong	Ind	4	wey	Grain	4	0	0	0
		2	wey	Malt	0	33	4	0
		1	lb	Silk, *Worked*	0	13	4	0
		1	lb	Saffron	0	10	0	0
		0.5	gross	Cutts	0	0	20	0

Bata Nicholas of Wexford, Nicholas Turner master, Entering, *26th February 1526*

Nicholas *Turner*	Ind	20	mease	Fish, Herring Red	0	100	0	0
		1	last	Fish, Herring white	0	60	0	0
		5	C	Fish, Hake	0	50	0	0
		1	barrel	Fish, Eels	0	13	4	0
		18	piece	Mantles	0	60	0	0
		6	C	Skins, Sheep	0	60	0	0
		2	pipe	Fish, Salmon	0	60	0	0

Merchant name	Origin	Qty	Unit	Commodity	£	s.	d.	f.

Bata Mary of Milford Haven, John Ries master, Exiting, 26th February 1526

| Philip Elyott | Ind | 5 | wey | Grain | 5 | 0 | 0 | 0 |
| | | 5 | wey | Malt | 4 | 3 | 4 | 0 |

Bata George of Malvern, [ ] Benett master, Entering, 27th February 1526

| Robert Powell | Ind | 9 | tun | Wine | 0 | 0 | 0 | 0 |

Bata Edward of Malvern, Thomas Hylle master, Entering, 27th February 1526

| Robert Powell | Ind | 5.5 | tun | Wine | 0 | 0 | 0 | 0 |

Bata Chrystofer of Cardiff, William Deyn master, Entering, 27th February 1526

| Thomas Wrynche | Ind | 6 | tun | Wine | 0 | 0 | 0 | 0 |

Bata George of Youghal, Nicholas Vele master, Exiting, 27th February 1526

Nicholas *Vele*	Ind	6	wey	Grain	6	0	0	0
		6	wey	Malt	0	100	0	0
		1.5	C	Hops	0	15	0	0
Richard Whyte	Ind	4	lb	Saffron	0	40	0	0
		4	lb	Silk, *Worked*	0	53	4	0
		3	gross	Points	0	3	0	0
		0.5	dozen	Caps	0	5	0	0
		0.25	C	Aniseed	0	0	20	0
		0.25	C	Alum	0	0	20	0
		1	piece	Cloth of Assize, Dozen Kersey	0	0	0	0

Navicula Mary Grace of *Bristol*, Richard Miller master, Exiting, 28th February 1526

| John Savage | Ind | 11.5 | dozen | Skins, Calf | 0 | 39 | 2 | 0 |

Bata Crantocke of Tenby, Evan Gough master, Exiting, 1st March 1526

| Walter Pypert | Ind | 12 | gross | Points | 0 | 12 | 0 | 0 |

Bata Kateryn of Milford Haven, William Wade master, Exiting, *1st March 1526*

| Thomas Whale | Ind | 12 | wey | Beans | 10 | 0 | 0 | 0 |

Bata Mary Baker, *Port Unknown*,[5] Robert Baker master, Exiting, 2nd March 1526

| William Murro | Ind | 4 | wey | Grain | 4 | 0 | 0 | 0 |
| | | 3 | wey | Malt | 0 | 50 | 0 | 0 |

Bata Crystofer of Longney, John Carter master, Entering, 3rd March 1526

| Thomas Brynche | Ind | 7.5 | tun | Wine | 0 | 0 | 0 | 0 |

5 Probably Bristol.

Merchant name	Origin	Qty	Unit	Commodity	£	s.	d.	f.
Bata Antony of Chepstow, Lewis Hayens master, Entering, 7th March 1526								
William Appowell	Ind	1	pipe	Wine	0	0	0	0
Bata Mary Garet of Elmore, William Ffox master, Exiting, 7th March 1526								
William *Ffox*	Ind	10	wey	Grain	10	0	0	0
		1	wey	Malt	0	16	8	0
		2.5	wey	Beans	0	41	8	0
Navicula Savyour of Bristol, William Deyn master, Entering, 7th March 1526								
John Shipman	Ind	11.5	tun	Wine	0	0	0	0
Roger Dawys	Ind	11.5	tun	Wine	0	0	0	0
		2	tun	Oil, *Olive*	8	0	0	0
John Ware	Ind	2.75	tun	Wine	0	0	0	0
William Shipman	Ind	9	tun	Wine	0	0	0	0
Thomas Pasey	Ind	4	tun	Wine	0	0	0	0
		2	tun	Oil, *Olive*	8	0	0	0
Robert Chapman	Ind	5	tun	Wine	0	0	0	0
Robert Avyntre	Ind	1	pipe	Oil, *Olive*	0	40	0	0
		6	C	Aniseed	4	0	0	0
William Ostryge	Ind	28	tun	Wine	0	0	0	0
		9.5	tun	Oil, *Olive*	38	0	0	0
		8	bale	Almonds	16	0	0	0
Nicholas Thorn	Ind	8	tun	Wine	0	0	0	0
		11.5	tun	Oil, *Olive*	46	0	0	0
John Thorn	Ind	6.75	tun	Wine	0	0	0	0
		1	pipe	Oil, *Olive*	0	40	0	0
		16.25	C	Soap	8	2	6	0
John Wynter	Ind	1.25	tun	Wine	0	0	0	0
William Rowley	Ind	5.5	tun	Wine	0	0	0	0
Richard Pryn	Ind	3	tun	Wine	0	0	0	0
		3	tun	Oil, *Olive*	12	0	0	0
Edward Pryn	Ind	6	tun	Wine	0	0	0	0
David Vaughan	Ind	6.25	tun	Wine	0	0	0	0
Thomas Hickys	Ind	6.25	tun	Wine	0	0	0	0
John Cappys	Ind	4	tun	Wine	0	0	0	0
John Jays	Ind	1.75	tun	Oil, *Olive*	7	0	0	0
John Bramton	Ind	4.5	tun	Oil, *Olive*	18	0	0	0
John Thomas	Ind	6.25	tun	Wine	0	0	0	0
John Ayleworth	Ind	5.5	tun	Oil, *Olive*	22	0	0	0
Thomas Hartt	Ind	4.5	tun	Wine	0	0	0	0
William Appowell	Ind	2.25	tun	Oil, *Olive*	9	0	0	0
William Spratt	Ind	1	tun	Wine	0	0	0	0
John Codder	Ind	2	tun	Wine	0	0	0	0
William Yate	Ind	1	tun	Wine	0	0	0	0
Richard Artur	Ind	1	tun	Wine	0	0	0	0
Thomas Vele	Ind	0.625	tun	Wine	0	0	0	0
William Deyn	Ind	1	tun	Wine	0	0	0	0
John Hilseys	Ind	0.75	tun	Wine	0	0	0	0
Roger Monox	Ind	2.5	tun	Wine	0	0	0	0

Merchant name	Origin	Qty	Unit	Commodity	£	s.	d.	f.
John Barett and assoc.	Ind	1.125	tun	Wine	0	0	0	0
John Maynerd	Ind	1	quarter	Pepper	0	28	0	0
		28	lb	Ginger	0	46	8	0
		28	lb	Graines	0	14	0	0
		2	lb	Nutmeg	0	6	8	0
		20	lb	Cloves and Mace	0	50	0	0

Navicula Sancti Maria of Juday,[6] Port Unknown, John Peers master, Entering, 7th March 1526

Simon Rodrigus & John Poers	Alien	17.125	ton	Fruit	34	5	0	0
		40	M	Oranges	6	13	4	0

Bata George of Tewkesbury, Roger Horus master, Entering, 8th March 1526

Roger Horus	Ind	2.5	tun	Wine	0	0	0	0

Bata George of Tidenham, Philip Hall master, Entering, 12th March 1526

John Coke and assoc.	Ind	7.91	tun	Wine	0	0	0	0
		7.5	balette	Woad	4	7	6	0

Bata Trynyte of Chepstow, William Heynes master, Entering, 13th March 1526

John Coke and assoc.	Ind	7	tun	Wine	0	0	0	0

Navicula Barbara of Pasajes de San Juan, Michael de Golde master, Entering, 14th March 1526

John Shipman	Ind	10	ton	Iron	25	0	0	0
William Shipman	Ind	10	ton	Iron	25	0	0	0
Gilbert Cogan	Ind	21	ton	Iron	52	10	0	0
John Thomas	Ind	9	ton	Iron	22	10	0	0
John Thorne	Ind	2.5	ton	Iron	6	5	0	0
John Bramton	Ind	2	ton	Iron	0	100	0	0
Nicholas Gay	Ind	3	ton	Iron	7	10	0	0
Thomas Hickys	Ind	1.5	ton	Iron	0	75	0	0
John Roland	Ind	1.5	ton	Iron	0	75	0	0
Thomas Harte	Ind	3.33	ton	Iron	8	6	8	0
Ralph Leche	Ind	10	ton	Iron	25	0	0	0
John Wynter	Ind	2	ton	Iron	0	100	0	0
Domingo Pilato	Alien	1.5 tun & 1 barrel		Sanie/Same?	7	6	8	0
		6	C	Rosin	0	8	0	0

Bata Myghell of St David's, Philip Stevyns master, Exiting, 14th March 1526

Philip Stevyns	Ind	6	wey	Grain	6	0	0	0
		8.5	wey	Malt & Barley	6	13	6	0
		1	wey	Rye	0	16	8	0
		7	wey	Beans and Peas	0	116	8	0

6 Presumably 'Juday' is a biblical reference rather than a port.

Merchant name	Origin	Qty	Unit	Commodity	£	s.	d.	f.
Bata Mary of Tenby, John Thomas master, Entering, 15th March 1526								
Richard Higons	Ind	2	tun	Wine	0	0	0	0
Bata Mawdelyn of Uphill, John Kettyngale master, Entering, 16th March 1526								
John Coke	Ind	5.66	tun	Wine	0	0	0	0
Bata Trynyte of Chepstow, William Hayens master, Entering, *16th March 1526*								
John Gurney and assoc.	Ind	7	tun	Wine	0	0	0	0
Bata Chrystofer of Cardiff, William Deyn master, Entering, *16th March 1526*								
Richard Williams	Ind	1	tun	Wine	0	0	0	0
Bata John of Milford Haven, Simon Watts master, Entering, *16th March 1526*								
John Williams and assoc.	Ind	2	last	Fish, Herring White	6	0	0	0
		2	C	Fish, Hake	0	20	0	0
Henry Caderne	Ind	1	pipe	Wine	0	0	0	0
Bata John of Milford Haven, William Gastarde master, Entering,*16th March 1526*								
Richard John	Ind	1	hogshead	Oil, *Olive*	0	20	0	0
Bata Nicholas of Wexford, Nicholas Turner master, Exiting, 17th March 1526								
Nicholas *Turner*	Ind	8	wey	Grain	8	0	0	0
		3	wey	Malt	0	50	0	0
		2	wey	Beans	0	33	4	0
Bata John of Bewdley, Thomas Trawth master, Entering, *17th March 1526*								
Edward Bawghe	Ind	1.25	tun	Wine	0	0	0	0
Bata Trynyte of Chepstow, William Hayens master, Entering, 21st March 1526								
John Hoper	Ind	5.75	tun	Wine	0	0	0	0
Evan Corre	Alien	1	hogshead	Vinegar	0	10	0	0
Bata Antony of Carmarthen, William Evans master, Entering, 21st March 1526								
Philip Davids	Ind	1	pipe	Wine	0	0	0	0
Navicula Mar*y* Crystofer of *Bristol*, John Welshe master, Entering, 22nd March 1526								
Robert Avyntre	Ind	48.75	ton	Salt	24	7	6	0

Merchant name	Origin	Qty	Unit	Commodity	£	s.	d.	f.

Navicula Kateryn of Bristol, John Barnarde master, Entering, 22nd March 1526

Merchant name	Origin	Qty	Unit	Commodity	£	s.	d.	f.
John Coke	Ind	17	tun	Wine	0	0	0	0
		2.5	balette	Woad	0	25	0	0
John Gurney	Ind	16.75	tun	Wine	0	0	0	0
Andrew Palmer	Ind	1.25	tun	Wine	0	0	0	0
John Halle	Ind	2.25	tun	Wine	0	0	0	0
William Woysley	Ind	1.75	tun	Wine	0	0	0	0
Richard Artur	Ind	2	tun	Wine	0	0	0	0
John Hoper	Ind	0.91	tun	Wine	0	0	0	0
Nicholas Walter &								
Thomas Shipman	Ind	1	C	Frankincense	0	3	4	0
		3	C	Rosin	0	4	0	0

Bata Mary of Gatcombe, Richard Whyte master, Entering, 23rd March 1526

Merchant name	Origin	Qty	Unit	Commodity	£	s.	d.	f.
Unknown Tucker	Ind	5.5	tun	Wine	0	0	0	0
	Ind	8.75	C	Soap	4	7	6	0

Bata Trynyte of Chepstow, William Hayens master, Entering, 24th March 1526

Merchant name	Origin	Qty	Unit	Commodity	£	s.	d.	f.
William Appowell	Ind	4.75	tun	Wine	0	0	0	0

Bata Mary Poldavy, *Port Unknown*, John Richards master, Entering, 26th March 1526

Merchant name	Origin	Qty	Unit	Commodity	£	s.	d.	f.
John *Richards*	Ind	7	piece	Poldavis *Cloth*	0	70	0	0

Bata St Kateryne of Mount Sinai,[7] *Port Unknown*, Peter de Jawrygy master, Entering, 26th March 1526

Merchant name	Origin	Qty	Unit	Commodity	£	s.	d.	f.
Roger Dawys	Ind	1.75	tun	Wine	0	0	0	0
		1	pipe	Oil, *Olive*	0	40	0	0
		2.5	C	Soap	0	25	0	0
John Shipman	Ind	4.5	tun	Wine	0	0	0	0
		12.5	C	Soap	6	5	0	0
Robert Avyntre	Ind	1	pipe	Oil, *Olive*	0	40	0	0
		1	tun	Wine	0	0	0	0
Robert Shipman	Ind	1	tun	Wine	0	0	0	0
John Kedermyster	Ind	14.25	tun	Oil, *Olive*	58	0	0	0
Nicholas Thorne	Ind	5	tun	Wine	0	0	0	0
		10	tun	Oil, *Olive*	40	0	0	0
		36	C	Soap	18	0	0	0
		18	C	Orchil	12	0	0	0
William Ostrige	Ind	2	tun	Wine	0	0	0	0
		13.75	C	Soap	6	17	6	0
Thomas Ashehurst	Ind	9	tun	Wine	0	0	0	0
William Spratt	Ind	2.75	tun	Oil, *Olive*	11	0	0	0
		14.5	C	Aniseed	7	5	0	0
		2.5	C	Soap	0	25	0	0
		10.5	tun	Wine	0	0	0	0
John Codar	Ind	7	tun	Wine	0	0	0	0

7 This is presumably a biblical reference rather than a port.

Merchant name	Origin	Qty	Unit	Commodity	£	s.	d.	f.
		2	tun	Oil, *Olive*	8	0	0	0
		7.5	C	Soap	0	75	0	0
		3	C	Cassia Fistula	9	0	0	0
Edward Pryn	Ind	1.75	tun	Wine	0	0	0	0
		2.5	C	Soap	0	25	0	0
John Ayleworth	Ind	17.5	tun	Wine	0	0	0	0
Thomas Yate	Ind	0.375	tun	Wine	0	0	0	0
John Cappys	Ind	1	pipe	Wine	0	0	0	0
Thomas Hickys	Ind	1	tun	Wine	0	0	0	0
John Thomas	Ind	1	pipe	Wine	0	0	0	0
Richard Pryn	Ind	4.25	tun	Oil, *Olive*	17	0	0	0
		25.25	C	Soap	12	12	6	0
		18	C	Orchil	12	0	0	0
		3	tun	Wine	0	0	0	0
Humphrey Cosgrove	Ind	1.25	tun	Wine	0	0	0	0
John Thorne	Ind	18	C	Orchil	12	0	0	0
		1	pipe	Oil, *Olive*	0	40	0	0
		1	hogshead	Wine	0	0	0	0
Richard Artur	Ind	2.5	tun	Wine	0	0	0	0
		1.5	tun	Oil, *Olive*	6	0	0	0
John Wynter	Ind	2	tun	Wine	0	0	0	0
		2.25	tun	Oil, *Olive*	9	0	0	0
		7.5	C	Soap	0	75	0	0
William Rowley	Ind	1	pipe	Wine	0	0	0	0
		2.5	C	Soap	0	25	0	0
Roger Monox	Ind	1.75	tun	Wine	0	0	0	0
		5	C	Soap	0	50	0	0
George Hall	Ind	1	pipe	Wine	0	0	0	0
John Bramton	Ind	1	pipe	Oil, *Olive*	0	40	0	0
		2.25	C	Soap	0	22	6	0
Thomas Vele	Ind	8.75	C	Soap	4	8	6	0
		1	hogshead	Vinegar	0	10	0	0
Thomas Harte	Ind	1.875	tun	Oil, *Olive*	7	10	0	0
		1	pipe	Wine	0	0	0	0
David Vaughan	Ind	3	tun	Wine	0	0	0	0
Nicholas Gay	Ind	1	tun	Wine	0	0	0	0
John Coke	Ind	0.83	tun	Wine	0	0	0	0
Humphrey Bradley	Ind	1	tun	Wine	0	0	0	0

Bata Jamys of Longney, Thomas Hyghyate master, Entering, 26th March 1526

Thomas *Hyghyate*	Ind	1	tun	Wine	0	0	0	0

Bata Kateryn of Tenby, Thomas Evanns master, Entering, *26th March 1526*

John Germen	Ind	2.25	tun	Wine	0	0	0	0
		1	barrel	Oil, *Olive*	0	7	6	0
		1	hogshead	Salt	0	2	6	0
John Barett	Ind	2.375	tun	Wine	0	0	0	0
Robert Shipman	Ind	1	tun	Wine	0	0	0	0
Richard Mower	Ind	1	tun	Wine	0	0	0	0
		1	ton	Salt	0	10	0	0

Merchant name	Origin	Qty	Unit	Commodity	£	s.	d.	f.
Mathew Hoper	Ind	1	pipe	Wine	0	0	0	0
Thomas Tanner	Ind	1	hogshead	Wine	0	0	0	0
		1	ton	Salt	0	10	0	0
		5	barrel	Prunes	0	66	8	0
Silvia Tucker,								
Maurice Powell &								
John Savage	Ind	1.5	tun	Wine	0	0	0	0

Bata George of Tewkesbury, Thomas Trawth master, Entering, *26th March 1526*

Patrick Welshe	Ind	7.5	tun	Wine	0	0	0	0

Bata John of Milford Haven, Simon Watts master, Exiting, *26th March 1526*

Nicholas Pypertt	Ind	1.5	gross	Cutts	0	5	0	0
		1.5	gross	Points	0	0	18	0
		1	dozen	Skins, Red	0	2	1	0
		1	dozen	Caps	0	10	0	0
		1.5	lb	Saffron	0	15	0	0
		3	lb	Pepper	0	2	6	0
		3	dozen	Combs	0	0	18	0
James Cordy	Ind	1	lb	Silk, *Worked*	0	13	4	0
		1	lb	Saffron	0	10	0	0
		0.5	dozen	Caps	0	5	0	0
		4	lb	Pepper	0	3	4	0
		1	lb	Ginger	0	0	20	0
Richard Welshe	Ind	2	gross	Points	0	2	0	0
		0.5	gross	Cutts	0	0	20	0
		6	dozen	Knives	0	10	0	0
		1	dozen	Caps	0	10	0	0
		4	dozen	Combs	0	2	6	0
		3	dozen	Girdles	0	5	0	0
		1	dozen	Skins, Red	0	2	1	0
		2	lb	Pepper	0	0	20	0
		1	lb	Kermes	0	0	18	0
Henry Doffe	Ind	36	gross	Points	0	36	0	0

Bata Mathew of Milford Haven, Pierce Robyns master, Exiting, *26th March 1526*

Nicholas Hamlyn	Ind	1	tun	Wine, Corrupt	0	30	0	0
		2	dozen	Caps	0	20	0	0
		3	gross	Points	0	3	0	0
		1	lb	Silk, *Worked*	0	13	4	0
		1	lb	Saffron	0	10	0	0

Navicula Mary Bonaventura of *Bristol*, Thomas Nungull master, Entering, *26th March 1526*

Thomas *Nungull*	Ind	37	ton	Salt	18	10	0	0

Bata Kateryn of Minehead, Robert Caly master, Exiting, 27th March 1526

Miles Roche	Ind	1.25	piece	Cloth of Assize	0	0	0	0

Merchant name	Origin	Qty	Unit	Commodity	£	s.	d.	f.
		1	dozen	Skins, Red	0	2	1	0
		1	lb	Saffron	0	10	0	0
William Crowley	Ind	2.5	piece	Cloth of Assize	0	0	0	0

Bata Edwarde of Tewkesbury, Walter Wotton master, Entering, *27th March 1526*

Patrick Welshe	Ind	8.5	tun	Wine	0	0	0	0

Bata Bonaventeura of Blavet, Nicholas Gemarron master, Entering, 28th March 1526

Nicholas *Gemarron*	Alien	34	ton	Salt	17	0	0	0
		50	yard?	Tower Canvas *Cloth*	0	8	4	0

Bata Trynyte of Chepstow, William Hayens master, Entering, 29th March 1526

John Coke &								
John Sparchford	Ind	6.5	tun	Wine	0	0	0	0

Navicula St Petro Kybadewe, *Port Unknown*, Peter Done the younger master, Entering, 31st March 1526

William Ostryge	Ind	22	tun	Wine	0	0	0	0
		60	C	Fruit	6	0	0	0
		4	C	Aniseed	0	54	4	0
		3	bale	Liquorice	0	10	0	0
Nicholas Gybeson	Ind	66	C	Fruit	6	12	0	0
		9	C	Aniseed	6	0	0	0
Nicholas Thorne	Ind	2.75	tun	Wine	0	0	0	0
John Thorne	Ind	1	tun	Wine	0	0	0	0
Edward Pryen	Ind	2	tun	Wine	0	0	0	0
		1	C	Liquorice	0	6	8	0
		1.5	C	Fruit	0	3	0	0

Navicula Anne of Bristol, George Hart master, Entering, 5th April 1526

Robert Ellyot and								
assoc.	Ind	48	ton	Salt	24	0	0	0

Bata Barbara of Youghal, [ ] Mongain master, Entering, *5th April 1526*

Unknown Mongain	Ind	8	burden	Fish, Salted	0	32	0	0

Bata Nicholas of Bristol, Thomas Bayly master, Entering, 9th April 1526

Peter Baron	Ind	5.5	C	Skins, Sheep	0	55	0	0
		1	C	Skins, Lamb	0	10	0	0
		18	piece	Mantles	3	0	0	0
Nicholas Harrys	Ind	2.6	M	Skins, Lamb	8	13	4	0
		25	piece	Skins, Fox	0	4	2	0
		7	C	Skins, Sheep	3	10	0	0
Thomas Sumpt*er*	Ind	4	C	Skins, Sheep	0	40	0	0
		6	C	Skins, Lamb	0	40	0	0

Merchant name	Origin	Qty	Unit	Commodity	£	s.	d.	f.
John More	Ind	1.75	tun	Wine	0	0	0	0
		2.66	C	Skins, Sheep	0	31	8	0
		2	C	Skins, Lamb	0	16	8	0
		1	piece	Mantles	0	3	4	0

Navicula Sant Espiryt of Bristol, John Roman master, Entering, *9th April 1526*

Merchant name	Origin	Qty	Unit	Commodity	£	s.	d.	f.
John Thorne	Ind	13	tun	Wine	0	0	0	0
		14.25	C	Orchil	9	10	0	0
		1	chest	Sugar	0	40	0	0
Richard Pryn	Ind	13	tun	Wine	0	0	0	0
		24.75	C	Orchil	16	10	0	0
Nicholas Thorne	Ind	9	tun	Wine	0	0	0	0
		15	C	Orchil	10	0	0	0
William Ostryge	Ind	4.25	tun	Wine	0	0	0	0
Edward Pryn	Ind	3.5	tun	Wine	0	0	0	0
John Code	Ind	1.75	tun	Wine	0	0	0	0
George Halle	Ind	1.75	tun	Wine	0	0	0	0
Nicholas Gay	Ind	1.5	tun	Wine	0	0	0	0
Humphrey Bosgrove	Ind	1	tun	Wine	0	0	0	0
Roger Monox	Ind	1	tun	Wine	0	0	0	0
John Roman	Alien	15	M	Oranges	0	50	0	0
		0.25	tun	Vinegar	0	10	0	0

Navicula Mathew of Bristol, Thomas Dowdyng master, Entering, *9th April 1526*

Merchant name	Origin	Qty	Unit	Commodity	£	s.	d.	f.
John Shipman	Ind	55	ton	Iron	137	10	0	0
William Shipman	Ind	34	ton	Iron	85	0	0	0
John Wyut	Ind	20	ton	Iron	50	0	0	0
William Appowell	Ind	8	ton	Iron	20	0	0	0
Ralph Leche	Ind	5	ton	Iron	12	10	0	0
John Smyth	Ind	5	ton	Iron	12	10	0	0
Thomas Dowdyng	Ind	2.5	bale	Woad	3	2	6	0
Lewis Grevell	Ind	2	dozen	Serches	0	8	4	0

Navicula Nicholas of Hondarribia, Raphael de Carbonera master, Entering, 10th April 1526

Merchant name	Origin	Qty	Unit	Commodity	£	s.	d.	f.
Roger Dawys	Ind	5	ton	Iron	12	10	0	0
John Shipman	Ind	3	ton	Iron	7	10	0	0
William Rowley	Ind	7	ton	Iron	17	10	0	0
William Shipman	Ind	3.5	ton	Iron	8	15	0	0
Ralph Leche	Ind	11	ton	Iron	27	10	0	0
William Cokke	Ind	3	ton	Iron	7	10	0	0
John Wyut	Ind	3	ton	Iron	7	10	0	0
Raphaell de Carbonera	Alien	10	bale	Liquorice	0	33	4	0
Peter de Prynsan	Alien	2	M	Combs	0	40	0	0
Peter de Solsedo	Alien	63.5	bale	Woad	76	17	6	0

Bata Edward of Elmore, Thomas Whyte master, Entering, 11th April 1526

Merchant name	Origin	Qty	Unit	Commodity	£	s.	d.	f.
John Bradsha	Ind	1	tun	Wine	0	0	0	0

Merchant name	Origin	Qty	Unit	Commodity	£	s.	d.	f.

Bata Antony of Bristol, Thomas Howell master, Entering, _11th April 1526_

Merchant name	Origin	Qty	Unit	Commodity	£	s.	d.	f.
Thomas _Howell_	Ind	60	piece	Mantles	10	0	0	0
		1	C	Fish, Salted	0	20	0	0
		60	yard	Check _Cloth_	0	20	0	0
		5	C	Skins, Lamb	0	33	4	0
		5	C	Skins, Sheep	0	50	0	0
Robert Morghe	Ind	3	M	Skins, Lamb	10	0	0	0

Bata Mary of Waterford, Patrick Ffytzjohn master, Entering, _11th April 1526_

Merchant name	Origin	Qty	Unit	Commodity	£	s.	d.	f.
Patrick _Ffytz_John	Ind	8.5	C	Skins, Sheep	4	5	0	0
		6	piece	Mantles	0	20	0	0
		0.5	C	Skins, Lamb	0	3	4	0
Thomas Kewe	Ind	6.5	C	Skins, Sheep	3	5	0	0
		0.5	C	Skins, Lamb	0	3	4	0
		0.5	pipe	Fish, Salmon	0	15	0	0
		30	piece	Fish, Salted	0	5	0	0
		6	stone	Wool, Flocks	0	2	6	0
		1	C	Irish Linen _Cloth_	0	10	0	0
		8	piece	Mantles	0	26	8	0
James Edward	Ind	3.5	C	Skins, Sheep	0	35	0	0
		1	C	Skins, Lamb	0	6	8	0
		1	piece	Mantles	0	3	4	0
		0.5	C	Scrof (rough wool clippings?)	0	5	0	0
Patrick Fflaman	Ind	1.5	C	Skins, Sheep	0	15	0	0
		1	C	Skins, Lamb	0	6	8	0
		1	dozen	Skins, Fox	0	2	0	0
		8	piece	Mantles	0	26	8	0
		1	hogshead	Wine	0	0	0	0
William Brene	Ind	2.5	C	Skins, Sheep	0	25	0	0
		1	C	Skins, Lamb	0	6	8	0
		3	dozen	Skins, Fox	0	6	0	0
		7	piece	Mantles	0	23	4	0
		60	yard	Check _Cloth_	0	20	0	0
William Rocke	Ind	2	C	Skins, Sheep	0	20	0	0
		6	piece	Mantles	0	20	0	0
John Dawny	Ind	80	piece	Skins, Sheep	0	6	8	0
		1.5	C	Skins, Lamb	0	10	0	0
		40	yard	Check _Cloth_	0	13	4	0
		2	piece	Mantles	0	6	8	0
		4	stone	Wool, Flocks	0	0	20	0

Bata Bonaventure of Blavet, Nicholas Gemeroy master, Exiting, 12th April 1526

Merchant name	Origin	Qty	Unit	Commodity	£	s.	d.	f.
Nicholas _Gemeroy_	Alien	12	lb	Thrums	0	6	8	0

Navicula Barbara of Pasajes de San Juan, Michael de Geldo master, Exiting, 12th April 1526

Merchant name	Origin	Qty	Unit	Commodity	£	s.	d.	f.
Gilbert Cogan	Ind	24	wey	Beans	20	0	0	0
		17	wey	Grain	17	0	0	0
		9	wey	Malt	7	10	0	0

Merchant name	Origin	Qty	Unit	Commodity	£	s.	d.	f.
		6	dozen	Skins, Calf	0	20	0	0
Thomas Whyte	Ind	10	piece	Cloth of Assize	0	0	0	0
William Foxley	Ind	1.25	piece	Cloth of Assize	0	0	0	0
William Cokke	Ind	4.5	dicker	Hides, Tanned	0	0	0	0
John Shipman	Ind	30	dozen	Skins, Calf	5	0	0	0
		18	piece	Cloth of Assize	0	0	0	0
William Shipman	Ind	9	piece	Cloth of Assize	0	0	0	0
Robert Ellyot	Ind	6	piece	Cloth of Assize	0	0	0	0
Michaell de Goldo	Alien	9	wey	Grain	9	0	0	0
Thomas Hart	Ind	7	piece	Cloth of Assize	0	0	0	0
Andrew Palmer	Ind	3	piece	Cloth of Assize	0	0	0	0

Navicula Nicholas of Hondarribia, Raphael de Carbonera master, Exiting, 13th April 1526

Merchant name	Origin	Qty	Unit	Commodity	£	s.	d.	f.
John Wyut	Ind	6	wey	Beans	5	0	0	0
John Shipman	Ind	8	wey	Beans	6	13	4	0
		19	piece	Cloth of Assize	0	0	0	0
Roger Dawys	Ind	4.5	dicker	Hides, Tanned	0	0	0	0
		12	dozen	Skins, Calf	0	40	0	0
Stephen Prymat	Alien	20	wey	Grain	20	0	0	0
William Rowley	Ind	8	piece	Cloth of Assize	0	0	0	0
William Shipman	Ind	2	piece	Cloth of Assize	0	0	0	0
Mathew Smyth	Ind	3	piece	Cloth of Assize	0	0	0	0

Bata Antony of Bristol, Thomas Howell master, Exiting, *13th April 1526*

Merchant name	Origin	Qty	Unit	Commodity	£	s.	d.	f.
Thomas Howell	Ind	7	wey	Grain	7	0	0	0
		8	wey	Malt	6	13	4	0

Navicula Santa Marya of Juda, *Port Unknown*, John Peers master, Exiting, 14th April 1526

Merchant name	Origin	Qty	Unit	Commodity	£	s.	d.	f.
John Peers	Alien	50	yard	Irish Woollen *Cloth*	0	16	8	0
		0.75	piece	Welsh *Cloth*	0	15	0	0
		2	wey	Grain	0	40	0	0
		12	modios	Grain	0	5	0	0
Symon Rodrigus	Alien	33	piece	Dunster *Cloth*	16	10	0	0
		0.495	piece	Cloth of Assize	0	20	0	0
John Rains	Alien	1	wey	Grain	0	20	0	0
		4	bushel	Grain	0	1	8	0
Dego Petrus	Alien	1.5	dicker	Hides, Tanned	0	0	0	0

Bata Barbara of Youghal, Germain Mangan, Exiting, *14th April 1526*

Merchant name	Origin	Qty	Unit	Commodity	£	s.	d.	f.
Germain Mangan	Ind	2	wey	Grain	0	40	0	0
		1	wey	Malt	0	16	8	0
		1	wey	Rye	0	16	8	0

Navicula Mary Christofer of Bristol, John Welshe master, Exiting, 16th April 1526

Merchant name	Origin	Qty	Unit	Commodity	£	s.	d.	f.
Robert Avyntre	Ind	2	C	Battery	4	0	0	0
		3	C	Hops	0	30	0	0
		3	barrel	Honey	0	50	0	0

Merchant name	Origin	Qty	Unit	Commodity	£	s.	d.	f.
		5	lb	Silk Worked	3	6	8	0
		5	lb	Saffron	0	50	0	0
		4	gross	Cutts	0	13	4	0
		4	dozen	Skins, Golden	0	16	8	0
		2	dozen	Skins, Red	0	4	2	0
		3	tun	Wine, Corrupt	4	10	0	0
		7	C	Alum	4	13	4	0
		30	gross	Points	0	30	0	0
		3	piece	Welsh Cloth	3	0	0	0
		0.5	piece	Stavlat Cloth with grains	0	0	0	0
		7	piece	Cloth of Assize	0	0	0	0

Bata Margret of Elmore, Henry Thorn master, Entering, *16th April 1526*

Merchant name	Origin	Qty	Unit	Commodity	£	s.	d.	f.
Philip Savage	Ind	5	C	Skins, Lamb	0	33	4	0
		8	C	Skins, Sheep	4	0	0	0
		2	dicker	Skins, Salted	0	26	8	0

Bata Mary Bonaventure of *Bristol*, Thomas Nongull master, Exiting, *16th April 1526*

Merchant name	Origin	Qty	Unit	Commodity	£	s.	d.	f.
Thomas *Nongull*	Ind	12	wey	Grain	12	0	0	0
		8	wey	Rye	6	13	4	0

Bata George of Bristol, Thomas Lee master, Entering, 20th April 1526

Merchant name	Origin	Qty	Unit	Commodity	£	s.	d.	f.
Thomas *Lee*	Ind	7	last	Fish, Herring White	21	0	0	0
Thomas Ashehurst	Ind	1	C	Thread, Irish Linen	0	30	0	0

Bata Tawdr of Gatcombe, John Drewis master, Entering, 21st April 1526

Merchant name	Origin	Qty	Unit	Commodity	£	s.	d.	f.
John Marks	Ind	2	tun	Wine	0	0	0	0

Bata Michaell of Tewkesbury, Henry Rogers master, Entering, 24th April 1526

Merchant name	Origin	Qty	Unit	Commodity	£	s.	d.	f.
Thomas Whyte	Ind	7	tun	Wine	0	0	0	0

Bata Jamys of Tewkesbury, John Andrews master, Entering, *24th April 1526*

Merchant name	Origin	Qty	Unit	Commodity	£	s.	d.	f.
Thomas Whyte	Ind	9	tun	Wine	0	0	0	0

Bata Kateryn of Tenby, Thomas Evanns master, Entering, *24th April 1526*

Merchant name	Origin	Qty	Unit	Commodity	£	s.	d.	f.
Edmund Body	Ind	1	tun	Wine	0	0	0	0
Richard More	Ind	4	C	Soap	0	40	0	0
		2.75	C	Prunes	0	18	4	0
Henry Whyte	Ind	4.125	C	Prunes	0	27	6	0

Bata Antony of Gloucester, Thomas Cokke master, Entering, *24th April 1526*

Merchant name	Origin	Qty	Unit	Commodity	£	s.	d.	f.
Thomas Whaley	Ind	1.5	tun	Wine	0	0	0	0
		1	hogshead	Oil, *Olive*	0	20	0	0

Merchant name	Origin	Qty	Unit	Commodity	£	s.	d.	f.

Bata Nicholas of Kidwelly, Owen Thomas master, Entering, *24th April 1526*

Merchant name	Origin	Qty	Unit	Commodity	£	s.	d.	f.
Silvia Tukkar	Ind	8.75	tun	Wine	0	0	0	0

Bata Mary of Waterford, Patrick Ffitzjohn master, Exiting, *24th April 1526*

Merchant name	Origin	Qty	Unit	Commodity	£	s.	d.	f.
Patrick *Ffitzjohn*	Ind	4	wey	Grain	4	0	0	0
		3	wey	Rye	0	50	0	0

Bata Kateryn of Youghal, William Colyns master, Entering, *24th April 1526*

Merchant name	Origin	Qty	Unit	Commodity	£	s.	d.	f.
William *Colyns*	Ind	0.5	pipe	Fish, Salmon	0	15	0	0
Henry Gall	Ind	12	piece	Mantles	0	40	0	0
		2	C	Skins, Lamb	0	13	4	0

Bata Antony of Waterford, John Strange master, Entering, *26th April 1526*

Merchant name	Origin	Qty	Unit	Commodity	£	s.	d.	f.
Richard Gall and assoc.	Ind	13	piece	Mantles	0	43	4	0
William Morghe	Ind	10	piece	Mantles	0	33	4	0

Bata Mary John of Bristol, Thomas Hart master, Entering, *26th April 1526*

Merchant name	Origin	Qty	Unit	Commodity	£	s.	d.	f.
William Shipman	Ind	2.75	tun	Wine	0	0	0	0
Robert Ellyot	Ind	3.75	tun	Wine	0	0	0	0
Robert Chapman	Ind	2.25	tun	Wine	0	0	0	0
George Hall	Ind	25.25	tun	Wine	0	0	0	0
		3.75	tun	Vinegar	7	10	0	0
		9	pipe	Woad	45	0	0	0
		3.5	balette	Woad	1	17	6	0
		33.75	C	Rosin	0	45	0	0
		2.5	last	Tar	0	50	0	0
William Yate	Ind	10	tun	Wine	0	0	0	0
		2	pipe	Woad	10	0	0	0
		6.5	balette	Woad	3	15	0	0
Thomas Hart	Ind	4	pipe	Woad	20	0	0	0
		4.5	balette	Woad	2	10	0	0
John Newport	Ind	7	bale	Woad	8	15	0	0
Auger de Noga	Alien	3.75	tun	Wine	0	0	0	0
Thomas Hykke	Ind	7.5	tun	Wine	0	0	0	0
John Cappys	Ind	3	tun	Wine	0	0	0	0
William Appowell	Ind	2.25	tun	Wine	0	0	0	0
Arthur Kennys	Ind	1	tun	Wine	0	0	0	0
Thomas Sompt*er*	Ind	8.5	tun	Wine	0	0	0	0
Thomas Ap Gwyllom	Ind	6.75	tun	Wine	0	0	0	0
Walter Rob*er*ts	Ind	1.5	tun	Wine	0	0	0	0
John Pyll	Ind	2.25	tun	Wine	0	0	0	0
John Davys	Ind	2.25	tun	Wine	0	0	0	0
		1	hogshead	Vinegar	0	10	0	0
William Ketche and assoc.	Ind	1	tun	Wine	0	0	0	0

Merchant name	Origin	Qty	Unit	Commodity	£	s.	d.	f.

Bata Mary John of Bristol, Evan Tyrr master, Entering, 26th April 1526

Merchant name	Origin	Qty	Unit	Commodity	£	s.	d.	f.
John Shipman	Ind	12	pipe	Woad	60	0	0	0
William Shipman	Ind	9	pipe	Woad	45	0	0	0
		7.5	balette	Woad	4	7	6	0
John Wyut	Ind	3	pipe	Woad	15	0	0	0
		5.5	balette	Woad	3	2	6	0
William Rowley	Ind	8	pipe	Woad	40	0	0	0
Thomas Sompter	Ind	3.25	tun	Wine	0	0	0	0
		12	barrel	Tar	0	20	0	0

Bata Jesus of Bristol, William Thomas master, Exiting, 26th April 1526

Merchant name	Origin	Qty	Unit	Commodity	£	s.	d.	f.
Howell Baker	Ind	3	wey	Grain	3	0	0	0
		2	wey	Malt	0	33	4	0
Dennis Baker	Ind	3	wey	Malt	0	50	0	0
James Travys	Ind	44	lb	*Pilus Tinctus*	0	14	8	0
		1	piece	Cloth of Assize	0	0	0	0
		0.5	piece	Cloth of Assize, Dozen Strait	0	0	0	0

Bata Trinite of Dublin, John Massy master, Entering, 26th April 1526

Merchant name	Origin	Qty	Unit	Commodity	£	s.	d.	f.
Thomas Ashehurst	Ind	15	dicker	Skins, Salted	10	0	0	0
		4	barrel	Tallow, Rendered	0	40	0	0
William Evans	Ind	6	dicker	Skins, Salted	4	0	0	0
		4	C	Skins, Sheep	0	40	0	0
		2	C	Skins, Lamb	0	13	4	0
		20	stone	Wool, Flocks	0	8	4	0

Bata Mary of Milford Haven, David Smyth master, Entering, 27th April 1526

Merchant name	Origin	Qty	Unit	Commodity	£	s.	d.	f.
Michael Boyes	Ind	18	C	Skins, Lamb	6	0	0	0
		14	C	Skins, Sheep	7	0	0	0
		6	piece	Skins, Fox	0	0	12	0
Thomas Ffosfert	Ind	14	C	Skins, Lamb	4	13	4	0
		6	C	Skins, Sheep	3	0	0	0
		1.5	C	Skins, Kid	0	7	6	0
		10	stone	Wool, Flocks	0	4	2	0
Oliver Cranysboro	Ind	28	C	Skins, Lamb	9	6	8	0
		6	C	Skins, Sheep	3	0	0	0
		2	C	Skins, Kid	0	10	0	0
		10	stone	Wool, Flocks	0	4	2	0
		12	piece	Skins, Fox	0	2	0	0
		4	piece	Mantles	0	13	4	0
Robert Murfyn	Ind	4	M	Skins, Lamb	13	6	8	0
		1	M	Skins, Sheep	5	0	0	0
		2	dozen	Skins, Fox	0	4	0	0

Bata Mary of Wexford, Robert Rothe master, Entering, 28th April 1526

Merchant name	Origin	Qty	Unit	Commodity	£	s.	d.	f.
Simon Marchant	Ind	4	ton	Salt	0	40	0	0
		3	dicker	Skins, Salted	0	40	0	0

Merchant name	Origin	Qty	Unit	Commodity	£	s.	d.	f.
		2	C	Skins, Lamb	0	13	4	0

Bata Kateryn of Tenby, Thomas Evans master, Exiting, 31st April 1526

Merchant name	Origin	Qty	Unit	Commodity	£	s.	d.	f.
Andrew Palmer	Ind	2	wey	Grain	0	40	0	0
		4	wey	Malt	3	6	8	0
		0.5	C	Hops	0	5	0	0
		0.5	C	Aniseed	0	6	8	0
		0.5	C	Alum	0	6	8	0
		2	lb	Silk Worked	0	26	8	0
Philip Ellyot	Ind	2	wey	Grain	0	40	0	0
		4	wey	Malt	3	6	8	0

Bata Vyncent of Morbihan, Ultan Moynoby master, Entering, 31st April 1526

Merchant name	Origin	Qty	Unit	Commodity	£	s.	d.	f.
Ultan Moynoby	Alien	25	ton	Salt	12	10	0	0
		1	C	Linen *Cloth*	0	33	4	0

Bata Antony of Waterford, John Strange master, Exiting, 31st April 1526

Merchant name	Origin	Qty	Unit	Commodity	£	s.	d.	f.
Henry Gall	Ind	8	wey	Grain	8	0	0	0
		8	wey	Rye	6	13	4	0
		1	wey	Malt	0	16	8	0

Bata Nicholas of Bristol, William of Bristoll master, Exiting, 2nd May 1526

Merchant name	Origin	Qty	Unit	Commodity	£	s.	d.	f.
Peter Baron	Ind	8	wey	Grain	8	0	0	0
		7	wey	Malt	5	16	8	0
		7	wey	Rye	5	16	8	0
Raymond Galshe	Ind	13	piece	Cloth of Assize	0	0	0	0
		24	gross	Points	0	24	0	0
		3	gross	Cutts	0	10	0	0
		2	dozen	Knives	0	3	4	0
		1	dozen	Skins, Red	0	2	1	0
		2	dozen	Skins, Golden	0	8	4	0
		8	lb	Thread	0	3	4	0
		2	lb	Silk Worked	0	26	8	0
		1	dozen	Caps	0	10	0	0
		2	C	Aniseed	0	26	8	0

Bata Mathew of Bristol, Thomas Dowdyng master, Exiting, 2nd May 1526

Merchant name	Origin	Qty	Unit	Commodity	£	s.	d.	f.
John Shipman	Ind	2.25	ton	Lead worked	11	5	0	0
John Sparchford	Ind	5	piece	Welsh *Cloth*	5	0	0	0

Bata Mary John of Bristol, Evan Tyrre master, Exiting, 2nd May 1526

Merchant name	Origin	Qty	Unit	Commodity	£	s.	d.	f.
Thomas Sumpter	Ind	6	wey	Malt	5	0	0	0
		2	wey	Grain	0	40	0	0
Andrew Palmer	Ind	2	wey	Grain	0	40	0	0

Merchant name	Origin	Qty	Unit	Commodity	£	s.	d.	f.
Bata George of Chepstow, William Gowgh master, Entering, 4th May 1526								
Patrick Welshe	Ind	1	tun	Wine	0	0	0	0
Bata Konolawgh of Kinsale, Nicholas Roche master, Entering, 5th May 1526								
Patrick Meagh	Ind	14	burden	Fish, Salted	0	58	4	0
		2.5	ton	Iron	6	5	0	0
		11	C	Skins, Lamb	3	13	4	0
		3.25	tun	Wine	0	0	0	0
Nicholas Roche	Ind	0.75	tun	Wine	0	0	0	0
		12	C	Skins, Lamb	4	0	0	0
		1.5	C	Shipboards	0	30	0	0
		10	stone	Wool, Flocks	0	4	2	0
		1	C	Iron	0	2	6	0
		1.5	C	Fish, Hake	0	15	0	0
Navicula Peter of Ribadeo, Peter Boneke master, Entering, 7th May 1526								
Peter *Boneke*	Alien	9	piece	Welsh *Cloth*	9	0	0	0
Navicula Sta Katerina of Mount Synay, *Port Unknown*, Peter Jawrgy master, Exiting, *7th May 1526*								
Peter Gyll	Alien	4	piece	Cloth of Assize, Dozen Northern	0	53	4	0
		3	piece	Welsh *Cloth*	3	0	0	0
		2.5	piece	Cloth of Assize	0	0	0	0
Peter de Gawregy	Alien	6.5	piece	Cloth of Assize, Dozen Northern	4	6	8	0
John Carpento	Alien	0.5	piece	Welsh *Cloth*	0	10	0	0
Bata Antony of Chepstow, Lewis Baugh master, Entering, 8th May 1526								
John Awode	Ind	1	tun	Wine	0	0	0	0
Thomas Veale	Ind	4	C	Rosin	0	5	4	0
Bata Margaret of Elmore, William Ffox master, Exiting, 9th May 1526								
William *Ffox*	Ind	11	wey	Grain	11	0	0	0
		0.5	wey	Beans	0	8	4	0
		0.5	wey	Malt	0	8	4	0
Bata Peryn of Youghal, Robert Sarsell master, Entering, *9th May 1526*								
Richard Gowgh	Ind	1.5	tun	Wine	0	0	0	0
		1	C	Skins, Sheep	0	10	0	0
		0.5	pipe	Fish, Salmon	0	15	0	0
		5	piece	Mantles	0	16	8	0
Bata Fawkon of Waterford, Nicholas Rothe master, Entering, 11th May 1526								
William Connow?	Ind	6	C	Skins, Sheep	3	0	0	0
		8	C	Skins, Lamb	0	53	4	0

Merchant name	Origin	Qty	Unit	Commodity	£	s.	d.	f.
		1	dozen	Skins, Fox	0	2	0	0
		1	piece	Mantles	0	3	4	0
		7	C	Skins, Sheep	3	10	0	0
		3.5	C	Skins, Lamb	0	23	4	0
		1.5	dozen	Skins, Fox	0	3	0	0
		1	piece	Mantles	0	3	4	0
Nicholas Welshe	Ind	6	C	Skins, Sheep	3	0	0	0
		2	C	Skins, Lamb	0	13	4	0
		6	piece	Skins, Fox	0	0	12	0
		2	piece	Mantles	0	6	8	0
Edmund Hewly	Ind	1.5	C	Skins, Sheep	0	15	0	0
		4	C	Skins, Lamb	0	26	8	0
Nicholas Barrow	Ind	6	C	Skins, Sheep	3	0	0	0
		4	C	Skins, Lamb	0	26	8	0
		6	piece	Mantles	0	20	0	0
Richard Donell	Ind	7	C	Skins, Sheep	3	10	0	0
		1	M	Skins, Lamb	3	6	8	0
		5	piece	Mantles	0	16	8	0

Bata Mary of Wexford, Robert Rothe master, Exiting, *11th May 1526*

Merchant name	Origin	Qty	Unit	Commodity	£	s.	d.	f.
Patrick Synot	Ind	3	wey	Grain	3	0	0	0
		2	wey	Malt	0	33	4	0

Bata Jamys of Hutton, William Benet master, Entering, *11th May 1526*

Merchant name	Origin	Qty	Unit	Commodity	£	s.	d.	f.
Patrick Welshe	Ind	2	tun	Wine	0	0	0	0

Navicula Sant Espyryt of Bristol, John Roman master, Exiting, *11th May 1526*

Merchant name	Origin	Qty	Unit	Commodity	£	s.	d.	f.
John *Roman*	Alien	1.75	piece	Cloth of Assize	0	0	0	0
		5	piece	Welsh *Cloth*	5	0	0	0
Roger Dawys	Ind	5	piece	Cloth of Assize	0	0	0	0
Nicholas Thorn	Ind	46	piece	Cloth of Assize	0	0	0	0
William Spratt	Ind	16	piece	Cloth of Assize	0	0	0	0
William Ostryge	Ind	21	piece	Cloth of Assize	0	0	0	0
Richard Pryn	Ind	7	piece	Cloth of Assize	0	0	0	0
William Bakar	Ind	10	piece	Cloth of Assize	0	0	0	0
Roger Monox	Ind	4	piece	Cloth of Assize	0	0	0	0

Bata Peryn of Youghal, Robert Serchfeld master, Exiting, *11th May 1526*

Merchant name	Origin	Qty	Unit	Commodity	£	s.	d.	f.
Richard Gowgh	Ind	4	wey	Grain	4	0	0	0
		2	wey	Malt	0	33	4	0
		2	wey	Malt	0	33	4	0

Bata Trinite of Chepstow, William Haynes master, Entering, *11th May 1526*

Merchant name	Origin	Qty	Unit	Commodity	£	s.	d.	f.
John Thomas	Ind	1	tun	Wine	0	0	0	0
Thomas Ashehurst	Ind	1.75	tun	Wine	0	0	0	0
Thomas Hykke	Ind	1	tun	Wine	0	0	0	0
Thomas Yate	Ind	3.25	tun	Wine	0	0	0	0

Merchant name	Origin	Qty	Unit	Commodity	£	s.	d.	f.
Bata Antony of Chepstow, Lewis Bawgh master, Entering, _11th May 1526_								
Robert Ellyot	Ind	2.25	tun	Wine	0	0	0	0
Bata Mary Penryce, _Port Unknown_, John Hyet master, Exiting, 12th May 1526								
Hugh Ellyot and assoc.	Ind	6	wey	Grain	6	0	0	0
		2	wey	Rye	0	33	4	0
		16	wey	Malt	13	6	8	0
Bata Mary of Milford Haven, David Smyth master, Exiting, 15th May 1526								
Philip Wydder	Ind	8	wey	Grain	8	0	0	0
		8	wey	Malt	6	13	4	4
Michael Boyes	Ind	1.5	piece	Cloth of Assize	0	0	0	0
		6	lb	Silk, _Worked_	4	0	0	0
		3	lb	Saffron	0	30	0	0
		1	gross	Cutts	0	3	4	0
		0.5	C	Aniseed	0	6	8	0
		8	gross	Points	0	8	0	0
		0.5	dozen	Caps	0	5	0	0
Oliver Cranysboro	Ind	4	piece	Cloth of Assize, Dozen Strait	0	0	0	0
		5	lb	Saffron	0	50	0	0
		4	lb	Silk, _Worked_	0	53	4	0
		1.5	gross	Cutts	0	5	0	0
		1	dozen	Caps	0	10	0	0
		10	gross	Points	0	10	0	0
		52	lb	_Pilus Tinctus_	0	17	4	0
		1	C	Aniseed	0	13	4	0
Thomas Ffosfort	Ind	1	piece	Cloth of Assize, Dozen Strait	0	0	0	0
		2	lb	Silk, _Worked_	0	26	8	0
		2	lb	Saffron	0	20	0	0
		1	gross	Cutts	0	3	4	0
		0.5	dozen	Caps	0	5	0	0
		0.5	C	Aniseed	0	6	8	0
		2	gross	Points	0	2	0	0
Bata Conolaugh of Kinsale, Nicholas Rothe master, Exiting, 16th May 1526								
Nicholas Roche	Ind	6	wey	Grain	6	0	0	0
		3	wey	Malt	0	50	0	0
		1	C	Hops	0	10	0	0
Bata Trinite of Dublin, John Massy master, Exiting, _16th May 1526_								
William Evers	Ind	3	wey	Grain	3	0	0	0
Bata Edward of Worcester, Richard Gowgh master, Entering, _16th May 1526_								
James Welshe	Ind	5	C	Skins, Lamb	0	33	4	0

Merchant name	Origin	Qty	Unit	Commodity	£	s.	d.	f.
Navicula Mary John of Bristol, John Davys master, Exiting, 18th May 1526								
George Hall	Ind	2	ton	Lead worked	10	0	0	0
		19	dozen	Skins, Calf	3	3	4	0
		10	piece	Welsh *Cloth*	10	0	0	0
Bata Trinite of Chepstow, William Haynes master, Entering, 19th May 1526								
John Aylworth	Ind	5.25	tun	Wine	0	0	0	0
Bata Mawdleyn of Magor, Robert Bakar master, Exiting, 19th May 1526								
John Manncell	Ind	1.5	tun	Wine, Corrupt	0	45	0	0
John Drewis	Ind	0.25	tun	Aqua vitae	0	26	8	0
Bata Sonday of Waterford, Walter Wodlok master, Entering, 24th May 1526								
Laurence Brewer	Ind	2.5	C	Skins, Lamb	0	16	8	0
		2.5	C	Skins, Sheep	0	25	0	0
		2	piece	Mantles	0	6	8	0
Walter Wodlok	Ind	12	lb	Pepper	0	12	0	0
		0.5	C	Skins, Sheep	0	5	0	0
Richard Lenagh	Ind	28	C	Skins, Lamb	9	6	8	0
		60	piece	Skins, Fox	0	10	0	0
		1	dozen	Skins, Marten	0	12	0	0
		3	piece	Mantles	0	10	0	0
Bata Vyncent of Morbihan, Ultan Moynoby master, Exiting, 25th May 1526								
Ultan Moynoby	Alien	1.75	piece	Cloth of Assize	0	0	0	0
Dennis Lynch	Ind	5	hogshead	Wood Ashes	0	33	4	0
Bata Mary Walsynghin of Tenby, William Walter master, Exiting, 26th May 1526								
John Marke	Ind	14	wey	Malt	11	13	4	0
Bata Jesus of Kinsale, Jordan Roche master, Entering, *26th May 1526*								
Jordan Roche	Ind	1.5	ton	Iron	3	15	0	0
		1.5	C	Shipboards	0	30	0	0
		8	C	Skins, Lamb	0	53	4	0
Bata Blase of Wexford, Nicholas Whytewall master, Entering, 28th May 1526								
Nicholas *Whytewall*	Ind	6	stone	Wool, Irish	0	16	0	0
		3	piece	Mantles	0	10	0	0
		1	stone	Wool, Flocks	0	0	5	0
		1	wey	Grain	0	20	0	0
		1	wey	Malt	0	16	8	0
		0.5	wey	Rye	0	8	4	0
Thomas Synot	Ind	1	wey	Malt	0	16	8	0
		0.5	wey	Grain	0	10	0	0

Merchant name	Origin	Qty	Unit	Commodity	£	s.	d.	f.
Bata Trinite of Chepstow, William Haynes master, Entering, *28th May 1526*								
John Thomas	Ind	2.5	tun	Wine	0	0	0	0
Bata Margaret of Newnham, Thomas Symond master, Entering, *28th May 1526*								
Thomas Symon	Ind	3	ton	Salt	0	30	0	0
Bata Chrystofer of Minsterworth, John Drewis master, Exiting, 29th May 1526								
Thomas Nongull	Ind	4	wey	Grain	4	0	0	0
		4	wey	Malt	3	6	8	0
		2	wey	Beans	0	33	4	0
Bata Antony of Chepstow, Lewis Baugh master, Entering, *29th May 1526*								
David Hutton	Ind	5.875	C	Soap	0	58	9	0
Bata Fawcon of Waterford, Maurice Welsh master, Exiting, 30th May 1526								
Maurice Welsh	Ind	12	wey	Rye	10	0	0	0
		2	wey	Grain	0	40	0	0
		2	wey	Malt	0	33	4	0
William Connow?	Ind	4	lb	Saffron	0	40	0	0
		3	lb	Silk, *Worked*	0	40	0	0
		3	gross	Cutts	0	10	0	0
		0.5	dozen	Skins, Red	0	0	12	0
		8	gross	Points	0	8	0	0
		2	gross	Lacquer	0	3	4	0
Nicholas Welsh	Ind	2	lb	Silk, *Worked*	0	26	8	0
		3	lb	Saffron	0	30	0	0
		1	dozen	Skins, Red	0	2	1	0
		1.5	gross	Cutts	0	5	0	0
		1	dozen	Aniseed	0	0	18	0
		6	gross	Points	0	6	0	0
		3	gross	Lacquer	0	5	0	0
Richard Donell	Ind	2	lb	Silk, *Worked*	0	26	8	0
		1	lb	Saffron	0	10	0	0
		0.5	gross	Cutts	0	0	20	0
		6	gross	Points	0	6	0	0
		2	gross	Lacquer	0	3	4	0
		2	dozen	Aniseed	0	3	0	0
		3.5	piece	Cloth of Assize, Dozen Strait	0	0	0	0
Tege Connow?	Ind	1	lb	Silk, *Worked*	0	13	4	0
		0.5	lb	Saffron	0	5	0	0
		2	gross	Lacquer	0	3	4	0
		6	gross	Points	0	6	0	0
		1.5	gross	Cutts	0	5	0	0
		1	lb	Mercury	0	0	18	0
		0.25	C	Thimbles	0	0	5	0

Merchant name	Origin	Qty	Unit	Commodity	£	s.	d.	f.

Bata Mary Bakar, *Port Unknown*, William Manyg master, Entering, *30th May 1526*

Merchant name	Origin	Qty	Unit	Commodity	£	s.	d.	f.
Gibbon Kelley	Ind	3	burden	Fish, Salted	0	12	0	0
Richard Barry	Ind	2	burden	Fish, Salted	0	8	0	0

Bata Nicholas of Swansea, Nicholas Jonys master, Exiting, 1st June 1526

Merchant name	Origin	Qty	Unit	Commodity	£	s.	d.	f.
Alan Ryant	Alien	2	piece	Cloth of Assize, Northern	0	53	4	0

Bata Kateryn of Tenby, Thomas Evans master, Entering, *1st June 1526*

Merchant name	Origin	Qty	Unit	Commodity	£	s.	d.	f.
Andrew Palmer	Ind	1.5	pipe	Fish, Salmon	0	45	0	0

Bata Sonday of Minehead, Gerald Barret master, Exiting, *1st June 1526*

Merchant name	Origin	Qty	Unit	Commodity	£	s.	d.	f.
Gibbon Kelley	Ind	12	wey	Grain	12	0	0	0
		8	wey	Malt	6	13	4	0
Thomas Fosfert	Ind	4	lb	Saffron	0	40	0	0
		5	lb	Silk, *Worked*	3	6	8	0
		1	dozen	Skins, Red	0	2	1	0
		1	dozen	Caps	0	10	0	0
		3	dozen	Knives	0	5	0	0
		1	gross	Cutts	0	3	4	0
		1	dozen	Girdles	0	0	5	0
		0.5	dozen	Lacquer	0	0	10	0
		1	piece	Cloth of Assize, Dozen Strait	0	0	0	0
Richard Loughar	Ind	1	lb	Silk, *Worked*	0	13	4	0
		1	lb	Saffron	0	10	0	0
		0.5	dozen	Skins, Red	0	0	12	0
		0.5	dozen	Girdles	0	0	3	0
		1	dozen	Playing Cards	0	0	15	0
		2	gross	Points	0	2	0	0

Bata Jesus of Kinsale, Jordan Roche master, Exiting, *1st June 1526*

Merchant name	Origin	Qty	Unit	Commodity	£	s.	d.	f.
Jordan Roche	Ind	5	wey	Grain	5	0	0	0
		4	wey	Malt	3	6	8	0

Bata Mary Bakar, *Port unknown*, William Mannyng master, Exiting, *1st June 1526*

Merchant name	Origin	Qty	Unit	Commodity	£	s.	d.	f.
Andrew Palmer	Ind	5	wey	Grain	5	0	0	0
		3	wey	Malt	0	50	0	0
		0.5	C	Hops	0	5	0	0

Bata George of Tidenham, Thomas Shipman master, Exiting, 2nd June 1526

Merchant name	Origin	Qty	Unit	Commodity	£	s.	d.	f.
John Strythe	Ind	5	wey	Grain	5	0	0	0
		5	wey	Malt	4	3	4	0

Bata Trinite of Carmarthen, Robert Dyo master, Entering, 4th June 1526

Merchant name	Origin	Qty	Unit	Commodity	£	s.	d.	f.
David Merydyth	Ind	1	tun	Wine	0	0	0	0

Merchant name	Origin	Qty	Unit	Commodity	£	s.	d.	f.
Bata Antony of Waterford, John Strange master, Entering, 4th June 1526								
Richard Lumbard	Ind	5	C	Skins, Lamb	0	33	4	0
		2	C	Skins, Sheep	0	20	0	0
		30	yard	Check Cloth	0	10	0	0
		4	piece	Mantles	0	13	4	0
		15	yard	Irish Canvas Cloth	0	0	15	0
		1	pipe	Wine	0	0	0	0
Henry Gall	Ind	1	pipe	Wine	0	0	0	0
		0.5	C	Skins, Sheep	0	5	0	0
		2	piece	Mantles	0	6	8	0
John Poer	Ind	2	piece	Mantles	0	6	8	0
Bata Mary of Wexford, Patrick Alyn master, Entering, 6th June 1526								
Patrick *Alyn*	Ind	0.5	C	Shipboards	0	10	0	0
		1.5	wey	Malt	0	25	0	0
		0.5	wey	Grain	0	10	0	0
Bata Kateryn of Bristol, John Gorwey master, Entering, 6th June 1526								
John Savage	Ind	2	tun	Wine	0	0	0	0
Bata John of Milford Haven, William Taskar master, Entering, 6th June 1526								
Andrew Palm*er*	Ind	1	butt	Fish, Salmon	0	15	0	0
Philip Ellyot	Ind	5.5	pipe	Fish, Salmon	8	5	0	0
		2	C	Skins, Sheep	0	20	0	0
Bata Trinite of Chepstow, William Haynes master, Entering, 7th June 1526								
Thomas Yate	Ind	3	tun	Wine	0	0	0	0
Bata Mary of Tenby, Patrick Grant master, Entering, 8th June 1526								
Evan Lloyd	Ind	7.5	tun	Wine	0	0	0	0
		4.5	C	Soap	0	45	0	0
Bata Cullumbe of Vannes, John de Barr master, Entering, 8th June 1526								
Philip Gowgh	Alien	23.75	tun	Wine	0	0	0	0
		4	piece	Oleron Cloth	0	26	8	0
		0.25	ton	Iron	0	12	6	0
Bata Frances of Waterford, John Le*e* master, Entering, 9th June 1526								
John Canlan[8]	Ind	1	C	Skins, Sheep	0	10	0	0
		2	piece	Mantles	0	6	8	0
		1	C	Skins, Lamb	0	6	8	0
David Whyte	Ind	22	piece	Skins, Sheep	0	2	6	0
		90	piece	Skins, Lamb	0	5	0	0

8 Possibly 'Caulan'

Merchant name	Origin	Qty	Unit	Commodity	£	s.	d.	f.
John Lee	Ind	0.5	C	Skins, Sheep	0	5	0	0
		2	piece	Mantles	0	6	8	0
		1	C	Iron	0	2	6	0

Bata Savior of Wexford, Robert Turnor master, Entering, 9th June 1526

Robert Turnor	Ind	2	dicker	Skins, Salted	0	26	8	0
		1	dicker	Skins, ? Ouprar	0	2	6	0
		1	C	Skins, Lamb	0	6	8	0
		1	C	Skins, Sheep	0	10	0	0
		5	piece	Mantles	0	16	8	0
		16	stone	Wool, Irish	0	42	8	0
		0.5	pipe	Fish, Salmon	0	15	0	0
		1	C	Shipboards	0	20	0	0
Mathew Smyth	Ind	6.5	dozen	Shipboards	0	13	0	0

Bata Antony of Waterford, John Strange master, Exiting, 11th June 1526

Henry Gall	Ind	6	wey	Grain	6	0	0	0
		10	wey	Rye	8	6	8	0
		1	wey	Malt	0	16	8	0

Bata Sonday of Waterford, Walter Wodlok master, Exiting, *11th June 1526*

Thomas Cotton	Ind	8	wey	Grain	8	0	0	0
		7.25	wey	Malt	6	10	0	0
Richard Stappoll	Ind	5	piece	Cloth of Assize	0	0	0	0
		1	dozen	Skins, Golden	0	4	2	0
		0.5	dozen	Skins, Red	0	0	12	0
		1	dozen	Caps	0	10	0	0
		2	gross	Cutts	0	6	8	0
		10	gross	Points	0	10	0	0
		3	lb	Saffron	0	30	0	0
John Verdon	Ind	3	piece	Cloth of Assize	0	0	0	0
		2	dozen	Skins, Golden	0	8	4	0
		2	dozen	Skins, Red	0	4	2	0
		10	gross	Points	0	10	0	0
		2	gross	Cutts	0	6	8	0
		6	lb	Saffron	3	0	0	0
		3	lb	Silk, *Worked*	0	40	0	0
		0.5	dozen	Caps	0	5	0	0
John Strych	Ind	2.75	piece	Cloth of Assize	0	0	0	0
		3	gross	Cutts	0	10	0	0
		2	dozen	Skins, Golden	0	8	4	0
		2	dozen	Skins, Red	0	4	2	0
		2	dozen	Knives	0	2	6	0
		12	gross	Points	0	12	0	0
		10	lb	Saffron	5	0	0	0
		8	lb	Silk Worked	5	6	8	0
Nicholas Ffox	Ind	6.75	piece	Cloth of Assize	0	0	0	0
		12	lb	Saffron	6	0	0	0
		6	lb	Silk Worked	4	0	0	0

Merchant name	Origin	Qty	Unit	Commodity	£	s.	d.	f.
		12	gross	Points	0	12	0	0
		1.5	gross	Cutts	0	5	0	0
		1	dozen	Skins, Golden	0	4	2	0
		1	lb	Thread	0	0	5	0
		1.5	C	Alum	0	20	0	0
		20	lb	*Pilus Tinctus*	0	6	8	0
		1.5	stone	Orchil	0	2	6	0
George Creagh	Ind	21.5	piece	Cloth of Assize	0	0	0	0
		16	lb	Saffron	8	0	0	0
		8	lb	Silk Worked	5	6	8	0
		3	dozen	Skins, Golden	0	12	6	0
		2	dozen	Cumin	0	2	6	0
		1	C	Aniseed	0	13	4	0
		6	lb	Pepper	0	6	0	0
		1	lb	Calamine	0	0	5	0
		4	dozen	Knives	0	6	8	0
		40	gross	Points	0	40	0	0
		1	gross	Lacquer	0	0	20	0
		2.5	gross	Cutts	0	8	4	0
		19	stone	Orchil	0	31	8	0
Dennis Whyte	Ind	13	piece	Cloth of Assize	0	0	0	0
		40	gross	Points	0	40	0	0
		3.5	gross	Cutts	0	11	8	0
		2	dozen	Knives	0	3	4	0
		2	lb	Mercury	0	0	10	0
		2	lb	Pepper	0	2	0	0
		12	lb	Cumin	0	0	15	0
		1	C	Aniseed	0	13	4	0
		4	dozen	Lacquer	0	6	8	0
		19	stone	Orchil	0	31	8	0
		1.5	dozen	Skins, Golden	0	6	3	0
		15.5	lb	Saffron	7	15	0	0
		4	lb	Silk Worked	0	53	4	0

Bata Peter of Tenby, Richard Webbe master, Exiting, *11th June 1526*

Thomas Cotton	Ind	5	wey	Malt	4	3	4	0

Bata Trinite George of Bristol, Gerald Hubbert master, Entering, 13th June 1526

Patrick Welshe	Ind	4	stone	Wool, Irish	0	10	8	0
		4	stone	Wool, Flocks	0	0	20	0

Bata Chrystofer of Cardiff, William Deane master, Entering, *13th June 1526*

Lewis Caddorn	Ind	4	ton	Salt	0	40	0	0
		4	tun	Wine	0	0	0	0

Bata Frances of Waterford, John Lee master, Exiting, *13th June 1526*

John Canlan	Ind	4.25	wey	Grain	4	5	0	0
		4.5	wey	Rye	3	15	0	0

Merchant name	Origin	Qty	Unit	Commodity	£	s.	d.	f.

Bata Mary John of Bristol, Evan Tarry master, Entering, *13th June 1526*

Thomas Sompter	Ind	5	C	Shipboards	5	0	0	0
		5	C	Skins, Lamb	0	33	4	0
		1	pipe	Iron	0	25	0	0
		15	stone	Wool, Flocks	0	6	3	0
		30	stone	Wool, Irish	4	0	0	0
		1.5	tun	Wine	0	0	0	0
Andrew Palmer	Ind	2.5	ton	Iron	6	5	0	0

Bata Antony of Bristol, Thomas Howell master, Entering, *13th June 1526*

Thomas Howell	Ind	2	tun	Wine	0	0	0	0
		7	piece	Mantles	0	23	4	0
		40	yard	Check *Cloth*	0	13	4	0
		10	stone	Wool, Flocks	0	4	2	0
Thomas Waddyng	Ind	8	C	Skins, Lamb	0	53	4	0
		2.66	C	Skins, Sheep	0	26	8	0

Bata Trinite of Chepstow, William Haynes master, Entering,*13th June 1526*

| John Jette | Ind | 1 | tun | Wine | 0 | 0 | 0 | 0 |

Navicula Mary Grace of Bristol, Richard Millar master, Entering, 14th June 1526

| John Savage | Ind | 7.75 | tun | Wine | 0 | 0 | 0 | 0 |

Bata Mary of Waterford, Patrick Ffitzjohn master, Entering, 15th June 1526

Patrick *Ffitzjohn*	Ind	1	C	Skins, Sheep	0	10	0	0
		10	stone	Wool, Flocks	0	4	2	0
		1	C	Skins, Lamb	0	6	8	0
		1	hogshead	Wine	0	0	0	0
John More	Ind	6	C	Skins, Sheep	3	0	0	0
Nicholas Ward	Ind	3.5	C	Skins, Sheep	0	35	0	0
		3	C	Skins, Lamb	0	20	0	0

Bata Mighell of Minehead, John Fyssher master, Entering, *15th June 1526*

| Thomas Mayo | Ind | 0.75 | tun | Wine | 0 | 0 | 0 | 0 |

Bata Peter of Wexford, Patrick Stafford master, Entering, *15th June 1526*

Patrick *Stafford*	Ind	0.75	tun	Wine	0	0	0	0
		0.5	C	Skins, Calf (rough)	0	0	20	0
		0.5	C	Skins, Sheep	0	5	0	0
		1.5	burden	Fish, Salted	0	6	3	0
		1.5	dicker	Skins, Salted	0	20	0	0

Bata Mighell of Minehead, Robert Makynglyng master, Exiting, 16th June 1526

| Robert *Makynglyng* | Ind | 12 | wey | Grain | 12 | 0 | 0 | 0 |

Merchant name	Origin	Qty	Unit	Commodity	£	s.	d.	f.
		2	wey	Malt	0	33	4	0

Bata Mary of Waterford, Patrick Fitzjohn master, Exiting, 18th June 1526

Merchant name	Origin	Qty	Unit	Commodity	£	s.	d.	f.
Patrick *Fitz*John	Ind	3	wey	Grain	3	0	0	0
		3	wey	Rye	0	50	0	0

Bata Patryk of Youghal, Edmond Fitzjohn master, Entering, 19th June 1526

Merchant name	Origin	Qty	Unit	Commodity	£	s.	d.	f.
William Condon	Ind	3	C	Skins, Sheep	0	30	0	0
		0.5	C	Skins, Lamb	0	3	4	0
		0.5	pipe	Fish, Salmon	0	15	0	0
		6	piece	Mantles	0	20	0	0
Patrick Flanynghin	Ind	1	C	Skins, Lamb	0	6	8	0
		0.5	C	Skins, Sheep	0	5	0	0

Navicula Seynt Kateryn of San Sebastián, [ ] Domyngo master, Exiting, *19th June 1526*

Merchant name	Origin	Qty	Unit	Commodity	£	s.	d.	f.
John Roland	Ind	7	piece	Cloth of Assize	0	0	0	0
John Shipman	Ind	16	piece	Cloth of Assize	0	0	0	0
		4	dicker	Hides, Tanned	0	0	0	0
William Shipman	Ind	16	piece	Cloth of Assize	0	0	0	0
		4	dicker	Hides, Tanned	0	0	0	0
John Wyut	Ind	13	piece	Cloth of Assize	0	0	0	0

Bata Mary of Wexford, Nicholas Launders master, Entering, 25th June 1526

Merchant name	Origin	Qty	Unit	Commodity	£	s.	d.	f.
Thomas Forlonnge	Ind	3.5	C	Skins, Lamb	0	23	4	0
		1	C	Skins, Sheep	0	10	0	0
		3	C	Skins, Kid	0	15	0	0
		50	yard	Irish Woollen *Cloth*	0	16	8	0
		0.5	dicker	Skins, Salted	0	6	8	0
		1	piece	Mantles	0	3	4	0
		3	stone	Wool, Irish	0	8	0	0
		1	tun	Wine	0	0	0	0

Bata Antony of Bristol, John Whyte master, Exiting, 26th June 1526

Merchant name	Origin	Qty	Unit	Commodity	£	s.	d.	f.
John *Whyte*	Ind	8	wey	Grain	8	0	0	0
		7	wey	Rye	0	116	8	0
Thomas Wadyng	Ind	1	gross	Cutts	0	3	4	0
		1	lb	Saffron	0	10	0	0
		5	piece	Caps	0	4	2	0

Navicula Anne of Bristol, Thomas Blake master, Entering, *26th June 1526*

Merchant name	Origin	Qty	Unit	Commodity	£	s.	d.	f.
Robert Chapman & assoc.	Ind	48	ton	Salt	24	0	0	0

Bata Mary John of *Bristol*, Evan Tyrry master, Exiting, *26th June 1526*

Merchant name	Origin	Qty	Unit	Commodity	£	s.	d.	f.
Thomas Sumpter	Ind	3	wey	Rye	0	50	0	0

Merchant name	Origin	Qty	Unit	Commodity	£	s.	d.	f.
		4	last	Sarnicia?	6	0	0	0
		4	wey	Grain	4	0	0	0

Bata Savyor of Wexford, Robert Turner master, Exiting, 26th June 1526

Merchant name	Origin	Qty	Unit	Commodity	£	s.	d.	f.
Robert Turner	Ind	4	wey	Grain	4	0	0	0
		3	wey	Malt	0	50	0	0

Bata Margarett of Elmore, William Ffox master, Exiting, 26th June 1526

Merchant name	Origin	Qty	Unit	Commodity	£	s.	d.	f.
William *Ffox*	Ind	7	wey	Grain	7	0	0	0
		5	wey	Malt	4	3	0	0

Bata Peter of Wexford, Patrick Stoke master, Exiting, 26th June 1526

Merchant name	Origin	Qty	Unit	Commodity	£	s.	d.	f.
Patrick *Stoke*	Ind	2	wey	Malt	0	33	4	0
		1	wey	Grain	0	20	0	0

Navicula Mathew of Bristol, Thomas Dawdyny master, Entering, 27th June 1526

Merchant name	Origin	Qty	Unit	Commodity	£	s.	d.	f.
John *Shipman*	Ind	103	ton	Salt	51	10	0	0

Navicula Savyor of Bristol, William Deyn master, Entering, 27th June 1526

Merchant name	Origin	Qty	Unit	Commodity	£	s.	d.	f.
John *Shipman*	Ind	186	ton	Salt	93	0	0	0

Navicula Mary John of Bristol, John Davys master, Entering, 27th June 1526

Merchant name	Origin	Qty	Unit	Commodity	£	s.	d.	f.
George Hall	Ind	120	ton	Salt	60	0	0	0
		1	C	Rosin	0	0	16	0

Bata Patricke of Youghal, Edmund Fitzjohn master, Exiting, 27th June 1526

Merchant name	Origin	Qty	Unit	Commodity	£	s.	d.	f.
William Conden	Ind	2.5	wey	Grain	0	50	0	0
		1	wey	Malt	0	16	8	0
		1	C	Alum	0	13	4	0
		1	gross	Cutts	0	3	4	0
		8	stone	Orchil	0	13	4	0
		1	piece	Cloth of Assize, Dozen Strait	0	0	0	0
Michael Crey	Alien	7	wey	Malt	0	116	8	0
		8	wey	Grain	8	0	0	0

Bata Mary Penryce, *Port Unknown*, Thomas Higyatt master, Entering, 28th June 1526

Merchant name	Origin	Qty	Unit	Commodity	£	s.	d.	f.
Thomas Higyatt	Ind	6.5	dicker	Skins, Salted	4	6	8	0
		19	piece	Mantles	0	63	4	0
		172	yard	Check Cloth	0	57	4	0
		84	piece	Shipboards	0	15	0	0
		7	piece	Skins, Deer	0	0	20	0

Merchant name	Origin	Qty	Unit	Commodity	£	s.	d.	f.

Bata Kateryn of Tenby, Thomas Yonnas? Master, Entering, *28th June 1526*

Merchant name	Origin	Qty	Unit	Commodity	£	s.	d.	f.
William Sutton	Ind	14	tun	Oil, *Olive*	56	0	0	0

Bata John of Milford Haven, William Tasker master, Exiting, *28th June 1526*

Merchant name	Origin	Qty	Unit	Commodity	£	s.	d.	f.
Philip Elyott	Ind	6	wey	Grain	6	0	0	0
		1	wey	Malt	0	16	8	0
Andrew Palmer	Ind	0.5	C	Hops	0	5	0	0

Bata George of Waterford, Robert Keyn master, Entering, *28th June 1526*

Merchant name	Origin	Qty	Unit	Commodity	£	s.	d.	f.
Richard Barkeley	Ind	8	C	Skins, Sheep	4	0	0	0
		3.5	C	Skins, Lamb	0	23	4	0
		7	piece	Mantles	0	23	4	0
Richard Edwarde	Ind	5.5	C	Skins, Sheep	0	55	0	0
		8	C	Skins, Lamb	0	53	4	0
		11	piece	Skins, Fox	0	0	22	0
		1	piece	Mantles	0	3	4	0
Raymond Nashe	Ind	3.5	C	Skins, Sheep	0	35	0	0
		8.5	C	Skins, Lamb	0	56	8	0
		7	piece	Mantles	0	23	4	0
		9	piece	Skins, Fox	0	0	18	0
Richard Maldony	Ind	1	hogshead	Wine	0	0	0	0
		2	piece	Mantles	0	6	8	0
Nicholas Comen	Ind	1	pipe	Wine	0	0	0	0
		4	piece	Mantles	0	13	4	0
John Marks	Ind	1	hogshead	Oil, *Olive*	0	20	0	0
		8	stone	Wool, Flocks	0	3	4	0

Bata Jhesus of Bristol, John Philips master, Entering, 30th June 1526

Merchant name	Origin	Qty	Unit	Commodity	£	s.	d.	f.
Howell Baker	Ind	3	tun	Wine	0	0	0	0
		1	virken	Fish, Salmon	0	7	6	0
Dennis Baker	Ind	1	tun	Wine	0	0	0	0
		14	piece	Fish, Salmon	0	3	4	0
William Kyssam	Ind	1	tun	Wine	0	0	0	0
		1.5	C	Shipboards	0	30	0	0
		2	C	Skins, Lamb	0	13	4	0
		1	butt	Fish, Salmon	0	15	0	0
		2.5	stone	Wool, Irish	0	6	8	0

Navicula Mawdelyn of Bristol, Antony Pykarde master, Entering, *30th June 1526*

Merchant name	Origin	Qty	Unit	Commodity	£	s.	d.	f.
Nicholas Gay	Ind	22	ton	Iron	55	0	0	0
		3	hogshead	Woad	5	0	0	0
		3.5	bale	Woad	4	7	6	0
		3	ton	Pitch & Rosin	4	0	0	0
Robert Elyott	Ind	2	ton	Iron	0	100	0	0
William Appowell	Ind	4	ton	Iron	10	0	0	0
John Shipman	Ind	5	ton	Iron	12	10	0	0

Merchant name	Origin	Qty	Unit	Commodity	£	s.	d.	f.
William Shipman	Ind	4	ton	Iron	10	0	0	0
John Welshe	Ind	15.5	ton	Iron	38	15	0	0
		3.5	ton	Rosin	4	13	4	0
John Cappys	Ind	5	ton	Iron	12	10	0	0
		3	dozen	Serches	0	12	6	0
John Brampton	Ind	1.5	ton	Iron	0	75	0	0
William Cockys	Ind	9.33	ton	Iron	23	6	8	0
		1	dozen	Serches	0	4	2	0
Philip Furbor	Ind	2	dozen	Serches	0	8	4	0

Bata Jamys of Dublin, Maurice Dyrram master, Entering, *30th June 1526*

Merchant name	Origin	Qty	Unit	Commodity	£	s.	d.	f.
David Edwards	Ind	1	hogshead	Fish, Salmon	0	30	0	0
		0.5	C	Skins, Sheep	0	5	0	0
		0.5	C	Skins, Calf (rough)	0	0	20	0
		12	yard	Check *Cloth*	0	4	2	0

Bata Mary of Wexford, Nicholas Launders, Exiting, *30th June 1526*

Merchant name	Origin	Qty	Unit	Commodity	£	s.	d.	f.
Thomas Forlonnge	Ind	2	wey	Grain	0	40	0	0
		3	wey	Malt	0	50	0	0

Bata Bonaventewre of Blavet, Colageinerew master, from *Blavet, 30th June 1526*

Merchant name	Origin	Qty	Unit	Commodity	£	s.	d.	f.
not stated								
Colageinerew?	Ind	37	ton	*Salt*	18	10	0	0

Bata Patrycke of New Ross, Thomas Shenell master, Entering, 2nd July 1526

Merchant name	Origin	Qty	Unit	Commodity	£	s.	d.	f.
Thomas *Shenell*	Ind	1.5	C	Skins, Sheep	0	15	0	0
		1	C	Skins, Lamb	0	6	8	0
		50	yard	Check *Cloth*	0	16	8	0
Thomas Highgate	Ind	2	dozen	Cork, for Bottles	0	8	4	0

Bata Trynyte of St David's, John Davys master, Entering, *2nd July 1526*

Merchant name	Origin	Qty	Unit	Commodity	£	s.	d.	f.
James Setgre	Ind	1		G[ ]cn?	0	13	4	0
		100	yard	Check *Cloth*	0	33	4	0
Hugh Norys	Ind	9	stone	Wool, Irish	0	24	0	0
Henry Tayler	Ind	5	C	Skins, Sheep	0	50	0	0
		3	C	Check *Cloth*	6	0	0	0
		3	C	Skins, Lamb	0	20	0	0
		1	C	Irish Linen *Cloth*	0	10	0	0
		6	piece	Skins, Fox	0	0	12	0
		3	dicker	Skins, Salted	0	40	0	0

Bata Jamys of Dublin, Maurice Dyrram master, Exiting, 4th July 1526

Merchant name	Origin	Qty	Unit	Commodity	£	s.	d.	f.
David Edwards	Ind	11	pair	Millstones	11	0	0	0

Merchant name	Origin	Qty	Unit	Commodity	£	s.	d.	f.

Bata Mary Baker, *Port Unknown*,[9] Robert Baker master, Entering, 5th July 1526

Merchant name	Origin	Qty	Unit	Commodity	£	s.	d.	f.
Robert Baker	Ind	2.5	C	Shipboards	0	50	0	0
Andrew Palmer	Ind	0.625	ton	Iron	0	28	9	0

Navicula Nicholas of Hondarribia, John de Jonata master, Entering, 9th July 1526

Merchant name	Origin	Qty	Unit	Commodity	£	s.	d.	f.
Roger Dawys	Ind	9	ton	Iron	22	10	0	0
John Shipman	Ind	26	ton	Iron	65	0	0	0
William Shipman	Ind	12	ton	Iron	30	0	0	0
Gilbert Cogan	Ind	1	C	Liquorice	0	6	8	0
John Roland	Ind	1.33	ton	Iron	0	66	8	0
John Jonata	Alien	1.33	ton	Iron	0	66	8	0
John Ware	Alien	0.66	ton	Iron	0	33	4	0
John de la Sard	Alien	0.5	C	Liquorice	0	3	4	0
		1.5	C	Skins, Sheep (from Spain)	0	20	0	0
John Thorne	Ind	1	pipe	Iron	0	25	0	0

Bata John of Wexford, Patrick Synott master, Entering, *9th July 1526*

Merchant name	Origin	Qty	Unit	Commodity	£	s.	d.	f.
Patrick *Synott*	Ind	3	dicker	Skins, Salted	0	40	0	0
		2	C	Skins, Lamb	0	13	4	0
		1	C	Skins, Sheep	0	10	0	0
		20	yard	Check *Cloth*	0	6	8	0
		6	stone	Wool, Irish	0	16	0	0
		8	piece	Mantles	0	26	8	0
		1.5	C	Skins, Kid	0	7	6	0
		0.5	C	Shipboards	0	10	0	0
		1	burden	Fish, Salted	0	4	2	0
		2.75	tun	Wine	0	0	0	0

Bata George of Waterford, Robert Keyn master, Exiting, *9th July 1526*

Merchant name	Origin	Qty	Unit	Commodity	£	s.	d.	f.
Richard Maldony	Ind	6.75	wey	Grain	6	15	0	0
		8.5	wey	Malt	7	0	20	0

Navicula Mawdelyn of Seville, John de St Laurance master, Entering, 10th July 1526

Merchant name	Origin	Qty	Unit	Commodity	£	s.	d.	f.
Nicholas Thomas	Ind	54	tun	Oil, *Olive*	116	0	0	0
		75	C	Soap	37	10	0	0
John de Salamanca	Alien	1	C	Soap	0	10	0	0

Bata Jamys of Berkeley, Henry Lynke master, Entering, 11th July 1526

Merchant name	Origin	Qty	Unit	Commodity	£	s.	d.	f.
Robert Elyott	Ind	6	ton	Iron	15	0	0	0
William Appowell	Ind	2	ton	Iron	0	100	0	0

Bata Colom*b* of Vannes, John Lybartt master, Exiting, *11th July 1526*

Merchant name	Origin	Qty	Unit	Commodity	£	s.	d.	f.
Philip Goe	Alien	6	piece	Cloth of Assize, Dozen Northern	4	0	0	0
		6	piece	Welsh *Cloth*	6	0	0	0
		2	C	Check *Cloth*	4	0	0	0

9 Probably Bristol.

Merchant name	Origin	Qty	Unit	Commodity	£	s.	d.	f.

Navicula Bonaventure[10] of Bristol, Thomas Nonull master, Entering, *11th July 1526*

Merchant name	Origin	Qty	Unit	Commodity	£	s.	d.	f.
Thomas *Nonull*	Ind	3	pipe	Fish, Salmon	4	10	0	0
		1	C	Skins, Sheep	0	10	0	0
		2	C	Shipboards	0	40	0	0
		8	stone	Wool, Flocks	0	3	4	0
		3	C	Rosin	0	4	0	0
Thomas Sarchell	Ind	1	hogshead	Fish, Salmon	0	30	0	0
		5	C	Skins, Sheep	0	50	0	0
		2	C	Skins, Lamb	0	13	4	0

Bata Myghell of Swansea, William Hoppekyns master, Entering, *11th July 1526*

Merchant name	Origin	Qty	Unit	Commodity	£	s.	d.	f.
Richard Evanns	Ind	7.5	tun	Wine	0	0	0	0
		3	ton	Salt	0	30	0	0

Bata Vyncent of Bristol, Thomas Webbe master, Entering, 13th July 1526

Merchant name	Origin	Qty	Unit	Commodity	£	s.	d.	f.
Katherine Woysley	Ind	20	ton	Iron	50	0	0	0
		1	pipe	Wine	0	0	0	0
Nicholas Thorne	Ind	5	pipe	Woad	25	0	0	0
Edward Pryn	Ind	2.5	ton	Iron	6	5	0	0
		4	pipe	Woad	20	0	0	0
Robert Elyott	Ind	2	ton	Iron	0	100	0	0
William Spratt	Ind	27	ton	Iron	67	10	0	0
		6	pipe	Woad	30	0	0	0
		6.5	balette	Woad	3	15	0	0

Bata George of Tidenham, Philip Hall master, Entering, 14th July 1526

Merchant name	Origin	Qty	Unit	Commodity	£	s.	d.	f.
George Brynnorke	Ind	24	piece	Mantles	4	0	0	0
		40	piece	Skins, Sheep	0	3	4	0
		36	piece	Skins, Lamb	0	2	2	2
John Streche	Ind	10	piece	Mantles	0	33	4	0

Bata John of Bristol, John Philips master, Exiting, *14th July 1526*

Merchant name	Origin	Qty	Unit	Commodity	£	s.	d.	f.
Henry Taylor	Ind	3	tun	Wine	0	0	0	0
		2.5	pair	Millstones	0	50	0	0
		8	wey	Grain	8	0	0	0
		4	wey	Malt	0	66	8	0
		1	C	Hops	0	10	0	0
		0.5	C	Aniseed	0	6	8	0

Bata Trynyte of St David's, John Towker master, Exiting, *14th July 1526*

Merchant name	Origin	Qty	Unit	Commodity	£	s.	d.	f.
James Setgre	Ind	10	wey	Grain	10	0	0	0
		4	wey	Malt	0	66	8	0
		10	lb	Saffron	0	100	0	0

10 This is likely to be the *Mary* Boneventure.

Merchant name	Origin	Qty	Unit	Commodity	£	s.	d.	f.

Bata Trynyte of Milford Haven, Thomas Reyneshe master, Entering, 16th July 1526

Merchant name	Origin	Qty	Unit	Commodity	£	s.	d.	f.
Thomas *illegible*	Ind	6	dicker	Skins, Salted	4	0	0	0
		5	C	Skins, Sheep	0	50	0	0
		60	yard	Irish Linen *Cloth*	0	5	0	0
		1	C	Skins, Calf (rough)	0	3	4	0
		1	dozen	Skins, Otter	0	5	0	0
		6	piece	Skins, Fox	0	0	12	0
		2	animal	Horses	0	26	8	0

Bata Antony of Waterford, John Strannge master, Entering, *16th July 1526*

Merchant name	Origin	Qty	Unit	Commodity	£	s.	d.	f.
John *Strannge*	Ind	1.5	C	Skins, Sheep	0	15	0	0
		3	piece	Mantles	0	10	0	0
Patrick Stoke	Ind	4	C	Skins, Sheep	0	40	0	0
		2.5	C	Skins, Lamb	0	16	8	0
		1	butt	Fish, Salmon	0	15	0	0
		14	piece	Mantles	0	46	8	0
Richard Lommberte	Ind	50	yard	Check *Cloth*	0	16	8	0
		1	C	Skins, Lamb	0	6	8	0
		1	piece	Mantles	0	3	4	0
John Power	Ind	4	piece	Mantles	0	13	4	0
		0.5	C	Skins, Lamb	0	3	4	0
Maurice Hay	Ind	4	piece	Mantles	0	13	4	0
Richard Gall	Ind	6	piece	Mantles	0	20	0	0
		1	C	Skins, Sheep	0	10	0	0
		1	C	Skins, Lamb	0	6	8	0
Tege Tyrry	Ind	4	piece	Mantles	0	13	4	0
John Streche	Ind	6	C	Skins, Sheep	0	60	0	0
		1.5	M	Skins, Lamb	0	100	0	0
		30	piece	Skins, Fox	0	5	0	0
		16	piece	Mantles	0	53	4	0
John Morthey	Ind	12	C	Skins, Sheep	6	0	0	0
		12	C	Skins, Lamb	4	0	0	0
		20	piece	Mantles	0	66	8	0
		6	piece	Skins, Fox	0	0	12	0
		0.25	C	Irish Linen *Cloth*	0	2	6	0
		13	yard	Check *Cloth*	0	4	4	0
		6	lb	Wax	0	2	0	0
John Quyrke	Ind	3	C	Skins, Sheep	0	30	0	0
		4	C	Skins, Lamb	0	26	8	0
		6	piece	Skins, Fox	0	0	12	0
Edmund Quyrke	Ind	5	piece	Mantles	0	16	8	0
		1	C	Skins, Lamb	0	6	8	0
William Verdon	Ind	4	M	Skins, Lamb	13	6	8	0
		6	dozen	Skins, Fox	0	12	0	0
		12	piece	Skins, Otter	0	5	0	0
		12	piece	Skins, Marten	0	12	0	0
Thomas Roche	Ind	10	C	Skins, Lamb	0	66	8	0
	Ind	12	piece	Mantles	0	40	0	0
	Ind	30	piece	Skins, Fox	0	5	0	0

Merchant name	Origin	Qty	Unit	Commodity	£	s.	d.	f.
Bata Trynte of Bristol, John Hay master, Entering, *16th July 1526*								
William Yonrough	Ind	2	ton	Salt	0	20	0	0
Richard Walker	Ind	4	tun	Wine	0	0	0	0
Bata John of Wexford, Patrick Synott master, Exiting, *16th July 1526*								
Patrick *Synott*	Ind	6	wey	Grain	6	0	0	0
		4	wey	Rye and Malt	0	66	8	0
Bata Fawkyn of Waterford, Maurice Welsh master, Entering, *16th July 1526*								
Maurice Welsh	Ind	5	C	Skins, Lamb	0	33	4	0
		4	C	Skins, Sheep	0	40	0	0
		1	pipe	Wine	0	0	0	0
Nicholas Carall	Ind	20	piece	Mantles	0	66	8	0
		1.5	C	Skins, Sheep	0	15	0	0
		1	C	Skins, Lamb	0	6	8	0
Walter Wodlocke	Ind	12	stone	Wool, Flocks	0	5	0	0
		8	piece	Mantles	0	26	8	0
		6	lb	Pepper	0	6	0	0
James Fetzwyll*ia*ms	Ind	6	C	Skins, Sheep	0	60	0	0
		2	C	Skins, Lamb	0	13	4	0
Bata Mary Barkett of Bristol, Robert Tawny master, Entering, *16th July 1526*								
John Hyer	Ind	7.5	tun	Wine	0	0	0	0
Bata Crystofer of Minsterworth (?), John Drew*is* master, Entering, *16th July 1526*								
John Welshe	Ind	9	C	Skins, Sheep	4	10	0	0
		2	M	Skins, Lamb	6	13	4	0
		10	piece	Mantles	0	33	4	0
John Lee	Ind	97	piece	Mantles	16	3	4	0
		5.5	C	Skins, Sheep	0	55	0	0
		7.5	C	Skins, Lamb	0	50	0	0
		6	piece	Skins, Fox	0	0	12	0
		20	yard	Check *Cloth*	0	6	8	0
Richard Fetzharry	Ind	152	piece	Mantles	25	6	8	0
		3	C	Skins, Sheep	0	30	0	0
		3	C	Skins, Lamb	0	20	0	0
		30	yard	Check *Cloth*	0	10	0	0
		18	piece	Skins, Fox	0	3	0	0
Thomas Ragid	Ind	48	piece	Mantles	8	0	0	0
		8	C	Skins, Sheep	4	0	0	0
Thomas Ragid	Ind	7	C	Skins, Lamb	0	46	8	0
		12	piece	Skins, Fox	0	2	0	0
		30	yard	Irish Linen *Cloth*	0	2	6	0
		12	yard	Check *Cloth*	0	4	0	0

Merchant name	Origin	Qty	Unit	Commodity	£	s.	d.	f.

Bata Mary of Tintern, Henry Tavar master, Entering, 17th July 1526

Merchant name	Origin	Qty	Unit	Commodity	£	s.	d.	f.
John Hewys	Ind	6	C	Woad	0	40	0	0

Bata Fawkyn of Waterford, Maurice Welshe master, Exiting, *17th July 1526*

Merchant name	Origin	Qty	Unit	Commodity	£	s.	d.	f.
Maurice Welshe	Ind	14	wey	Rye and Malt	11	13	4	0
		2	piece	Cloth of Assize	0	0	0	0
		3.5	lb	Saffron	0	35	0	0
		8.5	lb	Silk, *Worked*	0	113	4	0
		2.5	gross	Cutts	0	8	4	0
		2	dozen	Knives	0	3	4	0
		18	gross	Points	0	18	0	0
		1	gross	Lacquer	0	0	20	0
		3	lb	Thread	0	0	15	0
		1	dozen	Books, Primers	0	0	20	0
		1	dozen	Caps	0	10	0	0
John Quyrke	Ind	1.5	piece	Cloth of Assize	0	0	0	0
		1	lb	Saffron	0	10	0	0
		2	lb	Silk, *Worked*	0	26	8	0
		2	gross	Cutts	0	6	8	0
		4	gross	Points	0	4	0	0
		1	gross	Lacquer	0	0	20	0
John Fytzwilliams	Ind	1.5	piece	Cloth of Assize, Dozen Strait	0	0	0	0
		0.5	lb	Silk, *Worked*	0	6	8	0
		4	dozen	Aniseed	0	6	0	0
		4	lb	Cumin	0	0	5	0
		1	gross	Cutts	0	3	4	0
		5	piece	Caps	0	4	2	0
		6	gross	Points	0	6	0	0
		1	gross	Lacquer	0	0	20	0

Navicula Nicholas of Hondarribia, John de Jonate master, Exiting, *17th July 1526*

Merchant name	Origin	Qty	Unit	Commodity	£	s.	d.	f.
Roger Dawys	Ind	7.4	piece	Hides, Tanned	0	0	0	0
		6	wey	Grain	6	0	0	0
		51	dozen	Skins, Calf	8	10	0	0
John Jonate	Alien	8.5	wey	Grain	8	10	0	0
		15	dozen	Skins, Calf	0	50	0	0
		14	piece	Hides, Tanned	0	0	0	0
John Shipman	Ind	10	wey	Grain	10	0	0	0
		19.66	piece	Cloth of Assize	0	0	0	0
		3.5	dicker	Hides, Tanned	0	0	0	0
William Shipman	Ind	4	wey	Grain	4	0	0	0
		17.5	piece	Cloth of Assize	0	0	0	0
		3.5	dicker	Hides, Tanned	0	0	0	0
William Ffox	Ind	23	piece	Cloth of Assize	0	0	0	0
William Illegible	Ind	8	piece	Cloth of Assize	0	0	0	0
John Illegible	Ind	50	piece	Welsh *Cloth*, Dozen Strait	10	8	4	0

Merchant name	Origin	Qty	Unit	Commodity	£	s.	d.	f.

Bata Patrycke of New Ross, William Blake master, Entering, 18th July 1526

Merchant name	Origin	Qty	Unit	Commodity	£	s.	d.	f.
William *Blake*	Ind	1.5	pipe	Fish, Salmon	0	45	0	0
		6	piece	Mantles	0	20	0	0
William Lenarde	Ind	44	piece	Mantles	7	6	0	0
		4	C	Skins, Lamb	0	26	8	0
		40	yard	Check *Cloth*	0	13	4	0
Patrick Archer	Ind	70	piece	Mantles	11	13	4	0
		2	C	Skins, Sheep	0	20	0	0
		2	C	Skins, Lamb	0	13	4	0
		1	C	Check *Cloth*	0	40	0	0
Edward Lenarde	Ind	20	piece	Mantles	0	66	8	0
		5	C	Skins, Lamb	0	33	4	0
		1	C	Skins, Sheep	0	10	0	0
		2	dozen	Skins, Fox	0	4	0	0
Peter Roche	Ind	68	piece	Mantles	11	6	8	0
		4	C	Skins, Sheep	0	40	0	0
		13	C	Skins, Lamb	4	6	8	0
		18	piece	Skins, Fox	0	3	0	0
		70	yard	Check *Cloth*	0	23	4	0
James Ed*wards*	Ind	100	piece	Mantles	16	13	4	0
		1.25	C	Skins, Sheep	0	12	6	0
		4	C	Skins, Lamb	0	26	8	0

Navicula Mary Bonaventur*e* of Bristol, Thomas Nungull master, Exiting, 19th July 1526

Merchant name	Origin	Qty	Unit	Commodity	£	s.	d.	f.
Thomas *Nungull*	Ind	10	wey	Grain	10	0	0	0
		6	wey	Rye	0	100	0	0
		3	wey	Beans	0	50	0	0
		8	piece	Welsh *Cloth*	8	0	0	0
Robert Tyrry	Ind	16.5	piece	Cloth of Assize	0	0	0	0
		8	lb	Silk, *Worked*	0	106	8	0
		8	lb	Saffron	4	0	0	0
		8.5	gross	Cutts	0	28	4	0
		2.5	C	Aniseed	0	33	4	0
		4	dozen	Caps	0	40	0	0
		28	gross	Points	0	28	0	0
		1	gross	Lacquer	0	0	20	0
		8	stone	Orchil	0	13	4	0
Thomas Serche	Ind	4.75	piece	Cloth of Assize	0	0	0	0
		2	gross	Cutts	0	6	8	0
		6	lb	Saffron	0	60	0	0
		2	lb	Silk, *Worked*	0	26	8	0
		3	dozen	Caps	0	30	0	0
		2	gross	Points	0	2	0	0
Walter Tyrry	Ind	7	piece	Cloth of Assize	0	0	0	0
		1	piece	Cloth of Assize, Dozen Strait	0	0	0	0
		2	lb	Silk, *Worked*	0	26	8	0
		1	lb	Saffron	0	10	0	0
		5	gross	Points	0	5	0	0

Merchant name	Origin	Qty	Unit	Commodity	£	s.	d.	f.
Bata Mawdelyn of Morbihan, John de Levett master, Entering, 20th July 1526								
John de Levett	Alien	24	ton	Salt	12	0	0	0
Bata Trynyte of Dublin, John Masse master, Exiting, 21st July 1526								
William Evers	Ind	6	wey	Grain	6	0	0	0
Bata Margarett of Newnham, Henry Thorne master, Entering, *21st July 1526*								
Peter Henry	Ind	60	piece	Mantles	10	0	0	0
		15	C	Skins, Lamb	0	100	0	0
		12	C	Skins, Sheep	6	0	0	0
		24	piece	Skins, Fox	0	4	0	0
John Welshe	Ind	72	piece	Mantles	12	0	0	0
		1.5	C	Skins, Sheep	0	15	0	0
		3	C	Skins, Lamb	0	20	0	0
		3	C	Skins, Kid	0	15	0	0
		30	yard	Check *Cloth*	0	10	0	0
		24	piece	Skins, Fox	0	4	0	0
John Ley	Ind	3	C	Skins, Sheep	0	30	0	0
		4.5	C	Skins, Lamb	0	30	0	0
Nicholas Harrys	Ind	40	piece	Mantles	6	13	4	0
		1	C	Irish Linen *Cloth*	0	10	0	0
		1	C	Skins, Lamb	0	6	8	0
		6	piece	Skins, Fox	0	0	12	0
Thomas Mathew	Ind	2	pipe	Fish, Salmon	0	60	0	0
		2	C	Skins, Sheep	0	20	0	0
		2	C	Skins, Lamb	0	13	4	0
		10	yard	Check *Cloth*	0	3	4	0
John Blake	Ind	16	piece	Mantles	0	53	4	0
		3.5	C	Skins, Sheep	0	35	0	0
		2	pipe	Fish, Salmon	0	60	0	0
		3	virken	Fish, Salmon	1	2	6	0
Bata Patricke of New Ross, William Blake master, Exiting, 23rd July 1526								
Robert Pepwal	Ind	6	wey	Grain	6	0	0	0
Patrick Archer	Ind	2	piece	Cloth of Assize, Dozen Strait	0	0	0	0
		1	lb	Silk, *Worked*	0	13	4	0
		1	lb	Saffron	0	10	0	0
		1	gross	Knives	0	6	8	0
		0.5	gross	Cutts	0	0	20	0
		5	gross	Points	0	5	0	0
		0.5	gross	Lacquer	0	0	10	0
		2	dozen	Knives, Small	0	3	4	0
Thomas Roche	Ind	4	lb	Saffron	0	40	0	0
		1	gross	Knives	0	6	8	0
		1	dozen	Skins, Red	0	2	1	0
		8	gross	Points	0	8	0	0

Merchant name	Origin	Qty	Unit	Commodity	£	s.	d.	f.
Bata Peter of Waterford, John Ley master, Entering, *23rd July 1526*								
Robert Ley	Ind	13	C	Skins, Sheep	6	10	0	0
		8.25	C	Skins, Lamb	0	55	0	0
		2	pipe	Fish, Salmon	0	60	0	0
		1	virken	Fish, Salmon	0	7	6	0
		20	stone	Wool, Flocks	0	8	4	0
		30	piece	Mantles	0	100	0	0
		1	pipe	Wine	0	0	0	0
William Lenarde	Ind	24	piece	Mantles	4	0	0	0
		6	C	Skins, Sheep	0	60	0	0
		50	yard	Check *Cloth*	0	16	8	0
Bata Trynyte of Chepstow, William Hayens master, Entering, *23rd July 1526*								
John Davy	Ind	6.5	piece	Linen *Cloth*	6	10	0	0
Bata Peter of Milford Haven, John Coke master, Entering, 24rd July 1526								
John *Coke*	Ind	2	burden	Fish, Salted	0	8	4	0
		1	C	Fish, Hake	0	10	0	0
Bata Antony of Milford Haven, John Gryndam master, Entering, 25th July 1526								
Owen Ap Voen?	Ind	2.5	tun	Oil, *Olive*	10	0	0	0
Bata Gage of Portugal, John Hewys master, Entering, 25th July 1526								
John *Hewys*	Ind	4	dozen	Skins, Soetts (?stoat)	0	3	4	0
Bata Mary Walsyngin of Bristol/ Tenby,[11] Patrick Grannt master, Entering, 26th July 1526								
Rycy Williams	Ind	0.75	tun	Oil, *Olive*	0	55	0	0
Bata Antony of Carmarthen, Thomas Rogers master, Entering, 27th July 1526								
Lewis John	Ind	1.5	tun	Wine	0	0	0	0
Bata Mary of Carmarthen, Thomas Rogers master, Entering, *27th July 1526*								
Henry Taylor	Ind	2.875	tun	Wine	0	0	0	0
Bata Trynyte of Carmarthen, John Renoulld master, Entering, *27th July 1526*								
David Amerell	Ind	2	tun	Wine	0	0	0	0
Bata *Name Unknown* of Kinsale, Richard Colyns master, Entering, *27th July 1526*								
John Unknown	Ind	4	C	Fish, Unspecified	0	5	0	0
John Ilegible	Ind	1	C	Skins, Sheep	0	10	0	0

11 There are ships called the 'Mary Walsingham' from Bristol and Tenby in this account. Where the port of origin is unspecified it is most likely Bristol, but this is uncertain.

Merchant name	Origin	Qty	Unit	Commodity	£	s.	d.	f.

Bata Antony of Bristol, Thomas Howel master, Entering, 27th July 1526

Merchant name	Origin	Qty	Unit	Commodity	£	s.	d.	f.
Nicholas Harris	Ind	37	piece	Mantles	6	3	4	0
		9.5	C	Skins, Lamb	0	63	4	0
		5	C	Irish Linen *Cloth*	0	50	0	0
Thomas Howell	Ind	6	piece	Mantles	0	20	0	0
		1	C	Skins, Sheep	0	10	0	0
Nicholas Gysaytt	Ind	14	piece	Mantles	0	46	8	0
		1.5	C	Skins, Sheep	0	15	0	0
		20	yard	Check *Cloth*	0	6	8	0
Walter Grannt	Ind	3	piece	Mantles	0	10	0	0
		8	yard	Check *Cloth*	0	2	4	0

Bata Antony of Waterford, John Strannge master, Exiting, 27th July 1526

Merchant name	Origin	Qty	Unit	Commodity	£	s.	d.	f.
Richard Gaull	Ind	10	wey	Grain	10	0	0	0
		5	wey	Rye	4	3	4	0
		3	wey	Malt	0	66	8	0
		1.5	stone	Orchil	0	2	6	0
William Verdon	Ind	9.5	piece	Cloth of Assize	0	0	0	0
		5	gross	Cutts	0	16	8	0
		18	gross	Points	0	18	0	0
		2	dozen	Skins, Red	0	4	2	0
		2	dozen	Skins, Golden	0	8	4	0
		0.5	dozen	Caps	0	5	0	0
		2	lb	Thread	0	0	10	0
		8	lb	Silk, *Worked*	0	106	8	0
		9	lb	Saffron	4	10	0	0
		1	seam	Wood Ashes	0	4	0	0
		9	stone	Orchil	0	15	0	0
Nicholas Leynaugh	Ind	9.25	piece	Cloth of Assize	0	0	0	0
		3.5	gross	Cutts	0	11	8	0
		2	dozen	Skins, Red	0	4	2	0
		2	dozen	Skins, Golden	0	8	4	0
		1	dozen	Caps	0	10	0	0
		18	gross	Points	0	18	0	0
		2	gross	Lacquer	0	3	4	0
		2	lb	Cumin	0	0	5	0
		4	lb	Liquorice	0	0	10	0
		2	dozen	Combs	0	0	10	0
		1	lb	Thread	0	0	5	0
		8	lb	Mercury	0	2	0	0
		9	lb	Silk, *Worked*	6	0	0	0
		11	lb	Saffron	0	110	0	0
		9	stone	Orchil	0	15	0	0
		1	seam	Wood Ashes	0	4	0	0
Robert Hey	Ind	6.25	piece	Cloth of Assize	0	0	0	0
		4	dozen	Skins, Red	0	8	4	0
		4	dozen	Skins, Golden	0	16	8	0
		12	gross	Points	0	12	0	0
		10	lb	Saffron	0	100	0	0
		8	lb	Silk, *Worked*	0	106	8	0

Merchant name	Origin	Qty	Unit	Commodity	£	s.	d.	f.
		5	gross	Cutts	0	16	8	0
		1	C	Alum	0	13	4	0
		9	stone	Orchil	0	15	0	0
Pierce Whyte	Ind	6.25	piece	Cloth of Assize	0	0	0	0
		0.5	dozen	Skins, Golden	0	2	1	0
		12	gross	Points	0	12	0	0
		3	lb	Silk, *Worked*	0	40	0	0
		7	lb	Saffron	0	70	0	0
Richard Barkeley	Ind	1.75	piece	Cloth of Assize	0	0	0	0
		3	lb	Saffron	0	30	0	0
		2	lb	Silk, *Worked*	0	26	8	0
		2	gross	Cutts	0	6	8	0
		4	dozen	Aniseed	0	6	0	0
		1	dozen	Alum	0	0	18	0
		9	gross	Points	0	9	0	0
		1	gross	Lacquer	0	0	20	0
		2	lb	Verdigris	0	0	10	0
		4	piece	Caps	0	3	4	0
		0.5	dozen	Skins, Red	0	0	12	0
		2	dozen	Knives, in Pairs	0	3	4	0
Raymond Nashe	Ind	1	piece	Cloth of Assize	0	0	0	0
		3	lb	Silk, *Worked*	0	40	0	0
		2	lb	Saffron	0	20	0	0
		1	gross	Cutts	0	3	4	0
		6	gross	Points	0	6	0	0
		0.5	dozen	Caps	0	5	0	0
		2	dozen	Knives, in Pairs	0	3	4	0
		2	dozen	Aniseed	0	3	0	0
		1	dozen	Combs	0	0	18	0
		2	dozen	Alum	0	3	0	0
		1	dozen	*Oclem pro Seri*[12]	0	0	10	0
		1	gross	Lacquer	0	0	20	0
John Morthey	Ind	2.25	piece	Cloth of Assize	0	0	0	0
		5	lb	Silk, *Worked*	0	66	8	0
		4	lb	Saffron	0	40	0	0
		3	gross	Cutts	0	10	0	0
		12	gross	Points	0	12	0	0
Richard Everode	Ind	1	piece	Cloth of Assize	0	0	0	0
		3	lb	Silk, *Worked*	0	40	0	0
		2	lb	Saffron	0	20	0	0
		1	gross	Cutts	0	3	4	0
		12	piece	Knives, in Pairs	0	20	0	0
		6	gross	Points	0	6	0	0
		1	gross	Lacquer	0	0	20	0
		0.5	dozen	Caps	0	5	0	0
		6	lb	Verdigris	0	4	0	0
		12	lb	Wood, Brazil	0	4	2	0
		3	dozen	Aniseed	0	4	6	0
		2	dozen	Alum	0	3	0	0
		0.5	dozen	Skins, Golden	0	2	1	0
		0.5	dozen	Skins, Red	0	0	12	0

12 Unidentified.

Merchant name	Origin	Qty	Unit	Commodity	£	s.	d.	f.
Bata Trynyte of Milford Haven, Thomas Reynesthe master, Exiting, 28th July 1526								
Thomas Jurden	Ind	5	pair	Millstones	0	100	0	0
Bata Tawdre of Chepstow, Thomas Haye master, to Portugal, *28th July 1526*								
Consalus Vadants	Alien	38	piece	Cloth of Assize	0	0	0	0
		6.25	piece	Cloth of Assize	0	0	0	0
		3	piece	Cloth of Assize	0	0	0	0
		4.5	piece	Welsh *Cloth*	4	10	0	0
		2	C	Irish Linen *Cloth*	4	0	0	0
Bata Kateryn of Tenby, Thomas Evans master, Entering, 30th July 1526								
John Thomas	Ind	1	tun	Oil, *Olive*	4	0	0	0
Bata Antony of Chepstow, William Hayens master, Entering, *30th July 1526*								
Hugh Davy	Ind	4	C	Woad, Azores	0	26	8	0
Bata Mary Walsyngam of Tenby, William Walters master, Exiting, *30th July 1526*								
Antony Preda	Alien	31.5	piece	Cloth of Assize	0	0	0	0
		10	dozen	Skins, Calf	0	33	4	0
		2	dicker	Hides, Tanned	0	0	0	0
Bata Mary of Tenby, Watkin Taylor master, Exiting, *30th July 1526*								
George Thomas	Alien	3	piece	Welsh *Cloth*	3	0	0	0
		20	piece	Welsh *Cloth*, Dozen Strait	4	3	4	0
Dego Fanlerie	Alien	37	piece	Welsh *Cloth*, Dozen Strait	7	14	2	0
Bata Margarett of Elmore, William Ffox master, Exiting, *30th July 1526*								
William *Ffox*	Ind	8	wey	Grain	8	0	0	0
		4	wey	Rye	0	66	8	0
Bata Mary of Milford Haven, Hugh Nott master, Exiting, 31st July 1526								
Richard Cockesall	Ind	1	wey	Grain	0	20	0	0
		4	wey	Malt	0	66	8	0
Bata Peter of Waterford, John Lee master, Exiting, 31st July 1526								
Robert Lee	Ind	4	wey	Grain	4	0	0	0
		2	wey	Rye	0	33	4	0
		1	dozen	Caps	0	10	0	0
		0.5	lb	Silk, *Worked*	0	6	8	0
		0.25	gross	Cutts	0	0	10	0
		0.5	dozen	Aniseed	0	0	9	0
Geoffrey Foster	Ind	1.25	piece	Cloth of Assize	0	0	0	0
		0.5	gross	Cutts	0	0	20	0

Merchant name	Origin	Qty	Unit	Commodity	£	s.	d.	f.
		2	gross	Points	0	2	0	0

Bata Trynyte of Chepstow, William Hayens master, Entering, 4th August 1526

William Style	Ind	4.5	C	Woad, Azores	0	30	0	0

Bata Kateryn of Tenby, Thomas Evanns master, Entering, 6th August 1526

Robert Fowler	Ind	1.5	ton	Salt	0	15	0	0

Bata Bastian of St Ives, Robert Thomas master, Entering, *6th August 1526*

Robert Thomas	Ind	12	burden	Fish, Salted	0	50	0	0
		4	piece	Canvas *Cloth*	4	0	0	0

Bata Kateryn of Tenby, Thomas Evanns master, Exiting, *6th August 1526*

John Marting	Alien	36.25	piece	Cloth of Assize, Northern	48	6	8	0
		20	piece	Welsh *Cloth*, Dozen Strait	4	3	4	0
		0.5	piece	Welsh *Cloth*	0	10	0	0
Oliver Consalnus	Alien	35.75	piece	Cloth of Assize, Northern	47	13	4	0
		20	piece	Welsh *Cloth*, Dozen Strait	4	3	4	0
Unknown Consalnus	Alien	11.5	piece	Cloth of Assize, Northern	15	6	8	0
Antony Farnande	Alien	12	piece	Cloth of Assize, Northern	16	0	0	0
Emmanuel Barbosoe	Alien	21.75	piece	Cloth of Assize, Northern	29	0	0	0
Anthony Peers	Alien	18.75	piece	Cloth of Assize, Northern	25	0	0	0

Bata Mary of Waterford, Patrick Ffetzjohn master, Entering, 7th August 1526

Patrick *Ffetzjohn*	Ind	0.75	tun	Wine	0	0	0	0
		2	C	Skins, Sheep	0	20	0	0
		4	piece	Mantles	0	13	4	0

Bata Antony of Bristol, Thomas Howell master, Exiting, *7th August 1526*

John Lee	Ind	2	barrel	Honey	0	33	4	0
		1	lb	Pepper	0	0	12	0
		1	lb	Cloves	0	2	6	0
		4	lb	Silk, *Worked*	0	53	4	0
		3	lb	Liquorice	0	0	5	0
		3	gross	Cutts	0	10	0	0
		0.5	C	Hops	0	5	0	0
		5	dozen	Aniseed	0	7	6	0
		2	dozen	Caps	0	20	0	0
		24	lb	*Pilus Tinctus*	0	8	0	0
		4	lb	Verdigris	0	3	0	0
		2	dozen	Knives	0	3	4	0
		12	gross	Points	0	12	0	0
		1	gross	Lacquer	0	0	20	0
		3	piece	Cloth of Assize, Dozen Strait	0	0	0	0
Richard Ffetzharry	Ind	2.25	piece	Cloth of Assize	0	0	0	0
		4	lb	Silk, *Worked*	0	53	4	0

Merchant name	Origin	Qty	Unit	Commodity	£	s.	d.	f.
		2	lb	Saffron	0	20	0	0
		6	gross	Cutts	0	20	0	0
		4	dozen	Knives	0	6	8	0
		0.5	dozen	Caps	0	5	0	0
		1	C	Aniseed	0	13	4	0
		12	gross	Points	0	12	0	0
		1	gross	Lacquer	0	0	20	0
		1	barrel	Honey	0	16	8	0
		4	dozen	Girdles	0	6	8	0
		16	lb	*Pilus Tinctus*	0	5	4	0
		2	dozen	*Oclem Serptorn*[13]	0	2	6	0
		1	lb	Pepper	0	0	12	0
Thomas Kargyd	Ind	2	piece	Cloth of Assize	0	0	0	0
		4	lb	Silk, *Worked*	0	53	4	0
		5	lb	Saffron	0	50	0	0
		3	gross	Cutts	0	10	0	0
		16	gross	Points	0	16	0	0
		3	dozen	Playing Cards	0	2	6	0
		3	lb	Verdigris	0	2	6	0
		2	dozen	Girdles	0	3	4	0
		1.5	dozen	Caps	0	15	0	0
		4	dozen	Aniseed	0	6	0	0
		2	lb	Thread	0	0	10	0
		2	dozen	Knives	0	3	4	0
		0.5	lb	Ginger	0	0	6	0
John Welshe	Ind	6	piece	Cloth of Assize	0	0	0	0
		10	lb	Silk, *Worked*	6	12	4	0
		4	gross	Cutts	0	13	4	0
		2	gross	Lacquer	0	3	4	0
		24	gross	Points	0	24	0	0
		3	lb	Saffron	0	30	0	0
		1	lb	Pepper	0	0	12	0
		1	lb	Ginger	0	0	12	0
		1.5	dozen	Caps	0	15	0	0
		0.5	C	Hops	0	5	0	0
James Edwards	Ind	2	barrel	Honey	0	33	4	0
		5	lb	Silk, *Worked*	0	66	8	0
		4	lb	Saffron	0	40	0	0
		3	gross	Cutts	0	10	0	0
		6	gross	Points	0	6	0	0
		0.5	C	Aniseed	0	6	8	0
		4	lb	Verdigris	0	3	0	0
		1.5	dozen	Caps	0	15	0	0
		24	lb	*Pilus Tinctus*	0	8	0	0
		1	quarter	Hops	0	2	6	0
		1.5	piece	Cloth of Assize	0	0	0	0
Peter Rowth	Ind	3.5	piece	Cloth of Assize	0	0	0	0
		12	lb	Silk, *Worked*	8	0	0	0
		6	lb	Saffron	0	60	0	0
		2	dozen	Caps	0	20	0	0
		3	gross	Cutts	0	10	0	0

13 Unidentified.

Merchant name	Origin	Qty	Unit	Commodity	£	s.	d.	f.
		26	gross	Points	0	26	0	0
		1.5	lb	Cinnamon	0	3	0	0
		0.5	lb	Pepper	0	0	6	0
		0.5	lb	Ginger	0	0	6	0
		2	dozen	Knives	0	3	4	0
		2	gross	Lacquer	0	3	4	0
		4	dozen	Aniseed	0	6	0	0
William Lenarde	Ind	2	piece	Cloth of Assize	0	0	0	0
		4	lb	Silk, *Worked*	0	53	4	0
		2	lb	Saffron	0	20	0	0
		2	gross	Cutts	0	6	8	0
		1	dozen	Caps	0	10	0	0
		6	gross	Points	0	6	0	0
		1.5	dozen	Hops	0	0	20	0
		2	dozen	Aniseed	0	3	0	0
		24	lb	*Pilus Tinctus*	0	8	0	0
Thomas Purcell	Ind	4	lb	Silk, *Worked*	0	53	4	0
		2	gross	Cutts	0	6	8	0
		1	dozen	Caps	0	10	0	0
		0.5	C	Aniseed	0	6	8	0
		10	gross	Points	0	10	0	0
		2	dozen	Knives	0	3	4	0
Edward Lenarde	Ind	2	lb	Silk, *Worked*	0	26	8	0
		1	dozen	Caps	0	10	0	0
		3	gross	Cutts	0	10	0	0
		0.5	C	Aniseed	0	6	8	0
		4	dozen	Hops	0	4	8	0
		8	gross	Points	0	8	0	0
Peter Harrys	Ind	3	lb	Saffron	0	30	0	0
		6	lb	Silk, *Worked*	4	0	0	0
		2	gross	Cutts	0	6	8	0
		6	gross	Points	0	6	0	0
		2	dozen	Caps	0	20	0	0
		24	lb	*Pilus Tinctus*	0	8	0	0
		1	dozen	Aniseed	0	0	18	0
		2.5	piece	Cloth of Assize	0	0	0	0

Bata Kehocke of Milford Haven, John Whyte master, Entering, *7th August 1526*

Philip Elyott	Ind	10	stone	Wool, Irish	0	26	8	0

Bata George of Tidenham, Thomas Webbe master, Entering, 8th August 1526

Richard Hygons	Ind	3	tun	Wine	0	0	0	0

Bata Mary of Waterford, Patrick FfetzJohn master, Exiting, *8th August 1526*

Patrick *Ffetzjohn*	Ind	6.5	wey	Grain	6	10	0	0
		0.5	wey	Rye	0	8	4	0
		3	stone	Orchil	0	5	0	0

Merchant name	Origin	Qty	Unit	Commodity	£	s.	d.	f.

Navicula Chrystofer of Bristol, John Welshe master, Entering, 10th August 1526

Merchant name	Origin	Qty	Unit	Commodity	£	s.	d.	f.
Robert Avyntre	Ind	105.5	pipe	Fish, Salmon	158	5	0	0
		1	C	Fish, Hake	0	10	0	0
		1	C	Fish, Salted	0	20	0	0
		1.5	dicker	Skins, Salted	0	20	0	0
		2	C	Skins, Sheep	0	20	0	0
		3	animal	Horses	0	40	0	0
		1	piece	Knives	0	6	8	0
Mathew Smyth	Ind	3	pipe	Fish, Salmon	4	10	0	0

Bata, Name Unknown of Chepstow, Lewis ? master, Entering, 10th August 1526

Merchant name	Origin	Qty	Unit	Commodity	£	s.	d.	f.
William *Unknown*	*Unknown*	3	C	Woad, Azores	0	20	0	0

Bata Patryke of Kinsale, Richard Colyn master, Exiting, 12th August 1526

Merchant name	Origin	Qty	Unit	Commodity	£	s.	d.	f.
John Bathe	Ind	6	wey	Grain	6	0	0	0
		4	wey	Malt and Rye	0	66	8	0
		1	gross	Cutts	0	3	4	0
		3	gross	Points	0	3	0	0
		1	dozen	Caps	0	10	0	0
		1	C	Hops	0	10	0	0
		1	lb	Saffron	0	10	0	0
		8	piece	Cloth of Assize, Dozen Strait	0	0	0	0

Navicula Mawdelen of La Rochelle, John Stevan master, Entering, 12th August 1526

Merchant name	Origin	Qty	Unit	Commodity	£	s.	d.	f.
John *Stevan*	Alien	16	M	Fish, Newfoundland Salted	106	13	4	0
		20	hogshead	Whale Meat	0	100	0	0
		4	piece	Porpoise, little	0	6	8	0

Navicula Kateryn of Bristol, John Dal master, Exiting, 12th August 1526

Merchant name	Origin	Qty	Unit	Commodity	£	s.	d.	f.
Roger Dawys	Ind	20	piece	Cloth of Assize	0	0	0	0
John Cappys	Ind	20	piece	Cloth of Assize	0	0	0	0
		7	piece	Cloth of Assize, Strait	0	0	0	0
		30	piece	Welsh *Cloth*, Dozen Strait	6	5	0	0
William Rowley	Ind	8	piece	Cloth of Assize	0	0	0	0
Katherine Roland	Ind	10	piece	Cloth of Assize	0	0	0	0
		6	piece	Welsh *Cloth*	6	0	0	0
John Gurney	Ind	20	piece	Cloth of Assize	0	0	0	0
		hogshead & 1kilderkin		Cheese	0	10	0	0
Nicholas Thorne	Ind	15	C	Skins, Calf (rough)	0	50	0	0
		2	ton	Lead worked	10	0	0	0
John Gurney	Ind	18	piece	Cloth of Assize	0	0	0	0
John Welshe	Ind	32	piece	Cloth of Assize	0	0	0	0
William Ostrige	Ind	3	piece	Cloth of Assize	0	0	0	0
Thomas Blake	Ind	13	piece	Cloth of Assize	0	0	0	0
		3	dozen	Skins, Calf	0	10	0	0
John Shipman	Ind	11	piece	Cloth of Assize	0	0	0	0
William Shipman	Ind	7	piece	Cloth of Assize	0	0	0	0

Merchant name	Origin	Qty	Unit	Commodity	£	s.	d.	f.
Gryffith Joyns &								
Thomas Palmer	Ind	2.5	barrel	Butter	0	25	0	0
Richard Pryn	Ind	16	piece	Cloth of Assize	0	0	0	0

Bata Mary of Milford Haven, John Boullocke master, Entering, *12th August 1526*

John *Boullocke*	Ind	10	C	Fish, Hake	0	100	0	0

Bata Margarett of Milford Haven, Henry Wylle master, Entering, *12th August 1526*

Henry Wylle	Ind	13	C	Fish, Hake	6	10	0	0

Navicula Anne of Bristol, Thomas Harte master, Exiting, 13th August 1526

Thomas *Harte*	Ind	32	piece	Cloth of Assize	0	0	0	0
		1	piece	Welsh *Cloth*	0	20	0	0
Robert Elyott	Ind	110	piece	Welsh *Cloth*, Dozen Strait	22	18	4	0
		5	piece	Cloth of Assize	0	0	0	0
Thomas Roland	Ind	12	piece	Welsh *Cloth*	12	0	0	0
		8	piece	Cloth of Assize	0	0	0	0
John Davy	Ind	10	piece	Welsh *Cloth*, Dozen Strait	2	10	0	0
Nicholas Thorne	Ind	22	piece	Cloth of Assize	0	0	0	0
William Ostryge	Ind	14	piece	Cloth of Assize	0	0	0	0
Robert Chepman	Ind	27	piece	Cloth of Assize	0	0	0	0
Richard Pryn	Ind	8	piece	Cloth of Assize	0	0	0	0
Edward Pryn	Ind	10	piece	Cloth of Assize	0	0	0	0
John Thorne	Ind	8	piece	Cloth of Assize	0	0	0	0
John Coder	Ind	8	piece	Cloth of Assize	0	0	0	0
Philip Gryffyths	Ind	1	barrel	Butter	0	10	0	0

Bata Trynyte of Bristol, Pierce Roche master, Exiting, *13th August 1526*

Thomas Hartt	Ind	1	kilderkin	Aqua vitae	0	13	4	0
		0.5	piece	Welsh *Cloth*	0	10	0	0
		0.5	piece	Cloth of Assize	0	0	0	0

Bata Mary Walsyngam of Tenby, Richard Harrys master, Entering, *13th August 1526*

Cecilia Berforde	Ind	14	ton	Salt	7	0	0	0

Bata John of Milford Haven, Symon Watts master, Entering, *13th August 1526*

Symon Watts	Ind	7	C	Fish, Hake	0	70	0	0

Bata Mary of Tenby, Walter Taylor master, Entering, 15th August 1526

William Spere	Ind	13	ton	Salt	6	10	0	0

Bata Antony of Milford Haven, John Gryndam master, Entering, *15th August 1526*

John Gryndam	Ind	7	C	Fish, Hake	0	70	0	0

Merchant name	Origin	Qty	Unit	Commodity	£	s.	d.	f.

Bata Antony of Chepstow, Lewis Ball master, Entering, *15th August 1526*

Merchant name	Origin	Qty	Unit	Commodity	£	s.	d.	f.
Lewis Ball	Ind	2	C	Woad, Azores	0	13	4	0

Bata Mary of Carmarthen, Richard Davy master, Entering, *15th August 1526*

Merchant name	Origin	Qty	Unit	Commodity	£	s.	d.	f.
David Vaughin	Ind	2.5	balette	Woad	0	25	0	0

Bata Kateryn of Milford Haven, Thomas Wathen master, Entering, *15th August 1526*

Merchant name	Origin	Qty	Unit	Commodity	£	s.	d.	f.
Thomas *Wathen*	Ind	8	C	Fish, Hake	4	0	0	0

Navicula Mawdelen of Bristol, Antony Pygott master, Exiting, 21st August 1526

Merchant name	Origin	Qty	Unit	Commodity	£	s.	d.	f.
Nicholas Gay	Ind	20	piece	Welsh *Cloth*, Dozen Strait	4	3	4	0
		10	dozen	Skins, Calf	0	33	4	0
		13	piece	Cloth of Assize	0	0	0	0
John Cappys	Ind	4	piece	Cloth of Assize	0	0	0	0
Thomas Palmer	Ind	10	piece	Welsh *Cloth*	10	0	0	0
		5	barrel	Butter	0	50	0	0
		5	piece	Cloth of Assize	0	0	0	0
John Shipman	Ind	32	piece	Welsh *Cloth*, Dozen Strait	6	13	4	0
John Thorne	Ind	7	piece	Cloth of Assize	0	0	0	0
		3	dozen	Skins, Calf	0	10	0	0
		1	dicker	Hides, Tanned	0	0	0	0
Edward *Unknown*	Ind	3.5	piece	Cloth of Assize	0	0	0	0

Bata *Nicholas* of Youghal, William Hussey master, Entering, 19th August 1526[14]

Merchant name	Origin	Qty	Unit	Commodity	£	s.	d.	f.
Unknown Unknown	?	6	C	Fish, Hake	0	60	0	0
		5	burden	Fish, Salted	0	20	10	0
		1	pipe	Fish, Salmon	0	30	0	0
		6	piece	Mantles	0	20	0	0
John Pylls	Ind	8	piece	Cloth of Assize	0	0	0	0
Thomas Ashehurste	Ind	6	piece	Cloth of Assize	0	0	0	0
Richard Pryn	Ind	8	piece	Cloth of Assize	0	0	0	0

Navicula Peter of Bristol, Thomas Barett master, Entering, *19th August 1526*

Merchant name	Origin	Qty	Unit	Commodity	£	s.	d.	f.
Robert Chepman	Ind	5.5	tun	Wine	0	0	0	0
Walter Garway	Ind	12	tun	Wine	0	0	0	0
		1	tun	Oil, *Olive*	4	0	0	0
		16.5	C	Alum	8	5	0	0
		1	chest	Sugar	0	40	0	0
		1	ton	Salt	0	10	0	0
		1.5	C	Soap	0	15	0	0
Nicholas Thorne	Ind	27	C	Orchil	18	0	0	0
Richard Draper	Ind	3.5	tun	Wine	0	0	0	0
		1	pipe	Oil, *Olive*	0	40	0	0
Alice Smyth	Ind	1	tun	Wine	0	0	0	0
Thomas Barett	Ind	2.75	tun	Wine	0	0	0	0

14 The manuscript is damaged and part of this entry may be missing.

Merchant name	Origin	Qty	Unit	Commodity	£	s.	d.	f.
Richard Flemyng	Ind	2	tun	Wine	0	0	0	0
David Gloner?	Ind	2	tun	Wine	0	0	0	0
John Colyns	Ind	2	tun	Wine	0	0	0	0
Edward Pryn	Ind	3	C	Aniseed	0	40	0	0

Bata Mary of Carmarthen, Thomas Rogers master, Entering, 23rd August 1526

Thomas Hancoke	Ind	6	ton	Salt	0	60	0	0
David Amaredyth	Ind	8	ton	Salt	4	0	0	0

Bata Margarett of Milford Haven, Henry Willis master, Exiting, 25rd August 1526

Thomas Bowrey	Ind	1	pipe	Wine, Corrupt	0	15	0	0

Bata John of Bristol, John Philips master, Entering, 25th August 1526

Hugh Norys	Ind	26	C	Wool, Flocks	0	10	8	0

Bata Mawdelen of Seville, John de Salamanca master, Exiting, 27th August 1526

Petro Derkenygo	Alien	48.5	wey	Grain	48	10	0	0
John de Salamanca	Alien	1	piece	Cloth of Assize	0	0	0	0
		0.5	piece	Welsh *Cloth*	0	10	0	0
		1.75	C	Tin, Worked	0	52	6	0
William Spratt	Ind	45	dozen	Skins, Calf	7	10	0	0

Bata Nicholas of Youghal, William Hussey master, Exiting, 29th August 1526

William *Hussey*	Ind	3.5	wey	Grain	0	70	0	0
		3.5	wey	Malt	0	58	4	0
		2	lb	Saffron	0	20	0	0
		1	dozen	Skins, Red	0	2	1	0
		2	piece	Cloth of Assize, Dozen Strait	0	0	0	0
William Cumpton	Ind	4	wey	Grain	4	0	0	0
		4.5	wey	Malt	0	75	0	0
		4	lb	Saffron	0	40	0	0
		20	lb	*Pilus Tinctus*	0	6	8	0
		6	gross	Points	0	6	0	0
		2	piece	Cloth of Assize, Dozen Strait	0	0	0	0

Bata Carycke of Milford Haven, William Wade master, Entering, 30th August 1526

William *Wade*	Ind	10.5	C	Fish, Hake	0	105	0	0

Navicula Mary John of Bristol, John Davys master, Exiting, 30th August 1526

John Thorne	Ind	41	piece	Cloth of Assize	0	0	0	0
Thomas Ashehurste	Ind	2	piece	Cloth of Assize	0	0	0	0
John Williams	Ind	4	piece	Welsh *Cloth*	4	0	0	0
		2	barrel	Butter	0	20	0	0

Merchant name	Origin	Qty	Unit	Commodity	£	s.	d.	f.
John Roland	Ind	8	piece	Cloth of Assize	0	0	0	0
		1	piece	Welsh *Cloth*	0	20	0	0
Richard Donell	Ind	1	barrel	Butter	0	10	0	0
George Hall	Ind	64	piece	Cloth of Assize	0	0	0	0
John Davys &								
John Crocke	Ind	7	barrel	Butter	0	70	0	0
William Ostryge	Ind	16	piece	Cloth of Assize	0	0	0	0
John Cappys	Ind	4	piece	Cloth of Assize	0	0	0	0
		1	piece	Welsh *Cloth*	0	20	0	0
John Wynter	Ind	5	piece	Cloth of Assize	0	0	0	0
Robert Avyntre	Ind	29	piece	Cloth of Assize	0	0	0	0
Richard Artewre	Ind	14	piece	Cloth of Assize	0	0	0	0
William Budde	Ind	1	piece	Cloth of Assize	0	0	0	0
		1	piece	Welsh *Cloth*	0	20	0	0
		80	dozen	Welsh *Cloth*, Dozen Strait	16	13	4	0
		3	dozen	Skins, Calf	0	10	0	0
William Appowell	Ind	33	dozen	Skins, Calf	0	110	0	0
		7.5	piece	Cloth of Assize	0	0	0	0
Edmund Pope	Ind	1	piece	Welsh *Cloth*	0	20	0	0
Roger Dawys	Ind	1	piece	Cloth of Assize	0	0	0	0

Bata George of Bristol, John Whyte master, Exiting, *30th August 1526*

Merchant name	Origin	Qty	Unit	Commodity	£	s.	d.	f.
John *Whyte*	Ind	12	wey	Grain	12	0	0	0

Bata Trynyte of Chepstow, William Hayens master, Entering, *30th August 1526*

Merchant name	Origin	Qty	Unit	Commodity	£	s.	d.	f.
William Bocher	Ind	7	C	Woad, Azores	0	46	8	0

Bata Antony of Carmarthen, William Evanns master, Entering, 3rd September 1526

Merchant name	Origin	Qty	Unit	Commodity	£	s.	d.	f.
William *Evanns*	Ind	10	ton	Salt	0	100	0	0

Bata Myghell of Minehead, Robert Mackengely master, Exiting, *3rd September 1526*

Merchant name	Origin	Qty	Unit	Commodity	£	s.	d.	f.
Robert Mackengely	Ind	6	wey	Grain	6	0	0	0
		6	wey	Malt	0	100	0	0
Nicholas Warde	Ind	1	C	Alum	0	13	4	0
		1	C	Aniseed	0	13	4	0
		2	lb	Saffron	0	20	0	0
		1	lb	Silk, *Worked*	0	13	4	0

Bata Clement of Holt, Walter Bowrey master, Entering, *3rd September 1526*

Merchant name	Origin	Qty	Unit	Commodity	£	s.	d.	f.
Thomas Afflete	Ind	4	ton	Salt	0	40	0	0

Bata Elvew of Milford Haven, John Lee master, Exiting, *3rd September 1526*

Merchant name	Origin	Qty	Unit	Commodity	£	s.	d.	f.
Thomas Smyth	Ind	1.5	tun	Wine, Corrupt	0	45	0	0

Merchant name	Origin	Qty	Unit	Commodity	£	s.	d.	f.
Navicula Mathew of Bristol, Thomas Dowdyng master, Exiting, 4th September 1526								
Roger Dawys	Ind	4	dicker	Hides, Tanned	0	0	0	0
		96	dozen	Skins, Calf	16	0	0	0
William Rowley	Ind	14	piece	Cloth of Assize	0	0	0	0
		30	dozen	Skins, Calf	0	100	0	0
John Shipman	Ind	45	piece	Cloth of Assize	0	0	0	0
		50	dozen	Skins, Calf	8	6	8	0
William Shipman	Ind	43	piece	Cloth of Assize	0	0	0	0
		40	dozen	Skins, Calf	6	13	4	0
John Thomas	Ind	8	piece	Cloth of Assize	0	0	0	0
William Cocks	Ind	9	piece	Cloth of Assize	0	0	0	0
		18	dozen	Skins, Calf	0	60	0	0
		12	dicker	Hides, Tanned	0	0	0	0
William Appowell	Ind	15	dicker	Hides, Tanned	0	0	0	0
		70	dozen	Skins, Calf	11	13	4	0
Nicholas Gaye	Ind	27	piece	Cloth of Assize	0	0	0	0
John Roland	Ind	2	piece	Cloth of Assize	0	0	0	0
		2	piece	Welsh Cloth	0	40	0	0
		9	dicker	Hides, Tanned	0	0	0	0
John Wynter	Ind	12	piece	Cloth of Assize	0	0	0	0
		5	dicker	Hides, Tanned	0	0	0	0
John Ware	Ind	43	piece	Cloth of Assize	0	0	0	0
Andrew Palmer	Ind	4	piece	Cloth of Assize	0	0	0	0
Thomas Hicks	Ind	8.5	piece	Cloth of Assize	0	0	0	0
Thomas Whyte	Ind	6.5	piece	Cloth of Assize	0	0	0	0
Richard Evanns	Ind	3	piece	Cloth of Assize, Dozen Strait	0	0	0	0
Edward Pryn &								
Katerine Woysley	Ind	27	piece	Cloth of Assize	0	0	0	0
Bata Antony of Chepstow, Lewis Ball master, Entering, 4th September 1526								
William Glaskyryon	Ind	20	C	Woad, Azores	6	13	4	0
Roland Browyn	Ind	3	C	Woad, Azores	0	20	0	0
Navicula John of Pasajes de San Juan, Thomas de Neviges master, Entering, 5th September 1526								
John & William								
Shipman	Ind	27	ton	Iron	67	10	0	0
Thomas de Nevyges	Alien	3.5	C	Iron	0	9	9	0
Bata Chrystofer of Tintern, John Smyth master, Entering, 6th September 1526								
Roland Browyn &								
Thomas Lasingbe	Ind	91	C	Woad, Azores	30	6	8	0
Bata Gabryell of Bristol, George Reed master, Exiting, 6th September 1526								
Thomas Hickys	Ind	18	dozen	Skins, Calf	0	60	0	0
		13	wey	Beans	10	16	8	0
		12	wey	Grain	12	0	0	0

Merchant name	Origin	Qty	Unit	Commodity	£	s.	d.	f.
		10	piece	Cloth of Assize	0	0	0	0
William Appowell	Ind	3	dicker	Hides, Tanned	0	0	0	0
		2	dozen	Skins, Calf (Vabo?)	0	6	8	0
		2	piece	Cloth of Assize	0	0	0	0
John & William Shipman	Ind	60	dozen	Skins, Calf	10	0	0	0

Bata Mary of Carmarthen, Richard Davys master, Entering, 10th September 1526

Merchant name	Origin	Qty	Unit	Commodity	£	s.	d.	f.
Gryffyth Higons	Ind	4	tun	Wine	0	0	0	0

Navicula Mary Katherine of Bristol, John Gorway master, Exiting, 11th September 1526

Merchant name	Origin	Qty	Unit	Commodity	£	s.	d.	f.
William Nashe & Yate	Ind	9	piece	Cloth of Assize	0	0	0	0
		17	dozen	Skins, Calf	0	56	8	0
		0.5	piece	Welsh *Cloth*	0	10	0	0
John Cappys	Ind	8	piece	Cloth of Assize	0	0	0	0
		8	piece	Welsh *Cloth*	8	0	0	0
Auger de Noga	Alien	7	piece	Cloth of Assize	0	0	0	0
William Appowell	Ind	4.5	piece	Cloth of Assize	0	0	0	0
John Coke	Ind	55	piece	Cloth of Assize	0	0	0	0
		13	dozen	Skins, Calf	0	43	4	0
George Hall	Ind	19	piece	Cloth of Assize	0	0	0	0
William Ostryge	Ind	9	piece	Cloth of Assize	0	0	0	0
Andrew Palmer	Ind	4	piece	Cloth of Assize	0	0	0	0
		8	dozen	Skins, Calf	0	26	8	0
John Savage	Ind	5	dicker	Hides, Tanned	0	0	0	0
Richard *Unknown*	Ind	3.5	C	Fish, Hake	0	35	0	0
Roger *Unknown*	Ind	4	piece	Cloth of Assize	0	0	0	0

Navicula Mawdelen of La Rochelle, John de St Stephan master, Exiting, *11th September 1526*

Merchant name	Origin	Qty	Unit	Commodity	£	s.	d.	f.
John *de St Stephan*	Alien	30	wey	Grain	30	0	0	0

Navicula Rosmond of Barnstaple, William Wolley master, Exiting, 27th September 1526

Merchant name	Origin	Qty	Unit	Commodity	£	s.	d.	f.
John Ayleworthe	Ind	20	piece	Cloth of Assize	0	0	0	0
		20	piece	Welsh *Cloth*	20	0	0	0
		22	dozen	Skins, Calf	0	73	4	0
		1	last	Tallow, Rendered	6	0	0	0
		1	pipe	Cheese	0	20	0	0
		4	kilderkin	Butter	0	20	0	0
		28	piece	Oleron *Cloth*	9	6	8	0
Walter Garway	Ind	13	piece	Welsh *Cloth*	13	0	0	0
		4	piece	Welsh *Cloth*, Dozen Strait	0	16	8	0
		1	barrel	Butter	0	10	0	0
		2	piece	Cloth of Assize, Dozen Strait	0	0	0	0
		2	dicker	Hides, Tanned	0	0	0	0
Thomas Yatte	Ind	24	piece	Cloth of Assize	0	0	0	0
John Coke	Ind	7.33	piece	Cloth of Assize	0	0	0	0
Thomas Riley	Ind	0.5	piece	Cloth of Assize	0	0	0	0

1541/42

TNA E122/21/10 is an annual 'particular' customs account of collectors W.Goodwyn and R.Watkyns covering the period Michaelmas 1541 to Michaelmas 1542. Unlike the earlier accounts, it does not specify the ship type, recording simply the ship name. Neither does it contain the port of destination. It does record the custom and subsidy paid by the merchants, along with the nominal values for goods paying the poundage subsidy.

Merchant name	Origin	Qty	Unit	Commodity	£	s.	d.	f.

The John Baptist, *Port Unknown*, John de Irauso master, Exiting, 8th October 1541

Merchant name	Origin	Qty	Unit	Commodity	£	s.	d.	f.
John *de Irauso*	Alien	1.25	piece	Cloth of Assize	0	0	0	0
		8	piece	Welsh *Cloth*	8	0	0	0
		1	piece	Bristol Frieze *Cloth*	0	13	4	0
William Sprat	Ind	16	piece	Cloth of Assize	0	0	0	0
Alan Hill	Ind	6	piece	Cloth of Assize	0	0	0	0
		1	ton	Lead, worked	5	0	0	0
John Pryn	Ind	9	piece	Cloth of Assize	0	0	0	0
Francis Codryngton	Ind	6.5	ton	Lead, worked	32	10	0	0
		3	piece	Cloth of Assize	0	0	0	0
Robert Pycardye	Alien	0.5	piece	Cloth of Assize	0	0	0	0
John Smyth	Ind	4	piece	Cloth of Assize	0	0	0	0
Thomas Tyson	Ind	5	C	Wax	10	0	0	0
		0.75	ton	Lead, worked	3	15	0	0
		2	piece	Cloth of Assize	0	0	0	0
William Carr & Codryngton	Ind	10	dicker	Hides, Tanned	0	0	0	0

The Mary Gardelope, *Port Unknown*,[1] Peter Gylea master, Exiting, 9th October 1541

Merchant name	Origin	Qty	Unit	Commodity	£	s.	d.	f.
Peter *Gylea*	Alien	3	piece	Cloth of Assize	0	0	0	0

The Thomas Mawdelen of Bristol, Thomas Hardynge master, Exiting, 13th October 1541

Merchant name	Origin	Qty	Unit	Commodity	£	s.	d.	f.
Thomas Apbowen	Ind	5	piece	Cloth of Assize	0	0	0	0
Robert Thurban	Ind	20	piece	Cloth of Assize	0	0	0	0
Edward Pryn	Ind	20	piece	Cloth of Assize	0	0	0	0
		37	piece	Western *Cloth*	7	14	2	0

The Nicholas of Tewkesbury, William Rothe master, Entering, *13th October 1541*

Merchant name	Origin	Qty	Unit	Commodity	£	s.	d.	f.
William Alye	Ind	63	barrel	Fish, Herring White	15	15	0	0
		6	C	Fish, Hake	3	0	0	0
		3	piece	Skins, Salted	0	4	0	0

1 Our Lady of Guadalupe is a Marian Shrine in Extramadura Spain. This is likely to be a Spanish ship.

Merchant name	Origin	Qty	Unit	Commodity	£	s.	d.	f.
The Trynyte of Bristol, Walter Owen master, Entering, 17th October 1541								
Richard More & assoc.	Ind	114	barrel	Fish, Herring White	28	10	0	0
		7	C	Fish, Hake	3	10	0	0
The Sunday of Bristol, Peter Howell master, Entering, 17th October 1541								
William Gellye & assoc.	Ind	103.5	barrel	Fish, Herring White	25	17	6	0
		3	C	Fish, Hake	0	30	0	0
		10	C	Tallow, Rough	0	33	4	0
William Lord	Ind	6.5	barrel	Fish, Herring White	0	32	6	0
		3.25	C	Fish, Hake	0	32	6	0
The Anthonye of Waterford, Henry Gall master, Entering, 17th October 1541								
Lawrence Breuar	Ind	7	C	Check *Cloth*	14	0	0	0
Peter FfitzJohn	Ind	4	C	Check *Cloth*	8	0	0	0
		22	piece	Mantles	3	13	4	0
		1.5	C	Fish, Hake	0	15	0	0
		0.5	C	Skins, Sheep	0	5	0	0
Peter Danyell	Ind	5	C	Check *Cloth*	10	0	0	0
		16	piece	Mantles	2	13	4	0
		1.5	C	Skins, Sheep	0	15	0	0
William Whyte	Ind	4	C	Irish Frieze *Cloth*	8	0	0	0
		8	piece	Mantles	0	26	8	0
		0.25	C	Skins, Sheep	0	2	6	0
John Wyse	Ind	2	C	Check *Cloth*	4	0	0	0
		14	piece	Mantles	2	6	8	0
		1	C	Skins, Sheep	0	10	0	0
Edmund Clery	Ind	3	C	Irish Frieze *Cloth*	6	0	0	0
		6	piece	Mantles	0	20	0	0
		2	stone	Wool, Flocks	0	0	10	0
George Quenmerford	Ind	5	C	Check *Cloth*	10	0	0	0
		24	piece	Mantles	4	0	0	0
		4	stone	Wool, Flocks	0	0	20	0
		20	piece	Skins, Sheep	0	0	20	0
Edmund Grannt	Ind	1	C	Check *Cloth*	2	0	0	0
		12	piece	Mantles	2	0	0	0
		20	piece	Skins, Sheep	0	0	20	0
Thomas Grene & Clery	Ind	13	C	Check *Cloth*	26	0	0	0
		0.5	C	Skins, Sheep	0	5	0	0
Robert Wading & Gall	Ind	2.5	C	Check *Cloth*	5	0	0	0
		4	piece	Mantles	0	13	4	0
		0.25	C	Fish, Hake	0	2	6	0
Nicholas Rothe	Ind	30	yard	Irish Frieze *Cloth*	0	10	0	0
Edmund Seyse	Ind	4.25	C	Skins, Sheep	0	42	6	0
		0.5	C	Skins, Lamb	0	3	4	0
		12	piece	Mantles	2	0	0	0
		5.66	C	Check *Cloth*	11	6	8	0

Merchant name	Origin	Qty	Unit	Commodity	£	s.	d.	f.
		9	stone	Wool, Flocks	0	3	9	0
		20	yard	*Irish* Linen *Cloth*	0	0	20	0
		0.5	C	Fish, Sturgeon	0	5	0	0
Walter Flemyng &								
Butlar	Ind	4.66	C	Check *Cloth*	9	6	8	0
Richard Welshe	Ind	0.5	pipe	Fish, Salmon	0	15	0	0
		1.25	C	Fish, Hake	0	12	6	0
		2	C	Check *Cloth*	4	0	0	0
		0.5	C	Skins, Sheep	0	5	0	0
John Harold	Ind	1	C	Skins, Sheep	0	10	0	0
		1.5	C	Skins, Lamb	0	10	0	0
		9	piece	Skins, Fox	0	0	18	0
		2	piece	Skins, Marten	0	2	0	0
		16	yard	Check *Cloth*	0	5	4	0
Patrick Rychards	Ind	1.83	C	Skins, Sheep	0	18	4	0
		4	dozen	Skins, Lamb	0	3	0	0
		6	piece	Skins, Otter	0	2	6	0
		2	piece	Skins, Marten	0	2	0	0
David Creangh	Ind	1	C	Skins, Sheep	0	10	0	0
		7	dozen	Skins, Lamb	0	4	10	0
		3	piece	Skins, Fox	0	0	6	0
		2	piece	Skins, Otter	0	0	10	0
		70	yard	*Irish* Linen *Cloth*	0	5	10	0
Richard Verdon &								
Butlar	Ind	1.25	C	Skins, Sheep	0	12	6	0
		80	yard	Check *Cloth*	0	26	8	0

The Patryck of New Ross, Robert Senott master, Entering, *17th October 1541*

Merchant name	Origin	Qty	Unit	Commodity	£	s.	d.	f.
William Arthur	Ind	9	C	Check *Cloth*	18	0	0	0
		4	C	Skins, Sheep	0	40	0	0
		4	stone	Wool, Flocks	0	0	20	0
		20	lb	Wax	0	6	8	0
		3	piece	Mantles	0	10	0	0
		20	piece	Skins, Lamb	0	0	15	0
Walter Welshe	Ind	12	C	Check *Cloth*	24	0	0	0
		6	C	Skins, Sheep	3	0	0	0
		4	C	Skins, Kid	0	20	0	0
		0.5	C	Skins, Lamb	0	3	4	0
		4	piece	Mantles	0	13	4	0
David Sholwen	Ind	7	C	Check *Cloth*	14	0	0	0
		2	C	Skins, Sheep	0	20	0	0
		12	stone	Wool, Flocks	0	5	0	0
John Cotterell	Ind	1.5	pipe	Fish, Salmon	2	5	0	0
		3	C	Skins, Sheep	0	30	0	0
		3	C	Check *Cloth*	6	0	0	0
		2	piece	Mantles	0	6	8	0
		4	stone	Wool, Unspecified	0	10	8	0
		1	C	Fish, Hake	0	10	0	0
John Dowle &								
Hygbyd	Ind	3	C	Skins, Sheep	0	30	0	0
		2	dicker	Skins, Deer	0	4	2	0

287

Merchant name	Origin	Qty	Unit	Commodity	£	s.	d.	f.
		1	C	Check *Cloth*	2	0	0	0
		1	M	Skins, Lamb	3	6	8	0

The Anthony of Piltown, John Dymock master, Entering, 19th October 1541

John Burrell	Ind	117.5	barrel	Fish, Herring White	29	7	6	0

The Mary of Gloucester, John Llewwllyng master, Entering, *19th October 1541*

Thomas Cloturboke & assoc.	Ind	148.5	barrel	Fish, Herring White	37	2	6	0

The Mary George of Bristol, Cornell Andrew master, Entering, *19th October 1541*

Cornell Andrew & assoc.	Ind	143	barrel	Fish, Herring White	35	15	0	0
		5	barrel	Beef	0	25	0	0
		1	C	Fish, Hake	0	10	0	0

The Prymrose of Bristol, Thomas Large master, Entering, 24th October 1541

Edward Pryn & assoc.	Ind	19	tun	Woad, Azores	126	13	4	0
Francis Blankeley & assoc.	Alien	37.5	tun	Woad, Azores	250	0	0	0

The Jhesus of Mumbles, John Bragge master, Entering, *24th October 1541*

John *Bragg*	Ind	11	barrel	Fish, Herring White	2	15	0	0
		2	C	Fish, Hake	0	20	0	0
Patrick Bradwey & assoc.	Ind	5.5	last	Fish, Herring White	16	10	0	0
		1	barrel	Beef	0	5	0	0
		1.5	C	Tallow, Rough	0	5	0	0

The Bryde of Waterford, Maurice Welshe master, Entering, 24th October 1541

Thomas Savage	Ind	12	C	Check *Cloth*	24	0	0	0
		3	piece	Mantles	0	10	0	0
		11.5	C	Skins, Sheep	5	15	0	0
Thomas Rothe	Ind	13	C	Check *Cloth*	26	0	0	0
		2	C	Skins, Sheep	0	20	0	0
		1	piece	Mantles	0	3	4	0
Patrick Murfyn	Ind	3.5	C	Check *Cloth*	7	0	0	0
		4	C	Skins, Sheep	0	40	0	0
Richard Cantwell	Ind	3	C	Check *Cloth*	6	0	0	0
		24	piece	Mantles	4	0	0	0
		1	C	Skins, Sheep	0	10	0	0
Nicholas She*a*	Ind	7	C	Check *Cloth*	14	0	0	0
		3	C	Skins, Sheep	0	30	0	0
Walter Flemyng	Ind	6	C	Check *Cloth*	12	0	0	0
		12	C	Skins, Sheep	6	0	0	0
		1	C	Skins, Lamb	0	6	8	0

Merchant name	Origin	Qty	Unit	Commodity	£	s.	d.	f.
Walter Clerye	Ind	7	C	Check *Cloth*	14	0	0	0
		12	stone	Wool, Unspecified	0	32	0	0
		1	C	Skins, Sheep	0	10	0	0
Nicholas Balye	Ind	10	C	Check *Cloth*	20	0	0	0
		3	C	Skins, Sheep	0	30	0	0
		27	piece	Mantles	4	10	0	0
		12	stone	Wool, Flocks	0	5	0	0
Peter Butlar	Ind	3.5	C	Check *Cloth*	7	0	0	0
		2	C	Skins, Sheep	0	20	0	0
		10	piece	Mantles	0	33	4	0
Tibald Nashe	Ind	1.5	C	Check *Cloth*	3	0	0	0
		1.5	C	Skins, Sheep	0	15	0	0
		2	piece	Mantles	0	6	8	0
Peter Galsh	Ind	3.5	C	Skins, Sheep	0	35	0	0
		0.5	C	Fish, Sturgeon	0	5	0	0
		6	piece	Skins, Fox	0	0	12	0
Dennis Fyan &								
Dennis Richards	Ind	5	C	Check *Cloth*	10	0	0	0
		2.5	C	Skins, Sheep	0	25	0	0
Richard Arthur	Ind	1.6	C	Skins, Sheep	0	16	8	0
		0.6	C	Skins, Lamb	0	4	0	0
		12	piece	Skins, Fox	0	2	0	0
		4	piece	Skins, Otter	0	0	20	0
		0.25	C	*Irish* Linen *Cloth*	0	2	6	0
Oliver Harold	Ind	1.71	C	Skins, Sheep	0	17	6	0
		2	C	Skins, Lamb	0	13	4	0
Richard Verdon	Ind	6	C	Irish Linen *Cloth*	3	0	0	0
		24	piece	Skins, Sheep	0	2	0	0
		4	piece	Skins, Fox	0	0	8	0
		2	C	Skins, Lamb	0	13	4	0
		24	piece	Skins, Otter	0	10	0	0
		10	piece	Skins, Marten	0	10	0	0
		1	piece	Mantles	0	3	4	0
		2	piece	Skins, Marten	0	5	10	0

The Stenyons of Milford Haven, John Brother master, Entering, 25th October 1541

Merchant name	Origin	Qty	Unit	Commodity	£	s.	d.	f.
John Brother & Wogan	Ind	11	barrel	Fish, Herring White	2	15	0	0
John Hoper	Ind	29.5	barrel	Fish, Herring White	7	7	6	0
		3	C	Fish, Hake	0	30	0	0
Richard More	Ind	9.5	barrel	Fish, Herring White	2	7	6	0
		1	barrel	Beef	0	5	0	0

The Tabot of Milford Haven, Jenkin King master, Entering, 26th October 1541

Merchant name	Origin	Qty	Unit	Commodity	£	s.	d.	f.
William Chester	Ind	1	dicker	Skins, Deer	0	2	1	0
		7	C	Skins, Sheep	3	10	0	0
		1	C	Skins, Lamb	0	6	8	0
		0.5	pipe	Fish, Salmon	0	15	0	0
		0.5	C	Check *Cloth*	0	20	0	0

Merchant name	Origin	Qty	Unit	Commodity	£	s.	d.	f.

The Margaret of Mumbles, John Robyns master, Entering, 31st October 1541

Merchant name	Origin	Qty	Unit	Commodity	£	s.	d.	f.
John Robyns & John Kelly	Ind	16	barrel	Fish, Herring White	4	0	0	0
		1	C	Fish, Hake	0	10	0	0
Richard More & Appowell	Ind	1	C	Fish, Hake	0	10	0	0
		34	barrel	Fish, Herring White	8	10	0	0
		2	pipe	Fish, Salmon	3	0	0	0
Nicholas Thorn & Edy	Ind	25	barrel	Fish, Herring White	6	5	0	0
		3	barrel	Beef	0	15	0	0
		1	C	Fish, Hake	0	10	0	0
Robert Sternall & assoc.	Ind	34	barrel	Fish, Herring White	8	10	0	0
		1	barrel	Beef	0	5	0	0

The Jamys of Tewkesbury, Nicholas Harrys master, Entering, 2nd November 1541

Merchant name	Origin	Qty	Unit	Commodity	£	s.	d.	f.
Richard Tailor & Richard Kelly	Ind	52	barrel	Fish, Herring White	13	0	0	0

The Migall of Chepstow, John Wills master, Entering, *2nd November 1541*

Merchant name	Origin	Qty	Unit	Commodity	£	s.	d.	f.
Edmund Rogers	Ind	2	tun	Wine	0	0	0	0

The Jhesus of Bristol, Patrick Stephyns master, Entering, *2nd November 1541*

Merchant name	Origin	Qty	Unit	Commodity	£	s.	d.	f.
Robert Newborn & assoc.	Ind	41	barrel	Fish, Herring White	10	5	0	0

The Mary George of Bristol, Maurice Welsh master, Entering, 3rd November 1541

Merchant name	Origin	Qty	Unit	Commodity	£	s.	d.	f.
William Appowell & assoc.	Ind	150	barrel	Fish, Herring White	37	10	4	0
		3	barrel	Fish, Salmon	2	0	0	0
		4	pipe	Fish, Salmon	6	0	0	0
		10	barrel	Beef	2	10	0	0
		3	dicker	Skins, Salted	0	40	0	0
		2	C	Tallow, Rough	0	6	8	0

The Trynyte of Caerleon, Thomas Webb master, Entering, 4th November 1541

Merchant name	Origin	Qty	Unit	Commodity	£	s.	d.	f.
John Northall & assoc.	Ind	7.5	barrel	Fish, Herring White	0	37	6	0
		5	C	Fish, Hake	2	10	0	0
		1	barrel	Beef	0	5	0	0
		1	C	Tallow, Rough	0	3	4	0

The Anthonye of Waterford, Henry Gall master, Exiting, 5th November 1541

Merchant name	Origin	Qty	Unit	Commodity	£	s.	d.	f.
Edmund Seyse	Ind	8	stone	Orchil	0	13	4	0
		6	lb	Saffron	3	0	0	0

Merchant name	Origin	Qty	Unit	Commodity	£	s.	d.	f.
		4	lb	Silk, *Worked*	0	53	4	0
		1	gross	Knives	0	6	8	0
		12	gross	Points	0	12	0	0
		2	gross	Lacquer	0	3	4	0
		0.5	dozen	Aniseed	0	0	8	0
		4	dozen	Soap	0	5	0	0
		2	pair	Stock-Cards	0	2	0	0
Walter Clery	Ind	2	barrel	Honey	0	23	4	0
Lawrence Brewer	Ind	0.166	piece	Cloth of Assize, dyed with grain	0	0	0	0
		2	piece	Cloth of Assize, Dozen Strait	0	0	0	0
		0.5	gross	Knives	0	3	4	0
		0.5	dozen	Caps	0	5	0	0
Peter Danyell	Ind	1	gross	Knives	0	6	8	0
		1	gross	Lacquer	0	0	20	0
		1	gross	Points	0	0	12	0
		2	pair	Stock-Cards	0	2	0	0
		1	dozen	Soap	0	0	15	0
		1.5	piece	Cloth of Assize	0	0	0	0
Edmund Clery	Ind	0.5	piece	Cloth of Assize	0	0	0	0
		1.5	lb	Saffron	0	15	0	0
		2	gross	Points	0	2	0	0
Peter FitzJohn	Ind	1.5	piece	Cloth of Assize	0	0	0	0
		2	gross	Knives	0	13	4	0
		6	gross	Points	0	6	0	0
William Whyte	Ind	2	lb	Silk, *Worked*	0	26	8	0
		1.25	piece	Cloth of Assize	0	0	0	0
John Wyse & assoc.	Ind	15	lb	Seed, Onion	0	20	8	0
		1	lb	Silk, *Worked*	0	13	4	0
		0.5	gross	Knives	0	3	4	0
		2	dozen	Aniseed	0	2	6	0
		0.25	piece	Cloth of Assize	0	0	0	0

The Trynyte of Chepstow, Richard Mower master, Entering, 7th November 1541

Robert Pole	Ind	3.25	tun	Wine	0	0	0	0

The Trynyte of Gloucester, John Nashe master, Entering, *7th November 1541*

Robert Pole	Ind	3.5	last	Fish, Herring White	10	10	0	0
		4	C	Fish, Hake	2	0	0	0
		1.5	C	Spermaceti	7	10	0	0

The Nicholas of Cardiff, John Jeyne master, Entering, 8th November 1541

John Jonys & assoc.	Ind	77	barrel	Fish, Herring White	19	5	0	0
		5	barrel	Beef	1	5	0	0

The Trynyte of Chepstow, Roger Mower master, Entering, *8th November 1541*

William Ballard	Ind	1	tun	Wine	0	0	0	0

Merchant name	Origin	Qty	Unit	Commodity	£	s.	d.	f.

The Katryne of Tenby, William Philips master, Entering, 11th november 1541

Merchant name	Origin	Qty	Unit	Commodity	£	s.	d.	f.
Richard Tanner & assoc.	Ind	111.5	barrel	Fish, Herring White	27	17	6	0
		3	C	Fish, Hake	0	30	0	0

The Mary of Tewkesbury, Thomas Taylor master, Entering, 13th November 1541

Merchant name	Origin	Qty	Unit	Commodity	£	s.	d.	f.
John Hawkyns	Ind	7.75	tun	Wine	0	0	0	0

The Trynyte of Newnham, John Sparke master, Entering, *13th November 1541*

Merchant name	Origin	Qty	Unit	Commodity	£	s.	d.	f.
John Hawkyns	Ind	7	tun	Wine	0	0	0	0

The Trynyte of *Minsterford*,[2] Thomas Hyat master, Entering, *13th November 1541*

Merchant name	Origin	Qty	Unit	Commodity	£	s.	d.	f.
John Hawkyns	Ind	7.75	tun	Wine	0	0	0	0

The Bryde of Waterford, Maurice Welsh master, Exiting, *13th November 1541*

Merchant name	Origin	Qty	Unit	Commodity	£	s.	d.	f.
Nicholas Balye	Ind	1.83	piece	Cloth of Assize	0	0	0	0
		1	gross	Knives	0	6	8	0
		2	gross	Points	0	2	0	0
Walter Clery	Ind	1	pipe	Iron	0	40	0	0
		9	lb	Saffron	4	10	0	0
		2	gross	Knives	0	13	4	0
		4	barrel	Honey	3	6	8	0
		1	C	Hops	0	10	0	0
		12	gross	Points	0	12	0	0
		4	dozen	Knives, in Pairs	0	6	8	0
		3	lb	Silk, *Worked*	0	40	0	0
		2.25	piece	Cloth of Assize	0	0	0	0
Nicholas She*a*	Ind	2.25	piece	Cloth of Assize	0	0	0	0
		2	gross	Knives	0	13	4	0
		12	gross	Points	0	12	0	0
		1	gross	Lacquer	0	0	20	0
		1	barrel	Honey	0	16	8	0
		1	lb	Saffron	0	10	0	0
Thomas Savage	Ind	1.25	piece	Cloth of Assize	0	0	0	0
		9	lb	Saffron	4	10	0	0
		4	lb	Silk, *Worked*	0	53	4	0
		9	dozen	Knives, in Pairs	0	15	0	0
		4	dozen	Girdles	0	2	0	0
		2	lb	Thread	0	0	10	0
		2	dozen	Caps		20	0	0
		2	dozen	Skins, Golden	0	8	4	0
		3	dozen	Girdles	0	3	0	0
		4	dozen	Cumin	0	5	4	0
		1	C	Aniseed	0	13	4	0
		2	dozen	Wood, Brazil	0	6	8	0
		1	lb	Cinnamon	0	2	6	0

2 Possibly Minsterworth in Gloucestershire.

Merchant name	Origin	Qty	Unit	Commodity	£	s.	d.	f.
		3	dozen	Alum	0	3	9	0
		0.5	barrel	Honey	0	8	4	0
		0.5	gross	Knives	0	3	4	0
		6	gross	Points	0	6	0	0
		1	gross	Lacquer	0	0	20	0
		1	lot	Items, miscellaneous	0	6	8	0
Patrick Murphy	Ind	1.25	piece	Cloth of Assize	0	0	0	0
		2	lb	Silk, *Worked*	0	26	8	0
		4	lb	Saffron	2	0	0	0
		1	dozen	Skins, Golden	0	4	2	0
		2	gross	Knives	0	13	4	0
		12	gross	Points	0	12	0	0
		2	dozen	Aniseed	0	2	8	0
		1	dozen	Skins, Red	0	2	1	0
Richard Cantwell	Ind	1.5	piece	Cloth of Assize	0	0	0	0
		2	lb	Silk, *Worked*	0	26	8	0
		2	lb	Saffron	0	20	0	0
		0.5	C	Hops	0	5	0	0
		0.5	C	Aniseed	0	6	8	0
		1	barrel	Honey	0	16	8	0
		3	dozen	Alum	0	4	0	0
		0.5	gross	Knives	0	3	4	0
		6	dozen	Knives, in Pairs	0	10	0	0
		1	dozen	Skins, Red	0	2	1	0
		6	gross	Points	0	6	0	0
		1	dozen	Skins, Golden	0	4	2	0
		1	piece	Cloth of Assize	0	0	0	0
		14	lb	Saffron	7	0	0	0
		7	lb	Silk, *Worked*	4	13	4	0
		2	gross	Cutts	0	6	8	0
		2	gross	Knives	0	13	4	0
		3	dozen	Skins, Golden	0	12	6	0
		3	lb	Mace	0	7	6	0
		12	gross	Points	0	12	0	0
		2	lb	Verdigris	0	0	10	0
		2	lb	Thread	0	0	10	0
		2	dozen	Knives, in Pairs	0	3	4	0
Thomas Rothe	Ind	1	pipe	Iron	0	40	0	0
		4	lb	Silk, *Worked*	0	53	4	0
		16	lb	Saffron	8	0	0	0
		8	dozen	Knives, in Pairs	0	13	4	0
		1	dozen	Skins, Golden	0	4	2	0
		2	dozen	Cards, Playing	0	0	20	0
		3	dozen	Girdles	0	3	4	0
		1	lb	Mace	0	2	6	0
		4	dozen	Girdles	0	0	16	0
		1	gross	Points	0	0	12	0
		0.5	C	Aniseed	0	6	8	0
		0.5	C	Alum	0	6	8	0
		1	lot	Items, miscellaneous	0	6	8	0
		3	dozen	Malt	0	10	0	0
		1.5	piece	Cloth of Assize	0	0	0	0

Merchant name	Origin	Qty	Unit	Commodity	£	s.	d.	f.
Walter Flemyng	Ind	2.75	piece	Cloth of Assize	0	0	0	0
		6	lb	Silk, *Worked*	4	0	0	0
		16	lb	Saffron	8	0	0	0
		4	gross	Knives	0	26	8	0
		0.5	C	Aniseed	0	6	8	0
		1	dozen	Cumin	0	0	16	0
		0.5	dozen	Caps	0	5	0	0
		12	dozen	Girdles	0	4	0	0
		4	dozen	Cards, Playing	0	3	4	0
		12	dozen	Knives, in Pairs	0	20	0	0
		3	gross	Lacquer	0	5	0	0
		8	gross	Points	0	8	0	0
		1.5	C	Aniseed	0	20	0	0
		0.25	C	Hops	0	2	6	0
Tibald Nashe	Ind	3.5	piece	Cloth of Assize	0	0	0	0
		2	gross	Knives	0	13	4	0
		2	lb	Cinnamon	0	5	0	0
		1	lb	Mercury	0	0	5	0
		4	dozen	Cards, Playing	0	3	4	0
		4	lb	*Stygret*	0	0	20	0
		4	lb	Saffron	2	0	0	0
		1	lb	Pepper	0	0	12	0
		0.5	lb	Borax	0	0	20	0
		2	bolt	Thread	0	2	2	0
		8	dozen	Knives, in Pairs	0	13	4	0
		2	dozen	Cumin	0	2	8	0
		0.75	C	Aniseed	0	10	0	0
		8	gross	Points	0	8	0	0
		2	gross	Lacquer	0	3	4	0
		1	ton	Iron	4	0	0	0
		4	dozen	Girdles	0	2	0	0
		4	dozen	Combs	0	0	20	0
		6	lb	Liquorice	0	0	5	0
Peter Galsh	Ind	3	lb	Silk, *Worked*	0	40	0	0
		6	dozen	Knives, in Pairs	0	10	0	0
		1	dozen	Cumin	0	0	16	0
		5	gross	Points	0	5	0	0
		1	gross	Lacquer	0	0	20	0
		3	dozen	Cards, Playing	0	2	6	0
		0.5	dozen	Skins, Golden	0	2	1	0
		4	dozen	Combs	0	0	20	0
		2	lb	Saffron	0	20	0	0
		2	dozen	Girdles	0	3	0	0
		3	lb	Verdigris	0	0	15	0
		4	lb	Liquorice	0	0	5	0
Peter Butlar	Ind	1.25	piece	Cloth of Assize	0	0	0	0
		4	gross	Points	0	4	0	0
		1.5	C	Aniseed	0	20	0	0
		4	dozen	Soap	0	5	0	0
		1	C	Aniseed	0	13	4	0
John Harold	Ind	4.5	piece	Cloth of Assize	0	0	0	0
		15	lb	Saffron	7	10	0	0

Merchant name	Origin	Qty	Unit	Commodity	£	s.	d.	f.
		17	lb	Silk, *Worked*	11	6	8	0
		6	lb	Frankensense	0	0	10	0
		4	dozen	Knives, in Pairs	0	6	8	0
		8	dozen	Skins, Golden	1	13	4	0
		1	dozen	Nightcaps, Unspecified	0	3	4	0
		1	dozen	Caps	0	10	0	0
		2	lb	Senna	0	0	8	0
		1	lb	Cinnamon	0	2	6	0
		5	lb	Thread	0	2	1	0
		12	gross	Points	0	12	0	0
		2	dozen	Penners	0	0	14	0
		6	dozen	Glasses	0	3	0	0
		4	dozen	Cards, Playing	0	3	4	0
		3	lb	Verdigris	0	0	15	0
		4	gross	Knives	0	26	8	0
		2	piece	Cloth of Assize	0	0	0	0
		7	lb	Silk, *Worked*	4	13	4	0
		5	lb	Saffron	2	10	0	0
		12	gross	Points	0	12	0	0
		3	dozen	Girdles	0	4	2	0
		6	lb	Liquorice	0	0	5	0
		8	lb	Seed, Onion	0	3	4	0
		0.5	lb	Ginger	0	0	12	0
		2	dozen	Skins, Golden	0	8	4	0
		1	dozen	Hats	0	3	4	0
		0.5	dozen	Caps	0	5	0	0
		0.5	dozen	Nightcaps, Unspecified	0	2	0	0
		6	dozen	*Percular*	0	0	10	0
		12	dozen	Combs	0	3	4	0
		1	lb	Senna	0	0	10	0
		1	lb	Pepper	0	0	12	0
		2	lb	Verdigris	0	0	10	0
		5	dozen	Glasses	0	0	20	0
		0.5	gross	Lacquer	0	0	10	0
		2	dozen	Knives, in Pairs	0	3	4	0
		4	dozen	Cards, Playing	0	3	4	0
		2	lb	Mercury	0	0	10	0
Oliver Harold	Ind	4	piece	Cloth of Assize	0	0	0	0
		10	lb	Saffron	5	0	0	0
		10	lb	Silk, *Worked*	6	13	4	0
		3	bolt	Thread	0	3	1	2
		4	dozen	Knives, in Pairs	0	6	8	0
		3	dozen	Girdles	0	4	2	0
		3	gross	Knives	0	20	0	0
		3	dozen	Skins, Golden	0	12	6	0
		1	dozen	Skins, Red	0	2	1	0
		2	lb	Mercury	0	0	10	0
		3	lb	Verdigris	0	0	15	0
		3	dozen	Cards, Playing	0	2	6	0
		3	piece	Cloth of Assize	0	0	0	0
		4	lb	Silk, *Worked*	0	53	4	0
		5	dozen	Cards, Playing	0	4	2	0

Merchant name	Origin	Qty	Unit	Commodity	£	s.	d.	f.
		4	lb	Seed, Onion	0	0	20	0
		3	gross	Knives	0	20	0	0
		6	lb	Liquorice	0	0	5	0
		16	gross	Points	0	16	0	0
		7	dozen	Knives, in Pairs	0	11	8	0
		2	dozen	Girdles	0	3	0	0
		1	dozen	Caps	0	10	0	0
		0.5	dozen	Hats	0	4	0	0
		5	dozen	Skins, Golden	1	0	10	0
		1	bolt	Thread	0	0	12	2
		2.5	dozen	Glasses	0	0	10	0
		2	lb	Mercury	0	0	10	0
		2	dozen	Penners	0	0	14	0
		2	lb	Cinnamon	0	5	0	0
Richard Arthur	Ind	1.25	piece	Cloth of Assize	0	0	0	0
		4	lb	Silk, *Worked*	0	53	4	0
		8	gross	Points	0	8	0	0
		1	dozen	Skins, Golden	0	4	2	0
		2	dozen	Cards, Playing	0	0	20	0
		2	dozen	Girdles	0	0	15	0
		0.5	dozen	Caps	0	5	0	0
		6	lb	Liquorice	0	0	5	0
		12	dozen	*Percular*	0	0	15	0
		4	lb	Thread	0	0	20	0
		1	gross	Knives	0	6	8	0
		5	dozen	Knives, in Pairs	0	8	4	0
		2	lb	Verdigris	0	0	10	0
Richard Verdon	Ind	4	piece	Cloth of Assize	0	0	0	0
		16	lb	Saffron	8	0	0	0
		4	lb	Silk, *Worked*	0	53	4	0
		12	gross	Points	0	12	0	0
		8	lb	Verdigris	0	3	4	0
		12	dozen	Glasses	0	3	4	0
		8	dozen	Cards, Playing	0	6	8	0
		5	dozen	Skins, Golden	1	0	10	0
		1	dozen	Caps	0	10	0	0
		0.5	dozen	Hats	0	3	4	0
		5	dozen	Girdles	0	7	6	0
		4	dozen	Knives, in Pairs	0	6	8	0
		0.5	dozen	Crab-Locks	0	0	9	0
		0.5	dozen	Nightcaps, Unspecified	0	2	6	0
		6	lb	Pepper	0	6	0	0
		1	lb	Senna	0	0	5	0
		6	lb	Sulpher	0	0	15	0
		2	lb	Frankensense	0	0	5	0
		6	lb	Mercury	0	2	6	0
		0.5	dozen	Cumin	0	0	8	0
		1	lb	Cloves	0	2	6	0
		1	lb	Nutmeg	0	0	20	0
		1	lb	Ginger	0	0	18	0
		3	dozen	Inkhorns	0	0	20	0

Merchant name	Origin	Qty	Unit	Commodity	£	s.	d.	f.

The Patryck of New Ross, Robert Senot master, Exiting, *13th November 1541*

Merchant name	Origin	Qty	Unit	Commodity	£	s.	d.	f.
John Cotterell	Ind	3	lb	Saffron	0	30	0	0
		1	lb	Silk, *Worked*	0	13	4	0
		1	gross	Knives	0	6	8	0
		0.5	C	Hops	0	5	0	0
William Arthur	Ind	1.25	piece	Cloth of Assize	0	0	0	0
		6	lb	Saffron	3	0	0	0
		6	lb	Silk, *Worked*	4	0	0	0
		3	dozen	Skins, Red	0	6	3	0
		1	dozen	Skins, Golden	0	4	2	0
		7	dozen	Knives, in Pairs	0	11	8	0
		3	gross	Knives	0	20	0	0
		8	gross	Points	0	8	0	0
		0.5	C	Aniseed	0	6	8	0
		3	dozen	Girdles	0	2	0	0
		0.5	dozen	Caps	0	5	0	0
		1	lb	Pepper	0	0	12	0
		0.5	lb	Cinnamon	0	0	15	0
		2	dozen	Cards, Playing	0	0	20	0
		3	dozen	Combs	0	0	12	0
		3	dozen	Glasses	0	0	12	0
John Dowle	Ind	2.5	piece	Cloth of Assize, Dozen Strait	0	0	0	0
		1	lb	Silk, *Worked*	0	13	4	0
		1	lb	Saffron	0	10	0	0
		4	dozen	Knives, in Pairs	0	6	8	0
		2	gross	Points	0	2	0	0
		0.5	C	Hops	0	5	0	0
		0.25	C	Aniseed	0	3	4	0
		0.5	gross	Knives	0	3	4	0
Laurence Arthur	Ind	6	dozen	Knives, in Pairs	0	10	0	0
		6	dozen	Glasses	0	2	0	0
		4	dozen	Knives, in Pairs	0	6	8	0
		1	lb	Thread	0	0	5	0
		1	dozen	Cards, Playing	0	0	10	0
		2	lb	Silk, *Worked*	0	26	8	0
		2	dozen	Skins, Golden	0	8	4	0
		1	lb	Cinnamon	0	2	6	0
		1	dozen	Skins, Red	0	2	1	0
		6	gross	Points	0	6	0	0
		2	gross	Knives	0	13	4	0
David Sholwen	Ind	7	lb	Saffron	3	10	0	0
		5	lb	Silk, *Worked*	3	6	8	0
		2.5	gross	Knives	0	16	8	0
		5	dozen	Knives, in Pairs	0	8	4	0
		1	dozen	Skins, Golden	0	4	2	0
		6	gross	Points	0	6	0	0
		1	gross	Lacquer	0	0	20	0
		3	dozen	Girdles	0	2	0	0
		7	lb	Verdigris	0	2	11	0
		1	dozen	Aniseed	0	0	16	0
		4	dozen	Glasses	0	0	16	0

Merchant name	Origin	Qty	Unit	Commodity	£	s.	d.	f.
		2	dozen	Cards, Playing	0	0	20	0
		0.75	piece	Cloth of Assize	0	0	0	0
Walter Welsh	Ind	2.75	piece	Cloth of Assize	0	0	0	0
		10	lb	Silk, *Worked*	6	13	4	0
		8	lb	Saffron	4	0	0	0
		12	gross	Points	0	12	0	0
		2	gross	Lacquer	0	3	4	0
		8	dozen	Knives, in Pairs	0	13	4	0
		1	dozen	Caps	0	10	0	0
		6	lb	Verdigris	0	2	6	0
		6	lb	Senna	0	4	0	0
		2.5	gross	Knives	0	16	8	0
		2	lb	Cinnamon	0	5	0	0
		1	lb	Pepper	0	0	12	0
		4	dozen	Girdles	0	2	8	0
		2	dozen	Cards, Playing	0	0	20	0
Nicholas Kelly	Ind	1	hogshead	Iron	0	20	0	0

The Margarete of Bristol, John Williams master, Entering, 14th November 1541

Merchant name	Origin	Qty	Unit	Commodity	£	s.	d.	f.
Edward Butlar	Ind	14.5	tun	Wine	0	0	0	0
Thomas Whyte	Ind	7.75	tun	Wine	0	0	0	0
Nicholas Thorn	Ind	4.25	tun	Wine	0	0	0	0
John Smyth	Ind	8.75	tun	Wine	0	0	0	0
Richard Pryn	Ind	3.5	tun	Wine	0	0	0	0
William Rowley	Ind	4	tun	Wine	0	0	0	0
William Jaye	Ind	3.5	tun	Wine	0	0	0	0
Francis Codrington	Ind	4.25	tun	Wine	0	0	0	0
William Ballard	Ind	4.25	tun	Wine	0	0	0	0
Thomas Hycks	Ind	2.5	tun	Wine	0	0	0	0
John Welshe	Ind	1.75	tun	Wine	0	0	0	0
Robert Leyghton	Ind	4.5	tun	Wine	0	0	0	0
Robert Butlar	Ind	4.5	tun	Wine	0	0	0	0
Thomas Tyson	Ind	1.75	tun	Wine	0	0	0	0
William Blake	Ind	1	tun	Wine	0	0	0	0
James Bailey & assoc.	Ind	6.25	tun	Wine	0	0	0	0

The Jamys of Bristol, John Monmothe master, Entering, 15th November 1541

Merchant name	Origin	Qty	Unit	Commodity	£	s.	d.	f.
John Wynter	Ind	8.25	tun	Wine	0	0	0	0

The Bonaventure of Plymouth, John Thomsan master, Entering, *15th November 1541*

Merchant name	Origin	Qty	Unit	Commodity	£	s.	d.	f.
William Shipman	Ind	9.75	tun	Wine	0	0	0	0
John Smyth	Ind	8.75	tun	Wine	0	0	0	0
John Brampton	Ind	8	tun	Wine	0	0	0	0
William Cox	Ind	8.5	tun	Wine	0	0	0	0
Francis Codrington	Ind	9.75	tun	Wine	0	0	0	0
William Rowley	Ind	0.75	tun	Wine	0	0	0	0
John Wynter	Ind	17.5	tun	Wine	0	0	0	0
Mathew Kente	Ind	10.5	tun	Wine	0	0	0	0
		40.5	ballets	Woad	20	0	0	0

Merchant name	Origin	Qty	Unit	Commodity	£	s.	d.	f.
Edward Pryn	Ind	4	tun	Wine	0	0	0	0
Lewis Robyns	Ind	3	tun	Wine	0	0	0	0
George Smygg	Ind	3.5	tun	Wine	0	0	0	0
James Balis	Ind	1	pipe	Wine	0	0	0	0
William Preston & assoc.	Ind	2	tun	Wine	0	0	0	0

The Mawdelen of Errenteria, Martin de Alsega master, Entering, *15th November 1541*

Merchant name	Origin	Qty	Unit	Commodity	£	s.	d.	f.
Thomas Whyte & assoc.	Ind	2	K	Iron	40	5	0	0
Martin de Alsega	Alien	12	ton	Iron	30	0	6	0
		6	dozen	Serches	0	25	0	0

The John of Plymouth, Dennis Puffyn master, Entering, 16th November 1541

Merchant name	Origin	Qty	Unit	Commodity	£	s.	d.	f.
Thomas Tyson & Thomas Wynter	Ind	8.75	tun	Wine	0	0	0	0
		8	C	Rosin	0	10	8	0

The Bonaventure of Penmarch, Ryall Moyle master, Entering, *16th November 1541*

Merchant name	Origin	Qty	Unit	Commodity	£	s.	d.	f.
William Appowell	Ind	115	piece	Fruit	9	11	8	0
		4	tun	Wine	0	0	0	0
James Chester	Ind	12	C	Aniseed	8	0	0	0
		235	piece	Fruit	18	15	0	0
		9.5	tun	Wine	0	0	0	0

The Gabryele of Salcombe, John Tucker master, Entering, *16th November 1541*

Merchant name	Origin	Qty	Unit	Commodity	£	s.	d.	f.
William Ballard	Ind	28.75	tun	Wine	0	0	0	0
Thomas Whyte & Thomas Butlar	Ind	4.5	tun	Wine	0	0	0	0
Robert Leyghton	Ind	3.25	tun	Wine	0	0	0	0
Robert Newborn & assoc.	Ind	3.25	tun	Wine	0	0	0	0
William Rowley	Ind	3.5	tun	Wine	0	0	0	0
William Blake & William Kent	Ind	9.5	tun	Wine	0	0	0	0
William Cox	Ind	12.75	tun	Wine	0	0	0	0
Thomas Tyson	Ind	4.5	tun	Wine	0	0	0	0
Thomas Tyson	Ind	20	C	Rosin	0	26	8	0
John Channcelar & assoc.	Ind	7.5	tun	Wine	0	0	0	0

The Mary Forten of Gloucester, John Darby master, Entering, *16th November 1541*

Merchant name	Origin	Qty	Unit	Commodity	£	s.	d.	f.
Thomas Whyte	Ind	17	tun	Wine	0	0	0	0
John Smyth	Ind	8	tun	Wine	0	0	0	0
Robert Pole	Ind	21	tun	Wine	0	0	0	0
		10	ton	Iron	25	0	0	0
Lawrence Vyne & Jaye	Ind	3.5	tun	Wine	0	0	0	0

Merchant name	Origin	Qty	Unit	Commodity	£	s.	d.	f.
Thomas Tyson	Ind	1	tun	Wine	0	0	0	0
William Chester	Ind	1	pipe	Wine	0	0	0	0
John Darby	Ind	1	tun	Wine, Corrupt	0	30	0	0
William Rowley	Ind	3	tun	Wine	0	0	0	0
William Carr &								
William Codryntone	Ind	4.25	tun	Wine	0	0	0	0

The Bonaventure of Dublin, Richard Alen master, Entering, 22nd November 1541

Merchant name	Origin	Qty	Unit	Commodity	£	s.	d.	f.
Benedict Jaye	Ind	6.5	last	Fish, Herring White	19	10	0	0
		12	C	Tallow, Rough	2	0	0	0
		13	piece	Skins, Salted	0	17	4	0
William Evers	Ind	1	last	Fish, Herring White	3	0	0	0
		5	C	Fish, Hake	2	10	0	0

The Trynyte of Dartmouth, James Coke master, Entering, 22nd November 1541

Merchant name	Origin	Qty	Unit	Commodity	£	s.	d.	f.
John Brampton	Ind	6.5	tun	Wine	0	0	0	0
John Gurneye	Ind	29	tun	Wine	0	0	0	0
William Cox	Ind	4.75	tun	Wine	0	0	0	0
		20	C	Rosin	0	26	8	0
Lawrence Vyne &								
assoc.	Ind	5	tun	Wine	0	0	0	0

The Chrystopher of Dartmouth, John Harrys master, Entering, 22nd November 1541

Merchant name	Origin	Qty	Unit	Commodity	£	s.	d.	f.
John Brampton	Ind	8	tun	Wine	0	0	0	0
John Gurneye	Ind	42	tun	Wine	0	0	0	0
William Cox	Ind	7.5	tun	Wine	0	0	0	0
Lawrence Vyne &								
Rowley	Ind	2.5	tun	Wine	0	0	0	0
John Harrys	Ind	8	C	Rosin	0	10	8	0

The Migell of Bristol, William Mathew master, Entering, 22nd November 1541

Merchant name	Origin	Qty	Unit	Commodity	£	s.	d.	f.
William Spratt	Ind	5.25	tun	Wine	0	0	0	0
		8.5	ballets	Woad	4	0	0	0
		6	C	Rosin	0	8	0	0
Richard Williams	Ind	3.5	tun	Wine	0	0	0	0
		6.5	ballets	Woad	3	0	0	0
		10	C	Rosin	0	13	4	0
Alan Hyll	Ind	7	tun	Wine	0	0	0	0
		8.5	ballets	Woad	4	0	0	0
		10	C	Rosin	0	13	4	0

The Sundaye of Bristol, Thomas Walter master, Entering, 22nd November 1541

Merchant name	Origin	Qty	Unit	Commodity	£	s.	d.	f.
Thomas Walter &								
assoc.	Ind	28.5	barrel	Fish, Herring White	7	2	6	0

Merchant name	Origin	Qty	Unit	Commodity	£	s.	d.	f.

The Trinite of Bristol, Thomas Webb master, Entering, *22nd November 1541*

Merchant name	Origin	Qty	Unit	Commodity	£	s.	d.	f.
William Shipman	Ind	2	tun	Wine	0	0	0	0
		1	pipe	Wine, Corrupt	0	15	0	0
John Smyth	Ind	11.5	tun	Wine	0	0	0	0
		1.5	tun	Wine, Corrupt	0	45	0	0
Nicholas Thorn	Ind	5.25	tun	Wine	0	0	0	0
William Spratt	Ind	4	tun	Wine	0	0	0	0
		1	pipe	Wine, Corrupt	0	15	0	0
Edward Pryn	Ind	7	tun	Wine	0	0	0	0
		1	tun	Wine, Corrupt	0	30	0	0
Francis Codryngton	Ind	4.25	tun	Wine	0	0	0	0
		1	tun	Wine, Corrupt	0	30	0	0
William Ballard	Ind	4	tun	Wine	0	0	0	0
		1	pipe	Wine, Corrupt	0	15	0	0
William Cox &								
William Butlar	Ind	3.25	tun	Wine	0	0	0	0
Alan Hill &								
Alan Tyson	Ind	7.25	tun	Wine	0	0	0	0
		1	pipe	Wine, Corrupt	0	15	0	0
John Pryn &								
John Smyth	Ind	4	tun	Wine	0	0	0	0
Thomas Smyth &								
Thomas Thorburn	Ind	6.75	tun	Wine	0	0	0	0
		2	tun	Wine, Corrupt	3	0	0	0
James Balie	Ind	1.75	tun	Wine	0	0	0	0
Robert Gyttens	Ind	3.5	tun	Wine	0	0	0	0
John Welsh	Ind	4	tun	Wine	0	0	0	0
Johanna Carpynt*yr*	Ind	2.5	tun	Wine	0	0	0	0
Robert Leyhton	Ind	2.25	tun	Wine	0	0	0	0
Giles White	Ind	7	tun	Wine	0	0	0	0
Mathew Kent &								
Mathew Pygot	Ind	1	tun	Wine	0	0	0	0

The George of London, Thomas Candy master, Entering, *22nd November 1541*

Merchant name	Origin	Qty	Unit	Commodity	£	s.	d.	f.
Edward Pryn	Ind	6	tun	Wine	0	0	0	0
Mathew Kent	Ind	14.5	tun	Wine	0	0	0	0
Thomas Shipman	Ind	25	tun	Wine	0	0	0	0
Arthur Smyth &								
Shipman	Ind	4	tun	Wine	0	0	0	0
Francis Codryngtom								
& Hycks	Ind	3	tun	Wine	0	0	0	0

The Mary Bulleine of Barnstaple, Robert Whitstone master, Entering, *24th November 1541*

Merchant name	Origin	Qty	Unit	Commodity	£	s.	d.	f.
Edward Pryn	Ind	4.25	tun	Wine	0	0	0	0
William Ballard	Ind	5.25	tun	Wine	0	0	0	0
Thomas Tyson	Ind	13.25	tun	Wine	0	0	0	0
		9	C	Aniseed	6	0	0	0
Arthur Smyth	Ind	11	tun	Wine	0	0	0	0
Thomas Smyth	Ind	14.5	tun	Wine	0	0	0	0

Merchant name	Origin	Qty	Unit	Commodity	£	s.	d.	f.
		15	C	Aniseed	10	0	0	0
Robert Butlar	Ind	3.5	tun	Wine	0	0	0	0
William Blake	Ind	3.75	tun	Wine	0	0	0	0
Nicholas Tyson								
& Pryn	Ind	8	tun	Wine	0	0	0	0
Johanna Carpyntyr								
& Yonge	Ind	6.375	tun	Wine	0	0	0	0
		1	pipe	Wine, Corrupt	0	15	0	0
		1	ton	Fruit	0	40	0	0
		7.5	C	Soap	3	15	0	0
William Chester								
& Draper	Ind	4.25	tun	Wine	0	0	0	0
		1	tun	Wine, Corrupt	0	30	0	0
Giles White	Ind	4.25	tun	Wine	0	0	0	0

The Migell of Chepstow, William Barnes master, Entering, 26th November 1541

Merchant name	Origin	Qty	Unit	Commodity	£	s.	d.	f.
Richard Glover	Ind	2.5	C	Fish, Hake	0	25	0	0

The Trynyte of Caerleon, Sebastian Melyor master, Entering, 28th November 1541

Merchant name	Origin	Qty	Unit	Commodity	£	s.	d.	f.
Nicholas Thorn	Ind	8.75	tun	Wine	0	0	0	0
Thomas White	Ind	8.5	tun	Wine	0	0	0	0
William Shipman	Ind	3	tun	Wine	0	0	0	0
John Smyth	Ind	8.5	tun	Wine	0	0	0	0
Richard Pryn	Ind	5.25	tun	Wine	0	0	0	0
		15	C	Orchil	10	0	0	0
		17.5	C	Soap	8	15	0	0
William Yonge	Ind	3.5	tun	Wine	0	0	0	0
Henry White	Ind	8	tun	Wine	0	0	0	0
Francis Codryngton	Ind	6.75	tun	Wine	0	0	0	0
William Ballard	Ind	13	tun	Wine	0	0	0	0
Edward Butlar	Ind	8	tun	Wine	0	0	0	0
Robert Butlar	Ind	3.75	tun	Wine	0	0	0	0
Robert Leyhton	Ind	8	tun	Wine	0	0	0	0
Edward Pryn	Ind	5	tun	Wine	0	0	0	0
		3	tun	Wine, Corrupt	4	10	0	0
William Cox	Ind	3	tun	Wine	0	0	0	0
William Jonys &								
Blake & assoc.	Ind	5.25	tun	Wine	0	0	0	0
		2	tun	Wine, Corrupt	3	0	0	0
		12	C	Orchil	8	0	0	0
Watkyns, Jonys								
& Newborn	Ind	4.5	tun	Wine	0	0	0	0
Thomas Parker &								
assoc.	Ind	2	tun	Oil, Olive	8	0	0	0
		5	C	Soap	2	10	0	0
		0.25	tun	Fruit	0	10	0	0
		3.5	tun	Wine	0	0	0	0

Merchant name	Origin	Qty	Unit	Commodity	£	s.	d.	f.

The Prymrose of Bristol, Thomas Lack master, Exiting, *28th November 1541*

Thomas White &								
Tyson	Ind	18	piece	Cloth of Assize	0	0	0	0
John Pryn	Ind	3	piece	Welsh *Cloth*	3	0	0	0
		3	piece	Welsh *Cloth*, Dozen Strait	0	12	6	0
		2	piece	Cloth of Assize, Dozen Strait	0	0	0	0
Robert Sexe & Pryn	Ind	8.5	piece	Cloth of Assize	0	0	0	0
John Smyth &								
Codryngton	Ind	34	piece	Cloth of Assize	0	0	0	0

The Mary Anne of Tewkesbury, Robert Tawney master, Entering, 27th November 1541

Robert *Tawney*	Ind	14	barrel	Fish, Herring White	3	10	0	0

The Mary George of Bristol, Maurice Welsh master, Exiting, 1st December 1541

William Benet	Ind	1.25	tun	Wine, Corrupt	0	37	6	0

The Martyne of Milford Haven, Richard Brown master, Entering, *1st December 1541*

Richard *Brown*	Ind	21.5	barrel	Fish, Herring White	5	7	6	0

The Anthony of Milford Haven, John Steward master, Entering, 2nd December 1541

William Lye & assoc.	Ind	31	barrel	Fish, Herring White	7	15	0	0

The Migell of Bridgwater, Thomas Ryte master, Entering, *2nd December 1541*

William Appowell								
& Yonge	Ind	30	ton	Fruit	60	0	0	0
John Cutt & Capps	Ind	16.25	ton	Fruit	32	10	0	0
		1	hogshead	Oil, *Olive*	0	20	0	0
		50	dozen	Cork	4	3	4	0
William Rowley &								
assoc.	Ind	10.75	ton	Fruit	21	10	0	0
		0.5	C	Marmalade	0	6	8	0
		0.5	C	Conserves	0	10	0	0

The Jamys of Milford Haven, Richard Knetholl master, 3rd December 1541

William Lye & assoc.	Ind	67	barrel	Fish, Herring White	16	15	0	0

The Bonaventure of Penmarch, Ryall Moyle master, Exiting, *3rd December 1541*

Ryall Moyle	Alien	1.5	last	Coal	0	20	0	0

The Mawdelen of Errenteria, Martin de Alsega, master, Exiting, 3rd December 1541

Martin de Alsega	Alien	15	piece	Cloth of Assize	0	0	0	0
		9	piece	Welsh *Cloth*	9	0	0	0

Merchant name	Origin	Qty	Unit	Commodity	£	s.	d.	f.

The Sunday of Bristol, John Joynes master, Exiting, *3rd December 1541*

| Nicholas Rudsdale & Adams | Ind | 4 | wey | Beans | 3 | 6 | 8 | 0 |

The Mary Gyles of Tewkesbury, Robert Butlar master, Entering, 5th December 1541

| Robert *Butlar* | Ind | 2 | last | Fish, Herring White | 12 | 0 | 0 | 0 |

The Clement of Wexford, William Cormycke master, Entering, 5th December 1541

Thomas Forlong	Ind	5.5	barrel	Fish, Herring White	0	27	6	0
		9	C	Fish, Hake	4	10	0	0
		11	piece	Mantles	0	36	8	0
		1.5	C	Skins, Sheep	0	15	0	0
		1	C	Skins, Lamb	0	6	8	0
		2	dicker	Skins, Deer	0	4	2	0
		20	yard	Check *Cloth*	0	6	8	0
		1	dozen	Wood	0	2	0	0

The Mary Bonaventure of Bristol, Richard White master, Entering, *5th December 1541*

William Chester	Ind	3.25	tun	Wine	0	0	0	0
Nicholas Thorn	Ind	10	tun	Wine	0	0	0	0
		1.25	C	Kermes	10	0	0	0
John Smyth	Ind	7	tun	Wine	0	0	0	0
William Appowell	Ind	4.25	tun	Wine	0	0	0	0
Edward Butlar	Ind	7.5	tun	Wine	0	0	0	0
		8.75	C	Soap	4	7	6	0
William Ballard & Hycks	Ind	7.75	tun	Wine	0	0	0	0
William Carr & Codryngton	Ind	4.25	tun	Wine	0	0	0	0
John Welshe	Ind	10.25	tun	Wine	0	0	0	0
Robert Butlar & Smyth	Ind	6.5	tun	Wine	0	0	0	0
William Cox & Carpynt*yr*	Ind	3.5	tun	Wine	0	0	0	0
John Cutt & White	Ind	3.5	tun	Wine	0	0	0	0
Richard White	Ind	8.5	tun	Wine	0	0	0	0
John Sachefeld & Spilman	Ind	2.75	tun	Wine	0	0	0	0

The Jamys of Mundaka, John de Moreta master, Entering, *5th December 1541*

William Appowell & Yonge	Ind	496	piece	Fruit	41	6	8	0
		1	barrel	Marmalade	0	33	4	0
		4	tun	Wine	0	0	0	0
William Yonge	Ind	20.5	ton	Fruit	41	0	0	0
		4.25	tun	Wine	0	0	0	0

Merchant name	Origin	Qty	Unit	Commodity	£	s.	d.	f.

The Mary Conception of Bristol, John Bousher master, Entering, 6th December 1541

Merchant name	Origin	Qty	Unit	Commodity	£	s.	d.	f.
Thomas White & Chester	Ind	8	tun	Wine	0	0	0	0
Robert Eliot & Thorn	Ind	9.5	tun	Wine	0	0	0	0
John Brampton & Appowell	Ind	5.25	tun	Wine	0	0	0	0
Richard Pryn & Pole	Ind	7.75	tun	Wine	0	0	0	0
William Yonge & Rowley	Ind	9.5	tun	Wine	0	0	0	0
		0.5	ton	Fruit	0	20	0	0
William Jay & Leyghton	Ind	8.75	tun	Wine	0	0	0	0
		17	quart	Fruit	0	48	6	0
William Blake & Gyttens	Ind	0.75	ton	Fruit	0	30	0	0
		4.5	tun	Wine	0	0	0	0
William Jonys & Chancellar	Ind	5.25	tun	Wine	0	0	0	0
		2.5	C	Marmalade	0	33	4	0
William Spilman & Cutt	Ind	4	tun	Wine	0	0	0	0
John Boshar & Harrys	Ind	2.75	tun	Wine	0	0	0	0
		2.5	C	Marmalade	0	33	4	0
Richard Watkins & Broke	Ind	3	tun	Wine	0	0	0	0
		1	ton	Fruit	2	0	0	0

The Anne of London, John Gall master, Entering, 6th December 1541

Merchant name	Origin	Qty	Unit	Commodity	£	s.	d.	f.
William Shipman & Smyth	Ind	8.5	tun	Wine	0	0	0	0
		22.5	ballets	Woad	11	0	0	0
Richard Pryn & Rowley	Ind	6.25	tun	Wine	0	0	0	0
Francis Codryngton & Pryn	Ind	8.5	tun	Wine	0	0	0	0
John Gorney	Ind	3.5	tun	Wine	0	0	0	0
		79.5	ballets	Woad, Toulouse	39	10	0	0
Thomas Hycks	Ind	1	hogshead	Wine	0	0	0	0
		2.5	ballets	Woad, Toulouse	0	20	0	0
Lewis Robyns	Ind	8.75	tun	Wine	0	0	0	0
Robert Gyttens	Ind	5	tun	Wine	0	0	0	0
Robert Leyghton & Newborn	Ind	9.5	tun	Wine	0	0	0	0
John Welsh & Smyth	Ind	4	tun	Wine	0	0	0	0
Francis Wosley & Baly	Ind	2	tun	Wine	0	0	0	0
		4.5	ballets	Woad, Toulouse	0	40	0	0
Johanna Carpyntyr	Ind	2.5	tun	Wine	0	0	0	0

Merchant name	Origin	Qty	Unit	Commodity	£	s.	d.	f.
Mathew Kent	Ind	56.5	ballets	Woad, Toulouse	28	0	0	0
Lawrence Vyne	Ind	1	tun	Wine	0	0	0	0
		2.5	ballets	Woad, Toulouse	0	20	0	0
Alan Hylle	Ind	18.5	ballets	Woad, Toulouse	9	0	0	0
John Gall and assoc	Ind	4.75	tun	Wine	0	0	0	0
William Chester								
& Tyson	Ind	8.5	ballets	Woad, Toulouse	4	0	0	0
John Chancellar	Ind	1	pipe	Wine	0	0	0	0

The Mary Bryde of Bristol, John Hylsey master, Entering, 7th December 1541

Merchant name	Origin	Qty	Unit	Commodity	£	s.	d.	f.
Thomas White &								
Eliot	Ind	20	tun	Wine	0	0	0	0
Nicholas Thorn								
& Rowley	Ind	13.5	tun	Wine	0	0	0	0
William Jay	Ind	13.5	tun	Wine	0	0	0	0
		4	tun	Oil, *Olive*	16	0	0	0
		10	C	Soap	5	0	0	0
Robert Pole &								
Leyghton	Ind	12	tun	Wine	0	0	0	0
John Welsh	Ind	5	tun	Wine	0	0	0	0
		1.25	C	Aniseed	0	16	8	0
		2.5	C	Marmalade	0	33	4	0
Edward Pryn &								
Jonys	Ind	8.25	tun	Wine	0	0	0	0
John Chancellar								
& Harvest	Ind	7.5	tun	Wine	0	0	0	0
		12.5	C	Soap	6	5	0	0
William Blake &								
assoc.	Ind	8.125	tun	Wine	0	0	0	0
		1.25	C	Soap	0	12	6	0

The Migell of Chepstow, Roger Mower master, Entering, *7th December 1541*

Merchant name	Origin	Qty	Unit	Commodity	£	s.	d.	f.
Edmund Rogers	Ind	1.25	tun	Wine	0	0	0	0

The Trynyte of Bristol, Richard Baldwyn master, Entering, *7th December 1541*

Merchant name	Origin	Qty	Unit	Commodity	£	s.	d.	f.
William Appowell	Ind	13.75	tun	Wine	0	0	0	0
		1	tun	Wine, Corrupt	0	30	0	0
		4.5	C	Aniseed	3	0	0	0
		1	ton	Fruit	2	0	0	0
Thomas Whaley								
& Gyttens	Ind	13.25	tun	Wine	0	0	0	0
		1	pipe	Wine, Corrupt	0	15	0	0
John Capps	Ind	9.5	tun	Wine	0	0	0	0
		1.125	tun	Oil, *Olive*	4	10	0	0
		2	ton	Fruit	4	0	0	0

The Mary of Penmarch, John Kerbeleke master, Entering, *7th December 1541*

Merchant name	Origin	Qty	Unit	Commodity	£	s.	d.	f.
Francis Fowler	Ind	19.5	tun	Wine	0	0	0	0

Merchant name	Origin	Qty	Unit	Commodity	£	s.	d.	f.
George Snigg	Ind	12.5	tun	Wine	0	0	0	0
Francis Codryngton & Carpynter	Ind	6	tun	Wine	0	0	0	0
John Chancellar & Smyth	Ind	5.5	tun	Wine	0	0	0	0

The Savyour of Milford Haven, John Brother master, Entering, 12th December 1541

John *Brother*	Ind	1	last	Fish, Herring White	3	0	0	0

The Mary Forten of Gloucester, Lawrence Nunny master, Exiting, *12th December 1541*

Robert Pole	Ind	60	quart	Wheat	10	0	0	0

The Harry of Bristol, Anthony Pigot master, Entering, *12th December 1541*

Merchant name	Origin	Qty	Unit	Commodity	£	s.	d.	f.
William Shipman & Hycks	Ind	11	tun	Wine	0	0	0	0
		1	tun	Oil, *Olive*	4	0	0	0
		10	C	Soap	5	0	0	0
Francis Codryngton	Ind	1	pipe	Wine	0	0	0	0
		3	tun	Oil, *Olive*	12	0	0	0
		14	C	Aniseed	9	6	8	0
Nicholas Thorn & Smyth	Ind	19.5	tun	Wine	0	0	0	0
William Rowley & Shipman	Ind	7.25	tun	Wine	0	0	0	0
		1	tun	Oil, *Olive*	4	0	0	0
		13.75	C	Soap	6	17	6	0
Edward Pryn	Ind	5.75	tun	Wine	0	0	0	0
John Pryn	Ind	5	tun	Wine	0	0	0	0
		5	C	Soap	2	10	0	0
Alan Hyll & Sexe	Ind	7.75	tun	Wine	0	0	0	0
		2.5	C	Soap	0	25	0	0
Richard Pryn & Spratt	Ind	6.75	tun	Wine	0	0	0	0
William Ballard & White	Ind	12.75	tun	Wine	0	0	0	0
James Balye	Ind	1.75	tun	Oil, *Olive*	7	0	0	0
		5	C	Soap	2	10	0	0
		1.75	tun	Wine	0	0	0	0
Agnes Gaye	Ind	2.5	tun	Wine	0	0	0	0
		3.75	C	Soap	0	37	6	0
		2.5	C	Marmalade	0	33	4	0
George Snigg & Harrys	Ind	13.75	C	Soap	6	17	6	0
Walter Roberts	Ind	1	tun	Wine	0	0	0	0
John Pill & assoc.	Ind	27.5	C	Soap	13	15	0	0
Edward Butlar & assoc.	Ind	10.75	tun	Wine	0	0	0	0
		10	C	Soap	5	0	0	0
Robert Leyghton	Ind	2.5	C	Marmalade	0	33	4	0

Merchant name	Origin	Qty	Unit	Commodity	£	s.	d.	f.
William Champyn & Pygot	Ind	2.75	tun	Wine	0	0	0	0

The Mary Bonaventure of Dublin, Richard Alan master, Exiting, 13th December 1541

Merchant name	Origin	Qty	Unit	Commodity	£	s.	d.	f.
William Evers	Ind	1.5	last	Coal	0	20	0	0
		15	quart	Malt	0	41	8	0

The Anne of Gloucester, William Arthur master, Entering, *13th December 1541*

Merchant name	Origin	Qty	Unit	Commodity	£	s.	d.	f.
William *Arthur*	Ind	2	barrel	Fish, Herring White	0	10	0	0

The George of Barnstaple, John Lake master, Entering, 17th December 1541

Merchant name	Origin	Qty	Unit	Commodity	£	s.	d.	f.
Mark Averell	Ind	5.5	tun	Wine	0	0	0	0
		1	ton	Fruit	2	0	0	0
		1.25	C	Soap	0	12	6	0
John Monyng	Ind	16	tun	Wine	0	0	0	0
		1.25	C	Soap	0	12	6	0
		40	lb	Ginger	3	0	0	0
John Lake	Ind	17.75	tun	Wine	0	0	0	0
		12	lb	Ginger	0	18	0	0
		1.25	C	Soap	0	12	6	0
		18	lb	Pepper	0	18	0	0
William Lytylston	Ind	5	tun	Wine	0	0	0	0
		0.25	ton	Fruit	0	10	0	0
		1.25	C	Soap	0	12	6	0
Thomas Hunt	Ind	4.5	tun	Wine	0	0	0	0
John Mark	Ind	2.25	tun	Wine	0	0	0	0
William Appowell	Ind	12.5	tun	Wine	0	0	0	0
		1	tun	Wine, Corrupt	0	30	0	0
		6	C	Aniseed	4	0	0	0
John Satchfeld	Ind	0.75	tun	Wine	0	0	0	0
Edward Butlar	Ind	10	C	Soap	5	0	0	0
John Brampton	Ind	5.75	tun	Wine	0	0	0	0
John Capps	Ind	2.25	tun	Wine	0	0	0	0

The Mary of Pouldavid,[3] Lawrence Parnes master, Entering, 18th December 1541

Merchant name	Origin	Qty	Unit	Commodity	£	s.	d.	f.
Hugh Typton	Ind	14.5	tun	Wine	0	0	0	0

The Savyour of Northam, John Aung*er* master, Entering, *18th December 1541*

Merchant name	Origin	Qty	Unit	Commodity	£	s.	d.	f.
John Smyth	Ind	90	piece	Fruit	7	10	0	0
		1.25	tun	Wine	0	0	0	0
Francis Codrynngton	Ind	14.583	ton	Fruit	29	3	4	0
		5	tun	Wine	0	0	0	0
Thomas Shipman	Ind	90	piece	Fruit	7	10	0	0
John Aung*er*	Ind	5	ton	Fruit	10	0	0	0
		1	tun	Wine	0	0	0	0

3 Municipality of Douarnenez, France.

Merchant name	Origin	Qty	Unit	Commodity	£	s.	d.	f.

The Clement of Wexford, William Cornyck master, Exiting, 23rd December 1541

Merchant name	Origin	Qty	Unit	Commodity	£	s.	d.	f.
Thomas Forlong	Ind	3	lb	Silk, *Worked*	0	40	0	0
		1	stone	Aniseed	0	0	20	0
		0.5	gross	Knives	0	3	4	0
		3	weight	Hemp	0	7	6	0
		1	stone	Hops	0	0	15	0

The Jamys of Mundaka, John de Moreta master, Exiting, *23rd December 1541*

Merchant name	Origin	Qty	Unit	Commodity	£	s.	d.	f.
John *de Moreta*	Alien	2	piece	Cloth of Assize	0	0	0	0

The Trynyte of Bristol, Walter Owen master, Entering, 2nd January 1542

Merchant name	Origin	Qty	Unit	Commodity	£	s.	d.	f.
Richard More & Yate	Ind	4.25	C	Fish, Hake	2	2	6	0

The Mary George of Bristol, Maurice Welsh master, Exiting, *2nd January 1542*

Merchant name	Origin	Qty	Unit	Commodity	£	s.	d.	f.
William Appowell	Ind	0.5	piece	Cloth of Assize	0	0	0	0
		6	lb	Saffron	3	0	0	0
		1	C	Aniseed	0	13	4	0
		1	dozen	Cumin	0	0	16	0
		1	dozen	Liquorice	0	0	10	0
		1	C	Madder	0	6	8	0
		1	C	Alum	0	13	4	0
		2	C	Hops	0	20	0	0
		0.25	C	Wood, Brazil	0	8	4	0
		1	dozen	Skins, Golden	0	4	2	0
		2	gross	Knives	0	13	4	0
		3	dozen	Cards, Playing	0	2	6	0
William Benet & Welsh	Ind	4	piece	Cloth of Assize	0	0	0	0
		4	lb	Saffron	2	0	0	0
		3	lb	Silk, *Worked*	0	40	0	0

The Anthonye of Tintern, Walter Putley master, Entering, 7th January 1542

Merchant name	Origin	Qty	Unit	Commodity	£	s.	d.	f.
Leonard Coleman	Ind	2	last	Fish, Herring White	6	0	0	0
		3	C	Fish, Hake	0	30	0	0

The Mary of Penmarch, John Carbeleke master, Exiting, 11th January 1542

Merchant name	Origin	Qty	Unit	Commodity	£	s.	d.	f.
John *Carbeleke*	Alien	4	piece	Cloth of Assize	0	0	0	0

The Bonaventure of Penmarch, Ryall Moyle master, Exiting, *11th January 1542*

Merchant name	Origin	Qty	Unit	Commodity	£	s.	d.	f.
James Chest*er*	Ind	60	piece	Manchester *Cotton Cloth*	30	0	0	0
		4	piece	Welsh *Cloth*	4	0	0	0
		9	piece	Cloth of Assize	0	0	0	0
		4	dicker	Hides, Tanned	0	0	0	0

Merchant name	Origin	Qty	Unit	Commodity	£	s.	d.	f.
The Nicholas of Barnstaple, David Borow master, Entering, *11th January 1542*								
John Byrryman	Ind	0.25	tun	Vinegar	0	10	0	0
The Trynyte of Bristol, Thomas Webb master, Exiting, 13th January 1542								
John Smith	Ind	10	ton	Lead, worked	50	0	0	0
		33	piece	Cloth of Assize	0	0	0	0
		18	dicker	Hides, Tanned	0	0	0	0
Edward Pryn	Ind	4	piece	Cloth of Assize	0	0	0	0
		2	ton	Lead, worked	10	0	0	0
Robert Gyttens	Ind	14.833	piece	Cloth of Assize	0	0	0	0
William Spratt &								
Robyns	Ind	15	dicker	Hides, Tanned	0	0	0	0
Johanna Carpynt*er*	Ind	2.5	ton	Lead, worked	12	10	0	0
Nicholas Thorn								
& Sprat	Ind	19	piece	Cloth of Assize	0	0	0	0
The Sunday of Youghal, Thomas Davey master, Entering, 18th January 1542								
Thomas *Davey*	Ind	11	C	Fish, Hake	5	10	0	0
		0.5	C	Skins, Sheep	0	5	0	0
		0.5	burden	Fish, Salted	0	2	1	0
		30	yard	Check *Cloth*	0	10	0	0
		2	piece	Mantles	0	6	8	0
Richard Rownan	Ind	1	C	Check *Cloth*	2	0	0	0
		6	piece	Mantles	0	20	0	0
		1	C	Skins, Sheep	0	10	0	0
William Folon	Ind	12	C	Fish, Hake	6	0	0	0
		1	burden	Fish, Salted	0	4	2	0
		2	piece	Mantles	0	6	8	0
		2	piece	Seals	0	13	4	0
The Margaret of Newport, James Rothe master, Entering, *18th January 1542*								
William Sorth	Ind	90	yard	Check *Cloth*	0	30	0	0
		4.75	C	Fish, Hake	2	7	6	0
The Migell of Chepstow, Richard Mores master, Entering, 19th January 1542								
Leonard Coleman	Ind	2	C	Fish, Hake	0	20	0	0
The Julyan of Bristol, John Croke master, Entering, *19th January 1542*								
William Ches*ter*	Ind	1	pipe	Wine, Corrupt	0	15	0	0
William Jaye	Ind	8.5	tun	Wine	0	0	0	0
Richard Pryn &								
Yonge	Ind	5	tun	Wine	0	0	0	0
John Welsh & Tyson	Ind	4.5	tun	Wine	0	0	0	0
Richard Morse &								
assoc.	Ind	2.25	tun	Wine	0	0	0	0
John Croke & assoc.	Ind	15	tun	Wine	0	0	0	0

Merchant name	Origin	Qty	Unit	Commodity	£	s.	d.	f.
The Migell of Bristol, Nicholas Beffrest master, 20th January 1542								
William Sprat &								
Williams	Ind	15	dicker	Hides, Tanned	0	0	0	0
Robert Gyttens	Ind	1.66	piece	Cloth of Assize	0	0	0	0
The Anthonye of Waterford, Henry Gall master, Entering, 25th January 1542								
Henry Gall	Ind	1	C	Irish Frieze Cloth	2	0	0	0
		5	piece	Mantles	0	16	8	0
		1	C	Fish, Hake	0	10	0	0
Robert Tewe	Ind	3.5	C	Irish Frieze Cloth	7	0	0	0
		4	C	Skins, Sheep	0	40	0	0
		0.5	pipe	Fish, Salmon	0	15	0	0
		1	barrel	Fish, Herring White	0	5	0	0
		0.5	C	Fish, Hake	0	5	0	0
		6	piece	Mantles	0	20	0	0
James Fagan	Ind	4	C	Irish Frieze Cloth	8	0	0	0
		2	pipe	Fish, Salmon	3	0	0	0
		4	barrel	Fish, Herring White	0	20	0	0
		5	C	Fish, Hake	2	10	0	0
		1	burden	Fish, Salted	0	4	2	0
		3	piece	Mantles	0	10	0	0
		0.5	C	Skins, Sheep	0	5	0	0
William Grant	Ind	7.33	C	Irish Frieze Cloth	14	13	4	0
		4.5	C	Skins, Sheep	0	45	0	0
		1	butt	Fish, Salmon	0	15	0	0
James Morgan	Ind	2	barrel	Fish, Eels	0	26	8	0
		10	C	Irish Frieze Cloth	20	0	0	0
		6	piece	Mantles	0	20	0	0
		2	C	Skins, Sheep	0	20	0	0
		1	pipe	Fish, Salmon	0	30	0	0
Edmund Clery	Ind	4.33	C	Irish Frieze Cloth	8	13	4	0
		2.5	C	Skins, Sheep	0	25	0	0
Dennis Prendgret	Ind	1.16	C	Irish Frieze Cloth	2	6	8	0
		3	C	Skins, Sheep	0	30	0	0
Robert Maydell	Ind	6	barrel	Fish, Herring White	0	30	0	0
		2	C	Fish, Hake	0	20	0	0
		1	C	Irish Frieze Cloth	2	0	0	0
		6	piece	Mantles	0	20	0	0
		0.5	C	Skins, Sheep	0	5	0	0
William Madan	Ind	1.5	C	Irish Frieze Cloth	3	0	0	0
		4	piece	Mantles	0	13	4	0
		6	C	Skins, Sheep	3	0	0	0
		2	C	Fish, Hake	0	20	0	0
		2.5	barrel	Fish, Herring White	0	12	6	0
Peter Fitzjohn	Ind	4	C	Irish Frieze Cloth	8	0	0	0
		1	C	Skins, Sheep	0	10	0	0
William Doryn	Ind	0.5	C	Irish Frieze Cloth	0	20	0	0
		2	piece	Mantles	0	6	8	0
		1	virkin	Fish, Salmon	0	7	6	0
Edmund Grant	Ind	2	C	Irish Frieze Cloth	4	0	0	0

Merchant name	Origin	Qty	Unit	Commodity	£	s.	d.	f.
		2	piece	Mantles	0	6	8	0
		0.5	C	Skins, Sheep	0	5	0	0
John Wyse	Ind	5	C	Fish, Hake	2	10	0	0
		2	C	Skins, Sheep	0	20	0	0
		0.5	C	Irish Frieze *Cloth*	0	20	0	0
		1	barrel	Fish, Herring White	0	5	0	0

The Sunday of Bristol, John Jene master, Entering, 26th January 1542

William Gelly &								
Adams	Ind	6	barrel	Fish, Herring White	0	30	0	0
		4	C	Fish, Hake	2	0	0	0
		4	piece	Mantles	0	13	4	0
		1.16	C	Skins, Sheep	0	13	4	0

The George of Cork, Philip Barry master, Entering, 27th January 1542

William Sherchell	Ind	12	pipe	Fish, Salmon	18	0	0	0
		15	C	Fish, Hake	7	10	0	0
		2	barrel	Fish, Herring White	0	10	0	0
		2	barrel	Fish, Eels	0	26	8	0
		5	C	Wood	5	0	0	0
		11	C	Tree-Nails (Dowels)	0	3	4	0
		15	stone	Wool, Flocks	0	6	3	0
		3	piece	Mantles	0	10	0	0
		1	piece	Seals	0	6	8	0
Peter Creangh	Ind	3	pipe	Fish, Salmon	4	10	0	0
		6	C	Fish, Hake	3	0	0	0
		1.83	C	Skins, Sheep	0	18	4	0
		2	dicker	Skins, Deer	0	4	2	0
		24	stone	Wool, Flocks	0	10	0	0
		1	piece	Mantles	0	3	4	0
William Chest*er*								
& Verdon	Ind	8	pipe	Fish, Salmon	12	0	0	0
		1	kilderkin	Fish, Eels	0	6	8	0
		1	dicker	Skins, Deer	0	2	1	0
		8	C	Fish, Hake	4	0	0	0
		0.5	barrel	Fish, Herring White	0	2	6	0

The Sunday of Waterford, William Wodlock master, Entering, *27th January 1542*

Richard Conwey	Ind	3	C	Check *Cloth*	6	0	0	0
		4	C	Skins, Sheep	0	40	0	0
		4	barrel	Fish, Herring White	0	20	0	0
		10	piece	Mantles	0	33	4	0
		3	piece	Skins, Marten	0	3	0	0
Edmund Seyse	Ind	3	C	Check *Cloth*	6	0	0	0
		11	piece	Mantles	0	36	4	0
		6	stone	Wool, Flocks	0	2	6	0
		5	C	Skins, Sheep	0	40	0	0
		4	piece	Skins, Fox	0	0	8	0
Andrew Lyncoln	Ind	3	C	Check *Cloth*	6	0	0	0

Merchant name	Origin	Qty	Unit	Commodity	£	s.	d.	f.
		1	C	Fish, Hake	0	10	0	0
		3	piece	Mantles	0	10	0	0
		1	C	Skins, Sheep	0	10	0	0
Nicholas Balie	Ind	3	C	Skins, Sheep	0	30	0	0
		2	C	Check *Cloth*	4	0	0	0
		1	butt	Fish, Salmon	0	15	0	0
		0.5	C	Fish, Hake	0	5	0	0
		2	piece	Mantles	0	6	8	0
Patrick Strong	Ind	1.5	C	Check *Cloth*	3	0	0	0
		2	C	Skins, Sheep	0	20	0	0
		2	C	Fish, Hake	0	20	0	0
		2	barrel	Fish, Herring White	0	10	0	0
		1	kilderkin	Fish, Eels	0	6	8	0
		2	piece	Mantles	0	6	8	0
		6	piece	Skins, Deer	0	0	15	0
Peter Welsh	Ind	3	C	Check *Cloth*	6	0	0	0
		6	piece	Mantles	0	20	0	0
		2	C	Fish, Hake	0	20	0	0
		1	barrel	Fish, Herring White	0	5	0	0
Peter Grant	Ind	1.5	C	Check *Cloth*	3	0	0	0
		3	piece	Mantles	0	10	0	0
		1	virkin	Fish, Salmon	0	7	6	0
		0.5	C	Fish, Hake	0	5	0	0
Richard Guewe	Ind	1	C	Fish, Hake	0	10	0	0
		1	barrel	Fish, Herring White	0	5	0	0
		6	piece	Mantles	0	20	0	0
		1	C	Check *Cloth*	2	0	0	0
William Wodlock & assoc.	Ind	4	piece	Mantles	0	13	4	0
		0.5	barrel	Fish, Herring White	0	2	6	0
		6.5	C	Check *Cloth*	13	0	0	0

The George Butlar of Waterford, Edmund Medoll master, Entering, *27th January 1542*

Merchant name	Origin	Qty	Unit	Commodity	£	s.	d.	f.
Paul Butlar	Ind	0.75	pipe	Fish, Salmon	0	22	6	0
		3	barrel	Fish, Herring White	0	15	0	0
		3	C	Check *Cloth*	6	0	0	0
		1	C	Skins, Sheep	0	10	0	0
		2	piece	Mantles	0	6	8	0
		1.5	C	Fish, Hake	0	15	0	0
James Kyrk	Ind	6	barrel	Fish, Eels	4	0	0	0
		2.5	C	Check *Cloth*	5	0	0	0
		4.5	C	Skins, Sheep	0	45	0	0
John Rothe	Ind	11	C	Check *Cloth*	22	0	0	0
		10	C	Skins, Sheep	5	0	0	0
		2.5	stone	Wool, Flocks	0	0	12	2
James Savage	Ind	4	C	Skins, Sheep	0	40	0	0
		2	C	Check *Cloth*	4	0	0	0
Andrew Welsh & Nele	Ind	8	C	Check *Cloth*	16	0	0	0
		16	C	Skins, Sheep	8	0	0	0
		6	piece	Mantles	0	20	0	0

Merchant name	Origin	Qty	Unit	Commodity	£	s.	d.	f.
Edmund Medoll	Ind	1	butt	Fish, Salmon	0	15	0	0
		1	barrel	Fish, Herring White	0	5	0	0
		30	yard	Check *Cloth*	0	10	0	0
Patrick Knock	Ind	1	C	Fish, Hake	0	10	0	0
		1	barrel	Fish, Herring White	0	5	0	0
		0.5	C	Check *Cloth*	0	20	0	0
		4	piece	Mantles	0	13	4	0
John Hee & assoc.	Ind	2.5	C	Check *Cloth*	5	0	0	0
		10	piece	Mantles	0	33	4	0
		0.75	C	Fish, Hake	0	7	6	0

The Mary of Waterford, John Doryn master, Entering, 27th January 1542

Merchant name	Origin	Qty	Unit	Commodity	£	s.	d.	f.
John *Doryn*	Ind	6	barrel	Fish, Herring White	0	30	0	0
		1	C	Fish, Hake	0	10	0	0
		1	burden	Fish, Salted	0	4	2	0
Richard Kerry & Candy	Ind	10	C	Fish, Hake	5	0	0	0
		3	barrel	Fish, Herring White	0	15	0	0
		1	burden	Fish, Salted	0	4	2	0
Maurice Ley & Futtey	Ind	8	C	Fish, Hake	4	0	0	0
		1	barrel	Fish, Herring White	0	5	0	0
		0.5	burden	Fish, Salted	0	2	1	0
Maurice Greffyn & Williams	Ind	5	C	Fish, Hake	2	10	0	0
		1	barrel	Fish, Herring White	0	5	0	0
		0.4	burden	Fish, Salted	0	0	20	0

The Mary of Milford Haven, Patrick Holock master, Entering, 30th January 1542

Merchant name	Origin	Qty	Unit	Commodity	£	s.	d.	f.
Patrick *Holock*	Ind	4	C	Fish, Hake	2	0	0	0
		1	barrel	Fish, Herring White	0	5	0	0

The Sunday of Wexford, Thomas Coley master, Entering, 30th January 1542

Merchant name	Origin	Qty	Unit	Commodity	£	s.	d.	f.
Thomas *Coley*	Ind	1	last	Fish, Herring White	3	0	0	0
		20	mease	Fish, Herring Red	5	0	0	0
		6	C	Fish, Hake	3	0	0	0
		1	C	Skins, Sheep	0	10	0	0
Nicholas White	Ind	15	barrel	Fish, Herring White	3	15	0	0
		12	mease	Fish, Herring Red	3	0	0	0
		7	C	Fish, Hake	3	10	0	0
		2	piece	Mantles	0	6	8	0

The Brandon of Wexford, John Shennan master, Entering, 30th January 1542

Merchant name	Origin	Qty	Unit	Commodity	£	s.	d.	f.
John *Shennan*	Ind	17.5	mease	Fish, Herring Red	4	7	6	0
		19	barrel	Fish, Herring White	4	15	0	0
		16	C	Fish, Hake	8	0	0	0
		1	butt	Fish, Salmon	0	15	0	0
		6	C	Skins, Sheep	3	0	0	0

Merchant name	Origin	Qty	Unit	Commodity	£	s.	d.	f.
		5	piece	Mantles	0	16	8	0

The George of Waterford, Nicholas Colman master, Entering, *30th January 1542*

Merchant name	Origin	Qty	Unit	Commodity	£	s.	d.	f.
Nicholas *Colman*	Ind	1	C	Check *Cloth*	2	0	0	0
		1	barrel	Fish, Herring White	0	5	0	0
		1	C	Fish, Hake	0	10	0	0
Walter Shirlock	Ind	2	C	Check *Cloth*	4	0	0	0
		2	pipe	Fish, Salmon	3	0	0	0
		2	C	Fish, Hake	0	20	0	0
		2	C	Skins, Sheep	0	20	0	0
Richard Murfyn & Wadyng	Ind	4	C	Check *Cloth*	8	0	0	0
		6	piece	Mantles	0	20	0	0
Richard Wadyng	Ind	2.5	C	Check *Cloth*	5	0	0	0
		2.5	C	Skins, Sheep	0	25	0	0
James Snenerford	Ind	3.5	C	Check *Cloth*	7	0	0	0
		2	C	Skins, Sheep	0	20	0	0
		0.5	C	Fish, Hake	0	5	0	0
		7	stone	Wool, Flocks	0	2	11	0
Thomas Grene/ Row	Ind	7	C	Check *Cloth*	14	0	0	0
		2	barrel	Fish, Herring White	0	10	0	0
		1	virkin	Fish, Salmon	0	7	6	0
		1	C	Skins, Sheep	0	10	0	0
		1	C	Fish, Hake	0	10	0	0
George Snenerford	Ind	4	C	Check *Cloth*	8	0	0	0
		6	piece	Mantles	0	20	0	0
		5	C	Fish, Hake	2	10	0	0
		2	barrel	Fish, Herring White	0	10	0	0
		1.25	pipe	Fish, Salmon	0	37	6	0
		5	C	Skins, Sheep	2	10	0	0
		6	stone	Wool, Flocks	0	2	6	0
Nicholas Kett	Ind	3.5	C	Check *Cloth*	7	0	0	0
		1.5	C	Skins, Sheep	0	15	0	0
		6	piece	Mantles	0	20	0	0
		2	barrel	Fish, Herring White	0	10	0	0
John Snede & Brewer	Ind	2	C	Check *Cloth*	4	0	0	0
		1	C	Fish, Hake	0	10	0	0
		3	piece	Mantles	0	10	0	0
		1	C	Skins, Sheep	0	10	0	0
Maurice Power & Christopher	Ind	1	C	Check *Cloth*	2	0	0	0
		1	C	Fish, Hake	0	10	0	0
		2	piece	Mantles	0	6	8	0
Richard Fitzjohn & Shee	Ind	3	C	Check *Cloth*	6	0	0	0
		1	butt	Fish, Salmon	0	15	0	0
		2	barrel	Fish, Herring White	0	10	0	0
		5	piece	Mantles	0	16	8	0
		1	C	Fish, Hake	0	10	0	0

Merchant name	Origin	Qty	Unit	Commodity	£	s.	d.	f.
The Migell of Milford Haven, John Hyks master, Entering, *30th January 1542*								
John *Hyks*	Ind	3	barrel	Fish, Herring White	0	15	0	0
		1.5	C	Fish, Hake	0	15	0	0
The Migell of Waterford, Robert Ffytzjohn master, Entering, 31st January 1542								
John Hee	Ind	12	piece	Mantles	2	0	0	0
		2.5	C	Fish, Hake	0	25	0	0
		1.5	C	Check *Cloth*	3	0	0	0
		0.5	C	Skins, Sheep	0	5	0	0
James Tarrel & Nash	Ind	3.41	C	Check *Cloth*	6	16	8	0
		0.5	C	Skins, Sheep	0	5	0	0
		0.5	C	Fish, Hake	0	5	0	0
		2	piece	Mantles	0	6	8	0
David Welsh	Ind	9	C	Fish, Hake	4	10	0	0
		8	C	Skins, Sheep	4	0	0	0
		1.5	C	Check *Cloth*	3	0	0	0
		4	barrel	Fish, Herring White	0	20	0	0
		1	barrel	Fish, Eels	0	13	4	0
		1	virkin	Fish, Salmon	0	7	6	0
		0.5	burden	Fish, Salted	0	2	1	0
Nicholas She*a* & White	Ind	22	C	Fish, Hake	11	0	0	0
		13	C	Fish, Hake	6	10	0	0
Robert Butlar	Ind	6.5	C	Check *Cloth*	13	0	0	0
		7	C	Skins, Sheep	3	10	0	0
		8	piece	Mantles	0	26	8	0
		6	piece	Skins, Marten	0	6	0	0
Thomas Madan	Ind	5	C	Check *Cloth*	10	0	0	0
		8	piece	Mantles	0	26	8	0
		2	C	Fish, Hake	0	20	0	0
Robert Lu*m*bart	Ind	2.5	C	Check *Cloth*	5	0	0	0
		10	piece	Mantles	0	33	4	0
		3.66	C	Skins, Sheep	0	36	8	0
		0.5	C	Fish, Hake	0	5	0	0
John Hart	Ind	8	C	Skins, Sheep	4	0	0	0
		1.5	C	Check *Cloth*	3	0	0	0
		12	piece	Mantles	2	0	0	0
		1.5	C	Fish, Sturgeon	0	15	0	0
William Bretten	Ind	2	C	Skins, Sheep	0	20	0	0
		6	piece	Mantles	0	20	0	0
		70	yard	Check *Cloth*	0	23	4	0
The George of Youghal, William Donell master, Entering, 1st February 1542								
Edmund Rowley	Ind	14	C	Fish, Hake	7	0	0	0
		1	C	Skins, Sheep	0	10	0	0
		1	burden	Fish, Salted	0	4	2	0
Richard Hodney	Ind	5	C	Fish, Hake	2	10	0	0
		2	C	Skins, Sheep	0	20	0	0
		0.36	burden	Fish, Salted	0	0	18	0

Merchant name	Origin	Qty	Unit	Commodity	£	s.	d.	f.
Philip Rownan & assoc.	Ind	19	C	Fish, Hake	9	10	0	0
		2.25	pipe	Fish, Salmon	3	7	6	0
		1	C	Skins, Sheep	0	10	0	0
		1.5	dicker	Skins, Deer	0	3	1	2

The Mary Bryde of Bristol, John Hylsey master, Exiting, 3rd February 1542

Merchant name	Origin	Qty	Unit	Commodity	£	s.	d.	f.
William Jay & Codryngton	Ind	28	piece	Cloth of Assize	0	0	0	0
Thomas Shipman & Smyth	Ind	19	piece	Cloth of Assize	0	0	0	0
Thomas Tyson & Gyttens	Ind	12	piece	Cloth of Assize	0	0	0	0

The Mary of Milford Haven, William Hill master, Entering, 4th February 1542

Merchant name	Origin	Qty	Unit	Commodity	£	s.	d.	f.
William Hill	Ind	8	barrel	Fish, Herring White	2	0	0	0
Richard Saunders	Ind	1	tun	Wine	0	0	0	0

The Pawle of Newlyn, Alan Tailor master, Entering, 4th February 1542

Merchant name	Origin	Qty	Unit	Commodity	£	s.	d.	f.
Alan Taylor	Ind	20	stone	Wool, Spanish	5	6	8	0

The Jhesus of New Ross, Richard Doffe master, Entering, 4th February 1542

Merchant name	Origin	Qty	Unit	Commodity	£	s.	d.	f.
Richard Benet & Harrys	Ind	17	C	Check Cloth	34	0	0	0
		7	barrel	Fish, Herring White	0	35	0	0
		6	C	Skins, Sheep	3	0	0	0
William Benet	Ind	7	C	Check Cloth	14	0	0	0
		2	C	Skins, Sheep	0	20	0	0
		5	barrel	Fish, Herring White	0	25	0	0
		3	stone	Wool, Irish	0	8	0	0
Richard Nevell	Ind	3	C	Check Cloth	6	0	0	0
		1	piece	Mantles	0	3	4	0
		3	stone	Wool, Flocks	0	0	15	0
		1	stone	Wool, Irish	0	2	8	0
Tibald Blake & Francis	Ind	5.5	C	Check Cloth	11	0	0	0
		16	C	Skins, Sheep	8	0	0	0
Peter Asteken	Ind	7	C	Skins, Sheep	3	10	0	0
		6	C	Skins, Lamb	0	40	0	0
		1	stone	Wool, Irish	0	2	8	0
David Langhan	Ind	7	C	Fish, Hake	3	10	0	0
		1	burden	Fish, Salted	0	4	2	0
		2	stone	Wool, Flocks	0	0	10	0

The Mary of Cork, Philip Harrow master, Entering, 6th February 1542

Merchant name	Origin	Qty	Unit	Commodity	£	s.	d.	f.
Walter Harrow	Ind	15	C	Fish, Hake	7	10	0	0

Merchant name	Origin	Qty	Unit	Commodity	£	s.	d.	f.
The Francis of New Ross, John Brown master, Entering, *6th February 1542*								
Peter Harrys	Ind	15	C	Skins, Sheep	7	10	0	0
		1.33	C	Check *Cloth*	2	13	4	0
		3	piece	Mantles	0	10	0	0
		1.5	dicker	Skins, Deer	0	3	1	2
William Rothe	Ind	4	C	Check *Cloth*	8	0	0	0
		20	C	Skins, Sheep	10	0	0	0
		4	piece	Skins, Fox	0	0	8	0
		2	stone	Wool, Flocks	0	0	10	0
		0.5	C	Skins, Kid	0	2	6	0
		3	piece	Skins, Deer	0	0	10	0
John Cogan	Ind	5	C	Check *Cloth*	10	0	0	0
		7.5	C	Skins, Sheep	3	15	0	0
Thomas Comyn	Ind	11	C	Skins, Sheep	5	10	0	0
		1	C	Check *Cloth*	2	0	0	0
		4	stone	Wool, Flocks	0	0	20	0
		2	piece	Mantles	0	6	8	0
		2	barrel	Fish, Herring White	0	10	0	0
Patrick Kelly	Ind	3	C	Check *Cloth*	6	0	0	0
		10	stone	Wool, Flocks	0	4	2	0
Thomas Dowle	Ind	3	C	Skins, Sheep	0	30	0	0
		2.5	pipe	Fish, Salmon	3	15	0	0
		30	yard	Check *Cloth*	0	10	0	0
William Francis	Ind	0.75	pipe	Fish, Salmon	0	22	6	0
		11.5	stone	Wool, Unspecified	0	30	8	0
		4	C	Skins, Sheep	0	40	0	0
Nicholas Nevell & Kelly	Ind	2	C	Skins, Sheep	0	20	0	0
		4	stone	Wool, Unspecified	0	10	8	0
		0.5	C	Check *Cloth*	0	20	0	0

The Martyn of Milford Haven, Roger Brown master, Entering, *6th February 1542*

Merchant name	Origin	Qty	Unit	Commodity	£	s.	d.	f.
Roger *Brown*	Ind	3	barrel	Fish, Herring White	0	15	0	0

The George of Cork, Philip Barreye master, Exiting, 8th February 1542

Merchant name	Origin	Qty	Unit	Commodity	£	s.	d.	f.
Thomas Cloturboke	Ind	60	quart	Beans/Malt	8	6	8	0
		6	lb	Silk, *Worked*	4	0	0	0
		3	gross	Knives	0	20	0	0
		4	dozen	Skins, Golden	0	16	8	0
		2	dozen	Cards, Playing	0	0	20	0
		0.5	dozen	Caps	0	5	0	0
		4	gross	Lacquer	0	6	8	0
		9	gross	Points	0	9	0	0
		2	dozen	Wool-Cards	0	8	0	0
		2	weight	Hemp	0	4	0	0
		1	C	Iron	0	4	0	0
		1.5	piece	Cloth of Assize	0	0	0	0
Peter Creangh	Ind	4	piece	Cloth of Assize	0	0	0	0
		7	lb	Silk, *Worked*	4	13	4	0

Merchant name	Origin	Qty	Unit	Commodity	£	s.	d.	f.
		1	lb	Silk, *Worked*	0	13	4	0
		5	gross	Knives	0	33	4	0
		4	gross	Cutts	0	13	4	0
		1.5	dozen	Caps	0	15	0	0
		17	gross	Points	0	17	0	0
		1	lb	Cloves	0	2	6	0
		3	dozen	Cards, Playing	0	2	6	0
		2	lb	Thread	0	0	10	0
		1	dozen	Skins, Golden	0	4	2	0
		1.5	dozen	Knives, in Pairs	0	2	6	0
		1	C	Hops	0	10	0	0
Henry Verdon	Ind	0.75	piece	Cloth of Assize	0	0	0	0
		4.5	lb	Silk, *Worked*	3	0	0	0
		3.5	gross	Knives	0	23	4	0
		0.5	dozen	Caps	0	5	0	0
		6	gross	Points	0	6	0	0
		40	lb	Pewter	0	13	4	0
Edmund Fitzjohn	Ind	2	lb	Silk, *Worked*	0	26	8	0
		3	gross	Knives	0	20	0	0
		5	gross	Points	0	5	0	0
		1	dozen	Skins, Golden	0	4	2	0
		1	dozen	Cards, Playing	0	0	10	0
		2	piece	Caps	0	0	20	0
		1	gross	Lacquer	0	0	20	0

The Sunday of Youghal, Thomas Dawghe master, Exiting, 9th February 1542

Merchant name	Origin	Qty	Unit	Commodity	£	s.	d.	f.
Thomas *Dawghe*	Ind	0.25	piece	Cloth of Assize	0	0	0	0
		9	stone	Hops	0	11	3	0
		2	stone	Orchil	0	3	4	0
Richard Rownan	Ind	1	dozen	Skins, Golden	0	4	2	0
		3	dozen	Combs	0	0	12	0
		0.5	gross	Knives	0	3	4	0
		0.5	dozen	Alum	0	0	8	0
		1	gross	Points	0	0	12	0
		1	dozen	Purses	0	0	4	0
		1	dozen	Cards, Playing	0	0	10	0
		1	stone	Hops	0	0	15	0
William Folon	Ind	0.5	C	Hops	0	5	0	0
		1	C	Nails, Rouze	0	15	0	0

The George of London, Thomas Candy master, Exiting, *9th February 1542*

Merchant name	Origin	Qty	Unit	Commodity	£	s.	d.	f.
Anthony Fernandue	Alien	1.25	piece	Cloth of Assize	0	0	0	0

The Mary of Cork, Philip Harrow master, Exiting, *9th February 1542*

Merchant name	Origin	Qty	Unit	Commodity	£	s.	d.	f.
Walter Harrow	Ind	4	wey	Malt	3	6	8	0
		3	C	Hops	0	30	0	0
		1	gross	Knives	0	6	8	0
		2	gross	Points	0	2	0	0

Merchant name	Origin	Qty	Unit	Commodity	£	s.	d.	f.
The George Butlar of Waterford, Edmund Medoll master, Exiting, 10th February 1542								
John Kyrk	Ind	3	C	Iron	0	12	0	0
		2	dozen	Knives, in Pairs	0	3	4	0
		6	dozen	Knives, in Pairs	0	10	0	0
		4	gross	Points	0	4	0	0
		2	gross	Lacquer	0	3	4	0
		3.25	piece	Cloth of Assize	0	0	0	0
Andrew Welsh	Ind	1	pipe	Iron	2	0	0	0
		6	gross	Points	0	6	0	0
		1	gross	Lacquer	0	0	20	0
		2	dozen	Knives, in Pairs	0	3	4	0
		1	gross	Cutts	0	3	4	0
		3	lb	Cinnamon/Mace	0	7	6	0
		1	lb	Ginger	0	0	18	0
		0.5	C	Aniseed	0	6	8	0
		4.5	lb	Silk, *Worked*	3	0	0	0
		0.5	dozen	Caps	0	5	0	0
		2	piece	Fruit	0	3	4	0
		2	piece	Cloth of Assize	0	0	0	0
Thomas Neyle	Ind	1.5	lb	Silk, *Worked*	0	20	0	0
		1.25	gross	Knives	0	8	4	0
		6	gross	Points	0	6	0	0
		1	gross	Lacquer	0	0	20	0
		0.5	lb	Saffron	0	5	0	0
		2	dozen	Soap	0	2	6	0
		0.25	piece	Cloth of Assize	0	0	0	0
James Savage	Ind	12	gross	Points	0	12	0	0
		1	gross	Knives	0	6	8	0
		3	dozen	Knives, in Pairs	0	5	0	0
		2	lb	Thread	0	0	10	0
		2	piece	Caps	0	0	20	0
		2	dozen	*Percular*	0	2	0	0
		1	piece	Caps	0	0	12	0
		0.5	piece	Cloth of Assize	0	0	0	0
Paul Butlar	Ind	2	lb	Saffron	0	20	0	0
		1	lb	Silk, *Worked*	0	13	4	0
		2	gross	Points	0	2	0	0
		1	gross	Lacquer	0	0	20	0
John Rothe	Ind	0.25	C	Aniseed	0	3	4	0
		4	gross	Knives	0	26	8	0
		18	gross	Points	0	18	0	0
		1.5	gross	Lacquer	0	2	6	0
		2	dozen	Knives, in Pairs	0	3	4	0
		2	stone	Orchil	0	3	4	0
		0.5	dozen	Cards, Playing	0	0	5	0
		1	piece	Fruit	0	0	20	0
		1	dozen	Girdles	0	0	10	0
		1	dozen	Glasses	0	0	6	0
		1	dozen	Combs	0	0	6	0
		2	lb	Liquorice	0	0	5	0
		1.5	dozen	Soap	0	0	22	2

Merchant name	Origin	Qty	Unit	Commodity	£	s.	d.	f.
		2.75	piece	Cloth of Assize	0	0	0	0

The Mary of Waterford, John Doryn master, Exiting, *10th February 1542*

Merchant name	Origin	Qty	Unit	Commodity	£	s.	d.	f.
John *Doryn*	Ind	1	bolt	Poldavis *Canvas*	0	13	4	0
		3	C	Ropes	0	40	0	0
		1	C	Iron	0	4	0	0
Richard Kerry	Ind	1	bolt	Poldavis *Canvas*	0	13	4	0
		1	C	Nails, Rouze	0	13	4	0
		1	lb	Saffron	0	10	0	0
Richard Williams & assoc.	Ind	4	stone	Nails, Rouze & Cleuth	0	6	8	0
		0.5	lb	Saffron	0	5	0	0
		8	piece	Chest	0	20	0	0
		3	dozen	Knives, in Pairs	0	5	0	0

The Mary Conception of Bristol, John Bousher master, Exiting, 13th February 1542

Merchant name	Origin	Qty	Unit	Commodity	£	s.	d.	f.
Nicholas Thorn	Ind	42	ton	Lead, worked	210	0	0	0
		78	piece	Cloth of Assize	0	0	0	0
John Welsh	Ind	57.166	piece	Cloth of Assize	0	0	0	0
		3.625	ton	Lead, worked	18	2	6	0
Thomas Tyson & Snig	Ind	20	piece	Cloth of Assize	0	0	0	0
Robert Leyghton & White	Ind	22	piece	Cloth of Assize	0	0	0	0
		1	ton	Lead, worked	5	0	0	0
Thomas Shipman & Cutt	Ind	21.5	piece	Cloth of Assize	0	0	0	0
		4	piece	Bristol Frieze Cloth	2	13	4	0
William Appowell	Ind	16	piece	Cloth of Assize	0	0	0	0
		30	piece	Manchester *Cotton Cloth*	15	0	0	0
		15	piece	Dunster *Cloth*	7	10	0	0
		2	piece	Welsh *Cloth*	2	0	0	0
William Yonge	Ind	3	piece	Cloth of Assize	0	0	0	0
		3	piece	Welsh *Cloth*	3	0	0	0
		2	piece	Bristol Frieze Cloth	0	26	8	0

The Martyn of Newlyn, Benedict John master, Entering, *13th February 1542*

Merchant name	Origin	Qty	Unit	Commodity	£	s.	d.	f.
George Robert	Ind	2.5	C	Fish, Hake	0	25	0	0
		16	unknown	Fish, Newfoundland	0	16	0	0
		27.5	stone	Wool, Spanish	7	6	8	0
		1	barrel	Fish, Herring White	0	5	0	0

The Sunday of Waterford, William Wodlock master, Exiting, *13th February 1542*

Merchant name	Origin	Qty	Unit	Commodity	£	s.	d.	f.
Nicholas Baly	Ind	2	last	Coal	0	26	8	0
Tibald Nashe	Ind	1	pipe	Iron	2	0	0	0
		8	dozen	Wool-Cards	0	32	0	0
		0.5	gross	Knives	0	3	4	0
		2	dozen	Knives, in Pairs	0	3	4	0

Merchant name	Origin	Qty	Unit	Commodity	£	s.	d.	f.
		4	pair	Stock-Cards	0	4	0	0
		3	dozen	Soap	0	3	9	0
		1.5	C	Aniseed	0	20	0	0
		2	gross	Points	0	2	0	0
		1	piece	Cloth of Assize	0	0	0	0
Andrew Lyncoln	Ind	2.5	piece	Cloth of Assize	0	0	0	0
		1	gross	Knives	0	6	8	0
		6	gross	Points	0	6	0	0
		0.5	lb	Silk, *Worked*	0	6	8	0
		1	dozen	Soap	0	0	15	0
Edmund Seyse	Ind	2	lb	Silk, *Worked*	0	26	8	0
		4	lb	Saffron	2	0	0	0
		2.5	gross	Knives	0	16	8	0
		1	dozen	Knives, in Pairs	0	0	20	0
		2.5	gross	Lacquer	0	4	2	0
		10	gross	Points	0	10	0	0
		2	clout	Needles	0	2	6	0
		2	dozen	Soap	0	2	6	0
		1	dozen	Cards, Playing	0	0	10	0
Richard Conwey	Ind	0.5	lb	Saffron	0	5	0	0
		0.5	lb	Silk, *Worked*	0	6	8	0
		2	piece	Caps	0	0	20	0
		0.25	gross	Knives	0	0	20	0
		2	gross	Points	0	2	0	0
		1	dozen	Knives, in Pairs	0	0	20	0
Patrick Strange	Ind	0.75	piece	Cloth of Assize	0	0	0	0
		0.5	gross	Knives	0	3	4	0
		0.5	dozen	Caps	0	5	0	0
Peter Grannte	Ind	0.25	C	Hops	0	2	6	0
		2	pair	Stock-Cards	0	2	0	0
		4	piece	Caps	0	3	4	0
Peter Welsh	Ind	3	pair	Stock-Cards	0	3	0	0
		0.5	gross	Knives	0	3	4	0
		1	gross	Points	0	0	12	0

The Brandon of Wexford, John Shennan master, Exiting, 15th February 1542

John *Shennan*	Ind	3	C	Hops	0	30	0	0
		1	lb	Saffron	0	10	0	0
		2	lb	Silk, *Worked*	0	26	8	0
		1	gross	Knives	0	6	8	0
		0.25	C	Aniseed	0	3	4	0
		0.5	piece	Cloth of Assize	0	0	0	0

The George of Waterford, Nicholas Colman master, Exiting, 17th February 1542

Nicholas *Coleman*	Ind	9	quart	Beans/Malt	1	5	0	0
Richard Wadyng	Ind	2	lb	Saffron	0	20	0	0
		0.5	C	Hops	0	5	0	0
James Snererford	Ind	1.5	piece	Cloth of Assize	0	0	0	0
		4	pair	Stock-Cards	0	4	0	0
		0.5	gross	Knives	0	3	4	0

Merchant name	Origin	Qty	Unit	Commodity	£	s.	d.	f.
Nicholas Kett	Ind	1	lb	Saffron	0	10	0	0
		0.5	lb	Silk, *Worked*	0	6	8	0
		0.5	gross	Knives	0	3	4	0
		2	gross	Points	0	2	0	0
		1	gross	Lacquer	0	0	20	0
		3	pair	Stock-Cards	0	3	0	0
		3	piece	Caps	0	2	6	0
Walter Shirlock	Ind	1	gross	Knives	0	6	8	0
		3	gross	Lacquer	0	5	0	0
		2	pair	Stock-Cards	0	2	0	0
		1.5	piece	Cloth of Assize	0	0	0	0
Richard Fitzjohn	Ind	1	lb	Saffron	0	10	0	0
		0.25	piece	Cloth of Assize	0	0	0	0
William Benet	Ind	4	lb	Saffron	2	0	0	0
		4	lb	Silk, *Worked*	0	53	4	0
		1	barrel	Honey	0	16	8	0
		1	gross	Knives	0	6	8	0
		0.25	C	Hops	0	2	6	0
		2	lb	Thread	0	0	10	0
		2	lb	Mercury	0	0	10	0
		1	pair	Stock-Cards	0	0	12	0
		1	dozen	Soap	0	0	15	0
Peter Asteken	Ind	1	C	Hops	0	10	0	0
		12	gross	Points	0	12	0	0
		1	dozen	Skins, Golden	0	4	2	0
		1	dozen	Skins, Red	0	2	1	0
		2	stone	Orchil	0	3	4	0
		1	dozen	Cards, Playing	0	0	10	0
		4	dozen	Knives, in Pairs	0	6	8	0
		2	doz	Aniseed/Cumin	0	2	8	0
		1	dozen	Alum	0	0	16	0
		0.5	dozen	Caps	0	5	0	0
		1	dozen	Soap	0	0	15	0
		2	dozen	Knives, in Pairs	0	3	4	0
		1.25	piece	Cloth of Assize	0	0	0	0
George Snererford	Ind	1.75	piece	Cloth of Assize	0	0	0	0
		1	gross	Knives	0	6	8	0
		4	gross	Points	0	4	0	0
		2	dozen	Soap	0	2	6	0
Nicholas Roe	Ind	1	lb	Saffron	0	10	0	0
		1	lb	Silk, *Worked*	0	13	4	0
		2	dozen	Soap	0	2	6	0
		2	pair	Stock-Cards	0	2	0	0
		0.5	gross	Knives	0	3	4	0
		2	gross	Points	0	2	0	0
		0.5	piece	Cloth of Assize	0	0	0	0

The George of Youghal, William Donell master, Exiting, *17th February 1542*

Merchant name	Origin	Qty	Unit	Commodity	£	s.	d.	f.
Philip Rownan	Ind	0.75	piece	Cloth of Assize	0	0	0	0
		2	dozen	Skins, Red	0	4	2	0
		3	dozen	Skins, Golden	0	12	6	0

Merchant name	Origin	Qty	Unit	Commodity	£	s.	d.	f.
		0.5	C	Hops	0	5	0	0
		2	stone	Aniseed	0	3	4	0
		2	stone	Cumin	0	3	4	0
		2	stone	Liquorice	0	0	15	0
		3	lb	Cinnamon	0	7	6	0
		2.5	lb	Cloves	0	6	3	0
		2	lb	Ginger	0	3	0	0
		2	lb	Pepper	0	2	0	0
		3	gross	Knives	0	20	0	0
		6	gross	Points	0	6	0	0
		6	dozen	Combs	0	0	20	0
		3	lot	Items, miscellaneous	0	20	0	0
		3	dozen	Knives, in Pairs	0	5	0	0
		1	gross	Lacquer	0	0	20	0
		8	dozen	Purses	0	2	7	0
		0.5	lb	Nutmeg	0	0	12	0
		0.5	lb	Saffron	0	5	0	0
		2	dozen	Girdles	0	2	8	0
Edmund Rowley	Ind	1.5	piece	Cloth of Assize, Dozen Strait	0	0	0	0
		1	C	Hops	0	10	0	0
		0.5	C	Alum	0	6	8	0
		2	stone	Aniseed	0	3	4	0
		1	dozen	Skins, Red	0	2	1	0
		4	C	Iron	0	16	0	0
		4	stone	Orchil	0	6	8	0
		2	gross	Knives	0	13	4	0
		2	dozen	Knives, in Pairs	0	3	4	0
		0.5	lb	Saffron	0	5	0	0
		2	gross	Points	0	2	0	0
		6	dozen	Purses	0	0	18	0
		0.5	gross	Lacquer	0	0	10	0
Richard Hodney	Ind	1.5	C	Iron	0	6	0	0
		0.75	C	Hops	0	7	6	0

The Anthony of Waterford, Henry Gall master, Exiting, 18th February 1542

Merchant name	Origin	Qty	Unit	Commodity	£	s.	d.	f.
Robert Tewe	Ind	0.75	piece	Cloth of Assize	0	0	0	0
		1	lb	Saffron	0	10	0	0
		3	gross	Knives	0	20	0	0
		2	lb	Silk, *Worked*	0	26	8	0
James Savage	Ind	1	C	Liquorice	0	6	8	0
		1	C	Aniseed	0	13	4	0
		1	lb	Saffron	0	10	0	0
		1	lb	Silk, *Worked*	0	13	4	0
		0.5	gross	Knives	0	3	4	0
		2	gross	Points	0	2	0	0
		1	dozen	Cards, Playing	0	0	10	0
		2	dozen	Knives, in Pairs	0	3	4	0
		1	dozen	Girdles	0	0	20	0
		3.25	piece	Cloth of Assize	0	0	0	0
Edmund Clery	Ind	1.5	gross	Knives	0	10	0	0
		4	gross	Points	0	4	0	0

Merchant name	Origin	Qty	Unit	Commodity	£	s.	d.	f.
		1	gross	Lacquer	0	0	20	0
		3	piece	Fruit	0	5	0	0
		2	dozen	Flax	0	6	8	0
		3	pair	Stock-Cards	0	3	0	0
		1.5	piece	Cloth of Assize	0	0	0	0
William Grant	Ind	2.25	piece	Cloth of Assize	0	0	0	0
		0.5	lb	Silk, *Worked*	0	6	8	0
		6	gross	Points	0	6	0	0
		1.5	gross	Lacquer	0	2	6	0
		1	dozen	Knives, in Pairs	0	0	20	0
		0.25	C	Hops	0	2	6	0
		2	pair	Stock-Cards	0	2	0	0
Robert Maydell	Ind	0.5	lb	Silk, *Worked*	0	6	8	0
		6	gross	Points	0	6	0	0
		1	gross	Lacquer	0	0	20	0
		2	pair	Stock-Cards	0	2	2	0
		2	dozen	Soap	0	2	6	0
Peter Daniel	Ind	2	pair	Stock-Cards	0	2	0	0
		2	dozen	Soap	0	2	6	0
		0.5	gross	Knives	0	3	4	0
		1	gross	Lacquer	0	0	20	0
		6	gross	Points	0	6	0	0
		2	lb	Saffron	0	20	0	0
John Wyse	Ind	1	gross	Knives	0	6	8	0
		1	dozen	Knives, in Pairs	0	0	20	0
		6	gross	Points	0	6	0	0
James Morgan	Ind	2	lb	Saffron	0	20	0	0
		1.5	lb	Silk, *Worked*	0	20	0	0
		1	gross	Knives	0	6	8	0
		2	gross	Points	0	2	0	0
		1	dozen	Soap	0	0	15	0
Dennis Prendgret	Ind	0.5	gross	Knives	0	3	4	0
		2	gross	Points	0	2	0	0
		5	ell	Worsted *Cloth*	0	10	0	0
		1	dozen	Soap	0	0	15	0
		1	dozen	Knives, in Pairs	0	0	20	0
William Madan	Ind	3	dozen	Cards, Playing	0	2	6	0
		1	gross	Knives	0	6	8	0
		3	dozen	Girdles	0	2	6	0
		0.5	dozen	Caps	0	5	0	0
		1	dozen	Soap	0	0	15	0
		1	pair	Stock-Cards	0	0	12	0
Peter Fytzjohn	Ind	0.5	piece	Cloth of Assize	0	0	0	0
		0.5	gross	Knives	0	3	4	0
		4	gross	Points	0	4	0	0
		1	lb	Saffron	0	10	0	0
Edmund Grant	Ind	1	lb	Saffron	0	10	0	0

The Sunday of Wexford, Thomas Sholick master, Exiting, *18th February 1542*

Thomas *Sholick*	Ind	1	pipe	Iron	2	0	0	0
		1	lb	Silk, *Worked*	0	13	4	0

Merchant name	Origin	Qty	Unit	Commodity	£	s.	d.	f.
		4	C	Hops	2	0	0	0
		8	piece	Scythes	0	13	4	0
		0.75	C	Aniseed	0	10	0	0
		0.5	lb	Saffron	0	5	0	0
Nicholas White	Ind	0.25	piece	Cloth of Assize	0	0	0	0
		2	lb	Silk, *Worked*	0	26	8	0
		1	lb	Saffron	0	10	0	0
		4	piece	Caps	0	3	4	0
		1	lb	Cinnamon/Cloves	0	2	6	0
		0.5	C	Hops	0	5	0	0
		12	piece	Scythes	0	15	0	0
		2	lb	Thread	0	0	10	0
		4	weight	Hemp	0	8	0	0

The Migell of Waterford, Robert Fytzjohn master, Exiting, 19th February 1542

Merchant name	Origin	Qty	Unit	Commodity	£	s.	d.	f.
David Welsh	Ind	2	piece	Cloth of Assize	0	0	0	0
		1	tun	Wine, Corrupt	0	30	0	0
		2	lb	Saffron	0	20	0	0
		1	gross	Knives	0	6	8	0
Peter Butlar	Ind	3.75	piece	Cloth of Assize	0	0	0	0
		3	gross	Knives	0	20	0	0
		2	lb	Silk, *Worked*	0	26	8	0
		3	lb	Saffron	0	30	0	0
		2	gross	Lacquer	0	3	4	0
William Rothe	Ind	1.5	piece	Cloth of Assize	0	0	0	0
		1	gross	Knives	0	6	8	0
		1	hogshead	Iron	0	20	0	0
		3	lb	Saffron	0	30	0	0
		6	lb	Silk, *Worked*	4	0	0	0
		2	dozen	Skins, Red	0	4	2	0
		4	dozen	Skins, Golden	0	16	8	0
		8	stone	Orchil	0	13	4	0
		1.5	C	Alum/Aniseed	0	20	0	0
		0.5	C	Hops	0	5	0	0
		0.5	C	Wood, Brazil	0	16	8	0
		8	gross	Lacquer	0	13	4	0
		36	gross	Points	0	36	0	0
		0.5	dozen	Hats	0	2	0	0
		0.5	dozen	Caps	0	5	0	0
		3	gross	Knives	0	20	0	0
		2	gross	Cutts	0	6	8	0
		2	lb	Thread	0	0	10	0
		1	lb	Cinnamon	0	2	6	0
		18	dozen	Knives, in Pairs	0	30	0	0
		0.5	lb	Mace	0	0	15	0
		6	dozen	Glasses	0	2	0	0
		3	dozen	Girdles	0	0	18	0
		1	ream	Paper	0	0	20	0
		3	lb	Pepper	0	3	0	0
		1	clout	Needles	0	0	20	0
		1	dozen	Beads	0	0	6	0

Merchant name	Origin	Qty	Unit	Commodity	£	s.	d.	f.
		2	dozen	Cards, Playing	o	o	20	o
Thomas Madan & Cogan	Ind	4.5	piece	Cloth of Assize	o	o	o	o
		1	gross	Knives	o	6	8	o
		1	gross	Cutts	o	3	4	o
		9	lb	Silk, *Worked*	6	o	o	o
		1	barrel	Honey	o	16	8	o
		2	stone	Orchil	o	3	4	o
		2	lb	Thread	o	o	10	o
		3	lb	Pepper	o	3	o	o
		1	dozen	Skins, Golden	o	4	2	o
		2	dozen	Cards, Playing	o	o	20	o
		3	dozen	Knives, in Pairs	o	5	o	o
		0.25	C	Hops	o	2	6	o
John Hart	Ind	0.25	piece	Cloth of Assize	o	o	o	o
		0.5	lb	Silk, *Worked*	o	6	8	o
		1	gross	Knives	o	6	8	o
		2	gross	Lacquer	o	3	4	o
		1	dozen	Cards, Playing	o	o	10	o
		2	lb	Mercury	o	o	10	o

The Francis of New Ross, John Brown master, Exiting, *19th February 1542*

Merchant name	Origin	Qty	Unit	Commodity	£	s.	d.	f.
Thomas Comyn & Harrys	Ind	1.75	piece	Cloth of Assize	o	o	o	o
		1.5	C	Hops	o	15	o	o
		3	dozen	Skins, Golden	o	12	6	o
		3	lb	Thread	o	o	15	o
		0.5	dozen	Caps	o	5	o	o
		1	dozen	*Percular*	o	o	12	o
		5	dozen	Knives, in Pairs	o	8	4	o
		0.5	lb	Cinnamon	o	o	15	o
		1	lb	Kermes	o	o	12	o
		2	dozen	Glasses	o	o	8	o
		2	lb	Mercury	o	o	10	o
		1	dozen	Skins, Red	o	2	1	o
		10	dozen	Combs	o	3	4	o
		2	gross	Knives	o	13	4	o
		1	gross	Cutts	o	3	4	o
		36	gross	Points	o	36	o	o
		1.5	dozen	Soap	o	o	30	2
		2	clout	Needles	o	o	18	o
		11	dozen	Wool-Cards	2	4	o	o
		4	pair	Stock-Cards	o	4	o	o
		3	stone	Hops	o	3	9	o
		1	lb	Saffron	o	10	o	o
		1	pipe	Wine	o	o	o	o
Thomas Dewle	Ind	3	piece	Caps	o	2	6	o
		2	gross	Points	o	2	o	o
		2	lb	Saffron	o	20	o	o
		12	dozen	Knives, in Pairs	o	20	o	o
		1.5	gross	Knives	o	10	o	o

Merchant name	Origin	Qty	Unit	Commodity	£	s.	d.	f.
		12	gross	Points	0	12	0	0
		1	gross	Lacquer	0	0	20	0
		3	lb	Cinnamon/Cloves	0	7	6	0
		1	lb	Ginger	0	0	18	0
		2	dozen	Skins, Golden	0	8	4	0
		1	lb	Verdigris	0	0	5	0
		0.5	C	Hops	0	5	0	0
		3	dozen	Soap	0	3	9	0
		1	clout	Needles	0	0	10	0
		4	dozen	Combs	0	0	18	0
		0.25	piece	Cloth of Assize	0	0	0	0

The Peter of Milford Haven, Philip Smyth master, Entering, *19th February 1542*

Merchant name	Origin	Qty	Unit	Commodity	£	s.	d.	f.
Philip *Smyth*	Ind	10	C	Fish, Hake	5	0	0	0
		1	barrel	Fish, Herring White	0	5	0	0

The Katryn of Milford Haven, Richard Mower master, Entering, *19th February 1542*

Merchant name	Origin	Qty	Unit	Commodity	£	s.	d.	f.
Richard *Mower*	Ind	6	barrel	Fish, Herring White	0	30	0	0
		8	C	Fish, Hake	4	0	0	0
		0.5	burden	Fish, Salted	0	2	1	0

The Julian of Bristol, John Crocke master, Exiting, 20th February 1542

Merchant name	Origin	Qty	Unit	Commodity	£	s.	d.	f.
John Welsh & Jay	Ind	54	piece	Cloth of Assize	0	0	0	0
William Appowell	Ind	20	piece	Dunster *Cloth*	10	0	0	0
Thomas Tyson &								
Capps	Ind	25	piece	Cloth of Assize	0	0	0	0

The Mary Bonaventure of Bristol, John Williams master, Exiting, *20th February 1542*

Merchant name	Origin	Qty	Unit	Commodity	£	s.	d.	f.
Nicholas Thorn	Ind	8	ton	Lead, worked	40	0	0	0
John Darby &								
Chester	Ind	15	piece	Cloth of Assize	0	0	0	0
		20	piece	Northern *Cotton Cloth*	4	3	4	0
		1	piece	Welsh *Cloth*	0	20	0	0
		40	ell	Wadmal & Flannel *Cloth*	0	13	4	0
Edward Butlar &								
Chester	Ind	19	piece	Cloth of Assize	0	0	0	0
		1	ton	Lead, worked	5	0	0	0

The Jhesus of New Ross, Richard Doffe master, Exiting, 20th February 1542

Merchant name	Origin	Qty	Unit	Commodity	£	s.	d.	f.
Richard Nevell	Ind	1	lb	Silk, *Worked*	0	13	4	0
		1	dozen	Soap	0	0	15	0
		1	lb	Mercury	0	0	5	0
		1	gross	Points	0	0	12	0
		1	pair	Stock–Cards	0	0	12	0

Merchant name	Origin	Qty	Unit	Commodity	£	s.	d.	f.
The Dolphyn of Cardiff, John Watkyns master, Entering, *20th February 1542*								
Roland Coper	Ind	2	tun	Wine	o	o	o	o
The Mary of Dungarvan, John Fytzwilliam master, Entering, 22nd February 1542								
John *Fytzwilliam*	Ind	10	C	Fish, Hake	5	o	o	o
		1.5	burden	Fish, Salted	o	6	3	o
		1	stone	Wool, Flocks	o	o	5	o
		1	barrel	Fish, Gurnard	o	6	8	o
Robert Tobyn	Ind	12	C	Fish, Hake	6	o	o	o
		1.5	burden	Fish, Salted	o	6	3	o
		2	stone	Wool, Flocks	o	o	10	o
The Austen of Dungarvan, Walter Pore master, Entering, *22nd February 1542*								
Walter *Pore*	Ind	7	C	Fish, Hake	3	10	o	o
		2	burden	Fish, Salted	o	8	4	o
The Sunday of Dungarvan, John White master, Entering, *22nd February 1542*								
John *White*	Ind	25	C	Fish, Hake	12	10	o	o
		2	burden	Fish, Salted	o	8	4	o
Stephan Bathe	Ind	25	C	Fish, Hake	12	10	o	o
		2	burden	Fish, Salted	o	8	4	o
		0.5	C	Skins, Sheep	o	5	o	o
The Trynyte of Youghal, William Nele master, Entering, *22nd February 1542*								
John Jeffrey	Ind	30	C	Fish, Hake	15	o	o	o
		1	pipe	Fish, Salmon	o	30	o	o
		1	burden	Fish, Salted	o	4	2	o
Richard Annes	Ind	10	C	Fish, Hake	5	o	o	o
		0.5	C	Skins, Sheep	o	5	o	o
		20	lb	Battery	o	4	2	o
Maurice Tege	Ind	10	C	Fish, Hake	5	o	o	o
		0.5	C	Skins, Sheep	o	5	o	o
		2	piece	Mantles	o	6	8	o
		20	yard	Irish Frieze *Cloth*	o	6	8	o
		2	dicker	Skins, Deer	o	4	2	o
The Katryn of Youghal, Darby Greffithe master, Entering, *22nd February 1542*								
Darby Greffithe	Ind	15	C	Fish, Hake	7	10	o	o
		1	burden	Fish, Salted	o	4	2	o
William Hore	Ind	7	C	Fish, Hake	3	10	o	o
		0.5	burden	Fish, Salted	o	2	1	o
		0.5	C	Skins, Sheep	o	5	o	o
Richard Danell & Copyn*ger*	Ind	13	C	Fish, Hake	6	10	o	o
		1	C	Skins, Sheep	o	10	o	o
		1	piece	Mantles	o	3	4	o
		1	burden	Fish, Salted	o	4	2	o

Merchant name	Origin	Qty	Unit	Commodity	£	s.	d.	f.
The Mary of Youghal, Thomas Laurence master, Entering, *22nd February 1542*								
Thomas Laurence & assoc.	Ind	12	C	Fish, Hake	6	0	0	0
		1	burden	Fish, Salted	0	4	2	0
		8	C	Fish, Hake	4	0	0	0
		2	piece	Mantles	0	6	8	0
The Trynyte of Caerleon, Sebastian Melyor master, Exiting, 22nd February 1542								
Nicholas Thorn & White	Ind	20	ton	Lead, worked	100	0	0	0
		50	piece	Cloth of Assize	0	0	0	0
		1.5	dicker	Hides, Tanned	0	0	0	0
William Shipman & Codryngton	Ind	25	piece	Cloth of Assize	0	0	0	0
John Pryn	Ind	28.5	piece	Cloth of Assize	0	0	0	0
Edward Pryn & Hill	Ind	49	piece	Cloth of Assize	0	0	0	0
Johanna Carpynt*yr* & Sprat	Ind	42	piece	Cloth of Assize	0	0	0	0
James Balie & Hicks	Ind	17	piece	Cloth of Assize	0	0	0	0
Arthur Smyth & Butlar	Ind	6	piece	Cloth of Assize	0	0	0	0
Edward Pryn & Pryn	Ind	27	piece	Western *Cloth*	5	12	6	0
		17	piece	Cloth of Assize	0	0	0	0
William Carr	Ind	5	dicker	Hides, Tanned	0	0	0	0
The Anthony of Minsterworth (?), Thomas Hyat master, Entering, 23rd February 1542								
John Comeley	Ind	6	barrel	Fish, Herring White	0	30	0	0
The Savyour of Northam, John Aung*er* master, Exiting, 27th February 1542								
Thomas Shipman & Pressy	Ind	63	piece	Northern *Cotton Cloth*	13	2	6	0
		12.33	piece	Cloth of Assize	0	0	0	0
John Cutt, Pryn & assoc.	Ind	29	piece	Cloth of Assize	0	0	0	0
		18	piece	Cloth of Assize	0	0	0	0
The Nicholas of Bristol, John Lewellyn master, Entering, 28th February 1542								
Laurence Br*e*war & assoc.	Ind	15	C	Check *Cloth*	30	0	0	0
		10	C	Skins, Sheep	5	0	0	0
		1	barrel	Fish, Herring White	0	5	0	0
		16	burden	Fish, Salted	3	6	8	0
The John of Bideford, John Hychecocks master, Entering, 2nd March 1542								
William Helyng	Ind	1.5	ton	Fruit	3	0	0	0

Merchant name	Origin	Qty	Unit	Commodity	£	s.	d.	f.

The John of Kingswear, Nicholas Hochyns master, Entering, 3rd March 1542

Merchant name	Origin	Qty	Unit	Commodity	£	s.	d.	f.
Hugh Tipton & assoc.	Ind	16	tun	Wine	0	0	0	0
		3	tun	Honey	6	0	0	0
		202.5	C	Woad, Toulouse	81	0	0	0

The Sunday of Dungarvan, James Mawnger master, Entering, 3rd March 1542

Merchant name	Origin	Qty	Unit	Commodity	£	s.	d.	f.
Edmund Gowells	Ind	7	pipe	Fish, Salmon	10	10	0	0
		20	C	Fish, Hake	10	0	0	0
		1	burden	Fish, Salted	0	4	2	0

The Kerick of Milford Haven, John Andrew master, Entering, 3rd March 1542

Merchant name	Origin	Qty	Unit	Commodity	£	s.	d.	f.
John Ryte & assoc.	Ind	12.5	barrel	Fish, Herring White	3	2	6	0

The Nicholas of Plymouth, Thomas Deble master, Entering, 4th March 1542

Merchant name	Origin	Qty	Unit	Commodity	£	s.	d.	f.
Thomas Deble	Ind	35	burden	Fish, Salted	7	5	10	0

The Mary of Youghal, Thomas Laurence master, Exiting, 4th March 1542

Merchant name	Origin	Qty	Unit	Commodity	£	s.	d.	f.
Thomas Laurence	Ind	0.5	C	Hops	0	5	0	0
		0.5	dozen	Caps	0	5	0	0
		20	yard	Linen Cloth	0	15	0	0
		0.5	gross	Knives	0	3	4	0
		2	gross	Points	0	2	0	0
		8	lb	Flax	0	2	0	0
John Hore	Ind	0.75	lb	Saffron	0	7	6	0
		14	lb	Flax	0	4	2	0
		0.5	gross	Knives	0	3	4	0
		1	gross	Points	0	0	12	0
		0.5	stone	Aniseed	0	0	10	0

The Nicholas of Milford Haven, William Rothe master, Entering, 6th March 1542

Merchant name	Origin	Qty	Unit	Commodity	£	s.	d.	f.
William Rothe	Ind	11	barrel	Fish, Herring White	2	15	0	0

The Katryn of Youghal, Thomas Mongan master, Entering, 6th March 1542

Merchant name	Origin	Qty	Unit	Commodity	£	s.	d.	f.
Thomas Mongan	Ind	8	C	Fish, Hake	4	0	0	0
		1	virkin	Fish, Salmon	0	7	6	0
		0.25	C	Skins, Sheep	0	2	6	0
		4.5	burden	Fish, Salted	0	18	9	0
John Welsh	Ind	3	C	Fish, Hake	0	30	0	0
		1	burden	Fish, Salted	0	4	2	0

The Anthony of Milford Haven, John Steward master, Entering, 7th March 1542

Merchant name	Origin	Qty	Unit	Commodity	£	s.	d.	f.
John Steward	Ind	14	barrel	Fish, Herring White	3	10	0	0

Merchant name	Origin	Qty	Unit	Commodity	£	s.	d.	f.
The Mary of Stonehouse, Thomas Wynter master, Entering, 7th March 1542								
Thomas *Wynter*	Ind	34	burden	Fish, Salted	7	1	8	0
The Anthony of *Minsteford*, John Comeley master, Exiting, 12th March 1542								
John *Comeley*	Ind	4	wey	Malt	3	6	8	0
The Trynyte of Plymouth, John Sampson master, Entering, 13th March 1542								
John *Sampson*	Ind	35	burden	Fish, Salted	7	5	10	0
The Savyour of Youghal, John Shea master, Entering, 13th March 1542								
Richard Bluet	Ind	9	C	Fish, Hake	4	10	0	0
		1	C	Skins, Sheep	0	10	0	0
		1	C	Wood	0	20	0	0
		2	burden	Fish, Salted	0	8	4	0
		20	yard	Irish Frieze *Cloth*	0	6	8	0
William Drady	Ind	1.5	C	Skins, Sheep	0	15	0	0
		1	C	Skins, Lamb	0	6	8	0
		2	pipe	Fish, Salmon	3	0	0	0
		1	burden	Fish, Salted	0	4	2	0
The Bartholemew of 'Yealm', Edward Syme master, Entering, 13th March 1542								
Edward Syme	Ind	40	burden	Fish, Salted	8	6	8	0
The Mary of Dungarvan, John Fizwilliams master, Exiting, 13th March 1542								
John Fizwilliams & Tobin	Ind	4	wey	Malt	3	6	8	0
		1	C	Hops	0	10	0	0
		1	lb	Saffron	0	10	0	0
		60	lb	Flax	0	20	0	0
		1	dozen	Caps	0	10	0	0
William White	Ind	0.5	piece	Cloth of Assize	0	0	0	0
		3	gross	Knives	0	20	0	0
		12	gross	Points	0	12	0	0
		1	gross	Lacquer	0	0	20	0
		3	pair	Stock-Cards	0	3	0	0
		2	dozen	Soap	0	2	6	0
The Sunday of Dungarvan, John White master, Exiting, 13th March 1542								
John *White*	Ind	0.325	ton	Iron	0	26	0	0
		1	C	Hops	0	10	0	0
		1	C	Flax	0	33	4	0
		4	gross	Points	0	4	0	0
		1	lb	Saffron	0	10	0	0
		1	C	Aniseed	0	13	4	0
		0.5	piece	Cloth of Assize	0	0	0	0

Merchant name	Origin	Qty	Unit	Commodity	£	s.	d.	f.
Stephen Bathe	Ind	3	piece	Cloth of Assize, Dozen Strait	0	0	0	0
		0.33	piece	Cloth of Assize	0	0	0	0
		2	lb	Saffron	0	20	0	0
		1.5	C	Hops	0	15	0	0
		2	lb	Silk, *Worked*	0	26	8	0
		1	gross	Knives	0	6	8	0
		5	dozen	Flax	0	20	0	0
		2	dozen	Ribbons, Unspecified	0	3	4	0
		7	yard	Saye *Cloth*	0	10	0	0
		0.25	C	Aniseed	0	3	4	0

The Katryn of Youghal, Darby Greffithe master, Exiting, 14th March 1542

Merchant name	Origin	Qty	Unit	Commodity	£	s.	d.	f.
Saunders Attye	Ind	3.25	piece	Cloth of Assize	0	0	0	0
		4.5	lb	Silk, *Worked*	3	0	0	0
		20	lb	Saffron	10	0	0	0
		0.5	dozen	Skins, Red	0	0	13	2
		0.5	dozen	Skins, Golden	0	2	1	0
		20	lb	Cumin	0	2	0	0
		1	gross	Knives	0	6	8	0
		12	gross	Points	0	12	0	0
		6	dozen	Knives, in Pairs	0	10	0	0
Martin Founte	Ind	8	piece	Cloth of Assize	0	0	0	0
		25	lb	Cumin	0	2	8	0
		2	dozen	Skins, Golden	0	8	4	0
		1.5	dozen	Skins, Red	0	3	1	2
		4	lb	Silk, *Worked*	0	53	4	0
		25	lb	Saffron	12	10	0	0
		14	gross	Points	0	14	0	0
		2	lb	Thread	0	0	10	0
		12	dozen	Knives, in Pairs	0	20	0	0
		5	dozen	Cards, Playing	0	4	2	0
		4	gross	Knives	0	26	8	0
Darby Greffithe	Ind	1.5	piece	Cloth of Assize	0	0	0	0
		2	gross	Knives	0	13	4	0
		2	C	Iron	0	8	0	0
		0.5	C	Hops	0	5	0	0
		1	stone	Alum	0	0	20	0
		2	gross	Points	0	2	0	0
William Hore	Ind	3	lb	Saffron	0	30	0	0
		0.5	C	Hops	0	5	0	0
		2	dozen	Knives, in Pairs	0	3	4	0
		3	gross	Points	0	3	0	0
Richard Danell	Ind	0.75	piece	Cloth of Assize	0	0	0	0
		0.5	lb	Saffron	0	5	0	0
		1	gross	Knives	0	6	8	0
		4	gross	Points	0	4	0	0
		1	lb	Cinnamon/Cloves	0	2	6	0
		2	dozen	Knives, in Pairs	0	3	4	0
		1	gross	Purses	0	2	0	0
		2	C	Iron	0	8	0	0
		1	lb	Silk, *Worked*	0	13	4	0

Merchant name	Origin	Qty	Unit	Commodity	£	s.	d.	f.
		4	dozen	Cards, Playing	0	3	4	0
Thomas Copynger	Ind	1	hogshead	Iron	0	20	0	0
		2	gross	Knives	0	13	4	0
		4	gross	Points	0	4	0	0
		1	gross	Lacquer	0	0	20	0
		2	stone	Alum	0	3	4	0
		0.5	C	Hops	0	5	0	0
		3	stone	Orchil	0	5	0	0
		1	lb	Cloves	0	2	6	0
		0.5	lb	Nutmeg	0	0	6	0
Andrew Kerawan	Ind	2	dozen	Skins, Golden	0	8	4	0
		2	gross	Knives	0	13	4	0
		12	gross	Points	0	12	0	0
		9.5	piece	Cloth of Assize	0	0	0	0

The Trynyte of Youghal, William Nele master, Exiting, 14th March 1542

Merchant name	Origin	Qty	Unit	Commodity	£	s.	d.	f.
John Jeffres	Ind	1	C	Hops	0	10	0	0
		2	C	Alum	0	26	8	0
		2	lb	Saffron	0	20	0	0
		6	gross	Points	0	6	0	0
		0.25	piece	Cloth of Assize	0	0	0	0
Richard Annes & Tege	Ind	2	piece	Cloth of Assize	0	0	0	0
		2	lb	Saffron	0	20	0	0
		1	C	Hops	0	10	0	0
		1	C	Iron	0	4	0	0
		24	lb	Flax	0	8	0	0

The John of Kingswear, Nicholas Hochyns master, Exiting, 15th March 1542

Merchant name	Origin	Qty	Unit	Commodity	£	s.	d.	f.
Robert Newborn & Cogan	Ind	18	piece	Cloth of Assize	0	0	0	0
		12	piece	Narrow lining Cloth	2	10	0	0
		5	wey	Beans	4	3	4	0
		4	piece	Bristol Frieze Cloth	2	13	4	0
Robert Gyttens	Ind	11.66	piece	Cloth of Assize	0	0	0	0
Nicholas Ware	Ind	2	ton	Lead, worked	10	0	0	0

The Andrew Powdran, *Port Unknown*, John Martyn master, Entering, *15th March 1542*

Merchant name	Origin	Qty	Unit	Commodity	£	s.	d.	f.
John *Martyn*	Ind	45	burden	Fish, Salted	9	7	6	0

The Katryn of Youghal, Thomas Mongan master, Exiting, 16th March 1542

Merchant name	Origin	Qty	Unit	Commodity	£	s.	d.	f.
Thomas *Mongan*	Ind	2	wey	Malt	0	33	4	0
		0.5	wey	Beans	0	8	4	0
		3	piece	Caps	0	2	6	0
		2	gross	Lacquer	0	3	4	0
		16	lb	Flax	0	4	0	0

Merchant name	Origin	Qty	Unit	Commodity	£	s.	d.	f.

The Margarete of Milford Haven, John Reynolds master, Entering, *16th March 1542*

Merchant name	Origin	Qty	Unit	Commodity	£	s.	d.	f.
Robert Davye	Ind	1	barrel	Fish, Herring White	0	5	0	0
		1	mease	Fish, Herring Red	0	5	0	0

The Harry of Bristol, Anthony Pygot master, Exiting, 17th March 1542

Merchant name	Origin	Qty	Unit	Commodity	£	s.	d.	f.
Edward Pryn & assoc.	Ind	33	piece	Cloth of Assize	0	0	0	0
		3	piece	Welsh *Cloth*	3	0	0	0
		70	lb	Tin	0	23	4	0
		20	piece	Western *Cloth*	4	3	4	0
Francis Blankeley	Alien	40	piece	Cloth of Assize	0	0	0	0
John Cutt & Hycks	Ind	9	piece	Cloth of Assize	0	0	0	0
John Caps & Tyson	Ind	21.5	piece	Cloth of Assize	0	0	0	0

The Sunday of Bristol, Evan Brettan master, Exiting, *17th March 1542*

Merchant name	Origin	Qty	Unit	Commodity	£	s.	d.	f.
William Gelly	Ind	1	last	Coal	0	13	4	0

The Jhesus of Minehead, Dennis Macranghe master, Exiting, *17th March 1542*

Merchant name	Origin	Qty	Unit	Commodity	£	s.	d.	f.
William Appowell	Ind	6	dozen	Knives, in Pairs	0	10	0	0
		4	tun	Wine, Corrupt	6	0	0	0
		11	lb	Silk, *Worked*	7	6	8	0
		6	lb	Saffron	3	0	0	0
		4	C	Alum/Aniseed	2	13	4	0
		1	dozen	Cumin	0	0	16	0
		2	dozen	Liquorice	0	0	20	0
		1.25	C	Madder	0	8	4	0
		3	C	Hops	0	30	0	0
		3	gross	Knives	0	20	0	0
		36	gross	Points	0	36	0	0
		4	dozen	Glasses	0	0	20	0
		2	dozen	Cards, Playing	0	0	20	0
		12	dozen	Combs	0	6	8	0
		4	dozen	Skins, Golden	0	16	8	0
		2	dozen	Skins, Red	0	4	2	0
		0.5	C	Wood, Brazil	0	16	8	0
		2	ream	Paper	0	3	4	0
		1	dozen	Gloves	0	2	6	0
		1	piece	Welsh *Cloth*	0	20	0	0
		3.5	piece	Cloth of Assize	0	0	0	0
John Caps	Ind	2	tun	Wine, Corrupt	3	0	0	0
		10	lb	Silk, *Worked*	6	13	4	0
		18	gross	Points	0	18	0	0
		1.5	gross	Knives	0	10	0	0
		1	C	Alum	0	13	4	0
		0.5	C	Madder	0	3	4	0
		7	piece	Cloth of Assize	0	0	0	0

Merchant name	Origin	Qty	Unit	Commodity	£	s.	d.	f.

The Savyour of Youghal, John Shea master, Exiting, 18th March 1542

Merchant name	Origin	Qty	Unit	Commodity	£	s.	d.	f.
Richard Bluet	Ind	9	C	Iron	0	36	0	0
		1.5	gross	Knives	0	10	0	0
		12	dozen	Combs	0	4	0	0
		3	stone	Hops	0	3	9	0
		1	dozen	Skins, Red	0	2	1	0
		1	dozen	Skins, Golden	0	4	2	0
		12	dozen	Purses	0	3	0	0
		8	lb	Aniseed	0	0	8	0
		2	dozen	Liquorice	0	0	20	0
		2	dozen	Knives, in Pairs	0	3	4	0
		2	dozen	Cards, Playing	0	0	20	0
		1	lb	Cinnamon	0	2	6	0
		3	piece	Cloth of Assize, Dozen Strait	0	0	0	0

The Nicholas of Bristol, Bartholemew Garland master, Exiting, 20th March 1542

Merchant name	Origin	Qty	Unit	Commodity	£	s.	d.	f.
Bartholemew Garland	Ind	5	wey	Malt	4	3	4	0
		1	C	Hops	0	10	0	0
		1	gross	Knives	0	6	8	0

The George of Longney, Thomas Newman master, Exiting, *20th March 1542*

Merchant name	Origin	Qty	Unit	Commodity	£	s.	d.	f.
Hugh Pryn	Ind	2	wey	Malt	0	33	4	0

The James of Milford Haven, Richard Knetholl master, Entering, 21st March 1542

Merchant name	Origin	Qty	Unit	Commodity	£	s.	d.	f.
Richard *Knetholl*	Ind	5	barrel	Fish, Herring White	0	25	0	0

The John of Pasajes de San Juan, John de Lana master, Entering, 23rd March 1542

Merchant name	Origin	Qty	Unit	Commodity	£	s.	d.	f.
Thomas White	Ind	18	ton	Iron	45	0	0	0
John Perys	Alien	9	ton	Iron	22	10	0	0
		1	tun	Oil, Trane	2	13	4	0
		9	small bags	Liquorice	3	6	8	0
		5	dozen	Serches	0	20	10	0
		5.5	dozen	Skins, Fish	0	9	2	0

The Migell of Milford Haven, John Hycks master, Entering, 27th March 1542

Merchant name	Origin	Qty	Unit	Commodity	£	s.	d.	f.
John *Hycks*	Ind	3.5	barrel	Fish, Herring White	0	17	6	0

The Sunday of Dungarvan, James Mawnger master, Exiting, *27th March 1542*

Merchant name	Origin	Qty	Unit	Commodity	£	s.	d.	f.
Edmund Gowells	Ind	6	wey	Malt	5	0	0	0
		20	gross	Points	0	20	0	0
		30	lb	Flax	0	7	6	0
		1.33	piece	Cloth of Assize	0	0	0	0

Merchant name	Origin	Qty	Unit	Commodity	£	s.	d.	f.

The Mary Nashe of Milford Haven, Thomas Inon master, Entering, 29th March 1542

Merchant name	Origin	Qty	Unit	Commodity	£	s.	d.	f.
Thomas *Inon*	Ind	2	C	Fish, Hake	0	20	0	0

The Clement of Framilode, John Wade master, Entering, *29th March 1542*

Merchant name	Origin	Qty	Unit	Commodity	£	s.	d.	f.
William Shipman & assoc.	Ind	30	ton	Iron	75	0	0	0

The Mawdelen of Milford Haven, Richard Morice master, Entering, *29th March 1542*

Merchant name	Origin	Qty	Unit	Commodity	£	s.	d.	f.
Richard *Morice*	Ind	11	burden	Fish, Salted	2	5	10	0

The Bonaventure of Penmarch, Ryall Moyle master, Entering, 30th March 1542

Merchant name	Origin	Qty	Unit	Commodity	£	s.	d.	f.
James Chester	Ind	28	tun	Wine	0	0	0	0
		0.75	tun	Wine, Corrupt	0	22	6	0

The Mary George of Bristol, Cornell Andrew master, Entering, *30th March 1542*

Merchant name	Origin	Qty	Unit	Commodity	£	s.	d.	f.
Cornell Andrew	Ind	2.625	tun	Wine	0	0	0	0
		0.75	pipe	Fish, Salmon	0	22	6	0

The Trynyte of Bristol, Thomas David master, Exiting, *30th March 1542*

Merchant name	Origin	Qty	Unit	Commodity	£	s.	d.	f.
William Appowell	Ind	10	lb	Silk, *Worked*	6	13	4	0
		6	lb	Saffron	3	0	0	0
		5	C	Alum/Aniseed	3	6	8	0
		1.5	C	Madder	0	10	0	0
		2	C	Hops	0	20	0	0
		4	tun	Wine, Corrupt	6	0	0	0
		1	dozen	Cumin	0	0	16	0
		2	dozen	Liquorice	0	0	10	0
		0.5	C	Wood, Brazil	0	16	8	0
		2	dozen	Cards, Playing	0	0	20	0
		3	lb	Cinnamon/Cloves/Mace	0	7	6	0
		4	dozen	Skins, Golden	0	16	8	0
		2	dozen	Skins, Red	0	4	2	0
		3	gross	Knives	0	20	0	0
		36	gross	Points	0	36	0	0
		12	dozen	Combs	0	4	2	0
		2	ream	Paper	0	3	4	0
		12	yard	Damask *Cloth*	2	8	0	0
		11	yard	Velvet *Cloth*	4	2	6	0
		1	piece	Worsted *Cloth*	0	4	2	0
		5	yard	Satin *Cloth*	0	25	0	0
		3	lb	Cloves/Mace	0	7	6	
		1.833	piece	Cloth of Assize	0	0	0	0
		0.66	piece	Cloth of Assize, dyed with grain	0	0	0	0
John Caps	Ind	1	tun	Wine, Corrupt	0	30	0	0
		4	lb	Saffron	2	0	0	0
		15	lb	Silk, *Worked*	10	0	0	0

Merchant name	Origin	Qty	Unit	Commodity	£	s.	d.	f.
		2.5	gross	Knives	o	16	8	o
		24	gross	Points	o	24	o	o
		11	piece	Cloth of Assize	o	o	o	o

The Margarete of Mumbles, Thomas Ryte master, Exiting, 30th March 1542

Merchant name	Origin	Qty	Unit	Commodity	£	s.	d.	f.
William Appowell	Ind	5.5	tun	Wine, Corrupt	8	5	o	o
		1	piece	Welsh Cloth	o	20	o	o
		2	dozen	Skins, Red	o	4	2	o
		4	dozen	Skins, Golden	o	16	8	o
		1.25	C	Madder	o	8	4	o
		3	C	Alum/Aniseed	2	o	o	o
		0.5	C	Wood, Brazil	o	16	8	o
		2	C	Hops	o	20	o	o
		36	gross	Points	o	36	o	o
		3	gross	Knives	o	20	o	o
		2	dozen	Liquorice	o	o	10	o
		1	dozen	Cumin	o	o	16	o
		6	dozen	Combs	o	2	6	o
		4	lb	Silk, Worked	o	53	4	o
		3.5	piece	Cloth of Assize	o	o	o	o
John Caps	Ind	3	tun	Wine, Corrupt	4	10	o	o
		4	lb	Silk, Worked	o	53	4	o
		2	lb	Saffron	o	20	o	o
		2	gross	Knives	o	13	4	o
		12	gross	Points	o	12	o	o
		1	C	Alum	o	13	4	o
		3.75	piece	Cloth of Assize	o	o	o	o

The Sunday of St Ives, John Robyns master, Entering, 31st March 1542

Merchant name	Origin	Qty	Unit	Commodity	£	s.	d.	f.
John Robyns	Ind	30	burden	Fish, Salted	6	5	o	o

The Misericordia of Portugal, Jasper Famice master, Entering, 31st March 1542

Merchant name	Origin	Qty	Unit	Commodity	£	s.	d.	f.
Thomas Tyson	Ind	3	M	Oranges	o	10	o	o

The Sunday of Youghal, Thomas Daffy master, Entering, 1st April 1542

Merchant name	Origin	Qty	Unit	Commodity	£	s.	d.	f.
Thomas Daffy	Ind	1	butt	Fish, Salmon	o	15	o	o
		6	piece	Mantles	o	20	o	o
		30	yard	Check Cloth	o	10	o	o
		0.5	C	Skins, Sheep	o	5	o	o
		0.5	C	Skins, Lamb	o	3	4	o

The Migell of Mount's Bay, John Hickman master, Entering, 1st April 1542

Merchant name	Origin	Qty	Unit	Commodity	£	s.	d.	f.
John Hicks	Ind	5	ton	Pitch/Rosin	6	13	4	o
		8.75	stone	Wool, Spanish	2	6	8	o
		26	tun	Wine	o	o	o	o

Merchant name	Origin	Qty	Unit	Commodity	£	s.	d.	f.
The Mary of Gloucester, John Lewellyn master, Exiting, 3rd April 1542								
Thomas Cloturboke	Ind	8	wey	Beans/Malt	6	13	4	o
The George Butlar of Waterford, Edmund Medoll master, Entering, *3rd April 1542*								
Nicholas Balye	Ind	3	C	Check *Cloth*	6	0	0	o
		3	C	Skins, Sheep	o	30	0	o
Robert Ayleward	Ind	3	C	Skins, Sheep	o	30	0	o
		80	yard	Check *Cloth*	o	26	8	o
		4	piece	Mantles	o	13	4	o
Richard Vynyge	Ind	40	yard	Check *Cloth*	o	13	4	o
		3	burden	Fish, Salted	o	12	6	o
Patrick Wyse	Ind	7	C	Skins, Sheep	3	10	0	o
		80	yard	Irish Frieze *Cloth*	o	26	8	o
		60	yard	Irish Linen *Cloth*	o	5	0	o
		10	piece	Skins, Marten	o	10	0	o
		1	piece	Mantles	o	3	4	o
Nicholas Harold	Ind	7	C	Skins, Lamb	o	46	8	o
		22	piece	Skins, Marten	o	22	0	o
Andrew Wyse	Ind	1.16	C	Check *Cloth*	2	6	8	o
		0.25	C	Skins, Sheep	o	2	6	o
		1	piece	Mantles	o	3	4	o
Raymond Vale	Ind	3	burden	Fish, Salted	o	12	6	o
		3	C	Check *Cloth*	6	0	0	o
		0.5	C	Skins, Sheep	o	5	0	o
		2	piece	Mantles	o	6	8	o
Patrick Knock	Ind	1.16	C	Irish Frieze *Cloth*	2	6	8	o
		1	C	Skins, Sheep	o	10	0	o
		4	piece	Mantles	o	13	4	o
		1	burden	Fish, Salted	o	4	2	o
James Strech	Ind	1.66	C	Skins, Sheep	o	16	8	o
		8	C	Skins, Lamb	o	53	4	o
		40	piece	Skins, Fox	o	6	8	o
		18	piece	Skins, Otter	o	7	6	o
		30	piece	Skins, Marten	o	30	0	o
Richard Forstals & Fyan	Ind	7	C	Check *Cloth*	14	0	0	o
		1	C	Skins, Sheep	o	10	0	o
		1	burden	Fish, Salted	o	4	2	o
		3	piece	Mantles	o	10	0	o
The George of Waterford, Nicholas Colman master, Entering, 3rd April 1542								
Nicholas *Colman*	Ind	1	C	Check *Cloth*	2	0	0	o
		2	burden	Fish, Salted	o	8	4	o
		0.5	C	Skins, Sheep	o	5	0	o
James Welsh	Ind	10	C	Check *Cloth*	20	0	0	o
		2	C	Skins, Lamb	o	13	4	o
		4.5	C	Skins, Sheep	o	45	0	o
Maurice Pore	Ind	4	burden	Fish, Salted	o	16	8	o
		1	C	Check *Cloth*	2	0	0	o

Merchant name	Origin	Qty	Unit	Commodity	£	s.	d.	f.
Nicholas Bruar	Ind	1	C	Check *Cloth*	2	0	0	0
		0.5	C	Skins, Sheep	0	5	0	0
		1	C	Skins, Lamb	0	6	8	0
		5	piece	Mantles	0	16	8	0
Richard Knewe &								
Quede	Ind	2	C	Check *Cloth*	4	0	0	0
Thomas Christopher	Ind	2	C	Skins, Sheep	0	20	0	0
		0.5	C	Check *Cloth*	0	20	0	0
		2	piece	Mantles	0	6	8	0
William Bretten	Ind	6	C	Skins, Sheep	3	0	0	0
		3	C	Skins, Lamb	0	20	0	0
		40	yard	Check *Cloth*	0	13	4	0

The George of Stonehouse, Dennis Puffyn master, Entering, *3rd April 1542*

Dennis Puffyn	Ind	16	burden	Fish, Salted	3	6	8	0
		0.5	ton	Salt	0	5	0	0

The Stenyons of Milford Haven, David Sere master, Entering, *3rd April 1542*

David *Sere*	Ind	35	burden	Fish, Salted	7	5	10	0

The John of Pasajes de San Juan, John de Lana master, Exiting, 4th April 1542

John de Lana &								
Perys	Alien	0.5	piece	Cloth of Assize	0	0	0	0

The Peter of Mount's Bay, John Richards master, Entering, 5th April 1542

William Davy	Ind	11.25	stone	Wool, Spanish	2	17	0	0

The Andrew of Plymouth, John Andrew master, Entering, *5th April 1542*

John Shipman &								
assoc.	Ind	71	ton	Iron	177	10	0	0
		1	tun	Wine, Corrupt	0	30	0	0

The Sunday of Youghal, Thomas Daffe master, Exiting, 6th April 1542

Thomas *Daffe*	Ind	1.5	lb	Silk, *Worked*	0	20	0	0
		0.5	lb	Saffron	0	5	0	0
		1	gross	Knives	0	6	8	0
		3	stone	Hops	0	3	9	0
		2	stone	Alum	0	3	4	0
		0.5	stone	Cumin	0	0	10	0
		0.5	lb	Pepper	0	0	6	0
		1	stone	Aniseed	0	0	16	0
		2	gross	Points	0	2	0	0
		1	pipe	Wine, Corrupt	0	15	0	0
		1	dozen	Knives, in Pairs	0	0	20	0

Merchant name	Origin	Qty	Unit	Commodity	£	s.	d.	f.

The Trynyte of Bristol, Thomas Webbe master, Entering, 13th April 1542

| John Smyth & assoc. | Ind | 125 | ton | Iron | 312 | 10 | 0 | 0 |

The Mary James of Bristol, John Hilsye master, Entering, *13th April 1542*

| Thomas White & assoc. | Ind | 121 | ton | Iron | 302 | 10 | 0 | 0 |

The Migell of Bristol, Nicholas Waysheford master, Entering, 14th April 1542

Alan Hill & assoc.	Ind	36	ton	Iron	90	0	0	0
		1	dozen	Serches	0	4	2	0
John Dale	Ind	4	C	Liquorice	0	13	4	0
		2	dozen	Serches	0	8	4	0

The Bonaventure of Penmarch, Ryall Moyle master, Exiting, 15th April 1542

Ryall Moyle	Alien	4.5	last	Coal	3	0	0	0
		20	piece	Bristol Frieze Cloth	13	6	8	0
		15	piece	Manchester *Cotton Cloth*	7	10	0	0
		1.5	C	Wood, Bewdley	0	30	0	0
		0.75	tun	Lime	0	0	22	0

The Mary, *Port Unknown*, David Genyn master, Entering, 17th April 1542

| Maurice Geffreys | Ind | 4 | tun | Wine | 0 | 0 | 0 | 0 |
| | | 70 | C | Rosin | 4 | 13 | 4 | 0 |

The Anthony of *Minsterford*, John Comelye master, Entering, *17th April 1542*

| John *Comelye* | Ind | 8 | dicker | Skins, Deer | 0 | 16 | 8 | 0 |

The Clement of *Minsterford*, Robert Hyat master, Exiting, 22nd April 1542,

| Robert *Hyat* | Ind | 3 | wey | Beans/Malt | 2 | 10 | 0 | 0 |

The George of Waterford, Nicholas Colman master, Exiting, 26th April 1542

James Welsh	Ind	1	ton	Iron	4	0	0	0
		18	quart	Wheat	3	0	0	0
		26	quart	Beans/Malt	3	12	1	0
		1.75	C	Hops	0	17	6	0

The George Butlar of Waterford, Edmund Medoll master, Exiting, *26th April 1542*

James Strech	Ind	13.75	piece	Cloth of Assize	0	0	0	0
		11	lb	Silk, *Worked*	7	6	8	0
		42	gross	Points	2	2	0	0
		4	dozen	Skins, Golden	0	16	8	0
		1	dozen	Liquorice	0	0	10	0
		1	dozen	Knives, in Pairs	0	0	20	0

Merchant name	Origin	Qty	Unit	Commodity	£	s.	d.	f.
		6	gross	Knives	2	0	0	0
		1	gross	Lacquer	0	0	20	0
		5	dozen	*Percular*	0	0	10	0
		1	lb	Ginger	0	0	18	0
		4	doz	Ribbons, Unspecified	0	5	0	0
		3	bolt	Thread	0	2	6	0
		2	dozen	Cards, Playing	0	0	20	0
		0.5	dozen	Books, Primers	0	0	6	0
		0.5	lb	Cinnamon	0	0	15	0
		4	dozen	Glasses	0	0	16	0
		4	yard?	*Barrar*[4]	0	2	0	0
		1	dozen	Skins, Red	0	2	1	0
		4	dozen	Thimbles	0	0	12	0
Nicholas Harold	Ind	4	piece	Cloth of Assize	0	0	0	0
		9	lb	Silk, *Worked*	6	0	0	0
		9	lb	Saffron	4	10	0	0
		10	dozen	Skins, Golden	0	41	8	0
		13	gross	Knives	4	6	8	0
		10	dozen	Knives, in Pairs	0	16	8	0
		78	gross	Points	3	18	0	0
		25	lb	Thread	0	10	5	0
		16	dozen	Cards, Playing	0	13	4	0
		9	doz	Ribbons, Unspecified	0	12	9	0
		4	dozen	Skins, Red	0	8	4	0
		3.5	lb	Ginger	0	5	3	0
		7	lb	Pepper	0	7	0	0
		5	lb	Verdigris	0	2	1	0
		2	dozen	Books, Primers	0	2	0	0
		7	lb	Sulpher	0	0	10	0
		6	lb	Oil, Bay	0	3	0	0
		2	gross	Lacquer	0	3	4	0
		2	dozen	Caps	0	20	0	0
		1	lb	Senna	0	0	6	0
		14	dozen	*Percular*	0	0	20	0
		3	dozen	Girdles	0	0	12	0
		6	dozen	Glasses	0	2	0	0
		2	lb	Cinnamon/Cloves	0	5	0	0
		30	lb	Cumin	0	3	4	0
		24	lb	Incense	0	2	6	0
		42	lb	Liquorice	0	0	20	0
		6	lb	Mercury	0	2	6	0
		0.5	lb	Borax	0	4	0	0
		1	lb	Nutmeg	0	0	18	0
Walter Harold	Ind	4.25	piece	Cloth of Assize	0	0	0	0
		1	gross	Knives	0	6	8	0
		0.5	gross	Cutts	0	0	20	0
		1	bolt	Thread	0	0	13	0
		1	doz	Ribbons, Unspecified	0	0	16	0
		1	lb	Silk, *Worked*	0	13	4	0
		6	gross	Points	0	6	0	0
		1	dozen	Fubligar	0	0	18	0

4 Unidentified.

Merchant name	Origin	Qty	Unit	Commodity	£	s.	d.	f.
		4	dozen	Skins, Golden	0	16	8	0
Nicholas Balie & Forstall	Ind	7	C	Iron	0	28	0	0
		4	lb	Saffron	2	0	0	0
		2	lb	Silk, *Worked*	0	26	8	0
		1	dozen	Soap	0	0	15	0
Reonidus Vale and assoc.	Ind	3	C	Iron	0	12	0	0
		2	lb	Saffron	0	20	0	0

The John of Le Conquet, John Watts master, Entering, 27th April 1542

John Russell	Ind	25	ton	Salt	12	10	0	0

The Julyan of La Rochelle, William Gully master, Entering, *27th April 1542*

John Russell	Ind	16	ton	Salt	8	0	0	0

The Mary of Tenby, Watkyn Tailour master, Entering, 29th April 1542

Richard Retord & Prydie	Ind	4	tun	Oil, *Olive*	16	0	0	0
		3	tun	Wine	0	0	0	0

The George of Longney, Thomas Newman master, Entering, 2nd May 1542

John Rothe & assoc.	Ind	4	tun	Wine	0	0	0	0
		1	C	Skins, Lamb	0	6	8	0
		40	yard	Check *Cloth*	0	13	4	0

The Mary of Gloucester, John Lewllyn master, Entering, 4th May 1542

Thomas Cloturboke	Ind	1	C	Check *Cloth*	2	0	0	0

The Mary, *Port Unknown*, Gran*ville* Mayne master, Entering, 6th May 1542

John Russell	Ind	16	ton	Salt	8	0	0	0

The Prymrose of Bristol, Thomas White master, Entering, 8th May 1542

William Ballard & assoc.	Ind	80.5	ton	Iron	201	5	0	0

The John of Le Conquet, John Watts master, Exiting, 9th May 1542

John Watts	Alien	1.5	last	Coal	0	20	0	0
		0.825	piece	Welsh *Cloth*	0	16	5	0
		0.5	piece	Cloth of Assize	0	0	0	0

The Christopher of Chepstow, John Jene master, Entering, *9th May 1542*

William Jay & Draper	Ind	6	C	Woad, Azores	2	0	0	0

Merchant name	Origin	Qty	Unit	Commodity	£	s.	d.	f.
The Ann of St Ives, John Goodall master, Entering, 12th May 1542								
John *Goodall*	Ind	16	bolt	Poldavis *Canvas*	8	o	o	o
The Anthony of Waterford, Henry Gall master, Entering, 13th May 1542								
Jasper Harold	Ind	4	C	Skins, Sheep	o	40	o	o
		3	C	Skins, Lamb	o	20	o	o
		12	piece	Skins, Fox	o	2	o	o
		2.4	dicker	Skins, Deer	o	3	o	o
		12	piece	Skins, Marten	o	12	o	o
Roland Harold	Ind	8	C	Skins, Lamb	o	53	4	o
		1.33	C	Skins, Sheep	o	13	4	o
		58	piece	Skins, Marten	2	18	o	o
		36	piece	Skins, Fox	o	6	o	o
		10	piece	Skins, Otter	o	4	2	o
		6	piece	Skins, Wolf	o	2	o	o
		40	yard	*Irish* Linen *Cloth*	o	3	4	o
Thomas Creangh	Ind	3	C	Skins, Lamb	o	20	o	o
		2.5	C	Skins, Sheep	o	25	o	o
		19	piece	Skins, Fox	o	3	2	o
		22	piece	Skins, Otter	o	9	2	o
		3	piece	Skins, Marten	o	3	o	o
Thomas Skyllan	Ind	3	C	Skins, Sheep	o	30	o	o
		4	C	Skins, Lamb	o	26	8	o
		24	piece	Skins, Marten	o	24	o	o
		30	piece	Skins, Fox	o	5	o	o
		12	piece	Skins, Otter	o	5	o	o
		5	piece	Skins, Wolf	o	o	20	o
Edmund Draye	Ind	6	C	Check *Cloth*	12	o	o	o
		5	C	Skins, Sheep	2	10	o	o
		2	C	Skins, Lamb	o	13	4	o
		6	piece	Skins, Fox	o	o	12	o
		6	dicker	Skins, Deer	o	12	6	o
		2	piece	Mantles	o	6	8	o
Richard Donell	Ind	7	C	Skins, Sheep	3	10	o	o
		2	C	Skins, Lamb	o	13	4	o
		2.5	C	Check *Cloth*	5	o	o	o
		12	piece	Skins, Fox	o	2	o	o
Henry Gall	Ind	7	C	Check *Cloth*	14	o	o	o
		4	piece	Mantles	o	13	4	o
		0.5	C	Skins, Sheep	o	5	o	o
Robert Maidell	Ind	4	C	Check *Cloth*	8	o	o	o
		4	C	Skins, Sheep	o	40	o	o
		2	C	Skins, Lamb	o	13	4	o
		2	piece	Mantles	o	6	8	o
Peter Butlar	Ind	2	C	Check *Cloth*	4	o	o	o
		1.5	C	Skins, Sheep	o	15	o	o
		1	C	Skins, Lamb	o	6	8	o
		8	piece	Mantles	o	26	8	o

Merchant name	Origin	Qty	Unit	Commodity	£	s.	d.	f.

The Mary George of Bristol, Cornell Andrew master, Entering, 15th May 1542

| Cornell Andrew | Ind | 2 | C | Check *Cloth* | 4 | 0 | 0 | 0 |
| | | 2 | C | Skins, Sheep | 0 | 20 | 0 | 0 |

The Trynyte of Chepstow, Lewis Haynes master, Entering, 15th May 1542

| John White | Ind | 1.5 | tun | Wine | 0 | 0 | 0 | 0 |
| | | 5 | C | Rosin | 0 | 6 | 8 | 0 |

The Nicholas of Bristol, Bartholemew Garland master, Entering, 15th May 1542

Edward Pryn	Ind	1	pipe	Wine	0	0	0	0
		1	C	Skins, Sheep	0	10	0	0
		4	dicker	Skins, Deer	0	8	4	0
		1	virkin	Fish, Salmon	0	7	6	0
		1	C	Skins, Lamb	0	6	8	0

The Trynyte of Bristol, Thomas Webb master, Exiting, 19th May 1542

Nicholas Thorn	Ind	8	ton	Lead, worked	40	0	0	0
John Smyth	Ind	8	ton	Lead, worked	40	0	0	0
		45	piece	Cloth of Assize	0	0	0	0
		5	dicker	Hides, Tanned	0	0	0	0
Edward Pryn	Ind	1.5	ton	Lead, worked	7	10	0	0
		14	piece	Cloth of Assize	0	0	0	0
Thomas Shipman	Ind	1	ton	Lead, worked	5	0	0	0
		14.83	piece	Cloth of Assize	0	0	0	0
Thomas Tyson	Ind	10	piece	Cloth of Assize	0	0	0	0
Arthur Smyth	Ind	3.5	ton	Lead, worked	17	10	0	0
Robert Sexe	Ind	10	piece	Cloth of Assize	0	0	0	0
Thomas White	Ind	7	ton	Lead, worked	35	0	0	0
John Cutt	Ind	10	piece	Cloth of Assize	0	0	0	0
William Sprat	Ind	10	piece	Cloth of Assize	0	0	0	0
Thomas Webb	Ind	12	quart	Wheat	0	40	0	0
Robert Gyttens	Ind	7.66	piece	Cloth of Assize	0	0	0	0
		10	piece	Manchester *Cotton Cloth*	5	0	0	0
John Shipman	Ind	5	piece	Yellow lining *Cloth*	3	6	8	0

The Sunday of Bristol, Evan Brettan master, Entering, 20th May 1542

| William Gelly | Ind | 12 | ton | Salt | 6 | 0 | 0 | 0 |

The Anthony of Tintern, David Adams master, Entering, 22nd May 1542

Patrick Sarchesell	Ind	10	C	Check *Cloth*	20	0	0	0
		112	piece	Skins, Lamb	0	7	2	0
		33	piece	Skins, Kid	0	6	0	0
		5.2	C	Skins, Sheep	0	32	0	0
		3	piece	Skins, Deer	0	0	8	0
Thomas Fitzsymons	Ind	7	C	Check *Cloth*	14	0	0	0
		1	C	Skins, Sheep	0	10	0	0

Merchant name	Origin	Qty	Unit	Commodity	£	s.	d.	f.
		2	C	Skins, Lamb	0	13	4	0
		3.8	dicker	Skins, Deer	0	9	0	0
		12	piece	Skins, Fox	0	2	0	0
		7	piece	Mantles	0	23	4	0

The Nicholas of Waterford, Thomas Folan master, Entering, 22nd May 1542

Merchant name	Origin	Qty	Unit	Commodity	£	s.	d.	f.
Peter Fitzjohn & Madan	Ind	9	C	Check *Cloth*	18	0	0	0
		0.5	C	Skins, Lamb	0	3	4	0
		40	piece	Skins, Sheep	0	3	4	0
John Fleger	Ind	1.08	C	Check *Cloth*	2	3	4	0
		1.5	C	Skins, Sheep	0	15	0	0
		1.5	C	Skins, Lamb	0	10	0	0
		2	piece	Mantles	0	6	8	0

The Prymrose of Bristol, Thomas Lache master, Exiting, 25th May 1542

Merchant name	Origin	Qty	Unit	Commodity	£	s.	d.	f.
Edward Pryn	Ind	7	last	Coal	4	13	4	0
		2	piece	Welsh *Cloth*	2	0	0	0

The Patrick of New Ross, Thomas Colman master, Entering, 25th May 1542

Merchant name	Origin	Qty	Unit	Commodity	£	s.	d.	f.
Thomas *Colman*	Ind	7	C	Skins, Sheep	3	10	0	0
		10	C	Skins, Lamb	3	6	8	0
		1	C	Check *Cloth*	2	0	0	0
		4	stone	Wool, Flocks	0	0	20	0
		6	piece	Skins, Deer	0	0	18	0
William Butlar	Ind	7	C	Skins, Sheep	3	10	0	0
		5	C	Skins, Lamb	0	33	4	0
		1	C	Check *Cloth*	2	0	0	0
Thomas Dowle	Ind	3	C	Skins, Sheep	0	30	0	0
		3	C	Skins, Lamb	0	20	0	0
		2	dicker	Skins, Deer	0	4	2	0
		12	stone	Wool, Flocks	0	5	0	0
		30	yard	Check *Cloth*	0	10	0	0
John Coterell	Ind	2	C	Check *Cloth*	4	0	0	0
		0.5	C	Skins, Sheep	0	5	0	0
		1	dicker	Skins, Deer	0	2	1	0

The Myhell of Bristol, David Gyllam master, Exiting, 25th May 1542

Merchant name	Origin	Qty	Unit	Commodity	£	s.	d.	f.
Thomas White & Lyntley	Ind	13.8	ton	Lead, worked	69	0	0	0
		16	piece	Cloth of Assize	0	0	0	0
Edward Pryn & Sprat	Ind	1.5	ton	Lead, worked	7	10	0	0
		22	dicker	Hides, Tanned	0	0	0	0
Alan Hill	Ind	10	piece	Cloth of Assize	0	0	0	0
Richard Williams	Ind	2	piece	Welsh *Cloth*	2	0	0	0
		1	ton	Lead, worked	5	0	0	0

Merchant name	Origin	Qty	Unit	Commodity	£	s.	d.	f.

The George of Longney, William Rothe master, Exiting, *25th May 1542*

Merchant name	Origin	Qty	Unit	Commodity	£	s.	d.	f.
Hugh Pryn	Ind	12	quart	Wheat	0	40	0	0

The Trynyte Coke, *Port Unknown*, John Gratyan master, Exiting, 26th May 1542

Merchant name	Origin	Qty	Unit	Commodity	£	s.	d.	f.
Giles Fowlar	Ind	20	piece	Northern *Cotton Cloth*	4	3	4	0
		1	piece	Welsh *Cloth*	0	20	0	0
		3.75	piece	Cloth of Assize	0	0	0	0

The Savyour of Northam, John Aunger master, Entering, *26th May 1542*

Merchant name	Origin	Qty	Unit	Commodity	£	s.	d.	f.
Alan Hill & Pryn	Ind	17.25	tun	Woad, Azores	115	0	0	0
John Cutt & Shipman	Ind	18	tun	Woad, Azores	120	0	0	0
Francis Blankeley	Alien	10	tun	Woad, Azores	66	13	4	0

The John of Dartmouth, Nicholas Hythyns master, Entering, 1st June 1542

Merchant name	Origin	Qty	Unit	Commodity	£	s.	d.	f.
Robert Newborn & assoc.	Ind	38	ton	Iron	95	0	0	0

The Anthony of Waterford, Henry Gall master, Exiting, *1st June 1542*

Merchant name	Origin	Qty	Unit	Commodity	£	s.	d.	f.
Sir Anthony St Leger	Ind	60	quart	Wheat	10	0	0	0
		36	quart	Beans/Malt	5	0	0	0
Peter Butlar	Ind	0.1	ton	Lead, worked	0	10	0	0
Jasper Harold	Ind	11	piece	Cloth of Assize	0	0	0	0
		48	gross	Points	2	8	0	0
		8	lb	Liquorice	0	0	10	0
		6	dozen	Cards, Playing	0	5	0	0
		6	lb	Cumin	0	0	7	0
		0.5	dozen	Caps	0	5	0	0
		2	gross	Cutts	0	6	8	0
		2	lb	Mercury	0	0	10	0
Roland Harold	Ind	7	piece	Cloth of Assize	0	0	0	0
		3	lb	Saffron	0	30	0	0
		4.5	lb	Silk, *Worked*	3	0	0	0
		10	lb	Cumin	0	0	15	0
		5	gross	Knives	0	33	4	0
		1	gross	Cutts	0	3	4	0
		36	gross	Points	0	36	0	0
		10	lb	Mercury	0	4	2	0
		14	dozen	Glasses	0	0	20	0
		11	dozen	Cards, Playing	0	9	2	0
		2	dozen	Skins, Red	0	4	2	0
		3	lb	Cloves	0	7	6	0
		3	lb	Ginger	0	4	6	0
		3	lb	Sulpher	0	0	5	0
		17	lb	Thread	0	7	1	0
		10	lb	Pepper	0	10	0	0
		8	dozen	Skins, Golden	0	33	4	0
		4	dozen	Girdles	0	6	0	0

Merchant name	Origin	Qty	Unit	Commodity	£	s.	d.	f.
		4	lb	Verdigris	0	0	20	0
		2	dozen	Caps	0	20	0	0
		0.5	dozen	Hats	0	2	6	0
		1	gross	Lacquer	0	0	20	0
		1.5	dozen	Books, Primers	0	2	1	0
		3.5	lb	Cinnamon	0	8	9	0
		1	lb	Mace	0	2	6	0
		1	lb	Nutmeg	0	0	12	0
		2	dozen	Knives, in Pairs	0	3	4	0
		40	lb	Liquorice	0	0	20	0
		3	unknown	Drugs, Miscellaneous	0	3	4	0
Thomas Creangh	Ind	1.5	piece	Cloth of Assize	0	0	0	0
		2	lb	Silk, *Worked*	0	26	8	0
		3	gross	Knives	0	20	0	0
		1	gross	Cutts	0	3	4	0
		24	gross	Points	0	24	0	0
		2	dozen	Skins, Golden	0	8	4	0
		1	gross	Lacquer	0	0	20	0
		2.5	lb	Thread	0	0	12	2
		1	lb	Mercury	0	0	5	0
		1.5	dozen	Skins, Red	0	3	1	2
		10	lb	Cumin	0	0	15	0
		4	dozen	Cards, Playing	0	3	4	0
		2	dozen	Knives, in Pairs	0	3	4	0
Thomas Creangh	Ind	3	dozen	Girdles	0	0	8	0
		0.5	lb	Cinnamon	0	0	15	0
		1.5	lb	Pepper	0	0	18	0
		1	dozen	Girdles	0	0	15	0
Thomas Skyllan	Ind	3.5	piece	Cloth of Assize	0	0	0	0
		2	lb	Silk, *Worked*	0	26	8	0
		6	gross	Knives	2	0	0	0
		2	gross	Cutts	0	6	8	0
		8	dozen	Cards, Playing	0	6	8	0
		1	dozen	Books, Primers	0	0	10	0
		4	lb	Verdigris	0	0	20	0
		12.5	lb	Thread	0	5	2	0
		3	dozen	Knives, in Pairs	0	5	0	0
		4	dozen	Girdles	0	5	4	0
		6	dozen	Skins, Golden	0	25	0	0
		36	gross	Points	0	36	0	0
		1	gross	Lacquer	0	0	20	0
		1	dozen	Nightcaps, Unspecified	0	3	4	0
		1	lb	Cinnamon	0	2	6	0
		0.5	lb	Ginger	0	0	9	0
		2	lb	Pepper	0	2	0	0
		12	lb	Liquorice	0	0	5	0
		6	dozen	Glasses	0	0	9	0
		1	dozen	Hats	0	3	0	0
		1	lb	Mercury	0	0	5	0
		0.5	dozen	Skins, Red	0	0	13	0
		1	lb	Senna	0	0	8	0
		6	lb	Sulpher	0	0	8	0

Merchant name	Origin	Qty	Unit	Commodity	£	s.	d.	f.

The Nicholas of Waterford, Thomas Folan master, Exiting, *1st June 1542*

Merchant name	Origin	Qty	Unit	Commodity	£	s.	d.	f.
Sir Anthony St Leger	Ind	1.25	C	Beans/Malt	16	13	4	0
Edmund Dray	Ind	4.75	piece	Cloth of Assize	0	0	0	0
		3	lb	Saffron	0	30	0	0
		2	gross	Knives	0	13	4	0
		2	gross	Lacquer	0	3	4	0
		1	dozen	Skins, Golden	0	4	0	0
		3	dozen	Knives, in Pairs	0	5	0	0
		1	dozen	Caps	0	10	0	0
		0.5	dozen	Hats	0	5	0	0
		0.75	dozen	Nightcaps, Satin	0	12	0	0
		0.75	dozen	Nightcaps, Velvet	0	12	0	0
		1	dozen	Nightcaps, Cloth	0	4	0	0
Richard Donell	Ind	1.25	piece	Cloth of Assize	0	0	0	0
		1	dozen	Caps	0	10	0	0
		1	dozen	Nightcaps, Unspecified	0	4	0	0
		0.5	dozen	Hats	0	4	0	0
		1	dozen	Skins, Golden	0	4	2	0
		1	gross	Knives	0	6	8	0
		1.5	C	Hops	0	15	0	0
		2	gross	Lacquer	0	3	4	0
		2	gross	Points	0	2	0	0

The Patrycke of New Ross, Thomas Colman master, Exiting, *1st June 1542*

Merchant name	Origin	Qty	Unit	Commodity	£	s.	d.	f.
Sir Anthony St Leger	Ind	4	wey	Malt	3	6	8	0
		12	quart	Wheat	0	40	0	0
Thomas *Colman*	Ind	1.25	piece	Cloth of Assize	0	0	0	0
		0.75	gross	Knives	0	5	0	0
		12	gross	Points	0	12	0	0
		1	gross	Lacquer	0	0	20	0
		1	dozen	Skins, Golden	0	4	2	0
John Coterell	Ind	1.5	piece	Cloth of Assize, Dozen Strait	0	0	0	0
		0.5	piece	Cloth of Assize	0	0	0	0
Clement Fannyng	Ind	1.5	piece	Cloth of Assize	0	0	0	0
		24	gross	Points	0	24	0	0
		1	gross	Lacquer	0	0	20	0
		2	doz	Ribbons, Unspecified	0	3	0	0
		2	dozen	Caps	0	20	0	0
		6	dozen	Knives, in Pairs	0	10	0	0
		10	lb	Verdigris	0	4	2	0
		2.5	lb	Thread	0	0	12	0
		2	clout	Needles	0	0	18	0
		4	dozen	Skins, Golden	0	16	8	0

The Margarete of Bristol, John Jene master, Exiting, 3rd June 1542

Merchant name	Origin	Qty	Unit	Commodity	£	s.	d.	f.
Sir Anthony St Leger	Ind	37	quart	Wheat	6	0	0	0
		5	wey	Malt	4	3	4	0

349

Merchant name	Origin	Qty	Unit	Commodity	£	s.	d.	f.
The Sunday of Bristol, Nicholas Beverege master, Exiting, 10th June 1542								
Robert Newborn	Ind	18	quart	Wheat	3	0	0	0
		2.5	C	Hops	0	25	0	0
		0.5	C	Aniseed	0	6	8	0
		30	quart	Beans/Malt	4	3	4	0
The Mary of Nantes, Michael de New master, Exiting, _10th June 1542_								
Michael de New	Alien	2	last	Coal	0	26	8	0
		2	piece	Bristol Frieze Cloth	0	26	8	0
The Trynyte of Gloucester, William Coke master, Entering, 12th June 1542								
John Hawkyns	Ind	23.5	ton	Salt	11	15	0	0
		0.25	tun	Vinegar	0	10	0	0
The Thomas Mawdelen of Bristol, Thomas Hardyng master, Entering, 14th June 1542								
Robert Thurban	Ind	40	tun	Wine	0	0	0	0
		2	tun	Wine, Corrupt	3	0	0	0
		1	pipe	Oil, _Olive_	2	0	0	0
William Yonge	Ind	3	ton	Salt	0	30	0	0
		12	C	Aniseed	8	0	0	0
Thomas Apbowen & assoc.	Ind	13.5	C	Orchil	9	0	0	0
		16.25	C	Soap	8	2	6	0
		9	ton	Salt	4	10	0	0
		1	pipe	Wine	0	0	0	0
The John of Le Conquet, Mathew Legace master, Entering, _14th June 1542_								
Mathew Legace	Alien	24.5	ton	Salt	12	5	0	0
The Harry of Bristol, Anthony Pygot master, Entering, _14th June 1542_								
Peter Gonzales	Alien	30	tun	Woad, Azores	200	0	0	0
Edward Pryn & assoc.	Ind	84	tun	Woad, Azores	560	0	0	0
The Patryck of Cork, Robert Verdon master, Exiting, 15th June 1542								
Robert _Verdon_	Ind	0.25	piece	Cloth of Assize	0	0	0	0
		2	gross	Knives	0	13	4	0
		3	gross	Points	0	3	0	0
		0.25	C	Hops	0	2	6	0
		1	dozen	Wool-Cards	0	4	0	0
The Clement of Framilode, John Wade master, Entering, _15th June 1542_								
William Bullock	Ind	15	ton	Salt	7	10	0	0

Merchant name	Origin	Qty	Unit	Commodity	£	s.	d.	f.

The Martyn of San Antonio Abad, Martin Anthonius master, Entering, 16th June 1542

Merchant name	Origin	Qty	Unit	Commodity	£	s.	d.	f.
Martin Anthonius	Alien	75	M	Oranges	12	10	0	0

The Julyan of Bristol, John Croke master, Entering, 16th June 1542

Merchant name	Origin	Qty	Unit	Commodity	£	s.	d.	f.
John Welsh & assoc.	Ind	48.75	tun	Woad, Azores	333	6	8	0

The Trynyte of Chepstow, Lewis Haynes master, Entering, 17th June 1542

Merchant name	Origin	Qty	Unit	Commodity	£	s.	d.	f.
Nicholas Thorn	Ind	9.5	tun	Oil, Olive	38	0	0	0

The Peter of Gloucester, Thomas Smyth master, Entering, 17th June 1542

Merchant name	Origin	Qty	Unit	Commodity	£	s.	d.	f.
Robert Pole	Ind	6.5	tun	Wine	0	0	0	0
		4	tun	Oil, Olive	16	0	0	0
		6.25	C	Soap	3	2	6	0
		4	ton	Salt	2	0	0	0

The Margaret of Jersey, Dennis Jasper master, Entering, 19th June 1542

Merchant name	Origin	Qty	Unit	Commodity	£	s.	d.	f.
Dennis Jasper	Ind	24.75	ton	Salt	12	7	6	0

The John of Tewkesbury, John Madock master, Entering, 19th June 1542

Merchant name	Origin	Qty	Unit	Commodity	£	s.	d.	f.
Hugh Draper	Ind	10	tun	Woad, Azores	66	13	4	0
		2	chest	Sugar	4	0	0	0

The Clement of Bristol, Dennis Banghe master, Entering, 21st June 1542

Merchant name	Origin	Qty	Unit	Commodity	£	s.	d.	f.
Margannus? Mathen	Ind	49	C	Soap	24	10	0	0
Thomas Stanford	Ind	0.875	tun	Wine	0	0	0	0
William Appowell	Ind	2.5	C	Soap	0	25	0	0

The Jhesus of Wexford, John Stafford master, Entering, 23rd June 1542

Merchant name	Origin	Qty	Unit	Commodity	£	s.	d.	f.
John Stafford	Ind	3	C	Wood	3	0	0	0
		3	C	Skins, Sheep	0	30	0	0
		3	C	Skins, Lamb	0	20	0	0
		2	piece	Mantles	0	6	8	0
		40	yard	Check Cloth	0	13	4	0
		5	dicker	Skins, Deer	0	10	5	0

The Sunday of Bristol, Thomas Walter master, Entering, 26th June 1542

Merchant name	Origin	Qty	Unit	Commodity	£	s.	d.	f.
Stephen Mewghe	Ind	3.66	C	Skins, Sheep	0	36	8	0
		196	piece	Skins, Lamb	0	12	0	0
		18	piece	Skins, Fox	0	3	0	0
		3	piece	Skins, Wolf	0	2	6	0
		3	piece	Skins, Kid	0	0	10	0
		14	piece	Skins, Otter	0	5	10	0
		7	piece	Skins, Lamb	0	0	6	0

Merchant name	Origin	Qty	Unit	Commodity	£	s.	d.	f.
		6	yard	Check *Cloth*	0	2	0	0
Richard Malrony	Ind	3.9	C	Skins, Lamb	0	26	0	0
		32	piece	Skins, Fox	0	5	4	0
		31	piece	Skins, Otter	0	12	11	0
		40	piece	Skins, Marten	2	0	0	0
		65	yard	Check *Cloth*	0	21	8	0
David Richards	Ind	2.5	C	Skins, Sheep	0	25	0	0
		4	C	Skins, Lamb	0	26	8	0
		28	piece	Skins, Fox	0	4	8	0
		5	piece	Skins, Otter	0	2	1	0
		1	piece	Skins, Wolf	0	0	10	0
		0.5	C	Check *Cloth*	0	20	0	0
Richard White	Ind	2.5	C	Skins, Sheep	0	25	0	0
		1.5	C	Skins, Lamb	0	10	0	0
		1	dicker	Skins, Deer	0	2	1	0
		1	piece	Skins, Marten	0	0	12	0
		2	piece	Skins, Fox	0	0	4	0
		1	piece	Skins, Otter	0	0	5	0
		1	piece	Skins, Wolf	0	0	10	0
		20	yard	Check *Cloth*	0	6	8	0
Stephen White	Ind	3.28	C	Skins, Sheep	0	32	10	0
		7	C	Skins, Lamb	0	46	8	0
		29	piece	Skins, Fox	0	4	10	0
		14	piece	Skins, Otter	0	5	10	0
		2	piece	Skins, Wolf	0	0	20	0
		4	piece	Skins, Marten	0	4	0	0
		55	yard	Check *Cloth*	0	18	4	0
Thomas Stackpoll	Ind	3	C	Skins, Sheep	0	30	0	0
		324	piece	Skins, Lamb	0	21	6	0
		16	piece	Skins, Fox	0	2	8	0
		11	piece	Skins, Otter	0	4	7	0
		5	piece	Skins, Marten	0	5	0	0
		21	yard	Check *Cloth*	0	7	0	0

The Margaret of Jersey, Dennis Jasper master, Exiting, 27th June 1542

Dennis Jasper	Ind	3.5	last	Coal	2	6	8	0

The John of Le Conquet, Mathew Legace master, Exiting, 3rd July 1542

Mathew Legace	Alien	2.25	piece	Cloth of Assize	0	0	0	0
		1	tun	Lime	0	2	6	0
		3	piece	Dunster *Cloth*	0	30	0	0
		2	piece	Dunster *Cloth*	0	20	0	0

The Mary of Gloucester, Thomas Smyth master, Entering, *3rd July 1542*

Robert Pole	Ind	12	ton	Salt	6	0	0	0

The Bartholemew of Wexford, Richard Dawne master, Entering, 4th July 1542

Richard Dawne	Ind	1.5	C	Skins, Sheep	0	15	0	0
		30	yard	Check *Cloth*	0	10	0	0

Merchant name	Origin	Qty	Unit	Commodity	£	s.	d.	f.

The Mary of Gloucester, John Dymocke master, Exiting, *4th July 1542*

| Thomas Cloturboke | Ind | 4.5 | wey | Beans/Malt | 3 | 15 | 0 | 0 |

The Jhesus of Wexford, John Stafford master, Exiting, *4th July 1542*

| John Stafford | Ind | 12 | quart | Wheat | 0 | 40 | 0 | 0 |
| Sir Anthony St Leger | Ind | 2 | wey | Malt | 0 | 33 | 4 | 0 |

The Trynyte of Chepstow, Roger Mower master, Entering, 7th July 1542

| William Byford | Ind | 1 | pipe | Wine | 0 | 0 | 0 | 0 |

The Martyn of San Antonio *Abad*, Martin Anthonius master, Exiting, *7th July 1542*

| *Martin Anthonius* | Alien | 7 | piece | Welsh *Cloth* | 7 | 0 | 0 | 0 |
| | | 6.083 | piece | Cloth of Assize | 0 | 0 | 0 | 0 |

The Trynyte More of Bristol, John Gall master, Exiting, 9th July 1542

William Appowell	Ind	30	piece	Manchester *Cotton Cloth*	15	0	0	0
		10	piece	Dunster *Cloth*	5	0	0	0
		6	piece	Welsh *Cloth*	6	0	0	0
		20	piece	Cloth of Assize	0	0	0	0
Francis Codryngton	Ind	14	dicker	Hides, Tanned	0	0	0	0

The Christopher of Chepstow, Richard Jene, Entering, *9th July 1542*

| William Carey | Ind | 1.5 | chest | Sugar | 3 | 0 | 0 | 0 |
| William Yonge | Ind | 2.25 | chest | Sugar | 4 | 10 | 0 | 0 |

The Christopher of Chepstow, Richard Jene master, Exiting, *9th July 1542*

| William Carey | Ind | 2 | piece | Cloth of Assize | 0 | 0 | 0 | 0 |

The Bartholemew of Wexford, Richard Dawne master, Exiting, 10th July 1542

| Richard *Dawne* | Ind | 12 | quart | Wheat | 0 | 40 | 0 | 0 |

The Dowghen of Cardiff, John Merycke master, Entering, 13th July 1542

| John Fowlyng | Ind | 10.66 | C | Check *Cloth* | 21 | 6 | 8 | 0 |
| Richard Chancellor | Ind | 1 | pipe | Wine | 0 | 0 | 0 | 0 |

The Clement of *Minsterford*, Robert Hyat master, Entering, *13th July 1542*

| Robert *Hyat* | Ind | 3 | dicker | Skins, Deer | 0 | 6 | 6 | 0 |
| | | 0.5 | C | Check *Cloth* | 0 | 20 | 0 | 0 |

The Trynyte of Caerleon, Sebastian Melyor master, Entering, *13th July 1542*

| John Shipman | Ind | 2 | tun | Oil, *Olive* | 8 | 0 | 0 | 0 |
| William Shipman | Ind | 4.5 | tun | Oil, *Olive* | 18 | 0 | 0 | 0 |

Merchant name	Origin	Qty	Unit	Commodity	£	s.	d.	f.
Nicholas Thorn	Ind	9	tun	Oil, *Olive*	36	0	0	0
Henry White	Ind	2.75	tun	Oil, *Olive*	11	0	0	0
		16.5	C	Alum	13	5	0	0
William Sprat	Ind	6.5	tun	Oil, *Olive*	26	0	0	0
Robert Elyot	Ind	1	pipe	Oil, *Olive*	2	0	0	0
William Ballard	Ind	32	tun	Oil, *Olive*	128	0	0	0
		12	ton	Salt	6	0	0	0
		1	tun	Wine	0	0	0	0
Richard Pryn &								
Thomas Hicks	Ind	18	C	Orchil	12	0	0	0
		2	tun	Oil, *Olive*	8	0	0	0
Edward Pryn	Ind	7	tun	Oil, *Olive*	28	0	0	0
William Carr	Ind	10	tun	Oil, *Olive*	40	0	0	0
Edward Butlar	Ind	17.5	C	Soap	8	15	0	0
Lewis Robbyns	Ind	3.5	tun	Oil, *Olive*	14	0	0	0
Robert Butlar	Ind	6.5	tun	Oil, *Olive*	26	0	0	0
James Balie	Ind	3.75	tun	Oil, *Olive*	15	0	0	0
		3	C	Orchil	2	0	0	0
Giles White	Ind	3.5	tun	Oil, *Olive*	14	0	0	0
John Pryn	Ind	2.5	tun	Oil, *Olive*	10	0	0	0
Johanna Carpenter	Ind	5.75	tun	Oil, *Olive*	23	0	0	0
William Ostryche	Ind	1	tun	Oil, *Olive*	4	0	0	0
Arthur Smyth	Ind	2.75	tun	Oil, *Olive*	11	0	0	0
Thomas Jones	Ind	1	tun	Oil, *Olive*	4	0	0	0
		4.5	C	Orchil	3	0	0	0
John Appowell &								
assoc.	Ind	1.75	tun	Oil, *Olive*	7	0	0	0

The Bryde of Waterford, Nicholas Rothe master, Entering, 14th July 1542

Merchant name	Origin	Qty	Unit	Commodity	£	s.	d.	f.
Nicholas *Rothe*	Ind	6	piece	Mantles	0	20	0	0
Richard Welsh	Ind	2.5	C	Check *Cloth*	5	0	0	0
		5	piece	Mantles	0	16	8	0
John Bousher	Ind	8	C	Check *Cloth*	16	0	0	0
		27	piece	Mantles	4	10	0	0
		3	C	Skins, Lamb	0	20	0	0
		15	piece	Skins, Sheep	0	0	15	0
William Balie	Ind	0.25	C	Skins, Sheep	0	25	0	0
		1	C	Check *Cloth*	2	0	0	0
		3	C	Skins, Lamb	0	20	0	0
Clement Welsh	Ind	11.5	C	Check *Cloth*	23	0	0	0
		23	piece	Mantles	3	16	8	0
		3.5	C	Skins, Lamb	0	23	4	0
		3	C	Skins, Kid	0	15	0	0
		10	C	Skins, Sheep	5	0	0	0
		3	stone	Wool, Flocks	0	0	15	0
John Mawmesey	Ind	4	C	Check *Cloth*	8	0	0	0
		20	piece	Mantles	3	6	8	0
		4	C	Skins, Sheep	0	40	0	0
		1	C	Skins, Lamb	0	6	8	0
Oliver Rothe	Ind	10	C	Check *Cloth*	20	0	0	0
		5	C	Skins, Lamb	0	23	4	0

Merchant name	Origin	Qty	Unit	Commodity	£	s.	d.	f.
		6	C	Skins, Sheep	3	0	0	0
		6	stone	Wool, Flocks	0	2	6	0
		6	stone	Wool, Irish	0	16	0	0
		6	piece	Skins, Fox	0	0	12	0
		1	C	Skins, Kid	0	5	0	0
William Rothe	Ind	4	C	Check *Cloth*	8	0	0	0
		4	C	Skins, Sheep	0	40	0	0
		6	C	Skins, Lamb	0	40	0	0
		14	piece	Mantles	2	6	8	0
		4	stone	Wool, Flocks	0	0	20	0
		1	C	Skins, Kid	0	5	0	0
		1	piece	Skins, Marten	0	0	12	0
George Savage	Ind	7.5	C	Check *Cloth*	15	0	0	0
		10	C	Skins, Lamb	3	6	8	0
		2	C	Skins, Sheep	0	20	0	0
		83	piece	Mantles	13	16	8	0
		4	piece	Skins, Fox	0	0	8	0
		1	piece	Skins, Otter	0	0	5	0
		1	piece	Skins, Marten	0	0	12	0
Andrew Welsh	Ind	5	C	Skins, Sheep	2	10	0	0
		12.5	C	Check *Cloth*	25	0	0	0
		5	C	Skins, Lamb	0	33	4	0
		5	C	Skins, Kid	0	25	0	0
		12	piece	Skins, Fox	0	2	0	0
		6	piece	Mantles	0	20	0	0
		2	stone	Wool, Unspecified	0	5	4	0
James Donell	Ind	26	piece	Mantles	4	6	8	0
		8	C	Check *Cloth*	16	0	0	0
		4.5	C	Skins, Sheep	0	45	0	0
		2.5	C	Skins, Lamb	0	16	8	0
		6	piece	Skins, Fox	0	0	12	0
Nicholas Welsh	Ind	4	C	Skins, Sheep	2	0	0	0
		5	C	Skins, Lamb	0	33	4	0
		18	piece	Mantles	3	0	0	0
		3	C	Check *Cloth*	6	0	0	0
		6	piece	Skins, Fox	0	0	12	0
Nicholas Cranborow	Ind	6.5	C	Check *Cloth*	13	0	0	0
		8	piece	Skins, Fox	0	0	16	0
		1	piece	Mantles	0	3	4	0
		0.25	C	Skins, Sheep	0	2	6	0
		40	piece	Skins, Lamb	0	2	6	0
Patrick Strange	Ind	1	C	Check *Cloth*	2	0	0	0
		0.5	C	Skins, Sheep	0	5	0	0
William Bretten	Ind	3	C	Check *Cloth*	6	0	0	0
		1	C	Skins, Sheep	0	10	0	0
		0.5	C	Skins, Lamb	0	3	4	0

The John of Pasajes de San Juan, John de Lana master, Entering, 15th July 1542

Arnold Noll	Alien	23	ton	Iron	57	10	0	0
		4	tun	Wine, Corrupt	6	0	0	0

Merchant name	Origin	Qty	Unit	Commodity	£	s.	d.	f.

The George of Waterford, Nicholas Colman master, Entering, *15th July 1542*

Merchant name	Origin	Qty	Unit	Commodity	£	s.	d.	f.
Philip Quenmerford	Ind	24	C	Check *Cloth*	48	0	0	0
		3	dicker	Skins, Deer	0	6	6	0
		6	piece	Mantles	0	20	0	0
		0.25	C	Skins, Lamb	0	0	20	0
		2.5	C	Skins, Sheep	0	25	0	0
George Quenmerford	Ind	7	C	Check *Cloth*	14	0	0	0
		18	piece	Mantles	3	0	0	0
		0.25	C	Skins, Sheep	0	2	6	0
Andrew Lyncoln	Ind	5.5	C	Check *Cloth*	11	0	0	0
		5	piece	Mantles	0	16	8	0
		1	C	Skins, Lamb	0	6	8	0
		6	C	Skins, Sheep	3	0	0	0
Patrick Rothe	Ind	16.45	C	Skins, Sheep	8	4	7	0
		264	piece	Skins, Fox	2	4	0	0
		24	piece	Skins, Otter	0	10	0	0
		180	piece	Skins, Lamb	0	11	4	0
John Quyrke	Ind	1.5	C	Check *Cloth*	3	0	0	0
		12	piece	Mantles	2	0	0	0
		0.5	C	Skins, Sheep	0	5	0	0
		1	C	Skins, Lamb	0	6	8	0
John Marthyn	Ind	4.5	C	Skins, Sheep	0	45	0	0
		7	C	Skins, Lamb	0	46	8	0
		3	dicker	Skins, Deer	0	6	3	0
		6	piece	Skins, Fox	0	0	12	0
		4.5	C	Check *Cloth*	9	0	0	0
		6	piece	Mantles	0	20	0	0
Nicholas Garway	Ind	3	C	Skins, Sheep	0	30	0	0
		2	C	Check *Cloth*	4	0	0	0
		2	piece	Skins, Fox	0	0	4	0
Robert Moyne	Ind	36	piece	Skins, Fox	0	6	0	0
		10	C	Skins, Lamb	3	6	8	0
		12	piece	Skins, Marten	0	12	0	0
		12	piece	Skins, Otter	0	5	0	0
Nicholas Colman	Ind	2	C	Check *Cloth*	4	0	0	0
		6	piece	Mantles	0	20	0	0
Maurice Powre	Ind	1	C	Check *Cloth*	2	0	0	0
		16	piece	Mantles	2	13	4	0
Thomas Christofer	Ind	1	C	Check *Cloth*	2	0	0	0
		12	piece	Mantles	2	0	0	0
John Quede	Ind	2	C	Check *Cloth*	4	0	0	0
		6	piece	Mantles	0	20	0	0
Nicholas Brewer	Ind	2.5	C	Check *Cloth*	5	0	0	0
		8	piece	Mantles	0	26	8	0
Nicholas Malrony	Ind	9	C	Skins, Sheep	4	10	0	0
		3	C	Skins, Lamb	0	20	0	0
		1.5	C	Check *Cloth*	3	0	0	0
		4	piece	Mantles	0	13	4	0
James Braye	Ind	4	C	Skins, Sheep	0	40	0	0
		5	C	Skins, Lamb	0	23	4	0
		3	C	Check *Cloth*	6	0	0	0

Merchant name	Origin	Qty	Unit	Commodity	£	s.	d.	f.
		4	piece	Mantles	0	13	4	0
		6	piece	Skins, Fox	0	0	12	0
James Shyrlocke	Ind	3	C	Check *Cloth*	6	0	0	0
		1	piece	Mantles	0	3	4	0
		20	piece	Skins, Sheep	0	0	20	0
Maurice Quyrke	Ind	6	C	Check *Cloth*	12	0	0	0
		6	C	Skins, Lamb	0	40	0	0
		1	C	Skins, Sheep	0	10	0	0
Robert Wadyng	Ind	4	C	Check *Cloth*	8	0	0	0
Edmund Morres	Ind	72	piece	Skins, Fox	0	12	0	0
		10	piece	Skins, Otter	0	4	2	0
		5	piece	Skins, Marten	0	5	0	0
		0.25	C	*Irish* Linen *Cloth*	0	2	6	0
		23	C	Skins, Lamb	7	16	8	0
James Edye	Ind	33	piece	Mantles	5	10	0	0
		2	C	Skins, Sheep	0	20	0	0
		1	C	Skins, Lamb	0	6	8	0
		1.33	C	Check *Cloth*	2	13	4	0
		24	piece	Skins, Fox	0	4	0	0
		3	stone	Wool, Flocks	0	0	15	0
William She*a*	Ind	11	C	Check *Cloth*	22	0	0	0
		4	C	Skins, Sheep	0	40	0	0
		12	stone	Wool, Flocks	0	5	0	0
		80	yard	*Irish* Linen *Cloth*	0	6	8	0
		8	C	Skins, Lamb	0	53	4	0
		6	piece	Mantles	0	20	0	0
William Sholwen	Ind	9	C	Check *Cloth*	18	0	0	0
		5	C	Skins, Sheep	2	10	0	0
		5	C	Skins, Lamb	0	23	4	0
		2	C	Skins, Kid	0	10	0	0
		3	piece	Mantles	0	10	0	0

The George Butlar of Waterford, Edmund Medoll master, Entering, *15th July 1542*

Merchant name	Origin	Qty	Unit	Commodity	£	s.	d.	f.
Robert She*a*	Ind	16	C	Check *Cloth*	32	0	0	0
		48	piece	Mantles	8	0	0	0
		2	C	Skins, Lamb	0	13	4	0
		1.5	C	Skins, Sheep	0	15	0	0
		6	piece	Skins, Fox	0	0	12	0
Richard Creangh	Ind	16	C	Skins, Sheep	8	0	0	0
		4	C	Skins, Lamb	0	26	8	0
		2	C	Check *Cloth*	4	0	0	0
		12	piece	Skins, Fox	0	2	0	0
Edmund She*a*	Ind	8.5	C	Skins, Sheep	4	5	0	0
		3.25	C	Check *Cloth*	6	10	0	0
		12.5	C	Skins, Lamb	4	3	4	0
		15	piece	Mantles	0	50	0	0
Thomas Rothe	Ind	3.5	C	Check *Cloth*	7	0	0	0
		3	C	Skins, Sheep	0	30	0	0
		2	C	Skins, Lamb	0	13	4	0
		34	piece	Mantles	5	13	4	0
		3	stone	Wool, Flocks	0	0	15	0

Merchant name	Origin	Qty	Unit	Commodity	£	s.	d.	f.
		2	piece	Skins, Fox	0	0	4	0
		6	piece	Skins, Deer	0	0	15	0
James Shea	Ind	4.16	C	Check *Cloth*	8	6	4	0
		4	C	Skins, Sheep	0	40	0	0
		2.25	C	Skins, Lamb	0	15	0	0
		15	piece	Mantles	2	10	0	0
		3	stone	Wool, Unspecified	0	8	0	0
		2	stone	Wool, Flocks	0	0	10	0
		2	piece	Skins, Fox	0	0	4	0
Laurence Breuar	Ind	10	C	Check *Cloth*	20	0	0	0
		20	piece	Mantles	3	6	8	0
Richard Quemerford & Butlar	Ind	14	C	Check *Cloth*	28	0	0	0
		5	piece	Mantles	0	16	8	0
William Arthur	Ind	10	C	Skins, Sheep	5	0	0	0
		6	C	Check *Cloth*	12	0	0	0
		13	C	Skins, Lamb	4	6	8	0
		38	piece	Mantles	6	6	8	0
		12	stone	Wool, Flocks	0	5	0	0
		2	stone	Wool, Unspecified	0	5	4	0
Edmund Medell & assoc.	Ind	30	piece	Mantles	5	0	0	0
		2.75	C	Check *Cloth*	5	10	0	0

The Mary Conception of Bristol, John Bousher master, 17th July 1542

Merchant name	Origin	Qty	Unit	Commodity	£	s.	d.	f.
Thomas White	Ind	5.5	tun	Oil, *Olive*	22	0	0	0
		1.25	C	Soap	0	12	6	0
Nicholas Thorn	Ind	24.5	tun	Oil, *Olive*	98	0	0	0
		162.5	C	Soap	81	5	0	0
		9	C	Alum	4	10	0	0
John Shipman & Appowell	Ind	9.5	tun	Oil, *Olive*	38	0	0	0
		26.25	C	Soap	13	2	6	0
John Smyth & Yonge	Ind	4.625	tun	Oil, *Olive*	18	10	0	0
		2.5	C	Soap	0	25	0	0
William Jay & Brampton	Ind	1.875	tun	Oil, *Olive*	7	10	0	0
		2.5	C	Soap	0	25	0	0
Gilbert Cogan & Welsh	Ind	12.25	tun	Oil, *Olive*	49	0	0	0
		6.25	C	Soap	3	2	6	0
Thomas Harrys	Ind	2.25	tun	Oil, *Olive*	9	0	0	0
		1	chest	Sugar	0	40	0	0
		1.25	C	Soap	0	12	6	0
Thomas Tyson & Cutt	Ind	5	tun	Oil, *Olive*	20	0	0	0
		18	C	Orchil	12	0	0	0
		6.25	C	Soap	3	2	6	0
		1.5	C	Alum	0	15	0	0
Francis Fowler & Paresse	Ind	2.875	tun	Oil, *Olive*	11	10	0	0

Merchant name	Origin	Qty	Unit	Commodity	£	s.	d.	f.
		2.5	C	Soap	0	25	0	0
Thomas Howell & Chester	Ind	1	pipe	Oil, *Olive*	2	0	0	0
		17.5	C	Soap	8	15	0	0
		1	hogshead	Wine	0	0	0	0
Giles White & Pryn	Ind	1.875	tun	Oil, *Olive*	7	10	0	0
		17.5	C	Soap	8	15	0	0
Johanna Carpenter & assoc.	Ind	18.75	C	Soap	9	7	6	0
		2.5	tun	Oil, *Olive*	10	0	0	0
		1	chest	Sugar	0	40	0	0

The Chrystofer of Lübeck, Johannes Vynke master, Entering, 17th July 1542

Merchant name	Origin	Qty	Unit	Commodity	£	s.	d.	f.
Harinanus Soushens	Hansard	110.5	last	Tar	110	10	0	0
		9	C	Wainscot	18	0	0	0
		6	C	Wood, Clapholt	0	20	0	0
		1	C	Oars	0	40	0	0
		20	piece	Masts	1	0	0	0
Johannes Vynke	Hansard	85	piece	Wainscot	0	28	4	0
		11	last	Tar	11	0	0	0
		2	stone	Flax	0	3	4	0
		4	dozen	Tankards	0	3	4	0
		4	lb	Wax	0	0	16	0

The Anthony of Waterford, Henry Gall master, Entering, *17th July 1542*

Merchant name	Origin	Qty	Unit	Commodity	£	s.	d.	f.
Robert Gybb	Ind	24	piece	Mantles	4	0	0	0
		1	C	Check *Cloth*	2	0	0	0
Richard Wodlock	Ind	3	C	Check *Cloth*	6	0	0	0
		4	piece	Mantles	0	13	4	0
		1	C	Skins, Sheep	0	10	0	0
		1	C	Skins, Lamb	0	6	8	0
Edmund Grannt	Ind	1.5	C	Check *Cloth*	3	0	0	0
		8	piece	Mantles	0	26	8	0
		0.5	C	Skins, Sheep	0	5	0	0
Richard Hosnint	Ind	7	C	Check *Cloth*	14	0	0	0
		3.5	C	Skins, Sheep	0	35	0	0
		0.5	C	Skins, Lamb	0	3	4	0
Peter Fitzjohn	Ind	4.5	C	Check *Cloth*	9	0	0	0
		2	piece	Mantles	0	6	8	0
		40	piece	Skins, Sheep	0	3	4	0
Peter Danyell	Ind	14	C	Check *Cloth*	28	0	0	0
		4	C	Skins, Sheep	0	40	0	0
		2	C	Skins, Lamb	0	13	4	0
		16	piece	Mantles	2	13	4	0
Edmund Seyse	Ind	2.5	C	Skins, Sheep	0	25	0	0
		3.25	C	Skins, Lamb	0	21	8	0
		7	piece	Skins, Fox	0	0	14	0
		1	piece	Skins, Otter	0	0	5	0
		6	piece	Mantles	0	20	0	0
		9	C	Check *Cloth*	18	0	0	0

Merchant name	Origin	Qty	Unit	Commodity	£	s.	d.	f.
		4	stone	Wool, Flocks	0	0	20	0
Peter Welsh	Ind	4	C	Check *Cloth*	8	0	0	0
		12	piece	Mantles	2	0	0	0
Nicholas Deans	Ind	4	C	Check *Cloth*	8	0	0	0
		2	C	Skins, Sheep	0	20	0	0
		12	piece	Mantles	2	0	0	0
William Grannt	Ind	20	C	Check *Cloth*	40	0	0	0
		1.5	C	Skins, Lamb	0	10	0	0
		4	stone	Wool, Flocks	0	0	20	0
		2.5	stone	Wool, Unspecified	0	6	8	0
Robert Maydoll	Ind	2	C	Check *Cloth*	4	0	0	0
		2	piece	Mantles	0	6	8	0
Edmund Clery	Ind	3.5	C	Check *Cloth*	7	0	0	0
		21	piece	Mantles	3	10	0	0
		1.5	C	Skins, Sheep	0	15	0	0
Henry Gall	Ind	3	C	Check *Cloth*	6	0	0	0
		4	piece	Mantles	0	13	4	0
Peter Butlar	Ind	1	C	Check *Cloth*	2	0	0	0
		8	piece	Mantles	0	26	8	0
Nicholas Kelly	Ind	4	C	Check *Cloth*	8	0	0	0
		6	burden	Fish, Salted	1	5	0	0
Nicholas She*a*	Ind	7.5	C	Check *Cloth*	15	0	0	0
		1	C	Skins, Sheep	0	10	0	0
		2	piece	Mantles	0	6	8	0
Andrew Lyncolln & assoc.	Ind	4.58	C	Check *Cloth*	9	3	4	0
		24	piece	Mantles	4	0	0	0

The Sunday of Bristol, Nicholas Kyforest master, Entering, *17th July 1542*

Nicholas Kelly	Ind	10	stone	Wool, Flocks	0	4	2	0

The Kateryn of Waterford, Philip Doryn master, Entering, *17th July 1542*

Michael Penteny	Ind	57.3	C	Check *Cloth*	114	12	4	0
Thomas Madan	Ind	11	C	Check *Cloth*	22	0	0	0
		12	piece	Mantles	2	0	0	0
		1	C	Skins, Lamb	0	6	8	0
		0.5	C	Skins, Sheep	0	5	0	0
Bennett Sall	Ind	6	C	Check *Cloth*	12	0	0	0
		9	piece	Mantles	0	30	0	0
Richard Creangh	Ind	2	C	Check *Cloth*	4	0	0	0
		1	C	Skins, Lamb	0	6	8	0
		1.5	C	Skins, Sheep	0	15	0	0
William Madan	Ind	5	C	Check *Cloth*	10	0	0	0
		3	C	Skins, Lamb	0	20	0	0
		3	C	Skins, Sheep	0	30	0	0
		2	piece	Mantles	0	6	8	0
Richard Pore	Ind	6	C	Check *Cloth*	12	0	0	0
		15	piece	Mantles	2	10	0	0
		0.5	C	Skins, Sheep	0	5	0	0
William White	Ind	6	C	Check *Cloth*	12	0	0	0

Merchant name	Origin	Qty	Unit	Commodity	£	s.	d.	f.
		6	piece	Mantles	0	20	0	0
		1	C	Skins, Lamb	0	6	8	0
		1	C	Skins, Sheep	0	10	0	0
Nicholas Kett	Ind	3.5	C	Check *Cloth*	7	0	0	0
		40	piece	Skins, Sheep	0	3	4	0
		12	piece	Mantles	2	0	0	0
John Wyse	Ind	4	C	Check *Cloth*	8	0	0	0
		0.5	C	Skins, Lamb	0	3	4	0
		1	C	Skins, Sheep	0	10	0	0
		0.5	C	Skins, Kid	0	2	6	0
Philip Doryn	Ind	0.5	C	Check *Cloth*	0	20	0	0
		8	piece	Mantles	0	26	8	0
James Kenny	Ind	1	C	Check *Cloth*	2	0	0	0
		2	piece	Mantles	0	6	8	0
John Hee	Ind	4.5	C	Check *Cloth*	9	0	0	0
		1.5	C	Skins, Sheep	0	15	0	0
		7	piece	Mantles	0	23	4	0
Nicholas Quede	Ind	40	yard	Check *Cloth*	0	13	4	0
		6	piece	Mantles	0	20	0	0
William Hyde	Ind	100	yard	Check *Cloth*	0	23	4	0
		3	piece	Mantles	0	10	0	0
John Comyn	Ind	1	C	Skins, Sheep	0	10	0	0
		0.5	C	Check *Cloth*	0	20	0	0
		6	piece	Skins, Deer	0	0	15	0
John Forlonge	Ind	50	yard	Check *Cloth*	0	16	8	0
		1.5	C	Fish, Hake	0	15	0	0
		2	piece	Mantles	0	6	8	0
		24	piece	Skins, Sheep	0	2	0	0
Richard Wodlock	Ind	4	dicker	Skins, Deer	0	8	4	0
Peter Fitzjohn	Ind	9	piece	Mantles	0	30	0	0
		0.5	C	Skins, Lamb	0	3	4	0
		40	yard	Check *Cloth*	0	13	4	0

The Mary George of Bristol, Cornell Andrew master, Exiting, 18th July 1542

Merchant name	Origin	Qty	Unit	Commodity	£	s.	d.	f.
John Thomas & Kelly	Ind	1.5	tun	Wine, Corrupt	2	5	0	0
		1	ton	Iron	4	0	0	0
		16	lb	Silk, *Worked*	10	13	4	0
		1.25	piece	Cloth of Assize	0	0	0	0

The Patrick of New Ross, Richard Doffe master, Entering, 20th July 1542

Merchant name	Origin	Qty	Unit	Commodity	£	s.	d.	f.
Nicholas Cantwell	Ind	8	C	Check *Cloth*	16	0	0	0
		2.5	C	Skins, Sheep	0	25	0	0
		2.5	C	Skins, Lamb	0	16	8	0
		8	piece	Skins, Fox	0	0	16	0
		2	piece	Skins, Marten	0	2	0	0
		5	stone	Wool, Flocks	0	2	1	0
Thomas Barkeley	Ind	3	C	Check *Cloth*	6	0	0	0
		2	C	Skins, Sheep	0	20	0	0
		1	C	Skins, Lamb	0	6	8	0
		4	stone	Wool, Flocks	0	0	20	0

Merchant name	Origin	Qty	Unit	Commodity	£	s.	d.	f.
Thomas Comen	Ind	5	C	Check *Cloth*	10	0	0	0
		3	C	Skins, Sheep	0	30	0	0
		3	C	Skins, Lamb	0	20	0	0
		6	stone	Wool, Flocks	0	2	6	0
		3	dicker	Skins, Deer	0	6	3	0
		26	stone	Wool, Unspecified	3	9	4	0
Thomas Dowle	Ind	1	C	Skins, Sheep	0	10	0	0
		0.5	C	Check *Cloth*	0	20	0	0
		4	stone	Wool, Flocks	0	0	20	0
		1	dicker	Skins, Deer	0	2	1	0
John Coterell	Ind	1	C	Check *Cloth*	2	0	0	0
		1	C	Skins, Lamb	0	6	8	0
		2	C	Skins, Sheep	0	20	0	0

The Sunday of Waterford, Robert Fytzjohn master, Entering, 21st July 1542

Merchant name	Origin	Qty	Unit	Commodity	£	s.	d.	f.
Robert *Fytzjohn*	Ind	1	C	Check *Cloth*	2	0	0	0
Richard Barron	Ind	6	C	Check *Cloth*	12	0	0	0
		10	piece	Mantles	0	33	4	0
		0.25	C	Skins, Lamb	0	0	20	0
		24	piece	Skins, Sheep	0	2	0	0
		3	piece	Skins, Fox	0	0	6	0
Nicholas Balie	Ind	5	C	Check *Cloth*	10	0	0	0
		4	piece	Mantles	0	13	4	0
		1	C	Skins, Lamb	0	6	8	0
		12	piece	Skins, Sheep	0	0	12	0
James Goughe	Ind	8	C	Check *Cloth*	16	0	0	0
		6	piece	Mantles	0	20	0	0
		5	C	Skins, Lamb	0	3	4	0
		3	stone	Wool, Flocks	0	0	15	0
Thomas Nele	Ind	5	C	Check *Cloth*	10	0	0	0
		2	C	Skins, Sheep	0	20	0	0
		3	C	Skins, Lamb	0	20	0	0
		3	dicker	Skins, Deer	0	6	3	0
		3	piece	Mantles	0	10	0	0
		6	piece	Skins, Fox	0	0	12	0
Thomas Gorneye	Ind	6	C	Skins, Sheep	3	0	0	0
		2.66	C	Check *Cloth*	5	6	8	0
John Flay	Ind	4	C	Check *Cloth*	8	0	0	0
		10	piece	Mantles	0	33	4	0
Philip Welsh	Ind	3.5	C	Check *Cloth*	7	0	0	0
		2	C	Skins, Sheep	0	20	0	0
		4	piece	Mantles	0	13	4	0
		6	piece	Skins, Fox	0	0	12	0
Thomas Kyfe	Ind	3	C	Check *Cloth*	6	0	0	0
		6	piece	Mantles	0	20	0	0
Richard Guewe	Ind	2	C	Check *Cloth*	4	0	0	0
		16	piece	Mantles	2	13	4	0
Peter Grant & assoc.	Ind	7	C	Check *Cloth*	14	0	0	0
		23	piece	Mantles	3	16	8	0

Merchant name	Origin	Qty	Unit	Commodity	£	s.	d.	f.

The Sunday of Bristol, William Kelly master, Exiting, 21st July 1542

| John Greffithe | Ind | 1 | pipe | Wine, Corrupt | 0 | 15 | 0 | 0 |

The Mary of Gloucester, John Llewellyn master, Entering, 21st July 1542

| Richard Benet & Penteny | Ind | 38 | C | Check *Cloth* | 76 | 0 | 0 | 0 |
| | | 6 | C | *Irish* Linen *Cloth* | 3 | 0 | 0 | 0 |

The James of Milford Haven, John Wade master, Entering, 23rd July 1542

| Walter Clynton | Ind | 3 | C | Fish, Sturgeon | 0 | 30 | 0 | 0 |
| | | 0.75 | C | Skins, Sheep | 0 | 7 | 6 | 0 |

The Austen of Dungarvan, Robert Wry*ner* master, Entering, *23rd July 1542*

Robert Tobyn	Ind	28	burden	Fish, Salted	5	16	8	0
		5	C	Fish, Hake	2	10	0	0
		2	C	Skins, Lamb	0	13	4	0
		0.5	C	Skins, Sheep	0	5	0	0

The Nicholas of Milford Haven, William Rothe master, Entering, *23rd July 1542*

| John Phelps | Ind | 4 | C | Check *Cloth* | 8 | 0 | 0 | 0 |

The Stenyons of Milford Haven, David Sere master, Entering, *23rd July 1542*

Walter Burford	Ind	20	C	Check *Cloth*	40	0	0	0
		4.5	C	*Irish* Linen *Cloth*	2	5	0	0
		1	dicker	Skins, Deer	0	2	1	0

The Margaret of Bristol, John Jene master, Entering, *23rd July 1542*

| William Gall & assoc. | Ind | 5 | C | Check *Cloth* | 10 | 0 | 0 | 0 |
| | | 5 | burden | Fish, Salted | 1 | 0 | 10 | 0 |

The Migell of Bristol, David Gillam master, Entering, 26th July 1542

| Thomas White & assoc. | Ind | 36 | ton | Iron | 90 | 0 | 0 | 0 |

The Jhesus of Bristol, Lucas Kelly master, Exiting, *26th July 1542*

| Patrick Yonge & assoc. | Ind | 1.75 | tun | Wine, Corrupt | 2 | 12 | 6 | 0 |

The Trynyte of Carmarthen, William Walter master, Entering, *26th July 1542*

| James Balie | Ind | 9 | C | Orchil | 6 | 0 | 0 | 0 |

Merchant name	Origin	Qty	Unit	Commodity	£	s.	d.	f.

The Laurence of Barnstaple, Symon Davys master, Exiting, *26th July 1542*

Merchant name	Origin	Qty	Unit	Commodity	£	s.	d.	f.
William Carr & assoc.	Ind	20	piece	Cloth of Assize	0	0	0	0
		4	ton	Lead, worked	20	0	0	0
		30	piece	Manchester *Cotton Cloth*	15	0	0	0

The Dowgan of Cardiff, David Watkyns master, Entering, *26th July 1542*

Merchant name	Origin	Qty	Unit	Commodity	£	s.	d.	f.
John Roberts	Ind	2	tun	Wine	0	0	0	0

The Christofer of Chepstow, John Jene master, Exiting, 27th July 1542

Merchant name	Origin	Qty	Unit	Commodity	£	s.	d.	f.
Francis Carball	Alien	5	piece	Cloth of Assize	0	0	0	0

The John of San Sebastián, Predro de Lasaun master, Exiting, *27th July 1542*

Merchant name	Origin	Qty	Unit	Commodity	£	s.	d.	f.
Arnold de Vrobie	Alien	7	piece	Dunster *Cloth*	3	10	0	0
		2	piece	Welsh *Cloth*	2	0	0	0
		4	piece	Northern *Cotton Cloth*	0	16	8	0
		1	C	Skins, Sheep	0	10	0	0
		5.25	piece	Cloth of Assize	0	0	0	0

The Prymrose of Bristol, Thomas Lack master, Entering, 28th July 1542

Merchant name	Origin	Qty	Unit	Commodity	£	s.	d.	f.
William Balard	Ind	28	ton	Salt	14	0	0	0

The Nicholas of Bristol, Bartholemew Garland master, Entering, *28th July 1542*

Merchant name	Origin	Qty	Unit	Commodity	£	s.	d.	f.
Richard Sare	Ind	3.5	C	Fish, Hake	0	35	0	0
		5	burden	Fish, Salted	1	0	10	0

The George Butlar of Waterford, Edmund Medoll master, Exiting, *28th July 1542*

Merchant name	Origin	Qty	Unit	Commodity	£	s.	d.	f.
Paul Butlar	Ind	5	wey	Malt	4	3	4	0
		6	quart	Wheat	0	20	0	0
Robert Shea	Ind	7.75	piece	Cloth of Assize	0	0	0	0
		8	lb	Saffron	4	0	0	0
		2	lb	Silk, *Worked*	0	26	8	0
		2	dozen	Girdles, Silk	0	6	8	0
		4.5	dozen	Caps	2	5	0	0
		2.5	dozen	Nightcaps, Unspecified	1	0	0	0
		1.25	dozen	Hats	0	15	0	0
		2	dozen	Knives, in Pairs	0	3	4	0
		2	dozen	Soap	0	2	6	0
		2	gross	Points	0	2	0	0
		2	dozen	Girdles, Silk	0	2	6	0
Richard Creangh	Ind	4.25	piece	Cloth of Assize	0	0	0	0
		18	dozen	Knives, in Pairs	0	30	0	0
		7	gross	Knives	2	6	8	0
		3	lb	Saffron	0	30	0	0
		24	dozen	Combs	0	5	0	0
		2	bolt	Thread	0	2	2	0

Merchant name	Origin	Qty	Unit	Commodity	£	s.	d.	f.
		3	dozen	Cards, Playing	o	2	6	o
		3	dozen	Cumin	o	4	o	o
		1	lb	Cloves	o	2	6	o
		2	dozen	Liquorice	o	o	20	o
		12	dozen	Girdles	o	4	o	o
		6	dozen	Girdles	o	o	20	o
		0.5	dozen	Caps	o	5	o	o
		24	gross	Points	o	24	o	o
		2	gross	Lacquer	o	3	4	o
		2	dozen	Skins, Golden	o	8	4	o
		6	lb	Verdigris	o	2	6	o
Edmund Shea	Ind	2	piece	Cloth of Assize	o	o	o	o
		2	lb	Silk, *Worked*	o	26	8	o
		2	lb	Saffron	o	20	o	o
		2	dozen	Aniseed	o	2	8	o
		3	dozen	Glasses	o	o	5	o
		2	dozen	Girdles	o	o	15	o
		2	dozen	Combs	o	o	8	o
		1	dozen	Caps	o	10	o	o
		1	dozen	Skins, Golden	o	4	2	o
		3	dozen	Knives, in Pairs	o	5	o	o
Nicholas Dones	Ind	1	piece	Cloth of Assize, Dozen Strait	o	o	o	o
		1.5	lb	Silk, *Worked*	o	20	o	o
		0.25	gross	Knives	o	o	20	o
William Arthur	Ind	2.25	piece	Cloth of Assize	o	o	o	o
		7	lb	Saffron	3	10	o	o
		8	lb	Silk, *Worked*	5	6	8	o
		4	gross	Knives	o	26	8	o
		12	dozen	Knives, in Pairs	o	20	o	o
		2.5	dozen	Caps	o	25	o	o
		1	dozen	Nightcaps, Unspecified	o	8	o	o
		12	dozen	Girdles	o	8	o	o
		4	doz	Ribbons, Unspecified	o	5	o	o
		12	dozen	Combs	o	6	o	o
		1	bolt	Thread	o	o	13	o
		12	dozen	Glasses	o	4	o	o
		3	lb	Cinnamon/Cloves/Mace	o	7	6	o
		1	lb	Pepper	o	o	12	o
		1	lb	Kermes	o	o	12	o
		1	lb	Ginger	o	o	18	o
		1	dozen	Skins, Golden	o	4	2	o
		16	gross	Points	o	16	o	o
		4	gross	Lacquer	o	6	8	o
Thomas Rothe	Ind	3	gross	Knives	o	20	o	o
		6	stone	Orchil	o	10	o	o
		1	dozen	Caps	o	10	o	o
		4	dozen	Knives, in Pairs	o	6	8	o
		5	dozen	Girdles	o	3	4	o
		4	dozen	Glasses	o	o	16	o
		3	pair	Stock-Cards	o	3	o	o
		1	clout	Needles	o	o	20	o
		2	bolt	Thread	o	2	2	o

Merchant name	Origin	Qty	Unit	Commodity	£	s.	d.	f.
		2	dozen	Soap	0	2	6	0
		3	dozen	Combs	0	0	12	0
		1	piece	Cloth of Assize	0	0	0	0
James Shea	Ind	1	lb	Saffron	0	10	0	0
		1	gross	Knives	0	6	8	0
		2	dozen	Knives, in Pairs	0	3	4	0
		1	bolt	Thread	0	0	13	0
		3	dozen	Girdles	0	0	20	0
		1	dozen	Skins, Golden	0	4	2	0
		0.5	dozen	Glasses	0	2	0	0
		1	ream	Paper	0	0	20	0
		1	dozen	Cumin	0	0	16	0
		2	gross	Points	0	2	0	0
		1	gross	Lacquer	0	0	20	0
		1.5	piece	Cloth of Assize	0	0	0	0

The George of Waterford, Nicholas Colman master, Exiting, 28th July 1542

Merchant name	Origin	Qty	Unit	Commodity	£	s.	d.	f.
Sir Anthony St Leger	Ind	30	quart	Beans/Malt	4	3	4	0
Philip Quenmerford	Ind	12	quart	Wheat	0	40	0	0
		4	wey	Beans/Malt	3	6	8	0
		1	gross	Knives	0	6	8	0
		6	gross	Points	0	6	0	0
		1	gross	Lacquer	0	0	20	0
		6	piece	Caps	0	5	0	0
		2.33	piece	Cloth of Assize	0	0	0	0
Andrew Lyncoln	Ind	4.5	lb	Saffron	2	5	0	0
		1	gross	Knives	0	6	8	0
		5	gross	Points	0	5	0	0
		0.5	dozen	Caps	0	5	0	0
		2	dozen	Knives, in Pairs	0	3	4	0
		2	dozen	Soap	0	2	6	0
		1.5	lb	Silk, *Worked*	0	20	0	0
		12	lb	Glue	0	0	20	0
		0.5	piece	Cloth of Assize	0	0	0	0
Patrick Rothe	Ind	15	piece	Cloth of Assize, Dozen Strait	0	0	0	0
		4	dozen	Glasses	0	0	16	0
		8	dozen	Knives, in Pairs	0	13	4	0
		1	doz	Ribbons, Unspecified	0	0	18	0
		2	dozen	Skins, Golden	0	8	4	0
		1	bolt	Thread	0	0	13	0
		1	gross	Knives	0	6	8	0
		1	gross	Cutts	0	3	4	0
		8	lb	Silk, *Worked*	5	6	8	0
		0.5	dozen	Nightcaps, Unspecified	0	0	18	0
		0.5	dozen	Caps	0	5	0	0
		5	lb	Pepper	0	5	0	0
		2	lb	Mercury	0	0	10	0
		6	piece	Caps	0	5	0	0
		12	lb	Saffron	6	0	0	0
		0.5	C	Aniseed	0	6	8	0
		3	dozen	Cards, Playing	0	2	6	0

Merchant name	Origin	Qty	Unit	Commodity	£	s.	d.	f.
		2	clout	Needles	0	0	16	0
		18	gross	Points	0	18	0	0
		3	gross	Points	0	3	0	0
		2	dozen	Penners	0	0	8	0
		1	lot	Items, miscellaneous	0	7	6	0
		0.5	dozen	Hats	0	0	20	0
James Bray	Ind	1	lb	Silk, *Worked*	0	13	4	0
		1	lb	Saffron	0	10	0	0
		7	dozen	Knives, in Pairs	0	11	8	0
		4	gross	Knives	0	26	8	0
		1	dozen	Skins, Golden	0	4	2	0
		1	dozen	Cards, Playing	0	0	10	0
		8	dozen	Combs	0	2	8	0
		7	dozen	Girdles	0	2	4	0
		4	gross	Lacquer	0	6	8	0
		0.25	C	Hops	0	2	6	0
		8	gross	Points	0	8	0	0
		3	piece	Caps	0	2	6	0
		2	lb	Verdigris	0	0	10	0
		1	dozen	Aniseed	0	0	16	0
		1	piece	Cloth of Assize	0	0	0	0
George Quenmerford	Ind	1	lb	Saffron	0	10	0	0
Maurice Quyrke	Ind	2	gross	Knives	0	13	4	0
		4	gross	Lacquer	0	6	8	0
		0.5	dozen	Caps	0	5	0	0
		12	dozen	Combs	0	4	0	0
		6	dozen	*Percular*	0	0	6	0
		6	dozen	Knives, in Pairs	0	10	0	0
		1	dozen	Cumin	0	0	16	0
		0.25	C	Aniseed	0	3	4	0
		1	dozen	Skins, Golden	0	4	2	0
		6	dozen	Girdles	0	5	0	0
		1.5	piece	Cloth of Assize	0	0	0	0
William Shea	Ind	4	piece	Cloth of Assize	0	0	0	0
		3	lb	Saffron	0	30	0	0
		4	lb	Mace	0	10	0	0
		1	lb	Ginger	0	0	18	0
		1	lb	Pepper	0	0	12	0
		2	dozen	Caps	0	20	0	0
		2	gross	Knives	0	13	4	0
		6	gross	Points	0	6	0	0
		1	gross	Lacquer	0	0	20	0
		1	dozen	Hats	0	15	0	0
		4	lb	Verdigris	0	0	20	0
		1	dozen	Skins, Golden	0	4	2	0
		2	dozen	Knives, in Pairs	0	3	4	0
		2	dozen	Girdles	0	2	0	0
James Edy	Ind	1.75	piece	Cloth of Assize	0	0	0	0
		2	lb	Silk, *Worked*	0	26	8	0
		2	gross	Knives	0	13	4	0
		6	gross	Points	0	6	0	0
		1	dozen	Caps	0	10	0	0

Merchant name	Origin	Qty	Unit	Commodity	£	s.	d.	f.
		6	dozen	Girdles	0	3	6	0
		1	lb	Cinnamon/Cloves	0	2	6	0
		0.25	C	Aniseed	0	3	4	0
Nicholas Malrony	Ind	1.5	lb	Silk, *Worked*	0	20	0	0
		1.5	lb	Saffron	0	15	0	0
		3	gross	Knives	0	20	0	0
		1	lb	Pepper	0	0	12	0
		4	dozen	Knives, in Pairs	0	6	8	0
		3	gross	Lacquer	0	5	0	0
		8	gross	Points	0	8	0	0
		6	piece	Caps	0	5	0	0
		5	stone	Orchil	0	8	4	0
John Quyrke	Ind	2	gross	Knives	0	13	4	0
		2	gross	Lacquer	0	3	4	0
		0.5	C	Aniseed	0	6	8	0
		6	dozen	Knives, in Pairs	0	10	0	0
		3	dozen	Combs	0	0	12	0
		20	lb	Twine	0	4	0	0
John Murphy	Ind	0.5	piece	Cloth of Assize	0	0	0	0
		3.5	lb	Silk, *Worked*	0	46	8	0
		4	lb	Saffron	2	0	0	0
		2.5	gross	Knives	0	16	8	0
		4	dozen	Knives, in Pairs	0	6	8	0
		2	gross	Lacquer	0	3	4	0
		4	gross	Points	0	4	0	0
		1	dozen	Skins, Golden	0	4	2	0
		1.5	dozen	Cards, Playing	0	0	14	0
		2	lb	Mercury	0	0	10	0
		1	lot	Items, miscellaneous	0	12	0	0
Henry Mowghy	Ind	0.5	C	Aniseed	0	6	8	0
		2	dozen	Cards, Playing	0	0	20	0
		2.75	piece	Cloth of Assize	0	0	0	0
		2	dozen	Girdles	0	2	0	0
		1	lot	Items, miscellaneous	0	5	0	0
		2	dozen	Knives, in Pairs	0	3	4	0
		3	gross	Knives	0	20	0	0
		3	lb	Pepper	0	3	0	0
		3	dozen	*Percular*	0	0	8	0
		16	gross	Points	0	16	0	0
		3	lb	Saffron	0	30	0	0
		7	lb	Silk, *Worked*	4	13	4	0
		3	dozen	Skins, Golden	0	12	6	0
		2	bolt	Thread	0	2	2	0
David Sholwen	Ind	8	lb	Silk, *Worked*	5	6	8	0
		4	lb	Saffron	2	0	0	0
		1	gross	Knives	0	6	8	0
		2	dozen	Knives, in Pairs	0	3	4	0
		3	lb	Cinnamon/Cloves/Mace	0	7	6	0
		8	gross	Points	0	8	0	0
		0.25	C	Aniseed	0	3	4	0
		1	barrel	Honey	0	16	8	0
		0.25	C	Alum	0	3	4	0

Merchant name	Origin	Qty	Unit	Commodity	£	s.	d.	f.
		1	dozen	Skins, Golden	0	4	2	0
		6	pair	Stock-Cards	0	6	0	0
		0.5	C	Hops	0	5	0	0
		0.75	piece	Cloth of Assize	0	0	0	0
Peter Fitzjohn	Ind	0.5	gross	Knives	0	3	4	0
		4	gross	Points	0	4	0	0
Robert Gybb	Ind	2	lb	Silk, *Worked*	0	26	8	0
		0.5	gross	Knives	0	3	4	0
		2	gross	Points	0	2	0	0
		0.5	gross	Lacquer	0	0	10	0
		1	lb	Mercury	0	0	5	0
		6	lb	Sulpher	0	0	9	0
		4	piece	Caps	0	3	4	0
		1	dozen	Soap	0	0	15	0
Richard Wodlock	Ind	0.5	gross	Knives	0	3	4	0
		1	gross	Lacquer	0	0	20	0
		2	gross	Points	0	2	0	0
		1	lb	Saffron	0	10	0	0
		2	lb	Silk, *Worked*	0	26	8	0
		2	dozen	Soap	0	2	6	0
Richard Osmund	Ind	0.5	dozen	Caps	0	5	0	0
		1	gross	Points	0	0	12	0
		1	gross	Lacquer	0	0	20	0
		2	dozen	Soap	0	2	6	0

The Bryde of Waterford, Nicholas Rothe master, Exiting, *28th July 1542*

Merchant name	Origin	Qty	Unit	Commodity	£	s.	d.	f.
Peter Vynge	Ind	2	wey	Malt	0	33	4	0
John Bousher	Ind	4	piece	Cloth of Assize	0	0	0	0
		6	lb	Silk, *Worked*	4	0	0	0
		1	lb	Saffron	0	10	0	0
		4	gross	Knives	0	26	8	0
		0.75	dozen	Hats	0	3	0	0
		0.5	dozen	Caps	0	5	0	0
		6	gross	Points	0	6	0	0
		1	gross	Lacquer	0	0	20	0
		8	dozen	Girdles	0	4	8	0
		1	lot	Items, miscellaneous	0	4	10	0
Oliver Routhe	Ind	0.75	piece	Cloth of Assize	0	0	0	0
		2	gross	Knives	0	13	4	0
		3	dozen	Girdles	0	2	0	0
		6	lb	Silk, *Worked*	4	0	0	0
		3	lb	Silk, *Worked*	0	40	0	0
		3	lb	Saffron	0	30	0	0
		1	dozen	Skins, Golden	0	4	2	0
		1	dozen	Skins, Red	0	2	1	0
		3	dozen	Cards, Playing	0	2	6	0
		3	dozen	Knives, in Pairs	0	5	0	0
		2	lb	Verdigris	0	0	10	0
		2	lb	Mercury	0	0	10	0
		1	doz	Ribbons, Unspecified	0	0	18	0
		1	C	Alum	0	13	4	0

Merchant name	Origin	Qty	Unit	Commodity	£	s.	d.	f.
		0.5	C	Aniseed	0	6	8	0
		0.5	C	Hops	0	5	0	0
		3	stone	Orchil	0	5	0	0
		3	gross	Points	0	3	0	0
		1	gross	Lacquer	0	0	20	0
		1	lb	Cloves/Mace	0	2	6	0
		3	dozen	Glasses	0	0	12	0
William Routhe	Ind	0.75	piece	Cloth of Assize	0	0	0	0
		4	lb	Saffron	2	0	0	0
		1	dozen	Skins, Golden	0	4	2	0
		4	gross	Knives	1	6	8	0
		1	dozen	Alum	0	0	16	0
		6	dozen	Knives, in Pairs	0	10	0	0
		2	bolt	Thread	0	2	2	0
		0.5	C	Aniseed	0	6	8	0
		0.5	C	Hops	0	5	0	0
		1	dozen	Liquorice	0	0	10	0
		6	gross	Points	0	6	0	0
		2	gross	Lacquer	0	3	4	0
		1	hogshead	Iron	0	20	0	0
		1	lb	Pepper	0	0	12	0
		1	dozen	Cumin	0	0	16	0
		2	dozen	Girdles	0	0	14	0
		1	doz	Ribbons, Unspecified	0	0	18	0
John Mawmesey	Ind	1	C	Alum/Aniseed	0	13	4	0
		1	dozen	Cards, Playing	0	0	10	0
		1	piece	Cloth of Assize	0	0	0	0
		1.5	lb	Cloves/Mace	0	3	9	0
		3	dozen	Girdles	0	5	2	0
		0.5	C	Hops	0	5	0	0
		6	dozen	Knives, in Pairs	0	10	0	0
		1	gross	Knives	0	6	8	0
		1	gross	Lacquer	0	0	20	0
		3	lb	Mercury	0	0	15	0
		2	lb	Pepper	0	2	0	0
		6	gross	Points	0	6	0	0
		1	lb	Saffron	0	10	0	0
		4	lb	Silk, *Worked*	0	53	4	0
		1	dozen	Skins, Golden	0	4	2	0
		1	dozen	Skins, Red	0	2	1	0
Clement Welsh	Ind	3.5	lb	Silk, *Worked*	0	46	8	0
		3	lb	Saffron	0	30	0	0
		2	gross	Knives	0	13	4	0
		3	dozen	Knives, in Pairs	0	5	0	0
		12	gross	Points	0	12	0	0
		2	gross	Lacquer	0	3	4	0
		1.5	dozen	Caps	0	15	0	0
		4	dozen	Girdles	0	3	4	0
		2	lb	Cloves/Mace	0	5	0	0
		2	lb	Pepper	0	2	0	0
		0.5	C	Aniseed	0	6	8	0
		0.5	C	Hops	0	5	0	0

Merchant name	Origin	Qty	Unit	Commodity	£	s.	d.	f.
		3	bolt	Thread	0	3	3	0
		0.5	C	Alum	0	6	8	0
		1	dozen	Skins, Golden	0	4	2	0
		1	ream	Paper	0	0	20	0
		3	dozen	Cards, Playing	0	2	6	0
		5	pair	Stock-Cards	0	5	0	0
		2.5	piece	Cloth of Assize	0	0	0	0
George Savage	Ind	0.75	piece	Cloth of Assize	0	0	0	0
		6	lb	Silk, *Worked*	4	0	0	0
		1.5	lb	Saffron	0	15	0	0
		13	dozen	Knives, in Pairs	0	21	8	0
		3.5	gross	Knives	0	23	4	0
		0.75	C	Aniseed	0	10	0	0
		3	dozen	Alum	0	4	0	0
		12	dozen	Glasses	0	4	0	0
		12	gross	Points	0	12	0	0
		4	gross	Lacquer	0	6	8	0
		1.5	dozen	Skins, Golden	0	6	3	0
		0.25	C	Hops	0	2	6	0
		1	clout	Needles	0	0	8	0
		9	dozen	Combs	0	3	0	0
		1	gross	Beads	0	2	6	0
		2	dozen	Cards, Playing	0	0	20	0
		0.5	dozen	Books, Primers	0	0	15	0
		2	lb	Verdigris	0	0	10	0
		2	lb	Pepper	0	2	0	0
		1	lb	Ginger	0	0	18	0
		0.25	dozen	Hats	0	2	0	0
Nicholas Cranborow	Ind	1	piece	Cloth of Assize	0	0	0	0
		2	lb	Saffron	0	20	0	0
		0.5	gross	Knives	0	3	4	0
		0.5	gross	Lacquer	0	0	10	0
Andrew Welsh	Ind	1	ton	Iron	4	0	0	0
		3	lb	Saffron	0	30	0	0
		3	lb	Silk, *Worked*	0	40	0	0
		2	gross	Knives	0	13	4	0
		8	gross	Points	0	8	0	0
		1	gross	Lacquer	0	0	20	0
		0.5	piece	Fustian *Cloth*	0	8	4	0
		1	lb	Borax	0	8	0	0
		3	dozen	Soap	0	3	9	0
		3.25	piece	Cloth of Assize	0	0	0	0
Nicholas Welsh	Ind	2	lb	Saffron	0	20	0	0
		2	lb	Silk, *Worked*	0	26	8	0
		0.75	C	Alum/Aniseed	0	10	0	0
		0.25	C	Hops	0	2	6	0
		1	lb	Cloves/Mace	0	2	6	0
		1	gross	Knives	0	6	8	0
		4	dozen	Knives, in Pairs	0	6	8	0
		4	gross	Points	0	4	0	0
		1	gross	Lacquer	0	0	20	0
		1	dozen	Skins, Golden	0	4	2	0

Merchant name	Origin	Qty	Unit	Commodity	£	s.	d.	f.
		4	dozen	Girdles	0	2	6	0
		6	dozen	Combs	0	4	0	0
		1	dozen	Liquorice	0	0	5	0
		1	bolt	Thread	0	0	13	0
		1.5	piece	Cloth of Assize	0	0	0	0
James Danell	Ind	3	lb	Silk, *Worked*	0	40	0	0
		1	lb	Saffron	0	10	0	0
		2	dozen	Knives, in Pairs	0	3	4	0
		0.5	gross	Knives	0	3	4	0
		1	dozen	Aniseed	0	0	16	0
		3	gross	Points	0	3	0	0
		4	stone	Orchil	0	6	8	0
		0.75	piece	Cloth of Assize	0	0	0	0
Edmund Clery	Ind	3	lb	Saffron	0	30	0	0
		0.5	gross	Knives	0	3	4	0
		2	gross	Points	0	2	0	0
Peter Danell	Ind	1	gross	Knives	0	6	8	0
		1	gross	Lacquer	0	0	20	0
		7	gross	Points	0	7	0	0
		1	lb	Saffron	0	10	0	0
		1	dozen	Caps	0	10	0	0
		1	dozen	Soap	0	0	15	0
		2.25	piece	Cloth of Assize	0	0	0	0

The Kateryn of Waterford, Philip Doryn master, Exiting, 31st July 1542

Merchant name	Origin	Qty	Unit	Commodity	£	s.	d.	f.
Stephen Mewghe	Ind	14	piece	Cloth of Assize	0	0	0	0
		4	gross	Knives	0	26	8	0
		3	gross	Cutts	0	10	0	0
		26	gross	Points	0	26	0	0
		6	lb	Saffron	3	0	0	0
		5	lb	Silk, *Worked*	3	6	8	0
		1	gross	Lacquer	0	0	20	0
		1.5	dozen	Skins, Red	0	3	1	2
		8	dozen	Knives, in Pairs	0	13	4	0
		1	dozen	Penners	0	0	6	0
		1	dozen	Girdles	0	0	5	0
		4	doz	Ribbons, Unspecified	0	6	0	0
		1	dozen	Cards, Playing	0	0	10	0
		2	dozen	Skins, Golden	0	8	4	0
		2	lb	Cinnamon/Cloves	0	5	0	0
		2	lb	Pepper	0	2	0	0
		1	lb	Kermes	0	0	12	0
		2	lb	Ginger	0	3	0	0
		1	piece	Buckram *Cloth*	0	4	0	0
		1.5	dozen	Caps	0	15	0	0
		1	dozen	Liquorice	0	0	10	0
		0.5	C	Aniseed	0	6	8	0
Richard White	Ind	1.25	piece	Cloth of Assize	0	0	0	0
		13	lb	Saffron	6	10	0	0
		8	lb	Silk, *Worked*	5	6	8	0
		3	gross	Knives	1	0	0	0

Merchant name	Origin	Qty	Unit	Commodity	£	s.	d.	f.
		1.5	gross	Cutts	0	5	0	0
		26	gross	Points	0	26	0	0
		2	lb	Mercury	0	0	10	0
		4	dozen	Skins, Golden	0	16	8	0
		4	dozen	Knives, in Pairs	0	6	8	0
		2.5	lb	Thread	0	0	12	0
		4	dozen	Cards, Playing	0	3	4	0
		4	doz	Ribbons, Unspecified	0	6	0	0
		1	dozen	Caps	0	10	0	0
		1	dozen	Girdles	0	0	12	0
		1	dozen	Liquorice	0	0	10	0
		1.25	seam	Woad, Ashes	0	5	0	0
		2	lb	Pepper	0	2	0	0
Stephen White	Ind	0.5	piece	Cloth of Assize	0	0	0	0
		28	lb	Saffron	14	0	0	0
		14	lb	Silk, *Worked*	9	6	8	0
		3	dozen	Skins, Red	0	6	3	0
		6	dozen	Skins, Golden	0	25	0	0
		5	dozen	Glasses	0	0	10	0
		3	dozen	Knives, in Pairs	0	5	0	0
		7	dozen	Cards, Playing	0	5	10	0
		4	clout	Needles	0	2	6	0
		10	dozen	Thimbles	0	0	8	0
		9	doz	Ribbons, Unspecified	0	13	6	0
		3	dozen	*Percular*	0	2	6	0
		4	lb	Liquorice	0	0	5	0
		4	lb	Pepper	0	4	0	0
		4	lb	Cumin	0	0	5	0
		3	bolt	Thread	0	3	3	0
		2	dozen	Penners	0	0	12	0
		1	gross	Lacquer	0	0	20	0
		72	gross	Points	3	12	0	0
		8	gross	Knives	2	13	4	0
		1	C	Aniseed	0	13	4	0
Richard Malrony	Ind	11.75	piece	Cloth of Assize	0	0	0	0
		14	lb	Saffron	7	0	0	0
		10	lb	Silk, *Worked*	6	13	4	0
		30	lb	Cumin	0	3	4	0
		8	lb	Senna	0	3	4	0
		3	lb	Pepper	0	3	0	0
		4	lb	Cinnamon/Cloves	0	10	0	0
		2	lb	Ginger	0	3	0	0
		0.75	lb	Mace	0	0	22	0
		13	dozen	Knives, in Pairs	0	21	8	0
		6	dozen	Cards, Playing	0	5	0	0
		4	gross	Knives	0	26	8	0
		2	gross	Cutts	0	6	8	0
		24	gross	Points	0	24	0	0
		3	dozen	Caps	0	30	0	0
		5	bolt	Thread	0	5	5	0
		5	piece	Gart	0	0	15	0
		4	dozen	Skins, Red	0	8	4	0

Merchant name	Origin	Qty	Unit	Commodity	£	s.	d.	f.
		10	dozen	Skins, Golden	0	41	8	0
		5	doz	Ribbons, Unspecified	0	7	6	0
		1	C	Aniseed	0	13	4	0
		1	lot	Items, miscellaneous	0	5	0	0
Thomas Stackpoll	Ind	1	piece	Cloth of Assize	0	0	0	0
		12	lb	Saffron	6	0	0	0
		4	lb	Silk, *Worked*	0	53	4	0
		2.5	gross	Knives	0	16	8	0
		2	gross	Cutts	0	6	8	0
		18	gross	Points	0	18	0	0
		1.5	gross	Lacquer	0	2	6	0
		2	dozen	Skins, Golden	0	8	4	0
		3	dozen	Knives, in Pairs	0	5	0	0
		3	dozen	Cards, Playing	0	2	6	0
		2	lb	Pepper	0	2	0	0
		6	lb	Cumin	0	0	8	0
		2	bolt	Thread	0	2	2	0
		2	doz	Ribbons, Unspecified	0	3	0	0
		7	dozen	Glasses	0	0	14	0
		2	clout	Needles	0	0	16	0
		9	dozen	*Percular*	0	0	15	0
		4	lb	Verdigris	0	0	20	0
		1.5	dozen	Girdles for Penners	0	0	7	0
David Richards	Ind	4	piece	Cloth of Assize	0	0	0	0
		33	lb	Saffron	16	10	0	0
		16	lb	Silk, *Worked*	10	13	4	0
		10	dozen	Skins, Golden	0	41	8	0
		9	dozen	Knives, in Pairs	0	15	0	0
		3	dozen	Cards, Playing	0	2	6	0
		3	doz	Ribbons, Unspecified	0	4	6	0
		2	dozen	Girdles	0	0	10	0
		2	lb	Mercury	0	0	10	0
		4	lb	Incense	0	0	5	0
		6	lb	Verdigris	0	2	6	0
		4	bolt	Thread	0	4	4	0
		10	dozen	Glasses	0	0	20	0
		10	dozen	*Percular*	0	0	15	0
		2	dozen	Caps	0	20	0	0
		0.5	dozen	Nightcaps, Unspecified	0	0	20	0
		10	dozen	Thimbles	0	0	10	0
		12	dozen	Combs	0	3	4	0
		1.5	clout	Needles	0	0	12	0
		21	lb	Liquorice	0	0	10	0
		6	lb	Cumin	0	0	8	0
		6	lb	Pepper	0	6	0	0
		0.5	lb	Senna	0	0	5	0
		1.5	dozen	Penners	0	0	10	0
		12	lb	Soap	0	2	6	0
		6	lb	Soap, Black	0	0	5	0
		0.5	dozen	Skins, Red	0	0	12	2
		0.5	gross	Lacquer	0	0	10	0
		32	gross	Points	0	32	0	0

Merchant name	Origin	Qty	Unit	Commodity	£	s.	d.	f.
		5	gross	Knives	0	33	4	0
		1	gross	Cutts	0	3	4	0
		0.5	C	Aniseed	0	6	8	0
Thomas Madan	Ind	4	piece	Cloth of Assize	0	0	0	0
		1	gross	Knives	0	6	8	0
		1	dozen	Soap	0	0	15	0
Edward Arthur	Ind	0.5	piece	Cloth of Assize	0	0	0	0
		20	lb	Saffron	10	0	0	0
		10	lb	Silk, *Worked*	6	13	4	0
		3	gross	Knives	0	20	0	0
		0.5	gross	Cutts	0	0	20	0
		5	dozen	Cards, Playing	0	4	2	0
		5	doz	Ribbons, Unspecified	0	7	6	0
		0.5	dozen	Caps	0	5	0	0
		3	dozen	Knives, in Pairs	0	5	0	0
		20	gross	Points	0	20	0	0
		0.5	dozen	Hats	0	2	0	0
		0.5	C	Aniseed	0	6	8	0
		1	dozen	Skins, Golden	0	4	2	0
		1	dozen	Penners	0	0	17	0
Benedict Sall	Ind	0.75	piece	Cloth of Assize	0	0	0	0
		1	lb	Silk, *Worked*	0	13	4	0
		1	lb	Saffron	0	10	0	0
		4	dozen	Soap	0	5	0	0
		4	gross	Points	0	4	0	0
		1	gross	Lacquer	0	0	20	0
		1	gross	Knives	0	6	8	0
		2	dozen	Knives, in Pairs	0	3	4	0
		1	bolt	Thread	0	0	13	0
		3	dozen	Combs	0	0	10	0
John Mowghy	Ind	1	C	Aniseed	0	13	4	0
		3	piece	Cloth of Assize	0	0	0	0
		3	lb	Silk, *Worked*	0	40	0	0
Robert Moyne	Ind	1	piece	Cloth of Assize, Dozen Strait	0	0	0	0
		13	lb	Silk, *Worked*	8	13	4	0
		7	gross	Knives	2	6	8	0
		2	gross	Cutts	0	6	8	0
		42	gross	Points	2	2	0	0
		3	bolt	Thread	0	3	3	0
		1	doz	Balances	0	0	20	0
		1	dozen	Penners	0	0	5	0
		1.5	dozen	Caps	0	15	0	0
		9	dozen	Skins, Golden	0	37	6	0
		9	doz	Ribbons, Unspecified	0	13	4	0
		1	gross	Lacquer	0	0	20	0
		8	dozen	Knives, in Pairs	0	13	4	0
		4	dozen	Girdles	0	0	16	0
		1	lot	Items, miscellaneous	0	11	8	0
		5	dozen	Cards, Playing	0	4	2	0
Thomas Mower	Ind	3.25	piece	Cloth of Assize	0	0	0	0
		30	gross	Points	0	30	0	0
		7	lb	Verdigris	0	2	11	0

Merchant name	Origin	Qty	Unit	Commodity	£	s.	d.	f.
		12	dozen	Glasses	0	0	6	0
		1	gross	Diats	0	0	6	0
		1	gross	Knives	0	6	8	0
		3	lb	Mercury	0	0	15	0
		4	dozen	Girdles	0	3	4	0
		10	lb	Sulpher	0	0	10	0
William Madan	Ind	2	gross	Knives	0	13	4	0
		1	lb	Silk, *Worked*	0	13	4	0
		3	gross	Points	0	3	0	0
		0.5	lb	Saffron	0	5	0	0
		2	dozen	Knives, in Pairs	0	3	4	0
		1	gross	Lacquer	0	0	20	0
		2	dozen	Glasses	0	0	4	0
		1	piece	Cloth of Assize	0	0	0	0
Edmund Morres	Ind	1.25	piece	Cloth of Assize	0	0	0	0
		11	gross	Knives	3	13	4	0
		60	gross	Points	3	0	0	0
		1	dozen	Caps	0	10	0	0
		1	dozen	Skins, Golden	0	4	2	0
		2	dozen	Knives, in Pairs	0	3	4	0
		1.5	lb	Silk, *Worked*	0	20	0	0
Nicholas Kett	Ind	4	lb	Saffron	2	0	0	0
		2	lb	Silk, *Worked*	0	26	8	0
		0.5	gross	Knives	0	3	4	0
Richard Pore	Ind	3	lb	Saffron	0	30	0	0
		4	lb	Silk, *Worked*	0	53	4	0
		4	dozen	Caps	2	0	0	0
William White	Ind	2	lb	Saffron	0	20	0	0
		0.5	lb	Silk, *Worked*	0	6	8	0
		1	gross	Knives	0	6	8	0
		2	gross	Points	0	2	0	0
		4	pair	Stock-Cards	0	4	0	0
		6	dozen	Girdles	0	5	0	0
		2	dozen	Soap	0	2	6	0
		0.25	piece	Cloth of Assize	0	0	0	0
William Grant	Ind	4	piece	Cloth of Assize	0	0	0	0
		6	lb	Silk, *Worked*	4	0	0	0
		4	gross	Points	0	4	0	0
		8	gross	Lacquer	0	13	4	0
		3	gross	Knives	0	20	0	0
		7	dozen	Soap	0	8	9	0
John Hee & assoc.	Ind	1.5	piece	Cloth of Assize	0	0	0	0
		3	lb	Saffron	0	30	0	0
		1	lb	Silk, *Worked*	0	13	4	0

The Nicholas of Dungarvan, Richard Fizewilliams master, Entering, 2nd August 1542

Merchant name	Origin	Qty	Unit	Commodity	£	s.	d.	f.
Richard *Fizewilliams*	Ind	20	burden	Fish, Salted	4	3	4	0
		0.5	C	Skins, Sheep	0	5	0	0
		1	C	Skins, Lamb	0	6	8	0
		3.5	C	Fish, Hake	0	35	0	0
		1	stone	Wool, Flocks	0	0	5	0

Merchant name	Origin	Qty	Unit	Commodity	£	s.	d.	f.
		16	yard	Check *Cloth*	0	5	4	0
David Keryn	Ind	4	stone	Wool, Flocks	0	0	20	0
		0.5	C	Skins, Sheep	0	5	0	0

The Kateryn of Waterford, Edmund Morres master, Entering, *2nd August 1542*

Edmund Morres &

Pryn	Ind	1.66	dozen	Wood	0	5	0	0
		1	C	Check *Cloth*	2	0	0	0

The Austen of Dungarvan, Robert Royan master, Exiting, *2nd August 1542*

Robert Tobyn	Ind	3	piece	Cloth of Assize	0	0	0	0
		3	gross	Knives	0	20	0	0
		1	gross	Points	0	0	12	0
		0.5	C	Hops	0	5	0	0
		2	C	Iron	0	8	0	0

The Sunday of Waterford, Robert Fizejohn master, Exiting, *2nd August 1542*

John Gorney	Ind	1	hogshead	Iron	0	20	0	0
		1	barrel	Honey	0	16	8	0
		4	lb	Saffron	2	0	0	0
		3	lb	Silk, *Worked*	0	40	0	0
		8	gross	Points	0	8	0	0
		1	gross	Knives	0	6	8	0
		1	gross	Lacquer	0	0	20	0
Edmund Seyse	Ind	1	piece	Cloth of Assize	0	0	0	0
		1	dozen	Knives, in Pairs	0	0	20	0
		3	gross	Knives	0	20	0	0
		2	gross	Lacquer	0	3	4	0
		12	gross	Points	0	12	0	0
		1	lb	Saffron	0	10	0	0
		2	lb	Silk, *Worked*	0	26	8	0
Thomas Carall	Ind	2	lb	Saffron	0	20	0	0
		1	lb	Silk, *Worked*	0	13	4	0
		1	dozen	Caps	0	10	0	0
		2	dozen	Soap	0	2	6	0
		2	pair	Stock-Cards	0	2	0	0
		1	bolt	Thread	0	0	13	0
		2	dozen	Cards, Playing	0	0	20	0
Thomas Nele	Ind	0.25	piece	Cloth of Assize	0	0	0	0
		1	lb	Saffron	0	10	0	0
		1	lb	Silk, *Worked*	0	13	4	0
		0.5	dozen	Caps	0	5	0	0
		1	dozen	Soap	0	0	15	0
		0.5	gross	Knives	0	3	4	0
		3	gross	Points	0	3	0	0
		1	gross	Lacquer	0	0	20	0
		1	pair	Stock-Cards	0	0	12	0
James Goughe	Ind	0.25	piece	Cloth of Assize	0	0	0	0
		1	gross	Lacquer	0	0	20	0

Merchant name	Origin	Qty	Unit	Commodity	£	s.	d.	f.
		2	gross	Points	0	2	0	0
		2	dozen	Soap	0	2	6	0
		2	yard	Velvet *Cloth*	0	20	0	0
Richard Conwey	Ind	2	lb	Silk, *Worked*	0	26	8	0
		1	lb	Saffron	0	10	0	0
		1	gross	Lacquer	0	0	20	0
		1	dozen	Knives, in Pairs	0	0	20	0
		5	pair	Stock-Cards	0	5	0	0
		1	gross	Points	0	0	12	0
		2	dozen	Soap	0	2	6	0
Philip Welsh	Ind	1	gross	Knives	0	6	8	0
		0.5	gross	Lacquer	0	0	10	0
		6	gross	Points	0	6	0	0
		2.5	lb	Saffron	0	25	0	0
		2	dozen	Soap	0	2	6	0
		1	pair	Stock-Cards	0	0	12	0
John Fleye	Ind	1	lb	Saffron	0	10	0	0
		1	gross	Knives	0	6	8	0
		2	gross	Lacquer	0	3	4	0
		5	gross	Points	0	5	0	0
		1	bolt	Thread	0	0	13	0
		2	dozen	Soap	0	2	6	0
		4	pair	Stock-Cards	0	4	0	0
		3	piece	Caps	0	2	6	0
		1	dozen	Knives, in Pairs	0	0	20	0
		0.5	lb	Silk, *Worked*	0	6	8	0

The Jhesus of Barnstaple, John Skynner master, Exiting, 5th August 1542

Merchant name	Origin	Qty	Unit	Commodity	£	s.	d.	f.
William Appowell & Gerves	Ind	10	piece	Cloth of Assize	0	0	0	0
		17	piece	Dunster *Cloth*	8	10	0	0
		6	piece	Brecon *Cloth*	6	0	0	0
		2	piece	Bristol Frieze Cloth	0	26	8	0

The John of Pasajes de San Juan, John de Lana master, Exiting, *5th August 1542*

Merchant name	Origin	Qty	Unit	Commodity	£	s.	d.	f.
Arnold Noll	Alien	7	piece	Welsh *Cloth*	7	0	0	0
		1	piece	Dunster *Cloth*	0	10	0	0
		6	piece	Wodnall *Cloth*	4	10	0	0
		3	piece	Welsh *Cloth*, Dozen Strait	0	12	6	0
		3.5	piece	Cloth of Assize	0	0	0	0
John Shipman	Ind	0.5	piece	Cloth of Assize	0	0	0	0

The Margaret of Bristol, John Jene master, Exiting, *5th August 1542*

Merchant name	Origin	Qty	Unit	Commodity	£	s.	d.	f.
William Appowell	Ind	10	lb	Silk, *Worked*	6	13	4	0
		1	hogshead	Wine, Corrupt	0	7	6	0
		2	lb	Saffron	0	20	0	0
William Chester & assoc.	Ind	2.25	piece	Cloth of Assize	0	0	0	0

Merchant name	Origin	Qty	Unit	Commodity	£	s.	d.	f.
The Julian of Bristol, John Croke master, Exiting, 7th August 1542								
William Yonge	Ind	5	ton	Lead	25	0	0	0
		47.166	piece	Cloth of Assize	0	0	0	0
John Barbour	Ind	37	piece	Cloth of Assize	0	0	0	0
The Migell of Bristol, John Fesant master, Exiting, 9th August 1542								
William Appowell	Ind	10	lb	Silk, *Worked*	6	13	4	0
		2	lb	Saffron	0	20	0	0
		1	hogshead	Wine, Corrupt	0	7	6	0
Benedict Jay	Ind	4	piece	Cloth of Assize	0	0	0	0
Alan Hill	Ind	1	hogshead	Iron	0	20	0	0
The Trynyte of Padstow, John Sampson master, Entering, 10th August 1542								
Alexander Reynolds	Ind	5	C	Oakum	0	16	8	0
		5	dozen	Oars	0	20	0	0
The Mary Fortune of Gloucester, Laurence Nunny master, Exiting, *10th August 1542*								
Robert Pole	Ind	25	piece	Cloth of Assize	0	0	0	0
		4	dicker	Hides, Tanned	0	0	0	0
		4	ton	Lead	20	0	0	0
Alexander Packewod	Ind	10	piece	Cloth of Assize	0	0	0	0
Symon Grossin	Alien	12	piece	Cloth of Assize	0	0	0	0
The Anthony of Waterford, Henry Gall master, Entering, *10th August 1542*								
Henry *Gall*	Ind	2	burden	Fish, Salted	0	8	4	0
The John Baptist, *Port Unknown*, John de Irauso master, Entering, *10th August 1542*								
Rodrigo de Arthegure	Alien	77.66	ton	Iron	194	3	4	0
Francis Codryngton	Ind	10	ton	Iron	25	0	0	0
Stephen de Arbive & assoc.	Alien	16	dozen	Serches	3	6	8	0
		3	ton	Iron	7	10	0	0
The Nicholas of Dungarvan, Richard Fytzwilliams master, Exiting, 12th August 1542								
Richard *Fytzwilliams*	Ind	5	dozen	Flax	0	20	0	0
		1	C	Hops	0	10	0	0
		3	lb	Saffron	0	30	0	0
		3	gross	Knives	0	20	0	0
		2	gross	Points	0	2	0	0
		1	C	Iron	0	4	0	0
John Brown	Ind	1.25	piece	Cloth of Assize	0	0	0	0
		1	C	Flax	0	20	0	0
		4	bolt	Thread	0	4	4	0
		6	dozen	Cards, Playing	0	5	0	0

Merchant name	Origin	Qty	Unit	Commodity	£	s.	d.	f.

The Mary Bonaventure of Bristol, John Williams master, Entering, 14th August 1542

Merchant name	Origin	Qty	Unit	Commodity	£	s.	d.	f.
Johanna Carpenter	Ind	0.5	chest	Sugar	0	20	0	0
William Chester								
& Butlar	Ind	81	ton	Salt	40	10	0	0
		12	C	Alum	6	0	0	0

The Trynyte of Bristol, Thomas Webb master, Entering, *14th August 1542*

Merchant name	Origin	Qty	Unit	Commodity	£	s.	d.	f.
Thomas White &								
assoc.	Ind	122	ton	Iron	305	0	0	0

The Chrystofer of Lübeck, Johannes Vynk master, Exiting, *14th August 1542*

Merchant name	Origin	Qty	Unit	Commodity	£	s.	d.	f.
Johannes Vynk	Hansard	0.5	piece	Cloth of Assize	0	0	0	0

The Trynyte of Churcham, John Grason master, Entering, *14th August 1542*

Merchant name	Origin	Qty	Unit	Commodity	£	s.	d.	f.
Giles Fowlar	Ind	15	ton	Salt	7	10	0	0
		10	C	Rosin	0	13	4	0
		0.5	last	Tar	0	10	0	0
		4	C	Canvas *Cloth*	5	0	0	0
		7	C	Prunes	0	46	8	0
		3	C	Oakum	0	10	0	0
		3	C	Turpentine	0	40	0	0

The Trynyte of Bristol, Thomas Davys master, Entering, 16th August 1542

Merchant name	Origin	Qty	Unit	Commodity	£	s.	d.	f.
William Appowell								
& assoc.	Ind	116	pipe	Fish, Salmon	174	0	0	0
		3	C	Fish, Hake	0	30	0	0
		7	pipe	Fish, Salmon	9	6	8	0
		2	bird	Falcon	0	26	8	0
		4	bird	Hawk	0	26	8	0

The Trynyte of Gatcombe, Andrew Herne master, Entering, *16h August 1542*

Merchant name	Origin	Qty	Unit	Commodity	£	s.	d.	f.
Thomas FitzSymons								
& Sarchell	Ind	14.5	C	Check *Cloth*	29	0	0	0

The John of Milford Haven, William Taskar master, Entering, *16th August 1542*

Merchant name	Origin	Qty	Unit	Commodity	£	s.	d.	f.
Thomas Fitzsymons								
& assoc.	Ind	15.5	C	Check *Cloth*	31	0	0	0
		1	pipe	Oil, *Olive*	2	0	0	0
		6	piece	Skins, Marten	0	6	0	0

The George of Barnstaple, John Lake master, Exiting, 19th August 1542

Merchant name	Origin	Qty	Unit	Commodity	£	s.	d.	f.
William Appowell	Ind	4	piece	Dunster *Cloth*	2	0	0	0
		30	piece	Manchester *Cotton Cloth*	15	0	0	0
		10	piece	Cloth of Assize	0	0	0	0

Merchant name	Origin	Qty	Unit	Commodity	£	s.	d.	f.
Geoffrey Chantrell & Capps	Ind	18.5	piece	Cloth of Assize	0	0	0	0

The Dowghen of Cardiff, David Watkyns master, Entering, 26th August 1542

Merchant name	Origin	Qty	Unit	Commodity	£	s.	d.	f.
William Pycks & Hore	Ind	2	tun	Wine	0	0	0	0

The Mary James of Bristol, Richard White master, Exiting, 29th August 1542

Merchant name	Origin	Qty	Unit	Commodity	£	s.	d.	f.
John Welsh & Rowley	Ind	12.5	ton	Lead, worked	62	10	0	0
Thomas White & Jay	Ind	100	piece	Manchester *Cotton Cloth*	50	0	0	0
		41	piece	Cloth of Assize	0	0	0	0
Thomas Chancellor & Pryn	Ind	43	piece	Cloth of Assize	0	0	0	0
William Blake & Smyth	Ind	21	piece	Cloth of Assize	0	0	0	0
		30	piece	Manchester *Cotton Cloth*	15	0	0	0
Johanna Carpent*er*	Ind	5	piece	Cloth of Assize	0	0	0	0
		2.5	ton	Lead, worked	12	10	0	0

The John Baptist, *Port Unknown*, John de Irauso, Exiting, 6th September 1542

Merchant name	Origin	Qty	Unit	Commodity	£	s.	d.	f.
Thomas Harrys	Ind	60	dozen	Skins, Calf	10	0	0	0
Rodrigode Anthogore	Alien	55.25	piece	Cloth of Assize	0	0	0	0
		10	ton	Lead, worked	50	0	0	0
		30	yard	Flannel *Cloth*	0	15	0	0
Peter Andothe	Alien	12	yard	Yellow lining *Cloth*	0	6	8	0
		1	piece	Welsh *Cloth*	0	20	0	0
		0.25	piece	Cloth of Assize	0	0	0	0
Francis Dugard	Alien	36	piece	Cloth of Assize	0	0	0	0
Robert Picardie	Alien	1.5	piece	Cloth of Assize	0	0	0	0
		6.5	piece	Welsh *Cloth*	6	10	0	0
John De Irauso	Alien	25	dozen	Skins, Calf	4	3	4	0
William Car*r*	Ind	10	dicker	Hides, Tanned	0	0	0	0
		30	dozen	Skins, Calf	5	0	0	0

The Satar of *Royan*,[5] John Gerot master, Entering, 7th September 1542

Merchant name	Origin	Qty	Unit	Commodity	£	s.	d.	f.
John *Gerot*	Alien	27.7	M	Fish, Newfoundland	181	5	0	0
		1.33	tun	Oil, Trane	4	13	4	0

The Margarete of Mumbles, John Robyns master, Entering, 9th September 1542

Merchant name	Origin	Qty	Unit	Commodity	£	s.	d.	f.
William Appowell & assoc.	Ind	87	pipe	Fish, Salmon	130	10	0	0
		10	hogshead	Fish, Salmon	13	6	8	0
	4 hogshead & 1 barrel			Fish, Eels	6	0	0	0
		19	C	Fish, Hake	9	10	0	0
		2	C	Skins, Sheep	0	20	0	0
		29.5	barrel	Fish, Herring White	7	7	6	0

5 Could be Rouen or Royan, which is at the mouth of the Gironde. This ship may in fact be the Savyour of Rouen.

Merchant name	Origin	Qty	Unit	Commodity	£	s.	d.	f.

The Mary of Worcester, Thomas Afflete master, Entering, 12th September 1542

| Hugh Draper | Ind | 10 | tun | Woad, Azores | 66 | 13 | 4 | o |

The Mawdelen of St-Jean-de-Luz, Beltran Sugray master, Entering, *12th September 1542*

| *Beltran Sugray* | Alien | 27 | M | Fish, Newfoundland | 154 | 6 | 8 | o |
| | | 1 | tun | Oil, Trane | 4 | o | o | o |

The Jhesus of Padstow, John Beggyn master, Entering, 18th September 1542

| John *Beggyn* | Ind | 5.5 | C | Fish, Hake | 2 | 15 | o | o |

The Margaret of Mumbles, John Robbyns master, Exiting, *18th September 1542*

| Sir Anthony St Leger | Ind | 100 | quart | Malt | 13 | 16 | 9 | o |
| | | 100 | quart | Wheat | 16 | 13 | 4 | o |

The Mary of Chepstow, John Jene master, Entering, 21st September 1542

| Sebastian Flemyng | Ind | 10.166 | C | Fish, Hake | 5 | 1 | 8 | o |
| | | 12.33 | dicker | Skins, Salted | 8 | 5 | 4 | o |

The Trynyte of Bristol, Thomas Webb master, Exiting, 22nd September 1542

John Smyth	Ind	6	ton	Lead, worked	30	o	o	o
		8	wey	Wheat	8	o	o	o
		18	piece	Cloth of Assize	o	o	o	o

The Kateryn of Waterford, Edmund Morrese master, Entering, 24th September 1542

Henry Welsh	Ind	6.5	C	Check *Cloth*	13	o	o	o
		12	piece	Mantles	2	o	o	o
		48	piece	Skins, Sheep	o	4	o	o
John Wyse	Ind	1	C	Check *Cloth*	2	o	o	o
		12	piece	Mantles	2	o	o	o
		20	piece	Skins, Sheep	o	o	20	o
Edmund Morres & assoc.	Ind	10	piece	Mantles	o	33	4	o
Thomas Harrys	Ind	3	piece	Mantles	o	10	o	o
		1	stone	Wool, Flocks	o	o	5	o
Thomas White	Ind	12	piece	Skins, Fox	o	2	o	o
		0.5	C	Skins, Lamb	o	3	4	o
		12	piece	Skins, Otter	o	5	o	o
		6	C	Skins, Sheep	3	o	o	o

The John of *Angelett*, James Andersons master, Entering, *24th September 1542*

| William Sprat & assoc. | Ind | 22 | M | Fish, Newfoundland | 78 | 12 | 4 | o |
| | Ind | 3 | hogshead | Oil, Trane | 3 | o | o | o |

Merchant name	Origin	Qty	Unit	Commodity	£	s.	d.	f.
The Trynyte of Caerleon, John Darbye master, Exiting, *24th September 1542*								
William Balard	Ind	14	ton	Lead, worked	70	0	0	0
		54	piece	Cloth of Assize	0	0	0	0

1542/43

TNA E122/1994 is an annual 'particular' customs account of collectors W.Goodwyn and R.Watkyns covering the period Michaelmas 1542 to Michaelmas 1543. It contains the same information as the previous year.

Merchant name	Origin	Qty	Unit	Commodity	£	s.	d.	f.

The Margaret of Bristol, John Williams master, Exiting, 30th September 1542 £ s. d. f.

Merchant name	Origin	Qty	Unit	Commodity	£	s.	d.	f.
Thomas Payne	Ind	17	hogshead	Skins, Sheep Worked	8	10	0	0
		2.25	C	Lead, Worked	0	11	3	0
		20	piece	Cloth of Assize	0	0	0	0
Edward Butlar	Ind	28	dicker	Hides, Tanned	0	0	0	0
		40	dozen	Skins, Calf Tanned	6	13	4	0
		56	piece	Manchester Cotton *Cloth*	28	0	0	0
William Rowley	Ind	8	piece	Cloth of Assize	0	0	0	0
Thomas Tyson	Ind	10	piece	Cloth of Assize	0	0	0	0
Richard Pryn	Ind	4.5	piece	Cloth of Assize	9	0	0	0
		2	piece	Bristol Frieze Cloth	0	26	8	0
Edward Pryn	Ind	8	piece	Cloth of Assize	0	0	0	0
John Gurneye	Ind	3	ton	Lead, Worked	15	0	0	0
		16.66	piece	Cloth of Assize	0	0	0	0
		12	dicker	Hides, Tanned	0	0	0	0
Nicholas Thorn	Ind	33	piece	Manchester Cotton *Cloth*	16	10	0	0
William Yonge	Ind	25.5	piece	Cloth of Assize	0	0	0	0
William Chester	Ind	2.5	ton	Lead, Worked	12	10	0	0
		22	piece	Manchester Cotton *Cloth*	11	0	0	0
		3.33	piece	Cloth of Assize	0	0	0	0
Robert Thurban	Ind	3	piece	Cloth of Assize	0	0	0	0

The Prymrose of Bristol, Thomas Lache master, Exiting, *30th September 1542*

Merchant name	Origin	Qty	Unit	Commodity	£	s.	d.	f.
William Sprat	Ind	10	piece	Cloth of Assize	0	0	0	0
		30	dozen	Skins, Calf Tanned	5	0	0	0
Francis Codryngton	Ind	30	piece	Cloth of Assize	0	0	0	0
Hugh Typton	Ind	15	piece	Cloth of Assize	0	0	0	0
		70	piece	Northern *Cotton Cloth*	14	11	8	0
Edward Pryn	Ind	20	piece	Cloth of Assize	0	0	0	0
		2	piece	Bristol Frieze Cloth	0	26	8	0
		2	piece	Welsh *Cloth*, Dozen Strait	0	28	4	0
William Rowley	Ind	7	piece	Cloth of Assize	0	0	0	0
		3	piece	Welsh *Cloth*	3	0	0	0
Robert Gyttens	Ind	9	piece	Cloth of Assize	0	0	0	0
Alan Hyll	Ind	6	piece	Cloth of Assize	0	0	0	0
		3	piece	Bristol Frieze Cloth	2	0	0	0
Francis Wosley	Ind	11	dicker	Hides, Tanned	0	0	0	0

Merchant name	Origin	Qty	Unit	Commodity	£	s.	d.	f.
		30	dozen	Skins, Calf Tanned	5	0	0	0
		5	piece	Cloth of Assize	0	0	0	0
Thomas Tyson	Ind	4	piece	Cloth of Assize	0	0	0	0
William Chester	Ind	2	ton	Lead, Worked	10	0	0	0
Thomas Shipman	Ind	17	piece	Cloth of Assize	0	0	0	0

The Mary Conception of Bristol, John Champyon master, Exiting, 30th September 1542

Merchant name	Origin	Qty	Unit	Commodity	£	s.	d.	f.
Christine White	Ind	2	ton	Lead, Worked	10	0	0	0
		34	piece	Manchester Cotton *Cloth*	17	0	0	0
		8	piece	Cloth of Assize	0	0	0	0
Thomas Harrys	Ind	10	piece	Cloth of Assize	0	0	0	0
		15	dicker	Hides, Tanned	0	0	0	0
		22.5	dozen	Skins, Calf Tanned	3	15	0	0
George Snyg	Ind	17	piece	Cloth of Assize	0	0	0	0
John Smyth	Ind	60	piece	Manchester Cotton *Cloth*	30	0	0	0
Nicholas Thorn	Ind	6	ton	Lead, Worked	30	0	0	0
		12	C	Canvas *Cloth*	18	0	0	0
		100	bolt	Thread	5	8	4	0
		31	piece	Cloth of Assize	0	0	0	0
John Welshe	Ind	44	piece	Cloth of Assize	0	0	0	0
William Jonys	Ind	18	piece	Cloth of Assize	0	0	0	0
Robert Gyttens	Ind	6.5	piece	Cloth of Assize	0	0	0	0
		16	piece	Manchester Cotton *Cloth*	8	0	0	0
William Rowley	Ind	4	ton	Lead, Worked	20	0	0	0
William Appowell	Ind	10	piece	Dunster *Cloth*	5	0	0	0
		6	piece	Welsh *Cloth*	6	0	0	0
John Swetyng	Ind	4	ton	Lead, Worked	20	0	0	0
John Cutt	Ind	9	piece	Cloth of Assize	0	0	0	0
James Chester	Ind	3.33	piece	Cloth of Assize	0	0	0	0
		15	piece	Manchester Cotton *Cloth*	7	10	0	0
John Northall & Wosley	Ind	2	piece	Cloth of Assize	0	0	0	0

The Harry of Bristol, Anthony Pygot master, Exiting, 30th September 1542

Merchant name	Origin	Qty	Unit	Commodity	£	s.	d.	f.
Francis Codryngton	Ind	10	ton	Lead, Worked	50	0	0	0
		34.33	piece	Cloth of Assize	0	0	0	0
Edward Pryn & assoc.	Ind	40	piece	Cloth of Assize	0	0	0	0
Johanna Carpenter	Ind	8	piece	Cloth of Assize	0	0	0	0
Robert Butlar	Ind	30	piece	Manchester Cotton *Cloth*	15	0	0	0
		6	dicker	Hides, Tanned	0	0	0	0
Robert Gyttens	Ind	4	piece	Cloth of Assize	0	0	0	0
Robert Gyttens	Ind	20	piece	Manchester Cotton *Cloth*	10	0	0	0
William Appowell	Ind	26.16	piece	Cloth of Assize	0	0	0	0
		7	piece	Welsh *Cloth*	7	0	0	0
		30	piece	Manchester Cotton *Cloth*	15	0	0	0
		3	piece	Dunster *Cloth*	0	30	0	0
Thomas Hycks	Ind	5.5	piece	Cloth of Assize	0	0	0	0
Nicholas Tyson	Ind	5	piece	Cloth of Assize	0	0	0	0
James Balye	Ind	9	piece	Cloth of Assize	0	0	0	0
William Shipman	Ind	13	piece	Cloth of Assize	0	0	0	0

Merchant name	Origin	Qty	Unit	Commodity	£	s.	d.	f.
Nicholas Thorn	Ind	8	piece	Cloth of Assize	0	0	0	0
John Gurneye	Ind	15	piece	Cloth of Assize	0	0	0	0
Thomas Shipman	Ind	1.5	ton	Lead, Worked	7	10	0	0

The Trynyte of Caerleon, John Darby master, Exiting, *30th September 1542*

Merchant name	Origin	Qty	Unit	Commodity	£	s.	d.	f.
James Balye	Ind	9	piece	Cloth of Assize	0	0	0	0
William Balard	Ind	10	dicker	Hides, Tanned	0	0	0	0
		3	piece	Cloth of Assize	0	0	0	0
Francis Codryngton	Ind	10	piece	Cloth of Assize	0	0	0	0
Edward Pryn & assoc.	Ind	65	piece	Cloth of Assize	0	0	0	0
Robert Pressye	Ind	16	piece	Cloth of Assize	0	0	0	0
William Rowley	Ind	10	piece	Cloth of Assize	0	0	0	0
William Sprat	Ind	18	piece	Cloth of Assize	0	0	0	0
John Pryn	Ind	30.5	piece	Cloth of Assize	0	0	0	0
		8	dozen	Skins, Calf Tanned	1	6	8	0
John Channcelar	Ind	16	piece	Cloth of Assize	0	0	0	0
Robert Butlar	Ind	21	piece	Cloth of Assize	0	0	0	0
William Blake	Ind	11	piece	Cloth of Assize	0	0	0	0
Thomas Hycks	Ind	4	piece	Cloth of Assize	0	0	0	0
Alan Hyll	Ind	9	piece	Cloth of Assize	0	0	0	0
Thomas Lokyar	Ind	10	piece	Northern *Cotton Cloth*	2	1	8	0

The Trynyte of Bristol, Thomas Webbe master, Exiting, *30th September 1542*

Merchant name	Origin	Qty	Unit	Commodity	£	s.	d.	f.
William Rowley	Ind	20	piece	Manchester Cotton *Cloth*	10	0	0	0
Robert Pressye	Ind	8.5	piece	Cloth of Assize	0	0	0	0
John Gurneye	Ind	10	piece	Cloth of Assize	0	0	0	0
		24	dicker	Hides, Tanned	0	0	0	0
Thomas Tyson	Ind	10	piece	Cloth of Assize	0	0	0	0
Robert Gyttens	Ind	4	piece	Cloth of Assize	0	0	0	0
Arthur Smyth	Ind	16.5	piece	Cloth of Assize	0	0	0	0
John Cutt	Ind	35	piece	Manchester Cotton *Cloth*	17	10	0	0
Edward Pryn	Ind	25	piece	Cloth of Assize	0	0	0	0
		4	piece	Motley *Cloth*	4	0	0	0
Agnes Gay	Ind	3	piece	Cloth of Assize	0	0	0	0
Alan Hyll	Ind	4	piece	Cloth of Assize	0	0	0	0
Richard Sawnders	Ind	9	piece	Cloth of Assize	0	0	0	0

The Thomas Mawdelen of Bristol, William Mathewe master, Exiting, *30th September 1542*

Merchant name	Origin	Qty	Unit	Commodity	£	s.	d.	f.
Thomas Tyson & Snyg	Ind	2.8	ton	Lead, Worked	14	0	0	0

The Mary James of Bristol, Richard White master, Exiting, *2nd October 1542*

Merchant name	Origin	Qty	Unit	Commodity	£	s.	d.	f.
Arthur Smyth	Ind	11	piece	Cloth of Assize	0	0	0	0
		2	ton	Lead, Worked	10	0	0	0
Robert Leyghton	Ind	9	piece	Cloth of Assize	0	0	0	0

Merchant name	Origin	Qty	Unit	Commodity	£	s.	d.	f.

The Julyan of Bristol, John Crocke master, Exiting, 2nd October 1542

Merchant name	Origin	Qty	Unit	Commodity	£	s.	d.	f.
Thomas Tyson	Ind	12	piece	Cloth of Assize	0	0	0	0

The Mary Bonaventure of Bristol, Thomas Davys master, Exiting, 2nd October 1542

Merchant name	Origin	Qty	Unit	Commodity	£	s.	d.	f.
William Chester	Ind	15	piece	Manchester Cotton *Cloth*	7	10	0	0

The Trynyte of Bristol, John Hay master, Exiting, 2nd October 1542

Merchant name	Origin	Qty	Unit	Commodity	£	s.	d.	f.
John Capps	Ind	17	piece	Cloth of Assize	0	0	0	0
Robert Thurban	Ind	6	piece	Cloth of Assize	0	0	0	0
William Appowell	Ind	5	ton	Lead, Worked	25	0	0	0

The Savyour of Rouen,[1] John Gerot master, Exiting, 5th October 1542

Merchant name	Origin	Qty	Unit	Commodity	£	s.	d.	f.
John *Gerot*	Alien	8.5	last	Coal	5	13	4	0
		12	piece	Bristol Frieze *Cloth*	8	0	0	0
		6	barrel	Tar	2	0	0	0

The Kateryn of Waterford, Edmund Morres master, Exiting, 12th October 1542

Merchant name	Origin	Qty	Unit	Commodity	£	s.	d.	f.
Bastian Flemyng	Ind	11	C	Aniseed	7	6	8	0
		2	C	Alum	0	26	8	0
		2	piece	Bristol Frieze *Cloth*	0	26	8	0
Richard Lokar	Ind	10	lb	Saffron	5	0	0	0
		6	lb	Silk, *Worked*	4	0	0	0
		2	C	Aniseed	0	26	8	0
		2	piece	Cloth of Assize	0	0	0	0
Henry Welshe	Ind	6	lb	Saffron	3	0	0	0
		3	lb	Silk, *Worked*	2	0	0	0
		6	gross	Points	0	6	0	0
		3	dozen	Soap	0	3	9	0
		3.5	C	Aniseed	2	6	8	0
		1	piece	Raisins, *Great*	0	0	20	0
		1	piece	Cloth of Assize	0	0	0	0
John Wyse	Ind	2.5	C	Aniseed	0	33	4	0
		2	dozen	Knives, in Pairs	0	3	4	0
		2	dozen	Flax	0	0	20	0
		2	gross	Points	0	2	0	0
		1	piece	Northern *Cotton Cloth*	0	4	2	0
		1	piece	Cloth of Assize	0	0	0	0
Thomas Whyte	Ind	12	lb	Saffron	6	0	0	0
		8	lb	Silk, *Worked*	5	6	8	0
		0.5	gross	Knives	0	3	4	0
		6	gross	Points	0	6	0	0
		1.5	C	Aniseed	0	20	0	0
		2	lb	Verdigris	0	0	10	0
		2.25	piece	Cloth of Assize	0	0	0	0
Edmund Morres	Ind	0.25	piece	Cloth of Assize	0	0	0	0

1 Possibly Royan, at the mouth of the Gironde.

Merchant name	Origin	Qty	Unit	Commodity	£	s.	d.	f.
The Nicholas of Tewkesbury, John Butlar master, Entering, 20th October 1542								
John *Butlar*	Ind	13.5	barrel	Fish, Herring White	3	7	6	0
		1	C	Fish, Hake	0	10	0	0
The Trynyte More of *Bristol*, John Gall master, Entering, *20th October 1542*								
William Appowell	Ind	436	piece	Raisins, *Great*	36	6	8	0
		2.5	C	Marmalade	0	33	4	0
William Carr	Ind	120	piece	Raisins, *Great*	10	0	0	0
		10	ton	Fruit	20	0	0	0
		3.25	tun	Wine	0	0	0	0
Richard More & Gall	Ind	3.375	tun	Wine	0	10	0	0
The Trynyte of Gloucester, John Walleys master, Entering, *20th October 1542*								
Robert Pole	Ind	30	C	Fish, Hake	15	0	0	0
		1	kilderkin	Oil, Trane	0	5	0	0
The Mary George of Bristol, Cornell Andrew master, Entering, 22nd October 1542								
Nicholas Kelly & Smyth	Ind	7	last	Fish, Herring White	21	0	0	0
		7	C	Fish, Hake	3	10	0	0
Cornell Andrew & *assoc.*	Ind	32.5	barrel	Fish, Herring White	8	2	6	0
		1.5	C	Fish, Hake	0	15	0	0
The Migell of Bristol, Thomas Fesannt master, Entering, *22nd October 1542*								
William Sprat & assoc.	Ind	11.25	last	Fish, Herring White	33	15	0	0
		24.5	C	Fish, Hake	12	5	0	0
		1	pipe	Fish, Salmon	0	30	0	0
The Migell of Waterford, Robert Fyghejohn master, Entering, 22nd October 1542								
Robert *Fyghejohn*	Ind	8	piece	Mantles	0	26	8	0
Robert Tewe	Ind	5	C	Check *Cloth*	10	0	0	0
		5	C	Skins, Sheep	2	10	0	0
		20	piece	Mantles	3	6	8	0
Robert Butlar	Ind	5	C	Check *Cloth*	10	0	0	0
		7	C	Skins, Sheep	3	10	0	0
Walter White	Ind	4	C	Skins, Sheep	2	0	0	0
		7	dicker	Skins, Deer	0	14	7	0
		3.5	C	Skins, Sheep	0	35	0	0
Francis Felan	Ind	6	C	Skins, Sheep	3	0	0	0
		2.5	C	Check *Cloth*	5	0	0	0
		3	piece	Skins, Deer	0	0	7	0
		6	piece	Mantles	0	20	0	0
William Donohow	Ind	34	piece	Mantles	5	13	4	0
		1.5	C	Check *Cloth*	3	0	0	0
		1.5	C	Skins, Sheep	0	15	0	0

Merchant name	Origin	Qty	Unit	Commodity	£	s.	d.	f.
Patrick Connow	Ind	8	C	Skins, Sheep	4	0	0	0
		2	C	Check *Cloth*	4	0	0	0
		1	dicker	Skins, Deer	0	2	1	0
Patrick White	Ind	3	C	Check *Cloth*	6	0	0	0
		4.5	C	Check *Cloth*	9	0	0	0
		2	piece	Mantles	0	6	8	0
		6	piece	Mantles	0	20	0	0
William Grannt	Ind	7	C	Check *Cloth*	14	0	0	0
		30	piece	Mantles	5	0	0	0
		3	C	Skins, Sheep	0	30	0	0
David Welshe	Ind	8	C	Fish, Hake	4	0	0	0
		7	piece	Mantles	0	23	4	0
		150	yard	Check *Cloth*	2	10	0	0
		1	dicker	Skins, Deer	0	2	1	0
James Tarrell	Ind	8	piece	Mantles	0	26	8	0
		0.5	C	Skins, Sheep	0	5	0	0
		80	yard	Check *Cloth*	0	26	8	0
William Bruar & Grannt	Ind	3	piece	Mantles	0	10	0	0
		0.5	C	Check *Cloth*	0	20	0	0
		0.5	C	Skins, Sheep	0	5	0	0
Maurice Record & Quyrk	Ind	1	C	Check *Cloth*	2	0	0	0
		6	piece	Mantles	0	20	0	0
		0.5	C	Skins, Sheep	0	5	0	0
Jasper Harolde & White	Ind	3	C	Skins, Sheep	0	30	0	0
		65	lb	Spermaceti	5	8	4	0
		10	piece	Mantles	0	33	4	0
		0.5	C	Check *Cloth*	0	20	0	0

The Margaret of Bristol, John Jene master, Entering, *22nd October 1542*

William Gall & assoc.	Ind	9.5	last	Fish, Herring White	28	10	0	0
		7.5	C	Fish, Hake	3	15	0	0
		2	dicker	Skins, Deer	0	4	2	0

The Anthony of Waterford, Henry Gall master, Entering, *22nd October 1542*

Edmund Seyse	Ind	11.5	C	Check *Cloth*	23	0	0	0
		9	C	Skins, Sheep	4	10	0	0
		30	piece	Mantles	5	0	0	0
		1	dicker	Skins, Deer	0	2	1	0
		9	piece	Skins, Fox	0	0	18	0
		3	piece	Skins, Otter	0	0	15	0
		5	stone	Wool, Flocks	0	2	1	0
Peter Makar	Ind	30	yard	Check *Cloth*	0	10	0	0
		2	piece	Mantles	0	6	8	0
		6.33	C	Skins, Sheep	3	3	4	0
Robert Medoll	Ind	3	C	Check *Cloth*	6	0	0	0
		20	piece	Mantles	3	6	8	0
		1.5	C	Skins, Sheep	0	15	0	0

Merchant name	Origin	Qty	Unit	Commodity	£	s.	d.	f.
		0.5	C	Skins, Lamb	0	3	4	0
Edmund Clery	Ind	320	yard	Check *Cloth*	5	6	8	0
		3	piece	Mantles	0	10	0	0
		3.33	C	Skins, Sheep	0	3	4	0
		2	piece	Skins, Deer	0	0	5	0
William *Unknown*	Ind	1.5	C	Check *Cloth*	3	0	0	0
		0.5	C	Skins, Sheep	0	5	0	0
		2	C	Skins, Lamb	0	13	4	0
		1	C	Fish, Hake	0	10	0	0
		12	piece	Mantles	2	0	0	0
Patrick Strange	Ind	4	C	Check *Cloth*	8	0	0	0
		32	piece	Mantles	5	6	8	0
		0.5	C	Skins, Sheep	0	5	0	0
Peter Danyell	Ind	10	piece	Mantles	0	33	4	0
		2.5	C	Check *Cloth*	5	0	0	0
Henry Gall	Ind	3.5	C	Fish, Hake	0	35	0	0
		16	piece	Mantles	2	13	4	0
		30	yard	Check *Cloth*	0	10	0	0
George Quenmerford	Ind	1120	yard	Check *Cloth*	18	13	4	0
		50	piece	Mantles	8	6	8	0
		2	C	Skins, Sheep	0	20	0	0
John Fannyng	Ind	2	C	Skins, Sheep	0	20	0	0
		8	piece	Skins, Fox	0	0	16	0
Nicholas Harold	Ind	6	C	Skins, Sheep	3	0	0	0
		3	C	Skins, Lamb	0	20	0	0
		24	piece	Skins, Otter	0	10	0	0
		24	piece	Skins, Fox	0	4	0	0
		6	piece	Skins, Marten	0	6	0	0
		12	lb	Spermaceti	0	12	0	0

The Nicholas of Bristol, Bartholomew Garland master, Entering, *22nd October 1542*

Merchant name	Origin	Qty	Unit	Commodity	£	s.	d.	f.
Bartholomew Garland & assoc.	Ind	37	barrel	Fish, Herring White	9	5	0	0
		5.266	C	Fish, Hake	2	12	8	0
		1	barrel	Beef	0	5	0	0
		1	pipe	Fish, Salmon	0	30	0	0

The Bryde of Waterford, Nicholas Cornycke master, Entering, *22nd October 1542*

Merchant name	Origin	Qty	Unit	Commodity	£	s.	d.	f.
James Lunbart	Ind	5	C	Check *Cloth*	10	0	0	0
		4	piece	Mantles	0	13	4	0
		40	piece	Skins, Sheep	0	3	4	0
Fowke Quenmerford	Ind	8	C	Check *Cloth*	16	0	0	0
		2	piece	Mantles	0	6	8	0
Laurence Bruar	Ind	6	C	Check *Cloth*	12	0	0	0
		6	piece	Mantles	0	20	0	0
Patrick Bryn	Ind	40	yard	Check *Cloth*	0	13	4	0
		3	piece	Mantles	0	10	0	0
Hugh Pryn	Ind	2	C	Check *Cloth*	4	0	0	0
		4	stone	Wool, Flocks	0	0	20	0
		1	C	Fish, Hake	0	10	0	0

Merchant name	Origin	Qty	Unit	Commodity	£	s.	d.	f.
		6	piece	Mantles	0	20	0	0
		1	C	Skins, Sheep	0	10	0	0
		6	piece	Skins, Deer	0	0	14	0
Edward Rycheford	Ind	2	C	Check *Cloth*	4	0	0	0
George Walter	Ind	4	C	Skins, Sheep	2	0	0	0
		1	C	Skins, Lamb	0	6	8	0
		18	piece	Skins, Fox	0	3	0	0
		20	lb	Spermaceti	0	33	4	0
		2	piece	Skins, Wolf	0	0	8	0
James Styrche	Ind	2	C	Skins, Sheep	0	20	0	0
		2	piece	Skins, Wolf	0	0	10	0
		96	piece	Skins, Lamb	0	5	4	0
		4	piece	Mantles	0	13	4	0
		24	piece	Skins, Otter	0	10	0	0
		8	yard	Check *Cloth*	0	2	8	0
		18	piece	Skins, Fox	0	3	0	0
		11	lb	Spermaceti	0	11	0	0
		46	yard	Irish Linen *Cloth*	0	3	10	0
		2	piece	Skins, Marten	0	2	0	0

The Francis of New Ross, John Brown master, Entering, *22nd October 1542*

Merchant name	Origin	Qty	Unit	Commodity	£	s.	d.	f.
Peter Harrys	Ind	9	C	Skins, Sheep	4	10	0	0
		4	C	Check *Cloth*	8	0	0	0
		2.5	C	Skins, Lamb	0	16	8	0
		2	C	Skins, Kid	0	10	0	0
		4	piece	Mantles	0	13	4	0
Nicholas Kelly	Ind	3	C	Check *Cloth*	6	0	0	0
		7	C	Skins, Sheep	3	10	0	0
Richard Clery	Ind	7	C	Check *Cloth*	14	0	0	0
		3	C	Skins, Sheep	0	30	0	0
		8.5	stone	Wool, Irish	0	22	8	0
		2.5	stone	Wool, Flocks	0	0	12	2
		2	piece	Mantles	0	6	8	0
Thomas Rothe	Ind	4.5	C	Check *Cloth*	9	0	0	0
		4.5	C	Skins, Sheep	2	5	0	0
		0.25	C	Skins, Lamb	0	0	20	0
		4	piece	Skins, Fox	0	0	8	0
Peter Astekyn	Ind	4	C	Skins, Sheep	2	0	0	0
		1.5	C	Check *Cloth*	3	0	0	0
		1.5	C	Skins, Lamb	0	10	0	0
		7	stone	Wool, Irish	0	18	8	0
		4	stone	Wool, Flocks	0	0	20	0
		4	piece	Skins, Fox	0	0	8	0
		6	lb	Wax	0	2	0	0
William Ffrancis	Ind	3	C	Check *Cloth*	6	0	0	0
		0.5	dicker	Skins, Deer	0	0	14	0
		3	C	Skins, Sheep	0	30	0	0
		0.25	C	Skins, Lamb	0	0	20	0
		0.5	C	Skins, Kid	0	2	6	0
		3	piece	Mantles	0	10	0	0
William Rothe	Ind	2	C	Skins, Sheep	0	20	0	0

Merchant name	Origin	Qty	Unit	Commodity	£	s.	d.	f.
		30	yard	Check *Cloth*	0	10	0	0
		1	dicker	Skins, Deer	0	2	1	0
		12	stone	Wool, Flocks	0	5	0	0
		2	piece	Mantles	0	6	8	0
		0.5	dicker	Skins, Salted	0	6	8	0

The Sunday of Bristol, Master Unknown, Entering, 27th October 1542

William *Unknown*								
&White	Ind	45	barrel	Fish, Herring White	11	5	0	0

The Mary of Gloucester, John Llewelyn master, Entering, *27th October 1542*

John *Llewelyn*	Ind	7	barrel	Fish, Herring White	0	35	0	0
Thomas Cloturboke								
& Deans	Ind	12	last	Fish, Herring White	36	0	0	0
		2	C	Fish, Hake	0	20	0	0

The Savyour of Minehead, Henry Dale master, Entering, *27th October 1542*

William Appowell								
& Ca*p*ps	Ind	5	last	Fish, Herring White	15	0	0	0
		2	pipe	Fish, Salmon	3	0	0	0
		1	hogshead	Fish, Salmon	0	26	8	0
		5	dicker	Skins, Salted	3	6	8	0
		1	C	Tallow, Molten	0	10	0	0
		1	barrel	Tallow, rough	0	6	8	0
		8	barrel	Beef	2	0	0	0

The Bryde of Waterford, Nicholas Cornycke master, Exiting, *27th October 1542*

James Lu*n*bart	Ind	4.5	tun	Wine, Corrupt	6	15	0	0
George Quenm*e*rford	Ind	0.5	C	Aniseed	0	6	8	0
		1.75	piece	Cloth of Assize	0	0	0	0
		0.5	gross	Knives	0	3	4	0
		6	gross	Points	0	6	0	0
		2	lb	Saffron	0	20	0	0
Jasper Harold	Ind	20	lb	Saffron	10	0	0	0
		10	lb	Silk, *Worked*	6	13	4	0
		3	gross	Knives	0	20	0	0
		36	gross	Points	0	36	0	0
		6	lb	Cumin	0	0	8	0
		12	lb	Seed, Onion	0	10	0	0
		1	C	Aniseed	0	13	4	0
		2.5	piece	Cloth of Assize	0	0	0	0

The Magdalen of St-Jean-de-Luz, Beltran Suggraye master, Exiting, *27th October 1542*

Beltran Suggraye	Alien	13	piece	Bristol Frieze *Cloth*	8	13	4	0
		6	piece	Bristol Double Frieze *Cloth*	12	0	0	0
		15.33	piece	Cloth of Assize	0	0	0	0

Merchant name	Origin	Qty	Unit	Commodity	£	s.	d.	f.

The John Evangelyst, *Port Unknown*, William Edwards master, Exiting, 29th October 1542

Merchant name	Origin	Qty	Unit	Commodity	£	s.	d.	f.
Roger Jonys & Gybbyns	Ind	5	ton	Lead, Worked	25	0	0	0
		10	piece	Bristol Frieze *Cloth*	6	13	4	0
		3	last	Coal	0	40	0	0
		1	piece	Cloth of Assize	0	0	0	0

The Trynyte of *Castrow*,[2] Jordan Roche master, Entering, *29th October 1542*

Merchant name	Origin	Qty	Unit	Commodity	£	s.	d.	f.
Nicholas Kelly	Ind	7.5	C	Fish, Hake	3	15	0	0
		2	stone	Wool, Flocks	0	0	10	0
		0.5	C	Skins, Sheep	0	5	0	0
		1	C	Skins, Lamb	0	6	8	0
		1	barrel	Fish, Herring White	0	5	0	0

The Anthony of Waterford, Henry Gall master, Exiting, 30th October 1542

Merchant name	Origin	Qty	Unit	Commodity	£	s.	d.	f.
Sir Anthony St Leger	Ind	20	quart	Beans &Malt	0	55	6	0
		20	quart	Wheat	3	6	8	0
Peter Danyell	Ind	1	C	Aniseed	0	13	4	0
		2	gross	Points	0	2	0	0
		1	dozen	Soap	0	0	16	0
Edmund Seyse	Ind	2	dozen	Alum	0	0	16	0
		0.75	C	Aniseed	0	10	0	0
		2	lb	Cinnamon	0	5	0	0
		1	piece	Cloth of Assize	0	0	0	0
		4	dozen	Knives, in Pairs	0	6	8	0
		3	gross	Knives	0	20	0	0
		1	gross	Lacquer	0	0	20	0
		12	gross	Points	0	12	0	0
		24	gross	Points	0	24	0	0
		16	lb	Saffron	8	0	0	0
		1	lb	Saffron	0	10	0	0
		4	lb	Silk, *Worked*	2	13	4	0
		5	dozen	Soap	0	6	3	0
John Quyrke	Ind	30	lb	Saffron	15	0	0	0
		11	lb	Silk, *Worked*	7	6	8	0
		2	lb	Silk, *Worked*	0	26	8	0
		24	dozen	Knives, in Pairs	2	0	0	0
		4	gross	Knives	0	26	8	0
		4	gross	Cutts	0	13	4	0
		6	dozen	Skins, Golden	0	25	0	0
		6	dozen	Cards, Playing	0	5	0	0
		48	gross	Points	2	8	0	0
		4	lb	Seed, Onion	0	4	0	0
		1.5	piece	Cloth of Assize	0	0	0	0
Peter Makar	Ind	1.5	lb	Silk, *Worked*	0	20	0	0
		0.5	lb	Saffron	0	5	0	0
		1	gross	Knives	0	6	8	0
		2	gross	Points	0	2	0	0

2 Unidentified.

Merchant name	Origin	Qty	Unit	Commodity	£	s.	d.	f.
		1	gross	Lacquer	0	0	20	0
		6	lb	Verdigris	0	2	6	0
		3	piece	Caps	0	2	6	0
		1	dozen	Aniseed	0	0	16	0
		2	dozen	Knives, in Pairs	0	3	4	0
		0.5	lb	Pepper	0	0	6	0
Patrick Strange	Ind	1	piece	Cloth of Assize	0	0	0	0
		1	gross	Knives	0	6	8	0
Edmund Clery	Ind	1.5	gross	Knives	0	10	0	0
		1	gross	Lacquer	0	0	20	0
		3	gross	Points	0	3	0	0
Nicholas Harold	Ind	20	lb	Saffron	10	0	0	0
		3	lb	Silk, *Worked*	2	0	0	0
		3	dozen	Cards, Playing	0	2	6	0
		3	bolt	Thread	0	3	3	0
		3	dozen	Ribbons, Unspecified	0	4	0	0
		3	dozen	Knives, in Pairs	0	5	0	0
		24	gross	Points	0	24	0	0
		0.5	C	Aniseed	0	6	8	0
		6	dozen	Beads	0	0	9	0
		4	dozen	Skins, Golden	0	16	8	0
		5	gross	Knives	0	33	4	0
James Styrche	Ind	3	piece	Cloth of Assize	0	0	0	0
		4	dozen	Cards, Playing	0	3	4	0
		8	dozen	Knives, in Pairs	0	13	4	0
		4	dozen	Skins, Golden	0	16	8	0
		3	lb	Pepper	0	3	0	0
		6	dozen	Ribbons, Unspecified	0	8	0	0
		26	gross	Points	0	26	0	0
		1	gross	Lacquer	0	0	20	0
		4	gross	Knives	0	26	8	0
		2	gross	Cutts	0	6	8	0
		1	dozen	Cumin	0	0	16	0
		4	lb	Seed, Onion	0	4	0	0
		15	lb	Saffron	7	10	0	0
		4	lb	Silk, *Worked*	2	13	4	0
Edward Richeford	Ind	1.5	C	Aniseed	0	20	0	0
		4.5	lb	Saffron	2	5	0	0
		20	lb	Cumin	0	3	4	0
		6	lb	Liquorice	0	0	4	0
		3	lb	Pepper	0	3	0	0
		5	dozen	Knives, in Pairs	0	8	4	0
		4	gross	Points	0	4	0	0
		0.5	gross	Knives	0	3	4	0
		0.5	gross	Cutts	0	0	20	0

The Francis of New Ross, John Brown master, Exiting, 11th November 1542

Merchant name	Origin	Qty	Unit	Commodity	£	s.	d.	f.
Nicholas Cantwell	Ind	7	lb	Saffron	3	10	0	0
		4	lb	Silk, *Worked*	2	13	4	0
		1	C	Hops	0	10	0	0
		1	C	Alum	0	13	4	0

Merchant name	Origin	Qty	Unit	Commodity	£	s.	d.	f.
		7	dozen	Knives, in Pairs	0	11	8	0
		0.5	gross	Knives	0	3	4	0
		8	lb	Cinnamon &Cloves	0	20	0	0
		5	lb	Pepper	0	5	0	0
		6	gross	Points	0	6	0	0
		1	dozen	Cards, Playing	0	0	10	0
		7	piece	Cloth of Assize, Dozen Strait	0	0	0	0
Patrick Kelly	Ind	3	lb	Saffron	0	30	0	0
		4	lb	Silk, *Worked*	2	13	4	0
		2	dozen	Skins, Golden	0	8	4	0
		1	gross	Knives	0	6	8	0
		6	gross	Points	0	6	0	0
Thomas Rothe	Ind	1	hogshead	Iron	0	20	0	0
		3	lb	Saffron	0	30	0	0
		1.5	lb	Silk, *Worked*	0	20	0	0
		0.5	gross	Knives	0	3	4	0
		2	gross	Points	0	2	0	0
		8	lb	Seed, Onion	0	6	8	0
		1	bolt	Thread	0	0	13	0
		0.5	dozen	Skins, Red	0	0	13	0
		3	dozen	Girdles	0	2	0	0
		2.5	piece	Cloth of Assize, Dozen Strait	0	0	0	0
Martin Lege & Maynyng	Ind	12	lb	Saffron	6	0	0	0
Richard Corseye	Ind	2	piece	Cloth of Assize	0	0	0	0
		0.5	piece	Cloth of Assize	0	0	0	0
		8	lb	Saffron	4	0	0	0
		4	gross	Knives	0	26	8	0
		2	dozen	Caps	0	20	0	0
		1	dozen	Cards, Wool	0	4	0	0
		3	dozen	Cards, Playing	0	2	6	0
		10	dozen	Combs	0	0	20	0
		2	lb	Silk, *Worked*	0	26	8	0
		1	lb	Saffron	0	10	0	0
		3	gross	Points	0	3	0	0
		0.5	gross	Knives	0	3	4	0
William Francis	Ind	7	lb	Saffron	3	10	0	0
		2	lb	Silk, *Worked*	0	26	8	0
		2	dozen	Aniseed	0	2	8	0
		1.5	dozen	Cumin	0	2	0	0
		2	dozen	Knives, in Pairs	0	3	4	0
		0.5	gross	Knives	0	3	4	0
		6	lb	Seed, Onion	0	5	0	0
		2	gross	Points	0	2	0	0
		3	piece	Cloth of Assize, Dozen Strait	0	0	0	0
Peter Harrys	Ind	1.75	piece	Cloth of Assize	0	0	0	0
		6	lb	Saffron	3	0	0	0
		1	ream	Paper	0	0	20	0
		3	lb	Silk, *Worked*	2	0	0	0
		1	C	Aniseed	0	13	4	0
		6	gross	Points	0	6	0	0
		2	gross	Knives	0	13	4	0

Merchant name	Origin	Qty	Unit	Commodity	£	s.	d.	f.
		8	lb	Verdigris	0	3	4	0
		2	clout	Needles	0	2	8	0
		2	lb	Thread	0	0	10	0
		4	dozen	Glasses	0	0	12	0
Peter Asteken	Ind	1	piece	Cloth of Assize, Dozen Strait	0	0	0	0
		4	dozen	Knives, in Pairs	0	6	8	0
		0.5	gross	Knives	0	3	4	0
		1	lb	Cloves	0	2	6	0
		1	lb	Pepper	0	0	12	0
		1	lb	Saffron	0	10	0	0
Richard Clerye	Ind	1	gross	Knives	0	6	8	0
		2	dozen	Soap	0	2	6	0
		4	lb	Liquorice	0	0	8	0
		2	piece	Caps	0	0	20	0
		12	gross	Points	0	12	0	0
		0.5	C	Aniseed	0	6	8	0
		4	lb	Saffron	2	0	0	0
		1.75	piece	Cloth of Assize	0	0	0	0

The Margaret of Milford Haven, Philip Cabby master, Entering, 16th November 1542

Merchant name	Origin	Qty	Unit	Commodity	£	s.	d.	f.
Patrick Smyth & assoc.	Ind	13	C	Fish, Hake	6	10	0	0
		1	barrel	Fish, Herring White	0	5	0	0
		3	barrel	Beef	0	15	0	0
		2	stone	Wool, Flocks	0	0	10	0

The James of Milford Haven, William Philips master, Entering, 20th November 1542

Merchant name	Origin	Qty	Unit	Commodity	£	s.	d.	f.
Benedict Jay	Ind	10	barrel	Fish, Herring White	2	10	0	0

The Nicholas of Bristol, Bartholomew Garland master, Exiting, *20th November 1542*

Merchant name	Origin	Qty	Unit	Commodity	£	s.	d.	f.
John De Porres	Alien	3	lb	Silk, *Worked*	2	0	0	0
		12	lb	Saffron	6	0	0	0
Jordan Roche	Ind	1	lb	Saffron	0	10	0	0
		1	C	Hops	0	10	0	0
		6	stone	Orchil	0	10	0	0
		0.5	gross	Knives	0	3	4	0

The Mygell of Waterford, Robert Fyfgejohn master, Exiting, *20th November 1542*

Merchant name	Origin	Qty	Unit	Commodity	£	s.	d.	f.
David Welshe	Ind	2.25	piece	Cloth of Assize	0	0	0	0
		4	lb	Saffron	2	0	0	0
		1	C	Aniseed	0	13	4	0
		1	gross	Knives	0	6	8	0
William Donohow	Ind	0.5	lb	Saffron	0	5	0	0
		0.5	lb	Silk, *Worked*	0	6	8	0
		2	gross	Points	0	2	0	0
		1	gross	Lacquer	0	0	20	0
Robert Tewe	Ind	5	lb	Saffron	2	10	0	0
		2	lb	Silk, *Worked*	0	26	8	0

Merchant name	Origin	Qty	Unit	Commodity	£	s.	d.	f.
		1	gross	Knives	0	6	8	0
		1	gross	Cutts	0	3	4	0
		6	gross	Points	0	6	0	0
		1	gross	Lacquer	0	0	20	0
		6	dozen	Knives, in Pairs	0	10	0	0
		1	C	Aniseed	0	13	4	0
		4	piece	Caps	0	3	4	0
		2	dozen	Soap	0	2	6	0
		1.25	piece	Cloth of Assize	0	0	0	0
William Grannt	Ind	1	pipe	Iron	2	0	0	0
		2	gross	Lacquer	0	3	4	0
		1	piece	Cloth of Assize	0	0	0	0
Walter White	Ind	3	piece	Cloth of Assize, Dozen Strait	0	0	0	0
		1	lb	Saffron	0	10	0	0
		1	gross	Knives	0	6	8	0
Francis Felan	Ind	1	piece	Cloth of Assize	0	0	0	0
		2	gross	Knives	0	13	4	0
		4	gross	Points	0	4	0	0
		4	gross	Lacquer	0	6	8	0
		1	dozen	Skins, Golden	0	4	2	0
Patrick White	Ind	1.5	piece	Cloth of Assize	0	0	0	0
		1	lb	Saffron	0	10	0	0
		1	gross	Knives	0	6	8	0
		6	gross	Points	0	6	0	0
		1	gross	Lacquer	0	0	20	0
		2	pair	Stock-Cards	0	2	0	0
		12	lb	Liquorice	0	0	10	0
Patrick Connowe	Ind	1	piece	Cloth of Assize	0	0	0	0
		1	lb	Silk, *Worked*	0	13	4	0
		1	gross	Knives	0	6	8	0
		2	gross	Lacquer	0	3	4	0
		2	gross	Points	0	2	0	0
		2	lb	Saffron	0	20	0	0
		3	lb	Seed, Onion	0	3	0	0
		3	piece	Caps	0	2	6	0
Robert Butlar	Ind	2	piece	Cloth of Assize	0	0	0	0
		7	lb	Saffron	3	10	0	0
		2	gross	Knives	0	13	4	0
		12	gross	Points	0	12	0	0
		3	gross	Lacquer	0	5	0	0
		2	lb	Pepper	0	2	0	0
		0.25	lb	Cinnamon	0	0	7	0
		0.5	dozen	Caps, Night	0	2	0	0
		4	lb	Seed, Onion	0	4	0	0
John Yonge	Ind	1.5	piece	Cloth of Assize	0	0	0	0
		10	lb	Saffron	5	0	0	0
		2	lb	Silk, *Worked*	0	26	8	0
		2.5	gross	Knives	0	16	8	0
		12	gross	Points	0	12	0	0
		4	dozen	Skins, Golden	0	16	8	0
		0.5	dozen	Skins, Red	0	0	13	0
		2	dozen	Cards, Playing	0	0	20	0

Merchant name	Origin	Qty	Unit	Commodity	£	s.	d.	f.
		10	lb	Seed, Onion	0	8	0	0
		6	lb	Mercury	0	2	6	0
		6	lb	Verdigris	0	2	6	0
		1	bolt	Thread	0	0	13	0
George Walter	Ind	20	lb	Saffron	10	0	0	0
		5	lb	Silk, *Worked*	3	6	8	0
		30	gross	Points	0	30	0	0
		2	dozen	Skins, Red	0	4	2	0
		6	dozen	Skins, Golden	0	25	0	0
		4	dozen	Cards, Playing	0	3	4	0
		3	dozen	Girdles	0	3	0	0
		12	lb	Seed, Onion	0	8	4	0
		10	dozen	Knives, in Pairs	0	16	8	0
		3	gross	Knives	0	20	0	0
		2	lb	Mercury	0	0	10	0
		3	lb	Verdigris	0	0	15	0
		12	dozen	Beads	0	0	12	0
		8	lb	Liquorice	0	0	5	0
		6	lb	Frankincense	0	2	6	0
		6	lb	Sulpher	0	2	6	0
		10	dozen	Thimbles	0	0	8	0
		2	bolt	Thread	0	2	2	0
		6	lb	Cumin	0	0	8	0
		1	piece	Cloth of Assize	0	0	0	0

The Anthony of *Minsterford*, Nicholas Harrys master, Entering, 22nd November 1542

John Comleye	Ind	23	barrel	Fish, Herring White	5	15	0	0

The Mary of Tintern, Thomas ApJohn master, Entering, *22nd November 1542*

John Bysse	Ind	6	C	Woad, Azores	2	0	0	0

The Kateryn of Milford Haven, Richard Mower master, Entering, *22nd November 1542*

Richard *Mower* & assoc.	Ind	1.5	last	Fish, Herring White	4	10	0	0
		4	C	Fish, Hake	2	0	0	0

The Martyn of Milford Haven, Richard Brown master, Entering, 2nd December 1542

Richard *Brown*	Ind	6.5	barrel	Fish, Herring White	0	22	6	0

The Mary of Gloucester, John Llewelyn master, Exiting, *2nd December 1542*

Thomas Cloturboke	Ind	10	ton	Salt	5	0	0	0

The George of Gatcombe, William Hoper master, Entering, 22nd December 1542

John Nicholas & assoc.	Ind	2	C	Check *Cloth*	4	0	0	0
		12	piece	Mantles	0	40	0	0
		3	C	Fish, Sturgeon	0	30	0	0

Merchant name	Origin	Qty	Unit	Commodity	£	s.	d.	f.

The Prymrose of Bristol, Thomas Lache master, Entering, 29th December 1542

Christine White & assoc.	Ind	69.5	ton	Iron	173	15	0	0

The George of Elmore, John Dymocke master, Entering, 5th January 1543

John Goslynge	Ind	25	C	Fish, Hake	12	10	0	0

The Clement of Mumbles, Griffith ApDavid master, Entering, 10th January 1543

Richard White & Penteny	Ind	6.5	C	Check *Cloth*	13	0	0	0
		1.5	C	Fish, Salted	0	30	0	0
		4	C	Fish, Sturgeon	2	0	0	0
		1	barrel	Fish, Herring White	0	5	0	0

The Julyan of Dartmouth, Richard Cole master, Entering, 11th January 1543

John Gurneye	Ind	39.5	tun	Wine	0	0	0	0
William Balard & Chester	Ind	12	tun	Wine	0	0	0	0
		5.625	ton	Raisins, *Great*	11	5	0	0
		20	C	Aniseed	13	6	8	0
		1	C	Dates	0	13	4	0
Simon Wyllyng & Myllard	Ind	4.25	C	Alum	2	2	6	0
		1	piece	Raisins, *Great*	0	0	20	0
Nicholas Barnhowse	Ind	7.5	tun	Wine	0	0	0	0

The Brandon of Wexford, John Shennan master, Entering, 12th January 1543

John *Shennan*	Ind	2	last	Fish, Herring White	6	0	0	0
		12	C	Fish, Hake	6	0	0	0
		12	piece	Mantles	0	40	0	0
		5	C	Skins, Sheep	2	10	0	0
		1	C	Skins, Lamb	0	6	8	0
		1	dicker	Skins, Deer	0	2	1	0
		2	meise	Fish, Herring Red	0	10	0	0

The Saviour of Barnstaple, Richard Skynner master, Entering, *12th January 1543*

William Appowell & assoc.	Ind	52.125	ton	Fruit	104	5	0	0
		1.25	C	Soap	0	12	6	0

The Mary Smyth of Milford Haven, William Hyll master, Entering, 16th January 1543

Thomas Cadell	Ind	8	barrel	Fish, Herring White	2	0	0	0
		30	C	Fish, Hake	15	0	0	0
		2	C	Tallow, rough	0	6	8	0
		9	dicker	Skins, Salted	6	0	0	0

Merchant name	Origin	Qty	Unit	Commodity	£	s.	d.	f.

The Mary of Tewkesbury, Richard Cox master, Entering, 19th January 1543

Merchant name	Origin	Qty	Unit	Commodity	£	s.	d.	f.
Christopher Warren	Ind	10	ton	Woad, Azores	66	13	4	0

The Peter of Milford Haven, William Barker master, Entering, 20th January 1543

Merchant name	Origin	Qty	Unit	Commodity	£	s.	d.	f.
William *Barker*	Ind	5	barrel	Fish, Herring White	0	25	0	0

The Nicholas of Bristol, Bartholomew Garland master, Entering, 22nd January 1543

Merchant name	Origin	Qty	Unit	Commodity	£	s.	d.	f.
Edward Pryn & assoc.	Ind	62	C	Fish, Hake	31	0	0	0
		60	piece	Bowstaves	0	20	0	0
		2	barrel	Fish, Herring White	0	10	0	0
		1	hogshead	Fish, Salmon	0	26	8	0

The Mary of Tenby, Richard Whyte master, Entering, *22nd January 1543*

Merchant name	Origin	Qty	Unit	Commodity	£	s.	d.	f.
Richard *Whyte*	Ind	2	barrel	Fish, Herring White	0	10	0	0

The Mary of Gloucester, William Ilard master, Entering, *22nd January 1543*

Merchant name	Origin	Qty	Unit	Commodity	£	s.	d.	f.
Peter Creangh	Ind	10	C	Fish, Hake	5	0	0	0
		40	piece	Skins, Sheep	0	3	4	0
		6	piece	Skins, Deer	0	0	9	0
		6	piece	Skins, Fox	0	0	12	0
		20	lb	Pewter, broken	0	3	4	0
		1	C	Fish, Eels Small	0	0	20	0
		18.5	C	Fish, Hake	9	5	0	0
Christopher Tirry	Ind	16.5	C	Fish, Hake	8	5	0	0
		2	piece	Skins, Marten	0	2	0	0
		11	lb	Wax	0	3	8	0
Richard FigheJames & Saunders	Ind	31	C	Fish, Hake	15	10	0	0
		13	piece ?	Fish, Seals	0	20	0	0

The Sunday of Wexford, Nicholas Lunbart master, Entering, *22nd January 1543*

Merchant name	Origin	Qty	Unit	Commodity	£	s.	d.	f.
Nicholas White	Ind	20	barrel	Fish, Herring White	5	0	0	0
		8	C	Fish, Hake	4	0	0	0
		2	meise	Fish, Herring Red	0	10	0	0
		0.5	C	Skins, Sheep	0	5	0	0
Nicholas Lunbart	Ind	16	barrel	Fish, Herring White	4	0	0	0
		7	C	Fish, Hake	3	10	0	0
		2	piece	Mantles	0	6	8	0
		0.5	C	Skins, Sheep	0	5	0	0

The Jhesus of Wexford, John Stafford master, Entering, 23rd January 1543

Merchant name	Origin	Qty	Unit	Commodity	£	s.	d.	f.
John *Stafford*	Ind	20	barrel	Fish, Herring White	5	0	0	0
		12	C	Fish, Hake	6	0	0	0
		3	meise	Fish, Herring Red	0	15	0	0

Merchant name	Origin	Qty	Unit	Commodity	£	s.	d.	f.
		0.5	C	Skins, Sheep	0	5	0	0
		0.5	C	Skins, Lamb	0	3	4	0
		2	piece	Mantles	0	6	8	0
		2	barrel	Fish, Herring White	0	10	0	0

The Christofer of Youghal, Philip Morow master, Entering, 24th January 1543

Merchant name	Origin	Qty	Unit	Commodity	£	s.	d.	f.
Philip *Morow* & Morres	Ind	18	C	Fish, Hake	9	0	0	0
		0.5	barrel	Fish, Herring White	0	2	6	0
Robert Welshe & Hoberd	Ind	8.5	C	Fish, Hake	4	5	0	0
		70	yard	Check *Cloth*	1	3	4	0

The Jhesus of Youghal, Richard Hodney master, Entering, *24th January 1543*

Merchant name	Origin	Qty	Unit	Commodity	£	s.	d.	f.
Richard *Hodney*	Ind	9	C	Fish, Hake	4	10	0	0
		2.5	barrel	Fish, Herring White	0	12	6	0
		1.5	stone	Wool, Flocks	0	0	7	2
		65	yard	Check *Cloth*	0	21	8	0
		0.5	pipe	Fish, Salmon	0	15	0	0
		0.5	C	Skins, Sheep	0	5	0	0
Thomas Bluett	Ind	10	C	Fish, Hake	5	0	0	0
		1.5	C	Skins, Sheep	0	15	0	0
		0.5	C	Skins, Lamb	0	3	4	0
		2.5	barrel	Fish, Herring White	0	12	6	0
		3	piece	Mantles	0	10	0	0
Stephan Portyugall	Ind	7	C	Fish, Hake	3	10	0	0
		3	barrel	Fish, Herring White	0	15	0	0
Thomas Copyng*er*	Ind	4	C	Fish, Hake	2	0	0	0
		1	C	Skins, Sheep	0	10	0	0

The Trynyte of Dungarvan, Edmund Hore master, Entering, *24th January 1543*

Merchant name	Origin	Qty	Unit	Commodity	£	s.	d.	f.
Edmund *Hore*	Ind	10	C	Fish, Hake	5	0	0	0
		2	burden	Fish, Salted	0	8	4	0
Michael Hore	Ind	17	C	Fish, Hake	7	10	0	0
		3	burden	Fish, Salted	0	12	6	0
		4	stone	Wool, Flocks	0	0	20	0
		0.5	C	Skins, Sheep	0	5	0	0
		40	yard	Check *Cloth*	0	13	4	0
Thomas Colyn	Ind	11	C	Fish, Hake	5	10	0	0
		1	burden	Fish, Salted	0	4	2	0

Shipping Details Unknown, 25th January 1543

Merchant name	Origin	Qty	Unit	Commodity	£	s.	d.	f.
James Segerye	Ind	22	ton	Salt	11	0	0	0
		5	ton	Iron	20	0	0	0
		0.25	ton	Fruit	0	10	0	0
		1	tun	Wine	0	0	0	0

Merchant name	Origin	Qty	Unit	Commodity	£	s.	d.	f.

The Sunday of Bristol, John Jene master, Exiting, 26th January 1543

Merchant name	Origin	Qty	Unit	Commodity	£	s.	d.	f.
William Chester	Ind	12	ton	Salt	6	0	0	0
		2	tun	Wine, Corrupt	3	0	0	0
		3	C	Aniseed	2	0	0	0
		4	gross	Points	0	4	0	0

The Trynyte of Youghal, Maurice Bryan master, Entering, _26th January 1543_

Merchant name	Origin	Qty	Unit	Commodity	£	s.	d.	f.
Nicholas Forest	Ind	7	C	Fish, Hake	3	10	0	0
		36	yard	Check _Cloth_	0	12	0	0
		1.5	C	Skins, Sheep	0	15	0	0
Maurice Bryan	Ind	15	C	Fish, Hake	7	10	0	0
		6	piece	Mantles	0	20	0	0
		1	stone	Wool, Flocks	0	0	5	0
Thomas Mongan	Ind	9	C	Fish, Hake	4	10	0	0
		0.5	burden	Fish, Salted	0	2	1	0
John Colyns	Ind	0.5	barrel	Fish, Herring White	0	2	6	0
		1	virkyn	Fish, Eels	0	3	4	0
		40	yard	Check _Cloth_	0	13	4	0
		1.6	burden	Fish, Salted	0	6	8	0
		0.25	C	Fish, Sturgeon	0	2	6	0
		4	piece	Skins, Fox	0	0	8	0
		1	piece	Mantles	0	3	4	0
		2	C	Skins, Sheep	0	20	0	0
		1	C	Fish, Hake	0	10	0	0
Richard Amyas	Ind	5	C	Fish, Hake	2	10	0	0
		20	yard	Check _Cloth_	0	6	8	0
		2	piece	Mantles	0	6	8	0
		2	stone	Wool, Flocks	0	0	10	0
		0.5	C	Skins, Sheep	0	5	0	0

The Anthony of Milford Haven, John Steward master, Entering, _26th January 1543_

Merchant name	Origin	Qty	Unit	Commodity	£	s.	d.	f.
John _Steward_	Ind	14	barrel	Fish, Herring White	3	10	0	0

The Mary of Youghal, Robert Payne master, Entering, 27th January 1543

Merchant name	Origin	Qty	Unit	Commodity	£	s.	d.	f.
Philip Rownan & Payne	Ind	21.5	C	Fish, Hake	10	15	0	0
		0.5	pipe	Fish, Salmon	0	15	0	0
		3	C	Skins, Sheep	0	30	0	0
		6	piece	Skins, Fox	0	0	12	0
		2	piece	Skins, Deer	0	0	6	0
		12	yard	Check _Cloth_	0	4	0	0
		5	C	Fish, Hake	2	10	0	0
John Fitztege & Hore	Ind	30	C	Fish, Hake	15	0	0	0
		1.5	burden	Fish, Salted	0	6	3	0
		6	piece	Mantles	0	20	0	0
		6	yard	Check _Cloth_	0	2	0	0
		12	yard	Russet Lining _Cloth_	0	3	0	0

Merchant name	Origin	Qty	Unit	Commodity	£	s.	d.	f.

The Anthony of Waterford, Henry Gall master, Entering, 28th January 1543

Merchant name	Origin	Qty	Unit	Commodity	£	s.	d.	f.
Henry *Gall*	Ind	6	C	Fish, Hake	3	0	0	0
		6	piece	Mantles	0	20	0	0
David Creangh	Ind	1	C	Skins, Sheep	0	10	0	0
		7	piece	Skins, Deer	0	0	17	0
Robert Maydon	Ind	2.5	C	Skins, Sheep	0	25	0	0
		12	piece	Skins, Deer	0	2	6	0
		12	piece	Skins, Fox	0	2	0	0
		12	piece	Skins, Otter	0	5	0	0
		3	piece	Skins, Marten	0	3	0	0
		12	yard	Check *Cloth*	0	4	0	0
Patrick Richards	Ind	1.2	C	Skins, Sheep	0	12	0	0
		22	piece	Skins, Otter	0	9	2	0
		30	piece	Skins, Fox	0	5	0	0
		5	piece	Skins, Deer	0	0	15	0
		6	yard	Check *Cloth*	0	2	0	0
		2	piece	Skins, Wolf	0	0	8	0
Roland Harold	Ind	0.5	C	Skins, Sheep	0	5	0	0
		31	piece	Skins, Otter	0	12	11	0
		0.5	dicker	Skins, Deer	0	0	12	2
		24	piece	Skins, Fox	0	4	0	0
		6	piece	Skins, Marten	0	6	0	0
Richard Fizjohn	Ind	3	C	Check *Cloth*	6	0	0	0
		8	piece	Mantles	0	26	8	0
Thomas Sholwen	Ind	12	piece	Skins, Marten	0	12	0	0
		29	lb	Spermaceti	0	48	4	0
		42	piece	Skins, Fox	0	3	6	0
		19	piece	Skins, Otter	0	7	11	0
		14	yard	Check *Cloth*	0	4	8	0
		1	C	Skins, Sheep	0	10	0	0
		7	piece	Skins, Deer	0	0	17	0
Edmund Clery	Ind	1	pipe	Fish, Salmon	0	30	0	0
		260	yard	Check *Cloth*	4	6	8	0
		2	piece	Mantles	0	6	8	0
		0.5	C	Skins, Sheep	0	5	0	0
Peter Fizejohn	Ind	3.5	C	Check *Cloth*	7	0	0	0
		4	piece	Mantles	0	13	4	0
Peter Danyell	Ind	4	C	Check *Cloth*	8	0	0	0
		4	piece	Mantles	0	13	4	0
		80	piece	Skins, Sheep	0	6	8	0
Robert Maydell	Ind	2.5	C	Check *Cloth*	5	0	0	0
		2	piece	Mantles	0	6	8	0
Thomas Stackpoll	Ind	2	C	Skins, Sheep	0	20	0	0
		28	piece	Skins, Fox	0	4	8	0
		16	piece	Skins, Otter	0	6	8	0
		14	yard	Check *Cloth*	0	4	8	0

The George of Youghal, Patrick Rowley master, Entering, *28th January 1543*

Merchant name	Origin	Qty	Unit	Commodity	£	s.	d.	f.
Patrick *Rowley*	Ind	17	C	Fish, Hake	8	10	0	0
		0.5	barrel	Fish, Herring White	0	2	6	0

Merchant name	Origin	Qty	Unit	Commodity	£	s.	d.	f.
William Donell	Ind	15	C	Fish, Hake	7	10	0	0
		6	piece	Fish, Salted	0	0	12	0

The Saviour of Wexford, Patrick Alen master, Entering, *28th January 1543*

Patrick *Alen*	Ind	23	meise	Fish, Herring Red	5	15	0	0
		19	barrel	Fish, Herring White	4	15	0	0
		2	C	Fish, Hake	0	20	0	0
		3	piece	Mantles	0	10	0	0
		30	piece	Skins, Sheep	0	2	6	0

The George of Waterford, Nicholas Co*le*man master, Entering, 30th January 1543

Nicholas *Coleman*	Ind	1	C	Check *Cloth*	2	0	0	0
		2	C	Fish, Hake	0	20	0	0
		1	barrel	Fish, Herring White	0	5	0	0
		4	piece	Mantles	0	13	4	0
Richard Quen*mer*ford	Ind	4	C	Check *Cloth*	8	0	0	0
		12	piece	Mantles	0	40	0	0
Richard Wadyng	Ind	4.5	C	Check *Cloth*	9	0	0	0
		5	piece	Mantles	0	16	8	0
		4	C	Skins, Sheep	2	0	0	0
William Donohow	Ind	2.5	C	Check *Cloth*	5	0	0	0
		3	C	Skins, Sheep	0	30	0	0
		2	piece	Mantles	0	6	8	0
Edmund Quen*mer*ford	Ind	2.5	C	Check *Cloth*	5	0	0	0
		0.5	C	Skins, Sheep	0	5	0	0
		1	piece	Mantles	0	3	4	0
Nicholas Kett	Ind	3.5	C	Check *Cloth*	7	0	0	0
		1.5	C	Skins, Sheep	0	15	0	0
		6	piece	Mantles	0	20	0	0
Richard Welshe	Ind	1	C	Check *Cloth*	2	0	0	0
		8	piece	Mantles	0	26	8	0
		1	C	Skins, Sheep	0	10	0	0
Nicholas Bruar	Ind	2	C	Check *Cloth*	4	0	0	0
		6	piece	Mantles	0	20	0	0
		0.5	C	Skins, Sheep	0	5	0	0
Peter Welshe	Ind	3	C	Check *Cloth*	6	0	0	0
		2	piece	Mantles	0	6	8	0
John Quede	Ind	2	C	Check *Cloth*	4	0	0	0
		4	piece	Mantles	0	13	4	0
William Doren & assoc.	Ind	1.5	C	Check *Cloth*	3	0	0	0
		12	piece	Mantles	0	40	0	0
		8	C	Fish, Hake	4	0	0	0

The Sunday of Waterford, Maurice Power master, Entering, *30th January 1543*

Patrick Strange	Ind	4	C	Check *Cloth*	8	0	0	0
		2	C	Skins, Sheep	0	20	0	0
		3	barrel	Fish, Herring White	0	15	0	0
		3.5	C	Fish, Hake	0	35	0	0

Merchant name	Origin	Qty	Unit	Commodity	£	s.	d.	f.
		8	piece	Mantles	0	26	8	0
Richard Knewe	Ind	1.5	C	Check *Cloth*	3	0	0	0
		11	piece	Mantles	0	36	8	0
		0.5	C	Skins, Sheep	0	5	0	0
John Wyse	Ind	3	C	Check *Cloth*	6	0	0	0
		4	C	Fish, Hake	2	0	0	0
		0.5	C	Skins, Sheep	0	5	0	0
William Madan	Ind	3	C	Check *Cloth*	6	0	0	0
		0.5	C	Fish, Hake	0	5	0	0
		0.5	C	Skins, Sheep	0	5	0	0
Maurice Power & assoc.	Ind	3	C	Check *Cloth*	6	0	0	0
		4	piece	Mantles	0	13	4	0
		6	C	Skins, Sheep	3	0	0	0

The Brandon of Wexford, John Shennan master, Exiting, 1st February 1543

Merchant name	Origin	Qty	Unit	Commodity	£	s.	d.	f.
John *Shennan*	Ind	3	C	Iron	0	12	0	0
		2	lb	Saffron	0	20	0	0
		2	lb	Silk, *Worked*	0	26	8	0
		1	C	Hops	0	10	0	0
		2	gross	Knives	0	13	4	0
		6	gross	Points	0	6	0	0
		0.25	C	Aniseed	0	3	4	0
		1	piece	Cloth of Assize	0	0	0	0

The Kat*e*ryn of Milford Haven, Thomas Banam master, Entering, *1st February 1543*

Merchant name	Origin	Qty	Unit	Commodity	£	s.	d.	f.
Thomas *Banam*	Ind	3	butt	Fish, Salmon	2	5	0	0

The Mary of Gloucester, John Lewellen master, Entering, 3rd February 1543

Merchant name	Origin	Qty	Unit	Commodity	£	s.	d.	f.
Thomas Cloturboke	Ind	4	burden	Fish, Salted	0	16	8	0
		1	C	Check *Cloth*	2	0	0	0
		2	burden	Fish, Salted	0	8	4	0
James Savage	Ind	690	yard	Check *Cloth*	11	10	0	0
		7	C	Skins, Sheep	3	10	0	0
		9	stone	Wool, Flocks	0	3	9	0
		4	stone	Wool, Unspecified	0	10	8	0
		1	piece	Mantles	0	3	4	0
Andrew Welshe	Ind	8	C	Check *Cloth*	16	0	0	0
		18	C	Skins, Sheep	9	0	0	0
		1	piece	Mantles	0	3	4	0
John *Lewellen*	Ind	4	burden	Fish, Salted	0	16	8	0

The Mary of Milford Haven, John Raynolds master, Entering, *3rd February 1543*

Merchant name	Origin	Qty	Unit	Commodity	£	s.	d.	f.
Thomas Garnest	Ind	20.2	dicker	Skins, Salted	13	9	4	0
		1	barrel	Honey	0	16	8	0
		30	piece	Skins, Sheep	0	2	6	0
		1	piece	Anchor	0	5	0	0
Patrick Flemyng	Ind	16	dicker	Skins, Salted	10	13	4	0

Merchant name	Origin	Qty	Unit	Commodity	£	s.	d.	f.
Bastian Flemyng	Ind	9	C	Fish, Hake	4	10	0	0
Christopher Stocton	Ind	6	barrel	Beef	0	40	0	0
		2	barrel	Beef	0	10	0	0
		3	barrel	Fish, Herring White	0	15	0	0

The Anthony of Milford Haven, John Steward master, Exiting, *3rd February 1543*

Merchant name	Origin	Qty	Unit	Commodity	£	s.	d.	f.
Richard White	Ind	18	ton	Salt	9	0	0	0
		0.5	ton	Fruit	0	20	0	0
		1	piece	Cloth of Assize, Dozen Strait	0	0	0	0

The Francis of New Ross, John Brown master, Entering, *3rd February 1543*

Merchant name	Origin	Qty	Unit	Commodity	£	s.	d.	f.
Patrick Murfyn	Ind	5	C	Check *Cloth*	10	0	0	0
		8	C	Skins, Sheep	4	0	0	0
George Savage	Ind	8	C	Check *Cloth*	16	0	0	0
		11	C	Skins, Sheep	5	10	0	0
		6	piece	Skins, Fox	0	0	12	0
		4	piece	Skins, Otter	0	0	20	0
Thomas Crymyng	Ind	2.5	C	Check *Cloth*	5	0	0	0
		5.5	C	Skins, Sheep	2	15	0	0
		7	stone	Wool, Flocks	0	2	11	0
John Dowle	Ind	2	C	Check *Cloth*	4	0	0	0
		6	piece	Mantles	0	20	0	0
		12	piece	Skins, Fox	0	2	0	0
		9	C	Skins, Sheep	4	10	0	0
		6	piece	Skins, Deer	0	0	12	0
Thomas Dowle	Ind	4	C	Skins, Sheep	2	0	0	0
		0.5	C	Check *Cloth*	0	20	0	0

The Mary of Milford Haven, John Brother master, Entering, 5th February 1543

Merchant name	Origin	Qty	Unit	Commodity	£	s.	d.	f.
John Ryte	Ind	3	barrel	Fish, Herring White	0	15	0	0

The Patrick of New Ross, Richard Doffe master, Entering, *5th February 1543*

Merchant name	Origin	Qty	Unit	Commodity	£	s.	d.	f.
Richard *Doffe*	Ind	4	barrel	Fish, Herring White	0	20	0	0
		1	meise	Fish, Herring Red	0	5	0	0
Richard Ben*n*et	Ind	20	C	Check *Cloth*	40	0	0	0
		4	stone	Wool, Flocks	0	0	20	0
James Norres	Ind	3180	yard	Check *Cloth*	53	0	0	0
		3	C	Skins, Sheep	0	30	0	0
Thomas Co*l*eman	Ind	2	C	Fish, Hake	0	20	0	0
		2	C	Skins, Sheep	0	20	0	0
		4	stone	Wool, Irish	0	10	8	0

The George of Waterford, Edmund Medoll master, Entering, *5th February 1543*

Merchant name	Origin	Qty	Unit	Commodity	£	s.	d.	f.
Paul Butlar	Ind	3	C	Check *Cloth*	6	0	0	0
		1.5	C	Skins, Sheep	0	15	0	0
Richard Osmund	Ind	5	C	Check *Cloth*	10	0	0	0
		6	piece	Mantles	0	20	0	0

Merchant name	Origin	Qty	Unit	Commodity	£	s.	d.	f.
Andrew Lyncoln	Ind	1	C	Check *Cloth*	2	0	0	0
		16	piece	Mantles	2	13	4	0
		1	C	Skins, Sheep	0	10	0	0
Richard Forstall	Ind	4	C	Check *Cloth*	8	0	0	0
		3	piece	Mantles	0	10	0	0
Edmund Grannt	Ind	0.5	C	Skins, Sheep	0	5	0	0
		40	yard	Check *Cloth*	0	13	4	0
		3	piece	Mantles	0	10	0	0
Thomas Madan	Ind	3	C	Check *Cloth*	6	0	0	0
		12	piece	Mantles	0	40	0	0
		1	C	Skins, Sheep	0	10	0	0
Edmund Medoll	Ind	0.5	C	Check *Cloth*	0	20	0	0
		2	piece	Mantles	0	6	8	0
Raymond Vale	Ind	2	C	Check *Cloth*	4	0	0	0
		4	piece	Mantles	0	13	4	0
		30	piece	Skins, Sheep	0	2	6	0
Patrick Knock	Ind	1	butt	Fish, Salmon	0	15	0	0
		1	C	Fish, Hake	0	10	0	0
		1.5	C	Check *Cloth*	3	0	0	0
		6	piece	Mantles	0	20	0	0
Thomas White	Ind	3.5	barrel	Fish, Eels	0	46	8	0
		1	butt	Fish, Salmon	0	15	0	0
		1	C	Check *Cloth*	2	0	0	0
		3	piece	Mantles	0	10	0	0
William Balye	Ind	3	virken	Fish, Salmon	0	22	6	0

The Mary of Dungarvan, John Fizewilliams master, Entering, *5th February 1543*

John *Fizewilliams*	Ind	16	C	Fish, Hake	8	0	0	0
		6	burden	Fish, Salted	0	25	0	0
		4	stone	Wool, Flocks	0	0	20	0

The Anthony of Tintern, John Thomas master, Exiting, *5th February 1543*

Walter Putley	Ind	9	pair	Millstones	9	0	0	0

The George of Cork, Philip Barrey master, Entering, *5th February 1543*

William Sarchefell	Ind	10	pipe	Fish, Salmon	15	0	0	0
		30	C	Fish, Hake	15	0	0	0
		1	barrel	Fish, Eels	0	13	4	0
		2	dicker	Skins, Deer	0	4	2	0
		1.5	C	Skins, Sheep	0	15	0	0
Henry Verdon & Tirry	Ind	1.5	pipe	Fish, Salmon	2	5	0	0
		8	C	Fish, Hake	4	0	0	0
		0.75	barrel	Fish, Eels	0	10	0	0
		1	C	Skins, Sheep	0	10	0	0
		3	stone	Wool, Flocks	0	0	15	0
		12	piece	Skins, Deer	0	2	6	0
		3	hogshead	Fish, Salmon	4	0	0	0
		5	C	Fish, Hake	2	10	0	0
		3	piece	Skins, Deer	0	0	7	0

Merchant name	Origin	Qty	Unit	Commodity	£	s.	d.	f.
The Trynyte of Dungarvan, Edmund Hore master, Exiting, 6th February 1543								
Edmund *Hore*	Ind	3	ton	Salt	0	30	0	0
		1	pipe	Iron	2	0	0	0
Michael Hore	Ind	1	lb	Silk, *Worked*	0	13	4	0
		3	gross	Points	0	3	0	0
		1	C	Pitch	0	0	16	0
		1	piece	Cloth of Assize, Dozen Strait	0	0	0	0
Thomas Colyn	Ind	1	pipe	Iron	2	0	0	0
		80	lb	Flax	0	23	4	0
		2	gross	Knives	0	13	4	0
		1	lb	Silk, *Worked*	0	13	4	0
		6	piece	Caps	0	5	0	0
		12	dozen	Purses	0	4	2	0
The Leonard of Mount's Bay, John Barner master, Entering, 7th February 1543								
John *Barner*	Ind	5	C	Fish, Hake	2	10	0	0
The Trynyte of Youghal, Maurice Bryhan master, Exiting, *7th February 1543*								
John Colyns	Ind	0.5	dozen	Cards, Wool	0	2	0	0
		4	C	Iron	0	16	0	0
		0.5	gross	Knives	0	3	4	0
		2	gross	Points	0	2	0	0
Nicholas Forest	Ind	1	lb	Saffron	0	10	0	0
		1	gross	Knives	0	6	8	0
		6	lb	Flax	0	2	0	0
		3	C	Iron	0	12	0	0
		1	gross	Lacquer	0	0	20	0
		1	dozen	Cards, Wool	0	4	0	0
Richard Anyas	Ind	1	lb	Silk, *Worked*	0	13	4	0
		1	gross	Knives	0	6	8	0
		1	dozen	Aniseed	0	0	16	0
		1	Unknown	Drugs, Misc.	0	16	0	0
		2	gross	Points	0	2	0	0
		1	lb	Cinnamon	0	2	6	0
Thomas Mongan	Ind	1	C	Iron	0	4	0	0
		1	barrel	Tar	0	0	20	0
		6	lb	Flax	0	0	18	0
Maurice Bryhan	Ind	3	C	Iron	0	12	0	0
		1	barrel	Tar	0	0	20	0
		1	dozen	Flax	0	3	0	0
		0.5	C	Hops	0	5	0	0
The Christopher of Youghal, Philip Murhowe master, Exiting, *7th February 1543*								
David Artur	Ind	1	piece	Cloth of Assize	0	0	0	0
		5	lb	Silk, *Worked*	3	6	8	0
		2.5	gross	Knives	0	16	8	0
		1	dozen	Caps	0	10	0	0
		1	dozen	Flax	0	3	0	0

Merchant name	Origin	Qty	Unit	Commodity	£	s.	d.	f.
		4	lb	Saffron	2	0	0	0
Unknown	Ind	4	piece	Cloth of Assize, Dozen Strait	0	0	0	0
		1.5	lb	Saffron	0	15	0	0
		1	gross	Knives	0	6	8	0
		6	piece	Caps	0	5	0	0
		6	lb	Flax	0	0	20	0
Philip Murhowe	Ind	4	C	Pitch &Rosin	0	5	4	0
		0.5	lb	Saffron	0	5	0	0
		0.25	gross	Knives	0	0	20	0
		0.25	C	Hops	0	2	6	0
		1	dozen	Flax	0	3	0	0
		0.5	gross	Points	0	0	6	0
Richard Fizemorres	Ind	0.25	C	Aniseed	0	3	4	0
		0.25	C	Hops	0	2	6	0
		4	dozen	Combs	0	2	0	0
		1	lb	Verdigris	0	0	5	0
		4	dozen	Purses	0	0	16	0
		0.5	dozen	Skins, Red	0	0	13	0
		6	lb	Flax	0	0	18	0
		3	C	Pitch &Rosin	0	4	0	0
		1	barrel	Tar	0	0	20	0
Robert Nashe	Ind	240	yard	Linen Cloth	0	20	0	0
		5	lb	Aniseed	0	0	8	0
		0.25	C	Hops	0	2	6	0

The Nicholas of Bristol, Bartholomew Garland master, Exiting, 8th February 1543

Thomas Cadell	Ind	13	ton	Salt	6	10	0	0

The Mary of Milford Haven, John Raynolds master, Exiting, *8th February 1543*

Thomas Garnest	Ind	16	ton	Salt	8	0	0	0
		2	piece	Fruit	0	3	4	0
		6	gross	Points	0	6	0	0
		0.5	dozen	Skins, Red	0	0	13	0

The Mihell of Milford Haven, John Hicks master, Entering, *8th February 1543*

John Hicks	Ind	6	barrel	Fish, Herring White	0	30	0	0

The Sunday of Wexford, Nicholas Lunbart master, Exiting, *8th February 1543*

Nicholas Lunbart	Ind	15	C	Iron	3	0	0	0
		1	C	Hops	0	10	0	0
		2.5	dozen	Wood, Brazil	0	8	4	0
		1	barrel	Tar	0	0	20	0
		2	weight	Hemp	0	2	8	0
Nicholas White	Ind	4	piece	Cloth of Assize, Dozen Strait	0	0	0	0
		1.5	lb	Silk, Worked	0	20	0	0
		1	stone	Aniseed	0	0	20	0

Merchant name	Origin	Qty	Unit	Commodity	£	s.	d.	f.
The Sunday of Waterford, Maurice Power master, Exiting, 9th February 1543								
Patrick Strange	Ind	1	pipe	Iron	2	0	0	0
		2	gross	Knives	0	13	4	0
		9	gross	Points	0	9	0	0
		1.5	gross	Lacquer	0	2	6	0
		6	pair	Stock-Cards	0	6	0	0
William Madan	Ind	1	gross	Knives	0	6	8	0
		2	gross	Points	0	2	0	0
		0.5	gross	Lacquer	0	0	10	0
		26	lb	Pewter	0	10	0	0
Richard Knewe	Ind	5	pair	Stock-Cards	0	5	0	0
		2	dozen	Soap	0	2	6	0
		5	lb	Seed, Leek	0	3	4	0
		0.5	gross	Knives	0	3	4	0
		1	dozen	Alum	0	0	16	0
		2	gross	Points	0	2	0	0
		1	dozen	Soap	0	0	15	0
John Wyse	Ind	0.5	piece	Cloth of Assize	0	0	0	0
		1	gross	Points	0	0	12	0
The George of Youghal, Patrick Rowley master, Exiting, *9th February 1543*								
Patrick *Rowley*	Ind	6	C	Iron	0	24	0	0
		0.5	C	Hops	0	5	0	0
		1	gross	Knives	0	6	8	0
		4	gross	Points	0	4	0	0
William Donell	Ind	0.5	C	Hops	0	5	0	0
		1	lb	Saffron	0	10	0	0
		1	gross	Knives	0	6	8	0
		2	gross	Points	0	2	0	0
		1	stone	Liquorice	0	0	10	0
		1	stone	Aniseed	0	0	20	0
		1	stone	Alum	0	0	20	0
The Mary of Youghal, John Fizetege master, Exiting, *9th February 1543*								
John *Fizetege*	Ind	2	lb	Saffron	0	20	0	0
		1	C	Hops	0	10	0	0
		2.5	dozen	Flax	0	6	8	0
John Hore	Ind	1	lb	Saffron	0	10	0	0
		1	C	Hops	0	10	0	0
		1	stone	Alum	0	0	20	0
		1	stone	Flax	0	3	4	0
		1	C	Iron	0	4	0	0
		1	barrel	Tar	0	0	20	0
		1	C	Pitch	0	0	16	0
The Mary of Youghal, Robert Payne master, Exiting, 10th February 1543								
Philip Rownan	Ind	3	C	Iron	0	12	0	0
		2	lb	Saffron	0	20	0	0

Merchant name	Origin	Qty	Unit	Commodity	£	s.	d.	f.
		3	gross	Knives	0	20	0	0
		1	dozen	Caps	0	10	0	0
		12	gross	Points	0	12	0	0
		12	dozen	Combs	0	4	0	0
		12	dozen	Purses	0	4	0	0
		1	Unknown	Drugs, Misc.	0	20	0	0
		0.5	C	Aniseed &Cumin	0	6	8	0
		2.5	dozen	Liquorice	0	3	4	0
		4	dozen	Knives, in Pairs	0	6	8	0
		1	gross	Lacquer	0	0	20	0
		1	dozen	Girdles	0	0	18	0
		1	dozen	Flax	0	3	0	0
		2	dozen	Cards, Playing	0	0	20	0
		2	lb	Cinnamon &Cloves	0	5	0	0
		1	lb	Pepper	0	0	12	0
		0.66	piece	Cloth of Assize	0	0	0	0
Andrew Galwey	Ind	2.5	piece	Cloth of Assize	0	0	0	0
		2	lb	Silk, *Worked*	0	26	8	0
		2	gross	Knives	0	13	4	0
		1	dozen	Skins, Golden	0	4	2	0
		8	gross	Points	0	8	0	0
		1	bolt	Thread	0	0	12	0
		9	piece	Caps	0	7	6	0

The Mary George of Hasfield, David Adams master, Exiting, 11th February 1543

Merchant name	Origin	Qty	Unit	Commodity	£	s.	d.	f.
Patrick Flemyng	Ind	15	ton	Salt	7	10	0	0
		1	ton	Iron	4	0	0	0
		3	C	Aniseed	0	40	0	0
		24	gross	Points	0	24	0	0
		1	piece	Raisins, *Great*	0	0	20	0
		1	piece	Bristol Frieze *Cloth*	0	13	4	0

The Jhesus of Youghal, Richard Hodney master, Exiting, *11th February 1543*

Merchant name	Origin	Qty	Unit	Commodity	£	s.	d.	f.
Richard *Hodney*	Ind	0.5	lb	Silk, *Worked*	0	6	8	0
		1.5	gross	Knives	0	10	0	0
		8	gross	Points	0	8	0	0
		1	gross	Lacquer	0	0	20	0
		6	dozen	Purses	0	0	20	0
		6	dozen	Combs	0	0	20	0
		1	C	Pitch	0	0	16	0
		3.5	stone	Orchil	0	5	10	0
		2	stone	Aniseed	0	3	4	0
		1	stone	Alum	0	0	20	0
		1	lb	Cinnamon &Cloves	0	2	6	0
		0.25	C	Hops	0	2	6	0
		1	dozen	Skins, Golden	0	4	2	0
Thomas Bluet	Ind	4	piece	Cloth of Assize, Dozen Strait	0	0	0	0
		15	C	Iron	3	0	0	0
		0.5	C	Hops	0	5	0	0
		2	stone	Aniseed	0	3	4	0

Merchant name	Origin	Qty	Unit	Commodity	£	s.	d.	f.
		0.5	stone	Cumin	0	0	10	0
		1	stone	Alum	0	0	20	0
		3	stone	Orchil	0	5	0	0
		1	gross	Knives	0	6	8	0
		2	dozen	Knives, in Pairs	0	3	4	0
		1	lb	Cloves	0	2	6	0
		0.5	lb	Cinnamon	0	0	15	0
		0.5	lb	Ginger	0	0	9	0
		0.5	lb	Pepper	0	0	6	0
		0.5	stone	Liquorice	0	0	10	0
		6	gross	Points	0	6	0	0
		1	gross	Lacquer	0	0	20	0
		6	dozen	Combs	0	0	20	0
		6	dozen	Purses	0	0	20	0
		0.5	dozen	Caps	0	5	0	0
Stephan Portyngale	Ind	1	pipe	Iron	2	0	0	0
		18	lb	Flax	0	5	0	0
		1	gross	Knives	0	6	8	0

The Jhesus of Wexford, John Stafford master, Exiting, 13th February 1543

Merchant name	Origin	Qty	Unit	Commodity	£	s.	d.	f.
John Stafford	Ind	1	lb	Saffron	0	10	0	0
		1	lb	Silk, Worked	0	13	4	0
		3	C	Iron	0	12	0	0
		1	C	Hops	0	10	0	0
		0.5	C	Aniseed	0	6	8	0
		1	dozen	Knives	0	6	8	0
		3	weight	Hemp	0	5	0	0
		0.75	piece	Cloth of Assize	0	0	0	0

The Mary George of Barnstaple, John Lake master, Entering, 13th February 1543

Merchant name	Origin	Qty	Unit	Commodity	£	s.	d.	f.
William Appowell & Smyth	Ind	12.5	tun	Wine	0	0	0	0
Thomas Smyth & Cutt	Ind	2.25	tun	Wine	0	0	0	0
William Yonge & Barbour	Ind	4	tun	Wine	0	0	0	0
		10.5	C	Aniseed	7	0	0	0
Richard Pryn & Capps	Ind	20.5	tun	Wine	0	0	0	0
		1	tun	Oil, Olive	4	0	0	0
William Blake & Channcelar	Ind	9	tun	Wine	0	0	0	0
Geoffrey Chantrell & Hyll	Ind	10.5	tun	Wine	0	0	0	0
		5	piece	Raisins, Great	0	8	4	0
John Thomas	Ind	1.25	tun	Wine	0	0	0	0
		10	C	Soap	5	0	0	0
William Hyllyng & assoc.	Ind	2.75	tun	Wine	0	0	0	0
		4	piece	Raisins, Great	0	6	8	0

Merchant name	Origin	Qty	Unit	Commodity	£	s.	d.	f.
		5	C	Soap	2	10	0	0
		20	lb	Pepper	0	20	0	0
Mark Averell	Ind	8.75	C	Soap	4	7	6	0
		9	C	Alum	4	10	0	0
		4	piece	Raisins, *Great*	0	6	8	0
John Bonde	Ind	1.5	tun	Wine	0	0	0	0
		20	C	Soap	10	0	0	0
		100	lb	Pepper	5	0	0	0

The Mary Bulleyn of Bideford, Robert Whitstone master, Entering, *13th February 1543*

Merchant name	Origin	Qty	Unit	Commodity	£	s.	d.	f.
William Sprat & Balard	Ind	21.5	tun	Wine	0	0	0	0
William Cox & Butlar	Ind	6.75	tun	Wine	0	0	0	0
Edward & John Pryn	Ind	7.25	tun	Wine	0	0	0	0
William Blake & Chancelar	Ind	5	tun	Wine	0	0	0	0
Thomas Tyson & Carr	Ind	29.25	tun	Wine	0	0	0	0
William Shipman & Hycks	Ind	11.75	tun	Wine	0	0	0	0
Thomas Shipman	Ind	0.25	tun	Oil, *Olive*	0	20	0	0
John Haye	Ind	1	hogshead	Wine	0	0	0	0
Robert Whitstone	Ind	21.25	C	Soap	10	12	6	0

The Trynyte of Bristol, Thomas Webb master, Entering, *13th February 1543*

Merchant name	Origin	Qty	Unit	Commodity	£	s.	d.	f.
Nicholas Thorn & Smyth	Ind	20.5	tun	Wine	0	0	0	0
		2	tun	Oil, *Olive*	8	0	0	0
		17.5	C	Soap	8	15	0	0
		6	C	Alum	3	0	0	0
William Rowley & Sprat	Ind	5.5	tun	Wine	0	0	0	0
John Gurneye & Tyson	Ind	6.75	tun	Wine	0	0	0	0
Edward Pryn & Cox	Ind	6	tun	Wine	0	0	0	0
John Cutt & Gyttens	Ind	8.25	tun	Wine	0	0	0	0
		1	tun	Oil, *Olive*	4	0	0	0
Arthur Smyth & Pressye	Ind	5.5	tun	Wine	0	0	0	0
Thomas Harrys & Hyll	Ind	6.25	tun	Oil, *Olive*	25	0	0	0
Giles White & Saunders		2.5	tun	Wine	0	0	0	0
	Ind	7	tun	Wine	0	0	0	0
		0.5	tun	Oil, *Olive*	2	0	0	0
Mathew Kent & Tyson	Ind	6	tun	Wine	0	0	0	0
Alice Smyth & assoc.	Ind	1.875	tun	Oil, *Olive*	7	10	0	0
		1.75	tun	Wine	0	0	0	0

Merchant name	Origin	Qty	Unit	Commodity	£	s.	d.	f.

The George of Waterford, Nicholas Coleman master, Exiting, 14th February 1543

Merchant name	Origin	Qty	Unit	Commodity	£	s.	d.	f.
Richard Quenmerford	Ind	2.5	ton	Iron	10	0	0	0
Richard Wadyng & Doryn	Ind	15	C	Iron	3	0	0	0
		2	lb	Saffron	0	20	0	0
		1	gross	Knives	0	6	8	0
		6	gross	Points	0	6	0	0
		2	gross	Lacquer	0	3	4	0
		1	dozen	Knives, in Pairs	0	0	20	0
Andrew Lyncolne	Ind	1	piece	Cloth of Assize	0	0	0	0
		1	gross	Knives	0	6	8	0
		0.5	dozen	Caps, Night	0	2	0	0
William Donohowe	Ind	1.5	gross	Knives	0	10	0	0
		4	gross	Points	0	4	0	0
		1	gross	Lacquer	0	0	20	0
		0.5	dozen	Cumin	0	0	8	0
		2	dozen	Knives, in Pairs	0	3	4	0
Edmund Quenmerford & Kett	Ind	7	gross	Points	0	7	0	0
	Ind	2	gross	Lacquer	0	3	4	0
	Ind	1	gross	Knives	0	6	8	0
James Savage	Ind	3	lb	Silk, *Worked*	2	0	0	0
		3	lb	Saffron	0	30	0	0
		2.5	gross	Knives	0	16	8	0
		9	gross	Points	0	9	0	0
		9	dozen	Knives, in Pairs	0	15	0	0
		4	lb	Seed, Onion	0	6	8	0
		4	piece	Caps	0	2	8	0
		1	gross	Lacquer	0	0	20	0
James Savage	Ind	3	piece	Caps	0	2	6	0

The Mary of Northam, John Tyrrell master, Entering, *14th February 1543*

Merchant name	Origin	Qty	Unit	Commodity	£	s.	d.	f.
William Appowell & Carr	Ind	40	ton	Fruit	80	0	0	0
		8.5	tun	Wine	0	0	0	0
John Andres	Ind	6.416	ton	Fruit	12	16	8	0
		18.75	C	Soap	9	7	6	0
		6	C	Alum	3	0	0	0

The Trynyte Caps, *Port Unknown*, John Haye master, Entering, *14th February 1543*

Merchant name	Origin	Qty	Unit	Commodity	£	s.	d.	f.
Robert Thurban & Fowler	Ind	12.25	tun	Wine	0	0	0	0
Thomas Harrys & Smyth	Ind	8.75	tun	Wine	0	0	0	0
Robert Pressye & Smyth	Ind	3.5	tun	Wine	0	0	0	0
John Channcelar & Caps	Ind	4.75	tun	Wine	0	0	0	0
		0.5	chest	Sugar	0	20	0	0

Merchant name	Origin	Qty	Unit	Commodity	£	s.	d.	f.
William Appowell & assoc.	Ind	5.25	tun	Wine	0	0	0	0
		2.5	C	Marmalade	0	33	4	0

The Anthony of Waterford, Henry Gall master, Exiting, 15th February 1543

Merchant name	Origin	Qty	Unit	Commodity	£	s.	d.	f.
Peter Fizejohn	Ind	1.5	ton	Iron	6	0	0	0
Roland Harold	Ind	7.25	piece	Cloth of Assize	0	0	0	0
		3	lb	Saffron	0	30	0	0
		2	lb	Pepper	0	2	0	0
		3	lb	Mercury	0	0	15	0
		2	dozen	Girdles	0	4	0	0
		6	dozen	Knives, in Pairs	0	10	0	0
		3	bolt	Thread	0	3	0	0
		1	lb	Cinnamon	0	2	6	0
		0.5	C	Aniseed	0	6	8	0
		0.25	C	Alum	0	3	4	0
		16	lb	Cumin	0	0	20	0
		1	dozen	Cards, Playing	0	0	10	0
		1.5	gross	Knives	0	10	0	0
		0.5	gross	Cutts	0	0	20	0
		4	dozen	Skins, Golden	0	16	8	0
		1	gross	Points	0	0	12	0
Patrick Richards	Ind	3.5	piece	Cloth of Assize	0	0	0	0
		0.5	C	Aniseed	0	6	8	0
		0.25	C	Alum	0	3	4	0
		12	lb	Liquorice	0	0	5	0
		4	lb	Pepper	0	4	0	0
		2	dozen	Penners	0	0	15	0
		1	dozen	Cards, Playing	0	0	10	0
		2	bolt	Thread	0	2	1	0
		2	dozen	Girdles	0	0	10	0
		3	dozen	Knives, in Pairs	0	5	0	0
		1	dozen	Balances, Small	0	0	15	0
		12	gross	Points	0	12	0	0
		2	lb	Saffron	0	20	0	0
Thomas Stackpoll	Ind	1	piece	Cloth of Assize, Dozen Strait	0	0	0	0
		30	gross	Points	0	30	0	0
		1	lb	Mercury	0	0	5	0
		5	dozen	Cards, Playing	0	4	2	0
		5	dozen	Knives, in Pairs	0	8	4	0
		4	dozen	Skins, Golden	0	16	8	0
		2	dozen	Ribbons, Unspecified	0	2	6	0
		2	lb	Saffron	0	20	0	0
		0.5	C	Alum	0	6	8	0
		3	gross	Knives	0	20	0	0
		2	gross	Cutts	0	6	8	0
		10	lb	Verdigris	0	4	2	0
		2	dozen	Books, Primers	0	0	20	0
		4	lb	Cumin	0	0	5	0
		10	dozen	Thimbles	0	0	10	0
Thomas Sholweyn	Ind	1.25	piece	Cloth of Assize	0	0	0	0

Merchant name	Origin	Qty	Unit	Commodity	£	s.	d.	f.
		3.5	gross	Knives	0	23	4	0
		4	dozen	Girdles	0	16	8	0
		3	lb	Verdigris	0	0	15	0
		5	dozen	Cards, Playing	0	4	2	0
		6	dozen	*Percular*	0	0	10	0
		3	dozen	Girdles	0	4	2	0
		2	lb	Cloves	0	5	0	0
		20	dozen	Thimbles	0	0	20	0
		1	dozen	Penners	0	0	10	0
		34	gross	Points	0	34	0	0
		6	piece	Caps	0	5	0	0
		1	lb	Saffron	0	10	0	0
		1	dozen	Skins, Red	0	2	1	0
David Creangh	Ind	3.5	piece	Cloth of Assize	0	0	0	0
		1	dozen	Skins, Golden	0	4	2	0
		1.5	dozen	Glasses	0	0	5	0
		1	dozen	Girdles	0	0	5	0
		2	dozen	Knives, in Pairs	0	3	4	0
		1	gross	Knives	0	6	8	0
		1	gross	Cutts	0	3	4	0
Robert Manchowen	Ind	3	piece	Cloth of Assize, Dozen Strait	0	0	0	0
		0.5	C	Aniseed	0	6	8	0
		2	gross	Cutts	0	6	8	0
		4	dozen	Skins, Golden	0	16	8	0
		1	dozen	Skins, Red	0	2	1	0
		12	gross	Points	0	12	0	0
		1.5	dozen	Books, Primers	0	0	15	0
		3	dozen	Knives, in Pairs	0	5	0	0
		3	lb	Verdigris	0	0	15	0
		2	dozen	Girdles	0	0	10	0
		2	dozen	Cards, Playing	0	0	20	0
Peter Danyell	Ind	0.5	gross	Knives	0	3	4	0
		2	dozen	Soap	0	2	6	0
		0.5	gross	Lacquer	0	0	10	0

The Trynyte of Caerleon, John Darby master, Entering, *15th February 1543*

Merchant name	Origin	Qty	Unit	Commodity	£	s.	d.	f.
Christine White & Sprat	Ind	8.25	tun	Wine	33	0	0	0
William Balard & Rowley	Ind	5	C	Marmalade	3	6	8	0
		0.25	tun	Oil, *Olive*	0	20	0	0
		19.75	tun	Wine	0	0	0	0
William Jaye & Hycks	Ind	7.25	tun	Wine	0	0	0	0
Edward Pryn & Codryngton	Ind	11.75	tun	Wine	0	0	0	0
William Cox & Butlar	Ind	11.25	tun	Wine	0	0	0	0
		1.5	tun	Oil, *Olive*	6	0	0	0
		20	C	Soap	10	0	0	0
Alan Hyll & Kent	Ind	10.25	tun	Wine	0	0	0	0
John Pryn & Balye	Ind	1	tun	Oil, *Olive*	4	0	0	0

Merchant name	Origin	Qty	Unit	Commodity	£	s.	d.	f.
William Blake & Chancelar		8	tun	Wine	0	0	0	0
	Ind	9.75	tun	Wine	0	0	0	0
		1	tun	Wine, Corrupt	0	30	0	0
Robert Pressye & Jones	Ind	7.75	tun	Wine	0	0	0	0
Watkyns, Jones & Lockar	Ind	5	tun	Wine	0	0	0	0
John Appowell & Gyttens	Ind	2	tun	Wine	0	0	0	0
		5	C	Soap	2	10	0	0
Henry Mulberry & Harvest	Ind	1.25	tun	Wine	0	0	0	0
Thomas Harrys	Ind	7.5	tun	Wine	0	0	0	0
John Darby	Ind	5	C	Marmalade	3	6	8	0
		8.75	C	Soap	4	7	6	0

The Margaret of Bristol, John Williams master, Entering, 15th February 1543

Merchant name	Origin	Qty	Unit	Commodity	£	s.	d.	f.
Edward Butlar	Ind	15	tun	Wine	0	0	0	0
		1	ton	Fruit	2	0	0	0
		1	tun	Oil, Olive	4	0	0	0
Nicholas Thorn & White	Ind	17.75	tun	Wine	0	0	0	0
Richard Pryn & Rowley	Ind	4	tun	Wine	0	0	0	0
		7.5	C	Orchil	5	0	0	0
		3.5	tun	Oil, Olive	14	0	0	0
William Sprat & Yonge	Ind	12.5	tun	Wine	0	0	0	0
		2	tun	Oil, Olive	8	0	0	0
		20	C	Soap	10	0	0	0
William Balard & Codryngton	Ind	13.75	tun	Wine	0	0	0	0
Edward & John Pryn	Ind	3.25	tun	Wine	0	0	0	0
		1	tun	Oil, Olive	4	0	0	0
Robert Butlar & Robyns	Ind	13.75	tun	Wine	0	0	0	0
Thomas Tyson & Williams	Ind	5	tun	Wine	0	0	0	0
Thomas Shipman & assoc.	Ind	3	ton	Raisins, Great	6	0	0	0
		1	chest	Sugar	2	0	0	0
		7.5	C	Orchil	5	0	0	0
		0.75	tun	Wine	0	0	0	0

The Thomas of Tewkesbury, Richard Cox master, Entering, 15th February 1543

Merchant name	Origin	Qty	Unit	Commodity	£	s.	d.	f.
Christopher Warren	Ind	8.5	ton	Woad, Azores	56	13	4	0

Merchant name	Origin	Qty	Unit	Commodity	£	s.	d.	f.

The Michaell of Tewkesbury, John Hall master, Entering, *15th February 1543*

Merchant name	Origin	Qty	Unit	Commodity	£	s.	d.	f.
Christopher Warren	Ind	8.5	ton	Woad, Azores	56	13	4	0

The Mary James of Bristol, Richard Whyte master, Entering, *15th February 1543*

Merchant name	Origin	Qty	Unit	Commodity	£	s.	d.	f.
William Jay & White	Ind	28.5	tun	Wine	0	0	0	0
Richard Pryn	Ind	3	tun	Wine	0	0	0	0
		2	tun	Oil, *Olive*	8	0	0	0
William Rowley & Brampton	Ind	8.75	tun	Wine	0	0	0	0
William Balard & Leyghton	Ind	7	tun	Wine	0	0	0	0
Thomas Harrys & Wosley	Ind	3.75	tun	Wine	0	0	0	0
		1	chest	Sugar	2	0	0	0
William Jones & Smyth	Ind	12.25	tun	Wine	0	0	0	0
William Blake & Channcelar	Ind	5.5	tun	Wine	0	0	0	0
Johanna Carpenter & Kent	Ind	8	tun	Wine	0	0	0	0
		21.25	C	Soap	10	12	6	0
John Pryn & White	Ind	6.5	tun	Wine	0	0	0	0
		2	tun	Oil, *Olive*	8	0	0	0
John Draper	Ind	3.25	tun	Wine	0	0	0	0
William Appowell	Ind	1	chest	Sugar	2	0	0	0

The Mawdelen of Bristol, William Mathew master, Entering, *15th February 1543*

Merchant name	Origin	Qty	Unit	Commodity	£	s.	d.	f.
Thomas Apbowen & Jarves	Ind	4.5	tun	Wine	0	0	0	0
Thomas Tyson & Fowler	Ind	16.5	tun	Wine	0	0	0	0
William Blake & Snyg	Ind	10.5	tun	Wine	0	0	0	0
Robert Pressy & Channcelar	Ind	7.5	tun	Wine	0	0	0	0
Arthur Smyth & Fowler	Ind	6.75	tun	Wine	0	0	0	0
	Ind	4.5	tun	Wine	0	0	0	0
		8	piece	Raisins, *Great*	0	13	4	0

The Harry of Bristol, Anthony Pygot master, Entering, *15th February 1543*

Merchant name	Origin	Qty	Unit	Commodity	£	s.	d.	f.
William Shipman & Thorn	Ind	19.25	tun	Wine	0	0	0	0
John Smyth & Appowell	Ind	7.5	tun	Wine	0	0	0	0
		2.5	tun	Oil, *Olive*	10	0	0	0
William Sprat & Balard	Ind	16	tun	Wine	0	0	0	0

Merchant name	Origin	Qty	Unit	Commodity	£	s.	d.	f.
Francis Codryngton & Hycks	Ind	12	tun	Wine	0	0	0	0
Robert Gyttens & Pryn	Ind	5	tun	Wine	0	0	0	0
Christine White & Balie	Ind	1	chest	Sugar	2	0	0	0
		3.5	tun	Wine	0	0	0	0
Anthony Pygot & Carpenter	Ind	7.25	tun	Wine	0	0	0	0
Giles White & Tyson	Ind	1.75	tun	Oil, *Olive*	7	0	0	0
		6.75	tun	Wine	0	0	0	0
		1	tun	Wine, Corrupt	1	10	0	0
Thomas Roberts & Kyrke	Ind	8.25	tun	Wine	0	0	0	0
		1	tun	Oil, *Olive*	4	0	0	0
John Pryn & Kent	Ind	7.5	tun	Wine	0	0	0	0
John Satchfelde	Ind	12	C	Aniseed	8	0	0	0

The Nicholas of Pembroke, William Roche master, Entering, 16th February 1543

Merchant name	Origin	Qty	Unit	Commodity	£	s.	d.	f.
John Phyllyps	Ind	5	barrel	Fish, Herring White	0	25	0	0

The Mary Bonaventure of Bristol, Thomas Davys master, *16th February 1543*

Merchant name	Origin	Qty	Unit	Commodity	£	s.	d.	f.
William Chester & Thorn	Ind	15.75	tun	Wine	0	0	0	0
Richard Pryn & Balard	Ind	7.5	tun	Wine	0	0	0	0
Edward Butlar & Robbyns	Ind	11	tun	Wine	0	0	0	0
James Chester & Cutt	Ind	11.25	tun	Wine	0	0	0	0
Robert Gyttens & Lokyar	Ind	7	tun	Wine	0	0	0	0
		1	tun	Wine, Corrupt	0	30	0	0
John Pryn & White	Ind	7	tun	Wine	0	0	0	0
Richard White & assoc.	Ind	11.75	tun	Wine	0	0	0	0

The Mary Conception of Bristol, William Champyon master, 16th February 1543

Merchant name	Origin	Qty	Unit	Commodity	£	s.	d.	f.
Nicholas Thorn & Shipman	Ind	15.25	tun	Wine	0	0	0	0
John Smyth & Appowell	Ind	11.5	tun	Wine	0	0	0	0
William Rowley & Yonge	Ind	6.5	tun	Wine	0	0	0	0
Christine White & Welshe	Ind	12	tun	Wine	0	0	0	0
		1	pipe	Wine, Corrupt	0	15	0	0
Thomas Harrys & Cutt	Ind	8	tun	Wine	0	0	0	0

Merchant name	Origin	Qty	Unit	Commodity	£	s.	d.	f.
		1	pipe	Wine, Corrupt	0	15	0	0
Francis Codryngton & Jones	Ind	6	tun	Wine	0	0	0	0
		1	tun	Wine, Corrupt	0	30	0	0
James Chester & Gyttens	Ind	4	tun	Wine	0	0	0	0
		1	tun	Oil, Olive	4	0	0	0
		20	C	Soap	10	0	0	0
Richard Pryn & Carpenter	Ind	2.75	tun	Wine	0	0	0	0
Thomas Lokyar & Satchfeld	Ind	2	tun	Wine	0	0	0	0
William Cox & Vyne	Ind	1	tun	Wine	0	0	0	0
William Harvest & Vyne	Ind	1	tun	Oil, Olive	4	0	0	0
		10	C	Soap	5	0	0	0

The Kateryn of Bideford, Peter Dyrycke master, Entering, 16th February 1543

Merchant name	Origin	Qty	Unit	Commodity	£	s.	d.	f.
John Welshe & Brampton	Ind	20.5	tun	Wine	0	0	0	0
William Cox, Cutt & Harvest	Ind	11	tun	Wine	0	0	0	0
Francis Wosley & Smyth	Ind	4.5	tun	Wine	0	0	0	0
Robert Pressye & Snyg	Ind	2.5	tun	Wine	0	0	0	0
		37.5	C	Soap	18	15	0	0
		3	chest	Sugar	6	0	0	0
John Satchfeld & Barbour	Ind	10.5	tun	Wine	0	0	0	0
		1	ton	Fruit	2	0	0	0
Robert Minge, Patrick & Dyrycke	Ind	4.25	tun	Wine	0	0	0	0
		3.75	C	Soap	0	37	6	0
		1	chest	Sugar	2	0	0	0

The Leonard of Bewdley, William Benet, Entering, 16th February 1543

Merchant name	Origin	Qty	Unit	Commodity	£	s.	d.	f.
Simon Stone & assoc.	Ind	8	C	Soap	4	0	0	0
		0.375	tun	Oil, Olive	0	30	0	0
		3.5	tun	Wine	0	0	0	0

The Mary of Dungarvan, John Fizewilliams master, Exiting, 16th February 1543

Merchant name	Origin	Qty	Unit	Commodity	£	s.	d.	f.
John Fizewilliams	Ind	1	ton	Salt	0	10	0	0
		2	C	Iron	0	8	0	0
		2	barrel	Tar	0	3	4	0
		2	C	Pitch	0	2	8	0
		20	lb	Flax	0	6	8	0
		3	dozen	Knives, in Pairs	0	5	0	0
		2	C	Iron	0	8	0	0

Merchant name	Origin	Qty	Unit	Commodity	£	s.	d.	f.
		1	piece	Cloth of Assize, Dozen Strait	0	0	0	0

The Martyn of Milford Haven, Richard Brown master, Entering, 17th February 1543

Merchant name	Origin	Qty	Unit	Commodity	£	s.	d.	f.
Richard *Brown*	Ind	4	barrel	Fish, Herring White	0	20	0	0

The Savyour of Wexford, Patrick Alyn master, Exiting, 20th February 1543

Merchant name	Origin	Qty	Unit	Commodity	£	s.	d.	f.
Patrick *Alyn* & assot.	Ind	2	piece	Cloth of Assize	0	0	0	0
		2	C	Iron	0	8	0	0
		2	ton	Salt	0	20	0	0
		1	lb	Silk, *Worked*	0	13	4	0
		0.5	lb	Saffron	0	5	0	0

The George Butlar of Waterford, Edmund Medol master, Exiting, 20th February 1543

Merchant name	Origin	Qty	Unit	Commodity	£	s.	d.	f.
Richard Osmund	Ind	1	pipe	Iron	2	0	0	0
Paul Butlar	Ind	2	lb	Cinnamon &Cloves	0	5	0	0
		2	gross	Lacquer	0	3	4	0
		2	gross	Points	0	2	0	0
		3	stone	Orchil	0	5	0	0
		1	dozen	Soap	0	0	15	0
		0.5	piece	Cloth of Assize	0	0	0	0
Thomas Maydon	Ind	4	piece	Cloth of Assize, Dozen	0	0	0	0
Andrew Welshe	Ind	5	piece	Cloth of Assize, Dozen Strait	0	10	0	0
		2	piece	Cloth of Assize, Dozen	0	0	0	0
		11	lb	Silk, *Worked*	7	6	8	0
		6	lb	Saffron	3	0	0	0
		1	dozen	Cards, Playing	0	0	10	0
		1.5	gross	Knives	0	10	0	0
		9	gross	Points	0	9	0	0
		8	lb	Seed, Onion	0	6	8	0
		3	lb	Seed, Leek	0	0	20	0

The Patrycke of Cork, Philip Hore master, Entering, 21st February 1543

Merchant name	Origin	Qty	Unit	Commodity	£	s.	d.	f.
Dominic Roche & Williams	Ind	30	C	Fish, Hake	15	0	0	0
		3	virken	Fish, Salmon	0	22	6	0
		12	stone	Wool, Flocks	0	5	0	0
		2	C	Skins, Sheep	0	20	0	0
		1	dicker	Skins, Deer	0	2	1	0
		30	yard	Check *Cloth*	0	10	0	0
		4	piece	Mantles	0	13	4	0
Richard Fizejames & Golde	Ind	32.5	C	Fish, Hake	16	5	0	0
		2	dicker	Skins, Deer	0	4	2	0
		0.5	dicker	Skins, Salted	0	6	8	0

The Mawdelen of Gloucester, Thomas Morres master, Entering, 22nd February 1543

Merchant name	Origin	Qty	Unit	Commodity	£	s.	d.	f.
Robert Pole	Ind	8	tun	Wine	0	0	0	0
		0.25	tun	Oil, *Olive*	0	20	0	0

Merchant name	Origin	Qty	Unit	Commodity	£	s.	d.	f.

The Francis of New Ross, Robert Brown master, Exiting, 22nd February 1543

Merchant name	Origin	Qty	Unit	Commodity	£	s.	d.	f.
Patrick Murfie	Ind	5	lb	Saffron	2	10	0	0
		3	lb	Silk, *Worked*	2	0	0	0
		0.5	C	Aniseed	0	6	8	0
		6	dozen	Knives, in Pairs	0	10	0	0
		1	dozen	Skins, Red	0	2	1	0
George Savage	Ind	1.25	piece	Cloth of Assize	0	0	0	0
		8	lb	Saffron	4	0	0	0
		9	lb	Silk, *Worked*	6	0	0	0
		5	dozen	Knives, in Pairs	0	8	4	0
		6	dozen	Girdles	0	9	0	0
		0.5	C	Alum	0	6	8	0
		1	dozen	Skins, Golden	0	4	2	0
		1	lb	Ginger	0	0	18	0
		1	lb	Cinnamon &Mace	0	2	6	0
		1	gross	Knives	0	6	8	0
		1	dozen	Cards, Playing	0	0	10	0
		9	C	Iron	0	36	0	0
Thomas Crymyng	Ind	1.5	lb	Silk, *Worked*	0	20	0	0
		6	gross	Points	0	6	0	0
		1	gross	Lacquer	0	0	20	0
		1	gross	Knives	0	6	8	0
		1	dozen	Skins, Golden	0	4	2	0
		3	dozen	Knives, in Pairs	0	5	0	0
		4	dozen	Glasses	0	0	15	0
		1.5	dozen	Knives, Small	0	0	20	0
		4	dozen	Combs	0	0	18	0
		1.5	dozen	Cards, Playing	0	0	15	0
John Dowle	Ind	1.5	piece	Cloth of Assize	0	0	0	0
		1	lb	Silk, *Worked*	0	13	4	0
		1	lb	Saffron	0	10	0	0
		2	dozen	Aniseed	0	2	8	0
		4	stone	Orchil	0	6	8	0
		1	gross	Knives	0	6	8	0
		2	gross	Lacquer	0	3	4	0
		6	gross	Points	0	6	0	0
James Norres	Ind	2	piece	Cloth of Assize	0	0	0	0
		2	C	Aniseed	1	6	8	0
		1	lb	Cloves	0	2	6	0
		4	lb	Verdigris	0	0	20	0
		1.5	dozen	Liquorice	0	0	10	0
		4	lb	Silk, *Worked*	2	13	4	0
		2	pair	Stock-Cards	0	2	0	0
		1	gross	Knives	0	6	8	0
		1	lb	Pepper	0	0	12	0
Patrick Roghe	Ind	2	lb	Silk, *Worked*	0	26	8	0
		1	lb	Saffron	0	10	0	0
		4	stone	Orchil	0	6	8	0
		0.5	gross	Cutts	0	0	20	0
		1	dozen	Cards, Playing	0	0	10	0
		6	dozen	Glasses	0	0	20	0

Merchant name	Origin	Qty	Unit	Commodity	£	s.	d.	f.
		1	gross	Lacquer	0	0	20	0
		1	dozen	Knives, Small	0	0	15	0
		1	gross	Points	0	0	12	0
		0.25	lb	Silk, *Worked*	0	3	4	0
		1.5	gross	Knives	0	10	0	0
		0.5	dozen	Knives	0	0	20	0

The Bartholomew of 'Yealm', Edward Syman master, Entering, 23rd February 1543

Edward Syman	Ind	60	burden	Fish, Salted	12	10	0	0
		3	C	Fish, Hake	0	30	0	0

The Mary of Dublin (?), John Pyrrye master, Entering, 26th February 1543

John *Pyrrye*	Ind	18	burden	Fish, Salted	3	15	0	0
		1	C	Fish, Hake	0	10	0	0

Shipping Details Unknown, *Entering, 26th February 1543*

Unknown	Ind	1	pipe	Wine	0	0	0	0

The Sant John of Pasajes de San Juan, Thomas de Lanavesiae master, Entering, *26th February 1543*

Thomas *de Lanavesiae* *& assoc.*	Alien	42	ton	Iron	105	0	0	0
		3	C	Liquorice	0	10	0	0
		1	hogshead	Fish, Newfoundland	0	13	4	0
Nicholas Thorn & assoc.	Ind	25	ton	Iron	62	10	0	0

The Sant John of Errenteria, John de Garamen master, Entering, *26th February 1543*

Christine White & assoc.	Ind	28	ton	Iron	70	0	0	0
Peter de Salleo	Alien	56	ton	Iron	140	0	0	0
		4	dozen	Serches	0	16	8	0
		1	ell	Fletchers Fryshe[3]	0	3	4	0
		9	C	Liquorice	0	30	0	0

The Anthony of Milford Haven, Peter Bulloke master, Exiting, *26th February 1543*

Richard Benet	Ind	10	ton	Salt	5	0	0	0
		3	C	Aniseed	2	0	0	0
		1	dozen	Liquorice	0	0	10	0
		0.5	piece	Bristol Frieze *Cloth*	0	6	8	0
		4	dozen	Girdles	0	0	20	0
		1	lb	Pepper	0	0	12	0
		1	lb	Kermes	0	0	18	0
		1	Unknown	Unknown	0	0	12	0
		12	gross	Points	0	12	0	0

3 Probably a type of frieze cloth.

Merchant name	Origin	Qty	Unit	Commodity	£	s.	d.	f.
		3	dozen	Beads	0	0	20	0
		0.5	lb	Cinnamon	0	0	15	0
		1	Unknown	Unknown	0	2	0	0
		2	piece	Cloth of Assize, Dozen Strait	0	0	0	0

The Ffyell of Deusto,[4] Gonsauls Savander master, Entering, 27th February 1543

John Smyth & assoc.	Ind	56.5	tun	Wine	0	0	0	0
		10	ton	Salt	5	0	0	0
		14	piece	Raisins, Great	0	23	4	0

Unknown Ship of Plymouth, Benet Caughlon master, Entering, 27th February 1543

Benet Caughlon	Ind	14	burden	Fish, Salted	2	18	4	0

The John of Gatcombe, John Arthur master, Entering, 2nd March 1543

William Russemowre	Ind	0.85	C	Fish, Hake	0	8	6	0
		0.5	burden	Fish, Salted	0	2	1	0

The Sunday of Bristol, John Jeyn master, Entering, 2nd March 1543

William Benett	Ind	2	dicker	Skins, Salted	0	26	8	0
William Chester	Ind	4.5	tun	Wine	0	0	0	0

The George of Cork, Philip Barri master, Exiting, 2nd March 1543

William Sarsefill	Ind	6	piece	Cloth of Assize	0	0	0	0
		12	lb	Saffron	6	0	0	0
		6	lb	Silk, Worked	4	0	0	0
		1.2	ton	Iron	4	16	0	0
		5	dozen	Cards, Wool	1	0	0	0
		1.5	dozen	Caps	0	15	0	0
		2	dozen	Cards, Playing	0	0	20	0
		2	bolt	Thread	0	2	0	0
		4	dozen	Flax	0	10	0	0
		10	gross	Knives	3	6	8	0
		2	lb	Cloves & Mace	0	5	0	0
		24	gross	Points	0	24	0	0
Henry Verdon	Ind	10	lb	Silk, Worked	6	13	4	0
		7	gross	Knives	2	6	8	0
		17	gross	Points	0	17	0	0
		2	gross	Lacquer	0	3	4	0
		5.5	lb	Saffron	2	15	0	0
		1	Unknown	Unknown	0	9	4	0
[ ]ond Golde	Ind	10.25	piece	Cloth of Assize	0	0	0	0
		24	gross	Points	0	24	0	0
		1	dozen	Caps	0	10	0	0
		2	bolt	Thread	0	2	2	0
		4.5	dozen	Flax	0	8	4	0

4 Dews, as it appears in the account, is probably in Bilbao, Spain. Our thanks to Prof Wendy Childs (Leeds) for this suggestion.

Merchant name	Origin	Qty	Unit	Commodity	£	s.	d.	f.
Peter Creangh	Ind	4.5	piece	Cloth of Assize	0	0	0	0
		12	gross	Points	0	12	0	0
		3	gross	Lacquer	0	5	0	0
		3	dozen	Caps	0	30	0	0
		2	dozen	Cards, Wool	0	8	4	0
		4	gross	Knives	0	26	8	0
		2	gross	Cutts	0	6	8	0
		4	dozen	Flax	0	10	0	0
		5	lb	Silk, *Worked*	3	6	8	0
		6	lb	Saffron	3	0	0	0
		16.25	dozen	Aniseed	0	21	8	0
Christopher Tyrry	Ind	2.33	piece	Cloth of Assize	0	0	0	0
		1	dozen	Caps	0	10	0	0
		1	dozen	Skins, Golden	0	4	2	0
		2	dozen	Knives, in Pairs	0	3	4	0
		1	dozen	Cards, Playing	0	0	10	0
		1	lb	Silk, *Worked*	0	13	4	0
Unknown Coping*er*	Ind	0.75	C	Aniseed	0	10	0	0
		1.5	dozen	Cards, Wool	0	6	0	0
		2	dozen	Flax	0	5	0	0
		2	dozen	Skins, Golden	0	8	4	0
		2	lb	Saffron	0	20	0	0
		1	lb	Cinnamon &Cloves	0	2	6	0
		0.5	gross	Cutts	0	0	20	0
		1	dozen	Cards, Playing	0	0	10	0
		0.5	burden	Steel	0	0	20	0
Dominic Roche	Ind	3	piece	Cloth of Assize	0	0	0	0
		4	lb	Saffron	2	0	0	0
		5	dozen	Flax	0	10	0	0

The James *of* Milford Haven, Master Unknown, Entering, 9th March 1543

John Taylor	Ind	5	C	Fish, Hake	2	10	0	0

The George of Cork, Philip Barry master, Exiting, 12th March 1543

William Sarsfeld	Ind	8	wey	Malt	6	13	4	0

The Patrick of Cork, Philip Hore master, Exiting, *12th March 1543*

Richard Fetzjames	Ind	3	piece	Cloth of Assize	0	0	0	0
		2	lb	Saffron	0	20	0	0
		4	lb	Silk, *Worked*	3	0	0	0
		2	gross	Knives	0	13	4	0
		4	gross	Points	0	4	0	0
		0.5	dozen	Skins, Golden	0	2	1	0
		0.25	C	Aniseed	0	3	4	0
		1.5	dozen	Flax	0	4	2	0
Thomas Cloturboke	Ind	6	wey	Beans &Malt	5	0	0	0
Dominic Roche	Ind	30	dozen	Flax	3	0	0	0
		3	gross	Knives	0	20	0	0
		2	lb	Silk, *Worked*	0	26	8	0

Merchant name	Origin	Qty	Unit	Commodity	£	s.	d.	f.
		7	gross	Points	0	7	0	0
James Feitzwilliams	Ind	1.5	piece	Cloth of Assize	0	0	0	0
		9	lb	Silk, *Worked*	6	0	0	0
		4	gross	Knives	0	26	8	0
		1.5	dozen	Caps	0	15	0	0
		10	dozen	Flax	0	30	0	0
		3	lb	Saffron	0	30	0	0
		6	gross	Points	0	6	0	0

The Saynt John of Pasajes de San Juan, Thomas de Lanavesiae master, Exiting, 27th March 1543

Merchant name	Origin	Qty	Unit	Commodity	£	s.	d.	f.
Francis Codryngton	Ind	20	piece	Cloth of Assize	0	0	0	0
Peter Talhwell	Ind	7	piece	Welsh *Cloth*, Dozen Strait	0	29	2	0
Thomas de Lanavesiae	Alien	19.083	piece	Cloth of Assize	0	0	0	0
		7	piece	Welsh *Cloth*	7	0	0	0
		4.5	piece	Wadmal & Flannel *Cloth*	4	13	4	0
		74	lb	Tin	0	24	8	0
		2.2	C	Skins, Sheep	2	0	0	0
Edward Pryn	Ind	7	piece	Cloth of Assize	0	0	0	0
		20	piece	Cloth of Assize, Dozen Strait	0	0	0	0
John Smyth	Ind	9	piece	Cloth of Assize	0	0	0	0

The Kathern of Waterford, Edmund Morris master, Entering, 28th March 1543

Merchant name	Origin	Qty	Unit	Commodity	£	s.	d.	f.
Edmund *Morris*	Ind	2	C	Skins, Sheep	0	20	0	0
		2	C	Skins, Lamb	0	13	4	0
		10	piece	Mantles	0	33	4	0
Nicholas Coleman	Ind	0.5	C	Skins, Sheep	0	5	0	0
		0.5	C	Check *Cloth*	0	20	0	0
		2	C	Skins, Lamb	0	13	4	0
		3	piece	Mantles	0	10	0	0
Thomas Keff	Ind	6	piece	Mantles	0	20	0	0
		2	C	Skins, Lamb	0	13	4	0
		0.5	C	Skins, Sheep	0	5	0	0
John Flemyng	Ind	18	piece	Mantles	3	0	0	0
		2	C	Skins, Lamb	0	13	4	0
		0.5	C	Skins, Sheep	0	5	0	0
		1.5	C	Check *Cloth*	3	0	0	0
		1	piece	Mantles	0	3	4	0
Thomas Whill	Ind	1	C	Check *Cloth*	2	0	0	0
		7	burden	Fish, Salted	0	29	2	0
Nicholas Kelly	Ind	15	burden	Fish, Salted	3	2	6	0
		6	C	Fish, Hake	3	0	0	0
Nicholas Kelly	Ind	40	yard	Check *Cloth*	0	13	4	0
Nicholas S[ ]che?	Ind	12	burden	Fish, Salted	2	10	0	0
		1	C	Check *Cloth*	2	0	0	0
		2	piece	Mantles	0	6	8	0

Merchant name	Origin	Qty	Unit	Commodity	£	s.	d.	f.

The Clement of Framilode, John Wade master, Entering, 29th March 1543

Merchant name	Origin	Qty	Unit	Commodity	£	s.	d.	f.
William Carr	Ind	22	ton	Iron	55	0	0	0
Hugh Typton	Ind	8	ton	Iron	20	0	0	0

The Sunday of Bristol, John Jeynes, Exiting, *29th March 1543*

Merchant name	Origin	Qty	Unit	Commodity	£	s.	d.	f.
John Bowghan	Ind	10	pair	Millstones	10	0	0	0
Walter Clynton	Ind	4	lb	Pepper	0	4	0	0
		2	lb	Ginger	0	3	0	0
		1	lb	Cloves &Mace	0	2	6	0
		0.5	lb	Cinnamon	0	0	15	0
		1	lb	Nutmeg	0	0	12	0
		1	dozen	Cumin	0	0	16	0
		1	piece	Raisins, *Great*	0	0	20	0
		1	lot	Items, misc	2	13	4	0
		1.75	C	Aniseed	0	23	4	0

The Saynt John of Errenteria, John de Garamen master, Exiting, *29th March 1543*

Merchant name	Origin	Qty	Unit	Commodity	£	s.	d.	f.
Francis Codryngton	Ind	20	piece	Cloth of Assize	0	0	0	0
Peter de Sables	Alien	56	dozen	Skins, Calf	9	6	8	0
		1	piece	Bristol Frieze *Cloth*	0	13	4	0
		14	piece	Welsh *Cloth*	14	0	0	0
		12	piece	Wadmal & Flannel *Cloth*	7	10	0	0
		4.583	piece	Cloth of Assize	0	0	0	0
John Smyth	Ind	8	piece	Cloth of Assize	0	0	0	0
William Sprat	Ind	9	piece	Cloth of Assize	0	0	0	0

The Ffyell, Port Unknown, Gonnsauls Savander master, Exiting, 2nd April 1543

Merchant name	Origin	Qty	Unit	Commodity	£	s.	d.	f.
Gonsalus Savander	Alien	1	piece	Cloth of Assize	0	0	0	0

The Clement of Framilode, John Wade master, Exiting, 4th April 1543

Merchant name	Origin	Qty	Unit	Commodity	£	s.	d.	f.
John Smyth	Ind	3	dicker	Hides, Tanned	0	0	0	0
		5	wey	Wheat	5	0	0	0
		10	dozen	Skins, Calf	0	33	4	0

The Anthony of Tintern, John Thomas master, Entering, 5th April 1543

Merchant name	Origin	Qty	Unit	Commodity	£	s.	d.	f.
Walter Putlay	Ind	24	dicker	Skins, Salted	16	0	0	0

The Margaret of Bristol, Thomas Signet master, Entering, 6th April 1543

Merchant name	Origin	Qty	Unit	Commodity	£	s.	d.	f.
William Gale	Ind	2	C	Check *Cloth*	4	0	0	0

The George of Longney, William Dymmock master, Entering, 8th April 1543

Merchant name	Origin	Qty	Unit	Commodity	£	s.	d.	f.
William Taylor	Ind	0.75	tun	Wine	0	0	0	0
		0.5	C	Check *Cloth*	0	20	0	0

Merchant name	Origin	Qty	Unit	Commodity	£	s.	d.	f.
The Kathern of Waterford, Edmund Morris master, Exiting, *8th April 1543*								
Edmund *Morris*	Ind	1	C	Aniseed	0	13	4	0
		1	piece	Cloth of Assize, Dozen Strait	0	0	0	0
Nicholas Co*l*eman	Ind	1	hogshead	Iron	0	20	0	0
William Balye	Ind	3	piece	Cloth of Assize, Dozen Strait	0	0	0	0
		2	gross	Knives	0	13	4	0
The Mary George of Hasfield, Davyd Adams master, Entering, 10th April 1543								
William Fox	Ind	20	dicker	Skins, Salted	13	6	8	0
Thomas Hilcoke	Ind	10.4	dicker	Skins, Salted	6	18	8	0
		80	piece	Skins, Sheep	0	6	8	0
		0.25	C	Skins, Lamb	0	0	20	0
William Chester	Ind	2	tun	Wine	0	0	0	0
The Margeret of Chepstow, John Jeyns master, Entering, 16th April 1543								
Thomas Harris	Ind	2	ton	Woad, Azores	13	6	8	0
The Mary of Tewkesbury, John Cox master, Entering, 17th April 1543								
Robert Poole	Ind	9.5	tun	Wine	0	0	0	0
The Mary Smyth of Milford Haven, John Brother master, Entering, 18th April 1543								
William Balard	Ind	4	C	Check *Cloth*	8	0	0	0
The Mary of Gloucester, John Dymmock master, Exiting, 23rd April 1543								
Thomas Cloturboke	Ind	4	wey	Malt	3	6	8	0
The Julyan of Bristol, John Crocke master, Entering, *25th April 1543*								
William Jay, Yonge & assoc.	Ind	37.75	ton	Raisins, *Great*	75	10	0	0
		93.75	lb	Sugar	0	30	0	0
		0.5	C	Almonds	0	6	8	0
The Sunday of Bristol, John Jey*n*s master, Entering, 30th April 1543								
Robert Butler	Ind	1	tun	Wine	0	0	0	0
Lewis Robbyns	Ind	1	pipe	Wine	0	0	0	0
William Lewys	Ind	1	pipe	Wine	0	0	0	0
The Mary Gr*a*ce of Gloucester, John Ll*ewely*n master, Entering, *30th April 1543*								
Thomas Cloturboke	Ind	1	C	Check *Cloth*	2	0	0	0
Peter Astakyn	Ind	8	C	Skins, Sheep	4	0	0	0
		9	C	Check *Cloth*	18	0	0	0
		15	C	Skins, Lamb	5	0	0	0
		3	piece	Skins, Fox	0	0	6	0

Merchant name	Origin	Qty	Unit	Commodity	£	s.	d.	f.
		3.5	stone	Wool, Irish	0	9	4	0
		4	stone	Wool, Flocks	0	0	20	0
		9	piece	Skins, Deer	0	2	3	0
William Donohow	Ind	100	yard	Check *Cloth*	0	33	4	0

The Peter of Milford Haven, Philip Smyth master, Entering, *30th April 1543*

John Iryshe	Ind	5	tun	Wine	0	0	0	0

The Mary George of Hasfield, William Fox master, Exiting, 2nd May 1543

William Appowell	Ind	6	lb	Saffron	3	0	0	0

The George Butlar of Waterford, Edmund Medoll master, Entering, *2nd May 1543*

David Gromy	Ind	50	C	Skins, Lamb	16	13	4	0
		14	C	Skins, Sheep	7	0	0	0
		8	piece	Skins, Fox	0	0	16	0
		8	piece	Skins, Otter	0	3	4	0
John Yonge	Ind	1	C	Skins, Sheep	0	10	0	0
		2	C	Skins, Lamb	0	13	4	0
		24	piece	Skins, Marten	0	24	0	0
		6	piece	Skins, Otter	0	2	6	0
		6	piece	Skins, Fox	0	0	12	0
Edward Arture	Ind	4	C	Skins, Sheep	2	0	0	0
		10	C	Skins, Lamb	3	6	8	0
		12	piece	Skins, Fox	0	2	0	0
		6	piece	Skins, Otter	0	2	6	0
		1	piece	Mantles	0	3	4	0
Patrick Wyse	Ind	1	C	Check *Cloth*	2	0	0	0
		12	piece	Mantles	0	40	0	0
		5	C	Skins, Lamb	0	23	4	0
		1.5	C	Skins, Sheep	0	15	0	0
Richard Forstall	Ind	1.5	C	Check *Cloth*	3	0	0	0
		6	piece	Mantles	0	20	0	0
		0.5	C	Skins, Sheep	0	5	0	0
William Nele	Ind	0.5	C	Check *Cloth*	0	20	0	0
		2	piece	Mantles	0	6	8	0
		8	C	Skins, Lamb	2	13	4	0
		1.5	C	Skins, Sheep	0	15	0	0
Edmund Medoll & assoc.	Ind	14	piece	Mantles	2	6	8	0
Patrick Knock	Ind	6	piece	Mantles	0	20	0	0
		30	piece	Skins, Sheep	0	2	6	0
		0.5	C	Skins, Lamb	0	3	4	0
Robert Buschar	Ind	1	C	Skins, Lamb	0	6	8	0
		30	piece	Skins, Sheep	0	2	6	0
		6	piece	Mantles	0	20	0	0
		20	yard	Check *Cloth*	0	6	8	0
Thomas Rothe	Ind	820	yard	Check *Cloth*	13	13	4	0
		4	C	Skins, Sheep	2	0	0	0
		9	C	Skins, Lamb	3	0	0	0

Merchant name	Origin	Qty	Unit	Commodity	£	s.	d.	f.
David Savage	Ind	5	C	Check *Cloth*	10	0	0	0
		9	C	Skins, Lamb	3	0	0	0
John Harold	Ind	13	piece	Skins, Marten	0	13	0	0
		15	piece	Skins, Otter	0	6	3	0
		18	piece	Skins, Fox	0	3	0	0
		6.5	C	Skins, Lamb	2	3	4	0
		4.25	C	Skins, Sheep	0	4	3	0
		20	yard	Check *Cloth*	0	6	8	0
David Creangh	Ind	4	C	Skins, Sheep	2	0	0	0
		12	C	Skins, Lamb	4	0	0	0
		10	piece	Skins, Fox	0	0	20	0
		10	piece	Skins, Otter	0	4	2	0

The Nicholas of Bristol, Bartholomew Garland master, Entering, 4th May 1543

William Chester								
& assoc.	Ind	1.5	tun	Wine	0	0	0	0
		1.5	C	Check *Cloth*	3	0	0	0
Bartholomew Garland	Ind	1.5	tun	Wine	0	0	0	0
		2	C	Check *Cloth*	4	0	0	0
		2.5	dicker	Skins, Salted	0	33	4	0
		1	C	Skins, Kid	0	5	0	0
		1	C	Skins, Sheep	0	10	0	0

The Peter of Milford Haven, Philip Smyth master, Exiting, 4th May 1543

John Flemyng	Ind	8	C	Aniseed	5	6	8	0
		19.5	lb	Silk, *Worked*	13	0	0	0
		2	lb	*Silk*, Caddis	0	6	8	0
		14	lb	Saffron	7	0	0	0
		3.5	dozen	Liquorice	0	7	0	0
		2	gross	Cutts	0	6	8	0
		1	dozen	Cards, Playing	0	0	10	0
		4	piece	Cloth of Assize, Dozen Strait	0	0	0	0
		0.33	piece	Cloth of Assize	0	0	0	0

The Mary of Youghal, Robert Payne master, Entering, *4th May 1543*

Patrick Ronam	Ind	2	pipe	Fish, Salmon	3	0	0	0
		1.5	C	Skins, Lamb	0	10	0	0
		3	piece	Mantles	0	10	0	0
		1	C	Skins, Sheep	0	10	0	0
		40	yard	Check *Cloth*	0	13	4	0
		4	dozen	Wood, Irish	0	8	0	0
Robert *Payne*	Ind	40	yard	Check *Cloth*	0	13	4	0
		3	piece	Mantles	0	10	0	0
		0.5	C	Skins, Sheep	0	5	0	0
		1	C	Skins, Lamb	0	6	8	0
Hugh Jones	Ind	1	butt	Fish, Salmon	0	15	0	0

Merchant name	Origin	Qty	Unit	Commodity	£	s.	d.	f.

The Mary of Worcester, Thomas Coke master, Entering, 5th May 1543

| Christopher Warren | Ind | 9 | ton | Woad | 60 | o | o | o |
| | | 2 | tun | Wine | o | o | o | o |

The Mary James of Bristol, John Poscher master, Exiting, 7th May 1543

| Thomas Lokar | Ind | 1 | pipe | Wine | o | o | o | o |

The Nicholas of Bristol, Bartholomew Garland, Exiting, 11th May 1543

Patrick Flemyng	Ind	7	ton	Salt	3	10	o	o
		1	pipe	Iron	2	o	o	o
		1	tun	Wine, Corrupt	1	10	o	o
		3	wey	Coal	o	10	o	o
		1	C	Aniseed	o	13	4	o
		1	piece	Raisins, *Great*	o	o	20	o

The Mary of Youghal, Robert Payne master, Exiting, 18th May 1543

Patrick Ronam	Ind	1	lb	Pepper	o	o	12	o
		2	dozen	Flax	o	8	o	o
		1.5	lb	Saffron	o	15	o	o
		3	gross	Points	o	3	o	o
		0.5	gross	Lacquer	o	o	10	o
		1	clout	Needles	o	o	12	o
		1	lb	Cloves	o	2	6	o
		2	dozen	Purses	o	o	12	o
Robert *Payne*	Ind	1	lb	Saffron	o	10	o	o
		1	stone	Hops	o	o	15	o
		1	stone	Orchil	o	o	20	o

The Katheryn of Milford Haven, William Hill master, Entering, 23rd May 1543

| Nicholas Clynt | Ind | 20 | dicker | Skins, Salted | 13 | 6 | 8 | o |

The Sunday of Bristol, Peter Howell master, Exiting, 29th May 1543

| John Boughan | Ind | 8 | pair | Millstones | 8 | o | o | o |

The George of Waterford, Edmund Medoll master, Exiting, 31st May 1543

Peter Astaken	Ind	3	lb	Silk, *Worked*	2	o	o	o
		8	lb	Saffron	4	o	o	o
		6	dozen	Knives, in Pairs	o	10	o	o
		2	gross	Knives	o	13	4	o
		1	dozen	Caps	o	10	o	o
		1	dozen	Skins, Red	o	2	1	o
		0.5	dozen	Skins, Golden	o	2	1	o
		0.5	dozen	Caps, Night	o	3	4	o
		4	dozen	Girdles	o	5	o	o
		3	dozen	Glasses	o	o	20	o

Merchant name	Origin	Qty	Unit	Commodity	£	s.	d.	f.
		3	pair	Stock-Cards	0	3	0	0
		3	dozen	Cards, Playing	0	2	6	0
		0.5	dozen	Penners	0	0	12	0
		0.5	C	Aniseed	0	6	8	0
		2	dozen	Alum	0	2	8	0
		1	lb	Cloves	0	2	6	0
		1	lb	Pepper	0	0	12	0
		3	lb	Thread	0	0	15	0
		3	dozen	*Percular*	0	0	5	0
		12	gross	Points	0	12	0	0
		1	gross	Lacquer	0	0	20	0
		3	stone	Orchil	0	5	0	0
		3	piece	Cloth of Assize, Dozen Strait	0	0	0	0
		0.66	piece	Cloth of Assize	0	0	0	0
Thomas Roche	Ind	8	lb	Saffron	4	0	0	0
		2	lb	Silk, *Worked*	0	26	8	0
		0.75	C	Aniseed	0	10	0	0
		1	lb	Mercury	0	0	5	0
		3	dozen	Glasses	0	0	12	0
		2	dozen	Cards, Playing	0	0	20	0
		3	dozen	Combs	0	0	12	0
		0.5	dozen	Skins, Red	0	0	13	0
		0.5	dozen	Skins, Golden	0	2	1	0
		0.5	lb	Pepper	0	0	6	0
		3	dozen	Knives, in Pairs	0	5	0	0
		2	lb	Thread	0	0	10	0
		3	dozen	Girdles	0	2	0	0
		1	lb	Cloves	0	2	6	0
		1	dozen	Alum	0	0	16	0
		1	dozen	Caps	0	10	0	0
		0.5	dozen	Caps, Night	0	0	20	0
		0.5	lb	Urnate	0	0	10	0
		3	dozen	*Percular*	0	0	6	0
		1	dozen	Penners	0	2	0	0
		3	stone	Orchil	0	5	0	0
		0.5	gross	Knives	0	3	4	0
		1	piece	Cloth of Assize	0	0	0	0
David Savage	Ind	4	lb	Saffron	2	0	0	0
		0.5	gross	Knives	0	3	4	0
		1.5	dozen	Aniseed	0	2	0	0
		2.5	stone	Orchil	0	4	2	0
		0.5	lb	Silk, *Worked*	0	6	8	0
William Nele	Ind	1	lb	Saffron	0	10	0	0
		0.5	lb	Cloves &Mace	0	0	15	0
		0.25	lb	Ginger	0	0	5	0
		0.25	lb	Pepper	0	0	3	0
		1	gross	Lacquer	0	0	20	0
		1	gross	Points	0	0	12	0
		4	piece	Caps	0	3	4	0
		1	dozen	Soap	0	0	15	0
David Gromall	Ind	16	lb	Silk, *Worked*	10	13	4	0
		3	C	Aniseed	2	0	0	0

Merchant name	Origin	Qty	Unit	Commodity	£	s.	d.	f.
		0.5	C	Alum	0	6	8	0
		8	dozen	Ribbons, Unspecified	0	10	0	0
		3	gross	Knives	0	20	0	0
		2	gross	Cutts	0	6	8	0
		64	gross	Points	3	4	0	0
		4	dozen	Glasses	0	0	10	0
		3	lb	Cinnamon	0	7	6	0
		3	lb	Cloves	0	7	6	0
		2	lb	Ginger	0	3	0	0
		3	lb	Nutmeg	0	3	0	0
		8	dozen	Skins, Golden	0	33	4	0
		1	Unknown	Drugs, Misc.	0	20	0	0
		0.33	piece	Cloth of Assize	0	0	0	0
Edward Arthure	Ind	6	lb	Silk, *Worked*	4	0	0	0
		11	lb	Saffron	5	10	0	0
		4	dozen	Skins, Golden	0	16	8	0
		1	C	Aniseed	0	13	4	0
		4	gross	Knives	0	26	8	0
		7	lb	Pepper	0	7	0	0
		1	clout	Needles	0	0	8	0
		22	gross	Points	0	22	0	0
		4	dozen	Cards, Playing	0	3	4	0
		4	dozen	Knives, in Pairs	0	6	8	0
		6	lb	Cumin	0	0	5	0
		3	lb	Verdigris	0	0	15	0
		1	lb	Senna	0	0	8	0
		1	dozen	Caps	0	10	0	0
		2.33	piece	Cloth of Assize	0	0	0	0
John Yonge	Ind	4	piece	Cloth of Assize	0	0	0	0
		10	lb	Saffron	5	0	0	0
		13	lb	Silk, *Worked*	8	13	4	0
		3	C	Aniseed	2	0	0	0
		1.5	dozen	Caps	0	15	0	0
		2	lb	Cloves	0	5	0	0
		1	Unknown	Drugs, Misc.	0	2	0	0
		6	lb	Crossbow Thread	0	0	18	0
		5	lb	Pepper	0	5	0	0
		6	lb	Sugar	0	2	0	0
		1	lb	Thread	0	0	10	0
		12	lb	Liquorice	0	0	10	0
		2	dozen	Knives, in Pairs	0	3	4	0
		2	gross	Knives	0	13	4	0
		12	gross	Points	0	12	0	0
Richard Forstall	Ind	1.25	piece	Cloth of Assize	0	0	0	0
		1	C	Aniseed	0	13	4	0

The Patrycke of Tenby, William Flute master, Entering, 11th June 1543

Thomas Browne	Ind	2	ton	Salt	0	20	0	0

Merchant name	Origin	Qty	Unit	Commodity	£	s.	d.	f.

The Mary of Tenby, John Yougholl master, Entering, *11th June 1543*

Merchant name	Origin	Qty	Unit	Commodity	£	s.	d.	f.
Thomas Browne	Ind	2	ton	Salt	0	20	0	0

The Kathern of Waterford, Nicholas Parson master, Entering, 12th June 1543

Merchant name	Origin	Qty	Unit	Commodity	£	s.	d.	f.
James Wasche, Lee & assoc.	Ind	16	piece	Mantles	2	13	4	0
		440	yard	Check *Cloth*	7	6	8	0
		2	C	Skins, Sheep	0	20	0	0
		1	C	Skins, Lamb	0	6	8	0

The Trinite of Gatcombe, John Marks master, Entering, *12th June 1543*

Merchant name	Origin	Qty	Unit	Commodity	£	s.	d.	f.
Maurice Bocher	Ind	8	ton	Salt	4	0	0	0

The George of Waterford, Nicholas Coleman master, Entering, 13th June 1543

Merchant name	Origin	Qty	Unit	Commodity	£	s.	d.	f.
Nicholas Welche	Ind	9	C	Check *Cloth*	18	0	0	0
		5	C	Skins, Sheep	2	10	0	0
		20	C	Skins, Lamb	6	13	4	0
		18	piece	Skins, Fox	0	3	0	0
		2	stone	Wool, Irish	0	5	4	0
		5	stone	Wool, Flocks	0	2	1	0
Thomas Morre	Ind	98	C	Skins, Lamb	32	13	4	0
		20	dozen	Skins, Fox	0	20	0	0
		23	piece	Skins, Marten	0	23	0	0
		24	piece	Skins, Otter	0	10	0	0
Stephan White	Ind	10	C	Skins, Lamb	3	6	8	0
		2	C	Skins, Sheep	0	20	0	0
		12	piece	Skins, Fox	0	2	0	0
		6	piece	Skins, Otter	0	2	6	0
Edmund Clery	Ind	3	C	Check *Cloth*	6	0	0	0
		8	piece	Mantles	0	26	8	0
		1.5	C	Skins, Lamb	0	10	0	0
		0.5	C	Skins, Sheep	0	5	0	0
Nicholas Coleman	Ind	1	C	Check *Cloth*	2	0	0	0
		4	piece	Mantles	0	13	4	0
		1	C	Skins, Sheep	0	10	0	0
Thomas White	Ind	1.5	C	Check *Cloth*	3	0	0	0
		2	piece	Mantles	0	6	8	0
		3	C	Skins, Lamb	0	20	0	0
		1.5	C	Skins, Sheep	0	15	0	0
David Butlar	Ind	1.5	C	Check *Cloth*	3	0	0	0
		3	C	Skins, Lamb	0	20	0	0
Robert Maydan	Ind	2	C	Check *Cloth*	4	0	0	0
		3	C	Skins, Sheep	0	30	0	0
		1	C	Skins, Lamb	0	6	8	0
		2	piece	Mantles	0	6	8	0
Nicholas Bruar	Ind	8	piece	Mantles	0	26	8	0
		1.5	C	Skins, Lamb	0	10	0	0
		0.5	C	Skins, Sheep	0	5	0	0

Merchant name	Origin	Qty	Unit	Commodity	£	s.	d.	f.
John Quede	Ind	1	C	Check *Cloth*	2	0	0	0
		1	piece	Mantles	0	3	4	0
Maurice Power	Ind	30	yard	Check *Cloth*	0	10	0	0
		2	piece	Mantles	0	6	8	0
Nicholas Shea								
& Quyrke	Ind	2	C	Check *Cloth*	4	0	0	0
		15	C	Skins, Lamb	5	0	0	0
		4	C	Skins, Sheep	2	0	0	0
Thomas Bartholomew								
& assoc.	Ind	560	yard	Check *Cloth*	9	6	8	0
		19	piece	Mantles	3	3	4	0
		3	piece	Mantles, Waist	0	5	0	0
		4.5	C	Skins, Lamb	0	30	0	0
		3	dozen	Skins, Fox	0	6	0	0
		1	piece	Skins, Marten	0	0	12	0

The Nicholas of Milford Haven, William Roche master, Entering, 13th June 1543

David Glover	Ind	15	ton	Salt	7	10	0	0

The Anthony of Purton, John Saunders master, Entering, 13th June 1543

Robert Adams	Ind	5	ton	Salt	2	10	0	0

The Jhesus of Gatcombe, Thomas Hoper master, Entering, *13th June 1543*

Thomas Hoper	Ind	6	ton	Salt	3	0	0	0

The Sunday of Bristol, Thomas Walker master, Entering, 20th June 1543

Richard Grenwey	Ind	3	C	Skins, Lamb	0	20	0	0
		3	dicker	Skins, Deer	0	7	6	0

The George of Waterford, Nicholas Coleman master, Exiting, 26th June 1543

Robert Maydan	Ind	1	pipe	Iron	2	0	0	0
		1	dozen	Soap	0	0	15	0
		2	gross	Points	0	2	0	0
Nicholas Coleman	Ind	1	hogshead	Iron	0	20	0	0
Edmund Clery	Ind	0.5	piece	Cloth of Assize	0	0	0	0
Nicholas Bruar	Ind	1	pipe	Wine, Corrupt	0	15	0	0
Stephan White	Ind	3	piece	Cloth of Assize, Dozen Strait	0	0	0	0
		1	piece	Cloth of Assize	0	0	0	0
		1	C	Alum	0	13	4	0
		9	dozen	Girdles	0	12	0	0
		1	piece	Camlet *Cloth*	0	15	0	0
		1	dozen	Penners	0	2	0	0
		2	lb	Cinnamon	0	5	0	0
		12	dozen	Beads	0	0	12	0
		3	dozen	Penners	0	0	21	0
		2	dozen	Cards, Playing	0	0	20	0
		3	dozen	Knives, in Pairs	0	5	0	0

Merchant name	Origin	Qty	Unit	Commodity	£	s.	d.	f.
		6	dozen	Glasses	0	0	18	0
		4	dozen	Skins, Golden	0	16	8	0
		1	dozen	Skins, Red	0	2	1	0
		2	C	Aniseed	0	26	8	0
		2	gross	Knives	0	13	4	0
		6	lb	Pepper	0	6	0	0
		24	gross	Points	0	24	0	0
		0.5	lb	Ginger	0	0	9	0
		0.5	lb	Nutmeg	0	0	9	0
		1	C	Aniseed	0	13	4	0
Maurice Quyrke	Ind	3	piece	Cloth of Assize, Dozen Strait	0	0	0	0
		2	C	Aniseed	0	26	8	0
		2	C	Hops	0	20	0	0
		6	gross	Points	0	6	0	0
		2	gross	Lacquer	0	3	4	0
		1	dozen	Skins, Golden	0	4	2	0
		1	gross	*Percular*	0	5	0	0
		1	lb	Cinnamon	0	2	6	0
		2	dozen	Glasses	0	0	6	0
		1	lb	Pepper	0	0	12	0
		1	lb	Ginger	0	0	18	0
		1	lb	Nutmeg	0	0	20	0
		3	lb	Caddis	0	20	0	0
		3	lb	Silk, *Worked*	2	0	0	0
		1	lb	Saffron	0	10	0	0
David Creangh	Ind	4.5	piece	Cloth of Assize	0	0	0	0
		1	C	Aniseed	0	13	4	0
		1	C	Alum	0	13	4	0
		2	dozen	Skins, Golden	0	8	4	0
		6	lb	Cumin	0	0	8	0
		4	dozen	Knives, in Pairs	0	6	8	0
		5	dozen	Ribbons, Unspecified	0	6	8	0
		1	dozen	Penners	0	0	10	0
		2.5	dozen	Glasses	0	0	10	0
		2.5	lb	Pepper	0	2	6	0
		0.5	lb	Cinnamon	0	0	15	0
		0.5	lb	Cloves	0	0	15	0
		0.5	lb	Ginger	0	0	10	0
John Harrolde	Ind	6	piece	Cloth of Assize	0	0	0	0
		12	lb	Saffron	6	0	0	0
		2.5	lb	Cinnamon	0	6	3	0
		12	lb	Pepper	0	12	0	0
		15	lb	Silk, *Worked*	10	0	0	0
		6	lb	Verdigris	0	2	6	0
		1	lb	Cloves	0	2	6	0
		34	gross	Points	0	34	0	0
		20	lb	Cumin	0	2	0	0
		1	gross	Cutts	0	3	4	0
		9	gross	Knives	3	0	0	0
		2.75	C	Aniseed	0	36	8	0

Merchant name	Origin	Qty	Unit	Commodity	£	s.	d.	f.

The Nicholas of Bristol, Bartholomew Garland master, Entering, 27th June 1543

Merchant name	Origin	Qty	Unit	Commodity	£	s.	d.	f.
Bartholomew Garland	Ind	60	stone	Wool, Irish	8	0	0	0
		5	dicker	Skins, Salted	3	6	8	0
Henry Sandisord	Ind	10	dicker	Skins, Salted	6	13	4	0
		1	C	Skins, Lamb	0	6	8	0
John Iryshe	Ind	95	yard	Check *Cloth*	0	31	8	0
		6	piece	Mantles	0	20	0	0
		80	yard	Linen *Cloth*	0	6	8	0

The Katheryn of Waterford, Nicholas Parson master, Exiting, *27th June 1543*

Merchant name	Origin	Qty	Unit	Commodity	£	s.	d.	f.
William Waydyng	Ind	0.5	C	Aniseed	0	6	8	0
		5	dozen	Wood, Brazil	0	16	8	0
		0.5	C	Alum	0	6	8	0
		1	lb	Cinnamon	0	2	6	0
		0.5	lb	Cloves	0	0	15	0
		6	gross	Points	0	6	0	0
		2	gross	Lacquer	0	3	4	0
		2	pair	Stock-Cards	0	2	0	0
		2	dozen	Soap	0	2	6	0

The Clement of Framilode, John Wade master, Entering, 2nd July 1543

Merchant name	Origin	Qty	Unit	Commodity	£	s.	d.	f.
John Smyth & Pryn	Ind	28	ton	Iron	70	0	0	0
		2	dozen	Serches	0	8	4	0

The Sent John of Pasajes de San Juan, Stephan de Santa Clara master, Entering, *2nd July 1543*

Merchant name	Origin	Qty	Unit	Commodity	£	s.	d.	f.
William Schypman	Ind	74.166	ton	Iron	185	8	4	0
Stephan de Santa								
Clara	Alien	21	ton	Iron	52	10	0	0
		11	dozen	Serches	2	5	9	0
		0.5	bale	Woad	0	12	6	0
		5	dozen	Skins, Fish	0	20	0	0
		15	dozen	Skins, Budge Coarse	2	0	0	0
		4.5	C	Steel	2	5	0	0

The Mary of Errenteria Domingo de Lesso master, Entering, 2nd July 1543

Merchant name	Origin	Qty	Unit	Commodity	£	s.	d.	f.
William Schipman								
& assoc.	Ind	87.233	ton	Iron	218	1	8	0
		8	dozen	Serches	0	33	4	0
		60	dozen	Skins, Lamb Spanish	50	0	0	0
Domingo de Lesso								
& assoc.	Alien	39.5	ton	Iron	98	15	0	0
		7.5	balette	Woad	4	7	6	0
		10	dozen	Serches	2	1	8	0
		43.33	dozen	Skins, Budge (slawt[ ]r)?	4	6	8	0
		70	piece	Skins, Fish	0	23	4	0
		1	piece	Anchor	0	5	0	0

Merchant name	Origin	Qty	Unit	Commodity	£	s.	d.	f.
The Ann of Bristol, John Morris master, Entering, 6th July 1543								
Richard Morre	Ind	1	C	Check *Cloth*	2	0	0	0
The Mary of Errenteria, Domingo de Lesso master, Entering, 7th July 1543								
Christine White	Ind	10	ton	Lead, Worked	50	0	0	0
		20	dozen	Skins, Calf	3	6	8	0
		100	piece	Manchester Cotton *Cloth*	50	0	0	0
		5	dicker	Hides, Tanned	5	0	0	0
		20	piece	Cloth of Assize	0	0	0	0
John Smyth	Ind	18	piece	Cloth of Assize	0	0	0	0
		80	dozen	Skins, Calf	13	6	8	0
		5	dicker	Hides, Tanned	0	0	0	0
John Pryn	Ind	14	piece	Cloth of Assize	0	0	0	0
		8	piece	Bristol Frieze *Cloth*	5	6	8	0
		6	piece	Welsh *Cloth*, Dozen Strait	0	25	0	0
Martin Pers & Anthony Petrus	Alien	11	C	Wax	10	0	0	0
		0.55	C	Skins, Sheep Worked	0	7	4	0
		15	dozen	Skins, Calf	2	10	0	0
Francis Codryngton & Carr	Ind	10	ton	Lead, Worked	50	0	0	0
		40	dozen	Skins, Calf	6	13	4	0
		25	piece	Cloth of Assize	50	0	0	0
		3	dicker	Hides, Tanned	3	0	0	0
Domingo de Lesso	Alien	40	dozen	Skins, Calf	6	13	4	0
		0.66	piece	Cloth of Assize	0	0	0	0
William Schipman & Appowell	Ind	8	piece	Cloth of Assize	0	0	0	0
		2	piece	Welsh *Cloth*	2	0	0	0
Nicholas Thorn	Ind	10	piece	Cloth of Assize	0	0	0	0
John Cutt	Ind	9	piece	Cloth of Assize	0	0	0	0
		2	piece	Cloth of Assize, Dozen	0	0	0	0
		1	piece	Welsh *Cloth*	0	20	0	0
Giles White	Ind	10	piece	Cloth of Assize	0	0	0	0
William Sprat	Ind	18	piece	Cloth of Assize	0	0	0	0
		8	dicker	Hides, Tanned	0	0	0	0
		40	dozen	Skins, Calf	6	13	4	0
Francis Wosley	Ind	10	piece	Cloth of Assize	0	0	0	0
Peter de Sables	Alien	66	dozen	Skins, Calf	11	0	0	0
		6	piece	Narrow Lining *Cloth*	3	0	0	0
		4	piece	Cloth of Assize, Dozen	0	0	0	0
John de Bereby	Alien	30	dozen	Skins, Calf	5	0	0	0
		6	piece	Cloth of Assize, Dozen Strait	0	0	0	0
Stephan de Alsaty	Alien	75	dozen	Skins, Calf	12	10	0	0
		7	piece	Lining *Cloth*	7	0	0	0
		4.5	piece	Cloth of Assize	0	0	0	0
Laurence de Irauso	Alien	2.25	C	Wax	4	10	0	0
		6	piece	Welsh *Cloth*	6	0	0	0
		25	ell	Flannel *Cloth*	0	12	0	0
		4.5	piece	Cloth of Assize, Bridgwater	0	0	0	0

Merchant name	Origin	Qty	Unit	Commodity	£	s.	d.	f.
		2	piece	Cloth of Assize, Dozen Strait	0	0	0	0
John Jasy & Saune	Alien	15	piece	Welsh *Cloth*	15	0	0	0
		4	piece	Northern *Cotton Cloth*	0	20	0	0
		6	piece	Wadmal *Cloth*	5	0	0	0
		3.5	piece	Cloth of Assize	0	0	0	0
William Tyndale	Ind	8	piece	Cloth of Assize	0	0	0	0
Francis Fowler	Ind	19	piece	Cloth of Assize	0	0	0	0
		6	dicker	Hides, Tanned	0	0	0	0
Edward Pryn & Typton	Ind	19	piece	Cloth of Assize	0	0	0	0

The Laurence of Gloucester, John Carpenter master, Entering, *7th July 1543*

Merchant name	Origin	Qty	Unit	Commodity	£	s.	d.	f.
William Sprat	Ind	6	ton	Salt	3	0	0	0

The George of Gloucester, William Frape master, Entering, *7th July 1543*

Merchant name	Origin	Qty	Unit	Commodity	£	s.	d.	f.
John Greves	Ind	7	ton	Salt	3	10	0	0

The Anthony of Milford Haven, John Steward master, Entering, *7th July 1543*

Merchant name	Origin	Qty	Unit	Commodity	£	s.	d.	f.
Michael Grymway	Ind	19	ton	Salt	9	10	0	0

The Mary George of Hasfield, William Fox master, Entering, *7th July 1543*

Merchant name	Origin	Qty	Unit	Commodity	£	s.	d.	f.
William *Fox*	Ind	2	burden	Fish, Salted	0	8	4	0
		1	animal	Horse	0	26	8	0

The Sent John of Pasajes de San Juan, Stephan de Santa Clara master, Exiting, *7th July 1543*

Merchant name	Origin	Qty	Unit	Commodity	£	s.	d.	f.
John Smyth	Ind	9	piece	Cloth of Assize	0	0	0	0
		80	dozen	Skins, Calf	13	6	8	0
Christine White	Ind	20	piece	Cloth of Assize	0	0	0	0
		5	dicker	Hides, Tanned	0	0	0	0
Robert Gyttyns	Ind	25	unknown	Strats	5	4	2	0
		1.25	ton	Lead, Worked	6	5	0	0
Francis Codryngton	Ind	10	ton	Lead, Worked	50	0	0	0
		33	piece	Cloth of Assize	0	0	0	0
James Chester	Ind	4.5	ton	Lead, Worked	22	10	0	0
		60	piece	Manchester Cotton *Cloth*	30	0	0	0
William Shipman	Ind	9	piece	Cloth of Assize	0	0	0	0
William Appowell	Ind	60	piece	Manchester Cotton *Cloth*	30	0	0	f.
Nicholas Thorn	Ind	20	piece	Cloth of Assize	0	0	0	0
Edward Pryn	Ind	10	piece	Cloth of Assize	0	0	0	0
Michael de Avere	Alien	10	dicker	Hides, Tanned	0	0	0	0
William Sprat	Ind	10	dicker	Hides, Tanned	0	0	0	0
Giles White	Ind	22	piece	Cloth of Assize	0	0	0	0
		6	piece	Northern *Cotton Cloth*	0	25	0	0
Francis Fowler	Ind	45	dozen	Skins, Calf	7	10	0	0
		9	piece	Cloth of Assize	0	0	0	0
John de Lavagy	Alien	30	dozen	Skins, Calf	5	0	0	0
		18	dozen	Skins, Kid Rough	0	36	0	0

Merchant name	Origin	Qty	Unit	Commodity	£	s.	d.	f.
		1.5	C	Skins, Sheep Worked	0	20	0	0
Stephan de Santa Clara	Alien	11.25	piece	Cloth of Assize	0	0	0	0
		4	piece	Welsh Cloth	4	0	0	0
Peter de Lescano & Sebastian de Sant Sebastain	Alien	28	piece	Cloth of Assize, Dozen Strait	0	0	0	0
		4	piece	Cloth of Assize, Bridgwater	0	0	0	0
Stephan de Santa Clara	Alien	30.5	dozen	Skins, Calf	5	0	20	0
John de Lavagy	Alien	1	piece	Cloth of Assize, Bridgwater	0	0	0	0
		1.5	piece	Welsh Cloth	0	30	0	0
Thomas Tyson	Ind	14	piece	Cloth of Assize	0	0	0	0
		2	piece	Dunster Cloth	0	20	0	0
Robert Butlar	Ind	6	piece	Cloth of Assize	0	0	0	0

The Mary Gardilop (Guadalupe), Port Unknown, Thomas Howell master, Entering, *7th July 1543*

Thomas Whaley	Ind	1	pipe	Wine	0	0	0	0
		1.6	dicker	Skins, Salted	0	21	4	0

The Sonday of Bristol, William Gale master, Entering, 9th July 1543

Nicholas Kelly	Ind	5	dicker	Skins, Salted	3	6	8	0
		1	virken	Fish, Salmon	0	7	6	0
		0.25	C	Fish, Sturgeon	0	2	6	0
William Lewys	Ind	1.25	tun	Wine	5	0	0	0
		1.6	dicker	Skins, Salted	0	21	4	0

The Nicholas of Milford Haven, John Philypps master, Entering, *9th July 1543*

William Chester	Ind	12	ton	Salt	6	0	0	0

The Trinite of Longney, John Brother master, Entering, *9th July 1543*

William Brother	Ind	3.5	ton	Salt	0	35	0	0

The Mary of Gloucester, Richard Sugar master, Entering, 10th July 1543

William Saunders	Ind	10	ton	Salt	5	0	0	0

The Patrycke of Tenby, William Lloyd master, Entering, 11th July 1543

John Gough	Ind	3	ton	Salt	0	30	0	0

The Mary of Passage East, Richard Deryng master, Entering, 14th July 1543

John Malmesey	Ind	9	C	Check Cloth	18	0	0	0
		3	C	Skins, Sheep	0	30	0	0
		6	C	Skins, Lamb	0	40	0	0
David Garrod	Ind	27	piece	Mantles	4	10	0	0

Merchant name	Origin	Qty	Unit	Commodity	£	s.	d.	f.
		12	piece	Skins, Fox	0	2	0	0
		26	piece	Skins, Marten	0	26	0	0
Peter Roughe	Ind	3.5	C	Check *Cloth*	7	0	0	0
		11	C	Skins, Lamb	3	13	4	0
		20	piece	Mantles	3	6	8	0
		1.5	C	Skins, Sheep	0	15	0	0
		1.5	C	Skins, Kid	0	7	6	0
		6	piece	Skins, Fox	0	0	12	0
William Archer	Ind	4	C	Check *Cloth*	8	0	0	0
		7	C	Skins, Sheep	3	10	0	0
		1	C	Skins, Kid	0	5	0	0
		15	C	Skins, Lamb	5	0	0	0
		43	piece	Mantles	7	3	4	0
		4	stone	Wool, Flocks	0	0	20	0
		8	piece	Skins, Fox	0	1	4	0
		2	piece	Skins, Otter	0	0	10	0
Nicholas Cantwell	Ind	4	C	Check *Cloth*	8	0	0	0
		10	C	Skins, Lamb	3	6	8	0
		3	C	Skins, Sheep	0	30	0	0
		5	stone	Wool, Flocks	0	2	1	0
		2	piece	Mantles	0	6	8	0
Patrick Kelly & Pembroke	Ind	1636	yard	Check *Cloth*	27	5	4	0
		68	piece	Mantles	11	6	8	0
		18	C	Skins, Lamb	6	0	0	0
		3.83	C	Skins, Sheep	1	18	8	0
		5	piece	Skins, Fox	0	0	10	0
Walter Walshe	Ind	10	C	Check *Cloth*	20	0	0	0
		7.5	C	Skins, Lamb	2	10	0	0
		5	C	Skins, Sheep	2	10	0	0
		20	piece	Skins, Fox	0	3	4	0
		3	stone	Wool, Irish	0	8	0	0
		5	stone	Wool, Flocks	0	2	1	0
		3	piece	Mantles	0	10	0	0
		0.25	C	Skins, Kid	0	0	15	0
John Roughe & assoc.	Ind	8	C	Skins, Lamb	2	13	4	0
		1	C	Skins, Sheep	0	10	0	0
		2	piece	Mantles	0	6	8	0
		2	burden	Fish, Salted	0	8	4	0
Patrick Kelly	Ind	0.5	C	Check *Cloth*	0	20	0	0
		1.25	C	Skins, Lamb	0	8	4	0

The Trinite of Milford Haven, Owen Prendilgest master, Entering, 16th July 1543

William Chester	Ind	14	ton	Salt	7	0	0	0

The Anthony of Milford Haven, John Steward master, Exiting, *16th July 1543*

Nicholas Welshe	Ind	4	lb	Saffron	2	0	0	0
		4	lb	Silk, *Worked*	2	13	4	0
		1	dozen	Skins, Golden	0	4	2	0
		6	dozen	Knives, in Pairs	0	10	0	0

Merchant name	Origin	Qty	Unit	Commodity	£	s.	d.	f.
		4	dozen	Cards, Playing	0	3	4	0
		2	piece	Cloth of Assize, Dozen Strait	0	0	0	0
Edmund Morris	Ind	4	lb	Saffron	2	0	0	0
		12	dozen	Cards, Playing	0	10	0	0
		5	lb	Silk, *Worked*	3	6	8	0
		48	gross	Points	2	8	0	0
		5	lb	Verdigris	0	2	1	0
		12	dozen	Knives, in Pairs	0	20	0	0
		1	lb	Cinnamon	0	2	6	0
		4	lb	Mercury	0	0	20	0
		2	lb	Pepper	0	2	0	0
		2	dozen	Skins, Golden	0	8	4	0
		2	piece	Cloth of Assize, Dozen Strait	0	0	0	0
Thomas More	Ind	4	piece	Cloth of Assize	0	0	0	0
		6	lb	Silk, *Worked*	4	0	0	0
		11	lb	Verdigris	0	4	7	0
		2	lb	Mercury	0	0	10	0
		16	dozen	Knives, in Pairs	0	26	8	0
		5	lb	Pepper	0	5	0	0
		2	dozen	Skins, Golden	0	8	4	0
		1	lb	Cloves	0	2	6	0
		1	lb	Cinnamon	0	2	6	0
		6	lb	Oil, Bay	0	2	0	0
		14	lb	Cumin	0	0	18	0
		12	gross	Points	0	12	0	0

The Dowghen of Cardiff, John Roberts master, Entering, *16th July 1543*

John Roberts	Ind	1	tun	Wine	0	0	0	0

The Margaret of Tenby, Walter Bry*te* master, Entering, 18th July 1543

William Chester	Ind	29	ton	Salt	14	10	0	0
		270	yard	Check *Cloth*	4	10	0	0

The George of Milford Haven, John Alyn master, Entering, *18th July 1543*

John Adams	Ind	5	ton	Salt	2	10	0	0

The Mary Bryde of Milford Haven, John Folond master, Entering, *18th July 1543*

William Scarlet	Ind	8	ton	Salt	4	0	0	0

The Mary of Gloucester, John Smyth master, Entering, 19th July 1543

William Millward	Ind	13	piece	Mantles	2	3	4	0

The Michaell of Waterford, Robert Ffiztjohn master, Entering, 20th July 1543

Richard Donell	Ind	16	C	Skins, Sheep	8	0	0	0
		16	C	Skins, Lamb	5	6	8	0
		12	piece	Skins, Fox	0	2	0	0
		10	C	Check *Cloth*	20	0	0	0

Merchant name	Origin	Qty	Unit	Commodity	£	s.	d.	f.
		20	piece	Mantles	3	6	8	0
Richard Wadyng	Ind	7	C	Check *Cloth*	14	0	0	0
		16	piece	Mantles	2	13	4	0
		2	C	Skins, Sheep	0	20	0	0
		3.5	C	Skins, Lamb	0	23	4	0
		1	dicker	Skins, Deer	0	2	1	0
Benedict Saull	Ind	8	C	Check *Cloth*	16	0	0	0
		14	piece	Mantles	2	6	8	0
		1	C	Skins, Sheep	0	10	0	0
		2	C	Skins, Lamb	0	13	4	0
William Donohow	Ind	6	C	Check *Cloth*	12	0	0	0
		16	piece	Mantles	2	13	4	0
		0.5	C	Skins, Sheep	0	5	0	0
James Shee	Ind	5.5	C	Check *Cloth*	11	0	0	0
		28	piece	Mantles	4	13	4	0
		7	C	Skins, Lamb	2	6	8	0
		5	stone	Wool, Flocks	0	2	1	0
		4	piece	Skins, Fox	0	0	8	0
		2	C	Skins, Sheep	0	20	0	0
John Marshal	Ind	7	C	Check *Cloth*	14	0	0	0
		1.5	C	Skins, Lamb	0	10	0	0
		6	piece	Skins, Fox	0	0	12	0
		1	piece	Mantles	0	3	4	0
		1.16	C	Skins, Sheep	0	11	8	0
Henry Seyse	Ind	6	C	Check *Cloth*	12	0	0	0
		28	piece	Mantles	4	13	4	0
		3	C	Skins, Sheep	0	30	0	0
		9	C	Skins, Lamb	3	0	0	0
		6	piece	Skins, Fox	0	0	12	0
Richard Quenmerford	Ind	11	C	Check *Cloth*	22	0	0	0
		53	piece	Mantles	8	16	8	0
		4.5	C	Skins, Sheep	2	5	0	0
		6	C	Skins, Lamb	2	0	0	0
		12	piece	Skins, Fox	0	2	0	0
		2	piece	Skins, Otter	0	0	10	0
Thomas Maydan	Ind	4	C	Check *Cloth*	8	0	0	0
		6	piece	Mantles	0	20	0	0
		0.5	C	Skins, Sheep	0	5	0	0
		0.5	C	Skins, Lamb	0	3	4	0
John Murthy	Ind	2.5	C	Skins, Sheep	0	25	0	0
		1	piece	Mantles	0	3	4	0
		8	C	Skins, Lamb	2	13	4	0
		6	piece	Skins, Fox	0	0	12	0
		270	yard	Check *Cloth*	4	10	0	0
		2	C	Skins, Kid	0	10	0	0
James Bray	Ind	4	C	Skins, Sheep	2	0	0	0
		4	C	Skins, Lamb	0	26	8	0
		2	piece	Mantles	0	6	8	0
		0.5	C	Check *Cloth*	0	20	0	0
		6	piece	Skins, Fox	0	0	12	0
Laurence Brown & Wheland	Ind	9	C	Check *Cloth*	18	0	0	0

Merchant name	Origin	Qty	Unit	Commodity	£	s.	d.	f.
		7	C	Skins, Sheep	3	10	0	0
		3	C	Skins, Lamb	0	20	0	0
		2	piece	Mantles	0	6	8	0
Patrick Saull & assoc.	Ind	11.7	C	Skins, Sheep	5	17	0	0
		6.5	C	Skins, Lamb	2	3	4	0
		2060	yard	Check *Cloth*	34	6	8	0
		70	piece	Mantles	11	13	4	0
		0.5	C	Skins, Kid	0	2	6	0
Andrew Lyncoln & assoc.	Ind	12	C	Check *Cloth*	24	0	0	0
		3.5	C	Skins, Sheep	0	35	0	0
		16	piece	Mantles	2	13	4	0
		0.5	C	Skins, Lamb	0	3	4	0
		0.5	dicker	Skins, Deer	0	0	12	2

The Kateryn of Milford Haven, William Hyll master, Entering, *20th July 1543*

William Chester	Ind	2.75	tun	Wine	0	0	0	0
William Benet	Ind	2	tun	Wine	0	0	0	0
		2	C	Skins, Sheep	0	20	0	0
		1	C	Skins, Lamb	0	6	8	0
		4	stone	Wool, Irish	0	10	8	0
		0.5	C	Check *Cloth*	0	20	0	0

The Mary of Gloucester, John Smyth master, Entering, 21st July 1543

Robert Pole	Ind	8	tun	Wine	0	0	0	0

The Sunday of Waterford, Thomas Wheland master, Entering, 23rd July 1543

James Morris & Lincolne	Ind	42	C	Check *Cloth*	84	0	0	0
		10	C	Skins, Lamb	3	6	8	0
		4	C	Skins, Sheep	2	0	0	0
		8	piece	Mantles	0	26	8	0
James Lunbart & Strange	Ind	11	C	Check *Cloth*	22	0	0	0
		2	C	Skins, Sheep	0	20	0	0
		14	C	Skins, Lamb	4	13	4	0
		12	piece	Skins, Fox	0	2	0	0
		4	piece	Mantles	0	13	4	0
John Sale*nger*	Ind	3	C	Check *Cloth*	6	0	0	0
		12	piece	Mantles	0	40	0	0
		4	C	Skins, Sheep	2	0	0	0
		2	C	Skins, Lamb	0	13	4	0
Peter Walshe & Roche	Ind	4	C	Check *Cloth*	8	0	0	0
		12	piece	Mantles	0	40	0	0
		140	piece	Skins, Fox	0	21	8	0
		14	piece	Skins, Otter	0	5	10	0
		1	piece	Skins, Marten	0	0	12	0
		2	C	Skins, Lamb	0	13	4	0
		8	dozen	Purses	0	0	20	0

Merchant name	Origin	Qty	Unit	Commodity	£	s.	d.	f.
Roland Creangh	Ind	1	C	Skins, Sheep	0	10	0	0
		5	piece	Skins, Otter	0	2	1	0
		4	C	Skins, Lamb	0	26	8	0
		18	piece	Skins, Fox	0	3	0	0
Walter Mayahon	Ind	4	C	Skins, Sheep	2	0	0	0
		6	C	Skins, Lamb	2	0	0	0
		12	piece	Skins, Fox	0	2	0	0
		12	piece	Skins, Otter	0	5	0	0
		6	piece	Skins, Marten	0	6	0	0
		12	yard	Check *Cloth*	0	4	0	0
		40	yard	Irish Linen *Cloth*	0	3	4	0
Thomas Wheland & Gnew	Ind	16	piece	Mantles	2	13	4	0
		260	yard	Check *Cloth*	4	6	8	0
Thomas Maydan & Arthur	Ind	280	yard	Check *Cloth*	4	13	4	0
		6	piece	Mantles	0	20	0	0
		2	C	Skins, Lamb	0	13	4	0
		30	piece	Skins, Sheep	0	2	6	0
Roland Harold	Ind	7	C	Skins, Sheep	3	10	0	0
		12	C	Skins, Lamb	4	0	0	0
		1.5	C	Check *Cloth*	3	0	0	0
		27	piece	Skins, Otter	0	11	3	0
		4.5	dozen	Skins, Fox	0	9	0	0
		4	dicker	Skins, Deer	0	8	4	0
		3	piece	Skins, Marten	0	3	0	0
Nicholas Harold	Ind	10	C	Skins, Lamb	3	6	8	0
		4	C	Skins, Sheep	2	0	0	0
		5	dicker	Skins, Deer	0	10	5	0
		12	piece	Skins, Otter	0	5	0	0
		50	yard	Check *Cloth*	0	16	8	0
		8	piece	Skins, Marten	0	8	0	0
		40	lb	Spermaceti	2	0	0	0

The Saviour of Minehead, Master Unknown, Entering, *23rd July 1543*

Richard Kyng	Ind	2	burden	Fish, Salted	0	8	4	0

The Trinite of Carmarthen, William Walter master, Entering, *23rd July 1543*

William Malanghan	Ind	3	ton	Salt	0	30	0	0

The Mary Smyth of Milford Haven, John Parson master, Entering, 25th July 1543

William Saxsy	Ind	2.75	tun	Wine	0	0	0	0

The Mary Christopher of Tewkesbury, Nicholas Harris master, Exiting, 27th July 1543

Giles Gest	Ind	1.33	piece	Cloth of Assize	0	0	0	0

Merchant name	Origin	Qty	Unit	Commodity	£	s.	d.	f.

The Saviour of Minehead, Dennis Mauraughe master, Exiting, 27th July 1543

Merchant name	Origin	Qty	Unit	Commodity	£	s.	d.	f.
Nicholas Kelly	Ind	1.25	tun	Wine, Corrupt	0	37	6	0
		6	lb	Silk, *Worked*	4	0	0	0
		4	lb	Saffron	2	0	0	0
		2	ton	Iron	8	0	0	0
		1	piece	Bristol Frieze *Cloth*	0	13	4	0
		6	piece	Cloth of Assize	0	0	0	0
Patrick Smyth	Ind	3	piece	Cloth of Assize, Dozen Strait	0	0	0	0

The Mary of Passage East, John Deryn master, Exiting, 28th July 1543

Merchant name	Origin	Qty	Unit	Commodity	£	s.	d.	f.
John Malmesey	Ind	1	pipe	Iron	2	0	0	0
		5	lb	Saffron	2	10	0	0
		9	lb	Silk, *Worked*	6	0	0	0
		3	gross	Knives	0	20	0	0
		12	gross	Points	0	12	0	0
		2	gross	Lacquer	0	3	4	0
		1	C	Aniseed	0	13	4	0
		6	lb	Cumin	0	0	18	0
		0.5	C	Alum	0	6	8	0
		2	lb	Pepper	0	2	0	0
		0.5	lb	Cloves	0	0	15	0
		9	piece	Caps	0	7	6	0
		4	stone	Orchil	0	6	8	0
		0.5	dozen	Caps, Night	0	2	6	0
		6	dozen	Glasses	0	2	0	0
		1.5	dozen	Liquorice	0	0	20	0
		3	dozen	Knives, in Pairs	0	5	0	0
		2	dozen	Girdles	0	0	16	0
		2	piece	Cloth of Assize	0	0	0	0
Patrick Roughe	Ind	7.5	lb	Silk, *Worked*	5	0	0	0
		7.5	lb	Saffron	3	15	0	0
		2	gross	Knives	0	13	4	0
		0.5	gross	Cutts	0	0	20	0
		12	gross	Points	0	12	0	0
		1	dozen	Girdles	0	0	18	0
		3	dozen	Purse, Cord	0	2	0	0
		4	dozen	Girdles, Coarse	0	0	16	0
		1	dozen	Cards, Playing	0	0	10	0
		2	dozen	Knives, in Pairs	0	3	4	0
		2	gross	Lacquer	0	3	4	0
		1	dozen	Skins, Golden	0	4	2	0
		4	dozen	Spectacles	0	0	16	0
		6	dozen	Aniseed	0	8	0	0
		1	C	Taps	0	0	10	0
		1	dozen	Potol	0	0	10	0
		1	lb	Pepper	0	0	12	0
		3	pair	Stock-Cards	0	3	0	0
		3	pair	Hand-Cards	0	0	15	0
		2	dozen	Liquorice	0	0	5	0
		1	C	Nails	0	0	10	0

Merchant name	Origin	Qty	Unit	Commodity	£	s.	d.	f.
		1	lb	Thread	0	0	12	2
William Archer	Ind	2	piece	Cloth of Assize, Dozen	0	0	0	0
		6	piece	Cloth of Assize, Dozen Strait	0	0	0	0
		4	lb	Saffron	2	0	0	0
		5.5	lb	Silk, *Worked*	3	13	4	0
		7	gross	Knives	2	6	8	0
		16	gross	Points	0	16	0	0
		1.5	gross	Lacquer	0	2	6	0
		1	dozen	Girdles, Leather	0	0	7	0
		1	dozen	Girdles, Caddis	0	0	18	0
		7	dozen	Knives, in Pairs	0	11	8	0
		1	dozen	Cards, Playing	0	0	10	0
		0.5	dozen	Caps, Night	0	2	0	0
		0.5	dozen	Caps	0	5	0	0
		2	dozen	Rings, copper	0	0	8	0
		4	lb	Liquorice	0	0	4	0
		2	dozen	Aniseed	0	2	8	0
		1	dozen	Skins, Golden	0	4	2	0
		2	clout	Needles	0	2	0	0
		0.5	C	Quadrear	0	0	4	0
		3	pair	Stock-Cards	0	3	0	0
Walter Walshe	Ind	2	piece	Cloth of Assize	0	0	0	0
		6	lb	Silk, *Worked*	4	0	0	0
		2	gross	Knives	0	13	4	0
		4	dozen	Knives, in Pairs	0	6	8	0
		3	lb	Saffron	0	30	0	0
		1	dozen	Cards, Playing	0	0	10	0
		4	pair	Stock-Cards	0	4	0	0
		3	dozen	Girdles	0	2	4	0
		0.5	dozen	Skins, Red	0	0	13	0
		0.5	dozen	Skins, Golden	0	2	1	0
		0.5	dozen	Caps	0	5	0	0
		1	C	Aniseed	0	13	4	0
		0.5	C	Hops	0	5	0	0
		1	dozen	Liquorice	0	2	0	0
		8	gross	Points	0	8	0	0
		1	gross	Lacquer	0	0	20	0
		1	gross	Cutts	0	3	4	0
James Pembroke	Ind	6	lb	Saffron	3	0	0	0
		3	lb	Silk, *Worked*	2	0	0	0
		2	gross	Knives	0	13	4	0
		1	gross	Cutts	0	3	4	0
		3	dozen	Knives, in Pairs	0	5	0	0
		4	lb	Liquorice	0	0	8	0
		0.5	dozen	Caps	0	5	0	0
		0.5	dozen	Caps, Night	0	2	0	0
		2	lb	Pepper	0	2	0	0
		3	dozen	Spectacles	0	0	12	0
		1	dozen	Girdles	0	0	18	0
		0.5	lb	Cloves	0	0	15	0
		0.5	C	Aniseed	0	6	8	0
		8	gross	Points	0	8	0	0

447

Merchant name	Origin	Qty	Unit	Commodity	£	s.	d.	f.
		1	C	Nails	0	0	8	0
		1	dozen	Alum	0	0	16	0
		3	pair	Stock-Cards	0	3	0	0
		1	dozen	Cards, Playing	0	0	10	0
		5	stone	Orchil	0	8	4	0
		4	piece	Cloth of Assize, Dozen Strait	0	0	0	0
		1	piece	Cloth of Assize, Dozen	0	0	0	0
Predictus Pembroke & assoc.	Ind	2	lb	Saffron	0	20	0	0
		2	lb	Silk, *Worked*	0	26	8	0
		8	dozen	Aniseed	0	10	8	0
		1	dozen	Skins, Golden	0	4	2	0
		2	lb	Pepper	0	2	0	0
		5	dozen	Knives, in Pairs	0	8	4	0
		1.5	gross	Knives	0	10	0	0
		0.5	gross	Cutts	0	0	20	0
		2	dozen	Knives, Prage	0	2	0	0
		2	lb	Cumin	0	0	5	0
		4	dozen	Spectacles	0	0	16	0
		2	dozen	Girdles	0	2	4	0
		10	dozen	*Percular*	0	5	0	0
		1	dozen	Combs	0	0	4	0
		6	lb	Liquorice	0	0	10	0
		2.5	dozen	Cards, Playing	0	2	1	0
		8	gross	Points	0	8	0	0
		1.5	gross	Lacquer	0	2	6	0
		0.5	gross	Taps	0	0	4	0
		5	*piece*	Points, Silk	0	6	0	0
		24	yard	Ribbon, Unspecified	0	0	10	0
		2	C	Nails	0	0	16	0
		0.5	dozen	Sulpher	0	0	8	0
		0.25	C	Alum	0	3	4	0
		6	stone	Orchil	0	10	0	0
		1.5	piece	Cloth of Assize, Dozen Strait	0	0	0	0
James Shee	Ind	4	piece	Cloth of Assize, Dozen Strait	0	0	0	0
		0.5	piece	Cloth of Assize	0	0	0	0
		2.5	lb	Saffron	0	25	0	0
		2.5	lb	Silk, *Worked*	0	33	4	0
		1.5	C	Aniseed	0	20	0	0
		2	gross	Knives	0	13	4	0
		1	gross	Cutts	0	3	4	0
		7	gross	Points	0	7	0	0
		6	dozen	Girdles	0	4	0	0
		1	dozen	Girdles, Silk	0	0	20	0
		1	C	Nails	0	0	10	0
		4	dozen	Glasses	0	0	16	0
		1	dozen	Cards, Playing	0	0	10	0
		2	dozen	Knives, in Pairs	0	3	4	0
		2.5	lb	Cinnamon & Cloves & Mace	0	6	3	0
		1	lb	Pepper	0	0	12	0
		3	dozen	*Percular*	0	2	0	0
		1	clout	Needles	0	0	10	0

Merchant name	Origin	Qty	Unit	Commodity	£	s.	d.	f.
		1	lb	Sugar-Candy	0	0	8	0
		1	dozen	Soap	0	0	15	0
		0.5	dozen	Skins, Golden	0	2	1	0
		15	ell	Holland Linen *Cloth*	0	18	0	0
John Roughe	Ind	6	stone	Orchil	0	10	0	0
		0.5	lb	Saffron	0	5	0	0
		1	gross	Knives	0	6	8	0
		1	dozen	Cards, Playing	0	0	10	0
		2	gross	Points	0	2	0	0
		2	piece	Grid Irons	0	0	20	0
		2	piece	Pans, Dripping	0	0	20	0
John Marshal	Ind	8	piece	Cloth of Assize, Dozen Strait	0	0	0	0
		1	piece	Cloth of Assize, Dozen	0	0	0	0
		8	piece	Coifs, Velvet	0	20	0	0
		1	dozen	Caps	0	10	0	0
		0.5	Unknown	Unknown	0	0	0	0
Henry Seyse	Ind	3.5	piece	Cloth of Assize, Dozen Strait	0	0	0	0
		2.5	lb	Saffron	0	25	0	0
		2.5	lb	Silk, *Worked*	0	33	4	0
		1	dozen	Knives, in Pairs	0	0	20	0
		0.25	gross	Knives	0	0	20	0
		2	dozen	Aniseed	0	2	8	0
		2	gross	Points	0	2	0	0
		2	dozen	Combs	0	0	8	0
		0.5	dozen	Skins, Golden	0	2	1	0
		0.5	lb	Cinnamon &Mace	0	0	15	0
		2	pair	Stock-Cards	0	2	0	0
		6	lb	Liquorice	0	0	10	0

The Michaell of Waterford, Robert Ffiztjohn master, Exiting, 1st August 1543

Merchant name	Origin	Qty	Unit	Commodity	£	s.	d.	f.
Nicholas Kett	Ind	2	dozen	Soap	0	2	6	0
		3	pair	Stock-Cards	0	3	0	0
		1	gross	Points	0	0	12	0
Patrick Sall	Ind	2.5	piece	Cloth of Assize	0	0	0	0
		2	lb	Saffron	0	20	0	0
		16	dozen	Knives, in Pairs	0	26	8	0
		3	gross	Knives	0	20	0	0
		1	lb	Cloves	0	2	6	0
		1	lb	Pepper	0	0	12	0
		1	dozen	Skins, Golden	0	4	2	0
		12	gross	Points	0	12	0	0
		3	gross	Lacquer	0	5	0	0
		1	dozen	Liquorice	0	0	10	0
		10	lb	Cumin	0	0	14	0
		0.5	dozen	Caps	0	5	0	0
		6	dozen	Spectacles	0	0	20	0
		4	dozen	Girdles	0	0	8	0
		1	dozen	Girdles, Ribbon	0	0	16	0
		2	dozen	Cards, Playing	0	0	20	0
Thomas Madan	Ind	4	piece	Cloth of Assize, Dozen	0	0	0	0
		3	piece	Cloth of Assize, Dozen Strait	0	0	0	0

Merchant name	Origin	Qty	Unit	Commodity	£	s.	d.	f.
Richard Quenmerford	Ind	12	piece	Cloth of Assize, Dozen Strait	o	o	o	o
		2	piece	Cloth of Assize, Dozen Strait	o	o	o	o
		3	gross	Knives	o	20	o	o
		4	pair	Stock-Cards	o	4	o	o
		5	piece	Caps	o	4	2	o
		3	gross	Points	o	3	o	o
		2	gross	Lacquer	o	3	4	o
		3	bolt	Thread	o	3	o	o
		4	dozen	Cards, Playing	o	3	4	o
		3	lb	Silk, *Worked*	2	o	o	o
		4	lb	Saffron	2	o	o	o
		3	dozen	Soap	o	3	9	o
Richard Waydyng	Ind	0.25	piece	Cloth of Assize	o	o	o	o
		8	piece	Cloth of Assize, Dozen Strait	o	o	o	o
		0.5	C	Aniseed	o	6	8	o
		6	piece	Caps	o	5	o	o
		1	gross	Knives	o	6	8	o
		2	gross	Lacquer	o	3	4	o
		6	gross	Points	o	6	o	o
		1	dozen	Liquorice	o	o	10	o
		2	lb	Saffron	o	20	o	o
William Donohow	Ind	6	piece	Cloth of Assize, Dozen Strait	o	o	o	o
		4	lb	Saffron	2	o	o	o
		36	gross	Points	o	20	o	o
		5.5	lb	Silk, *Worked*	3	13	4	o
		3	gross	Lacquer	o	5	o	o
		0.75	C	Aniseed	o	10	o	o
		10	gross	Points	o	10	o	o
		0.5	C	Hops	o	5	o	o
Benedict Sall	Ind	2	piece	Cloth of Assize	o	o	o	o
		6	piece	Caps	o	5	o	o
		2	bolt	Thread	o	2	o	o
		1	gross	Knives	o	6	8	o
		2	lb	Saffron	o	20	o	o
		2	lb	Silk, *Worked*	o	26	8	o
		2	gross	Lacquer	o	3	4	o
James Bray	Ind	1	lb	Saffron	o	10	o	o
		1	lb	Silk, *Worked*	o	13	4	o
		3	gross	Knives	o	20	o	o
		3	dozen	Aniseed	o	4	o	o
John Murthy	Ind	3.5	piece	Cloth of Assize, Dozen Strait	o	o	o	o
		1.5	lb	Saffron	o	15	o	o
		2	gross	Knives	o	13	4	o
		1	bolt	Thread	o	o	12	o
		8	dozen	Purses	o	2	8	o
		8	dozen	Combs	o	o	16	o
		0.25	C	Aniseed	o	3	4	o
		4	dozen	Knives, in Pairs	o	6	8	o
		1	dozen	Skins, Red	o	2	1	o
		1	dozen	Caps, Night	o	4	o	o
		0.5	lb	Cinnamon	o	o	15	o
		3	lb	Liquorice	o	o	6	o

Merchant name	Origin	Qty	Unit	Commodity	£	s.	d.	f.
		4	gross	Lacquer	0	6	8	0
		4	gross	Points	0	4	0	0
		0.5	C	Hops	0	5	0	0
		1	dozen	Cards, Playing	0	0	10	0
Francis Felond	Ind	6.5	piece	Cloth of Assize, Dozen Strait	0	0	0	0
		1	lb	Silk, *Worked*	0	13	4	0
		6	dozen	Aniseed	0	8	0	0
		1.5	dozen	Skins, Golden	0	6	3	0
		1	dozen	Skins, Red	0	2	1	0
		2	gross	Knives	0	13	4	0
		5	gross	Lacquer	0	8	4	0
		7	dozen	Knives, in Pairs	0	11	8	0
		7	gross	Points	0	7	0	0
		12	dozen	Girdles	0	4	0	0
		1.5	lb	Thread	0	0	12	0
		3	lb	Liquorice	0	0	4	0
		4	dozen	Combs	0	0	6	0
		1	C	Hops	0	10	0	0
		1	lb	Saffron	0	10	0	0
		3	dozen	Spectacles	0	0	6	0
		4	dozen	*Percular*	0	0	5	0
		10	ell	Linen *Cloth*	0	10	0	0
		1	dozen	Cards, Playing	0	0	10	0
John Dony	Ind	5	lb	Silk, *Worked*	3	6	8	0
		3.5	lb	Saffron	0	35	0	0
		1.75	gross	Knives	0	11	8	0
		3	dozen	Knives, in Pairs	0	5	0	0
		6	gross	Points	0	6	0	0
		2	gross	Lacquer	0	3	4	0
		1	C	Aniseed	0	13	4	0
		0.25	C	Hops	0	2	6	0
		1	lb	Verdigris	0	0	5	0
Christopher Tyrry	Ind	14	C	Flax	14	0	0	0
		28	lb	Saffron	14	0	0	0
		4	lb	Silk, *Worked*	2	13	4	0
		4	dozen	Cards, Wool	0	16	0	0
		0.5	dozen	Skins, Golden	0	2	1	0
		0.5	dozen	Caps	0	5	0	0
		2	dozen	Cards, Playing	0	0	20	0
		6	gross	Points	0	6	0	0
		0.5	C	Aniseed	0	6	8	0
		4	piece	Cloth of Assize	0	0	0	0
Richard Donell	Ind	6.888	piece	Cloth of Assize	0	0	0	0
		4	lb	Silk, *Worked*	2	13	4	0
		4	lb	Saffron	2	0	0	0
		2	C	Hops	0	20	0	0
		0.75	C	Aniseed	0	10	0	0
		2	gross	Knives	0	13	4	0
		2	gross	Cutts	0	6	8	0
		3	dozen	Knives, in Pairs	0	5	0	0
		4	gross	Lacquer	0	6	8	0
		8	gross	Points	0	8	0	0

Merchant name	Origin	Qty	Unit	Commodity	£	s.	d.	f.
		2	dozen	Skins, Golden	0	8	4	0
		1	dozen	Skins, Red	0	2	1	0
		2	dozen	Combs	0	0	12	0

The Sunday of Waterford, Thomas Whelond master, Exiting, 1st August 1543

Merchant name	Origin	Qty	Unit	Commodity	£	s.	d.	f.
Patrick Roche	Ind	4.5	piece	Cloth of Assize	0	0	0	0
		5	lb	Saffron	2	10	0	0
		9.5	lb	Silk, *Worked*	6	6	8	0
		5	lb	Pepper	0	5	0	0
		1.5	lb	Senna	0	0	12	0
		2	dozen	Cards, Playing	0	0	20	0
		10	piece	Caps	0	8	4	0
		1	dozen	Ribbons, Caddis	0	0	18	0
		8	gross	Points	0	8	0	0
		5	dozen	Penners	0	5	0	0
		0.5	lb	Cinnamon	0	0	15	0
		0.5	C	Aniseed	0	6	8	0
		1	gross	Knives	0	6	8	0
Andrew Lincolne	Ind	7	piece	Cloth of Assize, Dozen Strait	0	0	0	0
		3	piece	Cloth of Assize, Dozen	0	0	0	0
		16	gross	Points	0	16	0	0
		1	C	Aniseed	0	13	4	0
		1	lb	Saffron	0	10	0	0
		1	lb	Silk, *Worked*	0	13	4	0
		1	lb	Cloves	0	2	6	0
		3	gross	Knives	0	20	0	0
		1.5	lb	Cinnamon	0	3	9	0
		2	gross	Lacquer	0	3	4	0
Patrick Strange	Ind	2.5	C	Aniseed	0	33	4	0
		3	gross	Points	0	3	0	0
		2	dozen	Soap	0	2	6	0
		0.5	gross	Knives	0	3	4	0
John Selynger	Ind	1	gross	Knives	0	6	8	0
		18	gross	Points	0	18	0	0
		4	C	Lead, Worked	0	20	0	0
James Lunbart	Ind	1	C	Aniseed	0	13	4	0
		1.5	gross	Knives	0	10	0	0
		5	gross	Points	0	5	0	0
		4	gross	Lacquer	0	6	8	0
		1	lb	Silk, *Worked*	0	13	4	0
		0.417	piece	Cloth of Assize	0	0	0	0
		4	piece	Cloth of Assize, Dozen Strait	0	0	0	0
Robert Maughan	Ind	1.5	piece	Cloth of Assize	0	0	0	0
		0.5	C	Alum	0	6	8	0
		2	C	Aniseed	0	26	8	0
		12	gross	Points	0	12	0	0
		2	gross	Knives	0	13	4	0
		2	dozen	Skins, Golden	0	8	4	0
		3	lb	Pepper	0	3	0	0
		5	dozen	Girdles, Caddis	0	5	10	0
		1	dozen	Caps	0	10	0	0

Merchant name	Origin	Qty	Unit	Commodity	£	s.	d.	f.
Nicholas Harold	Ind	5.25	piece	Cloth of Assize	o	o	o	o
		5	gross	Knives	1	13	4	o
		4	dozen	Skins, Golden	o	16	8	o
		0.5	dozen	Skins, Red	o	o	13	o
		1	lb	Nutmeg	o	o	16	o
		4	lb	Verdigris	o	o	20	o
		12	gross	Points	o	12	o	o
		6	lb	Saffron	3	o	o	o
		3	lb	Silk, *Worked*	2	o	o	o
		2	C	Aniseed	o	26	8	o
Roland Creangh	Ind	4	piece	Cloth of Assize, Dozen Strait	o	o	o	o
		2	gross	Knives	o	13	4	o
		3	dozen	Skins, Golden	o	12	6	o
		2	dozen	Girdles, Caddis	o	2	4	o
		6	gross	Points	o	6	o	o
		2	lb	Pepper	o	2	o	o
		1	C	Aniseed	o	13	4	o
Roland Harold	Ind	11.25	piece	Cloth of Assize	o	o	o	o
		4	dozen	Skins, Golden	o	16	8	o
		8	lb	Pepper	o	8	o	o
		4	dozen	Girdles, Caddis	o	4	8	o
		7	lb	Cloves	o	17	6	o
		1	lb	Ginger	o	o	18	o
		8	gross	Knives	2	13	4	o
		2.5	gross	Cutts	o	8	4	o
		24	gross	Points	o	24	o	o
		2	gross	Lacquer	o	3	4	o
		2	lb	Cinnamon	o	5	o	o
		6	lb	Saffron	3	o	o	o
		3	lb	Silk, *Worked*	2	o	o	o
		4	C	Aniseed	2	13	4	o

The Patryck of Cork, Patrick Ponnche master, Entering, *2nd August 1543*

Merchant name	Origin	Qty	Unit	Commodity	£	s.	d.	f.
Richard Fytzjames	Ind	6	C	Skins, Lamb	2	o	o	o
		2.75	C	Skins, Sheep	o	27	6	o
		9	stone	Wool, Flocks	o	3	9	o
		0.5	dicker	Skins, Deer	o	o	12	o
		7	piece	Skins, Marten	o	7	o	o
William Chest*er*	Ind	2.5	piece	Cloth of Assize	o	o	o	o
		1	gross	Knives	o	6	8	o
		4	gross	Points	o	4	o	o
		2	dozen	Skins, Golden	o	8	4	o
		0.5	C	Aniseed	o	6	8	o

The Dowghan of Cardiff, David Watkyns master, Entering, 8th August 1543

Merchant name	Origin	Qty	Unit	Commodity	£	s.	d.	f.
Peter Cowp*er*	Ind	1	pipe	Wine	o	o	o	o

The George of Hasfield, William Prydie master, Exiting, *8th August 1543*

Merchant name	Origin	Qty	Unit	Commodity	£	s.	d.	f.
William Appowell	Ind	1	tun	Wine, Corrupt	o	30	o	o

Merchant name	Origin	Qty	Unit	Commodity	£	s.	d.	f.
Unknown [ ] antwell	Ind	3	lb	Saffron	0	30	0	0
		3	lb	Silk, *Worked*	2	0	0	0
		1.666	dozen	Skins, Golden	0	7	0	0
		3	dozen	Girdles, Caddis	0	4	0	0
		10	dozen	Knives, in Pairs	0	16	8	0
		2	lb	Thread	0	0	10	0
		9	lb	Cloves	0	22	6	0
		1.5	dozen	Cumin	0	2	0	0
		1	C	Aniseed	0	13	4	0
		1	lb	Verdigris	0	0	5	0
		12	gross	Points	0	12	0	0
		2	gross	Lacquer	0	3	4	0
		1	gross	Knives	0	6	8	0
		2	dozen	Cards, Playing	0	0	20	0
		1	dozen	Cups	0	0	8	0
Unknown She	Ind	1	piece	Cloth of Assize	0	0	0	0
William Aly*n*	Ind	2	piece	Cloth of Assize	0	0	0	0
		2	lb	Saffron	0	20	0	0
		8	lb	Silk, *Worked*	5	6	8	0

The Michaell of Bristol, Maurice Welshe master, Exiting, 10th August 1543

Merchant name	Origin	Qty	Unit	Commodity	£	s.	d.	f.
William Appowell	Ind	3	tun	Wine, Corrupt	4	10	0	0
		2	dozen	Skins, Golden	0	8	4	0
		2	lb	Saffron	0	20	0	0
		1	C	Aniseed	0	13	4	0
		6.75	piece	Cloth of Assize	0	0	0	0
John Cappes	Ind	2	tun	Wine, Corrupt	3	0	0	0
		3	gross	Points	0	3	0	0
		0.5	gross	Knives	0	3	4	0
		6	piece	Cloth of Assize	0	0	0	0

The Mary of Tenby, Richard White master, Entering, 15th August 1543

Merchant name	Origin	Qty	Unit	Commodity	£	s.	d.	f.
Patrick Clynche	Ind	10	C	Irish Linen *Cloth*	5	0	0	0
		24	piece	Mantles	2	0	0	0
		4	piece	Mantles	0	13	4	0

The Trynite of Caerleon, Richard White master, Entering, 28th August 1543

Merchant name	Origin	Qty	Unit	Commodity	£	s.	d.	f.
William Benet	Ind	1	hogshead	Fish, Salmon	0	26	8	0

The Trinite Palard, Port Unknown, John Roche master, Exiting, *28th August 1543*

Merchant name	Origin	Qty	Unit	Commodity	£	s.	d.	f.
Richard Ffyztjames	Ind	5.5	dozen	Cards, Wool	0	22	0	0
		3.5	dozen	Flax	0	7	0	0
		1	gross	Knives	0	6	8	0
		0.5	gross	Cutts	0	0	20	0
		10	gross	Points	0	10	0	0
		2	C	Aniseed	0	26	8	0

Merchant name	Origin	Qty	Unit	Commodity	£	s.	d.	f.

The Trynite Pole of Gloucester, David Adams master, Entering, 31st August 1543

Merchant name	Origin	Qty	Unit	Commodity	£	s.	d.	f.
Robert Pole	Ind	16	C	Fish, Hake	8	0	0	0
		2	hogshead	Fish, Salmon	2	13	4	0

The Saviour of Bristol, Robert Brewys master, Entering, *31st August 1543*

Merchant name	Origin	Qty	Unit	Commodity	£	s.	d.	f.
William Sprat	Ind	5	hogshead	Fish, Salmon	6	13	4	0

The Mary George of Newport, Germain Saunders master, Exiting, 5th September 1543

Merchant name	Origin	Qty	Unit	Commodity	£	s.	d.	f.
Thomas Buttre	Ind	20	ton	Salt	10	0	0	0

The Sent John of Errenteria, Michael de Arasavlo master, Entering, 13th September 1543

Merchant name	Origin	Qty	Unit	Commodity	£	s.	d.	f.
Nicholas Thorn	Ind	12.25	tun	Wine	0	0	0	0
		10	ton	Iron	25	0	0	0
		2	tun	Wine, Corrupt	3	0	0	0
Michael *de Arasavlo* & assoc.	Alien	32.062	ton	Iron	80	3	1	2
		35.5	balette	Woad	20	17	6	0
		14	dozen	Serches	2	18	4	0
John Wells & White	Ind	13.5	ton	Iron	33	15	0	0
		1	hogshead	Wine	0	0	0	0

The Trynite Pole of Gloucester, David Adams master, Exiting, *13th September 1543*

Merchant name	Origin	Qty	Unit	Commodity	£	s.	d.	f.
Robert Pole	Ind	2	piece	Cloth of Assize	0	0	0	0

The James of Milford Haven, William Philyps master, Entering, *13th September 1543*

Merchant name	Origin	Qty	Unit	Commodity	£	s.	d.	f.
Peter Ffiztharry	Ind	7	C	Check *Cloth*	14	0	0	0
		5	C	Skins, Sheep	2	10	0	0
		4.75	C	Skins, Lamb	0	31	8	0
		2	dicker	Skins, Deer	0	4	2	0
		1	piece	Mantles	0	3	4	0
		2	stone	Wool, Flocks	0	0	10	0
Tibald Blake	Ind	7.5	C	Check *Cloth*	15	0	0	0
		2	C	Skins, Sheep	0	20	0	0
		3	dicker	Skins, Deer	0	6	3	0
		12	piece	Skins, Fox	0	2	0	0
		4	C	Skins, Lamb	0	26	8	0
Peter Bray & Flemyng	Ind	4	C	Check *Cloth*	8	0	0	0
		1	C	Skins, Lamb	0	6	8	0
		1	C	Skins, Sheep	0	10	0	0
		5	stone	Wool, Flocks	0	2	1	0

The Sent John of Errenteria, Michael de Arasavlo master, Exiting, 18th September 1543

Merchant name	Origin	Qty	Unit	Commodity	£	s.	d.	f.
Christine White Michael *de Arasavlo*	Ind	5	ton	Lead, Worked	25	0	0	0

Merchant name	Origin	Qty	Unit	Commodity	£	s.	d.	f.
& assoc.	Alien	22	dicker	Hides, Tanned	22	0	0	0
		20	piece	Cloth of Assize	0	0	0	0
Thomas Harris	Ind	4	piece	Bristol Frieze *Cloth*	2	13	4	0
		16	piece	Manchester Cotton *Cloth*	8	0	0	0
Thomas Tyson	Ind	5	ton	Lead, Worked	25	0	0	0
John Wells	Ind	60	dozen	Skins, Calf	10	0	0	0

1545/46

TNA E122/21/15 is an annual 'particular' customs account of controlment of customs and subsidies by John Wyke. It is written on a 'roll' in contrast to the other 1540s accounts, which are books. It contains the same level of detail.

Merchant name	Origin	Qty	Unit	Commodity	£	s.	d.	f.

The Nicholas of Orio, Domingo de Segura master, Entering, 28th September 1545

Merchant name	Origin	Qty	Unit	Commodity	£	s.	d.	f.
James Boyse & assoc.	Ind	12	C	Canvas *Cloth*	16	0	0	0
		8	*piece*	Poldavis *Cloth*	4	0	0	0
		6	ream	Paper	0	10	0	0

The Nicholas of Orio, Domingo de Segura master, Exiting, 6th October 1545

Merchant name	Origin	Qty	Unit	Commodity	£	s.	d.	f.
Martin Perys	Alien	10	dicker	Hides, Tanned	0	0	0	0
		10	piece	Cloth of Assize	0	0	0	0
John de Agnyrry	Alien	12	ton	Lead, Worked	60	0	0	0
		50	dozen	Skins, Calf	8	6	8	0
		2	piece	Bristol Frieze Cloth	0	26	8	0
		14	piece	Cloth of Assize	0	0	0	0
Martin de Sobeta	Alien	10	piece	Cloth of Assize	0	0	0	0
Christina Whyte	Ind	130	dozen	Skins, Calf	21	13	4	0
Domingo de Segura	Alien	80	piece	Manchester Cotton *Cloth*	40	0	0	0
		4.2	dicker	Hides, Tanned	0	0	0	0
		10	piece	Cloth of Assize	0	0	0	0
Christopher Valencia	Alien	5	piece	Cloth of Assize	0	0	0	0
Giles Whyte	Ind	20	piece	Northern Cotton *Cloth*	4	3	4	0
Francis de Mutela	Alien	17	piece	Cloth of Assize	0	0	0	0
Alonso de Castanetha	Alien	5	dicker	Hides, Tanned	0	0	0	0
		10	ton	Lead, Worked	50	0	0	0
Anthony Pivaras	Alien	23	piece	Cloth of Assize	0	0	0	0

The John of Errenteria, John de Beroby master, Exiting, *6th October 1545*

Merchant name	Origin	Qty	Unit	Commodity	£	s.	d.	f.
John de Agnyrry	Alien	12	ton	Lead, Worked	60	0	0	0
		35	dozen	Skins, Calf	5	16	8	0
John de Doda	Alien	12.75	piece	Cloth of Assize	0	0	0	0
		2	piece	Dunster *Cloth*	0	20	0	0
		80	piece	Manchester Cotton *Cloth*	40	0	0	0
		20	piece	Northern Cotton *Cloth*	4	3	4	0
		2.75	piece	Cloth of Assize	0	0	0	0
Martin de Sobeta	Alien	5	piece	Cloth of Assize	0	0	0	0
William Cary	Ind	117	dozen	Skins, Calf	17	16	8	0
		8	piece	Cloth of Assize	0	0	0	0

Merchant name	Origin	Qty	Unit	Commodity	£	s.	d.	f.
Laurence de Irauso	Alien	30	dozen	Skins, Sheep Worked	0	30	0	0
Peter de Alsata	Alien	15	dicker	Hides, Tanned	0	0	0	0
Edmund Jones	Ind	4	dicker	Hides, Tanned	0	0	0	0
John *de Beroby*	Alien	40	dozen	Skins, Calf	6	13	4	0
Richard Cary	Ind	8	piece	Welsh *Cloth*	8	0	0	0
Anthony Guaras	Alien	22	piece	Cloth of Assize	0	0	0	0

The Seynte Sebastian, Anthony Martinus master, Exiting, 9th October 1545

Merchant name	Origin	Qty	Unit	Commodity	£	s.	d.	f.
Anthony Guydoll	Alien	80.25	piece	Cloth of Assize	0	0	0	0
		17	ton	Lead, Worked	85	0	0	0
		35	piece	Manchester Cotton *Cloth*	17	10	0	0
		97	fother	Lead	0	0	0	0
Peter Carvailo & assoc.	Alien	106	piece	Cloth of Assize	0	0	0	0
		19	piece	Bristol Frieze Cloth	12	13	4	0
		40	dozen	Skins, Calf	6	13	4	0
Peter Gonsalo	Alien	3	ton	Lead, Worked	15	0	0	0
		2	piece	Bristol Frieze Cloth	0	26	8	0
		30	dozen	Skins, Calf	5	0	0	0
		74.416	piece	Cloth of Assize	0	0	0	0
		5.5	dicker	Hides, Tanned	0	0	0	0
Anthony Martinus	Alien	28	piece	Cloth of Assize	0	0	0	0
John Gerald	Alien	21.66	piece	Cloth of Assize	0	0	0	0
		46	piece	Manchester Cotton *Cloth*	23	0	0	0
		480	ell	Canvas *Cloth*	6	0	0	0
		1	bag	Feathers	0	13	4	0
		4	piece	Manchester Cotton *Cloth*	2	0	0	0
Peter Redrygus	Alien	13.5	piece	Cloth of Assize	0	0	0	0
Roderigo Janus	Alien	20	piece	Cloth of Assize	0	0	0	0
Manseo Cavalero	Alien	45	piece	Manchester Cotton *Cloth*	22	10	0	0

The Jhesus of Portugal, Gonsalo Dees master, Exiting, *9th October 1545*

Merchant name	Origin	Qty	Unit	Commodity	£	s.	d.	f.
Anthony Guydoll	Alien	29.75	ton	Lead, Worked	148	15	0	0
		35	piece	Manchester Cotton *Cloth*	17	10	0	0
		100.166	piece	Cloth of Assize	0	0	0	0
		97	fother	Lead	0	0	0	0
Peter Carvaylo	Alien	104.5	piece	Cloth of Assize	0	0	0	0
		19	piece	Bristol Frieze Cloth	12	13	4	0
Peter Piloll & assoc.	Alien	24	C	Lead, Worked	6	0	0	0
Peter Gonsalo	Alien	3	ton	Lead, Worked	15	0	0	0
		73	piece	Cloth of Assize	0	0	0	0
Gonsalo Dees	Alien	22	piece	Cloth of Assize	0	0	0	0
John Gerald	Alien	22.33	piece	Cloth of Assize	0	0	0	0
		23	piece	Manchester Cotton *Cloth*	11	10	0	0
John Robello	Alien	22	piece	Cloth of Assize	0	0	0	0
		9	piece	Welsh *Cloth*	9	0	0	0
		1	ton	Lead, Worked	5	0	0	0
Roderigo Janus	Alien	10	piece	Cloth of Assize	0	0	0	0
James Chester	Ind	4	unknown	Mees, brode	4	0	0	0
Manseo Cavalero	Alien	10	C	Tin, Worked	15	0	0	0

Merchant name	Origin	Qty	Unit	Commodity	£	s.	d.	f.
The Mary Norton, *Port Unknown*, David Adams master, Entering, 10th October 1545								
Richard Baynam	Ind	2	ton	Salt	0	20	0	0
The Margaret of Chepstow, John Pycher master, Entering, 14th October 1545								
Thomas Payne	Ind	1	ton	Salt	0	10	0	0
The *Christ*ofer of Chepstow, John Jeynes master, Entering, *14th October 1545*								
Robert Butlar	Ind	6	ton	Salt	3	0	0	0
The Trynyte of Chepstow, Lewis Haynes master, Entering, 15th October 1545								
William Butlar	Ind	5	ton	Salt	2	10	0	0
The Mychael of Chepstow, Roger Mower master, Entering, *15th October 1545*								
Robert Butlar	Ind	3	ton	Salt	0	30	0	0
The Margaret of Chepstow, John Jeynes master, Entering, 16th October 1545								
Robert Butlar	Ind	4	ton	Salt	2	0	0	0
The Sancta Maria of Pasajes de San Juan, Domingo de Areaga master, Entering, 20th October 1545								
William Yonge & assoc.	Ind	42	tun	Wine	0	0	0	0
		3	hogshead	Wine, Corrupt	0	22	6	0
Sebastian Sansowste	Alien	8	C	Rosin	0	10	8	0
The George of Waterford, Maurice Power master, Entering, 22nd October 1545								
James Welshe	Ind	17	C	Check *Cloth*	34	0	0	0
		22	piece	Mantles	3	13	4	0
		9	C	Skins, Sheep	4	10	0	0
		9.5	C	Skins, Lamb	3	3	4	0
		24	piece	Skins, Fox	0	4	0	0
		10	stone	Wool, Flocks	0	4	2	0
Patrick Sall & assoc.	Ind	12	C	Check *Cloth*	24	0	0	0
		9	C	Skins, Sheep	4	10	0	0
		10	piece	Mantles	0	33	4	0
Richard Hosman	Ind	7	C	Check *Cloth*	14	0	0	0
Nicholas Flaghe	Ind	5	C	Check *Cloth*	10	0	0	0
		20	piece	Mantles	3	6	8	0
		1	C	Skins, Lamb	0	6	8	0
		6	piece	Skins, Deer	0	0	12	0
Edmund Grawnte	Ind	3	C	Check *Cloth*	6	0	0	0
		20	piece	Mantles	3	6	8	0
		1	C	Skins, Lamb	0	6	8	0
		0.5	C	Skins, Sheep	0	5	0	0

Merchant name	Origin	Qty	Unit	Commodity	£	s.	d.	f.
		6	piece	Skins, Deer	0	2	0	0
Nicholas Kett	Ind	5	C	Check *Cloth*	10	0	0	0
		16	piece	Mantles	0	53	4	0
		30	piece	Skins, Sheep	0	2	6	0
Richard Creaghe	Ind	4	C	Check *Cloth*	8	0	0	0
		16	C	Skins, Sheep	8	0	0	0
		1	C	Skins, Lamb	0	6	8	0
		6	piece	Skins, Fox	0	0	12	0
		6	piece	Skins, Deer	0	2	0	0
Edmund Clery	Ind	3.5	C	Check *Cloth*	7	0	0	0
		20	piece	Mantles	3	6	8	0
Nicholas Brewar	Ind	2	C	Check *Cloth*	4	0	0	0
		15	piece	Mantles	2	10	0	0
		0.5	C	Skins, Lamb	0	3	4	0
John Qued & Bruer	Ind	36	piece	Mantles	6	0	0	0
		40	yard	Check *Cloth*	0	13	4	0
Walter Flemynge & assoc.	Ind	7	C	Check *Cloth*	14	0	0	0
		6	C	Skins, Sheep	3	0	0	0
		0.5	C	Skins, Lamb	0	3	4	0
		6	piece	Skins, Fox	0	0	12	0
Thomas Bray & assoc.	Ind	11	C	Check *Cloth*	22	0	0	0
		45	piece	Mantles	7	10	0	0
		6	C	Skins, Sheep	3	0	0	0
		0.5	C	Skins, Lamb	0	3	4	0
		6	piece	Skins, Fox	0	0	12	0
Patrick Maydan	Ind	4	C	Check *Cloth*	8	0	0	0
		40	piece	Mantles	6	13	4	0
		20	piece	Skins, Sheep	0	0	20	0
Thomas Stackpoll	Ind	6.5	C	Irish Linen *Cloth*	3	5	0	0
		2	C	Skins, Sheep	0	20	0	0
		1	C	Check *Cloth*	2	0	0	0
		4	piece	Skins, Marten	0	4	0	0
		12	piece	Skins, Fox	0	2	0	0
		5	piece	Mantles	0	16	8	0
Robert Arther	Ind	1.5	C	Check *Cloth*	3	0	0	0
		1	C	Skins, Sheep	0	10	0	0
		5	piece	Skins, Fox	0	0	10	0
		3	dozen	Skins, Lamb	0	0	20	0
John Brewar	Ind	2	C	Check *Cloth*	4	0	0	0
		2	piece	Mantles	0	6	8	0

The Sonday of Waterford, Robert Medoll master, Entering, *22nd October 1545*

Merchant name	Origin	Qty	Unit	Commodity	£	s.	d.	f.
Peter Fytzjohn	Ind	4	last	Fish, Herring White	12	0	0	0

The Trynyte George of Bristol, John Jeynes master, Entering, *22nd October 1545*

Merchant name	Origin	Qty	Unit	Commodity	£	s.	d.	f.
William Appowell & assoc.	Ind	12.5	last	Fish, Herring White	37	10	0	0
		2	C	Skins, Lamb	0	6	8	0

Merchant name	Origin	Qty	Unit	Commodity	£	s.	d.	f.

The Bryde of Waterford, Edmund Medoll master, Entering, 23rd October 1545

Merchant name	Origin	Qty	Unit	Commodity	£	s.	d.	f.
Robert Butlar & assoc.	Ind	6	C	Check *Cloth*	12	0	0	0
		9	C	Skins, Sheep	4	10	0	0
		24	piece	Mantles	4	0	0	0
		1	C	Skins, Lamb	0	6	8	0
James Wale & assoc.	Ind	8	C	Check *Cloth*	16	0	0	0
		2	C	Skins, Lamb	0	13	4	0
		2	piece	Mantles	0	6	8	0
Peter Welshe & assoc.	Ind	2	C	Check *Cloth*	4	0	0	0
		6	piece	Mantles	0	20	0	0
		7	C	Skins, Sheep	3	10	0	0
		2	C	Skins, Lamb	0	13	4	0
Thomas Vyne & assoc.	Ind	11.1	C	Skins, Sheep	5	11	0	0
		21	piece	Mantles	3	10	0	0
		6.25	C	Check *Cloth*	13	10	0	0
		8	C	Skins, Lamb	2	13	4	0
		3	stone	Wool, Flocks	0	0	15	0
Thomas Rothe & assoc.	Ind	20	C	Check *Cloth*	40	0	0	0
		18.5	C	Skins, Sheep	9	5	0	0
		3	C	Skins, Lamb	0	20	0	0
		4	piece	Skins, Deer	0	0	16	0
		6	piece	Skins, Fox	0	0	12	0
David Savage & assoc.	Ind	27.75	C	Skins, Sheep	13	17	6	0
		13.25	C	Check *Cloth*	26	10	0	0
		1	C	Skins, Kid	0	5	0	0
		1	piece	Mantles	0	3	4	0
		2.75	C	Skins, Lamb	0	18	4	0
		8	C	Irish Linen *Cloth*	4	0	0	0
		16	piece	Skins, Fox	0	2	8	0
		1.8	dicker	Skins, Deer	0	6	0	0

The George of Waterford, Nicholas Rownam master, Entering, *23rd October 1545*

Merchant name	Origin	Qty	Unit	Commodity	£	s.	d.	f.
Thomas Routh	Ind	4	dicker	Skins, Deer	0	13	4	0
		3	C	Check *Cloth*	6	0	0	0
		8	piece	Mantles	0	26	8	0
Nicholas Ley & assoc.	Ind	8.16	C	Check *Cloth*	16	6	8	0
		1	piece	Mantles	0	3	4	0
		0.5	C	Skins, Sheep	0	5	0	0
Oliver Stretche	Ind	2.5	C	Skins, Lamb	0	16	8	0
		6	C	Skins, Sheep	3	0	0	0
		2	C	Check *Cloth*	4	0	0	0
		6	piece	Skins, Marten	0	6	0	0
		8	piece	Skins, Otter	0	3	4	0
		5	piece	Skins, Deer	0	0	20	0
		80	yard	Irish Linen *Cloth*	0	6	8	0
Redmond Wale & assoc.	Ind	5	C	Check *Cloth*	10	0	0	0
		0.5	C	Skins, Sheep	0	5	0	0
		12	piece	Mantles	2	0	0	0

Merchant name	Origin	Qty	Unit	Commodity	£	s.	d.	f.
Oliver Roche & assoc.	Ind	2.16	C	Check *Cloth*	4	6	8	0
		20	piece	Skins, Sheep	0	0	20	0
		2	piece	Mantles	0	6	8	0
		4	C	Fish, Hake	0	40	0	0
John Turn*er*	Ind	1	unknown	Items, miscellaneous	16	0	0	0
Andrew Lyncoll*n*	Ind	2	C	Check *Cloth*	4	0	0	0
		3	C	Skins, Sheep	0	30	0	0
		30	piece	Mantles	5	0	0	0
		1	stone	Wool, Flocks	0	0	5	0
Walter Gromwell	Ind	1	C	Skins, Sheep	0	10	0	0
		3	C	Skins, Lamb	0	20	0	0
		6	piece	Skins, Fox	0	0	18	0
		0.5	C	Check *Cloth*	0	20	0	0
John Coke & assoc.	Ind	5.5	C	Skins, Sheep	2	15	0	0
		32	piece	Mantles	5	6	8	0
		6	C	Irish Linen *Cloth*	3	0	0	0
		7.16	C	Check *Cloth*	14	6	8	0
		4	C	Skins, Lamb	0	26	8	0

The Trynyte George, John Jeynes master, Exiting, 26th October 1545

Merchant name	Origin	Qty	Unit	Commodity	£	s.	d.	f.
Jeremy Sene & Worley	Ind	3	ton	Iron	12	0	0	0
		8	pair	Millstones	8	0	0	0
Nicholas Thorn & assoc.	Ind	2.5	ton	Iron	10	0	0	0
		1	tun	Wine, Corrupt	0	30	0	0
		4	C	Aniseed	0	53	4	0
		2	C	Rosin	0	2	8	0

The Nicholas of Tewkesbury, John Butlar master, Entering, 29th October 1545

Merchant name	Origin	Qty	Unit	Commodity	£	s.	d.	f.
John *Butlar*	Ind	51	barrel	Fish, Herring White	12	15	0	0

The Katheryn of Milford Haven, Peter Bollock master, Entering, *29th October 1545*

Merchant name	Origin	Qty	Unit	Commodity	£	s.	d.	f.
Henry Sameford & assoc.	Ind	64	barrel	Fish, Herring White	16	0	0	0

The Sonday of Waterford, Robert Medoll master, Exiting, 4th November 1545

Merchant name	Origin	Qty	Unit	Commodity	£	s.	d.	f.
Peter Fytzjohn	Ind	3	C	Hops	0	30	0	0
		3	C	Aniseed	0	40	0	0
		4	lb	Saffron	2	0	0	0
		1.25	piece	Cloth of Assize	0	0	0	0
Thomas Stackpoll	Ind	2	piece	Cloth of Assize	0	0	0	0
		1	lb	Silk, *Worked*	0	13	4	0
		16	lb	Saffron	8	0	0	0
		12	dozen	Skins, Golden	2	10	0	0
		1	dozen	Inkhorns	0	0	10	0
		2	bolt	Thread	0	2	2	0
		5	dozen	Cards, Playing	0	6	3	0
		6	dozen	*Stecull*	0	3	0	0

Merchant name	Origin	Qty	Unit	Commodity	£	s.	d.	f.
		1	dozen	Knives, in Pairs	0	0	20	0
		0.5	dozen	Books, Primers	0	0	6	0
		6	lb	Verdigris	0	2	6	0
		0.5	lb	Cinnamon	0	0	15	0
Robert Arther	Ind	2.25	piece	Cloth of Assize	0	0	0	0
		4	dozen	Skins, Golden	0	16	8	0
		4	lb	Silk, *Worked*	2	13	4	0
		2	dozen	Cards, Playing	0	2	6	0
		3	dozen	Glasses	0	0	9	0
		2	bolt	Thread	0	2	2	0
		2	dozen	Knives, in Pairs	0	3	4	0
		4	dozen	Girdles	0	6	0	0
		18	gross	Points	0	18	0	0
		10	lb	Saffron	5	0	0	0

The Mary of Gloucester, John Yonge master, Entering, 5th November 1545

Merchant name	Origin	Qty	Unit	Commodity	£	s.	d.	f.
Thomas Payne	Ind	8	ton	Salt	4	0	0	0

The Mary Nashe of Milford Haven, Thomas Ynon master, Entering, 6th November 1545

Merchant name	Origin	Qty	Unit	Commodity	£	s.	d.	f.
John Jeynes & assoc.	Ind	43	barrel	Fish, Herring White	10	15	0	0
		9	pipe	Fish, Salmon	13	10	0	0

The George Butlar of Waterford, Nicholas Rownam master, Exiting, *6th November 1545*

Merchant name	Origin	Qty	Unit	Commodity	£	s.	d.	f.
Paul Butlar	Ind	2	lb	Saffron	0	20	0	0
		0.5	C	Hops	0	5	0	0
Nicholas Devyshe	Ind	5	lb	Saffron	2	10	0	0
		4	dozen	Knives, in Pairs	0	6	8	0
		1	dozen	Caps	0	10	0	0
		0.5	C	Hops	0	5	0	0
		2.5	lb	Silk, *Worked*	0	33	4	0
		4	gross	Points	0	4	0	0
		1	gross	Lacquer	0	0	20	0
		2	pair	Stock-Cards	0	2	0	0
		15	lb	Sugar	0	15	0	0
		3	dozen	Liquorice	0	0	20	0
		0.5	piece	Cloth of Assize	0	0	0	0

The Andrew of Wexford, Nicholas Lambart master, Exiting, *6th November 1545*

Merchant name	Origin	Qty	Unit	Commodity	£	s.	d.	f.
Patrick Welshe	Ind	1	ton	Iron	4	0	0	0
		1	ton	Pitch	0	26	8	0
		2	lb	Saffron	0	20	0	0
		1	lb	Silk, *Worked*	0	13	4	0

The Sonday of Milford Haven, John Bottell master, Entering, *6th November 1545*

Merchant name	Origin	Qty	Unit	Commodity	£	s.	d.	f.
Robert Browne & assoc.	Ind	0.5	last	Fish, Herring White	0	30	0	0
		10.833	C	Fish, Hake	5	8	4	0
Giles Fowlar	Ind	2.5	last	Fish, Herring White	7	10	0	0

Merchant name	Origin	Qty	Unit	Commodity	£	s.	d.	f.

The Michaell of Minehead, WilliamThomas master, Entering, 6th November 1545

Merchant name	Origin	Qty	Unit	Commodity	£	s.	d.	f.
Henry Molbery	Ind	1	C	Fish, Hake	0	10	0	0

The Mary Norton, *Port Unknown*, William Adams master, Entering, 6th November 1545

Merchant name	Origin	Qty	Unit	Commodity	£	s.	d.	f.
Richard Baynam	Ind	1	pipe	Wine	0	0	0	0

The Katheryn of Milford Haven, John Froen master, Entering, 8th November 1545

Merchant name	Origin	Qty	Unit	Commodity	£	s.	d.	f.
Walter Doen	Ind	16	barrel	Fish, Herring White	4	0	0	0
		10	C	Fish, Hake	5	0	0	0

The Trynyte of Bridgwater, Bartholomew Garland master, Entering, 9th November 1545

Merchant name	Origin	Qty	Unit	Commodity	£	s.	d.	f.
Henry Sameford	Ind	8	pipe	Fish, Salmon	12	0	0	0
		3.5	last	Fish, Herring White	10	10	0	0
		1	C	Fish, Hake	0	10	0	0
Bartholomew Garland	Ind	8	barrel	Fish, Herring White	2	0	0	0
William Chester	Ind	3	last	Fish, Herring White	9	0	0	0
William Appowell	Ind	37	barrel	Fish, Herring White	9	5	0	0
		3	pipe	Fish, Salmon	4	10	0	0
		5	C	Fish, Hake	2	10	0	0
		1.5	dicker	Skins, Deer	0	5	0	0
Simon Wyllyng & Wykes	Ind	35	barrel	Fish, Herring White	8	15	0	0

The Santa Maria of Pasajes de San Juan, Domingo de Areaga master, Exiting, 10th November 1545

Merchant name	Origin	Qty	Unit	Commodity	£	s.	d.	f.
Paul de Aramboro	Alien	13	ton	Lead, Worked	65	0	0	0
Domingo de Areaga	Alien	6	dicker	Hides, Tanned	0	0	0	0
		6	piece	Cloth of Assize	0	0	0	0
Sebastian Sansowste	Alien	13.7	dicker	Hides, Tanned	0	0	0	0

The George of Waterford, Maurice Power master, Exiting, 16th November 1545

Merchant name	Origin	Qty	Unit	Commodity	£	s.	d.	f.
Benedict Sall	Ind	1	pipe	Iron	0	40	0	0
		1	ream	Paper	0	0	20	0
		1	dozen	Cards, Playing	0	0	15	0
		2	bolt	Thread	0	2	2	0
		5	lb	Liquorice	0	0	10	0
		2	gross	Lacquer	0	3	4	0
		8	gross	Points	0	8	0	0
		6	dozen	Knives, in Pairs	0	10	0	0
		6	dozen	Combs	0	2	6	0
		1.5	gross	Knives	0	10	0	0
		4	lb	Saffron	2	0	0	0
Nicholas Kett	Ind	12	lb	Saffron	6	0	0	0
		18	dozen	Knives, in Pairs	0	30	0	0
		1	gross	Knives	0	6	8	0
		1	gross	Points	0	0	12	0

Merchant name	Origin	Qty	Unit	Commodity	£	s.	d.	f.
		2	ream	Paper	0	3	4	0
		12	lb	Liquorice	0	0	20	0
		1	C	Aniseed	0	13	4	0
		2	C	Hops	0	20	0	0
		0.5	dozen	Cards, Playing	0	0	8	0
		1	dozen	Wool-Cards	0	4	0	0
		1	dozen	Soap	0	0	15	0
Richard Wadyng	Ind	1.25	piece	Cloth of Assize	0	0	0	0
		16	lb	Saffron	8	0	0	0
		3	lb	Silk, *Worked*	2	0	0	0
		1.5	dozen	Caps	0	15	0	0
		1	gross	Knives	0	6	8	0
		0.5	gross	Knives	0	3	4	0
		0.25	C	Hops	0	2	6	0
		1.5	dozen	Liquorice	0	0	20	0
		2	dozen	Aniseed	0	2	8	0
		8	gross	Points	0	8	0	0
		1	gross	Lacquer	0	0	20	0
Patrick Madan	Ind	2.75	piece	Cloth of Assize	0	0	0	0
		2	bolt	Thread	0	2	2	0
		3	gross	Points	0	3	0	0
		1	gross	Lacquer	0	0	20	0
		0.25	gross	Knives	0	0	20	0
		5	pair	Stock-Cards	0	5	0	0
		0.5	gross	Buttons	0	0	12	0
Edmund Clery	Ind	2	C	Hops	0	20	0	0
		12	dozen	Knives, in Pairs	0	20	0	0
		1	gross	Knives	0	6	8	0
		4	lb	Saffron	2	0	0	0
		1	lb	Silk, *Worked*	0	13	4	0
		8	gross	Points	0	8	0	0
		2	gross	Lacquer	0	3	4	0
James Welshe	Ind	1.25	piece	Cloth of Assize	0	0	0	0
		40	lb	Saffron	20	0	0	0
		24	dozen	Knives, in Pairs	2	0	0	0
		3	bolt	Thread	0	3	3	0
		4	lb	Silk, *Worked*	2	13	4	0
		8	gross	Points	0	8	0	0
		1	ream	Paper	0	0	20	0
		4	C	Hops	2	0	0	0
		1	gross	Cutts	0	3	4	0
Edmund Grawnt	Ind	2	lb	Saffron	0	20	0	0
		1	lb	Silk, *Worked*	0	13	4	0
		6	dozen	Knives, in Pairs	0	10	0	0
		4	gross	Points	0	4	0	0
		1	gross	Lacquer	0	0	20	0
		0.5	gross	Cutts	0	0	20	0
Richard Hosemonde	Ind	2	gross	Lacquer	0	3	4	0
		4	dozen	Knives, in Pairs	0	6	8	0
		6	lb	Liquorice	0	0	10	0
		0.5	gross	Knives	0	3	4	0
		6	gross	Points	0	6	0	0

Merchant name	Origin	Qty	Unit	Commodity	£	s.	d.	f.
Nicholas Flaghe	Ind	0.5	piece	Cloth of Assize	0	0	0	0
		6	pair	Stock-Cards	0	6	0	0
Richard Creaghe	Ind	3.5	piece	Cloth of Assize	0	0	0	0
		8	gross	Points	0	8	0	0
		3	gross	Lacquer	0	5	0	0
		6	dozen	Girdles	0	2	0	0
		4	dozen	Cumin	0	5	4	0
		3.5	gross	Cutts	0	11	8	0
		6	dozen	Knives, in Pairs	0	10	0	0
		2	dozen	Cards, Playing	0	2	6	0
		4	dozen	Knives, in Pairs	0	7	6	0
		2	lb	Silk, *Worked*	0	26	8	0
		0.5	C	Aniseed	0	6	8	0
		12	lb	Verdigris	0	5	0	0
		0.5	lb	Cinnamon	0	0	15	0
		8	lb	Saffron	4	0	0	0
		1	lb	Cloves	0	2	6	0
Edward Whyte	Ind	2	piece	Cloth of Assize, Dozen Strait	0	0	0	0
		8	lb	Saffron	4	0	0	0
		4	lb	Silk, *Worked*	2	13	4	0
		8	dozen	Knives, in Pairs	0	13	4	0
		12	gross	Points	0	12	0	0
		1.5	dozen	Caps	0	15	0	0
		0.5	C	Hops	0	5	0	0
Patrick Sall	Ind	16	lb	Saffron	8	0	0	0
		12	dozen	Knives, in Pairs	0	20	0	0
		3	gross	Knives	0	20	0	0
		2	bolt	Thread	0	2	2	0
		2	gross	Lacquer	0	3	4	0
		6	dozen	Girdles	0	4	0	0
		4	gross	Points	0	4	0	0
Nicholas Brewar	Ind	2	lb	Saffron	0	20	0	0
		0.5	gross	Knives	0	3	4	0
		2	stone	Orchil	0	3	4	0

The Sancta Maria of Errenteria, Julian de Gusseta master, Entering, *16th November 1545*

Merchant name	Origin	Qty	Unit	Commodity	£	s.	d.	f.
Christina Whyte	Ind	25	ton	Iron	62	10	0	0
Thomas Harrys	Ind	20	ton	Iron	50	0	0	0
		17	tun	Wine, Corrupt	25	10	0	0
William Appowell	Ind	17	tun	Wine, Corrupt	25	10	0	0
William Joanes	Ind	2.5	tun	Wine, Corrupt	3	15	0	0
John Smyth	Ind	1.5	tun	Wine	0	0	0	0
William Yonge & assoc.	Ind	20	ton	Iron	50	0	0	0
Julian de Gusseta & assoc.	Alien	22	ton	Iron	55	0	0	0
		6	M	Boxwood, for combs	6	0	0	0
		30	M	Oranges	5	0	0	0
		1	pipe	Wine	0	0	0	0

Merchant name	Origin	Qty	Unit	Commodity	£	s.	d.	f.

The Katheryn of Milford Haven, John Williams master, Entering, *16th November 1545*

Merchant name	Origin	Qty	Unit	Commodity	£	s.	d.	f.
John Pycks	Ind	1	virken	Fish, Herring White	0	0	15	0

The Mary of Hondarribia, Lewis de Avaria master, Entering, *16th November 1545*

Merchant name	Origin	Qty	Unit	Commodity	£	s.	d.	f.
John Smyth & assoc.	Ind	63.166	tun	Wine	0	0	0	0
		2	ton	Iron	5	0	0	0
Martin de Burbo	Alien	21	tun	Wine	0	0	0	0
		1.75	ton	Woad, Toulouse	17	10	0	0
Lewis de Avaria & assoc.	Alien	11.75	tun	Wine	0	0	0	0
		4.5	ton	Iron	11	5	0	0

The Peter of Pasajes de San Juan, Martin de Jarsa master, Entering, 17th November 1545

Merchant name	Origin	Qty	Unit	Commodity	£	s.	d.	f.
William Balard	Ind	31.5	tun	Wine	0	0	0	0
		10	ton	Iron	25	0	0	0
John Well	Ind	3	ton	Iron	7	10	0	0
Domingo de Chaby	Alien	2	ton	Iron	5	0	0	0

The Andrew of New Ross, William Jones master, Entering, *17th November 1545*

Merchant name	Origin	Qty	Unit	Commodity	£	s.	d.	f.
Alice Smyth	Ind	38	barrel	Fish, Herring White	9	10	0	0
Nicholas Kelly	Ind	3	last	Fish, Herring White	9	0	0	0
		2	pipe	Fish, Salmon	3	0	0	0
Robert Butlar & assoc.	Ind	2.5	last	Fish, Herring White	7	10	0	0
		1	barrel	Fish, Herring White	0	5	0	0
		3	pipe	Fish, Salmon	4	10	0	0

The John of Pasajes de San Juan, John Note master, Entering, *17th November 1545*

Merchant name	Origin	Qty	Unit	Commodity	£	s.	d.	f.
Martin de Burbo	Alien	44.75	tun	Wine	0	0	0	0
		60	C	Rosin	4	0	0	0
		36.25	C	Woad, Toulouse	18	2	6	0
John Well	Ind	8	ton	Iron	20	0	0	0

The Katheryn of Pasajes de San Juan, John Note de Villa Vaosa master, Entering, *17th November 1545*

Merchant name	Origin	Qty	Unit	Commodity	£	s.	d.	f.
Martin de Burbo	Alien	53.25	tun	Wine	0	0	0	0
John Note de Villa Vaosa & assoc.	Alien	10	ton	Iron	25	0	0	0
		4	C	Frankincense	0	13	4	0
		2	C	Turpentine	0	26	8	0

The Ann of Pembroke, Thomas Morgan master, Entering, *17th November 1545*

Merchant name	Origin	Qty	Unit	Commodity	£	s.	d.	f.
Thomas Morgan	Ind	9.5	barrel	Fish, Herring White	2	7	6	0

Merchant name	Origin	Qty	Unit	Commodity	£	s.	d.	f.
The Trynyte of Gloucester, Thomas Payne master, Entering, *17th November 1545*								
Thomas *Payne*	Ind	6	ton	Salt	3	0	0	0
The Peter of Tewkesbury, Thomas Veyse master, Entering, *17th November 1545*								
Thomas *Veyse*	Ind	4	ton	Salt	2	0	0	0
The Bryde of Waterford, Edmund Medoll master, Exiting, *17th November 1545*								
George Water	Ind	2	dozen	Liquorice	0	0	20	0
		1.5	gross	Knives	0	10	0	0
		0.5	dozen	Caps	0	5	0	0
		5	lb	Silk, *Worked*	3	6	8	0
		1	lb	Seed, Onion	0	0	12	0
		2	dozen	Knives, in Pairs	0	3	4	0
		4	gross	Points	0	4	0	0
		3	dozen	Girdles	0	3	0	0
		2	bolt	Thread	0	2	2	0
		1	lb	Thread	0	0	5	0
		1	dozen	Cards, Playing	0	0	15	0
		2	lb	Verdigris	0	0	10	0
		8	lb	Saffron	4	0	0	0
		4	dozen	Skins, Golden	0	16	8	0
		2	lb	Sulpher	0	0	3	0
		0.5	piece	Cloth of Assize	0	0	0	0
David Rychford	Ind	1.75	piece	Cloth of Assize	0	0	0	0
		5	lb	Silk, *Worked*	3	6	8	0
		6	lb	Pepper	0	6	0	0
		28	lb	Saffron	14	0	0	0
		1	C	Aniseed	0	13	4	0
		6	dozen	Cards, Playing	0	7	6	0
		12	dozen	Spectacles	0	2	0	0
		6	lb	Verdigris	0	2	6	0
		2	lb	Cumin	0	0	3	0
		3	clout	Needles	0	3	0	0
		16	dozen	Skins, Golden	3	6	8	0
		5	gross	Knives	0	33	4	0
		0.5	C	Liquorice	0	0	20	0
		2	gross	Lacquer	0	3	4	0
		5	dozen	Knives, in Pairs	0	8	4	0
		4	bolt	Thread	0	4	4	0
		44	gross	Points	2	4	0	0
		3	seam	Woad, Ashes	0	12	0	0
Sebastian Mahonud	Ind	1.5	piece	Cloth of Assize	0	0	0	0
		5	gross	Cutts	0	16	8	0
		16	dozen	Skins, Golden	3	6	8	0
		24	gross	Points	0	24	0	0
		5	lb	Silk, *Worked*	3	6	8	0
		2	bolt	Thread	0	2	2	0
		2	dozen	Girdles	0	2	0	0
		12	lb	Seed, Onion	0	12	0	0

Merchant name	Origin	Qty	Unit	Commodity	£	s.	d.	f.
		5	dozen	Knives, in Pairs	0	8	4	0
		0.5	C	Aniseed	0	6	8	0
		0.5	C	Liquorice	0	0	20	0
Oliver Stretche	Ind	0.5	piece	Cloth of Assize	0	0	0	0
		1	C	Aniseed	0	13	4	0
		6	dozen	Skins, Golden	0	25	0	0
		2	dozen	Skins, Red	0	4	2	0
		5	gross	Knives	0	33	4	0
		1	gross	Cutts	0	3	4	0
		12	lb	Seed, Onion	0	12	0	0
		10	lb	Cumin	0	0	15	0
		2	bolt	Thread	0	2	2	0
		40	lb	Saffron	20	0	0	0
		2	gross	Points	0	2	0	0
		2	lb	Silk, *Worked*	0	26	8	0
		2	lb	Silk, *Worked*	0	26	8	0
Henry Creaghe	Ind	0.5	piece	Cloth of Assize	0	0	0	0
		2	dozen	Skins, Golden	0	8	4	0
		1	dozen	Skins, Red	0	2	1	0
		16	gross	Points	0	16	0	0
		3	lb	Silk, *Worked*	2	0	0	0
		1	dozen	Cards, Playing	0	0	15	0
		1	dozen	Knives, in Pairs	0	0	20	0
		6	lb	Saffron	3	0	0	0
Patrick Rownam	Ind	2	dozen	Cards, Playing	0	2	6	0
		8	gross	Points	0	8	0	0
		1	gross	Cutts	0	3	4	0
		1	gross	Combs	0	5	0	0
		7	dozen	Girdles	0	3	4	0
		1	bolt	Thread	0	0	13	0
		0.5	gross	Lacquer	0	0	10	0
		2	dozen	Knives, in Pairs	0	3	4	0
		1	dozen	Aniseed	0	0	16	0
		0.5	doz	Liquorice	0	0	10	0
		2	dozen	Wool-Cards	0	8	0	0
Robert Butlar	Ind	2.5	piece	Cloth of Assize	0	0	0	0
		16	lb	Saffron	8	0	0	0
		1.5	dozen	Skins, Red	0	3	0	2
		1	ream	Paper	0	0	20	0
		1	dozen	Girdles	0	0	20	0
		6	dozen	Cards, Playing	0	7	6	0
		6	dozen	Knives, in Pairs	0	10	0	0
		2	gross	Cutts	0	6	8	0
		4	dozen	Skins, Golden	0	16	8	0
		2	bolt	Thread	0	2	2	0
		24	dozen	Girdles	0	12	0	0
		7	dozen	Caps	0	5	0	0
		3	gross	Lacquer	0	5	0	0
		4	gross	Points	0	4	0	0
		4	lb	Silk, *Worked*	2	13	4	0
		12	lb	Liquorice	0	0	10	0
Walter Flemyng	Ind	1.75	piece	Cloth of Assize	0	0	0	0

Merchant name	Origin	Qty	Unit	Commodity	£	s.	d.	f.
		5	gross	Lacquer	0	8	4	0
		6	gross	Points	0	6	0	0
		1	dozen	Cumin	0	2	0	0
		1	dozen	Liquorice	0	0	10	0
		1	dozen	Skins, Red	0	2	1	0
		10	lb	Saffron	5	0	0	0
		3	lb	Silk, *Worked*	2	0	0	0
		4	bolt	Thread	0	4	4	0
		2	gross	Knives	0	13	4	0
		1	ream	Paper	0	0	20	0
		6	dozen	Knives, in Pairs	0	10	0	0
		8	lb	Verdigris	0	3	4	0
		4	dozen	Cards, Playing	0	5	4	0
		6	dozen	Girdles	0	5	0	0
James Wale	Ind	1.33	piece	Cloth of Assize	0	0	0	0
		4	gross	Points	0	4	0	0
		1	dozen	Aniseed	0	0	16	0
		0.5	C	Hops	0	5	0	0
		1	dozen	Skins, Golden	0	4	2	0
		1	gross	Lacquer	0	0	20	0
		2	lb	Silk, *Worked*	0	26	8	0
		2	dozen	Cards, Playing	0	2	6	0
		0.5	gross	Cutts	0	0	20	0
		6	dozen	Knives, in Pairs	0	10	0	0
Nicholas Ley	Ind	10	lb	Saffron	5	0	0	0
		6	lb	Silk, *Worked*	4	0	0	0
		6	dozen	Knives, in Pairs	0	10	0	0
		4	dozen	Cards, Playing	0	5	0	0
		4	dozen	Hops	0	4	0	0
		8	piece	Skins, Golden	0	2	8	0
		0.5	C	Aniseed	0	6	8	0
		1	ream	Paper	0	0	20	0
		8	lb	Liquorice	0	0	15	0
		6	stone	Orchil	0	10	0	0
		2	dozen	Spectacles	0	0	8	0
		4	gross	Points	0	4	0	0
		1	gross	Lacquer	0	0	20	0
		0.5	lb	Pepper	0	0	6	0
		0.5	lb	Cloves	0	0	15	0
		5	lb	Seed, Onion	0	10	0	0
		1	lb	Seed, Leek	0	0	20	0
		1	gross	Cutts	0	3	4	0
Patrick Whyte	Ind	0.75	piece	Cloth of Assize	0	0	0	0
		3	lb	Silk, *Worked*	2	0	0	0
		5	gross	Points	0	5	0	0
		2	gross	Lacquer	0	3	4	0
		1.5	gross	Cutts	0	5	0	0
		3	dozen	Knives, in Pairs	0	5	0	0
		4	lb	Saffron	2	0	0	0
David Savage	Ind	0.5	piece	Cloth of Assize	0	0	0	0
		7	lb	Saffron	3	10	0	0
		2.5	dozen	Aniseed	0	3	4	0

Merchant name	Origin	Qty	Unit	Commodity	£	s.	d.	f.
		3	dozen	Knives, in Pairs	0	5	0	0
		0.5	lb	Cloves	0	0	15	0
		4	dozen	Spectacles	0	2	0	0
		1	dozen	Caps	0	10	0	0
		2	stone	Orchil	0	3	4	0
		1.5	lb	Silk, *Worked*	0	20	0	0
		3	dozen	Combs	0	0	15	0
Nicholas Bayly								
& Roche	Ind	13	lb	Saffron	6	10	0	0
		0.75	C	Hops	0	8	4	0
		1	lb	Silk, *Worked*	0	13	4	0
		0.5	gross	Knives	0	3	4	0
		2	dozen	Knives, in Pairs	0	3	4	0
		6	gross	Points	0	6	0	0
		2	dozen	Cards, Playing	0	2	6	0
		3	dozen	Combs	0	0	18	0
		6	dozen	Spectacles	0	2	0	0
		2	dozen	Girdles	0	0	12	0
		2.5	dozen	Aniseed	0	3	4	0
		6	lb	Liquorice	0	0	10	0
		2	pair	Stock-Cards	0	2	0	0
		2	dozen	Wool-Cards	0	8	0	0
		0.5	piece	Cloth of Assize	0	0	0	0
Clement Welshe	Ind	0.75	piece	Cloth of Assize	0	0	0	0
		1	dozen	Caps	0	10	0	0
		0.5	C	Hops	0	5	0	0
		0.5	C	Aniseed	0	6	8	0
		1	doz	Alum	0	0	16	0
		8	lb	Liquorice	0	0	15	0
		1	bolt	Thread	0	0	13	0
		0.5	gross	Cutts	0	0	20	0
		3	dozen	Wool-Cards	0	12	0	0
		6	pair	Stock-Cards	0	6	0	0
		4	dozen	Cards, Playing	0	5	0	0
		3	lb	Pepper	0	3	0	0
		1	lb	Cloves	0	2	6	0
		2	dozen	Knives, in Pairs	0	3	4	0
		1	C	Rosin	0	0	20	0
		5	gross	Points	0	5	0	0
		0.5	gross	Lacquer	0	0	10	0
		4	lb	Saffron	2	0	0	0
Thomas Vyn	Ind	1	lb	Saffron	0	10	0	0
		5	dozen	Knives, in Pairs	0	8	4	0
		2	gross	Knives	0	13	4	0
		3	dozen	Aniseed & Cumin	0	4	0	0
		1	dozen	Cards, Playing	0	0	15	0
		1	gross	Lacquer	0	0	20	0
		6	gross	Points	0	6	0	0
		0.5	lb	Silk, *Worked*	0	6	8	0
		6	lb	Liquorice	0	0	10	0
		0.5	lb	Cinnamon	0	0	15	0
		1	piece	Cloth of Assize, Dozen Strait	0	0	0	0

Merchant name	Origin	Qty	Unit	Commodity	£	s.	d.	f.
Patrick Kelly	Ind	1.5	piece	Cloth of Assize	0	0	0	0
		8	lb	Saffron	4	0	0	0
		5.5	lb	Silk, *Worked*	3	13	4	0
		8	dozen	Knives, in Pairs	0	13	4	0
		2.5	dozen	Aniseed	0	3	4	0
		6	dozen	Spectacles	0	2	0	0
		4	dozen	Combs	0	2	0	0
		1	lb	Verdigris	0	0	5	0
		2	lb	Thread	0	0	10	0
		1	lb	Pepper	0	0	12	0
		1.5	lb	Cloves & Ginger & Mace	0	3	9	0
		3	dozen	Caps	0	2	6	0
		3	piece	Nightcaps, Satin	0	3	0	0
		1	clout	Needles	0	0	16	0
		2	pair	Stock-Cards	0	2	0	0
		2	dozen	Wool-Cards	0	8	0	0
		0.5	gross	Knives	0	3	4	0
		4	piece	Hats	0	2	0	0
		6	gross	Points	0	6	0	0
		4	lb	Seed, Onion	0	6	8	0

The J*h*esus of Pasajes de San Juan, Anthony Althomira master, Entering, 18th November 1545

Merchant name	Origin	Qty	Unit	Commodity	£	s.	d.	f.
William Ca*rr*	Ind	20	tun	Wine	0	0	0	0
James Boyse	Ind	12.75	tun	Wine	0	0	0	0
		36.25	C	Woad, Toulouse	18	2	6	0
Francis Wosley	Ind	2.75	tun	Wine	0	0	0	0
Anthony Althomira								
& assoc.	Alien	2.75	tun	Wine	0	0	0	0

The Julian of Milford Haven, John Taylar master, Entering, 25th November 1545

Merchant name	Origin	Qty	Unit	Commodity	£	s.	d.	f.
Patrick Perslow	Ind	20	C	Fish, Hake	10	0	0	0

The *Christ*ofer of *Bokeslate*, Cornell Canyard master, Entering, *25th November 1545*

Merchant name	Origin	Qty	Unit	Commodity	£	s.	d.	f.
Cornell Canyard	Alien	17	tun	Wine	0	0	0	0
		18	tun	Wine, Corrupt	27	0	0	0
		37	ton	Salt	18	10	0	0
Martin Alownso	Alien	12	tun	Wine	0	0	0	0
		5	tun	Vinegar	10	0	0	0
		6	piece	Figs & Raisins	0	8	4	0
Frederick Marenar	Alien	2.5	tun	Wine	0	0	0	0
		6	piece	Raisins, *Great*	0	10	0	0
Christopher								
Flannders	Alien	15.5	tun	Wine	0	0	0	0
		3	tun	Vinegar	6	0	0	0
		30	piece	Figs	0	30	0	0
		8	C	Figs & Raisins	0	16	0	0
Miles Harrycks	Alien	0.875	tun	Oil, Train	2	4	10	0
		5	C	Marmalade	3	6	8	0
		0.5	ton	Figs	0	20	0	0

Merchant name	Origin	Qty	Unit	Commodity	£	s.	d.	f.
Francis Stephenart	Alien	56.25	tun	Wine	0	0	0	0
		53	tun	Wine, Corrupt	79	10	0	0
		12.5	ton	Figs	25	0	0	0

The Andrew of New Ross, William Jones master, Exiting, 26th November 1545

Merchant name	Origin	Qty	Unit	Commodity	£	s.	d.	f.
Thomas Rothe	Ind	1	piece	Cloth of Assize	0	0	0	0
		16	lb	Saffron	8	0	0	0
		8	lb	Silk, Worked	5	6	8	0
		6	lb	Seed, Onion	0	6	0	0
		13	piece	Caps	0	10	10	0
		1	dozen	Skins, Golden	0	4	2	0
		1	ream	Paper	0	0	20	0
		6	dozen	Knives, in Pairs	0	10	0	0
		2	dozen	Cards, Playing	0	2	6	0
		2	lb	Pepper	0	2	0	0
		6	gross	Points	0	6	0	0
		0.5	gross	Lacquer	0	0	10	0
		1	dozen	Cumin	0	0	16	0
		1	dozen	Books, Primers	0	2	0	0
		6	dozen	Vials	0	2	0	0
		3	lb	Verdigris	0	0	15	0
		0.5	gross	Knives	0	3	4	0
		7.5	dozen	Aniseed	0	10	0	0
		1	barrel	Honey	0	16	8	0
		1	C	Hops	0	10	0	0

The Lawrence of Holland, Cornell Harison master, Entering, 27th november 1545

Merchant name	Origin	Qty	Unit	Commodity	£	s.	d.	f.
Peter Martyn	Alien	1.5	tun	Wine	0	0	0	0
Henry Lyne	Alien	8.5	tun	Wine, Corrupt	13	10	0	0

The Mary of Tenby, Walter Bryte master, Entering, 2nd December 1545

Merchant name	Origin	Qty	Unit	Commodity	£	s.	d.	f.
Thomas Longhar & assoc.	Ind	10	ton	Salt	5	0	0	0

The James of Aveiro, George Hernandus master, Entering, 3rd December 1545

Merchant name	Origin	Qty	Unit	Commodity	£	s.	d.	f.
Nicholas Thorn & assoc.	Ind	43	tun	Wine	0	0	0	0

The Sonday of Bristol John Colyns master, Exiting, 4th December 1545

Merchant name	Origin	Qty	Unit	Commodity	£	s.	d.	f.
John Gryffythe	Ind	8	pair	Millstones	8	0	0	0
John Swan	Ind	1	tun	Wine, Corrupt	0	30	0	0
Leonard Sompter	Ind	1	tun	Wine, Corrupt	0	30	0	0
		1	C	Rosin	0	0	16	0

The Chrystopher of San Sebastián, William de Londres master, Entering, 4th December 1545

Merchant name	Origin	Qty	Unit	Commodity	£	s.	d.	f.
John de Lasara	Alien	33.33	ton	Iron	83	6	8	0
		6	ton	Pitch & Resin	8	0	0	0

Merchant name	Origin	Qty	Unit	Commodity	£	s.	d.	f.
Francis Wosley	Ind	2	ton	Iron	5	0	0	0
		1.75	tun	Wine, Corrupt	2	12	6	0

The Sancta Maria of Jutha, *Port Unknown*, Alonso Janus master, Entering, 5th December 1545

Merchant name	Origin	Qty	Unit	Commodity	£	s.	d.	f.
Nicholas Thorn & assoc.	Ind	68.5	tun	Wine	0	0	0	0
		24	ton	Raisins, *Great*	48	0	0	0
Nicholas Tyson	Ind	1.75	tun	Wine	0	0	0	0
William Balard	Ind	0.75	tun	Wine	0	0	0	0

The Peter of Pasajes de San Juan, Martin de Jarsa master, Exiting, *5th December 1545*

Merchant name	Origin	Qty	Unit	Commodity	£	s.	d.	f.
Martin de Jarsa	Alien	4	dicker	Hides, Tanned	0	0	0	0

The Jhesus of Pasajes de San Juan, Anthony Althomira master, Exiting, 7th December 1545

Merchant name	Origin	Qty	Unit	Commodity	£	s.	d.	f.
Anthony Althomira	Alien	1.2	ton	Lead, Worked	6	0	0	0
		10	piece	Bristol Frieze Cloth	6	13	4	0

The Sancta Maria of Errenteria, Julian de Gusseta master, Exiting, 9th December 1545

Merchant name	Origin	Qty	Unit	Commodity	£	s.	d.	f.
Julian de Gusseta	Alien	32.3	dicker	Hides, Tanned	0	0	0	0
		2	ton	Lead, Worked	10	0	0	0
Martin de Arysavlo	Alien	2	dicker	Hides, Tanned	0	0	0	0
Julian de Gusseta	Alien	80	dozen	Skins, Calf	13	6	8	0
		2	piece	Welsh *Cloth*	2	0	0	0
		20	dozen	Skins, Calf	5	0	0	0
		10	piece	Dunster *Cloth*	5	0	0	0
		15	piece	Welsh *Cloth*	15	0	0	0
		2	piece	Cloth of Assize	0	0	0	0

The Katheryn of Pasajes de San Juan, John Note master, Exiting, *9th December 1545*

Merchant name	Origin	Qty	Unit	Commodity	£	s.	d.	f.
John Dysense	Alien	1	piece	Bell	0	20	0	0
John *Note*	Alien	8.5	piece	Cloth of Assize	0	0	0	0
		4.5	piece	Welsh *Cloth*	4	10	0	0
		2	ton	Lead, Worked	10	0	0	0
		2	dicker	Hides, Tanned	0	0	0	0
William Carye	Ind	0.75	piece	Welsh *Cloth*	0	15	0	0
		2	dicker	Hides, Tanned	0	0	0	0

The Mary of Hondarribia, Lewis de Avaria master, Exiting, 14th December 1545

Merchant name	Origin	Qty	Unit	Commodity	£	s.	d.	f.
Louis de Avaria	Alien	16	dicker	Hides, Tanned	0	0	0	0
		2	piece	Cloth of Assize	0	0	0	0
		1	piece	Welsh *Cloth*	0	20	0	0
		2	piece	Bristol Frieze Cloth	0	26	8	0

Merchant name	Origin	Qty	Unit	Commodity	£	s.	d.	f.

The Conception of Aveiro, John Santis master, Entering, *14th December 1545*

Merchant name	Origin	Qty	Unit	Commodity	£	s.	d.	f.
Nicholas Thorn & assoc.	Ind	38	tun	Wine	0	0	0	0
		7	ton	Figs	14	0	0	0
Nicholas Tyson & Welshe	Ind	2.25	tun	Wine	0	0	0	0
		1	ton	Raisins, *Great*	2	0	0	0

The Conception of Viana do Castello, John Perrys master, Entering, 15th December 1545

Merchant name	Origin	Qty	Unit	Commodity	£	s.	d.	f.
John *Perrys*	Alien	20	ton	Figs	40	0	0	0

The Trynyte George of Bristol, John Jeyne master, Entering, 17th December 1545

Merchant name	Origin	Qty	Unit	Commodity	£	s.	d.	f.
William Gelly	Ind	3	wey	Wheat	3	0	0	0
		9	pipe	Fish, Salmon	13	10	0	0
		13.5	C	Fish, Hake	6	15	0	0
		0.5	C	Fish, Salted	0	10	0	0
Richard Whyte	Ind	10	pipe	Fish, Salmon	15	0	0	0
John Power	Ind	2	pipe	Fish, Salmon	3	0	0	0
		2	C	Fish, Hake	0	20	0	0.
		1	barrel	Fish, Herring White	0	5	0	0
Nicholas Kelly & Manereage	Ind	3	pipe	Fish, Salmon	4	10	0	0
		3	hogshead	Fish, Salmon	4	0	0	0
		2	barrel	Fish, Eels	0	26	8	0
George Walter & Jeynes	Ind	10.5	stone	Tallow, Rough	0	5	0	0
		1	pipe	Fish, Salmon	0	30	0	0
John Fyztesymons	Ind	5	barrel	Fish, Herring White	0	25	0	0
		80	yard	Irish Linen *Cloth*	0	13	4	0
		22	piece	Skins, Marten	0	22	0	0
Mathew Kente	Ind	1	C	Fish, Hake	0	10	0	0

The Christopher of San Sebastián, William de Londres master, Exiting, 18th December 1545

Merchant name	Origin	Qty	Unit	Commodity	£	s.	d.	f.
Peter de Sarage	Alien	31	dicker	Hides, Tanned	0	0	0	0
William *de Londres*	Alien	2	ton	Lead, Worked	10	0	0	0
		232	piece	Manchester Cotton *Cloth*	116	0	0	0
		8	piece	Cloth of Assize	0	0	0	0
		12	dicker	Hides, Tanned	0	0	0	0
Bartholemew de Lasranca	Alien	1.5	piece	Cloth of Assize	0	0	0	0
		26	piece	Northern Cotton *Cloth*	5	8	4	0

The Julyan of Milford Haven, John Taylar master, Exiting, 22nd December 1545

Merchant name	Origin	Qty	Unit	Commodity	£	s.	d.	f.
John Boughan	Ind	12	pair	Millstones	12	0	0	0

Merchant name	Origin	Qty	Unit	Commodity	£	s.	d.	f.

The Sancta Maria Gomar, *Port Unknown*, Hugh Lucas master, Entering, 23rd December 1545

Englebert Jacome & assoc.	Alien	17.75	tun	Wine	0	0	0	0
		30	tun	Wine, Corrupt	45	0	0	0
		66	piece	Raisins, *Great*	5	10	0	0
Nicholas Wares	Alien	150	piece	Raisins, *Great*	12	10	0	0
Bartholomew Lazonik	Alien	3	M	Oranges	0	10	0	0
Hugh Lucas	Alien	7	ton	Salt	3	10	0	0

The James of Aveiro, George Hernandus master, Exiting, *23rd December 1545*

George *Hernandus*	Alien	15	dozen	Skins, Calf	2	10	0	0
		2	piece	Welsh *Cloth*	2	0	0	0
		4	C	Lead, Worked	0	20	0	0
		6.416	piece	Cloth of Assize	0	0	0	0
Francis Rodrygus	Alien	3	piece	Bristol Frieze Cloth	2	0	0	0
		0.5	piece	Cloth of Assize	0	0	0	0

The Sancta Maria of Jutha, *Port Unknown*, Alonso Janus master, Exiting, 27th December 1545

Gonsalo Janus & assoc.	Alien	3	piece	Cloth of Assize	0	0	0	0
		1	piece	Welsh *Cloth*	0	20	0	0
Gonsalo Janus	Alien	0.5	piece	Cloth of Assize	0	0	0	0
Peter Janus	Alien	4	piece	Cloth of Assize, Northern Dozen	0	0	0	0
		2	piece	Welsh *Cloth*	2	0	0	0

The *Christ*ofer of *Bokeslate*, Cornell Canyard master, Exiting, 27th December 1545

Cornell Canyard	Alien	20	last	Coal	13	6	8	0
		4.5	C	Lead, Worked	0	22	6	0
		3	piece	Bristol Frieze Cloth	2	0	0	0
		90	dozen	Skins, Calf	15	0	0	0
		47	piece	Manchester Cotton *Cloth*	23	10	0	0
		14.5	piece	Cloth of Assize	0	0	0	0
		2.3	dicker	Hides, Kip	0	0	0	0

The Seynte John of Errenteria, John de Arasalvo master, Entering, 4th January 1546

Arnold & John de Arasavlo	Alien	29.75	tun	Wine	0	0	0	0
		0.75	tun	Vinegar	0	30	0	0
John Well & Bowerman	Ind	19.5	tun	Wine	0	0	0	0

The Conception of Aveiro, John Sanctis master, Exiting, 5th January 1546

John *Sanctis*	Alien	0.5	piece	Cloth of Assize	0	0	0	0

Merchant name	Origin	Qty	Unit	Commodity	£	s.	d.	f.
The Savyor of Errenteria, Francis de Sobeta master, Entering, 7th January 1546								
Francis de Sobeta	Alien	3	tun	Wine	0	0	0	0
John de Olasavall	Alien	7.75	tun	Wine	0	0	0	0
		7	ton	Raisins, *Great*	14	0	0	0
		1	pipe	Oil, *Olive*	2	0	0	0
John Smyth	Ind	12	tun	Wine	0	0	0	0
		100	piece	Raisins, *Great*	8	6	8	0
		2.5	tun	Wine, Corrupt	3	15	0	0
John Hamon	Ind	1	pipe	Wine	0	0	0	0
John Cutt	Ind	40	C	Alum	20	0	0	0
Anthony Payne & Pryn	Ind	1.5	tun	Wine	0	0	0	0
		3.25	tun	Oil, *Olive*	13	0	0	0
William Cox & Channcelar	Ind	3	tun	Wine	0	0	0	0
		1	tun	Wine, Corrupt	0	30	0	0
		1.5	tun	Oil, *Olive*	6	0	0	0
James Chester & Rowley	Ind	11.25	tun	Wine	0	0	0	0
		1	tun	Wine, Corrupt	0	30	0	0
Domingo de Salendia & Garrard	Alien	2	tun	Wine	0	0	0	0
		3	tun	Oil, *Olive*	12	0	0	0
		10	piece	Raisins, *Great*	0	16	8	0
		9	M	Oranges	0	30	0	0
John Well & Yonge	Ind	5.25	tun	Wine	0	0	0	0
		12	tun	Oil, *Olive*	48	0	0	0
		2	ton	Raisins, *Great*	4	0	0	0
		12.5	C	Soap	6	5	0	0
		1.5	chest	Sugar	3	0	0	0
		2.5	C	Marmalade	0	33	4	0
John Welshe	Ind	3.25	tun	Wine	0	0	0	0
		3.25	tun	Oil, *Olive*	13	0	0	0
		2	hogshead	Vinegar	0	20	0	0
		15	C	Alum	7	10	0	0
John Bayly & Harrys	Ind	9	tun	Wine	0	0	0	0
		15	tun	Oil, *Olive*	60	0	0	0
		1	tun	Wine, Corrupt	0	30	0	0
Hugh Gyttons & Pereman	Ind	8.25	tun	Wine	0	0	0	0
		1	tun	Oil, *Olive*	4	0	0	0
John Capps & Browne	Ind	2.75	tun	Oil, *Olive*	11	0	0	0
		50	piece	Raisins, *Great*	4	3	4	0
		1	tun	Wine	0	0	0	0
Thomas Hycks & Thorn	Ind	3.25	tun	Wine	0	0	0	0
Geoffrey Chawntrell	Ind	7.5	tun	Wine	0	0	0	0
		1	pipe	Oil, *Olive*	2	0	0	0
Dego de Gamon	Alien	1	hogshead	Oil, *Olive*	0	20	0	0

Merchant name	Origin	Qty	Unit	Commodity	£	s.	d.	f.

The Trynyte George, Richard Bryan master, Exiting, 11th January 1546

Merchant name	Origin	Qty	Unit	Commodity	£	s.	d.	f.
William Gelly &								
Chester	Ind	4	ton	Iron	16	0	0	0
		20	C	Wood, Laths	0	5	0	0
James Chester	Ind	2	tun	Wine	0	0	0	0
William Harvest &								
Dowtyng	Ind	1	ton	Iron	4	0	0	0
Nicholas Thorn &								
assoc.	Ind	5	tun	Wine	0	0	0	0
		1	hogshead	Vinegar	0	10	0	0

The Sancta Maria of Vila Do Conde, John Evans master, Entering, *11th January 1546*

Merchant name	Origin	Qty	Unit	Commodity	£	s.	d.	f.
John Welshe	Ind	34	tun	Wine	0	0	0	0
		36	piece	Raisins, *Great*	3	0	0	0
		10	C	Alum	5	0	0	0
John Smyth	Ind	12	tun	Wine	0	0	0	0
Geoffreyus Chantrell	Ind	16.5	tun	Wine	0	0	0	0
		2	little barrel	Olives	0	13	4	0
Hugh Gyttens &								
assoc.	Ind	8.25	tun	Wine	0	0	0	0
John Rypp & Peryman	Ind	5	tun	Wine	0	0	0	0
Sailors & assoc.	Alien	10	piece	Raisins, *Great*	0	16	8	0
		2	kilderkin	Woad, Azores	0	11	8	0

The Sonday of Bristol, John Gryffyth master, Entering, 13th January 1546

Merchant name	Origin	Qty	Unit	Commodity	£	s.	d.	f.
John *Gryffyth* &								
assoc.	Ind	6	C	Fish, Hake	3	0	0	0
		5	pipe	Fish, Salmon	7	10	0	0
		1	barrel	Fish, Herring White	0	5	0	0

The Conception of Viana do Castello, John Perrys master, Exiting, 14th January 1546

Merchant name	Origin	Qty	Unit	Commodity	£	s.	d.	f.
John Perrys	Alien	1.75	piece	Cloth of Assize	0	0	0	0
		12	yard	Bristol Frieze Cloth	0	10	0	0

The Michaell of Laugharne, William Gilford master, Entering, 18th January 1546

Merchant name	Origin	Qty	Unit	Commodity	£	s.	d.	f.
Gryffyth Jones	Ind	2	ton	Salt	0	20	0	0

The Sonday of Bristol, John Gryffyths master, Exiting, 18th January 1546

Merchant name	Origin	Qty	Unit	Commodity	£	s.	d.	f.
Nicholas Thorn &								
assoc.	Ind	7	tun	Wine	0	0	0	0
		25	C	Aniseed	16	13	4	0
		2	C	Soap	0	26	8	0
		5	C	Hops	2	10	0	0
		2.5	tun	Wine, Corrupt	3	15	0	0
		2.5	C	Marmalade	0	33	4	0
		3	C	Iron	0	12	0	0

Merchant name	Origin	Qty	Unit	Commodity	£	s.	d.	f.
		1	chest	Sugar	2	0	0	0
		48	gross	Points	2	8	0	0
		4	dozen	Girdles	0	6	0	0
		3	dozen	Knives, in Pairs	0	5	0	0
		10	lb	Cumin	0	0	12	0
		6	dozen	Skins, Calf	0	20	0	0

The Sparrow of Minehead, Thomas Veneam master, Entering, 19th January 1546

Merchant name	Origin	Qty	Unit	Commodity	£	s.	d.	f.
John Peter	Alien	48	ell	Holland *Cloth*	0	13	4	0

The Seynt John of Errenteria, John de Arasalvo master, Exiting, *19th January 1546*

Merchant name	Origin	Qty	Unit	Commodity	£	s.	d.	f.
Arnold de Alsata	Alien	25	dicker	Hides, Tanned	0	0	0	0
		20	dozen	Skins, Calf	3	6	8	0
Michael de Sanct								
Steven	Alien	23.5	dicker	Hides, Tanned	0	0	0	0

The Concepton of *Lasa*, John Martinus master, Entering, 20th January 1546

Merchant name	Origin	Qty	Unit	Commodity	£	s.	d.	f.
John Gurney	Ind	29	tun	Wine	0	0	0	0
John Smyth & assoc.	Ind	10.75	tun	Wine	0	0	0	0
William Ostrych &								
assoc.	Ind	8.5	tun	Wine	0	0	0	0
		1	tun	Wine, Corrupt	0	30	0	0
		3.75	tun	Oil, Train	10	0	0	0
		1.5	C	Irish Linen *Cloth*	0	15	0	0
		1	piece	Mantles	0	3	4	0
		15	yard	Check *Cloth*	0	5	0	0
Thomas Cutt	Ind	1.75	tun	Wine	0	0	0	0

The Sancta Maria Gomar, *Port Unknown*, Hugh Lucas master, Exiting, 1st February 1546

Merchant name	Origin	Qty	Unit	Commodity	£	s.	d.	f.
Hugh Lucas	Alien	10	last	Coal	6	13	4	0

The Salvador of Errenteria, Francis de Sobeta master, Exiting, *1st February 1546*

Merchant name	Origin	Qty	Unit	Commodity	£	s.	d.	f.
Dego de Gamon	Alien	7	dicker	Hides, Tanned	0	0	0	0
		0.5	dicker	Hides, Kip	0	0	0	0
		10	dozen	Skins, Calf	0	33	4	0
Martin Peris	Alien	2	dozen	Skins, Calf	0	6	8	0
		1	piece	Welsh *Cloth*	0	20	0	0
Anthony Garad &								
Martinus	Alien	9	dicker	Hides, Tanned	0	0	0	0
		15	C	*Candarn, bomy*	0	10	0	0
		1	piece	Bristol Frieze Cloth	0	13	4	0
Francis de Sobeta &								
assoc.	Alien	45	dicker	Hides, Tanned	0	0	0	0
		17	piece	Welsh *Cloth*	17	0	0	0
		118	dozen	Skins, Calf	19	13	4	0
		12	piece	Cloth of Assize	0	0	0	0
Anthony Garad	Alien	7.5	piece	Cloth of Assize	0	0	0	0

Merchant name	Origin	Qty	Unit	Commodity	£	s.	d.	f.
Domingo de Salendia	Alien	6	dozen	Skins, Calf	0	20	0	0
		6	C	Lead	0	30	0	0
Robert Gyttons	Ind	2	dicker	Hides, Tanned	0	0	0	0
		3	dicker	Hides, Kip	0	0	0	0
Francis de Sobeta	Alien	4	piece	Cloth of Assize	0	0	0	0
		29	dicker	Hides, Tanned	0	0	0	0
William Harvest	Ind	50	yard	Scottish Linen *Cloth*	0	16	8	0
Sebastian Sansowste	Alien	10	piece	Cloth of Assize, Dozen Strait	0	0	0	0
Thomas Cutt	Ind	5	piece	Cloth of Assize	0	0	0	0
John Michaell	Alien	26	piece	Manchester Cotton *Cloth*	13	0	0	0

The Marieta of Errenteria, Jeramus de Oyan Gorey master, Entering, 3rd February 1546

Merchant name	Origin	Qty	Unit	Commodity	£	s.	d.	f.
Martin Perys & assoc.	Alien	9.75	tun	Wine	0	0	0	0
		3	tun	Wine, Corrupt	4	10	0	0
		543	piece	Raisins, *Great*	41	0	12	0
John Welshe & Cutt	Ind	20	C	Alum	10	0	0	0

The Corpus Sancta of Bilbao, Domingo de Lunday master, Entering, 4th February 1546

Merchant name	Origin	Qty	Unit	Commodity	£	s.	d.	f.
Ralph Grenwey & assoc.	Ind	30	tun	Wine	0	0	0	0
		15	tun	Wine, Corrupt	22	10	0	0
		136	piece	Raisins, *Great*	11	6	8	0

The Nicholas of Orio, Domingo de Segura master, Entering, 8th February 1546

Merchant name	Origin	Qty	Unit	Commodity	£	s.	d.	f.
John Smyth & Rowley	Ind	30	ton	Iron	75	0	0	0
William Yonge & Tyndale	Ind	7	ton	Honey	18	13	4	0
		18	ton	Iron	45	0	0	0
		8	ballet	Viteri Canvas	12	0	0	0
John Smyth & Tyndale	Ind	7.25	tun	Wine	0	0	0	0
		5.75	tun	Wine, Corrupt	8	12	6	0
William Kyrk	Ind	6	ton	Iron	15	0	0	0
Edmund Joanes & Pryn	Ind	4.25	tun	Wine	0	0	0	0
		0.333	ton	Honey	0	20	0	0
		2	ton	Iron	5	0	0	0
Michael De Veroys & Agniry	Alien	24.75	tun	Wine	0	0	0	0
		8	tun	Wine, Corrupt	12	0	0	0
Henry Stafford & assoc.	Ind	10	M	Oranges	0	33	4	0
John Tuckar	Ind	12	C	Canes	0	5	0	0

The Trynyte of Bermeo, John Ithiago master, Entering, 9th February 1546

Merchant name	Origin	Qty	Unit	Commodity	£	s.	d.	f.
Peter Malwendo	Alien	28.5	tun	Oil, *Olive*	114	0	0	0
		125	C	Soap	62	10	0	0
		30	chest	Sugar	60	0	0	0

Merchant name	Origin	Qty	Unit	Commodity	£	s.	d.	f.
		12	C	Cassia Fistula	36	0	0	0
		40	C	Capers	20	0	0	0
		100	little barrel	Olives	8	6	8	0
		479	piece	Raisins, *Great*	39	18	4	0
John Peters & Ithiago	Alien	81	tun	Wine	0	0	0	0
		1	pipe	Wine, Corrupt	0	15	0	0
		4	C	Liquorice	0	26	8	0
		2	ton	Salt	0	20	0	0
		17	lb	Perfume	0	30	0	0
Nicholas Thorn	Ind	22.5	piece	Tissue *Cloth*	45	0	0	0

The John Baptyst, *Port Unknown*, Peter Nam master, Entering, 11th February 1546

Merchant name	Origin	Qty	Unit	Commodity	£	s.	d.	f.
Nicholas Thorn & assoc.	Ind	143	tun	Wine	0	0	0	0
		12.5	tun	Oil, *Olive*	50	0	0	0
		83.75	C	Soap	41	17	6	0
		43	piece	Raisins, *Great*	3	11	8	0
William Shipman & Coper	Ind	14.5	tun	Wine	0	0	0	0
		5	tun	Oil, *Olive*	20	0	0	0
		1	tun	Wine, Corrupt	0	30	0	0
Thomas Hycks & Payne	Ind	15.5	tun	Wine	0	0	0	0
		0.75	tun	Oil, *Olive*	3	0	0	0
John Channselar & Hyll	Ind	7	tun	Wine	0	0	0	0
		1	tun	Wine, Corrupt	0	30	0	0
Nicholas Teson	Ind	9.5	tun	Wine	0	0	0	0
		2	tun	Oil, *Olive*	8	0	0	0
Peter *Nam*	Alien	4.25	tun	Wine	0	0	0	0
		1	tun	Wine, Corrupt	0	30	0	0
		73	ton	Salt	36	10	0	0
James Bayly & Welshe	Ind	6	tun	Oil, *Olive*	24	0	0	0
		14.5	tun	Wine	0	0	0	0
John Broke & Smyth	Ind	5.5	tun	Wine	0	0	0	0
		3	C	Aniseed	0	40	0	0
		10.5	tun	Oil, *Olive*	42	0	0	0

The Trynyte of Berkeley, John Smyth master, Entering, 15th February 1546

Merchant name	Origin	Qty	Unit	Commodity	£	s.	d.	f.
Maurice Bocher	Ind	6	ton	Salt	3	0	0	0

The Seynt John of Errenteria, John Ward master, Entering, *15th February 1546*

Merchant name	Origin	Qty	Unit	Commodity	£	s.	d.	f.
Martin Peris	Alien	37	ton	Iron	92	10	0	0
		7	dozen	Serches	0	29	2	0
		10	M	Oranges	0	33	4	0
John Welshe & assoc.	Ind	17	tun	Wine	0	0	0	0
		35	ton	Iron	87	10	0	0
		40	C	Liquorice	6	13	4	0
		1.75	tun	Wine, Corrupt	2	12	6	0

Merchant name	Origin	Qty	Unit	Commodity	£	s.	d.	f.

The Marieta of Errenteria, Jeramus de Oyan Gorey master, Exiting, 17th February 1546

Merchant name	Origin	Qty	Unit	Commodity	£	s.	d.	f.
Martin Perrys & assoc.	Alien	28.5	dicker	Hides, Tanned	0	0	0	0
		14	piece	Manchester Cotton *Cloth*	7	0	0	0
		5	dozen	Skins, Calf	0	16	8	0
		1	piece	Cloth of Assize	0	0	0	0
Peter de Gyrrys	Alien	27	piece	Cloth of Assize	0	0	0	0
Jeremiah de Oyan, Gorey & assoc.	Alien	9	dicker	Hides, Tanned	0	0	0	0
		2	piece	Cloth of Assize, Dozen Strait	0	0	0	0

The Sonday of Milford Haven, William Phillypps master, Entering, *17th February 1546*

Merchant name	Origin	Qty	Unit	Commodity	£	s.	d.	f.
Christopher Jocham & Vaghan	Ind	6.5	C	Fish, Hake	3	5	0	0
		1	barrel	Fish, Herring White	0	5	0	0
		1	virken	Fish, Salmon	0	7	6	0
		80	yard	Check *Cloth*	0	26	8	0
		2	piece	Seal Pigs	0	6	8	0
		3	piece	Mantles	0	10	0	0
		20	piece	Skins, Marten	0	13	4	0

The Sancta Maria of Vila Do Conde, John Evyons master, Exiting, *17th February 1546*

Merchant name	Origin	Qty	Unit	Commodity	£	s.	d.	f.
John *Evyons* & assoc.	Alien	20	piece	Manchester Cotton *Cloth*	10	0	0	0
		0.5	piece	Bristol Frieze Cloth	0	6	8	0
		11	yard	Check *Cloth*	0	3	8	0
		6	dozen	Skins, Calf	0	20	0	0
		17.5	piece	Cloth of Assize	0	0	0	0

The Savyor of Minehead, Richard Langhar master, Entering, 20th February 1546

Merchant name	Origin	Qty	Unit	Commodity	£	s.	d.	f.
Nicholas Kelly	Ind	4	last	Fish, Herring White	12	0	0	0
		1.5	C	Tallow, Molten	0	6	8	0
		16	C	Fish, Hake	8	0	0	0
		2	pipe	Fish, Salmon	3	0	0	0
		9	barrel	Meat	2	5	0	0
Robert Butlar	Ind	5	last	Fish, Herring White	15	0	0	0
		10	C	Fish, Hake	5	0	0	0
		3	pipe	Fish, Salmon	4	10	0	0
William Appowell & assoc.	Ind	65	barrel	Fish, Herring White	16	5	0	0
		1	C	Fish, Hake	0	10	0	0

The Trynyte of Berkeley, John Smyth master, Entering, 22nd February 1546

Merchant name	Origin	Qty	Unit	Commodity	£	s.	d.	f.
Maurice Bocher	Ind	12	ton	Salt	6	0	0	0

The Concepton of *Lasa*, John Martinus master, Exiting, *22nd February 1546*

Merchant name	Origin	Qty	Unit	Commodity	£	s.	d.	f.
John Martinus	Alien	6.5	piece	Cloth of Assize	0	0	0	0

Merchant name	Origin	Qty	Unit	Commodity	£	s.	d.	f.

The Nicholas of Orio, Domingo de Segura master, Exiting, 25th February 1546

Merchant name	Origin	Qty	Unit	Commodity	£	s.	d.	f.
Alonso de Castanetha	Alien	4	ton	Lead, Worked	20	0	0	0
		30	dozen	Skins, Calf	5	0	0	0
Domingo de Segura	Alien	8	dicker	Hides, Tanned	0	0	0	0
		1	dozen	Skins, Calf	0	3	4	0
		7	piece	Cloth of Assize	0	0	0	0
Martin Perrys	Alien	3.75	dicker	Hides, Tanned	0	0	0	0
Sebastian de Orneta	Alien	17	piece	Cloth of Assize	0	0	0	0
Peter de Agyrra	Alien	27	piece	Cloth of Assize	0	0	0	0
William Carr	Ind	1	dicker	Hides, Tanned	0	0	0	0

The Seynt John of Errenteria, John Ward master, Exiting, 27th February 1546

Merchant name	Origin	Qty	Unit	Commodity	£	s.	d.	f.
John *Ward* & Michaell	Alien	7	dicker	Hides, Tanned	0	0	0	0
		7	piece	Cloth of Assize	0	0	0	0
		16	piece	Manchester Cotton *Cloth*	8	0	0	0
Peter de Agyrra	Alien	54	piece	Cloth of Assize	0	0	0	0
William Carye	Ind	6	dicker	Hides, Tanned	0	0	0	0
John *Ward*	Alien	30	piece	Northern Cotton *Cloth*	6	5	0	0
		4	ton	Lead, Worked	20	0	0	0
		10	dozen	Skins, Calf	0	33	4	0
Martin Perrys & assoc.	Alien	9.4	dicker	Hides, Tanned	0	0	0	0
		1.5	dicker	Hides, Kip	0	0	0	0
John de Olasawall	Alien	8	piece	Cloth of Assize, Northern Strait	0	0	0	0
Martin Perrys	Alien	39	dicker	Hides, Tanned	0	0	0	0
William Appowell	Ind	100	piece	Manchester Cotton *Cloth*	50	0	0	0
		23	piece	Dunster *Cloth*	11	10	0	0
		9	piece	Welsh *Cloth*	9	0	0	0
		1	piece	Cloth of Assize	0	0	0	0
Laurence de Aronoso	Alien	2	C	Skins, Sheep Worked	0	20	0	0

The Nicholas of San Sebastián, John Dorthayda master, Entering, 1st March 1546

Merchant name	Origin	Qty	Unit	Commodity	£	s.	d.	f.
John *Dorthayda*	Alien	51.75	tun	Wine	0	0	0	0
		8	tun	Vinegar	16	0	0	0
William Appowell & Yonge	Ind	58.5	tun	Wine	0	0	0	0
		5	tun	Wine, Corrupt	7	10	0	0

The Mary Nashe, *Port Unknown*, Thomas Baynam master, Entering, 3rd March 1546

Merchant name	Origin	Qty	Unit	Commodity	£	s.	d.	f.
Thomas Vowell	Ind	8.5	barrel	Fish, Herring White	2	2	6	0

The George of Waterford, Robert Medoll master, Entering, *3rd March 1546*

Merchant name	Origin	Qty	Unit	Commodity	£	s.	d.	f.
Robert *Medoll*	Ind	3	C	Check *Cloth*	6	0	0	0
		6	piece	Mantles	0	20	0	0
		1	pipe	Fish, Salmon	0	30	0	0
		1	C	Fish, Hake	0	10	0	0
George Lee	Ind	25	C	Fish, Hake	12	10	0	0

Merchant name	Origin	Qty	Unit	Commodity	£	s.	d.	f.
		4	barrel	Fish, Herring White	0	20	0	0
		0.5	C	Check *Cloth*	0	20	0	0
		3	piece	Mantles	0	10	0	0
		0.5	C	Skins, Sheep	0	5	0	0
John Craensburth	Ind	3.5	pipe	Fish, Salmon	5	5	0	0
		3	C	Fish, Hake	0	30	0	0
		1	C	Check *Cloth*	2	0	0	0
		1	C	Skins, Sheep	0	10	0	0
		12	piece	Mantles	2	0	0	0
		2	stone	Wool, Flocks	0	0	10	0
		2	barrel	Fish, Herring White	0	10	0	0
Edward Whyte	Ind	4	yard	Check *Cloth*	8	0	0	0
		2.5	C	Fish, Hake	0	25	0	0
		3.5	C	Skins, Sheep	0	35	0	0
		15	piece	Mantles	2	10	0	0
Edmund Grannte	Ind	5	yard	Check *Cloth*	10	0	0	0
		30	piece	Mantles	5	0	0	0
		3	C	Skins, Sheep	0	30	0	0
		3	stone	Wool, Flocks	0	0	15	0
		1	virken	Fish, Salmon	0	7	6	0
		6	piece	Skins, Fox	0	0	12	0
		0.5	C	Skins, Lamb	0	3	4	0
Thomas Skewlad	Ind	2	C	Skins, Sheep	0	20	0	0
		13	piece	Skins, Marten	0	13	0	0
		0.5	C	Irish Linen *Cloth*	0	5	0	0
		1	barrel	Fish, Herring White	0	5	0	0
Patrick Gybbe	Ind	1.5	pipe	Fish, Salmon	2	5	0	0
		4.5	C	Check *Cloth*	9	0	0	0
		8	C	Skins, Sheep	4	0	0	0
		2	barrel	Fish, Eels	0	26	8	0
		13	piece	Skins, Marten	0	13	0	0
		24	piece	Mantles	4	0	0	0
		9	piece	Skins, Fox	0	0	18	0
Patrick Carne	Ind	6	C	Skins, Sheep	3	0	0	0
		6	stone	Wool, Flocks	0	2	6	0
		3	stone	Wool, Irish	0	8	0	0
		5	piece	Skins, Fox	0	0	10	0
Edmund Clere	Ind	3	C	Skins, Sheep	0	30	0	0
		6.5	C	Check *Cloth*	13	0	0	0
		20	piece	Mantles	3	6	8	0
		1	barrel	Fish, Eels	0	13	4	0
		1	C	Fish, Hake	0	10	0	0
Leonard Bruar	Ind	1	C	Check *Cloth*	2	0	0	0
		10	piece	Mantles	0	33	4	0
Peter Welshe	Ind	1	C	Check *Cloth*	2	0	0	0
		6	piece	Mantles	0	20	0	0
		3	C	Fish, Hake	0	30	0	0
Nicholas Brewer & Pore	Ind	3	C	Check *Cloth*	6	0	0	0
		1.5	C	Fish, Hake	0	15	0	0
		4	C	Skins, Sheep	2	0	0	0
		2	barrel	Fish, Eels	0	26	8	0

484

Merchant name	Origin	Qty	Unit	Commodity	£	s.	d.	f.
		4	piece	Mantles	0	13	4	0
John Quede	Ind	6	C	Fish, Hake	3	0	0	0
		1	C	Check *Cloth*	2	0	0	0
		6	piece	Mantles	0	20	0	0
		1	burden	Fish, Salted	0	4	2	0
Peter Maydan	Ind	5	C	Check *Cloth*	10	0	0	0
		14	piece	Mantles	2	6	8	0
		0.5	C	Skins, Sheep	0	5	0	0
		5.5	C	Fish, Hake	2	15	0	0
		1	barrel	Fish, Herring White	0	5	0	0
		11	piece	Fish, Salted	0	0	22	0
Nicholas Mahan	Ind	100	yard	Check *Cloth*	0	33	4	0
		3	piece	Mantles	0	10	0	0
		1.25	C	Fish, Hake	0	12	6	0
		4.5	stone	Wool, Irish	0	12	0	0
Nicholas Flaghe	Ind	2	C	Fish, Hake	0	20	0	0
		0.5	C	Skins, Sheep	0	5	0	0
		3	C	Check *Cloth*	6	0	0	0
		6	piece	Mantles	0	20	0	0

The George Butlar of Waterford, Nicholas Rownam master, Entering, *3rd March 1546*

Merchant name	Origin	Qty	Unit	Commodity	£	s.	d.	f.
Nicholas Shee	Ind	45	C	Fish, Hake	22	10	0	0
		2	pipe	Fish, Salmon	3	0	0	0
		4	burden	Fish, Salted	0	16	8	0
		2	C	Check *Cloth*	4	0	0	0
		10	piece	Mantles	0	33	4	0
Mathew Wyse	Ind	14	C	Fish, Hake	7	0	0	0
		4	barrel	Fish, Herring White	0	20	0	0
		0.75	pipe	Fish, Salmon	0	22	6	0
		1	burden	Fish, Salted	0	4	2	0
		1.5	C	Skins, Sheep	0	15	0	0
		1.5	C	Check *Cloth*	3	0	0	0
		6	piece	Mantles	0	20	0	0
Paul Butlar	Ind	12	C	Fish, Hake	6	0	0	0
		12	piece	Mantles	2	0	0	0
		1.5	C	Check *Cloth*	3	0	0	0
		2	C	Skins, Sheep	0	20	0	0
Thomas Shee	Ind	8.5	C	Check *Cloth*	17	0	0	0
		6	stone	Wool, Irish	0	16	0	0
		10	C	Skins, Sheep	5	0	0	0
		0.5	C	Irish Linen *Cloth*	0	5	0	0
James Welshe	Ind	4	C	Check *Cloth*	8	0	0	0
		7	C	Skins, Sheep	3	10	0	0
		3	dicker	Skins, Deer	0	10	0	0

The Mary Jenny of Dungarvan, John Fytzwilliams master, Entering, *3rd March 1546*

Merchant name	Origin	Qty	Unit	Commodity	£	s.	d.	f.
John *Fytzwilliams* & Flyn	Ind	34	C	Fish, Hake	17	0	0	0
		4	burden	Fish, Salted	0	25	0	0
		3	stone	Wool, Flocks	0	0	15	0

Merchant name	Origin	Qty	Unit	Commodity	£	s.	d.	f.
Thomas Colyn	Ind	8	C	Fish, Hake	4	0	0	0
		3	stone	Wool, Flocks	0	0	15	0
		0.5	burden	Fish, Salted	0	2	1	0

The Sonday of Wexford, Thomas Scolyck master, Entering, 4th March 1546

Merchant name	Origin	Qty	Unit	Commodity	£	s.	d.	f.
Nicholas Whyte	Ind	26	barrel	Fish, Herring White	6	10	0	0
		10	C	Fish, Hake	5	0	0	0
		3	mease	Fish, Herring Red	0	15	0	0
		1.5	C	Skins, Sheep	0	15	0	0
Thomas *Scolyck*	Ind	10	barrel	Fish, Herring White	2	10	0	0
		3.5	C	Fish, Hake	0	35	0	0
		4	mease	Fish, Herring Red	0	20	0	0
		1	burden	Fish, Salted	0	4	2	0
		1	C	Skins, Sheep	0	10	0	0
		1	piece	Mantles	0	3	4	0
John Lamport	Ind	12	barrel	Fish, Herring White	3	0	0	0
		2	mease	Fish, Herring Red	0	10	0	0
		2	C	Fish, Hake	0	20	0	0
		0.5	pipe	Fish, Salmon	0	15	0	0
		3	piece	Mantles	0	10	0	0
Laurence Lawnders	Ind	5	barrel	Fish, Herring White	0	25	0	0
		1	mease	Fish, Herring Red	0	5	0	0
		1.25	C	Fish, Hake	0	12	6	0
		1	piece	Mantles	0	3	4	0
Henry Byllett	Ind	8	barrel	Fish, Herring White	2	0	0	0
		2.5	C	Fish, Hake	0	25	0	0
		3	mease	Fish, Herring Red	0	15	0	0
		1	burden	Fish, Salted	0	4	2	0

The Jhesus of Youghal, John Sheman master, Entering, *4th March 1546*

Merchant name	Origin	Qty	Unit	Commodity	£	s.	d.	f.
John Campyon & Rownam	Ind	6	M	Fish, Hake	30	0	0	0
		5.75	pipe	Fish, Salmon	8	11	0	0
		3	barrel	Fish, Herring White	0	15	0	0
		1	burden	Fish, Salted	0	4	2	0
		12	yard	Check *Cloth*	0	4	0	0
Thomas Blewett & Creaghe	Ind	29	barrel	Fish, Herring White	7	5	0	0
		7	C	Fish, Hake	3	10	0	0
		40	yard	Check *Cloth*	0	13	4	0
		1.5	C	Skins, Sheep	0	15	0	0
		1	kilderkin	Fish, Eels	0	6	8	0
Nicholas Shee & assoc.	Ind	15	C	Fish, Hake	7	10	0	0
		30	yard	Check *Cloth*	0	10	0	0
		1	burden	Fish, Salted	0	4	2	0

The Katheryn of Dungarvan, Robert Rowyn master, Entering, *4th March 1546*

Merchant name	Origin	Qty	Unit	Commodity	£	s.	d.	f.
Humphrey Wyse & Rowyn	Ind	38	C	Fish, Hake	19	0	0	0

Merchant name	Origin	Qty	Unit	Commodity	£	s.	d.	f.
		5.5	burden	Fish, Salted	1	2	1	0
		1	barrel	Fish, Seal (seal meat?)	0	6	8	0
		9	stone	Wool, Flocks	0	3	9	0
		12	yard	Check Cloth	0	4	0	0
		1	barrel	Fish, Mackerel	0	6	8	0
		2	barrel	Fish, Sprat	0	5	0	0

The Jhesus of Wexford, John Stafford master, Entering, 4th March 1546

Merchant name	Origin	Qty	Unit	Commodity	£	s.	d.	f.
John Stafford	Ind	2	last	Fish, Herring White	6	0	0	0
		6	C	Fish, Hake	3	0	0	0
		6	mease	Fish, Herring Red	0	30	0	0
		1	C	Skins, Lamb	0	6	8	0
		1	C	Skins, Sheep	0	10	0	0
		4	burden	Fish, Salted	0	16	8	0
Richard Maylar	Ind	1	last	Fish, Herring White	3	0	0	0
		5	C	Fish, Hake	2	10	0	0
		4	mease	Fish, Herring Red	0	20	0	0
		7	piece	Mantles	0	23	4	0
Philip Furlonge	Ind	1	last	Fish, Herring White	3	0	0	0
		6	C	Fish, Hake	3	0	0	0
		1.5	C	Skins, Sheep	0	15	0	0
		10	piece	Mantles	0	33	4	0

The Trynyte of Youghal, William Neale master, Entering, 4th March 1546

Merchant name	Origin	Qty	Unit	Commodity	£	s.	d.	f.
William Neale & Kelly	Ind	16	C	Fish, Hake	8	0	0	0
		14	barrel	Fish, Herring White	3	10	0	0
		3	pipe	Fish, Salmon	4	10	0	0
Francis Welshe & Copynger	Ind	14	C	Fish, Hake	7	0	0	0
		0.5	burden	Fish, Salted	0	2	1	0
		3	barrel	Fish, Herring White	0	15	0	0
Richard Annes	Ind	6	C	Fish, Hake	3	0	0	0
		1.5	C	Skins, Sheep	0	15	0	0
		0.5	barrel	Fish, Whiting	0	2	6	0
Maurice Broughan & assoc.	Ind	10	C	Fish, Hake	5	0	0	0
		1	last	Fish, Herring White	3	0	0	0
		4	C	Fish, Hake	0	40	0	0
		4	barrel	Fish, Herring White	0	20	0	0
		2	barrel	Fish, Eels	0	26	8	0

The Katheryn of Milford Haven, John Froen master, Entering, 4th March 1546

Merchant name	Origin	Qty	Unit	Commodity	£	s.	d.	f.
John Froen	Ind	5.5	C	Fish, Hake	2	15	0	0
		6	barrel	Fish, Herring White	0	30	0	0

The Andrew of New Ross, Richard Doffe master, Entering, 4th March 1546

Merchant name	Origin	Qty	Unit	Commodity	£	s.	d.	f.
Peter Harrys & Kelly	Ind	6	C	Skins, Sheep	3	0	0	0

Merchant name	Origin	Qty	Unit	Commodity	£	s.	d.	f.
		15	dicker	Skins, Deer	2	10	0	0
		6	piece	Mantles	0	20	0	0
		1	C	Skins, Lamb	0	6	8	0
		1	C	Irish Linen *Cloth*	0	10	0	0
		6	C	Check *Cloth*	12	0	0	0
		8	stone	Wool, Flocks	0	3	4	0
Robert Leonard	Ind	10	C	Skins, Sheep	5	0	0	0
		4	C	Check *Cloth*	8	0	0	0
		4	C	Skins, Lamb	0	26	8	0
		24	piece	Skins, Fox	0	4	0	0
		3	piece	Skins, Wolf	0	2	0	0
		20	stone	Wool, Flocks	0	8	4	0
		5	piece	Mantles	0	16	8	0
		1	dicker	Skins, Deer	0	3	4	0
Thomas Dowley	Ind	2	C	Check *Cloth*	4	0	0	0
		1	C	Skins, Lamb	0	6	8	0
		24	stone	Wool, Flocks	0	10	0	0
		10	stone	Wool, Irish	0	26	8	0
		4	piece	Skins, Fox	0	0	8	0
		8	piece	Mantles	0	26	8	0
		2	C	Skins, Sheep	0	20	0	0
		0.5	pipe	Fish, Salmon	0	15	0	0
		4	C	Fish, Hake	0	40	0	0
John Dowley & Chester	Ind	13.5	C	Skins, Sheep	6	15	0	0
		5.5	C	Check *Cloth*	11	0	0	0
		1	C	Skins, Lamb	0	6	8	0
		5	piece	Skins, Fox	0	0	10	0
		25	stone	Wool, Flocks	0	10	5	0
		9	stone	Wool, Irish	0	24	0	0
		40	lb	Fish, Sturgeon	0	3	4	0
		16	piece	Skins, Deer Tanned	0	7	1	0
		27	piece	Skins, Deer	0	9	0	0
		8	piece	Mantles	0	26	8	0

The Savior of Friesland, Firsopus Sybran master, Entering, *4th March 1546*

Merchant name	Origin	Qty	Unit	Commodity	£	s.	d.	f.
William Shypman	Ind	7	tun	Oil, *Olive*	28	0	0	0
Nicholas Thorn & assoc.	Ind	26	tun	Oil, *Olive*	104	0	0	0
		103.75	C	Soap	51	17	6	0
		23	tun	Wine	0	0	0	0
Anthony Payne & Smyth	Ind	13	tun	Wine	0	0	0	0
		1	pipe	Oil, *Olive*	2	0	0	0
John Broke & Vyne	Ind	34.5	tun	Wine	0	0	0	0
		34	C	Alum	17	0	0	0
William Rowley & Thorn	Ind	6.5	tun	Wine	0	0	0	0
		1	pipe	Wine, Corrupt	0	15	0	0
John Capps & Chester	Ind	16	tun	Wine	0	0	0	0
		4	tun	Wine, Corrupt	6	0	0	0

Merchant name	Origin	Qty	Unit	Commodity	£	s.	d.	f.
Henry Wyot & Tyson	Ind	23	tun	Wine	0	0	0	0
		4	tun	Wine, Corrupt	6	0	0	0
		314	piece	Raisins, *Great*	12	0	0	0
Thomas Harrys & Ostrydge	Ind	11	tun	Wine	0	0	0	0
		2	tun	Wine, Corrupt	3	0	0	0
William Pepwell & Chawncelar	Ind	6	tun	Wine	0	0	0	0
		1	hogshead	Oil, *Olive*	0	20	0	0
		2	ton	Raisins, *Great*	4	0	0	0
Thomas Teson & Leyton	Ind	13	tun	Wine	0	0	0	0
		5.5	tun	Wine, Corrupt	8	5	0	0
Thomas Cutt & Blake	Ind	25.25	tun	Wine	0	0	0	0
		1	pipe	Wine, Corrupt	0	15	0	0
		3	tun	Oil, *Olive*	12	0	0	0
Popius Sydron	Alien	47	ton	Salt	23	10	0	0
Peter Arnoll	Alien	17	tun	Wine	0	0	0	0
James Baylye & Gyttons	Ind	3.5	tun	Wine	0	0	0	0
William Jay & Hycks	Ind	32.75	tun	Wine	0	0	0	0
		8.5	tun	Oil, *Olive*	34	0	0	0
Thomas Hycks & assoc.	Ind	2.5	tun	Oil, *Olive*	10	0	0	0
		11	tun	Wine	0	0	0	0

The George of Bristol, Richard Bryan master, Entering, 5th March 1546

Merchant name	Origin	Qty	Unit	Commodity	£	s.	d.	f.
William Gelly & Brodway	Ind	30	wey	Tallow, Rough	5	0	0	0
		5	pipe	Fish, Salmon	7	10	0	0
		8	C	Fish, Hake	4	0	0	0
		1	wey	Grain	0	20	0	0
		0.5	wey	Wheat	0	8	4	0
		16	stone	Wool, Irish	2	2	8	0
		1.5	C	Skins, Sheep	0	15	0	0
		1	dicker	Skins, Salted	0	13	4	0
William Appowell & assoc.	Ind	5	barrel	Fish, Herring White	0	25	0	0
		2	pipe	Fish, Salmon	3	0	0	0
		79	lb	Brass, Broken	0	7	6	0
		0.5	C	Skins, Sheep	0	5	0	0
		5	dicker	Skins, Salted	3	6	8	0
		8.5	C	Tallow, Molten	2	16	8	0
		1	C	Tallow, Rough	0	3	4	0
		9	C	Fish, Hake	4	10	0	0

The Sonday of Dungarvan, James Manger master, Entering, *5th March 1546*

Merchant name	Origin	Qty	Unit	Commodity	£	s.	d.	f.
John Browne	Ind	5	last	Fish, Herring White	15	0	0	0

Merchant name	Origin	Qty	Unit	Commodity	£	s.	d.	f.
		15	C	Fish, Hake	7	10	0	0
		1	hogshead	Fish, Seal (seal meat?)	0	13	4	0

The Sonday of Waterford, William Wodlock master, Entering, 5th March 1546

Merchant name	Origin	Qty	Unit	Commodity	£	s.	d.	f.
Patrick Strannge	Ind	24	C	Fish, Hake	12	0	0	0
		1	burden	Fish, Salted	0	4	2	0
		40	piece	Mantles	6	13	4	0
		1.5	C	Check *Cloth*	3	0	0	0
		1	C	Skins, Sheep	0	10	0	0
Philip Welshe	Ind	9.5	C	Fish, Hake	4	15	0	0
		5.5	C	Skins, Sheep	2	15	0	0
		6	piece	Mantles	0	20	0	0
		2	C	Check *Cloth*	4	0	0	0
		2	piece	Skins, Marten	0	2	0	0
		4	piece	Skins, Fox	0	0	8	0
Robert Manghon &								
William Wodlock	Ind	9	C	Irish Linen *Cloth*	4	10	0	0
		1	C	Fish, Hake	0	10	0	0
		4	piece	Mantles	0	13	4	0
		2	stone	Wool, Flocks	0	0	10	0
Richard Turner	Ind	40	pipe	Fish, Salmon	60	0	0	0
		4	barrel	Fish, Eels	0	53	4	0
		12	C	Skins, Sheep	6	0	0	0
		3	C	Skins, Lamb	0	20	0	0
		2.5	C	Check *Cloth*	5	0	0	0
		27	piece	Mantles	4	10	0	0
		3	C	Skins, Rabbit	0	10	0	0
		40	piece	Skins, Otter	0	16	8	0
		32	piece	Skins, Marten	0	32	0	0
		50	piece	Skins, Fox	0	8	4	0
		2.5	C	Fish, Hake	0	25	0	0

The George of Cork, Philip Barry master, Entering, 5th March 1546

Merchant name	Origin	Qty	Unit	Commodity	£	s.	d.	f.
William Sarchefyld	Ind	12	pipe	Fish, Salmon	18	0	0	0
		7	last	Fish, Herring White	21	0	0	0
		2	dicker	Skins, Deer	0	6	8	0
		10	stone	Wool, Flocks	0	4	2	0
		0.5	C	Skins, Sheep	0	5	0	0
John Copynger	Ind	1.25	pipe	Fish, Salmon	0	37	6	0
		18	barrel	Fish, Herring White	4	10	0	0
		10	stone	Wool, Flocks	0	4	2	0
		20	yard	Check *Cloth*	0	6	8	0
		2	piece	Mantles	0	6	8	0
		6	stone	Fish, Sturgeon Broken	0	7	6	0

The Bryde of Waterford, Edmund Maydon master, Entering, 5th March 1546

Merchant name	Origin	Qty	Unit	Commodity	£	s.	d.	f.
Christopher Tyrry	Ind	8	last	Fish, Herring White	24	0	0	0
		2	pipe	Fish, Salmon	3	0	0	0
		10	C	Fish, Hake	5	0	0	0

Merchant name	Origin	Qty	Unit	Commodity	£	s.	d.	f.
		3	C	Skins, Sheep	0	30	0	0
		40	stone	Wool, Flocks	0	16	8	0
		1	dicker	Skins, Deer	0	3	4	0
		0.5	C	Wax	0	16	8	0
		3	last	Fish, Herring White	9	0	0	0

The Mawdelen of Errenteria, Peter de Sables master, Exiting, 6th March 1546

Merchant name	Origin	Qty	Unit	Commodity	£	s.	d.	f.
Peter *De Sables* & *assoc.*	Alien	14	dicker	Hides, Tanned	0	0	0	0

The Andrew of New Ross, Richard Doffe master, Exiting, 12th March 1546

Merchant name	Origin	Qty	Unit	Commodity	£	s.	d.	f.
Thomas Dowley	Ind	2.5	tun	Wine, Corrupt	3	15	0	0
		1	hogshead	Iron	0	20	0	0
		0.5	C	Hops	0	5	0	0
Peter Harrys	Ind	3.5	tun	Wine, Corrupt	5	5	0	0
		1	pipe	Iron	2	0	0	0
		0.5	C	Hops	0	5	0	0
		1	C	Aniseed	0	13	4	0
		1	gross	Knives	0	6	8	0
		1	kilderkin	Honey	0	8	4	0
		1	tun	Wine	0	0	0	0

The Trynyte of Bermeo, John Ithiago master, Exiting, 15th March 1546

Merchant name	Origin	Qty	Unit	Commodity	£	s.	d.	f.
John *Ithiago*	Alien	29.65	ton	Lead	148	5	0	0
		60	dozen	Skins, Calf	10	0	0	0
		13	unknown	Wire, *pole*	0	13	4	0
		2.25	piece	Cloth of Assize	0	0	0	0
John Holons	Alien	7.25	piece	Cloth of Assize	0	0	0	0
William Preston	Ind	22	dozen	Skins, Calf	3	13	4	0
Englebert *Unknown*	Alien	8.5	ton	Lead, Worked	42	10	0	0
John Browle	Ind	1	piece	*Stolorn Cloth*	0	10	4	0
		19	yard	Check *Cloth*	0	6	4	0
John Ithiago	Alien	12	piece	Cloth of Assize, Dozen Strait	0	0	0	0
		6	piece	Molton *Cloth*	0	25	0	0
William Harvest	Ind	20	piece	Manchester Cotton *Cloth*	10	0	0	0
		2	ton	Lead, Worked	10	0	0	0
James Chester & assoc.	Ind	79	piece	Cloth of Assize	0	0	0	0
		2.5	C	Check *Cloth*	5	0	0	0
		5	C	Tin	5	0	0	0
		7.2	dicker	Hides, Tanned	0	0	0	0
Richard Wigmore & assoc.	Ind	58.5	piece	Cloth of Assize	0	0	0	0
Domingo Eryso	Alien	80	ton	Lead	320	0	0	0

The Sonday of Wexford, Thomas Scolycke master, Exiting, 16th March 1546

Merchant name	Origin	Qty	Unit	Commodity	£	s.	d.	f.
Thomas *Scolycke*	Ind	1	hogshead	Iron	0	20	0	0
		0.5	C	Hops	0	5	0	0

Merchant name	Origin	Qty	Unit	Commodity	£	s.	d.	f.
		14	lb	Alum	0	0	20	0
		14	lb	Aniseed	0	0	20	0
		4	dozen	Knives, in Pairs	0	6	8	0
		1	lb	Saffron	0	10	0	0
		1	lb	Silk, *Worked*	0	13	4	0
		6	piece	Scythes	0	6	8	0
		0.25	gross	Knives	0	0	20	0
		1	*piece*	Poldavis *Cloth*	0	10	0	0
		1	stone	Wood, Brazil	0	0	20	0
Nicholas Whyte	Ind	1	hogshead	Iron	0	20	0	0
		0.5	C	Hops	0	5	0	0
		0.5	gross	Knives	0	3	4	0
		0.25	C	Alum	0	3	4	0
		2	M	Teazells	0	5	0	0
		1	lb	Saffron	0	10	0	0
		1	lb	Silk, *Worked*	0	13	4	0
		5	C	Pitch & Tar	0	3	4	0
		6	piece	Scythes	0	6	8	0
		1	bolt	Canvas *Cloth*	0	6	8	0
John Lamport	Ind	0.5	C	Hops	0	5	0	0
		0.5	gross	Knives	0	3	4	0
		3	C	Iron	0	12	0	0
		1.5	stone	Alum	0	2	6	0
		0.5	C	Wood, Brazil	0	16	8	0
		1	stone	Aniseed	0	0	20	0
		1	lb	Silk, *Worked*	0	13	4	0
		0.5	lb	Saffron	0	5	0	0
Lawrence Andros	Ind	0.5	C	Hops	0	5	0	0
		0.5	gross	Knives	0	3	4	0
		0.5	C	Iron	0	2	0	0
		1	barrel	Pitch	0	0	20	0
		1	lb	Kermes	0	0	20	0
		0.5	lb	Saffron	0	5	0	0
Henry Bennett	Ind	2	C	Iron	0	8	0	0
		0.5	C	Hops	0	5	0	0
		0.5	gross	Points	0	0	6	0
		0.5	lb	Silk, *Worked*	0	6	8	0
		1	stone	Aniseed	0	0	20	0
		1	lb	Saffron	0	10	0	0
		0.5	gross	Knives	0	3	4	0
James Lynch & assoc.	Ind	110	lb	Saffron	55	0	0	0
		9	lb	Silk, *Worked*	6	0	0	0

The Jhesus of Wexford, John Stafford master, Exiting, 16th March 1546

Merchant name	Origin	Qty	Unit	Commodity	£	s.	d.	f.
John *Stafford*	Ind	1	pipe	Iron	0	40	0	0
		1	C	Hops	0	10	0	0
		0.25	C	Alum	0	3	4	0
		0.5	gross	Knives	0	3	4	0
		1	M	Teazells	0	2	6	0
		1	ton	Salt	0	10	0	0
		9	C	Pitch	0	13	4	0

Merchant name	Origin	Qty	Unit	Commodity	£	s.	d.	f.
		4	lb	Saffron	2	0	0	0
		12	gross	Points	0	12	0	0
		1	lb	Silk, *Worked*	0	13	4	0
		1	dozen	Wool-Cards	0	4	0	0
		20	yard	Cloth of Assize	0	0	0	0
Richard Mayler	Ind	1	pipe	Iron	2	0	0	0
		1	C	Hops	0	10	0	0
		2.5	dozen	Aniseed	0	3	4	0
		10	C	Pitch & Tar	0	3	4	0
		2	lb	Saffron	0	20	0	0
		1	dozen	Wool-Cards	0	4	0	0
		1	last	*Barrels, Lear*	0	8	4	0
Philip Furlonge	Ind	1	pipe	Iron	2	0	0	0
		1	C	Hops	0	10	0	0
		1	gross	Combs	0	4	2	0
		1	lb	Saffron	0	10	0	0
		1	lb	Silk, *Worked*	0	13	4	0
		1	barrel	Pitch	0	3	4	0
		2	last	*Barrels, Lear*	0	16	8	0
		0.5	C	Alum & Aniseed	0	6	8	0
		1	C	Wood, Brazil	0	33	4	0
		2	weight	Hemp	0	8	0	0

The George Butler of Waterford, Nicholas Rownam master, Exiting, 17th March 1546

Merchant name	Origin	Qty	Unit	Commodity	£	s.	d.	f.
Paul Butler	Ind	1	C	Hops	0	10	0	0
		2	piece	Cloth of Assize	0	0	0	0

The Bryde of Waterford, Edmund Medall master, Exiting, *17th March 1546*

Merchant name	Origin	Qty	Unit	Commodity	£	s.	d.	f.
John Welshe & Dowley	Ind	1	pipe	Iron	2	0	0	0
		2	tun	Wine, Corrupt	3	0	0	0
		0.25	C	Hops	0	2	6	0
		8	lb	Liquorice	0	0	10	0
		2	gross	Knives	0	13	4	0
		8	dozen	Caps	0	6	8	0
		2	dozen	Wool-Cards	0	8	0	0
		4	pair	Stock-Cards	0	4	0	0
		1	dozen	Cards, Playing	0	0	15	0
		4	gross	Points	0	4	0	0
		6	lb	Aniseed	0	0	8	0
		1	pipe	Wine	0	0	0	0

The Sonday of Bristol, Henry Whyte master, Entering, 18th March 1546

Merchant name	Origin	Qty	Unit	Commodity	£	s.	d.	f.
John Gryffyth & assoc.	Ind	9	wey	Grain	9	0	0	0
		2	wey	Rye	0	33	4	0
		3	hogshead	Fish, Eels	4	0	0	0
		1.5	dicker	Skins, Deer	0	4	10	0
		8	piece	Skins, Fox	0	0	16	0

Merchant name	Origin	Qty	Unit	Commodity	£	s.	d.	f.
		2	piece	Skins, Otter	0	0	10	0
		7.25	stone	Wool, Irish	0	16	8	0
		1.466	C	Skins, Sheep	0	14	8	0
		13	piece	Skins, Kid	0	0	6	2

The Conception of *Lasaye*, John Martyn master, Entering, *18th March 1546*

Nicholas Thorn & assoc.	Ind	70	tun	Wine	0	0	0	0

The Santa Mary Conception of *Bristol*, James Lewse master, Exiting,*18th March 1546*

Nicholas Thorn & assoc.	Ind	10	tun	Wine	0	0	0	0
		43	ton	Salt	21	10	0	0
		25	C	Aniseed	16	13	4	0
		70	lb	Ginger	5	5	0	0
		7.66	ton	Iron	30	13	4	0

The Trynyte of Youghal, William Nele master, Exiting, 19th March 1546

Merchant name	Origin	Qty	Unit	Commodity	£	s.	d.	f.
William *Nele*	Ind	0.5	C	Hops	0	5	0	0
		1	pipe	Iron	2	0	0	0
		1	unknown	Payn?	0	10	0	0
James Roche	Ind	1.5	dozen	Wool-Cards	0	6	0	0
		0.5	C	Hops	0	5	0	0
		12	lb	Flax	0	3	4	0
		8	yard	Holland *Cloth*	0	10	0	0
		1	unknown	Payn?	0	10	0	0
		1	dozen	Caps	0	10	0	0
		1	dozen	Knives, in Pairs	0	0	20	0
		0.5	lb	Cinnamon & Cloves	0	0	15	0
Maurice Branghan	Ind	1	C	Iron	0	4	0	0
		0.5	C	Hops	0	5	0	0
		1	piece	Cable & Ropes	2	18	0	0
Richard Annes	Ind	1	lb	Saffron	0	10	0	0
		1	gross	Cutts	0	6	8	0
		3	stone	Hops	0	3	0	0
		2	gross	Points	0	2	0	0
		4	dozen	Combs	0	2	0	0
		0.5	gross	Lacquor	0	0	10	0
		5	dozen	Unknown	0	2	10	0
		1	dozen	Wool-Cards	0	4	0	0
		0.5	lb	Cinnamon & Cloves	0	0	15	0
		1	dozen	Knives, in Pairs	0	0	20	0
Francis Welshe	Ind	1	C	Hops	0	10	0	0
		1	stone	Aniseed	0	0	20	0
		1	gross	Knives	0	6	8	0
		2	gross	Points	0	2	0	0
		3	dozen	Caps	0	2	6	0
		1	lb	Saffron	0	10	0	0
		1	stone	Alum	0	0	20	0

Merchant name	Origin	Qty	Unit	Commodity	£	s.	d.	f.
Thomas Copynger	Ind	5	piece	Cloth of Assize, Dozen Strait	0	0	0	0
		1	gross	Knives	0	6	8	0
		12	gross	Points	0	12	0	0
		2	lb	Silk, *Worked*	0	26	8	0
		2	lb	Saffron	0	20	0	0

The Katheryn of Dungarvan, Robert Rowe master, Exiting, 21st March 1546

Merchant name	Origin	Qty	Unit	Commodity	£	s.	d.	f.
Robert *Rowe*	Ind	1	lb	Saffron	0	10	0	0
		1.5	C	Hops	0	15	0	0
		0.5	C	Aniseed	0	6	8	0
		2	dozen	Wool-Cards	0	8	0	0
		1	dozen	Soap	0	0	15	0
		1	C	Flax	0	33	4	0
		1	C	Iron	0	4	0	0
		4	bolt	Oleron *Cloth*	0	26	8	0
		0.5	C	Alum	0	6	8	0
		2	barrel	Tar	0	6	8	0
		1	piece	Cloth of Assize, Dozen Strait	0	0	0	0

The George Gelly, Richard Bryan master, Exiting, 21st March 1546

Merchant name	Origin	Qty	Unit	Commodity	£	s.	d.	f.
William Gelly & Romisey	Ind	2	tun	Wine	0	0	0	0
		1	pipe	Wine, Corrupt	0	15	0	0
		1	ton	Iron	4	0	0	0
		11	ton	Salt	5	10	0	0
		20	clout	Needles	0	2	6	0
		4	gross	Points, Silk	0	6	8	0
		4	lb	Cloves & Mace	0	10	0	0
		6	lb	Mail	0	3	0	0
		24	dozen	Girdles	0	6	0	0
		18	dozen	Fish-Hooks	0	5	0	0
		13	M	Fish-Hooks, Little	0	20	0	0
		2	gross	Combs	0	6	8	0
		6	bird	Game-birds	0	3	4	0
		20	gross	Trenchers	0	6	8	0
		6	lb	Kermes	0	5	0	0
		2	C	Hops	0	20	0	0
		1	C	Alum	0	13	4	0
		1	C	Wood, Brazil	0	33	4	0
Richard Barnard & Kelly	Ind	1.25	ton	Salt	0	12	6	0
		1	tun	Wine, Corrupt	0	30	0	0
		1	tun	Wine	0	0	0	0
Robert Burnell	Ind	13	M	Fish-Hooks, Little	0	32	0	0
		2	gross	Combs	0	6	13	0
		2	lb	Mail	0	0	12	0
		3.5	dozen	Books, Primers	0	6	0	0
		1	dozen	Hanging locks	0	6	0	0
		6	M	Pins	0	0	20	0
		1	piece	Cloth of Assize, Dozen Strait	0	0	0	0

Merchant name	Origin	Qty	Unit	Commodity	£	s.	d.	f.

The Mary of Dungarvan, John Fytzwilliams master, Exiting, 21st March 1546

Merchant name	Origin	Qty	Unit	Commodity	£	s.	d.	f.
Humphrey Wyes	Ind	1	tun	Wine	0	0	0	0
John Fytzwyllyams	Ind	0.5	C	Hops	0	5	0	0
		2	C	Iron	0	8	0	0
		4	dozen	Flax	0	12	0	0
		4	dozen	Caps	0	3	4	0
		1	C	Orchil	0	13	4	0
		1	stone	Alum	0	0	20	0
		2	dozen	Wool-Cards	0	8	0	0
Dennis Flen	Ind	2	C	Iron	0	8	0	0
		2	dozen	Flax	0	7	0	0
		1	dozen	Wool-Cards	0	4	0	0
		1	piece	Cauldrons, Brass	0	5	0	0
		1	stone	Hops	0	2	6	0
Thomas Scolyn	Ind	4	dozen	Caps	0	3	4	0
		2	dozen	Flax	0	6	0	0
		1	dozen	Wool-Cards	0	4	0	0
		1	piece	Pans, Brass	0	4	0	0
		0.25	C	Hops	0	2	6	0
		1	gross	Combs	0	6	0	0
		6	yard	Cloth of Assize	0	0	0	0

The Sonday of Waterford, William Wodlock master, Exiting, 21st March 1546

Merchant name	Origin	Qty	Unit	Commodity	£	s.	d.	f.
Patrick Strannge	Ind	2	ton	Iron	8	0	0	0
		2	C	Aniseed	0	26	8	0
		1	C	Hops	0	10	0	0
		1.5	gross	Knives	0	10	0	0
		12	gross	Points	0	12	0	0
		0.5	gross	Lacquer	0	0	10	0
Philip Welshe	Ind	1	C	Hops	0	10	0	0
		0.5	C	Aniseed	0	6	8	0
		6	gross	Knives	0	40	0	0
		21	dozen	Knives, in Pairs	1	15	0	0
		12	gross	Points	0	12	0	0
		1	burden	Steel	0	3	4	0
		4	bolt	Thread	0	4	2	0
		1	dozen	Liquorice	0	0	10	0
		5	dozen	Caps	0	4	2	0
		3	dozen	Soap	0	3	9	0
		2	dozen	Soap	0	2	6	0
		0.5	gross	Bowstrings	0	0	12	0
		0.25	piece	Cloth of Assize	0	0	0	0
Robert Manghan	Ind	2	piece	Cloth of Assize	0	0	0	0
		0.5	C	Aniseed	0	6	8	0
		4	dozen	Cumin	0	5	4	0
		4	gross	Knives	0	26	8	0
		0.5	gross	Cutts	0	0	20	0
		1	dozen	Liquorice	0	0	10	0
		2	lb	Kermes	0	2	0	0
		4	dozen	Glasses	0	0	12	0

Merchant name	Origin	Qty	Unit	Commodity	£	s.	d.	f.
		12	gross	Points	0	12	0	0
		1	lb	Nutmeg	0	0	12	0
		4	lb	Verdigris	0	0	20	0
		4	lb	Seed, Onion	0	3	4	0
		2	dozen	Cards, Playing	0	2	6	0
		2	dozen	Girdles, Caddis	0	2	4	0
		6	lb	Pepper	0	6	0	0
		4	dozen	Skins, Golden	0	16	8	0
		2	lb	Mace	0	5	0	0
		2	lb	Ginger	0	3	0	0
		2	lb	Mercury	0	0	10	0
James Maydan &								
Roche	Ind	3	piece	Cloth of Assize, Dozen Strait	0	0	0	0
		0.33	piece	Cloth of Assize	0	0	0	0
		2.5	C	Hops	0	25	0	0
		8	gross	Points	0	8	0	0
		4	dozen	Soap	0	5	0	0
		3	lb	Saffron	0	30	0	0
		2	lb	Silk, *Worked*	0	26	8	0
		0.5	dozen	Caps	0	5	0	0
		1	dozen	Wool-Cards	0	4	0	0
		1	dozen	Liquorice	0	0	15	0
		3	dozen	Girdles	0	2	0	0
		2	dozen	Spectacles	0	0	8	0
		2	pair	Stock-Cards	0	2	0	0
Thomas Shee	Ind	0.75	piece	Cloth of Assize	0	0	0	0
		1	pipe	Iron	2	0	0	0
		6	lb	Saffron	3	0	0	0
		3	lb	Silk, *Worked*	2	0	0	0
		5	gross	Knives	0	33	4	0
		1	C	Hops	0	10	0	0
		0.5	lb	Cinnamon	0	0	15	0
		12	gross	Points	0	12	0	0
		3	gross	Lacquer	0	5	0	0
		4	dozen	Girdles	0	2	8	0
		2	dozen	Cards, Playing	0	2	6	0
		1	dozen	Cumin	0	0	16	0
		1	doz	Alum	0	0	16	0
		1	bolt	Thread	0	0	12	0
		4	dozen	Spectacles	0	0	16	0
		3	dozen	Combs	0	2	0	0
		6	pair	Stock-Cards	0	6	0	0
		4	piece	Felts	0	2	8	0
		12	dozen	Knives, in Pairs	0	20	0	0
James Welshe	Ind	1.25	piece	Cloth of Assize	0	0	0	0
		1.5	gross	Knives	0	10	0	0
		6	dozen	Knives, in Pairs	0	10	0	0
		0.5	C	Alum	0	6	8	0
		0.5	C	Aniseed	0	6	8	0
		0.5	C	Hops	0	5	0	0
		5	dozen	Combs	0	4	0	0
		4	dozen	Girdles	0	2	0	0

Merchant name	Origin	Qty	Unit	Commodity	£	s.	d.	f.
		10	gross	Points	0	10	0	0
		1	gross	Lacquer	0	0	20	0
		2	dozen	Cards, Playing	0	2	6	0
		3	pair	Stock-Cards	0	3	0	0
		3	lb	Senna	0	2	0	0
		1	dozen	Cumin	0	0	16	0
		1	lb	Silk, *Worked*	0	13	4	0
		1	lb	Saffron	0	10	0	0
		2	lb	Cloves & Mace	0	5	0	0
		1	dozen	Caps	0	10	0	0
David Welshe	Ind	1	pipe	Wine	0	0	0	0
Henry Bonfeld	Ind	4	piece	Cloth of Assize	0	0	0	0
		6	lb	Silk, *Worked*	4	0	0	0
		6	lb	Saffron	3	0	0	0
		4	dozen	Skins, Golden	0	16	8	0
		2	gross	Combs	0	8	0	0
		0.5	lb	Borax	0	3	4	0
		0.5	lb	Nutmeg	0	0	6	0
		1	lb	Ginger	0	0	18	0
		10	lb	Thread	0	4	2	0
		4	dozen	Knives, in Pairs	0	6	8	0
		4	lb	Frankincense	0	0	10	0
		4	dozen	Cards, Playing	0	5	0	0
		1.5	lb	Cinnamon	0	3	9	0
		3	lb	Verdigris	0	0	15	0
		2	dozen	Glasses	0	0	16	0
		10	lb	Liquorice	0	0	20	0
		2	lb	Cumin	0	0	5	0
		24	gross	Points	0	24	0	0
		1	gross	Knives	0	6	8	0
		1	unknown	Drugs, miscellaneous	0	20	0	0
John Welshe	Ind	2.5	piece	Cloth of Assize	0	0	0	0
		0.5	C	Aniseed	0	6	8	0
		6	lb	Verdigris	0	2	6	0
		48	gross	Points	2	8	0	0
		1	dozen	Cards, Playing	0	0	15	0
		0.5	gross	Combs	0	2	4	0
		4	dozen	Spectacles	0	2	0	0
		2	lb	Pepper	0	2	0	0
		0.5	gross	Knives	0	3	4	0
		2	clout	Needles	0	2	0	0

The Jhesus of Youghal, John Sheman master, Exiting, *21st March 1546*

Merchant name	Origin	Qty	Unit	Commodity	£	s.	d.	f.
Robert Donell	Ind	1	lb	Saffron	0	10	0	0
		0.5	C	Hops	0	5	0	0
		1	gross	Knives	0	6	8	0
		9	gross	Points	0	9	0	0
		1	dozen	Knives, in Pairs	0	0	20	0
		0.5	gross	Lacquer	0	0	10	0
		6	dozen	Purses	0	2	0	0
		0.5	gross	Combs	0	3	0	0

Merchant name	Origin	Qty	Unit	Commodity	£	s.	d.	f.
		1	dozen	Wool-Cards	0	4	0	0
Philip Rownam	Ind	1	C	Hops	0	10	0	0
		3	stone	Aniseed	0	5	0	0
		0.25	C	Alum	0	3	4	0
		2	gross	Knives	0	13	4	0
		3	dozen	Knives, in Pairs	0	5	0	0
		12	gross	Points	0	12	0	0
		2	dozen	Wool-Cards	0	8	0	0
		2	lb	Cinnamon & Cloves	0	5	0	0
		1	lb	Pepper	0	0	12	0
		2	dozen	Caps	0	20	0	0
		12	dozen	Purses	0	4	0	0
		1	gross	Combs	0	5	0	0
		2	lb	Saffron	0	20	0	0
		1.25	dozen	Cumin	0	0	20	0
		2	dozen	Girdles	0	0	12	0
		1	pipe	Iron	2	0	0	0
		1	gross	Lacquer	0	0	20	0
Thomas Blewet	Ind	1	C	Hops	0	10	0	0
		1	gross	Knives	0	6	8	0
		1	gross	Lacquer	0	0	20	0
		8	gross	Points	0	8	0	0
		1	dozen	Wool-Cards	0	4	0	0
		2	dozen	Knives, in Pairs	0	3	4	0
		6	dozen	Purses	0	2	0	0
		1	dozen	Cards, Playing	0	0	15	0
		0.5	C	Ropes	0	8	0	0
		2	C	Iron	0	8	0	0
		1	barrel	Tar	0	3	4	0
		1	pipe	Wine, Corrupt	0	15	0	0
		4	piece	Cloth of Assize, Dozen Strait	0	0	0	0

The Mary of Milford Haven, Philip Smyth master, Entering, 26th March 1546

Merchant name	Origin	Qty	Unit	Commodity	£	s.	d.	f.
Philip *Smyth* & Putley	Ind	11	barrel	Fish, Herring White	2	15	0	0
		9	C	Fish, Hake	4	10	0	0

The Nicholas of Pembroke, John Phillypps master, Entering, *26th March 1546*

Merchant name	Origin	Qty	Unit	Commodity	£	s.	d.	f.
John Phyllypps	Ind	2	mease	Fish, Herring Red	0	10	0	0
		1	barrel	Fish, Herring White	0	5	0	0

The Nicholas of San Sebastián, John Dorthayda master, Exiting, 27th March 1546

Merchant name	Origin	Qty	Unit	Commodity	£	s.	d.	f.
Andrew de Lasara	Alien	2	piece	Cloth of Assize, Long	0	0	0	0
		8	piece	Cloth of Assize	0	0	0	0
John *Dorthayda* and two assoc.	Alien	34.5	dicker	Hides, Tanned	0	0	0	0
Martin de Burbo	Alien	62	dozen	Skins, Calf	10	6	8	0
		100	piece	Manchester Cotton *Cloth*	50	0	0	0
		3	piece	Cloth of Assize	0	0	0	0
		101.5	dicker	Hides, Tanned	0	0	0	0

Merchant name	Origin	Qty	Unit	Commodity	£	s.	d.	f.
Edmund Jones & Hammond	Ind	6	dozen	Skins, Calf	o	20	o	o
		10	piece	Dunster *Cloth*	5	o	o	o
		12	piece	Cloth of Assize	o	o	o	o
John Well	Ind	40	dicker	Hides, Tanned	o	o	o	o
		2.5	piece	Cloth of Assize	o	o	o	o
William Appowell	Ind	8	piece	Cloth of Assize, Northern Dozen	o	o	o	o
		14	piece	Welsh *Cloth*	14	o	o	o
		8	piece	Dunster *Cloth*	4	o	o	o
		1.75	dicker	Hides, Tanned	o	o	o	o
Andrew Burman	Ind	30	piece	Cloth of Assize	o	o	o	o
John Jakes & Newport	Ind	80	piece	Cloth of Assize	o	o	o	o
John Towlos & Gawardon	Ind	120	piece	Cloth of Assize	o	o	o	o
George Cassy & Cutt	Ind	67.75	piece	Cloth of Assize	o	o	o	o
		15	piece	Manchester Cotton *Cloth*	7	10	o	o

The Martin of Milford Haven, William Lewellyn master, Entering, 29th March 1546

Merchant name	Origin	Qty	Unit	Commodity	£	s.	d.	f.
William Lewellyn	Ind	2	barrel	Fish, Herring White	o	10	o	o

The *Christ*ofer of Waterford, John Strannge master, Entering, *29th March 1546*

Merchant name	Origin	Qty	Unit	Commodity	£	s.	d.	f.
David Welshe	Ind	10	burden	Fish, Salted	2	o	20	o
		43	piece	Mantles	7	3	4	o
		2.5	C	Skins, Sheep	o	25	o	o
		30	yard	Check *Cloth*	o	10	o	o
Nicholas Shee	Ind	4	pipe	Fish, Salmon	6	o	o	o
		21	burden	Fish, Salted	4	7	6	o
		1	C	Fish, Hake	o	10	o	o
		22	piece	Mantles	3	13	4	o
		1	hogshead	Olives	o	42	4	o
James Maydan	Ind	12	C	Fish, Hake	6	o	o	o
		7	piece	Mantles	o	23	4	o
		26	yard	Check *Cloth*	o	8	8	o
		1.5	C	Skins, Sheep	o	15	o	o
		3	barrel	Fish, Herring White	o	15	o	o
David Butlar	Ind	8.5	C	Skins, Sheep	4	5	o	o
		3	C	Check *Cloth*	6	o	o	o
		7	C	Skins, Lamb	2	6	8	o
Nicholas Harold	Ind	2	pipe	Fish, Salmon	3	o	o	o
		1	C	Skins, Sheep	o	10	o	o
		26	yard	Check *Cloth*	o	8	8	o
		30	piece	Skins, Fox	o	5	o	o
		8	piece	Skins, Otter	o	3	4	o
		40	yard	Linen *Cloth*	o	3	4	o
Philip Sawse	Ind	4	C	Skins, Sheep	2	o	o	o
		20	yard	Check *Cloth*	o	6	8	o
		20	lb	Fish, Sturgeon	o	o	20	o
John Welshe	Ind	10	C	Skins, Sheep	5	o	o	o
		1	C	Skins, Lamb	o	6	8	o

Merchant name	Origin	Qty	Unit	Commodity	£	s.	d.	f.
		4	C	Linen *Cloth*	0	40	0	0
		70	yard	Check *Cloth*	0	23	4	0
		18	piece	Skins, Fox	0	3	0	0
		1	piece	Skins, Otter	0	0	5	0

The Julyan of San Sebastián, Stephen de Venyeta master, Entering, 30th March 1546

Merchant name	Origin	Qty	Unit	Commodity	£	s.	d.	f.
Francis Wosley	Ind	6	tun	Wine	0	0	0	0
		30.833	ton	Iron	77	0	20	0
James Boyse	Ind	5	ton	Iron	12	10	0	0
		1	fardell	Canvas *Cloth*	0	40	0	0
Steven De Venyeta	Alien	10	M	Lemons & Oranges	0	35	0	0
		6	C	Canes	0	2	0	0

The John Baptyst, *Port Unknown*, Peter Nam master, Exiting, *30th March 1546*

Merchant name	Origin	Qty	Unit	Commodity	£	s.	d.	f.
Peter Gonsalo	Alien	62.5	piece	Cloth of Assize	0	0	0	0
		30	piece	Dunster *Cloth*	15	0	0	0
		320	piece	Molton and Tavestock *Cloth*	66	13	4	0
		2	ton	Lead, Worked	10	0	0	0
		10	piece	Bristol Frieze Cloth	6	13	4	0
		1	piece	Tin	0	50	0	0
		9	dozen	Skins, Calf	0	30	0	0
		3	dozen	Skins, Sheep Worked	0	3	4	0
Manuel Roderigo	Alien	28	piece	Cloth of Assize	0	0	0	0
Robert Halton	Ind	9.5	piece	Cloth of Assize	0	0	0	0
Edward Pryn & assoc.	Ind	164	piece	Cloth of Assize	0	0	0	0
Nicholas Thorn & assoc.	Ind	140	piece	Cloth of Assize	0	0	0	0
Nicholas Thorn & Pryn	Ind	6	last	Coal	4	0	0	0
		10	ton	Lead, Worked	50	0	0	0
		500	piece	Manchester Cotton *Cloth*	250	0	0	0
James Chester	Ind	25	piece	Cloth of Assize	0	0	0	0
Jasper Fownso	Alien	3	piece	Cloth of Assize	0	0	0	0

The George of Waterford, Robert Maydoll master, Exiting, *30th March 1546*

Merchant name	Origin	Qty	Unit	Commodity	£	s.	d.	f.
Robert *Maydoll*	Ind	1	C	Hops	0	10	0	0
		4	gross	Points	0	4	0	0
		1	gross	Lacquer	0	0	20	0
		2	dozen	Soap	0	2	6	0
		2	pair	Stock-Cards	0	2	0	0
William Skeryll	Ind	6	seam	Woad, Ashes	0	20	0	0
		40	lb	Saffron	20	0	0	0
		18	lb	Silk, *Worked*	12	0	0	0
		108	gross	Points	5	8	0	0
		2.5	gross	Knives	0	16	8	0
		15	lb	Verdigris	0	6	3	0
		1	dozen	Caps	0	10	0	0
		1	dozen	Skins, Golden	0	4	2	0
		1	dozen	Skins, Red	0	2	1	0

Merchant name	Origin	Qty	Unit	Commodity	£	s.	d.	f.
		4	dozen	Combs	0	2	0	0
		4	lb	Liquorice	0	0	10	0
		4	seam	Woad, Ashes	0	13	4	0
		7.25	piece	Cloth of Assize	0	0	0	0
Edmund Grannte	Ind	1	C	Hops	0	10	0	0
		1	lb	Silk, *Worked*	0	13	4	0
		1	lb	Saffron	0	10	0	0
		1	gross	Knives	0	6	8	0
		12	gross	Points	0	12	0	0
		1	gross	Lacquer	0	0	20	0
		0.5	C	Alum	0	6	8	0
Mathew Wyse	Ind	6	lb	Saffron	3	0	0	0
		3	lb	Silk, *Worked*	2	0	0	0
		0.5	gross	Knives	0	3	4	0
		2	piece	Cloth of Assize, Dozen Strait	0	0	0	0
Patrick Maydan	Ind	3	piece	Cloth of Assize	0	0	0	0
		3	bolt	Thread	0	3	0	0
		0.5	gross	Knives	0	3	4	0
Nicholas Maughan	Ind	1.5	lb	Saffron	0	15	0	0
		2	lb	Cinnamon	0	5	0	0
		2	pair	Stock-Cards	0	2	0	0
		2	lb	Kermes	0	2	6	0
		2	gross	Points	0	2	0	0
		0.5	gross	Knives	0	3	4	0
		1	gross	Lacquer	0	0	20	0
Edmund Clery	Ind	1.25	piece	Cloth of Assize	0	0	0	0
		0.5	C	Hops	0	5	0	0
		2	gross	Lacquer	0	3	4	0
		3	gross	Points	0	3	0	0
		1	lb	Saffron	0	10	0	0
Robert Leonard	Ind	2	C	Hops	0	20	0	0
		1	virkin	Honey	0	4	2	0
		4	gross	Knives	0	26	8	0
		12	gross	Points	0	12	0	0
		1.5	gross	Lacquer	0	2	6	0
		5	dozen	Skins, Golden	0	20	10	0
		1	dozen	Caps	0	10	0	0
		12	dozen	Knives, in Pairs	0	20	0	0
		12	dozen	Glasses	0	4	0	0
		12	dozen	*Percular*	0	6	0	0
		6	lb	Thread	0	2	6	0
		2	dozen	Girdles, Ribbon	0	3	4	0
		2	dozen	Cards, Playing	0	2	6	0
		4	dozen	Wool-Cards	0	16	0	0
		1	ream	Paper	0	0	20	0
		5	dozen	Soap	0	6	3	0
		4	lb	Seed, Onion	0	2	6	0
		3	stone	Aniseed & Cumin	0	5	0	0
		2	dozen	Liquorice	0	0	20	0
		0.5	C	Alum	0	6	8	0
		3	piece	Cloth of Assize, Dozen Strait	0	0	0	0
Robert Cranesborowe	Ind	12	dozen	Knives, in Pairs	0	20	0	0

Merchant name	Origin	Qty	Unit	Commodity	£	s.	d.	f.
		3	lb	Saffron	0	30	0	0
		12	pair	Stock-Cards	0	12	0	0
Nicholas Bruar	Ind	2	gross	Knives	0	13	4	0
		3	gross	Points	0	3	0	0
		0.5	C	Hops	0	5	0	0
		1	gross	Lacquer	0	0	20	0
Patrick Carney	Ind	3	lb	Saffron	0	30	0	0
		4	dozen	Knives, in Pairs	0	6	8	0
		1.5	gross	Knives	0	10	0	0
		2	dozen	Cards, Playing	0	2	6	0
		6	gross	Points	0	6	0	0
		1.5	gross	Lacquer	0	2	6	0
George Lee	Ind	2	piece	Cloth of Assize, Dozen Strait	0	0	0	0
		1	gross	Knives	0	6	8	0
		4	gross	Points	0	4	0	0
		1	C	Hops	0	10	0	0
		0.5	dozen	Caps	0	5	0	0
Thomas Skolyn	Ind	2	piece	Cloth of Assize	0	0	0	0
		0.5	C	Alum	0	6	8	0
		5	gross	Knives	0	33	4	0
		0.5	C	Aniseed	0	6	8	0
		4	lb	Verdigris	0	0	20	0
		2	dozen	Knives, in Pairs	0	3	4	0
		2	dozen	Cards, Playing	0	2	6	0
		6	dozen	Skins, Golden	0	25	0	0
		5	lb	Thread	0	2	1	0
		2	lb	Cinnamon	0	5	0	0
		1	lb	Kermes	0	0	12	0
		2	gross	Lacquer	0	3	4	0
		6	dozen	Glasses	0	0	18	0
		2	lb	Mercury	0	0	10	0
		0.5	lb	Mace	0	0	15	0
		24	gross	Points	0	24	0	0
		2	lb	Ginger	0	3	0	0
		2	clout	Needles	0	2	8	0
William Creaghe	Ind	3	gross	Knives	0	20	0	0
		0.5	C	Aniseed	0	6	8	0
		12	lb	Liquorice	0	0	20	0
		1	dozen	Cumin	0	0	16	0
		4	dozen	Skins, Golden	0	16	8	0
		2	dozen	Cards, Playing	0	2	6	0
		0.25	C	Alum	0	3	4	0
		2	dozen	Glasses	0	0	6	0
		1	bolt	Thread	0	0	12	0
		12	gross	Points	0	12	0	0
		2	lb	Silk, *Worked*	0	26	8	0
		2	lb	Saffron	0	20	0	0
		2	dozen	Cards, Playing	0	2	6	0
		1	dozen	Knives, in Pairs	0	0	20	0
		0.5	piece	Cloth of Assize	0	0	0	0
Patrick Fox	Ind	1.5	gross	Knives	0	10	0	0
		43	lb	Liquorice	0	5	0	0

Merchant name	Origin	Qty	Unit	Commodity	£	s.	d.	f.
		0.5	C	Aniseed	0	6	8	0
		10	lb	Thread	0	4	2	0
		0.5	dozen	Caps	0	5	0	0
		4	gross	Points	0	4	0	0
		10	lb	Saffron	5	0	0	0
		2	lb	Silk, *Worked*	0	26	8	0
		0.25	piece	Cloth of Assize	0	0	0	0
Nicholas Flaghe	Ind	1	lb	Saffron	0	10	0	0
		1	gross	Knives	0	6	8	0
Patrick Gybb	Ind	4	piece	Cloth of Assize, Dozen Strait	0	0	0	0
		12	dozen	Knives, in Pairs	0	20	0	0
		36	gross	Points	0	36	0	0
		12	gross	Lacquer	0	20	0	0
		1	lb	Saffron	0	10	0	0
		1	lb	Silk, *Worked*	0	13	4	0
		10	lb	Thread	0	4	2	0
		1	dozen	Caps	0	10	0	0
		4	C	Hops	2	0	0	0
		4	lb	Mercury	0	1	8	0
		1	lb	Nutmeg	0	0	12	0
		1	lb	Kermes	0	0	12	0
		1	gross	Combs	0	12	0	0
		0.25	lb	Mace	0	0	7	2
		1	dozen	Cumin	0	0	16	0
		1	dozen	Liquorice	0	0	20	0
		2	dozen	Cards, Playing	0	2	6	0
John Quede & Whyte	Ind	1.25	piece	Cloth of Assize	0	0	0	0
		1	barrel	Honey	0	16	8	0
		4	lb	Saffron	2	0	0	0
		4	lb	Silk, *Worked*	2	13	4	0
		0.5	C	Hops	0	5	0	0
		6	dozen	Knives, in Pairs	0	10	0	0
		2	gross	Knives	0	13	4	0
		2	dozen	Wool-Cards	0	8	0	0
		1	dozen	Caps	0	10	0	0
		6	pair	Stock-Cards	0	6	0	0
Patrick Sawse & Harold	Ind	4.5	piece	Cloth of Assize	0	0	0	0
		5	lb	Saffron	2	10	0	0
		3	lb	Silk, *Worked*	2	0	0	0
		3	dozen	Knives, in Pairs	0	5	0	0
		7	lb	Thread	0	2	9	0
		1	gross	Knives	0	6	8	0
		24	gross	Points	0	24	0	0
		1	unknown	Drugs, miscellaneous	0	10	0	0

The Sonday of Dungarvan, James Mang*er* master, Exiting, 30th March 1546

Merchant name	Origin	Qty	Unit	Commodity	£	s.	d.	f.
John Browne & assoc.	Ind	13	piece	Cloth of Assize	0	0	0	0
		1.25	C	Lead	0	6	3	0
		2	lb	Silk, *Worked*	0	26	8	0
		1	dozen	Caps	0	10	0	0

Merchant name	Origin	Qty	Unit	Commodity	£	s.	d.	f.

The Mary Grace of Bristol, John de Vusta master, Entering, 31st March 1546

Merchant name	Origin	Qty	Unit	Commodity	£	s.	d.	f.
Nicholas Thorn & assoc.	Ind	20.66	ton	Iron	51	13	4	0
		1.5	tun	Oil, *Olive*	6	0	0	0
Francis Wosley	Ind	1.25	tun	Oil, *Olive*	5	0	0	0
		2	ton	Iron	5	0	0	0
		1	hogshead	Olives	0	20	0	0
		3	balette	Paper	0	40	0	0
		1	C	Locks, small	0	16	8	0
Walter Roberts & assoc.	Ind	12.833	ton	Iron	32	0	20	0
		3	dozen	Serches	0	12	6	0

The *Christ*ofer of Waterford, John Strannge master, Entering, *31st March 1546*

Merchant name	Origin	Qty	Unit	Commodity	£	s.	d.	f.
Fulk Quemyrford	Ind	3	C	Check *Cloth*	6	0	0	0
		12	piece	Mantles	2	0	0	0
		1	virken	Fish, Salmon	0	7	6	0
Richard Turner & assoc.	Ind	11	pipe	Fish, Salmon	16	10	0	0
		2	C	Fish, Hake	0	20	0	0

The *Jhesus* of Pasajes de San Juan, Anthony de Althomira master, Entering, *31st March 1546*

Merchant name	Origin	Qty	Unit	Commodity	£	s.	d.	f.
John Betfyld & Whyte	Ind	5.75	tun	Wine	0	0	0	0
		1	hogshead	Vinegar	0	10	0	0
		30	ton	Salt	15	0	0	0

The Sonday of Bristol, John Brother master, Exiting, 5th April 1546

Merchant name	Origin	Qty	Unit	Commodity	£	s.	d.	f.
John Boughan	Ind	8	pair	Millstones	8	0	0	0
Richard Fyghan	Ind	38	lb	Sugar	0	12	8	0
		0.5	C	Liquorice	0	3	4	0
		36	gross	Points	0	36	0	0
		2	lb	Saffron	0	20	0	0
		3	dozen	Soap	0	3	9	0
		2.5	dozen	Books, Primers	0	3	4	0
Henry Smyth	Ind	1	piece	Bristol Frieze Cloth	0	13	4	0
		20	lb	Sugar	0	6	8	0
		4	M	Fish-Hooks	0	12	0	0

The Mary Rose of Newport, Watkin Thomas master, Entering, 6th April 1546

Merchant name	Origin	Qty	Unit	Commodity	£	s.	d.	f.
Watkin Thomas	Ind	6	ton	Salt	3	0	0	0

The Mary of Youghal, Germain Gryffyth master, Entering, *6th April 1546*

Merchant name	Origin	Qty	Unit	Commodity	£	s.	d.	f.
Germain Gryffyth	Ind	1.25	pipe	Fish, Salmon	0	37	6	0
		2	C	Skins, Sheep	0	20	0	0
		1.5	burden	Fish, Salted	0	6	3	0
William Blewett	Ind	4.25	pipe	Fish, Salmon	6	7	6	0

Merchant name	Origin	Qty	Unit	Commodity	£	s.	d.	f.
		0.5	burden	Fish, Salted	0	2	1	0
		10	C	Skins, Sheep	5	0	0	0
		2	C	Skins, Lamb	0	13	4	0
		1	C	Skins, Kid	0	5	0	0
		6	piece	Skins, Fox	0	0	12	0
Francis Welshe	Ind	1	barrel	Fish, Haddock	0	6	8	0
		2	burden	Fish, Salted	0	8	4	0

The Mary Rose of Newport, Watkin Thomas master, Exiting, 6th April 1546

Merchant name	Origin	Qty	Unit	Commodity	£	s.	d.	f.
Mathew Fernandus	Alien	1.25	piece	Cloth of Assize	0	0	0	0

The Christofer of Waterford, John Strannge master, Exiting, 10th April 1546

Merchant name	Origin	Qty	Unit	Commodity	£	s.	d.	f.
Nicholas Thorn & assoc.	Ind	30	ton	Salt	15	0	0	0
		4	C	Hops	2	0	0	0
		26	lb	Saffron	13	0	0	0
		16	lb	Silk, Worked	10	13	4	0
		12	gross	Points	0	12	0	0
		1	gross	Lacquer	0	0	20	0
		0.5	C	Aniseed	0	6	8	0
		7.5	piece	Cloth of Assize	0	0	0	0
William Tyndale	Ind	1	tun	Wine	0	0	0	0

The George of Cork, Philip Barry master, Exiting, 12th April 1546

Merchant name	Origin	Qty	Unit	Commodity	£	s.	d.	f.
William Sarchefyld	Ind	11.75	piece	Cloth of Assize	0	0	0	0
		3	dozen	Caps	0	30	0	0
		18	dozen	Wool-Cards	3	12	0	0
		3	C	Hops	0	30	0	0
		22	lb	Saffron	11	0	0	0
		1	C	Aniseed	0	13	4	0
		1	lb	Cloves	0	2	6	0
		40	gross	Points	2	0	0	0
		5	gross	Knives	0	33	4	0
		1	lb	Pepper	0	0	12	0
		2	gross	Lacquer	0	3	4	0
		6	lb	Silk, Worked	4	0	0	0
John Copynger & Jacobs	Ind	2	Clb	Twine, for Nets	4	0	0	0
		1	C	Hemp	0	23	4	0
		0.5	gross	Knives	0	3	4	0
		0.33	piece	Cloth of Assize	0	0	0	0
William Copynger	Ind	5	lb	Saffron	3	0	0	0
		5	lb	Silk, Worked	3	6	8	0
		12	gross	Points	0	12	0	0
		0.5	dozen	Caps	0	5	0	0
		2	gross	Lacquer	0	3	4	0
		1	stone	Aniseed	0	0	20	0
		1	piece	Cloth of Assize, Dozen Strait	0	0	0	0
John Browne	Ind	10	gross	Cutts	0	33	4	0

Merchant name	Origin	Qty	Unit	Commodity	£	s.	d.	f.
		10	gross	Points	0	10	0	0
		4	gross	Lacquer	0	6	8	0
Peter Creaghe	Ind	9	gross	Cutts	0	30	0	0
		1	gross	Combs	0	3	4	0
		6	dozen	Spectacles	0	0	18	0
		5	lb	Thread	0	2	1	0
		4	dozen	Knives, in Pairs	0	6	8	0
		2	dozen	Cards, Playing	0	2	6	0
Christopher Tyrry	Ind	14	lb	Silk, *Worked*	9	6	8	0
		0.5	dozen	Caps	0	5	0	0
		8	gross	Cutts	0	26	8	0
		3	C	Iron	0	12	0	0

The Mary of Youghal, Germain Gryffyth master, Exiting, 13th April 1546

Merchant name	Origin	Qty	Unit	Commodity	£	s.	d.	f.
William Blewet	Ind	4	lb	Silk, *Worked*	2	13	4	0
		12	gross	Points	0	12	0	0
		4	dozen	Knives, in Pairs	0	6	8	0
		4	stone	Aniseed	0	6	8	0
		2.5	dozen	Cumin	0	3	4	0
		2	C	Hops	0	20	0	0
		2	gross	Lacquer	0	3	4	0
		2	dozen	Cards, Playing	0	2	6	0
		12	dozen	Purses	0	4	0	0
		10	lb	Sugar	0	3	4	0
Germain Gryffyth	Ind	1	piece	Cloth of Assize, Dozen Strait	0	0	0	0
		2	stone	Orchil	0	3	4	0
		1	dozen	Wool-Cards	0	4	0	0
		1	dozen	Aniseed	0	1	4	0
		1	gross	Points	0	0	12	0
		1	lb	Saffron	0	10	0	0
		1	C	Hops	0	10	0	0
		2	C	Iron	0	8	0	0

The Ann of Milford Haven, Thomas Morgan master, Entering, 14th April 1546

Merchant name	Origin	Qty	Unit	Commodity	£	s.	d.	f.
George Piend	Ind	24	stone	Wool, Flocks	0	10	0	0

The Julian of San Sebastián, Stephende Venyeta master, Exiting, 15th April 1546

Merchant name	Origin	Qty	Unit	Commodity	£	s.	d.	f.
Hugh Hammond	Ind	4	ton	Lead, Worked	20	0	0	0
Stephen *de Venyeta*	Alien	1	ton	Lead, Worked	5	0	0	0
		0.5	piece	Bristol Frieze Cloth	0	6	8	0
Francis Wosley	Ind	5	ton	Lead, Worked	25	0	0	0
		14	dozen	Skins, Calf	2	6	8	0
		4	piece	Cloth of Assize, Dozen Strait	0	0	0	0
		1.5	piece	Cloth of Assize	0	0	0	0
Giles Whyte	Ind	30	piece	Northern Cotton *Cloth*	6	5	0	0

The Nicholas of San Sebastián, John Dorthayda master, Exiting, *15th April 1546*

Merchant name	Origin	Qty	Unit	Commodity	£	s.	d.	f.
Francis Wosley & assoc.	Ind	2	ton	Lead, Worked	10	0	0	0

Merchant name	Origin	Qty	Unit	Commodity	£	s.	d.	f.
	unknown		piece	Vestments	3	6	8	o
		52	piece	Manchester Cotton *Cloth*	26	o	o	o
		10	piece	Cloth of Assize	o	o	o	o

The Mary of Milford Haven, Philip Smyth master, Exiting, 19th April 1546

Merchant name	Origin	Qty	Unit	Commodity	£	s.	d.	f.
Philip *Smyth*	Ind	10	pair	Millstones	10	o	o	o

The Katheryn of Waterford, Peter Fytzjohn master, Entering, 21st April 1546

Merchant name	Origin	Qty	Unit	Commodity	£	s.	d.	f.
Peter Murthe & assoc.	Ind	38	C	Skins, Sheep	19	o	o	o
		4.15	C	Skins, Lamb	13	16	8	o
		34	piece	Skins, Fox	o	5	8	o
		29.5	C	Check *Cloth*	59	o	o	o
		14	piece	Mantles	2	6	8	o
		3.7	dicker	Skins, Deer	o	12	4	o
		18	piece	Skins, Marten	o	18	o	o
		1	piece	Skins, Otter	o	o	5	o
		5	stone	Wool, Flocks	o	2	1	o
Mathew Bossher & assoc.	Ind	8.33	C	Skins, Sheep	4	3	4	o
		1.93	C	Check *Cloth*	3	17	4	o
		20	piece	Skins, Fox	o	3	4	o
		20	piece	Skins, Fox	o	3	4	o
		26	piece	Mantles	4	6	8	o
		5.25	C	Skins, Lamb	o	35	o	o

The John Baptist, *Port Unknown*, Peter Nam master, Exiting, 26th April 1546

Merchant name	Origin	Qty	Unit	Commodity	£	s.	d.	f.
Thomas Hycks	Ind	60	dozen	Skins, Calf	10	o	o	o
		1	piece	Cloth of Assize	o	o	o	o
William Ballard	Ind	9.75	piece	Cloth of Assize	o	o	o	o
		44	piece	Manchester Cotton *Cloth*	22	o	o	o
George Eton	Ind	9	piece	Cloth of Assize	o	o	o	o
Nicholas Thorn & assoc.	Ind	40	piece	Cloth of Assize	o	o	o	o
John Whyte	Ind	200	piece	Manchester Cotton *Cloth*	100	o	o	o
William Shypman	Ind	10	piece	Cloth of Assize	o	o	o	o
Francis Codryngton	Ind	8	piece	Cloth of Assize	o	o	o	o
James Chester	Ind	20	piece	Welsh Cloth, Dozen Strait	4	3	4	o
John Pryn	Ind	28	piece	Manchester Cotton *Cloth*	14	o	o	o
		11	piece	Cloth of Assize	o	o	o	o
Amathere Perys	Alien	2	piece	Cloth of Assize	o	o	o	o
		1	piece	Bristol Frieze Cloth	o	13	4	o
John Pryn & Channceler	Ind	13	dozen	Skins, Calf	2	3	4	o

The Trynyte of Pasajes de San Juan, William de Londres master, Exiting, 31st April 1546

Merchant name	Origin	Qty	Unit	Commodity	£	s.	d.	f.
Martin Burbo	Alien	15.4	dicker	Hides, Tanned	o	o	o	o
Francis Wosley	Ind	1	ton	Lead, Worked	5	o	o	o
Giles Whyte	Ind	25	piece	Cloth of Assize, Northern Strait	5	4	2	o

Merchant name	Origin	Qty	Unit	Commodity	£	s.	d.	f.
John Jakes	Ind	54	piece	Cloth of Assize	0	0	0	0

The Dowghan of Cardiff, David Watkyns master, Entering, 3rd May 1546

Merchant name	Origin	Qty	Unit	Commodity	£	s.	d.	f.
John Roberts	Ind	1	tun	Oil, *Olive*	4	0	0	0
		60	lb	Sugar	0	20	0	0

The Trynyte of Chepstow, Lewis Haynes master, Entering, 3rd May 1546

Merchant name	Origin	Qty	Unit	Commodity	£	s.	d.	f.
William Harvest	Ind	5	ton	Salt	2	10	0	0

The Mychaell of Laugharne, William Gylford master, Entering, 3rd May 1546

Merchant name	Origin	Qty	Unit	Commodity	£	s.	d.	f.
John Pryn	Ind	60	lb	Sugar	0	20	0	0

The Mary Katheryn of Tenby, John Elyot master, Entering, 4th May 1546

Merchant name	Origin	Qty	Unit	Commodity	£	s.	d.	f.
Richard Baynam	Ind	3.5	chest	Sugar	3	0	0	0
		2	tun	Oil, *Olive*	8	0	0	0

The Katheryn of Pasajes de San Juan, John Note de Villa Vaosa master, Entering, 4th May 1546

Merchant name	Origin	Qty	Unit	Commodity	£	s.	d.	f.
John De Skyes	Alien	46	tun	Wine	0	0	0	0
		9	tun	Wine, Corrupt	13	10	0	0
		32.5	balette	Woad, Toulouse	20	0	0	0
		12	piece	Raisins, *Great*	0	13	4	0
		2	ton	Iron	5	0	0	0
		1.5	C	Frankincense	0	6	8	0

The Katheryn of Waterford, Robert Fyghtzjohn master, Exiting, 4th May 1546

Merchant name	Origin	Qty	Unit	Commodity	£	s.	d.	f.
James Kenny	Ind	1	gross	Lacquer	0	0	20	0
		0.5	C	Hops	0	5	0	0
Patrick Rothe	Ind	8.5	piece	Cloth of Assize	0	0	0	0
		36	gross	Points	0	36	0	0
		8	gross	Lacquer	0	13	4	0
		1	dozen	Caps	0	10	0	0
		3	stone	Aniseed	0	5	0	0
		6	lb	Liquorice	0	0	10	0
		7	gross	Knives	2	6	8	0
		2	C	Hops	0	20	0	0
John Browne	Ind	30	lb	Saffron	15	0	0	0
		20	lb	Silk, *Worked*	13	6	8	0
		7	dozen	Wool-Cards	0	28	0	0
Mathew Boysher	Ind	4	dozen	Girdles	0	2	0	0
		5	lb	Thread	0	2	1	0
		1	dozen	Skins, Red	0	2	1	0
		1	ream	Paper	0	0	20	0
		9	dozen	Cards, Playing	0	11	3	0
		4	dozen	Skins, Golden	0	16	8	0
		12	dozen	Spectacles, Pocket	0	3	0	0

Merchant name	Origin	Qty	Unit	Commodity	£	s.	d.	f.
		0.5	dozen	Books, Primers	0	0	8	0
		0.5	lb	Cinnamon	0	0	15	0
		1	dozen	Hats	0	3	0	0
		2	lb	Saffron	0	20	0	0
		40	lb	Wood, Brazil	0	12	6	0
		12	gross	Points	0	12	0	0
		1	gross	Lacquer	0	0	20	0
		1	dozen	Soap	0	0	15	0
		10	dozen	Knives, in Pairs	0	16	8	0
Richard Turnar	Ind	18.5	piece	Cloth of Assize	0	0	0	0
		38	lb	Silk, *Worked*	25	6	8	0
		2	lb	Saffron	0	20	0	0
		2	dozen	Nightcaps, Velvet	2	8	0	0
		0.5	dozen	Nightcaps, Satin	0	6	0	0

The Gryffyn of Middelburg, Stephen Stephens master, Entering, 5th May 1546

Merchant name	Origin	Qty	Unit	Commodity	£	s.	d.	f.
Michael de Possa	Alien	11.5	tun	Wine	0	0	0	0
		108	seron	Soap	80	0	0	0
		42.5	tun	Oil, *Olive*	170	0	0	0
Stephen Coole & Butlar	Alien	5	ton	Salt	2	10	0	0

The Sonday of Bristol, Henry Whyte master, Entering, 7th May 1546

Merchant name	Origin	Qty	Unit	Commodity	£	s.	d.	f.
John Gryffyth	Ind	0.5	wey	Grain	0	10	0	0
		3	stone	Wool, Irish	0	8	0	0

The Julyan of Tenby, Nicholas Harrys master, Entering, 10th May 1546

Merchant name	Origin	Qty	Unit	Commodity	£	s.	d.	f.
Amathere Perys	Alien	31.5	chest	Sugar	31	0	0	0
Thomas Langston	Ind	1.5	tun	Oil, *Olive*	6	0	0	0

The Trynyte of Bristol, John Jeynes master, Entering, 11th May 1546

Merchant name	Origin	Qty	Unit	Commodity	£	s.	d.	f.
William Butlar	Ind	3	ton	Salt	0	30	0	0

The Katheryn of Pasajes de San Juan, John Nott master, Exiting, 16th May 1546

Merchant name	Origin	Qty	Unit	Commodity	£	s.	d.	f.
John Well	Ind	3.5	dicker	Hides, Tanned	0	0	0	0
John *Note*	Alien	4	ton	Lead	20	0	0	0
		14	dozen	Skins, Calf	2	6	8	0
Andrew De Jarsa	Alien	12.5	dicker	Hides, Tanned	0	0	0	0
Giles Whyte	Ind	26	piece	Northern Cotton *Cloth*	5	8	4	0
Francis Codryngton	Ind	10	piece	Cloth of Assize	0	0	0	0
		88	piece	Manchester Cotton *Cloth*	44	0	0	0
		3.5	ton	Lead	17	10	0	0
William Harvest	Ind	30	piece	Manchester Cotton *Cloth*	15	0	0	0
William Cary	Ind	2	piece	Bristol Frieze Cloth	0	26	8	0
		3	piece	Brecon *Cloth*	3	0	0	0
		3.75	piece	Cloth of Assize	0	0	0	0

Merchant name	Origin	Qty	Unit	Commodity	£	s.	d.	f.

The Sancta Maria of Errenteria, Julian de Vocivita master, Entering, 18th May 1546

Merchant name	Origin	Qty	Unit	Commodity	£	s.	d.	f.
William Appowell	Ind	26	ton	Iron	65	0	0	0
		15.5	balette	Woad, Toulouse	9	7	6	0
		5	tun	Wine	0	0	0	0
William Ballard	Ind	7	ton	Iron	17	10	0	0
John Well	Ind	18	ton	Iron	45	0	0	0
William Yonge	Ind	13	tun	Wine	0	0	0	0
		1	tun	Wine, Corrupt	0	30	0	0
William Cary	Ind	10.5	tun	Wine	0	0	0	0
		4	ton	Iron	10	0	0	0
William Joanes	Ind	8.5	tun	Wine	0	0	0	0
		1	tun	Wine, Corrupt	0	30	0	0
Edmund Jones	Ind	1	tun	Wine	0	0	0	0
Robert Jeffreys	Ind	1	pipe	Iron	0	25	0	0
John Channceler	Ind	0.75	ton	Iron	0	37	6	0
Stephen de Olathola	Alien	2	hogshead	Vinegar	0	20	0	0
Julian de Vocivita	Alien	27	ton	Iron	67	10	0	0
		5	dozen	Serches	0	20	10	0
		3	M	Oranges	0	10	0	0
		22	piece	Skins, for Fletchers	0	6	8	0
		1	M	Canes	0	6	8	0
		30	dozen	Skins, Budge	3	0	0	0
Martin de Peragera	Alien	440	dozen	Skins, Budge	44	0	0	0
		6	piece	Skins, Marten	0	6	0	0
		1	piece	Skins, Beech Marten	0	0	12	0
		1	piece	Skins, Genet	0	0	12	0
		5	piece	Skins, Wildcat	0	0	10	0
		7	piece	Skins, Fox	0	0	14	0
Martin de Savala	Alien	320	dozen	Skins, Budge	32	0	0	0
		3.5	C	Skins, Lamb	0	23	4	0
		1.75	C	Skins, Sheep	0	20	0	0
		4	piece	Skins, Genet	0	4	0	0
		1	piece	Skins, Marten	0	0	12	0
		1	piece	Skins, Beech Marten	0	0	12	0
		4	piece	Skins, Fox	0	0	8	0

The Margerete of Caerleon, John Wyllyams master, Entering, 24th May 1546

Merchant name	Origin	Qty	Unit	Commodity	£	s.	d.	f.
Richard Davys	Ind	2	ton	Salt	0	20	0	0

The Mary of Tenby, William Harrys master, Entering, 24th May 1546

Merchant name	Origin	Qty	Unit	Commodity	£	s.	d.	f.
William Appowell	Ind	0.5	tun	Oil, Train	0	23	4	0

The Trynyte George of Bristol, Richard Bryan master, Entering, 26th May 1546

Merchant name	Origin	Qty	Unit	Commodity	£	s.	d.	f.
William Gelly	Ind	4.25	tun	Oil, *Olive*	17	0	0	0
		1.5	wey	Barley	0	25	0	0
		2	burden	Fish, Salted	0	8	4	0
		1.5	dicker	Skins, Salted	0	20	0	0

Merchant name	Origin	Qty	Unit	Commodity	£	s.	d.	f.

The Sancta Maria of Errenteria, John de Bereby master, Entering, 28th May 1546

Merchant name	Origin	Qty	Unit	Commodity	£	s.	d.	f.
William Rowley	Ind	2.33	ton	Iron	5	16	8	0
William Cary	Ind	4.833	ton	Iron	12	1	8	0
Richard Cary	Ind	4.666	ton	Iron	11	13	4	0
William & Robert Tyndale	Ind	33.5	ton	Iron	83	15	0	0
Simon Dowtyng	Ind	3.33	ton	Iron	8	6	0	0
John Hengod	Ind	2	ton	Iron	5	0	0	0
Giles Whyte	Ind	2.5	ton	Iron	6	5	0	0
		5.25	tun	Wine	0	0	0	0
		1	tun	Wine, Corrupt	0	30	0	0
Martin de Burbo	Alien	8	ton	Iron	20	0	0	0
John *de Bereby* & assoc.	Alien	9.5	ton	Iron	23	15	0	0
		4	M	Canes	0	13	4	0
		6	dozen	Skins, Budge	0	20	0	0
William Kyrk	Ind	1	ton	Iron	2	10	0	0
George Snygg	Ind	7	ton	Iron	17	10	0	0
William Yonge	Ind	2	ton	Iron	5	0	0	0
Hugh Gyttens	Ind	2.33	ton	Iron	5	16	8	0
John Newport	Ind	10	ton	Iron	25	0	0	0
William Ballard	Ind	1	hogshead	Iron	0	12	6	0
Thomas Cutt	Ind	9	C	Feathers	4	10	0	0
		4	bale	Woad, Toulouse	5	0	0	0

The Patrike of Youghal, Cornell Alan master, Entering, *28th May 1546*

Merchant name	Origin	Qty	Unit	Commodity	£	s.	d.	f.
Patrick Rownam	Ind	10	C	Skins, Lamb	3	6	8	0
		5	C	Skins, Sheep	2	10	0	0
		4	pipe	Fish, Salmon	6	0	0	0
		3	stone	Fish, Sturgeon Broken	0	6	0	0
		20	piece	Skins, Fox	0	3	4	0
Cornell Canyard & Blewet	Ind	2	pipe	Fish, Salmon	3	0	0	0
		6	piece	Mantles	0	20	0	0
		80	yard	Check *Cloth*	0	26	8	0
		4	stone	Wool, Flocks	0	0	20	0
		5	C	Skins, Lamb	0	33	4	0
Nicholas Shee	Ind	3.5	pipe	Fish, Salmon	5	5	0	0

The Margeret of Newport, John Thomas master, Entering, *28th May 1546*

Merchant name	Origin	Qty	Unit	Commodity	£	s.	d.	f.
John Thomas	Ind	5	ton	Salt	2	10	0	0

The Sancta Maria of Errenteria, Julian de Vocivita master, Exiting, 29th May 1546

Merchant name	Origin	Qty	Unit	Commodity	£	s.	d.	f.
Francis Codryngton	Ind	10	piece	Cloth of Assize	0	0	0	0
		44	piece	Manchester Cotton *Cloth*	22	0	0	0
		3	C	Lead	0	15	0	0
John Well	Ind	55	dicker	Hides, Tanned	0	0	0	0
		5	C	Lead, Worked	0	25	0	0
Thomas Harrys	Ind	24	dicker	Hides, Tanned	0	0	0	0
		8	piece	Cloth of Assize	0	0	0	0

Merchant name	Origin	Qty	Unit	Commodity	£	s.	d.	f.
William Yonge	Ind	2	dicker	Hides, Tanned	0	0	0	0
		8	dozen	Skins, Calf	0	26	8	0
Robert Gyttons	Ind	9	dicker	Hides, Tanned	0	0	0	0
Julian de Vocivita	Alien	0.33	piece	Cloth of Assize	0	0	0	0
John Cutt	Ind	2	ton	Lead	10	0	0	0
Edmund Joanes	Ind	20	dozen	Skins, Calf	3	6	8	0

The Sancta Maria of Errenteria, John de Beroby master, Exiting, 1st June 1546

Merchant name	Origin	Qty	Unit	Commodity	£	s.	d.	f.
William Tyndale	Ind	20	ton	Lead	100	0	0	0
		30	dozen	Skins, Calf	5	0	0	0
		3	piece	Brecon *Cloth*	3	0	0	0
		12	dozen	Skins, Calf	2	0	0	0
		27.75	dicker	Hides, Tanned	0	0	0	0
Laurence de Iraso	Alien	2	C	Skins, Sheep Worked	0	21	6	0
Francis Wosley	Ind	2	ton	Lead	10	0	0	0
William Yonge	Ind	13	piece	Cloth of Assize	0	0	0	0
		6	ton	Lead, Worked	30	0	0	0
Giles Whyte	Ind	2.5	piece	Cloth of Assize	0	0	0	0
Thomas Harrys	Ind	10	dicker	Hides, Tanned	0	0	0	0
William Cary	Ind	1.25	piece	Cloth of Assize	0	0	0	0
John Pryn	Ind	15	piece	Cloth of Assize	0	0	0	0
Hugh Gyttons	Ind	2	ton	Lead	10	0	0	0
		5	piece	Cloth of Assize	0	0	0	0
		6	dicker	Hides, Tanned	0	0	0	0
Robert Gyttons	Ind	20	dozen	Skins, Calf	3	6	8	0
		5	dicker	Hides, Tanned	0	0	0	0
William Appowell	Ind	10	piece	Cloth of Assize	0	0	0	0
		10	piece	Welsh *Cloth*	10	0	0	0
		10	piece	Dunster *Cloth*	5	0	0	0

The Sonday of Bristol, John Gryffyth master, Exiting, *1st June 1546*

Merchant name	Origin	Qty	Unit	Commodity	£	s.	d.	f.
John Worley	Ind	10	pair	Millstones	10	0	0	0
Nicholas Kelly	Ind	48	C	Quadrear	0	13	4	0
John Pavy	Ind	4	piece	Bristol Frieze Cloth	2	13	4	0

The Howbard of Arnemuiden, Peter Fryse master, Entering, 4th June 1546

Merchant name	Origin	Qty	Unit	Commodity	£	s.	d.	f.
Peter *Fryse*	Alien	22	tun	Wine	0	0	0	0

The Julyan of Wexford, Thomas Saint John master, Entering, 6th June 1546

Merchant name	Origin	Qty	Unit	Commodity	£	s.	d.	f.
Richard Hycksley	Ind	5	tun	Oil, *Olive*	20	0	0	0
Thomas *Saint* John	Ind	0.75	C	Skins, Sheep	0	7	6	0
		0.5	C	Skins, Lamb	0	3	4	0
		3	piece	Skins, Fox	0	0	6	0
John Stafford	Ind	3	piece	Mantles	0	10	0	0

The Mary of Milford Haven, Philip Smyth master, Entering, *6th June 1546*

Merchant name	Origin	Qty	Unit	Commodity	£	s.	d.	f.
John Boughan	Ind	7.5	C	Check *Cloth*	15	0	0	0

Merchant name	Origin	Qty	Unit	Commodity	£	s.	d.	f.
The Patrycke of Youghal, Cornell Alyn master, Exiting, 8th June 1546								
Patrick Rownam	Ind	5	gross	Knives	0	33	4	0
		5	dozen	Wool-Cards	0	20	0	0
		1.5	gross	Cutts	0	5	0	0
		8	dozen	Combs	0	4	0	0
		4	lb	Silk, *Worked*	2	13	4	0
		2	lb	Saffron	0	20	0	0
		2	dozen	Cards, Playing	0	2	6	0
		1	lb	Cinnamon & Cloves	0	2	6	0
		1	dozen	Knives, in Pairs	0	0	20	0
		6	dozen	Purses, belt	0	2	0	0
		1	lb	Mace	0	2	6	0
		1	lb	Verdigris	0	0	5	0
		12	gross	Points	0	12	0	0
		1	C	Hops	0	10	0	0
		1	stone	Aniseed	0	0	20	0
		0.5	dozen	Caps	0	5	0	0
Melchior Blewett	Ind	2	lb	Saffron	0	20	0	0
		1	dozen	Wool-Cards	0	4	0	0
		2	stone	Orchil	0	3	4	0
The Mary of Gloucester, William Hale master, Entering, 9th June 1546								
John Greves	Ind	5	ton	Salt	2	10	0	0
The Julyan of Wexford, Thomas Saint John master, Exiting, 10th June 1546								
Patrick Murthye & Rowth	Ind	10	piece	Cloth of Assize, Dozen Strait	0	0	0	0
		8	lb	Silk, *Worked*	5	6	8	0
		1	lb	Saffron	0	10	0	0
		2	C	Hops	0	20	0	0
		1	dozen	Caps	0	10	0	0
		1	dozen	Nightcaps, Velvet	0	26	8	0
		1	dozen	Nightcaps, Satin	0	12	0	0
		1	dozen	Nightcaps, Woollen	0	5	0	0
		3	dozen	Caps	0	30	0	0
		2	ream	Paper	0	3	4	0
		1	dozen	Skins, Red	0	2	1	0
		25	dozen	Knives, in Pairs	2	0	20	0
		12	dozen	Spectacles	0	3	0	0
		1	dozen	Cards, Playing	0	0	15	0
		4	lb	Thread, Blue	0	0	20	0
		48	gross	Points	2	8	0	0
		4	gross	Lacquer	0	6	8	0
		2	bolt	Thread	0	2	1	0
		3	dozen	Hats	0	15	0	0
The Mary Norton, Walter Bryte master, Entering, 15th June 1546								
Thomas Launsdown	Ind	1.5	tun	Wine	0	0	0	0
John Swan	Ind	2	ton	Salt	0	20	0	0

Merchant name	Origin	Qty	Unit	Commodity	£	s.	d.	f.

The John of Waterford, Richard Kyrry master, Entering, 21st June 1546

Merchant name	Origin	Qty	Unit	Commodity	£	s.	d.	f.
George Brydgis	Ind	410	dozen	Skins, Sheep Broken	10	5	0	0
		20	M	Skins, Rabbit	33	6	8	0
		36	C	Skins, Lamb	12	0	0	0
		4	piece	Skins, Fox	0	0	8	0
		2	piece	Skins, Wolf	0	0	20	0
Richard *Kyrry*	Ind	1	C	Skins, Sheep	0	10	0	0
		8	C	Skins, Lamb	2	13	4	0
		1	C	Skins, Kid	0	5	0	0
		4	piece	Mantles	0	13	4	0

The Bark Seymer of Bristol, John Boyssher master, Exiting, *21st June 1546*

Merchant name	Origin	Qty	Unit	Commodity	£	s.	d.	f.
William Sheryngton	Ind	7	last	Coal	4	13	4	0
		2	ton	Lead, Worked	10	0	0	0

The John of Waterford, Richard Kyrry master, Exiting, 26th June 1546

Merchant name	Origin	Qty	Unit	Commodity	£	s.	d.	f.
Richard *Kyrry*	Ind	1.25	C	Aniseed	0	16	8	0
		1.5	C	Hops	0	15	0	0

The Mary of Tenby, Harry William master, Entering, 30th June 1546

Merchant name	Origin	Qty	Unit	Commodity	£	s.	d.	f.
William Appowell & Butlar	Ind	15	ton	Salt	7	10	0	0
		1	tun	Vinegar	2	0	0	0

The Mary of Milford Haven, Philip Smyth master, Exiting, *30th June 1546*

Merchant name	Origin	Qty	Unit	Commodity	£	s.	d.	f.
Philip *Smyth*	Ind	10	pair	Millstones	5	0	0	0

The Mary Norton, *Port Unknown*, Walter Bryte master, Entering, *30th June 1546*

Merchant name	Origin	Qty	Unit	Commodity	£	s.	d.	f.
William Butlar	Ind	2.25	tun	Oil, *Olive*	9	0	0	0

The Dowghan of Cardiff, David Watkyns master, Entering, 3rd July 1546

Merchant name	Origin	Qty	Unit	Commodity	£	s.	d.	f.
John Northall & assoc.	Ind	5	ton	Woad, Toulouse	50	0	0	0
		5.15	ton	Iron	13	0	0	0

The Mary George of Moreton, Robert Tewe master, Entering, 8th July 1546

Merchant name	Origin	Qty	Unit	Commodity	£	s.	d.	f.
Robert *Tewe* & assoc.	Ind	5	ton	Salt	2	10	0	0

The Sonday of Bristol, Bartholomew Garland master, Entering, 12th July 1546

Merchant name	Origin	Qty	Unit	Commodity	£	s.	d.	f.
John Gryffyth & assoc.	Ind	12	burden	Fish, Salted	2	10	0	0
		12	stone	Wool, Irish	0	32	0	0
Henry Rownsell	Ind	1	wey	Barley	0	16	8	0
		2	burden	Fish, Salted	0	8	4	0
		10	stone	Wool, Irish	0	16	8	0

Merchant name	Origin	Qty	Unit	Commodity	£	s.	d.	f.

The Trynyte of Bristol, John Veneam master, Exiting, 14th July 1546

Merchant name	Origin	Qty	Unit	Commodity	£	s.	d.	f.
John Capps	Ind	3	tun	Wine, Corrupt	4	10	0	0

The Anthony of Milford Haven, John Brother master, Entering, 15th July 1546

Merchant name	Origin	Qty	Unit	Commodity	£	s.	d.	f.
Thomas Nayle	Ind	7	C	Skins, Lamb	2	6	8	0
		7	C	Skins, Sheep	3	10	0	0
		2	C	Check *Cloth*	4	0	0	0
		4	piece	Mantles	0	13	4	0
		2	piece	Skins, Marten	0	2	0	0
		4	piece	Skins, Wolf	0	3	4	0
Peter Astekyn	Ind	25	C	Skins, Lamb	8	6	8	0
		30	piece	Skins, Fox	0	5	0	0
		3	piece	Skins, Otter	0	0	15	0
		1	C	Irish Linen *Cloth*	0	10	0	0
		4.5	C	Check *Cloth*	9	0	0	0
		38	piece	Mantles	6	6	8	0

The Mysericordia of Vila Do Conde, Anthony Lews master, Entering, *15th July 1546*

Merchant name	Origin	Qty	Unit	Commodity	£	s.	d.	f.
Nicholas Thorn & assoc.	Ind	70	tun	Oil, *Olive*	280	0	0	0
		14	tun	Wine	0	0	0	0
John Whyte & assoc.	Ind	19	tun	Oil, *Olive*	76	0	0	0

The Trynyte of Bristol, Richard Wathen master, Exiting, 17th July 1546

Merchant name	Origin	Qty	Unit	Commodity	£	s.	d.	f.
William Harvest & Kelly	Ind	1.5	ton	Iron	6	0	0	0
		1	C	Hops	0	10	0	0
		1	piece	Cloth of Assize	0	0	0	0
William Chester	Ind	2	piece	Cloth of Assize, Dozen	0	0	0	0
		2	piece	Cloth of Assize, Dozen Strait	0	0	0	0
		2	dozen	Aniseed	0	3	0	0
		2	lb	Silk, *Worked*	0	26	8	0
		1	gross	Knives	0	6	8	0
Giles Rede	Ind	84	gross	Points	4	4	0	0
		12	gross	Lacquer	0	20	0	0
		3	lb	Saffron	0	30	0	0
Thomas Chester	Ind	1	pipe	Wine	0	0	0	0
Henry Rownsell	Ind	7	yard	Cloth of Assize	0	0	0	0
		2	M	Hooks, Small	0	3	4	0
		21	dozen	Hooks	0	7	0	0
		6	M	Assicul	0	2	0	0
		1	lb	Silk, *Worked*	0	13	4	0
		1	M	Pins	0	2	0	0
		2	dozen	Ribbons, Saye	0	8	0	0
		1	lb	Thread	0	0	5	0
		12	dozen	Glasses	0	4	0	0
		1	gross	Lacquer	0	0	20	0
		4	burden	Steel	0	13	4	0

Merchant name	Origin	Qty	Unit	Commodity	£	s.	d.	f.
		2	gross	Points, Silk	0	4	0	0
		60	gross	Points	3	0	0	0
		6	dozen	Girdles	0	4	0	0
		3	yard	Velvet *Cloth*	0	22	6	0

The George of Waterford, Robert Medoll master, Entering, 20th July 1546

Merchant name	Origin	Qty	Unit	Commodity	£	s.	d.	f.
Richard Donell	Ind	10	C	Skins, Sheep	5	0	0	0
		10	C	Skins, Lamb	3	6	8	0
		8	C	Check *Cloth*	16	0	0	0
		4	piece	Mantles	0	13	4	0
		6	piece	Skins, Fox	0	0	12	0
Francis Faylan	Ind	8	C	Skins, Sheep	4	0	0	0
		6	C	Skins, Lamb	2	0	0	0
		3	C	Check *Cloth*	6	0	0	0
Thomas Rothe	Ind	5	C	Check *Cloth*	10	0	0	0
		34	piece	Mantles	5	13	4	0
		7	C	Skins, Sheep	3	10	0	0
		2	dicker	Skins, Deer	0	6	8	0
		10	C	Skins, Lamb	3	6	8	0
		6	piece	Skins, Fox	0	0	12	0
		2	stone	Wool, Flocks	0	0	10	0
Percy Rowthe	Ind	45	piece	Mantles	7	10	0	0
		17	C	Skins, Lamb	5	13	4	0
		11	C	Skins, Sheep	5	10	0	0
		1.5	C	Check *Cloth*	3	0	0	0
		9	piece	Skins, Fox	0	0	18	0
		10	stone	Wool, Flocks	0	4	2	0
John Quott	Ind	1	C	Check *Cloth*	2	0	0	0
		24	piece	Mantles	4	0	0	0
		2	C	Skins, Lamb	0	13	4	0
		1	C	Skins, Sheep	0	10	0	0
		5	stone	Wool, Flocks	0	2	1	0
Edmund Grannte	Ind	3	C	Check *Cloth*	6	0	0	0
		20	piece	Mantles	3	6	8	0
		3	C	Skins, Lamb	0	20	0	0
		3	C	Skins, Sheep	0	30	0	0
		2	stone	Wool, Flocks	0	0	20	0
Walter Molrony	Ind	3	C	Skins, Sheep	0	30	0	0
		5	C	Skins, Lamb	0	33	4	0
		1.5	C	Check *Cloth*	3	0	0	0
		3	piece	Mantles	0	10	0	0
		12	piece	Skins, Fox	0	2	0	0
John Murthe	Ind	12	C	Skins, Sheep	6	0	0	0
		17	C	Skins, Lamb	5	13	4	0
		18	piece	Skins, Fox	0	3	0	0
		2.5	C	Check *Cloth*	5	0	0	0
		4	piece	Mantles	0	13	4	0
Peter Savage	Ind	9	C	Skins, Sheep	4	10	0	0
		5.5	C	Check *Cloth*	11	0	0	0
		1.6	dicker	Skins, Deer	0	5	4	0
		3	stone	Wool, Flocks	0	0	15	0

Merchant name	Origin	Qty	Unit	Commodity	£	s.	d.	f.
		2.5	stone	Wool, Irish	0	6	8	0
		20	piece	Skins, Fox	0	3	4	0
		2.5	C	Skins, Kid	0	12	6	0
		8	piece	Mantles	0	26	8	0
James Laynard	Ind	12	C	Skins, Lamb	4	0	0	0
George Savage	Ind	10	C	Skins, Sheep	5	0	0	0
		5.5	C	Check *Cloth*	9	0	0	0
		50	piece	Mantles	8	6	8	0
		20	piece	Skins, Fox	0	3	4	0
		17	C	Skins, Lamb	5	13	4	0
		3	piece	Skins, Otter	0	0	15	0
		8	stone	Wool, Flocks	0	3	4	0
		1	C	Skins, Kid	0	5	0	0
Benedict Sall	Ind	5.5	C	Check *Cloth*	11	0	0	0
		12	piece	Mantles	2	0	0	0
		2	C	Skins, Lamb	0	13	4	0
		1	C	Skins, Sheep	0	10	0	0
Nicholas Sepers	Ind	3	C	Check *Cloth*	6	0	0	0
		2	C	Skins, Lamb	0	13	4	0
		6	piece	Mantles	0	20	0	0
Henry Whyte	Ind	16	piece	Mantles	0	53	4	0
		1.5	C	Check *Cloth*	3	0	0	0
		0.5	C	Skins, Sheep	0	5	0	0
		0.5	C	Skins, Lamb	0	3	4	0
Nicholas Brewar & assoc.	Ind	30	piece	Mantles	5	0	0	0
		1	C	Check *Cloth*	0	40	0	0
Philip Rychards	Ind	24	piece	Skins, Marten	0	24	0	0
		0.5	C	Skins, Lamb	0	3	4	0
		4	piece	Skins, Otter	0	0	20	0
Edmund Clery	Ind	21	piece	Mantles	3	10	0	0
		0.5	C	Skins, Lamb	0	3	4	0
		1	C	Skins, Sheep	0	10	0	0
Robert Maydoll	Ind	2	C	Check *Cloth*	4	0	0	0
		1	C	Skins, Sheep	0	10	0	0
		12	piece	Mantles	2	0	0	0
		21	stone	Wool, Irish	2	16	0	0
Thomas Harold	Ind	6	C	Skins, Sheep	3	0	0	0
		3	C	Skins, Lamb	0	20	0	0
		2	C	Irish Linen *Cloth*	0	20	0	0
		28	yard	Check *Cloth*	0	9	4	0
		12	piece	Skins, Fox	0	2	0	0
		3	piece	Skins, Otter	0	0	15	0
Thomas Stackpoll	Ind	1.5	C	Irish Linen *Cloth*	0	15	0	0
		6	piece	Skins, Fox	0	0	12	0
		0.5	C	Skins, Sheep	0	5	0	0
Lewis Robyns	Ind	22.5	C	Skins, Lamb	7	10	0	0

The Michael of Milford Haven, John Hycks master, Entering, 20th July 1546

Merchant name	Origin	Qty	Unit	Commodity	£	s.	d.	f.
James Leonard	Ind	4	C	Check *Cloth*	8	0	0	0
		23	C	Skins, Lamb	7	13	4	0

Merchant name	Origin	Qty	Unit	Commodity	£	s.	d.	f.
		8	C	Skins, Kid	2	0	0	0
		6	piece	Mantles	0	20	0	0
		12	piece	Skins, Fox	0	2	0	0
Robert Laynard	Ind	8	C	Skins, Sheep	4	0	0	0
		40	yard	Irish Linen *Cloth*	0	3	4	0
		14	stone	Wool, Irish	0	37	4	0
		4	stone	Wool, Flocks	0	0	20	0
		1	dicker	Skins, Deer	0	3	4	0

The Sonday of Wexford, William Kynnaye master, Entering, 20th July 1546

Merchant name	Origin	Qty	Unit	Commodity	£	s.	d.	f.
William *Kynnaye*	Ind	3	pipe	Fish, Salmon	4	10	0	0
		5	stone	Wool, Irish	0	13	4	0
		5	C	Skins, Lamb	0	33	4	0
		1	C	Skins, Sheep	0	10	0	0
		8	piece	Mantles	0	26	8	0
		1	C	Check *Cloth*	2	0	0	0
		20	yard	Irish Linen *Cloth*	0	0	20	0
		20	yard	Check *Cloth*	0	5	0	0

The *Christ*ofer of Chepstow, Richard Jeynes master, Entering, 21st July 1546

Merchant name	Origin	Qty	Unit	Commodity	£	s.	d.	f.
David Harte	Ind	3	C	Woad, Azores	0	20	0	0

The Trynyte of Waterford, Thomas Butlar master, Entering, 21st July 1546

Merchant name	Origin	Qty	Unit	Commodity	£	s.	d.	f.
James Laynard	Ind	49	C	Skins, Lamb	16	6	8	0
		7.5	C	Check *Cloth*	14	6	0	0
		64	piece	Mantles	10	13	4	0
		4	piece	Skins, Fox	0	0	8	0
		2	piece	Skins, Marten	0	2	0	0
James Fagan	Ind	3	C	Skins, Sheep	0	30	0	0
		1.5	C	Skins, Lamb	0	10	0	0
		30	piece	Skins, Fox	0	5	0	0
		1	piece	Skins, Marten	0	0	12	0
		7	stone	Wool, Irish	0	18	8	0
		3	C	Check *Cloth*	6	0	0	0
		42	piece	Mantles	7	0	0	0
		1	pipe	Fish, Salmon	0	30	0	0
Edward Whyte	Ind	10.5	C	Skins, Sheep	5	5	0	0
		5	C	Check *Cloth*	10	0	0	0
		55	piece	Mantles	9	3	4	0
		5	piece	Skins, Fox	0	0	10	0
		1	piece	Skins, Otter	0	0	5	0
		3	C	Skins, Lamb	0	20	0	0
John Pecket	Ind	1.5	C	Check *Cloth*	3	0	0	0
		6	piece	Mantles	0	20	0	0
		0.5	C	Skins, Sheep	0	5	0	0
Richard Cantwell	Ind	68	piece	Mantles	11	6	8	0
		4	C	Check *Cloth*	8	0	0	0
		1	dicker	Skins, Deer	0	3	4	0
David Wadyng	Ind	1.5	C	Check *Cloth*	3	0	0	0

Merchant name	Origin	Qty	Unit	Commodity	£	s.	d.	f.
		4	piece	Mantles	0	13	4	0
		0.5	C	Skins, Lamb	0	3	4	0
		20	piece	Skins, Sheep	0	0	20	0
Robert Whyte	Ind	8	C	Skins, Sheep	4	0	0	0
		1	dicker	Skins, Deer	0	3	4	0
		12	C	Skins, Lamb	4	0	0	0
		18	piece	Skins, Fox	0	3	0	0
		2	piece	Skins, Otter	0	0	10	0
		8	C	Check *Cloth*	16	0	0	0
		0.5	C	Skins, Kid	0	2	6	0
Peter Creagh	Ind	10	C	Skins, Lamb	3	6	8	0
		2	C	Irish Linen *Cloth*	0	20	0	0
		4	C	Skins, Sheep	2	0	0	0
		3	piece	Skins, Fox	0	0	6	0
		2	piece	Skins, Wolf	0	0	20	0
Patrick Sall	Ind	10	C	Skins, Sheep	5	0	0	0
		7	C	Skins, Lamb	2	6	8	0
		1.83	C	Check *Cloth*	3	13	4	0
		9	piece	Skins, Fox	0	0	18	0
		2	piece	Mantles	0	6	8	0
John Marshall	Ind	3.66	C	Skins, Sheep	0	36	8	0
		21	piece	Mantles	3	10	0	0
		6	C	Irish Linen *Cloth*	3	0	0	0
		2.66	C	Check *Cloth*	5	6	8	0
		3	C	Skins, Lamb	0	20	0	0
Richard Arthur	Ind	3.33	C	Skins, Sheep	0	33	4	0
		7	stone	Wool, Irish	0	18	8	0
		1	stone	Wool, Flocks	0	0	5	0
		2	C	Check *Cloth*	4	0	0	0
		4	piece	Skins, Deer	0	0	16	0
		3	piece	Mantles	0	10	0	0
Richard Barron	Ind	3	C	Skins, Sheep	0	30	0	0
		3	C	Skins, Lamb	0	20	0	0
		1.5	C	Check *Cloth*	3	0	0	0
		2	piece	Mantles	0	6	8	0
David Connow	Ind	3	C	Skins, Sheep	0	30	0	0
		3	C	Skins, Lamb	0	20	0	0
		0.5	C	Check *Cloth*	0	20	0	0
		3	piece	Skins, Deer	0	0	12	0
Robert Medal	Ind	4.33	C	Skins, Lamb	0	28	2	0
		0.5	C	Skins, Sheep	0	5	0	0
Edmund Clery	Ind	22	piece	Mantles	3	13	4	0
		0.5	C	Check *Cloth*	0	20	0	0
Walter Malrony & Asteken	Ind	8	C	Skins, Sheep	4	0	0	0
		6	C	Skins, Lamb	2	0	0	0
		2	C	Check *Cloth*	4	0	0	0
Andrew Welshe	Ind	6	C	Check *Cloth*	12	0	0	0
		26	piece	Skins, Fox	0	4	4	0
		6	C	Skins, Sheep	3	0	0	0
		10.5	C	Skins, Lamb	3	10	0	0
		48	piece	Mantles	8	0	0	0

Merchant name	Origin	Qty	Unit	Commodity	£	s.	d.	f.
		1.5	C	Irish Linen *Cloth*	0	15	0	0
		3	piece	Skins, Marten	0	3	0	0
Henry Seyse	Ind	1.4	C	Check *Cloth*	2	16	8	0
		65	piece	Mantles	10	16	8	0
		11.33	C	Skins, Lamb	3	15	7	0
		6.5	C	Skins, Sheep	3	5	0	0
		4	stone	Wool, Flocks	0	0	20	0
James Troy	Ind	3.33	C	Check *Cloth*	6	13	4	0
		9	C	Skins, Lamb	3	0	0	0
		3	piece	Mantles	0	10	0	0
		24	piece	Skins, Fox	0	4	0	0
		1	piece	Skins, Marten	0	0	12	0
John Routhe	Ind	11	C	Skins, Lamb	3	13	4	0
		9	C	Skins, Sheep	4	10	0	0
		1.5	C	Check *Cloth*	3	0	0	0
		16	piece	Mantles	2	13	4	0
		19	piece	Skins, Fox	0	3	2	0
		1	piece	Skins, Marten	0	0	12	0
		4	stone	Wool, Flocks	0	0	20	0
Patrick Kelly	Ind	3	C	Check *Cloth*	6	0	0	0
		6	C	Skins, Lamb	2	0	0	0
		0.5	C	Skins, Sheep	0	5	0	0
Nicholas Welshe	Ind	8.5	C	Check *Cloth*	17	0	0	0
		9.5	C	Skins, Sheep	4	15	0	0
		21.5	C	Skins, Lamb	7	3	4	0
		10	piece	Skins, Fox	0	0	20	0
		60	piece	Mantles	10	0	0	0
		4	stone	Wool, Flocks	0	0	20	0
James Pembroke	Ind	20	C	Skins, Kid	5	0	0	0
		6	C	Skins, Sheep	3	0	0	0
		11	stone	Wool, Flocks	0	4	7	0
Vincent Stretch	Ind	32	yard	Check *Cloth*	0	10	8	0
		4.6	C	Skins, Lamb	0	31	0	0
		2.41	C	Skins, Sheep	0	24	2	0
		6	piece	Skins, Deer	0	2	0	0
		70	yard	Irish Linen *Cloth*	0	5	10	0
		13	piece	Skins, Fox	0	2	2	0
		2	piece	Skins, Marten	0	2	0	0
		3	piece	Skins, Otter	0	0	15	0
		2	piece	Mantles	0	6	8	0
John Creaghe	Ind	3.5	C	Skins, Sheep	0	35	0	0
		3	piece	Skins, Otter	0	0	15	0
		11	piece	Skins, Fox	0	1	10	0
		7.5	C	Irish Linen *Cloth*	3	15	0	0
		3	piece	Skins, Marten	0	3	0	0
		1.25	C	Check *Cloth*	2	10	0	0
		5.33	C	Skins, Lamb	0	35	10	0
		2	piece	Mantles	0	6	8	0
Francis Faylond & assoc.	Ind	5.5	C	Skins, Sheep	2	15	0	0
		16	C	Skins, Lamb	5	6	8	0
		6	C	Irish Linen *Cloth*	3	0	0	0

Merchant name	Origin	Qty	Unit	Commodity	£	s.	d.	f.
		3	piece	Skins, Otter	0	0	15	0
		4	piece	Skins, Marten	0	4	0	0
		70	piece	Skins, Fox	0	11	8	0
		1.4	dicker	Skins, Deer	0	4	8	0
		0.5	C	Check *Cloth*	0	20	0	0
Thomas Ferrys	Ind	30	C	Skins, Lamb	10	0	0	0
		1.5	dicker	Skins, Deer	0	5	0	0
		3	piece	Skins, Marten	0	3	0	0
		3	piece	Skins, Otter	0	0	15	0
		2.5	C	Skins, Sheep	0	25	0	0
		1	piece	Skins, Fox	0	0	2	0
		1	piece	Skins, Wolf	0	0	8	0
Nicholas Flaghan & Robyns	Ind	1	C	Check *Cloth*	2	0	0	0
		10	C	Skins, Lamb	3	6	8	0
Maurice Quyrke & Murthe	Ind	5	C	Check *Cloth*	10	0	0	0
		3.5	C	Skins, Sheep	0	35	0	0

The Michaell of Milford Haven, John Hycks master, Entering, 24th July 1546

Merchant name	Origin	Qty	Unit	Commodity	£	s.	d.	f.
Giles Fowler	Ind	8.5	C	Alum	4	5	0	0
		1	tun	Oil, *Olive*	4	0	0	0
John Bawkrey	Ind	1	pipe	Wine	0	0	0	0

The Jhesus of St David's, William Browne master, Entering, 24th July 1546

Merchant name	Origin	Qty	Unit	Commodity	£	s.	d.	f.
William Scarlett	Ind	1.5	tun	Wine	0	0	0	0

The Katheryn of Waterford, Edmund Morryce master, Entering, 24th July 1546

Merchant name	Origin	Qty	Unit	Commodity	£	s.	d.	f.
Edmund Morryce	Ind	80	yard	Check *Cloth*	0	26	8	0
		6	piece	Mantles	0	20	0	0
		2	pipe	Fish, Salmon	3	0	0	0
Nicholas Bayly	Ind	3	C	Check *Cloth*	6	0	0	0
		3	C	Skins, Sheep	0	30	0	0
		2	C	Skins, Lamb	0	13	4	0
		6	piece	Mantles	0	20	0	0
Redmond Wall	Ind	1	C	Check *Cloth*	2	0	0	0
		8	piece	Mantles	0	26	8	0
		0.25	C	Skins, Sheep	0	2	6	0
Nicholas Brewer & Kyff	Ind	2.5	C	Check *Cloth*	5	0	0	0
		4	piece	Mantles	0	13	4	0
William Caden & Marrys	Ind	1.33	C	Check *Cloth*	2	13	4	0
		3	piece	Mantles	0	10	0	0
		2	stone	Wool, Flocks	0	0	10	0
		4	C	Skins, Sheep	2	0	0	0
		2	C	Skins, Lamb	0	13	4	0
Edward Arthur	Ind	4	stone	Wool, Irish	0	10	8	0
		0.25	C	Skins, Sheep	0	2	6	0

Merchant name	Origin	Qty	Unit	Commodity	£	s.	d.	f.
		1	C	Skins, Lamb	0	6	8	0
		21	piece	Skins, Kid	0	0	10	0
Richard Turner	Ind	12	C	Skins, Sheep	6	0	0	0
		49	C	Skins, Lamb	16	6	8	0
		40	piece	Skins, Marten	2	0	0	0
		48	piece	Skins, Fox	0	8	0	0
		26	piece	Skins, Otter	0	10	10	0
		5.5	C	Linen *Cloth*	2	15	0	0
		1	C	Check *Cloth*	2	0	0	0
		28	C	Madder, green	2	6	8	0
		3	C	Skins, Rabbit	0	3	4	0
Michael de Posa	Alien	1	pipe	Oil, *Olive*	2	0	0	0

The Clement of Mumbles, Gryffyth Davys master, Entering, *24th July 1546*

John Russell	Ind	2.5	ton	Salt	0	25	0	0

The Nicholas of Carmarthen, William Walter master, Entering, *24th July 1546*

Robert Bryte	Ind	1	pipe	Oil, *Olive*	2	0	0	0

The Savyor of Friesland, Rayner Sybran master, Exiting, *24th July 1546*

Domingo Eryso	Alien	117	ton	Lead	468	0	0	0

The Trynyte More of Bristol, Thomas Sherwood master, Exiting, *24th July 1546*

John Welshe	Ind	17.5	ton	Lead	87	10	0	0
		27	piece	Manchester Cotton *Cloth*	13	10	0	0
Thomas *Sherwood*	Ind	13	piece	Cloth of Assize	0	0	0	0
John Capps	Ind	7.5	piece	Cloth of Assize	0	0	0	0
Geoffrey Chawntrell	Ind	4	dicker	Hides, Tanned	0	0	0	0

The Trynyte of Minehead, Thomas Walter master, Exiting, *28th July 1546*

James Lewell	Ind	2.25	piece	Cloth of Assize	0	0	0	0
		3.5	dozen	Caps	0	35	0	0
		30	gross	Points	0	30	0	0
		2	gross	Knives	0	13	4	0
		0.5	gross	Cutts	0	0	20	0
		2	gross	Lacquer	0	3	4	0

The Katheryn Bennett, Thomas Fowlar master, Exiting, *28th July 1546*

William Appowell	Ind	10	lb	Cinnamon	0	25	0	0
		12	lb	Pepper	0	12	0	0
		6	lb	Cloves	0	15	0	0
		3	lb	Mace	0	7	6	0
		6	lb	Nutmeg	0	6	0	0
		6	lb	Ginger	0	9	0	0
		6	lb	Kermes	0	6	0	0
		6	lb	Saffron	3	0	0	0
		5	C	Hops	2	10	0	0

Merchant name	Origin	Qty	Unit	Commodity	£	s.	d.	f.
William Chester								
& assoc.	Ind	4	tun	Wine, Corrupt	6	0	0	0
		1	pipe	Iron	2	0	0	0
		6	lb	Silk, *Worked*	4	0	0	0

The Sonday of Wexford, William Kennay master, Exiting, 31st July 1546

Merchant name	Origin	Qty	Unit	Commodity	£	s.	d.	f.
William *Kennay*	Ind	1.25	piece	Cloth of Assize	0	0	0	0
		4	lb	Saffron	2	0	0	0
		2	lb	Silk, *Worked*	0	26	8	0
		1	gross	Knives	0	6	8	0
		0.5	C	Wood, Brazil	0	16	8	0
		2	C	Iron	0	8	0	0
		0.5	C	Hops	0	5	0	0
		1	dozen	Wool-Cards	0	4	0	0
David Wadyng	Ind	0.25	piece	Cloth of Assize	0	0	0	0
		0.75	C	Hops	0	7	6	0
		0.25	gross	Knives	0	0	20	0
		1	gross	Combs	0	5	0	0
		4	dozen	Girdles	0	5	0	0
		6	piece	Hats	0	5	0	0
		2	gross	Points	0	2	0	0

The Trynyte of Waterford, Thomas Butlar master, Exiting, 2nd August 1546

Merchant name	Origin	Qty	Unit	Commodity	£	s.	d.	f.
Peter Asteken	Ind	3	piece	Cloth of Assize	0	0	0	0
		1.5	C	Hops	0	15	0	0
		0.75	C	Aniseed	0	10	0	0
		2	dozen	Cumin	0	2	8	0
		8	lb	Silk, *Worked*	5	6	8	0
		15	dozen	Knives, in Pairs	0	25	0	0
		2	dozen	Cards, Playing	0	2	6	0
		3	lb	Thread	0	0	15	0
		1.5	gross	Knives	0	10	0	0
		0.5	gross	Cutts	0	0	20	0
		1.5	lb	Cloves	0	3	9	0
		1	lb	Pepper	0	0	12	0
		10	dozen	Caps	0	8	4	0
		2	dozen	Wool-Cards	0	8	0	0
		6	pair	Stock-Cards	0	6	0	0
		1	dozen	Soap	0	0	15	0
		12	gross	Points	0	12	0	0
		6	lb	Saffron	3	0	0	0
James Fagan	Ind	3	piece	Cloth of Assize	0	0	0	0
		1	lb	Silk, *Worked*	0	13	4	0
		1	lb	Saffron	0	10	0	0
		4	dozen	Aniseed & Cumin	0	5	4	0
		3.5	C	Hops	0	35	0	0
		7	gross	Points	0	7	0	0
		0.5	gross	Lacquer	0	0	10	0
		2	gross	Combs	0	10	0	0
		1.5	gross	Knives	0	10	0	0

Merchant name	Origin	Qty	Unit	Commodity	£	s.	d.	f.
		2	dozen	Knives, in Pairs	0	3	4	0
		1	clout	Needles	0	0	15	0
		1	dozen	Cards, Playing	0	0	15	0
		1	ream	Paper	0	0	20	0
		0.25	gross	Beads	0	0	12	0
		3	lb	Verdigris	0	0	15	0
James Pembroke	Ind	9	stone	Orchil	0	15	0	0
		12.5	C	Aniseed	0	16	8	0
Edward Whyte	Ind	5	piece	Cloth of Assize, Dozen Strait	0	0	0	0
		3	lb	Saffron	0	30	0	0
		4	C	Hops	2	0	0	0
		2	gross	Knives	0	13	4	0
		0.5	dozen	Caps	0	5	0	0
		7	dozen	Soap	0	8	9	0
		8	pair	Stock-Cards	0	8	0	0
		8	gross	Points	0	8	0	0
		1.5	gross	Lacquer	0	2	6	0
Richard Barron	Ind	1	piece	Cloth of Assize, Dozen Strait	0	0	0	0
		2	lb	Saffron	0	20	0	0
		1	lb	Silk, *Worked*	0	13	4	0
		0.25	C	Aniseed	0	3	4	0
		2	gross	Knives	0	13	4	0
		4	dozen	Knives, in Pairs	0	6	8	0
		1	dozen	Cumin	0	0	16	0
		2	dozen	Cards, Playing	0	2	6	0
		1	bolt	Thread	0	0	12	0
		0.5	gross	Combs	0	2	0	0
		6	lb	Liquorice	0	0	10	0
		3	gross	Points	0	3	0	0
		3	gross	Lacquer	0	5	0	0
		1	ream	Paper	0	0	20	0
		6	dozen	Girdles	0	2	0	0
		1	C	Hops	0	10	0	0
Maurice Quyrke	Ind	3	piece	Cloth of Assize, Dozen Strait	0	0	0	0
		2	lb	Silk, *Worked*	0	26	8	0
		2	lb	Saffron	0	20	0	0
		4	dozen	Cards, Playing	0	5	0	0
		4	gross	Lacquer	0	6	8	0
		6	dozen	Girdles	0	2	0	0
		2	bolt	Thread	0	2	0	0
		2	gross	Points	0	2	0	0
		1	gross	Combs	0	3	4	0
		1	dozen	Cumin	0	0	16	0
		12	lb	Sulpher	0	0	12	0
		3	lb	Cloves	0	7	6	0
		1	lb	Nutmeg	0	0	20	0
		1	C	Hops	0	10	0	0
		1	C	Aniseed	0	13	4	0
Robert Whyte	Ind	3	piece	Cloth of Assize, Dozen Strait	0	0	0	0
		6	lb	Saffron	3	0	0	0
		4	lb	Silk, *Worked*	2	13	4	0
		5	gross	Knives	0	33	4	0

Merchant name	Origin	Qty	Unit	Commodity	£	s.	d.	f.
		6	dozen	Cards, Playing	0	7	6	0
		6	dozen	Girdles	0	3	0	0
		6	dozen	Spectacles	0	2	0	0
		0.5	gross	Combs	0	2	0	0
		1	C	Hops	0	10	0	0
		1	C	Aniseed	0	13	4	0
		1	dozen	Cumin	0	0	16	0
		3	gross	Lacquer	0	5	0	0
		6	gross	Points	0	6	0	0
		2	bolt	Thread	0	2	0	0
		0.5	doz	Liquorice	0	0	10	0
Henry Seyse	Ind	4.25	piece	Cloth of Assize	0	0	0	0
		1	lb	Saffron	0	10	0	0
		6	dozen	Cards, Playing	0	7	6	0
		3	dozen	Knives, in Pairs	0	5	0	0
		2	gross	Knives	0	13	4	0
		2	dozen	Aniseed	0	2	8	0
		1	dozen	Caps	0	10	0	0
		12	gross	Points	0	12	0	0
		2	dozen	Girdles	0	0	12	0
		0.5	gross	Lacquer	0	0	10	0
		2	lb	Cumin	0	0	6	0
James Troy	Ind	5	lb	Silk, *Worked*	3	6	8	0
		1	lb	Saffron	0	10	0	0
		2	gross	Knives	0	13	4	0
		12	gross	Points	0	12	0	0
		1	gross	Lacquer	0	0	20	0
		0.25	C	Aniseed	0	3	4	0
		6	gross	Knives	0	10	0	0
		1	dozen	Wool-Cards	0	4	0	0
		0.25	C	Hops	0	2	6	0
		1	dozen	Cards, Playing	0	0	15	0
		3	dozen	Girdles	0	0	16	0
		4	dozen	Caps	0	3	4	0
		2	piece	Hats	0	0	10	0
		1	lb	Pepper	0	0	12	0
		0.5	lb	Cinnamon	0	0	15	0
		0.25	lb	Cloves	0	0	7	2
Vincent Stretch	Ind	3	lb	Saffron	0	30	0	0
		5	lb	Silk, *Worked*	3	6	8	0
		4	dozen	Girdles, Caddis	0	5	0	0
		1	gross	Knives	0	6	8	0
		16	gross	Points	0	16	0	0
		2	clout	Needles	0	0	16	0
		3	dozen	Knives, in Pairs	0	5	0	0
		2	dozen	Cards, Playing	0	2	6	0
		6	lb	Liquorice	0	0	10	0
		2	lb	Mercury	0	0	10	0
		1	lb	Verdigris	0	0	5	0
		2	dozen	Girdles	0	0	8	0
		0.5	dozen	Girdles, Silk	0	0	16	0
		1	lb	Pepper	0	0	12	0

Merchant name	Origin	Qty	Unit	Commodity	£	s.	d.	f.
		0.5	lb	Nutmeg	0	0	10	0
		0.5	doz	Night-caps	0	0	14	0
		7	dozen	Combs	0	2	0	0
		1	lb	Thread	0	0	12	0
		0.5	lb	Cloves	0	0	15	0
		2	dozen	*Percular*	0	0	8	0
		1	lb	Ginger	0	0	18	0
		1.5	gross	Lacquer	0	2	6	0
		1	lb	Kermes	0	0	14	0
		0.5	lb	Cinnamon	0	2	0	0
Patrick Sall	Ind	3.5	piece	Cloth of Assize	0	0	0	0
		12	gross	Points	0	12	0	0
		2	gross	Lacquer	0	3	4	0
		12	lb	Liquorice	0	0	12	0
		3	gross	Knives	0	20	0	0
		6	piece	Hats	0	2	0	0
		1	bolt	Thread	0	0	12	0
		6	dozen	Girdles	0	3	0	0
		8	lb	Cumin	0	0	9	0
		1	dozen	Girdles, Caddis	0	0	20	0
		1	lb	Cloves	0	2	6	0
		4	lb	Saffron	2	0	0	0
		0.5	C	Aniseed	0	6	8	0
		10	dozen	Knives, in Pairs	0	16	8	0
		2	lb	Silk, *Worked*	0	26	8	0
		3	dozen	Cards, Playing	0	3	9	0
		6	dozen	Spectacles	0	0	20	0
David Connow	Ind	1	gross	Knives	0	6	8	0
		2	dozen	Cards, Playing	0	2	6	0
		0.5	gross	Combs	0	2	0	0
		6	dozen	Spectacles	0	2	0	0
		6	piece	Skins, Golden	0	2	1	0
		1	gross	Lacquer	0	0	20	0
		4	gross	Points	0	4	0	0
		1	lb	Silk, *Worked*	0	13	4	0
		1	bolt	Thread	0	0	12	0
		6	dozen	Girdles	0	2	6	0
		6	dozen	Knives, in Pairs	0	10	0	0
		0.25	C	Aniseed	0	3	4	0
		1	lb	Cloves	0	2	6	0
		2	lb	Saffron	0	20	0	0
		1	ream	Paper	0	0	20	0
James Pembroke	Ind	3.25	piece	Cloth of Assize	0	0	0	0
		14	lb	Saffron	7	0	0	0
		6	lb	Silk, *Worked*	4	0	0	0
		4	gross	Knives	0	26	8	0
		8	dozen	Knives, in Pairs	0	13	4	0
		1	dozen	Skins, Golden	0	4	2	0
		2	gross	Points	0	2	0	0
		2	gross	Lacquer	0	3	4	0
		3	dozen	Cards, Playing	0	3	9	0
Richard Cantwell	Ind	1	piece	Cloth of Assize	0	0	0	0

Merchant name	Origin	Qty	Unit	Commodity	£	s.	d.	f.
		7	lb	Saffron	3	10	0	0
		2	lb	Silk, *Worked*	0	26	8	0
		3	dozen	Wool-Cards	0	12	0	0
		0.25	C	Aniseed	0	3	4	0
		9.5	stone	Orchil	0	15	10	0
		12	gross	Points	0	12	0	0
		1	gross	Knives	0	6	8	0
		6	dozen	Knives, in Pairs	0	10	0	0
		4	pair	Stock-Cards	0	4	0	0
		1	clout	Needles	0	0	8	0
		2	lb	Cinnamon & Mace	0	5	0	0
Nicholas Welshe	Ind	3.5	piece	Cloth of Assize	0	0	0	0
		14	lb	Saffron	7	0	0	0
		6	lb	Silk, *Worked*	4	0	0	0
		0.5	C	Hops	0	5	0	0
		0.25	C	Aniseed	0	3	4	0
		1	dozen	Cumin	0	0	16	0
		4	dozen	Soap	0	5	0	0
		3	gross	Knives	0	20	0	0
		1	gross	Cutts	0	3	4	0
		0.5	piece	Fustian *Cloth*	0	7	0	0
		4	dozen	Knives, in Pairs	0	6	8	0
		4	lb	Thread	0	0	20	0
		1	lb	Pepper	0	0	12	0
		3	lb	Cloves	0	7	6	0
		1	lb	Kermes	0	0	12	0
		1	lb	Ginger	0	0	18	0
		1	dozen	Wool-Cards	0	4	0	0
		6	pair	Stock-Cards	0	6	0	0
Patrick Kelly	Ind	1.5	piece	Cloth of Assize, Dozen Strait	0	0	0	0
		6.5	lb	Silk, *Worked*	4	6	8	0
		3	lb	Cloves	0	7	6	0
		8	dozen	Knives, in Pairs	0	13	4	0
		2	lb	Thread	0	0	10	0
		1.5	gross	Knives	0	10	0	0
		0.25	C	Aniseed	0	3	4	0
		2	lb	Saffron	0	20	0	0
		4	lb	Liquorice	0	0	8	0
		6	gross	Points	0	6	0	0
		1	gross	Lacquer	0	0	20	0
		1	dozen	Skins, Golden	0	4	2	0
		2	piece	Worsted Russett *Cloth*	1	0	0	0
Richard Arthur	Ind	1	piece	Cloth of Assize, Dozen Strait	0	0	0	0
		0.5	C	Hops	0	5	0	0
		0.5	C	Aniseed	0	6	8	0
		4	lb	Silk, *Worked*	2	13	4	0
		1.5	lb	Saffron	0	15	0	0
		6	gross	Points	0	6	0	0
		1	gross	Lacquer	0	0	20	0
		2	gross	Knives	0	13	4	0
		10	dozen	Glasses	0	3	4	0
		2	pair	Stock-Cards	0	2	0	0

Merchant name	Origin	Qty	Unit	Commodity	£	s.	d.	f.
		4	dozen	Combs	o	o	20	o
		6	dozen	Girdles	o	3	4	o
		2	dozen	Knives, in Pairs	o	3	4	o
John Marshall	Ind	2.5	piece	Cloth of Assize	o	o	o	o
		6	gross	Points	o	6	o	o
		1	gross	Lacquer	o	o	20	o
		1	gross	Knives	o	6	8	o
		6	dozen	Spectacles	o	2	o	o
		1	dozen	Caps	o	10	o	o
		1	dozen	Felts	o	3	o	o
		6	lb	Cumin	o	o	8	o
		6	lb	Liquorice	o	o	5	o
		13	piece	Caps	o	10	10	o
		1	dozen	Soap	o	o	15	o
John Routhe	Ind	0.75	piece	Cloth of Assize	o	o	o	o
		2.5	lb	Silk, *Worked*	o	33	4	o
		1	lb	Saffron	o	10	o	o
		1.5	dozen	Skins, Golden	o	6	3	o
		4	gross	Knives	o	26	8	o
		4	dozen	Knives, in Pairs	o	6	8	o
		4	dozen	Combs	o	o	16	o
		12	gross	Points	o	12	o	o
		1	gross	Lacquer	o	o	20	o
		4	dozen	Girdles	o	2	o	o
		2	dozen	Cards, Playing	o	2	6	o
		2	lb	Thread	o	o	10	o
		3	dozen	Aniseed	o	4	o	o
		0.5	C	Hops	o	5	o	o
		8	dozen	Caps	o	6	8	o
		6	dozen	Glasses	o	2	o	o
		1	dozen	Girdles, Caddis	o	o	16	o
		1	lb	Mace	o	2	6	o
		1	dozen	Wool-Cards	o	4	o	o
Andrew Welshe	Ind	3.5	piece	Cloth of Assize	o	o	o	o
		6	lb	Silk, *Worked*	4	o	o	o
		7.5	lb	Saffron	3	15	o	o
		2.33	dozen	Caps	o	23	4	o
		4	piece	Nightcaps, Velvet	o	8	o	o
		1	dozen	Felts	o	4	o	o
		3	lb	Cloves & Mace	o	7	6	o
		1	lb	Ginger	o	o	18	o
		1	lb	Pepper	o	o	12	o
		0.5	lb	Nutmeg	o	o	12	o
		2	dozen	Skins, Golden	o	8	4	o
		2	dozen	Cards, Playing	o	2	6	o
		6	lb	Liquorice	o	o	10	o
		1	ream	Paper	o	o	20	o
		12	gross	Points	o	12	o	o
		3	gross	Knives	o	20	o	o
		1	gross	Lacquer	o	o	20	o
		9	dozen	Knives, in Pairs	o	15	o	o
		6	dozen	Girdles	o	3	o	o

Merchant name	Origin	Qty	Unit	Commodity	£	s.	d.	f.
		2	dozen	Wool-Cards	0	8	0	0
		6	pair	Stock-Cards	0	6	0	0
		1	pipe	Iron	2	0	0	0
		0.5	C	Hops	0	5	0	0
		1	clout	Needles	0	0	16	0
		2	lb	Thread	0	0	10	0
		1	lb	Sugar-Candy	0	0	8	0
		1	lb	Wax, Red	0	0	5	0

The Trynyte of Swansea, Nicholas Davy master, Entering, *2nd August 1546*

Merchant name	Origin	Qty	Unit	Commodity	£	s.	d.	f.
Roger Jenkyns	Ind	13	ton	Salt	6	10	0	0

The Francis of Blavet, Peter Froley master, Entering, *2nd August 1546*

Merchant name	Origin	Qty	Unit	Commodity	£	s.	d.	f.
Henry Petron	Alien	30	ton	Salt	15	0	0	0
		1090	ell	Canvas *Cloth*	13	10	0	0
		680	ell	Fine Canvas *Cloth*	10	6	8	0
		2	C	Rosin	0	2	8	0

The Ann of Penmarch, Evan Brenew master, Entering, *2nd August 1546*

Merchant name	Origin	Qty	Unit	Commodity	£	s.	d.	f.
John Alepewe & assoc.	Alien	645	C	Woad, Toulouse	322	10	0	0
		60	*piece*	Poldavis *Cloth*	30	0	0	0
		240	ell	Canvas *Cloth*	3	0	0	0
		280	ell	Fine Canvas *Cloth*	4	15	0	0
		8	C	Rosin	0	10	8	0

The Katheryn of Waterford, Edmund Morryce master, Exiting, *2nd August 1546*

Merchant name	Origin	Qty	Unit	Commodity	£	s.	d.	f.
Thomas Nele	Ind	3	lb	Saffron	0	30	0	0
		1	lb	Silk, *Worked*	0	13	4	0
		1	gross	Knives	0	6	8	0
		1	gross	Cutts	0	3	4	0
		0.5	dozen	Caps	0	5	0	0
		6	gross	Points	0	6	0	0
		2	gross	Lacquer	0	3	4	0
		6	pair	Stock-Cards	0	6	0	0
		1	hogshead	Iron	0	20	0	0
Thomas Merys	Ind	2	piece	Cloth of Assize, Dozen Strait	0	0	0	0
		1	ton	Iron	4	0	0	0
		2	gross	Knives	0	13	4	0
Nicholas Bayly	Ind	4	piece	Cloth of Assize, Dozen Strait	0	0	0	0
		3.5	lb	Silk, *Worked*	2	6	8	0
		9	gross	Points	0	9	0	0
		1	gross	Knives	0	6	8	0
Richard Langhan	Ind	2	lb	Saffron	0	20	0	0
		1	lb	Silk, *Worked*	0	13	4	0
		0.5	gross	Knives	0	3	4	0
		1	dozen	Soap	0	0	15	0
		0.5	gross	Points	0	0	6	0
		1	piece	Cloth of Assize, Dozen Strait	0	0	0	0

Merchant name	Origin	Qty	Unit	Commodity	£	s.	d.	f.
Richard Laynard	Ind	2.75	piece	Cloth of Assize	0	0	0	0
		2	gross	Points	0	2	0	0
		4	gross	Knives	0	26	8	0
		5	dozen	Knives, in Pairs	0	8	4	0
		1	C	Hops	0	10	0	0
		2	dozen	Liquorice	0	0	20	0
		1	lb	Nutmeg	0	0	16	0
		1	lb	Mace	0	2	6	0
		1	lb	Ginger	0	0	18	0
		1	lb	Kermes	0	0	12	0
		12	dozen	Spectacles	0	3	0	0
		4	lb	Sulpher	0	0	10	0
		4	lb	Thread	0	0	20	0
		1	gross	Combs	0	3	4	0
		4	dozen	Girdles	0	2	8	0
		40	lb	Wood, Brazil	0	5	0	0
		5	dozen	Soap	0	6	3	0
		4	lb	Glue	0	0	8	0
		4	dozen	Caps	0	3	4	0
		1	C	Hops	0	10	0	0
		1	gross	Knives	0	6	8	0
		1	dozen	Knives, in Pairs	0	0	20	0
		12	gross	Points	0	12	0	0
		1	gross	Lacquer	0	0	20	0
		1	ream	Paper	0	0	20	0
		0.5	gross	Combs	0	0	18	0
		6	dozen	Spectacles	0	0	18	0
Patrick Creaghe	Ind	7	piece	Cloth of Assize, Dozen Strait	0	0	0	0
		4	gross	Knives	0	26	8	0
		6	dozen	Spectacles	0	2	0	0
		2	dozen	Girdles	0	3	4	0
		8	dozen	Combs	0	3	0	0
		2	lb	Saffron	0	20	0	0
		16	gross	Points	0	16	0	0

The John of Le Conquet, Luke Caroryan master, Entering, 3rd August 1546

Merchant name	Origin	Qty	Unit	Commodity	£	s.	d.	f.
Mathew Legale	Alien	26	tun	Wine	0	0	0	0
Oliver & Luke								
Barroten & Carorian	Alien	1.5	C	Oakum	0	5	0	0
		120	ell	Canvas *Cloth*	0	31	8	0
		6	tun	Wine, Corrupt	9	0	0	0

The George of Waterford, Robert Medall master, Exiting, 4th August 1546

Merchant name	Origin	Qty	Unit	Commodity	£	s.	d.	f.
George Savage	Ind	1.25	piece	Cloth of Assize	0	0	0	0
		5	lb	Silk, *Worked*	3	6	8	0
		8	lb	Saffron	4	0	0	0
		1	c	Aniseed	0	13	4	0
		1	C	Hops	0	10	0	0
		3	stone	Orchil	0	5	0	0
		8	dozen	Knives, in Pairs	0	13	4	0

Merchant name	Origin	Qty	Unit	Commodity	£	s.	d.	f.
		2	gross	Knives	0	13	4	0
		1	dozen	Caps	0	10	0	0
		1.5	dozen	Skins, Golden	0	6	3	0
		1	dozen	Hats	0	5	0	0
		4	dozen	Girdles	0	6	8	0
		2	lb	Pepper	0	2	0	0
		1.5	lb	Cloves	0	3	9	0
		6	gross	Points	0	6	0	0
		1	gross	Lacquer	0	0	20	0
Peter Savage	Ind	6	lb	Silk, *Worked*	4	0	0	0
		2	lb	Saffron	0	20	0	0
		7	dozen	Knives, in Pairs	0	11	8	0
		1	bolt	Thread	0	0	12	0
		2	gross	Knives	0	13	4	0
		2	dozen	Girdles	0	4	0	0
		1	lb	Cloves & Mace	0	2	6	0
		1	ream	Paper	0	0	20	0
		6	gross	Points	0	6	0	0
		1	dozen	Cards, Playing	0	0	15	0
		1	dozen	Girdles, Leather	0	2	4	0
		3	dozen	Combs	0	0	12	0
		1	C	Hops	0	10	0	0
		4	dozen	Aniseed	0	5	4	0
		1	dozen	Skins, Golden	0	4	2	0
		3	stone	Orchil	0	5	0	0
Robert Tewe	Ind	1	dozen	Aniseed	0	0	16	0
		1	dozen	Cards, Playing	0	0	15	0
		2	piece	Cloth of Assize, Dozen Strait	0	0	0	0
		2	lb	Saffron	0	20	0	0
		4	lb	Silk, *Worked*	2	13	4	0
Edmund Clery	Ind	3	piece	Cloth of Assize, Dozen Strait	0	0	0	0
		0.5	gross	Knives	0	3	4	0
		0.5	C	Hops	0	5	0	0
		2	seam	Woad, Ashes	0	10	0	0
		0.5	lb	Saffron	0	5	0	0
		2	pair	Stock-Cards	0	2	0	0
		0.5	dozen	Caps	0	5	0	0
Leonard Brewer	Ind	1	piece	Cloth of Assize, Dozen Strait	0	0	0	0
Henry Whyte	Ind	1	C	Hops	0	10	0	0
		4	stone	Orchil	0	6	8	0
		1	gross	Knives	0	6	8	0
		0.5	dozen	Caps	0	5	0	0
John Codd	Ind	0.625	C	Hops	0	6	3	0
		0.5	lb	Silk, *Worked*	0	6	8	0
		4	pair	Stock-Cards	0	4	0	0
		2	piece	Cloth of Assize, Dozen Strait	0	0	0	0
John Murthye	Ind	1	piece	Cloth of Assize	0	0	0	0
		2	lb	Silk, *Worked*	0	26	8	0
		8	lb	Saffron	4	0	0	0
		3	gross	Knives	0	20	0	0
		3	dozen	Knives, in Pairs	0	5	0	0
		1	dozen	Caps	0	10	0	0

Merchant name	Origin	Qty	Unit	Commodity	£	s.	d.	f.
		1	dozen	Nightcaps	0	3	0	0
		3	dozen	Girdles, Leather	0	0	16	0
		3	dozen	Cards, Playing	0	3	9	0
		0.5	gross	Combs	0	0	16	0
		4	dozen	Spectacles	0	0	12	0
		6	gross	Lacquer	0	10	0	0
		8	gross	Points	0	8	0	0
		0.5	lb	Cinnamon	0	0	15	0
		0.5	lb	Ginger	0	0	9	0
		0.5	lb	Cloves	0	0	15	0
		0.5	lb	Mace	0	0	15	0
		1	lb	Nutmeg	0	0	12	0
		0.5	lb	Pepper	0	0	6	0
		2	clout	Needles	0	0	12	0
		6	lb	Cumin	0	0	8	0
		10	lb	Liquorice	0	0	10	0
		0.5	C	Aniseed	0	6	8	0
		1.5	C	Hops	0	15	0	0
Edmund Grawnte	Ind	1	C	Hops	0	10	0	0
		1	lb	Saffron	0	10	0	0
		1.5	lb	Silk, *Worked*	0	20	0	0
		3	gross	Points	0	3	0	0
		1	gross	Lacquer	0	0	20	0
		2	dozen	Soap	0	2	6	0
		2	bolt	Thread	0	2	1	0
		6	dozen	Knives, in Pairs	0	10	0	0
Nicholas Flaghe	Ind	7.5	C	Iron	0	30	0	0
		1.5	C	Hops	0	15	0	0
Walter Marony	Ind	2	piece	Cloth of Assize, Dozen Strait	0	0	0	0
		2	lb	Saffron	0	20	0	0
		1	lb	Silk, *Worked*	0	13	4	0
		3	dozen	Cards, Playing	0	3	9	0
		4	dozen	Combs	0	0	10	0
		6	dozen	Girdles	0	0	20	0
		1.5	gross	Knives	0	10	0	0
		3	dozen	Knives, in Pairs	0	5	0	0
		3	clout	Needles	0	0	21	0
		2	dozen	Aniseed	0	2	8	0
		1	dozen	Cumin	0	0	16	0
		6	lb	Liquorice	0	0	5	0
		1	ream	Paper	0	0	20	0
		1	bolt	Thread	0	0	12	0
		3	gross	Lacquer	0	5	0	0
		4	gross	Points	0	4	0	0
		2	C	Hops	0	20	0	0
		1	dozen	Soap	0	0	15	0
Richard Donell	Ind	4.5	piece	Cloth of Assize	0	0	0	0
		5.5	lb	Silk, *Worked*	3	13	4	0
		5	lb	Saffron	2	10	0	0
		4	gross	Knives	0	26	8	0
		3	dozen	Knives, in Pairs	0	5	0	0
		1	C	Aniseed	0	13	4	0

Merchant name	Origin	Qty	Unit	Commodity	£	s.	d.	f.
		1	C	Hops	0	10	0	0
		1	dozen	Cumin	0	0	16	0
		12	lb	Liquorice	0	0	12	0
		2	gross	Points	0	2	0	0
		2	gross	Lacquer	0	3	4	0
		6	lb	Silk, *Worked*	4	0	0	0
		2	lb	Saffron	0	20	0	0
		8	dozen	Girdles	0	2	8	0
		6	gross	Knives	0	10	0	0
		8	dozen	Combs	0	2	8	0
Francis Feland	Ind	3	piece	Cloth of Assize, Dozen Strait	0	0	0	0
		1	lb	Saffron	0	10	0	0
		1	lb	Silk, *Worked*	0	13	4	0
		2	gross	Knives	0	13	4	0
		6	dozen	Knives, in Pairs	0	10	0	0
		4	dozen	Girdles	0	4	0	0
		0.5	gross	Combs	0	5	0	0
		6	dozen	Girdles	0	2	0	0
		0.5	gross	Combs	0	3	0	0
		8	lb	Liquorice	0	0	10	0
		1	dozen	Cumin	0	0	16	0
		1	C	Aniseed	0	13	4	0
		1	C	Hops	0	10	0	0
Edward Arthur	Ind	4.75	piece	Cloth of Assize	0	0	0	0
		2	lb	Saffron	0	20	0	0
		1	lb	Silk, *Worked*	0	13	4	0
		4	gross	Knives	0	26	8	0
		1	gross	Cutts	0	3	4	0
		6	gross	Points	0	6	0	0
		1	lb	Ginger	0	0	18	0
		1	lb	Pepper	0	0	12	0
		1	dozen	Knives, in Pairs	0	0	20	0
		1	dozen	Spectacles	0	0	4	0
Peter Rowthe	Ind	8	lb	Saffron	4	0	0	0
		4	lb	Silk, *Worked*	2	13	4	0
		2.5	gross	Knives	0	16	8	0
		4	dozen	Knives, in Pairs	0	6	8	0
		3	lb	Cloves	0	7	6	0
		1	gross	Combs	0	4	0	0
		1	dozen	Cards, Playing	0	0	15	0
		6	gross	Points	0	6	0	0
		3	gross	Lacquer	0	5	0	0
		6	pair	Stock–Cards	0	6	0	0
		4	lb	Cumin	0	0	6	0
		1	dozen	Nightcaps	0	5	0	0
		6	dozen	Spectacles	0	2	0	0
		2	dozen	Wool–Cards	0	8	0	0
		0.75	C	Hops	0	7	6	0
Thomas Rowghe	Ind	6.375	piece	Cloth of Assize	0	0	0	0
		1	dozen	Knives, in Pairs	0	0	20	0
		0.5	gross	Combs	0	2	0	0
		1	gross	Knives	0	6	8	0

Merchant name	Origin	Qty	Unit	Commodity	£	s.	d.	f.
		4	lb	Cloves	0	10	0	0
		1	dozen	Cards, Playing	0	0	15	0
		4	lb	Turpentine	0	0	16	0
		1	dozen	Aniseed	0	1	4	0
		1	dozen	Hats	0	4	0	0
		1	gross	Lacquer	0	0	20	0
		6	gross	Points	0	6	0	0
		2	dozen	Books, Primers	0	5	0	0
		4	dozen	Knives, in Pairs	0	6	8	0
		6	dozen	Spectacles	0	2	0	0
		2	lb	Saffron	0	20	0	0
		1	dozen	Skins, Golden	0	4	2	0
		1	ream	Paper	0	0	20	0
		1	dozen	Knives, in Pairs	0	0	20	0
Benedict Sall	Ind	2.25	piece	Cloth of Assize	0	0	0	0
		1.5	gross	Knives	0	10	0	0
		3	gross	Lacquer	0	5	0	0
		8	gross	Points	0	8	0	0
		0.5	gross	Combs	0	2	0	0
		4	dozen	Girdles	0	0	16	0
		1	bolt	Thread	0	0	12	0
		0.5	C	Hops	0	5	0	0
		1	dozen	Caps	0	10	0	0
		4	dozen	Spectacles	0	0	16	0
		2	lb	Saffron	0	20	0	0
		0.5	lb	Silk, *Worked*	0	6	8	0
		1	dozen	Cards, Playing	0	0	20	0
		3	lb	Verdigris	0	0	15	0
		4	lb	Liquorice	0	0	4	0
Philip Richards	Ind	9.75	piece	Cloth of Assize	0	0	0	0
		3	seam	Woad, Ashes	0	12	0	0
		22	lb	Saffron	11	0	0	0
		11	lb	Silk, *Worked*	7	6	8	0
		48	gross	Points	2	8	0	0
		9	gross	Knives	3	0	0	0
		3	dozen	Cards, Playing	0	3	9	0
		3	bolt	Thread	0	3	0	0
		1	ream	Paper	0	0	20	0
		6	lb	Mercury	0	2	6	0
		3	lb	Cinnamon	0	7	6	0
		1	gross	Lacquer	0	0	20	0
		1	unknown	Drugs, miscellaneous	0	8	0	0
		1	dozen	Caps	0	10	0	0
		12	dozen	Knives, in Pairs	0	20	0	0
		1.75	C	Aniseed	0	24	4	0
		1	lb	Ginger	0	0	18	0
		0.5	lb	Nutmeg	0	0	10	0
Dominic Pollonghan & Breuar	Ind	2.5	dozen	Caps	0	25	0	0
		1	bolt	Thread	0	0	12	0
		2	lb	Mercury	0	0	10	0
		1	tun	Wine, Corrupt	0	30	0	0

535

Merchant name	Origin	Qty	Unit	Commodity	£	s.	d.	f.
Thomas Ferrys	Ind	2.5	piece	Cloth of Assize	0	0	0	0
		24	gross	Points	0	24	0	0
		4	gross	Knives	0	26	8	0
		13	lb	Silk, *Worked*	8	13	4	0
		2	gross	Points	0	2	0	0
John Creanghe	Ind	2.75	piece	Cloth of Assize	0	0	0	0
		10	gross	Knives	3	6	8	0
		1	dozen	Cumin	0	0	16	0
		24	gross	Points	0	24	0	0
		8	lb	Liquorice	0	0	10	0
		2	lb	Pepper	0	2	0	0
		1.5	dozen	Caps	0	15	0	0
		1	dozen	Nightcaps	0	5	0	0
		0.5	lb	Cloves	0	0	15	0
		0.5	lb	Ginger	0	0	9	0
		12	dozen	Spectacles	0	2	0	0
		2	dozen	Cards, Playing	0	2	6	0
		1.5	lb	Saffron	0	15	0	0
		2	dozen	Knives, in Pairs	0	3	4	0
		1	lb	Cinnamon	0	2	6	0
		11	lb	Silk, *Worked*	7	6	8	0
		1	bolt	Thread	0	0	12	0
		1	clout	Needles	0	0	7	0
Roger Everod	Ind	9	piece	Cloth of Assize	0	0	0	0
		6	gross	Knives	0	40	0	0
		2	gross	Cutts	0	6	8	0
		1	dozen	Knives, in Pairs	0	0	20	0
		12	lb	Silk, *Worked*	8	0	0	0
		13	lb	Saffron	6	10	0	0
		48	gross	Points	2	8	0	0
		1	gross	Lacquer	0	0	20	0
		4	lb	Frankincense	0	0	4	0
		1	bolt	Thread	0	0	12	0
		1.5	dozen	Caps	0	15	0	0
		1	dozen	Cards, Playing	0	0	15	0
		1	lb	Pepper	0	0	12	0
		0.5	lb	Cloves	0	0	15	0
		0.5	lb	Ginger	0	0	9	0
		0.5	lb	Nutmeg	0	0	10	0
		0.5	lb	Kermes	0	0	6	0
Thomas Stackpoll	Ind	3.25	piece	Cloth of Assize	0	0	0	0
		12	gross	Knives	4	0	0	0
		48	gross	Points	2	8	0	0
		2	gross	Lacquer	0	3	4	0
		7	dozen	Cards, Playing	0	8	9	0
		6	dozen	Knives, in Pairs	0	10	0	0
		1	C	Aniseed	0	13	4	0
		1	dozen	Cumin	0	0	16	0
		3	lb	Pepper	0	3	0	0
		1	lb	Nutmeg	0	0	20	0
		1.5	lb	Ginger	0	2	3	0
		1	lb	Cinnamon	0	2	6	0

Merchant name	Origin	Qty	Unit	Commodity	£	s.	d.	f.
		3	bolt	Thread	0	3	0	0
		1	ream	Paper	0	0	20	0
		9	lb	Saffron	4	10	0	0
		30	lb	Silk, *Worked*	20	0	0	0
		3	lb	Mercury	0	0	18	0
Thomas Harold & Gylbart	Ind	3.75	piece	Cloth of Assize	0	0	0	0
		6	gross	Knives	0	40	0	0
		1	gross	Cutts	0	3	4	0
		24	gross	Points	0	24	0	0
		1	gross	Lacquer	0	0	20	0
		4	dozen	Cards, Playing	0	5	0	0
		0.5	C	Aniseed	0	6	8	0
		2	lb	Cumin	0	0	3	0
		5	C	Hops	2	10	0	0

The Trynyte of Gloucester, John Dymmock master, Exiting, 6th August 1546

Merchant name	Origin	Qty	Unit	Commodity	£	s.	d.	f.
Thomas Cloterboke	Ind	1	ton	Iron	4	0	0	0
		1	pipe	Wine, Corrupt	0	15	0	0
		1.5	C	Hops	0	15	0	0

The Misercordiade of Vila Do Conde, Anthony Lews master, Exiting, *6th August 1546*

Merchant name	Origin	Qty	Unit	Commodity	£	s.	d.	f.
Anthony Lews	Alien	8	*piece*	Poldavis *Cloth*	4	0	0	0
John Whyte	Ind	3	dozen	Skins, Calf	0	10	0	0

The Jakes of Paimboef, Evan de Marrys master, Entering, 7th August 1546

Merchant name	Origin	Qty	Unit	Commodity	£	s.	d.	f.
Michael Parrett	Alien	5.5	ton	Salt	2	15	0	0

The Mary Conception of Bristol, Richard Whyte master, Exiting, 9th August 1546

Merchant name	Origin	Qty	Unit	Commodity	£	s.	d.	f.
John Smyth	Ind	20	ton	Lead	100	0	0	0
		40	piece	Tavestock *Cloth*	4	6	8	0
		120	piece	Manchester Cotton *Cloth*	60	0	0	0
John Swetynge	Ind	10.5	ton	Lead	52	10	0	0
		22	*piece*	Poldavis *Cloth*	11	0	0	0
		17	piece	Cloth of Assize	0	0	0	0
John Browne	Ind	3	dicker	Hides, Tanned	0	0	0	0
		1.5	dicker	Hides, Kip	0	0	0	0
Thomas Harrys	Ind	18	piece	Cloth of Assize	0	0	0	0
William Jay	Ind	20	piece	Cloth of Assize	0	0	0	0
		60	dozen	Skins, Calf	10	0	0	0
John Perryman & Pressy	Ind	15	piece	Cloth of Assize	0	0	0	0
		16	piece	Manchester Cotton *Cloth*	8	0	0	0
Henry Sandeford	Ind	6	dicker	Hides, Tanned	0	0	0	0
		2.5	dicker	Hides, Kip	0	0	0	0
		50	dozen	Skins, Calf	8	6	8	0
		25	piece	Manchester Cotton *Cloth*	13	0	0	0
		5	piece	Cloth of Assize	0	0	0	0

Merchant name	Origin	Qty	Unit	Commodity	£	s.	d.	f.
Nicholas Teson &								
Chester & Johns	Ind	74	piece	Manchester Cotton *Cloth*	37	0	0	0
		30	piece	Northern Cotton *Cloth*	6	5	0	0
		1.5	ton	Lead	7	10	0	0
		15	*piece*	Poldavis *Cloth*	7	10	0	0
		2	piece	Molton *Cloth*	0	8	4	0
		1	piece	Wadmal *Cloth*	0	10	0	0
William Harvest	Ind	18	piece	Manchester Cotton *Cloth*	9	0	0	0
James Baylye	Ind	9	piece	Cloth of Assize	0	0	0	0
William Sprat	Ind	100	dozen	Skins, Calf	16	13	4	0
		4	dicker	Hides, Tanned	0	0	0	0
		2	dicker	Hides, Kip	0	0	0	0
		9	piece	Cloth of Assize	0	0	0	0

The Jakes of Paimboef, Evan de Marrys master, Exiting, 10th August 1546

Merchant name	Origin	Qty	Unit	Commodity	£	s.	d.	f.
Michael Perrott	Alien	2	last	Coal	0	26	8	0
		21	dozen	Skins, Calf	3	10	0	0
		1	piece	Welsh *Cloth*	0	20	0	0
		36	yard	Check *Cloth*	0	12	0	0
		1	piece	White of Bristol Cloth	0	8	8	0
		6	dicker	Hides, Tanned	0	0	0	0
		6	piece	Cloth of Assize, Dozen Strait	0	0	0	0

The Yevan of Le Croisic, William Barnard master, Entering, *10th August 1546*

Merchant name	Origin	Qty	Unit	Commodity	£	s.	d.	f.
William *Barnard*	Alien	20	ton	Salt	10	0	0	0
		1.9	ton	Iron	4	15	0	0

The Mary of Le Croisic, Vincent Kynhemecke master, Entering, 11th August 1546

Merchant name	Origin	Qty	Unit	Commodity	£	s.	d.	f.
Vincent Kynhemecke	Alien	30.5	ton	Salt	15	5	0	0

The Jhesus of Mumbles, John Bragge master, Exiting, *11th August 1546*

Merchant name	Origin	Qty	Unit	Commodity	£	s.	d.	f.
John Swan	Ind	1	piece	Cloth of Assize	0	0	0	0
		4	tun	Wine, Corrupt	6	0	0	0
William Butlar &								
Kelly	Ind	1	piece	Cloth of Assize	0	0	0	0
		9	piece	Cloth of Assize, Dozen Strait	0	0	0	0
		1	ton	Iron	4	0	0	0
		4	dozen	Aniseed	0	5	4	0
		0.5	C	Liquorice	0	6	8	0
		12	lb	Kermes	0	12	0	0
		4	C	Hops	2	0	0	0
		1	tun	Wine, Corrupt	0	30	0	0
		3	lb	Saffron	0	30	0	0
		4	dozen	Aniseed	0	5	4	0
		12	lb	Pepper	0	12	0	0
		1	piece	Worsted Russett *Cloth*	0	13	4	0
Thomas Teson	Ind	1	pipe	Wine	0	0	0	0
John Reynolds	Ind	2	piece	Cloth of Assize	0	0	0	0

Merchant name	Origin	Qty	Unit	Commodity	£	s.	d.	f.

The Julyan of Marennes, Nicholas Oryo master, Entering, *11th August 1546*

| Nicholas *Oryo* | Alien | 30 | ton | Salt | 15 | 0 | 0 | 0 |

The Evan of Le Croisic, William Barnard master, Exiting, 14th August 1546

| William *Barnard* | Alien | 2 | last | Coal | 0 | 26 | 8 | 0 |
| | | 8 | piece | Bristol Frieze Cloth | 5 | 6 | 8 | 0 |

The Esabell of Blavet, Alan de Myrell master, Entering, 16th August 1546

| *Alan de Myrell* | Alien | 30 | ton | Salt | 15 | 0 | 0 | 0 |

The Julyan of Morbihan, John Corrow master, Entering, 17th August 1546

John *Corrow*	Alien	22	ton	Salt	11	0	0	0
		60	ell	Canvas *Cloth*	0	15	0	0
		15	british ell	White Cloth	0	6	8	0
		2	piece	Pitch	0	2	6	0

The Francis of Blavet, Peter Froley master, Exiting, *17th August 1546*

Robert Newborn & Harrys	Ind	1.75	last	Coal	0	23	4	0
		7	pipe	Fish, Salmon	10	10	0	0
		14	piece	Northern Cotton *Cloth*	2	18	4	0
		5	ton	Lead	25	0	0	0
		30	dozen	Skins, Calf	5	0	0	0
		8	dicker	Hides, Tanned	0	0	0	0
		8	piece	Cloth of Assize, Dozen Strait	0	0	0	0
Henry Petron	Alien	6	dicker	Hides, Tanned	0	0	0	0
		2	dicker	Hides, Kip	0	0	0	0

The Patrick of Tenby, Philip Thomas master, Entering, 20th August 1546

| Walter Lodbroke | Ind | 6.5 | chest | Sugar | 6 | 0 | 0 | 0 |

The Nicholas of Elmore, Thomas Hoper master, Entering, *20th August 1546*

| John Channcelar | Ind | 3 | C | Woad, Azores | 0 | 20 | 0 | 0 |

The Elysabeth of Quimperlé, William Gungelet master, Exiting, *21st August 1546*

| Roland Molen & William & Gungelet | Alien | 1.25 | piece | Cloth of Assize | 0 | 0 | 0 | 0 |
| | | 2 | piece | Bristol Frieze Cloth | 0 | 26 | 8 | 0 |

The Mary of Le Croisic, Vincent Kynhemecke master, Exiting, 25th August 1546

Vincent Kynhemecke	Alien	3	last	Coal	2	0	0	0
		6	piece	Bristol Frieze Cloth	4	0	0	0
		1	piece	Cloth of Assize	0	0	0	0

Merchant name	Origin	Qty	Unit	Commodity	£	s.	d.	f.
The Harry of Bristol, Thomas Webb master, Exiting, 25th August 1546								
Nicholas Thorn								
& assoc.	Ind	28	ton	Lead	140	0	0	0
		2	C	Hops	0	20	0	0
The Isabel of Blavet, Alan de Myrell master, Exiting, 25th August 1546								
Alan De Myrell	Alien	3.5	last	Coal	2	6	8	0
William & Robert								
Tyndale	Ind	13	piece	Cloth of Assize, Northern Strait	0	54	2	0
		2	piece	Manchester Cotton *Cloth*	1	0	0	0
The Margarete of Chepstow, Robert Botman master, Entering, 27th August 1546								
William Gale	Ind	3	C	Woad, Azores	0	20	0	0
The Sonday of Bristol, Thomas Walter master, Exiting, 27th August 1546								
John Bedfyld	Ind	1	tun	Wine	0	0	0	0
William Chester								
& assoc.	Ind	2.5	tun	Wine, Corrupt	3	15	0	0
		7.66	C	Hops	3	16	8	0
The Mary Conception, Richard Whyte master, Exiting, 28th August 1546								
John Capps	Ind	9	piece	Cloth of Assize	0	0	0	0
John Chancellar	Ind	15	piece	Cloth of Assize	0	0	0	0
Thomas Cutt	Ind	7	piece	Cloth of Assize	0	0	0	0
Thomas Teson	Ind	2	ton	Lead	10	0	0	0
The John of Le Conquet, Luke Carorian master, Exiting, 30th August 1546								
John Well	Ind	11.5	dicker	Hides, Tanned	0	0	0	0
		20	dozen	Skins, Calf	3	6	8	0
		10	piece	Cloth of Assize	0	0	0	0
Robert Gyttons	Ind	6	dicker	Hides, Tanned	0	0	0	0
William Pepwall	Ind	30	piece	Manchester Cotton *Cloth*	15	0	0	0
		2	ton	Lead	10	0	0	0
		7	dicker	Hides, Tanned	0	0	0	0
		1	piece	Cloth of Assize	0	0	0	0
The George of Milford Haven, Peter Bullock master, Entering, 30th August 1546								
Peter *Bullock* &								
Tanner	Ind	0.5	C	Fish, Hake	0	5	0	0
		6	barrel	Fish, Herring White	0	30	0	0
The Jhesus of Mumbles, Richard ApJohn master, Entering, 2nd September 1546								
John Clement	Ind	4	ton	Salt	2	0	0	0
		1	C	Oakum	0	3	4	0

Merchant name	Origin	Qty	Unit	Commodity	£	s.	d.	f.

The Savyor of Mumbles, John Hammon master, Entering, *2nd September 1546*

| David Gryffyth | Ind | 5 | ton | Salt | 2 | 10 | 0 | 0 |

The Michaell of Chepstow, Richard Jeyn master, Entering, *2nd September 1546*

| Thomas Selocumbe | Ind | 8 | C | Woad, Azores | 2 | 13 | 4 | 0 |

The Trynyte of Caerleon, ThomasBoyse master, Entering, 3rd September 1546

| William Ballard | Ind | 114 | ton | Salt | 57 | 0 | 0 | 0 |

The Julyan of Morbihan, John Corrow master, Exiting, 4th September 1546

| John *Corrow* | Alien | 1 | piece | Dunster *Cloth* | 0 | 10 | 0 | 0 |
| | | 3 | piece | Cloth of Assize, Dozen Strait | 0 | 0 | 0 | 0 |

The Mawdelen of Morbihan, John de Gayen master, Entering, *4th September 1546*

| George Jeffrey | Alien | 20 | ton | Salt | 10 | 0 | 0 | 0 |
| | | 150 | ell | Canvas *Cloth* | 2 | 0 | 0 | 0 |

The Ann of Penmarch, Evan Brynnowghe master, Exiting, *4th September 1546*

John Alepewe	Alien	22.7	dicker	Hides, Tanned	0	0	0	0
		17	dicker	Hides, Kip	0	0	0	0
		8	ton	Lead	40	0	0	0
		30	dozen	Skins, Calf	5	0	0	0
		20	piece	Manchester Cotton *Cloth*	10	0	0	0
		22	yard	Check *Cloth*	0	7	4	0
Evan Brynnowghe	Alien	1.5	last	Coal	0	20	0	0
		3	piece	Cloth of Assize, Dozen Strait	0	0	0	0
William Yonge	Ind	100	piece	Manchester Cotton *Cloth*	50	0	0	0
		2	piece	Brecon *Cloth*	2	0	0	0
		16	dozen	Skins, Calf	2	13	4	0
		5	piece	Cloth of Assize	0	0	0	0
William de le Vesero	Alien	126	piece	Manchester Cotton *Cloth*	63	0	0	0
Francis Methyck	Alien	8	piece	Manchester Cotton *Cloth*	4	0	0	0
		0.5	piece	Cloth of Assize	0	0	0	0
William de le Vesero	Alien	10	piece	Manchester Cotton *Cloth*	5	0	0	0
John Pryn	Ind	2.5	piece	Cloth of Assize	0	0	0	0

The Mary of Hondarribia, Alonso de Castanetha master, Entering, 6th September 1546

William Appowell & assoc.	Ind	28	ton	Iron	70	0	0	0
		8	ton	Salt	4	0	0	0
		5	C	Feathers, Down	10	0	0	0
		5	C	Turpentine	3	6	8	0
Alonso de Castanetha & assoc.	Alien	19.5	ton	Iron	48	15	0	0
	Alien	3	tun	Wine, Corrupt	4	10	0	0

Merchant name	Origin	Qty	Unit	Commodity	£	s.	d.	f.
	Alien	21	dozen	Serches	4	7	6	0
	Alien	6	C	Unknown	0	2	6	0

The Mary of Hondarribia, John de Bereby master, Exiting, 8th September 1546

Merchant name	Origin	Qty	Unit	Commodity	£	s.	d.	f.
William & Robert Tyndale	Ind	10	ton	Lead	50	0	0	0
		80	piece	Manchester Cotton *Cloth*	40	0	0	0
		20	dozen	Skins, Calf	3	6	8	0
		14	piece	Cloth of Assize	0	0	0	0
John Smyth	Ind	15	ton	Lead	75	0	0	0
		40	piece	Manchester Cotton *Cloth*	20	0	0	0
		6	piece	Bristol Frieze Cloth	4	0	0	0
		3.5	piece	Cloth of Assize	0	0	0	0
William Yonge	Ind	6	ton	Lead	30	0	0	0
		80	piece	Manchester Cotton *Cloth*	40	0	0	0
		10	piece	Northern Cotton *Cloth*	2	0	20	0
		8	piece	Cloth of Assize	0	0	0	0
John Cutt	Ind	4	ton	Lead	20	0	0	0
		8	piece	Cloth of Assize	0	0	0	0
Robert Gyttons	Ind	10	piece	Manchester Cotton *Cloth*	5	0	0	0
		8	piece	Cloth of Assize	0	0	0	0
Hugh Prowse	Ind	8	piece	Manchester Cotton *Cloth*	4	0	0	0
		2	ton	Lead	10	0	0	0
		2	piece	Cloth of Assize	0	0	0	0
Hugh Gyttons	Ind	30	piece	Cloth of Assize, Northern Strait	6	5	0	0
		6	piece	Cloth of Assize	0	0	0	0
		6	dicker	Hides, Tanned	0	0	0	0
William Appowell & Cutt	Ind	210	piece	Manchester Cotton *Cloth*	105	0	0	0
		5	piece	Welsh Cloth, Dozen Strait	0	20	10	0
		35	piece	Cloth of Assize	0	0	0	0
William Rowley & assoc.	Ind	28	piece	Cloth of Assize	0	0	0	0
John Browne	Ind	3	dicker	Hides, Tanned	0	0	0	0
		3	dicker	Hides, Kip	0	0	0	0
Francis Wosley & Brampton	Ind	15	piece	Cloth of Assize	0	0	0	0

The Martyne of Morbihan, George Truscat master, Entering, 8th September 1546

Merchant name	Origin	Qty	Unit	Commodity	£	s.	d.	f.
Mathew Falswen, Truscat & assoc.	Alien	330	ell	Canvas *Cloth*	2	15	0	0
		37	ton	Salt	18	10	0	0

The Nicholas of Errenteria, Martin de la Rendria master, Entering, *8th September 1546*

Merchant name	Origin	Qty	Unit	Commodity	£	s.	d.	f.
William Church	Ind	20	tun	Wine	0	0	0	0
		225	C	Woad, Toulouse	106	5	0	0
		70	tun	Wine, Corrupt	105	0	0	0
Peraton De Parry	Alien	5	tun	Wine	0	0	0	0
		6.5	tun	Wine, Corrupt	9	15	0	0

Merchant name	Origin	Qty	Unit	Commodity	£	s.	d.	f.

The Jamys of Nantes, John Davys master, Entering, 9th September 1546

| John *Davys* | Alien | 18 | ton | Salt | 9 | 0 | 0 | 0 |

The Bonaventure of Morbihan, John Fardell master, Entering, *9th September 1546*

| Evan Gyllett | Alien | 29 | ton | Salt | 14 | 10 | 0 | 0 |
| | | 126 | ell | Canvas *Cloth* | 0 | 30 | 0 | 0 |

The Michaell of Chepstow, Richard Mower master, Entering, *9th September 1546*

| David Hart | Ind | 3 | C | Woad, Azores | 0 | 20 | 0 | 0 |

The Fenix of Bristol, John Boysher master, Entering, 10th September 1546

| William Sheryngton | Ind | 31 | ton | Salt | 15 | 10 | 0 | 0 |

The Martyne of Morbihan, George Truscate master, Exiting, *10th September 1546*

| Mathew Falswen | Alien | 3 | last | Coal | 2 | 0 | 0 | 0 |

The Trynyte of Bristol, Thomas Boyse master, Exiting, *10th September 1546*

Nicholas Thorn								
& assoc.	Ind	31	ton	Lead	155	0	0	0
William Spratt	Ind	6.5	dicker	Hides, Tanned	0	0	0	0

The Sancta Maria of Errenteria, Julian de Gusseta master, Entering, 11th September 1546

John Well & assoc.	Ind	73	ton	Iron	182	10	0	0
Martin Perys & de								
Gusseta & assoc.	Alien	34	ton	Iron	85	0	0	0
		10	M	Lemons	0	33	4	0
		21	C	Rosin	0	28	0	0

The Jamys of Nantes, John Davys master, Exiting, *11th September 1546*

| John *Davys* | Alien | 7.5 | wey | Coal | 0 | 25 | 0 | 0 |

The Mary of Chepstow, John Jeynes master, Entering, 12th September 1546

| John Channceler | | | | | | | | |
| & Scloun | Ind | 9.5 | ton | Woad, Azores | 63 | 6 | 8 | 0 |

The Mawdlen of Bristol, Florence Typton master, Exiting, 13th September 1546

Henry Sandesford	Ind	27	dozen	Skins, Calf	4	10	0	0
		10	dicker	Hides, Tanned	0	0	0	0
		3.6	dicker	Hides, Kip	0	0	0	0
Walter Dowley	Ind	6	dozen	Skins, Calf	0	20	0	0
Henry Browne	Alien	35	dozen	Skins, Calf	5	16	8	0
John Swetynge	Ind	4.5	ton	Lead, Worked	22	10	0	0

Merchant name	Origin	Qty	Unit	Commodity	£	s.	d.	f.
James Chester	Ind	14	dozen	Skins, Calf	2	6	8	0
		4.5	ton	Lead	22	10	0	0
		10	piece	Molton *Cloth*	2	0	20	0
		5	dicker	Hides, Tanned	0	0	0	0
		2	dicker	Hides, Kip	0	0	0	0
John Cutt	Ind	6	*piece*	Poldavis *Cloth*	3	0	0	0
		8	pack	Oleron *Cloth*	0	53	4	0
Anthony Payne	Ind	5	ton	Lead, Worked	25	0	0	0

The Mary Richard of Tenby, John Moell master, Entering, 14th September 1546

William Butlar	Ind	1.25	tun	Wine, Corrupt	0	37	6	0

The Trynyte of Dublin, James Hey master, Entering, *14th September 1546*

Nicholas Kelly	Ind	40	ton	Salt	20	0	0	0

The Mary of Chepstow, John Johns master, Entering, 15th September 1546

John Gryffyth	Ind	6	C	Woad, Azores	2	0	0	0

The Martyne of Morbihan, George Truscat master, Exiting, 16th September 1546

Mathew Falswen & assoc.	Alien	2	piece	Cloth of Assize, Dozen Strait	0	0	0	0
		2	piece	Bristol Frieze Cloth	0	26	8	0
		1	piece	Tavestock *Cloth*	0	4	2	0

The Margaret of Chepstow, Richard Joyns master, Entering, 18th September 1546

David Harte	Ind	3	C	Woad, Azores	0	20	0	0

The Trynyte of Guernsey, Nicholas Grynam master, Exiting, 20th September 1546

Henry Wyott	Ind	22	piece	Cloth of Assize	0	0	0	0

The Bonaventure of Morbihan, John Fardell master, Exiting, *20th September 1546*

Evan Gyllett	Alien	2	last	Coal	0	26	8	0

The Harte of Bristol, John Boysher master, Exiting, 22nd September 1546

William Harvest	Ind	4	piece	Cloth of Assize	0	0	0	0
		10	piece	Manchester Cotton *Cloth*	5	0	0	0
		12	*piece*	Poldavis *Cloth*	6	0	0	0
		3	dicker	Hides, Kip	0	0	0	0
		2	dicker	Hides, Tanned	0	0	0	0
Edward Pryn	Ind	6.5	ton	Lead, Worked	32	0	0	0

The Margaret of Chepstow, Richard Jones master, Entering, 22nd September 1546

James Boyse	Ind	6	C	Woad, Azores	2	0	0	0

Merchant name	Origin	Qty	Unit	Commodity	£	s.	d.	f.

The Sancta Maria of Aveiro, Peter Thomas master, Entering, *22nd September 1546*

Merchant name	Origin	Qty	Unit	Commodity	£	s.	d.	f.
Gonsalo Enys	Alien	150	ropes	Onions	0	18	4	0

The Mawdlen of Morbihan, John de Gayen master, Exiting, 23rd September 1546

Merchant name	Origin	Qty	Unit	Commodity	£	s.	d.	f.
George Jeffreys	Alien	2	piece	Cloth of Assize, Dozen Strait	0	0	0	0
		1.5	piece	Worsted *Cloth*	0	30	0	0
John *De Gayen*	Alien	2	piece	Bristol Frieze Cloth	0	26	8	0
		1	piece	Worsted *Cloth*	0	20	0	0
		1	piece	Cloth of Assize, Dozen Strait	0	0	0	0

The Mary of Quimperlé, Evan de Bean master, Entering, 24th September 1546

Merchant name	Origin	Qty	Unit	Commodity	£	s.	d.	f.
Maurice Brewar	Alien	21	ton	Salt	10	10	0	0
		240	ell	Canvas *Cloth*	3	0	0	0
James & *Evan* Davy								
& *De Bean*	Alien	750	ell	Canvas *Cloth*	9	0	0	0

The Sancta Maria of Errenteria, Julian de Gussueta master, Exiting, *24th September 1546*

Merchant name	Origin	Qty	Unit	Commodity	£	s.	d.	f.
John Perrys	Alien	10	dozen	Skins, Calf	0	33	4	0

The Margaret of Chepstow, John Smyth master, Entering, 28th September 1546

Merchant name	Origin	Qty	Unit	Commodity	£	s.	d.	f.
John Chancellar	Ind	77	C	Woad, Azores	25	13	4	0

TNA E122/22/4 is an annual 'particular' customs account of Thomas Kelke & Henry Pomerey, collectors of customs and subsidies, running from Michaelmas 1550 to Michaelmas 1551. It contains the same level of detail as the 1540s accounts.

Merchant name	Origin	Qty	Unit	Commodity	£	s.	d.	f.
The George of Youghal, Maurice Fitzjohn master, Exiting, 1st October 1550								
Walter Grante	Ind	0.33	piece	Cloth of Assize	0	0	0	0
The Clement of Swansea, Griffith Davys master, Entering, *1st October 1550*								
William Fateras	Ind	5.5	tun	Wine	0	0	0	0
		43	ream	Paper	0	58	8	0
The *Christ*ofer of Minehead, Richard Cry[ ]an master, Exiting, 6th October 1550								
John Northall	Ind	5	piece	Bristol Frieze *Cloth*	0	66	8	0
The Savyou*r* of Bristol, John Fyshepyll master, Entering, 7th October 1550								
John *Fyshepyll*	Ind	2	ton	Woad, Azores	13	6	8	0
The George of Youghal, Maurice Fytzjohn master, Exiting, 7th October 1550								
Nicholas Shee	Ind	2.5	piece	Cloth of Assize	0	0	0	0
		15	lb	Saffron	7	10	0	0
		2	lb	Silk, *Worked*	0	26	8	0
		8	gross	Knives	0	53	4	0
		26	gross	Points	0	26	0	0
		0.5	dozen	Knives, in Pairs	0	0	10	0
David Mannd	Ind	1	gross	Knives	0	6	8	0
		2	gross	Points	0	2	0	0
The Hyend of Chepstow, John Corbett master, Exiting, 9th October 1550								
Edmund Weldon	Ind	6	fother	Lead	24	0	0	0
The Clement of Swansea, Thomas Whyte master, Exiting, *9th October 1550*								
William Fateras	Ind	3.08	piece	Cloth of Assize	0	0	0	0

Merchant name	Origin	Qty	Unit	Commodity	£	s.	d.	f.
The George of Youghal, Maurice Fytzjohn master, Exiting, 9th October 1550								
Edward Hyll	Ind	21	pair	Hose, Mens	4	0	0	0
The Sancta Maria of Hondarribia, John Beroby master, Entering, 10th October 1550								
John Smyth & assoc.	Ind	84	ton	Iron	210	0	0	0
		57	dozen	Gloves, Spanish	11	8	0	0
		4	dozen	Serches	0	16	8	0
John Beroby & assoc.	Alien	26.66	ton	Iron	66	13	4	0
		96	dozen	Felts, Spanish	32	0	0	0
		2	dozen	Skins, Red	0	20	0	0
The Sancta Maria of San Sebastián, Goveran Sebastian master, Entering, 10th October 1550								
Domyngo de Arso	Alien	2.5	M	Fish, Newfoundland (many sorts)	22	10	0	0
		92.25	C	Fish, Newfoundland (second sorte)	46	2	6	0
		447.8	C	Fish, Newfoundland (third sort)	89	11	0	0
		3	tun	Oil, Train	12	0	0	0
John Gordon	Ind	7.5	C	Fish, Newfoundland (big sort)	7	10	0	0
		39.25	C	Fish, Newfoundland (second sorte)	15	7	6	0
		149.3	C	Fish, Newfoundland *(third sort)*	29	17	0	0
		1	tun	Oil, Train	4	0	0	0
Martin de Layfrey	Alien	3	C	Fish, Dry Newfoundland	0	30	0	0
The Prymerose of Cork, John Nolan master, Entering, 14th October 1550								
James Rownan	Ind	7	tun	Wine, Corrupt	10	10	0	0
		1	barrel	Meat, Oxen	0	6	8	0
The Lady Pyttey of Aveiro, Peter Thome master, Entering, 14th October 1550								
Peter Rodrigus	Alien	65	ton	Woad, Azores	434	6	8	0
William Barrett	Ind	12	ton	Woad, Azores	80	0	0	0
The Mary Consepcyon of Portugal, Jasper Gonsalvys master, Entering, 14th October 1550								
Peter Rodrigus	Alien	115	ton	Woad, Azores	766	13	4	0
The Primrose of Bristol, John Howten master, Exiting, 16th October 1550								
John Rothemay	Ind	9	pair	Milstones	9	0	0	0
The Savyour of Bristol, Florence Typton master, Exiting, 21st October 1550								
Edward Weldon	Ind	10	piece	Cloth of Assize	0	0	0	0
William Pepwall	Ind	4	fother	Lead	16	0	0	0
William Cox & Pryn	Ind	39	piece	Cloth of Assize	0	0	0	0
George Knyght	Ind	5	piece	Cloth of Assize	0	0	0	0
George Snygge	Ind	9	piece	Cloth of Assize	0	0	0	0
		5	C	Lead	0	20	0	0
		1	piece	Bristol Frieze *Cloth*	0	13	4	0

Merchant name	Origin	Qty	Unit	Commodity	£	s.	d.	f.
Thomas Shypman	Ind	39	piece	Cloth of Assize	o	o	o	o
		17	fother	Lead	68	o	o	o
Robert Butler	Ind	8	piece	Cloth of Assize	o	o	o	o
John Pryn	Ind	13	piece	Cloth of Assize	o	o	o	o
Richard Pryn &								
Kyrke	Ind	9	piece	Cloth of Assize	o	o	o	o
Thomas Yonge	Ind	22	piece	Cloth of Assize	o	o	o	o
Thomas Hyckye								
& Baret	Ind	5.5	piece	Cloth of Assize	o	o	o	o
John Cutt & Harvest	Ind	13	piece	Cloth of Assize	o	o	o	o
Randal Wyllbra								
& Stone	Ind	13.33	piece	Cloth of Assize	o	o	o	o
William Balard								
& Nashe	Ind	14	piece	Cloth of Assize	o	o	o	o
Nicholas Kelley	Ind	1	piece	Bristol Frieze *Cloth*	o	13	4	o

The George & The *Christ*ofer of Gloucester, Nicholas Lynke & Horne masters, Entering, 23rd October 1550

Henry & William								
Horne	Ind	9.5	last	Fish, Herring White	28	10	o	o

The S*ancta* Maria of Hondarribia, John Beroby master, Exiting, *23rd October 1550*

Merchant name	Origin	Qty	Unit	Commodity	£	s.	d.	f.
John Smyth	Ind	15	piece	Cloth of Assize	o	o	o	o
		16	piece	Brecon *Cloth*	16	o	o	o
James Boyes &								
Woysley	Ind	29	piece	Cloth of Assize	o	o	o	o
Martin Pyrrys	Ind	3	C	Wax	6	o	o	o
John Wells	Ind	13	C	Wax	26	o	o	o
Andrew Assarayn	Alien	8	C	Wax	16	o	o	o
		2	piece	Welsh *Cloth*	o	40	o	o
		10	yard	Cloth of Assize	o	o	o	o
Francis Codryngton	Ind	66	piece	Cloth of Assize	o	o	o	o
Gruand Yeratta								
& assoc.	Alien	9	C	Wax	18	o	o	o
		2	piece	Cloth of Assize	o	o	o	o
William Yonge &								
assoc.	Ind	50	piece	Manchester Cotton *Cloth*	25	o	o	o
		30	piece	Northern Cotton *Cloth*	6	5	o	o
		5	C	Wax	10	o	o	o
		22.33	piece	Cloth of Assize	o	o	o	o
John Stone	Ind	5.33	piece	Cloth of Assize	o	o	o	o
		5	piece	Cotton *Cloth*	o	20	10	o
Martin Grevys	Ind	1.5	C	Wax	o	60	o	o
		0.33	piece	Cloth of Assize	o	o	o	o
William Cary	Ind	35.5	piece	Cloth of Assize	o	o	o	o
		9	piece	Welsh *Cloth*	9	o	o	o
John de Combere	Alien	2	piece	Cloth of Assize	o	o	o	o
Thomas Slocan	Ind	3	yard	Cloth of Assize, Bridgwater	o	o	o	o
		1	piece	Welsh *Cloth*	o	20	o	o
Richard Cary	Ind	16	piece	Cloth of Assize	o	o	o	o

1 Possibly a recording error.

Merchant name	Origin	Qty	Unit	Commodity	£	s.	d.	f.
John Pryn	Ind	7.5	piece	Cloth of Assize	0	0	0	0
Peter Sobleo &								
Martin Pirris	Alien	11	C	Wax	22	0	0	0
		4	piece	Cloth of Assize	0	0	0	0
John Stone & assoc.	Ind	10.75	piece	Cloth of Assize	0	0	0	0
		2	piece	Welsh *Cloth*	0	40	0	0
		1.25	C	Tin, Worked	0	37	6	0
		7.5	C	Wax	15	0	0	0

The Sonday of Bristol, William Gelly master, Entering, *23rd October 1550*

Merchant name	Origin	Qty	Unit	Commodity	£	s.	d.	f.
William Chester								
& assoc.	Ind	137	barrel	Fish, Herring White	34	5	0	0
		2	piece	Skins, Salted	0	2	6	0
		0.5	C	Tallow, Rough	0	0	20	0
		2	C	Fish, Hake	0	20	0	0

The Sonday of Bristol, James Williams master, Entering, 24th October 1550

Merchant name	Origin	Qty	Unit	Commodity	£	s.	d.	f.
Nicholas Kelley								
& assoc.	Ind	88	barrel	Fish, Herring White	19	0	0	0
		2	C	Fish, Hake	0	20	0	0

The Trynyte of Carleon, Robert Alyn master, Entering, 25th October 1550

Merchant name	Origin	Qty	Unit	Commodity	£	s.	d.	f.
Thomas Chester								
& assoc.	Ind	103.5	barrel	Fish, Herring White	25	17	6	0
		1.25	C	Fish, Hake	0	12	6	0

The John of Talmont, John Cornett master, Entering, 27th October 1550

Merchant name	Origin	Qty	Unit	Commodity	£	s.	d.	f.
Robert Saxcy & assoc.	Ind	22	tun	Wine	0	0	0	0

The Anthony of Tewkesbury, John Butler master, Entering, 29th October 1550

Merchant name	Origin	Qty	Unit	Commodity	£	s.	d.	f.
John *Butler*	Ind	122	barrel	Fish, Herring White	30	10	0	0

The Nicholas of Bristol, John Welshe master, Entering, *29th October 1550*

Merchant name	Origin	Qty	Unit	Commodity	£	s.	d.	f.
Nicholas Kelley								
& assoc.	Ind	220	barrel	Fish, Herring White	55	0	0	0
		3	C	Fish, Hake	0	30	0	0
		1	C	Skins, Sheep	0	10	0	0
		2	dicker	Skins, Salted	0	26	8	0

The Swan of Bristol, Nicholas Grynwey master, Entering, 30th October 1550

Merchant name	Origin	Qty	Unit	Commodity	£	s.	d.	f.
John Channceler								
& assoc.	Ind	25.25	tun	Wine	0	0	0	0

Merchant name	Origin	Qty	Unit	Commodity	£	s.	d.	f.

The Mary John of Waterford, John Strannge master, Entering, 3rd November 1550

Merchant name	Origin	Qty	Unit	Commodity	£	s.	d.	f.
David Brewer	Ind	6	C	Mantle, Frieze Cloth	12	0	0	0
		40	piece	Mantles	6	13	4	0
John Brewer	Ind	3	C	Mantle, Frieze Cloth	6	0	0	0
		10	piece	Mantles	0	33	4	0
Robert Whyte	Ind	3	C	Mantle, Frieze Cloth	6	0	0	0
		5	C	Skins, Sheep	0	50	0	0
		1	C	Skins, Kid	0	5	0	0
		6	piece	Mantles	0	20	0	0
Nicholas Harris	Ind	100	piece	Skins, Sheep	0	8	4	0
		44	yard	Mantle, Frieze Cloth	0	14	8	0
Edmund Waryng	Ind	1	C	Mantle, Frieze Cloth	0	40	0	0
		20	piece	Skins, Marten	0	20	0	0
		2.5	C	Skins, Sheep	0	25	0	0

The Mary of Waterford, Thomas Keryn master, Entering, *3rd November 1550*

Merchant name	Origin	Qty	Unit	Commodity	£	s.	d.	f.
Nicholas Bayley	Ind	2	C	Mantle, Frieze *Cloth*	4	0	0	0
		4	C	Skins, Sheep	0	40	0	0
		5	piece	Mantles	0	16	8	0
		1	C	Skins, Kid	0	5	0	0
John Flemyng	Ind	5	C	Mantle, Frieze *Cloth*	10	0	0	0
		8	piece	Mantles	0	26	8	0
		4	stone	Wool, Flocks	0	0	20	0
Nicholas Harrys	Ind	4	C	Skins, Sheep	0	40	0	0
		90	yard	Mantle, Frieze *Cloth*	0	30	0	0
		4	stone	Wool, Flocks	0	0	20	0
		0.5	C	Skins, Kid	0	2	6	0
		0.5	C	Skins, Lamb	0	3	4	0
Edward Whyte	Ind	4	C	Mantle, Frieze *Cloth*	8	0	0	0
		34	piece	Mantles	0	113	4	0
		0.5	C	Skins, Sheep	0	5	0	0
David Harrold	Ind	36	piece	Skins, Marten	0	36	0	0
		2	C	Irish Linen *Cloth*	0	20	0	0
		24	piece	Skins, Fox	0	7	4	0
		3	C	Skins, Sheep	0	30	0	0
		4	C	Skins, Otter	0	0	20	0
		20	yard	Check *Cloth*	0	6	8	0
		0.5	C	Skins, Lamb	0	3	4	0
David Haley	Ind	12	C	Skins, Sheep	6	0	0	0
		4	C	Skins, Lamb	0	26	8	0
		3.3	C	Skins, Kid	0	16	8	0
		9	piece	Skins, Fox	0	0	18	0
		4	piece	Skins, Otter	0	0	20	0
		210	yard	Mantle, Frieze *Cloth*	4	13	4	0
		40	yard	Irish Frieze *Cloth*	0	10	0	0
		3	piece	Mantles	0	10	0	0
		6	piece	Skins, Deer	0	2	0	0
Thomas Whyte	Ind	2.5	C	Check *Cloth*	0	113	4	0
		11	piece	Mantles	0	36	8	0
		1	piece	Skins, Otter	0	0	5	0

Merchant name	Origin	Qty	Unit	Commodity	£	s.	d.	f.
		2	piece	Skins, Fox	0	0	4	0
Peter Powell	Ind	3	C	Skins, Sheep	0	30	0	0
		13	piece	Mantles	0	43	4	0
		22	yard	Check *Cloth*	0	7	4	0
David Butler	Ind	4	C	Check *Cloth*	8	0	0	0
		2	C	Skins, Sheep	0	20	0	0
		2	piece	Mantles	0	6	8	0
		0.5	C	Skins, Kid	0	2	6	0
Nicholas Nashe	Ind	3	C	Mantle, Frieze *Cloth*	6	0	0	0
		0.5	C	Skins, Sheep	0	5	0	0
		8	piece	Mantles	0	26	8	0
		1	C	Skins, Lamb	0	6	8	0
		1	C	Skins, Kid	0	5	0	0
John Hyde	Ind	4	C	Skins, Sheep	0	40	0	0
		1.5	C	Check *Cloth*	0	60	0	0
Patrick Troy	Ind	9.5	C	Check *Cloth*	19	0	0	0
		8	piece	Mantles	0	26	8	0
		14	C	Skins, Sheep	7	0	0	0
		6	C	Skins, Kid	0	30	0	0
		6	piece	Skins, Fox	0	0	12	0
Laurence Bosher	Ind	4.375	C	Check *Cloth*	8	15	0	0
		1.33	C	Skins, Sheep	0	13	4	0
		10	piece	Skins, Deer	0	3	4	0
		24	piece	Mantles	4	0	0	0
Peter Savage	Ind	15	C	Skins, Sheep	7	10	0	0
		16	piece	Mantles	0	53	4	0
Nicholas Cantwell								
& Welshe	Ind	14.66	C	Check *Cloth*	29	10	0	0
		11	C	Skins, Sheep	0	110	0	0
		38	piece	Mantles	6	6	8	0
		3	C	Skins, Lamb	0	20	0	0
		6	piece	Skins, Deer	0	2	0	0

The Kathryn of Bristol, Thomas Bayley master, Entering, *3rd November 1550*

Leonard Sompter &								
assoc.	Ind	123.5	barrel	Fish, Herring White	30	17	6	0
		3	kilderkin	Fish, Eels	0	20	0	0

The George of Waterford, Robert Medall master, Entering, *3rd November 1550*

Edward Grannte	Ind	15	C	Check *Cloth*	30	0	0	0
		40	piece	Mantles	6	13	4	0
		1	C	Skins, Sheep	0	10	0	0
James Brever	Ind	15	C	Check *Cloth*	30	0	0	0
		18	piece	Mantles	0	60	0	0
		0.5	C	Skins, Sheep	0	5	0	0
Walter Whyte	Ind	2	C	Check *Cloth*	4	0	0	0
		6	C	Skins, Sheep	0	60	0	0
		16	piece	Mantles	0	53	4	0
		1	C	Skins, Kid	0	5	0	0
Nicholas Whyte	Ind	5	C	Check *Cloth*	10	0	0	0

Merchant name	Origin	Qty	Unit	Commodity	£	s.	d.	f.
		20	piece	Mantles	0	66	8	0
		3	C	Skins, Sheep	0	30	0	0
John Hyde & Hackett	Ind	8	C	Check *Cloth*	16	0	0	0
		48	piece	Mantles	8	0	0	0
		4	C	Skins, Sheep	0	40	0	0
		5	C	Skins, Lamb	0	33	4	0
		30	yard	Irish Linen *Cloth*	0	2	6	0
Thomas Whyte & Connowe	Ind	9.25	C	Skins, Sheep	4	12	6	0
		0.5	C	Skins, Lamb	0	3	4	0
Patrick Wodlocke	Ind	8	C	Check *Cloth*	16	0	0	0
		24	piece	Mantles	4	0	0	0
		15	C	Skins, Sheep	7	10	0	0
		1	C	Skins, Lamb	0	6	8	0
		4	piece	Skins, Fox	0	0	8	0
Patrick Madan	Ind	8	C	Check *Cloth*	16	0	0	0
		100	piece	Mantles	16	13	4	0
Robert Whyte	Ind	7	C	Check *Cloth*	14	0	0	0
		2	C	Skins, Sheep	0	20	0	0
		12	piece	Mantles	0	40	0	0
Henry Whyte	Ind	4	C	Check *Cloth*	8	0	0	0
		12	piece	Mantles	0	40	0	0
		0.5	C	Skins, Sheep	0	5	0	0
Richard Vyen	Ind	0.5	C	Check *Cloth*	0	20	0	0
		8	piece	Mantles	0	26	8	0
Richard Bryther	Ind	16	piece	Mantles	0	53	4	0
		30	yard	Check *Cloth*	0	10	0	0
Edmund Clere	Ind	8.5	C	Check *Cloth*	17	0	0	0
		22	piece	Mantles	0	73	0	0
Thomas Vyen	Ind	9	C	Skins, Sheep	4	10	0	0
		2	piece	Mantles	0	6	8	0
		16	yard	Check *Cloth*	0	5	4	0
		1.5	C	Check *Cloth*	0	60	0	0

The Margarett of Bristol, Maurice Welshe master, Entering, 4th November 1550

Robert Sternold	Ind	99.5	barrel	Fish, Herring White	23	17	6	0
		9	C	Fish, Hake	4	10	0	0
		1	pipe	Fish, Salmon	0	30	0	0
		1.5	C	Tallow, Rough	0	5	0	0

The Savyour of Minehead, John Kery master, Entering, 5th November 1550

John Pore & assoc.	Ind	183	barrel	Fish, Herring White	45	15	0	0
		3.5	C	Fish, Hake	0	35	0	0

The Sent John of Genoa, Henry de Maryndrega master, Entering, 6th November 1550

Francis Codryngton & assoc.	Ind	235.5	tun	Wine	0	0	0	0
James de Maring	Alien	12	tun	Wine, Malmysse	48	0	0	0
		23.5	C	Gall	15	6	8	0

Merchant name	Origin	Qty	Unit	Commodity	£	s.	d.	f.
		300.8	ell	Cotton *Cloth*	4	10	0	0
		2.25	tun	Oil, Olive	9	0	0	0
		28	dozen	Skins, Budge	0	112	0	0
		12.5	dozen	Skins, Sheep Worked	6	5	0	0
		25	C	Aniseed	16	13	4	0
		20	piece	Camlet *Cloth*	13	6	8	0
		1	nest	Chests	0	66	8	0

The Sonday of Bristol, William Kelley master, Exiting, 7th November 1550

Merchant name	Origin	Qty	Unit	Commodity	£	s.	d.	f.
William Mede	Ind	3	piece	Cloth of Assize	0	0	0	0
		20	lb	Saffron	10	0	0	0
		5	lb	Silk, *Worked*	0	66	8	0
		2	gross	Knives	0	13	4	0
		10	gross	Points	0	10	0	0
Patrick Rothe	Ind	50	lb	Saffron	25	0	0	0
		17	lb	Silk, *Worked*	11	6	8	0
		5	lb	Silk, *Worked*	0	66	8	0
		18	gross	Points	0	18	0	0
George Skyddy	Ind	36	lb	Saffron	18	0	0	0
		24	lb	Silk, *Worked*	16	0	0	0
		6	dozen	Girdles	0	6	0	0
		2	gross	Knives	0	13	4	0
		12	gross	Points	0	12	0	0
		3	dozen	Knives, in Pairs	0	5	0	0
		1	bolt	Thread	0	0	15	0
Walter Copynger	Ind	16	lb	Saffron	8	0	0	0
		12	lb	Silk, *Worked*	8	13	4	0
		1	gross	Knives	0	6	8	0
		6	dozen	Knives, in Pairs	0	10	0	0
		18	gross	Points	0	18	0	0
		1	gross	Lacquor	0	0	20	0
		2	lb	Cloves	0	5	0	0
		2	lb	Pepper	0	2	0	0
		1	lb	Ginger	0	0	18	0
		2	lb	Mercury	0	0	10	0
		6	lb	Gunpowder	0	2	0	0
		2	bolt	Thread	0	2	6	0
		1	piece	Bowkern	0	2	0	0
		4	dozen	Skins, Golden	0	16	8	0
		2	dozen	Skins, Red	0	4	2	0
Garrold Menghe	Ind	1	piece	Cloth of Assize, Dozen Strait	0	0	0	0
		6	lb	Silk, *Worked*	4	0	0	0
		6	lb	Saffron	0	60	0	0
		5	gross	Knives	0	33	4	0
		3	dozen	Glass, Looking	0	0	15	0
		3	lb	Girdles, Check	0	5	0	0
		6	dozen	Knives, in Pairs	0	10	0	0
		2	dozen	Playing Cards	0	2	6	0
		2	bolt	Thread	0	2	6	0
Roland Creanghe	Ind	6	lb	Saffron	0	60	0	0
		5	lb	Silk, *Worked*	0	65	8	0

Merchant name	Origin	Qty	Unit	Commodity	£	s.	d.	f.
		36	gross	Points	0	36	0	0
		1	lb	Cinnamon & Senna	0	0	5	0
		1	lb	Thread	0	0	5	0
		8	dozen	Girdles, Caddis	0	7	4	0
		12	lb	Seed, Onion	0	4	0	0
		1	dozen	Playing Cards	0	0	15	0
		10	dozen	Glass, Looking	0	4	2	0
		1	bolt	Thread	0	0	15	0
		1	seam	Wood Ashes	0	4	2	0
Thomas Whyte	Ind	1.75	piece	Cloth of Assize	0	0	0	0
		8	lb	Saffron	4	0	0	0
		6	lb	Silk, *Worked*	4	0	0	0
		1	ream	Paper	0	0	20	0
		2	bolt	Thread	0	2	6	0
		1	dozen	Skins, Golden	0	4	2	0
		4	gross	Knives	0	26	8	0
		24	gross	Points	0	24	0	0
		2	lb	Seed, Onion	0	0	10	0
		1	dozen	Sword Blades	0	13	4	0
Stephan Creanghe	Ind	1.5	piece	Cloth of Assize	0	0	0	0
		10	lb	Silk, *Worked*	6	13	4	0
		18	gross	Points	0	18	0	0
		4	dozen	Knives, in Pairs	0	6	8	0
		2	dozen	Girdles, Caddis	0	3	4	0
		8	lb	Saffron	4	0	0	0
		2.5	gross	Knives	0	16	8	0
		1	dozen	Knives, in Pairs	0	0	20	0
		1	bolt	Thread	0	0	15	0
		4	lb	Seed, Onion	0	0	20	0
Garrold Mengh	Ind	1.5	piece	Cloth of Assize	0	0	0	0
		18	lb	Saffron	9	0	0	0
		10	lb	Silk, *Worked*	6	13	4	0
		4	gross	Knives	0	26	8	0
		3	gross	Lacquor	0	5	0	0
		20	gross	Points	0	20	0	0
		1	bolt	Thread	0	0	15	0
		6	lb	Seed, Onion	0	2	6	0
		1	dozen	Skins, Golden	0	4	2	0
David Harold	Ind	1	piece	Cloth of Assize	0	0	0	0
		10	lb	Silk, *Worked*	6	13	4	0
		6	lb	Saffron	0	60	0	0
		4	bolt	Thread	0	5	0	0
		2	gross	Points	0	2	0	0
		2	dozen	Knives, in Pairs	0	3	4	0
		2	lb	Sulpher	0	0	2	0
		8	lb	Seed, Onion	0	3	4	0
		3	gross	Knives	0	20	0	0
		1	lb	Oil, Bay	0	0	9	2
		0.5	gross	Lacquor	0	0	10	0
		3	gross	Knives	0	20	0	0
		2	lb	Garters, Caddis	0	3	4	0

Merchant name	Origin	Qty	Unit	Commodity	£	s.	d.	f.

The Mary Conception of Portugal, Jasper Gounsalvys master, Exiting, 8th November 1550

Merchant name	Origin	Qty	Unit	Commodity	£	s.	d.	f.
Thomas Tyson	Ind	0.5	piece	Cloth of Assize	0	0	0	0
Jasper Gounsalvys	Alien	15	piece	Cloth of Assize	0	0	0	0
		1	piece	Cloth of Assize, Northern Dozen	0	13	4	0
Jasper Alverus	Alien	1	C	Flax	0	13	4	0

The John of Talmont, John Cornett master, Exiting, 10th November 1550

Merchant name	Origin	Qty	Unit	Commodity	£	s.	d.	f.
John *Cornett*	Alien	1.04	C	Check *Cloth*	0	41	8	0
		7	yard	Bristol Frieze *Cloth*	0	4	8	0

The Trynyte of Bristol, James Williams master, Exiting, 10th November 1550

Merchant name	Origin	Qty	Unit	Commodity	£	s.	d.	f.
Roland Harold	Ind	8lb 2 dickers[1]		Skins, Salted	101	6	8	0
		8	C	Gall	0	106	8	0

The Mary John of Waterford, John Strannge master, Exiting, 12th November 1550

Merchant name	Origin	Qty	Unit	Commodity	£	s.	d.	f.
William Harold	Ind	3	piece	Cloth of Assize	0	0	0	0
		6	lb	Saffron	0	60	0	0
		6	lb	Silk, *Worked*	4	0	0	0
		2	gross	Knives	0	13	3	0
		24	gross	Points	0	24	0	0
		2	dozen	Playing Cards	0	0	20	0
		4	dozen	Knives, in Pairs	0	6	8	0
		6	piece	Caps	0	5	0	0
Roland Harold	Ind	4.5	piece	Cloth of Assize	0	0	0	0
		4.5	dozen	Playing Cards	0	3	9	0
		11	dozen	Knives, in Pairs	0	18	4	0
		1	kippe	Skins, Golden	0	16	8	0
		1	bolt	Thread	0	0	15	0
Nicholas Welshe	Ind	2	piece	Cloth of Assize, Dozen Strait	0	0	0	0
		4.5	lb	Silk, *Worked*	0	60	0	0
		5	lb	Saffron	0	50	0	0
		1	ream	Paper	0	0	20	0
		3	gross	Points	0	3	0	0
		10	lb	Seed, Onion	0	3	4	0
		4	gross	Knives	0	26	8	0
		2	dozen	Knives, in Pairs	0	3	4	0
David Maughonnd	Ind	2	piece	Cloth of Assize, Dozen Strait	0	0	0	0
		1	gross	Knives	0	6	8	0
		1	ream	Paper	0	0	20	0
		6	lb	Silk, *Worked*	4	0	0	0
		10	lb	Saffron	0	100	0	0
		6	dozen	Knives, in Pairs	0	10	0	0
		3	gross	Points	0	3	0	0
		4	lb	Seed, Onion	0	0	16	0
		0.5	dozen	Playing Cards	0	0	5	0
Stephen Grommwell	Ind	8	lb	Saffron	4	0	0	0
		7	lb	Silk, *Worked*	4	13	4	0
		5	gross	Knives	0	33	4	0

Merchant name	Origin	Qty	Unit	Commodity	£	s.	d.	f.
		48	gross	Points	0	48	0	0
		4	dozen	Girdles, Caddis	0	4	0	0
		3	dozen	Glass, Looking	0	0	12	0
		1	dozen	Playing Cards	0	0	10	0
Peter Savage	Ind	1.75	piece	Cloth of Assize	0	0	0	0
		30	lb	Silk, *Worked*	20	0	0	0
		10	lb	Saffron	0	100	0	0
		1	gross	Knives, in Pairs	0	20	0	0
		1	lb	Cinnamon	0	2	6	0
		0.5	lb	Mace	0	0	15	0
		1.5	dozen	Caps	0	15	0	0
		1	gross	Knives	0	6	8	0
		18	gross	Points	0	18	0	0
		2	gross	Lacquor	0	3	4	0
		6	piece	Hats, Garnished	0	10	0	0
Thomas Rougth	Ind	1	piece	Cloth of Assize	0	0	0	0
		1	gross	Knives, in Pairs	0	20	0	0
		24	lb	Silk, *Worked*	16	0	0	0
		3	lb	Thread	0	0	15	0
		3	dozen	Nightcaps	0	10	0	0
		2	dozen	Caps	0	20	0	0
		1	doz	Hats, Little	0	0	20	0
		4	dozen	Knives, in Pairs	0	6	8	0
		1	dozen	Girdles, Sword	0	3	4	0
		4	gross	Lacquor	0	6	8	0
		12	gross	Points	0	12	0	0
		1	dozen	Daggers	0	6	8	0
		10	lb	Silk, *Worked*	6	13	4	0
		3	barrel	Honey	0	50	0	0
		2	dozen	Soap	0	2	6	0
		1	C	Alum	0	13	4	0
		0.5	C	Battery	0	16	8	0
David Brewer	Ind	9	lb	Saffron	4	10	0	0
		2	gross	Knives	0	13	4	0
		4	pair	Stock-Cards	0	4	0	0
		2	dozen	Soap	0	2	6	0
		1	gross	Lacquor	0	0	20	0
		6	gross	Points	0	6	0	0
James Walter	Ind	3	piece	Cloth of Assize	0	0	0	0
		10	lb	Silk, *Worked*	6	13	4	0
		4	lb	Saffron	0	40	0	0
James Walter	Ind	2	gross	Knives	0	13	4	0
		12	gross	Points	0	12	0	0
		3	dozen	Playing Cards	0	2	6	0
		5	dozen	Knives, in Pairs	0	8	4	0
		2	bolt	Thread	0	2	6	0
		24	bolt	String	0	0	6	0
		2	lb	Pepper	0	2	0	0
		1	lb	Cinnamon	0	2	6	0
		1	lb	Ginger	0	0	16	0
		1	lb	Nutmeg	0	0	12	0
William Hey	Ind	1.5	piece	Cloth of Assize	0	0	0	0

Merchant name	Origin	Qty	Unit	Commodity	£	s.	d.	f.
		14	lb	Silk, *Worked*	9	6	8	0
		2	lb	Saffron	0	20	0	0
		2	gross	Knives	0	13	4	0
		10	gross	Points	0	10	0	0
		4	dozen	Knives, in Pairs	0	6	8	0
Roland Harrold	Ind	7.25	piece	Cloth of Assize	0	0	0	0
		20	lb	Saffron	10	0	0	0
		20	lb	Silk, *Worked*	13	6	8	0
		12	dozen	Playing Cards	0	10	0	0
		4	gross	Knives	0	26	8	0
		2	gross	Cutts	0	6	8	0
		60	gross	Points	0	60	0	0
		7	lb	Seed, Onion	0	2	4	0
		2	dozen	Caps	0	20	0	0
		2	dozen	Skins, Golden	0	8	4	0

The Mary of Waterford, Thomas Keryn master, Exiting, *12th November 1550*

Merchant name	Origin	Qty	Unit	Commodity	£	s.	d.	f.
Peter Savage	Ind	1	barrel	Tar	0	0	20	0
		0.5	C	Rosin	0	0	10	0
		1	barrel	Honey	0	16	8	0
John Heyde	Ind	6	lb	Saffron	0	60	0	0
		3	lb	Silk, *Worked*	0	40	0	0
		1.5	gross	Knives	0	10	0	0
		4	dozen	Knives, in Pairs	0	6	8	0
		1	dozen	Flax	0	0	12	0
		4	gross	Points	0	4	0	0
		1	dozen	Knives, in Pairs	0	0	20	0
		1	barrel	Honey	0	16	8	0
Thomas Whyte	Ind	3	lb	Saffron	0	30	0	0
		1	gross	Knives	0	6	8	0
		4	dozen	Knives, in Pairs	0	6	8	0
		12	gross	Points	0	12	0	0
		4	gross	Lacquor	0	6	8	0
		1	gross	Combs	0	3	4	0
		1	gross	Girdles	0	10	0	0
		1	dozen	Girdles	0	0	10	0
		0.5	lb	Pepper	0	0	6	0
		0.5	ream	Paper	0	0	10	0
		1	piece	Cloth of Assize, Dozen Strait	0	0	0	0
Nicholas Harrys	Ind	6	yard	Cloth of Assize	0	0	0	0
		18	lb	Saffron	9	0	0	0
		1	C	Hops	0	10	0	0
		2	gross	Knives	0	13	4	0
		6	gross	Points	0	6	0	0
		2	dozen	Playing Cards	0	2	6	0
		2	dozen	Soap	0	2	6	0
		6	dozen	Knives, in Pairs	0	10	0	0
		3	pair	Stock-Cards	0	3	0	0
		0.5	ream	Paper	0	0	10	0
David Butler & Purcell	Ind	2	gross	Knives	0	13	4	0
		12	dozen	Knives, in Pairs	0	20	0	0

Merchant name	Origin	Qty	Unit	Commodity	£	s.	d.	f.
		1	dozen	Cumin	0	0	18	0
		12	gross	Points	0	12	0	0
		6	gross	Lacquor	0	10	0	0
		2	gross	Girdles	0	10	0	0
		6	dozen	Girdles, Wool	0	2	0	0
		6	dozen	Combs	0	0	20	0
		1	lb	Cinnamon	0	2	6	0
		1	lb	Silk, *Worked*	0	13	4	0
		2	barrel	Honey	0	33	4	0

The Grehounde of Waterford, William Wodlock master, Entering, 21st November 1550

Merchant name	Origin	Qty	Unit	Commodity	£	s.	d.	f.
Edmund Waryng	Ind	5	C	Skins, Sheep	0	50	0	0
		1	C	Skins, Lamb	0	6	8	0
William Sexton	Ind	12.5	C	Skins, Sheep	6	5	0	0
		4	C	Skins, Lamb	0	26	8	0
		0.916	C	Skins, Sheep	0	28	8	0
		26	piece	Skins, Fox	0	4	4	0
		2	piece	Skins, Otter	0	0	10	0
Richard Corre	Ind	7	C	Check *Cloth*	14	0	0	0
		1.5	C	Skins, Sheep	0	15	0	0
		30	piece	Mantles	0	100	0	0
Patrick Welshe	Ind	1.5	C	Check *Cloth*	0	50	0	0
		1.5	C	Skins, Sheep	0	15	0	0
		30	piece	Mantles	0	100	0	0
William Donell	Ind	0.5	C	Check *Cloth*	0	20	0	0
		4	piece	Mantles	0	13	4	0
		20	piece	Skins, Sheep	0	0	20	0
Peter Porcell	Ind	1.5	C	Skins, Sheep	0	15	0	0
		10	piece	Mantles	0	33	4	0
		30	yard	Check *Cloth*	0	10	0	0
		6	piece	Skins, Deer	0	2	0	0
Nicholas Hakett	Ind	2	C	Skins, Sheep	0	20	0	0
		2	C	Skins, Cimiclarn	0	6	8	0
		20	piece	Skins, Sheep	0	0	20	0
		1	C	Check *Cloth*	0	40	0	0
Thomas Whyte	Ind	0.5	C	Check *Cloth*	0	20	0	0
		1	C	Skins, Sheep	0	10	0	0
		6	piece	Mantles	0	20	0	0
James Leonard	Ind	12	C	Check *Cloth*	24	0	0	0
		97	piece	Mantles	16	3	4	0
Nicholas Connow	Ind	2	piece	Mantles	0	6	8	0
		0.75	C	Skins, Sheep	0	7	6	0
Roland Creangh	Ind	1	C	Skins, Sheep	0	10	0	0
		1	C	Skins, Lamb	0	6	8	0
		3	piece	Skins, Deer	0	0	12	0
		20	yard	Check *Cloth*	0	6	8	0

The Lady Pyttey of Aveiro, Peter Thome master, Exiting, 21st November 1550

Merchant name	Origin	Qty	Unit	Commodity	£	s.	d.	f.
Peter *Thome*	Alien	25	piece	Cloth of Assize, Bridgwater	0	0	0	0
		0.5	piece	Cloth of Assize, Dyed with Grainso	0	0	0	

Merchant name	Origin	Qty	Unit	Commodity	£	s.	d.	f.
		13	piece	Cloth of Assize	0	0	0	0
		140	dozen	Shovels	0	70	0	0

The Margaret of Bristol, Thomas Baynam master, Exiting, 22nd November 1550

Henry Smyth & Corre	Ind	11	pair	Milstones	11	0	0	0
		11	lb	Silk, *Worked*	7	6	8	0
		5	lb	Saffron	0	50	0	0
		8	dozen	Knives, in Pairs	0	13	4	0

The George of Waterford, Robert Medall master, Exiting, *22nd November 1550*

John Hyde	Ind	1	barrel	Honey	0	16	8	0
		3	dozen	Flax	0	3	0	0
		6	gross	Points	0	6	0	0
		3	lb	Silk, *Worked*	0	40	0	0
		4	lb	Saffron	0	40	0	0
		6	dozen	Knives, in Pairs	0	10	0	0
Edmund Clere	Ind	5	lb	Saffron	0	50	0	0
		2.5	gross	Knives	0	16	8	0
		0.5	C	Hops	0	5	0	0
		0.5	lb	Cinnamon	0	0	15	0
		4	gross	Points	0	4	0	0
		1	gross	Lacquor	0	0	20	0
		1	dozen	Flax	0	0	12	0
Edmund Grannte	Ind	3.5	piece	Cloth of Assize	0	0	0	0
		4	gross	Knives	0	20	0	0
		4	lb	Silk, *Worked*	0	53	0	0
		12	dozen	Knives, in Pairs	0	20	0	0
		3	lb	Saffron	0	30	0	0
		12	dozen	Knives, in Pairs	0	20	0	0
		5	dozen	Flax	0	15	0	0
Patrick Wodlock	Ind	2.83	piece	Cloth of Assize	0	0	0	0
		5	gross	Knives	0	33	4	0
		7	gross	Lacquor	0	11	8	0
		12	gross	Points	0	12	0	0
		4	dozen	Knives, in Pairs	0	6	8	0
		4	pair	Stock-Cards	0	4	0	0
		1	bolt	Thread	0	0	15	0
		4	lb	Saffron	0	40	0	0
		1	kilderkin	Honey	0	4	2	0
Richard Corre & Whyte	Ind	1.5	gross	Knives	0	10	0	0
		2	C	Flax	0	20	0	0
		10	lb	Saffron	0	100	0	0
		4	dozen	Knives, in Pairs	0	6	8	0
		12	gross	Points	0	12	0	0
		6	pair	Stock-Cards	0	6	0	0
		1	lb	Jhmblas (?*Jumb*)	0	2	1	0
		1	C	Flax	0	10	0	0
Walter Whyte	Ind	3	gross	Knives	0	20	0	0
		6	gross	Points	0	6	0	0

Merchant name	Origin	Qty	Unit	Commodity	£	s.	d.	f.
		1	gross	Lacquor	0	0	20	0
		3	pair	Stock-Cards	0	3	0	0
		8	dozen	Girdles	0	5	4	0
		1	dozen	Aniseed	0	0	20	0
		1	dozen	Liquorice	0	0	10	0
		1	dozen	Playing Cards	0	0	15	0
		1	dozen	Glass, Looking	0	0	4	0
		8	lb	Verdigris	0	3	4	0
		1	dozen	Soap	0	0	15	0
		3	dozen	Flax	0	13	0	0
Patrick Maydon	Ind	2	piece	Cloth of Assize	0	0	0	0
		8	lb	Saffron	4	0	0	0
		2	gross	Knives	0	13	4	0
		3	dozen	Knives, in Pairs	0	5	0	0
		2	bolt	Thread	0	2	6	0
		1	gross	Lacquor	0	0	20	0
		12	gross	Points	0	12	0	0
		1	C	Flax	0	10	0	0
		2	dozen	Soap	0	2	6	0
Henry Whyte	Ind	2	lb	Silk, *Worked*	0	26	8	0
		2	lb	Saffron	0	20	0	0
		1	gross	Knives	0	6	8	0
		2	gross	Lacquor	0	3	4	0
		2	gross	Points	0	2	0	0
		0.25	C	Hops	0	2	6	0
Robert Whyte	Ind	2	lb	Saffron	0	20	0	0
		1	lb	Silk, *Worked*	0	13	4	0
		6	gross	Knives	0	40	0	0
		6	lb	Verdigris	0	2	6	0
		1	lb	Cloves & Cinnamon	0	5	0	0
		10	dozen	Knives, in Pairs	0	16	8	0
		0.5	gross	Combs	0	2	2	0
		0.5	gross	Girdles, Wool	0	2	2	0
		2	C	Battery	4	0	0	0
		0.5	C	Hops	0	5	0	0
		6	pair	Stock-Cards	0	6	0	0
Edward Whyte	Ind	6	lb	Saffron	0	60	0	0
		8	lb	Silk, *Worked*	0	106	8	0
		4	dozen	Knives, in Pairs	0	6	8	0
		5	dozen	Knives, in Pairs	0	8	4	0
		2	gross	Knives	0	13	4	0
		1	great gross	Points	0	12	0	0
		1	gross	Lacquor	0	0	20	0
		1	bolt	Thread	0	0	15	0
Edmund Waryng	Ind	2	piece	Cloth of Assize	0	0	0	0
		10	lb	Silk, *Worked*	6	13	4	0
		8	lb	Saffron	4	0	0	0
		2	dozen	Skins, Golden	0	8	4	0
		3	gross	Knives	0	20	0	0
		4	dozen	Knives, in Pairs	0	6	8	0
		1	bolt	Thread	0	0	15	0
		2	gross	Points	0	2	0	0

Merchant name	Origin	Qty	Unit	Commodity	£	s.	d.	f.
		2	lb	Pepper	0	2	0	0
David Hayly	Ind	10	lb	Saffron	0	100	0	0
		8	lb	Silk, *Worked*	0	106	8	0
		6	lb	Girdles, Caddis	0	10	0	0
		60	gross	Points	0	60	0	0
		2	gross	Lacquor	0	3	4	0
		2	bolt	Thread	0	2	6	0
		6	lb	Cumin	0	0	8	0
		3	gross	Knives	0	20	0	0
		2	dozen	Knives, in Pairs	0	3	4	0
		6	dozen	G[ ]lte?	0	2	0	0
Patrick Troy	Ind	10	lb	Saffron	0	100	0	0
		8	lb	Silk, *Worked*	0	106	8	0
		10	gross	Knives	0	66	8	0
		6	gross	Lacquor	0	10	0	0
		20	lb	Seed, Onion	0	8	4	0
		12	pair	Hose, Womens	0	10	0	0
		2	lb	Pepper	0	2	0	0
		2	lb	Thread	0	0	20	0
		1	dozen	Playing Cards	0	0	15	0
Nicholas Cantwell	Ind	6	lb	Silk, *Worked*	4	0	0	0
		7	lb	Saffron	0	70	0	0
		4	lb	Cloves & Cinnamon	0	10	0	0
		1	lb	Pepper	0	0	12	0
		1	lb	Verdigris	0	0	5	0
		1	gross	Knives	0	6	8	0
		2	dozen	Knives, in Pairs	0	3	4	0
		12	gross	Points	0	12	0	0
Nicholas Nashe	Ind	1	dozen	Cumin	0	0	16	0
		8	lb	Silk, *Worked*	0	106	8	0
		6	dozen	Knives, in Pairs	0	10	0	0
		1	lb	Cinnamon & Cloves	0	2	6	0
		1	gross	Cutts	0	3	4	0
Maurice Quyrke & Brever	Ind	1	C	Battery	0	33	4	0
		40	lb	Saffron	20	0	0	0

The Julyan of Bristol, Richard Whyte master, Entering, 1st December 1550

Thomas Hyckes & assoc.	Ind	56.25	tun	Wine	0	0	0	0
		2.25	tun	Wine, Corrupt	0	67	6	0

The Margarett of Gloucester, John Snow master, Entering, *1st December 1550*

William Coper	Ind	6	ton	Salt	0	60	0	0

The Grehounde of Waterford, William Wodlock master, Exiting, *1st December 1550*

Nicholas Hackett	Ind	4	piece	Cloth of Assize, Dozen Strait	0	0	0	0
		4	lb	Silk, *Worked*	0	53	4	0
		2	lb	Cinnamon	0	5	0	0

Merchant name	Origin	Qty	Unit	Commodity	£	s.	d.	f.
		6	dozen	Knives, in Pairs	0	10	0	0
		1	ream	Paper	0	0	20	0
		3	gross	Lacquor	0	5	0	0
		6	gross	Points	0	6	0	0
		2	gross	Knives	0	13	4	0
Nicholas Connowe	Ind	3	piece	Cloth of Assize, Dozen Strait	0	0	0	0
		4	lb	Silk, *Worked*	0	53	4	0
		2	dozen	Skins, Golden	0	8	4	0
		2	dozen	Knives, in Pairs	0	3	4	0
		2	lb	Saffron	0	20	0	0
William Sexton	Ind	2	piece	Cloth of Assize, Dozen	0	0	0	0
		6	lb	Silk, *Worked*	4	0	0	0
		20	gross	Points	0	20	0	0
		2	lb	Saffron	0	20	0	0
		1	gross	Knives	0	6	8	0
Thomas Vynne	Ind	2.25	piece	Cloth of Assize	0	0	0	0
		1	lb	Saffron	0	10	0	0
		6	dozen	Knives, in Pairs	0	10	0	0
		4	lb	Silk, *Worked*	0	53	4	0
		2	dozen	Skins, Golden	0	8	4	0
		1	gross	Knives	0	6	8	0
		1	gross	Lacquor	0	0	20	0
		3	gross	Points	0	3	0	0
Nicholas Welshe	Ind	5	piece	Cloth of Assize	0	0	0	0
		4	lb	Silk, *Worked*	0	53	4	0
		6	lb	Saffron	0	60	0	0
		24	dozen	Knives, in Pairs	0	40	0	0
		2	bolt	Thread	0	2	6	0
		3	dozen	Caps	0	30	0	0
		1	dozen	Coifs, Velvet	0	26	8	0
		2	dozen	Playing Cards	0	2	6	0
		2	gross	Knives	0	13	4	0
		36	gross	Points	0	36	0	0
		3	gross	Lacquor	0	5	0	0
		2	barrel	Honey	0	33	4	0
		1	C	Alum	0	13	4	0
		1	C	Hops	0	10	0	0
Laurence Boussher	Ind	1	piece	Cloth of Assize, Dozen Strait	0	0	0	0
		1	barrel	Honey	0	16	8	0
		10	lb	Silk, *Worked*	6	13	4	0
		1.5	gross	Knives	0	10	0	0
		12	dozen	Knives, in Pairs	0	20	0	0
		6	gross	Points	0	6	0	0
		4	lb	Girdles, Caddis	0	6	8	0
		2	lb	Sugar Candy	0	0	15	0
		2	lb	Arsenic	0	0	12	0
		1	dozen	Crab-Locks	0	0	20	0
Thomas Whyte	Ind	3	lb	Saffron	0	30	0	0
		2	gross	Knives	0	13	4	0
		0.5	C	Hops	0	5	0	0
James Brewer	Ind	3	piece	Cloth of Assize, Dozen Strait	0	0	0	0
Patrick Welshe	Ind	3	lb	Saffron	0	30	0	0

Merchant name	Origin	Qty	Unit	Commodity	£	s.	d.	f.
		2.5	gross	Knives	0	16	4	0
		2	gross	Lacquor	0	3	4	0
		3	gross	Points	0	3	0	0
Richard Corre	Ind	7	lb	Saffron	0	70	0	0
		2.5	gross	Knives	0	16	8	0
		4	dozen	Knives, in Pairs	0	6	8	0
		2.5	gross	Lacquor	0	4	0	0
		4	gross	Points	0	4	0	0
		6.5	dozen	Soap	0	5	5	0
		8	pair	Stock-Cards	0	8	0	0

The Mary of St-Jean-de-Luz, Martin de Shevers master, Entering, 3rd December 1550

Merchant name	Origin	Qty	Unit	Commodity	£	s.	d.	f.
William Tyndale & assoc.	Ind	79.25	tun	Wine	0	0	0	0
		4	tun	Oil, Train	16	0	0	0
		1	pipe	Wine, Corrupt	0	15	0	0

The Magdelen of Sines, John Lewsey master, Entering, *3rd December 1550*

Merchant name	Origin	Qty	Unit	Commodity	£	s.	d.	f.
William Tyndale	Ind	109	tun	Wine	0	0	0	0

The Flower de Lewys of Fécamp, Nicholas Michel master, Entering, 4th December 1550

Merchant name	Origin	Qty	Unit	Commodity	£	s.	d.	f.
John Brampton & assoc.	Ind	60.75	tun	Wine	0	0	0	0

The Angeleu of Fécamp, Peter Dewdycke master, Entering, 4th December 1550

Merchant name	Origin	Qty	Unit	Commodity	£	s.	d.	f.
William Spratt & assoc.	Ind	53.75	tun	Wine	0	0	0	0

The Santa Maria of San Sebastián, Sebastian de Govoran master, Exiting, 8th December 1550

Merchant name	Origin	Qty	Unit	Commodity	£	s.	d.	f.
Domingo de Arsey	Alien	5	C	Wax	10	0	0	0
Nicholas Ware & Stone	Ind	9	piece	Cloth of Assize	0	0	0	0
		24	piece	Northern Cotton *Cloth*	0	100	0	0
William Yonge	Ind	10	piece	Northern Cotton *Cloth*	0	41	8	0
		4	piece	Brecon *Cloth*	4	0	0	0
John Gordowne	Ind	17	piece	Cloth of Assize	0	0	0	0
William Capps & Codryngton	Ind	24	piece	Cloth of Assize	0	0	0	0
		17	C	Wax	34	0	0	0
James Chester	Ind	3	piece	Cloth of Assize	0	0	0	0
		6	piece	Bristol Frieze *Cloth*	4	0	0	0
Gilbert Robtys	Ind	9	piece	Cloth of Assize	0	0	0	0

Merchant name	Origin	Qty	Unit	Commodity	£	s.	d.	f.

The Santa Maria of Lantringuier, Evan Lodowyke master, Entering, 9th December 1550

Merchant name	Origin	Qty	Unit	Commodity	£	s.	d.	f.
Henry Manyng & assoc.	Ind	31	tun	Wine	0	0	0	0

The Mary of Milford Haven, Richard Browne master, Entering, 10th December 1550

Merchant name	Origin	Qty	Unit	Commodity	£	s.	d.	f.
Richard *Browne*	Ind	8	barrel	Fish, Herring White	0	40	0	0

The Sonday of Bristol, John Walter master, Exiting, 11th December 1550

Merchant name	Origin	Qty	Unit	Commodity	£	s.	d.	f.
John Gryffyth & Taylor	Ind	12	pair	Milstones	12	0	0	0
		1.5	C	Alum	0	20	0	0

The Prymerose of Bristol, Thomas Waryn master, Entering, 12th December 1550

Merchant name	Origin	Qty	Unit	Commodity	£	s.	d.	f.
William Pepwell	Ind	367	piece	Raisins, *Great*	30	11	8	0
		35	C	Aniseed	23	6	8	0
		3	C	Almonds	0	40	0	0
		2	ton	Figs	4	0	0	0
		3.5	tun	Wine	0	0	0	0
Nicholas Sowdeley & assoc.	Ind	445	piece	Raisins, *Great*	37	0	20	0
Lewis Robyns & assoc.	Ind	1	ton	Figs	0	40	0	0
		5	C	Comfits, Sugar	0	50	0	0
		1	pipe	Wine, Corrupt	0	15	0	0
		15	piece	Raisins, *Great*	0	25	0	0
		2.5	tun	Wine	0	0	0	0

The Kathryn of St-Jean-de-Luz, Sampson de Halden master, Entering, 15th December 1550

Merchant name	Origin	Qty	Unit	Commodity	£	s.	d.	f.
George Shawe & assoc.	Ind	62.75	tun	Wine	0	0	0	0
		3	tun	Oil, Train	15	0	0	0
		4.75	tun	Vinegar	9	10	0	0
		2	tun	Wine, Corrupt	0	60	0	0
Sampson de Halden	Alien	0.5	tun	Oil, Train	0	40	0	0
		18	C	Raisins, *Great*	0	24	0	0
Nicholas Kelley	Ind	5	piece	Cloth of Assize	0	0	0	0
		7.5	piece	Cloth of Assize	0	0	0	0
		1	C	Irish Frieze *Cloth*	0	30	0	0
		0.5	C	Check *Cloth*	0	20	0	0
John Shreve	Ind	4	piece	Cloth of Assize	0	0	0	0
		4	piece	Welsh *Cloth*	4	0	0	0
Richard Mansell	Ind	18	piece	Welsh *Cloth*, Strait	0	75	0	0
Robert Jones	Ind	1	piece	Bristol Frieze *Cloth*	0	13	4	0
		1	piece	Welsh *Cloth*, Strait	0	4	2	0
Robert Saxsy	Ind	20	piece	Manchester *Cotton Cloth*	10	0	0	0

Merchant name	Origin	Qty	Unit	Commodity	£	s.	d.	f.

The George of New Ross, William Blake master, Entering, 16th December 1550

Merchant name	Origin	Qty	Unit	Commodity	£	s.	d.	f.
Patrick Archer	Ind	19	C	Skins, Sheep	9	10	0	0
		6	C	Check *Cloth*	12	0	0	0
		4	C	Skins, Sheep, Broken	0	20	0	0
		0.5	C	Skins, Lamb	0	3	4	0
		19	piece	Mantles	0	53	4	0
		2	stone	Wool, Irish	0	5	4	0
		4	piece	Skins, Fox	0	0	8	0
		10	piece	Skins, Deer	0	3	4	0
Walter Dofe, Archer & assoc.	Ind	2	tun	Wine	0	0	0	0
		4.75	C	Skins, Sheep	0	47	6	0
		0.5	barrel	Fish, Herring White	0	2	6	0
		1	stone	Wool, Irish	0	2	8	0
		5.5	C	Check *Cloth*	11	0	0	0
		1	C	Skins, Lamb	0	6	8	0
		0.5	C	Skins, Kid	0	2	6	0
		4	piece	Mantles	0	13	4	0

The Mary Norton, *Port Unknown*, Nicholas Longe master, Entering, 16th December 1550

Merchant name	Origin	Qty	Unit	Commodity	£	s.	d.	f.
David Palmer	Ind	22	barrel	Fish, Herring White	0	110	0	0

The Mawdelyn of Errenteria, Martin Beroby master, Entering, 17th December 1550

Merchant name	Origin	Qty	Unit	Commodity	£	s.	d.	f.
John Smyth	Ind	10	tun	Wine	0	0	0	0
		4	tun	Wine, Corrupt	6	0	0	0
		68	piece	Raisins, *Great*	0	116	8	0
Thomas Paycey & Balard	Ind	2	tun	Wine	0	0	0	0
		2	tun	Wine, Corrupt	0	60	0	0
Edward Pryn	Ind	10.5	tun	Wine	0	0	0	0
		3	tun	Wine, Corrupt	4	10	0	0
		74	piece	Raisins, *Great*	6	3	4	0
John Cutt & Carr	Ind	4	tun	Wine	0	0	0	0
		5	tun	Wine, Corrupt	7	10	0	0
		150	piece	Raisins, *Great*	12	10	0	0
Thomas Sheward & Shipman	Ind	3.75	tun	Wine	0	0	0	0
		3	tun	Wine, Corrupt	4	10	0	0
William Yonge & Boydell	Ind	6	tun	Wine	0	0	0	0
		4	tun	Wine, Corrupt	6	0	0	0
Robert Pressey & Kyrke	Ind	3.5	tun	Wine	0	0	0	0
		75	piece	Raisins, *Great*	6	5	0	0
		2	tun	Wine, Corrupt	0	60	0	0
Robert Butler	Ind	1	tun	Wine, Corrupt	0	30	0	0
Thomas Hycks & Cox	Ind	4.5	tun	Wine	0	0	0	0
		1	tun	Wine, Corrupt	0	30	0	0

Merchant name	Origin	Qty	Unit	Commodity	£	s.	d.	f.
Thomas Symons	Ind	5	tun	Wine, Corrupt	7	10	0	0
Nicholas Crosby &								
Morese	Ind	4.5	tun	Wine	0	0	0	0
		3	tun	Wine, Corrupt	4	10	0	0
		2.5	tun	Oil, Olive	0	10	0	0
		1	ton	Figs	0	40	0	0
		0.5	chest	Sugar	0	20	0	0
Edward Weldon	Ind	3	tun	Wine, Corrupt	4	10	0	0
Martin Beroby	Alien	2	tun	Oil, Olive	8	0	0	0
		1	hogshead	Wine	0	0	0	0

The Trynyte of Errenteria John Michell master, Entering, *17th December 1550*

Merchant name	Origin	Qty	Unit	Commodity	£	s.	d.	f.
James Chester &								
assoc.	Ind	57	ton	Figs	114	0	0	0
		2.5	tun	Wine, Corrupt	0	75	0	0
John *Michell*	Alien	3	ton	Figs	6	0	0	0

The Mynyon of Bristol, John Williams master, Entering, 18th December 1550

Merchant name	Origin	Qty	Unit	Commodity	£	s.	d.	f.
Edward Prynn & Carr	Ind	19.75	tun	Wine, Corrupt	29	12	6	0
William Tyndale								
& Balard	Ind	5.5	tun	Wine	0	0	0	0
		5.5	tun	Wine, Corrupt	8	5	0	0
Thomas Sheward								
& Shipman	Ind	1.75	tun	Wine	0	0	0	0
		15	tun	Wine, Corrupt	22	10	0	0
		4.5	tun	Oil, Olive	18	0	0	0
Robert Butler & Cutt	Ind	5	tun	Wine, Corrupt	7	10	0	0
		4	tun	Oil, Olive	16	0	0	0
John Capps & Hicks	Ind	1.25	tun	Wine	0	0	0	0
		4	tun	Wine, Corrupt	6	0	0	0
William Cox &								
Chester	Ind	2.5	tun	Wine	0	0	0	0
		4	tun	Wine, Corrupt	6	0	0	0
John Pryn	Ind	2	tun	Wine	0	0	0	0
		3	tun	Wine, Corrupt	4	10	0	0
Robert Pressy &								
Whyte	Ind	5.5	tun	Wine	0	0	0	0
		4.5	tun	Wine, Corrupt	6	15	0	0
William Kyrke &								
Harvest	Ind	1.5	tun	Wine	0	0	0	0
		2	tun	Wine, Corrupt	0	60	0	0
Ralph Richemon*d*	Ind	1.5	tun	Wine, Corrupt	0	45	0	0
		3.75	tun	Oil, Olive	15	0	0	0
John Boydell &								
Halton	Ind	1	tun	Wine	0	0	0	0
		2	tun	Wine, Corrupt	0	60	0	0
John Browne &								
Bayley	Ind	2	tun	Wine	0	0	0	0
		2	tun	Wine, Corrupt	0	60	0	0
		13.5	C	Orchil	9	0	0	0

Merchant name	Origin	Qty	Unit	Commodity	£	s.	d.	f.
Thomas Hemyng &								
Badram	Ind	1.75	tun	Wine	0	0	0	0
		2.75	tun	Wine, Corrupt	4	2	6	0
Nicholas Crosby &								
assoc.	Ind	2.25	tun	Wine	0	0	0	0
		4.5	tun	Wine, Corrupt	6	15	0	0
		1	chest	Sugar	0	40	0	0
Nicholas Cowman &								
assoc.	Ind	1.5	tun	Wine, Corrupt	0	45	0	0
		4	tun	Oil, Olive	16	0	0	0
		22	piece	Raisins, Great	0	36	8	0
Lewis Robyns &								
assoc.	Ind	8	piece	Raisins, Great	0	13	4	0
		54	piece	Raisins, Great	0	54	0	0
		2	tun	Wine, Corrupt	0	60	0	0
Nicholas Shee	Ind	1	pipe	Wine	0	0	0	0

The Sonday of Bristol, William Gelley master, Entering, 19th December 1550

Merchant name	Origin	Qty	Unit	Commodity	£	s.	d.	f.
William *Gelley*	Ind	1	C	Wood, Irish	0	20	0	0
		30	yard	Check *Cloth*	0	10	0	0
John Evanns	Ind	8.5	C	Skins, Sheep	4	5	0	0
Arthur Richards	Ind	8.5	dicker	Skins, Deer	0	28	4	0
		10	stone	Wool, Flocks	0	4	2	0
		1	barrel	Honey	0	13	4	0
		50	piece	Skins, Sheep	0	4	2	0
Maurice Welshe	Ind	6	dicker	Skins, Deer	0	20	0	0
		0.5	C	Skins, Sheep	0	5	0	0

The Mare of Penmarch, Harve Ledree master, Entering, *19th December 1550*

Merchant name	Origin	Qty	Unit	Commodity	£	s.	d.	f.
William Carr & assoc.	Ind	62.25	tun	Wine	0	0	0	0

The Crowsannte of Bordeaux, Raymond de Tyras master, Entering, *19th December 1550*

Merchant name	Origin	Qty	Unit	Commodity	£	s.	d.	f.
Henry Sandyforde								
& Fylde	Ind	53.75	tun	Wine	0	0	0	0
		3	tun	Vinegar	6	0	0	0
Raymond de Tyras	Alien	23	piece	Rosin	0	30	8	0

The Trynyte of Barnstaple, Simon Davys master, Entering, 20th December 1550

Merchant name	Origin	Qty	Unit	Commodity	£	s.	d.	f.
Thomas Sheward	Ind	1	tun	Wine	0	0	0	0
William Pepwall	Ind	3	tun	Wine, Corrupt	4	10	0	0
John Cutt	Ind	2	tun	Wine	0	0	0	0
		1	tun	Wine, Corrupt	0	30	0	0
James Chester &								
Butler	Ind	6	tun	Wine, Corrupt	9	0	0	0
Henry Sandyforde	Ind	2.75	tun	Wine	0	0	0	0
		2.5	tun	Vinegar	0	100	0	0
		33	piece	Raisins, Great	0	55	0	0
George Bear*ie*	Ind	6.25	tun	Wine	0	0	0	0

Merchant name	Origin	Qty	Unit	Commodity	£	s.	d.	f.
		10	C	Alum	6	13	4	o
William Balard & Yonge	Ind	3	ton	Alum	40	o	o	o
		1	C	Alum	o	13	4	o
		196	piece	Raisins, *Great*	16	6	8	o
		1	tun	Wine, Corrupt	o	30	o	o
William Harvest	Ind	0.75	tun	Wine	o	o	o	o

The Mare of Milford Haven, Philip Smyth master, Entering, *20th December 1550*

Gwylygo Spynyoley	Alien	8	tun	Wine, Malmysse	32	o	o	o
		1.5	tun	Oil, Olive	6	o	o	o

The Mary of Chepstow, Richard Howys master, Entering, *22nd December 1550*

William Jones	Ind	5	tun	Wine	o	o	o	o
		3	tun	Wine, Corrupt	4	10	o	o
		1	ton	Figs	o	40	o	o

The Harte of Chepstow, John Hyggons master, Entering, *22nd December 1550*

William Jones	Ind	5	tun	Wine	o	o	o	o
		3	tun	Wine, Corrupt	4	10	o	o
		6.75	ton	Figs	13	10	o	o

The Peryn of Nantes, Dennis Pycto master, Entering, *22nd December 1550*

Robert Newburne	Ind	6	ton	Salt	o	60	o	o
Francis Olyver	Alien	6	ton	Salt	o	60	o	o

The Mare Jamys of Bristol, David Gyllyn master, Entering, *23rd December 1550*

William Jaye & Balard	Ind	3	tun	Oil, Olive	12	o	o	o
		1	hogshead	Wine, Corrupt	o	7	6	o
		3	tun	Wine	o	o	o	o
John Cutt & Symonds	Ind	3.5	tun	Wine	o	o	o	o
		3	tun	Wine, Corrupt	4	10	o	o
		1.75	tun	Oil, Olive	7	o	o	o
William Yonge	Ind	4.25	tun	Oil, Olive	17	o	o	o
		1	tun	Wine, Corrupt	o	30	o	o
		37	C	Alum	24	13	4	o
John Bronne & Draper	Ind	2	tun	Wine	o	o	o	o
		4.25	tun	Wine, Corrupt	6	7	8	o
		46	piece	Raisins, *Great*	o	76	8	o
Richard Lynke & Yonge	Ind	17	tun	Wine	o	o	o	o
		3	tun	Wine, Corrupt	4	10	o	o
Sampson Foley & Ambrose Greyn	Ind	2.5	tun	Wine	o	o	o	o

Merchant name	Origin	Qty	Unit	Commodity	£	s.	d.	f.
		3	tun	Wine, Corrupt	4	10	0	0
		1	tun	Oil, Olive	4	0	0	0
Thomas Cutt & assoc.	Ind	4.75	tun	Oil, Olive	19	0	0	0
		20	C	Alum	13	6	8	0
		1	pipe	Wine, Corrupt	0	15	0	0
		0.75	tun	Wine	0	0	0	0
Roland Wilbram & assoc.	Ind	5.5	tun	Wine	0	0	0	0
		1.5	tun	Wine, Corrupt	0	45	0	0
		1	chest	Sugar	0	40	0	0
William Jones & assoc.	Ind	12.25	C	Alum	8	3	4	0
		1	tun	Wine, Corrupt	0	30	0	0
		2.75	tun	Oil, Olive	11	0	0	0
		5.5	tun	Wine	0	0	0	0
Robert Jefferys & assoc.	Ind	3.75	tun	Wine	0	0	0	0
		5.5	tun	Wine, Corrupt	8	5	0	0

The George of New Ross, William Blake master, Entering, *23rd December 1550*

Merchant name	Origin	Qty	Unit	Commodity	£	s.	d.	f.
Thomas Barcley	Ind	1	C	Fish, Hake	0	10	0	0
		20	piece	Fish, Salted	0	0	20	0
		62	yard	Check *Cloth*	0	20	8	0
Thomas Howell	Ind	0.75	C	Fish, Hake	0	7	6	0
		1	burden	Fish, Salted	0	4	2	0

The Jhesus of Chepstow, John Hewys master, Entering, *23rd December 1550*

Merchant name	Origin	Qty	Unit	Commodity	£	s.	d.	f.
William Jones	Ind	3	tun	Wine	0	0	0	0
		4	tun	Wine, Corrupt	6	0	0	0

The Sancta Maria of San Sebastián, Sebastian de Govoran master, Exiting, 26th December 1550

Merchant name	Origin	Qty	Unit	Commodity	£	s.	d.	f.
William Tyndall	Ind	14	C	Wax	28	0	0	0
		8	piece	Cloth of Assize	0	0	0	0

The Flowre de Luce of Fécamp, Nicholas Michell master, Exiting, 29th December 1550

Merchant name	Origin	Qty	Unit	Commodity	£	s.	d.	f.
John Wells	Ind	60	piece	Northern Cotton *Cloth*	12	10	0	0
		16	piece	Bristol Frieze *Cloth*	10	13	4	0
		10	piece	Cloth of Assize, Kersey	0	0	0	0
		6	piece	Cloth of Assize, Dyed with Grainso	0	0	0	0
		9.33	piece	Cloth of Assize	0	0	0	0

The Nicholas of Bristol, John Welshe master, Exiting, *29th December 1550*

Merchant name	Origin	Qty	Unit	Commodity	£	s.	d.	f.
Richard Manncell	Ind	7	piece	Bristol Frieze *Cloth*	4	13	4	0
		1	piece	Cloth of Assize	0	0	0	0

Merchant name	Origin	Qty	Unit	Commodity	£	s.	d.	f.
The Katherina of Lezo, Pero Gonsalus master, Entering, *29th December 1550*								
Robert Sothall & assoc.	Ind	5.25	tun	Wine	0	0	0	0
		2	tun	Wine, Corrupt	3	0	0	0
Peter Daries	Alien	32.5	tun	Wine	0	0	0	0
		8	tun	Vinegar	16	0	0	0
		6	tun	Wine	0	0	0	0
		1	tun	Vinegar	0	40	0	0
The Harte of Chepstow, John Higgins master, Entering, *29th December 1550*								
William Barrett & assoc.	Ind	2.5	tun	Wine	0	0	0	0
		2	tun	Wine, Corrupt	3	0	0	0
The George of New Ross, William Blake master, Exiting, *30th December 1550*								
Patrick Archer	Ind	2	barrel	Honey	0	33	4	0
		4.5	C	Hops	0	45	0	0
		1	barrel	Honey	0	16	8	0
		7	lb	Saffron	3	10	0	0
		27	dozen	Knives, in Pairs	0	45	0	0
		1	dozen	Girdles	0	0	10	0
		33	lb	Seed, Onion	0	5	6	0
		2	dozen	Aniseed	0	3	0	0
		0.5	burden	Steel	0	0	20	0
		0.5	lb	Sugar, of Roses	0	0	15	0
		1	lb	Wax	0	0	5	0
		0.5	lb	Cinnamon	0	0	15	0
		1.5	dozen	Girdles	0	3	9	0
		1	dozen	Caps	0	10	0	0
		1	dozen	Spurs, pair	0	2	6	0
		2	bolt	*Thread*	0	2	6	0
		0.5	gross	Lacquor	0	0	10	0
		4	piece	Hats	0	0	20	0
		36	gross	Points	0	36	0	0
		4	gross	Lacquor	0	6	8	0
		385	lb	Lead, Worked	0	18	3	0
		25	pair	Stock-Cards	0	25	0	0
		2	dozen	Soap	0	2	6	0
		0.5	ream	Paper	0	0	10	0
		0.33	piece	Cloth of Assize	0	0	0	0
James Butler	Ind	3.5	barrel	Honey	0	58	4	0
		2	C	Hops	0	20	0	0
		5	piece	Hats	0	4	2	0
		1	dozen	Soap	0	0	15	0
		6	piece	Caps	0	5	0	0
		1	dozen	Knives, in Pairs	0	0	20	0
John Dowle	Ind	1	kilderkin	Honey	0	8	4	0
		1.5	C	Hops	0	15	0	0
		3	dozen	Knives, in Pairs	0	5	0	0

Merchant name	Origin	Qty	Unit	Commodity	£	s.	d.	f.
		1	C	Battery	0	40	0	0
		3	dozen	Knives	0	0	20	0
		4	gross	Points	0	4	0	0
		1	dozen	Soap	0	0	15	0
		4	pair	Stock-Cards	0	4	0	0
		1	bolt	Thread	0	0	15	0
		3	dozen	Combs	0	0	12	0
		1	dozen	Playing Cards	0	0	15	0
		4	dozen	Spert	0	0	16	0
		2	dozen	Girdles	0	0	16	0
		1	clout	Needles	0	2	0	0
		10	piece	Caps	0	8	4	0
		2	gross	Lacquor	0	3	4	0
		1	dozen	Aniseed	0	0	16	0
		1	dozen	Alum	0	0	16	0
		0.5	C	Flax	0	6	8	0
		1	dozen	Aniseed	0	0	18	0
		1	dozen	Soap	0	0	15	0
		1	lb	Mercury	0	0	5	0
Peter Porsell & assoc.	Ind	1	C	Battery	0	40	0	0
		10	lb	Saffron	5	0	0	0
		4	lb	Silk, *Worked*	0	53	4	0
		2	piece	Cloth of Assize, Dozen Strait	0	0	0	0

The Francis of St-Malo, Gillermo Bretton master, Entering, 31st December 1550

Merchant name	Origin	Qty	Unit	Commodity	£	s.	d.	f.
William Jonys & assoc.	Ind	39.75	tun	Wine	0	0	0	0
		13.5	tun	Wine, Corrupt	20	5	0	0
		1.75	tun	Oil, Olive	7	0	0	0
		15	C	Canes	0	25	0	0
		13	piece	Figs, Green	2	3	0	0
Gillermo Bretton & *assoc.*	Alien	4.5	C	Aniseed	2	6	8	0
		9	piece	Figs	0	9	0	0
		1	C	Aniseed	0	13	4	0

The Mary of St-Jean-de-Luz, Martin de Shevero master, Exiting, *31st December 1550*

Merchant name	Origin	Qty	Unit	Commodity	£	s.	d.	f.
William Tyndall	Ind	50	piece	Northern Cotton *Cloth*	10	8	4	0
		6	C	Wax	12	0	0	0

The Mawdelen of Sines, John de Cusshe master, Exiting, *31st December 1550*

Merchant name	Origin	Qty	Unit	Commodity	£	s.	d.	f.
William Tyndall & assoc.	Ind	25	piece	Northern Cotton *Cloth*	5	4	2	0
		4	C	Wax	8	0	0	0

The George of Chepstow, William Hugher master, Entering, 8th January 1551

Merchant name	Origin	Qty	Unit	Commodity	£	s.	d.	f.
William Jones	Ind	3.5	tun	Wine	0	0	0	0

Merchant name	Origin	Qty	Unit	Commodity	£	s.	d.	f.
The Sancta Maria of Lantringuier, Evan Lodick master, Exiting, 8th January 1551								
Evan Lodick	Alien	6	piece	Bristol Frieze *Cloth*	4	o	o	o
The Sancta Crux of Bordeaux, Raymond de Tiras master, Exiting, 9th January 1551								
Martin Affeld & assoc.	Ind	90	piece	Manchester Cotton *Cloth*	45	o	o	o
		32	piece	Cloth of Assize	o	o	o	o
Raymond de Tiras	Alien	1	piece	Welsh *Cloth*	o	20	o	o
The Sonday of Bristol, Maurice Welshe master, Exiting, *9th January 1551*								
William Golde	Ind	1	piece	Cloth of Assize, Dozen Strait	o	o	o	o
		4	gross	Knives	o	26	8	o
		16	gross	Points	o	16	o	o
		2	dozen	Caps	o	20	o	o
		0.5	burden	Steel	o	o	20	o
		5	lb	Saffron	2	10	o	o
		15	lb	Saffron	7	10	6	o
		6	piece	Caps	o	5	o	o
The Angell of Fécamp, Peter Dewdycke master, Exiting, *9th January 1551*								
Peter Dudick	Alien	2.5	piece	Cloth of Assize	o	o	o	o
		1	piece	Bristol Frieze *Cloth*	o	13	4	o
		1	C	Check *Cloth*	o	40	o	o
The Katryne of St-Jean-de-Luz, Sampson de Halden master, Exiting, 12th January 1551								
Bartholemew Poyner & assoc.	Ind	35.5	piece	Cloth of Assize	o	o	o	o
		70	piece	Manchester Cotton *Cloth*	35	o	o	o
		1	C	Wax	2	o	o	o
The Mary of Penmarch, Henry le Dryo master, Exiting, *12th January 1551*								
Henry *le Dryo*	Alien	4	piece	Bristol Frieze *Cloth*	o	53	4	o
		5	piece	Welsh *Cloth*	5	o	o	o
		1.5	piece	Cloth of Assize	o	o	o	o
The Mawdelen of Errenteria, Martin de Berobie master, *Exiting,* 13th January 1551								
Alexander Case & assoc.	Ind	41.83	piece	Cloth of Assize	o	o	o	o
		12	C	Wax	24	o	o	o
		1	piece	Bristol Frieze *Cloth*	o	13	4	o
John Sans & assoc.	Alien	18	C	Wax	36	o	o	o
The Frances of St Malo, Gillermo Brytton master, Exiting, 14th January 1551								
Gillermo Brytton & assoc.	Alien	20	piece	Bristol Frieze *Cloth*	13	6	8	o
		2.83	piece	Cloth of Assize	o	o	o	o

Merchant name	Origin	Qty	Unit	Commodity	£	s.	d.	f.

The Saviour of Milford Haven, Thomas Watt master, Entering, *14th January 1551*

Merchant name	Origin	Qty	Unit	Commodity	£	s.	d.	f.
William Pepwall	Ind	8.5	tun	Wine	0	0	0	0

The Swanne of Bristol, Nicholas Grenehin master, Exiting, *14th January 1551*

Merchant name	Origin	Qty	Unit	Commodity	£	s.	d.	f.
John Swanne & assoc.	Ind	36.66	piece	Cloth of Assize	0	0	0	0
		84	piece	Manchester Cotton *Cloth*	42	0	0	0
		1.5	C	Check *Cloth*	3	0	0	0
		12	piece	Mantles	0	40	0	0
		8	piece	Bristol Frieze *Cloth*	5	6	8	0

The Katerina of Lezo, Pero Gonsalus master, Exiting, 25th January 1551

Merchant name	Origin	Qty	Unit	Commodity	£	s.	d.	f.
Pero Gonsalus	Alien	5.33	piece	Cloth of Assize	0	0	0	0

The Cristopher of Gloucester, William Horne master, Entering, 27th January 1551

Merchant name	Origin	Qty	Unit	Commodity	£	s.	d.	f.
Robert Lovedaye	Ind	4	pair	Milstones	4	0	0	0

The Julian of Bristol, Richard White master, Exiting, *27th January 1551*

Merchant name	Origin	Qty	Unit	Commodity	£	s.	d.	f.
Francis Woseley & assoc.	Ind	124.8	piece	Cloth of Assize	0	0	0	0
		8	piece	Dunster *Cloth*	4	0	0	0
		117	piece	Northern Cotton *Cloth*	24	7	6	0
		75	piece	Manchester Cotton *Cloth*	37	10	0	0
		20.25	C	Wax	40	10	0	0

The Paule of Bristol, Ralph Browne master, Exiting, *27th January 1551*

Merchant name	Origin	Qty	Unit	Commodity	£	s.	d.	f.
John Stone & assoc.	Ind	86.5	piece	Cloth of Assize	0	0	0	0
		16	piece	Bristol Frieze *Cloth*	10	13	4	0
		10	piece	Manchester Cotton *Cloth*	5	0	0	0
		41	piece	Northern Cotton *Cloth*	8	10	10	0
		5	C	Wax	10	0	0	0
		20	piece	Welsh *Cloth*, Dozen Strait	4	3	4	0

The Trinite of Ilfracombe, John Phelipp master, Entering, 3rd February 1551

Merchant name	Origin	Qty	Unit	Commodity	£	s.	d.	f.
Edmund Roche	Ind	6	piece	Skins, Salted	0	8	4	0

The Marye of Milford Haven, Richard Browne master, Entering, *3rd February 1551*

Merchant name	Origin	Qty	Unit	Commodity	£	s.	d.	f.
Richard Browne	Ind	5	barrel	Fish, Herring White	0	25	0	0

The Trinyte of Youghal, William Nele master, Entering, *3rd February 1551*

Merchant name	Origin	Qty	Unit	Commodity	£	s.	d.	f.
William *Nele & assoc.*	Ind	25	C	Fish, Hake	12	10	0	0
		29.95	C	Skins, Sheep	14	19	6	0
		5.66	C	Skins, Lamb	0	37	10	0
		7.5	C	Skins, Kid	0	37	6	0

Merchant name	Origin	Qty	Unit	Commodity	£	s.	d.	f.
		23	piece	Skins, Deer	0	7	8	0
		41	piece	Skins, Fox	0	6	10	0
		9	piece	Mantles	0	30	0	0
		32	piece	Skins, Otter	0	13	4	0
		10	piece	Skins, Marten	0	10	0	0
		2.258	C	Check *Cloth*	4	10	4	0
		10	stone	Wool, Flocks	0	4	2	0
		4	piece	Skins, *Greis*[2]	0	0	20	0

The Onyon of *Laverte*, Bernard Wortyn master, Entering, *3rd February 1551*

John de la Rockett	Alien	29	tun	Wine	0	0	0	0

The Sant *Christ*ofer of Viana do Castelo, Sebastian Gonsalus master, Entering, *3rd February 1551*

Sebastian Gonsalus & assoc.	Alien	90	M	Oranges	15	0	0	0

The Marie of Youghal, William Donell master, Entering, 4th February 1551

William *Donell*	Ind	27	C	Fish, Hake	13	10	0	0
		6	C	Skins, Sheep	3	0	0	0
		2	barrel	Fish, Herring White	0	10	0	0
		20	yard	Check *Cloth*	0	6	8	0
		1	pipe	Fish, Salmon	0	30	0	0

The Trynite of Youghal, Maurice Morghe master, Entering, *4th February 1551*

Maurice Morghe	Ind	36.5	C	Fish, Hake	18	5	0	0
		6	barrel	Fish, Herring White	0	30	0	0
		3.5	C	Skins, Sheep	0	35	0	0

The George of Youghal, Maurice Fitzjohn master, Entering, *4th February 1551*

John Sherlock & assoc.	Ind	10.5	M	Fish, Hake	52	10	0	0
		3	burden	Fish, Salted	0	12	6	0
		1	barrel	Fish, Herring White	0	5	0	0

The Mawdelen of Viana do Castelo, Martin Alvus master, Entering, 5th February 1551

Martin Alvus	Alien	50	M	Oranges	8	6	8	0

The Jesus of Youghal, Thomas Duffins master, Entering, 11th February 1551

Thomas *Duffins &* assoc.	Ind	11	C	Fish, Hake	5	10	0	0
		11.5	C	Skins, Sheep	5	15	0	0
		3	piece	Skins, Deer	0	0	12	0
		3	C	Skins, Lamb	0	20	0	0
		40	yard	Check *Cloth*	0	13	4	0

2 Possibly a deer skin.

574

Merchant name	Origin	Qty	Unit	Commodity	£	s.	d.	f.
		2	stone	Wool, Flocks	0	0	10	0

The Marie of Milford Haven, Philip Smyth master, Entering, *11th February 1551*

Merchant name	Origin	Qty	Unit	Commodity	£	s.	d.	f.
Philip Smyth	Ind	1	pipe	Fish, Salmon	0	30	0	0

The Trynite of Barnstaple, Simon Sherman master, Exiting, 13th February 1551

Merchant name	Origin	Qty	Unit	Commodity	£	s.	d.	f.
Robert Saxei	Ind	16.5	piece	Cloth of Assize	0	0	0	0

The Katryne of Dungarvan, Robert Royne master, Entering, *13th February 1551*

Merchant name	Origin	Qty	Unit	Commodity	£	s.	d.	f.
Robert *Royne & assoc.*	Ind	49	C	Fish, Hake	24	10	0	0
		5	burden	Fish, Salted	0	20	10	0
		0.25	C	Skins, Sheep	0	2	6	0

The Mary of Dungarvan, John Fitzwilliams master, Entering, *13th February 1551*

Merchant name	Origin	Qty	Unit	Commodity	£	s.	d.	f.
John *Fitzwilliams*	Ind	53	C	Fish, Hake	26	10	0	0
		10.5	burden	Fish, Salted	0	43	10	0
		0.75	C	Skins, Sheep	0	7	6	0

The Sancta Maria of Penmarch, Donarte de Britton master, Entering, *13th February 1551*

Merchant name	Origin	Qty	Unit	Commodity	£	s.	d.	f.
William Spratt & assoc.	Ind	71.25	tun	Wine	0	0	0	0
		4.25	tun	Wine, Corrupt	6	7	6	0

The Marie of Penmarch, James Laurennce master, Entering, *13th February 1551*

Merchant name	Origin	Qty	Unit	Commodity	£	s.	d.	f.
John Smyth & assoc.	Ind	61	tun	Wine	0	0	0	0
		1	hogshead	Wine, Corrupt	0	7	6	0
Harvy Gravalion	Alien	12	piece	Pitch & Rosin	0	12	0	0

The Jaques of Penmarch, Gillam Hambrone master, Entering, *13th February 1551*

Merchant name	Origin	Qty	Unit	Commodity	£	s.	d.	f.
John Smyth & assoc.	Ind	84.5	tun	Wine	0	0	0	0
		1.5	tun	Wine, Corrupt	0	45	0	0
		21	C	Rosin	0	28	0	0
Gillam Hambrone	Alien	4	C	Rosin	0	5	4	0

The Trinite of Youghal, William Nele master, Exiting, *13th February 1551*

Merchant name	Origin	Qty	Unit	Commodity	£	s.	d.	f.
William *Nele*	Ind	2	piece	Pans (5lb)	0	12	0	0
		0.5	gross	Knives	0	3	4	0
		12	lb	Flax	0	4	0	0
		0.25	C	Hops	0	2	6	0
		5	piece	Caps	0	4	2	0
		1	dozen	Skins, Golden	0	4	2	0
Maurice White	Ind	1	lb	Saffron	0	10	0	0
		0.5	C	Hops	0	5	0	0
		0.5	C	Aniseed	0	6	8	0

Merchant name	Origin	Qty	Unit	Commodity	£	s.	d.	f.
		2	lb	Cinnamon	0	5	0	0
		1	lb	Cloves	0	2	6	0
		1	stone	Cumin	0	2	6	0
		1	lb	Nutmeg	0	0	20	0
		3	gross	Knives	0	20	0	0
		3	dozen	Knives, in Pairs	0	5	0	0
		6	piece	Caps	0	5	0	0
		14	gross	Points	0	14	0	0
John Teke	Ind	3	lb	Saffron	0	30	0	0
		2	lb	Silk, *Worked*	0	26	8	0
		0.75	C	Hops	0	7	6	0
		4	stone	Orchil	0	6	8	0
		1	gross	Knives	0	6	8	0
		2	gross	Points	0	2	0	0
		1	stone	Alum	0	0	20	0
		5	piece	Pans (91lb)	0	30	0	0
John Foxam	Ind	1	C	Hops	0	10	0	0
		2	dozen	Flax	0	0	20	0
		3	stone	Alum	0	5	0	0
		1	lb	Saffron	0	10	0	0
Edmund Roche	Ind	2	gross	Knives	0	13	4	0
		0.5	burden	Steel	0	2	6	0
		1	lb	Saffron	0	10	0	0
		2	gross	Points	0	2	0	0
		1	dozen	Skins, Golden	0	4	2	0
		1	bolt	Thread	0	0	15	0
		2	lb	Silk, *Worked*	0	26	8	0
		10	pair	Playing Cards	0	0	10	0
		0.5	C	Hops	0	5	0	0
		3	stone	Orchil	0	5	0	0

The Harte of Bristol, William Mors*e* master, Entering, 14th February 1551

John Smyth & assoc.	Ind	8.5	tun	Wine	0	0	0	0
		34.5	tun	Wine, Corrupt	51	15	0	0
		22	seron	Soap	13	15	0	0
		68	tun	Oil, Olive	272	0	0	0
		21	C	Orchil	14	0	0	0
		3	chest	Sugar	6	0	0	0
		16	piece	Raisins, *Great*	0	26	8	0
		5	sorte	Figs	0	20	0	0

The Mary of Youghal, William Donell master, Exiting, 16th February 1551

William *Donell*	Ind	100	lb	Battery	0	33	4	0
		1	C	Hops	0	10	0	0
Thomas Blewett	Ind	1	C	Hops	0	10	0	0
		1.5	gross	Knives	0	10	0	0
		6	dozen	Knives, in Pairs	0	10	0	0
		3	stone	Alum	0	5	0	0
		2	stone	Aniseed	0	3	4	0
		7	gross	Points	0	7	0	0

Merchant name	Origin	Qty	Unit	Commodity	£	s.	d.	f.
		2	lb	Cinnamon	0	5	0	0
		0.5	gross	Lacquor	0	0	10	0
		5	C	Nails	0	0	20	0
		0.5	C	Battery	0	18	8	0
		1	lb	Verdigris	0	0	5	0
Robert Donell	Ind	1.5	gross	Knives	0	10	0	0
		4	dozen	Knives, in Pairs	0	6	8	0
		8	gross	Points	0	8	0	0
		2	stone	Hops	0	2	6	0
		1	stone	Alum	0	0	20	0
		1	stone	Aniseed	0	0	20	0
		0.5	C	Battery	0	18	8	0
		2	dozen	Flax	0	5	0	0

The Trynyte of Youghal, Maurice Morghe master, Exiting, *16th February 1551*

Merchant name	Origin	Qty	Unit	Commodity	£	s.	d.	f.
Maurice Morghe	Ind	1	C	Hops	0	10	0	0
		2	lb	Saffron	0	20	0	0
		2	dozen	Flax	0	5	0	0
		50	lb	Battery	0	16	8	0
		1	stone	Alum	0	0	20	0
Francis Welshe	Ind	2	lb	Saffron	0	20	0	0
		0.5	C	Hops	0	5	0	0
		0.25	gross	Knives	0	0	20	0
Francis Welshe	Ind	2	gross	Points	0	2	0	0
Philip Ronam	Ind	2	lb	Silk, *Worked*	0	26	8	0
		1	lb	Cinnamon	0	2	6	0
		1	gross	Knives	0	6	8	0
		6	dozen	Knives, in Pairs	0	10	0	0
		6	piece	Caps	0	5	0	0
		2	dozen	Playing Cards	0	0	20	0
		0.5	dozen	Skins, Golden	0	2	1	0
		8	gross	Points	0	8	0	0
		0.5	C	Hops	0	5	0	0
		4	dozen	Combs	0	0	20	0
		4	dozen	Spert	0	0	20	0
		60	lb	Battery	0	20	0	0
		1.5	piece	Cloth of Assize	0	0	0	0

The Jupbiter of Bideford, Robert Bense master, Entering, *16th February 1551*

Merchant name	Origin	Qty	Unit	Commodity	£	s.	d.	f.
Ralph Richmond & assoc.	Ind	17.5	tun	Wine	0	0	0	0
		12.75	tun	Wine, Corrupt	19	2	6	0
		18	tun	Oil, Olive	72	0	0	0
		1	chest	Sugar	0	40	0	0
		3	seron	Soap	0	30	0	0

The George of Youghal, Maurice Fitzjohn master, Exiting, 19th February 1551

Merchant name	Origin	Qty	Unit	Commodity	£	s.	d.	f.
John Shurlock & assoc.	Ind	4.25	piece	Cloth of Assize	0	0	0	0
		4	lb	Saffron	0	40	0	0

Merchant name	Origin	Qty	Unit	Commodity	£	s.	d.	f.

The Margaret of Bristol, Thomas Baynam master, Entering, 20th February 1551

Merchant name	Origin	Qty	Unit	Commodity	£	s.	d.	f.
Arthur Jenkyns	Ind	1	C	Check *Cloth*	0	40	0	0
		3	stone	Wool, Flocks	0	0	15	0
		17	yard	Check *Cloth*	0	5	8	0

The Trynite of Youghal, William Nele master, Exiting, 22nd February 1551

Merchant name	Origin	Qty	Unit	Commodity	£	s.	d.	f.
Thomas Harrolde	Ind	1	piece	Cloth of Assize	0	0	0	0
		2	lb	Saffron	0	20	0	0
		3	gross	Knives	0	20	0	0
		0.5	gross	Knives, in Pairs	0	10	0	0
		3	dozen	Playing Cards	0	3	9	0
		2	dozen	Skins, Golden	0	8	4	0
		12	gross	Points	0	12	0	0
		3	dozen	Girdles	0	4	6	0
		30	lb	Seed, Onion	0	10	0	0
		6	lb	Cumin	0	0	10	0
		3	stone	Sulpher	0	0	3	0
		4	bolt	Thread	0	5	0	0
		4	lb	Thread	0	0	20	0
		0.5	gross	Lacquor	0	0	10	0
		6	piece	Caps	0	5	0	0
		1	C	Woad, Azores	0	6	8	0
		1	seam	Wood Ashes	0	4	0	0

The Jesus of Youghal, Thomas Duffie master, Exiting, 22nd February 1551

Merchant name	Origin	Qty	Unit	Commodity	£	s.	d.	f.
Thomas *Duffie*	Ind	3	lb	Saffron	0	30	0	0
		1	gross	Knives	0	6	8	0
		4	gross	Points	0	4	0	0
		4	dozen	Purses	0	0	20	0
		1.5	C	Hops	0	15	0	0
		48	lb	Battery	0	16	0	0
		0.5	gross	Lacquor	0	0	10	0
		1	stone	Alum	0	0	20	0
		2	stone	Orchil	0	3	4	0
Dominic Welshe	Ind	1	lb	Silk, *Worked*	0	13	4	0
		0.5	C	Hops	0	5	0	0
		32	lb	Battery	0	10	8	0
William Blewett	Ind	2.75	piece	Cloth of Assize	0	0	0	0
		1	gross	Knives	0	6	8	0
		1	gross	Cutts	0	3	4	0
		24	lb	Battery	0	8	0	0
		3	gross	Points	0	3	0	0
		0.5	C	Hops	0	5	0	0
		1	dozen	Skins, Golden	0	4	2	0
		2	stone	Orchil	0	3	4	0
		2	stone	Cumin & Aniseed	0	3	4	0
		0.5	stone	Alum	0	0	10	0
		1	stone	Liquorice	0	0	20	0
		1	dozen	Wool-Cards	0	4	0	0

Merchant name	Origin	Qty	Unit	Commodity	£	s.	d.	f.
		2	dozen	Playing Cards	0	0	20	0
Henry Verdon	Ind	26	gross	Knives	8	13	4	0
		15	lb	Saffron	7	10	0	0
		14	dozen	Girdles, Leather	0	9	4	0
		42	gross	Points	2	2	0	0
Peter Hackett	Ind	4	piece	Cloth of Assize	0	0	0	0
		12	lb	Silk, *Worked*	8	0	0	0
		4	lb	Saffron	0	40	0	0
		5	lb	Girdles, Caddis	0	8	4	0
		6	bolt	Thread	0	7	6	0
		24	gross	Points	0	24	0	0
		3	dozen	Caps	0	30	0	0
		7	gross	Knives	0	46	8	0
Cornell Hallye	Ind	3.5	piece	Cloth of Assize	0	0	0	0
		3	lb	Silk, *Worked*	0	40	0	0
		24	gross	Points	0	24	0	0
		3	lb	Saffron	0	30	0	0
		5	gross	Knives	0	33	4	0
		6	dozen	Knives, in Pairs	0	10	0	0
		3	lb	Girdles, Caddis	0	4	6	0
		2	dozen	Playing Cards	0	2	6	0

The Fawcon Grey of Chepstow, Thomas Davis master, Exiting, 25th February 1551

Merchant name	Origin	Qty	Unit	Commodity	£	s.	d.	f.
William Spratt & assoc.	Ind	63.83	piece	Cloth of Assize	0	0	0	0
		14	piece	Bristol Frieze *Cloth*	9	6	8	0
		5	C	Wax	10	0	0	0
		50	piece	Northern Cotton *Cloth*	10	8	4	0

The Sonday of Bristol, Maurice Welshe master, Entering, 26th February 1551

Merchant name	Origin	Qty	Unit	Commodity	£	s.	d.	f.
Henry Verdon	Ind	17	barrel	Fish, Herring White	4	5	0	0
		1	barrel	Fish, Eels	0	13	4	0
		21.5	C	Skins, Sheep	10	15	0	0
		1.5	pipe	Fish, Salmon	0	45	0	0
		38	stone	Wool, Irish	5	0	16	0
		23	stone	Wool, Flocks	0	9	7	0
		16	C	Fish, Hake	8	0	0	0
		24.4	dicker	Skins, Deer	4	0	16	0
		0.375	tun	Oil, Train	0	30	0	0
		1	hogshead	Meat	0	10	0	0
		4	piece	Fish, Seal	0	26	8	0
		1	C	Skins, Lamb	0	6	8	0
		24	piece	Skins, Marten	0	24	0	0
		1	C	Wood, Irish	0	20	0	0

The Katherina of Dungarvan, Robert Ronam master, Exiting, 28th February 1551

Merchant name	Origin	Qty	Unit	Commodity	£	s.	d.	f.
Morgan Kellie	Ind	1	dozen	Knives, in Pairs	0	0	20	0
		9	lb	Girdles, Caddis	0	12	0	0
		1	gross	Combs	0	4	0	0

Merchant name	Origin	Qty	Unit	Commodity	£	s.	d.	f.
		1	ream	Paper	0	0	20	0
		2	dozen	Playing Cards	0	2	6	0
		8	gross	Knives	0	53	4	0
		72	gross	Points	3	12	0	0
Robert Rowen	Ind	1	lb	Saffron	0	10	0	0
		0.5	C	Battery	0	16	8	0
		4	dozen	Flax	0	20	0	0
		0.5	gross	Knives	0	3	4	0
		2	stone	Alum	0	3	4	0
Robert Nogle	Ind	3	lb	Silk, *Worked*	0	40	0	0
		1	lb	Saffron	0	10	0	0
		3	stone	Alum	0	5	0	0
		0.5	gross	Knives	0	3	4	0
		0.25	C	Flax	0	10	0	0
		3	C	Hops	0	30	0	0
		1	dozen	Caps	0	10	0	0
		4	barrel	Pitch & Tar	0	6	8	0
		6	gross	Points	0	6	0	0
Nicholas Shee & assoc.	Ind	7	C	Battery	11	13	4	0
		15	dozen	Flax	0	15	0	0

The Mary of Milford Haven, Philip Smyth master, Exiting, *28th February 1551*

Merchant name	Origin	Qty	Unit	Commodity	£	s.	d.	f.
Philip *Smyth*	Ind	1	pair	Milstones	0	20	0	0

The Mary of Dungarvan, John Fitzwilliams master, Exiting, *28th February 1551*

Merchant name	Origin	Qty	Unit	Commodity	£	s.	d.	f.
John *Fitzwilliams*	Ind	1	lb	Saffron	0	10	0	0
		90	lb	Battery	0	30	0	0
		1	C	Hops	0	10	0	0
William Nyngell	Ind	1	lb	Saffron	0	10	0	0
		1	gross	Knives	0	6	8	0
		2	stone	Flax	0	0	20	0
		0.5	C	Battery	0	16	8	0
		0.5	C	Hops	0	5	0	0
		1	dozen	Caps	0	10	0	0
James Mangner	Ind	2	lb	Saffron	0	20	0	0
		3	barrel	Pitch & Tar	0	5	0	0
		3	C	Iron	0	12	0	0
		6	piece	Caps	0	5	0	0

The Anthony of Carmarthen, Thomas Hanrake master, Entering, 2nd March 1551

Merchant name	Origin	Qty	Unit	Commodity	£	s.	d.	f.
Thomas Tizon & assoc.	Ind	5	tun	Wine	0	0	0	0
		1	tun	Wine, Corrupt	0	30	0	0

The Margett of Bristol, William Histocke master, Exiting, *2nd March 1551*

Merchant name	Origin	Qty	Unit	Commodity	£	s.	d.	f.
John Channcellor & assoc.	Ind	6	tun	Wine	0	0	0	0
		15	tun	Wine, Corrupt	22	10	0	0

Merchant name	Origin	Qty	Unit	Commodity	£	s.	d.	f.
		28.75	tun	Oil, Olive	115	0	0	0
		11.08	ton	Raisins, *Great*	22	3	4	0
		6	C	Figs	0	24	0	0
		26	seron	Soap	23	10	0	0
		1	sack	Orchil	0	20	0	0

The Minion of Bristol, John Williams master, Exiting, *2nd March 1551*

Edward Weldon & assoc.	Ind	418.2	piece	Cloth of Assize	0	0	0	0
		12	fother	Lead	48	0	0	0
		59	piece	Manchester Cotton *Cloth*	29	10	0	0
		7	piece	Bristol Frieze *Cloth*	4	13	4	0
		13.5	piece	Welsh *Cloth*	13	10	0	0
		145	piece	Northern Cotton *Cloth*	30	4	2	0
George Dres	Alien	20	piece	Cloth of Assize	0	0	0	0

The George Butlar of Waterford, John Deris master, Entering, *2nd March 1551*

Leonard Harrolde & assoc.	Ind	85.5	C	Skins, Sheep	42	15	0	0
		80	piece	Skins, Marten	4	0	0	0
		10	piece	Skins, Otter	0	4	2	0
		5	piece	Skins, Fox	0	0	10	0
		3.5	C	Skins, Lamb	0	23	4	0
		1.5	C	Skins, Kid	0	7	6	0
		200	piece	Mantles	33	6	8	0
		2	stone	Wool, Flocks	0	0	10	0
		4	stone	Wool, Irish	0	10	8	0
		37	C	Check *Cloth*	74	0	0	0
		14	C	Fish, Hake	7	0	0	0
		1.75	burden	Fish, Salted	0	7	4	0

The Christopher of Gloucester, William Horne master, Entering, 3rd March 1551

Walter Grannt & assoc.	Ind	9	C	Skins, Sheep	4	10	0	0
		21	piece	Mantles	3	10	0	0
		80	yard	Check *Cloth*	0	26	8	0
		12	C	Fish, Hake	6	0	0	0
		2	burden	Fish, Salted	0	8	4	0

The Katheryne of St Ives, Henry Thomas master, Entering, *3rd March 1551*

Henry Thomas	Ind	16	burden	Fish, Salted	3	6	8	0

The St Sebastian of Vila do Conde, Lewis Fornandus master, Entering, 5th March 1551

Edward Prynne & assoc.	Ind	9	tun	Wine	0	0	0	0
		438	piece	Raisins, *Great*	36	10	0	0
		3.5	tun	Vinegar	7	0	0	0

Merchant name	Origin	Qty	Unit	Commodity	£	s.	d.	f.
		69.75	tun	Wine, Corrupt	104	12	6	0
		11	bag	Orchil	11	0	0	0
		7	ton	Raisins, *Great*	14	0	0	0

The Jesus of Youghal, Thomas Duffye master, Exiting, 7th March 1551

Merchant name	Origin	Qty	Unit	Commodity	£	s.	d.	f.
Peter Creanghe	Ind	2	piece	Cloth of Assize	0	0	0	0
		6	gross	Knives	0	40	0	0
		12	dozen	Knives, in Pairs	0	20	0	0
		12	gross	Points	0	12	0	0
		1	lb	Saffron	0	10	0	0
		0.5	gross	Lacquor	0	0	10	0
		12	dozen	Spert	0	3	0	0
Nicholas Shee & assoc.	Ind	3	piece	Cloth of Assize	0	0	0	0

The John of Kinsale, Henry Rothe master, Entering, 8th March 1551

Merchant name	Origin	Qty	Unit	Commodity	£	s.	d.	f.
Henry *Rothe*	Ind	23	C	Fish, Hake	11	10	0	0
		18	barrel	Fish, Herring White	4	10	0	0
		1	barrel	Porpoise	0	6	8	0
		3	burden	Fish, Salted	0	12	6	0
		3	barrel	Oil, Train	0	30	0	0
		2	barrel	Meat	0	13	4	0

The Nicholas of Plymouth, Walter Harris master, Entering, *8th March 1551*

Merchant name	Origin	Qty	Unit	Commodity	£	s.	d.	f.
Walter *Harris &* assoc.	Ind	56	burden	Fish, Salted	11	13	4	0

The Sancta Maria of Penmarch, Donarte de Brytton master, Exiting, 10th March 1551

Merchant name	Origin	Qty	Unit	Commodity	£	s.	d.	f.
Donarte de Brytton	Alien	4.25	piece	Cloth of Assize	0	0	0	0
		5	piece	Welsh *Cloth*	5	0	0	0
		30	piece	Mantles	5	0	0	0

The Marye of Penmarch, James Laurennce master, Exiting, 11th March 1551

Merchant name	Origin	Qty	Unit	Commodity	£	s.	d.	f.
James *Laurence*	Alien	5.825	piece	Cloth of Assize	0	0	0	0
		15	piece	Mantles	2	10	0	0

The Jaques of Penmarch, Gillam Lambrero master, Exiting, *11th March 1551*

Merchant name	Origin	Qty	Unit	Commodity	£	s.	d.	f.
Gillam Lambrero	Alien	1.33	piece	Cloth of Assize	0	0	0	0
		8	piece	Bristol Frieze *Cloth*	5	6	8	0
		1.5	piece	Welsh *Cloth*	0	30	0	0
		16	piece	Mantles	0	53	4	0
		1.25	piece	Cloth of Assize	0	0	0	0

Merchant name	Origin	Qty	Unit	Commodity	£	s.	d.	f.

The Kateryne of Youghal, John Lere master, Entering, 12th March 1551

John *Lere & assoc.*	Ind	33	burden	Fish, Salted	7	4	1	0
		0.5	barrel	Fish, Seal	0	3	4	0

The Julian of Wexford, Laurence Landresse master, Entering, *12th March 1551*

Laurence Landresse	Ind	12.5	barrel	Fish, Herring White	3	2	6	0
		2.5	C	Skins, Sheep	0	25	0	0
		0.5	C	Skins, Lamb	0	3	4	0
		4	piece	Mantles	0	13	4	0
		15	yard	Check *Cloth*	0	5	0	0

The Jesus of Youghal, Richard Gryffyn master, Entering, *12th March 1551*

Richard *Gryffyn &* assoc.	Ind	52	burden	Fish, Salted	10	16	8	0
		76	stone	Wool, Flocks	0	31	8	0
		7	C	Skins, Sheep	3	10	0	0
		0.5	C	Skins, Lamb	0	3	4	0
		1	piece	Mantles	0	3	4	0
		77	stone	Wool, Irish	10	5	4	0

The Mawdelen of Youghal, Darby Gryffyn master, Entering, 13th March 1551

Darby *Gryffyn &* assoc.	Ind	30	burden	Fish, Salted	6	5	0	0
		15	stone	Wool, Flocks	0	6	3	0
		0.5	C	Fish, Hake	0	5	0	0

The John of Kinsale, Henry Rothe master, Exiting, 16th March 1551

Henry *Rothe*	Ind	2	lb	Silk, *Worked*	0	26	8	0
		2	C	Hops	0	20	0	0
		2	lb	Saffron	0	20	0	0
		2	C	Orchil	0	26	8	0
		1	gross	Knives	0	6	8	0
		3	gross	Points	0	3	0	0

The Mighell of Kenton, Simon Gyles master, Entering, 17th March 1551

Simon Gyles	Ind	40	burden	Fish, Salted	8	6	8	0

The Julian of Wexford, Laurence Landresse master, Exiting, 18th March 1551

Laurence Landresse	Ind	2.5	C	Hops	0	25	0	0
		1	lb	Saffron	0	10	0	0
		2	gross	Knives	0	13	4	0
		1	gross	Combs	0	3	4	0
		1	dozen	Aniseed	0	0	16	0
		12	gross	Points	0	12	0	0
		0.5	C	Hops	0	5	0	0

Merchant name	Origin	Qty	Unit	Commodity	£	s.	d.	f.
		2	lb	Saffron	0	20	0	0
		2	lb	Silk, *Worked*	0	26	8	0
		3	gross	Knives	0	20	0	0
		0.5	dozen	Wool–Cards	0	2	0	0
		1	barrel	Tar	0	0	20	0
		3	weight	Hemp	0	9	0	0
		1	last	Lime	0	5	0	0
		1	lb	Saffron	0	10	0	0

The Jesus of Youghal, Richard Gryffyn master, Exiting, 20th March 1551

Merchant name	Origin	Qty	Unit	Commodity	£	s.	d.	f.
Nicholas Shee & assoc.	Ind	2.5	tun	Wine	0	0	0	0
		4	piece	Cloth of Assize	0	0	0	0
		8	gross	Knives	0	53	4	0
		1.5	C	Hops	0	15	0	0
		5	lb	Saffron	0	50	0	0
		2	stone	Orchil	0	3	4	0
		6	gross	Points	0	6	0	0

The Kat*e*ryne of Youghal, John Lere master, Exiting, *20th March 1551*

Merchant name	Origin	Qty	Unit	Commodity	£	s.	d.	f.
John *Lere*	Ind	1.5	lb	Saffron	0	15	0	0
		1	gross	Lacquor	0	0	20	0
		1	C	Hops	0	5	0	0

The George Butlar of Waterford, John Deris master, Exiting, *20th March 1551*

Merchant name	Origin	Qty	Unit	Commodity	£	s.	d.	f.
Nicholas White & assoc.	Ind	2	C	Hops	0	20	0	0
		8	stone	Orchil	0	13	4	0
		8	dozen	Soap	0	10	0	0
		1	lb	Saffron	0	10	0	0
		2	gross	Knives	0	13	4	0
		12	gross	Points	0	12	0	0
		3	gross	Lacquor	0	5	0	0
		3	dozen	Knives, in Pairs	0	5	0	0
		7	C	Iron	0	17	6	0
		12	lb	Cumin	0	0	16	0
		16	pair	Stock–Cards	0	16	0	0
		2	lb	Starch	0	0	8	0
		8.58	piece	Cloth of Assize	0	0	0	0
Nicholas She*e*	Ind	1	pipe	Wine	0	0	0	0
		2	C	Hops	0	20	0	0
		0.5	C	Liquorice	0	0	20	0
		0.5	C	Aniseed	0	6	8	0
Edmund Mollronye	Ind	2	lb	Saffron	0	20	0	0
		3	lb	Silk, *Worked*	0	40	0	0
		8	dozen	Knives, in Pairs	0	11	8	0
		0.5	gross	Knives	0	16	8	0
		0.25	C	Hops	0	2	6	0
		0.25	C	Alum	0	3	4	0
		1	C	Battery	0	33	4	0

Merchant name	Origin	Qty	Unit	Commodity	£	s.	d.	f.
		8	piece	Caps	0	6	8	0
		4	gross	Lacquor	0	6	8	0
		6	gross	Points	0	6	0	0
		3	clout	Needles	0	2	0	0
Paul Butlar & assoc.	Ind	5	C	Hops	0	50	0	0
		1	lb	Saffron	0	10	0	0
		0.5	C	Battery	0	16	8	0
		0.75	C	Flax	0	10	0	0
		1	bolt	Thread	0	0	15	0
		1	gross	Knives	0	6	8	0
		2	dozen	Knives, in Pairs	0	3	4	0
		3	gross	Points	0	3	0	0
		0.5	gross	Lacquor	0	0	10	0
		1	dozen	Caps	0	10	0	0
		1	gross	Buttons	0	0	20	0
		2	pair	Stock-Cards	0	2	0	0
		4	ell	Worsted *Cloth*	0	10	0	0
		1	C	Hops	0	10	0	0
		1	lb	Saffron	0	10	0	0
		1.5	C	Potol	0	50	0	0
		4	dozen	Playing Cards	0	3	4	0
		14	lb	Flax	0	5	0	0
		2	C	Battery	3	6	8	0
		1	C	Hops	0	10	0	0
		2	lb	Saffron	0	20	0	0
		4	lb	Silk, *Worked*	0	53	4	0
		0.5	dozen	Hats	0	10	0	0
		5	gross	Knives	0	33	4	0
		2	gross	Knives, Bumbard	2	0	0	0
Peter Brewer & assoc.	Ind	2	C	Hops	0	20	0	0
		10	stone	Orchil	0	16	8	0
		4	dozen	Flax	0	12	0	0
		10.5	gross	Points	0	10	10	0
		4	dozen	Soap	0	5	0	0
		5	pair	Stock-Cards	0	5	0	0
		1.5	lb	Saffron	0	15	0	0
		3	gross	Lacquor	0	5	0	0
		6	gross	Knives	0	6	8	0
Edward White & assoc.	Ind	6	C	Flax	4	0	0	0
		1.5	C	Battery	3	0	0	0
		1	gross	Knives, Almaine	0	20	0	0
		6	gross	Knives	0	40	0	0
		2.5	gross	Points	0	2	6	0
		5	lb	Saffron	0	50	0	0
		12	lb	Cumin	0	0	16	0
		6	bolt	Thread	0	7	6	0
		2.5	gross	Lacquor	0	4	2	0
		0.5	C	Hops	0	5	0	0
		12	pair	Stock-Cards	0	12	0	0
		1.5	dozen	Hand Cards	0	6	0	0

Merchant name	Origin	Qty	Unit	Commodity	£	s.	d.	f.

The Mawdelen of Youghal, Darby Gryffyn master, Exiting, 21st March 1551

Merchant name	Origin	Qty	Unit	Commodity	£	s.	d.	f.
Darby Gryffyn	Ind	6	lb	Saffron	3	0	0	0
		60	lb	Battery	0	20	0	0
		0.5	C	Madder	0	5	0	0
		1	piece	Pans (10lb)	0	3	4	0

The Mawdelen of Viana do Castelo, Martin Alvus master, Exiting, 22nd March 1551

Merchant name	Origin	Qty	Unit	Commodity	£	s.	d.	f.
Martin Alvus	Alien	3	piece	Manchester Cotton *Cloth*	0	30	0	0
		4	piece	Welsh *Cloth*	4	0	0	0
	1 hogshead & 3	bag	Lists	0	40	0	0
		4	piece	Northern Cotton *Cloth*	0	16	8	0
		7.66	piece	Cloth of Assize	0	0	0	0

The Sant *Christ*ofer of Viana do Castelo, Sebastian Gonsaluus master, Exiting, 23rd March 1551

Merchant name	Origin	Qty	Unit	Commodity	£	s.	d.	f.
Sebastian Gonsalnus & assoc.	Alien	1.5	piece	Cloth of Assize	0	0	0	0
		20	yard	Check *Cloth*	0	6	8	0
		0.75	piece	Welsh *Cloth*	0	15	0	0

The Jesus of Bideford, Robert Byatt, Exiting, *23rd March 1551*

Merchant name	Origin	Qty	Unit	Commodity	£	s.	d.	f.
Henry Sandiford & assoc.	Ind	22.5	piece	Cloth of Assize	0	0	0	0
		46	piece	Manchester Cotton *Cloth*	23	0	0	0
		95	piece	Northern Cotton *Cloth*	19	15	10	0

The Mighell of Crozon, John de Pres master, Entering, *23rd March 1551*

Merchant name	Origin	Qty	Unit	Commodity	£	s.	d.	f.
William Carre & assoc.	Ind	27	tun	Wine	0	0	0	0
		45	tun	Wine, Corrupt	67	10	0	0
John de Pres	Alien	30	piece	Poldavis *Cloth*	15	0	0	0

The Sonday of Bristol, William Kellie master, Exiting, 26th March 1551

Merchant name	Origin	Qty	Unit	Commodity	£	s.	d.	f.
Walter Coppyng*er*	Ind	4	lb	Silk, *Worked*	0	53	4	0
		4	lb	Saffron	0	40	0	0
		1.5	C	Battery	3	0	0	0
		2	C	Hops	0	20	0	0
		3	unknown	Flax	0	40	0	0
		0.5	C	Alum	0	6	8	0
		16	lb	Cumin	0	0	20	0
		3	gross	Knives	0	20	0	0
		18	gross	Points	0	18	0	0
		2	gross	Lacquor	0	3	4	0
		1	dozen	Skins, Golden	0	4	2	0
		1	burden	Steel	0	0	20	0
		1	bolt	Thread	0	0	15	0

Merchant name	Origin	Qty	Unit	Commodity	£	s.	d.	f.
		2	lb	Thread	0	0	20	0
		6	dozen	Knives, Bumbard	0	10	0	0
		15	dozen	Spert	0	3	4	0
		2	dozen	Girdles, Caddis	0	0	10	0
		0.5	piece	Cloth of Assize	0	0	0	0
Henry Verdon	Ind	2	lb	Silk, *Worked*	0	26	8	0
		2	gross	Knives	0	13	4	0
		1	burden	Steel	0	0	30	0
		1	dozen	Knives, in Pairs	0	0	20	0
		2	gross	Lacquor	0	3	4	0
		1	C	Flax	0	13	4	0
		3	stone	Hops	0	5	0	0
		1	C	Battery	2	0	0	0
		2	dozen	Alum	0	2	6	0
Edmund Sacheford	Ind	1	C	Battery	2	0	0	0
		4	lb	Silk, *Worked*	0	53	4	0
		4	stone	Orchil	0	6	8	0
		1	dozen	Knives, in Pairs	0	0	20	0
		24	lb	Flax	0	2	0	0
		1	gross	Knives	0	6	8	0
Christopher Lumard	Ind	4	lb	Silk, *Worked*	0	53	4	0
		4	lb	Saffron	0	40	0	0
		3	gross	Knives	0	20	0	0
		12	dozen	Knives, in Pairs	0	20	0	0
		4	dozen	Knives, in Pairs	0	6	8	0
		6	bolt	Thread	0	7	6	0
		1	dozen	Caps	0	10	0	0
		3	burden	Steel	0	5	0	0
		1	C	Flax	0	13	4	0
		3	gross	Lacquor	0	5	0	0
		20	gross	Points	0	20	0	0
William Chester & assoc.	Ind	4	lb	Saffron	2	0	0	0
		6	gross	Knives	0	40	0	0
		1	dozen	Playing Cards	0	2	6	0
		10	gross	Points	0	10	0	0
		1	bolt	Thread	0	0	15	0
		6	dozen	Spert	0	2	6	0
		2	dozen	Girdles	0	0	8	0
		10	lb	Cumin	0	2	1	0
		1	dozen	Skins, Golden	0	4	2	0
		2	lb	Silk, *Worked*	0	26	8	0
		2	lb	Saffron	0	20	0	0
		7.75	piece	Cloth of Assize	0	0	0	0

The Trynyte of Bristol, James Williams master, Entering, 26th March 1551

Merchant name	Origin	Qty	Unit	Commodity	£	s.	d.	f.
Hugh Draper	Ind	13	punches	Prunes & Packet Thread & Habedashery Ware	196	8	0	0

Merchant name	Origin	Qty	Unit	Commodity	£	s.	d.	f.

The St Sebastian of Vila do Conde, Lewis Fornando master, Exiting, 26th March 1551

Lewis Fornando	Alien	3.33	piece	Cloth of Assize	0	0	0	0
		4	piece	Manchester Cotton *Cloth*	2	0	0	0
		2	piece	Cloth of Assize, Northern Dozen	0	26	8	0

The Trinite of Bristol, James Williams master, Exiting, 26th March 1551

| John Flemynge | Ind | 14 | piece | Cloth of Assize | 0 | 0 | 0 | 0 |

The St John of Genoa, Henry de Maryndrega master, Exiting, 27th March 1551

John Richards & assoc.	Ind	23	fother	Lead	92	0	0	0
		30	piece	Northern cotton *Cloth*	6	5	0	0
		36	piece	Manchester Cotton *Cloth*	18	0	0	0
		51.25	piece	Cloth of Assize	0	0	0	0

The Onyon of *Laverte*, Bernard Worton master, Exiting, 22nd February 1551[3]

| John de La Rocketa | Alien | 9 | piece | Cloth of Assize | 0 | 0 | 0 | 0 |

***The Christ*ofer of Chepstow, Richard Jene master, Entering, 27th March 1551**

| Peter de Alsara | Alien | 2.5 | ton | Walnuts | 0 | 22 | 6 | 0 |

The John of Genoa, Henry de Maryndrega master, Exiting, 1st April 1551

| John Whyte & assoc. | Ind | 12 | piece | Cloth of Assize | 0 | 0 | 0 | 0 |
| John Richards | Ind | 20 | piece | Northern cotton *Cloth* | 4 | 3 | 4 | 0 |

The Mawdelyn of Viana do Castelo, Martin Alvys master, Exiting, 1st April 1551

| John Alsonne & Deys | Alien | 1.5 | piece | Cloth of Assize | 0 | 0 | 0 | 0 |

The Trynyte of Fécamp, Jovands de Sanse master, Exiting, 1st April 1551

Jovands de Sanse	Alien	1	piece	Cloth of Assize	0	0	0	0
		2	piece	Bristol Frieze *Cloth*	0	26	8	0
		20	yard	Bristol Frieze *Cloth*	0	10	0	0

The Michill of Crozon, John de Pres master, Exiting, 2nd April 1551

John *de Pres*	Alien	14	piece	Bristol Frieze *Cloth*	9	6	8	0
		4	piece	Cloth of Assize, Northern Dozen	0	53	4	0
		1	piece	Cloth of Assize, Dozen Strait	0	0	0	0

The Mare Jamys of Bristol, David Gyllam master, Exiting, 3rd April 1551

| William Barett | Ind | 5.5 | piece | Cloth of Assize | 0 | 0 | 0 | 0 |
| John Welsh | Ind | 8 | C | Hops | 4 | 0 | 0 | 0 |

3 A recording error or perhaps this entry was entered at a later date.

Merchant name	Origin	Qty	Unit	Commodity	£	s.	d.	f.

The Kathryn of Penmarch, John le Clee master, Entering, 6th April 1551

Martin Afylde & Caeson	Alien	88	tun	Wine	0	0	0	0
		10	tun	Wine, Corrupt	15	0	0	0

The Sent Sebastián of Vila do Conde, Lewis Farnando master, Exiting, 6th April 1551

John Pyssye & assoc.	Alien	9	piece	Cloth of Assize	0	0	0	0
		1	piece	Bristol Frieze *Cloth*	0	13	4	0
William Barret & Souche	Ind	5	piece	Cloth of Assize	0	0	0	0

The Trynyte of Penmarch, Evan Gelley master, Entering, 6th April 1551

John Wells & assoc.	Ind	57.5	tun	Wine	0	0	0	0
		3	tun	Wine, Corrupt	4	10	0	0
		1	pipe	Rosin	0	13	4	0

The Jenett of *Lettewry*, Gillam de Oderny master, Entering, 6th April 1551

John Wells & assoc.	Ind	24.5	tun	Wine	0	0	0	0
		2.75	tun	Wine, Corrupt	0	77	6	0
		1	pipe	Rosin	0	13	4	0
		16	piece	Poldavis *Cloth*	8	0	0	0
Robert Nashe & assoc.	Ind	31	tun	Wine	0	0	0	0
		2	tun	Wine, Corrupt	0	60	0	0

The Nicho*las* of Waterford, Nicholas Strannge master, Entering, 6th April 1551

John Swan & assoc.	Ind	34.25	tun	Wine	0	0	0	0
		4	tun	Wine, Corrupt	6	0	0	0
		3.5	ton	Rosin & Pitch	4	13	4	0

The Lyvon of Penmarch, Bryon Tolond master, Entering, 7th April 1551

George Shawe & Bartholome	Ind	47.5	tun	Wine	0	0	0	0
		3	tun	Wine, Corrupt	4	10	0	0
		5.5	tun	Oil, Train	22	0	0	0
		15	C	Feathers	7	10	0	0

The Mary of Penmarch, Harvy de Drewe master, Entering, 7th April 1551

Jenott Doyorean	Alien	80	tun	Wine	0	0	0	0
		2	tun	Vinegar	4	0	0	0

The Trynyte of Bristol, James Wyll*i*ams master, Exiting, 8th April 1551

John Arthure	Ind	2	piece	Cloth of Assize, Dozen Strait	0	0	0	0
		4	dozen	Glass, Looking	0	0	12	0
		2	gross	Points	0	2	0	0

Merchant name	Origin	Qty	Unit	Commodity	£	s.	d.	f.
		1	gross	Lacquor	0	0	20	0
		2	dozen	Books, Primers	0	2	6	0
		6	piece	Caps	0	5	0	0
Thomas Marton & Welshe	Ind	14	piece	Bristol Frieze *Cloth*	9	6	8	0
		1.5	piece	Cloth of Assize	0	0	0	0

The Santa Clare of Biscay, John de Morot master, Exiting, *8th April 1551*

Merchant name	Origin	Qty	Unit	Commodity	£	s.	d.	f.
Peter de Alsa	Alien	0.125	piece	Cloth of Assize	0	0	0	0
		2.5	piece	Welsh *Cloth*	0	50	0	0
		2.5	piece	Manchester Cotton *Cloth*	0	25	0	0

The Mare John of Bideford, John Worthe master, Entering, 9th April 1551

Merchant name	Origin	Qty	Unit	Commodity	£	s.	d.	f.
Francis Codryngton & assoc.	Ind	37	ton	Iron	92	10	0	0
		4	M	Oranges	0	13	4	0

The Heyende of Bristol, John Corbett master, Entering, 9th April 1551

Merchant name	Origin	Qty	Unit	Commodity	£	s.	d.	f.
Miles Wylton & assoc.	Ind	15.25	tun	Oil, Olive	61	0	0	0
		1	tun	Wine, Corrupt	0	30	0	0
		1	tun	Wine	0	0	0	0
John Pryn & assoc.	Ind	2.25	tun	Wine, Corrupt	0	67	6	0
		5	tun	Oil, Olive	20	0	0	0
		2	tun	Wine	0	0	0	0
William Cox & assoc.	Ind	1	pipe	Wine	0	0	0	0
		7.25	tun	Oil, Olive	29	0	0	0
		1	tun	Wine, Corrupt	0	30	0	0
John Channceler & assoc.	Ind	4.25	tun	Oil, Olive	17	0	0	0
		4.25	tun	Wine, Corrupt	6	7	6	0
Roland Wilbra & assoc.	Ind	3.5	tun	Oil, Olive	14	0	0	0
		21	C	Orchil	14	0	0	0
		1	tun	Wine	0	0	0	0
Thomas Wyllyng	Ind	0.25	tun	Oil, Olive	0	20	0	0
		12	dozen	Hats	8	0	0	0
		30	pair	Buskins, Spanish	0	60	0	0
		20	dozen	Gloves, Pairs	0	40	0	0

The Santa Crews of Viana do Castelo, Roderigo Alvera master, Entering, 10th April 1551

Merchant name	Origin	Qty	Unit	Commodity	£	s.	d.	f.
Roderigo Alveris	Alien	50	M	Oranges	8	6	8	0

The George of Wexford, Richard Bossher master, Entering, *10th April 1551*

Merchant name	Origin	Qty	Unit	Commodity	£	s.	d.	f.
Richard *Bossher*	Ind	5	C	Skins, Sheep	0	50	0	0
		0.5	C	Skins, Lamb	0	3	4	0
		3	piece	Mantles	0	10	0	0

Merchant name	Origin	Qty	Unit	Commodity	£	s.	d.	f.

The Nicholas of Bristol, John Welshe master, Entering, _10th April 1551_

Merchant name	Origin	Qty	Unit	Commodity	£	s.	d.	f.
John Shrevye & assoc.	Ind	14.5	tun	Wine	0	0	0	0

The Prymrose of Bristol, Thomas Warne master, Exiting, _10th April 1551_

Merchant name	Origin	Qty	Unit	Commodity	£	s.	d.	f.
Lewis Robyns & Watley	Ind	120	piece	Manchester Cotton _Cloth_	60	0	0	0
		18	piece	Bristol Frieze _Cloth_	12	0	0	0
		18	piece	Worsted _Cloth_	0	75	0	0
Robert Yonge	Ind	18	piece	Cloth of Assize, Strait Dyed with Grains	0	0	0	0
		3	piece	Cloth of Assize	0	0	0	0

The Savyour of Bristol, Florence Typton master, Entering, _12th April 1551_

Merchant name	Origin	Qty	Unit	Commodity	£	s.	d.	f.
John Smyth & assoc.	Ind	13.25	tun	Oil, Olive	53	0	0	0
		26.25	C	Soap	13	2	6	0
		5	tun	Wine, Corrupt	7	10	0	0
		30	C	Orchil	20	0	0	0
		2.5	tun	Wine	0	0	0	0
William Tyndale & assoc.	Ind	10.5	tun	Wine	0	0	0	0
		14.5	tun	Oil, Olive	58	0	0	0
		11.5	tun	Wine, Corrupt	17	5	0	0
		1	seron	Soap	0	12	6	0
		1	C	Marmalade	0	13	4	0
James Chester & assoc.	Ind	18	tun	Oil, Olive	72	0	0	0
		5	tun	Wine, Corrupt	7	10	0	0
		2	tun	Wine	0	0	0	0
George Knyght & assoc.	Ind	7	tun	Oil, Olive	28	0	0	0
		4	tun	Wine, Corrupt	6	0	0	0
		18.75	C	Soap	9	7	6	0
		6.25	tun	Wine	0	0	0	0
George Snygge & assoc.	Ind	8.25	tun	Oil, Olive	33	0	0	0
		22.5	C	Soap	11	5	0	0
		1	tun	Wine, Corrupt	0	30	0	0
		2	chest	Sugar	4	0	0	0
		15	C	Alum	10	0	0	0
		8.25	tun	Wine	0	0	0	f.
William Spratt & assoc.	Ind	2.25	tun	Oil, Olive	9	0	0	0
		3.75	C	Soap	0	37	6	0
Thomas Hickes & assoc.	Ind	2.75	tun	Oil, Olive	11	0	0	0
		2.25	tun	Wine, Corrupt	0	67	6	0
		25	C	Soap	12	10	0	0
		16.5	C	Aniseed	11	0	0	0
Edward Grannt & assoc.	Ind	6.75	tun	Wine	0	0	0	0

Merchant name	Origin	Qty	Unit	Commodity	£	s.	d.	f.

The Savyour of Errenteria, Julian de Gosoweta master, Entering, 12th April 1551

Merchant name	Origin	Qty	Unit	Commodity	£	s.	d.	f.
William Carre & assoc.	Ind	179	ton	Iron	447	10	0	0
		2	quintal	Iron	0	30	20	0
		13.5	tun	Oil, Train	54	0	0	0
Julian de Gosoweta & assoc.	Alien	69	ton	Iron	172	10	0	0
		4	quintal	Iron	0	20	0	0
		0.75	tun	Oil, Train	0	60	0	0
		9	dozen	Serches	0	37	6	0
		4	M	Canes	0	13	4	0

The Mary of Pouldavid, Gillam Glewdewyke master, Entering, 15th April 1551

Merchant name	Origin	Qty	Unit	Commodity	£	s.	d.	f.
Arnold de Lalane	Alien	30	tun	Wine	0	0	0	0
Gillam Glewdewyke	Alien	1.5	piece	Poldavis *Cloth*	0	15	0	0
		1	C	Canvas *Cloth*	0	26	8	0

The George of Wexford, Richard Bossher master, Exiting, 17th April 1551

Merchant name	Origin	Qty	Unit	Commodity	£	s.	d.	f.
Richard *Bossher*	Ind	1.5	C	Hops	0	15	0	0
		1	C	Battery	0	33	4	0
		1	lb	Silk, *Worked*	0	13	4	0
		1.5	gross	Knives	0	10	0	0
		12	gross	Points	0	12	0	0

The Mary of Milford Haven, Richard Alyn master, Entering, 18th April 1551

Merchant name	Origin	Qty	Unit	Commodity	£	s.	d.	f.
James Barett & Fowler	Ind	2	tun	Wine	0	0	0	0
		0.25	tun	Vinegar	0	10	0	0

The Margarett of Longney, Thomas Pyesse master, Entering, *18th April 1551*

Merchant name	Origin	Qty	Unit	Commodity	£	s.	d.	f.
Richard Awyntyll	Ind	2.5	ton	Salt	0	25	0	0

The Lyvon of Penmarch, Bryon Tolond master, Exiting, *18th April 1551*

Merchant name	Origin	Qty	Unit	Commodity	£	s.	d.	f.
Bryon Tolond & assoc.	Alien	13	C	Wax	26	0	0	0
		50	piece	Manchester Cotton *Cloth*	25	0	0	0
		110	piece	Cloth of Assize, Northern Dozen	73	6	8	0

The Hartt of Bristol, William Moorse master, Exiting, 21st April 1551

Merchant name	Origin	Qty	Unit	Commodity	£	s.	d.	f.
George Wynter	Ind	17	piece	Cloth of Assize	0	0	0	0

The Nicholas of Waterford, Nicholas Strannge master, Exiting, 22nd April 1551

Merchant name	Origin	Qty	Unit	Commodity	£	s.	d.	f.
Richard Uxley	Ind	76	lb	Saffron	38	0	0	0
Nicholas Strannge & assoc.	Ind	2.5	piece	Cloth of Assize	0	0	0	0

Merchant name	Origin	Qty	Unit	Commodity	£	s.	d.	f.
		1	pipe	Iron	0	25	0	0
		16	lb	Saffron	8	0	0	0
		30	C	Orchil	20	0	0	0
		1	piece	Worsted Cloth	0	4	2	0

The Anthony of Tewkesbury, John Butler master, Entering, 22nd April 1551

Merchant name	Origin	Qty	Unit	Commodity	£	s.	d.	f.
John *Butler*	Ind	6	tun	Wine	0	0	0	0

The Trynyte of Bideford, Walter Davys master, Exiting, 23rd April 1551

Merchant name	Origin	Qty	Unit	Commodity	£	s.	d.	f.
John Northall & Cappys	Ind	4.5	piece	Cloth of Assize	0	0	0	0
		40	lb	Saffron	20	0	0	0
		60	lb	Silk, *Worked*	40	0	0	0
		10	kippe	Skins, Golden	8	6	8	0
		15	tun	Wine, Corrupt	22	10	0	0
		2	C	Madder	0	13	4	0
		2	C	Alum	0	26	8	0
		10	ton	Salt	0	100	0	0
		1	C	Aniseed	0	13	4	0
Manus Quegley	Ind	14	lb	Aniseed	0	0	20	0
		1	dozen	Playing Cards	0	0	15	0
		6	dozen	Glass, Looking	0	2	0	0
		4	gross	Points	0	4	0	0
		4	dozen	Purses	0	0	16	0
		0.5	gross	Combs	0	0	16	0
		0.5	lb	Saffron	0	5	0	0

The Andrew of Newport, Andrew Apryes master, Exiting, *23rd April 1551*

Merchant name	Origin	Qty	Unit	Commodity	£	s.	d.	f.
John Northall & Cappys	Ind	2.5	piece	Cloth of Assize	0	0	0	0
		40	lb	Silk, *Worked*	26	13	8	0
		20	lb	Saffron	10	0	0	0
		3	tun	Wine, Corrupt	4	10	0	0
		2	C	Alum	0	26	8	0
		2	C	Madder	0	13	4	0
		1	C	Aniseed	0	13	4	0
		10	kippe	Skins, Golden	8	6	8	0

The Salvadur of Errenteria, Julian *de* Gosoweta master, Exiting, 29th April 1551

Merchant name	Origin	Qty	Unit	Commodity	£	s.	d.	f.
Andrew de Seron & assoc.	Alien	14.5	piece	Cloth of Assize	0	0	0	0
		4	piece	Welsh *Cloth*	4	0	0	0
		24	C	Silk, *Worked*	48	0	0	0
		1	piece	Cloth of Assize	0	0	0	0
William Tyndale	Ind	44	piece	Cloth of Assize	0	0	0	0
		20	piece	Welsh *Cloth*, Dozen Strait	4	3	4	0
John Wells	Ind	22	piece	Cloth of Assize	0	0	0	0
		100	piece	Northern Cotton *Cloth*	20	16	8	0

Merchant name	Origin	Qty	Unit	Commodity	£	s.	d.	f.
		20	piece	Manchester Cotton *Cloth*	10	0	0	0
John Pryn & assoc.	Ind	33.5	piece	Cloth of Assize	0	0	0	0
Nicholas Ware & assoc.	Ind	40	piece	Northern Cotton *Cloth*	8	6	8	0
		32.5	piece	Cloth of Assize	0	0	0	0
William Flecher & assoc.	Ind	51.25	piece	Cloth of Assize	0	0	0	0
		15	piece	Welsh *Cloth*	15	0	0	0
		5	C	Wax	10	0	0	0
George Snygge & assoc.	Ind	25	piece	Northern Cotton *Cloth*	0	104	2	0
		9	piece	Welsh *Cloth*	9	0	0	0
		7	fother	Lead	28	0	0	0
		36	piece	Cloth of Assize	0	0	0	0
John Smyth & assoc.	Ind	49.5	piece	Cloth of Assize	0	0	0	0
		13	piece	Welsh *Cloth*	13	0	0	0
William Carri & assoc.	Ind	180.5	piece	Cloth of Assize	0	0	0	0
		1	C	Wax	0	40	0	0

The Kathryn of Penmarch, John de Clerke master, Entering,[4] 2nd May 1551

Merchant name	Origin	Qty	Unit	Commodity	£	s.	d.	f.
John *de Clerke*	Alien	7.08	piece	Cloth of Assize	0	0	0	0
		1.5	piece	Bristol Frieze *Cloth*	0	20	0	0
Alex*ander* Caes*e*	Ind	1.66	piece	Cloth of Assize	0	0	0	0

The Jenett of *Lottewre*, Gillam de Oderne master, Exiting, *2nd May 1551*

Merchant name	Origin	Qty	Unit	Commodity	£	s.	d.	f.
Gill*am* de Oderne	Alien	2.66	piece	Cloth of Assize	0	0	0	0
		8	piece	Bristol Frieze *Cloth*	0	106	8	0

The Mar*y* of Penmarch, Harvy Le Drew master, Exiting, *2nd May 1551*

Merchant name	Origin	Qty	Unit	Commodity	£	s.	d.	f.
Harvy le Drew	Alien	4.16	piece	Cloth of Assize	0	0	0	0
		40	yard	Irish Frieze *Cloth*	0	13	4	0

The Mary John of Tenby, William Adams master, Entering, 4th May 1551

Merchant name	Origin	Qty	Unit	Commodity	£	s.	d.	f.
Thomas Chester	Ind	2	tun	Wine	0	0	0	0

The S*anta* Crucke of Viana do Castelo, Roderigo Alvera master, Exiting, 4th May 1551

Merchant name	Origin	Qty	Unit	Commodity	£	s.	d.	f.
Roderigo Alvera & Molcher	Alien	26	piece	Manchester Cotton *Cloth*	13	0	0	0

The Blacke Pynnes of Tenby, Philip Gybbons master, Entering, *4th May 1551*

Merchant name	Origin	Qty	Unit	Commodity	£	s.	d.	f.
George Bear*ie*	Ind	3	tun	Wine	0	0	0	0

4 This is probably an error as the cargo suggests that this ship was exiting and not entering the port.

Merchant name	Origin	Qty	Unit	Commodity	£	s.	d.	f.
The Mary John of Bideford, John Lake master, Exiting, 6th May 1551								
Thomas Teson	Ind	18	piece	Manchester Cotton *Cloth*	9	0	0	0
		42	piece	Northern Cotton *Cloth*	8	15	0	0
Thomas Shipman & assoc.	Ind	30.5	piece	Cloth of Assize	0	0	0	0
The George of Chepstow, John Hygons master, Entering, 6th May 1551								
John Pyssye	Ind	1	tun	Wine	0	0	0	0
The Mary of Waterford, Thomas Rowgth master, Entering, 6th May 1551								
Nicholas Harrys	Ind	1.5	C	Check *Cloth*	0	60	0	0
		3.5	C	Skins, Sheep	0	35	0	0
		8	C	Skins, Lamb	0	53	4	0
		4	C	Skins, Kid	0	20	0	0
		12	stone	Wool, Flocks	0	5	0	0
		5	stone	Wool, Irish	0	13	4	0
John Tomyn	Ind	2	C	Skins, Sheep	0	20	0	0
		3	C	Skins, Lamb	0	20	0	0
		2	C	Skins, Kid	0	10	0	0
		40	lb	Ceruse	0	3	4	0
Nicholas Baylley	Ind	10	C	Skins, Sheep	0	100	0	0
		2	C	Skins, Lamb	0	13	4	0
		1	C	Skins, Kid	0	5	0	0
		12	piece	Mantles	0	40	0	0
		40	yard	*Irish* Frieze *Cloth*	0	13	4	0
		0.25	tun	Vinegar	0	10	0	0
Nicholas Shee	Ind	2	C	*Irish* Frieze *Cloth*	4	0	0	0
		30	piece	Mantles	0	100	0	0
James Tyrrell & Shurlocke	Ind	1	C	Skins, Sheep	0	10	0	0
		6	piece	Mantles	0	20	0	0
		1	stone	Wool, Irish	0	2	8	0
Richard Serche & assoc.	Ind	20	burden	Fish, Salted	4	3	4	0
		4	C	Check *Cloth*	8	0	0	0
		2	dozen	Skins, Lamb	0	0	20	0
The Mary of Pouldavid, Gillam Glewdewyke master, Exiting, 8th May 1551								
Gillam Glewdewyke	Alien	2.5	piece	Cloth of Assize	0	0	0	0
		3.5	piece	Bristol Frieze *Cloth*	0	46	8	0
		50	yard	Irish Frieze *Cloth*	0	16	8	0
		4	piece	Welsh *Cloth*	4	0	0	0
Alexander Cays	Ind	10	piece	Cloth of Assize, Strait	0	0	0	0
The George & The Peter of Roosendaal, Simon Cornelyson master, Exiting, 8th May 1551								
Thomas Alyn	Ind	8.5	M	Skins, Lamb	28	6	8	0
		0.75	C	Skins, Kid	0	3	9	0

Merchant name	Origin	Qty	Unit	Commodity	£	s.	d.	f.
Cornell Daimker	Alien	164	fother	Lead	656	0	0	0
Henry Mannyng	Ind	12	piece	Cloth of Assize	0	0	0	0
		3	piece	Organ Pipes, Old	0	40	0	0

The Antony of Carmarthen, Thomas Hankey master, Entering, *8th May 1551*

David Morris & Gryffithe	Ind	7.75	tun	Wine	0	0	0	0

The Trynyte of Penmarch, Evan Geley master, Exiting, 9th May 1551

Evan Geley	Alien	1	piece	Frieze *Cloth*	0	20	0	0
		3	piece	Mantles	0	10	0	0
		9	hogshead	Lime	0	5	8	0

The Trynyte of Chepstow, Richard Watkyns master, Entering, *9th May 1551*

William Jonas	Ind	2.5	tun	Wine	0	0	0	0

The Nicho*las* of Carmarthen, William Walker master, Entering, *9th May 1551*

William Walter	Ind	7.5	tun	Wine	0	0	0	0

The Sonday of Bristol, William Gelly master, Entering, 12th May 1551

Nicholas Welshe	Ind	21	C	Skins, Lamb	7	0	0	0
		16	C	Skins, Kid	4	0	0	0
		27	piece	Skins, Marten	0	27	0	0
		6.5	C	Skins, Sheep	0	65	0	0
		7	piece	Mantles	0	23	4	0
		6	piece	Skins, Deer	0	2	0	0
John Sexton	Ind	22	C	Skins, Lamb	7	6	8	0
		30	yard	Check *Cloth*	0	10	0	0
		12	C	Skins, Sheep	6	0	0	0
		4	C	Skins, Kid	0	20	0	0
		24	piece	Skins, Fox	0	4	0	0
		5	stone	Wool, Flocks	0	2	1	0
		40	piece	Skins, Marten	0	40	0	0
		12	piece	Skins, Otter	0	5	0	0
		4	lb	Spermaceti	0	6	5	0
Stephan Gromewell	Ind	20	C	Skins, Lamb	6	13	4	0
		1.5	C	Skins, Kid	0	7	6	0
		4	piece	Skins, Fox	0	0	8	0
		3	piece	Skins, Otter	0	0	15	0
		6	C	Skins, Sheep	0	60	0	0
		6	piece	Skins, Deer	0	2	0	0
William Medy	Ind	8	C	Skins, Lamb	0	53	5	0
		97	piece	Skins, Marten	4	17	0	0
		1	piece	Mantles	0	3	4	0
Edmund Jones	Ind	4	C	Skins, Sheep	0	40	0	0
		13	stone	Wool, Irish	0	34	8	0
		1	piece	Mantles	0	3	4	0

Merchant name	Origin	Qty	Unit	Commodity	£	s.	d.	f.
		2	stone	Wool, Flocks	o	o	10	o
		12	piece	Skins, Marten	o	12	o	o
		80	yard	Check *Cloth*	o	26	8	o
William Chester	Ind	4.5	C	Skins, Sheep	o	45	o	o
		2	dicker	Skins, Deer	o	6	8	o
		1	tun	Wine	o	o	o	o
Arthur Richards & Brodwey	Ind	12	piece	Skins, Deer	o	4	o	o
		1.5	C	Skins, Sheep	o	15	o	o
		1.5	C	Skins, Lamb	o	10	o	o
		12	lb	Wax	o	4	o	o

The Salvador*e* of Errenteria, Julian *de* Gosoweta master, Exiting, 15th May 1551

John Cutt & assoc.	Ind	58.66	piece	Cloth of Assize	o	o	o	o
		12	piece	Welsh *Cloth*	12	o	o	o
		1	C	Wax	o	40	o	o
Robert Southall & assoc.	Ind	2	piece	Bristol Frieze *Cloth*	o	26	8	o
		3	piece	Dunster *Cloth*	o	30	o	o
		13	piece	Northern Cotton *Cloth*	o	54	2	o
		2	C	Wax	4	o	o	o
		21.5	piece	Cloth of Assize	o	o	o	o

The Doe of Bristol, Thomas Webb master, Entering, 15th May 1551

Francis Codryngton	Ind	36	tun	Wine	o	o	o	o
		1	ton	Rosin	o	40	o	o
		19.75	tun	Vinegar	39	10	o	o

The Margarett of Elmore, John Snowe master, Entering, *15th May 1551*

Richard Wyntyll	Ind	1.5	C	Salt	o	15	o	o

The Jenett of Penmarch, Alyn Dycke master, Entering, 22nd May 1551

Robert Yonge & assoc.	Ind	81	tun	Wine	o	o	o	o
		0.75	ton	Rosin	o	20	o	o
		3	tun	Vinegar	6	o	o	o

The Mar*y* of Penmarch, John de Sala master, Entering, *22nd May 1551*

Martin Afylde & assoc.	Ind	45.5	tun	Wine	o	o	o	o
		9.5	tun	Vinegar	19	o	o	o

The Nicho*las* of Bristol, Nicholas Gry*ndam* master, Exiting, *22nd May 1551*

Nicholas Kelley	Ind	1	piece	Bristol Frieze *Cloth*	o	13	4	o
		12	piece	Mantles	o	40	o	o
		0.5	C	*Irish* Frieze Cloth	o	20	o	o

Merchant name	Origin	Qty	Unit	Commodity	£	s.	d.	f.
The Margarett of Bristol, Ralph Bronne master, Exiting, *22nd May 1551*								
John Stone & Barett	Ind	8.75	piece	Cloth of Assize	0	0	0	0
		17	piece	Northern Cotton *Cloth*	0	70	10	0
William Tyndale	Ind	120	dozen	Skins, Calf	20	0	0	0
		8	dicker	Hides, Tanned	0	0	0	0
		8	piece	Cloth of Assize	0	0	0	0
John Keyen & assoc.	Ind	13.83	piece	Cloth of Assize	0	0	0	0
The Jenett & The Mary of Penmarch, Alan Dycke master, Exiting, 25th May 1551								
Alan Dycke	Alien	6	piece	Cloth of Assize	0	0	0	0
		2	piece	Bristol Frieze *Cloth*	0	26	8	0
		2	fother	Lead	8	0	0	0
The Mary of Waterford, Thomas Rougth master, Exiting, 25th May 1551								
Nicholas Harris	Ind	2	C	Hops	0	20	0	0
		4	dozen	Knives, in Pairs	0	6	8	0
		2	dozen	Playing Cards	0	2	6	0
		12	gross	Points	0	12	0	0
		6	pair	Stock-Cards	0	6	0	0
		1	dozen	Soap	0	0	15	0
John Tomyn	Ind	1	piece	Cloth of Assize, Dozen Strait	0	0	0	0
		1	C	Battery	0	40	0	0
		0.5	C	Hops	0	5	0	0
		2	dozen	Playing Cards	0	2	6	0
		2	dozen	Knives, in Pairs	0	3	4	0
		2	dozen	Soap	0	2	6	0
		6	stone	Orchil	0	10	0	0
		0.5	gross	Knives	0	3	4	0
		2	gross	Points	0	2	0	0
		3	dozen	Combs	0	0	15	0
The Julyan of New Ross, Richard Dofe master, Exiting, 30th May 1551								
Nicholas Cantwell	Ind	11	lb	Silk, *Worked*	7	6	8	0
		2	lb	Saffron	0	20	0	0
		3	lb	Cloves & Cinnamon	0	7	6	0
		6	dozen	Knives, in Pairs	0	10	0	0
		2.5	lb	Verdigris	0	0	12	2
		5	dozen	Combs	0	3	4	0
		2	clout	Needles	0	0	20	0
		1	lb	Hedlack	0	0	12	0
		1	lb	Girdles, Check	0	0	12	0
		4	C	Hooks, Fish	0	0	10	0
		1	C	Nail Blades	0	0	12	0
		6	dozen	Girdles	0	2	6	0
		1	gross	Buttons	0	2	6	0
		12	pair	Stock-Cards	0	12	0	0
		1	dozen	Wool-Cards	0	4	0	0
		0.5	C	Alum	0	6	8	0

Merchant name	Origin	Qty	Unit	Commodity	£	s.	d.	f.
		1	gross	Knives	0	6	8	0
		6	piece	Knives, in Pairs	0	0	10	0
		4	dozen	Knives	0	5	0	0
		12	gross	Points	0	12	0	0
		1	gross	Lacquor	0	0	20	0
		1	bolt	Thread	0	0	15	0

The Sonday of Bristol, William Kelley master, Exiting, *30th May 1551*

Thomas Gryffyth	Ind	8	pair	Milstones	8	0	0	0
		12	pair	Quern Stones	0	10	0	0

The Jhesus of Barnstaple, John Beapull master, Entering, 2nd June 1551

Martin Afylde & assoc.	Alien	40	tun	Wine	0	0	0	0
		10	tun	Vinegar	20	0	0	0

The George of Chepstow, John Higgons master, Entering, 3rd June 1551

John Bedyll & assoc.	Ind	7.5	tun	Wine	0	0	0	0

The Mary Gray of Tenby, John Glone master, Entering, *3rd June 1551*

Richard Whyte	Ind	4	M	Oranges	0	13	4	0

The Marri Palmer of Tenby, Philip Thomas master, Entering, *3rd June 1551*

Thomas Parett	Ind	2	tun	Wine	0	0	0	0
		2	chest	Sugar	4	0	0	0

The Julyan of Bristol, Thomas Martyn master, Entering, 4th June 1551

Francis Codryngton	Ind	68	ton	Iron	170	0	0	0
		8	tun	Oil, Train	32	0	0	0
		4.5	tun	Wine	0	0	0	0

The Paull of Bristol, Thomas Whyte master, Entering, *4th June 1551*

William Tyndale & assoc.	Ind	72	ton	Iron	180	0	0	0
		21.5	tun	Oil, Train	86	0	0	0
		1.75	tun	Wine	0	0	0	0
John Debara & Perigri	Alien	535	dozen	Skins, Budge	105	16	8	0
		100	dozen	Skins, Budge Rough	8	16	8	0
		3	piece	Skins, Genet	0	3	4	0

The Christofer of Gdańsk, Thomas Tyme master, Entering, 5th June 1551

Arnold Van Holde & assoc.	Hansard	12	pack	Flax	48	0	0	0

Merchant name	Origin	Qty	Unit	Commodity	£	s.	d.	f.
		41	last	Pitch & Tar	41	0	0	0
		7.5	C	Wainscot	15	0	0	0
		2.5	great hundred	Wood, Clapholt	10	0	0	0
		19	piece	Mast	19	0	0	0
		9	piece	Sail Yards	4	10	0	0
		60	piece	Wood, Deal	0	100	0	0
		14	nest	Chests	7	0	0	0
		2	last	Rye Meal	0	33	4	0

The Mare Jamys of Bristol, David Gyllam master, Entering, 5th June 1551

Merchant name	Origin	Qty	Unit	Commodity	£	s.	d.	f.
Robert Yonge & assoc.	Ind	1.5	C	Skins, Lamb	0	10	0	0
		2	C	Skins, Sheep	0	20	0	0

The George of Chepstow, Walter Gryffyth master, Entering, 5th June 1551

Merchant name	Origin	Qty	Unit	Commodity	£	s.	d.	f.
Sampson Amsley & assoc.	Ind	7.5	tun	Wine	0	0	0	0

The Sonday of Bristol, William Gylley master, Exiting, 8th June 1551

Merchant name	Origin	Qty	Unit	Commodity	£	s.	d.	f.
Edmund Jones	Ind	6.5	piece	Cloth of Assize	0	0	0	0
		8	bolt	Thread	0	10	0	0
		12	lb	Silk, *Worked*	8	0	0	0
		11	lb	Pepper	0	11	0	0
		2	lb	Cloves	0	5	0	0
		3	dozen	Caps	0	30	0	0
		2	dozen	Skins, Golden	0	8	4	0
		6	gross	Knives	0	40	0	0
		36	gross	Points	0	36	0	0
		18	dozen	Knives, in Pairs	0	30	0	0
Nicholas Wolfe	Ind	6	piece	Cloth of Assize	0	0	0	0
		4	lb	Saffron	0	40	0	0
		8	lb	Silk, *Worked*	0	106	8	0
		12	gross	Points	0	12	0	0
		4	lb	Cinnamon	0	10	0	0
		2	lb	Nutmeg	0	2	0	0
		2	bolt	Thread	0	2	6	0
		8	dozen	Knives, in Pairs	0	13	4	0
		5	gross	Knives	0	33	4	0
		6	dozen	Glass, Looking	0	2	0	0
		2	lb	Girdles, Caddis	0	3	4	0
		1	dozen	Playing Cards	0	0	15	0
		6	piece	Skins, Golden	0	2	1	0
John Sexton & Gromewell	Ind	3.75	piece	Cloth of Assize	0	0	0	0
		24	gross	Points	0	24	0	0
		8	dozen	Knives, in Pairs	0	13	4	0
		7	gross	Knives	0	46	8	0
		4	lb	Girdles, Caddis	0	6	8	0
		3	bolt	Thread	0	3	9	0
		6	piece	Skins, Golden	0	2	1	0

Merchant name	Origin	Qty	Unit	Commodity	£	s.	d.	f.
		9	lb	Silk, *Worked*	6	0	0	0
		2	lb	Saffron	0	20	0	0
		1	dozen	Playing Cards	0	0	15	0

The *Christ*ofer of Chepstow, Thomas Bronne master, Entering, 12th June 1551

Sampson Amseley & assoc.								
	Ind	7	tun	Wine	0	0	0	0
		1.5	tun	Vinegar	0	45	0	0
		2	C	Rosin	0	2	8	0

The Antony of Elmore, Thomas Norrys master, Entering, 16th June 1551

Henry Charleton & assoc.								
	Ind	5.5	C	Check *Cloth*	11	0	0	0
		0.5	chest	Sugar	0	20	0	0
		88	piece	Mantles	14	13	4	0
		4	burden	Fish, Salted	0	16	8	0

The Voracks of Gdańsk, Hans Brose master, Entering, 18th June 1551

Benedict Heytfylde	Hansard	42	last	Pitch & Tar	42	0	0	0
		9	barrel	Pitch & Tar	0	15	0	0
		26.5	last	Pitch	26	10	0	0
		12.5	ton	Iron	41	13	4	0
		480	piece	Wood, Fir	40	0	0	0
		42	C	Wainscot	84	0	0	0
		1	great hundred	Wood, Clapholt	4	0	0	0
		4	sack	Hops (?)	8	0	0	0
		29	nest	Chests	14	10	0	0
		13	single	Chests	0	65	0	0
		2	nest	Counters	0	40	0	0
		14	nest	Coffers	4	13	4	0
		16	bundle	Bowstaves	4	0	0	0
		13	C	Bowers	0	8	4	0
		20	piece	Trenchers, Painted	0	8	4	0
		80	piece	Tankards	0	10	0	0
		1	unknown	Beer*er*	0	40	0	0
		20	piece	Dish, Painted	0	10	0	0

The Faucone Graye of Chepstow, John Davis master, Entering, 20th June 1551

William Spratt	Ind	14	tun	Wine	0	0	0	0
		4.5	ton	Iron	11	5	0	0
		24.5	balette	Woad, Tolouse	15	0	0	0

The Antony of Cork, Patrick Staunton master, Entering, 22nd June 1551

Richard Creanngh	Ind	1	M	Skins, Sheep	0	100	0	0
		1	M	Skins, Lamb	0	66	8	0
		1	M	Skins, Kid	0	50	0	0
		18	piece	Skins, Marten	0	18	0	0

Merchant name	Origin	Qty	Unit	Commodity	£	s.	d.	f.
		7	piece	Skins, Otter	0	2	11	0
		4	piece	Skins, Deer	0	0	16	0
		4	piece	Skins, Fox	0	0	8	0
John Bronght	Ind	2	M	Skins, Lamb	6	13	4	0
		5	C	Skins, Sheep	0	50	0	0
		5	C	Skins, Kid	0	25	0	0
		12	piece	Skins, Fox	0	2	0	0
		6	piece	Skins, Marten	0	6	0	0
		2	piece	Skins, Deer	0	0	8	0
Edmund Duell								
& Gryffyth	Ind	3.5	C	Skins, Sheep	0	35	0	0
		8	C	Skins, Lamb	0	53	4	0
		4	C	Skins, Kid	0	20	0	0
		24	piece	Skins, Fox	0	4	0	0
		6	piece	Skins, Otter	0	2	6	0
		10	piece	Skins, Deer	0	3	4	0
		3	piece	Skins, Marten	0	3	0	0
		1.5	burden	Fish, Salted	0	6	3	0
Richard Boyley	Ind	29	C	Skins, Lamb	9	13	4	0
		25	C	Skins, Kid	6	5	0	0
		95	piece	Skins, Marten	4	15	0	0
		2.83	C	Skins, Sheep	0	28	4	0
		17	piece	Skins, Deer	0	5	8	0
		3	dozen	Skins, Kid	0	0	20	0
		2	piece	Skins, Fox	0	0	4	0

The Jenett of Penmarch, Evan Calacke master, Exiting, *22nd June 1551*

Evan Calacke	Alien	6	piece	Bristol Frieze *Cloth*	4	0	0	0

The *Christ*ofer of Gdańsk, Thomas Tyme master, Exiting, 23rd June 1551

Luke Hartema &								
assoc.	Hansard	10	piece	Cloth of Assize, Dozen Strait	0	0	0	0

The Paule of Bristol, Thomas Whyte master, Exiting, 24th June 1551

George Snygge	Ind	34	piece	Northern Cotton *Cloth*	7	20	0	0
		68	piece	Bristol Frieze *Cloth*	45	6	8	0
		2	fother	Lead	8	0	0	0
		10	piece	Manchester Cotton *Cloth*	5	0	0	0
		80	dozen	Skins, Worked	0	26	8	0
		23	piece	Cloth of Assize	0	0	0	0
Janof de Yerian	Alien	15	piece	Cloth of Assize	0	0	0	0
		20	piece	Northern Cotton *Cloth*	4	3	4	0

The Fawkyn Graye of Chepstow, John Davys master, Entering, 25th June 1551

John Heugot & assoc.	Ind	6.5	ton	Iron	16	5	0	0

Merchant name	Origin	Qty	Unit	Commodity	£	s.	d.	f.

The Antony of Cork, Patrick Staunton master, Exiting, *25th June 1551*

Merchant name	Origin	Qty	Unit	Commodity	£	s.	d.	f.
Dominic Skeddey & assoc.	Ind	12.33	lb	Soap	0	15	0	0
		1	dozen	Wool-Cards	0	4	0	0
		6	piece	Caps	0	5	0	0

The Mary of Chepstow, John Morgan master, Entering, 26th June 1551

Merchant name	Origin	Qty	Unit	Commodity	£	s.	d.	f.
Lewis Bowlles	Ind	5.5	tun	Wine	0	0	0	0

The Mineon of Bristol, John Williams master, Entering, *26th June 1551*

Merchant name	Origin	Qty	Unit	Commodity	£	s.	d.	f.
John Smyth & assoc.	Ind	6	chest	Sugar	12	0	0	0
		10.5	C	Pepper	52	10	0	0
		210	ton	Woad	1400	0	0	0

The Margaret of Chepstow, David Williams master, Entering, 27th June 1551

Merchant name	Origin	Qty	Unit	Commodity	£	s.	d.	f.
William Spratt	Ind	7	tun	Wine	0	0	0	0

The Julian of Tenby, Lewis Botrell master, Entering, 30th June 1551

Merchant name	Origin	Qty	Unit	Commodity	£	s.	d.	f.
James Barret	Ind	3	tun	Wine	0	0	0	0

The Mathew of Penmarch, John Codron master, Entering, 2nd July 1551

Merchant name	Origin	Qty	Unit	Commodity	£	s.	d.	f.
Laurence Vyne & assoc.	Ind	11.5	tun	Wine	0	0	0	0
		4	tun	Vinegar	8	0	0	0

The Michell of Chepstow, John Higens master, Entering, 3rd July 1551

Merchant name	Origin	Qty	Unit	Commodity	£	s.	d.	f.
Laurence Vyne	Ind	8	tun	Wine	0	0	0	0

The Primrose of Bristol, Thomas Warrey master, Entering, 5th July 1551

Merchant name	Origin	Qty	Unit	Commodity	£	s.	d.	f.
Lewis Robyns	Ind	9.5	tun	Wine	0	0	0	0
		5	ton	Iron	12	10	0	0
		13	ton	Salt	6	10	0	0
		2	chest	Sugar	4	0	0	0

The Mychell of Chepstow, John Higens master, Entering, *5th July 1551*

Merchant name	Origin	Qty	Unit	Commodity	£	s.	d.	f.
Laurence Vyne	Ind	8	tun	Wine	0	0	0	0

The Cloyden of *Odiem*,[5] Giles Mychellet master, Entering, *5th July 1551*

Merchant name	Origin	Qty	Unit	Commodity	£	s.	d.	f.
William Corke & assoc.	Ind	18	tun	Wine	0	0	0	0

5 Possibly Odemira or Odeceixe in Portugal.

Merchant name	Origin	Qty	Unit	Commodity	£	s.	d.	f.
The Mary George of Newport, William Butler master, Entering, _5th July 1551_								
Laurence Vyne	Ind	7.5	tun	Wine	0	0	0	0
The George of Carmarthen, Robert Brise master, Entering, 6th July 1551								
Walter Dale	Ind	8	ton	Salt	4	0	0	0
		1	pipe	Wine	0	0	0	0
The Mary John of Bideford, John _Lake_ master, Entering, 11th July 1551								
Francis Codrington & assoc.	Ind	65.5	ton	Iron	163	15	0	0
		8	dozen	Serches	0	33	4	0
		1	hogshead	Oil, Train	0	20	0	0
		3	tun	Wine	0	0	0	0
The Hart of Bristol, William Morse master, Entering, 14th July 1551								
Arthur Wynter	Ind	100	ton	Salt	50	0	0	0
The Mathew of Penmarch, John Codroy master, Exiting, 16th July 1551								
John _Codroy_	Alien	20	piece	Bristol Frieze _Cloth_	13	6	8	0
		0.5	C	Check _Cloth_	0	20	0	0
The Cloydon of _Odyery_, Giles Mychell master, Exiting, 17th July 1551								
Giles Mychell	Alien	13	piece	Bristol Frieze _Cloth_	8	13	4	0
		18	yard	Welsh _Cloth_	0	41	0	0
The Sonday of Bristol, William Gelley master, Entering, 18th July 1551								
William _Gelley_	Ind	11.5	C	Check _Cloth_	23	0	0	0
		52	piece	Mantles	8	13	4	0
		8.25	tun	Wine	0	0	0	0
The Sancta _Maria_ of Camarinas, Martin Domyngo master, Entering, 20th July 1551								
Thomas Pacty & assoc.	Ind	22.5	tun	Oil, Olive	90	0	0	0
		46	C	Alum	30	13	4	0
		4	M	Canes	0	13	4	0
The Margaret of Bristol, Maurice Welshe master, Entering, 23rd July 1551								
Henry Smyth & assoc.	Ind	8	burden	Fish, Salted	0	33	4	0
		6	C	Fish, Hake	3	0	0	0
		74	piece	Mantles	12	6	8	0
		9.91	C	Check _Cloth_	19	16	8	0
		14	C	Skins, Kid	3	10	0	0

Merchant name	Origin	Qty	Unit	Commodity	£	s.	d.	f.
		10	C	Skins, Lamb	3	10	0	0
		1.5	C	Skins, Sheep	0	15	0	0

The Mary of Minsterworth, Thomas Pewgat master, Entering, 23rd July 1551

Merchant name	Origin	Qty	Unit	Commodity	£	s.	d.	f.
Thomas Flemynge & assoc.	Ind	24	C	Check *Cloth*	48	0	0	0
		1.16	C	Skins, Sheep	0	11	8	0
		18	C	Skins, Lamb	6	0	0	0
		6	piece	Skins, Deer	0	2	0	0
		85	piece	Mantles	14	3	4	0
		1	tun	Wine, Corrupt	0	30	0	0
		1	tun	Wine	0	0	0	0

The Jhesus of New Ross, Richard Duffye master, Entering, 23rd July 1551

Merchant name	Origin	Qty	Unit	Commodity	£	s.	d.	f.
Thomas Barkeley	Ind	28.73	C	Check *Cloth*	57	9	4	0
		164	piece	Mantles	27	6	8	0
		45	C	Skins, Sheep	22	10	0	0
		32	C	Skins, Lamb	10	13	4	0
		29	C	Skins, Kid	9	15	0	0
		5	stone	Wool, Flocks	0	2	1	0
		29	piece	Skins, Deer	0	9	8	0
		16	piece	Skins, Fox	0	2	8	0
		3	piece	Skins, Otter	0	0	15	0

The Nicholas of Bristol, William Walter master, Entering, 23rd July 1551

Merchant name	Origin	Qty	Unit	Commodity	£	s.	d.	f.
Robert Sternall	Ind	5.25	tun	Wine	0	0	0	0

The Mari of Waterford, Thomas Fowler master, Entering, 24th July 1551

Merchant name	Origin	Qty	Unit	Commodity	£	s.	d.	f.
James Leonarde & assoc.	Ind	16.33	C	Skins, Kid	6	11	8	0
		26.75	C	Skins, Lamb	12	5	0	0
		30	piece	Skins, Fox	0	5	0	0
		15	piece	Skins, Otter	0	6	8	0
		60	piece	Skins, *Greis*	0	5	0	0
		14.5	C	Check *Cloth*	29	0	0	0
		85	piece	Mantles	14	3	4	0
		2	tun	Vinegar	4	0	0	0

The Leonarde of Ballyhack, John Baylle master, Entering, 24th July 1551

Merchant name	Origin	Qty	Unit	Commodity	£	s.	d.	f.
John Peket & assoc.	Ind	20.5	C	Check *Cloth*	41	0	0	0
		75	piece	Mantles	12	10	0	0
			C	Skins, Sheep	0	28	4	3
		3.5	C	Skins, Kid	0	17	6	0
		4.4	C	Skins, Lamb	0	29	2	0
		2	piece	Skins, Deer	0	0	8	0
		10	stone	Wool, Irish	0	26	8	0
		1	piece	Skins, Fox	0	0	2	0

Merchant name	Origin	Qty	Unit	Commodity	£	s.	d.	f.
		4.25	tun	Wine	0	0	0	0

The Kathern of Tenby, John Glover master, Entering, 24th July 1551

| John Dekyn & assoc. | Ind | 1 | ton | Salt | 0 | 10 | 0 | 0 |
| | | 1.75 | tun | Wine | 0 | 0 | 0 | 0 |

The Nicholas of Bristol, Nicholas Gryndam master, Entering, 24th July 1551

| Nicholas Kelley & assoc. | Ind | 24 | ton | Salt | 12 | 0 | 0 | 0 |
| | | 16 | C | Rosin | 0 | 21 | 4 | 0 |

The Katherine of Waterford, Nicholas Fitzrobert master, Entering, 24th July 1551

Thomas Morrys & assoc.	Ind	15.33	C	Skins, Sheep	7	13	4	0
		100	piece	Mantles	16	13	4	0
		15.5	C	Skins, Lamb	5	3	4	0
		15.5	C	Check Cloth	31	0	0	0
		8.75	C	Skins, Kid	2	3	9	0
		2	piece	Skins, Deer	0	0	8	0
		7	tun	Wine	0	0	0	0

The Fawkon of Waterford, Robert Medwell master, Entering, 25th July 1551

Robert Walshe & assoc.	Ind	57.5	C	Check Cloth	115	3	4	0
		425	piece	Mantles	70	16	8	0
		119.7	C	Skins, Sheep	59	16	8	0
		99	C	Skins, Lamb	33	3	0	0
		9.5	C	Skins, Kid	9	17	6	0
		14	piece	Skins, Fox	0	2	4	0
		40	doz	Hides, Unspecified	0	13	4	0
		4	stone	Wool, Irish	0	10	8	0
		4	stone	Wool, Flocks	0	0	20	0
		2	piece	Skins, Wolf	0	0	20	0
		3	piece	Skins, Otter	0	0	15	0
		27	piece	Skins, Marten	0	27	0	0

The Trenyte of Bristol, James Williams master, Entering, 27th July 1551

| Thomas Martyn | Ind | 9.5 | tun | Wine | 0 | 0 | 0 | 0 |
| | | 4 | ton | Rosin | 5 | 6 | 8 | 0 |

The George of Gloucester, Henry Joens master, Exiting, 27th July 1551

| John Donell | Ind | 4 | piece | Cloth of Assize | 0 | 0 | 0 | 0 |

The St Stevyn of San Sebastián, Martin Peris master, Entering, 27th July 1551

| Martin Peris & assoc. | Alien | 44.33 | ton | Iron | 110 | 16 | 8 | 0 |

Merchant name	Origin	Qty	Unit	Commodity	£	s.	d.	f.
		2.25	tun	Oil, Train	9	0	0	0
		8 & 1.5	dozen	Skins, Budge Coarse & Fine	0	35	0	0
William Carry & assoc.	Ind	12	ton	Iron	30	0	0	0

The Peter of Elmore, John Bulloke master, Exiting, 28th July 1551

Thomas Lane	Ind	2	piece	Cloth of Assize	0	0	0	0

The Trenyte of Bideford, Simon Beapull master, Exiting, 31st July 1551

William Preston & assoc.	Ind	83.66	piece	Cloth of Assize	0	0	0	0

The Jhesus of New Ross, Richard Duff master, Exiting, *31st July 1551*

John Osmonde	Ind	4	dozen	Knives, in Pairs	0	6	8	0
		2	dozen	Knives	0	6	0	0
		1	gross	Girdles	0	0	20	0
				Habedashery ware	47	7	4	0
		4.5	piece	Cloth of Assize	0	0	0	0

The Fawkon of Waterford, Robert Medwell master, Exiting, 3rd August 1551

John Fleatt & assoc.	Ind	8.33	dozen	Petticoat	10	0	0	0
		6	dozen	Skins, Spanish	6	0	0	0
		80	pair	Buskins	6	13	4	0
		3.33	dozen	Girdles, Seal	0	32	6	0
		7.66	dozen	Flasket	5	2	3	0
				Miscellaneous Merchandise	236	4	0	0
		30	piece	Cloth of Assize	0	0	0	0

The Kathern of Penmarch, John de Clerke master, Entering, *3rd August 1551*

John *de Clerke*	Alien	101	ton	Salt	50	10	0	0

The Mary of Penmarch, John de Rie master, Exiting, *3rd August 1551*

John *de Rie*	Alien	75	ton	Salt	37	10	0	0

The Mari of Waterford, Thomas Rothe master, Exiting, *3rd August 1551*

William Donforde & assoc.	Ind	6.5	piece	Cloth of Assize	0	0	0	0
		3	lb	Saffron	0	30	0	0
		6	lb	Silk, *Worked*	4	0	0	0
		1.5	C	Hops	0	15	0	0
		4	stone	Orchil	0	6	8	0
				Miscellaneous Merchandise	5	4	6	0

Merchant name	Origin	Qty	Unit	Commodity	£	s.	d.	f.
The Nicholas of Bristol, John Welshe master, Exiting, *3rd August 1551*								
Henry Sandyford & assoc.	Ind	1.75	ton	Iron	7	0	0	0
		1	pipe	Wine, Corrupt	0	15	0	0
				Miscellaneous Merchandise	18	1	6	0
		2.5	piece	Cloth of Assize	0	0	0	0
The Trenyte of Bristol, James Williams master, Exiting, 4th August 1551								
John Griffithe	Ind	1	ton	Iron	4	0	0	0
The Savior of Minehead, Patrick Fowler master, Exiting, *4th August 1551*								
Leonard Sumpter	Ind	1	tun	Wine, Corrupt	0	30	0	0
The Leonardus of Ballyhack, John Baylly master, Exiting, *4th August 1551*								
Thomas Madan & assoc.	Ind	1	tun	Wine, Corrupt	0	30	0	0
		1	lb	Silk, *Worked*	0	13	4	0
		9	stone	Orchil	0	15	0	0
		1	gross	Knives	0	6	8	0
		0.5	C	Hops	0	5	0	0
		1.5	piece	Cloth of Assize	0	0	0	0
The Margret of Bristol, Maurice Welshe master, Exiting, *4th August 1551*								
Robert Sternall & assoc.	Ind	2	ton	Iron	8	0	0	0
The Trinety Prowse, *Port Unknown*, Thomas Marrey master, Exiting, *4th August 1551*								
Nicholas Shee	Ind	30.83	piece	Cloth of Assize	0	0	0	0
		6	piece	Mantles	0	20	0	0
The Sonday of Bristol, William Gellei master, Exiting, 6th August 1551								
Philip Carwell	Ind	1	tun	Wine, Corrupt	0	**40**	0	0
The Myneon of Bristol, John Williams master, Exiting, *6th August 1551*								
Thomas Shipman & assoc.	Ind	240	dozen	Skins, Calf	41	0	0	0
		77.33	piece	Cloth of Assize	0	0	0	0
Peter Redericus	Alien	120	piece	Cloth of Assize	0	0	0	0
The Mary George of Tenby, Anthony Dene master, Exiting, 8th August 1551								
George Snygge & assoc.	Ind	20	dozen	Skins, Calf	3	6	8	0
		7	piece	Welsh *Cloth*	7	0	0	0

Merchant name	Origin	Qty	Unit	Commodity	£	s.	d.	f.
		58	piece	Cloth of Assize	0	0	0	0

The Mary Jamys of Bristol, Florence Typton master, Exiting, 10th August 1551

Merchant name	Origin	Qty	Unit	Commodity	£	s.	d.	f.
William Pepwall & assoc.	Ind	12	dicker	Hides, Tanned	0	0	0	0
		220	dozen	Skins, Calf	36	13	4	0
		145	piece	Northern Cotton *Cloth*	30	4	2	0
		11	piece	Manchester Cotton *Cloth*	5	10	0	0
		50	dozen	Skins, Sheep Worked	0	25	0	0
		3	piece	Bristol Frieze *Cloth*	0	40	0	0
		6	piece & 1 C ells	Cloth, Unknown	3	6	8	0
		7	piece	Welsh *Cloth*	7	0	0	0
		120.5	piece	Cloth of Assize	0	0	0	0

The Margaret of Bristol, Ralph Brown master, Entering, *10th August 1551*

Merchant name	Origin	Qty	Unit	Commodity	£	s.	d.	f.
William Tyndall & assoc.	Ind	78	ton	Iron	192	10	0	0
		8.75	tun	Oil, Train	35	0	0	0
		0.75	tun	Wine, Corrupt	0	22	6	0
		3.5	tun	Vinegar	7	0	0	0
		8.5	tun	Wine	0	0	0	0
Fernando de Sola	Alien	104	dozen	Felts, Spanish	52	0	0	0
		13.91	dozen	Skins, Spanish	13	18	4	0
		3	dozen	Gloves, Spanish	0	14	0	0
William Tyndall & assoc.	Ind	96	dozen	Skins, Calf	16	0	0	0
		21	piece	Northern Cotton *Cloth*	4	7	6	0
		24	piece	Manchester Cotton *Cloth*	12	0	0	0
		161.8	piece	Cloth of Assize	0	0	0	0

The S*anta* Maria of Camarinas, Martin Domyngo master, Exiting, 11th August 1551

Merchant name	Origin	Qty	Unit	Commodity	£	s.	d.	f.
Thomas Pacty & assoc.	Ind	26	piece	Manchester Cotton *Cloth*	13	0	0	0
		60	piece	Northern Cotton *Cloth*	12	10	0	0
		7	piece	Welsh *Cloth*	7	0	0	0
		27.66	piece	Cloth of Assize	0	0	0	0
Martin Domyngo & assoc.	Alien	5.33	piece	Cloth of Assize	0	0	0	0

The Flow*er*delice of Le Conquet, Christopher Peto master, Exiting, *11th August 1551*

Merchant name	Origin	Qty	Unit	Commodity	£	s.	d.	f.
Christopher Peto & assoc.	Alien	5	piece	Welsh *Cloth*	5	0	0	0
		1.125	C	Check *Cloth*	2	5	0	0
		15.5	piece	of Bristol, Frieze Cloth	10	6	8	0
		37	piece	Manchester Cotton *Cloth*	18	10	0	0
		80	yard	Flannel *Cloth*	2	13	4	0
		10.66	piece	Cloth of Assize	0	0	0	0
		14	piece	Cloth of Assize, Northern Dozen	9	13	4	0

Merchant name	Origin	Qty	Unit	Commodity	£	s.	d.	f.

The Kathryn of Penmarch, John de Clerke master, Exiting, 13th August 1551

Merchant name	Origin	Qty	Unit	Commodity	£	s.	d.	f.
John de Clerke & assoc.	Alien	2	piece	Cloth of Assize	0	0	0	0
		4	piece	Mantles	0	16	0	0
		3	piece	Vestment	5	0	0	0
		1	piece	Bristol Frieze Cloth	0	13	4	0

The Mary of Penmarch, John de Rie master, Exiting, 13th August 1551

Merchant name	Origin	Qty	Unit	Commodity	£	s.	d.	f.
John de Rie & assoc.	Alien	20	piece	Welsh Cloth	20	0	0	0
		4	piece	Bristol Frieze Cloth	0	53	4	0
		1	piece	Bristol Frieze Cloth	0	13	4	0

The St Stevyn of San Sebastián, Martin Perys master, Exiting, 14th August 1551

Merchant name	Origin	Qty	Unit	Commodity	£	s.	d.	f.
Stephen Delshaque Humphrey Colle & assoc.	Alien	11	dicker	Hides, Tanned	0	0	0	0
	Ind	6	fother	Lead	24	0	0	0
		4	piece	Welsh Cloth	4	0	0	0
		2	piece	Bristol Frieze Cloth	0	26	8	0
		120	ell	Wadmal Cloth	4	0	0	0
		25	piece	Cloth of Assize	0	0	0	0
Martin Perys & assoc.	Alien	12	piece	Cloth of Assize	0	0	0	0

The Doe of Bristol, William Tayler master, Exiting, 16th August 1551

Merchant name	Origin	Qty	Unit	Commodity	£	s.	d.	f.
John Brown & assoc.	Ind	12	dozen	Skins, Calf	0	40	0	0
		28	piece	Manchester Cotton Cloth	14	0	0	0
		5	piece	Welsh Cloth	5	0	0	0
		45	piece	Northern Cotton Cloth	9	7	6	0
		166.3	piece	Cloth of Assize	0	0	0	0

The Julyan of Bristol, Richard Whyte master, Exiting, 17th August 1551

Merchant name	Origin	Qty	Unit	Commodity	£	s.	d.	f.
William Pepwall & assoc.	Ind	12.5	fother	Lead	50	16	0	0
		36	dozen	Skins, Calf	6	0	0	0
		2.5	C	Wax	5	0	0	0
		73	piece	Manchester Cotton Cloth	36	10	0	0
		70	piece	Northern Cotton Cloth	14	11	8	0
		17	piece	Bristol Frieze Cloth	11	6	8	0
		700	lb	Tin, Worked	10	10	0	0
		3.33	dicker	Hides, Tanned	0	0	0	0
		126.2	piece	Cloth of Assize	0	0	0	0

The Barke Shermgton of Bristol, John Williams master, Exiting, 18th August 1551

Merchant name	Origin	Qty	Unit	Commodity	£	s.	d.	f.
Martin Grevis & assoc.	Ind	72	dozen	Skins, Calf	12	0	0	0
		80.5	fother	Lead	322	0	0	0
		40	piece	Welsh Cloth	40	0	0	0

Merchant name	Origin	Qty	Unit	Commodity	£	s.	d.	f.
		151	piece	Northern Cotton *Cloth*	31	9	2	0
		37	piece	Bristol Frieze *Cloth*	24	13	4	0
		30	piece	Manchester Cotton *Cloth*	15	0	0	0
		0.5	C	Wax	0	20	0	0
		?	dozen	Skins, Sheep Worked	0	51	8	0
		7.5	dicker	Hides, Tanned	0	0	0	0
		451.5	piece	Cloth of Assize	0	0	0	0

The Rosse of Newport, William Robarde master, Exiting, 19th August 1551

Merchant name	Origin	Qty	Unit	Commodity	£	s.	d.	f.
John Swan & assoc.	Ind	36	dozen	Skins, Calf	6	0	0	0
		33.66	piece	Cloth of Assize	0	0	0	0

The Salvador of Errenteria, Julian *de* Gosoweta master, Entering, 25th August 1551

Merchant name	Origin	Qty	Unit	Commodity	£	s.	d.	f.
John Cutt & assoc.	Ind	210.5	ton	Iron	526	4	2	0
		1	M	Canes	0	3	4	0
		8.5	tun	Vinegar	18	0	0	0
		7.75	tun	Oil, Train	31	0	0	0
Julian Gowsoweta								
& assoc.	Alien	51.66	ton	Iron	129	3	4	0
		18	dozen	Skins, Budge Fine	4	10	0	0
		25	dozen	Skins, Budge Coarse	4	3	4	0
		162	dozen	Serches	33	15	0	0
		50	gross	Combs	10	0	0	0

The George of Milford Haven, John Thorn master, Entering, 27th August 1551

Merchant name	Origin	Qty	Unit	Commodity	£	s.	d.	f.
John Leonarde	Ind	22.25	C	Check *Cloth*	44	10	0	0

The Savior of Bristol, John Lodwike master, Exiting, *27th August 1551*

Merchant name	Origin	Qty	Unit	Commodity	£	s.	d.	f.
John Wells & assoc.	Ind	216	piece	Northern Cotton *Cloth*	45	0	0	0
		30	piece	Manchester Cotton *Cloth*	15	0	0	0
		95	piece	Bristol Frieze *Cloth*	63	6	8	0
		3.1	dicker	Hides, Tanned	0	0	0	0
		88	piece	Cloth of Assize	0	0	0	0

The Mary John of Bideford, John Lake master, Exiting, *27th August 1551*

Merchant name	Origin	Qty	Unit	Commodity	£	s.	d.	f.
John Capps & assoc.	Ind	30	piece	Northern Cotton *Cloth*	6	5	0	0
		2	piece	Bristol Frieze *Cloth*	0	26	8	0
		4	dicker	Hides, Tanned	0	0	0	0
		11.33	piece	Cloth of Assize	0	0	0	0

The Salvador of Errenteria, Julian *de* Gosoweta master, Exiting, 31st August 1551

Merchant name	Origin	Qty	Unit	Commodity	£	s.	d.	f.
Martin Grevys &								
assoc.	Ind	5	dicker	Hides, Tanned	0	0	0	0
		168	dozen	Skins, Calf	28	0	0	0
		20	piece	Manchester Cotton *Cloth*	10	0	0	0
		30	piece	Northern Cotton *Cloth*	6	5	0	0

Merchant name	Origin	Qty	Unit	Commodity	£	s.	d.	f.
Andrew de Sara & assoc.	Alien	24	dozen	Skins, Calf	4	0	0	0
		11	piece	Cloth of Assize	0	0	0	0
John Pryn & assoc.	Ind	40.33	piece	Cloth of Assize	0	0	0	0

The Prymrosse of Bristol, Thomas Sherwodd master, Exiting, 8th September 1551

Lewis Robins & assoc.	Ind	22	piece	Worsted *Cloth*	7	6	8	0
		5	piece	Bristol Frieze *Cloth*	3	6	8	0
		4	piece	Bristol Frieze *Cloth*	2	13	4	0
		5.5	piece	Cloth of Assize	0	0	0	0

The *Christ*opher of Antwerpen, Adrian de Warde master, Exiting, *8th September 1551*

Cornell Dankarde	Alien	58	fother	Lead	232	0	0	0

The Powle of Minsterworth, Robert Hiet master, Entering, *8th September 1551*

Robert Hiet	Ind	2	ton	Salt	0	20	0	0

The John of Pasajes de San Juan, John de Mores master, Entering, 14th September 1551

Richard Darrell & assoc.	Ind	79	seron	Soap	49	7	6	0
		52	tun	Oil, Olive	208	0	0	0
		2	M	Canes	0	6	8	0

The Mawdlyn of Milford Haven, Philip Pollard master, Entering, 16th September 1551

John Kyttingall	Ind	6	tun	Wine	0	0	0	0
		7	C	Skins, Sheep	3	10	0	0
		0.5	C	Check *Cloth*	0	20	0	0
		4	piece	Mantles	0	16	8	0

The Andrewe of Newport, Andrew Prowse master, Entering, 18th September 1551

John Northall & assoc.	Ind	10	pipe	Fish, Salmon	15	0	0	0
		7	hogshead	Fish, Salmon	9	6	8	0
		2	barrel	Fish, Herring White	0	10	0	0

The *Christ*offer of Gloucester, Roger Horn master, Entering, 18th September 1551

Roger *Horn* & assoc.	Ind	51.5	barrel	Fish, Herring White	12	17	6	0
		16	burden	Fish, Salted	3	6	8	0
		1	C	Check *Cloth*	0	40	0	0

The Vorax of Gdańsk, Hans Brawse master, Entering, 25th September 1551

Hans Brawse	Hansard	200	ton	Salt	100	0	0	0

Merchant name	Origin	Qty	Unit	Commodity	£	s.	d.	f.

The Andrewe of Newport, Andrew Prowse master, Exiting, 28th September 1551

Merchant name	Origin	Qty	Unit	Commodity	£	s.	d.	f.
Thomas Gillons & assoc.	Ind	6	C	Soap	3	0	0	0
		2	C	Flax	0	30	0	0
		12	C	Hops	6	0	0	0
		30	lb	Pepper	0	30	0	0
		23	bolt	Thread	0	28	9	0

1563/64

TNA E122/199/9 is a 'particular' account of Thomas Robertes, collector of customs and subsidies on exports. It covers all the recorded exports from Bristol for the period Michaelmas 1563 to Michaelmas 1564

TNA E122/24/12 is the annual account of G. Jones, the controller of import duties, for the period Michaelmas 1563 to Michaelmas 1564.

The values in the 1563/4 accounts are based on a new book of rates that was issued in 1558. This book was issued because, due to inflation, the values in the old rates book no longer bore any relation to actual prices and, furthermore, it did not contain many of the new goods which had entered the trade in the interim. Apart from this, the accounts contain the same type of detail as the 1540s and 1550/1 accounts, including nominal values and duties paid.

EXPORTS

Merchant name	Origin	Qty	Unit	Commodity	£	s.	d.	f.
The Fawkon of Bristol, James Webb master, Exiting, 29th September 1563								
Robert Smyth	Ind	4	piece	Cloth of Assize	0	0	0	0
Robert Sax/ie	Ind	3	piece	Cloth of Assize	0	0	0	0
		2	piece	Brecon *Cloth*	0	40	0	0
Lettice Shee	Ind	9	piece	Mantles	0	45	0	0
		0.5	C	Frieze *Cloth*	0	20	0	0
The Primrose of Bristol, Richard Cothrell master, Exiting, *29th September 1563*								
Robert Smyth	Ind	6	piece	Cloth of Assize	0	0	0	0
		6	piece	Brecon *Cloth*	6	0	0	0
Thomas Rowland	Ind	1	piece	Cloth of Assize	0	0	0	0
John Sowche	Ind	2	piece	Cloth of Assize	0	0	0	0
		4	piece	Frieze *Cloth*	4	0	0	0
Richard Carie	Ind	2	piece	Cloth of Assize	0	0	0	0
William Tyler	Ind	3	piece	Cloth of Assize	0	0	0	0
		2	piece	Brecon *Cloth*	0	40	0	0
William Hycke	Ind	1.5	C goad	Cotton *Cloth*	0	100	0	0
John Carre	Ind	12.33	piece	Cloth of Assize	0	0	0	0
Robert Halton	Ind	1	fother	Lead	8	0	0	0

Merchant name	Origin	Qty	Unit	Commodity	£	s.	d.	f.

The Mary Fortune of Bristol, William Gwilliam master, Exiting, 29th September 1563

Merchant name	Origin	Qty	Unit	Commodity	£	s.	d.	f.
John Cutte	Ind	4	piece	Cloth of Assize	0	0	0	0
William Pepwall	Ind	4	piece	Cloth of Assize	0	0	0	0
Philip Kytchen	Ind	3	piece	Cloth of Assize	0	0	0	0
		3	piece	Frieze *Cloth*	0	60	0	0
John Boydle	Ind	1.33	piece	Cloth of Assize	0	0	0	0
Richard Hentley	Ind	1.33	piece	Cloth of Assize	0	0	0	0
Philip Blake	Ind	2	piece	Cloth of Assize	0	0	0	0
John Bradshowe	Ind	3.33	piece	Cloth of Assize	0	0	0	0
John Bisse	Ind	5	C goad	Cotton *Cloth*	16	13	4	0
		12	piece	Frieze *Cloth*	12	0	0	0
		1	piece	Cloth of Assize	0	0	0	0
Robert Halton	Ind	28	piece	Cloth of Assize	0	0	0	0
John Brown & Wood	Ind	24	piece	Cloth of Assize	0	0	0	0
John Goldesmyth	Ind	1	piece	Cloth of Assize	0	0	0	0
		6	piece	Frieze *Cloth*	6	0	0	0
William Kircke & Morse	Ind	7	piece	Cloth of Assize	0	0	0	0
John Bigge & Keyns	Ind	8.83	piece	Cloth of Assize	0	0	0	0
		14	piece	Brecon *Cloth*	14	0	0	0
		2	C goad	Cotton *Cloth*	6	13	4	0

The Julian of Bristol, Thomas Moris master, Exiting, 29th September 1563

Merchant name	Origin	Qty	Unit	Commodity	£	s.	d.	f.
Thomas Williams & Pepwall	Ind	10.66	piece	Cloth of Assize	0	0	0	0
Robert Halton & Smyth	Ind	10	piece	Cloth of Assize	0	0	0	0

The Margaret of Bristol, William Morse master, Exiting, 29th September 1563

Merchant name	Origin	Qty	Unit	Commodity	£	s.	d.	f.
John Cutte & Holden	Ind	10.33	piece	Cloth of Assize	0	0	0	0
George Katheram & Tyndall	Ind	9.66	piece	Cloth of Assize	0	0	0	0
George Page & Blake	Ind	7	piece	Cloth of Assize	0	0	0	0
John Bisse	Ind	26	piece	Frieze *Cloth*	26	0	0	0
Robert Halton & Browne	Ind	22	piece	Cloth of Assize	0	0	0	0

The Peter of Bristol, David Gillen master, Exiting, 29th September 1563

Merchant name	Origin	Qty	Unit	Commodity	£	s.	d.	f.
Andrew Cottrell & Hicke	Ind	4.66	piece	Cloth of Assize	0	0	0	0
Richard Hentley	Ind	1.66	piece	Cloth of Assize	0	0	0	0

The Hope of Bristol, John Cottrell master, Exiting, 29th September 1563

Merchant name	Origin	Qty	Unit	Commodity	£	s.	d.	f.
Andrew Cotrell & Sowche	Ind	4	piece	Cloth of Assize	0	0	0	0
Michael Pepwall & Bisse	Ind	3.33	piece	Cloth of Assize	0	0	0	0

Merchant name	Origin	Qty	Unit	Commodity	£	s.	d.	f.
		2	C goad	Cotton *Cloth*	6	13	4	0
		4	piece	Brecon *Cloth*	4	0	0	0
		2	fother	Lead	16	0	0	0
Robert Sanford								
& Swetnam	Ind	3	piece	Cloth of Assize	0	0	0	0
Anthony Memford	Ind	1	piece	Brecon *Cloth*	0	20	0	0
John Bigge	Ind	3	C goad	Cotton *Cloth*	10	0	0	0

The Marten Bonaventure of Bristol, Thomas Kynglen master, Exiting, *29th September 1563*

Edward Cullimore								
& Cutt	Ind	3	piece	Cloth of Assize	0	0	0	0
Richard Yonge	Ind	3	piece	Cloth of Assize	0	0	0	0
Rendall Wilbram	Ind	4	C goad	Cotton *Cloth*	13	6	8	0

The Angell of Bristol, Thomas Corbet master, Exiting, *29th September 1563*

John Cutt & Warden	Ind	11	piece	Cloth of Assize	0	0	0	0
Richard Carie &								
Halton	Ind	9	piece	Cloth of Assize	0	0	0	0
		1	piece	Brecon *Cloth*	0	20	0	0
		2	piece	Frieze *Cloth*	0	40	0	0

The Tobye of Bristol, John Baker master, Exiting, *29th September 1563*

Edward Cullimore &								
Yonge	Ind	6	piece	Cloth of Assize	0	0	0	0
William Pepwall &								
Wynter	Ind	11.66	piece	Cloth of Assize	0	0	0	0
		1	fother	Lead	8	0	0	0
		1	piece	Frieze *Cloth*	0	20	0	0
William Jones &								
Sowche	Ind	6.33	piece	Cloth of Assize	0	0	0	0
John Carre & Pollard	Ind	6	piece	Cloth of Assize	0	0	0	0
William Kytchen								
& Pepwall	Ind	3	piece	Cloth of Assize	0	0	0	0
		2	C	Wax	6	0	0	0
		4	piece	Brecon *Cloth*	4	0	0	0
George Wilson	Ind	2	piece	Cloth of Assize	0	0	0	0

The George of Bristol, Walter Dull*es* master, Exiting, *29th September 1563*

John Brown	Ind	2	fother	Lead	16	0	0	0
John Souche & Blake	Ind	6	piece	Cloth of Assize	0	0	0	0
Robert Boydell	Ind	7	piece	Cloth of Assize	0	0	0	0
		2	piece	Brecon *Cloth*	0	40	0	0

The Edwarde of Bristol, John Overey master, Exiting, *29th September 1563*

Edward Cullimore	Ind	2	C goad	Cotton *Cloth*	6	13	4	0
John Browne	Ind	1	fother	Lead	8	0	0	0
Robert Ambreslen								
& Souche	Ind	5.33	piece	Cloth of Assize	0	0	0	0

Merchant name	Origin	Qty	Unit	Commodity	£	s.	d.	f.
Richard Mackerets	Ind	2	C goad	Cotton *Cloth*	6	13	4	0
Robert Saxtie	Ind	8.33	piece	Cloth of Assize	0	0	0	0
		1	piece	Frieze *Cloth*	0	20	0	0
		1	fother	Lead	8	0	0	0
		4	C goad	Cotton *Cloth*	13	6	8	0
		1	C	Wax	0	60	0	0
Robert Halton & Grevis	Ind	2.5	C goad	Cotton *Cloth*	8	6	8	0
John Carre & Pendegrace	Ind	7	piece	Cloth of Assize	0	0	0	0
William Huke	Ind	1.5	C goad	Cotton *Cloth*	0	100	0	0
		2	piece	Cloth of Assize	0	0	0	0

The John of Bristol, Edmund Perkyns master, Exiting, *29th September 1563*

John Currt & Halton	Ind	10.5	C goad	Cotton *Cloth*	35	0	0	0
Edmund Perkyns	Ind	6	piece	Frieze *Cloth*	6	0	0	0

The Tryamore of Bristol, Thomas Monnen master, Exiting, *29th September 1563*

Richard Mackerets	Ind	2	C goad	Cotton *Cloth*	6	13	4	0

The Michell of Bristol, William Sumpter master, Exiting, 19th October 1563

Robert Halton & Tyndale	Ind	1	fother	Lead	8	0	0	0
		1	C goad	Cotton *Cloth*	0	66	8	0

The Grace of God of Bristol, Thomas Davis master, Exiting, *19th October 1563*

William Yonge & Grevis	Ind	3	C goad	Cotton *Cloth*	10	0	0	0
Richard Yonge & Smyth	Ind	20	C	Wax	60	0	0	0
		1	fother	Lead	8	0	0	0
John Serche & Sowche	Ind	0.66	piece	Cloth of Assize	0	0	0	0
		1	piece	Frieze *Cloth*	0	20	0	0
		2	piece	Brecon *Cloth*	0	40	0	0
George Higons & Hentley	Ind	2	piece	Cloth of Assize	0	0	0	0
		1	C goad	Cotton *Cloth*	0	66	8	*f.*
		10	piece	Brecon *Cloth*	10	0	0	0
Thomas Amershen & Atkins	Ind	1.5	piece	Cloth of Assize	0	0	0	0
		2	piece	Brecon *Cloth*	0	40	0	0
		1	piece	Frieze *Cloth*	0	20	0	0
John Draper	Ind	2	C goad	Cotton *Cloth*	6	13	4	0
Robert Saxtie & Snowe	Ind	3.5	piece	Cloth of Assize	0	0	0	0

Merchant name	Origin	Qty	Unit	Commodity	£	s.	d.	f.
The James of Youghal, Cornell Gerran master, Exiting, 20th October 1563								
Richard Lawallen	Ind	12	gross	Cutts	0	60	0	0
		11	lb	Saffron	7	6	8	0
		3	M	Teazles	0	5	0	0
		3	dozen	Girdles, Leather (1d.)	0	3	4	0
		3	great gross	Points	0	24	0	0
		1.5	lb	Seed, Onion	0	2	6	0
		5	piece	Cloth of Assize	0	0	0	0
Thomas Affarmin	Ind	11	lb	Silk, Raw	0	73	4	0
		1	dozen	Hats	0	12	0	0
		1	dozen	Caps	0	16	8	0
		3	gross	Cutts	0	15	0	0
		5	small gross	Points	0	3	4	0
		1	dozen	Girdles, Leather (1d.)	0	0	10	0
		1	piece	Cloth of Assize	0	0	0	0
Jasper Rowthe	Ind	2.33	dozen	Liquorice	0	4	8	0
		28	lb	Sugar	0	23	4	0
		6	gross	Cutts	0	30	0	0
		2	great gross	Points	0	16	0	0
		4	small gross	Points	0	2	8	0
		2	gross	Points, Leather	0	3	4	0
		1.5	M	Nails	0	2	6	0
		1.5	dozen	Penhorns	0	2	6	0
		1.5	dozen	Soap, White	0	6	0	0
		2	gross	Trenchers	0	0	8	0
		0.5	dozen	Soap, Black	0	0	9	0
		1	lb	Thread	0	0	15	0
		0.5	gross	Bowstrings	0	0	15	0
		0.5	lb	Pepper	0	0	10	0
		0.25	lb	Mercury	0	0	12	0
		2	lb	Seed, Senna	0	3	0	0
		1	lb	Terra Sigillab?	0	0	3	0
		5	lb	Twine	0	5	0	0
		4	dozen	Girdles, Leather (1d.)	0	3	4	0
		3	gross	Buttons, Silk	0	5	0	0
		3	gross	Buttons, Thread	0	3	0	0
		1.5	C	Orchil	0	30	0	0
		4	M	Teazles	0	6	8	0
		29.75	lb	Silk, Raw	9	18	4	0
		16	lb	Saffron	10	13	4	0
		1	M	*Smgynge bred?*	0	0	12	0
		2	burden	Steel	0	8	0	0
		1.16	piece	Cloth of Assize	0	0	0	0
The Clement of Bristol, Hugh Willis master, Exiting, *20th October 1563*								
David Drilinge & Rowth	Ind	2	C	Aniseed	0	53	4	0
		1.5	gross	Cutts	0	7	6	0
		1	gross	Knives, in Pairs	0	24	0	0
		1	gross	Merells	0	4	0	0

Merchant name	Origin	Qty	Unit	Commodity	£	s.	d.	f.
		0.5	gross	Knives, Prage	0	8	4	0
		6	dozen	Playing Cards	0	10	0	0
		6	dozen	Girdles, Leather (1d.)	0	8	4	0
		2	lb	Check	0	2	0	0
		4	small gross	Points	0	2	8	0
		1	ream	Paper	0	2	8	0
		6	lb	Seed, Onion	0	10	0	0
		4	lb	Seed, Leek	0	3	4	0
		4.75	piece	Cloth of Assize	0	0	0	0

The Jeshus of New Ross, John Peerse master, Exiting, 23rd November 1563

Merchant name	Origin	Qty	Unit	Commodity	£	s.	d.	f.
Richard Marshall	Ind	1	barrel	Honey	0	30	0	0
		0.5	C	Aniseed	0	13	4	0
		1.5	gross	Knives, Almaine	0	45	0	0
		2	gross	Cutts	0	10	0	0
		1	gross	Knives, in Pairs	0	24	0	0
		4	dozen	Playing Cards	0	6	8	0
		4	lb	Check	0	4	0	0
		1	gross	Combs (ob.)	0	5	0	0
		5	lb	Girdles, Leather (1d.)	0	4	2	0
		2	dozen	Liquorice	0	4	0	0
		4	dozen	Flax	0	10	8	0
		1	piece	Raisins	0	3	4	0
		4	pair	Stock-Cards	0	4	0	0
		5	lb	Silk, Raw	0	33	4	0
		1	lb	Saffron	0	13	4	0
		3	lb	Seed, Onion	0	5	0	0
		4	lb	Seed, Leek	0	3	4	0
		0.5	great gross	Points	0	4	0	0
		1	gross	Trenchers	0	0	4	0
		0.5	gross	Taps	0	0	3	0
John Rowthe	Ind	2	gross	Cutts	0	10	0	0
		1	gross	Knives, in Pairs	0	24	0	0
		1	gross	Knives, Almaine	0	30	0	0
		6	dozen	Playing Cards	0	10	0	0
		4	lb	Check	0	4	0	0
		1	gross	Combs (ob.)	0	5	0	0
		11	dozen	Girdles, Leather (1d.)	0	9	2	0
		2	dozen	Liquorice	0	4	0	0
		0.5	C	Aniseed	0	13	4	0
		1	dozen	Flax	0	2	8	0
		2	pair	Artisons	0	6	8	0
		6	pair	Stock-Cards	0	6	0	0
		13	lb	Silk, Raw	4	6	8	0
		2	lb	Saffron	0	26	8	0
		4	lb	Seed, Leek	0	3	4	0
		8	lb	Seed, Onion	0	13	4	0
		1	great gross	Points	0	8	0	0
		1	gross	Points, Leather	0	0	20	0
		0.5	dozen	Skins, Golden	0	2	6	0
		1	piece	Cloth of Assize	0	0	0	0

Merchant name	Origin	Qty	Unit	Commodity	£	s.	d.	f.
Philip Ragged	Ind	16	lb	Silk, Raw	0	106	8	0
		10	gross	Knives, Almaine & Bumbard	15	0	0	0
		5	gross	Cutts	0	25	0	0
		1	gross	Knives, Prage	0	16	8	0
		2	C	Aniseed	0	53	4	0
		2	dozen	Liquorice	0	4	0	0
		2	great gross	Points	0	16	0	0
		2	gross	Points, Leather	0	3	4	0
		1	ream	Paper	0	2	8	0
		1	gross	Playing Cards	0	20	0	0
		6	dozen	Skins, Golden	0	30	0	0
		1	gross	Combs (ob.)	0	5	0	0
		6	dozen	Flax	0	16	0	0
		6	lb	Seed, Leek	0	5	0	0
		6	lb	Seed, Onion	0	10	0	0
		3	lb	Saffron	0	40	0	0
		2	gross	Merells	0	8	0	0
		0.5	piece	Cloth of Assize	0	0	0	0
John Archer	Ind	2	pair	Stock-Cards	0	2	0	0
		6	dozen	Girdles, Leather (1d.)	0	5	0	0
		6	lb	Check	0	6	0	0
		0.5	gross	Combs (ob.)	0	2	6	0
		0.5	gross	Knives, Almaine	0	15	0	0
		1	great gross	Points	0	8	0	0
		3	lb	Silk, Raw	0	20	0	0
		0.5	gross	Merells	0	2	0	0
		0.58	piece	Cloth of Assize	0	0	0	0

The Katheryne of Waterford, Thomas Kene master, Exiting, *23rd November 1563*

Merchant name	Origin	Qty	Unit	Commodity	£	s.	d.	f.
John Wolf	Ind	1	gross	Cutts	0	5	0	0
		6	lb	Seed, Onion	0	10	0	0
		6	lb	Seed, Leek	0	5	0	0
		1	small gross	Points	0	0	8	0
		1	unknown	Fubligar ?	0	16	8	0
		2	dozen	Knives, Bumbard	0	5	0	0
		1	lb	Ginger	0	0	18	0
		0.75	piece	Cloth of Assize	0	0	0	0
Daniel Arther	Ind	4	lb	Saffron	0	53	4	0
		1	gross	Cutts	0	5	0	0
		2	dozen	Girdles, Leather (1d.)	0	0	20	0
		3	lb	Pepper	0	5	0	0
		2	lb	Ginger	0	3	0	0
		8	lb	Seed, Onion	0	13	4	0
		10	lb	Seed, Leek	0	4	2	0
		3	lb	Thread	0	3	9	0
		1.5	great gross	Points	0	12	0	0
		8	lb	Liquorice	0	0	16	0
		0.25	piece	Cloth of Assize	0	0	0	0
Dominic Crewghe	Ind	8	lb	Saffron	0	106	8	0
		4	lb	Silk, Raw	0	26	8	0
		10	lb	Pepper	0	16	8	0

Merchant name	Origin	Qty	Unit	Commodity	£	s.	d.	f.
		2	lb	Cloves	0	10	0	0
		2	lb	Ginger	0	3	0	0
		2	lb	Nutmeg	0	6	8	0
		12	lb	Seed, Leek	0	10	0	0
		12	lb	Seed, Onion	0	20	0	0
		0.5	C	Aniseed	0	13	4	0
		0.25	C	Alum	0	8	4	0
		0.5	C	Lead	0	4	0	0
		0.5	great gross	Points	0	4	0	0
		1	gross	Cutts	0	5	0	0
		4	lb	Thread	0	5	0	0
		4	dozen	Bowstrings	0	0	10	0
		6	lb	Cross-Bow Thread	0	2	0	0
		2	lb	Mercury	0	8	0	0
		6	lb	Soap, White	0	3	0	0
		1	bolt	Thread	0	3	4	0
		13	lb	Gun Powder	0	8	8	0
		2	gross	Points, Leather	0	3	4	0
		2	lb	Check	0	2	0	0
		2	dozen	Knives, Bumbard	0	5	0	0
		0.5	piece	Cloth of Assize	0	0	0	0
Patrick Ffox	Ind	0.5	gross	Cutts	0	2	6	0
		3	small gross	Points	0	2	0	0
		2	ell	Sarcenet *Cloth*	0	8	0	0
		13	lb	Seed, Onion	0	21	8	0
		13	lb	Seed, Leek	0	10	10	0
		1	bolt	Thread	0	3	4	0
		1	dozen	Skins, Golden	0	5	0	0
		2	dozen	Knives, Bumbard	0	5	0	0
		1	lb	Nutmeg	0	3	4	0
		1	lb	Pepper	0	0	20	0
		3	lb	Liquorice	0	0	6	0
		0.5	burden	Steel	0	2	0	0
		1	dozen	Skins, Budge	0	13	4	0
		0.25	piece	Chamlet *Cloth*	0	5	0	0
		0.5	gross	Trenchers	0	0	2	0
		0.75	piece	Cloth of Assize	0	0	0	0
Nicholas Moromen	Ind	4	lb	Saffron	0	53	4	0
		2	lb	Silk, Raw	0	13	4	0
		0.5	gross	Knives, in Pairs	0	12	0	0
		1	gross	Cutts	0	5	0	0
		6	lb	Seed, Leek	0	5	0	0
		2.5	lb	Thread	0	3	1	2
		0.5	C	Aniseed	0	13	4	0
		12	lb	Seed, Onion	0	20	0	0
		0.5	dozen	Caps	0	8	4	0
		2	dozen	Girdles, Ribbon	0	3	4	0
		0.5	dozen	Skins, Golden	0	2	6	0
		1	dozen	Girdles, Leather (1*d.*)	0	0	10	0
		4	dozen	Merells	0	0	16	0
		2	lb	Verdigris	0	0	16	0
		1	C	Thimbles	0	0	16	0

Merchant name	Origin	Qty	Unit	Commodity	£	s.	d.	f.
		2	lb	Ginger	0	3	0	0
		8	small gross	Points	0	5	4	0
		1	lb	Pepper	0	0	20	0
		1	gross	Points, Leather	0	0	20	0
		1	lb	Nutmeg	0	3	4	0
		1	lb	Mercury	0	4	0	0
		2	lb	Liquorice	0	0	4	0
		1	piece	Cloth of Assize	0	0	0	0
William Welshe	Ind	1.5	C	Flax	0	20	0	0
		2	gross	Cutts	0	10	0	0
		0.5	gross	Girdles, Leather (1d.)	0	5	0	0
		0.25	lb	Check	0	0	3	0
		6	lb	Seed, Leek	0	5	0	0
		2	lb	Seed, Fennel	0	0	4	0
		2	lb	Seed, Porcelic	0	0	6	0
		0.5	dozen	Aniseed	0	0	16	2
		1	dozen	Alum	0	4	0	0
		2	small gross	Points	0	0	16	0
Patrick Handrefell	Ind	3	lb	Saffron	0	40	0	0
		1	lb	Silk, Raw	0	6	8	0
		4.5	gross	Cutts	0	22	6	0
		1.5	gross	Knives, Almaine	0	45	0	0
		1.5	gross	Knives, Bumbard	0	45	0	0
		0.5	gross	Knives, Bumbard	0	15	0	0
		1	dozen	Knives	0	0	20	0
		3	dozen	Girdles, Leather (2d.)	0	5	0	0
		2	dozen	Girdles, Leather (1d.)	0	0	20	0
		4	gross	Combs (ob.)	0	20	0	0
		5	lb	Packet Thread	0	0	20	0
		1	bolt	Thread	0	3	4	0
		4	dozen	Playing Cards	0	6	8	0
		3	gross	Points, Leather	0	5	0	0
		6	small gross	Points	0	4	0	0
		4	lb	Seed, Onion	0	6	6	0
		12	lb	Seed, Leek	0	10	0	0
Edmund Power	Ind	1	lb	Saffron	0	13	4	0
		0.5	C	Flax	0	6	8	0
		1	gross	Cutts	0	5	0	0
		6	lb	Seed, Leek	0	5	0	0
		1	gross	Points, Leather	0	0	20	0
		1	small gross	Points	0	0	8	0
Richard Wale	Ind	1	lb	Saffron	0	13	4	0
		6	lb	Seed, Onion	0	10	0	0
		8	lb	Seed, Leek	0	6	8	0
		4	dozen	Girdles, Leather (2d.)	0	6	8	0
		6	dozen	Girdles, Leather (1d.)	0	5	0	0
		4	dozen	Knives, Almaine	0	10	0	0
		3	gross	Cutts	0	15	0	0
		0.25	C	Flax	0	3	4	0
Edmund Clirie	Ind	4	pair	Stock-Cards	0	4	0	0
		0.5	gross	Cutts	0	2	6	0
		2	dozen	Aniseed	0	6	0	0

Merchant name	Origin	Qty	Unit	Commodity	£	s.	d.	f.
		1	dozen	Skins, Cunirub	0	6	0	0
		8	piece	Skins, Lamb Worked	0	5	4	0
		2	small gross	Points	0	0	16	0
		4	lb	Seed, Leek	0	3	4	0
Maurice Browne & Sawle	Ind	1.5	C	Flax	0	19	0	0
		1	lb	Saffron	0	13	4	0
		12	lb	Seed, Onion	0	20	0	0
		12	lb	Seed, Leek	0	10	0	0
		0.5	gross	Cutts	0	2	6	0
		1	small gross	Points	0	0	8	0
		2	dozen	Knives, Almaine	0	5	0	0
		6	lb	Liquorice	0	0	12	0
Patrick White	Ind	2	lb	Saffron	0	26	8	0
		0.5	lb	Silk, Raw	0	3	4	0
		1.5	gross	Cutts	0	7	6	0
		0.5	gross	Knives, in Pairs	0	12	0	0
		2	dozen	Brasers	0	2	6	0
		1	gross	Knives, Almaine	0	30	0	0
		6	lb	Seed, Onion	0	10	0	0
		6	lb	Seed, Leek	0	5	0	0
		0.5	gross	Combs (ob.)	0	2	6	0
		4	dozen	Soap	0	6	0	0
		4	pair	Stock-Cards	0	4	0	0
		1	dozen	Playing Cards	0	0	20	0
		5	dozen	Girdles, Leather (1d.)	0	4	2	0
		1.5	dozen	Aniseed	0	4	6	0
		0.5	dozen	Cumin	0	0	20	0
		2	dozen	Girdles, Ribbon	0	3	4	0
		2	dozen	Liquorice	0	4	0	0
		0.5	stone	Alum	0	2	1	0
		2	gross	Points, Leather	0	3	4	0
		6	small gross	Points	0	4	0	0

The James of Youghal, Cornell Gerran master, Exiting, *23rd November 1563*

Merchant name	Origin	Qty	Unit	Commodity	£	s.	d.	f.
Roland Creanghe	Ind	3	lb	Seed, Onion	0	5	0	0
		1.5	lb	Seed, Leek	0	0	15	0
		4	lb	Liquorice	0	0	8	0
		0.5	dozen	Soap	0	0	9	0
		2	lb	*Orchement*	0	0	16	0
		2	dozen	Merells	0	0	8	0
		1	piece	Cloth of Assize	0	0	0	0
Andrew Creawghe	Ind	0.5	C	Aniseed	0	13	4	0
		1	gross	Cutts	0	5	0	0
		1	great gross	Points	0	8	0	0
		3	gross	Points, Leather	0	5	0	0
		5	lb	Liquorice	0	0	10	0
		2	dozen	Girdles, Leather (1d.)	0	0	20	0
		3	dozen	Merells	0	0	12	0
		3	lb	Seed, Onion	0	5	0	0
		2.5	piece	Cloth of Assize	0	0	0	0

Merchant name	Origin	Qty	Unit	Commodity	£	s.	d.	f.
Thomas Verdon	Ind	25	lb	Saffron	16	13	4	0
		8	lb	Silk, Raw	0	53	4	0
		5	gross	Cutts	0	25	0	0
		1	pipe	Iron	4	0	0	0
		0.5	C	Pewter	0	23	4	0
		0.58	piece	Cloth of Assize	0	0	0	0

The Anne of Pembroke, Thomas Follent master, Exiting, 23rd November 1563

Merchant name	Origin	Qty	Unit	Commodity	£	s.	d.	f.
Thomas Doffe	Ind	2	ton	Iron	16	0	0	0
		12	M	Teazles	0	40	0	0
		3	C	Soap, Black	0	20	0	0

The Sancta Maria of Hondarribia, John Swaris master, Exiting, 3rd January 1564

Merchant name	Origin	Qty	Unit	Commodity	£	s.	d.	f.
Richard Smyth	Ind	7	piece	Cloth of Assize	0	0	0	0
William Yonge & Kitchen	Ind	12	C	Wax	36	0	0	0
Mighell Deifuren & Derangavell	Alien	8.5	C	Wax	25	10	0	0
John Griffithe & Aldeworth	Ind	15	piece	Brecon *Cloth*	15	0	0	0
		8	piece	Cloth of Assize	0	0	0	0
John Bradshowe & Ashe	Ind	4	piece	Cloth of Assize	0	0	0	0
		1	C goad	Cotton *Cloth*	0	66	8	0
		1	C	Wax	0	60	0	0
		13	piece	Brecon *Cloth*	13	0	0	0
John Carre	Ind	20	piece	Brecon *Cloth*	20	0	0	0
		4	C	Wax	12	0	0	0
		2	piece	Cloth of Assize	0	0	0	0

The St Mighell of Errenteria, Michael de Gurobi master, Exiting, 3rd January 1564

Merchant name	Origin	Qty	Unit	Commodity	£	s.	d.	f.
Thomas Chester & Jene	Ind	9	C goad	Cotton *Cloth*	30	0	0	0
		2	fother	Lead	16	0	0	0
		3	piece	Cloth of Assize	0	0	0	0
George Higons & Rowlond	Ind	6	piece	Cloth of Assize	0	0	0	0
Philip Kitchens & Gittons	Ind	26	piece	Frieze *Cloth*	26	0	0	0
Peter de Rino & Ourobi	Alien	5	piece	Frieze *Cloth*	0	100	0	0
John Browne	Ind	1	fother	Lead	8	0	0	0
Philip Carne	Ind	6.5	piece	Cloth of Assize	0	0	0	0

The Salvator of Errenteria, Sebastian de Suebetuan master, Exiting, 3rd January 1564

Merchant name	Origin	Qty	Unit	Commodity	£	s.	d.	f.
Domingo de Salamander & Dega	Alien	7	C	Wax	21	0	0	0
Robert Sayne & Sherwodde	Ind	2.5	C	Wax	7	10	0	0

Merchant name	Origin	Qty	Unit	Commodity	£	s.	d.	f.
		6	piece	Brecon *Cloth*	6	0	0	0
John de Sara & Samora	Alien	9	C	Wax	27	0	0	0
John Carre & Ashe	Ind	4	fother	Lead	32	0	0	0
Thomas Rowland	Ind	1	fother	Lead	8	0	0	0
Man*uel?* Curobi & Assara	Alien	14	C	Wax	42	0	0	0
		21	C	Wax	63	0	0	0

The John of San Sebastián, Bartholemew Hernando master, Exiting, *3rd January 1564*

Merchant name	Origin	Qty	Unit	Commodity	£	s.	d.	f.
Thomas Rowland & Hammond	Ind	6	piece	Cloth of Assize	0	0	0	0
		6	piece	Wadmal *Cloth*	6	0	0	0
		8	piece	Brecon *Cloth*	8	0	0	0
John Bradshowe & Chester	Ind	1	piece	Cloth of Assize	0	0	0	0
		3.5	C	Wax	10	10	0	0
		2	C goad	Cotton *Cloth*	6	13	4	0
Bartholemew Hernando & Passolone	Alien	9	piece	Cloth of Assize	0	0	0	0
		14	C	Wax	42	0	0	0

The Phage of Dungarvan, Thomas Fitzjohn master, Exiting, 15th January 1564

Merchant name	Origin	Qty	Unit	Commodity	£	s.	d.	f.
Thomas Fitzricharde	Ind	1	ton	Salt	0	20	0	0
		1	hogshead	Iron	0	40	0	0
		3	dozen	Flax	0	8	0	0
		3	dozen	Hemp	0	7	0	0
		0.5	lb	Saffron	0	6	8	0
		1	small gross	Points	0	0	8	0
		1	gross	Points, Red	0	0	20	0
		0.5	gross	Cutts	0	2	6	0

The George of Wexford, James Sare master, Exiting, 11th February 1564

Merchant name	Origin	Qty	Unit	Commodity	£	s.	d.	f.
James Sare	Ind	0.25	C	Battery	0	10	0	0
		4	weight	Hemp	0	20	0	0
		1	hogshead	Salt	0	5	0	0
		0.25	C	Hops	0	2	6	0
		1	C	Iron	0	8	0	0
		0.5	lb	Saffron	0	6	8	0

The Grace of God of Waterford, Darby Harte master, Exiting, 17th February 1564

Merchant name	Origin	Qty	Unit	Commodity	£	s.	d.	f.
James Rowe	Ind	1	pipe	Iron	4	0	0	0
		1	dozen	Flax	0	2	8	0
		6	pair	Stock-Cards	0	6	0	0

Merchant name	Origin	Qty	Unit	Commodity	£	s.	d.	f.

The Salvator of Viana do Castello, Sebastian de Costuaner master, Exiting, *17th February 1564*

Merchant name	Origin	Qty	Unit	Commodity	£	s.	d.	f.
Sebastian de Costuaner	Alien	1	fother	Lead	8	o	o	o

The Trynytie of Dublin, John Langhan master, Exiting, *17th February 1564*

Merchant name	Origin	Qty	Unit	Commodity	£	s.	d.	f.
Patrick Lymbricke & White	Ind	9	C	Soap, Black	3	o	o	o
		5	great gross	Points	o	40	o	o
Thomas Meawghe & White	Ind	3	C	Soap, Black	o	20	o	o
		1	great gross	Points	o	8	o	o
		1.72	tun	Vinegar	4	o	o	o
		2	piece	Calico *Cloth*	o	13	4	o

The Peter of Wexford, Nicholas Hewe master, Exiting, 20th February 1564

Merchant name	Origin	Qty	Unit	Commodity	£	s.	d.	f.
William Launders	Ind	1	ton	Iron	8	o	o	o
		1.5	ton	Salt	o	30	o	o
		2	dozen	Aniseed	o	5	8	o
		0.5	dozen	Scythes	o	6	8	o
		2	weight	Hemp	o	10	o	o

The Jesus of Youghal, Richard Griffin master, Exiting, 27th February 1564

Merchant name	Origin	Qty	Unit	Commodity	£	s.	d.	f.
Pierce Lincolne & Rotche	Ind	1.5	gross	Cutts	o	7	6	o
		2	dozen	Wool-Cards	o	20	o	o
		1	lb	Saffron	o	13	4	o
		17	stone	Orchil	o	34	o	o
		9	dozen	Hemp	o	22	6	o
Philip Rotche & Browne	Ind	2	lb	Saffron	o	26	8	o
		6	stone	Orchil	o	12	o	o
		4	gross	Cutts	o	20	o	o
		16	dozen	Hemp	o	40	o	o
		14	lb	Battery	o	10	o	o
		1	great gross	Points	o	8	o	o

The Trynytie of Youghal, William Nele master, Exiting, 8th March 1564

Merchant name	Origin	Qty	Unit	Commodity	£	s.	d.	f.
William Dredie & *Nele*	Ind	4	lb	Saffron	o	53	4	o
		4	gross	Cutts	o	20	o	o
		0.5	great gross	Points	o	4	o	o
		2	M	Teazles	o	3	4	o
		2	C	Aniseed	o	53	4	o
		0.5	small gross	Points	o	o	4	o
		2	stone	Orchil	o	4	o	o
James Galwaie	Ind	6	gross	Cutts	o	30	o	o
		3	great gross	Points	o	24	o	o
		4	dozen	Flax	o	10	8	o

Merchant name	Origin	Qty	Unit	Commodity	£	s.	d.	f.

The Jeshus of Dungarvan, David Jones master, Exiting, 11th March 1564

David *Jones*	Ind	2	C	Iron	0	16	0	0
		1	dozen	Flax	0	2	8	0
		1	dozen	Wool-Cards	0	10	0	0

The Katherne of Waterford, Pierce Hoore master, Exiting, 3rd April 1564

George Gromwell	Ind	1	gross	Knives, Bumbard	0	35	0	0
		6	lb	Silk, Raw	0	40	0	0
		6	lb	Saffron	4	0	0	0
		6.5	C	Aniseed	8	13	4	0
		28	lb	Pepper	0	46	8	0
		6	lb	Verdigris	0	4	0	0
		6	lb	Mercury	0	24	0	0
		3	bolt	Thread	0	10	0	0
		3	M	Nails	0	5	0	0
		4	dozen	Girdles, Ribbon	0	6	8	0
		6	lb	Lead, Red	0	0	12	0
		2	gross	Merells	0	8	0	0
		1	lb	Wax, Red	0	0	8	0
		1	dozen	Crab-Locks	0	3	4	0
		4	gross	Cutts	0	20	0	0
		3	great gross	Points	0	24	0	0
		1	lb	Cloves	0	5	0	0
		1	lb	Nutmeg	0	3	4	0
		2	lb	Ginger	0	3	0	0
		6	lb	Cumin	0	0	20	0
		8	lb	Sulpher	0	0	8	0
		1	lb	Arsenic	0	0	5	0
		2	dozen	Wool-Cards	0	20	0	0
		6	lb	Sugar	0	4	0	0
		2	lb	Twine	0	0	16	0
		2	lb	Unknown	0	0	8	0
		5	lb	Soap, White	0	0	20	0
		1	gross	Combs, (1*d*.)	0	10	0	0
		7	piece	Cloth of Assize	0	0	0	0
Nicholas Shyrtche	Ind	2	lb	Saffron	0	26	8	0
		6	dozen	Merells	0	2	0	0
		0.5	gross	Cutts	0	2	6	0
		2	dozen	Knives, Bumbard	0	5	0	0
		0.5	great gross	Points	0	4	0	0
		2	dozen	Bowstrings	0	0	5	0
		1	lb	Mercury	0	4	0	0
		2	dozen	Combs, (1*d*.)	0	0	20	0
		3	lb	Lead, Red	0	0	6	0
		0.5	ream	Paper	0	0	16	0
		1	lb	Sugar	0	0	10	0
		2	dozen	Wool-Cards	0	30	0	0
		2	piece	Cloth of Assize	0	0	0	0
Walter Welshe	Ind	10	dozen	Flax	0	26	8	0
		0.5	gross	Girdles, Leather (1*d*.)	0	5	0	0

Merchant name	Origin	Qty	Unit	Commodity	£	s.	d.	f.
		3	dozen	Soap, Black	0	4	6	0
		4	dozen	Knives, Almaine	0	10	0	0
		2	ream	Paper	0	5	4	0
Henry Browne & Butler	Ind	6	C	Flax	6	0	0	0

The George of Fethard-on-Sea, John Brytton master, Exiting, *3rd April 1564*

Francis Reymond	Ind	4	weight	Hemp	0	20	0	0

The Jeshus of New Ross, John Peers master, Exiting, *3rd April 1564*

William Collen	Ind	1	C	Soap	0	6	8	0
		2	pair	Stock-Cards	0	2	0	0
		3	M	Teazles	0	5	0	0

The Sondaye of Wexford, Philip Stafford master, Exiting, 4th April 1564

Philip *Stafford*	Ind	4	C	Iron	0	32	0	0
		2.5	weight	Hemp	0	12	6	0
		0.5	C	Battery	0	20	0	0
		0.5	dozen	Aniseed	0	0	18	0
		0.25	C	Pewter	0	11	8	0

The Anne of Waterford, Thomas [ ]enner master, Exiting, *4th April 1564*

Stephen Leonard	Ind	3	C	Iron	0	24	0	0
		1	gross	Cutts	0	5	0	0
		1.5	dozen	Girdles, Leather (1d.)	0	0	15	0
		2.5	dozen	Soap, Black	0	3	9	0
		3	pair	Stock-Cards	0	3	0	0
		2	lb	Starch	0	0	4	0
		1	lb	Seed, Onion	0	0	20	0
		2	lb	Seed, Leek	0	0	20	0
		3	C	Oakum	0	15	0	0
Andrew Lyncolln	Ind	3	C	Flax	3	0	0	0
David Dryling & Turbeck	Ind	1.5	C	Oakum	0	7	6	0
		2	gross	Cutts	0	10	0	0
		0.5	dozen	Girdles, Leather (1d.)	0	0	5	0
		2	C	Soap, Black	0	13	4	0
		2	pair	Stock-Cards	0	2	0	0
		2.5	dozen	Hemp	0	6	8	0

The Goosechecken of *Nostradame,* Claus Peter master, Exiting, 16th April 1564

Claus Peter	Alien	20	wey	Coal, Smith	6	13	4	0

The Jonas of *Browsse Haven,* Andrew Cornell master, Exiting, 21st April 1564

Andrew Cornell	Alien	10	wey	Coal, Smith	3	6	8	0

Merchant name	Origin	Qty	Unit	Commodity	£	s.	d.	f.
The Mackerell of Dungarvan, Philip Hore master, Exiting, 21st April 1564								
Philip *Hore*	Ind	1	barrel	Tar	0	3	4	0
		0.25	C	Battery	0	10	0	0
Geoffrey Stirche	Ind	10	lb	Pepper	0	16	8	0
		0.5	C	Aniseed	0	13	4	0
		2	dozen	Wool-Cards	0	20	0	0
		2	dozen	Playing Cards	0	3	4	0
		0.5	gross	Cutts	0	2	6	0
		2	lb	Verdigris	0	0	16	0
		1	lb	Ginger	0	0	18	0
		2	dozen	Combs (*ob.*)	0	0	10	0
		2	dozen	Girdles, Ribbon	0	3	4	0
		4	lb	Sugar	0	2	8	0
		2	piece	Cloth of Assize	0	0	0	0
The Nicholas of Mutriku, Domingo de Torica master, Exiting, 3rd May 1564								
Domingo de Torica	Alien	1	fother	Lead	8	0	0	0
		2.25	C	Tin, Worked	5	5	0	0
The Tobye of Bristol, Philip Baker master, Exiting, 3rd May 1564								
John Carr	Ind	5	fother	Lead	40	0	0	0
The Prymrose of Bristol, Richard Cottrell master, Exiting, 3rd May 1564								
John Browne	Ind	2	C	Wax, Red	6	0	0	0
Richard Yonge & Symons	Ind	4	piece	Brecon *Cloth*	4	0	0	0
		1	pipe	Iron	4	0	0	0
		10	piece	Cloth of Assize	0	0	0	0
Robert Halton & Aldworth	Ind	2	piece	Brecon *Cloth*	0	40	0	0
		9	C goad	Cotton *Cloth*	30	0	0	0
		5	piece	Cloth of Assize	0	0	0	0
William Sherwood & Sowche	Ind	16	piece	Brecon *Cloth*	16	0	0	0
		1	C	Wax	3	0	0	0
		8.5	piece	Cloth of Assize	0	0	0	0
Anthony Monnford	Ind	6.33	piece	Cloth of Assize	0	0	0	0
John Boydell & Saxye	Ind	2	C goad	Cotton *Cloth*	6	13	4	0
		7.5	piece	Frieze *Cloth*	7	10	0	0
		2	piece	Brecon *Cloth*	0	40	0	0
		3.75	piece	Cloth of Assize	0	0	0	0
Nicholas Thorne & Hentley	Ind	5	C	Wax	15	0	0	0
		10	piece	Brecon *Cloth*	10	0	0	0
		1	piece	Frieze *Cloth*	0	20	0	0
		2	piece	Cloth of Assize	0	0	0	0
Robert Smyth & Kytchen	Ind	6	piece	Brecon *Cloth*	6	0	0	0

Merchant name	Origin	Qty	Unit	Commodity	£	s.	d.	f.
		2	C goad	Cotton *Cloth*	6	8	4	0
		5	piece	Cloth of Assize	0	0	0	0
Edmund Smyth & Colymore	Ind	13	piece	Brecon *Cloth*	13	0	0	0
		20	piece	Frieze *Cloth*	20	0	0	0
		2	piece	Cloth of Assize	0	0	0	0
Dominic Chester & Higgons	Ind	6	piece	Frieze *Cloth*	6	0	0	0
		3	C goad	Cotton *Cloth*	10	0	0	0
Philip Ashe & Hykke	Ind	12	piece	Brecon *Cloth*	12	0	0	0
		1	C goad	Cotton *Cloth*	3	6	8	0
		8	piece	Cloth of Assize	0	0	0	0
John Bradshawe	Ind	2	piece	Brecon *Cloth*	0	40	0	0
		0.5	C	Wax	0	30	0	0
		3	piece	Cloth of Assize	0	0	0	0

The Faulcon of Bristol, Thomas Morrys master, Exiting, *3rd May 1564*

Merchant name	Origin	Qty	Unit	Commodity	£	s.	d.	f.
Dominic Chester & Cutt	Ind	2	piece	Frieze *Cloth*	0	40	0	0
		3	C goad	Cotton *Cloth*	10	0	0	0
		3	piece	Cloth of Assize	0	0	0	0
William Yonge & Sowche	Ind	6	piece	Brecon *Cloth*	6	0	0	0
		12	piece	Cloth of Assize	0	0	0	0
Thomas Chester & Watford	Ind	7	C goad	Cotton *Cloth*	23	6	8	0
		4	piece	Brecon *Cloth*	4	0	0	0
		5	piece	Frieze *Cloth*	5	0	0	0
Robert Smythe & Wilson	Ind	5	piece	Brecon *Cloth*	5	0	0	0
		5	C goad	Cotton *Cloth*	16	13	4	0
		6	piece	Cloth of Assize	0	0	0	0
Robert Tyndall & Browne	Ind	2	piece	Brecon *Cloth*	0	40	0	0
		6	piece	Cloth of Assize	0	0	0	0
John Bradshawe & Saunders	Ind	3	C goad	Cotton *Cloth*	10	0	0	0
		6	piece	Frieze *Cloth*	6	0	0	0

The Julyan of Bristol, James Webbe master, Exiting, 6th May 1564

Merchant name	Origin	Qty	Unit	Commodity	£	s.	d.	f.
Thomas Symons	Ind	2	fother	Lead	16	0	0	0
		8	wey	Coal, Smith	0	53	4	0

The Marten Bonaventure of Bristol, William More master, Exiting, 7th May 1564

Merchant name	Origin	Qty	Unit	Commodity	£	s.	d.	f.
Thomas Chester	Ind	2	fother	Lead	16	0	0	0

The Unicorne of Bristol, William Hyscocke master, Exiting, 9th May 1564

Merchant name	Origin	Qty	Unit	Commodity	£	s.	d.	f.
William Ryswell	Ind	10	wey	Coal, Smith	3	6	8	0

Merchant name	Origin	Qty	Unit	Commodity	£	s.	d.	f.

The Peter of Bristol, John Cottrell master, Exiting, 12th May 1564

Merchant name	Origin	Qty	Unit	Commodity	£	s.	d.	f.
John Carr & Aldworth	Ind	15	wey	Coal, Smith	5	0	0	0
		10	C goad	Cotton *Cloth*	33	6	8	0
		5	fother	Lead	40	0	0	0
		6	piece	Brecon *Cloth*	6	0	0	0
		44	piece	Cloth of Assize	0	0	0	0
Thomas Symons & Ashe	Ind	10	piece	Brecon *Cloth*	10	0	0	0
		8	piece	Cloth of Assize	0	0	0	0
Lettice Chester & Hentley	Ind	1	C	Frieze *Cloth*	0	40	0	0
		0.5	C	Wax	0	30	0	0
		2	piece	Brecon *Cloth*	0	40	0	0
		2	piece	Frieze *Cloth*	0	40	0	0

The Grace of God of Waterford, Darby Harte master, Exiting, 13th May 1564

Merchant name	Origin	Qty	Unit	Commodity	£	s.	d.	f.
Pierce Raccett	Ind	2	C	Soap, Black	0	13	4	0
		2	small gross	Cutts	0	10	0	0
		4	dozen	Girdles, Leather (1*d.*)	0	3	4	0
		2	dozen	Girdles, Leather (2*d.*)	0	3	4	0
James Brenocke	Ind	1.5	gross	Cutts	0	7	6	0
		1	great gross	Points	0	8	0	0
		3	pair	Stock-Cards	0	3	0	0
		2.5	dozen	Aniseed	0	7	6	0
		1	dozen	Alum	0	4	2	0
		4	dozen	Girdles, Leather (1*d.*)	0	3	4	0
Thomas Lynche	Ind	1	C	Soap, Black	0	6	8	0
		3	pair	Stock-Cards	0	3	0	0
Edmund Butler	Ind	1.5	gross	Cutts	0	7	6	0
		2	small gross	Points, Leather	0	3	4	0
		2	small gross	Points	0	0	16	0
		1	dozen	Aniseed	0	3	0	0
		0.5	dozen	Cumin	0	0	20	0
		4	dozen	Girdles, Leather (1*d.*)	0	3	4	0
		0.5	dozen	Alum	0	2	0	0
		3	dozen	Knives, Almaine	0	7	6	0
Morgan Rede	Ind	0.5	dozen	Aniseed	0	0	18	0
		0.25	C	Alum	0	8	4	0
		2	dozen	Knives, Bumbard	0	5	0	0
		2	lb	Check	0	2	0	0
		1	lb	Cloves	0	5	0	0
		2	lb	Mail	0	0	20	0
		1	C	Awl Blades	0	0	8	0

The Dragon of Bristol, John Clodye master, Exiting, 23rd May 1564

Merchant name	Origin	Qty	Unit	Commodity	£	s.	d.	f.
Philip Colemen	Ind	1	gross	Cutts	0	5	0	0
		0.5	gross	Combs, (1*d.*)	0	5	0	0
		0.5	gross	Merells	0	2	0	0
		1	ream	Paper	0	2	8	0

Merchant name	Origin	Qty	Unit	Commodity	£	s.	d.	f.
		0.5	gross	Knives, in Pairs	0	12	0	0
		1.25	C	Aniseed	0	33	4	0
		4	piece	Cloth of Assize	0	0	0	0
		3	piece	Cloth of Assize, Kersey	0	0	0	0
Thomas Lynche	Ind	0.25	C	Oakum	0	0	15	0

The Swanne of Bristol, Edmond Philips master, Exiting, 27th May 1564

Merchant name	Origin	Qty	Unit	Commodity	£	s.	d.	f.
William P[ ]ffett	Ind	10	wey	Coal, Smith	3	6	8	0
		10	piece	Frieze *Cloth*	10	0	0	0
John Atkyns	Ind	5	piece	Frieze *Cloth*	5	0	0	0

The Katherne of Wexford, William Stafford master, Exiting, 7th June 1564

Merchant name	Origin	Qty	Unit	Commodity	£	s.	d.	f.
William *Stafford*	Ind	1	lb	Saffron	0	13	4	0
		1	dozen	Aniseed	0	3	0	0
		1	gross	Knives, in Pairs	0	24	0	0
		2	dozen	Soap, Black	0	3	0	0
		0.5	great gross	Points	0	4	0	0
		1	lb	Pepper	0	0	20	0
		1	lb	Graines	0	0	8	0

The Katherne of Waterford, John Roster master, Exiting, 8th June 1564

Merchant name	Origin	Qty	Unit	Commodity	£	s.	d.	f.
Nicholas Morffey	Ind	0.5	piece	Cloth of Assize	0	0	0	0
		1	piece	Cloth of Assize, Dozen Strait	0	0	0	0
Walter Marshall	Ind	3	lb	Saffron	0	40	0	0
		4	lb	Silk, Raw	0	26	8	0
		0.5	gross	Knives, Almaine	0	15	0	0
		2	gross	Points, Leather	0	3	4	0
		0.5	dozen	Caps	0	8	4	0
		3	dozen	Girdles, Leather (1d.)	0	2	6	0
		1	lb	Thread	0	0	15	0
		0.5	dozen	Cumin	0	0	20	0
		0.5	C	Flax	0	5	0	0
		1	C	Oakum	0	5	0	0
		0.5	C	Corn Powder	0	16	8	0
		2	dozen	Liquorice	0	4	0	0
		1	ream	Paper	0	2	8	0
		1	C	Soap, Black	0	6	8	0
		1	piece	Cloth of Assize, Dozen Strait	0	0	0	0

The Jeshus of New Ross, Edmund Kellye master, Exiting, 11th June 1564

Merchant name	Origin	Qty	Unit	Commodity	£	s.	d.	f.
Jasper Striche	Ind	1	C	Aniseed	0	26	8	0
		1	gross	Cutts	0	5	0	0
		2	dozen	Playing Cards	0	3	4	0
		1	lb	Check	0	0	12	0
		0.5	gross	Merells	0	2	0	0
		0.5	great gross	Points	0	4	0	0
		1	bolt	Thread	0	3	4	0
John Archer	Ind	3	lb	Silk, Raw	0	20	0	0

Merchant name	Origin	Qty	Unit	Commodity	£	s.	d.	f.
		1	gross	Cutts	0	5	0	0
		0.5	gross	Girdles, Leather (1d.)	0	5	0	0
		2	ream	Paper	0	5	4	0
		1	gross	Combs, (1d.)	0	8	0	0
		2	dozen	Playing Cards	0	3	4	0
		1	gross	Trenchers	0	0	4	0
		2	small gross	Points	0	0	16	0
		1	dozen	Soap	0	0	18	0
		2	pair	Stock-Cards	0	2	0	0
Richard Raggett	Ind	2	dozen	Knives, in Pairs	0	5	0	0
		2	ream	Paper	0	5	4	0
		2	dozen	Playing Cards	0	3	4	0
		4	piece	Hats	0	4	0	0
		6	lb	Cloves	0	30	0	0
		3	pair	Stock-Cards	0	3	0	0
		6	small gross	Points	0	4	0	0
		5	dozen	Soap, Black	0	7	6	0
		0.5	piece	Cloth of Assize	0	0	0	0
		1	piece	Cloth of Assize, Dozen Strait	0	0	0	0

The Grace of God of Cork, David Fitzwilliam master, Exiting, 26th June 1564

Merchant name	Origin	Qty	Unit	Commodity	£	s.	d.	f.
David Golding	Ind	60	quart	Malt	20	0	0	0
William Golde	Ind	4	gross	Cutts	0	20	0	0
		3	great gross	Points	0	24	0	0
		2	gross	Points, Leather	0	3	4	0
		1	burden	Steel	0	4	0	0
		4	lb	Cloves	0	20	0	0
		1	lb	Saffron	0	13	4	0
		3	dozen	Playing Cards	0	5	0	0
		1	lb	Mercury	0	4	0	0
		1	ream	Paper	0	2	8	0
		3	M	Teazles	0	5	0	0
		0.5	piece	Cloth of Assize	0	0	0	0
		0.5	piece	Cloth of Assize, Kersey	0	0	0	0
George Rothe	Ind	3.5	lb	Cloves	0	17	6	0
		1	lb	Pepper	0	0	20	0
		2	gross	Cutts	0	10	0	0
		1	gross	Points, Leather	0	0	20	0
		2	M	Teazles	0	3	4	0
		1	lb	Saffron	0	13	4	0
		1	dozen	Flax	0	2	8	0
		0.5	piece	Cloth of Assize	0	0	0	0
		1	piece	Cloth of Assize, Kersey	0	0	0	0

The Jesus of Morbihan, Dominic Bryan master, Exiting, 10th July 1564

Merchant name	Origin	Qty	Unit	Commodity	£	s.	d.	f.
Dominic Chester	Ind	8	piece	Cloth of Assize	0	0	0	0
		4	piece	Frieze Cloth	4	0	0	0
James de Morowe	Ind	3	piece	Frieze Cloth	3	0	0	0
		2	piece	Cloth of Assize, Kersey	0	0	0	0

Merchant name	Origin	Qty	Unit	Commodity	£	s.	d.	f.

The John of Combe Martin, John Wyott master, Exiting, 11th July 1564

Merchant name	Origin	Qty	Unit	Commodity	£	s.	d.	f.
Aldrean de Gr[ ]dote	Alien	2	ton	Ashes, Soap	0	40	0	0

The Mary of Tintern, Howell Apprece master, Exiting, 11th July 1564

Merchant name	Origin	Qty	Unit	Commodity	£	s.	d.	f.
Lyvon de Blenett	Alien	0.75	piece	Cloth of Assize	0	0	0	0

The Mighell of Newport, John Harrys master, Exiting, 11th July 1564

Merchant name	Origin	Qty	Unit	Commodity	£	s.	d.	f.
Bartholemew Rottus?	Alien	5	piece	Cloth of Assize	0	0	0	0
		2	piece	Cloth of Assize, Kersey	0	0	0	0

The Margarett of Bristol, John Pollarde master, Exiting, 19th July 1564

Merchant name	Origin	Qty	Unit	Commodity	£	s.	d.	f.
William Pepwall & Browne	Ind	7	fother	Lead	56	0	0	0
		30	piece	Brecon *Cloth*	30	0	0	0
		25	piece	Cloth of Assize	0	0	0	0
Edmund Smithe & Halton	Ind	17	piece	Cloth of Assize	0	0	0	0
		3	piece	Brecon *Cloth*	3	0	0	0
Richard Cary & Higgons	Ind	9	piece	Frieze *Cloth*	9	0	0	0
		8	piece	Brecon *Cloth*	8	0	0	0
		2	C goad	Cotton *Cloth*	6	13	4	0
		18.66	piece	Cloth of Assize	0	0	0	0
John Cutt & Kytchyn	Ind	3	C goad	Cotton *Cloth*	10	0	0	0
		4	piece	Brecon *Cloth*	4	0	0	0
		8	piece	Cloth of Assize	0	0	0	0
Robert Tyndall & Aldworth	Ind	6	piece	Brecon *Cloth*	6	0	0	0
		9.5	piece	Cloth of Assize	0	0	0	0
John Sowche & Smythe	Ind	4	piece	Brecon *Cloth*	4	0	0	0
		1	piece	Frieze *Cloth*	0	20	0	0
		5	piece	Cloth of Assize	0	0	0	0
Thomas Kelke	Ind	2.5	C goad	Cotton *Cloth*	8	6	8	0
John Bysse & Gyttons	Ind	4	C goad	Cotton *Cloth*	13	6	8	0

The Angell of Newport, William Watkyn master, Exiting, 21st July 1564

Merchant name	Origin	Qty	Unit	Commodity	£	s.	d.	f.
Dego Gonsalis	Alien	3.33	piece	Cloth of Assize	0	0	0	0
Thomas Rowland	Alien	1	fother	Lead	8	0	0	0

The Marye Gryffyth of Bristol, William Hawkyns master, Exiting, 26th July 1564

Merchant name	Origin	Qty	Unit	Commodity	£	s.	d.	f.
Robert Halton & Griffith	Ind	4	fother	Lead	32	0	0	0
		8	piece	Brecon *Cloth*	8	0	0	0
John Carr & Chester	Ind	2	C goad	Cotton *Cloth*	6	13	4	0
		15	fother	Lead	120	0	0	0
		8.5	piece	Cloth of Assize	0	0	0	0

Merchant name	Origin	Qty	Unit	Commodity	£	s.	d.	f.
The Katherne of Waterford, John Coscrowe master, Exiting, 26th July 1564								
John Gromwell	Ind	1	great gross	Points	0	8	0	0
		6	lb	Pepper	0	10	0	0
		2	C	Aniseed	0	53	4	0
		2	lb	Check	0	2	0	0
		2	lb	Ginger	0	3	0	0
		4	lb	Thread	0	5	0	0
		2	bolt	Thread	0	6	8	0
		4	dozen	Girdles, Leather (1d.)	0	3	4	0
		4	dozen	Playing Cards	0	6	8	0
		2	dozen	Skins, Golden	0	10	0	0
		0.5	gross	Knives, Bumbard	0	15	0	0
		0.5	dozen	Combs (ob.)	0	0	20	0
		4	lb	Soap, White	0	0	20	0
		2	gross	Cutts	0	10	0	0
		1.33	piece	Cloth of Assize	0	0	0	0
Richard Hoore	Ind	1	C	Aniseed	0	26	8	0
		3	gross	Cutts	0	15	0	0
		1	C	Soap, Black	0	6	8	0
		1	gross	Knives, Almaine	0	30	0	0
		1	dozen	Liquorice	0	2	0	0
		0.5	dozen	Cumin	0	0	20	0
		0.5	gross	Playing Cards	0	10	0	0
		1	lb	Cloves	0	5	0	0
		2	lb	Pepper	0	3	4	0
		1	great gross	Points	0	8	0	0
		1	gross	Combs (ob.)	0	5	0	0
		0.5	gross	Girdles, Leather (1d.)	0	5	0	0
		7	lb	Sugar	0	4	8	0
		1	C	Hops	0	10	0	0
Thomas Welshe	Ind	1	lb	Silk, Raw	0	6	8	0
		1	gross	Cutts	0	5	0	0
		0.5	gross	Cutts, in pairs	0	15	0	0
		0.25	C	Hops	0	2	6	0
		4	clout	Needles	0	3	4	0
		1	gross	Girdles, Leather (1d.)	0	10	0	0
Nicholas Whyte	Ind	1	gross	Cutts	0	5	0	0
		1	dozen	Caps	0	16	8	0
		2	gross	Points, Leather	0	3	4	0
		1	great gross	Points	0	8	0	0
		2	lb	Saffron	0	26	8	0
		12	pair	Stock-Cards	0	12	0	0
		0.5	C	Hops	0	5	0	0
		5	C	Aniseed	6	13	4	0
		15	C	Teazles	0	2	6	0
		0.5	C	Soap, Black	0	3	4	0
Michael Whyte	Ind	1	dozen	Aniseed	0	3	0	0
		1	gross	Cutts	0	5	0	0
		1	lb	Saffron	0	13	4	0
		1	gross	Points, Leather	0	0	20	0
		2	dozen	Knives, Almaine	0	5	0	0

Merchant name	Origin	Qty	Unit	Commodity	£	s.	d.	f.
		5	dozen	Girdles, Leather (1d.)	0	4	2	0
		0.5	gross	Combs, (1d.)	0	5	0	0
		0.25	C	Hops	0	2	6	0
		4	lb	Soap, Black	0	6	0	0
		4	pair	Stock-Cards	0	4	0	0
		7.25	piece	Cloth of Assize	0	0	0	0
John Braye	Ind	0.5	gross	Cutts	0	2	6	0
		1	dozen	Soap, Black	0	0	18	0
		1	gross	Points, Leather	0	0	20	0
		1	small gross	Points	0	0	8	0
		4	lb	Mail	0	3	4	0
		0.5	piece	Cloth of Assize	0	0	0	0
Walter Welshe	Ind	0.5	C	Soap, Black	0	3	4	0
		0.5	C	Hops	0	5	0	0
		12	pair	Stock-Cards	0	12	0	0
		0.5	piece	Cloth of Assize	0	0	0	0
Henry Fagan	Ind	1	lb	Saffron	0	13	4	0
		2	lb	Silk, Raw	0	13	4	0
		8	dozen	Girdles, Leather (1d.)	0	6	8	0
		1.5	gross	Cutts	0	7	6	0
		4	dozen	Knives, Almaine	0	10	0	0
		4	gross	Points, Leather	0	3	4	0
		4	small gross	Points	0	2	8	0
		2	bolt	Thread	0	6	8	0
		2	small gross	Combs (ob.)	0	10	0	0
		5	dozen	Playing Cards	0	8	4	0
		1	dozen	Aniseed	0	3	0	0
		1	dozen	Liquorice	0	2	0	0
		4	lb	Check	0	4	0	0
		4	dozen	Soap, Black	0	6	0	0
		1	gross	Merells	0	4	0	0
		3	lb	Mail	0	2	6	0
		1	piece	Frieze *Cloth*	0	20	0	0
		1.25	piece	Cloth of Assize	0	0	0	0

The Julyan of Bristol, James Webbe master, Exiting, *26th July 1564*

Merchant name	Origin	Qty	Unit	Commodity	£	s.	d.	f.
Thomas Symons	Ind	6	wey	Coal, Smith	0	40	0	0
Thomas Pepwall	Ind	19	piece	Brecon *Cloth*	19	0	0	0
		35	piece	Cloth of Assize	0	0	0	0
Thomas Aldworthe & Higgons	Ind	12	piece	Brecon *Cloth*	12	0	0	0
		13	piece	Cloth of Assize	0	0	0	0
William Gyttons & Cutt	Ind	10	piece	Brecon *Cloth*	10	0	0	0
		11	piece	Cloth of Assize	0	0	0	0
Robert *Pressey* & Cox	Ind	18	piece	Cloth of Assize	0	0	0	0
William Yonge & Smythe	Ind	14	piece	Brecon *Cloth*	14	0	0	0
		11	piece	Cloth of Assize	0	0	0	0
John Sowche & Carr	Ind	22	piece	Cloth of Assize	0	0	0	0

Merchant name	Origin	Qty	Unit	Commodity	£	s.	d.	f.
Robert Halton &								
Jones	Ind	2	C goad	Cotton *Cloth*	6	13	4	o
		5	piece	Frieze *Cloth*	5	o	o	o
Thomas Williams								
& Symons	Ind	15	piece	Cloth of Assize	o	o	o	o

The Tremore of Bristol, David Guggan master, Exiting, 28th July 1564

Merchant name	Origin	Qty	Unit	Commodity	£	s.	d.	f.
William Pepwall &								
Sowche	Ind	4	fother	Lead	32	o	o	o
		2	piece	Cloth of Assize	o	o	o	o
Robert Smyth &								
Saxtey	Ind	5	piece	Cloth of Assize	o	o	o	o
		1	piece	Frieze *Cloth*	o	40	o	o

The Salomone of Bristol, Richard Richardes master, Exiting, *28th July 1564*

Merchant name	Origin	Qty	Unit	Commodity	£	s.	d.	f.
Nicholas Blake &								
Smythe	Ind	9	piece	Frieze *Cloth*	9	o	o	o
		3	piece	Cloth of Assize	o	o	o	o
William Kyrke &								
Yonge	Ind	5	piece	Fricze *Cloth*	5	o	o	o
		7	piece	Brecon *Cloth*	7	o	o	o
		5	piece	Cloth of Assize	o	o	o	o
Richard Cary &								
Gyttons	Ind	10	piece	Frieze *Cloth*	10	o	o	o
		5	piece	Brecon *Cloth*	5	o	o	o
Richard Hentley	Ind	10	piece	Frieze *Cloth*	10	o	o	o

The Phenix of Bristol, Thomas Corbett master, Exiting, 29th July 1564

Merchant name	Origin	Qty	Unit	Commodity	£	s.	d.	f.
John Cutt & Bysse	Ind	2	fother	Lead	16	o	o	o
		2	C goad	Cotton *Cloth*	6	13	4	o
		18	piece	Frieze *Cloth*	18	o	o	o
William Sherwoode	Ind	6	piece	Brecon *Cloth*	6	o	o	o

The Swanne of Bristol, John Allen master, Exiting, 2nd August 1564

Merchant name	Origin	Qty	Unit	Commodity	£	s.	d.	f.
Edmund Stones	Ind	1.7	ton	Iron	13	12	o	o
		1.5	tun	Vinegar	3	10	o	o

The Starre of Bristol, William Come(?) master, Exiting, 3rd August 1564

Merchant name	Origin	Qty	Unit	Commodity	£	s.	d.	f.
Maurice Warforde	Ind	1	C goad	Cotton *Cloth*	3	6	8	o
		5	piece	Frieze *Cloth*	5	o	o	o

The Marye Fortune of Bristol, Edmund Wodde master, Exiting, 4th August 1564

Merchant name	Origin	Qty	Unit	Commodity	£	s.	d.	f.
Giles Wodde & Coxe	Ind	23	piece	Cloth of Assize	o	o	o	o
John Browne &								
Chester	Ind	10	piece	Brecon *Cloth*	10	o	o	o
		17	piece	Cloth of Assize	o	o	o	o

Merchant name	Origin	Qty	Unit	Commodity	£	s.	d.	f.
Robert Hamblyne & Rowland	Ind	15	piece	Brecon *Cloth*	15	0	0	0
		2	piece	Frieze *Cloth*	0	40	0	0
		4	C goad	Cotton *Cloth*	13	6	8	0
Richard Cary & Higons	Ind	4	piece	Brecon *Cloth*	4	0	0	0
		3	C goad	Cotton *Cloth*	10	0	0	0
		14	piece	Cloth of Assize	0	0	0	0
Robert Halton & Kytchyn	Ind	1	fother	Lead	8	0	0	0
		6	piece	Brecon *Cloth*	6	0	0	0
		11	piece	Cloth of Assize	0	0	0	0
Nicholas Blake & Sowche	Ind	6	piece	Brecon *Cloth*	6	0	0	0
		19	piece	Cloth of Assize	0	0	0	0
John Cutt & Aldworth	Ind	4	piece	Brecon *Cloth*	4	0	0	0
		11	piece	Cloth of Assize	0	0	0	0
John Bysse & Sandford	Ind	4	C goad	Cotton *Cloth*	13	6	8	0
		21	piece	Cloth of Assize	0	0	0	0
Robert Smyth & Saxtey	Ind	18	piece	Cloth of Assize	0	0	0	0
William Gyttons & Dulle	Ind	6	piece	Brecon *Cloth*	6	0	0	0
		5	piece	Cloth of Assize	0	0	0	0

The Jeshus of New Ross, Edmund Kellye master, Exiting, 5th August 1564

Merchant name	Origin	Qty	Unit	Commodity	£	s.	d.	f.
Patrick Mathewe	Ind	1	hogshead	Iron	0	40	0	0
		2	dozen	Soap, Black	0	3	0	0
		4	pair	Stock-Cards	0	4	0	0
		0.5	C	Hops	0	5	0	0
Walter Whyte & Whyte	Ind	1.5	C	Aniseed	0	40	0	0
		0.75	C	Hops	0	7	6	0
		3.25	dozen	Soap, Black	0	7	10	0
		1	dozen	Caps	0	16	0	0
Nicholas Raggett	Ind	1.5	gross	Knives, in Pairs	0	36	0	0
		1	C	Thimbles	0	0	21	0
		2	ream	Paper	0	5	4	0
		4	dozen	Playing Cards	0	6	8	0
		1	dozen	Caps	0	16	8	0
		9	piece	Felts	0	10	0	0
		0.5	C	Aniseed	0	13	4	0
		6	dozen	Soap, Black	0	9	0	0
		1	dozen	Cumin	0	3	4	0
		1	lb	Saffron	0	13	4	0
		2	lb	Silk, Raw	0	13	4	0
		3	dozen	Girdles, Leather (*ob.*)	0	0	15	0
		3	dozen	Girdles, Leather (*2d.*)	0	5	0	0
		6	lb	Sulpher	0	0	6	0

Merchant name	Origin	Qty	Unit	Commodity	£	s.	d.	f.
		1	lb	Ginger	0	0	18	0
		1	lb	Pepper	0	0	20	0
		3	lb	Cloves	0	15	0	0
		1	lb	Mace	0	6	8	0
		1	dozen	Penhorns	0	0	12	0
		2	C	Awl Blades	0	0	16	0
		1	lb	Mail	0	0	10	0
		0.75	piece	Cloth of Assize	0	0	0	0
Richard Savage	Ind	1	gross	Cutts	0	5	0	0
		8	dozen	Girdles, Leather (2d.)	0	13	4	0
		10	dozen	Girdles, Leather (1d.)	0	8	4	0
		4	dozen	Playing Cards	0	6	8	0
		1	gross	Combs, (1d.)	0	10	0	0
		2	lb	Pepper	0	3	4	0
		2	lb	Cloves	0	10	0	0
		1	lb	Saffron	0	13	4	0
		0.25	C	Hops	0	2	6	0
		0.25	C	Aniseed	0	6	8	0
		2	dozen	Soap, Black	0	3	0	0
		2	bolt	Thread	0	6	8	0
		0.5	gross	Bowstrings	0	2	0	0
		0.5	gross	Knives, in Pairs	0	12	0	0
		2	lb	Silk, Raw	0	13	4	0
		0.5	great gross	Points	0	4	0	0
		1	dozen	Prunes	0	0	20	0
Thomas Rafter	Ind	1	pipe	Iron	4	0	0	0
		7	yard	Sarcenet *Cloth*	0	23	4	0
		8	lb	Silk, Raw	0	53	4	0
		2	ream	Paper	0	5	4	0
		2	piece	Night Caps, Velvet	0	5	0	0
		2	piece	Skins, Golden	0	2	2	0
		3	dozen	Penhorns	0	2	6	0
		3	bolt	Thread	0	10	0	0
		4	lb	Check	0	4	0	0
		8	lb	Sugar	0	5	4	0
		3	lb	Pepper	0	5	0	0
		3	lb	Cloves	0	15	0	0
		3	gross	Cutts	0	15	0	0
		1	dozen	Caps	0	16	8	0
		0.5	C	Hops	0	5	0	0
		0.5	lb	Saffron	0	6	8	0
		3	dozen	Aniseed	0	9	0	0
		3	dozen	Soap	0	4	6	0
		4	dozen	Girdles, Leather (2d.)	0	6	8	0
		3	dozen	Playing Cards	0	5	0	0
		2	gross	Points, Leather	0	3	4	0
		1	great gross	Points	0	8	0	0
		2	lb	Mercury	0	8	0	0
		1.5	piece	Cloth of Assize	0	0	0	0
John Seyte	Ind	2	gross	Cutts	0	10	0	0
		3	gross	Knives, in Pairs	3	12	0	0
		3	ream	Paper	0	8	0	0

Merchant name	Origin	Qty	Unit	Commodity	£	s.	d.	f.
		0.5	gross	Merells	0	2	0	0
		2	great gross	Points	0	16	0	0
		1	gross	Taps	0	0	6	0
		3	lb	Pepper	0	5	0	0
		3	lb	Cloves	0	15	0	0
		1	lb	Nutmeg	0	3	4	0
		0.5	C	Aniseed	0	13	4	0
		0.5	C	Hops	0	5	0	0
		4	dozen	Liquorice	0	8	0	0
		2	lb	Mail	0	0	20	0
		3	lb	Silk, Raw	0	20	0	0
		4	dozen	Playing Cards	0	6	8	0
		1	bolt	Thread	0	3	4	0
		2	lb	Check	0	2	0	0
		0.5	piece	Cloth of Assize	0	0	0	f.

The Grace of God of Waterford, Darby Harte master, Exiting, 5th August 1564

Merchant name	Origin	Qty	Unit	Commodity	£	s.	d.	f.
Merchant Unknown	Ind	1	dozen	Playing Cards	0	0	20	0
		1	bolt	Thread	0	3	4	0
		1	dozen	Penhorns	0	0	10	0
		1	ream	Paper	0	2	8	0
		1	dozen	Skins, Golden	0	5	0	0
		1	gross	Combs, (1d.)	0	8	0	0
		9	dozen	Girdles, Leather (2d.)	0	7	6	0
		2	piece	Hats	0	2	2	0
		1	gross	Points, Leather	0	0	20	0
James Lynche	Ind	1	dozen	Girdles, Sword	0	7	0	0
		1.5	great gross	Points	0	12	0	0
		1	dozen	Liquorice	0	2	0	0
		4	dozen	Playing Cards	0	6	8	0
		1.5	dozen	Caps	0	25	0	0
		3	dozen	Wool-Cards	0	30	0	0
		0.5	lb	Check	0	0	6	0
		1	ream	Paper	0	2	8	0
		1	dozen	Cumin	0	3	4	0
		2	lb	Mercury	0	8	0	0
		6	lb	Verdigris	0	4	0	0
		10	dozen	Buttons, Thread	0	0	10	0
		4	lb	Lead, Red	0	0	8	0
		2.25	piece	Cloth of Assize	0	0	0	0
		1	dozen	Girdles, Sword	0	7	0	0
		2	lb	Saffron	0	26	8	0
		2	lb	Silk, Raw	0	13	4	0
		1	gross	Knives, Bumbard	0	30	0	0
		3	great gross	Points	0	24	0	0
		1	lb	Mercury	0	4	0	0
		4	lb	Liquorice	0	0	8	0
		1	dozen	Caps	0	16	8	0
		1	dozen	Girdles, Leather (1d.)	0	0	10	0
		1	dozen	Skins, Golden	0	5	0	0
		3	dozen	Playing Cards	0	5	0	0

Merchant name	Origin	Qty	Unit	Commodity	£	s.	d.	f.
		1	dozen	Purses, Women	0	8	0	0
		1	piece	Chamlet *Cloth*	0	20	0	0
		1	ream	Paper	0	2	8	0
		2.25	piece	Cloth of Assize	0	0	0	0
Thomas Byrwen	Ind	4	lb	Saffron	0	53	4	0
		4	dozen	Cumin	0	14	4	0
		2	bolt	Thread	0	6	8	0
		4	piece	Night Caps, Velvet	0	10	0	0
		3	yard	Taffeta *Cloth*	0	20	0	0
		1	great gross	Points	0	8	0	0
		1	gross	Merells	0	4	0	0
		2	lb	Borax	0	26	8	0
		3.5	dozen	Caps	0	58	4	0
		4	dozen	Buttons, Thread	0	0	4	0
		0.5	dozen	Skins, Golden	0	2	6	0
		6	dozen	Girdles, Ribbon	0	10	0	0
		3	lb	Thread	0	3	10	0
		5	lb	Silk, Raw	0	33	4	0
		1.5	dozen	Knives, Almaine	0	3	9	0
		3	great gross	Points	0	24	0	0
		2	ream	Paper	0	5	4	0
		2	dozen	Playing Cards	0	3	4	0
		3	lb	Ryceres (?)	0	0	16	0
		2	dozen	Wool-Cards	0	20	0	0
		2	gross	Knives, Bumbard	3	0	0	0
		4	piece	Cloth of Assize	0	0	0	0
Nicholas Ffrenche	Ind	6	lb	Silk, Raw	0	40	0	0
		1	gross	Knives, Bumbard	0	30	0	0
		2	dozen	Cumin	0	6	8	0
		8	dozen	Girdles, Ribbon	0	13	4	0
		4	lb	Bornby	0	8	4	0
		6	lb	Mercury	0	24	0	0
		2	bolt	Thread	0	6	8	0
		0.5	gross	Playing Cards	0	10	0	0
		1	ream	Paper	0	2	8	0
		4	dozen	Merells	0	0	16	0
		0.5	dozen	Gloves, Venice	0	4	0	0
		0.5	dozen	Skins, Golden	0	2	6	0
		10	lb	Verdigris	0	6	8	0
		4	piece	Night Caps, Velvet	0	10	0	0
		2	gross	Cutts	0	10	0	0
		2.5	piece	Cloth of Assize	0	0	0	0
Walter Sawle	Ind	1	C	Hops	0	10	0	0
		1.5	C	Soap, Black	0	10	0	0
		1	dozen	Caps	0	16	8	0
		1.5	dozen	Stock-Cards	0	18	0	0
		1	gross	Cutts	0	5	0	0
		1	great gross	Points	0	8	0	0
		1	gross	Points, Leather	0	0	20	0
		4	M	Teazles	0	6	8	0
Stephen Whyte	Ind	2	dozen	Knives, Bumbard	0	5	0	0
		4	lb	Pepper	0	6	8	0

Merchant name	Origin	Qty	Unit	Commodity	£	s.	d.	f.
		0.5	small gross	Points	0	0	4	0
		1	lb	Soap, White	0	0	4	0
		1	bolt	Thread	0	3	4	0
		1	lb	Thread	0	0	15	0
		1	lb	Girdles, Ribbon	0	0	20	0
		0.5	gross	Merells	0	2	0	0
		2.25	piece	Cloth of Assize	0	0	0	0
James Water	Ind	1	gross	Cutts	0	5	0	0
		1	great gross	Points	0	8	0	0
		6	dozen	Knives, Bumbard	0	15	0	0
		1	dozen	Playing Cards	0	0	20	0
		4	lb	Thread	0	5	0	0
		1	dozen	Girdles, Leather (1d.)	0	0	10	0
		1	bolt	Thread	0	3	4	0
		2	lb	Saffron	0	26	8	0
		8	lb	Pepper	0	13	4	0
		4	yard	Chamlet *Cloth*	0	8	0	0
		0.5	piece	Frieze *Cloth*	0	10	0	0
		2.5	piece	Cloth of Assize	0	0	0	0
Peter Hacket	Ind	20	lb	Pepper	0	33	4	0
		1	gross	Cutts	0	5	0	0
		2	bolt	Thread	0	6	8	0
		2	lb	Check	0	2	0	0
		2	lb	Thread	0	2	6	0
		2	dozen	Knives, Bumbard	0	5	0	0
		2.5	piece	Cloth of Assize	0	0	0	0
David Dryling	Ind	2	C	Oakum	0	10	0	0
		1	C	Hops	0	10	0	0
		1	gross	Cutts	0	5	0	0
		2	bolt	Thread	0	6	8	0
		1	lb	Saffron	0	13	4	0
		0.5	lb	Cinnamon	0	2	0	0
		3	dozen	Hose, Womens	0	20	0	0
		1.25	piece	Cloth of Assize	0	0	0	0
Stephen Leonarde	Ind	5	ton	Iron	40	0	0	0
		1	lb	Saffron	0	13	4	0
		1	C	Hops	0	10	0	0
		2	C	Oakum	0	10	0	0
		0.75	piece	Cloth of Assize	0	0	0	0

The John of Bristol, Edmund Perkyns master, Exiting, 6th August 1564

Merchant name	Origin	Qty	Unit	Commodity	£	s.	d.	f.
John Carre & Kelke[ ]	Ind	4	fother	Lead	32	0	0	0
		3	C goad	Cotton *Cloth*	10	0	0	0
Thomas Diconson & Bysse	Ind	7	C	Tin, Worked	16	6	8	0
		2	C goad	Cotton *Cloth*	6	13	4	0

The Margarett of Morbihan, Lewis Baron master, Exiting, 15th August 1564

Merchant name	Origin	Qty	Unit	Commodity	£	s.	d.	f.
Evan Ffalcon & *Lewis Baron*	Alien	15	wey	Coal, Smith	5	0	0	0

Merchant name	Origin	Qty	Unit	Commodity	£	s.	d.	f.
		20	piece	Frieze *Cloth*	20	0	0	0
		2	piece	Flannel *Cloth*	0	40	0	0
		0.5	piece	Cloth of Assize	0	0	0	0

The Tobye of Bristol, John Baker master, Exiting, 23rd August 1564

Merchant name	Origin	Qty	Unit	Commodity	£	s.	d.	f.
William Yonge & Yonge	Ind	7.5	C goad	Cotton *Cloth*	25	0	0	0
		20	piece	Brecon *Cloth*	20	0	0	0
		31	piece	Cloth of Assize	0	0	0	0
Nicholas Blake & Ashe	Ind	10	piece	Brecon *Cloth*	10	0	0	0
		3	C goad	Cotton *Cloth*	10	0	0	0
		10	piece	Frieze *Cloth*	10	0	0	0
		14	piece	Cloth of Assize	0	0	0	0
James Dowle & Hentley	Ind	11	piece	Brecon *Cloth*	11	0	0	0
		12	piece	Cloth of Assize	0	0	0	0
Robert Halton & Carr	Ind	3	piece	Brecon *Cloth*	3	0	0	0
		8.66	piece	Cloth of Assize	0	0	0	0
John Puyck? & Baddram	Ind	11	piece	Brecon *Cloth*	11	0	0	0
		3	C goad	Cotton *Cloth*	10	0	0	0
		2	piece	Cloth of Assize	0	0	0	0

The Dragon of Bristol, William Apgwilliam master, Exiting, 1st September 1564

Merchant name	Origin	Qty	Unit	Commodity	£	s.	d.	f.
William Gyttons & Roberts	Ind	32	piece	Frieze *Cloth*	32	0	0	0
		1	piece	Brecon *Cloth*	0	20	0	0
		7	piece	Cloth of Assize	0	0	0	0
Robert Kytchyn & Higgons	Ind	4	C goad	Cotton *Cloth*	13	6	8	0
Richard Band & Shee	Ind	3	piece	Frieze *Cloth*	3	0	0	0
		8	C	Irish Frieze *Cloth*	16	0	0	0
John Bradshaw & Atkyns	Ind	1	C goad	Cotton *Cloth*	3	6	8	0
		5	piece	Frieze *Cloth*	5	0	0	0

The George of Bristol, Henry Nelson master, Exiting, 2nd September 1564

Merchant name	Origin	Qty	Unit	Commodity	£	s.	d.	f.
Unknown Langton	Ind	4	lb	Silk, Raw	0	26	8	0
		1	lb	Saffron	0	13	4	0
		1	gross	Knives, Almaine	0	30	0	0
		1	great gross	Points	0	8	0	0
		1.5	piece	Cloth of Assize	0	0	0	0
George Owen	Ind	8	lb	Silk, Raw	0	53	4	0
		8	lb	Saffron	5	6	8	0
		6	lb	Cloves	0	30	0	0
		2	dozen	Caps	0	33	4	0

Merchant name	Origin	Qty	Unit	Commodity	£	s.	d.	f.
		3	lb	Pepper	0	5	0	0
		2	gross	Cutts	0	10	0	0
		1	great gross	Points	0	8	0	0
		2	lb	Borax	0	26	8	0
		1	bolt	Thread	0	3	4	0
		4	lb	Verdigris	0	2	8	0
		4	dozen	Playing Cards	0	6	8	0
		3	dozen	Flax	0	8	0	0
		3	dozen	Girdles, Leather (1d.)	0	2	6	0
		2	lb	Mercury	0	8	0	0
		1	dozen	Skins, Golden	0	5	0	0
		3.5	piece	Cloth of Assize	0	0	0	0
Robert Walter	Ind	2	lb	Saffron	0	26	8	0
		6	lb	Silk, Raw	0	40	0	0
		1	dozen	Caps	0	16	8	0
		2	gross	Cutts	0	10	0	0
		1	great gross	Points	0	8	0	0
		1	gross	Points, Leather	0	0	20	0
		2	piece	Calico Cloth	0	13	4	0
		1	lb	Cloves	0	5	0	0
		1	lb	Pepper	0	0	20	0
		1	dozen	Twine	0	8	0	0
		1	dozen	Penhorns	0	0	20	0
		1	lb	Mercury	0	4	0	0
		1	clout	Needles	0	0	10	0
		0.5	piece	Cloth of Assize	0	0	0	0

The Savyor of Milford Haven, John Wade master, Exiting, 2nd September 1564

Merchant name	Origin	Qty	Unit	Commodity	£	s.	d.	f.
Thomas Duffe & Baddram	Ind	3	C goad	Cotton Cloth	10	0	0	0
		6	C	Soap, Black	0	40	0	0
		1.5	C	Aniseed	0	40	0	0
		3	M	Teazles	0	5	0	0

The Flower de Luce of Bristol, Thomas Nailer master, Exiting, *2nd September 1564*

Merchant name	Origin	Qty	Unit	Commodity	£	s.	d.	f.
John Browne & Saxtye	Ind	1	fother	Lead	8	0	0	0
		4	piece	Brecon Cloth	4	0	0	0
		9	piece	Cloth of Assize	0	0	0	0

The Trinitye of Topsham, William Hystocke master, Exiting, 4th September 1564

Merchant name	Origin	Qty	Unit	Commodity	£	s.	d.	f.
Thomas Rowland & Chester	Ind	4	fother	Lead	32	0	0	0
		4	C goad	Cotton Cloth	13	6	8	0
		9	piece	Brecon Cloth	9	0	0	0
		3	piece	Wadmal Cloth	3	0	0	0
John Roberts	Ind	6	piece	Brecon Cloth	6	0	0	0
		1	C goad	Cotton Cloth	3	6	8	0
		6	piece	Cloth of Assize	0	0	0	0

Merchant name	Origin	Qty	Unit	Commodity	£	s.	d.	f.

The Angell of Bristol, Henry Money master, Exiting, 4th September 1564

Merchant name	Origin	Qty	Unit	Commodity	£	s.	d.	f.
George Higgons								
& Cary	Ind	3	piece	Brecon *Cloth*	3	0	0	0
		4	piece	Frieze *Cloth*	4	0	0	0
		8	piece	Cloth of Assize	0	0	0	0
Robert Saxty &								
Standfast	Ind	6	piece	Frieze *Cloth*	6	0	0	0
		5	piece	Cloth of Assize	0	0	0	0
John Bradshaw &								
Snowe	Ind	4	piece	Brecon *Cloth*	4	0	0	0
		3	piece	Frieze *Cloth*	3	0	0	0

The *Marye* of San Sebastián, Julian Dollonds master, Exiting, 4th September 1564

Merchant name	Origin	Qty	Unit	Commodity	£	s.	d.	f.
Merchant Unknown	Ind	5	piece	Wadmal *Cloth*	5	0	0	0
			Unknown	Unknown	6	0	0	0
		12.5	piece	Cloth of Assize	0	0	0	0
		1	piece	Frieze *Cloth*	0	20	0	0
		5.83	piece	Cloth of Assize	0	0	0	0
John de S[ ]	Alien	1.5	C	Wax	4	10	0	0
		5	piece	Wadmal *Cloth*	5	0	0	0
		0.5	piece	Cloth of Assize	0	0	0	0
Robert Tyndall &								
Bradshaw	Ind	4	piece	Brecon *Cloth*	4	0	0	0
Robert Ravell	Ind	6	piece	Cloth of Assize	0	0	0	0
William Gyttons &								
Atkyns	Ind	2	piece	Brecon *Cloth*	0	40	0	0
		3	piece	Frieze *Cloth*	3	0	0	0
		2	piece	Cloth of Assize	0	0	0	0

The Prymrose of Bristol, Thomas Morrys master, Exiting, 6th September 1564

Merchant name	Origin	Qty	Unit	Commodity	£	s.	d.	f.
Robert Kytchyn &								
Ashe	Ind	28	piece	Frieze *Cloth*	28	0	0	0
Thomas Rowland	Ind	26	piece	Frieze *Cloth*	26	0	0	0
		4	C	Tin, Devon	6	0	0	0
		3	piece	Cloth of Assize	0	0	0	0
Robert Smyth &								
Southe	Ind	4	piece	Frieze *Cloth*	4	0	0	0
		1	piece	Brecon *Cloth*	0	20	0	0
		4	piece	Cloth of Assize	0	0	0	0
Thomas Dyconson								
& Saxcty	Ind	4	C	Tin, Devon	6	0	0	0
		1	piece	Cloth of Assize	0	0	0	0

The [ ] of Bristol, David Seyte master, Exiting, 6th September 1564

Merchant name	Origin	Qty	Unit	Commodity	£	s.	d.	f.
John Roberts &								
Unknown	Ind	19	piece	Frieze *Cloth*	19	0	0	0

Merchant name	Origin	Qty	Unit	Commodity	£	s.	d.	f.
The Jeshus of Liverpool, John Cocks master, Exiting, 7th September 1564								
Lettice Shee	Ind	10	ton	Ashes, Ore	3	6	8	0
		2	M	Horns, Unspecified	3	0	0	0
		2	C	Lead	0	24	0	0
The Francys of Le Conquet, John Ladrysack master, Exiting, 7th September 1564								
John *Ladrysack*	Ind	3	piece	Frieze *Cloth*	3	0	0	0
		2	piece	Wadmal *Cloth*	0	40	0	0
Robert Ams[ ]	Ind	10	wey	Coal, Smith	3	6	8	0
		1	C goad	Cotton *Cloth*	3	6	8	0
		1	piece	Brecon *Cloth*	0	20	0	0
		6	piece	Frieze *Cloth*	6	0	0	0
		1.5	piece	Cloth of Assize	0	0	0	0
The Katherne of Le Conquet, William Levesrane master, Exiting, 7th September 1564								
Unknown Pollard	Ind	10	wey	Coal, Smith	3	6	8	0
		2	C goad	Cotton *Cloth*	6	13	4	0
The Mawdelen of San Sebastián, Martin [ ], master, Exiting, 12th September 1564								
John de Grattson	Alien	3	piece	Cloth of Assize	0	0	0	0
Unknown Roberts & Lye	Ind	2	piece	Wadmal *Cloth*	0	40	0	0
		1.5	C	Wax	4	10	0	0
Robert Saxtye & Bradshawe	Ind	3	C goad	Cotton *Cloth*	10	0	0	0
The Faulcon of Bristol, John Slyght master, Exiting, 18th September 1564								
John Sowche & Smyth	Ind	4	piece	Brecon *Cloth*	4	0	0	0
		6	piece	Cloth of Assize	0	0	0	0
Robert Pressye	Ind	3	piece	Cloth of Assize	0	0	0	0
The Margarett of Bridgwater, John Mowrse master, Exiting, 18th September 1564								
David Jones	Ind	0.5	C	Aniseed	0	13	4	0
		1	C	Iron	0	8	0	0
		0.25	C	Hops	0	2	6	0
		1	lb	Silk, Raw	0	6	8	0

Merchant name	Origin	Qty	Unit	Commodity	£	s.	d.	f.

IMPORTS

The Trinite of Combwich, William Sumpter master, Entering, 1st October 1563 £ s. d. f.

Merchant name	Origin	Qty	Unit	Commodity	£	s.	d.	f.
William Crosse, Sumpter & Baylie	Ind	125	C	Fish, Cole	25	0	0	0
		2.5	last	Fish, Salmon	45	0	0	0

The James of Youghal, Cornell Geren master, Entering, 3rd October 1563

Merchant name	Origin	Qty	Unit	Commodity	£	s.	d.	f.
Richard Lavalen	Ind	1.5	last	Fish, Herring White	9	0	0	0
		2	hogshead	Fish, Salmon	6	0	0	0
		44	stone	Wool, Irish	5	17	4	0
		10	stone	Wool, Flocks	0	19	2	0
		7	C	Skins, Lamb	5	16	8	0
		15	piece	Skins, Otter	0	30	0	0
		3.5	C	Tallow	0	58	4	0
		3	C	Skins, Sheep	0	40	0	0
		12	piece	Skins, Fox	0	8	0	0
James Rotche	Ind	5	C	Skins, Lamb	4	3	4	0
		2.5	C	Skins, Sheep	0	33	4	0
		15	piece	Skins, Deer	0	5	0	0
		1	C	Skins, Sheep Broken	0	5	0	0
		8	piece	Skins, Otter	0	16	0	0
		15	piece	Skins, Fox	0	10	0	0
		7	stone	Wool, Irish	0	18	8	0
		20	stone	Wool, Flocks	0	38	4	0
		0.5	C	Tallow	0	8	4	0

The Jeshus of New Ross, John Peers master, Entering, 2nd November 1563

Merchant name	Origin	Qty	Unit	Commodity	£	s.	d.	f.
John Rotche & Archer	Ind	8.5	C	*Irish* Frieze *Cloth*	17	0	0	0
		9.5	C	Skins, Sheep	6	6	8	0
		8	piece	Skins, Fox	0	5	4	0
		3	stone	Wool, Flocks	0	5	9	0
		1	piece	Skins, Otter	0	2	0	0
		1	barrel	Fish, Herring White	0	10	0	0
Richard Marshall & Ragged	Ind	11	C	*Irish* Frieze *Cloth*	21	0	0	0
		10	C	Skins, Sheep	6	13	4	0
		3	piece	Mantles	0	15	0	0
		2	piece	Skins, Fox	0	0	16	0
		0.5	C	Skins, Sheep Broken	0	2	6	0

The Katheren of Waterford, Pierce Hoore master, Entering, 24th November 1563

Merchant name	Origin	Qty	Unit	Commodity	£	s.	d.	f.
Edmund Power & Clerye	Ind	8.5	C	*Irish* Frieze *Cloth*	17	0	0	0
		12	piece	Mantles	3	0	0	0
		3.5	C	Skins, Sheep	0	46	8	0
Pierce Hoore & Duffe	Ind	4	barrel	Fish, Herring White	0	40	0	0

Merchant name	Origin	Qty	Unit	Commodity	£	s.	d.	f.
		4	C	*Irish* Frieze *Cloth*	8	0	0	0
Pierce White & Keren	Ind	5.5	C	*Irish* Frieze *Cloth*	11	0	0	0
		6	C	Skins, Sheep	4	0	0	0
		6	stone	Wool, Flocks	0	11	6	0
		4	piece	Mantles	0	20	0	0
		2	barrel	Fish, Herring White	0	10	0	0
Patrick Hanraughan & Wale	Ind	21	C	Skins, Sheep	14	0	0	0
		6	C	*Irish* Frieze *Cloth*	12	0	0	0
		20	piece	Skins, Fox	0	13	4	0
		2	C	Skins, Kid	0	10	0	0
		2	C	Skins, Lamb	0	33	4	0
Andrew Creangh & Welshe	Ind	10	C	Skins, Sheep	6	13	4	0
		4	C	Skins, Lamb	3	6	8	0
		12	stone	Wool, Irish	0	32	0	0
		8	stone	Wool, Flocks	0	15	4	0
		6	piece	Skins, Otter	0	12	0	0
		36	piece	Skins, Fox	0	12	0	0
		23	piece	Skins, Deer	0	11	0	0
		1	C	*Irish* Frieze *Cloth*	0	40	0	0
		1	barrel	Fish, Herring White	0	10	0	0
		12	piece	Mantles	3	0	0	0
		0.5	C	Skins, Sheep Broken	0	2	6	0
Nicholas Morewey & Wulfe	Ind	4.5	C	Skins, Sheep	3	0	0	0
		30	piece	Skins, Deer	0	10	0	0
		6	piece	Skins, Fox	0	4	0	0
		14	piece	Skins, Otter	0	28	0	0
		0.5	C	Skins, Lamb	0	8	4	0
Dominic Crewghe & Crewghe	Ind	4	C	Skins, Sheep	0	53	4	0
		1.5	C	Skins, Lamb	0	25	0	0
		31	piece	Skins, Fox	0	20	8	0
		44	yard	Irish Linen *Cloth*	0	7	4	0
		13	piece	Skins, Marten	0	43	4	0
		50	piece	Skins, Otter	5	0	0	0
		0.5	C	Skins, Sheep Broken	0	2	6	0

The Maria of Pasajes de San Juan, Michael Deisaste master, Entering, 2nd December 1563

Merchant name	Origin	Qty	Unit	Commodity	£	s.	d.	f.
George *Hopton* & Barnes	Ind	18	tun	Wine	0	0	0	0
Richard Hill & Yonge	Ind	18	tun	Wine	0	0	0	0
John de Salavilia	Alien	1	pipe	Wine	0	0	0	0

The Savior of Errenteria, Sebastian de Subrieta master, Entering, 10th December 1563

Merchant name	Origin	Qty	Unit	Commodity	£	s.	d.	f.
William Carre & Hentley	Ind	54	tun	Wine	0	0	0	0
John Ashe & Yonge	Ind	11	tun	Wine	0	0	0	0
Thomas Bonas	Ind	30	C	Alum	50	0	0	0

Merchant name	Origin	Qty	Unit	Commodity	£	s.	d.	f.
John de Petie & Dearana	Alien	12	tun	Wine	0	0	0	0

The Sancta Maria of Hondarribia, John Swane master, Entering, 13th December 1563

Merchant name	Origin	Qty	Unit	Commodity	£	s.	d.	f.
Robert Sexie & Yonge	Ind	9	ton	Iron	36	0	0	0
Gabriel Derangavell & Munsabay	Alien	8.3	ton	Iron	33	6	8	0
Laurence de Ewyengeron & Deifurem	Alien	8.3	ton	Iron	33	6	8	0
		1	ton	Rosin	0	40	0	0
William Yonge & assoc.	Ind	5	tun	Wine	0	0	0	0

The St Michaell of Errenteria, Michael de Beroby master, Entering, 13th December 1563

Merchant name	Origin	Qty	Unit	Commodity	£	s.	d.	f.
Stephen de Sastie & de Labaia	Alien	6	ton	Iron	24	0	0	0
Martin Suabar & Derobie	Alien	3	ton	Iron	12	0	0	0
Robert Tindall & Carye	Ind	7	ton	Iron	28	0	0	0
Domingo de Joa & de Gee	Alien	2	ton	Iron	8	0	0	0
Michael de Samora & de Sara	Alien	6	ton	Iron	24	0	0	0
Francis de Passalour	Alien	8	ton	Iron	32	0	0	0
Thomas Chester & assoc.	Ind	4	tun	Wine	0	0	0	0
Francis de Passalour	Alien	4	tun	Wine	0	0	0	0

The James of Youghal, Cornell Geren master, Entering, 14th December 1563

Merchant name	Origin	Qty	Unit	Commodity	£	s.	d.	f.
Thomas Verdon	Ind	10	barrel	Fish, Herring White	5	0	0	0
		6	barrel	Fish, Salmon	9	0	0	0
		4	C	Tallow	3	6	8	0
		5	C	Fish, Hake	5	0	0	0
		2.5	C	Skins, Lamb	0	41	8	0
		2.5	C	Skins, Sheep	0	33	4	0
		2.5	C	Hops	0	25	0	0
		2	hoghead	Meat	4	0	0	0

The Anne of Pembroke, Thomas Folland master, Entering, 16th December 1563

Merchant name	Origin	Qty	Unit	Commodity	£	s.	d.	f.
Thomas Duffe & Folland	Ind	5	last	Fish, Herring White	30	0	0	0

The St John of San Sebastián, Bartholemew Hernandus master, Entering, 16th December 1563

Merchant name	Origin	Qty	Unit	Commodity	£	s.	d.	f.
Thomas Chester & assoc.	Ind	9	tun	Wine	0	0	0	0
		10	ton	Rosin	20	0	0	0

Merchant name	Origin	Qty	Unit	Commodity	£	s.	d.	f.

The Trenete of Tintern, John Getinge master, Entering, 17th December 1563

Merchant name	Origin	Qty	Unit	Commodity	£	s.	d.	f.
Richard Carye	Ind	2.5	ton	Iron	10	0	0	0

The Angell of Chepstow, Thomas Longe master, Entering, *17th December 1563*

Merchant name	Origin	Qty	Unit	Commodity	£	s.	d.	f.
Robert Saxie & Bishoppe	Ind	9	ton	Iron	36	0	0	0
Domingo de Salavaria	Alien	2	ton	Iron	8	0	0	0

The Clement of Bristol, Hugh Willis master, Entering, 19th December 1563

Merchant name	Origin	Qty	Unit	Commodity	£	s.	d.	f.
Walter Standfaste & Winter	Ind	14	barrel	Fish, Herring White	7	0	0	0
Thomas Edie & Benett	Ind	10	barrel	Fish, Herring White	5	0	0	0
John Thorne & Phelpe	Ind	10	barrel	Fish, Herring White	5	0	0	0
Walter Cox & Edye	Ind	4	barrel	Fish, Herring White	0	40	0	0

The Michaell of Chepstow, David Jones master, Entering, 23rd December 1563

Merchant name	Origin	Qty	Unit	Commodity	£	s.	d.	f.
James Dowle & Carre	Ind	1	ton	Rosin	0	40	0	0
		5	tun	Vinegar	11	13	4	0

The Fage of Dungarvan, Thomas Ffitzrichard master, Entering, 24th December 1563

Merchant name	Origin	Qty	Unit	Commodity	£	s.	d.	f.
Thomas *Ffitzrichard*	Ind	20	barrel	Fish, Herring White	10	0	0	0
		3	C	Fish, Hake	3	0	0	0
Thomas Ffitzjohn	Ind	10	barrel	Fish, Herring White	5	0	0	0
		1	C	Fish, Hake	0	20	0	0
		0.5	C	Skins, Sheep	0	6	8	0

The Salvator of Viana do Castello, Sebastian de Costo master, Entering, 24th January 1564

Merchant name	Origin	Qty	Unit	Commodity	£	s.	d.	f.
Sebastian de Costo	Alien	40	M	Oranges	13	6	8	0

The George of Wexford, James Sayes master, Entering, 27th January 1564

Merchant name	Origin	Qty	Unit	Commodity	£	s.	d.	f.
Patrick Chever & Sayes	Ind	20	barrel	Fish, Herring White	10	0	0	0
		20	mease	Fish, Herring Red	5	0	0	0

The Grace of God of Waterford, Darby Harte master, Entering, 28th January 1564

Merchant name	Origin	Qty	Unit	Commodity	£	s.	d.	f.
James *Rotche* & Madden	Ind	7	last	Fish, Herring White	42	0	0	0
		4	piece	Mantles	0	20	0	0
Darby Harte & assoc.	Ind	2	last	Fish, Herring White	12	0	0	0

Merchant name	Origin	Qty	Unit	Commodity	£	s.	d.	f.

The Katheren of Waterford, John Coscrowe master, Entering, 28th January 1564

Merchant name	Origin	Qty	Unit	Commodity	£	s.	d.	f.
John Browne & Morfey	Ind	82	barrel	Fish, Herring White	41	0	0	0
Maurice Fitzharry & Nele	Ind	26	barrel	Fish, Herring White	13	0	0	0

The Trenetie of Dublin, Philip Langhan master, Entering, 12th February 1564

Merchant name	Origin	Qty	Unit	Commodity	£	s.	d.	f.
Jasper Chonder & White	Ind	9	last	Fish, Herring White	54	0	0	0
		2	barrel	Fish, Salmon	3	0	0	0
Walter White & Meangh	Ind	3.5	last	Fish, Herring White	21	0	0	0
Edward Brawe & *Philip Langhan*	Ind	3	stone	Wool, Flocks	0	5	9	0
		2	hoghead	Fish, Herring White	0	40	0	0

The Jeshus of Youghal, Richard Griffan master, Entering, 15th February 1564

Merchant name	Origin	Qty	Unit	Commodity	£	s.	d.	f.
Peter Lyncolln, Roche & assoc.	Ind	1	M	Fish, Hake	10	0	0	0
		7.5	last	Fish, Herring White	45	0	0	0
		20	stone	Wool, Flocks	0	28	4	0
		0.5	C	Skins, Sheep	0	6	8	0
		1	dicker	Skins, Deer	0	3	4	0

The Peter of Wexford, Nicholas Haye master, Entering, 15th February 1564

Merchant name	Origin	Qty	Unit	Commodity	£	s.	d.	f.
Patrick Chever & assoc.	Ind	4.5	last	Fish, Herring White	22	0	0	0
		40	mease	Fish, Herring Red	10	0	0	0
		2	C	Skins, Sheep	0	26	8	0
		6	piece	Mantles	0	30	0	0

The George of Gloucester, Thomas Carewell master, Entering, 17th February 1564

Merchant name	Origin	Qty	Unit	Commodity	£	s.	d.	f.
William Tyler	Ind	28	barrel	Fish, Herring White	14	0	0	0

The Andrewe James of London, John Borell master, Entering, 22nd February 1564

Merchant name	Origin	Qty	Unit	Commodity	£	s.	d.	f.
James Hawes	Ind	40	tun	Oil, *Olive*	320	0	0	0
		55	C	Aniseed	73	6	8	0
Robert Dove & Underwood	Ind	5.5	ton	Raisins, *Great*	33	0	0	0
		8	pair	Hose, Silk	10	13	4	0
		3.8	dozen	Skins, Spanish	11	10	0	0
		105	yard	Taffeta *Cloth*	21	0	0	0
		1	lb	Stiching silk coler	0	26	8	0

Merchant name	Origin	Qty	Unit	Commodity	£	s.	d.	f.

The Anne of Milford Haven, Thomas Folland master, Entering, 25th February 1564

Merchant name	Origin	Qty	Unit	Commodity	£	s.	d.	f.
William Dodall	Ind	3.5	last	Fish, Herring White	21	0	0	0
		3.5	C	Tallow	0	58	4	0

The Triamor of Bristol, Thomas Monndy master, Entering, 25th February 1564

Merchant name	Origin	Qty	Unit	Commodity	£	s.	d.	f.
George Snigge	Ind	8	ton	Iron	24	0	0	0
		2.8	tun	Oil, Train	13	15	0	0
		2	ton	Pitch	4	0	0	0
William Coxe & White	Ind	5.5	ton	Iron	22	0	0	0
Peter Hamlyn & Pope	Ind	19	ton	Iron	76	0	0	0
Robert Byshoppe & Walton	Ind	4	ton	Iron	16	0	0	0
Rowland Northall & Sherwode	Ind	6	C	Iron	0	24	0	0
		1.3	tun	Oil, Train	6	5	0	0
Thomas Monndy	Ind	1	hogshead	Oil, Train	0	25	0	0

The John of Bristol, Edmund Perkins master, Entering, 25th February 1564

Merchant name	Origin	Qty	Unit	Commodity	£	s.	d.	f.
John Carre & Halton	Ind	14	tun	Wine	0	0	0	0

The George of Bristol, Walter Dulles master, Entering, 25th February 1564

Merchant name	Origin	Qty	Unit	Commodity	£	s.	d.	f.
Robert Saxie & Souche	Ind	10	ton	Iron	40	0	0	0
Nicholas Blake & Sheward	Ind	9	ton	Iron	36	0	0	0
		1.5	tun	Wine	12	0	0	0
Walter Dulles & White	Ind	13	ton	Iron	52	0	0	0
John Griffeth	Ind	1.5	tun	Wine	12	0	0	0

The Trenytie of Youghal, William Neele master, Entering, 25th February 1564

Merchant name	Origin	Qty	Unit	Commodity	£	s.	d.	f.
William Neele & Dradye	Ind	18	barrel	Fish, Herring White	9	0	0	0
		12	C	Skins, Sheep	8	0	0	0
		1	barrel	Fish, Salmon	0	30	0	0
		1	virken	Fish, Salmon	0	15	0	0
		33	stone	Wool, Flocks	3	16	0	0
		4	stone	Wool, Irish	0	10	8	0

The Jeshus of Dungarvan, David Ffitzjohn master, Entering, 25th February 1564

Merchant name	Origin	Qty	Unit	Commodity	£	s.	d.	f.
James Hore	Ind	3	last	Fish, Herring White	18	0	0	0
		1	C	Fish, Hake	0	20	0	0
		1	C	Skins, Sheep	0	13	4	0

Merchant name	Origin	Qty	Unit	Commodity	£	s.	d.	f.
The Ellen of Newnham, John Spratt master, Entering, 10th March 1564								
Thomas Weston	Ind	6.5	C	Tallow	6	5	0	0
The Katheren of Waterford, Patrick Hoore master, Entering, 11th March 1564								
Patrick *Hoore* & Luicolle?	Ind	2.5	last	Fish, Herring White	15	0	0	0
		1	C	*Irish* Frieze *Cloth*	0	40	0	0
		3	piece	Mantles	0	15	0	0
Pierce Sharlocke & Browne	Ind	3	last	Fish, Herring White	18	0	0	0
		0.5	C	*Irish* Frieze *Cloth*	0	20	0	0
		1	C	Skins, Sheep	0	13	4	0
		6	piece	Mantles	0	30	0	0
		10	piece	Skins, Deer	0	3	4	0
Walter Welshe & Power	Ind	3	C	Skins, Sheep	0	40	0	0
		12	barrel	Fish, Herring White	6	0	0	0
		1	C	*Irish* Frieze *Cloth*	0	40	0	0
Edmund Clere & Turbecke	Ind	3	C	Skins, Sheep	0	40	0	0
		22	barrel	Fish, Herring White	11	0	0	0
		190	yard	*Irish* Frieze *Cloth*	3	3	4	0
		1	piece	Mantles	0	5	0	0
The Anne of Waterford, Thomas Kerren master, Entering, 13th March 1564								
Thomas Kerren, Butler & Bruer	Ind	5	last	Fish, Herring White	30	0	0	0
		4	C	Skins, Sheep	0	53	4	0
Stephen Leonard & Gromwell	Ind	30	barrel	Fish, Herring White	15	0	0	0
		7	C	Skins, Sheep	4	13	4	0
		1	hogshead	Cute	3	0	0	0
		1	C	Skins, Lamb	0	16	8	0
The George of Fethard-on-Sea, John Brytton master, Entering, 16th March 1564								
Francis Rammond & Langton	Ind	4	last	Fish, Herring White	24	0	0	0
		30	mease	Fish, Herring Red	7	10	0	0
		5	stone	Wool, Irish	0	14	8	0
The Sonday of Wexford, Philip Stafford master, Entering, *16th March 1564*								
Philip *Stafford*	Ind	1.5	last	Fish, Herring White	9	0	0	0
The Jeshus of New Ross, John Peers master, Entering, 18th March 1564								
Jasper Stafford	Ind	4	last	Fish, Herring White	24	0	0	0
		5	C	Skins, Sheep	3	6	8	0

Merchant name	Origin	Qty	Unit	Commodity	£	s.	d.	f.
		1	piece	Mantles	0	5	0	0
		1	virken	Fish, Salmon	0	15	0	0

The Marye of Wexford, Gareth Fortune master, Entering, 24th March 1564

Merchant name	Origin	Qty	Unit	Commodity	£	s.	d.	f.
Thomas Whitehall	Ind	1	last	Fish, Herring White	6	0	0	0
		2	mease	Fish, Herring Red	0	10	0	0
		1	barrel	Fish, Salmon	0	30	0	0
		3	piece	Mantles	0	15	0	0
		1	stone	Wool, Irish	0	2	8	0
		2	stone	Wool, Flocks	0	3	10	0

The Julyan of Bristol, Thomas Morryce master, Entering, 7th April 1564

Merchant name	Origin	Qty	Unit	Commodity	£	s.	d.	f.
Thomas Aldworth & Smyth	Ind	5.8	tun	Wine	0	0	0	0
Thomas Symons & Willyams	Ind	4.5	tun	Wine	0	0	0	0
		1.5	tun	Oil, *Olive*	12	0	0	0
		2	ton	Raisins, *Great*	12	0	0	0
		7	C	Soap	5	5	0	0
Richard Yonge & Fownes	Ind	4	tun	Wine	0	0	0	0
Edmund Smyth & Atkins	Ind	2.5	tun	Wine	0	0	0	0
George Higgons & Ashe	Ind	4.5	tun	Wine	0	0	0	0
William Coxe & Yonge	Ind	3.5	tun	Wine	0	0	0	0
Robert Halton & Boydell	Ind	3	tun	Wine	0	0	0	0
Andrew Cottrell	Ind	2	tun	Wine	0	0	0	0
William Pepwall	Ind	7	tun	Oil, *Olive*	56	0	0	0
John Cutt & Samford	Ind	4.3	tun	Oil, *Olive*	34	0	0	0

The Mackerell of Dungarvan, John Hore master, Entering, *7th April 1564*

Merchant name	Origin	Qty	Unit	Commodity	£	s.	d.	f.
John *Hore*	Ind	14	burden	Fish, Salted	0	58	4	0
		4	barrel	Fish, Herring White	0	40	0	0

The Tobye of Bristol, John Baker master, Entering, *7th April 1564*

Merchant name	Origin	Qty	Unit	Commodity	£	s.	d.	f.
William Yonge & Ashe	Ind	8.5	tun	Wine	0	0	0	0
Thomas Aldworth & Presye	Ind	5.3	tun	Oil, *Olive*	42	0	0	0
Thomas Rowlande & Fowens	Ind	2	tun	Oil, *Olive*	16	0	0	0
		1	tun	Wine	0	0	0	0
John Carre & Dorre	Ind	2.5	tun	Oil, *Olive*	20	0	0	0
		12	C	Soap	9	0	0	0
John Souche & Wynter	Ind	3.5	tun	Oil, *Olive*	28	0	0	0

Merchant name	Origin	Qty	Unit	Commodity	£	s.	d.	f.
		14	C	Alum	23	6	8	0
John Ashe & Sherwoode	Ind	14	C	Soap	10	10	0	0
William Pepwall & Gyttons	Ind	6.5	tun	Oil, *Olive*	52	0	0	0
		5.5	tun	Wine	0	0	0	0
William Jones & Brodeshowe	Ind	2	tun	Vinegar	4	13	4	0
		3	barrel	Oil, *Olive*	0	60	0	0
Michaell Pepwall & Langleye	Ind	1.9	tun	Oil, *Olive*	15	0	0	0
		6	C	Soap	4	10	0	0
Robert Samford & Powell	Ind	6	C	Soap	4	10	0	0
		1.8	tun	Oil, *Olive*	14	0	0	0
Edmund Smyth & Drap*er*	Ind	3	tun	Wine	0	0	0	0
Richard Yonge & Wilbrone	Ind	7	tun	Wine	0	0	0	0
		3	tun	Vinegar	7	0	0	0
John Pollard & Blake	Ind	1.8	tun	Oil, *Olive*	14	0	0	0
Thomas Willyams & Wynter	Ind	4	tun	Vinegar	9	6	8	0
		3	C	Sugar	10	0	0	0

The Prymrose of Bristol, Richard Cottrell master, Entering, *7th April 1564*

Merchant name	Origin	Qty	Unit	Commodity	£	s.	d.	f.
Robert Smyth & Symons	Ind	10	tun	Wine	0	0	0	0
		1.5	tun	Oil, *Olive*	12	0	0	0
William Yonge & Willyams	Ind	3	tun	Wine	0	0	0	0
		3	tun	Vinegar	7	0	0	0
		1	pipe	Oil, *Olive*	4	0	0	0
John Souche & Rowland	Ind	9	tun	Wine	0	0	0	0
Thomas Aldworth & Kirke	Ind	4.5	tun	Wine	0	0	0	0
		3	C	Sugar	10	0	0	0
Thomas Kelke & Hentley	Ind	15	C	Soap	11	5	0	0
		3.5	tun	Oil, *Olive*	28	0	0	0
John Ashe & Hicke	Ind	4.8	tun	Wine	0	0	0	0
Robert HaltonPrecye	Ind	5.5	tun	Wine	0	0	0	0
Anthony Momford & Brodshewe	Ind	1	pipe	Oil, *Olive*	4	0	0	0
		10	C	Alum	16	13	4	0

The Angell of Bristol, Thomas Corbett master, Entering, *7th April 1564*

Merchant name	Origin	Qty	Unit	Commodity	£	s.	d.	f.
George Higgons & Carre	Ind	14	tun	Wine	0	0	0	0

Merchant name	Origin	Qty	Unit	Commodity	£	s.	d.	f.
Dominic Chester								
& Gittons	Ind	8	tun	Wine	0	0	0	0
Robert Shewarde								
& Samford	Ind	8	tun	Wine	0	0	0	0
Robert Kitchen								
& Crosbye	Ind	6	tun	Wine	0	0	0	0
		1.5	ton	Raisins, *Great*	9	0	0	0
John Cutt & Smyth	Ind	4	tun	Wine	0	0	0	0
		3.5	tun	Oil, *Olive*	28	0	0	0
		1	tun	Vinegar	0	46	8	0
William Pepwall	Ind	12	tun	Wine	0	0	0	0

The Marye Fortune of Bristol, William Agwilliams master, Entering, 8th April 1564

Merchant name	Origin	Qty	Unit	Commodity	£	s.	d.	f.
John Cutte & Kelke	Ind	9	tun	Oil, *Olive*	72	0	0	0
Robert Halton &								
Yonge	Ind	4	tun	Wine	0	0	0	0
		2.5	tun	Oil, *Olive*	20	0	0	0
		15	C	Alum	25	0	0	0
		9	C	Aniseed	12	0	0	0
Edmund Woode &								
Hamlyn	Ind	6.5	tun	Wine	0	0	0	0
Richard Fowens &								
Yonge	Ind	7	tun	Wine	0	0	0	0
George Higgons &								
Coxe	Ind	8	tun	Wine	0	0	0	0
		3	C	Sugar	10	0	0	0
Dominic Chester &								
Browne	Ind	6	tun	Oil, *Olive*	48	0	0	0
Giles Codrington &								
Brodeshowe	Ind	3.8	tun	Oil, *Olive*	30	0	0	0
Randal Wilborne &								
Williams	Ind	3.5	tun	Wine	0	0	0	0
William Gittons &								
Pepwall	Ind	6	tun	Wine	0	0	0	0
		2.5	tun	Oil, *Olive*	20	0	0	0
Nicholas Blake &								
Bygge	Ind	2	tun	Wine	0	0	0	0
		4	tun	Oil, *Olive*	32	0	0	0
John Atkyns &								
Chester	Ind	8.5	tun	Wine	0	0	0	0
John Keynes &								
Smyth	Ind	2	tun	Wine	0	0	0	0
		3.5	tun	Oil, *Olive*	28	0	0	0

The Margarett of Bristol, William Morse master, Entering, 8th April 1564

Merchant name	Origin	Qty	Unit	Commodity	£	s.	d.	f.
George Higgons &								
Fowens	Ind	4	tun	Wine	0	0	0	0
Robert Halton &								
Hamlyn	Ind	6.5	tun	Wine	0	0	0	0
Robert Presye &								
Smyth	Ind	2.5	tun	Wine	0	0	0	0

Merchant name	Origin	Qty	Unit	Commodity	£	s.	d.	f.
John Brodeshowe & Willyams	Ind	3	tun	Wine	0	0	0	0
Randal Wilbronne & Gittons	Ind	4.8	tun	Wine	0	0	0	0
Nicholas Blake & Yonge	Ind	2.8	tun	Wine	0	0	0	0
Thomas Aldworth & Badram	Ind	12	tun	Wine	0	0	0	0
		0.3	tun	Oil, *Olive*	0	26	8	0
William Wynter	Ind	30	C	Alum	50	0	0	0
John Gryffyth & Souche	Ind	2	tun	Wine	0	0	0	0
Edmund Smyth & Tyndall	Ind	3.8	tun	Wine	0	0	0	0
Thomas Kelke & Kitchen	Ind	4.5	tun	Wine	0	0	0	0

The Gooscheken of *Nostrodame*, Claus Peters master, Entering, *8th April 1564*

Merchant name	Origin	Qty	Unit	Commodity	£	s.	d.	f.
Simon de Sterke, de Hayes & de la Cluse	Alien	93	tun	Wine	0	0	0	0

The Peter of Bristol, John Pollard master, Entering, *8th April 1564*

Merchant name	Origin	Qty	Unit	Commodity	£	s.	d.	f.
Thomas Aldworth & Yonge	Ind	6	tun	Wine	0	0	0	0
Robert Precye & Hicke	Ind	2	tun	Wine	0	0	0	0
		0.8	tun	Oil, *Olive*	6	0	0	0
Thomas Rowland & Ashe	Ind	3.8	tun	Wine	0	0	0	0
John Carre & Cottrell	Ind	5.5	tun	Wine	0	0	0	0
		1	tun	Oil, *Olive*	8	0	0	0
		1	ton	Raisins, *Great*	6	0	0	0
William Wynter & Yonge	Ind	20	C	Alum	33	6	8	0
		3	ton	Raisins, *Great*	18	0	0	0
Robert Smyth & Willyams	Ind	4.5	tun	Wine	0	0	0	0
Thomas Pentegrece & Hentley	Ind	2	tun	Wine	0	0	0	0
William Pepwall	Ind	6	tun	Wine	0	0	0	0

The Marlyn of London, Robert Revelle*r* master, Entering, *8th April 1564*

Merchant name	Origin	Qty	Unit	Commodity	£	s.	d.	f.
William Garret, Chester & assoc.	Ind	40	C	Graines	133	6	8	0
		15	C	Elephant Tusks	50	0	0	0

The Marten Bonaventure of Bristol, John Slight (?) master, Entering, *8th April 1564*

Merchant name	Origin	Qty	Unit	Commodity	£	s.	d.	f.
William Yonge & Cutte	Ind	6	tun	Wine	0	0	0	0

Merchant name	Origin	Qty	Unit	Commodity	£	s.	d.	f.
		5	tun	Oil, *Olive*	40	0	0	0
Richard Fowens & Rowland	Ind	5	tun	Wine	0	0	0	0
William Coxe & White	Ind	3.5	tun	Wine	0	0	0	0
Giles Codrington & Ashe	Ind	2.8	tun	Wine	0	0	0	0
Richard Yonge & Dra*per*	Ind	7.5	tun	Wine	0	0	0	0
George Higgons & Hamlyn	Ind	5.5	tun	Wine	0	0	0	0
		1.8	tun	Oil, *Olive*	14	0	0	0
Thomas Symons & Chester	Ind	7.8	tun	Wine	0	0	0	0
Randal Wilbrone & Swetnam	Ind	4	tun	Wine	0	0	0	0
Dominic Chester & Halton	Ind	6.5	tun	Wine	0	0	0	0
Edmund Woode & Morse	Ind	2.5	tun	Wine	0	0	0	0
Nicholas Blake & Kyrke	Ind	2	tun	Oil, *Olive*	16	0	0	0
Edmund Smyth & Bysse	Ind	1	tun	Wine	0	0	0	0
		8	C	Soap	6	0	0	0

The Salomon of Bristol, Richard Ricarde master, Entering, *8th April 1564*

Merchant name	Origin	Qty	Unit	Commodity	£	s.	d.	f.
Thomas Chester	Ind	4	tun	Oil, *Olive*	32	0	0	0
		1.5	tun	Vinegar	3	10	0	0
William Kirke & Smyth	Ind	1	pipe	Wine	0	0	0	0
		3	tun	Oil, *Olive*	24	0	0	0
		7	C	Soap	5	5	0	0
		3	C	Sumach	0	40	0	0
John Souche & Smyth	Ind	3.5	tun	Wine	0	0	0	0
William Pepwall & Pepwall	Ind	2	tun	Wine	0	0	0	0
		2.5	tun	Oil, *Olive*	20	0	0	0
George Higgons & Halton	Ind	2.5	tun	Wine	0	0	0	0
Thomas Kelke & Blake	Ind	1	tun	Wine	0	0	0	0
		4.5	tun	Oil, *Olive*	36	0	0	0

The Nicholas of Mutriku, Domingo de Astorico master, Entering, 11th April 1564

Merchant name	Origin	Qty	Unit	Commodity	£	s.	d.	f.
John Browne & Bysse	Ind	8.5	tun	Wine	0	0	0	0
Nicholas Williams & Pepwell	Ind	0.8	tun	Oil, *Olive*	6	0	0	0
		2	C	Sugar	6	13	4	0
		5	C	Alum	8	6	8	0

Merchant name	Origin	Qty	Unit	Commodity	£	s.	d.	f.
Robert Samford & Presye	Ind	1.5	tun	Wine	0	0	0	0
James Langhton & Gyttons	Ind	6.8	tun	Wine	0	0	0	0
Richard Swetnam & Higgons	Ind	4	tun	Wine	0	0	0	0
Anthony Momford & Smyth	Ind	7.5	tun	Wine	0	0	0	0
William Coxe & Taylor	Ind	1	pipe	Wine	0	0	0	0
		2.5	tun	Oil, *Olive*	20	0	0	0
Giles White & Willyams	Ind	3	tun	Wine	0	0	0	0
James Souche & Cutte	Ind	13	tun	Wine	0	0	0	0
Thomas Jones & Cottrell	Ind	5	tun	Wine	0	0	0	0
John Roberts & Kitchen	Ind	4.5	tun	Wine	0	0	0	0
		2.3	tun	Oil, *Olive*	18	0	0	0
George Batheram & Jeyne	Ind	10	tun	Wine	0	0	0	0
Robert Amersleye	Ind	60	C	Alum	100	0	0	0

The Fawlcon of Bristol, James Webbe master, Entering, *11th April 1564*

Merchant name	Origin	Qty	Unit	Commodity	£	s.	d.	f.
George Higgons & Souche	Ind	3	tun	Vinegar	7	0	0	0
Robert Kitchen & Saxie	Ind	2	tun	Wine	0	0	0	0
		1	tun	Oil, *Olive*	8	0	0	0
Dominic Chester & Rowland	Ind	2	tun	Vinegar	4	13	4	0
		1.3	tun	Oil, *Olive*	10	0	0	0
Richard Hentley & Cox	Ind	2	tun	Wine	0	0	0	0
		5	C	Soap	0	75	0	0
William Pepwall & Aldworth	Ind	2	tun	Vinegar	4	13	4	0
Edmund Smyth & Precye	Ind	1.5	tun	Vinegar	0	70	0	0
Robert Smyth & Spratt	Ind	1.5	tun	Wine	0	0	0	0
Nicholas Blake & Momford	Ind	1.5	tun	Vinegar	0	70	0	0
		1.5	tun	Oil, *Olive*	12	0	0	0
Robert Halton & Brodeshewe	Ind	1	tun	Wine	0	0	0	0
		8	C	Soap	6	0	0	0
John Carre & Yonge	Ind	5.5	tun	Oil, *Olive*	44	0	0	0
William Warford & Bysse	Ind	4	C	Sumach	0	53	4	0

Merchant name	Origin	Qty	Unit	Commodity	£	s.	d.	f.
		1	pipe	Cute	6	0	0	0
Thomas Smyth &								
James Webb	Ind	1	hogshead	Wine	0	0	0	0
		2	C	Soap	0	30	0	0

The Grace of God of Waterford, Darby Harte master, Entering, 5th May 1564

Merchant name	Origin	Qty	Unit	Commodity	£	s.	d.	f.
Thomas Affarnam								
& Jones	Ind	15	C	Skins, Sheep	9	13	4	0
		2.3	C	*Irish* Frieze *Cloth*	4	10	0	0
		1	C	Skins, Lamb	0	16	8	0
		2	pipe	Mantles	0	10	0	0
James Brenocke								
& Rede	Ind	14	C	Skins, Sheep	9	6	8	0
		4	C	*Irish* Frieze *Cloth*	8	0	0	0
		4	piece	Mantles	0	20	0	0
		5	piece	Skins, Marten	0	16	8	0
		13	C	Skins, Lamb	10	16	8	0
		3	C	Skins, Sheep Broken	0	15	0	0
Thomas Lynche								
& Marshall	Ind	8	C	Skins, Sheep	5	6	8	0
		6.5	C	Skins, Lamb	5	8	4	0
		2	C	Skins, Sheep Broken	0	10	0	0
		9	piece	Skins, Fox	0	6	0	0
		2.4	C	*Irish* Frieze *Cloth*	4	16	8	0
		3	piece	Skins, Marten	0	10	0	0
Patrick Hackett								
& Butler	Ind	21	C	Skins, Sheep	14	0	0	0
		30	C	Skins, Lamb	25	0	0	0
		83	yard	*Irish* Frieze *Cloth*	0	27	4	0
		10	C	Skins, Sheep Broken	0	50	0	0
		5	piece	Skins, Fox	0	3	4	0
		3	C	Skins, Cunirub?	0	7	0	0
		15	yard	Check *Cloth*	0	5	0	0
		2	piece	Mantles	0	10	0	0
William Grannt	Ind	12	C	Skins, Sheep	8	0	0	0
		6	C	Skins, Lamb	5	0	0	0
		0.5	C	*Irish* Frieze *Cloth*	0	20	0	0

The Grace of God of Cork, David Ffizthwilliam master, Entering, 20th May 1564

Merchant name	Origin	Qty	Unit	Commodity	£	s.	d.	f.
William Golie &								
Roche	Ind	8	C	Skins, Sheep	5	6	8	0
		17	C	Skins, Lamb	14	3	4	0
		12	C	Skins, Sheep Broken	3	0	0	0
		2	dicker	Skins, Deer	0	6	8	0
		42	piece	Skins, Fox	0	28	0	0
		11	piece	Skins, Otter	0	22	0	0
		75	yard	*Irish* Frieze *Cloth*	0	25	0	0
		9	C	Tallow	7	10	0	0
		3	piece	Mantles	0	15	0	0
		4	piece	Skins, Marten	0	13	4	0

Merchant name	Origin	Qty	Unit	Commodity	£	s.	d.	f.
		1.3	ton	Wood, Brazil	41	13	4	0
		1	pipe	Fish, Salmon	6	0	0	0
		1	virken	Fish, Salmon	0	15	0	0
		18	stone	Wool, Flocks	0	34	6	0
		12	stone	Wool, Irish	0	32	0	0
David Meanghe	Ind	4	C	Skins, Sheep	0	53	4	0
		4	C	Skins, Lamb	0	66	8	0
		0.5	C	Skins, Sheep Broken	0	2	6	0
		6	piece	Skins, Deer	0	2	0	0
		1	piece	Skins, Otter	0	2	0	0
		4	stone	Wool, Flocks	0	7	8	0
		4	burden	Fish, Salted	0	16	8	0

The Peter of St David's, Lewis Roberts master, Entering, 23rd May 1564

Merchant name	Origin	Qty	Unit	Commodity	£	s.	d.	f.
George Shilnell	Ind	5	C	Skins, Sheep	0	66	8	0
		10	C	Skins, Lamb	8	6	8	0
		8	piece	Skins, Deer	0	2	8	0
		4	piece	Skins, Fox	0	2	8	0
		2	stone	Wool, Irish	0	5	4	0
		2	C	Skins, Sheep Broken	0	10	0	0
Philip Cayen	Ind	1	tun	Wine	0	0	0	0

The Katheren of Waterford, John Roster master, Entering, 25th May 1564

Merchant name	Origin	Qty	Unit	Commodity	£	s.	d.	f.
Michael White	Ind	8	C	Skins, Sheep	5	6	8	0
		4	C	Skins, Lamb	0	66	8	0
		4	stone	Wool, Irish	0	10	8	0
		0.5	C	*Irish* Frieze *Cloth*	0	20	0	0
		2	burden	Fish, Salted	0	8	4	0
		10	piece	Skins, Fox	0	6	8	0
Jasper Streche & Reane	Ind	8	C	Skins, Sheep	5	6	8	0
		8	C	Skins, Lamb	6	13	4	0
		4	stone	Wool, Irish	0	10	8	0

The Katheren of Wexford, David Roche master, Entering, 27th May 1564

Merchant name	Origin	Qty	Unit	Commodity	£	s.	d.	f.
David *Roche*	Ind	4	C	Skins, Sheep	0	53	4	0
		10	C	Skins, Lamb	8	6	8	0
		12	C	Skins, Sheep Broken	3	0	0	0
		4	stone	Wool, Irish	0	10	8	0
		3	piece	Mantles	0	15	0	0
		2	stone	Wool, Flocks	0	3	10	0

The Dolfen of Uphill, John Dyer master, Entering, 29th May 1564

Merchant name	Origin	Qty	Unit	Commodity	£	s.	d.	f.
Thomas Hyde	Ind	10	C	Skins, Lamb	8	6	8	0
		2.5	C	Skins, Sheep	0	33	4	0
		5	piece	Skins, Fox	0	3	4	0

Merchant name	Origin	Qty	Unit	Commodity	£	s.	d.	f.

The Katheren of Wexford, William Stafford master, Entering, 30th May 1564

Merchant name	Origin	Qty	Unit	Commodity	£	s.	d.	f.
William *Stafford*	Ind	5	C	Skins, Sheep	0	66	8	0
		8	C	Skins, Sheep Broken	0	40	0	0
		5	C	Skins, Cunirub?	0	12	6	0
		10	C	Skins, Lamb	8	6	8	0

The Jeshus of New Ross, Edmund Kellye master, Entering, 31st May 1564

Merchant name	Origin	Qty	Unit	Commodity	£	s.	d.	f.
Richard Ragged & Archer	Ind	15	C	Skins, Lamb	12	10	0	0
		20	C	Skins, Sheep	13	6	8	0
		3	C	Skins, Sheep Broken	0	15	0	0
		1	C	*Irish* Frieze *Cloth*	0	40	0	0

The Maudelena of Errenteria, Martin de Suasuaber master, Entering, 15th June 1564

Merchant name	Origin	Qty	Unit	Commodity	£	s.	d.	f.
Thomas Dickenson & Tyndale	Ind	7.5	ton	Iron	30	0	0	0
		3	tun	Wine	0	0	0	0
Nicholas Thorn & Draper	Ind	4.5	ton	Iron	14	0	0	0
John Griffeth & Jeyne	Ind	4	ton	Iron	16	0	0	0
Domingo de Salavaria	Alien	5	ton	Iron	20	0	0	0
		12	dozen	Hopes for Serches	0	20	0	0

The George of Chepstow, Philip Stringer master, Entering, 16th June 1564

Merchant name	Origin	Qty	Unit	Commodity	£	s.	d.	f.
Thomas Chester	Ind	2	tun	Wine	0	0	0	0
		1	tun	Vinegar	0	46	8	0

The Angell of Chepstow, Morgan Howell master, Entering, 21st June 1564

Merchant name	Origin	Qty	Unit	Commodity	£	s.	d.	f.
Dominic Chester	Ind	1	tun	Wine	0	0	0	0
		1	tun	Vinegar	0	46	8	0

The Ellen of Bristol, William Fage master, Entering, *21st June 1564*

Merchant name	Origin	Qty	Unit	Commodity	£	s.	d.	f.
Robert Halton	Ind	4.5	tun	Wine	0	0	0	0

The Clement of Bristol, John Williams master, Entering, 22nd June 1564

Merchant name	Origin	Qty	Unit	Commodity	£	s.	d.	f.
Edmund Warren	Ind	2.5	tun	Vinegar	5	16	8	0
John Warren	Ind	3	C	Sumach	0	40	0	0

The Markes of Barnstaple, Robert Hollye master, Entering, *22nd June 1564*

Merchant name	Origin	Qty	Unit	Commodity	£	s.	d.	f.
John Pearde & Pearde	Ind	20	ton	Iron	80	0	0	0

Merchant name	Origin	Qty	Unit	Commodity	£	s.	d.	f.

The Jeshus of Morbihan, Denis Bryan master, Entering, 26th June 1564

James de Maren								
& *Denis Bryan*	Alien	40	ton	Salt	40	0	0	0

The Trenetie Smyth of Bristol, William Come master, Entering, *26th June 1564*

Henry Smyth								
& *Pursell*	Ind	20	ton	Salt	20	0	0	0
		2.5	tun	Vinegar	5	16	8	0
James Dowle								
& *Warford*	Ind	1	ton	Pitch	0	40	0	0
		20	C	Madder	18	13	4	0

The Julyan of Bristol, James Webbe master, Entering, *26th June 1564*

Thomas Symons								
& assoc.	Ind	40	ton	Salt	40	0	0	0

The Salomon of Bristol, Richard Ricarde master, Entering, *26th June 1564*

Thomas Chester								
& Smyth	Ind	30	ton	Salt	30	0	0	0
		12	barrel	Tar	0	40	0	0

The George of Chepstow, Philip Strenger master, Entering, *26th June 1564*

Dominic Chester	Ind	2	tun	Wine	0	0	0	0
		1.5	tun	Vinegar	0	70	0	0

The Dragon of Bristol, John Cloddye master, Entering, 29th June 1564

John Gromwell	Ind	5	C	Skins, Sheep	0	66	8	0
		10	C	Skins, Lamb	8	6	8	0
		48	piece	Skins, Fox	0	32	0	0
		5	piece	Skins, Deer	0	20	0	0
		3	piece	*Skins, Otter*	0	6	0	0

The Dragon of Bristol, Ralph Browne master, Entering, 30th June 1564

George Higgons								
& assoc.	Ind	25	ton	Salt	25	0	0	0

The Marten Bonaventure of Bristol, William Morse master, Entering, 3rd July 1564

William Yonge								
& Kelke	Ind	18	ton	Iron	72	0	0	0
John Ashe & Jeyne	Ind	14	ton	Iron	54	0	0	0
Thomas Chester								
& Boydell	Ind	31	ton	Iron	124	0	0	0
William Yonge &								
Browne	Ind	7	ton	Iron	28	0	0	0

Merchant name	Origin	Qty	Unit	Commodity	£	s.	d.	f.
Dominic Chester & Tindall	Ind	7	ton	Iron	28	0	0	0
Thomas Dykenson & Yonge	Ind	11	ton	Iron	44	0	0	0
Walter Morse & Halton	Ind	4	ton	Iron	16	0	0	0
Randal Wilbran & Langley	Ind	5	ton	Iron	20	0	0	0

The Katheren of Tenby, Thomas Kynge master, Entering, *3rd July 1564*

Francis Deisdyes	Alien	7	M	Oranges	0	46	8	0

The Angell of Chepstow, Morgan Howell master, Entering, 7th July 1564

Richard Newton	Ind	4	ton	Iron	16	0	0	0
		1	pipe	Vinegar	0	23	4	0
		1	tun	Wine	0	0	0	0
Peter Derett	Alien	2	ton	Iron	8	0	0	0

The Ellen of Bristol, William Fage master, Entering, 12th July 1564

Dominic Chester	Ind	2	tun	Vinegar	4	13	4	0

The George of Chepstow, Philip Stringer master, Entering, 14th July 1564

John Atkins	Ind	1	pipe	Vinegar	0	23	4	0

The Trenytie of Topsham, John Dymerd master, Entering, 17th July 1564

Richard Strobridge & Wells	Ind	35	ton	Iron	140	0	0	0
		12	C	Alum	20	0	0	0

The Katheren of Waterford, John Koscrowe master, Entering, *17th July 1564*

Richard Lee & White	Ind	15	C	Skins, Sheep	10	0	0	0
		1	piece	Mantles	0	5	0	0
		15	C	*Irish* Frieze *Cloth*	30	8	4	0
		5	C	Skins, Sheep Broken	0	25	0	0
John Braye & Fagan	Ind	24	C	Skins, Sheep	16	0	0	0
		11	C	Skins, Lamb	9	3	4	0
		8.8	C	*Irish* Frieze *Cloth*	17	13	4	0
		3	piece	Mantles	0	15	0	0
		1	piece	Skins, Fox	0	0	8	0
		1	C	Skins, Sheep Broken	0	5	0	0
		1	piece	Skins, Marten	0	3	4	0
James Lyncolne	Ind	0.5	C	Skins, Sheep	0	6	8	0
		3	piece	Mantles	0	15	0	0
		1	stone	Wool, Flocks	0	0	23	0

Merchant name	Origin	Qty	Unit	Commodity	£	s.	d.	f.

The Jeshus of New Ross, John Blake master, Entering, 20th July 1564

Merchant name	Origin	Qty	Unit	Commodity	£	s.	d.	f.
Nicholas Ragged, Seyes & Rafter	Ind	18	C	*Irish* Frieze *Cloth*	37	0	0	0
		4.8	C	Skins, Sheep	0	63	4	0
		1	piece	Skins, Fox	0	0	8	0
		4.8	C	Skins, Lamb	3	19	2	0
		1	piece	Skins, Otter	0	2	0	0
		2	piece	Mantles	0	10	0	0
		1	C	Skins, Sheep Broken	0	5	0	0

The Jeshus of New Ross, Edmund Cavham master, Entering, 21st July 1564

Merchant name	Origin	Qty	Unit	Commodity	£	s.	d.	f.
William Langton & Langton	Ind	6.5	C	*Irish* Frieze *Cloth*	13	0	0	0
		3	C	Skins, Sheep	0	40	0	0
		2	C	Skins, Lamb	0	33	4	0
		2	C	Skins, Sheep Broken	0	10	0	0
		4		*Caste Mlyons*	0	26	8	0
Richard Savage & Raston	Ind	5	C	*Irish* Frieze *Cloth*	10	0	0	0
		13	C	Skins, Sheep	8	13	4	0
		4	C	Skins, Lamb	0	66	8	0
		1	C	Skins, Sheep Broken	0	5	0	0
		2	stone	Wool, Flocks	0	3	10	0
		2	piece	Skins, Fox	0	0	16	0
		1	piece	Skins, Otter	0	2	0	0
		1	piece	Mantles	0	5	0	0

The Clement of Bristol, Hugh Willys master, Entering, *21st July 1564*

Merchant name	Origin	Qty	Unit	Commodity	£	s.	d.	f.
Walter Standfaste	Ind	5	ton	Salt	0	100	0	0
		1	ton	Iron	4	0	0	0
		15	C	Pitch	0	30	0	0
		6	barrel	Tar	0	20	0	0

The Grace of God of Waterford, Darby Harte master, Entering, *21st July 1564*

Merchant name	Origin	Qty	Unit	Commodity	£	s.	d.	f.
Andrew Lincolne & Grannte	Ind	5	C	Skins, Sheep	0	66	8	0
		8	piece	Mantles	0	40	0	0
		1	C	Skins, Sheep Broken	0	5	0	0
		3	C	*Irish* Frieze *Cloth*	6	0	0	0
		1		*Caste Mlyons*	0	6	8	0
James Rowe & Payne	Ind	4	C	*Irish* Frieze *Cloth*	8	0	0	0
		12	piece	Mantles	0	60	0	0
		3.5	C	Skins, Sheep	0	46	8	0
Stephen White & White	Ind	12	C	Skins, Sheep	8	0	0	0
		1	C	Skins, Lamb	0	16	8	0
		1	C	*Irish* Frieze *Cloth*	0	40	0	0
		6	piece	Skins, Deer	0	2	0	0

Merchant name	Origin	Qty	Unit	Commodity	£	s.	d.	f.
Patrick Madden								
& Welshe	Ind	7	C	Skins, Sheep	4	13	4	0
		4	C	Skins, Lamb	0	66	8	0
		6	piece	Skins, Deer	0	2	0	0
		1	C	*Irish* Frieze *Cloth*	0	40	0	0
		10	piece	Mantles	0	50	0	0
David Drylenge	Ind	2	C	Skins, Sheep	0	26	8	0
		1	piece	Mantles	0	5	0	0
		20	stone	Wool, Flocks	0	38	4	0

The Mary Tasker of Milford Haven, William Tasker master, Entering, 22nd July 1564

Merchant name	Origin	Qty	Unit	Commodity	£	s.	d.	f.
Patrick White &								
White	Ind	7	C	Skins, Sheep	4	13	4	0
		2	C	*Irish* Frieze *Cloth*	4	0	0	0
		1	C	Skins, Sheep Broken	0	5	0	0
		5	piece	Mantles	0	25	0	0
Walter Sawle &								
Hungar	Ind	10	C	Skins, Sheep	6	13	4	0
		4	C	Skins, Lamb	3	6	8	0
		13	piece	Mantles	0	65	0	0
		2	piece	Skins, Marten	0	6	8	0
John Swanne	Ind	5	C	Skins, Sheep	0	66	8	0
		4	C	Skins, Lamb	0	66	8	0
		0.2	C	*Irish* Frieze *Cloth*	0	8	0	0

The Tobye of Bristol, John Baker master, Entering, 22nd July 1564

Merchant name	Origin	Qty	Unit	Commodity	£	s.	d.	f.
John Carre & assoc.	Ind	60	ton	Salt	60	0	0	0
		2	tun	Wine	0	0	0	0
		13	tun	Vinegar	29	3	4	0

The Angell of Bristol, Thomas Mondy master, Entering, 22nd July 1564

Merchant name	Origin	Qty	Unit	Commodity	£	s.	d.	f.
John Brodeshowe								
& Kitchen	Ind	34	ton	Salt	34	0	0	0
		5	tun	Vinegar	11	13	4	0

The Swanne of Bristol, John Purkins master, Entering, 22nd July 1564

Merchant name	Origin	Qty	Unit	Commodity	£	s.	d.	f.
William Pursell								
& Sumpter	Ind	25	ton	Salt	25	0	0	0
		1.5	last	Tar	0	60	0	0
		10	C	Pitch	0	20	0	0
		2	tun	Wine	*16*	*0*	*0*	*0*
		3	tun	Vinegar	7	0	0	0

The Sondaye of Boscastle, John Kirton master, Entering, 24th July 1564

Merchant name	Origin	Qty	Unit	Commodity	£	s.	d.	f.
Patrick Welshe	Ind	1.5	C	*Irish* Frieze *Cloth*	0	60	0	0
		4	piece	Mantles	0	20	0	0

Merchant name	Origin	Qty	Unit	Commodity	£	s.	d.	f.

The George of Bristol, Thomas Watkins master, Entering, *24th July 1564*

Merchant name	Origin	Qty	Unit	Commodity	£	s.	d.	f.
Robert Water	Ind	8	C	Skins, Sheep	5	6	8	0
		9	C	Skins, Lamb	7	10	0	0
		20	stone	Wool, Flocks	0	38	4	0
		2	C	Skins, Sheep Broken	0	10	0	0
		16	piece	Skins, Deer	0	5	4	0
		7	piece	Skins, Otter	0	14	0	0
		12	piece	Skins, Fox	0	8	0	0
		8	stone	Wool, Irish	0	21	4	0
		1	C	Wood, Brazil	0	33	4	0
		30	yard	*Irish* Frieze *Cloth*	0	10	0	0
		5	C	Madder, Mul	0	5	0	0

The Unicorne of Bristol, William Histcocke master, Entering, 27th July 1564

Merchant name	Origin	Qty	Unit	Commodity	£	s.	d.	f.
Hugh Brooke & Bovett	Ind	24	ton	Salt	24	0	0	0
		1	tun	Wine	0	0	0	0
		2.5	tun	Vinegar	5	16	8	0

The Angell of Chepstow, Morgan Howell master, Entering, *27th July 1564*

Merchant name	Origin	Qty	Unit	Commodity	£	s.	d.	f.
William Jeyne	Ind	1	tun	Wine	0	0	0	0

The Mawdelena of Morbihan, Mathew Furra master, Entering, 3rd August 1564

Merchant name	Origin	Qty	Unit	Commodity	£	s.	d.	f.
Evan Falwhin	Alien	35	ton	Salt	35	0	0	0

The Margett of Morbihan, Lewis Baron master, Entering, *3rd August 1564*

Merchant name	Origin	Qty	Unit	Commodity	£	s.	d.	f.
John de Vusurke	Alien	40	ton	Salt	40	0	0	0

The Primrose of Bristol, Richard Cottrell master, Entering, 11th August 1564

Merchant name	Origin	Qty	Unit	Commodity	£	s.	d.	f.
John Souche & assoc.	Ind	50	tun	Woad, Azores	500	0	0	0

The George of Chepstow, Philip Stringer master, Entering, *11th August 1564*

Merchant name	Origin	Qty	Unit	Commodity	£	s.	d.	f.
Richard (surname unknown)	Ind	1	tun	Vinegar	0	46	8	0

The Marye of San Sebastián, Julian Dellondo master, Entering, *11th August 1564*

Merchant name	Origin	Qty	Unit	Commodity	£	s.	d.	f.
John Carre & Henley	Ind	12	ton	Iron	48	0	0	0
John de Sara & de Berobie	Alien	10	ton	Iron	40	0	0	0
Robert Tindall	Ind	6	ton	Iron	24	0	0	0
Stephen Deisaste	Alien	4	ton	Iron	16	0	0	0

Merchant name	Origin	Qty	Unit	Commodity	£	s.	d.	f.

The Fawkon of Bristol, Thomas Morrys master, Entering, 22nd August 1564

Merchant name	Origin	Qty	Unit	Commodity	£	s.	d.	f.
Dominic Chester & assoc.	Ind	32	tun	Woad, Azores	320	0	0	0

The Peter of Bristol, John Cottrell master, Entering, *22nd August 1564*

Merchant name	Origin	Qty	Unit	Commodity	£	s.	d.	f.
John Grannte & Aldworth	Ind	40	ton	Salt	40	0	0	0
		9	tun	Oil, *Olive*	72	0	0	0
		6.5	C	Pepper	54	3	4	0
		0.8	C	Cloves	13	15	0	0
		2	C	Ginger	15	0	0	0
		10	lb	Cinnamon	0	40	0	0
		14	lb	Mace	4	13	4	0
Thomas Simons, Kekke & Hicke	Ind	5	tun	Oil, *Olive*	40	0	0	0
John Ashe	Ind	10	C	Pepper	83	6	8	0
		1	C	Cloves	18	6	8	0
		60	lb	*Illegible*	20	0	0	0
		80	lb	Cinnamon	16	0	0	0
		2	C	Ginger	15	0	0	0

The Maudelena of San Sebastián, Martin de Swasuaber master, Entering, 4th September 1564

Merchant name	Origin	Qty	Unit	Commodity	£	s.	d.	f.
William Wynter & Kirke	Ind	18	ton	Iron	72	0	0	0
Martin Greves & Wilbrane	Ind	3	ton	Iron	12	0	0	0
Robert Tindall & Wilson	Ind	5	ton	Iron	20	0	0	0
Francis Amboro & de Cratson	Alien	2.5	ton	Iron	10	0	0	0
		26	dozen	Hopes for Serches	0	30	0	0
Gregory de Turriega	Alien	2	ton	Iron	8	0	0	0
John Boydell	Ind	2	ton	Iron	8	0	0	0

The Katheren of Le Conquet, William de Laseva master, Entering, 5th September 1564

Merchant name	Origin	Qty	Unit	Commodity	£	s.	d.	f.
John Pollard	Ind	25	ton	Salt	25	0	0	0
William *de Laseva* & assoc.	Alien	1	tun	Oil, *Olive*	8	0	0	0
		100	yard	Dowlas *Cloth*	0	33	4	0
		100	yard	Canvas *Cloth*	0	30	0	0
		8	ream	Paper	0	21	4	0
		0.5	C	Turpentine	0	5	0	0
		1	C	Oakum	0	5	0	0

The Francis of Le Conquet, John Latrisarke master, Entering, *5th September 1564*

Merchant name	Origin	Qty	Unit	Commodity	£	s.	d.	f.
Robert Amersley	Ind	25	ton	Salt	25	0	0	0

Merchant name	Origin	Qty	Unit	Commodity	£	s.	d.	f.
John *Latrisarke*	Alien	1	tun	Oil, *Olive*	8	0	0	0
		1.5	C	Canvas *Cloth*	0	45	0	0
		3	piece	Rosin	0	10	0	0
		0.5	C	Turpentine	0	5	0	0

The Mastris of Le Conquet, Peter Devalle master, Entering, 6th September 1564

James Hangton	Ind	30	ton	Salt	30	0	0	0

The Margaret of Bridgwater, Master unknown, Entering, 28th September 1564

Merchant Unknown		7	C	Fish, Hake	7	0	0	0
		6	barrel	Fish, Herring White	0	60	0	0
		0.3	C	Skins, Sheep	0	3	4	0
		2	burden	Fish, Salted	0	8	4	0

PART 2

The Port Books

The 'Port Book' series resulted from an Exchequer Order of November 1564, which required all customs officials in England and Wales thenceforth to make their entries in Blank books issued by the Exchequer.

In terms of their value as a source for the analysis of Bristol's trade, the Port Books are far more detailed records than the 'particular' accounts of the earlier century. In addition to the information contained in the earlier accounts, they record: the tonnage of each ship, the exact port of destination, the name, domicile and occupation of the merchant, for example, draper, soap-maker etc., along with the signature of the merchant or his factor, and specific details regarding the packaging of commodities, for example, the number of chests, bundles, fardels etc.

All of these details have been included in this transcription, with the exception of the packaging details and merchants signatures, which are available in the electronic versions. The transcriptions also include any additional information regarding licenses, warrants or irregularities in customs payments etc. found in the accounts. These are supplied in the footnotes.

The accounts have been transcribed as closely as possible to the original documents, therefore in cases where the account omits values because an item was exempt from custom for some reason, for example because it cleared custom at another port, it is also omitted here.

1575/6

TNA E190/1129/12 is the account of the controller for outward duties for the period Michaelmas 1575 to Michaelmas 1576.

Of note in this account is the general absence of nominal values for grains including malt, barley, rye and wheat. The 1582 rates book values malt at 6s. 8d. per quart (£2 per wey). It is found in the 1575/6 account paying 4s. per wey custom (along with beans, barley and rye) which based on the poundage subsidy of 1s. per pound works out at £4 per wey. In the case of grains, however, after 1571, this is a meaningless figure. An act 'for the increase of tyllage' in that year decreed that it was lawful to transport any grain or wheat only from a port with a resident customs officer and that the new rate of custom would be 12*d*. per quarter for wheat and 8*d*. per quarter for all other grains (peas, malt, beans, barley).[1] The figures seen in the account reflect this custom and in some cases the officer has back projected to provide a value which explains why sometimes the value in the accounts seems to be twice that of the rates book.[2] In most cases however there is no value included for grains, just the custom payment. The transcription follows the manuscript in this regard.

TNA E190/1129/11 is the account of the controller for inwards duties for the same period. Wine imports are recorded together separately at the end of the manuscript.

EXPORTS

Merchant name	Qty	Unit	Commodity	£	s.	d.	f.

The Peter of Bristol, burden 100 tons, Philip Whitinge master, to Bayonne, 30th September 1575

Merchant name	Qty	Unit	Commodity	£	s.	d.	f.
Mark Wardford of Bristol, Merchant Ind	8	piece	Cloth of Assize, Short Somerset	0	0	0	0
	10	piece	Bay *Cloth*	10	0	0	0
	4	C goad	Manchester Cotton Cloth	13	6	8	0
John Barnes of Bristol, Clothier Ind	9	piece	Tenby Cotton *Cloth*	9	0	0	0
Thomas Williams of Bristol, Merchant Ind	6	piece	Cloth of Assize, Short Somerset	0	0	0	0
	8	piece	Brecon *Cloth*	8	0	0	0
	10	piece	Bristol Frieze *Cloth*	10	0	0	0
Alice Roberts of Bristol, Widow Ind	18	piece	Tenby Frieze *Cloth*	18	0	0	0

The Conney of Bristol, burden 20 tons, Richard Lollett master, to San Sebastián, 9th October 1575

Merchant name	Qty	Unit	Commodity	£	s.	d.	f.
Thomas Aldworth of Bristol, Merchant Ind	8	wey	Beans[3]	0	0	0	0
Thomas Merrike of Bristol, Merchant Ind	1	C	Irish Rugg Frieze *Cloth*	0	40	0	0

The Grasshoper of Bristol, burden 26 tons, John Durban mster, to La Rochelle, 28th November 1575

Merchant name	Qty	Unit	Commodity	£	s.	d.	f.
Thomas Pitte of Bristol, Merchant Ind	2	fother	Lead	16	0	0	0
	10	wey	Coal, Smith	3	6	8	0

The Mynikin of Bristol, burden 40 tons, Richard Ricards master, to Biscay, *28th November 1575*

Merchant name	Qty	Unit	Commodity	£	s.	d.	f.
Thomas Aldworth of Bristol, Merchant Ind	60	quart	Wheat[4]	0	0	0	0

---

1 Statutes of the Realm, (1571) Vol. 4, Chapter XIII, p. 547. 2 See, for example, the Katherine of Wexford, TNA E190/1129/12 f20r. 3 Custom exempt. 4 Custom exempt.

Merchant name	Qty	Unit	Commodity	£	s.	d.	f.

The Cheritie of Lanherne, burden 28 tons, Hugh Gwilliam master, to San Sebastián, 18th December 1575

Robert Allin of Bristol, Merchant Ind	6	C	Wax	18	0	0	0
William Prewett of Bristol, Draper Ind	40	unknown	Wax	12	0	0	0
	4	C goad	Manchester Cotton Cloth	13	6	8	0

The Mynikin of Bristol, burden 40 tons, Richard Ricards master, to Biscay, 20th December 1575

Thomas Allin of London, Merchant Ind	20	dozen	Skins, Calf	10	0	0	0

The Julian of Bristol, burden 28 tons, Richard Lullett master, to La Rochelle, 11th January 1576

Thomas Diconsone of Bristol, Merchant Ind	2	C goad	Manchester Cotton Cloth	6	13	4	0
	6	piece	Brecon Cloth	6	0	0	0
	1	piece	Cloth of Assize, Short Somerset	0	0	0	0
	2	piece	Cloth of Assize, Bridgwater	0	0	0	0

The Nightingale of Bristol, burden 25 tons, John Jones master, to La Rochelle, 13th January 1575

Francis Rowley of Bristol, Merchant Ind	2	fother	Lead	16	0	0	0
	12	wey	Coal, Smith	4	0	0	0

The Thobie of Bristol, burden 100 tons, John Baker master, to Bayonne, 19th January 1576

Thomas Simons of Bristol, Merchant Ind	4	fother	Lead	32	0	0	0
	10	C	Wax	30	0	0	0
	5	piece	Cloth of Assize, Short Somerset	0	0	0	0
John Hollester of Bristol, Merchant Ind	3.5	fother	Lead	28	0	0	0
Richard Yonnge of Bristol, Merchant Ind	7	fother	Lead	56	0	0	0
Thomas Kelke of Bristol, Merchant Ind	16	piece	Cloth of Assize, Western Dozen Kersey	0	0	0	0
Henry Goughe of Bristol, Merchant Ind	2	fother	Lead	16	0	0	0
William Cutt of Bristol, Merchant Ind	12	piece	Cloth of Assize, Northern Kersey	0	0	0	0
	10	piece	Cloth of Assize, Devonshire Kersey	0	0	0	0
Giles Bitfilde of Bristol, Merchant Ind	4	piece	Cloth of Assize, Short Somerset	0	0	0	0
Thomas Sawle of Bristol, Merchant Ind	3	piece	Cloth of Assize, Short Somerset	0	0	0	0
	1	piece	Grasier Cloth	0	20	0	0
Nicholas Hick of Bristol, Merchant Ind	1	fother	Lead	8	0	0	0

Merchant name	Qty	Unit	Commodity	£	s.	d.	f.
William Gittons of Bristol, Merchant Ind	20	piece	Cloth of Assize, Devonshire Dozen	0	0	0	0

The Trinitie of Cork, burden 10 tons, James Welsh master, to Cork, 21st January 1576

Merchant name	Qty	Unit	Commodity	£	s.	d.	f.
James Creanghe of Cork, Merchant Ind	2	C	Hops	0	20	0	0
	9	stone	Orchil	0	22	6	0
	3	gross	Cutts	0	15	0	0
	20	lb	Cumin	0	6	8	0
	12	lb	Flax	0	2	8	0
	2	burden	Steel	0	5	0	0
	30	dozen	Combs (ob.)	0	12	6	0
	1	gross	Merells	0	4	0	0
	2	lb	Seed, Leek	0	0	8	0
	1.5	great gross	Points	0	12	0	0
	10	piece	Hats	0	10	10	0
	1	stone	Prunes	0	2	2	0
	1	ream	Paper	0	2	8	0
	3	dozen	Girdles, Leather (1d.)	0	2	6	0
	3	clout	Needles	0	2	6	0
	2	dozen	Ribbons	0	2	0	0
	2	lb	Saffron	0	26	8	0

The Foxe of Bristol, burden 45 tons, Richard White master, to Lisbon, 24th January 1576

Merchant name	Qty	Unit	Commodity	£	s.	d.	f.
John Alkyn of Bristol, Merchant Ind	1	fother	Lead	8	0	0	0
Thomas Kelke of Bristol, Merchant Ind	3	quart	Lead	14	0	0	0
Robert Halton of Bristol, Merchant Ind	2	fother	Lead	16	0	0	0
	10	piece	Bay *Cloth*	10	0	0	0
	12	piece	Cloth of Assize, Northern Kersey	0	0	0	0
	8	piece	Cloth of Assize, Western Dozen	0	0	0	0
Thomas Aldworth of Bristol, Merchant Ind	60	piece	Cloth of Assize, Hampshire Kersey	0	0	0	0
	20	piece	Bay *Cloth*	20	0	0	0
Anthony Robins of Bristol, Merchant Ind	6	piece	Cloth of Assize, Redinge Kersey	0	0	0	0
John Browne of Bristol, Merchant Ind	8	piece	Cloth of Assize, Devonshire Dozen	0	0	0	0
John Walron of Tiverton, Merchant Ind	60	piece	Cloth of Assize, Devonshire Dozen	0	0	0	0
John Ashe of Bristol, Merchant Ind	20	piece	Cloth of Assize, Redinge Kersey	0	0	0	0
	6	piece	Grasier *Cloth* White	6	0	0	0

The Hare of Bristol, burden 55 tons, Robert Davies master, to Sanlúcar de Barrameda, 9th February 1575

Merchant name	Qty	Unit	Commodity	£	s.	d.	f.
John Alkin of Bristol, Merchant Ind	4	piece	Cloth of Assize, Short Somerset	0	0	0	0

Merchant name	Qty	Unit	Commodity	£	s.	d.	f.

The Peter & Pawle of Lübeck, burden 200 ton, Hanndridge Datkins master, Destination Unknown, 10th February 1576

William Gittons of Bristol, Merchant Ind	5	piece	Bay *Cloth*	5	0	0	0
	40	wey	Coal, Smith	13	6	8	0

The Conney of Bristol, burden 20 tons, Thomas Pheleps master, to San Sebastián, 16th February 1576

Thomas Aldworth of Bristol, Merchant Ind	8	wey	Beans[5]	0	0	0	0
Thomas Merrike of Bristol, Merchant Ind	3	piece	Cloth of Assize, Short Somerset	0	0	0	0
	2	C goad	Manchester Cotton *Cloth*	6	13	4	0

The Golden Lion of Bristol, burden 350 tons, John Sheppard master, to Bayonne, 27th February 1576

Thomas Warren of Bristol, Merchant Ind	5	fother	Lead	40	0	0	0
John Barnes of Bristol, Merchant Ind	3	fother	Lead	24	0	0	0
Richard Ashehurst of Bristol, Merchant Ind	8	fother	Lead	64	0	0	0
Michael Pepwall of Bristol, Merchant Ind	4	fother	Lead	32	0	0	0
Francis Knight of Bristol, Merchant Ind	2	fother	Lead	16	0	0	0

The Falcon of Bristol, burden 50 tons, Humphrey Heyward master, to La Rochelle, 10th March 1576

Thomas Lacy of Bristol, Merchant Ind	10	piece	Bay *Cloth*	10	0	0	0
	20	wey	Coal, Smith	6	13	4	0

The Dominicke of Bristol, burden 100 tons, John Silley master, to La Rochelle, 17th March 1576

Edward Chester of Bristol, Merchant Ind	5	piece	Cloth of Assize, Northern Kersey	0	0	0	0
	8	piece	Bay *Cloth*	8	0	0	0

The Katherine Morfey of Waterford, burden 10 tons, John Aileworth master, to Waterford, 20th March 1576

Dominic Arther of Limerick, Merchant Ind	1	dozen	Hats, Felt	0	16	8	0
	0.5	gross	Cutts	0	2	6	0
	0.5	gross	Combs (1*d*.)	0	5	0	0
	0.5	piece	Cloth of Assize, Short Somerset	0	0	0	0
	1	piece	Cloth of Assize, Devonshire Kersey	0	0	0	0

The Julian of Wexford, burden 16 tons, Francis Rothe master, to Wexford, 21st March 1576

John Chambers of Marshfield, Yeoman Ind	3	wey	Malt/Barley	0	0	0	0

5 Custom exempt.

Merchant name	Qty	Unit	Commodity	£	s.	d.	f.

The Katherin of Barnstaple, burden 40 tons, Richard Westland master, to Bordeaux, *21st March 1576*

Merchant name	Qty	Unit	Commodity	£	s.	d.	f.
John Sallysbury of Bristol, Merchant Ind	4	piece	Cloth of Assize, Short Somerset	0	0	0	0
Richard Strobridge of Bristol, Merchant Ind	4	C goad	Manchester Cotton *Cloth*	13	6	8	0

The Margett of Kinsale, burden 18 tons, Richard Roche master, to Kinsale, *21st March 1576*

Merchant name	Qty	Unit	Commodity	£	s.	d.	f.
Henry Roche of Kinsale, Merchant Ind	50	lb	Iron	0	15	0	0
	1	C	Orchil	0	20	0	0
	40	*unknown*	*Pics*	0	13	4	0
	2	gross	Cutts	0	10	0	0
	2	great gross	Points, Red (1d.)	0	8	0	0
	1	burden	Steel	0	2	6	0
	1	stone	Aniseed	0	3	6	0
	28	lb	Liquorice	0	4	8	0

The Katherin Morfey of Waterford, burden 10 tons, John Ayleworth master, to Waterford, *21st March 1576*

Merchant name	Qty	Unit	Commodity	£	s.	d.	f.
Edward Brenam of Waterford, Merchant Ind	2	dozen	Knives, Cappe	0	5	0	0
	1.5	gross	Cutts, Cutler	0	7	6	0
	0.5	gross	Knives, Flemish	0	15	0	0
	1	dozen	Hats	0	6	8	0
	3	ell	Holland *Cloth*	0	6	0	0
	0.5	dozen	Hilt and Pomells	0	6	8	0
	2	ell	Sarcenet *Cloth*, Coarse	0	10	0	0
	4	dozen	Points, Small Copper	0	4	0	0
	1	ream	Paper	0	2	8	0
	6	dozen	Combs (1d.)	0	5	0	0
	1	gross	Girdles (1d.)	0	10	0	0
	1	dozen	Spurs, Single	0	2	6	0
	2	lb	Lace, Check	0	3	4	0
	3	clout	Needles	0	2	6	0
	0.5	C	Thimbles	0	0	8	0
	0.75	C	Battery	0	30	0	0
	8	dozen	Garters, Check	0	6	0	0
	3	gross	Buttons, Steel	0	40	0	0
	3	big gross	Buttons, Thread	0	7	6	0
	1	dozen	Girdles, Waist	0	0	12	0
	1	lb	Crewel Fringe	0	4	0	0
	12.5	dozen	Merells	0	6	0	0
	0.5	dozen	Purses, Children	0	2	0	0
	9	lb	Silk, Paris	3	0	0	0
	1	lb	Saffron	0	13	4	0

The Katherin of Barnstaple, burden 40 tons, Richard Westland master, to Bordeaux, 23rd March 1576

Merchant name	Qty	Unit	Commodity	£	s.	d.	f.
John Brasier of Barnstaple, Merchant Ind	4	piece	Cloth of Assize, Short Somerset	0	0	0	0

Merchant name	Qty	Unit	Commodity	£	s.	d.	f.

The Richard of Kinsale, burden 15 tons, Richard John master, to Kinsale, 23rd March 1576

Richard John of Kinsale, Merchant Ind	3	C	Orchil	3	0	0	0
	6	dozen	Hemp	0	15	0	0
	3	C	Pitch?	0	10	0	0
	6	C	Iron	0	48	0	0
	1.5	gross	Cutts	0	8	6	0

The Michaell of Youghal burden 17 tons, Maurice Gayre master, to Youghal, 26th March 1576

| James Bleweth of Youghal, Merchant Ind | 3 | C | Pitch | 0 | 10 | 0 | 0 |
| | 0.5 | C | Hops | 0 | 5 | 0 | 0 |

The Julian of Wexford, burden 16 tons, Francis Roth master, to Wexford, 28th March 1576

| Francis Roth of Wexford, Merchant Ind | 3 | wey | Malt/Barley | 0 | 0 | 0 | 0 |

The Anne of Waterford, burden 20 tons, Patricke Brannocke master, to Waterford, 28th March 1576

Thomas Balliff of Waterford, Merchant Ind	2	lb	Counters, Lattene	0	0	20	0
	4	C	Hops	0	40	0	0
	6	C	Oakum	0	30	0	0
	3	lb	Silk, Paris	0	20	0	0
	6	dozen	Flax	0	0	16	0
	36	dozen	Lace, Statute	0	36	0	0
	12	dozen	Combs (ob.)	0	5	0	0
	11	lb	Mail	0	9	2	0
	2	clout	Needles	0	0	20	0
	18	dozen	Girdles (1d.)	0	15	0	0
	12	piece	Funnels	0	0	12	0
	2	gross	Buttons, Silk	0	20	0	0

The Katherin of Wexford, burden 8 tons, Nicholas Haie master, to Wexford, 29th March 1576

Nicholas Haye of Wexford, Merchant Ind	1	piece	Pans, Brass (60lb)	0	20	0	0
	120	lb	Pots, Brass	0	40	0	0
	2	C	Iron	0	16	0	0
	2	C	Pitch?	0	6	8	0
	0.5	C	Hops	0	5	0	0
	40	lb	Pewter	0	16	8	0
	4	weight	Hemp	0	20	0	0
	3	dozen	Soap, Black	0	4	6	0

The Fage of Dungarvan, burden 9 tons, David Marlyn master, to Dungarvan, 29th March 1576

| David Marlyn of Dungarvan, Merchant Ind | 1.25 | wey | Malt/Barley | 0 | 0 | 0 | 0 |

The Julian of Wexford, burden 16 tons, Francis Roth master, to Wexford, 30th March 1576

| Gareth Sinnote of Wexford, Merchant Ind | 21 | lb | Iron, Flanders | 7 | 0 | 0 | 0 |

Merchant name	Qty	Unit	Commodity	£	s.	d.	f.
	1	lb	Points, Broad (1*d.*)	0	6	0	0
	3	lb	Crewel Fringe	0	12	0	0
	3	lb	Saffron	0	40	0	0
	3	lb	Girdeling, Coarse	0	7	6	0
	8	lb	Senna	0	8	0	0
	6	lb	Cumin	0	0	20	0
	3	dozen	Gloves, Coarse	0	5	6	0
	3	dozen	Girdles (2*d.*)	0	5	0	0
	0.5	great gross	Points	0	4	0	0
	1.5	dozen	Hats, Felt	0	25	0	0
	4	M	Nails	0	6	8	0
	1	dozen	Seed, Onion	0	4	0	0
	1.5	gross	Cutts	0	7	6	0
	1	gross	Girdles (*ob.*)	0	10	0	0
	1	gross	Playing Cards	0	20	0	0
	3	dozen	Combs (*ob.*)	0	15	0	0
	3	ream	Paper	0	8	0	0
	3	lb	Thread, Ynkle	0	3	4	0
	0.5	M	Awl Blades	0	3	4	0
	1.5	C	Battery	3	0	0	0
	5	burden	Steel	0	12	6	0
	2	C	Hops	0	20	0	0
	8	lb	Sulpher	0	0	8	0
	12	lb	Bole Armeniac	0	0	18	0
	12	lb	Turpentine	0	2	0	0
	20	yard	Levant Taffeta Cloth	0	30	0	0
	1.5	dozen	Spurs, Single	0	5	0	0
	8	lb	Graines	0	5	4	0
	2	piece	Cloth of Assize, Devonshire Kersey	0	0	0	0
Francis Rothe of Wexford, Merchant Ind	1.5	C	Battery	3	0	0	0
	10	lb	Iron, Flanders	3	6	8	0
	4	lb	Girdles, Silk	0	10	0	0
	0.5	C	Orchil	0	10	0	0
	0.5	C	Soap, Black	0	3	4	0
	2	dozen	Hats	0	26	8	0
	0.5	lb	Saffron	0	6	8	0
	10	yard	Levant Taffeta Cloth	0	15	0	0
	8	ell	Coarse Holland *Cloth*	0	12	0	0
	2.5	gross	Cutts	0	12	6	0
	1	yard	Velvet	0	15	0	0
	39	piece	Wool-Cards, Paris	0	32	6	0
	0.5	burden	Steel	0	0	15	0
	1	great gross	Points	0	8	0	0
	6	pair	Quern Stones	0	6	0	0
	1	piece	Pan, Brass (40lb)	0	16	8	0
	26	lb	Pewter	0	11	8	0
	2	C	Iron	0	16	0	0
	0.5	last	Calx	0	3	0	0
	0.75	piece	Cloth of Assize	0	0	0	0

Merchant name	Qty	Unit	Commodity	£	s.	d.	f.

The Katherine Hore of Waterford, burden 24 tons, Thomas Ryce master, to Waterford, *30th March 1576 (?)*[6]

Merchant name	Qty	Unit	Commodity	£	s.	d.	f.
Martin Archer of Kilkenny, Merchant Ind	6	C	Hops	3	0	0	0
	1	piece	Pan, Brass (100lb)	0	40	0	0
	1	C	Soap, Black	0	6	8	0
	12	lb	Soap, White	0	4	0	0
	12	lb	Cumin	0	4	0	0
	1	dozen	Hats	0	13	4	0
	6	ream	Paper	0	16	0	0
	6	dozen	Playing Cards	0	10	0	0
	3	C	Tapps and Cannells	0	0	18	0
	3	dozen	Bibs	0	0	18	0
	1	dozen	Funnels	0	2	0	0
	3	pair	Stock-Cards	0	3	0	0
	0.75	piece	Cloth of Assize	0	0	0	0
	1	piece	Cloth of Assize, Kersey	0	0	0	0
Thomas Archer of Kilkenny, Merchant Ind	4	C	Hops	0	40	0	0
	1	piece	Pan, Brass (100lb)	0	40	0	0
	1	C	Soap, Black	0	6	8	0
	1	C	Ochre, Yellow	0	10	0	0
	4	C	Towe, Coarse	0	26	8	0
	3	C	Tapps and Cannells	0	0	18	0
	3	gross	Trenchers, Coarse	0	10	0	0
	4	dozen	Glue	0	10	0	0
	6	lb	Soap, White	0	2	0	0
	1	C	Liquorice	0	10	0	0
	1	dozen	Combs, Horse	0	4	0	0
	1	ream	Paper	0	2	8	0
	1	dozen	Funnels, Tin	0	2	0	0
	6	pair	Stock-Cards	0	6	0	0
	1	C	Flax, Coarse	0	20	0	0

The Margett of Wexford, burden 9 tons, Robert Bromigham master, to Wexford, 2nd April 1576

Merchant name	Qty	Unit	Commodity	£	s.	d.	f.
Stephen Stafford of Wexford, Merchant Ind	1	last	Calx	0	6	0	0
	12	pair	Quern Stones	0	12	0	0
	40	lb	Battery	0	13	4	0
	1	hogshead	Oil, Train	0	25	0	0
	1	dozen	Soap, Black	0	0	18	0
	0.5	C	Hops	0	5	0	0
	2	C	Iron	0	16	0	0
	4.5	wey	Malt/Barley	0	0	0	0
John Holland of Wexford, Merchant Ind	2	wey	Malt/Barley	0	0	0	0

The Katherin Hayward of Waterford, burden 20 tons, Thomas Ryce master, to Waterford, *2nd April 1576*

Merchant name	Qty	Unit	Commodity	£	s.	d.	f.
Pierce Hore of Waterford, Merchant Ind	80	lb	Battery	0	26	8	0

6 Date omitted in the original account.

Merchant name	Qty	Unit	Commodity	£	s.	d.	f.

The Anthony of Milford Haven, burden 15 tons, Philip Folland master, to Drogheda, 4th April 1576

Richard Flemynge of Drogheda,

Merchant Ind	3	ton	Iron	24	0	0	0
	1	C	Soap, Black	0	6	8	0
	2	C	Hops	0	20	0	0
	0.5	M	Trenchers	0	2	6	0

The Anne of Waterford, burden 16 tons, Henry Mayne master, to Waterford, *4th April 1576*

David Dobin of Waterford, Merchant Ind	2	C	Orchil	0	40	0	0
	2	C	Oakum	0	10	0	0
	2	gross	Cutts	0	10	0	0
	2	gross	Knives, In Pairs	3	0	0	0
	12	pair	Stock–Cards	0	12	0	0
	0.5	C	Soap, Black	0	3	4	0
	0.5	gross	Girdles, Leather (1d.)	0	5	0	0
	1.5	great gross	Points	0	12	0	0
	1	lb	Lace, *Billim*	0	20	0	0
	0.5	lb	Saffron	0	6	8	0
	2	lb	Seed, Leek	0	0	8	0
	2	lb	Seed, Onion	0	0	8	0
	12	lb	Hemp	0	2	6	0
	12	lb	Cumin	0	3	4	0
	6	lb	Argol	0	0	15	0
	1.5	lb	Silk, Caddis	0	10	0	0
	3	bolt	Thread	0	10	0	0
	12	yard	Bay *Cloth*	0	6	8	0
	2	piece	Cloth of Assize, Devonshire Kersey	0	0	0	0
	0.5	piece	Cloth of Assize, Short	0	0	0	0

The Katherin of Wexford, burden 8 tons, Nicholas Haie master, to Wexford, *4th April 1576*

Thomas Aldworth of Bristol, Merchant Ind	3	wey	Beans[7]	0	0	0	0

The Sondaye of Wexford, burden 3 tons, Robert Maylor master, to Wexford, 5th April 1576

Robert Maylor of Wexford, Merchant Ind	0.5	weight	Hemp	0	2	6	0
	1.5	stone	Hops	0	2	0	0
	1.5	flitch	Bacon	0	6	0	0
	3	M	Teazles	0	5	0	0

The Domynicke of Bristol, burden 100 tons, John Silley master, to La Rochelle, 7th April 1576

John Ashe of Bristol, Merchant Ind	20	piece	Bay *Cloth*	20	0	0	0

7 Custom exempt.

Merchant name	Qty	Unit	Commodity	£.	s.	d.	f.

The Julian of Barry, burden 45 tons, William Gall master, to Saõ Miguel, *7th April 1576*

| George Higgins of Bristol, Merchant Ind | 60 | quart | Wheat | 0 | 0 | 0 | 0 |
| | 60 | quart | Rye | 0 | 0 | 0 | 0 |

The Mary Fortune of Wexford, burden 7 tons, William Butler master, to Wexford, 9th April 1576

William Butler of Wexford, Merchant Ind	4	C	Iron	0	32	0	0
	100	lb	Battery	0	40	0	0
	6	stone	Hops	0	8	0	0
	24	lb	Pewter	0	10	0	0
	1.5	weight	Hemp	0	7	6	0
	10	piece	Grind -Stones	0	8	4	0
	5	pair	Quern Stones	0	5	0	0

The Domynicke of Bristol, burden 100 tons, John Silley master, to La Rochelle, *9th April 1576*

John Barker of Bristol, Merchant Ind	3	piece	Cloth of Assize, Short	0	0	0	0
	3	C goad	Manchester Cotton *Cloth*	10 0	0	0	0
	3	fother	Lead	24	0	0	0
William Prewett of Bristol, Merchant Ind	10	piece	Bristol Frieze *Cloth*	10	0	0	0
Richard Salterne of Bristol, Merchant Ind	2.5	fother	Lead	20	0	0	0
	6	piece	Tin, Worked	18	0	0	0
	2	C goad	Manchester Cotton *Cloth*	6	13	4	0
	2	piece	Cloth of Assize Short Somerset	0	0	0	0

The Anne of Waterford, burden 20 tons, Patrick Bronocke master, to Waterford, *9th April 1576*

Henry Neale of Waterford, Merchant Ind	0.5	gross	Cutts	0	2	6	0
	12	yard	Mockado *Cloth*	0	10	0	0
	2	gross	Buttons, Thread	0	5	0	0
	1	piece	Holland *Cloth*	0	21	0	0
	2	C	Oakum	0	10	0	0
	0.5	C	Liquorice	0	5	0	0
	1.5	C	Hops	0	15	0	0
	0.5	great gross	Points	0	4	0	0
	0.5	gross	Girdles	0	5	0	0
	1	cribbe	Glass	0	20	0	0

The Katherin Hore of Waterford, burden 20 tons, Thomas Rice master, to Waterford, *9th April 1576*

David Hackett, of Limerick, Merchant Ind	5.5	lb	Silk, Flanders	0	36	8	0
	1	ream	Paper	0	2	8	0
	1	gross	Playing Cards	0	20	0	0
	1	dozen	Hats	0	13	4	0
	1	gross	Combs (*ob.*)	0	5	0	0
	2	lb	Thread, Black	0	2	6	0
	1	dozen	Penners	0	0	20	0

Merchant name	Qty	Unit	Commodity	£	s.	d.	f.
	1	gross	Merrells	0	4	0	0
	1	gross	Cutts	0	5	0	0
	0.5	piece	Bay *Cloth*	0	10	0	0
	1	piece	Cloth of Assize, Short Somerset	0	0	0	0
	0.5	piece	Cloth of Assize, Hampshire Kersey	0	0	0	0

The Golden Lion of Bristol, burden 350 tons, John Shepard master, to Cadiz, 10th April 1576

Merchant name	Qty	Unit	Commodity	£	s.	d.	f.
Thomas Pitt of Bristol, Draper Ind	20	piece	Cloth of Assize, Hampshire Kersey	0	0	0	0
	20	piece	Bay *Cloth*	20	0	0	0
Philip Langley of Bristol, Grocer Ind	9	piece	Cloth of Assize, Short Somerset	0	0	0	0
	20	piece	Cloth of Assize, Hampshire Kersey	0	0	0	0
	15	piece	Bay *Cloth*	15	0	0	0
	40	dozen	Flax	5	6	8	0

The Domynicke of Bristol, burden 100 tons, John Silloy master, to La Rochelle, *10th April 1576*

Merchant name	Qty	Unit	Commodity	£	s.	d.	f.
Robert Sherwode of Bristol, Merchant Ind	3	piece	Cloth of Assize, Short Somerset	0	0	0	0
	10	piece	Bristol Frieze *Cloth*	10	0	0	0
	2	C goad	Manchester Cotton *Cloth*	6	13	4	0

The Margett of Milford Haven, burden 16 tons, John Fisher master, to Drogheda, 11th April 1576

Merchant name	Qty	Unit	Commodity	£	s.	d.	f.
Richard Flemynge of Drogheda, Merchant Ind	8	pair	Milstones	8	0	0	0
	2	M	Teazles	0	3	4	0
	3	M	Trenchers, Coarse	0	15	0	0
	18	M	Teazles	0	30	0	0
	10	pair	Quern Stones	0	10	0	0
	1	C	Madder	0	13	4	0
	2	C	Soap, Black	0	13	4	0
	2	C	Hops	0	20	0	0

The Golden Lion of Bristol, burden 350 tons, John Shepard master, to Cadiz, *11th April 1576*

Merchant name	Qty	Unit	Commodity	£	s.	d.	f.
Benjamin Boydle of Bristol, Merchant Ind	3	piece	Cloth of Assize, Short Somerset	0	0	0	0

The Julian of Barry, burden 45 tons, William Gall master, to Saõ Miguel, *11th April 1576*

Merchant name	Qty	Unit	Commodity	£	s.	d.	f.
Miles Diconsone of Bristol Merchant, Ind	40	piece	Bay *Cloth*	40	0	0	0
	7	piece	Brecon *Cloth*	7	0	0	0
	3	piece	Cloth of Assize, Short Somerset	0	0	0	0

Merchant name	Qty	Unit	Commodity	£	s.	d.	f.

The Domynicke of Bristol, burden 100 tons, John Silloy master, to La Rochelle, 12th April 1576

Merchant name	Qty	Unit	Commodity	£	s.	d.	f.
John Gittons of Bristol, Merchant Ind	4	C goad	Manchester Cotton Cloth	13	6	8	0
Thomas Rowland of Bristol, Merchant Ind	1	fother	Lead	8	0	0	0
William Hicke of Bristol, Merchant Ind	2	fother	Lead	16	0	0	0

The Golden Lion of Bristol, burden 350 tons, John Shepard master, to Cadiz, *12th April 1576*

Merchant name	Qty	Unit	Commodity	£	s.	d.	f.
Nicholas Blake of Bristol, Merchant Ind	3	piece	Cloth of Assize, Short Somerset	0	0	0	0
	6	piece	Bristol Frieze *Cloth*	6	0	0	0
Michael Pepwall of Bristol, Merchant Ind	6	piece	Welsh Cotton *Cloth*	6	0	0	0
William Chester of Bristol, Merchant Ind	5	piece	Cloth of Assize, Short Somerset	0	0	0	0
William Hicke of Bristol, Merchant Ind	20	piece	Cloth of Assize, Hampshire Kersey	0	0	0	0
John Ashe of Bristol, Merchant Ind	9	piece	Cloth of Assize, Short Somerset	0	0	0	0
William Gittons of Bristol, Merchant Ind	5	piece	Cloth of Assize, Short Somerset	0	0	0	0
Robert Kitchinge of Bristol, Merchant Ind	18	piece	Cloth of Assize, Short Somerset	0	0	0	0
Alice Roberts of Bristol, Widow Ind	30	piece	Tenby Cotton *Cloth*	30	0	0	0

The Minikin of Tenby, burden 14 tons, Thomas Kinge master, to Fethard-on-Sea, 13th April 1576

Merchant name	Qty	Unit	Commodity	£	s.	d.	f.
Bartholemew Ramond of Fethard-on Sea, Merchant Ind	0.5	C	Hops	0	5	0	0
	2	weight	Hemp	0	10	0	0
	1	piece	Pan, Brass (20lb)	0	6	8	0

The George of Milford Haven, burden 14 tons, John Gutter master, to Waterford, *13th April 1576*

Merchant name	Qty	Unit	Commodity	£	s.	d.	f.
James Maddane of Waterford, Merchant Ind	8	C	Hops	4	0	0	0
	2	C	Soap, Black	0	13	4	0
Michael Bray of New Ross, Merchant Ind	0.5	gross	Playing Cards	0	10	0	0
	1	gross	Combs (1d.)	0	10	0	0
	1	bolt	Thread, Paris	0	3	4	0
	1	dozen	Penners	0	0	20	0
	1	gross	Points, Crewel	0	12	0	0
	0.5	gross	Garters, Plain Coloured	0	6	0	0
	2	lb	Wax, Red	0	0	16	0
	1	role	Gartering, Worsted	0	3	2	0
	2	dozen	Lace, Black Stole	0	2	0	0
	4	dozen	Glasses, Round	0	2	0	0
	2	gross	Points, Thread	0	0	16	0
	1	gross	Merells	0	4	0	0
	5	clout	Needles	0	4	2	0

Merchant name	Qty	Unit	Commodity	£	s.	d.	f.
	4	lb	Thread	0	5	0	0
	4	piece	Glasses, Hour	0	0	12	0
	6	pair	Bells, Sparrow Hawk	0	0	12	0
	6	pair	Bells, Tassel	0	0	12	0
	2	dozen	Knives, In Pairs	0	4	0	0
	1	dozen	Knives, Flanders	0	2	6	0
	2	ream	Paper	0	5	4	0
	1	C	Awl Blades	0	0	8	0
	18	gross	Buttons, Thread	0	45	0	0
	4	lb	Biskett	0	6	8	0
	4	lb	Seed, Caraway	0	6	8	0
	4	lb	Comfits	0	4	0	0
	4	lb	Coriander	0	4	0	0
	2	lb	Comfits, Spice	0	5	0	0
	12	lb	Almonds	0	4	4	0
	4	lb	Sugar Candy	0	4	0	0
	6	lb	Sugar	0	4	0	0
	7	lb	Currants	0	2	4	0
	0.5	dozen	Sword Blades	0	13	0	0
	0.5	dozen	Hilt and Pomells	0	10	0	0
	0.5	dozen	Spurs, Pairs	0	0	20	0
	0.5	dozen	Spurs, Pairs White	0	0	15	0
	1	gross	Buttons, Brass	0	13	4	0
	1	gross	Buttons, Steel	0	13	4	0
	3	piece	Bits	0	0	20	0
	1	lb	Counters, Yellow	0	0	10	0
	27	C	Nails, Board	0	11	6	0
	0.5	burden	Steel	0	0	15	0
	1	dozen	Knives (1d.)	0	0	12	0
	6	piece	Bells, Sheep	0	0	10	0
	6	piece	Combs, Horse	0	0	22	0
	6	pair	Hinges, Portal (gate)	0	0	20	0
	1.5	lb	Counters, White	0	0	10	0
	18	piece	Books, for Children	0	8	10	0
	2	gross	Cutts	0	10	0	0
	1.75	C	Towe, Coarse	0	20	0	0
	0.5	C	Battery	0	20	0	0
	2	dozen	Flax	0	5	4	0
	1	C	Soap, Black	0	6	8	0
	12	lb	Aniseed	0	3	0	0
	5	piece	Scythe	0	6	0	0
	0.25	C	Seed, Cumin	0	6	8	0
	0.25	C	Prunes	0	6	0	0
	1.33	dozen	Stock-Cards	0	16	0	0
	1	C	Hops	0	10	0	0
	0.75	piece	Cloth of Assize, Short Somerset	0	0	0	0
	0.75	piece	Cloth of Assize, Hampshire Kersey	0	0	0	0
	1	piece	Cloth of Assize, Devonshire Kersey	0	0	0	0

Merchant name	Qty	Unit	Commodity	£	s.	d.	f.

The Mynikin of Bristol, burden 45 tons, Philip Smith master, to La Rochelle, 19th April 1576

Merchant name	Qty	Unit	Commodity	£	s.	d.	f.
Robert Kitchinge of Bristol, Merchant Ind	12	wey	Coal, Smith	4	0	0	0

The Peter of Youghal, burden 28 tons, Darby John master, to Cork, *19th April 1576*

Merchant name	Qty	Unit	Commodity	£	s.	d.	f.
Patrick Galwaye of Cork, Merchant Ind	2	wey	Malt/Barley	0	0	0	0
James Myaghe of Cork, Merchant Ind	2,5	wey	Malt/Barley	0	0	0	0

The Mary Deringe of Passage East, burden 30 tons, William Gall master, to Waterford, 27th April 1576

Merchant name	Qty	Unit	Commodity	£	s.	d.	f.
George Purkell of London, Merchant Ind	1	piece	Cloth of Assize, Short Northern	0	0	0	0
	5	piece	Cloth of Assize, Devonshire Kersey	0	0	0	0
	1	piece	Bay *Cloth*	0	20	0	0
	10	dozen	Hose, for Women	3	6	8	0
	10	dozen	Hose, for Men	5	0	0	0
	1	dozen	Doublet, Canvas	0	30	0	0
	1	dozen	Doublet, Sack Cloth	0	40	0	0
John Archer of Kilkenny, Merchant Ind	4	dozen	Hats	0	53	4	0
	3	dozen	Locks, small	0	5	0	0
	1	gross	Girth Web	0	6	8	0
	1	gross	Buckles, Girth	0	0	20	0
	1	burden	Steel	0	2	6	0
	4	dozen	Spurs, Single	0	13	4	0
	2	lb	*Corten Ruige*	0	0	20	0
	0.5	lb	Wire, Virginal	0	0	10	0
	1	dozen	Saw Files	0	0	18	0
	1	dozen	Chisels	0	0	18	0
	1	gross	Buckles, Boot	0	0	20	0
	1	dozen	Scabbards	0	2	0	0
	6	piece	Scythe	0	6	8	0
	1	dozen	Saws	0	16	0	0
	6	piece	Sword Blades	0	6	8	0
	4	ream	Paper	0	10	8	0
	0.5	gross	Combs (*ob.*)	0	2	6	0
	0.5	C	Prunes	0	9	4	0
	1	C	Ochre	0	3	4	0
	12	lb	Cotton Wool	0	8	0	0
	0.25	C	Madder	0	3	4	0
	2	lb	Starch	0	0	4	0
	1	lb	Wormseed	0	2	0	0
	12	lb	Crossbow Thread	0	5	0	0
	4	lb	Wax	0	2	8	0
	1	gross	Buttons, Thread	0	2	6	0
	6	lb	Thread, Packet	0	2	0	0
	1	bolt	Thread, Black	0	3	4	0
	3	dozen	Bells, Hawk	0	3	0	0
	1	dozen	Bottles, Pewter	0	12	0	0
	2	dozen	Pewter Salt	0	10	0	0

Merchant name	Qty	Unit	Commodity	£	s.	d.	f.
	1	dozen	Candlesticks, Pewter	0	12	0	0
	1	piece	Bay *Cloth*	0	20	0	0
	1.25	piece	Cloth of Assize, Short	0	0	0	0
	2	piece	Cloth of Assize,				
			Hampshire Kersey	0	0	0	0

The Trinitie of Cork, burden 12 tons, James Welsh master, to Cork, 27th April 1576

Geoffrey Galwey of Cork, Merchant Ind	4	gross	Cutts	0	20	0	0
	4	lb	Silk, Paris	0	26	8	0
	3	gross	Points, Paris Red	0	2	0	0
	1	gross	Points, Leather	0	0	20	0
	3	dozen	Hemp	0	7	6	0
	3	piece	Hats	0	3	3	0
	3	piece	Caps	0	3	3	0
	2	piece	Caps, Velvet	0	10	0	0
	6	dozen	Merells	0	2	0	0
	4	dozen	Girdles	0	3	4	0
	1.5	burden	Steel	0	3	9	0
	0.25	C	Hops	0	2	6	0
	1	gross	Combs (1*d*.)	0	10	0	0
	2	clout	Needles	0	0	20	0
	3	stone	Pewter	0	11	8	0
	1	ream	Paper	0	2	8	0
	1	bolt	Thread	0	3	4	0

The Mary Deringe of Passage East, burden 30 tons, William Gawle master, to Waterford, *27th April 1576*

John Archer of Kilkenny, Merchant Ind	3	hogshead	Vinegar	0	35	0	0
	0.5	C	Liquorice	0	5	0	0
	1.5	C	Soap, Black	0	10	0	0
	0.5	C	Unknown	0	8	0	0

The Grashoper of Bristol, burden 25 tons, John Tegge master, to La Rochelle, 30th April 1576

Richard Jones of Bristol, Merchant Ind	4	fother	Lead	32	0	0	0

The William Bonaventure of London, burden 30 tons, John Rickma*n* master, to Waterford, 8th May 1576

Thomas White of Waterford, Merchant Ind	1	dozen	Brushes, Small	0	4	0	0
	9	lb	Almonds	0	3	2	0
	1	dozen	Penners and Inkhorns	0	0	20	0
	4	pair	Hilts, Single	0	4	4	0
	2	dozen	Girdles, Leather (1d.)	0	3	4	0
	2	dozen	Spurs, Single	0	6	8	0
	4	small gross	Points	0	2	8	0
	0.5	C	Liquorice	0	5	0	0
	1	gross	Combs (*ob*.)	0	5	0	0
	2	lb	Thread	0	2	6	0
	3	dozen	Knives	0	7	6	0

Merchant name	Qty	Unit	Commodity	£	s.	d.	f.
	3	piece	Hatchets, Dansk	0	3	0	0
	2	piece	Knives, Shope?	0	0	16	0
	4	lb	Arsenic	0	0	20	0
	1	piece	Towe, Coarse	0	10	0	0
	4	piece	Sword Blades	0	4	4	0
	1	dozen	Hose, for Women	0	6	8	0
	1.5	dozen	Hats	0	25	0	0
	4	piece	Cap Cases	0	4	0	0
	2	dozen	Girth Web	0	4	0	0
	1	dozen	Hose, for Men	0	10	0	0
	20	lb	Sugar	0	13	4	0
	0.25	C	Glue	0	2	6	0
	2	dozen	Soap, Black	0	3	0	0
	20	lb	Soap, White	0	6	8	0
Darby Hungerford of Waterford, Merchant Ind	10	C	Oakum	0	50	0	0
	2	C	Battery	4	0	0	0
	3	C	Liquorice	0	30	0	0
	1	C	Soap, Black	0	6	8	0
	2	gross	Cutts	0	10	0	0
	1	dozen	Stock-Cards	0	12	0	0
	8	gross	Points	0	5	4	0
	3	C	Hops	0	30	0	0
	1	dozen	Serches	0	8	0	0
	2	dozen	Glue	0	4	0	0
Patrick Welsh of Limerick, Merchant Ind	3	ream	Paper	0	8	0	0
	1	gross	Cutts	0	5	0	0
	6	dozen	Girdles, Leather	0	6	8	0
	4	dozen	Girdles, Ribbon	0	5	0	0
	2	dozen	Playing Cards	0	3	4	0
	2	bolt	Thread	0	6	8	0
	2	dozen	Penners and Inkhorns	0	3	4	0
	6	lb	Thread	0	7	6	0
	6	lb	Frankinscense	0	0	12	0
	1	dozen	Crab -locks	0	3	4	0
	0.5	dozen	Hats, for Children	0	6	8	0
	1	gross	Combs (ob.)	0	5	0	0
	1	gross	Points, Leather	0	0	20	0
	1	gross	Merells	0	4	0	0
	1.5	dozen	Soap, White	0	6	0	0
	1	dozen	Seed, Cumin	0	3	4	0
	4	lb	Crewel	0	20	0	0
	0.5	great gross	Points	0	4	0	0
	2	lb	Silk, Paris	0	13	4	0
John Welsh of Waterford, Merchant Ind	2	dozen	Playing Cards	0	3	4	0
	1	ream	Paper	0	2	8	0
	6	dozen	Merells	0	2	0	0
	9	dozen	Combs (ob.)	0	3	9	0
	4	piece	Hats, for Children	0	4	0	0
	1	dozen	Penners and Inkhorns	0	0	20	0
	1	bolt	Thread	0	3	4	0
	0.5	C	Hops	0	5	0	0

Merchant name	Qty	Unit	Commodity	£	s.	d.	f.
	2	stone	Liquorice	0	2	6	0
	1	small gross	Points	0	0	8	0

The Peter of Youghal, burden 30 tons, Darby John master, to Cork, 9th May 1576

Merchant name	Qty	Unit	Commodity	£	s.	d.	f.
Robert Breckley of Limerick, Merchant Ind	2	lb	Silk, Paris	0	13	4	0
	1	great gross	Points	0	8	0	0
	1	ream	Paper	0	2	8	0
	2	dozen	Playing Cards	0	3	4	0
	0.5	gross	Merells	0	2	0	0
	4	piece	Hats	0	4	4	0
	1	dozen	Penners and Inkhorns	0	0	20	0
	3	dozen	Girdles, Leather (1d.)	0	2	6	0
	8	dozen	Bowstrings	0	2	8	0
	0.5	dozen	Spurs, Pairs	0	0	15	0
	4	lb	Soap, White	0	0	16	0
	3	lb	Cumin	0	0	12	0
	3	lb	Ochre	0	0	2	0
	1	lb	Wax	0	0	8	0
	12	dozen	Combs (ob.)	0	5	0	0
Richard Mahownde of Limerick, Merchant Ind	4	lb	Silk, Paris	0	26	8	0
	5	gross	Cutts	0	25	0	0
	2	dozen	Knives, in Pairs (2d.)	0	4	0	0
	1.5	great gross	Points	0	12	0	0
	2	small gross	Points, Red	0	3	4	0
	0.5	C	Hops	0	5	0	0
	0.5	C	Liquorice	0	5	0	0
	2	ream	Paper	0	5	4	0
	7	box	Combs (ob.)	0	9	0	0
	1	bolt	Thread	0	3	4	0
	4	dozen	Playing Cards	0	6	8	0
	20	lb	Seed, Cumin	0	6	8	0
	2	stone	Turpentine	0	0	4	0
	1.5	gross	Merells	0	6	0	0
	2	dozen	Penners	0	3	4	0
	4	lb	Frankinscense	0	0	8	0
	2	piece	Hats	0	2	2	0
	1	lb	Senna	0	0	12	0
	8	lb	Bole Armeniac	0	0	16	0
	6	dozen	Girdles (ob.)	0	3	0	0
	3	dozen	Fell Fonnells[8]	0	3	0	0
	1.5	great gross	Points, Red	0	5	0	0
	2	lb	Thread	0	2	6	0
	6	lb	Sulpher	0	0	6	0
	2	gross	Points, Thread	0	0	8	0
	2	dozen	Locks	0	3	4	0
	2	lb	Wax	0	0	16	0
	1	lb	Thread, White	0	0	20	0
	1	lb	Graines	0	0	8	0
	2	lb	Arsenic	0	0	10	0

8 Perhaps funnels of some type.

Merchant name	Qty	Unit	Commodity	£	s.	d.	f.
	2	dozen	Garters, Crewel	0	3	0	0
John Strech of Limerick, Merchant Ind	2	clout	Needles	0	0	20	0
	4	dozen	Playing Cards	0	6	8	0
	4	box	Combs (ob.)	0	5	0	0
	6	piece	Hats, for Children	0	6	0	0
	1.5	dozen	Penners	0	0	20	0
	3	ream	Paper	0	8	0	0
	3	stone	Liquorice	0	7	0	0
	0.5	gross	Merells	0	2	0	0
	2	lb	Wax, Red	0	0	16	0
	8	lb	Soap, White	0	2	8	0
	3	lb	Seed, Cumin	0	0	12	0
	1	dozen	Girdles	0	0	5	0
	0.5	gross	Cutts	0	2	6	0
	1	dozen	Locks	0	0	20	0
	0.5	dozen	Spurs, Pairs	0	0	15	0
	1	small gross	Points	0	0	8	0
	1	dozen	Skins, Golden	0	5	0	0
	1	bolt	Thread	0	3	4	0
Patrick Galwey of Cork, Merchant Ind	1	C	Hops	0	10	0	0
	3	lb	Silk, Raw	0	20	0	0
	12	lb	Silk, Paris	4	0	0	0
	2	lb	Thread, Brown	0	2	6	0
	1	lb	Saffron	0	13	4	0
	1	gross	Girdles (1d.)	0	10	0	0
	4	gross	Cutts	0	20	0	0
	2	small gross	Points	0	0	16	0
	8	piece	Caps	0	8	8	0
	2	burden	Steel	0	5	0	0
	3	piece	Hats	0	3	3	0
	6	lb	Glue	0	0	8	0
	2	gross	Trenchers	0	6	8	0
	1	gross	Points, Leather	0	0	8	0
	6	lb	Sugar	0	4	0	0
	1	dozen	Spurs	0	3	4	0
	1	dozen	Girth	0	0	12	0
	0.5	dozen	Serches	0	4	0	0
	0.5	gross	Merells	0	2	0	0

The Trinitie of Bristol, burden 30 tons, Leonard Shereman master, to La Rochelle, 14th May 1576

Richard Strobridge of Bristol, Merchant Ind	16	wey	Coal, Smith	5	6	8	0
Richard Ashehurst of Bristol, Merchant Ind	1	C goad	Manchester Cotton				
			Cloth	3	6	8	0

The Julian of Bristol, burden 30 tons, Thomas Jennynge master, to La Rochelle, 18th May 1576

Thomas Deconsone of Bristol, Merchant Ind	3	fother	Lead	24	0	0	0
	2	C goad	Manchester Cotton				
			Cloth	6	13	4	0

Merchant name	Qty	Unit	Commodity	£	s.	d.	f.

The Jesus of Bideford burden 25 tons, Robert Lunbery master, to Saõ Miguel, 22nd May 1576

Merchant name	Qty	Unit	Commodity	£	s.	d.	f.
Thomas Aldworth of Bristol, Merchant Ind	20	piece	Bay *Cloth*	20	0	0	0
	4	piece	Brecon *Cloth*	4	0	0	0
	8	C	Flax	8	0	0	0
	3	piece	Cloth of Assize, Short Somerset	0	0	0	0
Robert Hatton of Bristol, Merchant Ind	4	piece	Cloth of Assize, Short Somerset	0	0	0	0
William Salterne of Bristol, Merchant Ind	9	piece	Cloth of Assize, Short Somerset	0	0	0	0
	10	piece	Brecon *Cloth*	10	0	0	0
	10	dozen	Flax	0	26	8	0
Thomas Rowland of Bristol, Merchant Ind	2	piece	Cloth of Assize, Short Somerset	0	0	0	0
	7	piece	Brecon *Cloth*	7	0	0	0
	1.75	C	Wax	5	5	0	0
John Browne of Bristol, Merchant Ind	3	C	Wax	9	0	0	0

The Margett of Kinsale, burden 15 tons, Henry Roche master, to Kinsale, 24th May 1576

Merchant name	Qty	Unit	Commodity	£	s.	d.	f.
Henry Roche of Kinsale, Merchant Ind	1	wey	Barley/Beans[9]	0	0	0	0

The Pleasure of Marennes, burden 50 tons, John Provote master, to Marennes, 15th June 1576

Merchant name	Qty	Unit	Commodity	£	s.	d.	f.
John Provote of Marennes, Merchant Alien	3	piece	Cloth of Assize, Short Somerset	0	0	0	0
	2.5	piece	Cloth of Assize, Short	0	0	0	0
	0.33	piece	Cloth of Assize, Short	0	0	0	0
	1.5	piece	Cloth of Assize, Devonshire Kersey	0	0	0	0
	1	piece	Bay *Cloth*	0	20	0	0
	10	wey	Coal, Smith	3	6	8	0
	6	ton	Calx	0	12	0	0

The France of Marennes, burden 40 tons, John Martine master, to Marennes, 15th June 1576

Merchant name	Qty	Unit	Commodity	£	s.	d.	f.
John Martine of Marennes, Merchant Alien	5	piece	Cloth of Assize, Short Somerset	0	0	0	0
	2.5	piece	Cloth of Assize, Short	0	0	0	0
	1	piece	Cloth of Assize, Devonshire Kersey	0	0	0	0
	8	wey	Coal, Smith	0	53	4	0
	6	ton	Calx	0	12	0	0
	1	piece	Frieze *Cloth*	0	20	0	0

The Margett of Bristol, burden 20 tons, William Morrice master, to Dublin, 18th June 1576

Merchant name	Qty	Unit	Commodity	£	s.	d.	f.
Mathew Gedon & Alexander Barnwell of Dublin, Merchants Ind	4	ton	Iron	32	0	0	0
	10	C	Soap, Black	3	6	8	0

9 Custom exempt.

Merchant name	Qty	Unit	Commodity	£	s.	d.	f.
	3	C	Soap, White	0	40	0	0
	4	C	Hops	0	40	0	0
	4	C	Liquorice	0	40	0	0

The Jesus of Pembroke, burden 20 tons, James Dic[] master, to Cork, 20th June 1576

Dominic Waters of Cork, Merchant Ind	1	lb	Saffron	0	13	4	0
	3	gross	Cutts	0	15	0	0
	6	dozen	Girdles (1d.)	0	6	0	0
	1.5	burden	Steel	0	3	9	0
	0.5	lb	Cloves	0	2	6	0
	0.5	great gross	Points	0	4	0	0
	0.5	dozen	Serches	0	4	0	0
	6	lb	Sulpher	0	0	6	0

The Mary Fortune of Wexford, burden 8 tons, Robert Butler master, to Wexford, *20th June 1576*

Richard Synote of Wexford, Merchant Ind	2	wey	Malt/Barley/Beans	0	0	0	0

The Nicholas of Fécamp, burden 60 tons, John Basiro master, to Fécamp, *20th June 1576*

John Basiro of Fécamp, Merchant Alien	20	wey	Coal, Smith	6	13	4	0

The Anne Gallant, *of Bristol*, burden 26 tons, Humphrey Dic[] master, to La Rochelle, 22nd June 1576

William Smith of Bristol, Merchant Ind	8	wey	Coal, Smith	0	53	4	0
	2	C goad	Manchester Cotton				
			Cloth	6	12	4	0

The Gabriel of Mortain, burden 40 tons, Michael Durant master, to Mortain, 25th June 1576

Michael Durant of Mortain, Merchant Alien	3	fother	Lead	24	0	0	0
	35	wey	Coal, Smith	11	13	4	0
	3	piece	Bay *Cloth*	3	0	0	0
	2	piece	Frieze *Cloth*	0	40	0	0
	1	ton	Calx	0	2	0	0
	5	piece	Cloth of Assize, Devonshire Kersey	0	0	0	0

The Mary Fortune of Bristol, burden 30 tons, Walter Doll[] master, to Cork, 30th June 1576

David Harolde of Limerick, Merchant Ind	6	dozen	Points, Silk	0	6	8	0
	1	bolt	Thread	0	3	4	0
	0.5	gross	Combs (*ob.*)	0	2	6	0
	1	clout	Needles	0	0	10	0
	0.5	dozen	Penners and Inkhorns	0	0	10	0
	1	lb	Knives, Bombard	0	0	12	0
	0.5	gross	Cutts	0	2	6	0
	2	dozen	Knives	0	2	0	0
	1	small gross	Points	0	5	4	0

Merchant name	Qty	Unit	Commodity	£	s.	d.	f.
	0.5	gross	Merells	0	2	0	0
	0.5	C	Cuttlebones	0	0	6	0
	1	lb	Wax	0	0	8	0
	2	dozen	*Cathurhisin*	0	2	0	0
	2	unknown	Silk, Paris	0	2	0	0
	5	unknown	Girth, Paris	0	0	10	0
	6	gross	Levant Taffeta Cloth	0	9	0	0
	1	ream	Paper	0	2	8	0
	0.66	piece	Cloth of Assize, Short	0	0	0	0
Leonard Stackpole of Limerick, Merchant Ind	1	C	Hops	0	10	0	0
	2	lb	Silk, Paris	0	13	4	0
	6	piece	Hats	0	6	8	0
	4	dozen	Girdles, Waist	0	3	4	0
	1	dozen	Ribbons	0	0	12	0
	0.5	clout	Needles	0	0	5	0
	0.5	gross	Cutts	0	2	6	0
	8.5	small gross	Points	0	5	4	0
	1	dozen	Spurs	0	2	6	0
	1	ream	Paper	0	2	8	0
	1	lb	Crewel, Red	0	0	20	0
	2	dozen	Knives (1d.)	0	2	0	0
	3	gross	Buttons, Thread	0	7	6	0
	1	dozen	Playing Cards	0	0	20	0
	3	piece	Hats, for Children	0	3	3	0
	9	yard	Black Buckram *Cloth*	0	6	0	0

The Mary of Fécamp, burden 68 tons, Stephen Mabire master, to Fécamp, 4th July 1576

Stephen Mabire of Fécamp, Merchant Alien	20	wey	Coal, Smith	6	13	4	0

The Hope of Fécamp, burden 40 tons, Thomas Lebert master, to Fécamp, *4th July 1576*

Thomas Lebert of Fécamp, Merchant Alien	8	wey	Coal, Smith	0	53	4	0
	18	ton	Calx Vive	0	36	8	0

The Bonaventure of Fécamp, burden 50 tons, Nicholas Bertiere master, to Fécamp, *4th July 1576*

Nicholas Bertiere of Fécamp, Merchant Alien	20	wey	Coal, Smith	6	13	4	0
	4	ton	*Calx (Vine)*	0	8	0	0

The Cony of Bristol, burden 20 tons, Walter Phelpes master, to San Sebastián, 13th July 1576

Richard Langford of Bristol, Merchant Ind	2	fother	Lead	16	0	0	0
Thomas Merricke of Bristol, Merchant Ind	3	fother	Lead	24	0	0	0

The Lewys of Crozon, burden 26 tons, Harvey Harvell master, to Crozon, 18th July 1576

Harvey Harvell of Crozon, Merchant Alien	18	wey	Coal, Smith	6	0	0	0

Merchant name	Qty	Unit	Commodity	£	s.	d.	f.

The Greyhounde of Bristol, burden 40 tons, James Whitinge master, to the Azores, 21st July 1576

Merchant name	Qty	Unit	Commodity	£	s.	d.	f.
Robert Kitchinge of Bristol, Merchant Ind	4	piece	Cloth of Assize, Short Somerset	0	0	0	0
William Gittons of Bristol, Merchant Ind	18	piece	Trucker *Cloth*	18	0	0	0
Thomas Aldworth of Bristol, Merchant Ind	100	piece	Bay *Cloth*	100	0	0	0
	60	piece	Cloth of Assize, Hampshire Kersey	0	0	0	0
Miles Diconsone of Bristol, Merchant Ind	12	piece	Cloth of Assize, Short Somerset	0	0	0	0
	70	piece	Cloth of Assize, Northern Kersey	0	0	0	0
	2	piece	Brecon *Cloth*	0	40	0	0
	2	C goad	Manchester Cotton *Cloth*	6	13	4	0
Botholl Holder of London, Merchant Ind	18	piece	Cloth of Assize, Redinge Long	0	0	0	0
John Alkin of Bristol, Soapmaker Ind	6	piece	Cloth of Assize, Short	0	0	0	0
Thomas Rowland of Bristol, Merchant Ind	2	piece	Cloth of Assize, Short Somerset	0	0	0	0
	1	piece	Trucker *Cloth*	0	20	0	0
Andrewe Cottrell of Bristol, Merchant Ind	6	piece	Grasier and Trucker *Cloth*	6	0	0	0

The Katherin of Wexford, burden 9 tons, Nicholas Haie master, to Wexford, 28th July 1576

Merchant name	Qty	Unit	Commodity	£	s.	d.	f.
Patrick Chevers of Wexford, Merchant Ind	5	ton	Salt	5	0	0	0
	2	C	Iron	0	16	0	0
	2	C	Battery	4	0	0	0
	1	C	Pots, Brass	0	33	4	0
	2	C	Hops	0	20	0	0
	4	lb	Silk, Paris	0	26	8	0
	3	gross	Cutts	0	15	0	0
	2	dozen	Hats	0	26	8	0
	1	C	Orchil	0	20	0	0
	1	C	Soap, Black	0	6	8	0
	1	lb	Saffron	0	13	4	0
	0.75	piece	Cloth of Assize, Short	0	0	0	0
	2	piece	Cloth of Assize, Western Kersey	0	0	0	0

The Julian of Bristol, burden 30 tons, Robert Spoddle, to Galway, 30th July 1576

Merchant name	Qty	Unit	Commodity	£	s.	d.	f.
Ronald French of Galway, Merchant Ind	8	lb	Silk, Paris	0	53	4	0
	6	bolt	Thread	0	20	0	0
	2	C	Alum	3	6	8	0
	4	C	Lead	0	32	0	0
	1	gross	Playing Cards	0	20	0	0
	3	dozen	Wool–Cards	0	30	0	0
	6	gross	Garters, Crewel	0	20	0	0
	4	gross	Lace, Statute	0	48	0	0

Merchant name	Qty	Unit	Commodity	£	s.	d.	f.
	18	dozen	Combs (*ob.*)	0	7	6	0
	6	gross	Cutts	0	30	0	0
	2	ream	Paper	0	5	4	0
	40	lb	Soap, White	0	13	4	0
	20	lb	Liquorice	0	3	4	0
	8	dozen	Girdles, Leather (1*d.*)	0	6	8	0
	3	gross	Merells	0	12	0	0
	5	great gross	Points	0	40	0	0
	10	lb	Cumin	0	3	4	0
	1	piece	Cloth of Assize, Short Somerset	0	0	0	0
	3	piece	Cloth of Assize, Devonshire Kersey	0	0	0	0

The Katherin of Waterford, burden 16 tons, John Gall master, to Waterford, 31st July 1576

Merchant name	Qty	Unit	Commodity	£	s.	d.	f.
Thomas Strech of Limerick, Merchant Ind	6	lb	Silk, Paris	0	40	0	0
	6	gross	Cutts	0	30	0	0
	3	gross	Merells	0	12	0	0
	16	small gross	Points	0	10	8	0
	2	gross	Points, Leather	0	0	16	0
	4	lb	Cumin	0	0	16	0
	3	dozen	Girdles, Leather (1*d.*)	0	2	6	0
	3	dozen	Playing Cards	0	5	0	0
	6	lb	Frankinscense	0	0	12	0
	9	dozen	Combs (*ob.*)	0	3	9	0
	1	dozen	Knives, Prage	0	0	16	0

The Julian of Elmore, burden 15 tons, Thomas Windane master, to Cork, 1st August 1576

Merchant name	Qty	Unit	Commodity	£	s.	d.	f.
Christopher Meaghe of Cork, Merchant Ind	5	lb	Silk, Paris	0	33	4	0
	1	lb	Saffron	0	13	4	0
	2	gross	Cutts	0	10	0	0
	2.5	dozen	Girdles (1*d.*)	0	2	6	0
	1	gross	Merells	0	4	0	0
	1	ream	Paper	0	2	8	0
	2.5	stone	Pewter	0	11	8	0
	1	gross	Combs	0	5	0	0
	1	burden	Steel	0	2	6	0
	2	dozen	Points, Silk	0	2	0	0
	2	stone	Hops	0	2	6	0
	2	clout	Needles	0	0	20	0
	4	lb	Cumin	0	0	16	0
	0.5	great gross	Points	0	4	0	0

The Jesus of Bristol, burden 9 tons, Richard Knight master, to Dublin, 2nd August 1576

Merchant name	Qty	Unit	Commodity	£	s.	d.	f.
Patrick Dowdall of Dublin, Merchant Ind	8	ton	Iron	64	0	0	0
	5	C	Hops	2	10	0	0
	2	C	Orchil	0	40	0	0
	2	C	Alum	3	6	8	0

Merchant name	Qty	Unit	Commodity	£	s.	d.	f.

The Katherin of Waterford, burden 16 tons, John Gall master, to Waterford, 7th August 1576

Merchant name	Qty	Unit	Commodity	£	s.	d.	f.
John Welsh of Waterford, Merchant Ind	0.5	lb	Silk, Paris	0	3	4	0
	3	pair	Stock-Cards	0	3	0	0
	0.5	C	Soap, Black	0	3	4	0
	1.5	dozen	Skins, Cony Black	0	10	0	0
	1	dozen	Cruses, Stone	0	0	14	0
	0.5	lb	Thread	0	0	20	0
	2	piece	Russett Fustian *Cloth*	0	30	0	0
David Dobin of Waterford, Merchant Ind	0.5	gross	Cutts	0	2	6	0
	0.5	gross	Knives	0	2	6	0
	12	pair	Stock-Cards	0	12	0	0
	0.25	gross	Playing Cards	0	5	0	0
	7&8	piece	*Balches/Lins?*	0	8	0	0
	1	dozen	Hats, for Children	0	13	0	0
	8	lb	Sugar	0	5	4	0
	0.5	C	Battery	0	20	0	0
	1	dozen	Wick Yarn	0	0	18	0
	5	lb	Biskett	0	0	20	0
	4	M	Nails, Lath	0	4	0	0
	1	piece	Cloth of Assize, Short	0	0	0	0
	2.5	piece	Cloth of Assize, Devonshire Kersey	0	0	0	0
Pierce Quirke of Clonmel, Merchant Ind	2	piece	Calico *Cloth*	0	13	4	0
	2	gross	Cutts	0	10	0	0
	1.5	lb	Silk, Paris	0	8	0	0
	1	lb	Cinnamon	0	4	0	0
	1	lb	Cloves	0	5	0	0
	10	piece	Hats	0	10	10	0
	4	piece	Candlesticks	0	4	0	0
	3	pair	Stock-Cards	0	3	0	0
	2	dozen	Playing Cards	0	3	4	0
	2	dozen	Girdles (1*d.*)	0	0	20	0
	1	ream	Paper	0	2	8	0
	1	dozen	Penners and Inkhorns	0	0	20	0
	1	lb	Pepper	0	0	20	0
	2	lb	Mail	0	0	12	0
	9	dozen	Unknown	0	4	9	0
	12	lb	Aniseed	0	4	0	0
	2	*lb*	Serches	0	2	0	0
Jeremiah Lumbard of Waterford, Merchant Ind	6.5	gross	Cutts	0	32	6	0
	0.5	gross	Knives (1*d.*)	0	10	0	0
	1	gross	Knives (2*d.*)	0	30	0	0
	10	dozen	Knives, Cullen	0	25	0	0
	2	gross	Girdles (1*d.*)	0	20	0	0
	1	gross	Girdles (*ob.*)	0	5	0	0
	8	dozen	Girdles, Waist (1*d.*)	0	8	4	0
	2	gross	Merells	0	8	0	0
	2	gross	Garters, Ribbon	0	16	0	0
	3	great gross	Points	0	24	0	0
	4	ream	Paper	0	10	8	0

Merchant name	Qty	Unit	Commodity	£	s.	d.	f.
	2	clout	Needles	0	0	20	0
	10	ounce	Lace, Black Silk	0	4	2	0
	4	ounce	Silk, Paris	0	0	20	0
	4	lb	Mail	0	2	0	0
	1	lb	Saffron	0	13	4	0
	0.5	gross	Combs (ob.)	0	2	6	0
	12	pair	Stock-Cards	0	12	0	0
	1.25	C	Soap, Black	0	8	4	0

The Mary Deringe of Waterford, burden 30 tons, Philip Deringe master, to Waterford, 7th August 1576

Merchant name	Qty	Unit	Commodity	£	s.	d.	f.
Patrick White of Waterford, Merchant Ind	2	gross	Cutts	0	10	0	0
	1	gross	Girdles (ob.)	0	5	0	0
	2	dozen	Aniseed	0	6	0	0
	1	dozen	Seed, Cumin	0	3	4	0
	12	lb	Liquorice	0	2	0	0
	1	lb	Senna	0	0	12	0
	2	dozen	Knives (1d.)	0	5	0	0
	3	dozen	Playing Cards	0	5	0	0
	0.25	C	Soap, Black	0	0	20	0
	6	dozen	Combs (ob.)	0	2	6	0
	1	clout	Needles	0	0	10	0
	6	lb	Glue	0	0	12	0
	1	lb	Luxanom[10]	0	3	4	0
	2	lb	Electuary	0	3	4	0
	1	C	Hops	0	10	0	0
Thomas Braynocke of Waterford, Merchant Ind	1	gross	Cutts	0	5	0	0
	2	dozen	Playing Cards	0	3	4	0
	2	pair	Stock-Cards	0	2	0	0
	1	gross	Points, Leather	0	0	20	0
	1	dozen	Seed, Cumin	0	3	4	0
	3	dozen	Combs (ob.)	0	0	15	0
	2	lb	Mail	0	0	12	0
	1	clout	Needles	0	0	10	0
	2	dozen	Soap, Black	0	3	0	0
	1	lb	Wax	0	0	8	0
Nicholas Brever of Waterford, Merchant Ind	12	pair	Stock-Cards	0	12	0	0
	1	gross	Cutts	0	5	0	0
	0.5	gross	Knives (1d.)	0	5	0	0
	4	piece	Caps	0	2	4	0
	5	pair	Hose, for Men	0	4	2	0
	2	piece	Hats	0	2	2	0
	2	lb	Mail	0	0	12	0
	3	dozen	Hooks, Hake	0	0	18	0
	8	ell	Holland *Cloth*	0	16	0	0
	8	yard	Sack *Cloth*	0	4	8	0
	1	ell	Changable Taffeta *Cloth*	0	8	4	0

10 Unidentified.

Merchant name	Qty	Unit	Commodity	£	s.	d.	f.
George Quemerford of Waterford, Merchant Ind	1	gross	Girdles (1d.)	0	10	0	0
	1	pipe	Iron	4	0	0	0
	2	C	Soap, Black	0	13	4	0
	24	lb	Sugar	0	16	0	0
	4	piece	Hats, for Children	0	4	0	0
	6	gross	Cutts	0	30	0	0
	24	pair	Wool-Cards	0	20	0	0
	6	dozen	Points, Leather	0	0	10	0
	2	great gross	Points	0	16	0	0
	12	pair	Hose, for Women	0	6	8	0
	3	piece	Saws, Hand	0	0	18	0
	2	dozen	Seed, Cumin	0	6	8	0
	1	C	Hops	0	10	0	0
Thomas Corkeram of Waterford, Merchant Ind	1	gross	Girdles (1d.)	0	10	0	0
	1	gross	Cutts	0	5	0	0
	0.5	gross	Knives, Cullen	0	15	0	0
	1	dozen	Hats, for Children	0	12	0	0
	12	lb	Almonds	0	4	3	0
	0.25	C	Ure	0	5	10	0
	1	gross	Combs (ob.)	0	5	0	0
	3	lb	Silk, Paris	0	20	0	0
	12	pair	Stock-Cards	0	12	0	0
	2	piece	Cloth of Assize, Devonshire Kersey	0	0	0	0
Geoffrey Roth of Kilkenny, Merchant Ind	1	C	Soap, Black	0	6	8	0
	6	pair	Stock-Cards	0	6	0	0
	2	C	Lead	0	16	0	0
	1	clout	Needles	0	0	10	0
	3	lb	Silk, Paris	0	20	0	0
	1	lb	Cinnamon	0	4	0	0
	1	lb	Ginger	0	0	18	0
	2	ream	Paper	0	5	4	0
	0.5	great gross	Points	0	4	0	0
	2	gross	Cutts	0	10	0	0
	2	gross	Girdles (1d.)	0	20	0	0
	1	gross	Bowstrings	0	3	0	0
	6	piece	Hats, for Children	0	6	0	0
	12	lb	Seed, Cumin	0	3	4	0
	2	bolt	Thread	0	6	8	0
	3	dozen	Combs (ob.)	0	0	15	0
	4	dozen	Soap, White	0	16	0	0
	3	dozen	Crewel Fringe	0	12	0	0
	1	animal	Jenet	0	25	8	0
	1	piece	Mockado Tuffed Cloth	0	10	0	0
	1	unknown	Skins Budge, Fine	0	10	0	0
	1	piece	Skins, Cony Fine	0	10	0	0
	4.5	yard	Satin	0	9	0	0
	3.5	yard	Velvet	0	52	6	0
	6	lb	Biskett	0	10	0	0
	6	lb	Comfits	0	6	0	0

Merchant name	Qty	Unit	Commodity	£	s.	d.	f.
John Archer of Kilkenny, Merchant Ind	2	C	Hops	0	20	0	0
	12	pair	Stock–Cards	0	12	0	0
	1	hogshead	Vinegar	0	11	8	0
	1	C	Soap, Black	0	6	8	0
	12	piece	Hats, for Children	0	12	0	0
	1	gross	Cutts	0	5	0	0
	4	lb	Silk, Paris	0	26	8	0
	0.5	gross	Playing Cards	0	10	0	0
	1	ream	Paper	0	2	8	0
	1	ream	Paper, Brown	0	2	6	0
	1	gross	Girth Web	0	6	8	0
	1	gross	Buckles	0	3	4	0
	6	lb	Wax	0	6	8	0
	0.5	gross	Girdles (1d.)	0	5	0	0
	1	gross	Bowstrings	0	3	0	0
	0.5	gross	Combs (ob.)	0	5	0	0
	10	lb	Sugar	0	6	8	0
	1	lb	Pepper	0	0	20	0
	3	clout	Needles	0	2	6	0
	0.5	C	Battery	0	20	0	0
	10	ell	Holland Cloth	0	15	0	0
	0.5	piece	Cloth of Assize, Short	0	0	0	0
John Roth of Waterford, Merchant Ind	11	lb	Silk, Paris	3	13	4	0
	2	dozen	Hats	0	33	4	0
	5.5	gross	Cutts	0	27	6	0
	2	bolt	Thread	0	6	8	0
	2	ream	Paper	0	5	4	0
	0.5	gross	Merells	0	2	0	0
	1	dozen	Penners and Inkhorns	0	0	20	0
	2	lb	Thread, Packet	0	0	12	0
	1	gross	Playing Cards	0	20	0	0
	2.5	lb	Cinnamon	0	10	0	0
	1	C	Hops	0	10	0	0
	17.5	lb	Cloves	0	12	6	0
	3	ell	Sarcenet Cloth	0	15	0	0
	1.5	piece	Calico Cloth	0	10	0	0
	1	piece	Cloth of Assize, Short Somerset	0	0	0	0
	2	piece	Cloth of Assize, Devonshire Kersey	0	0	0	0
James Savers of Waterford, Merchant Ind	4	bolt	Thread	0	13	4	0
	1	gross	Combs (ob.)	0	5	0	0
	1	dozen	Balches	0	12	0	0
	1	dozen	Penners and Inkhorns	0	0	20	0
	12	lb	Thread, Packet	0	4	0	0
	1	C	Hops	0	10	0	0
	1	dozen	Stock–Cards	0	12	0	0
	2	gross	Cutts	0	10	0	0
	1	gross	Merells	0	4	0	0
	2	small gross	Points	0	0	16	0
	2	dozen	Hats, for Children	0	24	0	0
	2	piece	Cloth of Assize, Devonshire Kersey	0	0	0	0

Merchant name	Qty	Unit	Commodity	£	s.	d.	f.
Maurice Brown of Waterford, Merchant Ind	1	C	Soap, Black	0	6	8	0
	3	bolt	Thread	0	10	0	0
	4	gross	Cutts	0	20	0	0
	1	gross	Knives (1d.)	0	10	0	0
	0.5	gross	Knives (2d.)	0	10	0	0
	3	lb	Mail	0	2	6	0
	1	gross	Combs (ob.)	0	5	0	0
	1	dozen	Cumin	0	3	1	0
	0.5	gross	Girdles (ob.)	0	2	6	0
	3	dozen	Stock-Cards	0	36	0	0
	1	great gross	Points	0	8	4	0
	1	small gross	Points	0	2	8	0
	3	lb	Check	0	3	0	0
	3	lb	Ceruse	0	0	6	0
	0.5	lb	Saffron	0	6	8	0
	2	dozen	Skins, Cony Black	0	12	0	0
	3	lb	Soap, White	0	0	12	0

The Katherin of Waterford, burden 12 tons, John Aileworth master, to Waterford, *7th August 1576*

Merchant name	Qty	Unit	Commodity	£	s.	d.	f.
John Welsh of Waterford, Merchant Ind	0.5	dozen	Stock-Cards	0	6	0	0
	0.5	gross	Cutts	0	2	6	0
	0.5	lb	Saffron	0	6	8	0
	2	M	Nails, Lath	0	2	8	0
	2	C	Nails, Bord	0	0	12	0
	4	dozen	Soap, Black	0	6	0	0
Thomas White of Waterford, Merchant Ind	1	pipe	Iron	4	0	0	0
	1	gross	Cutts	0	5	0	0
	1	gross	Girdles (1d.)	0	10	0	0
	2	lb	Crewel Fringe	0	8	0	0
	3	lb	Almonds	0	0	13	0
	0.25	C	Rice	0	2	6	0
	2	dozen	Penners and Inkhorns	0	3	4	0
	12	lb	Cumin	0	2	0	0
	2	dozen	Soap, Black	0	3	0	0
	2	lb	Twine	0	0	16	0
	12	lb	Glue	0	0	14	0
	3	dozen	Playing Cards	0	5	0	0
	1	dozen	Merells	0	0	4	0
Robert Wise of Waterford, Merchant Ind	1	C	Hops	0	10	0	0
	2	C	Towe	0	16	0	0
	20	lb	Seed, Cumin	0	6	8	0
	1	lb	Points, Silk	0	12	0	0
	2,3	bolt, lb	Thread	0	10	5	0
	4.5	gross	Buttons, Thread	0	11	3	0
	1	gross	Girdles (1d.)	0	10	0	0
	12	lb	Mail	0	6	0	0
	3	piece	Hats, for Children	0	3	0	0
	3	clout	Needles	0	0	20	0
	3	pair	Hose, for Women	0	0	20	0

Merchant name	Qty	Unit	Commodity	£	s.	d.	f.
	1	C	Alum	0	33	4	0
	4	pair	Stock-Cards	0	4	0	0
John Morsey of Waterford Merchant Ind	1	C	Hops	0	10	0	0
	1	C	Battery	0	40	0	0
	1	C	Alum	0	33	4	0
	4	lb	Silk, Paris	0	26	8	0
	1	lb	Cloves	0	5	0	0
	1	lb	Pepper	0	0	20	0
	2	dozen	Locks, small	0	3	4	0
	2	dozen	Knives, Cullen	0	5	0	0
	2	gross	Cutts	0	10	0	0
	1.5	gross	Girdles (1*d.*)	0	15	0	0
	6	pair	Stock-Cards	0	6	0	0
	3	dozen	Playing Cards	0	5	0	0
	6	piece	Hats, for Children	0	6	0	0
	6	dozen	Soap, White	0	24	0	0
	2	lb	Wax	0	0	16	0
	1	dozen	Penners and Inkhorns	0	0	20	0
	3	dozen	Combs (*ob.*)	0	0	15	0
	1	barrel	Vinegar	0	6	2	0

The Margaret of Milford Haven, burden 16 tons, John Fisher master, to Drogheda, 9th August 1576

Richard Flemynge of Drogheda, Merchant Ind	8	pair	Milstones	8	0	0	0
	10	pair	Quern Stones	0	10	0	0
	5	M	Teazles	0	8	4	0
	2	C	Soap, Black	0	13	4	0
	2	C	Hops	0	20	0	0
	1	hogshead	Iron	0	40	0	0

The Makarell of Dungarvan, burden 12 tons, Thomas Solivan master, to Dungarvan, *9th August 1576*

Edmund Lynche of Waterford, Merchant Ind	0.5	great gross	Points	0	4	0	0
	1	dozen	*Balches*	0	12	0	0
	10	pair	Stock-Cards	0	10	0	0
	1	ream	Paper	0	2	8	0
	1	gross	Cutts	0	5	0	0
	1	hogshead	Vinegar	0	11	8	0
	1	lb	Thread	0	0	15	0
	0.5	dozen	Hats, for Children	0	6	0	0
	1	gross	Merells	0	4	0	0
	0.5	lb	Check	0	0	6	0
	1	burden	Steel	0	2	6	0
	2	C	Hops	0	20	0	0
	1	C	Oakum	0	5	0	0

The Greyhounde of Bristol, burden 40 tons, James Whitinge master, to Lisbon, 10th August 1576

John Ball of Bristol, Merchant Ind	36	piece	Cloth of Assize, Northern Dozen	0	0	0	0

Merchant name	Qty	Unit	Commodity	£	s.	d.	f.

The Thobie of Bristol, burden 100 tons, Robert Davies master, to Sanlúcar de Barrameda, 11th August 1576

Merchant name	Qty	Unit	Commodity	£	s.	d.	f.
Thomas Simons of Bristol, Merchant Ind	2	fother	Lead	16	0	0	0
	9	piece	Cloth of Assize, Short Somerset	0	0	0	0
Richard Younge of Bristol, Merchant Ind	3	fother	Lead	24	0	0	0
	27	piece	Cloth of Assize, Short Somerset	0	0	0	0

The Mynion of Bristol, burden 100 tons, William AgWilliam master, to Lisbon, 13th August 1576

Merchant name	Qty	Unit	Commodity	£	s.	d.	f.
Henry Goughe of Bristol, Merchant Ind	5	fother	Lead	40	0	0	0
William Gittons of Bristol, Merchant Ind	11	piece	Cloth of Assize, Short	0	0	0	0
	5	fother	Lead	40	0	0	0

The Fage of Dungarvan, burden 13 tons, John Power master, to Dungarvan, *13th August 1576*

Merchant name	Qty	Unit	Commodity	£	s.	d.	f.
John Welsh of Waterford, Merchant Ind	4	lb	Silk, Paris	0	26	8	0
	3	dozen	Hemp	0	7	6	0
	3	dozen	Flax	0	8	0	0
	1	C	Oakum	0	5	0	0
	2	gross	Cutts	0	10	0	0
	0.5	gross	Girdles (1d.)	0	5	0	0
	0.5	C	Hops	0	5	0	0
	12	lb	Thread, Packet	0	4	0	0
	1	dozen	Playing Cards	0	0	20	0
	3	*lb*	Serches	0	2	0	0

The James of Dungarvan, burden 4 tons, Nicholas Magner master, to Dungarvan, *13th August 1576*

Merchant name	Qty	Unit	Commodity	£	s.	d.	f.
Nicholas Magner of Dungarvan, Merchant Ind	0.5	wey	Malt/Barley	0	0	0	0

The Conney of Bristol, burden 20 tons, William Pheleps master, to San Sebastián, 14th August 1576

Merchant name	Qty	Unit	Commodity	£	s.	d.	f.
Thomas Mericke of Bristol, Merchant Ind	2.5	fother	Lead	12	0	0	0
	2	C goad	Manchester Cotton *Cloth*	6	13	4	0
	39	lb	Wax	2	0	0	0
	1	C	Irish Rugg Frieze *Cloth*	2	0	0	0

The Julian of Workington, burden 90 tons, Hugh Bowiner master, to Drogheda, 15th August 1576

Merchant name	Qty	Unit	Commodity	£	s.	d.	f.
John Wotton of Drogheda, Merchant Ind	11	pair	Milstones	11	0	0	0
	24	pair	Wool-Cards	0	20	0	0
	0.5	gross	*P[]tergm[]t*	0	10	0	0
	0.5	gross	Points, Thread	0	0	10	0

Merchant name	Qty	Unit	Commodity	£	s.	d.	f.
	1	gross	Garters, Crewel	0	5	0	0
	3	lb	Crewel Fringe	0	12	0	0
	2.5	C	Hops	0	25	0	0
	0.25	gross	Buttons, Glass	0	0	12	0
	2.5	dozen	Stockings, Coarse	0	25	0	0
	3	hogshead	Vinegar	0	35	0	0
	6	C	Soap, Black	0	40	0	0
	1	small gross	Points	0	0	8	0
	2	dozen	Caps	0	24	0	0
	3	dozen	Spectacle Cases, Ungilted	0	0	20	0
	0.5	gross	Spectacles	0	5	0	0
Arthur Wilson of Workington, Merchant Ind	1	C	Hops	0	10	0	0
	1	C	Soap, Black	0	6	8	0
	5	lb	Saffron	3	6	8	0
	10	wey	Coal, Smith	3	6	8	0
	2	gross	Trenchers, Coarse	0	6	8	0

The Sondaye of New Ross, burden 15 tons, John Perse master, to New Ross, *15th August 1576*

Walter White of Waterford, Merchant Ind	6	pair	Stock-Cards	0	6	0	0
	1	gross	Cutts	0	5	0	0
Mark Dormer of New Ross, Merchant Ind	1	C	Liquorice	0	10	0	0
	1.5	C	Hops	0	15	0	0
	6	ell	Spanish Taffeta *Cloth*	0	56	8	0
	0.5	C	Soap, Black	0	3	4	0
	1	dozen	Hats	0	13	4	0
	2.5	lb	Silk, Paris	0	16	8	0
	1	C	Mail	0	0	8	0
	2	clout	Needles	0	0	20	0
	1	dozen	Penners	0	0	20	0
	2	gross	Merells	0	8	0	0
	12	lb	Twine	0	8	0	0
	1	dozen	Stock-Cards	0	12	0	0
	2	ream	Paper	0	5	4	0
	6	dozen	Combs (*ob.*)	0	2	6	0
	1	lb	Pepper	0	0	20	0
	1	lb	Cinnamon	0	4	0	0
	1	lb	Cloves	0	5	0	0
	1	lb	Ginger	0	0	12	0
	12	lb	Seed, Cumin	0	4	0	0
	6.5	gross	Cutts	0	32	6	0
	1	gross	Girdles	0	5	0	0
	12	pair	Hose, for Men	0	6	8	0

The Admirall of Bristol, burden burden 20 tons, Richard Croke master, to Cork, 16th August 1576

Edmund Roth of Cork, Merchant Ind	2	lb	Saffron	0	26	8	0
	6	lb	Silk, Paris	0	40	0	0
	4.08	gross	Cutts	0	20	6	0
	4	great gross	Points	0	32	0	0

Merchant name	Qty	Unit	Commodity	£	s.	d.	f.
	1	C	Hops	0	10	0	0
	4	dozen	Penners and Inkhorns	0	6	8	0
	1	dozen	Hemp	0	2	6	0
	0.5	gross	Combs (*ob.*)	0	2	6	0
	2	dozen	Liquorice	0	4	0	0
	1	burden	Steel	0	2	6	0
	0.5	dozen	Caps	0	6	0	0
	0.5	dozen	Hats, for Children	0	6	0	0
	20	lb	Soap, White	0	6	8	0
	1	clout	Needles	0	0	10	0
	1	dozen	Girth	0	0	16	0
	1	lb	Wax	0	0	8	0
	0.5	gross	Points, Leather	0	0	10	0
	1	pair	Stock-Cards	0	0	12	0
	1	dozen	Books, Primers	0	0	20	0
	9	dozen	Girdles, Leather	0	3	9	0
	0.5	lb	Thread	0	0	7	2
	9	piece	*Balches*	0	9	0	0
	0.25	C	Alum	0	8	4	0
	12	yard	Hair *Cloth*	0	8	0	0
	2	dozen	Spurs, Single	0	6	8	0
	5	lb	Sugar	0	3	4	0
	24	dozen	Trenchers, Coarse	0	6	8	0
	1	dozen	Urnalls[11]	0	0	16	0
	1	piece	Cloth of Assize, Short Somerset	0	0	0	0
	1	piece	Cloth of Assize, Devonshire Kersey	0	0	0	0
	1	piece	Cloth of Assize, Hampshire Kersey	0	0	0	0

The Minion of Bristol, burden 100 tons, William AgWilliam master, to Lisbon, *16th August 1576*

Botholl Holder of London, Merchant Ind	72	piece	Cloth of Assize, Redinge and Kentish Long	0	0	0	0
	30	piece	Holland *Cloth*	36	0	0	0
	20	piece	Bay *Cloth*	20	0	0	0
	300	lb	Mercury	76	0	0	0

The Margett of Tenby, burden 20 tons, Richard Homand master, to Waterford, 21st August 1576

James Boyton of Kinsale, Merchant Ind	4	gross	Cutts	0	20	0	0
	6	lb	Silk, Paris	0	40	0	0
	2	gross	Girdles (1*d.*)	0	20	0	0
	1	ream	Paper	0	2	8	0
	13	lb	Points, Crewel	0	5	0	0
	1	dozen	Hats, Felt	0	16	8	0
	3	box	Combs (*ob.*)	0	3	9	0
	6	lb	Sulpher	0	0	6	0

11 Probably urinals, which, according to the OED, were small vessels used to collect urine for medical examination.

Merchant name	Qty	Unit	Commodity	£	s.	d.	f.
	1	gross	Merells	0	4	0	0
	2	lb	Fringe	0	6	0	0
	2	gross	Buttons, Brass	0	40	0	0
	1	lb	Mail	0	0	6	0
	2	clout	Needles	0	0	20	0
	8	dozen	Garters, Crewel	0	8	0	0
	1	dozen	Penners and Inkhorns	0	0	20	0
	3	bolt	Thread	0	10	0	0
	0.5	lb	Pepper	0	0	10	0
	2	dozen	Funnels	0	8	0	0
	1	dozen	Spurs, Single	0	2	6	0
	6	dozen	Trenchers	0	0	20	0
	2	dozen	Soap, Black	0	3	0	0
	6	unknown	Glasses	0	7	0	0
Martin Archer of Kilkenny, Merchant Ind	0.5	dozen	Hats	0	6	0	0
	2	C	Oakum	0	10	0	0
	1	gross	Cutts	0	5	0	0
	10	lb	Sugar	0	6	8	0
	3	C	Hops	0	30	0	0
	2	bolt	Thread	0	6	8	0
	2	gross	Trenchers	0	6	8	0
	4	C	Tapps and Cannells	0	2	0	0
	1	dozen	Spurs, Single	0	2	6	0
	4	piece	Jerkins, Leather	0	12	0	0
	0.5	C	Soap, Black	0	3	4	0
	4	piece	Boxes, Painted	0	3	4	0
	12	pair	Stock-Cards	0	12	0	0
	1	doz	Bibs	0	0	6	0
	1	piece	Holland *Cloth*	0	24	0	0
	3	barell	Honey	4	10	0	0
	6	pairs	Knives, Paring	0	0	12	0
	1	dozen	Awl Hafte	0	0	12	0
	2	C	Pewter	4	13	4	0
	0.5	piece	Cloth of Assize, Short	0	0	0	0
Edmund Vale of Clonmel, Merchant Ind	4	C	Hops	0	40	0	0
	1	C	Battery	0	40	0	0
	3	C	Oakum	0	15	0	0
	0.25	C	Aniseed	0	6	8	0
	0.25	C	Rice	0	5	0	0
	1	ream	Paper	0	2	8	0
	2	gross	Cutts	0	10	0	0
	0.5	gross	Merells	0	2	0	0
	3	dozen	Playing Cards	0	5	0	0
	3	box	Combs (*ob.*)	0	3	9	0
	1	gross	Buttons, Thread	0	2	6	0
	2	bolt	Thread	0	6	8	0
	2	lb	Mail	0	0	12	0
	0.5	gross	Girdles (1*d.*)	0	5	0	0
	0.5	dozen	Twine	0	4	0	0
	1	dozen	Hats	0	12	0	0
	2	pair	Stock-Cards	0	2	0	0
	2	dozen	Soap, Black	0	3	0	0

Merchant name	Qty	Unit	Commodity	£	s.	d.	f.

The Katherin of Waterford, burden 18 tons, John Gall master, to Waterford, *21st August 1576*

Adam Drolie of Kilkenny, Merchant Ind	2.5	gross	Cutts	0	12	6	0
	0.5	gross	Knives, Almaine	0	15	0	0
	1	gross	Merells	0	4	0	0
	1	dozen	Penners and Inkhorns	0	0	20	0
	5	lb	Check	0	5	0	0
	4	piece	Sword Hilt	0	3	4	0
	3	gross	Buttons, Steel	0	40	0	0
	1	lb	Fringe	0	4	0	0
	3	dozen	Garters, Crewel	0	3	0	0
	1	box	Combs (*ob.*)	0	0	15	0
	1	lb	Thread	0	0	15	0
	4	dozen	Knives, Flemish	0	10	0	0
	8.5	dozen	Girdles (1*d.*)	0	7	1	0
	2	piece	Candlesticks, Pewter	0	2	0	0
	1	dozen	Spurs, Single	0	2	6	0
	2	lb	Mail	0	0	12	0
	0.5	M	Awl Blades	0	3	4	0
	1	ream	Paper	0	2	8	0
	1	clout	Needles	0	0	10	0
	3	C	Nails, Bord	0	0	12	0
	3	M	Nails, Lath	0	3	0	0
	0.5	M	*Seny?*	0	0	6	0
	0.5	gross	Playing Cards	0	10	0	0
	2	dozen	Locks	0	3	4	0
	1	C	Tapps and Cannells	0	0	6	0
	8	piece	Hats	0	8	0	0
	2	stone	Hops	0	2	6	0

The Sondaye of Wexford, burden 10 tons, Thomas Stafford master, to Wexford, 23rd August 1576

Michael Braye of New Ross, Merchant Ind	7	lb	Silk, Paris	0	46	8	0
	1	lb	Points, Silk	0	12	0	0
	0.5	gross	Points, Crewel	0	0	20	0
	2	lb	Points, Crewel	0	8	0	0
	1.3	gross	Cutts	0	6	8	0
	1	dozen	Penners and Inkhorns	0	0	20	0
	1	dozen	Hawk Hoods	0	2	0	0
	3	lb	Thread, Packet	0	6	8	0
	2	gross	Buttons, Brass	0	26	8	0
	1	small role	Garters, Crewel	0	0	12	0
	1	ream	Paper	0	2	8	0
	3	dozen	Playing Cards	0	5	0	0
	3	piece	Boxes, Painted	0	2	0	0
	4	clout	Needles	0	3	4	0
	2	bolt	Thread	0	6	8	0
	2	box	Combs (*ob.*)	0	2	6	0
	2	dozen	Spectacles	0	0	20	0
	1	C	Orchil	0	20	0	0
	0.5	lb	Pepper	0	0	10	0

Merchant name	Qty	Unit	Commodity	£	s.	d.	f.
	2	dozen	Hats	0	26	8	0
	1	lb	Mail	0	0	6	0
	0.5	C	Battery	0	20	0	0
	6	lb	Twine	0	4	0	0
	2	C	Towe, *Coarse*	0	13	4	0
	1	C	Hops	0	10	0	0
	3	hogshead	*Verinis*	0	30	0	0
	6	pair	Hose, for Women	0	5	0	0
	1	pair	Bows	0	20	0	0
	0.5	piece	Cloth of Assize, Short	0	0	0	0
	0.5	piece	Cloth of Assize, Hampshire Kersey	0	0	0	0

The Thobie of Bristol, burden 100 tons, Robert Davies master, to Sanlúcar de Barrameda, 25th August 1576

Merchant name	Qty	Unit	Commodity	£	s.	d.	f.
John Hollester of Bristol, Merchant Ind	12	piece	Cloth of Assize, Short Somerset	0	0	0	0
	2	piece	Cloth of Assize, Northern Kersey	0	0	0	0

The Mynion of Bristol, burden 100 tons, William AgWilliam master, to Lisbon, 26th August 1576

Merchant name	Qty	Unit	Commodity	£	s.	d.	f.
Thomas Merricke of Bristol, Merchant Ind	4	piece	Cloth of Assize, Short Somerset	0	0	0	0

The Florance of Falmouth, burden 40 tons, Robert Carthyvike master, to Bordeaux, *26th August 1576*

Merchant name	Qty	Unit	Commodity	£	s.	d.	f.
William Gittons of Bristol, Merchant Ind	2	piece	Cloth of Assize, Short Somerset	0	0	0	0
	8	piece	Bristol Frieze *Cloth*	8	0	0	0
	3	fother	Lead	24	0	0	0
Edward Chester of Bristol, Merchant Ind	3	fother	Lead	24	0	0	0

The Katherin of Wexford, burden 10 tons, John Huler master, to Wexford, 27th August 1576

Merchant name	Qty	Unit	Commodity	£	s.	d.	f.
James Turner of Wexford, Merchant Ind	2	ton	Salt	0	40	0	0
	0.5	wey	Malt/Barley	0	40[12]	0	0
	2	C	Iron	0	16	0	0
	1.5	C	Pots, Brass	2	10	0	0
	1	last	Calx	0	3	0	0
	0.5	C	Hops	0	5	0	0
	0.5	C	Orchil	0	10	0	0
	1	C	Soap, Black	0	6	8	0

The Domynicke of Bristol, burden 100 tons, John Silly master, to Cadiz, 28th August 1576

Merchant name	Qty	Unit	Commodity	£	s.	d.	f.
Henry Goughe of Bristol, Merchant Ind	8	fother	Lead	64	0	0	0
John Ashe of Bristol, Merchant Ind	6	fother	Lead	48	0	0	0

12 See introductory note regarding this valuation.

Merchant name	Qty	Unit	Commodity	£	s.	d.	f.

The Dellinge of Padstow, burden 40 tons, Thomas Sarc[] master, to Bordeaux, *28th August 1576*

Merchant name	Qty	Unit	Commodity	£	s.	d.	f.
Richard Longford of Bristol, Merchant Ind	4	fother	Lead	32	0	0	0

The Margett of Bristol, burden 20 tons, William Morriche master, to Biscay, *28th August 1576*

Merchant name	Qty	Unit	Commodity	£	s.	d.	f.
John Porter of Bristol, Merchant Ind	3	piece	Tenby Cotton *Cloth*	3	0	0	0
	3	piece	Wadmal *Cloth*	3	0	0	0
	1.5	C goad	Manchester Cotton *Cloth*	5	0	0	0
	1	piece	Cloth of Assize, Western Dozen	0	0	0	0

The Florance of Falmouth, burden 40 tons, Robert Cartewike master, to Bordeaux, *28th August 1576*

Merchant name	Qty	Unit	Commodity	£	s.	d.	f.
Edward Chester of Bristol, Merchant Ind	1	fother	Lead	8	0	0	0
	7	C	Tin, Cornish Unwrought	11	13	4	0
	2	piece	Cloth of Assize, Short Somerset	0	0	0	0

The Dellinge of Padstow, burden 40 tons, Thomas Sarc[ ] master, to Bordeaux, *29th August 1576*

Merchant name	Qty	Unit	Commodity	£	s.	d.	f.
Richard Ashehurst of Bristol, Merchant Ind	7	C goad	Manchester Cotton *Cloth*	23	6	8	0
	1	piece	Cloth of Assize, Short Somerset	0	0	0	0

The Thobie of Bristol, burden 100 tons, Robert Davies master, to Sanlúcar de Barrameda, *29th August 1576*

Merchant name	Qty	Unit	Commodity	£	s.	d.	f.
Richard Ashehurst of Bristol, Merchant Ind	4	C goad	Manchester Cotton *Cloth*	13	6	8	0
John Salterne of Bristol, Merchant Ind	40	dozen	Hemp	5	0	0	0
	5	dozen	Buckram *Cloth*	7	10	0	0
Mathew Haviland of Bristol, Merchant Ind	3	piece	Cloth of Assize, Short Somerset	0	0	0	0
	3	piece	Bay *Cloth*	3	0	0	0
Thomas Pitt of Bristol, Merchant Ind	27	piece	Cloth of Assize, Newbery Kersey	0	0	0	0
Robert Kitchinge of Bristol, Merchant Ind	72	piece	Cloth of Assize, Hampshire Kersey	0	0	0	0
	9	piece	Cloth of Assize, Short Somerset	0	0	0	0
John Dray of Bristol, Merchant Ind	11	piece	Cloth of Assize, Short Somerset	0	0	0	0

Merchant name	Qty	Unit	Commodity	£	s.	d.	f.

The Mynion of Bristol, burden 100 tons, William AgWilliam master, to Lisbon, 29th August 1576

Merchant name	Qty	Unit	Commodity	£	s.	d.	f.
Thomas Pitt of Bristol, Merchant Ind	9	piece	Cloth of Assize, Short Somerset	0	0	0	0
Thomas Kelke of Bristol, Merchant Ind	36	piece	Cloth of Assize, Redinge Kersey	0	0	0	0
Miles Diconsone of Bristol, Merchant Ind	9	piece	Cloth of Assize, Short Somerset	0	0	0	0
	18	piece	Cloth of Assize, Northern Dozen	0	0	0	0
Robert Kitchinge of Bristol, Merchant Ind	108	piece	Cloth of Assize, Hampshire Kersey	0	0	0	0
Richard Jones of Bristol, Merchant Ind	18	piece	Cloth of Assize, Short Somerset	0	0	0	0
William Ellies of Bristol, Merchant Ind	13.5	piece	Cloth of Assize, Short Somerset	0	0	0	0
Hector Nonnz? of London, Merchant Alien	47	piece	Bay *Cloth*	47	0	0	0
	20	piece	Mockado *Cloth*	13	6	8	0

The Golden Lion of Bristol, burden 300 tons, John Shep*ard* master, to Cadiz, *29th August 1576*

Merchant name	Qty	Unit	Commodity	£	s.	d.	f.
Thomas Warren of Bristol, Merchant Ind	10	fother	Lead	80	0	0	0

The Domynicke of Bristol, burden 100 tons, John Silly master, to Cadiz, *29th August 1576*

Merchant name	Qty	Unit	Commodity	£	s.	d.	f.
Richard Cole of Bristol, Merchant Ind	8	fother	Lead	64	0	0	0
William Ellies of Bristol, Merchant Ind	1.5	fother	Lead	12	0	0	0

The Greyhounde of Bristol, burden 40 tons, James Whitinge master, to Lisbon, 30th August 1576

Merchant name	Qty	Unit	Commodity	£	s.	d.	f.
John Webbe of Bristol, Merchant Ind	1	piece	Cloth of Assize, Short Somerset	0	0	0	0
	5	piece	Mockado *Cloth*	3	6	8	0
Hector Nonnz? of London, Merchant Alien	50	lb	Beads, Amber	33	6	8	0

The Nightingale of Bristol, burden 24 tons, John Jones master, to Ayamonte, *30th August 1576*

Merchant name	Qty	Unit	Commodity	£	s.	d.	f.
William Ellies of Bristol, Merchant Ind	2	piece	Cloth of Assize, Short Somerset	0	0	0	0
	20	piece	Cloth of Assize, Short Somerset Streit	0	0	0	0
	3	C goad	Manchester Cotton *Cloth*	10	0	0	0

The Domynicke of Bristol, burden 100 tons, John Silloy master, to Cadiz, *30th August 1576*

Merchant name	Qty	Unit	Commodity	£	s.	d.	f.
Nicholas Cutt of Bristol, Merchant Ind	4	fother	Lead	32	0	0	0

Merchant name	Qty	Unit	Commodity	£	s.	d.	f.

The Thobie of Bristol, burden 100 tons, Robert Davies master, to Sanlúcar de Barrameda, 1st September 1576

Richard Cole of Bristol, Merchant Ind	9	piece	Cloth of Assize, Short Somerset	o	o	o	o
Thomas Aldworth of Bristol, Merchant Ind	18	piece	Cloth of Assize, Northern Kersey	o	o	o	o
	5	piece	Cloth of Assize, Short Somerset	o	o	o	o

The Mynion of Bristol, burden 100 tons, William AgWilliam master, to Lisbon, *1st September 1576*

Thomas Mellin of Bristol, Merchant Ind	18	piece	Cloth of Assize, Northern Dozen	o	o	o	o
	1	piece	Cloth of Assize, Short Somerset	o	o	o	o
	4	C goad	Manchester Cotton *Cloth*	13	6	8	o
William Jones of Bristol, Merchant Ind	5	piece	Cloth of Assize, Short Somerset	o	o	o	o
	12	piece	Bay *Cloth*	12	o	o	o
Bennett Meryfilde of Bristol, Merchant Ind	2	C goad	Manchester Cotton *Cloth*	6	13	4	o
Thomas James of Bristol, Merchant Ind	24	piece	Bay *Cloth*	24	o	o	o
Thomas Rowland of Bristol, Merchant Ind	5	piece	Cloth of Assize, Short Somerset	o	o	o	o
	1	piece	Trucker *Cloth*	o	20	o	o
Richard Fowyns of Bristol, Merchant Ind	4	piece	Cloth of Assize, Short Somerset	o	o	o	o
William Cutt of Bristol, Merchant Ind	5	piece	Cloth of Assize, Short Somerset	o	o	o	o
Michael Pepwall of Bristol, Merchant Ind	9	piece	Cloth of Assize, Short Somerset	o	o	o	o
	9	piece	Brecon *Cloth*	9	o	o	o
John Alkin of Bristol, Merchant Ind	9	piece	Cloth of Assize, Short Somerset	o	o	o	o
Richard Langford of Bristol, Merchant Ind	9	piece	Cloth of Assize, Short Somerset	o	o	o	o
Robert Halton of Bristol, Merchant Ind	1	piece	Cloth of Assize, Short Somerset	o	o	o	o
	4	piece	Cloth of Assize, Western Kersey	o	o	o	o
	22	piece	Cloth of Assize, Newbery Kersey	o	o	o	o
	45	piece	Bay *Cloth*	45	o	o	o
John Ashe of Bristol, Merchant Ind	9	piece	Cloth of Assize, Short Somerset	o	o	o	o
	18	piece	Cloth of Assize, Redinge Kersey	o	o	o	o
	18	piece	Bay *Cloth*	18	o	o	o

Merchant name	Qty	Unit	Commodity	£	s.	d.	f.

The Domynicke of Bristol, burden 100 tons, John Selly master, to Cadiz, 5th September 1576

Merchant name	Qty	Unit	Commodity	£	s.	d.	f.
Thomas Rowland of Bristol, Merchant Ind	3	fother	Lead	24	0	0	0
	1	piece	Trucker *Cloth*	0	20	0	0
	1	piece	Cloth of Assize, Short Somerset	0	0	0	0
Richard Langford of Bristol, Merchant Ind	4	fother	Lead	32	0	0	0
Edward Chester of Bristol, Merchant Ind	1.5	C goad	Manchester Cotton Cloth	5	0	0	0
Richard Ashehurst of Bristol, Merchant Ind	4	C goad	Manchester Cotton Cloth	13	6	8	0
John Webbe of Bristol, Merchant Ind	10	piece	Bay *Cloth*	10	0	0	0
William Cutt of Bristol, Merchant Ind	1	fother	Lead	8	0	0	0
	8	piece	Bay *Cloth*	8	0	0	0
	1	piece	Cloth of Assize, Short Somerset	0	0	0	0
	10	piece	Cloth of Assize, Northern Kersey	0	0	0	0

The Foxe of Bristol, burden 45 tons, Richard White master, to Ayamonte, 7th September 1576

Merchant name	Qty	Unit	Commodity	£	s.	d.	f.
William Parfett of Bristol, Merchant Ind	2	fother	Lead	16	0	0	0
John Webbe of Bristol, Merchant Ind	7	piece	Bay *Cloth*	7	0	0	0
	1	piece	Cloth of Assize, Redinge Kersey	0	0	0	0

The Nightingale of Bristol, burden 24 tons, John Jones master, to Ayamonte, *7th September 1576*

Merchant name	Qty	Unit	Commodity	£	s.	d.	f.
Thomas Pollington of Bristol, Merchant Ind	2	C goad	Manchester Cotton Cloth	6	13	4	0

The John of Bristol, burden 25 tons, William Meage master, to Saõ Miguel, *7th September 1576*

Merchant name	Qty	Unit	Commodity	£	s.	d.	f.
Thomas Aldworth of Bristol, Merchant Ind	25	piece	Cloth of Assize, Northern Kersey	0	0	0	0
	4	piece	Brecon *Cloth*	4	0	0	0
	6	C	Flax	6	0	0	0
	10	piece	Saddles	3	6	8	0

The Grashoper of Bristol, burden 24 tons, John Tege master, to La Rochelle, *10th September 1576*

Merchant name	Qty	Unit	Commodity	£	s.	d.	f.
Richard Jones of Bristol, Merchant Ind	5	fother	Lead	40	0	0	0

Merchant name	Qty	Unit	Commodity	£	s.	d.	f.

The Hounde of Gloucester, burden 26 tons, David Davies master, to Cadiz,[13] *10th September 1576*

| Christopher Huntley of Gloucester, Merchant Ind | 9 | piece | Cloth of Assize, Short Somerset | 0 | 0 | 0 | 0 |

The Lion of Bristol, burden 30 tons, Richard Lullett master, to La Rochelle, 11th September 1576

| John Ball of Bristol, Merchant Ind | 18 | piece | Cloth of Assize, Bridgwater | 0 | 0 | 0 | 0 |
| | 6 | C goad | Manchester Cotton *Cloth* | 20 | 0 | 0 | 0 |

The Gabriell of Bristol, burden 30 tons, John Williams master, to Madeira, 12th September 1576

Richard Cole of Bristol, Merchant Ind	5	C	Wax	15	0	0	0
	6	C	Normandy Brown Canvas *Cloth*	15	0	0	0
Thomas Aldworth of Bristol, Merchant Ind	25	piece	Cloth of Assize, Northern & Hampshire Kersey	0	0	0	0
	40	piece	Bay *Cloth*	40	0	0	0

The Domynicke of Bristol, burden 100 tons, John Silloy master, to Cadiz, *12th September 1576*

| Philip Langley of Bristol, Merchant Ind | 50 | dozen | Flax | 0 | 0 | 0 | 0 |

The Gabriell of Bristol, burden 30 tons, John Williams master, to Madeira, *13th September 1576*

William Salterne of Bristol, Merchant Ind	11	piece	Trucker *Cloth*	11	0	0	0
Anthony Robins of Bristol, Merchant Ind	6	piece	Grasier *Cloth*	6	0	0	0
	4	piece	Bay *Cloth*	4	0	0	0
	1	piece	Cloth of Assize, Short Somerset	0	0	0	0
William Gittons of Bristol, Merchant Ind	3	piece	Cloth of Assize, Short Somerset	0	0	0	0
	2	piece	Trucker *Cloth*	0	40	0	0
	1	piece	Brecon *Cloth*	0	20	0	0
	4	piece	Frieze *Cloth*	4	0	0	0

The Nightingale of Bristol, burden 24 tons, John Jones master, to Ayamonte, *13th September 1576*

| William Gittons of Bristol, Merchant Ind | 1 | piece | Cloth of Assize, Short Somerset | 0 | 0 | 0 | 0 |
| | 2 | piece | Bristol Frieze *Cloth* | 0 | 40 | 0 | 0 |

13 From Gatcombe.

Merchant name	Qty	Unit	Commodity	£	s.	d.	f.

The Sallomon of Bristol, burden 50 tons, James Webbe master, to Bordeaux, *13th September 1576*

| Robert Allen of Bristol, Merchant Ind | 2.5 | fother | Lead | 20 | 0 | 0 | 0 |

The Gabriell of Bristol, burden 30 tons, John Williams master, to Madeira, 17th September 1576

| John Ashe of Bristol, Merchant Ind | 12 | piece | Bay *Cloth* | 12 | 0 | 0 | 0 |
| | 5 | piece | Trucker *Cloth* | 5 | 0 | 0 | 0 |

The Swallowe of Bristol, burden 80 tons, Thomas Jennynge master, to Livorno, 20th September 1576

| Henry Goughe of Bristol, Merchant Ind | 1.5 | fother | Lead | 12 | 0 | 0 | 0 |
| William Salterne of Bristol, Merchant Ind | 10 | fother | Lead | 80 | 0 | 0 | 0 |

The Swallowe of Bristol, burden 80 tons, Thomas Jennynge master, to Livorno, 22nd September 1576

| Thomas Rowland of Bristol, Merchant Ind | 4 | fother | Lead | 32 | 0 | 0 | 0 |

The Julian of Barry, burden 40 tons, Humphrey Dic[] master, to La Rochelle, 25th September 1576

| Thomas Kelke of Bristol, Merchant Ind | 2.5 | fother | Lead | 20 | 0 | 0 | 0 |

The Sallomon of Bristol, burden 50 tons, James Webbe master, to Bordeaux, 26th September 1576

| Anthony Pil[] of Bristol, Merchant Ind | 1 | fother | Lead | 8 | 0 | 0 | 0 |

The Golden Lion of Bristol, burden 300 tons, John Shepard master, to Cadiz, 28th September 1576

| Thomas Warren of Bristol, Merchant Ind | 4 | fother | Lead | 32 | 0 | 0 | 0 |

IMPORTS

The Minikin of Bristol, burden 40 tons, Richard Rikarde master, from Lisbon, 2nd October 1575

Hugh Andrewes of Taunton, Merchant Ind	20	C	Pepper	166	13	4	0
	2	C	Cloves	50	0	0	0
	1	C	Cinnamon	20	0	0	0
	3	C	Ginger	22	10	0	0
John Cottrell of Bristol, Merchant Ind	6	C	Pepper	50	0	0	0
	1	C	Ginger	7	10	0	0
	1	C	Cloves	25	0	0	0
	10	C	Alum	16	13	4	0
Richard Dodrigge of Barnstaple, Merchant Ind	3	C	Pepper	25	0	0	0

Merchant name	Qty	Unit	Commodity	£	s.	d.	f.
	2	C	Ginger	15	0	0	0
	1	C	Cloves	25	0	0	0
	150	piece	Calico *Cloth*	50	0	0	0
John Walron of Tiverton, Merchant Ind	7	C	Pepper	58	6	8	0
	50	C	Soap	37	10	0	0
	60	piece	Calico *Cloth*	20	0	0	0
Thomas Pitt of Bristol, Merchant Ind	4	C	Pepper	33	6	8	0
	20	C	Soap	15	0	0	0
	50	piece	Calico *Cloth*	16	13	4	0
Thomas Sawle of Bristol, Merchant Ind	6	C	Pepper	50	0	0	0
	1	C	Ginger	7	10	0	0
	30	piece	Calico *Cloth*	10	0	0	0
Robert Kitching of Bristol, Merchant Ind	14	C	Pepper	116	13	4	0
	65	piece	Calico *Cloth*	21	13	4	0
	10	ton	Salt	10	0	0	0
John Ashe of Bristol, Merchant Ind	120	piece	Calico *Cloth*	40	0	0	0
Richard Langford of Bristol, Merchant Ind	2	C	Soap	0	30	0	0
	40	piece	Calico *Cloth*	13	6	8	0
	2	C	Pepper	16	13	4	0

The Swallowe of Bristol, burden 80 tons, Anthony Robins master, from the Azores, *2nd October 1575*

Thomas Aldworth, Diconson & Williams of Bristol, Merchants Ind	50	ton	Woad, Green	500	0	0	0

The Peter & Pawle of Lübeck, burden 300 tons, Henry Goctgens master, from Lisbon, 6th October 1575

Henry Goctgens of Lübeck, Merchant Hansard	200	ton	Salt	200	0	0	0
Melcher Englebert of Lübeck Merchant Alien	26	C	Pepper	216	13	4	0

The Golden Lyon of Bristol, burden 350 tons, John Sheppard master, from Cadiz, 29th November 1575

Philip Langley & Michael Pepwall of Bristol, Merchants Ind	200	ton	Salt	200	0	0	0

The Anne Gallant of Bristol, burden 24 tons, William Morrice master, from San Sebastián, *29th November 1575*

Thomas Pollington & Richard Dedmister of Bristol, Merchants Ind	40	M	Oranges and Lemons	13	6	8	0
	2	ton	Iron	8	0	0	0
	5	ton	Pitch and Rosin	10	0	0	0
John Lange of Bristol, Merchant Ind	0.875	tun	Oil, Train	4	7	6	0

The Thobie of Bristol, burden 90 tons, John Baker master, from Sanlúcar de Barrameda, 1st December 1575

Thomas Kelke, Thomas Simons & Henry Goughe of Bristol, Merchants Ind	14	tun	Oil, *Olive*	112	0	0	0
	46	ton	Salt	46	0	0	0

Merchant name	Qty	Unit	Commodity	£	s.	d.	f.

The Edward of Bristol, burden 28 tons, William Skore master, from San Sebastián, 2nd December 1575

William Hopkins & John Griffyth of Bristol, Merchants Ind	11	ton	Iron	44	0	0	0
	3.5	tun	Oil, Train	17	10	0	0
	30	M	Oranges and Lemons	10	0	0	0
	1	ton	Pitch, Hearth	2	0	0	0

The Nightingale of Bristol, burden 26 tons, Thomas Nailor master, from Ayamonte, 5th December 1575

Philip Richard, Richard Fowyns & William Ellies of Bristol, Merchants, Ind	15	ton	Figs	75	0	0	0

The Hare of Bristol, burden 50 tons, Robert Davies master, from Cadiz, 13th December 1565

Randal Wilbram & Richard Swetnam of Bristol, Merchants Ind	30	ton	Salt	30	0	0	0

The Conney of Bristol, burden 25 tons, Richard Lollett master, from Biscay, 15th December 1575

Richard Langford, Nicholas Hicke & Thomas Mericke of Bristol, Merchants Ind	7.5	ton	Iron	30	0	0	0
	20	M	Oranges	6	13	4	0
Thomas Pollington of Bristol, Merchant Ind	1	tun	Oil, Train	5	0	0	0
John Gittons of Bristol, Merchant Ind	1	ton	Pitch, Hearth	2	0	0	0

The Dominick of Bristol, burden 120 tons, William Morrice master, from Lisbon, 17th December 1575

Botholl Holder of London, Merchant Ind	121.1	C	Pepper	1009	16	8	0
	8	C	Ginger	60	0	0	0
	1.5	C	Cinnamon	30	0	0	0
	3	quart	Mace	25	0	0	0
	1	C	Nutmeg	16	13	4	0
Thomas Kelke of Bristol, Merchant Ind	1	C	Ginger	7	10	0	0
	50	lb	Mace	16	13	4	0
	4.5	C	Pepper	37	10	0	0
	60	lb	Cloves	15	0	0	0
	5	C	Soap, White	3	15	0	0
	12	C	Alum	20	0	0	0
	40[14]	piece	Calico *Cloth*	13	6	8	0
John Walron of Tiverton, Merchant Ind	16	C	Pepper	133	6	8	0
	1	C	Cinnamon	20	0	0	0
	1	C	Ginger	7	10	0	0
	50	lb	Mace	16	13	4	0
	60[15]	piece	Calico *Cloth*	20	0	0	0
Richard Yonnge of Bristol, Merchant Ind	18	C	Soap	13	0	0	0
	40	lb	Mace	13	6	8	0

14 Sixty pieces laded; twenty wet and of no value.   15 Eighty pieces laded; twenty wet and of no value.

Merchant name	Qty	Unit	Commodity	£	s.	d.	f.
	80	lb	Cloves	20	0	0	0
	7	C	Pepper	58	6	8	0
	1	C	Ginger	7	10	0	0
	100[16]	piece	Calico *Cloth*	33	6	8	0
	2	ton	Woad, Green	20	0	0	0
Thomas Pitt of Bristol, Merchant Ind	8	C	Soap	6	0	0	0
	3	C	Pepper	25	0	0	0
	1	ton	Woad, Green	10	0	0	0
Benedict Spinnolan of London, Merchant of Genoa							
	13	C	Pepper	108	6	8	0
John Ashe of Bristol, Merchant Ind	100[17]	piece	Calico *Cloth*	33	6	8	0
	140	lb	Pepper	11	13	4	0
	7	ton	Woad, Green	70	0	0	0
William Hix of Bristol, Merchant Ind	1	C	Pepper	8	6	8	0
	60	piece	Calico *Cloth*	20	0	0	0
	6	ton	Woad, Green	60	0	0	0
Thomas Rowland of Bristol, Merchant Ind	1	C	Pepper	8	6	8	0
	60	piece	Calico *Cloth*	20	0	0	0
	6	ton	Woad, Green	60	0	0	0
Thomas Aldworth of Bristol, Merchant Ind	3	C	Pepper	25	0	0	0
	80[18]	piece	Calico *Cloth*	26	13	4	0
	4	ton	Woad, Green	40	0	0	0
Robert Halton of Bristol, Merchant Ind	50	lb	Cinnamon	10	0	0	0
	376	lb	Pepper	28	6	8	0
	1	C	Ginger	7	10	0	0
	40	piece	Calico *Cloth*	13	6	8	0
	4	ton	Woad, Green	40	0	0	0
Robert Kitching of Bristol, Merchant Ind	8	ton	Woad, Green	80	0	0	0
Hugh Andrewes of Taunton, Merchant Ind	18	ton	Woad, Green	180	0	0	0
John Cottrell of Bristol, Merchant Ind	6	ton	Woad, Green	60	0	0	0
	13	C	Soap	9	15	0	0
	14	C	Pepper	116	13	4	0
	6.5	C	Ginger	48	15	0	0
	84	lb	Cinnamon	16	16	0	0
	150[19]	piece	Calico *Cloth*	50	0	0	0
	2	C	Cloves	50	0	0	0
William Salterne of Bristol, Merchant Ind	4	C	Pepper	33	6	8	0
	50	piece	Calico *Cloth*	16	13	4	0
	4.5	ton	Woad, Green	45	0	0	0
Mark Wardforde of Bristol, Merchant Ind	3	C	Pepper	25	0	0	0
	0[20]	piece	Calico *Cloth*	0	0	0	0
Thomas Warren of Bristol, Merchant Ind	30	piece	Calico *Cloth*	10	0	0	0
	1.5	C	Pepper	12	10	0	0
John Barnes of Bristol, Clothier Ind	30	piece	Calico *Cloth*	10	0	0	0
Edward Wilson of Bristol, Merchant Ind	18	C	Pepper	150	0	0	0
	4	C	Ginger	30	0	0	0
	120	lb	Cloves	30	0	0	0
	4	C	Cotton Wool	13	6	8	0

16 One hundred pieces laded; fifty wet and of no value.   **17** One hundred and forty pieces laded; forty wet and of no value.   **18** One hundred and twenty pieces laded; forty wet and of no value.   **19** Two hundred pieces laded; fifty wet and of no value.   **20** Thirty pieces laded; all wet and of no value.

Merchant name	Qty	Unit	Commodity	£	s.	d.	f.
	8	C	Soap	6	0	0	0
	30	piece	Calico *Cloth*	10	0	0	0
	4	ton	Woad, Green	40	0	0	0
Edward Morrice of Bristol, Merchant Ind	20	C	Soap	15	0	0	0
	5.5	C	Pepper	45	16	8	0
	1	C	Cloves	25	0	0	0
	4	C	Ginger	30	0	0	0
	0.5	C	Cinnamon	10	0	0	0
	60	piece	Calico *Cloth*	13	6	8	0
	8	ton	Woad, Green	80	0	0	0
William Salterne of London, Merchant Ind	8	C	Pepper	66	13	4	0

The Grasshopar of Bristol, burden 24 tons, John Tegge master, from San Sebastián, 17th March 1576

Thomas Pitte & John Saundars of Bristol Merchants Ind	4	tun	Oil, Train	20	0	0	0
	15	ton	Salt	15	0	0	0

The Jesus of Bideford, burden 25 tons, Robert Limbery master, from San Sebastián, 20th March 1576

Alonso Ordicke of San Antonio, Merchant Alien	95	M	Oranges & Lemons	31	13	4	0

The Mynikin of Bristol, burden 40 tons, Richard Richards master, from San Sebastián, 2nd April 1576

Robert Kitching of Bristol, Merchant Ind	19	tun	Oil, Train	95	0	0	0
Richard Jones of Bristol, Merchant Ind	8	tun	Oil, Train	40	0	0	0
Richard Dedmister of Bristol, Merchant Ind	2.5	tun	Oil, Train	12	10	0	0

The Julian of Bristol, burden 30 tons, Richard Lullet master, from La Rochelle, 4th April 1576

Thomas Diconson & John Bawle of Bristol, Merchants Ind	12	ton	Salt	12	0	0	0

The Mary Deringe of Waterford, burden 30 tons, William Garole master, from Waterford, 16th April 1576

David Querke of Waterford, Merchant Ind	12	C	Skins, Sheep Broken	4	5	0	0

The Peter of Youghal, burden 30 tons, Darby Johnes master, from Cork, 17th April 1575

Patrick Galway of Cork, Merchant Ind	8	C	Skins, Lamb	6	0	0	0
	10	C	Skins, Sheep Broken	2	10	0	0
	24	piece	Skins, Fox	0	20	0	0

Merchant name	Qty	Unit	Commodity	£	s.	d.	f.

The Half Mone of Lübeck, burden 200 tons, Thomas Gatcott master, from Lisbon, *17th April* 1576

| Thomas Gatcott of Lübeck, Master Hansard | 15 | ton | Salt | 15 | 0 | 0 | 0 |

The Grace Dei of Milbrook, burden 28 tons, Edward Ride master, from Bordeaux, *Date Unknown*

| Thomas Diconson of Bristol, Merchant Ind | 8 | ton | Salt | 8 | 0 | 0 | 0 |

The Lion of Bristol, burden 26 tons, Thomas Jennynge master, from La Rochelle, 26th April 1576

| Thomas Diconson of Bristol, Merchant Ind | 8 | ton | Salt | 8 | 0 | 0 | 0 |

The Pawle of Teignmouth, burden 27 tons, John Mylbrowghe master, from Bordeaux, 2nd May 1576

| Edward Gowlde of Totnes, Merchant Ind | 10 | ton | Pitch and Rosin | 20 | 0 | 0 | 0 |

The Elizabeth of Tewkesbury, burden 36 tons, Bonaventure Audy master, from Bordeaux, 10th May 1576

| John Dowre of Totnes, Merchant Ind | 10 | ton | Salt | 10 | 0 | 0 | 0 |

The Trinitie of Bristol, burden 40 tons, Raymond Shereman master, from Bordeaux, 12th May 1576

William Gittons & Richard Strobridge of Bristol Merchants Ind	4	tun	Oil, Train	20	0	0	0
	4	ton	Iron	16	0	0	0
	10	ton	Salt	10	0	0	0

The John Baptist of Newnham, burden 8 tons, Thomas Norries master, from Wexford, *12th May 1576*

Leonard Sutton of Wexford, Merchant Ind	5	dicker	Hides, Salted	16	13	4	0
	7	C	Skins, Lamb	5	16	8	0
	2	C	Skins, Sheep Broken	0	10	0	0

The Hare of Bristol, burden 50 tons, Robert Davies master, from Andalusia, *12th May 1576*

Richard Yonnge of Bristol, Merchant Ind	1.75	tun	Oil, Train	14	0	0	0
John Hawkins of Bristol, Merchant Ind	3	tun	Oil, *Olive*	24	0	0	0
Randal Wilbram of Bristol, Merchant Ind	3	ton	Salt	3	0	0	0

The Rose of Bristol, burden 26 tons, William Estman master, from La Rochelle, 14th May 1576

| Myles Diconson of Bristol, Merchant Ind | 20 | ton | Salt | 20 | 0 | 0 | 0 |

Merchant name	Qty	Unit	Commodity	£ s. d. f.

The Spedwell of Bristol, burden 30 tons, Thomas Cornish master, from Puerto de Santa Maria, 17th May 1576

William Salterne of Bristol, Merchant Ind	6.5	tun	Oil, *Olive*	52 0 0 0
	3	ton	Salt	3 0 0 0

The Margarett of Kinsale, burden 14 tons, James Dongon master, from Kinsale, *17th May 1576*

James Dongon of Kinsale, Merchant Ind	1.5	ton	Wood, Brazil	50 0 0 0
	2	C	Skins, Sheep Broken	0 10 0 0

The Mary Fortune of Bristol, burden 30 tons, Walter Dowle master, from La Rochelle, *17th May 1576*

Walter Dowle of Bristol, Merchant Ind	20	ton	Salt	20 0 0 0

The Mynion of Bristol, burden 120 tons, William AgWilliam master, from Cadiz, *17th May 1576*

Thomas Kelke of Bristol, Merchant Ind	5.25	tun	Oil, *Olive*	42 0 0 0
William Gittons of Bristol, Merchant Ind	2.5	tun	Oil, *Olive*	20 0 0 0
Robert Sandford of Bristol, Merchant Ind	5.25	tun	Oil, *Olive*	42 0 0 0
Robert Halton of Bristol, Merchant Ind	5.25	tun	Oil, *Olive*	42 0 0 0
William Salterne of Bristol, Merchant Ind	2.5	tun	Oil, *Olive*	20 0 0 0
John Hopkins of Bristol, Merchant Ind	0.875	tun	Oil, *Olive*	7 0 0 0
Henry Goughe of Bristol, Merchant Ind	2.5	tun	Oil, *Olive*	20 0 0 0
Thomas Mellin of Bristol, Merchant Ind	2.125	tun	Oil, *Olive*	17 0 0 0
William Cutt of Bristol, Merchant Ind	1.25	tun	Oil, *Olive*	10 0 0 0
John Gittons of Bristol, Merchant Ind	1.75	tun	Oil, *Olive*	14 0 0 0
Thomas Merricke of Bristol, Merchant Ind	1.75	tun	Oil, *Olive*	14 0 0 0
John Bisse of Bristol, Merchant Ind	1.75	tun	Oil, *Olive*	14 0 0 0
William Jones of Bristol, Merchant Ind	6	tun	Oil, *Olive*	48 0 0 0

The Pleasure of Marennes, burden 40 tons, John Provote master, from Marennes, 20th May 1576

John Provote of Marennes, Merchant Alien	35	ton	Salt	35 0 0 0

The France of Marennes, burden 30 tons, John Martinus master, from Marennes, *20th May 1576*

John Martinus of Marennes, Merchant Alien	25	ton	Salt	25 0 0 0
	4	tun	Vinegar	9 6 8 0

The Fox of Bristol, burden 45 tons, Richard White master, from Lisbon, *20th May 1576*

Robert Done of London, Merchant Ind	12	C	Pepper	100 0 0 0
	1	C	Cinnamon	20 0 0 0
Botholl Holder of London, Merchant Ind	10	M	Soap	75 0 0 0
	3	C	Pepper	25 0 0 0
	6	ton	Salt	6 0 0 0

Merchant name	Qty	Unit	Commodity	£	s.	d.	f.
William Gittons of Bristol, Merchant Ind	12	C	Pepper	100	0	0	0
	0.5	C	Cloves	12	10	0	0
	1	C	Ginger	7	10	0	0
Robert Kitchinge of Bristol, Merchant Ind	18	C	Pepper	150	0	0	0
John Ashe of Bristol, Merchant Ind	1.5	C	Cloves	37	10	0	0
	0.75	C	Ginger	5	12	6	0
	3.5	C	Pepper	29	3	4	0
	0.75	C	Cinnamon	15	0	0	0
Thomas Kelke of Bristol, Merchant Ind	1.5	C	Cloves	37	10	0	0
	1.5	C	Pepper	12	10	0	0
	0.5	C	Cinnamon	10	0	0	0
John Webbe of Bristol, Merchant Ind	1.5	C	Cloves	37	10	0	0
	2.5	C	Pepper	20	16	8	0
John Hopkins of Bristol, Merchant Ind	0.75	C	Cloves	18	15	0	0
	0.75	C	Pepper	6	5	0	0
Robert Halton of Bristol, Merchant Ind	6.5	C	Pepper	54	3	4	0
Richard Jones of Bristol, Merchant Ind	1.75	C	Pepper	14	11	8	0
William Olboroughe of London, Merchant Ind	6	C	Pepper	50	0	0	0
	60	piece	Calico *Cloth*	20	0	0	0
	5	ton	Salt	5	0	0	0
Randal Wilbram of Bristol, Merchant Ind	4.5	C	Pepper	37	10	0	0
Michael Pepwall of Bristol, Merchant Ind	3	C	Pepper	25	0	0	0
	0.5	C	Cloves	12	10	0	0
Edward Chester of Bristol, Merchant Ind	3	C	Pepper	25	0	0	0
	0.5	C	Cloves	12	10	0	0

The Nicholas of Fécamp, burden 60 tons, John Basin master, from La Rochelle, 23rd May 1576

Robert Showard & Richard Salterne of Bristol, Merchants Ind	54	ton	Salt	54	0	0	0

The Minikin of Bristol, burden 40 tons, Philip Smith master, from La Rochelle, 1st June 1576

Robert Kitchinge of Bristol, Merchant Ind	30	ton	Salt	30	0	0	0

The Domynicke of Bristol, burden 120 tons, John Syle master, from La Rochelle, *1st June 1576*

Robert Kitchinge, John Ashe & Edward Chester of Bristol, Merchants Ind	100	ton	Salt	100	0	0	0

The Nightingale of Bristol, burden 28 tons, John Jones master, from Biscay, 2nd June 1576

Peter Stevans of Spain, Merchant Alien	60	M	Oranges & Lemons	20	0	0	0

The Boneventure of Fécamp, burden 60 tons, Nicholas Berture master, from La Rochelle, 5th June 1576

John Barker of Bristol, Merchant Ind	50	ton	Salt	50	0	0	0

Merchant name	Qty	Unit	Commodity	£	s.	d.	f.

The John of Bristol, burden 28 tons, William Skore master, from Biscay, *5th June 1576*

Merchant name	Qty	Unit	Commodity	£	s.	d.	f.
Nicholas Blake & William Hopkins of Bristol, Merchants Ind	8.5	tun	Oil, Train	45	0	0	0
	6.5	ton	Iron	26	0	0	0

The Margarett of Bristol, burden 20 tons, William Morrice master, from Biscay, *5th June 1576*

Merchant name	Qty	Unit	Commodity	£	s.	d.	f.
Nicholas Hicks & Richard Didmister of Bristol, Merchants Ind	3.5	tun	Oil, Train	7	10	0	0
	1	ton	Iron	4	0	0	0
	13	ton	Salt	13	0	0	0

The Conney of Bristol, burden 20 tons, William Phelpes master, from Biscay, *5th June 1576*

Merchant name	Qty	Unit	Commodity	£	s.	d.	f.
Thomas Merricke of Bristol, Merchant Ind	50	M	Oranges and Lemons	16	13	4	0
	3	ton	Salt	3	0	0	0

The Ricke Smith of Bristol, burden 30 tons, William Molgraye master, from Biscay, 6th June 1576

Merchant name	Qty	Unit	Commodity	£	s.	d.	f.
Richard Ashehurste of Bristol, Merchant Ind	3	ton	Iron	12	0	0	0
	2	ton	Rosin	4	0	0	0
Thomas Aldworth & Thomas Kelke of Bristol, Merchant Ind	4	tun	Oil, Train	20	0	0	0
Lewis Jenckin of Carleon, Merchant Ind	3	ton	Iron	12	0	0	0
William Smith of Bristol, Merchant Ind	5	ton	Pitch and Rosin	10	0	0	0
	9	ton	Salt	9	0	0	0

The Anne Gallant of Bristol, burden 25 tons, Humphrey Dier master, from Biscay, 7th June 1576

Merchant name	Qty	Unit	Commodity	£	s.	d.	f.
Richard Ashehurste & Nicholas Hicks of Bristol, Merchants Ind	8	tun	Oil, Train	40	0	0	0
	3	ton	Iron	12	0	0	0
William Smith of Bristol, Merchant Ind	1	ton	Iron	4	0	0	0
	10	C	Rosin	0	20	0	0
	12	ton	Salt	12	0	0	0

The Tobie of Bristol, burden 100 tons, Thomas Cottrell master, from Cadiz, *7th June 1576*

Merchant name	Qty	Unit	Commodity	£	s.	d.	f.
Henry Goughe of Bristol, Merchant Ind	5.25	tun	Oil, *Olive*	42	0	0	0
William Ellies of Bristol, Merchant Ind	1.75	tun	Oil, *Olive*	14	0	0	0
Richard Jones of Bristol, Merchant Ind	4.375	tun	Oil, *Olive*	35	0	0	0
John Hawes of London, Merchant Ind	14	tun	Oil, *Olive*	112	0	0	0
Thomas Simons of Bristol, Merchant Ind	7.25	tun	Oil, *Olive*	58	0	0	0
Richard Yonnge of Bristol, Merchant Ind	3.5	tun	Oil, *Olive*	28	0	0	0
Thomas Pollington of Bristol, Merchant Ind	1.25	tun	Oil, *Olive*	10	0	0	0
Thomas Griffith of Bristol, Merchant Ind	7	barrel	Oil, *Olive*	7	0	0	0
Thomas Kelke of Bristol, Merchant Ind	4.375	tun	Oil, *Olive*	35	0	0	0
Thomas Rowland of Bristol, Merchant Ind	1.75	tun	Oil, *Olive*	14	0	0	0

Merchant name	Qty	Unit	Commodity	£	s.	d.	f.
John Ashe of Bristol, Merchant Ind	2.125	tun	Oil, *Olive*	17	0	0	0
William Hicke of Bristol, Merchant Ind	7	barrel	Oil, *Olive*	7	0	0	0
Nicholas Hicke of Bristol, Merchant Ind	1.75	tun	Oil, *Olive*	14	0	0	0
Thomas Pitt of Bristol, Merchant Ind	7	barrel	Oil, *Olive*	7	0	0	0
	8	ton	Salt	8	0	0	0
	1	ton	Raisins, *Great*	6	5	0	0
Richard Swetnam of Bristol, Merchant Ind	3	tun	Oil, *Olive*	24	0	0	0

The Gabriell of *Mortamo (?)*, burden 50 tons, Michael Duran master, from Marennes, 9th June 1576

Michael Duran of Marennes, Merchant Alien	38	ton	Salt	38	0	0	0

The Hope of Fécamp, burden 25 tons, Thomas Lebert master, from La Rochelle, 13th June 1576

Edward Chester of Bristol, Merchant Ind	25	ton	Salt	25	0	0	0

The Julian of *Barre*, burden 50 tons, William Gawle master, from the Azores, *13th June 1576*

Thomas Aldworth of Bristol, Merchant Ind	9	ton	Woad, Green	90	0	0	0
Miles Diconson of Bristol, Merchant Ind	17	ton	Woad, Green	170	0	0	0
Henry Nayler of Bristol, Merchant Ind	2.75	ton	Woad, Green	27	10	0	0
Thomas Lane of Bristol, Merchant Ind	5.25	ton	Woad, Green	52	10	0	0

The Trinitie of Bristol, burden 100 tons, William Poolen master, from Majorca, *13th June 1576*

Nicholas Blake, William Hopkins & Thomas Pitt of Bristol, Merchants Ind	21	tun	Oil, *Olive*	168	0	0	0
Philip Langley of Bristol, Merchant Ind	19	tun	Oil, *Olive*	152	0	0	0
Richard Strobridge of Bristol, Merchant Ind	40	tun	Oil, *Olive*	320	0	0	0

The Julian of Bristol, burden 28 tons, Thomas Jennynge master, from La Rochelle, 20th June 1576

Miles Diconson of Bristol, Merchant Ind	20	ton	Salt	20	0	0	0

The Michaell of Fowey, burden 26 tons, Henry Martin master, from Bordeaux, *20th June 1576*

John Fo[]d of Plymouth, Merchant Ind	10	ton	Salt	10	0	0	0

The Grashoper of Bristol, burden 30 tons, John Tegge master, from San Sebastián, 3rd July 1576

William Prewett of Bristol, Merchant Ind	10	ton	Iron	40	0	0	0
Thomas Pitt of Bristol, Merchant Ind	6	ton	Iron	24	0	0	0
Richard Jones of Bristol, Merchant Ind	6	ton	Iron	24	0	0	0
Geoffrey Eton of Bristol, Merchant Ind	4	tun	Oil, Train	20	0	0	0

Merchant name	Qty	Unit	Commodity	£	s.	d.	f.

The Henry Sidney of *Apsam*, burden 40 tons, James Coxe master, from Andalusia, 6th July 1576

Merchant name	Qty	Unit	Commodity	£	s.	d.	f.
John Carr of Bristol, Merchant Ind	30	ton	Salt	30	0	0	0

The Katherin of Wexford, burden 12 tons, Nicholas Haie master, from Wexford, 10th July 1576

Merchant name	Qty	Unit	Commodity	£	s.	d.	f.
Richard Signett of Wexford, Ireland, Merchant Ind	2	dicker	Hides, Salted	6	13	4	0
	4	C	Skins, Sheep Broken	0	20	0	0
	1	dozen	Oars	0	5	0	0
	1	C	Boards	0	5	0	0

The Margett of Waterford, burden 5 tons, Nicholas Welsh master, from Waterford, 14th July 1576

Merchant name	Qty	Unit	Commodity	£	s.	d.	f.
John Lincolne of Waterford, Merchant Ind	5	C	Skins, Sheep Broken	0	25	0	0
	25	stone	Wool, Flocks	2	1	8	0
	1	stone	Wool, Irish	0	2	8	0

The James of Pembroke, burden 28 tons, John Devonishe master, from Cork, 16th July 1576

Merchant name	Qty	Unit	Commodity	£	s.	d.	f.
Henry Welshe of Cork, Merchant Ind	4	C	Skins, Lamb	3	6	8	0
	2	C	Skins, Sheep Broken	0	10	0	0
	30	piece	Skins, Fox	0	25	0	0
	3	piece	Skins, Marten	0	15	0	0
James Crewghe of Clonmel, Merchant Ind	10	C	Skins, Lamb	8	6	8	0
	15	C	Skins, Sheep Broken	3	15	0	0
	30	piece	Skins, Fox	0	25	0	0
	6	piece	Skins, Otter	0	10	0	0
	6	piece	Skins, Marten	0	30	0	0

The Lewys of Crozon, burden 26 tons, Harvie Harnell master, from La Rochelle, 16th July 1576

Merchant name	Qty	Unit	Commodity	£	s.	d.	f.
William Prewett & Richard Langford of Bristol Merchants Ind	24	ton	Salt	24	0	0	0

The Margarett of Bristol, burden 20 tons, William Morrice master, from Dublin, *16th July 1576*

Merchant name	Qty	Unit	Commodity	£	s.	d.	f.
John Porter of Bristol, Merchant Ind	100	stone	Wool, Irish	12	10	0	0

The Mary of Waterford, burden 24 tons, Philip Deringe master, from Waterford, *16th July 1576*

Merchant name	Qty	Unit	Commodity	£	s.	d.	f.
Thomas Kernysbroughe of Kilkenny, Merchant Ind	8	C	Irish Frieze *Cloth*	16	0	0	0
	8	piece	Caddows	4	0	0	0
James Deverier of Kilkenny, Merchant Ind	8	C	Irish Frieze *Cloth*	16	0	0	0
	18	piece	Mantles	4	10	0	0

Merchant name	Qty	Unit	Commodity	£	s.	d.	f.
Samuel Plunckett of London, Merchant Ind	6	C	Irish Frieze *Cloth*	12	0	0	0
Thomas Breuar of Kilkenny, Merchant Ind	5	C	Irish Frieze *Cloth*	10	0	0	0
	6	piece	Mantles	0	30	0	0
	1	C	Skins, Sheep Broken	0	5	0	0
Thomas Branocke of Kilkenny, Merchant Ind	3	C	Irish Frieze *Cloth*	6	0	0	0
	6	piece	Skins, Fox	0	5	0	0
	10	C	Skins, Sheep Broken	2	10	0	0
	3	piece	Skins, Otter	0	5	0	0

The Grace Dei of Tewkesbury, burden 6 tons, John Davies master, from Waterford, *16th July 1576*

Merchant name	Qty	Unit	Commodity	£	s.	d.	f.
Maurice Browne of Waterford, Merchant Ind	2	C	Irish Frieze *Cloth*	4	0	0	0
	24	piece	Mantles	6	0	0	0
John Welshe of Waterford, Merchant Ind	2	C	Irish Frieze *Cloth*	4	0	0	0
	4	piece	Coverlet	2	0	0	0
	6	piece	Mantles	0	30	0	0

The Katherin Hore of Waterford, burden 16 tons, John Gawle master, from Waterford, *16th July 1576*

Merchant name	Qty	Unit	Commodity	£	s.	d.	f.
Patrick Welshe of Waterford, Merchant Ind	5	C	Irish Frieze *Cloth*	10	0	0	0
	7	piece	Blankets	3	10	0	0
	7	piece	Mantles	0	35	0	0
Edmund Rowth of Waterford, Merchant Ind	3	C	Irish Frieze *Cloth*	6	0	0	0
	0.5	C	Skins, Lamb	0	8	4	0
	3	piece	Blankets	0	30	0	0
John Morfin of Waterford, Merchant Ind	3	C	Irish Frieze *Cloth*	6	0	0	0
	1	C	Skins, Sheep Broken	0	5	0	0
	6	piece	Skins, Fox	0	5	0	0
	2	piece	Blankets, White	0	20	0	0
John Welshe of Waterford, Merchant Ind	3	C	Irish Frieze *Cloth*	6	0	0	0
	6	piece	Blankets	3	0	0	0
Peter White of Waterford, Merchant Ind	3	C	Irish Frieze *Cloth*	6	0	0	0
	1	M	Skins, Sheep Broken	2	10	0	0
	2	piece	Mantles	0	10	0	0

The Trinitie of Bristol, burden 40 tons, Richard Sherman master, from La Rochelle, 26th July 1576

Merchant name	Qty	Unit	Commodity	£	s.	d.	f.
Richard Strobridge of Bristol, Merchant Ind	20	ton	Salt	20	0	0	0

The Sondaye of New Ross, burden 15 tons, John Perre master, from New Ross, *26th July 1576*

Merchant name	Qty	Unit	Commodity	£	s.	d.	f.
George Synet of New Ross, Merchant Ind	9	C	Skins, Sheep Broken	0	45	0	0
	3.5	C	Irish Frieze *Cloth*	7	0	0	0
	1	C	Skins, Lamb	0	16	8	0
	6	stone	Wool, Flocks	0	15	0	0
	8	piece	Coverlet, Coarse	4	0	0	0

Merchant name	Qty	Unit	Commodity	£	s.	d.	f.

The Fage of Dungarvan, burden 8 tons, John Poolen master, from Dungarvan, *26th July 1576*

Merchant name	Qty	Unit	Commodity	£	s.	d.	f.
John Mulbroughe of Dungarvan, Merchant Ind	2	M	Skins, Sheep Broken	5	0	0	0
	0.5	C	Irish Frieze *Cloth*	0	20	0	0
	10	stone	Wool, Flocks	0	25	0	0

The Katherin Morfey of Waterford, burden 9 tons, John Aileworth master, from Waterford, *26th July 1576*

Merchant name	Qty	Unit	Commodity	£	s.	d.	f.
Robert Wise of Waterford, Merchant Ind	6	piece	Coverlet	3	0	0	0
	15	piece	Mantles, Grey	3	15	0	0
	0.5	C	Irish Frieze *Cloth*	0	20	0	0
	1	C	Check *Cloth*	2	0	0	0
Geoffrey Porson of Waterford, Merchant Ind	1	C	Irish Frieze *Cloth*	2	0	0	0
	4	piece	Mantles	0	20	0	0
	5	piece	Caddows	2	10	0	0
Edward Aileworth of Waterford, Merchant Ind	9	C	Irish Frieze *Cloth*	18	0	0	0
	23	piece	Coverlet	11	10	0	0
	3	piece	Mantles	0	15	0	0
	40	yard	Check *Cloth*	0	13	4	0

The James of Dungarvan, burden 6 tons, Nicholas Magnor master, from Dungarvan, 28th July 1576

Merchant name	Qty	Unit	Commodity	£	s.	d.	f.
Nicholas Magner of Dungarvan, Merchant Ind	8	C	Skins, Sheep Broken	2	0	0	0

The Mackarell of Dungarvan, burden 12 tons, Thomas Sholland master, from Dungarvan, 29th July 1576

Merchant name	Qty	Unit	Commodity	£	s.	d.	f.
James Warde of Clonmel, Merchant Ind	5	C	Skins, Lamb	4	3	4	0
	9	C	Skins, Sheep Broken	2	5	0	0
	2	piece	Caddows	0	20	0	0
	1	C	Irish Frieze *Cloth*	2	0	0	0
Pierce Querke of Clonmel, Merchant Ind	4	C	Irish Frieze *Cloth*	8	0	0	0
	2	piece	Mantles	0	10	0	0
	2	piece	Blankets	0	20	0	0
Edmond Vale of Clonmel, Merchant Ind	5	C	Irish Frieze *Cloth*	10	0	0	0
	4	piece	Blankets	2	0	0	0
	3	C	Skins, Sheep Broken	0	15	0	0
	8	piece	Blankets, Grey	2	0	0	0

The Jesus of Bideford, burden 25 tons, Robert Limbery master, from Terceira, 30th July 1576

Merchant name	Qty	Unit	Commodity	£	s.	d.	f.
Thomas Alldworth of Bristol, Merchant Ind	13	ton	Woad, de Surries	130	0	0	0
Thomas Rowland, William Salterne & Robert Halton of Bristol, Merchants Ind	13	ton	Woad, de Surries	130	0	0	0

Merchant name	Qty	Unit	Commodity	£	s.	d.	f.

The Swallowe of Weymouth, burden 12 tons, Robert Gibbes master, from New Ross, 4th August 1576

John Chapell of Bristol, Merchant Ind	10	stone	Wool, Flocks	0	16	8	0
	19	piece	Hides, Salted	6	6	8	0
	1	C	Irish Frieze *Cloth*	2	0	0	0
	8	stone	Wool, Irish	0	20	0	0
	6	piece	Hides, Deer, with hair	0	6	8	0
	1	hogshead	Oil, Train	0	25	0	0

The Trinitie of Cork, burden 10 tons, John Welshe master, from Cork, 8th August 1576

Geoffrey Galwaye of Cork Merchant Ind	5	C	Skins, Sheep Broken	0	25	0	0
	2	dozen	Boards, small	0	10	0	0
	20	yard	Coverlet	0	6	8	0

The Gabriell of Bristol, burden 30 tons, Anthony Roberts master, from the Island of Madeira, 10th August 1576

| Thomas Aldworth, John Ashe & Anthony Roberts of Bristol, Merchants Ind | 80 | C | Sugar | 266 | 13 | 4 | 0 |
| | 5 | ton | Sumach | 66 | 13 | 4 | 0 |

The Katherin of Wexford, burden 10 tons, John Horrind master, from Wexford, 15th August 1576

James Turner of Wexford, Merchant Ind	3	C	Boards, Small	0	20	0	0
	10	piece	Hides, Salted	3	6	8	0
	1	C	Pipe Staves	0	5	0	0
	3	C	Skins, Sheep Broken	0	15	0	0

The Cheritie of Tewkesbury, burden 8 tons, John Bishope master, from Youghal, 16th August 1576

James *Ranen* of Wexford, Ireland, Merchant Ind	6	C	Skins, Sheep Broken	0	30	0	0
	24	yard	Irish Frieze *Cloth*	0	6	8	0
	2	piece	Hides, Deer	0	3	4	0

The Florance of Falmouth, burden 45 tons, John Daniell master, from *Lasroye, 16th August 1576*

| William Gittons & William Hopkins of Bristol, Merchants Ind | 30 | dicker | Hides, Salted | 100 | 0 | 0 | 0 |

The Corke of Dublin, burden 40 tons, Nicholas Quyne master, from Dublin, 21st August 1576

| Robert Brandon of Dublin, Merchant Ind | 2 | last | Soap Ashes | 7 | 10 | 0 | 0 |

Merchant name	Qty	Unit	Commodity	£	s.	d.	f.

The Golden Lion of Bristol, burden 350 tons, John Shepard master, from Cadiz, _21st August 1576_

Merchant name	Qty	Unit	Commodity	£	s.	d.	f.
Nicholas Blake of Bristol, Merchant Ind	33	ton	Salt	33	0	0	0
	1.75	tun	Oil, _Olive_	14	0	0	0
	1.25	tun	Aquavitae	20	0	0	0
	8	C	Alum	13	6	8	0
Michael Pepwall of Bristol, Merchant Ind	15	ton	Salt	15	0	0	0
	5.25	tun	Oil, _Olive_	42	0	0	0
Philip Langley of Bristol, Merchant Ind	33	ton	Salt	33	0	0	0
	4.75	tun	Oil, _Olive_	38	0	0	0
	3	barrel	Aquavitae	6	0	0	0
	2	hogshead	Olives	5	6	8	0
Thomas Warren of Bristol, Merchant Ind	5	ton	Salt	5	0	0	0
	4	tun	Oil, _Olive_	32	0	0	0
	4	ton	Alum	133	6	8	0
John Barnes of Bristol, Merchant Ind	7	ton	Salt	7	0	0	0
	3.5	tun	Oil, _Olive_	28	0	0	0
Thomas Pitt of Bristol, Merchant Ind	9	ton	Salt	9	0	0	0
	6.125	tun	Oil, _Olive_	49	0	0	0
	7	hogshead	Aquavitae	28	0	0	0
Richard Ashehurste of Bristol, Merchant Ind	11	ton	Salt	11	0	0	0
	5.25	tun	Oil, _Olive_	42	0	0	0
Alice Roberts of Bristol, Widow Ind	12	ton	Salt	12	0	0	0
	4.375	tun	Oil, _Olive_	35	0	0	0
Elizabeth Bondle of Bristol, Widow Ind	18	ton	Salt	18	0	0	0
Francis Knight of Bristol Merchant Ind	0.875	tun	Oil, _Olive_	7	0	0	0
Thomas Griffith of Bristol, Merchant Ind	7	ton	Salt	7	0	0	0
	1.75	tun	Oil, _Olive_	14	0	0	0
William Hicks of Bristol, Merchant Ind	4.375	tun	Oil, _Olive_	35	0	0	0
George Snigge of Bristol, Merchant Ind	3.5	tun	Oil, _Olive_	28	0	0	0
John Alkins of Bristol, Merchant Ind	7	tun	Oil, _Olive_	56	0	0	0
Giles Bitfilde of Bristol, Merchant Ind	4	tun	Oil, _Olive_	32	0	0	0
Nicholas Hicke of Bristol, Merchant Ind	1.75	tun	Oil, _Olive_	14	0	0	0
Roger Wike of Bristol, Merchant Ind	3.5	tun	Oil, _Olive_	28	0	0	0
	2	hogshead	Aquavitae	8	0	0	0
Robert Cable of Bristol, Merchant Ind	1.25	tun	Oil, _Olive_	10	0	0	0
Richard Jones of Bristol, Merchant Ind	0.875	tun	Oil, _Olive_	7	0	0	0
John Oliver of Bristol, Merchant Ind	2	hogshead	Olives	5	6	8	0
	0.875	tun	Oil, _Olive_	7	0	0	0

The White Bere of London, burden 200 tons, Robert Davies master, from Andalusia, 24th August 1576

Merchant name	Qty	Unit	Commodity	£	s.	d.	f.
Henry Roberts of Bristol, Merchant Ind	100	ton	Salt	100	0	0	0

The White Lion of Bristol, burden 45 tons, William Hawle master, from Andalusia, _24th August 1576_

Merchant name	Qty	Unit	Commodity	£	s.	d.	f.
Henry Roberts of Bristol, Merchant Ind	10	ton	Salt	10	0	0	0
	20	tun	Oil, _Olive_	160	0	0	0

Merchant name	Qty	Unit	Commodity	£	s.	d.	f.

The Anne Gallant of Bristol, burden 25 tons, Humphrey Dier master, from La Rochelle, 6th September 1576

| William Smith of Bristol, Merchant Ind | 16 | ton | Salt | 16 | 0 | 0 | 0 |

The John of Bristol, burden 24 tons, William Skore master, from San Sebastián, 20th September 1576

| William Hopkins & Richard Langford of Bristol, Merchants Ind | 10 | ton | Iron | 40 | 0 | 0 | 0 |
| Thomas Pollington of Bristol, Merchant Ind | 1.5 | tun | Oil, Train | 7 | 10 | 0 | 0 |

WINE IMPORTS

Golden Lion of Bristol, burden 350 tons, John Shepard master, from Cadiz, 29th November 1575

	Qty	Unit	Commodity	£	s.	d.	f.
Robert Kitching of Bristol, Merchant Ind	50	tun	Wine, Seck	0	0	0	0
	10	tun	Wine, Corrupt	0	0	0	0
	20	tun	Wine, Leakage	0	0	0	0
Philip Langton of Bristol, Merchant Ind	5	tun	Wine, Seck	0	0	0	0
	1	tun	Wine, Leakage	0	0	0	0
	1	tun	Wine, Corrupt	0	0	0	0
John Hopkins of Bristol, Merchant Ind	8	tun	Wine, Seck	0	0	0	0
	2	tun	Wine, Prisage	0	0	0	0
	2	tun	Wine, Leakage	0	0	0	0
	1.5	tun	Wine, Corrupt	0	0	0	0

The Thobie of Bristol, burden 90 tons, John Baker master, from Sanlúcar de Barrameda, 2nd December 1575

Thomas Simons & John Hopkins of Bristol Merchants Ind	9	tun	Wine, Seck	0	0	0	0
	1.5	tun	Wine, Corrupt	0	0	0	0
	1.5	tun	Wine, Leakage	0	0	0	0

The Hare of Bristol, burden 50 tons, Robert Davies master, from Cadiz, 13th December 1575

Richard Hamity & John Rowland of Bristol, Merchant Ind	5	tun	Wine, Seck	0	0	0	0
	1	tun	Wine, Corrupt	0	0	0	0
	1	tun	Wine, Leakage	0	0	0	0

The Nightingale of Bristol, burden 26 tons, Thomas Naylor master, from Ayamonte, *13th December 1575*

Richard Fowynes & William Ellies of Bristol Merchants Ind	6.5	tun	Wine, Bastard	0	0	0	0
	1.5	tun	Wine, Corrupt	0	0	0	0
	1	tun	Wine, Leakage	0	0	0	0

Merchant name	Qty	Unit	Commodity	£	s.	d.	f.

The Cony of Bristol, burden 25 tons, Richard Lullet master, from Biscay, 15th December 1575

Thomas Merricke of Bristol, Merchant Ind	3.25	tun	Wine, French	o	o	o	o
	1.25	tun	Wine, Corrupt	o	o	o	o
	0.75	tun	Wine, Leakage	o	o	o	o
Richard Langford of Bristol, Merchant Ind	2	hogshead	Wine, French	o	o	o	o
	1	hogshead	Wine, Corrupt	o	o	o	o
	1	hogshead	Wine, Leakage	o	o	o	o

The Julian of Bristol, burden 30 tons, Richard Lullet master, from La Rochelle, 4th April 1576

Thomas Diconson & John Bawle of Bristol Merchants Ind	9	tun	Wine, Rochell	o	o	o	o
	1	tun	Wine, Prisage	o	o	o	o
	2	tun	Wine, Corrupt[21]	o	o	o	o
	1.5	tun	Wine, Leakage	o	o	o	o

The White Falcon of London, burden 120 tons, John Keller master, from Sanlúcar de Barrameda, 25th April 1576

Edward Osborne of London, Merchant Ind	50	tun	Wine, Seck	o	o	o	o
	3	tun	Wine, Corrupt	o	o	o	o
	7	tun	Wine, Leakage	o	o	o	o
Laurence Mellowe of London, Merchant Ind	25	tun	Wine, Seck	o	o	o	o
	2	tun	Wine, Corrupt	o	o	o	o
	3	tun	Wine, Leakage	o	o	o	o
Maria Hills of London, Widow Ind	3.5	tun	Wine, Seck	o	o	o	o
	3	hogshead	Wine, Leakage	o	o	o	o
	3	hogshead	Wine, Corrupt	o	o	o	o

The Grace of God of Milbrook, Devon, burden 28 tons, Edward Eide master, from La Rochelle, *25th April 1576*

Thomas Diconson of Bristol, Merchant Ind	11.5	tun	Wine, Rochell	o	o	o	o
	1	pipe	Wine, Provision	o	o	o	o
	1	tun	Wine, Rochell	o	o	o	o
	1	tun	Wine, Prisage	o	o	o	o
	2.5	tun	Wine, Leakage	o	o	o	o
	2	tun	Wine, Corrupt[22]	o	o	o	o
Edward Eide of Bristol, Merchant Ind	1	tun	Wine, Rochell	o	o	o	o

The Lion of Bristol, burden 26 tons, Thomas Jennynge master, from La Rochelle, 26th April 1576

Thomas Diconson of Bristol, Merchant Ind	11	tun	Wine, Rochell	o	o	o	o
	1	tun	Wine, Prisage	o	o	o	o
	2	tun	Wine, Corrupt[23]	o	o	o	o
	2	tun	Wine, Leakage	o	o	o	o

21 Sold to William Parfett. 22 Sold to Thomas Best. 23 Sold to William Parfett.

Merchant name	Qty	Unit	Commodity	£	s.	d.	f.

The Pawle of Teignmouth, burden 27 tons, John Milbroughe master, from Bordeaux, 2nd May 1576

Edward Goulde of Totnes, Merchant Ind	9.5	tun	Wine, French	o	o	o	o
	2	tun	Wine, Corrupt[24]	o	o	o	o
	1.5	tun	Wine, Leakage	o	o	o	o

The Elizabeth of Tewkesbury, burden 36 tons, Bonaventure Aude master, from Bordeaux, 10th May 1576

John Dowre of Totnes, Merchant Ind	16	tun	Wine, French	o	o	o	o
	0.25	tun	Wine, French	o	o	o	o
	1	tun	Wine, Prisage	o	o	o	o
	3	tun	Wine, Corrupt[25]	o	o	o	o
	2.75	tun	Wine, Leakage	o	o	o	o

The Trinitie of Bristol, burden 40 tons, Ronald Sharmin master, from Bordeaux, 12th May 1576

Richard Strobridge of Bristol, Merchant Ind	4.25	tun	Wine, French	o	o	o	o
	1	hogshead	Wine, French	o	o	o	o
	1	tun	Wine, Corrupt[26]	o	o	o	o
	3	hogshead	Wine, Leakage	o	o	o	o
John Ashe of Bristol, Merchant Ind	3.75	tun	Wine, French	o	o	o	o
	2	hogshead	Wine, Corrupt	o	o	o	o
	3	hogshead	Wine, Leakage	o	o	o	o
Nicholas Blake of Bristol, Merchant Ind	2	hogshead	Wine, French	o	o	o	o
	1	tun	Wine, French	o	o	o	o
	1	hogshead	Wine, Corrupt[27]	o	o	o	o
	1	hogshead	Wine, Leakage	o	o	o	o
William Gittons of Bristol, Merchant Ind	3.75	tun	Wine, French	o	o	o	o
	2	hogshead	Wine, Corrupt[28]	o	o	o	o
	3	hogshead	Wine, Leakage	o	o	o	o

The Hare of Bristol, burden 50 tons, Robert Davies master, from Andalusia, 12th May 1576

George Collyncor of London, Merchant Ind	31	tun	Wine, Seck	o	o	o	o
	3	tun	Wine, Corrupt	o	o	o	o
	6	tun	Wine, Leakage	o	o	o	o

The Spedewell of Bristol, burden 25 tons, Thomas Cornish master, from Puerto de Santa Maria, 17th May 1576

William Salterne of Bristol, Merchant Ind	6	tun	Wine, Seck	o	o	o	o
	1	tun	Wine, Leakage	o	o	o	o
	1	butt	Wine, Corrupt	o	o	o	o

24 Sold to Robert Allin. 25 Sold to Robert Allin. 26 Sold to John Alkin. 27 Sold to Nicholas Crosbie. 28 Sold to William Parfett.

Merchant name	Qty	Unit	Commodity	£	s.	d.	f.

The Mynion of Bristol, burden 120 tons, William AgWilliam master, from Cadiz, *17th May* 1576

Merchant name	Qty	Unit	Commodity	£	s.	d.	f.
Thomas Kelke of Bristol, Merchant Ind	4.125	tun	Wine, Seck	o	o	o	o
	0.875	tun	Wine, Leakage	o	o	o	o
William Gittons of Bristol, Merchant Ind	27.5	tun	Wine, Seck	o	o	o	o
	5.5	tun	Wine, Leakage	o	o	o	o
Robert Sandford of Bristol, Merchant Ind	21	tun	Wine, Seck	o	o	o	o
	4	tun	Wine, Leakage	o	o	o	o
Richard Langford of Bristol, Merchant Ind	4.125	tun	Wine, Seck	o	o	o	o
	0.875	tun	Wine, Leakage	o	o	o	o
John Hopkins of Bristol, Merchant Ind	6.25	tun	Wine, Seck	o	o	o	o
	1.25	tun	Wine, Leakage	o	o	o	o
William Ellies of Bristol, Merchant Ind	7	tun	Wine, Seck	o	o	o	o
	2	tun	Wine, Prisage	o	o	o	o
	2	tun	Wine, Leakage	o	o	o	o

The Fox of Bristol, burden 45 tons, Richard White master, from Lisbon, 20th May 1576

Merchant name	Qty	Unit	Commodity	£	s.	d.	f.
Botholl Holder & Randal Wilbram of London & Bristol, Merchants	4	tun	Wine, Muscadell	o	o	o	o

The France of Marennes, burden 40 tons, John Martine master, from Marennes, *20th May* 1576

Merchant name	Qty	Unit	Commodity	£	s.	d.	f.
John Martino of Marennes, Merchant Alien	3.5	tun	Vinegar	8	3	4	o

The Thobie of Bristol, burden 100 tons, Thomas Cottrell master, from Cadiz, 7th June 1576

Merchant name	Qty	Unit	Commodity	£	s.	d.	f.
George Cullymore of London, Merchant Ind	16.75	tun	Wine, Seck	o	o	o	o
William Hicke & John Hopkins, of Bristol, Merchants Ind	8	tun	Wine, Seck	o	o	o	o
	1.5	tun	Wine, Leakage	o	o	o	o

The Mary of Fécamp, burden 65 tons, Estiman? Mabene master, from Bordeaux, *7th June* 1576

Merchant name	Qty	Unit	Commodity	£	s.	d.	f.
Thomas Warren of Bristol, Merchant Ind	1	tun	Wine, French[29]	o	o	o	o
Michael Pepwall of Bristol, Merchant Ind	1	tun	Wine, French[30]	o	o	o	o
William Hicke of Bristol, Merchant Ind	4	tun	Wine, French	o	o	o	o
	3	hogshead	Wine, French[31]	o	o	o	o
	2	tun	Wine, Corrupt	o	o	o	o
	3	hogshead	Wine, Leakage	o	o	o	o
Thomas Rowland of Bristol, Merchant Ind	1	tun	Wine, French	o	o	o	o
	3	hogshead	Wine, French[32]	o	o	o	o
	2	hogshead	Wine, Corrupt[33]	o	o	o	o
	1	hogshead	Wine, Leakage	o	o	o	o

29 Allowed for his provision.   30 Allowed for the provision of his house.   31 Allowed for his provision.   32 Allowed for his provision.   33 Sold to William M[]te[ ], Bristol Soapmaker.

Merchant name	Qty	Unit	Commodity	£	s.	d.	f.
John Ashe of Bristol, Merchant Ind	4.5	tun	Wine, French	0	0	0	0
	1.75	tun	Wine, Corrupt	0	0	0	0
	3	hogshead	Wine, Leakage	0	0	0	0
Nicholas Jobbes of Bristol, Vintener Ind	4	tun	Wine, French	0	0	0	0
	1.5	tun	Wine, Corrupt	0	0	0	0
	3	hogshead	Wine, Leakage	0	0	0	0
Thomas Kelke of Bristol, Merchant Ind	3	hogshead	Wine, French	0	0	0	0
William Prewett of Bristol, Merchant Ind	2.66	tun	Wine, French	0	0	0	0
	2.5	tun	Wine, Corrupt	0	0	0	0
	2	hogshead	Wine, Leakage	0	0	0	0
Robert Showard of Bristol, Merchant Ind	4	tun	Wine, French	0	0	0	0
	2	tun	Wine, Prisage	0	0	0	0
	2	hogshead	Wine, French[34]	0	0	0	0
	2.5	tun	Wine, Corrupt[35]	0	0	0	0
	1	tun	Wine, Leakage	0	0	0	0
Mathewe Haviland of Bristol, Merchant Ind	2.625	tun	Wine, French	0	0	0	0
	0.75	tun	Wine, Corrupt[36]	0	0	0	0
	2	hogshead	Wine, Leakage	0	0	0	0
John Barker of Bristol, Merchant Ind	2.5	tun	Wine, French	0	0	0	0
	1	tun	Wine, Corrupt[37]	0	0	0	0
	2	hogshead	Wine, Leakage	0	0	0	0
Richard Salterne of Bristol, Merchant Ind	3.875	tun	Wine, French	0	0	0	0
	1.5	tun	Wine, Corrupt[38]	0	0	0	0
	2	hogshead	Wine, Leakage	0	0	0	0
William Salterne of Bristol, Merchant Ind	3.41	tun	Wine, French	0	0	0	0
	2	hogshead	Wine, French[39]	0	0	0	0
	1.5	tun	Wine, Corrupt[40]	0	0	0	0
	2	hogshead	Wine, Leakage	0	0	0	0
Richard Langford of Bristol, Merchant Ind	2	tun	Wine, French	0	0	0	0
	2	hogshead	Wine, French[41]	0	0	0	0
	1	tun	Wine, Corrupt[42]	0	0	0	0
	2	hogshead	Wine, Leakage	0	0	0	0

The Michaell of Fowey, burden 30 tons, Henry Martin master, from Bordeaux, 20th June 1576

Merchant name	Qty	Unit	Commodity	£	s.	d.	f.
John F[ ]ind & Humfrey Freyns of Plymouth Merchants Ind	13	tun	Wine, French	0	0	0	0
	1	tun	Wine, Prisage	0	0	0	0
	3	tun	Wine, Corrupt[43]	0	0	0	0
	2	tun	Wine, Leakage	0	0	0	0

The Henry Sidney of *Apsam*, burden 40 tons, James Coxe master, from Puerto de Santa Maria, 6th July 1576

Merchant name	Qty	Unit	Commodity	£	s.	d.	f.
John Carr of Bristol, Merchant Ind	5	tun	Wine, Seck	0	0	0	0
	1	tun	Wine, Leakage	0	0	0	0

34 Allowed for his provision. 35 Sold to William Yate, soapmaker. 36 Sold to Henry Shee. 37 Sold to Edward Chester. 38 Sold to Nicholas Crosbie. 39 Allowed for his provision. 40 Sold to John Alkin. 41 Allowed for his provision. 42 Sold to Edward Chester. 43 Sold to Nicholas Crosbie.

Merchant name	Qty	Unit	Commodity	£	s.	d.	f.

The Katherin of Barnstaple, burden 40 tons, John Williams master, from Bordeaux, *6th July 1576*

Richard Strobridge & William Prewett of Bristol, Merchants Ind	13	tun	Wine, French	0	0	0	0
	1	tun	Wine, Prisage	0	0	0	0
	3	tun	Wine, Corrupt[44]	0	0	0	0
	2	tun	Wine, Leakage	0	0	0	0
	15	ton	Salt	15	0	0	0

The Gabriell of Bristol, burden 30 tons, Anthony Robins master, from the Island of Madeira, 10th August 1576

Thomas Aldworth & John Ashe of Bristol Merchants Ind	7.5	tun	Wine, Madeira	0	0	0	0
	1	tun	Wine, Leakage	0	0	0	0

The Golden Lion of Bristol, burden 350 tons, John Shepard master, from Andalusia, 21st August 1576

Nicholas Blake of Bristol, Merchant Ind	3.5	tun	Wine, Seck	0	0	0	0
	1	butt	Wine, Leakage	0	0	0	0
Michael Pepwall of Bristol, Merchant Ind	3.5	tun	Wine, Seck	0	0	0	0
	1	butt	Wine, Leakage	0	0	0	0
Philip Langley of Bristol, Merchant Ind	7	tun	Wine, Seck	0	0	0	0
	2	tun	Wine, Prisage	0	0	0	0
William Gittons of Bristol, Merchant Ind	8	tun	Wine, Seck	0	0	0	0
	2	tun	Wine, Leakage	0	0	0	0
William Hicks of Bristol, Merchant Ind	2.5	tun	Wine, Seck	0	0	0	0
	1	tun	Wine, Leakage	0	0	0	0
Giles Bitfilde of Bristol, Merchant Ind	4.25	tun	Wine, Seck	0	0	0	0
	3	hogshead	Wine, Leakage	0	0	0	0
Richard Jones of Bristol, Merchant Ind	3	tun	Wine, Seck	0	0	0	0
	0.5	tun	Wine, Leakage	0	0	0	0

44 Sold to John Caro.

1594/95

TNA E190/1131/10 is an annual surveyor's account, covering both inwards and outwards trade during the period Michaelmas 1594 to Michaelmas 1595. Overall, it contains the same level of detail as the 1575/6 account, with the exception of the fact that it does not always record nominal values for each item. This is particularly the case with respect to long lists of exports to Ireland, where the surveyor usually includes the subsidy paid on each item, and then gives a total nominal value at the end, in addition to recording the total duty paid in the right hand margin. This is potentially confusing as, on a cursory inspection, the value of the poundage subsidy could be mistaken for the nominal value. Also sometimes the total value given by the surveyor includes a 'value' for goods not actually paying poundage, such as cloth of assize.

In this transcription, where nominal values occur, they have been transcribed as in the manuscript. To avoid confusion, and maintain continuity throughout the series, in cases where an item is paying poundage, but the poundage subsidy is recorded instead of the nominal value, the nominal value has been inputted and italicised. As with the other accounts, items not paying poundage, such as cloth of assize and wine are transcribed without values.

Worthy of note in this account are the number of errors in terms of the 'total values' arrived at by the surveyor. While the total duty is usually correct, there are strong indications that the lists of commodities, at least, are being copied (somewhat inaccurately at times) from another source. There are numerous instances where the list of goods, when totalled using EXCEL, come to a slightly lower value than that given by the surveyor, suggesting that he has omitted various small items from his lists. Comparing this account with the customer's accounts for the same year is instructive.[1] On some occasions the customer's account helps to identify the missing objects and where this is possible, items have been entered in the transcription. On other occasions however, it is interesting to note that the surveyor and customer record matching lists of commodities but each comes to a different total value, neither of which appears to be correct based on the commodities recorded.[2] This of course raises questions about the roles of

---

1 TNA E190/1131/11: customer's outward Michaelmas 1594 – Easter 1595 and TNA E190/1131/13 customers outward, Easter 1595 – Michaelmas 1595. 2 For example TNA E190/1131/10 f39v, the Mary of Wexford.

the various customs officials and the level of independence involved in their recording procedures.[3]

Of further note in this account is that a number of ships are recorded as coming from 'a mare', which appears to mean from 'the sea'. The term is written in English in the 1600/1 account, and usually denotes a prize ship carrying confiscated goods. In the 1594/5 account however, it is applied also to certain ships, such as the Daisy of Bristol, which are clearly not prize ships. It may be that the term in this case relates to the goods on board the vessel and not the vessel itself or perhaps 'a mare' is an abbreviation for Marennes, in France. This is unlikely however as this port, where it appears in generally written in full.

IMPORTS

Merchant name	Qty	Unit	Commodity	£	s.	d.	f.
The Hare of Cherbourg, burden 30 tons, Francis Garre master, from La Rochelle, 30th September 1594							
Thomas Hopkins of Bristol, Merchant Ind	25	ton	Salt	25	0	0	0
The Peter of Middelburg, burden 100 tons, James Symons master, from _Burniffe_,[4] _30th September 1594_							
Christopher Harlonson of Middelburg, Merchant Alien	60	ton	Salt	60	0	0	0
	125	piece	_Metlerniptes_[5]_Cloth_	60	0	0	0
	20	fardel	Vitry Canvas _Cloth_	100	0	0	0
The Mary of Bristol, burden 18 tons, John Wattes master, from Cork, _30th September 1594_							
Edward Roche of Cork, Merchant Ind	16	C	Skins, Morkin & Sheep Broken	5	6	8	0
The Rose of Bristol, burden 16 tons, William Davis master, from Waterford, 1st October 1594							
William Hallie of Limerick, Merchant Ind	12	C	Skins, Morkin & Sheep Broken	4	0	0	0
The Henry of Bayonne, burden 40 tons, John Furnewe master, from Bayonne, _1st October 1594_							
Geoffrey Gittins of Bristol, Merchant Ind	15	ton	Salt	15	0	0	0
The Henry aforesaid							
John Furnewe of Bayonne, Merchant Alien	15	ton	Salt	15	0	0	0

3 For a detailed discussion on the roles of various officials see Gras, _Early English customs system._   4 Possibly Bourgneuf, France.   5 Unidentified.

Merchant name	Qty	Unit	Commodity	£	s.	d.	f.

The Thought of Bayonne, burden 40 tons, Clement Davy master, from *Larmuster*,[6] 1st October 1594

Maria Gittins of Bristol, Widow Ind	8.5	ton	Salt	8	10	0	0
	0.5	fardel	Vitry Canvas *Cloth*	2	10	0	0
	1	hogshead	Oil, *Olive*	2	0	0	0

The Thought aforesaid, 1st October 1594

| John Collimore of Bristol, Merchant Ind | 1 | hogshead | Oil, *Olive* | 2 | 0 | 0 | 0 |
| | 1.5 | fardel | Vitry Canvas *Cloth* | 7 | 10 | 0 | 0 |

The Thought aforesaid, 1st October 1594

Benedict Harvy of Bristol, Merchant Ind	22.5	ton	Salt	22	10	0	0
	1	hogshead	Oil, *Olive*	2	0	0	0
	1	fardel	Vitry Canvas *Cloth*	5	0	0	0
	8	bushel	Seed, Mustard	0	13	4	0
	3.5	tun	Wine, Corrupt	0	0	0	0

The Rose aforesaid, 4th October 1594

| Robert Gardener of Bristol, Grocer Ind | 1 | C | *Irish* Frieze *Cloth* | 2 | 0 | 0 | 0 |

The Elizabeth of Bristol, burden 40 tons, John Crose master, from Newfoundland, 7th October 1594

| Abraham Davis of Bristol, Merchant Ind | 4 | tun | Oil, Train | 20 | 0 | 0 | 0 |

The Mayeflower of Bristol, burden 90 tons, Tobias Parris master, from Newfoundland, 15th October 1594

| Thomas James of Bristol, Merchant & Company Ind | 7.5 | tun | Oil, Train | 37 | 10 | 0 | 0 |

The Roa of Bristol, burden 40 tons, Henry Ellis master, from Newfoundland, 17th October 1594

| William Ellis & John Barker of Bristol, Merchant & Company Ind | 8 | tun | Oil, Train | 40 | 0 | 0 | 0 |

The Dove of Bristol, burden 40 tons, Thomas Bennet master, from Newfoundland, 18th October 1594

| Thomas Bromley of Bristol, Merchant & Company Ind | 3 | tun | Oil, Train | 15 | 0 | 0 | 0 |

---

6 This is very likely to be Noirmoutier off Les Sables d'Olonne as 'muster' or 'mister' in the English form is often 'moustier' in the French form. The fact the the ship is from Bayonne further suggests this identification.

Merchant name	Qty	Unit	Commodity	£	s.	d.	f.

The Daysey of Bristol, burden 30 tons, *from the Sea*,[7] 19th October 1594

| John Hopkins of Bristol, Merchant Ind | 17.04 | ton | Iron[8] | 68 | 3 | 4 | 0 |

The Lillie of Bristol, burden 25 tons, John Peckham master, from Newfoundland, 21st October 1594

| John Browne of Bristol, Merchant & Company Ind | 2 | tun | Oil, Train | 10 | 0 | 0 | 0 |

The Dyamound of Bristol, burden 50 tons, Christopher Taylor master, from Brest, 4th November 1594

| John Love of Bristol, Merchant Ind | 80 | piece | Dowlas and Lockram Cloth | 133 | 6 | 8 | 0 |

The Diamound aforesaid, 4th November 1594

| George Lane of Bristol, Merchant Ind | 20 | piece | Dowlas and Lockram Cloth | 33 | 6 | 4 | 0 |

The Diamound aforesaid, *4th November 1594*

| John Webbe of Bristol, Merchant Ind | 15 | piece | Dowlas & Lockram Cloth | 25 | 0 | 0 | 0 |

The Diamound aforesaid, 4th November 1594

| Thomas Hewett of Bristol, Merchant Ind | 17.5 | piece | *Dowlas & Lockram* Cloth | 29 | 3 | 4 | 0 |

The Diamound aforesaid, *4th November 1594*

| John Parker of Bristol, Merchant Ind | 8 | piece | Dowlas & Lockram Cloth | 13 | 6 | 8 | 0 |

The Diamound aforesaid, *4th November 1594*

| John Higins of Bristol, Merchant Ind | 5 | piece | Dowlas & Lockram Cloth | 8 | 6 | 8 | 0 |

The Diamound aforesaid, *4th November 1594*

| John Collimore of Bristol, Merchant Ind | 20 | piece | Dowlas & Lockram Cloth | 33 | 6 | 8 | 0 |

The Diamound aforesaid, *4th November 1594*

| Edward Bentley of Bristol, Merchant Ind | 30 | piece | Dowlas & Lockram Cloth | 50 | 0 | 0 | 0 |

7 Usually 'a mare' is used to denote a prize ship taken from 'the sea'. This is confirmed by the 1600 accounts, where the term is written in English. This, however, is not a prize ship. A possibility is that 'Mare' is an abbreviation for Marennes. Elsewhere, however, Marennes this is usually written in full.   8 On the lighter of the Globe of London.

Merchant name	Qty	Unit	Commodity	£	s.	d.	f.

The Diamound aforesaid, *4th November 1594*

| Richard Batt of Bristol, Merchant Ind | 45 | piece | Dowlas & Lockram Cloth | 83⁹ | 6 | 8 | 0 |

The Diamound aforesaid, *4th November 1594*

| William Walles of Bristol Merchant Ind | 50 | piece | Dowlas & Lockram Cloth | 83 | 6 | 8 | 0 |

The Diamound aforesaid, *4th November 1594*

| John Merrick of Bristol Merchant Ind | 25 | piece | Dowlas & Lockram Cloth | 41 | 13 | 4 | 0 |

The Nicholas of Padstow, burden 40 tons, John Davis master, from Newfoundland, 13th November 1594

| Nicholas Yeo of Padstow, , Merchant Ind | 3 | tun | Oil, Train | 15 | 0 | 0 | 0 |

The Sallomon of Bristol, burden 18 tons, Peter Dine? Master, from Galway, 18th November 1594

| William Chappell of Bristol, Merchant Ind | 10 | barrel | Fish, Herring White | 5 | 0 | 0 | 0 |
| | 43 | stone | Wool, Flocks | 3 | 11 | 8 | 0 |

The Sallomon aforesaid, *18th November 1594*

| Thomas Wakely of Bristol, Merchant Ind | 3 | C | Skins, Morkin & Sheep Broken | 1 | 0 | 0 | 0 |

The John of Bristol, burden 12 tons, Christopher Burkett master, from Youghal, *18th November 1594*

| Christopher Burkett of Bristol, Merchant Ind | 4 | barrel | Fish, Herring White | 2 | 0 | 0 | 0 |
| | 6 | C | Skins, Morkin | 2 | 0 | 0 | 0 |

Robert of Marennes, burden 20 tons, Peter Jubert master, from Bordeaux, 30th November 1594

| William Ellis of Bristol, Merchant Ind | 9.75 | tun | Wine, Gascon | 0 | 0 | 0 | 0 |

The Robert of Marennes aforesaid, *30th November 1594*

| John Whittson of Bristol, Merchant Ind | 7.5 | tun | Wine, Gascon | 0 | 0 | 0 | 0 |

The Robert of Marennes aforesaid, *30th November 1594*

| Hugh Griffith of Bristol, Merchant Ind | 3.25 | tun | Wine, Gascon | 0 | 0 | 0 | 0 |

---

9 This appears to be an erroneous total value. The total custom paid is entered at £3 15s.

Merchant name	Qty	Unit	Commodity	£	s.	d.	f.

The Pellican of Marennes, burden 40 tons, Saye? Gautier master, from Bordeaux, 2nd December 1594

| Richard Coole of Bristol, Merchant Ind | 10 | tun | Wine, Gascon | o | o | o | o |

The Pellican aforesaid, 2nd December 1594

| John Barber of Bristol, Merchant Ind | 11 | tun | Wine, Gascon | o | o | o | o |

The Pellican aforesaid, *2nd December 1594*

| Hugh Griffith of Bristol, Merchant Ind | 11 | tun | Wine, Gascon | o | o | o | o |

The Pellican aforesaid, *2nd December 1594*

| John Bowlton of Bristol, Merchant Ind | 4 | tun | Wine, Gascon | o | o | o | o |

The Pellican aforesaid, *2nd December 1594*

| Michael Pepwall of Bristol, Merchant Ind | 2 | tun | Wine, Gascon | o | o | o | o |

The Hercules of Bristol, burden 50 tons, James Barton master, from Saõ Miguel, *2nd December 1594*

| Robert Aldworth of Bristol, Merchant Ind | 40 | ton | Woad, Green | 400 | o | o | o |

The Greenfild of Vlissingen, burden 100 tons, Derek Petterson Prince master, from Cadiz, *2nd December 1594*

| Tobias Vanasall of London, Merchant Ind | 700 | piece | Raisons, Shoeris & Rotta | 166 | 13 | 4 | o |

The Greenfild aforesaid, *2nd December 1594*

| Derek Petterson Prince of Vlissingen, Merchant Alien | 16 | ton | Salt | 16 | o | o | o |

The Greenfild aforesaid, *2nd December 1594*

| Roger Vancolge of London, Merchant Alien | 28 | butt | Wine, Seck | o | o | o | o |
| | 12 | butt | Wine, Corrupt | o | o | o | o |

The Greenfild aforesaid, 10th December 1594

| Dirick Petterson Prince of Vlissingen, Merchant Alien | 21 | butt | Wine, Seck | o | o | o | o |

The Greenfild aforesaid, *10th December 1594*

| Daniel Pointes of London Merchant & Company Ind | 29 | butt | Wine, Seck | o | o | o | o |

Merchant name	Qty	Unit	Commodity	£	s.	d.	f.

The Greenfild aforesaid, *10th December 1594*

| Tobias Vanassell of London, Merchant Ind | 14 | C | Raisins, of the Sun | 11 | 13 | 4 | 0 |

The Sallomon of Minsterwood, burden 14 tons, John Wooles master, from Youghal, 19th December 1594

| Ralph Culbert of Bristol, Merchant Ind | 10 | C | Skins, Morkin & Sheep Broken | 3 | 6 | 8 | 0 |

The Rose of Bristol, burden 14 tons, Thomas Davis master, from Youghal 20th December 1594

| William Mercer of Gloucester, Merchant Ind | 3 | hogshead | Fish, Herring White | 3 | 0 | 0 | 0 |

The Rose aforesaid, *20th December 1594*

| Thomas Slade of Bristol, Merchant Ind | 7 | piece | Caddows | 3 | 10 | 0 | 0 |
| | 5 | piece | Check *Cloth* | 2 | 10 | 0 | 0 |

The Rose aforesaid

Richard Comerford of Waterford, Merchant Ind	4	C	Irish Frieze *Cloth*	8	0	0	0
	12	piece	Caddows	6	0	0	0
	10	C	Skins, Morkin & Sheep Broken	3	6	8	0

The Fullia of Saõ Vicente, burden 16 tons, Martin Deoyarsiver master, from *Alatheroe, 20th December 1594*

| William Ellis of Bristol, Merchant Ind | 20 | M | Oranges & Lemons | 6 | 13 | 4 | 0 |

The Fullia aforesaid, *20th December 1594*

| Martin Deoyarsiver of Saõ Vicente, Master Alien | 30 | M | Oranges & Lemons | 10 | 0 | 0 | 0 |
| | 1 | ton | Iron | 4 | 0 | 0 | 0 |

The Anne of Marennes, burden 30 tons, Evan Evans master, from Charente, 23rd December 1594

| Peter Jubert of La Rochelle, Merchant Alien | 30 | tun | Wine, Charente | 0 | 0 | 0 | 0 |

The Katheren of Alderney, 25 tons, Michael Cork master, from St Malo, 2nd January 1595

| James Bevoyre of Jersey, Merchant Alien | 19 | butt | Wine, Seck | 0 | 0 | 0 | 0 |

The Katheren aforesaid, *2nd January 1595*

| James Bevoyre of Jersey, Merchant Alien | 15 | ton | Raisins, *Great* | 100 | 0 | 0 | 0 |
| | 25 | C | Figs | 16 | 13 | 4 | 0 |

Merchant name	Qty	Unit	Commodity	£	s.	d.	f.

The Pellican of Bremen, burden 80 tons, Henry Vanleighe master, from Sanlúcar de Barrameda, *2nd January 1595*

Abraham Vanherwick of London,
Merchant & Company Alien

	60	tun	Oil, Seville[10]	600	0	0	0

The Pellican of Bremen aforesaid, *2nd January 1595*

Christopher Gatsede of Middelburg,
Merchant Alien

	16	butt	Wine, Seck	0	0	0	0
	2	pipe	Wine, Bastard	0	0	0	0

The Red Lyon of Haarlem, burden 130 ton, Simon Clawson master, from Sanlúcar de Barrameda, *2nd January 1595*

Richard Stap[ ] of London, Merchant Ind

	130	butt	Wine, Seck	0	0	0	0
	28	hogshead	Wine, Bastard	0	0	0	0

The Red Lyon aforesaid, *2nd January 1595*

Richard Powell of Bristol, Merchant Ind

	10	butt	Wine, Seck	0	0	0	0

The Red Lyon aforesaid, *2nd January 1595*

Simon Clawson, *Master* Alien

	4	butt	Wine, Seck	0	0	0	0
	2	pipe	Wine, Bastard	0	0	0	0

The Red Lyon aforesaid, *2nd January 1595*

Richard Stap of London, Merchant Ind

	15	ton	Raisins, *Great*	100	0	0	0
	11.75	ton	Figs	156	13	4	0
	7.5	ton	Figs	100	0	0	0

The Red Lyon aforesaid, *2nd January 1595*

Simon Clawson, Master Alien

	300	piece	Raisins, *Rotta*	85	0	0	0
	25	C	Figs	16	13	4	0
	2	M	Canes[11]	0	0	0	0

The John of Barnstaple, burden 40 tons, Richard Haynes master, from Bordeaux, *2nd January 1595*

John Barker & Hugh Griffiths of Bristol
Merchants & Company Ind

	29	tun	Wine, Bordeaux	0	0	0	0

The John aforesaid, 2nd January 1595

John Barker & John Griffiths of Bristol
Merchants Ind

	3	tun	Honey	36	0	0	0
	1	tun	Vinegar	2	6	8	0

10 Another apparent error in the total value given by the surveyor. This should be £480.   11 Custom exempt.

Merchant name	Qty	Unit	Commodity	£	s.	d.	f.
The John aforesaid, *2nd January 1595*							
Hugh Griffiths of Bristol, Merchant Ind	3	tun	Honey	36	0	0	0
The John aforesaid, *2nd January 1595*							
Daniel Baker of Bristol, Merchant Ind	2	tun	Honey	24	0	0	0
The Pellican of Bristol, burden 40 tons, Mathew Whittson master, from Bordeaux, *2nd January 1595*							
William Ellis & John Oliver of Bristol, Merchants & Company Ind	27	tun	Wine, Bordeaux	0	0	0	0
The Pellican aforesaid, *2nd January 1595*							
John Barker of Bristol Merchants & Company Ind	1	tun	Vinegar	2	6	8	0
The Pellican aforesaid, *2nd January 1595*							
William Ellis of Bristol, Merchant Ind	3	tun	Honey	36	0	0	0
The Pellican aforesaid, *2nd January 1595*							
Mathew Hickman of Bristol, Merchant Ind	5	tierce	Honey	10	0	0	0
The Pellican of Bremen aforesaid, 7th January 1595							
Abraham Vanherwick of London, Merchants & Company Alien	30	tun	Oil, Seville[12]	300	0	0	0
The Amity of Bristol, burden 20 tons, James Whittinge master, from St-Jean-de-Luz, 13th January 1595							
Hugh Griffiths of Bristol, Merchant Ind	12	cake	Pitch & Rosin	2	0	0	0
	3	C	Wool, Spanish Hat	12	10	0	0
	1	ton	Iron, Spanish	4	0	0	0
The Amity of Bristol aforesaid, *13th January 1595*							
John Barker of Bristol, Merchant Ind	4.5	C	Wool, Spanish Hat	18	15	0	0
	12	cake	Pitch & Rosin	2	0	0	0
	1	ton	Iron, Spanish	4	0	0	0
The Amity of Bristol aforesaid, *13th January 1595*							
John Draper of Bristol, Merchant Ind	0.5	tun	Honey	6	0	0	0

12 Probable error for £240. The total custom appears to be correct at £12.

Merchant name	Qty	Unit	Commodity	£	s.	d.	f.

The Amity of Bristol aforesaid, *13th January 1595*

| John Boulton of Bristol, Merchant Ind | 2 | tun | Honey | 24 | 0 | 0 | 0 |

The Amity of Bristol aforesaid, *13th January 1595*

| John Whittson of Bristol, Merchant Ind | 0.5 | tun | Honey | 6 | 0 | 0 | 0 |

The Amity of Bristol aforesaid, *13th January 1595*

| Mathew Haviland of Bristol, Merchant Ind | 0.5 | tun | Honey | 6 | 0 | 0 | 0 |
| | 1 | C | Fish Teeth | 1 | 0 | 0 | 0 |

The Amity of Bristol aforesaid, *13th January 1595*

| John Younge of Bristol, Merchant Ind | 0.5 | tun | Honey | 6 | 0 | 0 | 0 |

The Amity aforesaid, *13th January 1595*

| William Coole of Bristol, Merchant Ind | 0.5 | tun | Honey | 6 | 0 | 0 | 0 |

The Amity aforesaid, *13th January 1595*

| Thomas Hopkins of Bristol, Merchant Ind | 1 | tun | Honey | 12 | 0 | 0 | 0 |

The Amity aforesaid, *13th January 1595*

William Ellis of Bristol, Merchant Ind	48	cake	Pitch & Rosin	8	0	0	0
	5	ton	Iron, Spanish	20	0	0	0
	3.5	C	Liquorice	1	15	0	0
	4	C	Sumach	2	13	4	0
	3	C	Wool, Spanish Hat	12	10	0	0
	3.5	tun	Honey	42	0	0	0

The Petter of Middelburg, burden, 100 tons, Peter Kinge master, from Cadiz, *13th January 1595*

| Cornell Monox of Middelburg, Merchant Alien | 150 | piece | Raisins, *Rotta* | 30 | 0 | 0 | 0 |

The Petter aforesaid, *13th January 1595*

| Cornell Monox of Middelburg, Merchant Alien | 176 | butt | Wine, Seck | 0 | 0 | 0 | 0 |
| | 2 | butt | Wine, Seck[13] | 0 | 0 | 0 | 0 |

The Red Lyon aforesaid, *13th January 1595*

| Simon Clawson, Alien | 28 | C | Canes | 4 | 13 | 4 | 0 |

13 Custom exempt.

Merchant name	Qty	Unit	Commodity	£	s.	d.	f.

The Blacke Swane, *Port Unknown*, William Swanley master, from Waterford, 15th January 1595

Thomas Hasell of London, Merchant Ind	7	C	Skins, Morkin & Sheep Broken	2	6	8	0
	1	C	*Irish* Frieze *Cloth*	2	0	0	0
	1	C	*Irish* Linen *Cloth*	0	25	0	0
	7	piece	Caddows	3	10	0	0

The Mary of Bristol, burden 16 tons, John Wattes master, from Cork, 16th January 1595

John Wattes of Bristol, Merchant Ind	1	last	Fish, Hake	6	0	0	0

The Mary aforesaid, *16th January 1594*

William Borne of Bristol, Merchant Ind	6	barrel	Fish, Hake	3	0	0	0

The Elizabeth Bonaventure, *Port Unknown*, burden 50 tons, John Genet master, from the Sea,[14] *16th January 1595*

John Hopkins of Bristol, Merchant & Company Ind	5	pipe	Wine, Robe Davy	0	0	0	0

The Minikin of Bristol, burden 18 tons, William Slack master, from Waterford, *16th January 1595*

Adam Benion of Bristol, Merchant Ind	6	barrel	Fish, Hake	3	0	0	0

The Minikin aforesaid, *16th January 1595*

Thomas Edye of Bristol, Merchant Ind	10	barrel	Fish, Hake	5	0	0	0

The Daysey of Bristol, burden 30 tons, Richard Presons master, from Saõ Miguel, *16th January 1594*

John Gittins of Bristol, Merchant & Company Ind	23	ton	Woad, Green	230	0	0	0

The Blacke Swane aforesaid, *16th January 1595*

Giles Harris of Westbury, Merchant Ind	6	barrel	Fish, Hake	3	0	0	0

The Blacke Swane aforesaid, *16th January 1595*

Francis Garway of London, Merchant Ind	20	barrel	Fish, Hake	16	0	0	0
	24	piece	Caddows	12	0	0	0
	2	piece	Caddows[15]	0	20	0	0
	1	C	Check *Cloth*	2	0	0	0

14 See note 7.   15 Custom exempt.

Merchant name	Qty	Unit	Commodity	£	s.	d.	f.

The Elizabeth of Gloucester, burden 30 tons, John Swanley master, from Youghal, 17th January 1594

| John Swanley of Youghal, Master Ind | 1 | last | Fish, Hake | 6 | 0 | 0 | 0 |

The Blacke Swane aforesaid, *17th January 1595*

| James Goodman of Bristol, Merchant Ind | 6 | barrel | Fish, Hake | 3 | 0 | 0 | 0 |

The Martha of Bristol, 92 tons, John Baker master, from Bordeaux, *17th January 1594*

| John Barnes, John Younge & Robert Aldworth of Bristol, Merchants & Company Ind | 78.41 | tun | Wine, Bordeaux | 0 | 0 | 0 | 0 |

The Martha aforesaid, *17th January 1595*

| John Barnes of Bristol, Merchant Ind | 4 | tun | Honey | 48 | 0 | 0 | 0 |
| | 3 | ton | Iron | 12 | 0 | 0 | 0 |

The Martha aforesaid, *17th January 1595*

| John Fownes of Bristol, Merchant Ind | 1 | tun | Honey | 12 | 0 | 0 | 0 |

The Martha aforesaid, *17th January 1595*

| Thomas Whitt of Bristol, Merchant Ind | 1 | tun | Honey | 12 | 0 | 0 | 0 |

The Martha aforesaid, *17th January 1595*

| William Wickam of Bristol, Merchant Ind | 3 | tun | Honey | 36 | 0 | 0 | 0 |

The Martha aforesaid, *17th January 1595*

| Arthur Hibbons of Bristol, Merchant Ind | 1 | tun | Honey | 12 | 0 | 0 | 0 |
| | 1 | ton | Prunes | 10 | 0 | 0 | 0 |

The John of Bristol, burden 16 tons, Christopher Burckett master, from Youghal, *17th January 1594*

| Christopher Burkett of Bristol, Merchant Ind | 10 | stone | Wool, Irish | 2 | 10 | 0 | 0 |
| | 30 | stone | Wool, Flocks | 2 | 10 | 0 | 0 |

The Blacke Swane aforesaid, *17th January 1595*

| Christopher Scalles of London, Merchant Ind | 2 | C | Check *Cloth* | 4 | 0 | 0 | 0 |
| | 8 | piece | Caddows | 4 | 0 | 0 | 0 |

The Blacke Swane aforesaid, *17th January 1595*

| Richard Hughes of Tewkesbury, Merchant Ind | 13 | barrel | Fish, Hake | 6 | 10 | 0 | 0 |

Merchant name	Qty	Unit	Commodity	£	s.	d.	f.
The Blacke Swane aforesaid, *17th January 1595*							
John A[]rpin of Tewkesbury, Merchant Ind	3	barrel	Fish, Hake	1	10	0	0
The Blacke Swane aforesaid, *17th January 1595*							
John Cave of Tewkesbury, Merchant Ind	3	barrel	Fish, Hake	1	10	0	0
The Blacke Swane aforesaid, *17th January 1595*							
Hugh Aldworth of Tewkesbury, Merchant Ind	3	barrel	Fish, Hake	1	10	0	0
The Blacke Swane aforesaid, 17th January 1595							
Henry Howell of Tewkesbury, Merchant Ind	10	barrel	Fish, Hake	5	0	0	0
The Josephe of Bristol, burden 80 tons, Thomas Rice master, from Toulon, 20th January 1595							
Mathew Haviland & William Ellis of Bristol Merchants & Company Ind	6	ton	Alum	200	0	0	0
	12	tun	Oil, *Olive*	96	0	0	0
	8	M	Canes	13	6	8	0
	26	C	Seed, Cumin	34	13	4	0
	20	C	Cotton *Cloth*	66	13	4	0
	5	C	Aniseed	6	13	4	0
The Josephe aforesaid, 20th January 1595							
George Allam of Bristol, Merchant & Company Ind	35	C	Raisins, Gallipola	11	13	4	0
	1	tun	Oil, *Olive*	8	0	0	0
	3.9	M	Canes	6	10	0	0
The Petter aforesaid, *20th January 1595*							
Peter Kinge Unknown, Master Ind	18	butt	Wine, Seck	0	0	0	0
The Jonas of Jersey, burden 18 tons, Peter Brocke master, from St Malo, 23rd January 1595							
John Mercer of Hampton, Merchant Alien	140	piece	Raisins, Malaga	36	13	8	0
The Jonas aforesaid, *23rd January 1595*							
Michael Mingartt of St Malo, Merchant Alien	260	piece	Raisins, Malaga	70	0	0	0
	8	C	Raisins, of the Sun	6	13	4	0
	13	C	Aniseed	17	6	8	0
	25	C	Soap, Castille	18	15	0	0

Merchant name	Qty	Unit	Commodity	£	s.	d.	f.

The Seaflower of Jersey, burden 18 tons, George Buttler master, from St Malo, *23rd January 1595*

James Beavoyre of Jersey, Merchant Ind?	24	C	Figs	16	0	0	0
	7.5	tun	Oil, *Olive*	60	0	0	0
	4	fardel	Vitry Canvas *Cloth*	20	0	0	0

The Seaflower of Jersey aforesaid, 23rd January 1595

| James Beavoyre of Jersey, Merchant Ind? | 18 | butt | Wine, Seck | 0 | 0 | 0 | 0 |

The Dove of Bristol, burden 40 tons, Tobias Pis? from Alderney, 4th February 1595

| Thomas Brumley & Benedict Harvey of Bristol Merchants Ind | 25 | ton | Salt | 25 | 0 | 0 | 0 |

The Jonas of Dungarvan, burden 30 tons, Philip Nogle master, from Dungarvan, 10th February 1595

| Philip Nogle of Dungarvan, Merchant Ind | 5 | C | Skins, Morkin & Sheep Broken | 1 | 13 | 8 | 0 |

The Mary of Wexford, burden 6 tons, Philip Roche master, from Wexford, 17th February 1595

Philip Kettinge of Wexford, Merchant Ind	9	stone	Wool, Flocks	0	15	0	0
	6	stone	Wool, Irish	1	10	0	0
	6	piece	Coveringe	3	0	0	0
	1.5	C	Skins, Morkin & Sheep Broken	0	10	0	0
	1	hogshead	Fish, Salmon	3	0	0	0

The Hope of Emden, burden 120 tons, Gareth Egber master, from Kinsale, *17th February 1595*

| William Chapell of Bristol, Merchant Ind | 170 | quart | Wheat/Rye | 46 | 13 | 4 | 0 |

The Mary of Wexford, burden 8 tons, Richard Cod[] master, from Wexford, 18th February 1595

Melcher Stafford of Wexford, Merchant Ind	8	barrel	Fish, Hake	4	0	0	0
	14	stone	Wool, Flocks	1	3	2	0
	4.5	C	Skins, Morkin & Sheep Broken	1	10	0	0

The Sallomon of Bristol, burden 16 tons, Thomas Coblin master, from Glandore, 19th February 1595

| William Chapell of Bristol, Merchant Ind | 40 | stone | Wool, Flocks | 3 | 6 | 8 | 0 |
| | 50 | yard | Irish Frieze *Cloth*, Raw | 1 | 0 | 0 | 0 |

Merchant name	Qty	Unit	Commodity	£	s.	d.	f.

The Sallomon aforesaid, *19th February 1595*

Coronall? Williams, Merchant Ind	40	stone	Wool, Irish	10	0	0	0

The Lilly of Bristol, burden 30 tons, Hugh Jones master, from La Rochelle, *19th February 1595*

John Gourninge of Bristol, Merchant & Company Ind	300	piece	Raisins, Malaga	75	0	0	0
	3	hogshead	Oil, *Olive*	6	0	0	0

The Lilly aforesaid, *19th February 1595*

John Browne of Bristol, Merchant Ind	160	cake	Pitch & Rosin	26	13	4	0
	2	hogshead	Oil, *Olive*	4	0	0	0

The Lilly aforesaid, *19th February 1595*

Robert Colstone of Bristol, Merchant Ind	1	last	Tar	2	0	0	0
	18	C	Prunes	9	0	0	0
	1	ton	Iron, Spanish	4	0	0	0
	2	tun	Oil, *Olive*	16	0	0	0

The Lilly aforesaid, *19th February 1595*

Hugh Jones of London, Merchant Ind	1	tun	Oil, *Olive*	8	0	0	0

The Trinittie of Bristol, burden 12 tons, Thomas Davis master, from Youghal, 21st February 1595

William Horley of Kilmallock, Merchant Ind	11	C	Skins, Morkin & Sheep Broken	3	13	4	0
	6	piece	Rugg, *Irish*	3	0	0	0
	0.5	C	*Irish* Linen *Cloth*	0	13	4	0
	20	yard	Canvas *Cloth*	0	5	0	0

The Trinittie of Bristol aforesaid, 21st February 1595

Henry Exa[]m of Mallow, Merchant Ind	6	C	Skins, Coney	0	15	0	0

The Trinittie of Bristol aforesaid, 21st February 1595

William Hughes of Carleon, Merchant Ind	5	stone	Wool, Flocks	0	8	4	0
	2	stone	Wool, Irish	0	10	0	0

The Sallomon of Elmore, burden 14 tons, William Griffiths master, from Youghal, 24th February 1595

John Kernie of Youghal, Merchant Ind	24	stone	Wool, Flocks	2	0	0	0
	6	C	Skins, Morkin & Sheep Broken	2	0	0	0
	6	barrel	Fish, Hake	3	0	0	0

Merchant name	Qty	Unit	Commodity	£	s.	d.	f.

The Hercules of Bristol, burden 50 tons, Thomas Bennet master, from *Larmoster*, 25th February 1595

Merchant name	Qty	Unit	Commodity	£	s.	d.	f.
Mary Gitton of Bristol, Widow Ind	1	fardel	Vitry Canvas *Cloth*	5	0	0	0

The Hercules aforesaid, *25th February 1595*

Merchant name	Qty	Unit	Commodity	£	s.	d.	f.
John Collimore of Bristol, Merchant Ind	2	fardel	Vitry Canvas *Cloth*	10	0	0	0

The Hercules aforesaid, *25th February 1595*

Merchant name	Qty	Unit	Commodity	£	s.	d.	f.
Christopher Pitt, of Bristol, Merchant Ind	8	ton	Salt	8	0	0	0

The Mayflower of Bristol, burden 90 tons, Andrew Batten master, from Youghal, *25th February 1595*

Merchant name	Qty	Unit	Commodity	£	s.	d.	f.
Edward Lewis of Bristol, Merchant & Company Ind	6	tun	Wine, French	0	0	0	0

The Mayflower of Bristol aforesaid, *25th February 1595*

Merchant name	Qty	Unit	Commodity	£	s.	d.	f.
Richard & Edward Lewis of Bristol, Merchants & Company Ind	100	barrel	Tar	16	13	4	0
	3	C	Prunes	1	10	0	0
	100	cake	Pitch & Rosin	16	13	4	0

The Mayflower of Bristol aforesaid, *25th February 1595*

Merchant name	Qty	Unit	Commodity	£	s.	d.	f.
William Ellis of Bristol, Merchant Ind	1.5	tun	Oil, *Olive*	12	0	0	0

The Mayflower of Bristol aforesaid, *25th February 1595*

Merchant name	Qty	Unit	Commodity	£	s.	d.	f.
Edward Lewis of Bristol, Merchant Ind	8	ton	Salt	8	0	0	0

The Falcon of Milford Haven, burden 20 tons, Hugh Moore master, from Ayamonte, 1st March 1595

Merchant name	Qty	Unit	Commodity	£	s.	d.	f.
George Whitt of Bristol, Merchant & Company Ind	6	tun	Oil, Seville	48	0	0	0
	3.75	ton	Figs	50	0	0	0
	19	butt	Wine, Seck	0	0	0	0

The John of Bristol, burden 14 tons, Christopher Burkett master, from Youghal, 3rd March 1595

Merchant name	Qty	Unit	Commodity	£	s.	d.	f.
Christopher Burkett of Bristol, Merchant & Company Ind	4	C	*Melton & Luige*[16]	4	0	0	0
	15	C	Skins, Coney	2	1	0	0
	15	stone	Wool, Irish	3	15	0	0

16 Unidentified.

Merchant name	Qty	Unit	Commodity	£	s.	d.	f.

The John of Bristol aforesaid, *3rd March 1595*

John Kernie of Youghal, Merchant Ind	2	C	Skins, Morkin	0	13	4	0
	9	barrel	Fish, Hake	4	10	0	0

The William of London, burden 40 tons, Nathan Harrison master, *from the Sea*, 4th March 1595

Merchant name	Qty	Unit	Commodity	£	s.	d.	f.
William Savill of London, Merchant & Company Ind	307	piece	Hides, India	153	10	0	0
	386	ell	Hamborough & Portingale *Cloth*	13	10	0	0
	1115	ell	Vitry Canvas *Cloth*	18	10	0	0
	43	yard	Stiped Canvas Cloth	1	15	0	0
	1	sutt?	Curtains & Testers, Network	0	13	4	0
	3	piece	Cauls of Fine Lawns for Women	0	10	0	0
	8	yard	White Buffin *Cloth*	0	13	4	0
	18.5	yard	Testers & Curtains, Coarse Drapery	2	0	0	0
	21	pair	Chappines, of gilt & leather for women's slippers	0	10	0	0
	1	pair	Blace bendels?	0	3	4	0
	9	dozen	Knives, Coarse	1	0	0	0
	14	dozen	Venice Earthen Dishes	0	0	0	0
	2	piece	Basins, Large	0	0	0	0
	34	piece	Dishes & Saucers	6	6	8	0
	9	ream	Paper, Coarse	1	0	0	0
	42	M	Pins	1	13	4	0
	18	ell	Coarse Holland *Cloth*	6	13	4	0
	1	piece	Woollen Russett Portingale *Cloth*	11	0	0	0
	0.5	C	Soap, Castille	0	7	6	0
	0.5	C	Raisins, of the Sun	0	8	4	0
	12	piece	Spanish Shirts	1	6	8	0
	7	piece	Doublets	3	10	0	0
	7	pair	Sheets, Coarse	0	16	8	0
	2	dozen	Girdles & Hangers	1	0	0	0
	40	unknown	Kerchers[17] for women of *ntadell* Cloth	1	0	0	0
	3	piece	Tape, Coarse	0	3	4	0
	8	piece	Table Napkins	0	3	4	0
	11	piece	Diaper Cloth	2	1	8	0
	2	lb	Pepper	0	3	4	0
	4	dozen	Cards	0	5	0	0
	3	pair	Sheets	1	5	0	0
	1	pair	Sheets, Holland	1	6	8	0
	1	cake	Pitch & Rosin	0	3	4	0

17 Kerchiefs.

Merchant name	Qty	Unit	Commodity	£	s.	d.	f.

The Mary of Bristol, burden 16 tons, William Manfield master, from Cork, 7th March 1595

Richard Aylise of Overton, Merchant Ind	40	stone	Wool, Flocks	3	6	8	0
	2	piece	Irish Fustian *Cloth*	1	6	8	0

The Peter of Milford Haven, burden 16 tons, John Devery master, from Waterford, 14th March 1595

Nicholas Lea of Waterford, Merchant Ind	4	C	*Irish* Frieze *Cloth*	8	0	0	0
	3	C	*Irish* Linen *Cloth*	3	15	0	0
	20	piece	Coveringe	10	0	0	0
	2	M	Skins, Morkin & Sheep Broken	6	13	4	0
	50	lb	Marmalade	2	6	8	0

The Younge Tobias of Gdańsk, burden 200 tons, Nicholas Asbrand master, from the Canary Islands, 21st March 1595

Thomas Cottellis of London, Merchant & Company Alien	100	pipe	Wine, Canaries	0	0	0	0

The Younge Tobias aforesaid, *21st March 1595*

George Collimore of London, Merchant Ind	40	pipe	Wine, Canaries	0	0	0	0

The Younge Tobias aforesaid, 3rd April 1595

Veronius Martine of London, Merchant & Company Alien	18	pipe	Wine, Canaries	0	0	0	0
	3	hogshead	Wine, Canaries	0	0	0	0

The Younge Tobias aforesaid, 4th April 1595

Veronius Martine of London, Merchant & Company Alien	50	pipe	Wine, Canaries	0	0	0	0
	1	hogshead	Molasses[18]	0	0	0	0
	1	case	Sugar, Panele[19]	0	0	0	0

The Younge Tobias aforesaid, 8th April 1595

Veronius Martine of London, Merchant & Company Alien	60	pipe	Wine, Canaries	0	0	0	0

The Younge Tobias aforesaid, 10th April 1595

Veronius Martine of London, Merchant & Company Alien	60	pipe	Wine, Canaries	0	0	0	0

The Petter of Cardiff, burden 18 tons, Thomas Robins master, from Cardiff, 11th April 1595

Philip Nicholas of Cardiff, Merchant Ind	5	barrel	*Iare*[20]	0	16	4	0

18 Custom exempt. 19 Custom exempt. 20 Unidentified.

Merchant name	Qty	Unit	Commodity	£	s.	d.	f.

The Grace of Bristol, burden 18 tons, Stephen Buckhall, from St-Jean-de-Luz, 24th April 1595

William Ellis of Bristol, Merchant Ind	4	ton	Iron, Spanish	16	0	0	0
	6	C	Wool, Spanish Hat	25	0	0	0

The Grace aforesaid, *24th April 1595*

John Samford of Bristol, Merchant Ind	3	ton	Iron, Spanish	12	0	0	0

The Grace aforesaid, *24th April 1595*

Michael Pepwall of Bristol, Merchant Ind	3	ton	Iron, Spanish	12	0	0	0

The Grace aforesaid, *24th April 1595*

John Barker of Bristol, Merchant Ind	7.5	C	Wool, Spanish Hat	31	5	0	0

The Grace aforesaid, *24th April 1595*

William Powell & Mathew Hickman of Bristol, Merchants Ind	160		*Cakes*	26	13	4	0

The Grace aforesaid, *24th April 1595*

William Powell & Mathew Hickman of Bristol, Merchants Ind	3	C	Liquorice	1	10	0	0

The Minikine of Bristol, burden 18 tons, William Slack master, from Waterford, *24th April 1595*

Thomas Pembrocke of Kilkenny, Merchant Ind	5	M	Skins, Morkin & Sheep Broken	16	13	4	0
	2	C	Check *Cloth*	4	0	0	0
	0.5	C	*Irish* Frieze *Cloth*	1	0	0	0
	1	C	Whale Fins	1	13	4	0
	5	C	Unknown	1	13	4	0
	2	piece	Coveringe	1	0	0	0

The Minikine aforesaid, *24th April 1595*

John Howlett of Bristol, Merchant Ind	10[21]	M	Skins, Morkin & Sheep Broken	3	6	8	0

The Minikine aforesaid, *24th April 1595*

Edward Walshe of Waterford, Merchant Ind	0.5	C	*Irish* Frieze *Cloth*	1	0	0	0
	10	piece	Caddows	5	0	0	0
	4	piece	Mantles	1	0	0	0

21 Error in the value or the quantity as 10 M would have a value of £33. 6s. 8d.

Merchant name	Qty	Unit	Commodity	£	s.	d.	f.

The Whitt Beare of Hull, burden 50 tons, William Pheleps master, from Bordeaux, 24th April 1595

| Thomas Whitt & John Fownes of Bristol, Merchants & Company Ind | 38 | tun | Wine, Gascon | 0 | 0 | 0 | 0 |

The Whitt Beare aforesaid, *24th April 1595*

| William Vawer of Bristol, Merchant Ind | 28 | C | Prunes | *14* | *0* | *0* | *0* |
| | 60 | cake | Rosin | *10* | *0* | *0* | *0* |

The Whitt Beare aforesaid, *24th April 1595*

| John Samford of Bristol, Merchant Ind | 14 | C | Prunes | 7 | 0 | 0 | 0 |

The Whitt Beare aforesaid, *24th April 1595*

| Mary Gitton of Bristol, Widow Ind | 6.5 | C | Prunes | 3 | 5 | 0 | 0 |

The Whitt Beare aforesaid, *24th April 1595*

| John Fownes of Bristol, Merchant Ind | 4 | C | Prunes | 2 | 0 | 0 | 0 |

The Whitt Beare aforesaid, *24th April 1595*

| John Angell of Bristol, Merchant Ind | 8.5 | C | Prunes | *4* | *5* | *0* | *0* |
| | 20 | cake | Rosin | *3* | *6* | *8* | *0* |

The Rose of Bristol, burden 16 tons, Robert Venicombe master, from Waterford, *24th April 1595*

Nicholas Everet of Limerick, Merchant Ind	1	M	Skins, Morkin & Sheep Broken	*3*	*6*	*8*	*0*
	2	C	*Irish* Linen *Cloth*	*2*	*10*	*0*	*0*
	1	C	Canvas *Cloth*	*1*	*5*	*0*	*0*
	3	piece	Mantles	*0*	*15*	*0*	*0*

The Rose aforesaid, *24th April 1595*

George Richards of Bristol, Glover Ind	1.5	C	Skins, Morkin	0	10	0	0
	2	pipe	Wines	0	0	0	0
	1	butt	Wine, Seck	0	0	0	0

The Keale of Brest, burden 30 tons, Peter John master, from *Larmuster*, *24th April 1595*

| Christopher Harlinson of Middelburg, Merchant Alien | 25 | ton | Salt | *25* | *0* | *0* | *0* |
| | 2 | hogshead | Oil, Train | *2* | *10* | *0* | *0* |

Merchant name	Qty	Unit	Commodity	£	s.	d.	f.

The John of Bristol, burden 18 tons, Christopher Burkett master, from Youghal, *24th April 1595*

Merchant name	Qty	Unit	Commodity	£	s.	d.	f.
Tessicke Berii of Youghal, Merchant Alien	6.5	case	Glass	3	0	0	0
	4	C	Skins, Coney	0	10	0	0
	2	C	Skins, Morkin	0	13	4	0

The St Anthony of Lisbon, burden 40 tons, Thomas Haltin master, from the Sea, *24th April 1595*

Merchant name	Qty	Unit	Commodity	£	s.	d.	f.
Alan Tompson of London, Merchant & Company Ind	100	chest	Sugar, Moscavado & White	1000	0	0	0
	300	C	Sugar, Panele de Brasell	500	0	0	0
	3	C	*Orrice*[22]	2	5	0	0
	1.5	C	Conserves	6	18	4	0
	15	C	Molasses	7	10	0	0
	18	C	Sugar, Panele[23]	0	0	0	0

The Diamount of Bristol, burden 50 tons, Christopher Taillor master, from Ilfracombe, 30th April 1595

Merchant name	Qty	Unit	Commodity	£	s.	d.	f.
George Whitt of Bristol, Merchant Ind	20	cake	Pitch & Rosin	3	6	8	0
	3	tierce	Honey	6	0	0	0

The Diamount aforesaid, *30th April 1595*

Merchant name	Qty	Unit	Commodity	£	s.	d.	f.
Thomas Hopkins of Bristol, Merchant Ind	20	cake	Pitch & Rosin	3	6	8	0

The Diamount aforesaid, *30th April 1595*

Merchant name	Qty	Unit	Commodity	£	s.	d.	f.
John Slye of Bristol, Soapmaker Ind	20	cake	Pitch & Rosin	3	6	8	0

The Angell of Fethard-on-Sea, burden 16 tons, Mathew Hawlen master, from Fethard-on-Sea, 2nd March 1595

Merchant name	Qty	Unit	Commodity	£	s.	d.	f.
John Roche of Limerick, Merchant Ind	1	M	Skins, Morkin & Sheep Broken	3	6	8	0
	3	C	*Irish* Linen *Cloth*	3	15	0	0
	3	piece	Mantles	0	15	0	0

The Dove of Bristol, burden 40 tons, Richard P[]sons master, from La Rochelle, 8th May 1595

Merchant name	Qty	Unit	Commodity	£	s.	d.	f.
John Barker of Bristol, Merchant & Company Ind	30.5	tun	Wine, French	0	0	0	0

The Dove aforesaid, *8th May 1595*

Merchant name	Qty	Unit	Commodity	£	s.	d.	f.
William Hopkins of Bristol, Merchant Ind	8	C	Prunes	4	0	0	0
	2	ton	Iron	8	0	0	0
	4	bale	Writing Paper	5	6	8	0

22 Unidentified.　23 Wet & spoiled.

Merchant name	Qty	Unit	Commodity	£	s.	d.	f.
The Dove aforesaid, *8th May 1595*							
Thomas Hopkins of Bristol, Merchant Ind	8	C	Prunes	4	0	0	0
The Dove aforesaid, *8th May 1595*							
Vincent Collson of Bristol, Merchant Ind	8	C	Prunes	*4*	*0*	*0*	*0*
	3	bale	Paper	*4*	*0*	*0*	*0*
The Dove aforesaid, *8th May 1595*							
Robert Pendigrese of Bristol, Merchant Ind	12	C	Prunes	6	0	0	0
The Dove aforesaid, *8th May 1595*							
George Whitt of Bristol, Merchant Ind	8	C	Prunes	4	0	0	0
The Dove aforesaid, *8th May 1595*							
Thomas Brumley of Bristol, Merchant Ind	4	C	Prunes	*2*	*0*	*0*	*0*
	3	ton	Iron	*12*	*0*	*0*	*0*
The Lillie of Bristol, burden 30 tons, Hugh Jones master, from La Rochelle, *8th May 1595*							
John Browne of Bristol, Merchant Ind	1	ton	Iron	4	0	0	0
The Lillie aforesaid, *8th May 1595*							
John Gunninge of Bristol, Merchant Ind	10	C	Prunes	*5*	*0*	*0*	*0*
	5	bale	Paper	*6*	*13*	*4*	*0*
	40	piece	Rosin	*6*	*13*	*4*	*0*
	14	ton	Salt	*14*	*0*	*0*	*0*
The Lillie aforesaid, *8th May 1595*							
William Ellis of Bristol, Merchant Ind	1.5	tun	Oil, *Olive*	12	0	0	0
The Lillie aforesaid, *8th May 1595*							
John Barker of Bristol, Merchant & Company Ind	9.25	tun	Wine, French	0	0	0	0
The Jane of *Ile de Ars*, **burden 40 tons, Peter Rowland master, from** *Burnife,* 10th May 1595							
Geoffrey Gitton of Bristol, Merchant Ind	30	ton	Salt	*30*	*0*	*0*	*0*
	4	fardel	Vitry Canvas *Cloth*	*20*	*0*	*0*	*0*
The Jane of *Ile de Ars*, **burden 30 tons, Lewis Lodowick master, from** *Burnife,* 10th May 1595							
Geoffrey Gitton of Bristol, Merchant Ind	25	ton	Salt	25	0	0	0

Merchant name	Qty	Unit	Commodity	£	s.	d.	f.

The Petter of *Ile de Ars*, burden 25 tons, Bernard Bennett master, from *Burnife*, 10th May 1595

Geoffrey Gitton of Bristol, Merchant Ind	20	ton	Salt	20	0	0	0

The Petter of Barnstaple, burden 20 tons, Richard Westiford master, from St Jean-de-Luz, 12th May 1595

William Ellis, William Vavre, John Draper, Hugh Griffith, John Coliberde, of Bristol & Barnstaple

Merchants Ind	10	ton	Iron	40	0	0	0

The Petter aforesaid, *12th May 1595*

Mathew Haviland of Bristol, Merchant Ind	3	C	Sea Horse Teeth[24]	3	0	0	0
	2	C	Soap, Castille	1	10	0	0

The Petter aforesaid, *12th May 1595*

Thomas Taillor of Bristol, Merchant Ind	15	cake	Pitch	2	10	0	0

The Rowe Buck of Bristol, burden 40 tons, Morgan Howell master, from Penmarch, 13th May 1595

William Ellis & John Whittson of Bristol,

Merchants Ind	6	ton	Alum	200	0	0	0
	14.75	tun	Oil, *Olive*	118	0	0	0
	20	C	Currants	30	0	0	0
	25	C	Liquorice	12	10	0	0
	15	C	Aniseed	20	0	0	0
	3.5	M	Canes	5	16	4	0

The Daisey of Bristol, burden 40 tons, Henry Lewis master, from Brest, *13th May 1595*

Edward Benttley of Bristol, Merchant Ind	47.5	piece	Dowlas & Lockram Cloth	79	3	4	0

The Daisey aforesaid, *13th May 1595*

Christopher Carry of Bristol, Merchant Ind	15	piece	Dowlas & Lockram Cloth	25	0	0	0

The Daisey aforesaid, *13th May 1595*

John Collimore of Bristol, Merchant Ind	20	piece	Dowlas & Lockram Cloth	33	6	8	0

24 Hippopothamus teeth, for ivory

Merchant name	Qty	Unit	Commodity	£	s.	d.	f.
The Daisey aforesaid, *13th May 1595*							
William Benger of Bristol, Merchant Ind	35	piece	Dowlas & Lockram *Cloth*	58	6	8	0
The Daisey aforesaid, *13th May 1595*							
John Love of Bristol, Merchant Ind	40	piece	Dowlas & Lockram *Cloth*	66	13	4	0
The Daisey aforesaid, *13th May 1595*							
Richard Batt of Bristol, Merchant Ind	70	piece	Dowlas & Lockram *Cloth*	116	13	8	0
The Daisey aforesaid, *14th May 1595*							
John Redinge & Benjamin Mannsell of Bristol Merchants Ind	25	piece	Dowlas & Lockram *Cloth*	41	13	4	0
The Daisey aforesaid, *14th May 1595*							
William Walles of Bristol, Merchant Ind	17	piece	Dowlas & Lockram *Cloth*	29	3	4	0
The Daisey aforesaid, *14th May 1595*							
Edward Benttley of Bristol, Merchant Ind	27.5	piece	Dowlas & Lockram *Cloth*	45	16	8	0
The Mary of Bristol, burden 16 tons, Thomas Neale master, from Cork, *14th May 1595*							
William Craghe of Cork, Merchant Ind	18	C	Skins, Morkin & Sheep Broken	6	0	0	0
The George of Wexford, burden 8 tons, David Xevre master, from Wexford, *17th May 1595*							
Paul Furlonge of Wexford, Merchant Ind	3	tun	Wine, Seck	0	0	0	0
	1	butt	Wine, Seck	0	0	0	0
The Falcon of Gdańsk, burden 200 tons, *Master & Destination Unknown,* **20th May 1595**							
Conrad Zerenbridge, Merchant & Consort Alien	338	quart	*Cereals*	84	6	8	0
	80	quart	*Cereals* (Corrupt)	0	0	0	0
	383	quart	Wheat	127	13	4	0
	60	quart	Wheat (Corrupt)	0	0	0	0
The Jonothan of St Ives, burden 8 tons, Robert Alberie master, from St Ives, *21st May 1595*							
Robert Dudlie of Kenilworth Castle, Esquire Ind	1	tun	Wine, Spanish	0	0	0	0

Merchant name	Qty	Unit	Commodity	£	s.	d.	f.

The Nicholas of Milford Haven, burden 18 tons, William Harris master, from Waterford, 23rd May 1595

| John Whittson of Bristol, Merchant Ind | 15 | butt | Wine, Seck | 0 | 0 | 0 | 0 |

The Nicholas aforesaid, 23rd May 1595

| Thomas Wackelis of Bristol, Merchant Ind | 10 | C | Skins, Morkin & Sheep Broken | 3 | 6 | 8 | 6 |

The Nicholas aforesaid, 23rd May 1595

| John Howlett of Bristol, Glover Ind | 6 | C | Skins, Morkin & Sheep Broken | 2 | 0 | 0 | 0 |

The Minikine of Bristol, burden 18 tons, William Slacke master, from Waterford, 23rd May 1595

| John Whittson of Bristol, Merchant Ind | 16 | butt | Wine, Seck | 0 | 0 | 0 | 0 |

The Minikine aforesaid, 23rd May 1595

| Walter Archer of New Ross, Merchant Ind | 13 | piece | Caddows | 6 | 10 | 0 | 0 |
| | 6 | piece | Mantles | 1 | 10 | 0 | 0 |

The Petter of Milford Haven, burden 14 tons, John Deverx master, from Waterford, 23rd May 1595

| John Whittson of Bristol, Merchant Ind | 15 | butt | Wine, Seck | 0 | 0 | 0 | 0 |

The Thomas of Bristol, burden 23 tons, James Whittinge master, from Saõ Miguel, 23rd May 1595

| John Whittson of Bristol, Merchant Ind | 5 | ton | Woad, Green | 50 | 0 | 0 | 0 |

The Thomas of Bristol aforesaid, 23rd May 1595

| George Whitt of Bristol, Merchant Ind | 6 | ton | Woad, Green | 60 | 0 | 0 | 0 |

The Thomas of Bristol aforesaid, 23rd May 1595

| William Co[ ] of Bristol, Merchant Ind | 4 | ton | Woad, Green | 40 | 0 | 0 | 0 |

The Thomas of Bristol aforesaid, 23rd May 1595

| John Pitt of Bristol, Merchant Ind | 8 | ton | Woad, Green | 80 | 0 | 0 | 0 |

The John of Waterford, burden 18 tons, Maurice Cleere master, from Waterford, 23rd May 1595

| Thomas Baron of Clonmel, Merchant Ind | 6 | C | Skins, Morkin & Sheep Broken | 2 | 0 | 0 | 0 |
| | 2 | C | Skins, Coney | 0 | 5 | 0 | 0 |

Merchant name	Qty	Unit	Commodity	£	s.	d.	f.
The John aforesaid, *23rd May 1595*							
Thomas Daniell of Limerick, Merchant Ind	11	C	Skins, Morkin & Sheep Broken	3	13	4	0
The John aforesaid, *23rd May 1595*							
Walter Harold of Limerick, Merchant Ind	4	C	*Irish* Linen *Cloth*	5	0	0	0
	11	C	Skins, Morkin & Sheep Broken	3	13	4	0
	3	C	Kre Skins?	1	13	4	0
	3	piece	Skins, Otter	0	5	0	0
The John aforesaid, *23rd May 1595*							
Robert Roche of Limerick, Merchant Ind	10	C	Skins, Morkin & Sheep Broken	3	6	8	0
	0.5	C	*Irish* Linen *Cloth*	0	13	4	0
	3	piece	Mantles	0	15	0	0
	7	yard	White Frieze Cloth	0	5	0	0
The John aforesaid, *23rd May 1595*							
Nicholas Murphie of Kilkenny, Merchant Ind	3.5	C	Skins, Morkin & Sheep Broken	1	3	4	0
The Mary of *St Surnie,* burden 26 tons, John Movellenis, from Marennes, 30th May 1595							
John Movellenis, Merchant Alien	22	ton	Salt	22	0	0	0
The Doe of Bristol, burden 18 tons, John Lullet master, from Youghal, *30th May 1595*							
George Richards of Bristol, Merchant Ind	12	C	Skins, Morkin & Sheep Broken	4	0	0	0
	6	stone	Wool, Flocks	0	10	0	0
The Minikine aforesaid, *30th May 1595*							
George Richards of Bristol, Merchant Ind	6	C	Skins, Morkin & Sheep Broken	2	0	0	0
The Minikine aforesaid, *30th May 1595*							
John Howlett of Bristol, Glover Ind	20	C	Skins, Morkin & Sheep Broken	6	13	4	0
	3	C	*Lase*	1	6	8	0
The Mary of Wexford, burden 12 tons, John Lumbart master, from Wexford, 3rd June 1595							
David Hayes of Wexford, Merchant Ind	10	butt	Wine, Seck	0	0	0	0

Merchant name	Qty	Unit	Commodity	£	s.	d.	f.
The Mary of Wexford aforesaid, *3rd June 1595*							
David Hayes of Wexford, Merchant Ind	11	C	Skins, Morkin & Sheep Broken	3	13	4	0
	4	piece	Coveringe	2	0	0	0
	14	yard	*Irish* Frieze *Cloth*	0	5	0	0
The Elizabeth of Gloucester, burden 18 tons, Nicholas Dureinge master, from Wexford, 9th June 1595							
George Richards of Bristol, Glover Ind	11.5	M	Skins, Morkin & Sheep Broken	38	6	8	0
The Mary of Wexford, burden 6 tons, Nicholas Dureinge master, from Wexford, 12th June 1595							
Hugh Griffiths & John Barker of Bristol, Merchant Ind	9	butt	Wine, Seck	0	0	0	0
The John of Bristol, burden 16 tons, Thomas Lattim*er* master, from Youghal, 13th June 1595							
William Borne of Bristol, Merchant Ind	2	C	Skins, Cony Grey	0	5	0	0
	14	stone	Wool, Irish	3	10	0	0
	3	dozen	Glass Bottles, Coloured	1	10	0	0
The John aforesaid, *13th June 1595*							
James Copenge*r* of Bristol, Weaver Ind	10	C	Skins, Morkin & Sheep Broken	3	6	8	0
The George of Wexford, burden 8 tons, David Ewer master, from Wexford, 23rd June 1595							
Paul Furlonge of Wexford, Merchant Ind	9	butt	Wine, Seck	0	0	0	0
The George aforesaid, *23rd June 1595*							
Martin Esmound of Wexford, Merchant Ind	40	stone	Wool, Irish	10	0	0	0
	4	C	Skins, Coney Grey	0	10	0	0
	1.5	C	Skins, Sheep Broken	0	10	0	0
The Diana of Bristol, burden 22 tons, Robert Patterson master, from St Malo, 27th June 1595							
John Love & William Walles of Bristol, Merchant Ind	8	tun	Wine, *Alegant?*	0	0	0	0
The Diana aforesaid, 27th June 1595							
John Love of Bristol, Merchant Ind	3	tun	Oil, *Olive*	24	0	0	0
The Diana aforesaid, 27th June 1595							
John Merricke of Bristol, Merchant Ind	2	tun	Oil, *Olive*	16	0	0	0
	1.5	ton	Alum	50	0	0	0

Merchant name	Qty	Unit	Commodity	£	s.	d.	f.

The Diana aforesaid, 27th June 1595

| John Bisse of Bristol, Merchant Ind | 6 | tun | Oil, *Olive* | 48 | 0 | 0 | 0 |

The Diana aforesaid, 27th June 1595

| George Wilkinson of Bristol, Merchant Ind | 1 | tun | Oil, *Olive* | 8 | 0 | 0 | 0 |

The Angell of Waterford, burden 16 tons, Mathew Howlen, from Waterford, 30th June 1595

| George Richards of Bristol, Glover Ind | 4 | M | Skins, Morkin & Sheep Broken | 13 | 6 | 8 | 0 |

The Angell aforesaid, 30th June 1595

| William Wiett of Bristol, Glover Ind | 15 | C | Skins, Morkin & Sheep Broken | 5 | 0 | 0 | 0 |

The Catherine of Wexford, burden 4 tons, David Wadden master, from Wexford, 7th July 1595

Richard Deale of Wexford, Merchant Ind	2	tun	Wine, Seck	0	0	0	0
	1	butt	Wine, Corrupt	0	0	0	0
	1	butt	Wine (Hollocke?)	0	0	0	0

The Mary Catherine of Amsterdam, burden 50 tons, Andrew Tompson master, from Bordeaux, 7th July 1595

| Richard Coole & Mathew Haviland of Bristol Merchants & Company Ind | 50 | tun | Wine, Gascon | 0 | 0 | 0 | 0 |
| | 5 | tun | Wine, Gascon Leakage | 0 | 0 | 0 | 0 |

The Margarett of Padstow, burden 18 tons, John Burdwood master, from *Laseroy*, 9th July 1595

| William & Thomas Hopkins, of Bristol, Merchants Ind | 10 | hogshead | Fish, Salmon Grilse | 15 | 0 | 0 | 0 |

The Mary of La Tremblade, burden 18 tons, John de Beinon master, from La Rochelle, 9th July 1595

| John de Beinon, Merchant Alien | 15 | ton | Salt | 15 | 0 | 0 | 0 |

The Ellephaunt of *Messes*[25], burden 40 tons, Hillary Woodward master, from *Messes*, 14th July 1595

| Hillary Woodward, Merchant & Company Alien | 5 | tun | Wine, French | 0 | 0 | 0 | 0 |

25 Unidentified.

Merchant name	Qty	Unit	Commodity	£	s.	d.	f.

The Ellephaunt aforesaid, *14th July 1595*

Hillary Woodward, Merchant Alien	25	ton	Salt	25	0	0	0

The Mathewe of Fremington, burden 12 tons, James Witheredge master, from Waterford, *14th July 1595*

Hugh Griffith & John Barker of Bristol, Merchant Ind	9.5	tun	Wine, Seck	0	0	0	0

The Trinitie Smith of Milford Haven, burden 20 tons, John Stome Master, from Waterford, 15th July 1595

George Richards of Bristol, Glover Ind	54	C	Skins, Morkin & Sheep Broken	18	0	0	0

The Trinitie Smith aforesaid, *15th July 1595*

Michael Browne of Waterford, Merchant Ind	44	C	Skins, Morkin & Sheep Broken	14	13	4	0
	1	M	Skins, Coney	1	5	0	0

The Trinitie Smith aforesaid, *15th July 1595*

Francis Garway of London, Merchant Ind	100	piece	Caddows	50	0	0	0
	1.5	C	*Irish* Linen *Cloth*	1	18	4	0
	4	piece	Mantles	1	0	0	0

The Trinitie of Fethard-on-Sea, burden 8 tons, John Chever master, from Waterford, *15th July 1595*

John Lincole of Waterford, Merchant Ind	3	C	*Irish* Frieze *Cloth*	6	0	0	0
	1.5	C	Check *Cloth*	3	0	0	0
	40	piece	Coveringe	20	0	0	0
	1	M	Skins, Coney	1	5	0	0
	6	C	Skins, Morkin & Sheep Broken	2	0	0	0

The Trinitie aforesaid, *15th July 1595*

John Howlett of Bristol, Merchant Ind	4	C	Skins, Morkin & Sheep Broken	1	6	8	0

The Rose of Bristol, burden 18 tons, John Fine master, from Waterford, 16th July 1595

James Lea of Waterford, Merchant Ind	12	C	Skins, Morkin & Sheep Broken	4	0	0	0
	3	C	*Irish* Frieze *Cloth*	6	0	0	0
	20	piece	Caddows	10	0	0	0

The Rose aforesaid, *16th July 1595*

John Whitt of Clonmel, Merchant Ind	8	C	Skins, Morkin & Sheep Broken	2	13	4	0

Merchant name	Qty	Unit	Commodity	£	s.	d.	f.
	4	C	Check *Cloth*	8	0	0	0
	0.5	C	*Irish* Frieze *Cloth*	1	0	0	0
	4	C	*Irish* Linen *Cloth*	5	0	0	0

The Rose aforesaid, *16th July 1595*

George Richards of Bristol, Glover Ind	38	C	Skins, Morkin & Sheep Broken	12	13	4	0

The Rose aforesaid, *16th July 1595*

Richard Comerford of Waterford, Merchant Ind							
	3	C	*Irish* Frieze *Cloth*	6	0	0	0
	7	C	Skins, Sheep Broken	2	6	8	0
	20	piece	Caddows	10	0	0	0
	0.5	C	Check *Cloth*	1	0	0	0
	2	piece	Mantles	0	10	0	0

The Rose aforesaid, *16th July 1595*

James Buttler of Galway, Merchant Ind							
	3	C	*Irish* Linen *Cloth*	3	75	0	0
	5	C	Skins, Sheep Broken	1	13	4	0
	1	C	Check *Cloth*	2	0	0	0
	0.5	C	*Irish* Frieze *Cloth*	1	0	0	0

The Rose aforesaid, *16th July 1595*

John Oliver of Bristol, Merchant Ind	2	tun	Wine, Seck	0	0	0	0

The Elizabeth of Gloucester, burden 18 tons, John Swanley master, from Waterford, *16th July 1595*

John Whittson of Bristol, Merchant Ind	4	tun	Wine, Seck	0	0	0	0

The Elizabeth aforesaid, *16th July 1595*

William Arthur of Limerick, Merchant Ind	17	C	Skins, Morkin & Sheep Broken	5	13	4	0
	1	C	*Irish* Linen *Cloth*	1	5	0	0
	2	C	Skins, Coney	0	5	0	0

The Elizabeth aforesaid, *16th July 1595*

John Scoland of Limerick, Merchant Ind	7	C	Skins, Morkin & Sheep Broken	2	6	8	0
	1	M	Skins, Morkin & Sheep Broken	3	6	8	0
	180	yard	*Irish* Linen *Cloth*	2	10	0	0
	1	piece	Mantles	0	5	0	0

Merchant name	Qty	Unit	Commodity	£	s.	d.	f.

The Elizabeth aforesaid, *16th July 1595*

| Richard Glewe of Bristol, Merchant Ind | 1 | butt | Wine, Seck | 0 | 0 | 0 | 0 |

The Elizabeth aforesaid, *16th July 1595*

Alexander Whitt of Waterford, Merchant Ind	4	C	*Irish* Frieze *Cloth*	8	0	0	0
	10	piece	Caddows	5	0	0	0
	3	C	Skins, Morkin & Sheep Broken	1	0	0	0
	0.5	C	Check *Cloth*	1	0	0	0

The Elizabeth aforesaid, *16th July 1595*

David Neale of Waterford, Merchant Ind	5	C	*Irish* Frieze *Cloth*	10	0	0	0
	16	piece	Caddows	8	0	0	0
	1	C	Check *Cloth*	2	0	0	0
	6	C	Skins, Sheep Broken	2	0	0	0
	2	piece	Mantles	0	10	0	0

The Francis of London, burden 40 tons, Edmund Bon[ ]man master, from La Rochelle, *16th July 1595*

| Benedict Harvy of Bristol, Merchant Ind | 30 | ton | Salt | 30 | 0 | 0 | 0 |

The Adventure of Ilfracombe, burden 18 tons, Philip Emett master, from Waterford, 17th July 1595

Peter Whitt of Clonmel, Merchant Ind	6	C	*Irish* Frieze & Check *Cloth*	12	0	0	0
	18	C	Skins, Morkin & Sheep Broken	6	0	0	0
	1	C	Skins, Coney Grey	0	2	6	0
	30	piece	Coveringe	15	0	0	0
	4	piece	Mantles	1	0	0	0
	30	yard	Canvas *Cloth*	0	6	8	0

The Adventure aforesaid, *17th July 1595*

Babtharius Whittie of Waterford, Merchant Ind	6	C	*Irish* Frieze *Cloth*	12	0	0	0
	15	piece	Mantles	3	15	0	0
	7	piece	Coveringe	3	10	0	0
	16	C	Skins, Morkin & Sheep Broken	5	6	8	0
	5	C	Skins, Kid	2	10	0	0

The Adventure aforesaid, *17th July 1595*

John Whitt of Waterford, Merchant Ind	36	C	Skins, Morkin & Sheep Broken	12	0	0	0
	4	C	*Irish* Frieze *Cloth*	8	0	0	0
	30	piece	Coveringe	15	0	0	0
	5	piece	Mantles	1	5	0	0

Merchant name	Qty	Unit	Commodity	£	s.	d.	f.
	1	C	Check *Cloth*	2	0	0	0
	15	piece	Mantles	3	15	0	0
	1	C	*Irish* Frieze *Cloth*	2	0	0	0
	1	firkin	Fish, Salmon	0	15	0	0

The Adventure aforesaid, *17th July 1595*

Edward Leonard of Waterford, Merchant Ind	8	C	*Irish* Frieze & Check Cloth	16	0	0	0
	20	piece	Coveringe	10	0	0	0
	14	piece	Mantles	3	10	0	0
	15	C	Skins, Morkin & Sheep Broken	5	0	0	0

The Adventure aforesaid, *17th July 1595*

James Daniell of Clonmel, Merchant Ind	5	C	*Irish* Frieze *Cloth*	10	0	0	0
	14	C	Skins, Morkin & Sheep Broken	4	13	4	0
	20	piece	Coveringe	10	0	0	0
	4	piece	Mantles	1	0	0	0

The Adventure aforesaid, *17th July 1595*

Lancellot Lucar of Waterford, Merchant Ind	8	butt	Wine, Seck	0	0	0	0

The John of Bristol, burden 16 tons, Thomas Lattim*er* master, from Youghal, *17th July 1595*

William Pitt, Merchant Ind	10	C	Sumach	6	13	4	0

The John aforesaid, *17th July 1595*

Christopher Burckett of Bristol, Merchant Ind	8.5	case	Glass	4	0	0	0

The Mary of Bristol, burden 16 tons, John Lulett master, from Cork, 19th July 1595

Thomas Stanfast & Richard Gould of Bristol & Cork, Merchants Ind	5.25	tun	Wine, French	0	0	0	0
	1	tun	Wine, French (Tayutt)	0	0	0	0

The Mary aforesaid, 19th July 1595

John Younge of Cork, Merchant Ind	12	C	Skins, Morkin & Sheep Broken	4	0	0	0

The Clement of Bristol, burden 18 tons, John Banister master, from Cork, *19th July 1595*

Dominick Copinger of Cork, Merchant Ind	10	C	Skins, Morkin & Sheep Broken	3	6	8	0

Merchant name	Qty	Unit	Commodity	£	s.	d.	f.

The Clement aforesaid, *19th July 1595*

Ralph Nuwgent of Cork, Merchant Ind	6	C	Skins, Morkin & Sheep Broken	2	0	0	0

The Clement aforesaid, *19th July 1595*

Peter Goughe of Bristol, Merchant Ind	1	tun	Wine, French	0	0	0	0

The Anne Synnott of Waterford, burden 50 tons, John Synnott master, from Waterford, 21st July 1595

John Roth of Kilkenny, Merchant Ind	31	piece	Caddows	15	10	0	0
	8	C	*Irish* Frieze & Check *Cloth*	16	0	0	0
	0.5	C	*Irish* Linen *Cloth*	0	13	4	0
	29	C	Skins, Morkin & Sheep Broken	9	13	4	0

The Anne aforesaid, 21st July 1595

Martin Archer of Kilkenny, Merchant Ind	40	piece	Coveringe	20	0	0	0
	4	C	*Irish* Frieze & Check *Cloth*	8	0	0	0
	1	M	Skins, Morkin & Sheep Broken	3	6	8	0

The Anne aforesaid, 21st July 1595

Walter Dowley of Kilkenny, Merchant Ind	2	M	Skins, Morkin & Sheep Broken	6	13	4	0
	1	C	Check *Cloth*	2	0	0	0
	0.5	C	*Irish* Frieze *Cloth*	1	0	0	0

The Anne aforesaid, 21st July 1595

Edward Cuff of Waterford, Merchant Ind	1	M	Skins, Morkin & Sheep Broken	3	6	8	0
	20	piece	Mantles	5	0	0	0
	4	C	Check *Cloth*	8	0	0	0
	24	piece	Coveringe	12	0	0	0

The Anne aforesaid, 21st July 1595

Richard Walsh of Waterford, Merchant Ind	2	C	*Irish* Frieze *Cloth*	4	0	0	0
	12	piece	Caddows	6	0	0	0
	6	piece	Mantles	1	10	0	0
	0.5	C	Check *Cloth*	1	0	0	0
	3	C	Skins, Morkin & Sheep Broken	1	0	0	0

Merchant name	Qty	Unit	Commodity	£	s.	d.	f.

The Anne aforesaid, 21st July 1595

Edward Roth of Kilkenny, Merchant Ind	20	piece	Coveringe	10	0	0	0
	3	C	*Irish* Frieze & Check				
			Cloth	6	0	0	0
	8	C	Skins, Sheep Broken	2	13	4	0

The Anne aforesaid, 21st July 1595

David Dobine of Waterford, Merchant Ind	12	C	*Irish* Frieze *Cloth*	24	0	0	0
	40	piece	Coveringe	20	0	0	0

The Anne aforesaid, *21st July 1595*

James Quem*er*ford of Waterford, Merchant Ind	6	C	*Irish* Frieze *Cloth*	12	0	0	0
	50	piece	Coveringe	25	0	0	0
	5	piece	Mantles	1	5	0	0
	2	C	Check *Cloth*	4	0	0	0
	10	gallons	Aquavitae	1	0	0	0

The Anne aforesaid, 21st July 1595

Edward Hackett of Fethard-on-Sea, Merchant Ind	6	C	*Irish* Frieze *Cloth*	12	0	0	0
	16	piece	Caddows	8	0	0	0
	8	C	Skins, Sheep Broken	2	13	4	0
	1	C	Skins, Morkin	0	6	8	0

The Anne aforesaid, 21st July 1595

Richard Roth of Kilkenny, Merchant Ind	4	C	*Irish* Frieze *Cloth*	8	0	0	0
	16	piece	Caddows	8	0	0	0
	24	C	Skins, Morkin	8	0	0	0

The Anne aforesaid, *21st July 1595*

Oliver Shortoll of Kilkenny, Merchant Ind	8	piece	Caddows	4	0	0	0
	1.5	C	*Irish* Frieze *Cloth*	3	0	0	0
	1.5	C	Check *Cloth*	3	0	0	0
	8	C	Skins, Morkin & Sheep Broken	2	13	4	0
	2	C	Skins, Lamb	1	0	0	0

The Anne aforesaid, *21st July 1595*

George St Lenger of Kilkenny, Merchant Ind	6	C	*Irish* Frieze *Cloth*	12	0	0	0
	20	piece	Coveringe	10	0	0	0
	16	C	Skins, Morkin	5	6	8	0

The Anne aforesaid, *21st July 1595*

Walter Daniell of Kilkenny, Merchant Ind	1	M	*Irish* Frieze & Check				

Merchant name	Qty	Unit	Commodity	£	s.	d.	f.
			Cloth	20	0	0	0
	20	piece	Coveringe	10	0	0	0
	3	M	Skins, Morkin &				
			Sheep Broken	10	0	0	0

The Anne Synnott aforesaid, *21st July 1595*

Walter Ryan of Kilkenny, Merchant Ind	15	piece	Caddows	7	10	0	0
	2.5	C	Check *Cloth*	5	0	0	0
	16	C	Skins, Morkin &				
			Sheep Broken	5	6	8	0

The Anne aforesaid, *21st July 1595*

George Comerford of Kilkenny, Merchant Ind	6	C	*Irish* Frieze & Check				
			Cloth	12	0	0	0
	24	piece	Caddows	12	0	0	0
	15	C	Skins, Sheep Broken	5	0	0	0
	4	piece	Skins, Otter	0	8	4	0
	4	piece	Hides, Dry Bull	1	0	0	0

The Anne aforesaid, *21st July 1595*

Pierce Hackett of Fethard-on-Sea, Merchant Ind	16	piece	Caddows	8	0	0	0
	5	C	*Irish* Frieze & Check				
			Cloth	10	0	0	0
	8	C	Skins, Sheep Broken	2	13	4	0

The Grace of Northam, burden 12 tons, William Adger master, from Waterford, *21st July 1595*

John Lincole of Waterford, Merchant Ind	18	C	Skins, Sheep Broken	6	3	2	0
	6	C	*Irish* Frieze & Check				
			Cloth	12	0	0	0
	2	piece	Coveringe	1	0	0	0
	30	yard	*Irish* Linen *Cloth*	0	6	8	0

The Mary Grace aforesaid, *21st July 1595*

Hugh Griffeth of Bristol, Merchant Ind	2.5	tun	Wine, French	0	0	0	0

The Speedwell of New Ross, burden 40 tons, Tobias Whitt master, from Waterford, *21st July 1595*

John Whittson of Bristol, Merchant Ind	11	tun	Oil, *Olive*	88	0	0	0
	4	tun	Wine, Seck	0	0	0	0

The Speedwell aforesaid, *21st July 1595*

Nicholas Lea of Waterford, Merchant Ind	1	M	*Irish* Frieze *Cloth*	20	0	0	0
	2	C	Check *Cloth*	4	0	0	0
	50	piece	Blankets	25	0	0	0

Merchant name	Qty	Unit	Commodity	£	s.	d.	f.
	16	C	Skins, Morkin	5	6	8	0
	40	yard	*Irish* Frieze *Cloth*	0	13	4	0
	2.5	C	*Irish* Frieze & Check				
			Cloth	5	0	0	0
	14	piece	Coveringe	7	0	0	0
	1	M	Skins, Morkin &				
			Sheep Broken	3	6	8	0

The Speedwell aforesaid, *21st July 1595*

James Wealshe of Waterford, Merchant Ind	1	M	Skins, Morkin &				
			Sheep Broken	3	6	8	0
	3	C	*Irish* Frieze *Cloth*	6	0	0	0
	18	piece	Caddows	9	0	0	0

The Speedwell aforesaid, *21st July 1595*

John Roth of Kilkenny, Merchant Ind	13	C	Skins, Morkin &				
			Sheep Broken	4	6	8	0
	2	C	*Irish* Frieze *Cloth*	4	0	0	0
	2	C	Check *Cloth*	4	0	0	0
	10	piece	Caddows	5	0	0	0
	0.5	C	*Irish* Frieze *Cloth*	1	0	0	0

The Speedwell aforesaid, *21st July 1595*

John Skidie of Waterford, Merchant Ind	18	C	Skins, Morkin &				
			Sheep Broken	6	0	0	0
	5	C	*Irish* Frieze & Check				
			Cloth	10	0	0	0
	30	piece	Coveringe	15	0	0	0
	15	piece	Mantles	3	15	0	0

The Speedwell aforesaid, *21st July 1595*

William Whitt of Waterford, Merchant Ind	30	piece	Coveringe	15	0	0	0
	2	C	Check *Cloth*	4	0	0	0
	3	yard	Rugg, Irish	8	0	0	0
	6	C	Skins, Morkin &				
			Sheep Broken	2	0	0	0

The Speedwell aforesaid, *21st July 1595*

Edward Lycar? of Waterford, Merchant Ind	60	piece	Coveringe	30	0	0	0
	4	C	*Irish* Frieze *Cloth*	8	0	0	0
	4	C	Skins, Morkin &				
			Sheep Broken	1	6	8	0

The Speedwell aforesaid, *21st July 1595*

Edward Everet of Limerick, Merchant Ind	11	C	Skins, Morkin &				
			Sheep Broken	3	13	4	0
	80	yard	*Irish* Linen *Cloth*	1	5	0	0

Merchant name	Qty	Unit	Commodity	£	s.	d.	f.

The Speedwell aforesaid, *21st July 1595*

Merchant name	Qty	Unit	Commodity	£	s.	d.	f.
Robert Strange of Waterford, Merchant Ind	3	C	*Irish* Frieze *Cloth*	6	0	0	0
	20	piece	Coveringe	10	0	0	0
	5	M	Skins, Morkin & Sheep Broken	16	13	4	0

The Gift of Waterford, burden 25 tons, John Gall master, from Waterford, *21st July 1595*

Merchant name	Qty	Unit	Commodity	£	s.	d.	f.
Thomas Whitt of Clonmel, Merchant Ind	6	C	*Irish* Frieze *Cloth*	12	0	0	0
	40	piece	Caddows	20	0	0	0
	2	M	Skins, Sheep Broken	6	13	4	0

The Gift aforesaid, *21st July 1595*

Merchant name	Qty	Unit	Commodity	£	s.	d.	f.
Thomas Donohewe of Clonmel, Merchant Ind	8	C	*Irish* Frieze *Cloth*	16	0	0	0
	16	piece	Coveringe	8	0	0	0
	2	M	Skins, Sheep Broken	6	13	4	0

The Gift aforesaid, *21st July 1595*

Merchant name	Qty	Unit	Commodity	£	s.	d.	f.
Henry Pembrocke of Kilkenny, Merchant Ind	20	piece	Caddows	10	0	0	0
	2	C	Check *Cloth*	4	0	0	0
	12	C	Skins, Sheep Broken	4	0	0	0

The Gift aforesaid, *21st July 1595*

Merchant name	Qty	Unit	Commodity	£	s.	d.	f.
Richard Hart of Waterford, Merchant Ind	3	C	*Irish* Frieze *Cloth*	6	0	0	0
	12	piece	Coveringe	6	0	0	0
	4	piece	Mantles	1	0	0	0
	1	M	Skins, Sheep Broken	3	6	8	0

The Gift aforesaid, *21st July 1595*

Merchant name	Qty	Unit	Commodity	£	s.	d.	f.
Edward Lucar of Waterford, Merchant Ind	40	piece	Coveringe	20	0	0	0
	2	C	*Irish* Frieze *Cloth*	4	0	0	0
	3	C	Skins, Morkin	1	0	0	0
	2	hogshead	Aquavitae	8	0	0	0

The Gift aforesaid, *21st July 1595*

Merchant name	Qty	Unit	Commodity	£	s.	d.	f.
Edward Vale of Clonmel, Merchant Ind	6	C	*Irish* Frieze *Cloth*	12	0	0	0
	4	C	Check *Cloth*	8	0	0	0
	2	M	Skins, Sheep Broken	6	13	4	0
	40	piece	Coveringe	20	0	0	0
	1.5	C	*Irish* Linen *Cloth*	1	18	0	0

The Gift aforesaid, *21st July 1595*

Merchant name	Qty	Unit	Commodity	£	s.	d.	f.
Nicholas Murphie of Kilkenny, Merchant Ind	6	C	*Irish* Frieze & Check *Cloth*	12	0	0	0
	12	C	Skins, Morkin & Sheep Broken	4	0	0	0

Merchant name	Qty	Unit	Commodity	£	s.	d.	f.
	13	piece	Mantles	3	5	0	0
	70	yard	*Irish* Linen *Cloth*	1	0	0	0

The Gift aforesaid, *21st July 1595*

Richard Bucher of Waterford, Merchant Ind	2	butt	Wine, Seck	0	0	0	0
	2	hogshead	Wine, French	0	0	0	0

The Gift aforesaid, *21st July 1595*

Patrick Lea of Waterford, Merchant Ind	3	butt	Wine, Seck	0	0	0	0

The Gift aforesaid, *21st July 1595*

Patrick Bucher of Waterford, Merchant Ind	2	tun	Wine, French	0	0	0	0

The Mary Dearinge of Waterford, burden 30 tons, Richard Coney master, from Waterford, *21st July 1595*

James Knowles of Waterford, Merchant Ind	40	piece	Coveringe	20	0	0	0
	1.5	C	*Irish* Frieze *Cloth*	3	0	0	0

The Mary Dearinge aforesaid, *21st July 1595*

Nicholas Goughe of Waterford, Merchant Ind	3	C	*Irish* Frieze *Cloth*	6	0	0	0
	12	piece	Coveringe	6	0	0	0
	6	piece	Mantles	1	10	0	0

The Mary Dearinge aforesaid, *21st July 1595*

Edmund Walshe of Waterford, Merchant Ind	18	C	Skins, Morkin	6	0	0	0
	1	C	*Irish* Frieze *Cloth*	2	0	0	0
	12	piece	Coveringe	6	0	0	0
	4	piece	Mantles	1	0	0	0

The Mary Dearinge aforesaid, *21st July 1595*

Michael Browne of Waterford, Merchant Ind	28	piece	Coveringe	14	0	0	0
	6	C	*Irish* Frieze & Check Cloth	12	0	0	0
	14	C	Skins, Morkin & Sheep Broken	4	13	4	0

The Mary Dearinge aforesaid, *21st July 1595*

Patrick Sherlock of Waterford, Merchant Ind	6	C	Skins, Morkin	2	0	0	0
	4	C	*Irish* Frieze *Cloth*	8	0	0	0
	12	piece	Coveringe	6	0	0	0
	20	piece	Mantles	5	0	0	0

Merchant name	Qty	Unit	Commodity	£	s.	d.	f.
The Mary Dearinge aforesaid, _21st July 1595_							
Nicholas Briver of Waterford, Merchant Ind	6	C	_Irish_ Frieze _Cloth_	12	0	0	0
	32	piece	Coveringe	16	0	0	0
	6	piece	Mantles	1	10	0	0
	3	M	Skins, Morkin &				
			Sheep Broken	10	0	0	0
The Mary Dearinge aforesaid, _21st July 1595_							
Richard Buttler of Waterford, Merchant Ind	32	piece	Coveringe	16	0	0	0
	4	C	_Irish_ Frieze _Cloth_	8	0	0	0
	2	C	Check _Cloth_	4	0	0	0
	16	C	Skins, Morkin	5	6	8	0
The Mary Dearinge aforesaid, _21st July 1595_							
John Sutton of Waterford, Merchant Ind	5	C	_Irish_ Frieze _Cloth_	10	0	0	0
	20	piece	Coveringe	10	0	0	0
	10	C	Skins, Morkin	3	6	8	0
	3	M	Skins, Sheep Broken	10	0	0	0
	1	barrel	Aquavitae	2	0	0	0
The Mary Dearinge aforesaid, _21st July 1595_							
David Dobine of Waterford, Merchant Ind	3	C	_Irish_ Frieze _Cloth_	6	0	0	0
	10	piece	Coveringe	5	0	0	0
The James of Northam, burden 18 tons, John Pu[]rey master, from Youghal, _21st July 1595_							
Walter Williams of London, Merchant Ind	20.5	case	Glass	10	0	0	0
The James aforesaid, 21st July 1595							
Dominick Galway of Cork, Merchant Ind	4	C	Skins, Morkin &				
			Sheep Broken	1	6	8	0
	1	tun	Wine, French	0	0	0	0
The John of Waterford, burden 14 tons, John Keron master, from Waterford, 22nd July 1595							
Richard Neale of Kilkenny, Merchant Ind	2	C	_Irish_ Frieze _Cloth_	4	0	0	0
	24	piece	Coveringe	12	0	0	0
	2	M	Skins, Morkin	6	13	4	0
	2	M	Skins, Sheep Broken	6	13	4	0
	15	C	Skins, Cony	1	18	0	0
The John aforesaid, _22nd July 1595_							
Thomas Whitt of Waterford, Merchant Ind	3	C	_Irish_ Frieze _Cloth_	6	0	0	0
	3	C	Check _Cloth_	6	0	0	0
	18	piece	Coveringe	9	0	0	0
	14	C	Skins, Sheep Broken	4	13	4	0

Merchant name	Qty	Unit	Commodity	£	s.	d.	f.

The John aforesaid, *22nd July 1595*

Nicholas Moulroney of London,
Merchant Ind

	2	C	*Irish* Frieze *Cloth*	4	0	0	0
	5	C	Skins, Morkin	1	13	4	0
	1	M	Skins, Sheep Broken	3	6	8	0
	11	piece	Caddows	5	10	0	0
	0.5	C	*Irish* Linen *Cloth*	0	13	4	0

The John aforesaid, *22nd July 1595*

Thomas Whitt of Clonmel, Merchant Ind

	6	C	*Irish* Frieze & Check Cloth	12	0	0	0
	5	M	Skins, Sheep Broken	16	13	4	0

The John of Waterford, burden 16 tons, Maurice Cleere master, from Waterford, *22nd July 1595*

James Duffe of Waterford, Merchant Ind

	30	piece	Coveringe	15	0	0	0
	22	piece	Mantles	5	10	0	0
	2	C	*Irish* Frieze & Check Cloth	4	0	0	0
	3	M	Skins, Sheep Broken	10	0	0	0

The John aforesaid, *22nd July 1595*

Nicholas Roth of New Ross, Merchant Ind

	3	C	*Irish* Frieze *Cloth*	6	0	0	0
	40	piece	Mantles	10	0	0	0
	40	piece	Caddows	20	0	0	0
	15	C	Skins, Morkin & Sheep Broken	5	0	0	0
	1	M	Skins, Sheep Broken	3	6	8	0

The Trinittie of Waterford, burden 14 tons, Walter Keney master, from Waterford, *22nd July 1595*

Michael Browne of Waterford, Merchant Ind

	4	C	*Irish* Frieze *Cloth*	8	0	0	0
	8	piece	Coveringe	4	0	0	0
	8	piece	Mantles	2	0	0	0
	12	C	Skins, Morkin	4	0	0	0

The Trinittie aforesaid, *22nd July 1595*

Edward Hackett of Fethard-on-Sea,
Merchant Ind

	2	C	*Irish* Frieze *Cloth*	4	0	0	0
	16	C	Skins, Sheep Broken	5	6	8	0

The Trinittie aforesaid, *22nd July 1595*

Patrick Lea of Waterford, Merchant Ind

	4	C	*Irish* Frieze *Cloth*	8	0	0	0
	3	C	Skins, Morkin	1	0	0	0
	17	piece	Caddows	8	10	0	0
	6	piece	Mantles	1	10	0	0

Merchant name	Qty	Unit	Commodity	£	s.	d.	f.

The Trinittie aforesaid, *22nd July 1595*

James Gibson of Waterford, Merchant Ind	3	C	*Irish* Frieze *Cloth*	6	0	0	0
	9	piece	Coveringe	4	10	0	0
	6	piece	Mantles	1	10	0	0
	1	M	Skins, Morkin	3	13	4	0

The Trinittie aforesaid, *22nd July 1595*

Geoffrey Foster of Waterford, Merchant Ind	5	C	*Irish* Frieze & Check *Cloth*	10	0	0	0
	10	piece	Coveringe	5	0	0	0
	6	piece	Mantles	1	10	0	0
	2	C	Skins, Morkin & Sheep Broken	0	13	4	0

The Margarett of Wexford, burden 5 tons, John Chevers master, from Wexford, 24th July 1595

| John Chevers of Wexford, Merchant Ind | 9 | butt | Wine, Seck | 0 | 0 | 0 | 0 |

The James of Dungarvan, burden 9 tons, Walter Hore master, from Dungarvan, *24th July 1595*

Robert Lea of Waterford, Merchant Ind	1.5	C	*Irish* Frieze *Cloth*	3	0	0	0
	11	C	Skins, Morkin & Sheep Broken	3	13	4	0
	11	C	Skins, Coney	1	10	0	0

The *Ieorke* of Youghal, burden 12 tons, Maurice Gurrie? master, from Youghal, 26th July 1595

| Dominick Galway of Youghal, Merchant Ind | 5 | C | Skins, Morkin & Sheep Broken | 1 | 13 | 4 | 0 |

The Clement of Ilfracombe, burden 18 tons, Walter Palin master, from Kinsale, *26th July 1595*

| Dominick Copinger of Kinsale, Merchant Ind | 30 | C | Wool, Spanish Hat | 125 | 0 | 0 | 0 |

The *Ieorke* aforesaid, *26th July 1595*

| Walter Williams of London, Merchant Ind | 8.5 | case | Glass | 4 | 0 | 0 | 0 |

The George of Wexford, burden 6 tons, Nicholas Roche master, from Wexford, 8th August 1595

| Philip Gettinge of Wexford, Merchant Ind | 4 | piece | Coveringe | 2 | 0 | 0 | 0 |
| | | | Check *Cloth* | 1 | 0 | 0 | 0 |

The George aforesaid, *8th August 1595*

| Walter Turner of Wexford, Merchant Ind | 1 | tun | Wine, Seck | 0 | 0 | 0 | 0 |

Merchant name	Qty	Unit	Commodity	£	s.	d.	f.

The Minion of Jersey, burden 14 tons, John Rouse master, from St Malo, 11th August 1595

James Beavoier of Jersey, Merchant							
	12.25	tun	Oil, *Olive*	98	0	0	0

The Minion aforesaid, *11th August 1595*

George Watkins of Bristol, Merchant Ind	16	C	Alum	26	13	4	0

The Pellican of Bristol, burden 40 tons, Andrew Batten master, from La Rochelle, *11th August 1595*

Peter Goughe & Andrew Batten of Bristol, Merchant Ind	25	ton	Salt	25	0	0	0

The Dove of Bristol, burden 40 tons, William Pheleps master, from La Rochelle, *11th August 1595*

Robert & Vincent Colston, John Younge & Richard Paine of Bristol, Merchants Ind	25	ton	Salt	25	0	0	0
	16	C	Prunes	8	0	0	0
	60	piece	Rosin	10	0	0	0
	1	bale	Paper	2	13	4	0

The Margarett of Jersey, burden 18 tons, Nicholas Maistor master, from St Malo, 13th August 1595

John Whittson of Bristol, Merchant Ind	36	C	Alum	60	0	0	0
	1.5	C	Soap, Castille	1	3	4	0
	1	pipe	Oil, *Olive*	4	0	0	0

The Margarett aforesaid, *13th August 1595*

John Love of Bristol, Merchant Ind	8	butt	Wine, Seck	0	0	0	0
	5	ton	Woad, Green	50	0	0	0

The Prize called the Fox of *Arcuzauires,* burden 100 tons, Mathew Whittson master, from the Sea, 22nd August 1595

William Wattson & *Mountsea* of Weymouth, Merchant Ind			Unknown	0	0	0	0
			Unknown	0	0	0	0
			Unknown	320	0	0	0
	8	C	Aniseed	10	13	4	0

The Peter of Bristol, burden 18 tons, Richard Westerot master, from St Malo, 25th August 1595

Mathew Haviland of Bristol, Merchant Ind	5	pipe	Oil, *Olive*	20	0	0	0
	1	hogshead	Oil, *Olive*	2	0	0	0

Merchant name	Qty	Unit	Commodity	£	s.	d.	f.

The Peter aforesaid, *25th August 1595*

| William Ellis of Bristol, Merchant Ind | 5 | pipe | Oil, *Olive* | 20 | 0 | 0 | 0 |
| | 1 | hogshead | Oil, *Olive* | 2 | 0 | 0 | 0 |

The Peter aforesaid, *25th August 1595*

| John Whittson of Bristol, Merchant Ind | 6 | pipe | Oil, *Olive* | 24 | 0 | 0 | 0 |

The Peter aforesaid, *25th August 1595*

| John Younge of Bristol, Merchant Ind | 1 | pipe | Oil, *Olive* | 4 | 0 | 0 | 0 |

The Peter aforesaid, *25th August 1595*

| John Drap of Bristol, Merchant Ind | 1 | pipe | Oil, *Olive* | 4 | 0 | 0 | 0 |

The Peter aforesaid, *25th August 1595*

| George Whitt of Bristol, Merchant Ind | 2 | pipe | Oil, *Olive* | 8 | 0 | 0 | 0 |

The Hercules of Bristol, burden 50 tons, Thomas Bennett master, from Newfoundland, 27th August 1595

| Christopher Pitt & Thomas Bennet of Bristol Merchants & Consort Ind | 4 | tun | Oil, Train | 20 | 0 | 0 | 0 |

The Spreadegle of Emden, burden 300 tons, Bennet Albertus master, from the Sea, 10th September 1595

Bennett Albertus, *Bernard Sate,* Jaques Vonstonhold & Peter Puie, Merchants Alien	64	chest	Sugar, White	640	0	0	0
	34	chest	Sugar, Moscavado	330	0	0	0
	36	chest	Sugar, Panele	180	0	0	0
	22	C	Brazil & *Furnando Bucke*	70	0	0	0
	3.25	C	Elephant's Tusks	10	16	8	0

The Spreadegle aforesaid, 11th September 1595

| Lucas Vandravena of Amsterdam, Merchant Alien | 32 | chest | Sugar, Moscavado & White | 320 | 0 | 0 | 0 |
| | 19 | chest | Sugar, Panele | 95 | 0 | 0 | 0 |

The Spreadegle aforesaid, 12th September 1595

| Daniel Whitt of Bristol, Merchant & Consort Ind | 156 | chest | Sugar, White & Muscavado | 1560 | 0 | 0 | 0 |
| | 81 | chest | Sugar, Panele | 403 | 6 | 8 | 0 |

Merchant name	Qty	Unit	Commodity	£	s.	d.	f.
	4	ton	Wood, Brazil	133	6	8	0
	6	chest	Sugar, White[26]	0	0	0	0

The Fox aforesaid, *12th September 1595*

Daniel Whitt of Bristol, Merchant & Consort Ind	4	C	Aniseed	5	6	8	0
	116	bags	Rice	160	0	0	0
	3	C	Elephant's Tusks	10	0	0	0

The Unicorne of Bristol, burden 110 tons, James Powell master, from Newfoundland, 16th September 1595

John Barker of Bristol, Merchant & Consort Ind	10	tun	Oil, Train	50	0	0	0

The Spreadegle aforesaid, *16th September 1595*

William Merodeth & Michael Pepwall of Bristol, Merchants & Consort Ind	154	chest	Sugar, White	1540	0	0	0
William Merodeth & Michael Pepwall of Bristol, Merchants & Consort Ind	81	chest	Sugar, Panele	405	0	0	0
William Merodeth & Michael Pepwall of Bristol, Merchants & Consort Ind	4	ton	Wood, Brazil	133	6	8	0
William Merodeth & Michael Pepwall of Bristol, Merchants & Consort Ind	3	C	Elephant's Tusks	10	0	0	0
William Merodeth & Michael Pepwall of Bristol, Merchants & Consort Ind	6	chest	Sugar, White[27]	0	0	0	0

The Fox aforesaid, *16th September 1595*

William Merodeth & Michael Pepwall of Bristol, Merchants & Consort Ind	116	bags	Rice	160	0	0	0
	4	C	Aniseed	5	6	8	0

The Spreadegle aforesaid, *16th September 1595*

Thomas Webb & Walter Pashon, Merchant Ind	156	chest	Sugar, Moscavado & White	1560	0	0	0
Thomas Webb & Walter Pashon, Merchant Ind	81	chest	Sugar, Panele	405	0	0	0
Thomas Webb & Walter Pashon, Merchant Ind	4	ton	Wood, Brazil	133	6	8	0
Thomas Webb & Walter Pashon, Merchant Ind	3	C	Elephant's Tusks	10	0	0	0
Thomas Webb & Walter Pashon, Merchant Ind	6	chest	Sugar, Moscavado & White[28]	0	0	0	0

26 Custom exempt.   **27** Custom exempt.   **28** Custom exempt.

Merchant name	*Qty*	Unit	Commodity	£	s.	d.	f.

The Fox aforesaid, *16th September 1595*

Thomas Webb & Walter Pashon,
Merchant Ind

| | 116 | bags | Rice | *160* | 0 | 0 | 0 |
| | 4 | C | Aniseed | *5* | *6* | *8* | *0* |

The Abraham of Gdańsk, burden 200 tons, John Aboutt master, from La Rochelle, 17th September 1595

Veronius Martine of London,
Merchant Alien

| | 100 | ton | Salt | 100 | 0 | 0 | 0 |

The Abraham aforesaid, *17th September 1595*

Henry Pine, Merchant Ind

| | 60 | ton | Salt | 60 | 0 | 0 | 0 |

The John of Bristol, burden 60 tons, Thomas Barker master, from Newfoundland, 18th September 1595

John Barnes of Bristol, Merchant Ind

| | 6 | tun | Oil, Train | 30 | 0 | 0 | 0 |

The Mayflower of Bristol, burden 90 tons, John Flecher master, from Newfoundland, 20th September 1595

Thomas James & Jennings of Bristol
Merchant & Consort Ind

| | 8 | tun | Oil, Train | 40 | 0 | 0 | 0 |

EXPORTS

The Martha of Bristol, burden 60 tons, John Baker master, to La Rochelle, 30th September 1594

John Barns? of Bristol, Merchant Ind

| | 5 | ton | Lead | *40* | 0 | 0 | 0 |

The Unicorne of Bristol, burden 110 tons, James Powell master, to Livorno, *30th September 1594*

Baptiste Hasell of London, Merchant Ind

| | 9 | C | Sugar, Powder de Brasil | *30* | 0 | 0 | 0 |

The Unicorne aforesaid, *30th September 1594*

Giovanni Francisco Soprani of London,
Merchant Alien

	25	cases	Glass	*25*	0	0	0
	24	C	Sugar	*76*	*13*	*4*	*0*
	5	ton	Lead	*40*	0	0	0
	1	ton	Iron	*8*	0	0	0
	54	piece	Cloth of Assize, Bridgwater	0	0	0	0

Merchant name	Qty	Unit	Commodity	£	s.	d.	f.
	6	piece	Cloth of Assize, Bridgwater[29]	0	0	0	0

The Martha aforesaid, *30th September 1594*

Merchant name	Qty	Unit	Commodity	£	s.	d.	f.
John Younge of Bristol, Merchant Ind	3	ton	Lead	24	0	0	0
	9	piece	Cloth of Assize, Penistone[30]	15	0	0	0
	1	piece	Cloth of Assize, Penistone[31]	0	0	0	0
William Wickam of Bristol, Merchant Ind	5	ton	Lead	40	0	0	0

The Daysey of Bristol, burden 30 tons, Richard Parsons master, to St-Jean-de-Luz, *30th September 1594*

Merchant name	Qty	Unit	Commodity	£	s.	d.	f.
John Hopkins of Bristol, Merchant Ind	3	piece	Bay Cloth	6	0	0	0
	2.5	piece	Bay Cloth	5	0	0	0
	3	piece	Cloth of Assize, Bridgwater	0	0	0	0
	5	piece	Cloth of Assize	0	0	0	0
	2	M	Fish, Dry Newfoundland	10	0	0	0
		piece	Cloth of Assize, Overlengths	0	0	0	0

The Daysey aforesaid, 30th September 1594

Merchant name	Qty	Unit	Commodity	£	s.	d.	f.
John Gittins of Bristol, Merchant Ind	10	piece	*Bristol* Frieze *Cloth*[32]	11	0	0	0
	1	piece	*Bristol* Frieze *Cloth*[33]	0	0	0	0
	4	piece	Cloth of Assize, Coarse	0	0	0	0
			Cloth of Assize, Overlenghts	0	0	0	0

The Daysey aforesaid, 1st October 1594

Merchant name	Qty	Unit	Commodity	£	s.	d.	f.
John Roberowe of Bristol, Merchant Ind	8	piece	Cloth of Assize, Devonshire Dozen	0	0	0	0

The Pellican of Bristol, burden 40 tons, Andrew Batten master, to La Rochelle, *1st October 1594*

Merchant name	Qty	Unit	Commodity	£	s.	d.	f.
John Aldworth of Bristol, Merchant Ind	3	C	Wax	9	0	0	0

The Daysey aforesaid, *1st October 1594*

Merchant name	Qty	Unit	Commodity	£	s.	d.	f.
John Aldworth of Bristol, Merchant Ind	8	piece	Cloth of Assize, Streit	0	0	0	0

---

29 Custom exempt.   30 Has been given a poundage value by the customs officer.   31 Custom exempt.   32 Seems to be an error in value, should be £10 if 1 piece is custom exempt.   33 Custom exempt.

Merchant name	Qty	Unit	Commodity	£	s.	d.	f.

The Daysey aforesaid, 1st October 1594

Merchant name	Qty	Unit	Commodity	£	s.	d.	f.
John Gittins of Bristol, Merchant Ind	2	piece	Cloth of Assize, Kersey	o	o	o	o
	2	piece	Cloth of Assize, Kersey	o	o	o	o
	3	piece	Cloth of Assize, Devonshire Dozen	o	o	o	o
	0.5	piece	Cloth of Assize	o	o	o	o
			Cloth of Assize, Overlengths	o	o	o	o
	1	C	Flax, Unwrought	o	13	4	o

The Mary Rose of Newport, burden 16 tons, Thomas Williams master, to Newport,[34] 3rd October 1594

Merchant name	Qty	Unit	Commodity	£	s.	d.	f.
John Samford of Bristol, Merchant Ind	4	piece	Cloth of Assize, Devonshire Dozen	o	o	o	o
	3	piece	Cloth of Assize	o	o	o	o
			Cloth of Assize, Overlengths	o	o	o	o

The Mary Rose aforesaid,

Merchant name	Qty	Unit	Commodity	£	s.	d.	f.
John Samford of Bristol, Merchant Ind	50	C	Rice[35]	o	o	o	o

The Unicorne aforesaid, 3rd October 1594

Merchant name	Qty	Unit	Commodity	£	s.	d.	f.
Baptist Hasell of London, Merchant Ind	36	piece	Cloth of Assize, Bridgwater	o	o	o	o
	4	piece	Cloth of Assize, Bridgwater[36]	o	o	o	o

The Unicorne aforesaid, 4th October 1594

Merchant name	Qty	Unit	Commodity	£	s.	d.	f.
Hugh Griffith of Bristol, Merchant Ind	6	piece	Cloth of Assize	o	o	o	o
			Cloth of Assize, Overlengths	o	o	o	o

The Martha aforesaid, 5th October 1594

Merchant name	Qty	Unit	Commodity	£	s.	d.	f.
Arthur Hibbons of Bristol, Merchant Ind	17	C	Wax	51	o	o	o
	29	piece	Bristol Frieze Cloth	29	o	o	o
	3	piece	Bristol Frieze Cloth[37]	o	o	o	o

The Pellican aforesaid, 5th October 1594

Merchant name	Qty	Unit	Commodity	£	s.	d.	f.
John Oliver of Bristol, Merchant Ind	2	ton	Lead	16	o	o	o
	2	piece	Cloth of Assize	o	o	o	o
			Cloth of Assize, Overlengths	o	o	o	o

34 Then on the White Bear of Hull, burden 50 tons, William Philips master, to La Rochelle. 35 Custom and subsidy paid in the Diamond of Bristol, burden 50 tons, William Meager master, from Tolone, 25th May 1594. 36 Custom exempt. 37 Custom exempt.

Merchant name	Qty	Unit	Commodity	£	s.	d.	f.

The Martha aforesaid,

John Younge of Bristol, Merchant Ind	6	C	Rice[38]	0	0	0	0

The Martha of Bristol aforesaid, 5th October 1594

John Fownes of Bristol, Merchant Ind	4	C	Wax	12	0	0	0

The Mary Rose aforesaid, 8th October 1594

John Angell of Bristol, Merchant Ind	4	C	Wax	12	0	0	0
	8	piece	Bristol Frieze Cloth	8	0	0	0
	1	piece	Cloth of Assize	0	0	0	0
			Cloth of Assize, Overlengths	0	0	0	0

The Gabriell of Bristol, burden 50 tons, Thomas Nethway master, to Livorno, 10th October 1594

John Aldworth of Bristol, Merchant Ind	8	ton	Lead	64	0	0	0

The Thought of Bayonne, burden 50 tons, Clement Davy master, to Larmester, 11th October 1594

Benedict Harvy of Bristol, Merchant Ind	17	wey	Coal	5	13	4	0

The St Peter of Middelburg, burden 100 tons, James Symons master, to La Rochelle, 11th October 1594

Christopher Harlingson of Middelburg, Merchant Alien	40	wey	Coal	13	6	8	0

The Harry of Bayonne, burden 40 tons, John Furnewe master, to Bayonne, 11th October 1594

John Furnewe of Bayonne, Merchant Alien	15	wey	Coal	5	0	0	0

The Thomas of Bristol, burden 18 tons, William Johans, to St Jean-de-Luz, 12th October 1594

John Barker of Bristol, Merchant Ind	1	dicker	Skins, Calf[39]	1	0	0	0
	3	piece	Cloth of Assize	0	0	0	0
			Cloth of Assize, Overlengths	0	0	0	0

The Thomas of Bristol aforesaid, 12th October 1594

John Drap of Bristol, Merchant Ind	2	piece	Cloth of Assize	0	0	0	0
			Cloth of Assize, Overlengths	0	0	0	0

38 See 26. 39 License dated 4th March 1586.

Merchant name	Qty	Unit	Commodity	£	s.	d.	f.

The Rose of Bristol, burden 16 tons, Thomas Davis master, to Waterford, 15th October 1594

Merchant name	Qty	Unit	Commodity	£	s.	d.	f.
George Woodlock of Waterford, Merchant Ind	2	C	Hops	1	0	0	0
	1	C	Soap, Black	0	10	0	0
	1	hogshead	Vinegar	0	11	6	0

The Hare of Cherbourg, burden 70 tons, Francis Garry master, to La Rochelle, *15th October 1594*

Merchant name	Qty	Unit	Commodity	£	s.	d.	f.
Francis Garry of Cherbourg, *Master* Alien	20	wey	Coal	6	13	4	0

Rose of Bristol aforesaid, *15th October 1594*

Merchant name	Qty	Unit	Commodity	£	s.	d.	f.
John Hopkins of Bristol, Merchant Ind	4	butt	Wine, Rob Davy Corrupt	4	0	0	0

The Roe of Bristol, burden 40 tons, Mathew Honywell master, to Livorno & Marseille, 19th October 1594

Merchant name	Qty	Unit	Commodity	£	s.	d.	f.
William Ellis & John Whittson of Bristol, Merchant Ind	4	ton	Lead	32	0	0	0
	9	piece	Cloth of Assize	0	0	0	0
	1	piece	Cloth of Assize[40]	0	0	0	0
			Cloth of Assize, Overlengths	0	0	0	0

The Elizabeth of *Glon[ ]a?*, burden 50 tons, Stephen Julian master, to *Glon[ ]a, 19th October 1594*

Merchant name	Qty	Unit	Commodity	£	s.	d.	f.
Stephen Jullian, Merchant Alien	12	wey	Coal	4	0	0	0

The Gabriell aforesaid, 23rd October 1594

Merchant name	Qty	Unit	Commodity	£	s.	d.	f.
John Aldworth of Bristol, Merchant Ind	1	piece	Cloth of Assize	0	0	0	0
			Cloth of Assize, Overlengths	0	0	0	0

The Petter of Middelburg aforesaid, 26th October 1594

Merchant name	Qty	Unit	Commodity	£	s.	d.	f.
Christopher Harlinson of Middelburg, Merchant Alien	45	piece	*Bristol* Frieze *Cloth*	45	0	0	0
	5	piece	*Bristol* Frieze *Cloth*[41]	0	0	0	0
	15	piece	Cloth, French (Serge)	30	0	0	0
	14	piece	Cloth of Assize	0	0	0	0
	1	piece	Cloth of Assize[42]	0	0	0	0
			Cloth of Assize, Overlengths	0	0	0	0

The Thought of Bayonne aforesaid, *26th October 1594*

Merchant name	Qty	Unit	Commodity	£	s.	d.	f.
Benedict Harvy of Bristol, Merchant Ind	8	piece	Cloth, French (Serge)	16	0	0	0
	6	piece	*Bristol* Frieze *Cloth*	6	0	0	0

40 Custom exempt.   41 Custom exempt.   42 Custom exempt.

Merchant name	Qty	Unit	Commodity	£	s.	d.	f.
The Thought aforesaid, _26th October 1594_							
John Roberowe of Bristol, Merchant Ind	1.5	C goad	Cotton _Cloth_	5	0	0	0
	4	piece	Cloth of Assize, Devonshire Dozen	0	0	0	0
The Thought aforesaid, _26th October 1594_							
John Cullimore of Bristol, Merchant Ind	4	C goad	Cotton _Cloth_	13	6	8	0
	9	piece	Wadmal Cloth	9	0	0	0
	1	piece	Wadmal Cloth[43]	0	0	0	0
	2	piece	Cloth of Assize	0	0	0	0
			Cloth of Assize, Overlengths	0	0	0	0
The Dove of Bristol, burden 40 tons, Tobias Parry master, to _Larmuster_,[44] 31st October 1594							
Benedict Harvy of Bristol, Merchant Ind	6	piece	_Bristol_ Frieze _Cloth_	6	0	0	0
	10	wey	Coal	3	6	8	0
The Roe of Bristol aforesaid, 2nd November 1594							
John Barker of Bristol, Merchant Ind	5	ton	Lead	40	0	0	0
	5	piece	Cloth of Assize	0	0	0	0
			Cloth of Assize, Overlengths	0	0	0	0
The Roe of Bristol aforesaid, 4th November 1594							
John Drap of Bristol, Merchant Ind	2	piece	Cloth of Assize	0	0	0	0
			Cloth of Assize, Overlengths	0	0	0	0
The Roe of Bristol aforesaid, _4th November 1594_							
Thomas Watkins of Bristol, Draper Ind	4	piece	Cloth of Assize	0	0	0	0
			Cloth of Assize, Overlengths	0	0	0	0
The Roe of Bristol aforesaid, _4th November 1594_							
Walter Williams of Bristol, Draper Ind	5	piece	Cloth of Assize	0	0	0	0
			Cloth of Assize, Overlengths	0	0	0	0
The Roe of Bristol aforesaid, 6th November 1594							
John Webe of Bristol, Merchant Ind	3	piece	Cloth of Assize	0	0	0	0
			Cloth of Assize, Overlengths	0	0	0	0

43 Custom exempt.   44 Possibly Noirmoutier, France.

Merchant name	*Qty*	Unit	Commodity	£	*s.*	*d.*	*f.*
The Roe of Bristol aforesaid, 6th November 1594							
Hugh Griffeths of Bristol, Merchant Ind	9	piece	Cloth of Assize, Kersey	0	0	0	0
	1	piece	Cloth of Assize, Kersey[45]	0	0	0	0
The Roe of Bristol aforesaid, 6th November 1594							
Thomas Whitt of Bristol, Merchant Ind	30	C	Copperas, Green	*15*	0	0	0
	2	ton	Lead	*16*	0	0	0
	2	piece	Cloth of Assize	0	0	0	0
	9	piece	Cloth of Assize, Kersey	0	0	0	0
			Cloth of Assize, Overlengths	0	0	0	0
The Grace of Bristol, burden 18 tons, Stephen Buckhall master, to La Rochelle, 26th November 1594							
John Samford of Bristol, Merchant Ind	8	wey	Coal	2	*13*	*4*	0
The Grace aforesaid, *26th November 1594*							
John Samford of Bristol, Merchant Ind	8	C	Rice	6	*13*	*4*	0
	4	C	Sulpher[46]	*0*	*0*	*0*	*0*
The Diamound of Bristol, burden 50 tons, Christopher Taylor master, to La Rochelle, 27th November 1594							
John Aldworth of Bristol, Merchant Ind	2	ton	Lead	*16*	0	0	0
	6	C	Wax	*18*	0	0	0
The Diamound aforesaid, 28th November 1594							
John Barker of Bristol, Merchant Ind	5	ton	Lead	40	0	0	0
The Diamound aforesaid, 28th November 1594							
George Lane & John Love of Bristol, Merchant Ind	6	ton	Lead	*48*	0	0	0
	6	C	Wax	*18*	0	0	0
The Diamound aforesaid, 28th November 1594							
John Oliver of Bristol, Merchant Ind	2	ton	Lead	*16*	0	0	0
	3	C	Wax	9	0	0	0
The Grace of Bristol aforesaid, 28th November 1594							
John Barker of Bristol, Merchant Ind	2	ton	Lead	*16*	0	0	0
	7	C	Wax	*21*	0	0	0

45 Custom exempt.   **46** See note 35.

Merchant name	Qty	Unit	Commodity	£	s.	d.	f.
The Diamound aforesaid, 29th November 1594							
John Roberowe of Bristol, Merchant Ind	4	piece	Cloth of Assize, Devonshire Dozen	0	0	0	0
The Grace aforesaid, *29th November 1594*							
John Drap of Bristol, Merchant Ind	5	C	Wax	15	0	0	0
The Lilllie of Bristol, burden 25 tons, Hugh Jones master, to La Rochelle, *29th November 1594*							
John Browne of Bristol, Merchant Ind	3	ton	Lead	24	0	0	0
The John of Bristol, burden 16 tons, Christopher Burkett master, to Youghal, *29th November 1594*							
Thomas Darrell of London, Merchant Ind	3	C	Pans, Frying	2	0	0	0
The Grace aforesaid, 30th November 1594							
William Ellis of Bristol, Merchant Ind	3.5	C	Wax	10	10	0	0
The John of Bristol aforesaid, *30th November 1594*							
Richard Hackett of Waterford, Merchant Ind	1	dozen	Galer	1	10	0	0
	2	lb	Silk, Nobs	0	0	20	0
	1	gross	Points, Thread	0	0	10	0
	2	lb	Mail	0	0	15	0
	2	piece	Lanterns	0	0	15	0
	1	gross	Girdles, Leather (1d.)	0	10	0	0
	1	lb	Wax	0	0	10	0
	0.5	dozen	Penners	0	0	10	0
	1	gross	Trenchers	0	3	4	0
	2	piece	Brushes	0	0	20	0
	1	ream	Paper	0	3	4	0
	1	gross	Knives	1	0	0	0
	1	M	Pins	0	0	10	0
	6	piece	Bottles, Leather small	0	3	4	0
	2	piece	Candlesticks, Small Brass	0	3	4	0
	6	yard	Levant Taffeta Cloth	0	10	0	0
	21	lb	Pewter	0	4	2	0
	2	pair	Bellows	0	0	20	0
	2	lb	Thread, Packet	0	0	10	0
	1	clout	Needles	0	0	10	0
	1.5	lb	Silk, Paris	0	10	0	0
	6	piece	Setting Sticks	0	0	20	0
	0.5	gross	Combs, Wooden	0	2	6	0
	1	dozen	Playing Cards	0	0	20	0
	1	dozen	Wool-Cards	0	10	0	0

Merchant name	Qty	Unit	Commodity	£	s.	d.	f.

The Grace of Bristol aforesaid, 2nd December 1594

| Mathew Haviland of Bristol, Merchant Ind | 2 | C | Wax | 6 | 0 | 0 | 0 |

The Diamound aforesaid, *2nd December 1594*

| John Barker of Bristol, Merchant Ind | 5 | ton | Lead | 40 | 0 | 0 | 0 |

The Sallomon of Barnstaple, burden 15 tons, Robert Patenson master, to Cork, *2nd December 1594*

| William Clappell of Bristol, Merchant Ind | 1 | ton | Iron | 8 | 0 | 0 | 0 |

The Diamound aforesaid, *2nd December 1594*

| George Whitt of Bristol, Merchant Ind | 3.5 | C | Wax | 10 | 10 | 0 | 0 |
| | 4 | piece | *Bristol* Frieze *Cloth* | 4 | 0 | 0 | 0 |

The Sallomon aforesaid, *2nd December 1594*

William Haley of Limerick, Merchant Ind	1	C	Hops	0	10	0	0
	3	dozen	Wool-Cards, Old	1	0	0	0
	9	piece	Hats, Coarse	1	2	6	0
	2	ream	Paper	0	6	8	0
	4	small gross	Buttons, Thread	0	0	20	0
	2	small gross	Buttons, Glass	0	0	20	0
	6	dozen	Drinking Glasses, Coarse	0	5	0	0
	0.5	gross	**Peeres**	0	2	6	0
	0.5	gross	Cutts (*ob.*)	0	2	6	0
	3	small gross	Points, Thread	0	2	6	0
	1	dozen	Spurs, Small	0	0	20	0
	4	small gross	Points, Red	0	3	4	0
	1	burden	Steel	0	5	0	0
	4	lb	Mail	0	0	25	0
	2	clout	Needles	0	0	20	0
	6	dozen	Combs, Wooden	0	2	6	0
	4	nests	Boxes, Painted	0	0	20	0
	4	lb	Thread, Packet	0	0	20	0
	1	dozen	Glasses, Looking	0	0	10	0
	4	gross	Trenchers, Wooden	0	13	4	0
	2	dozen	Cups, Wooden	0	0	20	0
	3	dozen	Bottles, Sucking	0	0	20	0

The Sallomon aforesaid, *2nd December 1594*

Edward Roche of Cork, Merchant Ind	4	dozen	Wool-Cards	2	0	0	0
	0.5	piece	Holmes Fustian *Cloth*	0	6	8	0
	2	burden	Tin	0	10	0	0
	4	dozen	Girdles (1*d.*)	0	3	4	0
	2	dozen	Girdles, Waist	0	0	20	0

Merchant name	Qty	Unit	Commodity	£	s.	d.	f.
	1	C	Hops	0	10	0	0
	28	lb	Soap, Black	0	0	30	0
	7	dozen	Knives, Pocket	0	11	6	0
	8	dozen	Cutts (1d.)	0	6	8	0
	2	dozen	Knives, in Pairs	0	3	4	0
	2	dozen	Knives, Prage	0	3	4	0
	0.5	gross	Combs, Wooden	0	0	30	0
	6	M	Pins	0	3	4	0
	2	gross	Trenchers	0	6	8	0
	3	gross	Points, Thread	0	0	30	0
	4	gross	Points, Red	0	3	4	0
	2	piece	Nickel	0	0	20	0
	2	rolls	Gartering	0	3	4	0
	1	lb	Silk, Paris	0	6	8	0
	3	dozen	Glasses, Looking	0	0	30	0
	2	lb	Thread,Black	0	0	20	0
	2	dozen	Books, School of Virtue	0	0	20	0
	0.25	lb	Saffron	0	3	4	0
	6	yard	Levant Taffeta Cloth	0	10	0	0
	1	ell	Broad Taffeta Cloth	0	8	4	0
	4	piece	Brushes	0	0	10	0
	0.5	C	Orchil	0	10	0	0
	3	lb	Mail	0	0	20	0
	2	dozen	Girth-Web	0	0	20	0
	8	lb	Sugar	0	5	0	0
	6	lb	Soap, White	0	0	20	0
	6	unknown	Skins, Parchment	0	0	20	0
	0.5	lb	Cloves	0	2	6	0
	12	lb	Liquorice	0	0	20	0
	1	ream	Paper	0	3	4	0
	0.5	dozen	Candlesticks	0	0	20	0
	1	dozen	Penners	0	0	10	0
	1	lb	Silk, Nobs	0	0	10	0
	12	lb	Bombas	0	5	0	0
	12	piece	Felts	1	10	0	0
	2	clout	Needles	0	0	20	0

The Mayflower of Bristol, burden 80 tons, Andrew Battine master, to La Rochelle, 3rd December 1594

Thomas James of Bristol, Merchant Ind	15	wey	Coal	5	0	0	0

The Diamound aforesaid, 4th December 1594

Thomas Hopkins of Bristol, Merchant Ind	1	ton	Lead	8	0	0	0

The Hercules of Bristol, burden 50 tons, Thomas Bennett master, to La Rochelle, 4th December 1594

Christopher Pitt of Bristol, Merchant Ind	24	wey	Coal	8	0	0	0

Merchant name	Qty	Unit	Commodity	£	s.	d.	f.

The Pellican of Marennes, burden 40 tons, Isaiah Gottier master, to Marennes, 6th December 1594

| Isaiah Gottier of Marennes, ,Merchant Alien | 10 | wey | Coal | 3 | 6 | 8 | 0 |

The Robert of Marennes, burden 20 tons, Peter Jubert master, to Marennes, *6th December 1594*

| Peter Jubert of Marennes, Merchant Alien | 10 | wey | Coal | 3 | 6 | 8 | 0 |

The Mayflower aforesaid, 12th December 1594

| Edward Lewis of Bristol, Merchant Ind | 13 | piece | *Bristol* Frieze *Cloth* | 13 | 0 | 0 | 0 |
| | 9 | C | Rice | 7 | 4 | 2 | 0 |

The Mayflower aforesaid, *12th December 1594*

| Maria Gittins of Bristol, Merchant Ind | 3 | C | Rice | 2 | 8 | 0 | 0 |

The Mayflower aforesaid, *12th December 1594*

| William Dawer of Bristol, Merchant Ind | 2 | ton | Lead | 16 | 0 | 0 | 0 |

The Mayflower aforesaid, *12th December 1594*

| William Coale of Bristol, Merchant Ind | 4 | C | Wax | 12 | 0 | 0 | 0 |

The Mayflower aforesaid, 16th December 1594

William Ellis of Bristol, Merchant Ind	1	ton	Lead	8	0	0	0
	4	piece	Cloth of Assize	0	0	0	0
			Cloth of assize, Overlengths	0	0	0	0

The Doe of Bristol, burden 18 tons, John Everett master, to Cork, 21st December 1594

William Copenger of Cork, Merchant Ind	2	C	Hops	*1*	*0*	*0*	*0*
	12	yard	Cotton *Cloth*	*0*	*10*	*0*	*0*
	12	yard	Levant Taffeta Cloth	*1*	*0*	*0*	*0*
	0.5	gross	Wool-Cards	*3*	*0*	*0*	*0*
	0.5	piece	Holmes Fustian *Cloth*	*0*	*6*	*8*	*0*
	0.5	C	Orchil	*0*	*10*	*0*	*0*
	24	lb	Bombas	*0*	*6*	*8*	*0*
	2	dozen	Girdles (1*d.*)	*0*	*0*	*20*	*0*
	2	ream	Paper	*0*	*6*	*8*	*0*
	1	gross	Knives (1*d.*)	*0*	*10*	*0*	*0*
	2	gross	Trenchers, Common	*0*	*0*	*20*	*0*
	12	lb	Liquorice	*0*	*0*	*15*	*0*
	2	small gross	*Points*, Thread	*0*	*0*	*20*	*0*
	1	gross	***Points, Red***	*0*	*0*	*10*	*0*
	2	gross	Combs, Wooden	*0*	*10*	*0*	*0*
	2	dozen	Hats, Coarse	*3*	*0*	*0*	*0*

Merchant name	Qty	Unit	Commodity	£	s.	d.	f.
	1	dozen	Stockings, Short	0	8	4	0
	1	gross	Girth-Web	0	6	8	0
	4	dozen	Girdles (1d.)	0	3	4	0
	1	lb	Silk, Paris	0	6	8	0
	1	dozen	Lanterns	0	6	8	0
	1	dozen	Serches	0	6	8	0
	4	dozen	Glasses (ob.)	0	0	20	0
	4	lb	Gales	0	0	10	0
	6	lb	Copperas	0	0	10	0
	2	lb	Pepper	0	3	4	0
	2	lb	Ginger	0	3	4	0
	2	dozen	Snuffers	0	6	8	0
	2	dozen	Glasses, Hour	0	3	4	0
	4	lb	Mail	0	0	25	0
	6	yard	Cloth of Assize, Northern	0	0	0	0

The Doe aforesaid, 21st December 1594

Merchant name	Qty	Unit	Commodity	£	s.	d.	f.
Patrick Meagh of Cork, Merchant Ind	1	dozen	Hats	1	10	0	0
	1	C	Hops	0	10	0	0
	6	yard	Levant Taffeta Cloth	0	10	0	0
	9	yard	Cotton *Cloth*	0	7	6	0
	1	gross	Wool-Cards, Old	4	0	0	0
	1	ream	Paper	0	3	4	0
	2	lb	Mail	0	0	15	0
	12	lb	Liquorice	0	0	15	0
	3	small gross	Points, Thread	0	2	6	0
	9	dozen	Points, Red	0	0	15	0
	6	pairs	Stockings, Short	0	4	2	0
	0.5	gross	Girth-Web	0	3	4	0
	3	dozen	Girth Buckles	0	0	20	0
	6	dozen	Girdles (1d.)	0	5	0	0
	1	lb	Silk, Slewe	0	6	8	0
	1	small gross	Glasses, Looking (ob.)	0	4	2	0
	3	lb	Gales	0	0	10	0
	6	lb	Copperas	0	0	10	0
	3	dozen	Cups, Wooden	0	2	6	0
	2	lb	Pepper	0	3	4	0
	2	lb	Ginger	0	3	4	
	3	lb	Mercury	0	6	8	0
	3	pair	Playing Cards	0	2	6	0
	1	dozen	Snuffers	0	3	4	0
	1	dozen	Glasses, Hour	0	0	20	0
	0.5	dozen	Brushes	0	0	10	0
	12	bale	Dice	0	3	4	0
	3	lb	Girdles, Nobs Silk	0	2	6	0
	4	clout	Needles	0	3	4	0
	2	dozen	Spurs, Coarse	0	6	8	0
	4	C	Awl Blades	0	3	4	0
	2	lb	Counters	0	0	20	0
	6	small gross	Buttons, Thread	0	5	0	0

Merchant name	Qty	Unit	Commodity	£	s.	d.	f.
	6	dozen	Shoe Horns	0	0	10	0
	6	pair	Bellows	0	5	0	0
	2	lb	Thread, Brown	0	3	4	0
	1	burden	Steel	0	5	0	0
	5	yard	New *Cloth*	1	7	6	0

The Kathern of Alderney, burden 25 tons, Nicholas Coke master, to Guernsey, 7th January 1595

James Bevoire of Jersey, Merchant	14	wey	Coal	4	13	4	0

The Follia of Saõ Vicente, burden 16 tons, Martin Deoyarsiver master, to Saõ Vicente, 14th January 1595

John Barker of Bristol, Merchant Ind	2	ton	Lead	16	0	0	0
	2	C	Wax	6	0	0	0

The Follia aforesaid, 14th January 1595

Martin Deoyarsiver of Saõ Vicente, Merchant Alien	6.5	C	Wax	19	10	0	0

The Anne of Marennes, burden 30 tons, Evan Evans master, to La Rochelle, 15th January 1595

James Goder of La Rochelle, Merchant Alien	16	wey	Coal	5	6	8	0

The Follia aforesaid, 17th January 1595

Thomas James of Bristol, Merchant Ind	8	dicker	Skins, Calf	8	0	0	0

The Follia aforesaid, 18th January 1595

William Ellis of Bristol, Merchant Ind	1	piece	Cloth of Assize	0	0	0	0
			Cloth of Assize, Overlengths	0	0	0	0

The Follia aforesaid, 18th January 1595

Martin Deoyarsiver of Saõ Vicente, Merchant Alien	4.5	C	Wax	13	10	0	0

The Follia aforesaid, 18th January 1595

Thomas James of Bristol, Merchant Ind	4	dicker	Skins, Calf	4	0	0	0

The Peter of Milford Haven, burden 16 tons, John Devorex master, to Waterford, 28th January 1595

Patrick Sall of Waterford, Merchant Ind	4	C	Hops	2	0	0	0

Merchant name	Qty	Unit	Commodity	£	s.	d.	f.

The Peter aforesaid, 28th January 1595

Patrick Lea of Waterford, Merchant Ind	1	C	Currants	1	10	0	0
	0.5	C	Prunes	0	5	0	0
	0.5	C	Aniseed	0	13	4	0
	0.5	C	Sugar	1	13	4	0
	1	C	Alum	1	13	4	0

The Peter aforesaid, 28th January 1595

Nicholas Rice of Limerick, Merchant Ind	1	dozen	Hats, Black	1	10	0	0
	3	C	Hops	1	10	0	0
	6	pair	Playing Tables	0	6	8	0
	0.5	gross	Wool-Cards	3	0	0	0
	3	gross	Trenchers, Wooden	0	3	4	0
	6	lb	Mail	0	3	4	0
	1	C	Figs	0	13	4	0
	1	dozen	Hats, Childrens	1	0	0	0
	4	gross	Buttons, Thread	0	3	4	0
	0.25	C	Currants	0	4	2	0
	2	gross	Buttons, Glass	0	0	20	0
	2	lb	Thread, Piecing	0	5	0	0
	0.5	gross	Points, Red	0	0	10	0
	4	lb	Succado & Marmalade	0	4	2	0
	4	clout	Needles	0	3	4	0
	10	papers[47]	Pins	0	0	20	0
	23	lb	Sugar	0	13	4	0
	4	dozen	Glasses, Looking	0	3	4	0
	6	piece	Brushes	0	0	20	0
	23	lb	Seed, Onion	0	5	0	0
	18	lb	Seed, Leek	0	3	4	0
	1	dozen	Penners	0	0	20	0
	4	dozen	Girdles (1d.)	0	3	4	0
		unknown	Glasses (1d.)	0	10	0	0
	1	gross	Knives	0	10	0	0
	1	gross	Knives, Pocket	1	0	0	0
	2	gross	Points, Thread	0	3	4	0
			Apothecary Wares	0	10	0	0
	9	yard	Cloth of Assize, Remnants	0	0	0	0

The George of Milford Haven, burden 16 tons, David Proutt master, to Drogheda, 31st January 1595

| Edward Bath of Drogheda, Merchant Ind | 16 | pair | Millstones, small called Dogstones | 16 | 0 | 0 | 0 |

47 Ie. a clout.

Merchant name	Qty	Unit	Commodity	£	s.	d.	f.

The Pellican of Bremen, burden 100 tons, Henry Vanleighe master, to La Rochelle, 1st February 1595

Abraham Vanherwicke of London, Merchant Alien	20	wey	Coal	6	13	4	o

The John of Bristol, burden 16 tons, Christopher Burckett master, to Youghal, 3rd February 1595

Christopher Burckett of Bristol, Merchant Ind	11	pair	Quern-Stones	1	16	8	o
	1	pair	Millstones, small called Dogstones	1	o	o	o
	3	piece	Grind- Stones	o	5	o	o
	3	C	Iron	o	6	8	o

The Mary of Bristol, burden 16 tons, William Mansfield master, to Youghal, 5th February 1595

John Wattes of Bristol, Merchant Ind	25	piece	Raisins, *Great*	6	5	o	o

Pellican of Bremen aforesaid, 10th February 1595

Hug[]bright Jonson of Antwerp, Merchant Alien	8	C	Cork	2	13	4	o

The Thomas of Bristol, burden 20 tons, James Whittinge master, to La Rochelle, *10th February 1595*

Thomas Hopkins of Bristol, Merchant Ind	3	piece	*Bristol* Frieze *Cloth*	3	o	o	o
	4	piece	Cloth of Assize, Bridgwater	o	o	o	o
	7	piece	Cloth of Assize	o	o	o	o
			Cloth of Assize, Overlengths	o	o	o	o

The Thomas aforesaid, *10th February 1595*

George Whitt of Bristol, Merchant Ind	4	piece	Cloth of Assize	o	o	o	o
			Cloth of Assize, Overlengths	o	o	o	o

The Thomas aforesaid, *10th February 1595*

Thomas Rowe & John Pitt of London & Bristol, Merchants Ind	11	piece	Cloth of Assize, Northern Dozen Single	o	o	o	o
	1	piece	Cloth of Assize, Northern Dozen Single[48]	o	o	o	o

48 Custom exempt.

Merchant name	Qty	Unit	Commodity	£	s.	d.	f.
	4	piece	Cloth of Assize	0	0	0	0
			Cloth of Assize, Overlengths	0	0	0	0
	3	C	Soap, Black	1	10	0	0

The Thomas aforesaid, 10th February 1595

Merchant name	Qty	Unit	Commodity	£	s.	d.	f.
John Aldworth of Bristol, Merchant Ind	11	piece	Cloth of Assize, Streit	0	0	0	0
	1	piece	Cloth of Assize, Streit[49]	0	0	0	0
	0.75	C	Wax	2	5	0	0

The Thomas aforesaid, 10th February 1595

Merchant name	Qty	Unit	Commodity	£	s.	d.	f.
William Cole of Bristol, Merchant Ind	2	piece	Cloth of Assize	0	0	0	0
			Cloth of Assize, Overlengths	0	0	0	0

The Thomas aforesaid, 10th February 1595

Merchant name	Qty	Unit	Commodity	£	s.	d.	f.
William Ellis of Bristol, Merchant Ind	7	piece	Cloth of Assize	0	0	0	0
			Cloth of Assize, Overlengths	0	0	0	0

The Thomas aforesaid, 10th February 1595

Merchant name	Qty	Unit	Commodity	£	s.	d.	f.
John Robero of Bristol, Merchant Ind	6	piece	Cloth of Assize, Streit	0	0	0	0

The Rose of Bristol, burden 16 tons, Robert U[]ien (?) master, to Waterford, 12th February 1595

Merchant name	Qty	Unit	Commodity	£	s.	d.	f.
Richard Comerford of Waterford, Merchant Ind	4	C	Battery	8	0	0	0
	0.5	dozen	Stock-Cards	0	6	8	0
	20	rolls	Coarse Cyprus *Cloth*	0	16	6	0
	2	gross	Lace, Statute	0	13	4	0
	2	lb	Girdles, Nobs Silk	0	0	20	0
	1.5	dozen	Knives, Pocket	0	2	6	0
	8	dozen	Cruses, Stone Uncovered	0	5	0	0
	0.5	dozen	Pots, Iron	0	5	0	0
	2	dozen	Locks Hanging, Small	0	3	4	0
	2	lb	Seed, Cumin	0	0	10	0
	18	lb	Mail	0	9	2	0
	1	dozen	Penners	0	0	10	0
	3	lb	Silk, Paris	1	0	0	0
	1.5	piece	Holmes Fustian *Cloth*	1	0	0	0
	0.5	C	Rice	0	8	4	0
	2	dozen	Hats	3	0	0	0
	1	dozen	Hats, Childrens	1	0	0	0

49 Custom exempt.

Merchant name	Qty	Unit	Commodity	£	s.	d.	f.
	1	piece	Jeane Fustian *Cloth*	0	13	4	0
	1	dozen	Stockings, Short Knit	0	10	0	0
	1	dozen	Hose, Womens	0	8	4	0
	0.5	lb	Kermes	0	0	20	0
			Points, Broad[50]	0	3	4	0
	4	small gross	Buttons, Thread	0	0	20	0
	2	small gross	Points, Thread	0	0	20	0
	7	C	Hops	3	10	0	0
	6	*lb*	Serches	0	3	4	0
	12	lb	Thread, Packet	0	4	2	0
	3	lb	Turnsole	0	0	20	0
	14	lb	Alum	0	5	0	0
	8	lb	Currants	0	0	20	0
	0.5	lb	Wormseed	0	0	15	0
	1	M	Lath Nails	0	3	4	0
	8	piece	Hats, Coarse	1	0	0	0

The Petter of Cardiff, burden 14 tons, John Blethen master, to Cardiff, 17th February 1595[51]

Nicholas Ningartt of St Malo, Merchant Alien	12	piece	Kidwelly Frieze Cloth	11	0	0	0

The Black Swane of Bristol, burden 50 tons, Peter Dine master, to La Rochelle, *17th February 1595*

	Qty	Unit	Commodity	£	s.	d.	f.
Robert Aldworth of Bristol, Merchant Ind	18	piece	Bay *Cloth*	36	0	0	0
	2	piece	Bay *Cloth*[52]	0	0	0	0
	9	piece	Saye *Cloth*	9	0	0	0
	1	piece	Saye *Cloth*	0	0	0	0
	1.5	C	Wax	4	10	0	0
	44	piece	Cloth of Assize, Penistone, Unfriezed	0	0	0	0
	4	piece	Cloth of Assize, Penistone[53]	0	0	0	0
	5	piece	Cloth of Assize, Pin White	0	0	0	0
	14	piece	Cloth of Assize, Streit	0	0	0	0
	1	piece	Cloth of Assize, Streit[54]	0	0	0	0
	18	piece	Cloth of Assize, Dozen Devonshire Single	0	0	0	0
	2	piece	Cloth of Assize, Dozen Devonshire Single[55]	0	0	0	0
	8	piece	Cloth of Assize	0	0	0	0
			Cloth of Assize, Overlengths	0	0	0	0

50 Listed as broad lace. This may be points or lace.   51 From there to be transported in the Ange of Cardiff, burden 40 tons, Peter Balan master, to St Malo.   52 Custom exempt.   53 Custom exempt.   54 Custom exempt.   55 Custom exempt.

Merchant name	Qty	Unit	Commodity	£	s.	d.	f.

The Fortune of Bristol, burden 25 tons, Henry Hogaskins master, to La Rochelle, *17th February 1595*

John Marshall of Bristol, Merchant Ind	12	wey	Coal	4	0	0	0

The Daisey of Bristol, burden 30 tons, Henry Lewis master, to Brest, 18th February 1595

John Love of Bristol, Merchant Ind	8	C goad	Cotton *Cloth*	26	13	4	0
	22	piece	Wadmal Cloth	22	0	0	0
	2	piece	Wadmal Cloth[56]	0	0	0	0
	9	piece	Bay *Cloth*	18	0	0	0
	1	piece	Bay *Cloth*	2	0	0	0

The Daisey aforesaid, *18th February 1595*

Edward Bentley of Bristol, Merchant Ind	6	C goad	Cotton *Cloth*	20	0	0	0
	22	piece	Wadmal Cloth	22	0	0	0
	2	piece	Wadmal Cloth[57]	0	0	0	0
	18	piece	Dunster Cotton *Cloth*	18	0	0	0
	2	piece	Dunster Cotton *Cloth*[58]	0	0	0	0

The Daisey aforesaid, *18th February 1595*

John Redinge of Bristol, Merchant Ind	2	C goad	Cotton *Cloth*	6	13	4	0
	11	piece	Wadmal Cloth	11	0	0	0
	1	piece	Wadmal Cloth[59]	0	0	0	0

The Daisey aforesaid, *18th February 1595*

John Collimore of Bristol, Merchant Ind	9	piece	Serge called Paris Cloth	18	0	0	0
	4	piece	Cloth of Assize	0	0	0	0
			Cloth of Assize, Overlengths	0	0	0	0

The Daisey aforesaid, *18th February 1595*

Richard Batt of Bristol, Merchant Ind	24	piece	Wadmal Cloth	24	0	0	0
	2	piece	Wadmal Cloth[60]	0	0	0	0
	4	C goad	Cotton *Cloth*	13	6	8	0
	6	piece	Coloured Cotton *Cloth*	6	0	0	0
	2	piece	Cloth of Assize	0	0	0	0
			Cloth of Assize, Overlengths	0	0	0	0

The Pellican aforesaid, 19th February 1595

Abraham Vanherwicke of London, Merchant Alien	6	wey	Coal	2	0	0	0

56 Custom exempt. 57 Custom exempt. 58 Custom exempt. 59 Custom exempt. 60 Custom exempt.

Merchant name	Qty	Unit	Commodity	£	s.	d.	f.

The Daisey aforesaid, 20th February 1595

Merchant name	Qty	Unit	Commodity	£	s.	d.	f.
William Ben[]ger of Bristol, Merchant Ind	4	C goad	Cotton *Cloth*	13	6	8	0
		piece	*Bristol* Frieze *Cloth*	8	0	0	0
		piece	Cloth of Assize	0	0	0	0
			Cloth of Assize, Overlengths	0	0	0	0

The Daisey aforesaid, *20th February 1595*

Merchant name	Qty	Unit	Commodity	£	s.	d.	f.
Christopher Carry of Bristol, Merchant Ind	9.5	piece	Milan Fustian *Cloth*	9	10	0	0
	18	piece	Cloth of Assize, Kersey	0	0	0	0
	1	piece	Cloth of Assize, Kersey[61]	0	0	0	0

The Daisey aforesaid, *20th February 1595*

Merchant name	Qty	Unit	Commodity	£	s.	d.	f.
George Lane of Bristol, Merchant Ind	2.5	piece	Cloth of Assize	0	0	0	0
			Cloth of Assize, Overlengths	0	0	0	0

The Daisey aforesaid, *20th February 1595*

Merchant name	Qty	Unit	Commodity	£	s.	d.	f.
William Walles of Bristol, Merchant Ind	4	C goad	Cotton *Cloth*	13	6	8	0
	4	piece	Cloth of Assize	0	0	0	0
			Cloth of Assize, Overlengths	0	0	0	0

The Dove of Bristol, burden 40 tons, Richard Parsons master, to La Rochelle, *20th February 1595*

Merchant name	Qty	Unit	Commodity	£	s.	d.	f.
Daniel Baker of Bristol, Merchant Ind	6	C goad	Cotton *Cloth*	20	0	0	0
	9	piece	*Bristol* Frieze *Cloth*	9	0	0	0
	1	piece	*Bristol* Frieze *Cloth*[62]	0	0	0	0

The St Petter of Middelburg, burden 100 tons, Petter Kinge master, to Livorno, 20th February 1595

Merchant name	Qty	Unit	Commodity	£	s.	d.	f.
Peter Kinge of Middelburg, Merchant Alien	10	M	Fish, Dry Newfoundland	50	0	0	0

The Red Lyon of Haarlem, burden 110 tons, Symon Clawson master, to Livorno, *20th February 1595*

Merchant name	Qty	Unit	Commodity	£	s.	d.	f.
Symon Clawson of Middelburg, Merchant Alien	8	M	Fish, Dry Newfoundland	40	0	0	0

61 Custom exempt.   62 Custom exempt.

Merchant name	Qty	Unit	Commodity	£	s.	d.	f.

The Daisey aforesaid, 21st February 1595

Merchant name	Qty	Unit	Commodity	£	s.	d.	f.
John Hopkins of Bristol, Merchant Ind	40	yard	Portingale *Cloth*	2	0	0	0
	1	piece	*Bristol* Frieze *Cloth*	*1*	0	0	0
	9	piece	Wadmal Cloth	9	0	0	0
	1	piece	Wadmal Cloth[63]	0	0	0	0

The Margaret of Milford Haven, burden 16 tons, Patrick Savers master, to Dundalk, 21st February 1595

Merchant name	Qty	Unit	Commodity	£	s.	d.	f.
Patrick Cashall of Dundalk, Merchant Ind	12	piece	Millstones, small called Dogstones	12	0	0	0

The Fortune aforesaid, 22nd February 1595

Merchant name	Qty	Unit	Commodity	£	s.	d.	f.
Richard Tovy of Bristol, Merchant Ind	8	piece	*Bristol* Frieze *Cloth*	8	0	0	0

The Red Lyon aforesaid, 28th February 1595

Merchant name	Qty	Unit	Commodity	£	s.	d.	f.
Tobias Van Assan of London, Merchant Ind	5	piece	Cloth of Assize	0	0	0	0
			Cloth of Assize, Overlengths	0	0	0	0

The Red Lyon aforesaid, 28th February 1595

Merchant name	Qty	Unit	Commodity	£	s.	d.	f.
Roger Van Colge of London, Merchant Ind	2	M ell	Narrow Hamborough Linen *Cloth*	50	0	0	0

The St Petter of Middelburg aforesaid, burden 100 tons, 28th February 1595

Merchant name	Qty	Unit	Commodity	£	s.	d.	f.
Christopher Harlinson of Middelburg, Merchant Alien	16.5	fardel	Vitry Canvas *Cloth*	0	0	0	0
	60	piece	**Methernix Cloth**[64]	*0*	*0*	*0*	*0*

The Red Lyon aforesaid, *28th February 1595*

Merchant name	Qty	Unit	Commodity	£	s.	d.	f.
Christopher Harlinson of Middelburg, Merchant Alien	60	piece	**Methernix Cloth**[65]	*0*	*0*	*0*	*0*

The Red Lyon aforesaid, *28th February 1595*

Merchant name	Qty	Unit	Commodity	£	s.	d.	f.
Christopher Harlinson of Middelburg, Merchant Alien	14	balette	Vitry Canvas *Cloth*	*0*	*0*	*0*	*0*

The Dove aforesaid, 1st March 1595

Merchant name	Qty	Unit	Commodity	£	s.	d.	f.
John Barker of Bristol, Merchant Ind	4	dicker	Hides, Calf[66]	4	0	0	0

---

63 Custom exempt. **64** Custom paid in the Peter of Middelburg, burden 100 tons, James Symonds master, from *Burniffe*, 30th Sept. 1594. **65** As above. **66** License dated 4th March 1586.

Merchant name	Qty	Unit	Commodity	£	s.	d.	f.

The Elizabeth Bonaventure of Bristol, burden 50 tons, Thomas Horwell master, to Brest, 3rd March 1595

Merchant name	Qty	Unit	Commodity	£	s.	d.	f.
Richard Cole & Arthur Hibons of Bristol, Merchants Ind	30	C	Wax	90	0	0	0

The Elizabeth Bonaventure aforesaid, 3rd March 1595

Merchant name	Qty	Unit	Commodity	£	s.	d.	f.
Arthur Hibons of Bristol, Merchant Ind	18	piece	Cloth of Assize, Devonshire Kersey	0	0	0	0
	2	piece	Cloth of Assize, Devonshire Kersey[67]	0	0	0	0
	3	M	Fish, Dry Newfoundland	15	0	0	0

The Elizabeth Bonaventure aforesaid, 3rd March 1595

Merchant name	Qty	Unit	Commodity	£	s.	d.	f.
William Ellis of Bristol, Merchant Ind	11	piece	Bay *Cloth*	22	0	0	0
	1	piece	Bay Cloth[68]	0	0	0	0

The Pellican aforesaid, *3rd March 1595*

Merchant name	Qty	Unit	Commodity	£	s.	d.	f.
John Whittson of Bristol, Merchant Ind	18	piece	Cloth of Assize, Kersey	0	0	0	0
	2	piece	Cloth of Assize, Kersey[69]	0	0	0	0

The Pellican aforesaid, *3rd March 1595*

Merchant name	Qty	Unit	Commodity	£	s.	d.	f.
Peter Kinge of Middelburg, Merchant Ind	18	piece	Bay *Cloth*	36	0	0	0
	2	piece	Bay *Cloth*[70]	0	0	0	0

The Pellican aforesaid, *3rd March 1595*

Merchant name	Qty	Unit	Commodity	£	s.	d.	f.
Christopher Harlinson of Middelburg, Merchant Alien	11	piece	Serge called Paris Cloth	22	0	0	0
	1	piece	Serge called Paris Cloth[71]	0	0	0	0
	54	piece	Cloth of Assize, Kersey	0	0	0	0
	6	piece	Cloth of Assize, Kersey[72]	0	0	0	0
	4	piece	Cloth of Assize	0	0	0	0
	9	piece	Cloth of Assize, Streit	0	0	0	0
			Cloth of Assize, Overlengths	0	0	0	0

67 Custom exempt. 68 Custom exempt. 69 Custom exempt. 70 Custom exempt. 71 Custom exempt. 72 Custom exempt.

Merchant name	Qty	Unit	Commodity	£	s.	d.	f.
The Pellican of Bremen aforesaid, 4th March 1595							
John Collimore of Bristol, Merchant Ind	4	C goad	Cotton *Cloth*	13	6	8	0
The Elizabeth Bonaventure aforesaid, 4th March 1595							
Thomas Tailor of Bristol, Merchant Ind	2	piece	Cloth of Assize	0	0	0	0
			Cloth of Assize, Overlengths	0	0	0	0
	6	piece	*Bristol* Frieze *Cloth*	6	0	0	0
The Dove aforesaid, 7th March 1595							
William Ellis of Bristol, Merchant Ind	5	piece	Cloth of Assize	0	0	0	0
			Cloth of Assize, Overlengths	0	0	0	0
The Pellican aforesaid, *7th March 1595*							
William Ellis of Bristol, Merchant Ind	5	piece	Cloth of Assize	0	0	0	0
			Cloth of Assize, Overlengths	0	0	0	0
The Elizabeth Bonaventure aforesaid, *7th March 1595*							
Arthur Hibons of Bristol, Merchant Ind	4	C	Soap, White	3	0	0	0
The Jonas of Dungarvan, burden 30 tons, Philip Nogle master, to Dungarvan, *7th March 1595*							
James Hoare of Dungarvan, Merchant Ind	1	C	Hops	0	10	0	0
	3	dozen	Knives (1d.)	0	0	30	0
	4	lb	Girdles, Nobs Silk	0	3	4	0
	1	gross	Thread, Inkle	0	6	8	0
	1.5	C	Battery	3	0	0	0
	28	lb	Pots, Brass	0	10	0	0
The Salloman of Bristol, burden 16 tons, Thomas Davis master, to Cork, 13th March 1595							
William Chappell of Bristol, Merchant Ind	2	ton	Iron	16	0	0	0
	1	pair	Millstones, small called Dogstones	1	0	0	0
The Salloman aforesaid, 14th March 1595							
Edward Roche of Cork, Merchant Ind	1	C	Hops	0	10	0	0
	0.5	dozen	*Hats, Coarse*	0	15	0	0
	0.5	dozen	Hats, Childrens	0	10	0	0
	2	burden	Tin	0	10	0	0
	4	gross	Trenchers	0	3	4	0
	3	dozen	Wool-Cards	1	10	0	0
	1	gross	Cutts (1d.)	0	10	0	0
	6	dozen	Knives (1d.)	0	5	0	0

Merchant name	Qty	Unit	Commodity	£	s.	d.	f.
	3	dozen	Cups, Wooden	0	2	6	0
	3	M	Nails, Board	1	0	0	0
	3	M	Nails, Lath	0	10	0	0
	6	dozen	Girdles (1d.)	0	5	0	0
	14	lb	Rice	0	3	4	0
	0.25	C	Soap, Black	0	2	6	0
	3	dozen	*Girdles, Penny Leather*[73]	0	2	6	0
	2	lb	Silk, Paris	0	13	4	0
	2	ell	Broad Taffeta Cloth	0	13	4	0
	2	lb	Girdles, Nobs Silk	0	0	20	0
	8	lb	Sugar	0	6	8	0
	0.5	C	Orchil	0	10	0	0
	6	yard	Levant Taffeta Cloth	0	10	0	0
	0.5	dozen	Spurs	0	3	4	0
	4	lb	Copperas	0	0	20	0
	4	lb	Gales	0	2	6	0
	4	clout	Needles	0	3	4	0
	4	dozen	*Girth-Web*[74]	0	2	6	0
	6	dozen	*Drinking Glasses, French*[75]	0	6	8	8
	0.5	dozen	Pans, Frying	0	6	8	0
	0.5	dozen	Bellows	0	5	0	0
	6	dozen	Glasses, Drinking	0	6	8	0
			Trifles	2	0	0	0

The Salloman aforesaid, *14th March 1595*

Stephen Skidie of Cork, Merchant Ind	1	C	Hops	0	10	0	0
	4	dozen	Wool-Cards	2	0	0	0
	6	unknown	Skins, Parchment	0	0	20	0
	6	piece	Felts, Black	0	15	0	0
	6	piece	Felts, Childrens	0	10	0	0
	4	lb	Thread, Packet	0	0	20	0
	1	dozen	Cups, Wooden	0	0	10	0
	6	yard	Levant Taffeta Cloth	0	10	0	0
	18	lb	Flax	0	2	6	0
	8	M	Pins	0	2	6	0
	1	dozen	Locks Hanging, Small	0	0	20	0
	12	yard	Hair *Cloth*	0	3	4	0
	6	pair	Stockings, Short	0	4	2	0
	1	lb	Girdles, Nobs Silk	0	0	10	0
	4	dozen	Girdles (1d.)	0	3	4	0
	4	dozen	Knives, Pocket	0	6	8	0
	2	gross	Trenchers, Common	0	0	20	0
	1	gross	Knives (1d.)	0	10	0	0
	0.5	C	Orchil	0	10	0	0
	0.5	C	Soap, Black	0	5	0	0
	1	burden	Tin	0	5	0	0
	1	clout	Needles	0	0	10	0
	4	gross	Buttons, Glass	0	3	4	0

73 TNA E190/1131/13.   **74** As above.   **75** As above.

Merchant name	Qty	Unit	Commodity	£	s.	d.	f.
	1	small gross	Points, Thread	0	0	10	0
	2	small gross	Points, Red	0	0	20	0
	2	lb	Mail	0	0	15	0
	3	lb	Wire	0	0	10	0
	1	dozen	Locks, Small	0	3	4	0
	6	lb	Turpentine	0	0	10	0
	3.25	yard	Cloth of Assize	0	0	0	0

The Lillie of Bristol, burden 30 tons, Hugh Jones master, to *Burniffe, 14th March 1595*

John Browne of Bristol, Merchant Ind	16	wey	Coal	5	6	8	0

The John of Bristol, burden 16 tons, Christopher Burkett master, to Youghal, 19th March 1595

John Keren of Youghal, Merchant Ind	3	dozen	Hats, Coarse	4	10	0	0
	6	gross	Trenchers, Common	0	5	0	0
	2	gross	Cups, Wooden	1	0	0	0
	1.5	C	Hops	0	15	0	0
	3	ream	Paper	0	10	0	0
	2	gross	Knives (1*d.*)	1	0	0	0
	1	gross	Knives, Pocket	1	0	0	0
	3	dozen	Spurs	0	10	0	0
	4	gross	Points, Red	0	3	4	0
	4	gross	Points, White Leather	0	3	4	0
	4	dozen	Wool-Cards	2	0	0	0
	11	lb	Sugar	0	8	4	0
	0.25	C	Aniseed	0	6	8	0
	6	gross	Buttons, Thread	0	5	0	0
	1	M	Nails, Board	0	6	8	0
	2	burden	Steel	0	10	0	0
	1	gross	Girdles (1*d.*)	0	10	0	0
	2	lb	Girdles, Round Silk	0	0	20	0
	3	dozen	Girdles, Waist	0	0	30	0
	0.75	C	Raisins, *Great*	0	5	0	0
	0.5	C	Soap, Black	0	5	0	0
	2	gross	Glasses, Drinking	0	16	8	0

The Mary of Wexford, burden 8 tons, Richard []od master, to Wexford, 19th March 1595

Michael Stafford of Wexford, Merchant Ind	2	last	Lime	0	10	10	0
	10	pair	Quern-Stones, *Small*	0	12	6	0
	7	C	Battery	14	0	0	0
	1.5	C	Hops	1	5	0	0
	3	dozen	Wool-Cards	1	10	0	0
	1	C	Soap, Black	0	10	0	0

The Mary of Wexford, burden 8 tons, Philip Roche master, to Wexford, *19th March 1595*

Richard Roche of Kilkenny, Merchant Ind	1	C	Alum	1	13	4	0
	0.75	C	Orchil	0	15	0	0
	6	dozen	Wool-Cards	3	0	0	0

Merchant name	Qty	Unit	Commodity	£	s.	d.	f.
	1	gross	Knives (1d.)	0	10	0	0
	1	C	Battery	2	0	0	0
	5	piece	Cloth of Assize	0	0	0	0

The Mary aforesaid, *19th March 1595*

Philip Kettinge of Wexford, Merchant Ind	3	C	Hops	1	10	0	0
	1	C	Soap, Black	0	15	0	0
	2	dozen	Wool-Cards	1	0	0	0
	3	pair	Quern-Stones, Small	0	3	9	0
	2	last	Lime	0	8	4	0
	1	C	Battery	2	0	0	0

The Mary of Bristol, burden 16 tons, Thomas Neve master, to Youghal, 31st March 1595

Andrew Meaghe of Cork, Merchant Ind	1.5	dozen	Hats	2	5	0	0
	0.5	dozen	Hats, Childrens	0	10	0	0
	1	dozen	Stockings, Short	0	8	4	0
	6	dozen	Wool-Cards	3	0	0	0
	1	piece	Osborne Fustian *Cloth*	0	13	4	0
	2	dozen	Girdles, Silk	0	0	20	0
	2	ream	Paper	0	6	8	0
	12	yard	Cotton *Cloth*	0	10	0	0
	6	pair	Bellows	0	5	0	0
	0.5	gross	Knives, Pocket	0	10	0	0
	0.5	gross	Knives (1d.)	0	5	0	0
	1	C	Orchil	1	0	0	0
	1	burden	Tin	0	5	0	0
	15	lb	Sugar	0	8	14	0
	1	dozen	Horse Combs	0	0	25	0
	0.5	gross	Girdles (1d.)	0	5	0	0
	0.5	gross	Combs, Wooden	0	0	30	0
	6	dozen	Glasses, French Drinking	0	4	2	0
			Small Wares	3	0	0	0
	0.5	piece	Cloth of Assize, Northern Dozen Single	0	0	0	0
	3	yard	Cloth of Assize	0	0	0	0

The Mary aforesaid, 31st March 1595

George Meaghe of Limerick, Merchant Ind	0.5	piece	Holmes Fustian *Cloth*	0	6	8	0
	2	ell	Coarse Holland *Cloth*	0	0	20	0
	1	dozen	Hats	1	10	0	0
	0.5	dozen	Hats, Childrens	0	10	0	0
	1	dozen	Penners & Inkhorns	0	0	10	0
	6	pair	Stockings, Short	0	4	2	0
	2	dozen	Girdles (1d.)	0	0	20	0
	4	dozen	*Wool-Cards, Old*	1	6	8	0
	2	ell	Broad Taffeta Cloth	0	16	8	0
	8	yard	Cotton *Cloth*	0	6	8	0

Merchant name	Qty	Unit	Commodity	£	s.	d.	f.
	0.5	C	Raisins, *Great*	0	3	4	0
	12	lb	Prunes	0	0	10	0
	2	lb	Silk, Nobs	0	0	20	0
	4	dozen	Knives (1*d*.)	0	3	4	0
	6	yard	Levant Taffeta Cloth	0	10	0	0
	1	gross	Trenchers, Common	0	0	10	0
	4	dozen	Combs, Wooden	0	0	20	0
	6	pair	Candlesticks, Small	0	0	20	0
	2	dozen	Points, Broad (1*d*.)	0	0	20	0
	1	dozen	Cups, Wooden	0	0	10	0
	2	lb	Mail	0	0	10	0
	2	dozen	Girdles, Waist	0	0	20	0

The Petter of Milford Haven, burden 15 tons, John Devorey master, to Waterford, 5th April 1595

Merchant name	Qty	Unit	Commodity	£	s.	d.	f.
Andrew Luccar of Waterford, Merchant Ind	6.5	C	Battery	13	0	0	0
	12	yard	Cotton *Cloth*	0	10	0	0
	12	yard	Bay *Cloth*	1	0	0	0
	3	dozen	Hats	4	10	0	0
	3	dozen	Stockings, Short Woollen	1	5	0	0
	0.5	C	Seed, Onion	0	16	4	0
	6	lb	Indigo	2	0	0	0
	0.5	piece	Milan Fustian *Cloth*	0	10	0	0
	0.5	piece	Jeane Fustian *Cloth*	0	6	8	0
	6	M	Pins	0	0	20	0
	2	clout	Needles	0	0	20	0
	1.5	C	Sugar	5	0	0	0
	0.5	C	Rice	0	8	4	0
	20	lb	Almonds	0	8	4	0
	1	dozen	Grainte?	0	5	0	0
	1	gross	Knives (1*d*.)	0	10	0	0
	2	piece	White Cyprus Cloth	0	0	20	0
	2	dozen	Thimbles	0	0	20	0
	2	lb	Girdles, Round silk	0	0	20	0
	6	M	Cox Lace	0	10	0	0
	6	lb	Thread, Packet	0	2	6	0
	2	lb	Thread, Black	0	3	4	0
	2	gross	Trenchers	0	0	20	0
	0.25	C	Soap, Black	0	2	6	0
	8	yard	Cloth of Assize	0	0	0	0

The Petter of Milford Haven aforesaid, 5th April 1595

Merchant name	Qty	Unit	Commodity	£	s.	d.	f.
Philip Linch of Waterford, Merchant Ind	1	piece	Milan Fustian *Cloth*	1	0	0	0
	1.25	lb	Cox Lace	0	10	0	0
	2	dozen	Girdles, Waist	0	3	4	0
	9	dozen	Gartering, Norwich	0	5	0	0
	2.5	lb	Points, Coarse[76]	0	10	0	0
	2	dozen	Ink Horns	0	0	20	0
	1	quarter	Thread, Inkle	0	5	0	0

76 Possibly lace.

Merchant name	Qty	Unit	Commodity	£	s.	d.	f.
	1	butt	Thread	0	2	6	0
	6	small gross	Buttons, Thread	0	0	20	0
	6	small gross	Buttons, Silk	0	2	6	0
	3	lb	Nutmeg	0	10	0	0
	28	lb	Currants	0	7	6	0
	22	lb	Seed, Onion	0	7	6	0
	0.75	C	Rice	0	12	6	0
	6	dicker	Bracelets	0	2	6	0
	2.75	C	Battery	5	10	0	0
	0.5	lb	Lace (2d.)	0	3	4	0
	2	dozen	Hawk Hoods	0	0	20	0
	2	C	Hops	1	0	0	0
	1	small gross	Points, Red	0	0	20	0
	1.25	lb	Fringe, Crewel & Silk	0	6	8	0
		bale	Dice & small ropes for scales	0	0	20	0
	1	dozen	Locks, Hanging	0	3	4	0
	132	lb	Sugar	4	0	0	0
	32	pairs	Stockings, Short	1	3	4	0
	16	yard	Bologna Sarcenet *Cloth*	2	13	4	0
	6.25	yard	Broad Taffeta Cloth	2	0	0	0
	4.16	dozen	Hats	6	5	0	0
	24	yard	Silk Cyprus *Cloth*	1	0	0	0
	6	lb	Indigo	2	0	0	0

The Nicholas of Milford Haven, burden 14 tons, William Harris master, to Waterford, 15th April 1595

Merchant name	Qty	Unit	Commodity	£	s.	d.	f.
John Sutton of Waterford, Merchant Ind	4.25	C	Battery	8	10	0	0
	6.5	C	Hops	3	5	0	0
	1.5	C	Aniseed	2	0	0	0
	2	dozen	Stockings, Short	0	16	8	0
	3	dozen	Hats	4	10	0	0
	4	dozen	Girdles (1d.)	0	3	4	0
	1	gross	Gold Paper	0	6	8	0
	12	lb	Thread, Packet	0	4	2	0
	14	lb	Sugar	0	15	0	0
	0.5	gross	Knives (1d.)	0	5	0	0
	0.5	gross	Knives (2d.)	0	10	0	0
	3	dozen	Wool-Cards	1	10	0	0
	3	C	Blockwood	1	10	0	0
	2	lb	Girdles, Nobs *Silk*	0	0	20	0
	6	gross	Trenchers, Common	0	5	0	0
	2	burden	Tin	0	10	0	0
	3	C	Taps & Cannells	0	2	6	0
	12	lb	Mail	0	6	8	0
	14	lb	Currants	0	3	9	0
	1	C	Soap, Black	0	10	0	0
	2	small gross	Buttons, Thread	0	0	20	0
	7	dozen	Glasses, French Drinking	0	6	8	0
	1	ton	Iron	8	0	0	0

Merchant name	Qty	Unit	Commodity	£	s.	d.	f.

The Nicholas of Milford Haven aforesaid, 16th April 1595

Merchant name	Qty	Unit	Commodity	£	s.	d.	f.
Simon Salle of Cashel, Merchant Ind	1	ton	Iron	8	o	o	o

The Parvo Diana of Bristol, burden 18 tons, Robert Pattenson master, to Brest, 17th April 1595

Merchant name	Qty	Unit	Commodity	£	s.	d.	f.
John Bisse of Bristol, Merchant Ind	9	piece	Cloth of Assize, Streit	o	o	o	o
	1	piece	Cloth of Assize, Streit[77]	o	o	o	o
	5	piece	Cloth of Assize	o	o	o	o
			Cloth of Assize, Overlengths	o	o	o	o

The Parvo Diana aforesaid, 17th April 1595

Merchant name	Qty	Unit	Commodity	£	s.	d.	f.
George Lane & Willkinson of Bristol, Merchants Ind	8	piece	*Bristol* Frieze *Cloth*	8	o	o	o
	5	piece	Cloth of Assize	o	o	o	o
			Cloth of Assize, Overlengths	o	o	o	o

The Parvo Diana aforesaid, 17th April 1595

Merchant name	Qty	Unit	Commodity	£	s.	d.	f.
Philip Bisse of Bristol, Merchant Ind	4	C goad	Cotton *Cloth*	13	6	8	o
	4	piece	Cloth of Assize	o	o	o	o
			Cloth of Assize, Overlengths	o	o	o	o

The Parvo Diana aforesaid, 17th April 1595

Merchant name	Qty	Unit	Commodity	£	s.	d.	f.
John Merrick of Bristol, Merchant Ind	6	piece	Cloth of Assize	o	o	o	o
			Cloth of Assize, Overlengths	o	o	o	o

The Parvo Diana aforesaid, 17th April 1595

Merchant name	Qty	Unit	Commodity	£	s.	d.	f.
John Love of Bristol, Merchant Ind	5	piece	*Bristol* Frieze *Cloth*	5	o	o	o
	3	piece	Cloth of Assize	o	o	o	o
			Cloth of Assize, Overlengths	o	o	o	o

The Parvo Diana aforesaid, 18th April 1595

Merchant name	Qty	Unit	Commodity	£	s.	d.	f.
Philip Bisse of Bristol, Merchant Ind	3	piece	Cloth of Assize	o	o	o	o
			Cloth of Assize, Overlengths	o	o	o	o

77 Custom exempt.

Merchant name	Qty	Unit	Commodity	£	s.	d.	f.

The Margarett of Padstow, burden 18 tons, John Burdwood master, to Sligo, 18th April 1595

William Hopkins of Bristol, Merchant Ind	2	tun	Cider	2	0	0	0
	1	C	Alum	1	13	4	0
	1	piece	Cloth of Assize, Kersey	0	0	0	0
	2.5	piece	Cloth of Assize	0	0	0	0
			Cloth of Assize, Overlengths	0	0	0	0

The Keele of Brest, burden 40 tons, Peter John master, to Brest, 30th April 1595

Christopher Harlinson of Middelburg, Merchant Alien	13	wey	Coal	4	6	8	0

The Minikin of Bristol, burden 16 tons, Hugh Troy master, to Waterford, 1st May 1595

John Whittson of Bristol, Merchant Ind	1	ton	Iron	8	0	0	0
	1	C	Soap, Black	0	10	0	0
	2	C	Orchil	2	0	0	0

The Parvo Elizabeth of Gloucester, burden 18 tons, John Swanley master, to Waterford, 8th May 1595

Richard Glewe of Bristol, Merchant Ind	1	ton	Iron	8	0	0	0

The John of Bristol, burden 16 tons, Thomas Lattimer master, to Youghal, *8th May 1595*

Giles Baynard of Bristol, Merchant Ind	5	C	Hops	2	10	0	0

The Parvo Elizabeth aforesaid, 10th May 1595

Simon Sall of Cashel, Merchant Ind	4	C	Hops	2	0	0	0
	1	gross	Lace, Statute	0	6	8	0
	1	gross	Knives (1d.)	0	10	0	0
	6	lb	Mail	0	3	4	0
	4	dozen	Cups, Wooden	0	3	4	0
	2	C	Awl Blades	0	0	20	0
	1	gross	Trenchers, Common	0	0	10	0
	1	ream	Paper	0	3	4	0
	3	clout	Needles	0	0	30	0
	1	C	Blockwood	0	10	0	0
	1	C	Taps & Cannells	0	0	10	0
	1	dozen	Penners	0	0	10	0
	4	gross	Buttons, Hair	0	3	4	0
	3	gross	Points	0	0	30	0
	1	lb	Points, Green[78]	0	6	8	0

The Parvo Elizabeth aforesaid, 10th May 1595

John Mortine of Waterford, Merchant Ind	4	lb	Mail	0	0	20	0

78 Possibly green lace.

Merchant name	Qty	Unit	Commodity	£	s.	d.	f.
	4	dozen	Girdles (1*d*.)	0	3	4	0
	0.5	gross	Knives (1*d*.)	0	5	0	0
	3	clout	Needles	0	0	30	0
	3	dozen	Urinalls	0	0	30	0
	3	dozen	Thread, Packet	0	11	6	0
	2	lb	Girdles, Nobs *Silk*	0	0	20	0
	3	small gross	Points	0	0	30	0
	1	gross	Lace, Statute	0	6	8	0
	10	lb	Sugar	0	6	8	0
	3	dozen	Bibs	0	0	20	0
	6	gross	Buttons, Thread	0	5	0	0
	6	gross	Buttons, Hair	0	5	0	0
	1	dozen	Locks Hanging, Small	0	3	4	0
	1	C	Aniseed	1	6	8	0
	1	lb	Green Silk Lace	0	6	8	0
	1	dozen	*Arridence*	0	3	4	0
	1	C	Soap, Black	0	10	0	0

The Parvo Elizabeth aforesaid, 14th May 1595

Merchant name	Qty	Unit	Commodity	£	s.	d.	f.
Christopher Comen of London, Fruterer Ind	4	pairs	Stockings, Short	0	3	4	0
	3	dozen	Combs, Wooden	0	0	15	0
	1	dozen	Bands, Falling	0	3	4	0
	2	dozen	Wool-Cards, Old	0	13	4	0
	3	dozen	Girdles	0	2	6	0
	12	lb	Sugar	0	8	4	0
	1.5	dozen	Knives, Pocket	0	2	6	0
	8	*lb*	Galer	1	0	0	0
	2	gross	Trenchers	0	0	20	0
	3	yard	Gentish Carpen *Cloth*	0	7	6	0
	2	piece	Caddows	1	0	0	0
	1	piece	Mantles	0	5	0	0
	6	yard	Cloth of Assize	0	0	0	0

The Parvo Elizabeth aforesaid, 14th May 1595

Merchant name	Qty	Unit	Commodity	£	s.	d.	f.
Nicholas Everett of Limerick, Merchant Ind	2	dozen	Hats	3	0	0	0
	1	piece	Holmes Fustian *Cloth*	0	13	4	0
	3	dozen	Wool-Cards	1	0	0	0
	15	lb	Sugar	0	8	4	0
	0.5	gross	Knives (1*d*.)	0	5	0	0
	6	yard	Cotton *Cloth*	0	5	0	0
	6	gross	Trenchers, Common	0	5	0	0
	2	dozen	Penners & Inkhorns	0	0	20	0
	1	lb	Thread, Coloured	0	0	20	0
	1	lb	Thread, Blue	0	0	20	0
	2	lb	Wax	0	0	20	0
	3	M	Lath Nails	0	10	0	0
	1	gross	*Buttons, Thread*[79]	0	0	20	0
	2	small gross	Points, Thread	0	2	6	0
	3	small gross	Points, Leather	0	2	6	0

79 TNA E190/1131/13.

Merchant name	Qty	Unit	Commodity	£	s.	d.	f.
	3	lb	Mail	0	0	20	0
	3	clout	Needles	0	2	6	0
	1	dozen	Points, Inkle	0	0	20	0
	1	ream	Paper	0	3	4	0
	4	dozen	Glasses, French Drinking	0	2	11	0
	2	lb	Flax	0	3	4	0
	2	piece	Girdles, Nobs Silk	0	0	25	0
	6	pair	Stockings, Short	0	4	2	0
	6	yard	Cloth of Assize	0	0	0	0

The Parvo Elizabeth aforesaid, 15th May 1595

William Ellis of Bristol, Merchant Ind	2	ton	Iron[80]	0	0	0	0

The Angell of Fethard-on-Sea, burden 16 tons, Mathew Howlinge master, to Waterford, 17th May 1595

Merchant name	Qty	Unit	Commodity	£	s.	d.	f.
George Sent Linger of Kilkenny, Merchant Ind	1	C	Sugar	3	6	8	0
	3	C	Battery	6	0	0	0
	1	C	Lead	0	8	4	0
	1	C	Gun Powder	1	13	4	0
	30	C	Pewter	0	9	2	0
	8	unknown	Cider	0	13	4	0
	3	C	Hops	1	10	0	0
	4	lb	Sandalwood	0	6	8	0
	3	lb	Senna	0	5	0	0
	12	dozen	Wool-Cards, Old	4	0	0	0
	2.5	gross	Knives (1d.)	1	5	0	0
	1	dozen	Hats, Coarse	1	10	0	0
	0.5	C	Soap, Black	0	5	0	0
	2.5	gross	Trenchers, Common	0	0	25	0
	6	lb	Silk, Paris	2	0	0	0
	2	lb	Silk, Raw	0	13	4	0
	6	piece	Halberts, Ungilted	0	10	0	0
	1	barrel	Honey	1	10	0	0
	1	C	Alum	1	13	4	0
	2	dozen	Stock-Cards	1	6	8	0
	3	C	*Battery*	6	0	0	0

The Angell aforesaid, 19th May 1595

Merchant name	Qty	Unit	Commodity	£	s.	d.	f.
Thomas Pembrock of Kilkenny, Merchant Ind	6	C	Hops	3	0	0	0
	3	dozen	Hats	4	10	0	0
	2	gross	Knives (1d.)	1	0	0	0
	8	dozen	Wool-Cards	4	0	0	0
	2	dozen	Stock-Cards	1	6	8	0
	1	dozen	Stockings, Short	0	8	4	0
	8	lb	Girdles, Nobs Silk	0	6	8	0
	2	gross	Girdles (1d.)	1	0	0	0

80 Custom and subsidy paid in the Grace of Bristol, burden 18 tons, Stephen Burkall master, from St-Jean-de-Luz, 14th April 1595.

Merchant name	Qty	Unit	Commodity	£	s.	d.	f.
	6	lb	Nails, Yellow	0	3	4	0
	2	gross	Lace, Statute	0	13	4	0
	20	lb	Sugar	0	12	4	0
	2	dozen	Locks Hanging, Small	0	3	4	0
	6	dozen	Bibs	0	3	4	0
	4	C	Taps & Cannells	0	3	4	0
	0.5	C	Orchil	0	10	0	0
	2	clout	Needles	0	3	4	0
	6	yard	Cloth of Assize, Green Kersey	0	0	0	0

The Dorethie of Tewkesbury, burden 8 tons, Richard Lullet master, to Swansea, 19th May 1595[81]

Merchant name	Qty	Unit	Commodity	£	s.	d.	f.
Henry Ottred of Brest, Merchant Alien	2.5	gross	Combs, Wooden	0	12	6	0
	2	dozen	Girdles, Leather	0	0	20	0
	50	lb	Iron Wire	0	16	8	0
	4	piece	Ribbon, Crewel	0	3	4	0
	2	lb	Thread, Black	0	3	4	0
	6	dozen	Lace, Statute	0	3	4	0
	24	small gross	Points, Leather	0	16	8	0
	1	small gross	Points, Thread	0	3	4	0
	4	dozen M	Pins	0	13	4	0
	6	lb	Jeane Treackle?	0	4	2	0
	6	pair	Hose, Worsted	2	0	0	0
	6	dozen	Skins, Cony Black	1	17	6	0
	6	piece	Skins, Parchment	0	0	20	0
	12	lb	Unknown	0	0	20	0
	12	small gross	Buttons, Silk	0	5	0	0
	6	lb	*Sugar Candy*[82]	0	4	2	0
	12	ream	*Paper*[83]	1	10	0	0
	6	lb	Latine for Points	0	5	0	0
	6	yard	Lil*l*e Buffine *Cloth*	0	10	0	0
	11	yard	Saye, Hunskolt	1	6	8	0

The Gabriell of Gloucester, burden 16 tons, Walter Rawlen master, to La Rochelle, 20th May 1595

Merchant name	Qty	Unit	Commodity	£	s.	d.	f.
Walter Rawlen of St Ives, Merchant Ind	75	yard	Cloth of Assize, Remnants	0	0	0	0

The Rose of Bristol, burden 18 tons, John Fyone master, to Waterford, 24th May 1595

Merchant name	Qty	Unit	Commodity	£	s.	d.	f.
John Hiron of London, Skiner Ind	12	C	Battery	24	0	0	0
	29	C	Aniseed	38	13	4	0
	40	C	Hops	20	0	0	0
	10	dozen	Wool-Cards	5	0	0	0
	0.5	C	Match Cords	0	9	2	0

81 This seems to be going via Swansea to another port, but the name of the port is not listed. 82 This has been added from the Customer's account for the same period (TNA E190/1131/13). It is interesting that his 'total value' includes items that he seemingly fails to record which suggests that he is in fact copying from another source. 83 As above.

Merchant name	Qty	Unit	Commodity	£	s.	d.	f.
	10	C	Orchil	10	0	0	0
	2	C	Hops[84]	1	0	0	0

The George of Wexford, burden 8 tons, David Ever master, to Wexford, 28th May 1595

Paul Furlonge of Wexford, Merchant Ind	2	dozen	Wool-Cards	1	0	0	0
	2	C	Ropes, White	1	13	4	0
	3	Piece	Hats, Childrens	0	5	0	0

The Mary of St Surnie,[85] burden 26 tons, John Moveline master, to St Surnie, 30th May 1595

John Moveline, Master Alien	10	wey	Coal	3	6	8	0

The Clement of Bristol, burden 18 tons, John Barne master, to Cork, 31st May 1595

William Hore of Cork, Merchant Ind	15	lb	Sugar	0	8	4	0
	1	C	Hops	0	10	0	0
	3	dozen	Knives	0	2	6	0
	3	ell	Holland Cloth	0	3	4	0
	6	yard	Levant Taffeta Cloth	0	10	0	0
	?	ell	Broad Taffeta Cloth	0	10	0	0
	1	lb	Gales	0	0	10	0
	2	lb	Copperas	0	0	10	0
	0.5	piece	Milan Fustian Cloth	0	10	0	0
	1	dozen	Hats	1	8	4	0
	1	dozen	Books, Grammar	0	3	4	0
	6	lb	Unknown	0	3	6	0
	3.25	yard	Cloth of Assize	0	0	0	0

The Rose of Bristol aforesaid, 3rd June 1595

Nicholas Linche of Limerick, Merchant Ind	2	piece	Jeane Fustian *Cloth*	0	13	4	0
	0.5	piece	Holmes Fustian *Cloth*	0	6	8	0
	1	butt	Thread	0	0	25	0
	1	dozen	Girdles, Leather	0	0	10	0
	2	dozen	Girdles, Leather (*ob.*)	0	0	10	0
	1	lb	Crewel, French	0	0	20	0
	1	lb	Wax	0	0	10	0
	6	lb	Candles, Wax	0	5	0	0
	16	lb	Bombas	0	8	4	0
	2	ream	Paper	0	6	8	0
	2	bundle	Paper, Brown	0	0	20	0
	16	small gross	Buttons, Thread & Hair	0	0	20	0
	8	small gross	Points, Thread	0	6	8	0
	6	gross	Points, Red	0	5	0	0
	4	gross	Points, Leather	0	3	4	0
	6	lb	Starch	0	0	20	0
	3	M	Pins	0	0	10	0
	0.5	gross	Combs	0	2	6	0
	1	lb	Mail	0	0	10	0
	5	dozen	Hats	7	10	0	0

84 As above. 85 Unidentified port.

Merchant name	Qty	Unit	Commodity	£	s.	d.	f.
	4	dozen	Hats, Boys	4	0	0	0
	60	yard	Bay *Cloth*	3	6	8	0
	15	yard	Dornick Cloth	0	10	0	0
	20	yard	*Bristol* Frieze *Cloth*	0	15	0	0
	1	dozen	Headstalls	0	5	0	0
	3	dozen	Girth-Web	0	0	20	0
	6	piece	Striapes	0	5	0	0
	6	unknown	Snaffees?	0	2	6	0
	1	dozen	Spurs	0	3	4	0
	1	dozen	Books, Horn	0	0	10	0
	6	piece	Knives, Shoemaker	0	0	10	0
	4	piece	Horse Combs	0	0	10	0
	3	C	Taps	0	2	6	0
	1	dozen	Cups, Wooden	0	0	10	0
	10	lb	Glue	0	0	10	0
	1.5	dozen	Wool-Cards	1	5	0	0
	4	gross	Trenchers, Common	0	3	4	0
	1	M	Nails, Board	0	3	4	0
	4	M	Tape, Small	0	6	8	0
	4	clout	Needles	0	3	4	0

The Rose of Bristol aforesaid, 3rd June 1595

Merchant name	Qty	Unit	Commodity	£	s.	d.	f.
John Bodkine of Limerick, Merchant Ind	5.5	piece	Holmes Fustian *Cloth*	1	13	4	0
	3.5	piece	Jeane Fustian *Cloth*	1	0	0	0
	30	lb	Bombas	0	16	8	0
	3	small gross	Buttons, Thread & Hair	0	3	4	0
	1	dozen	Stockings, Short	0	8	4	0
	10	small gross	Points, Thread	0	8	4	0
	7	M	Pins	0	0	25	0
	5	ream	Paper	0	13	4	0
	0.5	ream	Paper, Painted	0	3	4	0
	2	dozen	Trenchers, Painted	0	0	15	0
	3	dozen	Penners & Inkhorns	0	2	6	0
	1	bundle	Paper Brown	0	0	10	0
	4	lb	Mail	0	0	25	0
	6	clout	Needles	0	5	0	0
	4	dozen	Hats	6	0	0	0
	2	dozen	Hats, Childrens	2	0	0	0
	10	small gross	Points, White & Red	0	8	4	0
	3	small gross	Knives (2d.)	3	0	0	0
	50	yard	Bay *Cloth*	2	13	4	0
	24	yard	Dornick Cloth	0	15	0	0
	40	yard	*Bristol* Frieze *Cloth*	1	10	0	0
	4	dozen	Parchment *Skins*	0	13	4	0
	6	piece	Horse Combs	0	0	15	0
	0.5	gross	Girth-Web	0	3	4	0
	0.5	gross	Girth Buckles	0	3	4	0
	2	dozen	Cap Hooks	0	3	4	0
	2	dozen	Cap-Case Locks	0	3	4	0
	3	dozen	Snaffles	0	15	0	0

Merchant name	Qty	Unit	Commodity	£	s.	d.	f.
	3	dozen	Headstalls	0	15	0	0
	1	dozen	Stirrups, Iron	0	3	4	0
	6	pair	Balances, Small	0	6	8	0
	1	dozen	Candlesticks, Small Brass	0	3	4	0
	6	piece	Brushes, Heath	0	0	20	0
	1.5	gross	Combs, Wooden	0	7	6	0
	10	lb	Verdegris	0	4	2	0
	2	gross	Knives (1d.)	1	0	0	0
	3	pair	Bellows	0	5	0	0
	5	dozen	Wool-Cards	2	10	0	0
	3	dozen	Stock-Cards	2	0	0	0
	8	dozen	Trenchers, Common	0	0	10	0
	4	C	Taps	0	3	4	0
	20	lb	Glue	0	0	20	0
	1	dozen	Cups, Wooden	0	0	10	0
	6	M	Nails, Board	1	0	0	0
	1	burden	Tin	0	5	0	0
	3	M	Nails, Small	0	5	0	0

The Rose of Bristol aforesaid, 4th June 1595

Merchant name	Qty	Unit	Commodity	£	s.	d.	f.
David Rice of Limerick, Merchant Ind	4	C	Hops	2	0	0	0
	4	dozen	Wool-Cards	2	0	0	0
	2	dozen	Hats	3	0	0	0
	1	small gross	Knives (1d.)	0	10	0	0
	8	yard	Cotton *Cloth*	0	6	8	0
	1	lb	Thread, Piecing	0	2	6	0
	3	small gross	Points, Thread	0	10	0	0
	4	lb	Mail	0	0	25	0
	3	C	Awl Blades	0	2	6	0
	2	gross	Buttons, Glass	0	0	20	0
	8	lb	Sugar	0	5	0	0
	6	lb	Thread, Packet	0	0	25	0
	2	gross	Trenchers, Common	0	0	20	0
	2	dozen	Glasses, Looking (1d.)	0	0	20	0
	3	gross	Points, Red	0	2	6	0
	12	lb	Glue	0	0	20	0
	0.5	gross	Combs, Wooden	0	2	6	0
	8	lb	Gun Powder	0	3	4	0
	12	lb	Matches	0	0	25	0
	0.5	C	Lead	0	4	2	0
	6	lb	Rice	0	0	20	0
	1	ream	Paper, Brown	0	0	10	0
	0.5	gross	Girth-Web	0	3	4	0
	1	pair	Bellows	0	0	20	0
	4	gross	Buttons, Thread	0	3	4	0
	2	gross	Buttons, Hair	0	0	20	0
	28	lb	Aniseed	0	6	8	0
	3	lb	Lead, Red	0	0	10	0
	1	C	Taps	0	0	10	0
	3	dozen	Cups, Wooden	0	2	6	0

Merchant name	Qty	Unit	Commodity	£	s.	d.	f.
	2	C	Nails, Board	0	0	10	0
	3	piece	Lanterns	0	0	20	0
	1	dozen	Bibs	0	0	10	0
	0.5	burden	Tin	0	2	6	0
	3	lb	Gales	0	0	10	0
	6	lb	Copperas	0	0	10	0
	1	clout	Needles	0	0	10	0
	28	lb	Prunes	0	2	6	0
	28	lb	Currants	0	7	6	0
	6	lb	Seed, Cumin	0	0	20	0
	4	lb	Almonds	0	0	20	0
	1	dozen	Girdles, Waist	0	0	20	0
	4	lb	Indigo	1	6	8	0
	0.5	piece	Holmes Fustian *Cloth*	0	6	8	0
	4	pair	Stockings, Short	0	3	4	0
	2	M	Taps, Small	0	3	4	0
	4	pair	Stock-Cards	0	5	0	0
	2	dozen	Shoe Horns	0	0	20	0
	2	dozen	Awl Hafts	0	0	20	0
	8	lb	Turpentine	0	0	10	0
	6	piece	Bands, Falling	0	3	4	0
	1	dozen	Combes ? Marie	0	3	4	0
	1	dozen	Spurs	0	3	4	0
	4	dozen	Girth Buckles	0	2	6	0
	1	C	Chalk	0	0	20	0

The John of Waterford, burden 16 tons, Maurice Cleere master, to Waterford, 6th June 1595

Merchant name	Qty	Unit	Commodity	£	s.	d.	f.
Patrick Stronge of Waterford, Merchant Ind	84	lb	Pewter	1	5	0	0
	2	C	Hawser	1	13	4	0
	9	piece	Hats	1	2	6	0
	2	pair	Stock-Cards	0	2	6	0
	1	yard	Cloth of Assize, Kersey	0	0	0	0

The Rose of Bristol aforesaid, 11th June 1595

Merchant name	Qty	Unit	Commodity	£	s.	d.	f.
Thomas Symondes, Merchant Ind[86]	260	lb	Indigo[87]	0	0	0	0

The Keele of Brest aforesaid, *11th June 1595*

Merchant name	Qty	Unit	Commodity	£	s.	d.	f.
John Collimore of Bristol, Merchant Ind	2	C goad	Cotton *Cloth*	6	13	4	0
	8	piece	Wadmal Cloth	8	0	0	0
	3	piece	Serge *Cloth* (Paris Cloth)	6	0	0	0
	9	piece	Cloth of Assize, Kersey	0	0	0	0

86 For Humphrey Hamford Ind.   87 Subsidy paid in London and certificate shown. Value not given but would be £86.87

Merchant name	Qty	Unit	Commodity	£	s.	d.	f.

The Mary of Bristol, burden 16 tons, Robert Vinicomb master, to Cork, 18th June 1595

Merchant name	Qty	Unit	Commodity	£	s.	d.	f.
William Creaghe of Cork, Merchant Ind	3.5	C	Hops	1	15	0	0
	4	dozen	Wool-Cards	2	0	0	0
	6	pair	Stockings, Short	0	4	2	0
	1	dozen	Penners	0	0	10	0
	4	dozen	Urinalls	0	3	4	0
	1	dozen	Hats	1	10	0	0
	0.5	dozen	Hats, Childrens	0	10	0	0
	5	gross	Trenchers, Common	0	4	2	0
	1	burden	Tin	0	5	0	0
	1	gross	Knives	0	10	0	0
	0.5	gross	Knives, Pocket[88]	0	10	0	0
	1	gross	Points, Leather[89]	0	10	0	0
	1	dozen	Spurs	0	3	4	0
	0.5	C	Orchil	0	10	0	0
	4	dozen	Glue	0	5	0	0
			Apothecary Wares	2	0	0	0
			Small Wares	2	10	0	0
	4	M	Nails, Board	0	13	4	0
	12	M	Nails, Lath	1	0	0	0
	2	dozen	Stock Locks	0	10	0	0

The Jane of *Insula de Ars*, burden 40 tons, Peter Rowland master, to *Insula de Ars*, 19th June 1595

Merchant name	Qty	Unit	Commodity	£	s.	d.	f.
Geoffrey Gitton of Bristol, Merchant Ind	15	wey	Coal	5	0	0	0

The Jane of *Insula de Ars*, burden 30 tons, Lewis Lodowicke master, to *Insula de Ars*, 19th June 1595

Merchant name	Qty	Unit	Commodity	£	s.	d.	f.
Geoffrey Gitton of Bristol, Merchant Ind	15	wey	Coal	5	0	0	0

The Petter of *Insula de Ars*, burden 25 tons, Bernard Bennet master, to *Insula de Ars*, 19th June 1595

Merchant name	Qty	Unit	Commodity	£	s.	d.	f.
Geoffrey Gitton of Bristol, Merchant Ind	10	wey	Coal	3	6	8	0

The Whitt Falcon of Gda_sk, burden 200 tons, John Windelkine master, to Youghal, 24th June 1595

Merchant name	Qty	Unit	Commodity	£	s.	d.	f.
Roger Vancolege of London, Merchant Alien	14	piece	Bay *Cloth*	28	0	0	0
	1	piece	Bay *Cloth*[90]	0	0	0	0
	11	piece	Saye *Cloth*	11	0	0	0
	1	piece	Saye *Cloth*[91]	0	0	0	0
	8.5	piece	Canvas *Cloth*, Striped	1	13	4	0
	170	piece	Table Cloths & Diapers[92]	34	0	0	0

88 See note 68. 89 As above. 90 Custom exempt. 91 Custom exempt. 92 Containing 340 yards.

Merchant name	Qty	Unit	Commodity	£	s.	d.	f.

The Dove of Bristol, burden 40 tons, William Pheleps master, to La Rochelle, 24th June 1595

Robert Colston of Bristol, Merchant Ind	20	wey	Coal	6	13	4	0

The Mary of Wexford, burden 12 tons, John Lamport master, to Wexford, 25th June 1595

David Haye of Wexford, Merchant Ind	3	dozen	Hats	4	10	0	0
	0.5	C	Hops	0	5	0	0
	0.5	C	Aniseed	0	13	4	0
	2.25	C	Battery/Brass	4	10	0	0
	0.5	C	Soap, Black	0	5	0	0
	1	dozen	Stock-Cards	0	13	4	0
	7	C	Ropes	5	16	8	0
	3	barrel	Lime	0	0	20	0
	6	C	Blockwood	3	0	0	0
	0.5	C	Orchil	0	10	0	0

The Parvo Elizabeth of Gloucester, burden 18 tons, John Swanley master, to Waterford, 26th June 1595

Thomas Daniell of Limerick, Merchant Ind	1	C	Hops	0	10	0	0
	0.5	dozen	Hats	0	15	0	0
	0.5	dozen	Wool-Cards	1	10	0	0
	1	gross	Trenchers, Common	0	0	10	0
	3	stone	Soap, White	0	5	15	0
	4	dozen	Combs, Wooden	0	0	20	0
	2	lb	Mail	0	0	15	0
	1	lb	Thread, Packet	0	0	5	0
	1	dozen	Penners & Inkhorns	0	0	10	0
	3	lb	Gales	0	0	10	0
	4	lb	Copperas	0	0	10	0
	0.5	gross	Lace, Statute	0	3	4	0
	1	small gross	Buttons, Thread	0	0	10	0
	1	gross	Knives (1d.)	0	10	0	0
	0.5	gross	Knives, Pocket	0	10	0	0
	0.5	gross	Girdles (1d.)	0	5	0	0
	6	lb	Starch	0	0	35	0
	1	M	Nails, Lath	0	0	20	0
	6	yard	Cotton *Cloth*	0	10	0	0
	1	dozen	Combs, Wooden	0	0	10	0

The Parvo Elizabeth aforesaid, 26th June 1595

Walter Harold of Limerick, Merchant Ind	1.5	C	Hops	0	15	0	0
	6	dozen	Wool-Cards	3	0	0	0
	4	pair	Stock-Cards	0	5	0	0
	1.5	gross	Trenchers, Common	0	0	15	0
	1	C	Orchil	1	0	0	0
	12	lb	Sugar	0	8	4	0
	1	gross	Knives, Pocket	1	0	0	0
	1	gross	Knives (1d.)	0	10	0	0
	1	gross	Girdles (1d.)	0	10	0	0

Merchant name	Qty	Unit	Commodity	£	s.	d.	f.
	12	lb	Gales & Copperas	0	3	4	0
	2	M	Nails, Lath	0	3	4	0
	1	burden	Tin	0	5	0	0
	4	small gross	Points, Red	0	3	4	0
	2	clout	Needles	0	0	20	0
	2	dozen	Hats	3	0	0	0
	1	dozen	Hats, Childrens	1	0	0	0
	2	stone	Aniseed	0	6	8	0
	2	vettir	Soap, White	0	4	2	0
	8	lb	Starch	0	3	4	0
	6	lb	Rice	0	0	20	0
	1	lb	Thread, Piecing	0	2	6	0
	2	nests	Boxes, Painted	0	3	4	0
	2	M	Pins	0	0	10	0
	1	dozen	Penners	0	0	10	0
	4	lb	Thread, Packet	0	0	20	0
	1	dozen	Glasses, Looking small	0	0	10	0
	4	piece	Brushes	0	0	10	0
	1	gross	Points, Crewel	0	6	8	0
	1	gross	Buttons, Thread	0	10	0	0
	2	roll	Gartering, Crewel	0	0	20	0
	2	lb	Mail, Red	0	0	15	0
	6	lb	Ginger	0	9	2	0

The Parvo Elizabeth aforesaid, 26th June 1595

Merchant name	Qty	Unit	Commodity	£	s.	d.	f.
Robert Roche of Limerick, Merchant Ind	1	dozen	Hats	1	10	0	0
	4	dozen	Wool-Cards, Old	1	6	8	0
	2	stone	Soap, Castile	0	4	2	0
	2	gross	Knives, Pocket	2	0	0	0
	8	dozen	Girdles (1d.)	0	6	8	0
	1	gross	Knives (1d.)	0	10	0	0
	2	dozen	Bristol Pairs[93]	0	3	4	0
	6	small gross	Points, Red	0	5	0	0
	0.5	lb	Thread, Sisters	0	4	2	0
	4	gross	Points, Crewel	1	6	8	0
	4	oz	Lace, Chain	0	0	20	0
	2	lb	Thread, Piecing	0	5	0	0
	0.5	M	Nails, Board	0	0	20	0
	4	lb	Mail	0	0	25	0
	5	lb	Thread, Packet	0	0	20	0
	2	lb	Copperas	0	0	5	0
	7	lb	Starch	0	0	20	0
	1	dozen	Girdles	0	0	10	0
	2	dozen	Cups, Wooden	0	0	20	0
	2	dozen	Bibs	0	0	10	0

The Nicholas of Wexford, burden 18 tons, Nicholas Dorney master, to La Rochelle, 27th June 1595

Merchant name	Qty	Unit	Commodity	£	s.	d.	f.
Nicholas Dowrey of Wexford, Merchant Ind	7	wey	Coal	2	6	8	0

93 Probably knives.

Merchant name	Qty	Unit	Commodity	£	s.	d.	f.

The Petter of Bristol, burden 18 tons, Richard Westicott master, to La Rochelle, 27th June 1595

William Ellis of Bristol, Merchant Ind	9	wey	Coal	3	0	0	0
	12	piece	Cloth of Assize	0	0	0	0
	1	piece	Cloth of Assize[94]	0	0	0	0
			Cloth of Assize, Overlengths	0	0	0	0

The Petter aforesaid, 28th June 1595

John Younge of Bristol, Merchant Ind	1.5	C	Wax	4	10	0	0
	3	piece	Cloth of Assize, Bridgwater	0	0	0	0
	2	piece	Cloth of Assize	0	0	0	0

The Petter aforesaid, 28th June 1595

George Lane of Bristol, Merchant Ind	2	C goad	Cotton *Cloth*	6	13	8	0

The George of Wexford, burden 8 tons, David E[]ner master, to Wexford, 30th June 1595

Martin Esmound of Wexford, Merchant Ind	1	C	Hops	0	10	0	0
	0.5	C	Aniseed	0	13	4	0
	0.5	C	Soap, Black	0	5	0	0
	0.5	C	Orchil	0	10	0	0
	1	dozen	Wool-Cards	0	10	0	0
	0.5	M	Trenchers, Common	0	2	6	0
	0.5	last	Lime	0	2	6	0

The Dove of Bristol, burden 18 tons, Robert Vinicombe master, to Cork, 1st July 1595

Henry Gold of Cork, Merchant Ind	6	C	Hops	3	0	0	0
	6	dozen	Wool-Cards	3	0	0	0
	2	lb	Cloves	0	6	8	0
	8	dozen	Penners	0	6	8	0
	2	dozen	Hats	3	0	0	0
	2	dozen	Hats, Childrens	2	0	0	0
	3	ream	Paper	0	10	0	0
	1	dozen	Parchment *Skins*	0	3	4	0
	3	dozen	Candlesticks, Small	0	10	0	0
	12	gross	Trenchers, Common	0	10	0	0
	20	lb	Sugar	0	11	6	0
	12	lb	Thread, Brown	1	0	0	0
	6	gross	Combs	1	10	0	0
	7	dozen	Locks Hanging, Small	0	11	6	0
	5	dozen	Brushes	0	7	6	0
	2	burden	Tin	0	10	0	0
	1	M	Nails, Board	0	3	4	0
	4	dozen	Flax	0	6	8	0

94 Custom exempt.

Merchant name	Qty	Unit	Commodity	£	s.	d.	f.
The Dove aforesaid, 1st July 1595							
Stephen Galway of Cork, Merchant Ind	0.5	ton	Iron	4	0	0	0
	9	C	Hops	4	10	0	0
	5	dozen	Wool-Cards	2	10	0	0
	3	lb	Pepper	0	5	0	0
	2	lb	N[]ptmicks?	0	6	8	0
	4	dozen	Penners	0	3	4	0
	1	dozen	Hats	1	10	0	0
	2	dozen	Hats, Childrens	2	0	0	0
	2	ream	Paper	0	6	8	0
	1	dozen	Parchment *Skins*	0	3	4	0
	3	dozen	Candlesticks	0	10	0	0
	2	C	Orchil	2	0	0	0
	9	lb	Sugar	0	5	0	0
	10	lb	Thread, Brown	0	16	8	0
	14	yard	Bay *Cloth*	0	13	4	0
	6	gross	Combs, Wooden	1	10	0	0
	5	dozen	Crab- Locks	0	8	4	0
	3	dozen	Brushes	0	5	0	0
	2	burden	Tin	0	10	0	0
	2	M	Nails, Board	0	6	8	0
	5	dozen	Flax	0	8	4	0
	1	dozen	Girths	0	3	4	0
	6	dozen	Girdles	0	5	0	0
	20	lb	Thread, Packet	0	6	8	0
	15	yard	Cloth of Assize	0	0	0	0
	1	piece	Cloth of Assize, Kersey	0	0	0	0
The Dove aforesaid, 1st July 1595							
Robert Arthur of Limerick, Merchant Ind	1	C	Aniseed	1	6	8	0
	2	C	Hops	1	0	0	0
	1	dozen	Hats	1	10	0	0
	12	lb	Sugar	0	6	8	0
	1	burden	Tin	0	5	0	0
	1	gross	Girdles	0	10	0	0
	20	lb	Thread, Packet	0	6	8	0
	1	gross	Combs, Wooden	0	5	0	0
	1	C	Rice	0	16	8	0
	12	yard	Cotton *Cloth*	0	10	0	0
	3	ream	Paper	0	10	0	0
	2	dozen	Wool-Cards	1	0	0	0
	4	dozen	Penners	0	3	4	0
	4	lb	Unknown ? Black soap	0	3	4	0
	0.5	C	Alum	0	16	8	0
	5	gross	Trenchers, Common	0	4	2	0
	4	yard	Cloth of Assize	0	0	0	0

Merchant name	Qty	Unit	Commodity	£	s.	d.	f.

The Whitt Beare of Bristol, burden 40 tons, Alexander Chapman master, to *Larmister*, 9th July 1595

Alexander Chapman of Bristol, Merchant Ind	20	wey	Coal	6	13	4	0

The Rose of Bristol, burden 16 tons, Hugh Troy master, to Dublin, *9th July 1595*

George Ken of Temple Haydon, Som., Merchant Ind	5	wey	Coal	1	13	4	0
	2	C	Soap, Black	1	0	0	0
	2	dozen	Wool-Cards	1	0	0	0
	1	C	Hops	0	10	0	0

The Diamount of Bristol, burden 50 tons, Tobias Parris master, to La Rochelle, 11th July 1595

John Barker of Bristol, Merchant Ind	5	piece	Cloth of Assize	0	0	0	0
			Cloth of Assize, Overlengths	0	0	0	0

The Diamount aforesaid, 12th July 1595

William Ellis of Bristol, Merchant Ind	9	piece	Cloth of Assize	0	0	0	0
			Cloth of Assize, Overlengths	0	0	0	0

The Diamount aforesaid, *12th July 1595*

Daniel Barker of Bristol, Merchant Ind	4	C goad	Cotton *Cloth*	13	6	8	0

The Mary of La Tremblade, burden 15 tons, John de Benio master, to La Rochelle, 17th July 1595

John de Benio of La Tremblade, Merchant Alien	6	wey	Coal	2	0	0	0

The Ellephant of *Messes*, burden 40 tons, Hilary Oddard master, to *Messes*, 21st July 1595

Hillary Oddard, Merchant Alien	10	wey	Coal	3	6	8	0

The Catherine of Wexford, burden 4 tons, David Wadinge master, to Wexford, 22nd July 1595

David Waddinge of Wexford, Merchant Ind	50	lb	Pots, Brass	0	18	4	0
	2	dozen	Cards, Hand	1	0	0	0
	3	piece	Hats	0	7	6	0
	2	dozen	Knives	0	0	20	0
	6	pair	Quern-Stones, Small	0	6	8	0
	2	piece	Grind-Stones, Small	0	0	20	0
	24	lb	Soap, Black	0	0	25	0
	30	*lb*	Pewter	0	8	4	0

Merchant name	Qty	Unit	Commodity	£	s.	d.	f.

The Francis of London, burden 40 tons, Edmund Bonnerto La Rochelle, 28th July 1595

Benedict Webbe of Kingswood, Wilts.

Merchant Ind	11	piece	Paris *Cloth*	33	0	0	0
	1	piece	Paris Cloth[95]	0	0	0	0
	18	piece	Serge *Cloth*	36	0	0	0
	2	piece	Serge *Cloth*[96]	0	0	0	0

The Mary Whitt of Wexford, burden 16 tons, Balcher Patricke master, to Wexford, 30th July 1595

Balcher Pattrick of Wexford, Merchant Ind	1	C	Soap, Black	0	10	0	0
	1	C	Hops	0	10	0	0
	0.5	last	Lime	0	0	20	0
	1	dozen	Hats	1	10	0	0
	1	C	Pots, Brass	2	0	0	0

The Gift of Waterford, burden 30 tons, John Gall master, to Waterford, 31st July 1595

Richard Comerford of Waterford, Merchant Ind	2	C	Wax	6	0	0	0

The Gift aforesaid, 31st July 1595

John Lincole of Waterford, Merchant Ind	14	C	Hops	7	0	0	0
	0.5	C	Soap, Black	0	5	0	0
	20	yard	Bay *Cloth*	1	0	0	0

The Gift aforesaid, 31st July 1595

Andrew Linche of Galway, Merchant Ind	3	dozen	Stockings, Woollen	1	5	0	0
	1	dozen	Stockings, Worsted	2	0	0	0
	4	great gross	Points, Thread & Leather	2	0	0	0
	5	dozen	Wool-Cards	2	10	0	0
	3	gross	Trenchers, Common	0	2	6	0
	5	lb	Crewel, French	1	13	4	0
	6	piece	Pin Purses	0	0	20	0
	2	gross	Buttons, Scottish	0	3	4	0
	1	dozen	Girdles	0	0	20	0
	4	dozen	Penners & Inkhorns	0	3	4	0
	6	bolts	Thread, Black	0	15	0	0
	4	ream	Paper	0	13	4	0
	1	dozen	Brushes, Heath	0	0	20	0
	1	dozen	Brushes, Rubbing	0	0	10	0
	12	piece	Laces, Coarse for knives	0	6	8	0
	6	M	Beads, Bugle	0	3	4	0
	5	C	Buttons, *Copper*	0	5	0	0
	6	piece	Neck Bracelets	0	0	10	0
	5?	M	Pins	0	0	20	0
	20	dicker	Bracelets	0	5	0	0

95 Custom exempt.   96 Custom exempt.

Merchant name	Qty	Unit	Commodity	£	s.	d.	f.
	5	dozen	Glasses, Looking	0	4	2	0
	1	nest	Boxes, Painted	0	0	20	0
	2	dozen	Dials	0	3	4	0
	8	dozen	Knives, Coarse	1	0	0	0
	3	dozen	Horse Combs	0	6	8	0
	30	small gross	Buttons, Glass	0	3	4	0
	1	gross	Knives, Pocket	1	0	0	0
	6	dozen	Knives, Prage	0	8	4	0
	5	dozen	Hats	7	10	0	0
	2	dozen	Hats, Childrens	2	0	0	0
	3	piece	Portmanteau	0	5	0	0
	2	piece	Cap-Cases	0	3	4	0
	2	gross	Lace, Statute	0	13	4	0
	1	piece	Milan Fustian *Cloth*	1	0	0	0
	43	yard	Levant Taffeta Cloth	3	11	6	0
	1	bolt	Silk, Ferett	0	16	8	0
	2	bolt	Silk, Paris	1	13	4	0
	6	piece	Cauls, for Children	0	0	20	0
	9	dozen	Books	2	2	0	0
	4	gross	Combs, Light Wooden	1	0	0	0
	10	yard	Dornick Cloth	0	6	8	0
	40	yard	Bay *Cloth*	2	0	0	0
	2	piece	Welsh Frieze *Cloth*	2	0	0	0
	0.5	C	Pans, Frying	0	6	8	0
	1	C	Hops	0	10	0	0
	2	dozen	Chest locks	0	6	8	0
	6	lb	Mail	0	3	4	0
	6	yard	Cloth of Assize	0	0	0	0

The Gift aforesaid, 1st August 1595

Richard Madan of Waterford, Merchant Ind	20	C	Lead	9	0	0	0

The John of Waterford, burden 14 tons, John Kernie master, to Waterford, *1st August 1595*

Edmund Aleworth of Waterford, Merchant Ind	6	C	Hops	3	0	0	0
	6	piece	Diaper Napkins	0	4	2	0
	1	C	Pewter	0	16	4	0

The John of Waterford, burden 16 tons, Maurice Cleare master, to Waterford, 1st August 1595

Patrick Burcher of Waterford, Merchant Ind	1	M	Hops	5	0	0	0
	4	yard	Taffeta Cloth	1	6	8	0
	42	lb	Pewter	0	16	8	0

The John aforesaid, 1st August 1595

Edmund Nellis of Callan, Merchant Ind	4	C	Hops	2	0	0	0

Merchant name	Qty	Unit	Commodity	£	s.	d.	f.

The Gift aforesaid, 2nd August 1595

Merchant name	Qty	Unit	Commodity	£	s.	d.	f.
Pierce Hackett of Fethard-on-Sea, Merchant Ind	4	C	Hops	2	0	0	0

The Francis aforesaid, *2nd August 1595*

Merchant name	Qty	Unit	Commodity	£	s.	d.	f.
John Collimore of Bristol, Merchant Ind	2	C goad	Cotton *Cloth*	6	13	4	0

The Margarett of Milford Haven, burden 16 tons, Patrick Savord master, to Dublin, *2nd August 1595*

Merchant name	Qty	Unit	Commodity	£	s.	d.	f.
William Cattchemy of Gloucester, Ind	10	pair	Millstones, small called Dogstones	10	0	0	0

The John of Waterford aforesaid, *2nd August 1595*

Merchant name	Qty	Unit	Commodity	£	s.	d.	f.
Richard Butler of Waterford, Merchant Ind	0.5	C	Alum	0	16	8	0
	2	stone	Soap, Black	0	2	6	0
	2	piece	Hats	0	5	0	0
	0.5	gross	Knives	0	5	0	0
	1	ream	Paper	0	3	4	0
	1	lb	Girdles, Nobs Silk	0	0	10	0
	1	M	Nails, Lath	0	0	20	0

John of Bristol, burden 16 tons, Christopher Birckehead master, to Youghal, 5th August 1595

Merchant name	Qty	Unit	Commodity	£	s.	d.	f.
Robert Ashfeld of Kerry, Armiger Ind	4	piece	Cloth of Assize	0	0	0	0
			Cloth of Assize, Overlengths	0	0	0	0

The Francis aforesaid, 7th August 1595

Merchant name	Qty	Unit	Commodity	£	s.	d.	f.
John Collimore of Bristol, Merchant Ind	12	wey	Coal	4	0	0	0
	4	piece	Cloth of Assize	0	0	0	0
			Cloth of Assize, Overlengths	0	0	0	0

The George of Wexford, burden 6 tons, Nicholas Roche master, to Wexford, 8th August 1595

Merchant name	Qty	Unit	Commodity	£	s.	d.	f.
Philip Kettinge of Wexford, Merchant Ind	1	last	Lime	0	4	2	0
	4	C	Hops	2	0	0	0
	4	C	Soap, Black	2	0	0	0
	28	lb	Orchil	0	5	0	0
	3	dozen	Hats, Childrens	3	0	0	0
	12	lb	Aniseed	0	3	4	0
	1	C	Battery/Brass	2	0	0	0
	0.5	gross	Knives, Cuttlers	0	10	0	0
	1.5	M	Trenchers, Common	0	7	6	0

Merchant name	*Qty*	Unit	Commodity	£	s.	d.	f.

The Mary of Bristol, burden 16 tons, John Lullet master, to Cork, *8th August 1595*

| Roger Aliblaster of Youghal, Merchant & Undertaker Ind | 10 | C | Hops | 5 | 0 | 0 | 0 |

The Margarett of Wexford, burden 4 tons, Christopher Chevers to Wexford, *8th August 1595*

John Chevers of Wexford, Merchant Ind	3	barrel	Lime	0	0	20	0
	1	pair	Grind- Stones, *Small*	0	0	20	0
	1	C	Ropes	0	16	8	0
	12	yard	Green Irish Frieze Cloth	0	5	0	0
	28	lb	Pots, Brass	0	10	0	0

The Mary aforesaid, 9th August 1595

David Lewis of Cork, Merchant Ind	4	yard	Bay *Cloth*	0	6	8	0
	2.5	lb	Silk, Paris	0	16	8	0
	2.5	yard	Taffeta Cloth	0	16	8	0
	5	yard	Levant Taffeta Cloth	0	8	4	0
	4	dozen	Wool-Cards	2	0	0	0
	3	gross	Trenchers, Common	0	2	6	0
	6	dozen	Glasses, Drinking	0	5	0	0
	4	dozen	Urinalls	0	3	4	0
	1	gross	Knives (1d.)	0	10	0	0
	5	lb	Thread	0	0	20	0
	3	small gross	Points, Thread	0	2	6	0
	3	small gross	Points, Red	0	2	6	0
	0.5	burden	Tin	0	2	6	0
	3	lb	Thread, Packet	0	0	15	0
	3	dozen	Cups, Wooden	0	2	6	0
	9	dozen	Combs, Wooden	0	3	9	0
	1	ream	Paper, Brown	0	0	10	0
	2	lb	Mail	0	0	15	0
	12	lb	Liquorice	0	0	15	0
	6	lb	Glue	0	0	10	0
	2	nest	Boxes, Painted	0	0	20	0
	1	ream	Paper	0	3	4	0
	1	dozen	Penners	0	0	10	0
	4	dozen	Girdles (1d.)	0	3	4	0
	2	small gross	Buttons, Glass	0	0	20	0
	1	M	Nails, Lath	0	0	20	0
	2	stone	Soap, Black	0	2	6	0
	6	pair	Spurs	0	0	20	0
	2	dozen	Knives, Pocket	0	3	4	0
	1	C	Hops	0	10	0	0
	5	lb	Sugar	0	3	4	0
	7	yard	Cloth of Assize, Northern Dozen	0	0	0	0

Merchant name	Qty	Unit	Commodity	£	s.	d.	f.

The Speedwell of New Ross, burden 40 tons, Tibald Whitt master, to New Ross, *9th August 1595*

Merchant name	Qty	Unit	Commodity	£	s.	d.	f.
William Whitt of New Ross, Merchant Ind	3	dozen	Girth-Web	0	0	20	0
	3	small gross	Points, Thread	0	2	6	0
	12	lb	Indigo, Coarse	4	0	0	0
	1	dozen	Wool-Cards	0	10	0	0
	6	pair	Stock-Cards	0	6	8	0
	4	dozen	Knives	0	3	4	0
	3	dozen	Gartering	0	2	6	0
	4	piece	Purses, Taffeta	0	3	4	0
	4	M	Nails, Lath	0	6	8	0
	3	C	Nails, Board	0	0	20	0
	1	dozen	Crab-Locks	0	0	20	0
	1	lb	Mail	0	0	10	0
	2	lb	Thread, Packet	0	0	10	0
	1	lb	Thread	0	0	20	0
	4	pair	Stockings, Short	0	3	4	0
	1	piece	Holmes Fustian *Cloth*	0	13	4	0
	3	gross	Buttons, Thread	0	2	6	0
	1	gross	Buttons, Shell	0	0	10	0
	10	C	Hops	5	0	0	0
	1	C	Awl Blades	0	0	10	0
	0.5	clout	Needles	0	0	5	0
	1.5	C	Blockwood	1	10	0	0
	3	dozen	Girdles	0	2	6	0
	1	C	Soap	0	10	0	0
	1	pipe	Iron	4	0	0	0
	12	lb	Ginger	0	18	4	0
	6	yard	Cloth of Assize, Green Kersey	0	0	0	0

The Elizabeth of Gloucester, burden 18 tons, John Swanley master, to Waterford, *9th August 1595*

Merchant name	Qty	Unit	Commodity	£	s.	d.	f.
Peter Whitt of Clonmel, Merchant Ind	1	C	Hops	0	10	0	0
	0.5	burden	Tin	0	2	6	0
	1	gross	Trenchers, Common	0	0	10	0
	20	lb	Pewter	0	6	8	0
	9	pair	Stock-Cards	0	10	15	0
	1	C	Iron Work	0	13	4	0
	2	piece	Locks	0	0	20	0
	2	piece	Chafing Dishes	0	0	20	0
	4	yard	Dornick Cloth	0	4	2	0
	3.5	yard	Fustian *Cloth*	0	5	0	0
	6	yard	Unknown	0	5	0	0
	28	lb	Soap, Black	0	2	6	0
	20	lb	Pots, Brass	0	6	8	0
	3	piece	Cloth of Assize	0	0	0	0

Merchant name	Qty	Unit	Commodity	£	s.	d.	f.

The Elizabeth aforesaid, 11th August 1595

Merchant name	Qty	Unit	Commodity	£	s.	d.	f.
Nicholas Lea of Waterford, Merchant Ind	8	C	Hops	4	0	0	0
	1	C	Orchil	1	0	0	0
	2	dozen	Wool–Cards	1	0	0	0
	1	dozen	Stockings	0	13	4	0
	4	yard	Bay *Cloth*	0	6	8	0
	2	C	Soap, Black	1	0	0	0
	13	yard	Cloth of Assize, Kersey	0	0	0	0

The Mary Dearinge of Waterford, burden 30 tons, Richard Coney master, to Waterford, 12th August 1595

Merchant name	Qty	Unit	Commodity	£	s.	d.	f.
Nicholas Briver of Waterford, Merchant Ind	7	C	Hops	3	10	0	0

The Ann Synott of Waterford, burden 50 tons, John Synott master, to Waterford, *12th August 1595*

Merchant name	Qty	Unit	Commodity	£	s.	d.	f.
John Whitt of Waterford, Merchant Ind	4	C	Hops	2	0	0	0
	1.5	gross	Knives (1*d.*)	0	15	0	0
	1	C	Towe	0	6	8	0
	1.5	dozen	Wool–Cards	0	15	0	0
	1	*sone?*	Nails, Lath	0	16	8	0
	1	M	Nails, Board	0	3	4	0
	1	piece	Calico *Cloth*	0	6	8	0
	6	piece	Balches	0	3	4	0
	1.5	dozen	Aniseed	0	5	0	0
	4	yard	Dornick Cloth	0	3	4	0
	5	piece	Hats, Boys	0	8	4	0
	3	*lb*	Serches	0	0	10	0
	1	stone	Blockwood	0	2	6	0

The Ann Synott aforesaid, 14th August 1595

Merchant name	Qty	Unit	Commodity	£	s.	d.	f.
Edward Hackett of Fethard-on-Sea, Merchant Ind	4	C	Hops	2	0	0	0
	2.25	C	Aniseed	3	0	0	0
	24	dozen	Glasses, Green	1	5	0	0
	2.75	dozen	Hats	4	2	6	0
	0.5	piece	Osborne Fustian *Cloth*	0	6	8	0
	5	gross	Knives (1*d.*)	2	10	0	0
	1	gross	Girdles (1*d.*)	0	10	0	0
	4	lb	Girdles, Nobs Silk	0	3	4	0
	0.5	C	Raisins, *Great*	0	3	4	0
	0.5	C	Prunes	0	5	0	0
	10	dozen	Drinking Horns	0	6	8	0
	12	lb	Sugar	0	6	8	0
	3	lb	Silk, Paris	1	0	0	0
	1	lb	Silk, Slewe	0	6	8	0
	1	lb	Points, Broad (1*d.*)	0	6	8	0
	2	gross	Points, Crewel	0	13	4	0

Merchant name	Qty	Unit	Commodity	£	s.	d.	f.
	4	dicker	Bracelets	0	3	4	0
	6	lb	Mail	0	3	4	0
	5	clout	Needles	0	4	2	0
	2.5	yard	Taffeta Cloth	0	16	8	0
	2	ream	Paper, Brown	0	0	20	0
	1	piece	Calico *Cloth*	0	6	8	0
	2	lb	Cloves	0	10	0	0
	1	lb	Ivory	0	5	0	0
	6	dozen	Playing Cards	0	10	0	0
	1	dozen	Gloves, Pairs	0	3	4	0
	4	ell	Holland *Cloth*	0	4	2	0
	2	ell	Levant Taffeta Cloth	0	4	2	0
	2	gross	Trenchers	0	0	20	0
	2	stone	Soap, Black	0	2	6	0
	6	lb	Thread, Packet	0	2	6	0
	1	dozen	Wool-Cards	0	10	0	0

The Speedwell of New Ross aforesaid, 14th August 1595

Merchant name	Qty	Unit	Commodity	£	s.	d.	f.
Nicholas Rothe of New Ross, Merchant Ind	1	ton	Iron	8	0	0	0
	6	C	Hops	3	0	0	0
	6	dozen	Wool-Cards	3	0	0	0
	1	dozen	Stock-Cards	0	13	4	0
	3	C	Wood, Brazil	5	0	0	0
	2	dozen	Penners & Inkhorns	0	0	20	0
	2	gross	Trenchers, Common	0	0	20	0
	1	dozen	Brushes, Heath	0	0	10	0
	12	lb	Thread, Packet	0	4	2	0
	3	gross	Points, Thread	1	10	0	0
	6	small gross	Buttons, Thread	0	5	0	0
	12	pair	Stockings, Woollen	0	8	4	0
	3	dozen	Hats	4	10	0	0
	14	lb	Currants	0	3	9	0
	4	gross	Lace, Statute	1	6	8	0
	12	lb	Mail	0	6	8	0
	4.5	lb	Silk, Paris	1	10	0	0
	1	gross	Gartering, Crewel	0	6	8	0
	1	C	Drinking Glasses, French	0	8	4	0
	1	C	Soap, Black	0	10	0	0
	1.5	C	Battery	3	0	0	0
	6	yard	Cloth of Assize	0	0	0	0

The Speedwell aforesaid, 14th August 1595

Merchant name	Qty	Unit	Commodity	£	s.	d.	f.
James Hore of New Ross, Merchant Ind	4	C	Hops	2	0	0	0
	4	C	Wool-Cards	2	0	0	0
	1	dozen	Stock-Cards	0	13	4	0
	2	gross	Lace, Statute	0	13	4	0
	2	gross	Knives (1*d.*)	1	0	0	0
	1	gross	Girdles	0	10	0	0
	12	piece	Hats	1	10	0	0

Merchant name	Qty	Unit	Commodity	£	s.	d.	f.
	2	C	Taps	0	0	20	0
	1	gross	Points, Thread	0	10	0	0
	1	dozen	Brushes, Heath	0	0	10	0
	28	lb	Lead	0	0	25	0
	1	gross	Trenchers, Common	0	0	10	0
	30	lb	Pewter	0	8	4	0
	20	dozen	Drinking Glasses, French	0	16	8	0

The Speedwell aforesaid, *14th August 1595*

James Duffe of New Ross, , Merchant Ind	5	C	Hops	2	10	0	0
	1	C	Blockwood	0	10	0	0
	1	C	Alum	1	13	4	0
	1.5	C	Soap, Black	0	15	0	0
	0.5	C	Orchil	0	10	0	0
	3	dozen	Wool-Cards	1	10	0	0
	1.5	dozen	Hats	2	5	0	0
	2	gross	Lace, Statute	0	13	4	0
	4	gross	Trenchers	0	3	4	0
	1	barrel	Verg[]l	0	3	4	0
	1.5	C	Battery/Brass	3	0	0	0
	3	unknown	Starces?	0	2	6	0
	1	gross	Knives (1d.)	0	10	0	0
	6	dozen	Drinking Glasses, French	0	5	0	0
			Earthen Ware	0	2	6	0
	3	lb	Mail	0	0	20	0
	2	gross	Buttons, Glass	0	0	20	0

The Speedwell aforesaid, 15th August 1595

Andrew Archer of Kilkenny, Merchant Ind	5	C	Hops	2	10	0	0
	5	gross	Trenchers, Common	0	4	2	0
	1	C	Pewter	1	13	4	0
	1	gross	Gartering, Crewel	0	6	8	0
	2	gross	Lace, Statute	0	13	4	0
	1	gross	Beads, Bugle	0	0	10	0
	1	M	Nails, Lath	0	0	20	0
	1	M	Nails, Board	0	3	4	0
	6	lb	Thread, Black	0	12	6	0

The Ann Synott aforesaid, 15th August 1595

Richard Walsh Fitznicholas of Waterford, Merchant Ind	1	C	Orchil	1	0	0	0
	1.5	C	Soap, Black	0	15	0	0
	12	M	Nails, Lath	1	0	0	0
	1	pipe	Iron	4	0	0	0
	1	burden	Tin	0	5	0	0
	1	dozen	Hats	1	10	0	0
	0.5	dozen	Hats, Childrens	0	10	0	0

Merchant name	Qty	Unit	Commodity	£	s.	d.	f.
	18	yard	Flannel *Cloth*	0	10	0	0
	12	clout	Needles	0	10	0	0
	2	C	Awl Blades	0	0	20	0
	1	bolt	Thread, Black	0	2	6	0
	1	C	Aniseed	1	6	8	0
	0.5	C	Rice	0	8	4	0
	1	lb	Mercury	0	0	20	0
	2	lb	Verdegris	0	0	20	0
	1	dozen	Wool-Cards	0	10	0	0
	6	yard	Cloth of Assize, Kersey	0	0	0	0

The Mary Dearinge aforesaid, 15th August 1595

John Soutton of Waterford, Merchant Ind	3	C	Aniseed	4	0	0	0
	2	piece	Bay *Cloth*	4	0	0	0
	5	gross	Knives (2*d.*)	5	0	0	0
	3	gross	Knives (1*d.*)	1	10	0	0
	2	gross	Girdles	1	0	0	0
	16	lb	Sugar	0	9	4	0
	0.5	C	Orchil	0	10	0	0
	2	M	Nails, Board Single	0	6	8	0
	1	M	Nails, Lath	0	0	20	0
	12	lb	Mail	0	6	8	0
	6	gross	Points	0	5	0	0
	9	yard	Cloth of Assize, Kersey	0	0	0	0

The Ann Synott aforesaid, 15th August 1595

Robert Hackett of Cashel, Merchant Ind	1	C	Aniseed	1	6	8	0
	8	dozen	Glasses, Coarse	0	6	8	0
	2	gross	Knives (1*d.*)	1	0	0	0
	1	gross	Girdles (1*d.*)	0	10	0	0
	0.5	C	Pewter	0	16	8	0
	1	lb	Girdles, Nobs Silk	0	0	10	0
	1	gross	Lace, Statute	0	6	8	0
	1	small gross	Points, Thread	0	0	20	0
	1	dozen	Hats	1	10	0	0
	2	lb	Mail, Red	0	0	20	0
	1	ream	Paper	0	3	4	0
	1	gross	Trenchers	0	0	10	0
	0.5	dozen	Bottles, Leather small	0	5	0	0
	2	stone	Soap, Black	0	2	6	0
	3	dozen	Stone Inges?	0	3	4	0
	1	dozen	Wool-Cards	0	10	0	0

The Elizabeth of Gloucester, burden 18 tons, John Swanley master, to Waterford, 15th August 1595

John Hoore of Limerick, Merchant Ind	1	C	Hops	0	10	0	0
	4	dozen	Wool-Cards, Old	1	6	8	0

Merchant name	Qty	Unit	Commodity	£	s.	d.	f.
	2	dozen	Hats	3	0	0	0
	3	ream	Paper	0	10	0	0
	5	small gross	Buttons, Thread	0	4	2	0
	6	small gross	Buttons, Glass	0	5	0	0
	6	dozen	Glasses, Drinking	0	5	0	0
	8	dozen	Knives, in Pairs	0	13	4	0
	0.5	small gross	Girdles (1d.)	0	5	0	0
	13	dozen	Knives, Pocket	1	1	8	0
	4	small gross	Points, Thread	0	3	4	0
	4	small gross	Points, Red	0	3	4	0
	3	dozen	Spurs	0	5	0	0
	3	burden	Tin	0	15	0	0
	8	lb	Mail	0	4	2	0
	8	clout	Needles	0	6	8	0
	5	boxes	Combs, Wooden	0	6	8	0
	3	nest	Boxes, Painted	0	0	30	0
	4	lb	Thread, Packet	0	0	20	0
	6	piece	Glasses, Looking small	0	10	0	0
	6	dozen	Thimbles	0	0	20	0
	5	gross	Trenchers, Common	0	4	2	0
	4	dozen	Bibs	0	3	4	0
	9	lb	Sulpher	0	0	20	0
	0.5	gross	Girth-Web	0	3	4	0
	1	dozen	Girth Buckles	0	0	10	0
	4	lb	Rice	0	0	10	0
	16	yard	Cotton *Cloth*	0	13	4	0
	2	lb	Thread, Coloured	0	3	4	0
	1	bolt	Thread, Black	0	0	30	0
	6	piece	Brushes	0	0	10	0
	4	dozen	Cups, Wooden	0	3	4	0
	1	dozen	Candlesticks, Small	0	10	0	0

The Elizabeth aforesaid, 15th August 1595

Merchant name	Qty	Unit	Commodity	£	s.	d.	f.
William Arthur of Limerick, Merchant Ind	2	C	Aniseed	2	13	4	0
	8	dozen	Glasses, Brace	0	11	6	0
	17	dozen	Urinalls	0	5	10	10
	7	dozen	Girdles	0	5	10	0
	3.5	dozen	Hats, Childrens	3	10	0	0
	26	yard	Bay Cloth	1	3	4	0
	30	lb	Sugar	0	17	8	0
	2	piece	Holmes Fustian *Cloth*	1	6	8	0
	3	gross	Knives (1d.)	1	10	0	0
	1	C	Soap, Black	0	10	0	0
	2	gross	Knives (2d.)	2	0	0	0
	1	gross	Knives, Pocket	1	0	0	0
	1	dozen	Stockings, Short	0	8	4	0
	0.5	C	Orchil	0	10	0	0
			Apothecary Wares	0	30	0	0
	12	yard	Cloth of Assize	0	0	0	0
	2	piece	Cloth of Assize, Kersey	0	0	0	0

Merchant name	Qty	Unit	Commodity	£	s.	d.	f.

The Adventure of Ilfracombe, burden 18 tons, Philip Emett master, to Brest, 18th August 1595

Richard Batt of Bristol, Merchant Ind	12	C goad	Cotton *Cloth*	40	0	0	0
	11	piece	Wadmal Cloth	11	0	0	0
	1	piece	Wadmal Cloth[97]	0	0	0	0
	6	piece	*Bristol* Frieze *Cloth*	6	0	0	0
	4	piece	Cloth of Assize	0	0	0	0
			Cloth of Assize, Overlengths	0	0	0	0

The Adventure aforesaid, 18th August 1595

Edward Bentely of Bristol, Merchant Ind	6	C goad	Cotton *Cloth*	20	0	0	0
	8	piece	Cloth of Assize	0	0	0	0
			Cloth of Assize, Overlengths	0	0	0	0

The Mary Dearinge aforesaid, 19th August 1595

Andrew Lucar of Waterford, Merchant Ind	1	C	Sugar	3	6	8	0
	2	piece	*Bristol* Frieze *Cloth*	2	0	0	0
	1	piece	Cotton *Cloth*	1	0	0	0
	36	yard	Bay *Cloth*	2	0	0	0
	1	piece	Sack *Cloth*	0	13	4	0
	2	gross	Knives (1*d.*)	1	0	0	0
	2	dozen	Knives, Fine	0	5	0	0
	1	dozen	Stockings, Woollen	0	8	4	0
	0.5	dozen	Stockings, Worsted	1	10	0	0
	1	dozen	Hats, Black	1	10	0	0
	1	dozen	Hats, Childrens	1	0	0	0
	0.5	dozen	Hats, Womens	0	15	0	0
	0.5	piece	Osborne Fustian *Cloth*	0	6	8	0
	0.5	piece	Milan Fustian *Cloth*	0	10	0	0
	1	piece	Jeane Fustian *Cloth*	0	13	4	0
	2	dozen	Girdles	0	0	20	0
	1	piece	Buffin *Cloth*	0	13	4	0
	0.5	C	Currants	0	15	0	0
	2	dozen	Locks, Hanging	0	6	8	0
	1	dozen	Horse Combs	0	3	4	0
	12	lb	Mail	0	6	8	0
	1	sone?	Nails, Lath	0	16	8	0
	2	dozen	Wool-Cards	1	0	0	0
	2	ream	Paper	0	6	8	0
	6	clout	Needles	0	5	0	0
	1	dozen	Hat Bands	0	0	20	0
	3	lb	Isinglass	0	0	10	0
	4	lb	Turnsole	0	0	30	0
	18	yard	Levant Taffeta Cloth	1	10	0	0
	2	dozen	Ink Horns	0	0	20	0
	1	M	Nails, Scopp	0	0	20	0

[97] Custom exempt.

Merchant name	Qty	Unit	Commodity	£	s.	d.	f.
	1	C	Soap, Black	0	10	0	0
	20	lb	Starch	0	5	0	0
	6	small gross	Points	0	2	6	0
	2	gross	Girth-Web	0	13	4	0
	6	pair	Stock-Cards	0	6	8	0
	1	gross	Playing Cards	1	0	0	0
	1	ream	Paper, Brown	0	0	10	0
	3.5	dozen	Books, Small	0	11	6	0
	15	ells	Coarse Holland Cloth	0	12	6	0
	2.5	dozen	Drinking Glasses	0	0	30	0
	3	dozen	Crest *Cloth*	0	0	30	0
	1	gross	Gartering, Norwich	0	6	8	0
	6	piece	Snaffles	0	3	4	0
	1	dozen	Snuffers	0	3	4	0
	6	pair	Bellows	0	5	0	0
	6	pair	Candlesticks, Small	0	0	20	0
	30	yard	Cloth of Assize	0	0	0	0

The Speedwell aforesaid, 19th August 1595

Merchant name	Qty	Unit	Commodity	£	s.	d.	f.
Edward Rothe of Kilkenny, Merchant Ind	3.5	C	Hops	1	15	0	0
	2	C	Aniseed	2	13	4	0
	12	dozen	Drinking Glasses	0	10	0	0
	12	dozen	Violles	0	10	0	0
	12	dozen	Violles, Square	0	10	0	0
	8	dozen	Wool-Cards	4	0	0	0
	1.5	dozen	Stock-Cards	1	0	0	0
	0.5	C	Soap, Black	0	5	0	0
	2	gross	Trenchers	0	0	20	0
	2	dozen	Hats	3	0	0	0
	1	dozen	Hats, Childrens	1	0	0	0
	1	piece	Osborne Fustian *Cloth*	0	13	4	0
	12	yard	Cotton *Cloth*	0	10	0	0
	6	yard	Bay *Cloth*	0	10	0	0
	1	gross	Knives (1*d.*)	0	10	0	0
	1	gross	Knives, Pocket	1	0	0	0
	2	small gross	Points	0	0	20	0
	7	lb	Mail	0	3	4	0
	2	lb	Nails, Daysy?	0	0	20	0
	2	butt	Thread, Black	0	4	2	0
	2	C	Awl Blades	0	0	20	0
	24	lb	Rice	0	3	4	0
	24	lb	Matches	0	4	2	0
	3	dozen	Locks	0	10	0	0
	3	dozen	Locks, Plate	0	10	0	0
	9	lb	Silk, Paris	3	0	0	0
	2	lb	Girdles, Nobs Silk	0	0	20	0
	1	lb	Silk, Slewe	0	6	8	0
	2	gross	Lace, Statute	0	13	4	0
	6	dozen	Locks Hanging, Small	0	10	0	0
	2	dozen	Files	0	3	0	0
	2	small gross	Buttons, *Tin*	0	0	20	0

Merchant name	Qty	Unit	Commodity	£	s.	d.	f.
	1	dozen	Gouge & Formes	0	3	4	0
	3	piece	Scythes	0	0	30	0
	3	piece	Saws, Hand	0	0	30	0
	2	piece	Vice, Hand	0	3	4	0
	2	C	Nails, Board	0	0	20	0
	6	C	Nails, Lath	0	0	20	0
	2	C	Hooks, Fish	0	0	20	0
	3	dozen	Shewers?	0	3	4	0
	6	piece	Bottles, Leather small	0	5	0	0
	2	gross	Wire	0	0	10	0
	2	dozen	Parchment *Skins*	0	6	8	0
	2	C	Taps & Cannells	0	0	20	0
	12	yard	Cloth of Assize, Kersey	0	0	0	0
	9	yard	Cloth of Assize	0	0	0	0

The Ann Synott aforesaid, 19th August 1595

Thomas Donohowe of Clonmel, Merchant Ind	1	gross	Girdles (1*d*.)	0	10	0	0
	2	gross	Knives (1*d*.)	1	0	0	0
	12	lb	Mail	0	6	8	0
	1	dozen	Locks, Small	0	0	20	0
	1.5	lb	Senna	0	0	10	0
	6	lb	Thread, Packet	0	0	25	0
	10	lb	Sulpher	0	0	10	0
	1	dozen	Penners	0	0	10	0
	0.5	gross	Girth-Web	0	3	4	0
	0.5	gross	Girdles, Crewel	0	6	8	0
	2	dozen	Candlesticks, Small	0	6	8	0
	2	C	Hops	1	0	0	0
	2	lb	Thread	0	3	4	0
	1.5	lb	Silk, Raw	0	10	0	0
	2	lb	Silk, Paris	0	13	4	0
	3	ream	Paper	0	10	0	0
	3	lb	Pepper	0	5	0	0
	16	lb	Sugar	0	10	10	0
	20	lb	Rice	0	3	9	0
	1.5	dozen	Hats	2	5	0	0
	1	lb	Ginger	0	0	20	0

The Ann Synott aforesaid, *19th August 1595*

Walter Hackett of Fethard-on-Sea, Merchant Ind	0.5	gross	Girth-Web	0	3	4	0
	1	gross	Knives	0	10	0	0
	1	dozen	Spurs	0	0	20	0
	1	dozen	Girdles	0	0	10	0
	0.5	gross	Girdles	0	6	8	0
	0.5	gross	Ribbon	0	3	4	0
	3	lb	Mail	0	0	20	0
	0.5	clout	Needles	0	0	10	0
	4	small gross	Buttons, Copper	0	3	4	0

Merchant name	Qty	Unit	Commodity	£	s.	d.	f.
	1	butt	Thread, Black	0	0	25	0
	1	dozen	Penners	0	0	10	0
	4	piece	Inkle	0	5	10	0
	0.5	gross	Gartering, Norwich	0	3	4	0
	2	lb	Girdles, Nobs Silk	0	0	20	0
	1	dozen	Candlesticks, Small	0	3	4	0
	1.5	C	Hops	0	15	0	0
	1	lb	Thread	0	0	20	0
	1	lb	Silk, Slewe	0	6	8	0
	1	ream	Paper	0	3	4	0
	1	dozen	Locks Hanging, Small	0	0	20	0
	2	gross	Buttons, Silk	0	0	10	0
	1	lb	Ribbon, Broad (1d.)	0	6	8	0
	1	dozen	Horse Bells, Coarse	0	0	5	0
	1	gross	Lace, Statute	0	6	8	0
	4	stone	Aniseed	0	13	4	0
	6	pair	Playing Tables	0	4	2	0
	1	dozen	Hats	1	10	0	0
	1	dozen	Glasses, Looking (1d.)	0	0	10	0
	4	lb	Rice	0	0	10	0

The Ann Synott aforesaid, 19th August 1595

Merchant name	Qty	Unit	Commodity	£	s.	d.	f.
Pierce Vine of Fethard-on-Sea, Merchant Ind	1.5	dozen	Hats	2	5	0	0
	1	gross	Knives	0	10	0	0
	2	small gross	Buttons	0	0	10	0
	1	clout	Needles	0	0	10	0
	1	gross	Points	0	0	10	0
	1	dozen	Locks, Small	0	0	20	0
	3	lb	Mail	0	0	20	0
	1	small gross	Girdles, Leather	0	10	0	0
	1	lb	Thread	0	0	20	0
	0.5	gross	Gartering, Norwich	0	3	4	0
	2	dozen	Glasses, Looking (1d.)	0	0	20	0
	1	piece	Osborne Fustian *Cloth*	0	13	4	0
	6	pair	Stock-Cards	0	4	2	0
	6	ell	Holland *Cloth*	0	5	0	0
	1.5	lb	Silk, Paris	0	10	0	0
	0.5	lb	Ribbon, Broad (1d.)	0	3	4	0
	2	lb	Thread, Packet	0	0	10	0
	3	lb	Girdles, Nobs Silk	0	2	6	0
	6	lb	Rice	0	0	15	0
	3	dozen	Drinking Glasses, French	0	2	6	0
	1	piece	Canykine	0	10	0	0
	1	pipe	Iron	4	0	0	0
	1	ream	Paper	0	3	4	0
	1	burden	Tin	0	5	0	0

Merchant name	Qty	Unit	Commodity	£	s.	d.	f.

The Mary Dearinge aforesaid, 21st August 1595

Merchant name	Qty	Unit	Commodity	£	s.	d.	f.
Patrick Lea of Waterford, Merchant Ind	30	yard	Cotton *Cloth*	1	5	0	0
	10	dozen	Knives, Pocket	0	16	8	0
	6	dozen	Knives (1d.)	0	5	0	0
	2	dozen	Stockings, Short	0	16	8	0
	4	gross	Trenchers, Common	0	3	4	0
	3	dozen	Girdles	0	2	6	0
	3	lb	Girdles, Nobs Silk	0	2	6	0
	6	dozen	Drinking Glasses	0	5	0	0
	20	ell	Holland *Cloth*	0	16	8	0
	3.5	piece	Osborne Fustian *Cloth*	1	0	0	0
	6	lb	Thread, Black	0	5	0	0
	12	lb	Almonds	0	5	0	0
	2	ream	Paper	0	6	8	0
	6	small gross	*Buttons, Silk*[98]	0	2	6	0
	6	small gross	*Points*[99]	0	5	0	0
	3	dozen	Ribbon, Silk	0	4	2	0
	2	dozen	Points, Bugle	0	3	4	0
	16	dozen	Lace, Statute	0	8	4	0
	4	piece	Brushes	0	0	10	0
	4	lb	Seed, Cumin	0	0	20	0
	2	lb	Senna	0	3	4	0
	3	lb	Sugar Candy	0	0	20	0
	6	dozen	Gartering	0	3	4	0
	1	lb	Thread, Coloured	0	0	20	0
	6	lb	Mail	0	3	4	0
	1	dozen	Locks, Cap Cases	0	0	20	0
	1	gross	Knives	0	10	0	0
	1	dozen	Spurs	0	0	20	0
	2	gross	Trenchers	0	0	20	0
	1	dozen	Glue	0	0	20	0
	6	small gross	Buttons, Thread	0	0	20	0
	16	piece	Hats	2	0	0	0
	24	yard	Cloth of Assize	0	0	0	0

The Ann Synott aforesaid, *21st August 1595*

Merchant name	Qty	Unit	Commodity	£	s.	d.	f.
Nicholas Langton of Kilkenny, Merchant Ind	31	yard	Bay *Cloth*	1	13	4	0
	4	C	Hops	2	0	0	0
	0.5	C	Aniseed	0	13	4	0
	0.5	C	Rice	0	8	4	0
	1	C	Currants	1	10	0	0
	4	dozen	Wool-Cards	2	0	0	0
	12	dozen	Knives (1d.)	0	10	0	0
	1	dozen	Stock-Cards	0	13	4	0
	4	ream	Paper	0	10	10	0
	4	lb	Girdles, Nobs Silk	0	3	4	0
	1	piece	Osborne Fustian *Cloth*	0	13	4	0
	1	piece	Jeane Fustian *Cloth*	0	13	4	0
	1	piece	Holland *Cloth*	1	4	2	0

98 See note 68.   **99** As above.

Merchant name	Qty	Unit	Commodity	£	s.	d.	f.
	1	dozen	Hats	1	10	0	0
	1	dozen	Penners	0	0	10	0
	1	dozen	Horse Combs	0	0	25	0
	1	stone?	Nails, Lath	0	16	8	0
	1	M	Nails, Board	0	3	4	0
	16	dozen	Drinking Glasses	0	13	4	0
	12	lb	Mail	0	6	8	0
	1	barrel	Chalk	0	0	20	0
	1	dozen	Locks, Small	0	3	4	0
	1	C	Awl Blades	0	0	10	0
	2	lb	Counters	0	0	20	0
	6	lb	Senna	0	9	2	0
	20	lb	Tin	0	5	0	0
	2	gross	Trenchers	0	0	20	0
	0.5	C	Soap, Black	0	5	0	0
	2	clout	Needles	0	0	20	0
	0.5	C	Matches	0	8	4	0
	3	lb	Isinglass	0	0	10	0
	2	lb	Turnsole	0	0	20	0
	6	piece	Girth-Web	0	3	4	0
	24	yard	Cloth of Assize	0	0	0	0
	1	piece	Cloth of Assize, Kersey	0	0	0	0

The Ann Synott aforesaid, *21st August 1595*

Thomas Cransborowe of Waterford,
Merchant Ind

	Qty	Unit	Commodity	£	s.	d.	f.
	85	yard	Cotton *Cloth*	3	15	0	0
	1	C	Almonds	2	0	0	0
	0.5	C	Currants	0	15	0	0
	2	piece	Osborne Fustian *Cloth*	1	6	8	0
	5	piece	Jeane Fustian *Cloth*	3	6	8	0
	8	dozen	Drinking Glasses	0	6	8	0
	3	dozen	Bottles, Glass	0	10	0	0
	4	butt	Thread, Black	0	8	4	0
	2	gross	Gartering, Coarse	0	13	4	0
	4	lb	Thread, Piecing	0	10	0	0
	6	lb	Girdles, Nobs Silk	0	5	0	0
	3	gross	Points, Thread	0	2	6	0
	2	dozen	Horse Combs	0	4	2	0
	3	dozen	Spurs	0	5	0	0
	1	dozen	Pans, Plate Dripping	0	5	0	0
	64	yard	Cloth of Assize	0	0	0	0

The Ann Synott aforesaid, *21st August 1595*

Walter Reyan of Kilkenny, Merchant Ind	Qty	Unit	Commodity	£	s.	d.	f.
	0.5	piece	Osborne Fustian *Cloth*	0	6	8	0
	6	yard	Cotton *Cloth*	0	5	0	0
	2	lb	Girdles, Nobs Silk	0	0	20	0
	1	lb	Silk, Paris	0	6	8	0
	2	lb	Thread	0	3	4	0
	1	gross	Lace, Statute	0	6	8	0

Merchant name	Qty	Unit	Commodity	£	s.	d.	f.
	1	lb	Crewel, French	0	2	6	0
	1	dozen	Hats, Childrens	1	10	0	0
	6.5	gross	Gold Paper	0	6	8	0
	2	gross	Buttons, Glass	0	0	20	0
	1	gross	Buttons, Silk	0	2	6	0
	1	gross	Buttons, Pewter	0	0	10	0
	2	pair	Candlesticks, Brass	0	3	4	0
	1	C	Hops	0	10	0	0
	4	dozen	Wool-Cards, Old	1	6	8	0
	6	pair	Stock-Cards	0	6	8	0
	6	lb	Mail	0	3	4	0
	3	C	Awl Blades	0	2	6	0
	2	clout	Needles	0	0	20	0
	2	stone	Aniseed	0	6	8	0
	1	stone	Currants	0	3	9	0
	3	lb	Turpentine	0	0	10	0
	2	lb	Treacle	0	0	20	0
	1	lb	Sandlewood	0	0	20	0
	1	stone	Rice	0	0	25	0
	2	unknown	Morions Plain	0	6	8	0
	1	dozen	Bibs	0	0	10	0
	1	gross	Knives (1d.)	0	10	0	0
	2	small gross	Points, Thread	0	0	20	0
	1	dozen	Gloves, Pairs	0	3	4	0
	1	dozen	Locks, Small	0	3	4	0
	1	dozen	Spurs	0	0	20	0
	1	dozen	Thimbles	0	0	5	0
	6	piece	Neck Bands/ Necklaces	0	0	10	0
	1	dozen	Girdles (1d.)	0	0	10	0
	1	dozen	Bands Plain	0	3	4	0
	2	ream	Paper	0	5	10	0
	5	lb	Comfits	0	5	0	0
	11.25	yard	Cloth of Assize	0	0	0	0
	4	yard	Cloth of Assize, Kersey	0	0	0	0

The Elizabeth of Gloucester aforesaid, *21st August 1595*

David Dobin of Waterford, Merchant Ind	3.5	C	Hops	1	15	0	0
	0.5	piece	Milan Fustian *Cloth*	0	10	0	0
	6	pair	Stockings, Short	0	4	2	0
	1	lb	Silk, Ferett	0	8	4	0
	12	piece	Hats	1	10	0	0
	1	gross	Lace, Statute	0	6	8	0
	12	yard	Bay *Cloth*	1	0	0	0
	0.5	dozen	Stock-Cards	0	6	8	0

The Ann Synott aforesaid, *21st August 1595*

Walter Dowley of Kilkenny, Merchant Ind	3	C	Hops	1	10	0	0
	4	dozen	Wool-Cards	2	0	0	0

Merchant name	Qty	Unit	Commodity	£	s.	d.	f.
	1	piece	Jeane Fustian *Cloth*	0	13	4	0
	2	C	Lead	0	16	8	0
	28	lb	Prunes	0	2	6	0
	1	gross	Knives (1*d.*)	0	10	0	0
	6	piece	Hats, Childrens	0	10	0	0
	6	piece	Hats	0	15	0	0
	6	lb	Turpentine	0	0	10	0
	28	lb	Alum	0	8	4	0
	1	gross	Knives, Pocket	1	0	0	0
	2	dozen	Playing Cards	0	3	4	0
	28	lb	Aniseed	0	6	8	0
	1	dozen	Knives, Prage	0	0	20	0
	28	lb	Soap, Black	0	2	6	0
	3	lb	Mail	0	2	6	0
	10	lb	Frankinsense	0	3	4	0
	1	burden	Tin	0	5	0	0
	1	small gross	Buttons, Hair	0	0	10	0
	2	gross	Points	0	0	20	0
	3	M	Pins	0	0	25	0
	2	C	Arrow Heads	0	0	20	0
	1	dozen	Spectacles	0	0	10	0
	6	piece	Books, Grammar	0	3	4	0
	4	dozen	Drinking Glasses	0	3	4	0
	2	C	Chalk	0	0	20	0
	3	yard	Cloth of Assize	0	0	0	0

The Ann Synott aforesaid, *21st August 1595*

Merchant name	Qty	Unit	Commodity	£	s.	d.	f.
George St Lenger of Kilkenny, Merchant Ind	0.5	C	Rice	0	8	4	0
	8	dozen	Wool-Cards	4	0	0	0
	4	dozen	Stock-Cards	2	13	4	0
	2	lb	Girdles, Nobs Silk	0	0	20	0
	6	lb	Silk, Paris	2	0	0	0
	0.5	small gross	Buttons, Hair	0	0	10	0
	1	gross	Trenchers, Common	0	0	10	0
	1	M	Pins	0	0	10	0
	6	piece	Lanterns	0	3	4	0
	3	C	Hops	1	10	0	0
	2	gross	Knives, Cuttlers	2	0	0	0
	1	small gross	Points, Thread	0	0	10	0
	1	dozen	Hats	1	10	0	0
	2	C	Taps & Cannells	0	0	20	0
	3	dozen	Girdles (1*d.*)	0	2	6	0
	4	piece	Morions Plain	0	13	4	0
	2	dozen	Cruses, Stone	0	0	20	0
	3	C	Battery	6	0	0	0

The Ann Synott aforesaid, *21st August 1595*

Merchant name	Qty	Unit	Commodity	£	s.	d.	f.
Oliver Shortall of Kilkenny, Merchant Ind	2	C	Hops	1	0	0	0
	6	lb	Girdles, Nobs Silk	0	5	0	0
	1	gross	Gold Paper	0	6	8	0

Merchant name	Qty	Unit	Commodity	£	s.	d.	f.
	2	C	Chalk	0	0	20	0
	1	gross	Playing Cards	1	0	0	0
	6	lb	Mail	0	3	4	0
	2	gross	Knives (1d.)	1	0	0	0
	6	dozen	Bibs	0	5	0	0
	4	nest	Boxes, Painted	0	3	4	0
	3	C	Awl Blades	0	2	6	0
	1	M	Pins	0	0	10	0
	1	C	Pewter	1	13	4	0

The Ann Synott aforesaid, 22nd August 1595

Merchant name	Qty	Unit	Commodity	£	s.	d.	f.
John Rothe of Kilkenny, Merchant Ind	6	C	Hops	2	10	0	0
	0.5	C	Aniseed	0	13	4	0
	0.5	C	Rice	0	8	4	0
	20	yard	Bay *Cloth*	1	0	0	0
	1	piece	Milan Fustian *Cloth*	1	0	0	0
	1	piece	Jeane Fustian *Cloth*	0	13	4	0
	1.5	dozen	Hats	2	5	0	0
	3	dozen	Wool-Cards	1	10	0	0
	1	dozen	Stock-Cards	0	13	4	0
	12	dozen	Knives (1d.)	0	10	0	0
	3	ream	Paper	0	8	4	0
	12	?	Penners & Inkhorns	0	0	10	0
	5	lb	Girdles, Nobs Silk	0	4	2	0
	1	dozen	Horse Combs	0	0	25	0
	1	sone?	Nails, Lath	0	16	8	0
	5	C	Nails, Board	0	0	20	0
	1	C	Lead	0	8	4	0
	12	piece	Setting Sticks	0	3	4	0
	6	piece	Garters, Broad	0	0	25	0
	1	dozen	Spurs	0	0	20	0
	1	dozen	Girdles (1d.)	0	0	10	0
	12	dozen	Drinking Glasses	0	10	0	0
	6	dozen	Urinalls	0	5	0	0
	3.5	C	Chalk	0	5	0	0
	1	lb	Senna	0	0	20	0
	6	lb	Starch	0	0	10	0
	28	lb	Soap, Black	0	2	6	0
			Apothecary Wares	3	0	0	0
	31	yard	Cloth of Assize	0	0	0	0
	2.5	piece	Cloth of Assize, Kersey	0	0	0	0

The Ann Synott aforesaid, 22nd August 1595

Merchant name	Qty	Unit	Commodity	£	s.	d.	f.
Walter Daniell of Kilkenny, Merchant Ind	12	lb	Thread, Packet	0	4	2	0
	5	C	Hops	2	10	0	0
	3	dozen	Wool-Cards	1	10	0	0
	20	yard	Cotton *Cloth*	0	16	8	0
	0.5	C	Rice	0	8	4	0
	3	lb	Girdles, Nobs Silk	0	2	6	0

Merchant name	Qty	Unit	Commodity	£	s.	d.	f.
	2	lb	Silk, Paris	0	13	4	0
	2	dozen	Spurs	0	3	4	0
	1	dozen	Hats	1	10	0	0
	3	lb	Mail	0	0	20	0
	10	dozen	Drinking Glasses	0	8	4	0
	1	small gross	Points, Thread	0	0	10	0
	1	dozen	Penners & Inkhorns	0	0	10	0
	3	ream	Paper	0	8	4	0
	28	lb	Matches	0	5	0	0
	1	gross	Knives (1d.)	0	10	0	0
	5	C	Taps & Cannells	0	4	2	0
	1	gross	Glasses, Looking (ob.)	0	8	4	0
	30	lb	Sugar	0	18	4	0
	30	lb	Soap,	0	0	35	0
	10	dozen	Girdles (1d.)	0	8	4	0
	6	dozen	Bibs(1d.)	0	5	0	0
	20	lb	Comfits	1	0	0	0
	6	piece	Hats, Childrens	0	10	0	0
	20	yard	Cloth of Assize	0	0	0	0

The Ann Synott aforesaid, 22nd August 1595

Merchant name	Qty	Unit	Commodity	£	s.	d.	f.
Richard Rothe of Kilkenny, Merchant Ind	30	yard	Cotton *Cloth*	1	5	0	0
	12	lb	Girdles, Nobs Silk	0	10	0	0
	3	C	Hops	1	10	0	0
	4	dozen	Wool-Cards	1	6	8	0
	5	gross	Trenchers, Common	0	4	2	0
	1.5	dozen	Hats	2	5	0	0
	1.5	gross	Knives (1d.)	0	15	0	0
	13	small gross	Buttons, Thread	0	5	5	0
	2	ream	Paper	0	5	5	0
	6	piece	Bed Cords, Small	0	3	4	0
	2	lb	Mail	0	0	15	0
	4	C	Taps & Cannells	0	3	4	0
	6	dozen	Drinking Glasses	0	5	0	0
	28	lb	Matches	0	5	0	0
	0.5	C	Soap, Black	0	5	0	0
	2	barrel	Vinegar	0	11	6	0
	6	yard	Cloth of Assize	0	0	0	0
	12	yard	Cloth of Assize, Kersey	0	0	0	0

The Ann Synott aforesaid, 22nd' August 1595

Merchant name	Qty	Unit	Commodity	£	s.	d.	f.
George Comerford of Kilkenny, Merchant Ind	2	C	Hops	1	0	0	0
	2	dozen	Stock-Cards	1	6	8	0
	4	dozen	Wool-Cards	2	0	0	0
	28	lb	Rice	0	4	2	0
	0.5	C	Aniseed	0	13	4	0
	2	lb	Silk, Nobs	0	0	20	0
	1	gross	Paper, Gold	0	6	7	0
	1	gross	Knives, Cuttlers	1	0	0	0

Merchant name	Qty	Unit	Commodity	£	s.	d.	f.
	1	dozen	Hats	1	10	0	0
	3	lb	Mail	0	0	20	0
	1	C	Awl Blades	0	0	10	0
	1	clout	Needles	0	0	10	0
	1	dozen	Locks, Small	0	0	20	0
	0.5	gross	Gartering, Norwich	0	3	4	0
	2	gross	Points, Thread	0	0	20	0
	6	dozen	Knives	0	5	0	0
	0.5	piece	Dornick Cloth	0	5	0	0
	6	piece	Candlesticks, Small	0	0	20	0
	5	C	Battery	10	0	0	0
	6	yard	Cloth of Assize	0	0	0	0
	44	yard	Bay Cloth	2	13	4	0
	1	piece	*Bristol* Frieze *Cloth*	1	0	0	0
	2.5	piece	Cotton *Cloth*	1	0	0	0

The Ann Synott aforesaid, *22nd^t August 1595*

Robert Black & Patrick French of Galway, Merchants

	Qty	Unit	Commodity	£	s.	d.	f.
Ind	46	yard	Levant Taffeta Cloth	3	16	8	0
	3	piece	Sack *Cloth*	2	0	0	0
	16	pair	Stockings, Short Worsted	4	0	0	0
	4	pair	Stockings, Short	1	0	0	0
	0.5	dozen	Stockings, Short Womens	0	4	2	0
	1	gross	Lace, Statute	0	6	8	0
	1	gross	Points, Crewel	0	6	8	0
	2	dozen	Parchment Skins	0	13	4	0
	12	dozen	Penners & Inkhorns	0	10	0	0
	4	butt	Thread, Black	0	8	4	0
	50	lb	Combs, Bone	0	5	0	0
	20	M	Pins	0	10	10	0
	12	gross	Knives (*ob.*)	3	0	0	0
	0.5	gross	Knives, in Pairs	0	10	0	0
	4	gross	Knives, Pocket	4	0	0	0
	13	gross	Girth-Web	4	6	8	0
	1	gross	Knives, Prage	0	16	8	0
	6	dozen	Girdles (1*d.*)	0	5	0	0
	7	dozen	Girdles (*ob.*)	0	3	4	0
	2	C	Hops	1	0	0	0
	20	small gross	Buttons, Glass	0	8	4	0
	2.5	dozen	Snuffers	0	8	4	0
	1	C	Glue	0	10	0	0
	8	lb	Silk, Paris	2	13	4	0
	4	dozen	Gloves, Coarse	1	0	0	0
	1.5	dozen	Gloves, *Coarse*	0	7	6	0
	1	dozen	Portmanteau	1	0	0	0
	9	dozen	Shoe Horns	0	6	8	0
	3.5	piece	Milan Fustian Cloth	3	10	0	0
	4	piece	Osborne Fustian Cloth	2	13	4	0

Merchant name	Qty	Unit	Commodity	£	s.	d.	f.
	2.5	piece	Jeane Fustian Cloth	1	13	4	0
	12	small gross	Buttons, Silk	0	5	0	0
	20	gross	Buttons, Crewel & Silk	0	8	4	0
	8	ounces	Silk, Coloured	0	10	0	0
	3	ounces	Silk, Black	0	4	2	0
	40	lb	Thread, Packet	0	13	4	0
	12	dozen	Glasses, Looking	0	8	4	0
	12	pair	Garters, Coarse	1	0	0	0
	3	dozen	Brushes, Coarse Heath	0	5	5	0
	5	dozen	Laces for Knives	0	4	2	0
	13	small gross	Points, Thread	0	10	10	0
	10	nest	Boxes, Painted	0	8	4	0
	62	piece	Books, Small	0	11	6	0
	6	dozen	Locks, Cap Cases	0	10	0	0
	3	dozen	Spurs	0	5	0	0
	3	clout	Needles	0	2	6	0
	5	dozen	Hats	7	10	0	0
	3	dozen	Bands, Coarse Cyprus	0	15	0	0
	13	gross	Trenchers, Common	0	11	6	0
	8	dozen	Wool-Cards	4	0	0	0
	1	dozen	Ribbon	0	5	0	0
	6	lb	Wax	0	5	0	0
	1.25	gross	Points, Saye	0	8	4	0
	1	gross	Points, Small Silk	0	5	0	0
	3	roles	Buckram *Cloth*	0	7	6	0
	2	lb	Mail	0	0	20	0
	7	dozen	Drinking Glasses	0	5	10	0
	2	dozen	Purses	0	6	8	0
	4	dozen	Spectacles	0	3	4	0
	4	dozen	Knives, Pocket	0	6	8	0
	20	lb	Starch	0	5	0	0
	1	piece	Cloth of Assize	0	0	0	0
	24	yard	Cloth of Assize	0	0	0	0
	1	piece	Cloth of Assize, Northern Dozen Single	0	0	0	0
	3	yard	Cloth of Assize, Northern	0	0	0	0

The Mary Dearinge aforesaid, 22nd August 1595

Merchant name	Qty	Unit	Commodity	£	s.	d.	f.
James Lea of Waterford, Merchant Ind	2	dozen	Balches	0	13	4	0
	1	sone?	Nails, Lath	0	16	8	0
	12	yard	Bay *Cloth*	1	0	0	0
	6	small gross	Buttons, Thread	0	5	0	0
	1	dozen	Girdles (1d.)	0	0	10	0
	1	dozen	Stockings, Woollen	0	8	4	0
	1	gross	Knives, Cuttlers	1	0	0	0
	1	dozen	Hats	1	10	0	0
	1	dozen	Urinalls	0	0	10	0
	7	dozen	Drinking Glasses	0	5	10	0

Merchant name	Qty	Unit	Commodity	£	s.	d.	f.
	1	C	Chalk	0	0	20	0
	1	dozen	Brushes, Coarse *Heath*	0	0	20	0
	2	C	Taps	0	0	20	0
	2	small gross	Points, Thread	0	0	20	0
	6	ell	Sarcenet *Cloth*	2	0	0	0
	12	yard	Levant Taffeta Cloth	1	0	0	0
	2	ell	Taffeta Cloth	0	16	8	0
	?	dozen	Books, Fable?	0	6	8	0
	1	C	Hops	0	10	0	0
	1	dozen	Spurs	0	0	20	0
	1	piece	Jeane Fustian *Cloth*	0	13	4	0
	2	butt	Thread, Black	0	4	2	0
	1.5	dozen	Penners	0	0	20	0
	9	piece	Lanterns	0	5	0	0
	2	clout	Needles	0	0	20	0
	1	dozen	Locks, Small	0	0	20	0
	2	C	Awl Blades	0	0	20	0
	6	piece	Saws, Hand	0	5	0	0
	6	lb	Thread, Packet	0	0	25	0
	20	yard	Cotton *Cloth*	0	16	8	0
	6	yard	Cloth of Assize, Kersey	0	0	0	0
	6	yard	Cloth of Assize	0	0	0	0

The Lillie of Bristol, burden 30 tons, Hugh Jones master, to La Rochelle, *22nd August 1595*

Nicholas Barnesley of Bristol, Merchant Ind	12	wey	Coal	4	0	0	0
	4	C	Wax	12	0	0	0
	4	piece	*Bristol* Frieze *Cloth*	4	0	0	0

The Diamount aforesaid, *22nd August 1595*

Mathew Havilland of Bristol, Merchant Ind	5	piece	Cloth of Assize	0	0	0	0
			Cloth of Assize, Overlengths	0	0	0	0

The Ann Synott aforesaid, *22nd August 1595*

Henry Pembrocke of Kilkenny, Merchant Ind	2	C	Hops	1	0	0	0
	2	dozen	Wool-Cards	1	0	0	0
	1	dozen	Stock-Cards	0	13	4	0
	3	lb	Silk, Nobs	0	2	6	0
	0.5	gross	Knives (1*d.*)	0	5	0	0
	2	ream	Paper	0	5	5	0
	6	lb	Mail	0	3	4	0
	2	C	Awl Blades	0	0	20	0
	6	piece	Hats	0	15	0	0
	0.5	piece	Osborne Fustian *Cloth*	0	6	8	0
	2	dozen	Locks, Small	0	6	8	0
	0.5	gross	Knives, Pocket	0	10	0	0
	1	dozen	Spurs	0	0	20	0
	6	dozen	Gold Paper	0	3	4	0

Merchant name	Qty	Unit	Commodity	£	s.	d.	f.
	2	lb	Silk, Paris	0	13	4	0
	2	stone	Aniseed	0	6	8	0

The Mary Dearinge aforesaid, 22nd August 1595

Edmund Walsh of Waterford, Merchant Ind	1	piece	Bay *Cloth*	2	0	0	0
	1	gross	Knives (2d.)	1	0	0	0
	0.5	gross	Knives (1d.)	0	5	0	0
	1	dozen	Stockings, Short	0	12	6	0
	12	yard	Cotton *Cloth*	0	10	0	0
	6	small gross	Buttons, Thread	0	2	6	0
	1	sone?	Nails, Lath	0	16	8	0
	6	M	Nails *(2d.)*	0	10	0	0
	2	dozen	Spurs	0	3	4	0
	1	dozen	Girdles (1d.)	0	0	10	0
	1	dozen	Girdles (2d.)	0	0	20	0
	3	lb	Girdles, Nobs Silk	0	2	6	0
	4	lb	Thread	0	6	8	0
	3	M	Pins	0	0	20	0
	6	yard	Levant Taffeta Cloth	1	0	0	0
	0.5	piece	Milan Fustian *Cloth*	0	10	0	0
	1	piece	Jeane Fustian *Cloth*	0	13	4	0
	5	lb	Silk, Slewe	**0**	**6**	**8**	**0**
	1	dozen	Books, Horn	0	0	10	0
	4	lb	Mail	0	0	25	0
	1	gross	Trenchers, Common	0	0	10	0
	11	yard	Cloth of Assize, Kersey	0	0	0	0
	6	yard	Cloth of Assize	0	0	0	0

The Mary Dearinge aforesaid, 25th August 1595

Nicholas Molronie of London, Merchant Ind	3.75	C	Hops	1	18	4	0
	14	dozen	Glasses	0	11	6	0
	30	lb	Prunes	0	5	5	0
	30	lb	Currants	0	7	11	0
	0.5	C	Soap, Black	0	5	0	0
	2	dozen	Hats	3	0	0	0

The Ann Synott aforesaid, 25th August 1595

Martin Archer of Kilkenny, Merchant Ind	8	C	Hops	4	0	0	0
	3	C	Aniseed	4	0	0	0
	1	C	Rice	0	16	8	0
	12	ream	Paper	1	13	4	0
	1	piece	Raisins, *Great*	0	5	0	0

The Diamound aforesaid, 25th August 1595

Thomas Picherde of Bristol, Merchant Ind	19	piece	Cloth of Assize, Devonshire Dozen	0	0	0	0

Merchant name	Qty	Unit	Commodity	£	s.	d.	f.
	1	piece	Cloth of Assize, Devonshire Dozen[100]	0	0	0	0
	1	piece	Cloth of Assize	0	0	0	0
			Cloth of Assize, Overlengths	0	0	0	0

The Adventure aforesaid, 26th August 1595

John Collimore of Bristol, Merchant Ind	4	piece	Cloth of Assize	0	0	0	0
			Cloth of Assize, Overlengths	0	0	0	0

The Lillie aforesaid, 26th August 1595

Thomas James of Bristol, Merchant Ind	2	dicker	Skins, Calf[101]	2	0	0	0

The Adventure aforesaid, 27th August 1595

William Benger of Bristol, Merchant Ind	4	C goad	Cotton *Cloth*	13	6	8	0
	4	C goad	Cotton *Cloth*	13	6	8	0
	11	piece	Wadmal Cloth	11	0	0	0
	1	piece	Wadmal Cloth[102]	0	0	0	0
	6	piece	*Bristol* Frieze *Cloth*	6	0	0	0
	6	piece	Cloth of Assize	0	0	0	0
			Cloth of Assize, Overlengths	0	0	0	0

The Adventure aforesaid, *27th August 1595*

John Dierrick of Bristol, Merchant Ind	3	piece	Cloth of Assize	0	0	0	0
			Cloth of Assize, Overlengths	0	0	0	0

The Adventure aforesaid, *27th August 1595*

John Webbe of Bristol, Merchant Ind	2	C goad	Cotton *Cloth*	6	13	4	0

The Adventure aforesaid, *27th August 1595*

George Lane of Bristol, Merchant Ind	2	C goad	Cotton *Cloth*[103]	6	13	4	0

The Adventure aforesaid, *27th August 1595*

John Redinge of Bristol, Merchant Ind	11	piece	Wadmal Cloth	11	0	0	0
	1	piece	Wadmal Cloth[104]	0	0	0	0
	7	piece	*Bristol* Frieze *Cloth*	7	0	0	0

The Adventure aforesaid, *27th August 1595*

Christopher Carry of Bristol, Merchant Ind	18	piece	Wadmal Cloth	18	0	0	0

100 Custom exempt. **101** License dated 4th March 1586. **102** Custom exempt. **103** Custom and subsidy paid in the Peter of Bristol, burden 18 tons, to Brest, 27th August. **104** Custom exempt.

Merchant name	Qty	Unit	Commodity	£	s.	d.	f.
	2	piece	Wadmal Cloth[105]	0	0	0	0
	4	piece	Cloth of Assize	0	0	0	0
			Cloth of Assize, Overlengths	0	0	0	0

The Rose of Bristol, burden 18 tons, to Waterford, 27th August 1595

Lancelot Lucar of Waterford, Merchant Ind	1	C	Sugar	3	6	8	0

The Adventure aforesaid, *27th August 1595*

Peter Gough of Bristol, Merchant Ind	2	piece	*Bristol* Frieze *Cloth*	2	0	0	0
	5	piece	Cloth of Assize	0	0	0	0
			Cloth of Assize, Overlengths	0	0	0	0

The Adventure aforesaid, 1st September 1595

John Reedinge of Bristol, Merchant Ind	3	piece	Cloth of Assize	0	0	0	0
			Cloth of Assize, Overlengths	0	0	0	0

The Mary Edwards of Barnstaple, burden 60 tons, John Millard master, to La Rochelle, 4th September 1595

Benedict Webbe of Kingswood, Wilts. Merchant Ind	18	piece	Serge *Cloth*	36	0	0	0
	2	piece	Serge Cloth[106]	0	0	0	0

The Mary Katherine of London, burden 60 tons, John Gold master, to La Rochelle, 5th September 1595

William Harrison of London, Merchant Ind	20	ton	Lead	160	0	0	0
	5	ton	Lead	40	0	0	0

The Mary Edwards aforesaid, 5th September 1595

William Ellis of Bristol, Merchant Ind	13	piece	Cloth of Assize[107]	0	0	0	0

The Mary Edwards aforesaid, 5th September 1595

Mathew Havilland of Bristol, Merchant Ind	6	C	Sugar	21	13	4	0

The Mary Edwards aforesaid, 5th September 1595

John Roberowe of Bristol, Merchant Ind	4	piece	Cloth of Assize	0	0	0	0
			Cloth of Assize, Overlengths	0	0	0	0

105 Custom exempt.   **106** Custom exempt.   **107** Custom and subsidy paid in the Peter of Bristol

Merchant name	Qty	Unit	Commodity	£	s.	d.	f.

The Rose aforesaid, 7th September 1595

Merchant name	Qty	Unit	Commodity	£	s.	d.	f.
Nicholas Browne of Waterford, Merchant Ind	0.5	piece	Jeane Fustian *Cloth*	0	6	8	0
	1	piece	Osborne Fustian *Cloth*	0	13	4	0
	1	piece	Holmes Fustian *Cloth*	0	13	4	0
	3	butt	Thread, Black	0	6	8	0
	0.5	gross	Points, Crewel	0	3	4	0
	3	piece	Portmanteau	0	5	0	0
	3	lb	*Girdles, Nobs Silk*[108]	0	2	6	0
	2.5	dozen	*Hats*[109]	2	5	0	0
	2	piece	Inkle	0	3	4	0
	5.5	yard	Buckram *Cloth*	0	2	6	0
	0.5	gross	Knives	0	5	0	0
	0.5	gross	Thread, Fibulor?	0	0	10	0
	16	yard	Bay *Cloth*	1	0	0	0
	7	yard	Cotton *Cloth*	0	5	0	0
	1	C	Hops	1	0	0	0
	6	pair	Wool-Cards	0	5	0	0
	12	yard	Cloth of Assize	0	0	0	0
	6	yard	Cloth of Assize, Kersey	0	0	0	0

The Adventure aforesaid, 7th September 1595

Merchant name	Qty	Unit	Commodity	£	s.	d.	f.
William Wardford of Bristol, Merchant Ind	4	C goad	Cotton *Cloth*	13	6	8	0
	11	piece	Wadmal Cloth	11	0	0	0
	1	piece	Wadmal Cloth[110]	0	0	0	0

The Adventure aforesaid, *7th September 1595*

Merchant name	Qty	Unit	Commodity	£	s.	d.	f.
Thomas Jewell of Bristol, Merchant Ind	2	piece	Cloth of Assize	0	0	0	0
			Cloth of Assize, Overlengths	0	0	0	0

The Adventure aforesaid, 7th September 1595

Merchant name	Qty	Unit	Commodity	£	s.	d.	f.
Hugh Griffeth & John Barker of Bristol, Merchants Ind	10	C goad	Cotton *Cloth*	33	6	8	0
	4	piece	Cloth of Assize	0	0	0	0
			Cloth of Assize, Overlengths	0	0	0	0

The Adventure aforesaid, 7th September 1595

Merchant name	Qty	Unit	Commodity	£	s.	d.	f.
John Love of Bristol, Merchant Ind	2	C goad	Cotton *Cloth*	6	13	4	0
	6	piece	Cloth of Assize, Streit	0	0	0	0

---

108 From the customer's account (TNA E190/1131/13 f15r) Presumably erroneously omitted in the surveyor's account. **109** As above. **110** Custom exempt.

Merchant name	Qty	Unit	Commodity	£	s.	d.	f.

The Adventure aforesaid, 8th September 1595

Merchant name	Qty	Unit	Commodity	£	s.	d.	f.
William Harrison of London, Merchant Ind	5	ton	Lead	40	0	0	0

The Clement of Bristol, burden 18 tons, William Leighton master, to Cork, *8th September 1595*

Merchant name	Qty	Unit	Commodity	£	s.	d.	f.
Richard Gold of Cork, Merchant Ind	2	C	Hops	1	0	0	0
	10	dozen	Wool-Cards	5	0	0	0
	2	dozen	Hats	3	0	0	0
	1	piece	Osborne Fustian *Cloth*	0	13	4	0
	1	gross	Girdles (1d.)	0	10	0	0
	1.5	gross	Knives	0	15	0	0
	2	burden	Tin	0	10	0	0
	2	gross	Lace, Statute	0	13	4	0
	1	dozen	Penners	0	0	10	0
	3	small gross	Points	0	2	6	0
	1	ream	Paper	0	3	4	0
	9	lb	Sugar	0	6	8	0
	1	lb	Cloves	0	5	0	0
	6	ell	Holland *Cloth*	0	5	0	0
	1.5	lb	Silk, Paris	0	10	0	0
	2	butt	Thread, Black	0	4	2	0
	4	lb	Thread	0	6	8	0
	9	yard	Levant Taffeta Cloth	0	15	0	0
	1	gross	Trenchers, Common	0	0	10	0
	0.5	gross	Playing Cards	0	10	0	0
	1	dozen	Spurs	0	0	20	0
	1	dozen	Skins, Budge	0	13	4	0
	8	yard	Bay *Cloth*	0	13	4	0
	1	dozen	Paper, Gold	0	6	8	0
	1	dozen	Locks	0	3	4	0
	1	piece	Cotton *Cloth*	1	0	0	0
	1	lb	Silk, Slewe	0	6	8	0
	1	piece	Cloth of Assize, Single Northern	0	0	0	0
	11	yard	Cloth of Assize	0	0	0	0

The Mary Edwards aforesaid, 10th September 1595

Merchant name	Qty	Unit	Commodity	£	s.	d.	f.
Benedict Webbe of Kingswood, Wilts., Merchant Ind	9	piece	Paris *Cloth*	27	0	0	0
	1	piece	Paris *Cloth*[111]	0	0	0	0
	4	piece	Serge *Cloth*	8	0	0	0

The Mary Edwards aforesaid, 11th September 1595

Merchant name	Qty	Unit	Commodity	£	s.	d.	f.
Thomas James of Bristol, Merchant Ind	3	dicker	Skins, Calf[112]	3	0	0	0

111 Custom exempt.   112 License for Peter Newells dated 4th March 1586.

Merchant name	Qty	Unit	Commodity	£	s.	d.	f.

The Diana of Bristol, burden 18 tons, William Meager master, to La Rochelle, *11th September 1595*

Merchant name	Qty	Unit	Commodity	£	s.	d.	f.
Christopher Cary of Bristol, Merchant Ind	4	piece	Cloth of Assize[113]	0	0	0	0

The Vantage of Barnstaple, burden 48 tons, Richard Haynes master, to La Rochelle, 13th September 1595

Merchant name	Qty	Unit	Commodity	£	s.	d.	f.
John Barker of Bristol, Merchant Ind	5	C goad	Cotton *Cloth*	16	13	4	0

The Vantage aforesaid, 15th September 1595

Merchant name	Qty	Unit	Commodity	£	s.	d.	f.
John Rober[]ro of Bristol, Merchant Ind	10	piece	Cloth of Assize, Northern Plains & Checks	0	0	0	0
	1	piece	Cloth of Assize, Northern Plains & Checks[114]	0	0	0	0

The Vantage aforesaid, 16th September 1595

Merchant name	Qty	Unit	Commodity	£	s.	d.	f.
John Oliver of Bristol, Merchant Ind	3	piece	Cloth of Assize	0	0	0	0
			Cloth of Assize, Overlengths	0	0	0	0

The Vantage aforesaid, 16th September 1595

Merchant name	Qty	Unit	Commodity	£	s.	d.	f.
Thomas James of Bristol, Merchant Ind	4	dicker	Skins, Calf[115]	4	0	0	0

The Elizabeth of Gloucester, burden 18 tons, John Swanley master, to Waterford, 17th September 1595

Merchant name	Qty	Unit	Commodity	£	s.	d.	f.
John Whitt of Clonmel, Merchant Ind	6	C	Battery	12	0	0	0
	8	C	Hops	4	0	0	0
	8	dozen	Wool-Cards, Old	2	13	4	0
	3	dozen	Hats	4	10	0	0
	2	dozen	Hats, Childrens	2	0	0	0
	10	yard	Dornick Cloth	0	6	8	0
	2	dozen	Belts	0	6	8	0
	3	dozen	Candlesticks, Small	0	10	0	0
	8	dozen	Girdles, Leather	0	6	8	0
	0.5	gross	Gartering	0	3	4	0
	0.5	lb	Combs, Ivory	0	2	6	0
	3	gross	Lace, Statute	1	0	0	0
	28	lb	Pewter (in small [ ])	0	8	4	0
	22	dozen	Combs, Wooden	0	9	2	0
	2	small gross	Buttons, Silk	0	0	10	0
	6	small gross	Buttons, Thread	0	0	10	0
	6	small gross	Buttons, Hair	0	0	10	0
	4	ream	Paper	0	10	10	0
	6	small gross	Points, Thread	0	5	0	0

113 Custom paid in the Peter of Bristol on 27th August.   114 Custom exempt.   115 See note 99.

Merchant name	Qty	Unit	Commodity	£	s.	d.	f.
	3	lb	Thread	0	5	0	0
	6	dozen	Glasses, Looking[116]	0	5	0	0
	1	dozen	Gloves, Coarse[117]	0	3	4	0
	6	pair	Stockings, Short	0	4	2	0
	1	dozen	Bands, Falling	0	3	4	0
	1	lb	Senna	0	0	20	0
	0.5	lb	Gom??	0	0	10	0
	1	lb	Gales	0	0	5	0
	3	lb	Copperas	0	0	5	0
	2.5	piece	Osborne Fustian Cloth	0	13	4	0
	1	gross	Knives	0	10	0	0
	5	dozen	Knives, Pocket	0	8	4	0
	4	dozen	Knives, Cuttlers	0	6	8	0
	0.5	gross	Girdles (1d.)	0	5	0	0
	3	dozen	Girdles (2d.)	0	5	0	0
	6	dozen	Penners & Inkhorns	0	5	0	0
	6	piece	Brushes	0	0	10	0
	6	lb	Mail	0	3	4	0
	4	dozen	Crab-Locks	0	13	4	0
	6	dozen	Hinges	0	10	0	0
	1	dozen	Locks, Cupboard	0	5	0	0
	1	dozen	Scissors	0	2	6	0
	3	dozen	Snuffers	0	8	4	0
	1	dozen	Horse Combs	0	0	25	0
	2	dozen	Headstalls	0	10	0	0
	1	dozen	Bits	0	3	4	0
	1	gross	Girth-Web	0	6	8	0
	4	gross	Buckles	0	6	8	0
	4	unknown	Unknown	1	6	8	0
	2	lb	Pile Weights	0	0	20	0
	8	yard	Levant Taffeta Cloth	0	13	4	0
	0.5	lb	Points, Broad (1d.)	0	3	4	0
	1.5	yard	Taffeta Cloth	0	10	0	0
	3	lb	Girdles, Nobs Silk	0	2	6	0
	6	lb	Mercury	0	11	11	0
	6	lb	Thread, Packet	0	0	25	0
	8	dozen	Bibs	0	6	8	0
	6	piece	Visors	0	6	8	0
	9	yard	Cotton Cloth	0	7	6	0
	12	yard	Bay Cloth	1	0	0	0
	2	piece	Calico Cloth	0	13	4	0
	3	lb	Pepper	0	5	0	0
	3	ell	Holland Cloth	0	3	4	0
	6	lb	Starch	0	0	20	0
	21	lb	Sugar	0	13	4	0
	5	M	Beads, Bugle	0	4	2	0
	1	dozen	Necklaces	0	2	6	0
	1	dozen	Bracelets	0	0	20	0
	4	gross	Trenchers	0	3	4	0
	6	piece	Swords	1	0	0	0
	1	dozen	Bellows	0	6	8	0

116 TNA E190/1131/13. 117 As above.

Merchant name	Qty	Unit	Commodity	£	s.	d.	f.
	2	dozen	Boxes	0	3	4	0
	4	gross	Buttons, Glass	0	3	4	0
	2	dozen	Parchment *Skins*	0	6	8	0
	12	dozen	Drinking Glasses	0	10	0	0
	2	piece	Cloth of Assize, Northern Dozen	0	0	0	0
	11	yard	Cloth of Assize	0	0	0	0
	6	yard	Cloth of Assize, Penistone	0	0	0	0

The Vantage aforesaid, 19th September 1595

Merchant name	Qty	Unit	Commodity	£	s.	d.	f.
William Ellis of Bristol, Merchant Ind	2	piece	Cloth of Assize	0	0	0	0
	2	piece	Cloth of Assize, Overlengths	0	0	0	0

The Petter of Bristol, burden 18 tons, Richard Westerott master, to La Rochelle, 19th September 1595

Merchant name	Qty	Unit	Commodity	£	s.	d.	f.
William Ellis of Bristol, Merchant Ind	6	piece	Cloth of Assize	0	0	0	0
			Cloth of Assize, Overlengths	0	0	0	0

The Petter aforesaid, 20th September 1595

Merchant name	Qty	Unit	Commodity	£	s.	d.	f.
John Whitson of Bristol, Merchant Ind	5	piece	Cloth of Assize, Streit	0	0	0	0

The Vantage aforesaid, *20th September 1595*

Merchant name	Qty	Unit	Commodity	£	s.	d.	f.
Benedict Webe of Kingswood, Wilts., Merchant Ind	10	piece	Serge *Cloth*	20	0	0	0
	1	piece	Serge Cloth[118]	0	0	0	0

The Petter aforesaid, *20th September 1595*

Merchant name	Qty	Unit	Commodity	£	s.	d.	f.
John Barker of Bristol, Merchant Ind	18	piece	Cloth of Assize, Streit	0	0	0	0
	2	piece	Cloth of Assize, Streit[119]	0	0	0	0

The Petter aforesaid, *20th September 1595*

Merchant name	Qty	Unit	Commodity	£	s.	d.	f.
Mathew Haviland of Bristol, Merchant Ind	5	piece	Cloth of Assize, Streit	0	0	0	0

The Petter aforesaid, *20th September 1595*

Merchant name	Qty	Unit	Commodity	£	s.	d.	f.
John Younge of Bristol, Merchant Ind	3	piece	Cloth of Assize, Penistone Unfriezed	0	0	0	0
	5	piece	Cloth of Assize, Bridgwater	0	0	0	0

118 Custom exempt.   119 Custom exempt.

Merchant name	Qty	Unit	Commodity	£	s.	d.	f.

The Petter aforesaid, 20th September 1595

| John Pitt of Bristol, Merchant Ind | 5 | piece | Cloth of Assize, Penistone Unfriezed | 0 | 0 | 0 | 0 |

The Dove of Bristol, burden 40 tons, William Pheleps master, to La Rochelle, *20th September 1595*

| William Harrison of London, Merchant Ind | 5 | ton | Lead[120] | 40 | 0 | 0 | 0 |

The Dove aforesaid, *20th September 1595*

Arthur Hibbins of Bristol, Merchant Ind	2	C goad	Cotton *Cloth*	6	13	4	0
	11	piece	Cloth of Assize, Streit	0	0	0	0
	1	piece	Cloth of Assize, Streit[121]	0	0	0	0

The Minikine of Bristol, burden 18 tons, William Slacke master, to Brest, 22nd September 1595

| Thomas Hopkins of Bristol, Merchant Ind | 30 | piece | Cloth of Assize, Streit | 0 | 0 | 0 | 0 |
| | 17.5 | yard | Cloth of Assize | 0 | 0 | 0 | 0 |

The Minikine aforesaid, *22nd September 1595*

| John Love of Bristol, Merchant Ind | 17 | piece | Cloth of Assize, Streit | 0 | 0 | 0 | 0 |
| | 1 | piece | Cloth of Assize, Streit[122] | 0 | 0 | 0 | 0 |

The Diana aforesaid, *22nd September 1595*

| John Love of Bristol, Merchant Ind | 6 | C goad | Cotton *Cloth* | 20 | 0 | 0 | 0 |

---

120 Warrant dated 21ˢᵗ June.   121 Custom exempt.   122 Custom exempt.

TNA E190/1132/11 is the account of the surveyor for the overseas trade of Bristol during the period Michaelmas 1600 to Michaelmas 1601.

It contains the same level of detail as the 1594/5 account. Again, a detailed comparison of the surveyor and controller accounts for the same period raises questions about the level of independence involved in the creation of these records. An interesting example, found on f31r., shows both officials listing goods, that when totalled using EXCEL, come to the modern equivalent of £28.92, while both accounts give a total value of £29.92, which suggests that they are both missing an item, or items, of the same value, and indicates copying at some point in the recording procedure.[1] Where any missing items have been identified in this comparative examination of the accounts they have been imputed into this transcription and are clearly identified as such.

IMPORTS

Merchant name	Qty	Unit	Commodity	£	s.	d.	f.
The Desier of La Rochelle, burden 30 tons, Nicholas John master, from La Rochelle, 2nd October 1600							
Sebastian Fleminge of Dublin, Merchant Ind	30	ton	Salt	30	0	0	0
The Roase of Lübeck, burden 70 tons, Henry Kerosa master, from Sanlúcar de Barrameda, 6th October 1600							
Henry Kerosa of Lübeck, Merchant Stranger	40	ton	Salt	40	0	0	0
The Roase of Bristol, burden 18 tons, John Marks master, from Madeira, 7th October 1600							
William Ellis of Bristol, Merchant Ind	18	C	Sugar	60	0	0	0
	10	C	Sumach	6	13	4	0
The Sygnett of London, burden 18 tons, John Hale master, from Le Croisic, 11th October 1600							
George Lane & Alexander Creswell of Bristol, Merchants Ind	14	ton	Salt	14	0	0	0

---

1 TNA E190/1132/11 f31r., the Mary Busher of Waterford, merchant Philip Linch and see also the corresponding entry in TNA E190/1132/12 f15v.

Merchant name	*Qty*	*Unit*	Commodity	£	s.	d.	f.

The Roase of Bristol abovesaid, 16th October 1600

John Salsburie & James Downe of Barnstaple,
Merchants Ind

| | 42 | C | Sugar | 140 | 0 | 0 | 0 |
| | 31 | C | Sumach | 20 | 13 | 4 | 0 |

The Tobias of Lübeck, burden 60 tons, George Snoore master, from Lübeck, 27th October 1600

George Snoore of Lübeck, Merchant Stranger 30 ton Salt 30 0 0 0

The Barbara of Brest, burden 25 tons, Lucas Cororell master, from Brest, 28th October 1600

Lucas Cororell of Brest, Merchant Stranger 22 ton Salt 22 0 0 0

The Salomon of Barnstaple, burden 20 tons, Richard Elliott master, from La Rochelle, 31st October 1600

John Barker of Bristol, Merchant Ind 2 tun Vinegar 4 13 4 0

The Bonaventure of *Olone*[2] burden 50 tons, John Febora master, from Málaga, *31st October 1600*

Andrew Pearde, Merchant Stranger

| | 880 | piece | Raisins, Malaga | 220 | 0 | 0 | 0 |
| | 12 | C | Raisins, of the Sun | 10 | 0 | 0 | 0 |

The Huntsman of Amsterdam, burden 100 tons, Leonard Petterson master, from Gdansk, 3rd November 1600

John Fearne of London, Merchant Ind

	40	last	Tar and Pitch	80	0	0	0
	4	ton	Hemp	*80*	*0*	*0*	*0*
	1.5	ton	Flax	*20*	*0*	*0*	*0*

The Elizabeth of Jersey, burden 55 tons, John Balhatch master, from Cadiz, 6th November 1600

Laurence Porry of St Malo, Merchant
Stranger

| | 30 | ton | Raisins, Rotta | 200 | 0 | 0 | 0 |
| | 3 | ton | Figs | 40 | 0 | 0 | 0 |

The Charitie of Bristol, burden 18 tons, John Watts master, from Waterford, 7th November 1600

Patrick Mayler of Waterford, Merchant Ind 1 butt Vinegar *1* *3* *4* *0*

The George of Barnstaple, burden 35 tons, John Hawkins master, from Saõ Miguel, 24th November 1600

William Ellis, John Butcher, William
Colstone & John Roberts of Bristol,
Merchants & Company Ind 31.8 ton Woad, Green 318 0 0 0

2 Possibly Ile d' Oleron, France.

Merchant name	Qty	Unit	Commodity	£	s.	d.	f.
Nicholas Buggens & Ferdinand Burke of Bristol, Merchants Ind	1.5	ton	Woad, Green	15	0	0	0

The Roase of Bristol, burden 18 tons, William Brooke master, from Waterford, 29th November 1600

George Richards of Bristol, Merchant Ind	18	C	Skins, Morkin	6	0	0	0
Jasper Butler of Waterford, Merchant Ind	5	dicker	Hides	16	13	4	0
	10	dicker	Hides, Kip	16	13	4	0
Nicholas Hollonbrigge of Bristol, Pewterer Ind	5	dicker	Hides, Kip	8	6	8	0

The Dove of Bristol, burden 40 tons, Richard Parsons master, from Le Croisic, 3rd December 1600

William Cole of Bristol, Merchant Ind	36	ton	Salt	36	0	0	0

The Spedwell of Millbrook, burden 42 tons, Harry Warwicke master, from Bordeaux, 16th December 1600

Nicholas Buggens of Bristol, Merchant Ind	24	C	Prunes	12	0	0	0

The Marie of Roscoff, burden 30 tons, Alan Bezian master, from Málaga, 16th December 1600

Nicholas Buggens & Richard Powle of Bristol, Merchants Ind	450	piece	Raisins, Great	112	10	0	0

The Amitie of Bristol, burden 80 tons, William Worgan master, from Le Croisic, 18th December 1600

William Hopkins & George Lane of Bristol, Merchants Ind	60	ton	Salt	60	0	0	0

The Flower of St Malo, burden 60 tons, William Hamline master, from Cadiz, 18th December 1600

Michael Quirke of Bristol, Merchant & Company Ind	20	piece	Raisins, Great	5	0	0	0
	11.25	C	Figs	7	10	0	0
William Hamlin of Bristol, Merchant & Company Stranger	50.25	C	Figs	33	10	0	0
	4	C	Raisins, of the Sun	3	6	8	0

The Royall Defence of Bristol, burden 100 tons, Christopher Tailor master, from Bordeaux, 22nd December 1600

Christopher Tailor of Bordeaux, Merchant Ind	2	ton	Rosin	6	13	4	0
John Fownes of Bristol, Merchant Ind	5	ton	Prunes	50	0	0	0

Merchant name	Qty	Unit	Commodity	£	s.	d.	f.

The White Swan of Bristol, burden 50 tons, William Browne master, from La Rochelle, 23rd December 1600

John Roberts & George White of Bristol, Merchant Ind	30	ton	Salt	30	0	0	0
	4	tun	Oil, *Olive*	32	0	0	0

The Jennett of St-Jean-de-Luz, burden 70 tons, Peter de Peraxa master, from Bordeaux, 23rd December 1600

Thomas Anthonie of Bristol, Merchant Ind	1	ton	Prunes	10	0	0	0
John Prestine, Merchant Stranger	1	ton	Prunes	10	0	0	0
Peter de Peraxa of Bordeaux, Merchant & Company Stranger	35	C	Prunes	17	10	0	0

The Margarett of Milford Haven, burden 24 tons, John Evans master, from La Rochelle, 29th December 1600

John Gunninge & Francis Dirrecke of Bristol, Merchants Ind	14	ton	Salt	14	0	0	0
	7	tun	Vinegar	16	6	8	0

The Longe Barke of Hoorn, burden 120 tons, Cornell Anthonie master, from Aveiro, 30th December 1600

Cornell Anthonie of Hoorn, Merchant Stranger	88	ton	Salt	88	0	0	0

The Recompence of St Malo, burden 50 tons, Brian le Dean master, from Cadiz, 30th December 1600

Mathew Haviland & James Beavoire of Bristol & Guernsey, Merchants Ind	938	piece	Raisins, Malaga	234	10	0	0
James Briant of St Malo, Merchant Stranger	5	ton	Raisins, of the Sun	83	6	8	0

The William of Bristol, burden 40 tons, William Meager master, from La Rochelle, 30th December 1600

Richard James, Moore, Burkine of Bristol, Merchants Ind	20	ton	Salt	20	0	0	0

The Daniell of Newcastle, burden 94 tons, John Johnson master, from Bordeaux, 31st December 1600

Harry Addams & John Hopkins of Bristol, Merchants Ind	2.25	ton	Prunes	22	10	0	0
Richard Teage of Bristol, Merchant Ind	3.75	ton	Prunes	37	10	0	0

The John of Glasgow, burden 40 tons, John Hopkins master, from Málaga, 7th January 1601

Richard Jones, James Coble & Thomas Lambert of Plymouth, Merchants Ind	400	piece	Raisins, Malaga	100	0	0	0
	4	ton	Raisins, of the Sun	66	13	4	0

Merchant name	Qty	Unit	Commodity	£	s.	d.	f.

The Mathew of Berkeley, burden 18 tons, Richard Daniell master, from Waterford, 12th January 1601

| George Richards of Bristol, Merchant Ind | 16 | C | Skins, Morkin | 5 | 6 | 8 | 0 |

The White Falcon of Denmark, burden 80 tons, Bartholemew Hellinge master, from Sanlúcar de Barrameda, 12th January 1601

| Bartholemew Hellinge, Merchant Stranger | 60 | ton | Salt | 60 | 0 | 0 | 0 |

The Jesus of Elmore, burden 18 tons, Richard Hooper master, from Waterford, 3rd February 1601

George Richards of Bristol, Merchant Ind	12	C	Skins, Morkins & Sheep Skins Broken	4	0	0	0
Francis Lumberte of Waterford, Merchant Ind	6	C	Skins, Morkins & Sheep Skins Broken	2	0	0	0
	15	stone	Wool, Flocks	1	5	0	0
	12	piece	Coverlet	6	0	0	0
	1	C	Irish Frieze Cloth	2	0	0	0

The Maie Flower of Bristol, burden 100 tons, Richard Mogglege master, from Le Croisic, *3rd February 1601*

| Thomas James of Bristol, Merchant Ind | 30 | ton | Salt | 30 | 0 | 0 | 0 |

The Dove of Bristol, burden 40 tons, Richard Parsonns master, from Le Croisic, 5th February 1601

| William Cole of Bristol, Merchant Ind | 35 | ton | Salt | 35 | 0 | 0 | 0 |
| | 30 | cake | Pitch, Hearth | 5 | 0 | 0 | 0 |

The Doe of Bristol, burden 18 tons, John Frinde master, from Waterford, 11th February 1601

Richard Cumberford of Waterford, Merchant Ind	20	piece	Caddows	10	0	0	0
	1	C	*Irish* Frieze and Check *Cloth*	2	0	0	0
	6	C	Skins, Morkins & Sheep Skins Broken	2	0	0	0
	6	C	Skins, Coney	0	15	0	0

The Prize called the St Anne of Seville, burden 30 tons, Richard Lloyde master, from the Sea, 12th February 1601

| John & William Bowrell of London, Merchants & Company Ind | 333.5[3] | C | Ginger | 838 | 8 | 4 | 0 |

3 Out of the gross volume (342.5C) 7.5C is allowed for tar and dust and a twentieth (16.75C) is allowed to the queen by order of the treasurer of England at £2 10s. per cwt.

Merchant name	Qty	Unit	Commodity	£	s.	d.	f.

The Mathew of Berkeley, burden 18 tons, John Smithe master, from Cork, 12th February 1601

George Richards of Bristol, Merchant Ind	12	C	Skins, Morkin	4	0	0	0
	5	stone	Wool, Flocks	0	8	4	0
	5	animal	Horses, Garones	3	6	8	0

The Samnalena of Brest, burden 70 tons, Asker le Mayer master, from Cadiz, *12th February 1601*

| William Ellis, John Aldworth & Nicholas Buggens of Bristol, Merchants Ind | 90 | C | Figs | 60 | 0 | 0 | 0 |

The Perle of Le Conquet, burden 50 tons, John Bardicke master, from Bordeaux, 16th February 1601

| Mathew Haviland of Bristol, Merchant Ind | 1.5 | tun | Vinegar | 3 | 10 | 0 | 0 |
| John Bardicke of Bordeaux, Merchant Stranger | 175 | ell | Dowlas *Cloth* | 21 | 8 | 4 | 0 |

The Daisie of Bristol, burden 34 tons, Andrew Batten master, from Madeira, 4th March 1601

| John Hopkins, William Ellis, John Barker & Robert Aldworth of Bristol, Merchants & Company Ind | 159 | C | Sugar | 531 | 8 | 4 | 0 |
| | 19 | C | Sumach | 12 | 13 | 8 | 0 |

The Bonavanture of Ile d' Oleron,[4] burden 55 tons, John Febra master, from Málaga, *4th March 1601*

| Nicholas Buggens, John Gunninge & Christopher Webb of Bristol, Merchants Ind | 300 | piece | Raisins, Malaga | *75* | *0* | *0* | *0* |
| | 2.5 | ton | Raisins, of the Sun | *41* | *13* | *4* | *0* |

The Desier of Bristol, burden 60 tons, Mathew Rice master, from Toulon, 6th March 1601

| John Barker, Mathew Haviland & John Fowens of Bristol, Merchants and Company Ind | 57.87[5] | tun | Oil, *Olive* | *479* | *6* | *8* | *0* |
| | 12.5 | C | Aniseed | *10* | *6* | *8* | *0* |

The Marie of Brest, burden 50 tons, Gooldenhen le Meyre master, from Cadiz, 7th March 1601

| Nicholas Buggins of Bristol, Merchant Ind | 2 | ton | Wood, Brazil | 66 | 13 | 4 | 0 |

The Gabriell of Barnstaple, burden 30 tons, Stephen le Meroos master, from Saõ Miguel, 9th March 1601

| Robert Aldworth of Bristol, Merchant Ind | 26 | ton | Woad, Green | *260* | *0* | *0* | *0* |
| | 4.5 | ton | Wood, Brazil | *150* | *0* | *0* | *0* |

4 This port is found in the account as Oolone, Oleron & Wolone. It is presumably Oleron in France, but this may be a mis-translation.   5 Possibly a recording error as the value suggests this should be 59.87 tuns.

Merchant name	Qty	Unit	Commodity	£	s.	d.	f.

The Beniamyne of London, burden 135 tons, William Rickes master, from La Rochelle, 9th March 1601

Merchant name	Qty	Unit	Commodity	£	s.	d.	f.
Giles Fleminge & Thomas Hollowood of London, Merchant Ind	80	ton	Salt, French	80	0	0	0
Henry Addams of Bristol, Merchant Ind	20	barrels	Tar	3	6	8	0
	2	tun	Vinegar	4	13	4	0

The Blacke Swan of Bristol, burden 60 tons, Thomas Rockwell master, from *Saffolana*, 18th March 1601

Merchant name	Qty	Unit	Commodity	£	s.	d.	f.
Robert Aldworth of Bristol, Merchants and Company Ind	50.35	ton	Currants	1510	10	0	0

The Blacke Swan aforesaid, 21st March 1601

Merchant name	Qty	Unit	Commodity	£	s.	d.	f.
Zuane? Cymera, *domicile unknown*, Merchant Stranger	8	ton	Currants	240	0	0	0

The Mathew of Berkeley, burden 18 tons, William Grene master, from Cork, 26th March 1601

Merchant name	Qty	Unit	Commodity	£	s.	d.	f.
John Howlett of Bristol, Glover Ind	16	C	Skins, Morkins & Sheep Skins Broken	5	6	8	0
	10	piece	Skins, Deer	2	10	0	0
Thomas Phelps of Bristol, Glover Ind	4	stone	Wool, Flocks	0	6	8	0
	2.5	C	Tallow	2	1	8	0
	4	C	Skins, Morkin	1	6	8	0

The Recoverie of Bristol, burden 18 tons, John Shepward master, from Cork, 28th March 1601

Merchant name	Qty	Unit	Commodity	£	s.	d.	f.
Nicholas Routhe of New Ross, Merchant Ind	12	C	Skins, Morkins & Sheep Skins Broken	4	0	0	0
	20	stone	Wool, Flocks	1	13	4	0

The Speedwell of Milford Haven, burden 30 tons, Henry Warren master, from La Rochelle, 30th March 1601

Merchant name	Qty	Unit	Commodity	£	s.	d.	f.
John Barker of Bristol, Merchant Ind	18	ton	Salt	18	0	0	0
	10	C	Liquorice	5	0	0	0
	4	tun	Vinegar	9	6	8	0
Hugh Pearde of Bristol, Grocer Ind	15	C	Wool, Spanish Hat	62	10	0	0
	22.5	C	Liquorice	11	5	0	0
John Griffiths of Bristol, Merchant Ind	2.5	C	Wool, Spanish Hat	10	8	4	0
Thomas White of Bristol, Merchant Ind	2	tun	Vinegar	4	13	4	0

Merchant name	Qty	Unit	Commodity	£	s.	d.	f.

The Prize called the Marie of Pasajes de San Juan, burden 80 tons, George Kellie master, from the Seas, *30th March 1601*

Christopher Hubbard & Robert Aldworth of Bristol, Merchant & Company Ind	48	M	Fish, Newfoundland Small	240	0	0	0
	2.75	tun	Oil, Train[6]	13	15	0	0

The Desier of Bristol, burden 40 tons, William Hicks master & captain, from the Sea,[7] *30th March 1601*

William Hicks of Bristol, Captain and Company Ind	2120	lb	Wax, Unrefined[8]	60	0	0	0

The Jane of Plymouth, burden 40 tons, John Pyke master, from Candalaria, 15th April 1601

Richard & John Newman of London & *Diggery* Holman of Plymouth, Merchant Ind	3	ton	Currants	90	0	0	0

The Fawlcon of Millbrook, burden 18 tons, Thomas Searell master, from Bayonne, 15th April 1601

William Ellis of Bristol, Merchant Ind	18	C	Wool, Spanish Hat	75	0	0	0
	10	C	Liquorice	5	0	0	0
Nicholas Buggens of Bristol, Merchant Ind	9	C	Wool, Spanish Hat	37	10	0	0
	20	C	Liquorice	10	0	0	0
	30	cake	Pitch	5	0	0	0
Thomas Searell, *domicile unknown*, Master Ind	30	cake	Pitch	5	0	0	0

The Charitie of Bristol, burden 18 tons, John Fynne master, from Cork, 15th April 1601

William Goold of Cork, Merchant Ind	4	M	Coney Staggers	5	0	0	0
	10	C	Skins, Morkins & Sheep Skins Broken	3	6	8	0
	4	stone	Wool, Flocks	0	6	8	0

The Patricke of Dungarvan, burden 14 ton, Gilbert Noggle master, from Dungarvan, 15th April 1601

James Hoore of Dungarvan, Merchant Ind	5	C	Skins, Morkin	1	13	4	0

The Marie of Wexford, burden 8 tons, Thomas Busher master, from Wexford, 15th April 1601

Melcher Stafforde of Wexford, Merchant Ind	1	M	Barrel Staves	0	0	0	0
	7	dozen	*Clonen* Boards	1	0	0	0
	1	dozen	Oar Staves	0	13	4	0
	10	stone	Wool, Flocks	0	16	8	0
	1	C	Skins, Morkin	0	6	8	0

6 The twentieth part allowed to her majesty.   7 Taken from the sea by reprisal.   8 The twentieth part allowed to her majesty.

Merchant name	Qty	Unit	Commodity	£	s.	d.	f.

The Marie Fortune of Bristol, burden 90 tons, Alexander Seward master, from *Saffolana*, 16th April 1601

William Ellis, John Webb & Whitson of Bristol, Merchants & Company Ind	76.35	ton	Currants	2291	5	0	0
	80	lb	Nutmeg	13	6	8	0
Edward Lewes, *domicile unknown*, Factor of the Ship Ind	1	ton	Currants[9]	0	0	0	0

The John of Bristol, burden 16 tons, William Moore master, from Cork, 21st April 1601

George Richards of Bristol, Glover Ind	21	C	Skins, Morkins & Sheep Skins Broken	7	0	0	0
Thomas Mytchell of Bristol, Glover Ind	16	C	Skins, Morkins & Sheep Skins Broken	5	6	8	0

The Sune of Bristol, burden 25 tons, Thomas Latymer master, from Galicia, 22nd April 1601

Thomas Latymer, Master Ind	10	M	Oranges	3	6	8	0
Thomas & James Rice of Dingle, Merchants Ind	30	M	Oranges and Lemons	10	0	0	0

The Lyon of Gdansk, burden 80 tons, Jasper Demayne master, from *Tovells*, 22nd April 1601

Jasper Demayne, *domicile unknown*, Merchant Alien	54	ton	Salt	54	0	0	0

The Mynikine of Bristol, burden 17 tons, Richard Moggrige master, from Bordeaux, 22nd April 1601

John Gunnynge & Roger Grenehill of Bristol, Merchant Ind	3.6	ton	Prunes	36	0	0	0
	2	tun	Vinegar	4	13	4	0
	8	cakes	Rosin	1	6	8	0

The Primeroase of Combe Martin, burden 5 tons, Anthonye Skymer master, from Combe Martin, 25th April 1601

Paul Callen of Bristol Ind & John Beaker alien, Merchants	2	C	Cinnamon[10]	0	0	0	0
	2	C	Cinnamon	40	0	0	0

The Guye of Le Croisic, burden 30 tons, John Fooker master, from Le Croisic, 4th May 1601

Alexander Kersewell of Bristol, Merchant Ind	20	ton	Salt	20	0	0	0

The Pane of Le Croisic, burden 16 tons, Peter Lucett master, from Le Croisic, 4th May 1601

Alexander Kersewell of Bristol, Merchant Ind	10	ton	Salt	10	0	0	0

9 Allowed to Edward Lewis being factor of the ship (ie. custom exempt and therefore no value is given in the account)
10 Custom & subsidy paid for 2C by the said Paul Callan at Combe at the first discharge, certificate dated 7th April; the other 2C weight for John Beaker.

Merchant name	Qty	Unit	Commodity	£ s. d. f.

The Marie of Roscoff, burden 37 tons, Alien Bezian master, from Málaga, 5th May 1601

| Nicholas Buggens of Bristol, Merchant Ind | 32 | C | Sumach | 21 6 8 0 |

The Gabriell of Bristol, burden 70 tons, William Brooke master, from Guinea, 18th May 1601

Robert, John & Thomas Aldworth of Bristol, Merchants Ind	2	C	Hides, Ginney,[11] with hair	66 13 4 0
	4	C	Hides, Ginney Kips, with hair	66 13 4 0
	33	dozen	Hides, Ginney Calf, with hair	16 10 0 0
	16	ton	Salt	16 0 0 0
	14.07	C	Elephants Tusks	46 18 8 0

The Antloppe of Crail, burden 70 tons, Thomas Devonson master, from Puerto de Santa Maria, 22nd May 1601

| John Simple, *domicile unknown*, Merchant Stranger | 3 | ton | Salt | 3 0 0 0 |

The Joseph of Bristol, burden 100 tons, Mathew Honnywell master, from Toulon, 22nd May 1601

| William Ellis, John Whitson, Thomas James & William Kellett of Bristol & London, Merchants and Company Ind | 93.25 | tun | Oil, *Punice* | 1862 10 0 0 |

The Unicorne of Bristol, burden 130 tons, James Powell master, from Toulon, 22nd May 1601

John Whitson, Thomas James, Thomas Pitcher, Able Kitchine & Mathew Haviland of Bristol, Merchants and Company Ind	123.25	tun	Oil, *Punice*	2465 0 0 0
John Guy, Ind	3.5	ton	Soap, White	52 10 0 0
James Apowell of Bristol, Merchant Ind	15	C	Aniseed	20 0 0 0

The Charitie of Bristol, burden 18 tons, John Ffyn master, from Waterford, 5th June 1601

| George Richards of Bristol, Merchant Ind | 30 | C | Skins, Morkins & Sheep Skins Broken | 10 0 0 0 |

The Marie of Marennes, burden 30 tons, John Harvay master, from Marennes, 5th June 1601

| John Pedcoole, *domicile unknown*, Merchant Alien | 9 | ton | Salt | 9 0 0 0 |
| Richard Tege of Bristol, Merchant Ind | 9 | ton | Salt | 9 0 0 0 |

11 Guinea hides.

Merchant name	Qty	Unit	Commodity	£	s.	d.	f.

The Mariegoulde of Gatcombe, burden 20 tons, Christopher Raye master, from Cork, 5th June 1601

Merchant name	Qty	Unit	Commodity	£	s.	d.	f.
Thomas Wilcocks of Bristol, Merchant Ind	14	animal	Horses and Mares, Garones	9	6	8	0
	1	C	Skins, Morkins & Sheep Skins Broken	0	6	8	0

The Roase of Bristol, burden 18 tons, William Meager master, from Cork, 5th June 1601

Merchant name	Qty	Unit	Commodity	£	s.	d.	f.
Morris Silver of Cork, Yeoman Ind	5	animal	Horses, Garones	3	6	8	0
William Slade of Bristol, Grocer Ind	10	C	Skins, Sheep Broken	3	6	8	0

The Lyon of Amsterdam, burden 200 tons, Isbrane Tyson master, from Norway, 6th June 1601

Merchant name	Qty	Unit	Commodity	£	s.	d.	f.
John Fearne of London, Merchant Ind	70	piece	Masts (great)	23	6	8	0
	2	M	Boards, Deal	66	13	4	0

The Guifte of God of Barnstaple, burden 60 tons, John Wize master, from Toulon, 6th June 1601

Merchant name	Qty	Unit	Commodity	£	s.	d.	f.
William Ellis, John Barker, John Fowens & William Chapel of Bristol & Barnstaple, Merchants and Company Ind	25.25	tun	Oil, Punice	500	5	0	0
William Chapel of Barnstaple, Merchant Ind	18	C	Galls	24	0	0	0
	6	ton	Salt	6	0	0	0
	7	tun	Vinegar	16	13	4	0
John Barker of Bristol, Merchant Ind	4.5	C	Cotton Wool	15	0	0	0
Walter Oldfeild of Bristol, Merchant Ind	4.5	C	Cotton Wool	15	0	0	0
Thomas Davis of Bristol, Merchant Ind	4.5	C	Cotton Wool	15	0	0	0

The Grace of Bristol, burden 18 tons, Walter Daniell master, from Youghal, 17th June 1601

Merchant name	Qty	Unit	Commodity	£	s.	d.	f.
William Bouren of Bristol, Merchant Ind	5	animal	Horses, Garones	3	6	8	0
John Burkeberry of Bristol, Merchant Ind	4	C	Skins, Morkins & Sheep Skins Broken	1	6	8	0
John Rowberrowe of Bristol, Merchant Ind	11	M	Barrel Staves, New	16	10	0	0

The Elizabeth of Newnham, burden 10 tons, Richard Daniell master, from Waterford, 22nd June 1601

Merchant name	Qty	Unit	Commodity	£	s.	d.	f.
Thomas Mytchell of Bristol, Glover Ind	10	C	Skins, Morkins & Sheep Skins Broken	3	6	8	0

The Rooebuck of Bristol, burden 16 tons, William Swanley master, from Waterford, 22nd June 1601

Merchant name	Qty	Unit	Commodity	£	s.	d.	f.
George Richards of Bristol, Merchant Ind	20	C	Skins, Morkins & Sheep Skins Broken	6	13	4	0

Merchant name	Qty	Unit	Commodity	£	s.	d.	f.

The James of Bristol, burden 18 tons, Walter Daniell master, from Cork, *22nd June 1601*

| James Coppenger of Bristol, Glover Ind | 10 | stone | Wool, Flocks | 0 | 16 | 4 | 0 |
| | 4 | animal | Horses, Garones | 2 | 13 | 4 | 0 |

The Clement of Bristol, burden 30 tons, John Smythe master, from Dublin, 3rd July 1601

| Thomas Allen & Walter Wilson of London, Merchant Ind | 25.5 | pipes | Oil, Seville | 102 | 0 | 0 | 0 |

The Spedewell of Millbrook, burden 40 tons, Henry Warwicke master, from Le Croisic, 6th July 1601

| Nicholas Williams of Plymouth, Merchant Ind | 20 | ton | Salt | 20 | 0 | 0 | 0 |

In the Prize called the Savior of Portugal, burden 30 tons, Ambros Birch from the Sea, 6th July 1601[12]

| Simon Harvie of London, Merchant & Company Ind | 508.75 | C | Sugar | 1694 | 2 | 6 | 0 |
| | 144.25[13] | C | Sugar | 0 | 0 | 0 | 0 |

The Mathew of Berkeley, burden 18 tons, William Grene master, from Cork, 16th July 1601

| William Keate | 9 | animal | Horses, Garones | 6 | 0 | 0 | 0 |
| | 1 | animal | Horses, Garones[14] | 0 | 0 | 0 | 0 |

The Antloppe of Crail, burden 60 tons, Thomas Devonson master, from *Oloone of Barges*, 18th July 1601

| Thomas Devonson, *domicile unknown*, Master *Ind* | 35 | ton | Salt | 35 | 0 | 0 | 0 |

The Nicholas of Milford Haven, burden 16 tons, William Kinn[ ] master, from Waterford, 25th July 1601

Edward Cuffe of Waterford, Merchant Ind	6	C	Skins, Morkins & Sheep Skins Broken	2	0	0	0
	12	piece	Caddows	6	0	0	0
	1	C	*Irish* Frieze *Cloth*	2	0	0	0
John Browne of Waterford, Merchant Ind	5	M	Coney Staggers	6	5	0	0
	15	C	Skins, Morkins & Sheep Skins Broken	5	0	0	0
	6	C	Coverlet	3	0	0	0
James Gibson of Waterford, Merchant Ind	4	M	Skins, Morkins & Sheep Skins Broken	13	6	8	0
	20	piece	Caddows	10	0	0	0
	2	C	*Irish* Frieze and Check *Cloth*	4	0	0	0

12 Taken by the Carles of London.   13 Of the gross amount, 146.25 lbs allowed for tar and dust.   14 Allowed for his provision.

Merchant name	Qty	Unit	Commodity	£	s.	d.	f.
Garrett Wale of Clonmel, Merchant Ind	16	C	Coverlet	8	0	0	0
	4	C	Skins, Morkins & Sheep Skins Broken	1	6	8	0

The Emanuell of Tenby, burden 20 tons, Henry Feilde master, from La Rochelle, 23rd July 1601[15]

Richard Barrett of Tenby, Merchant Ind	15	ton	Salt	15	0	0	0

The Mathew of Milford Haven, burden 16 tons, William Younge master, from *Traughrdaghe*, 23rd July 1601

Michael Quirke of Bristol, Merchant Ind	10	tun	Oil, Seville	80	0	0	0

The Good Luck of Bristol, burden 18 tons, Simon Bowman master, from Waterford, *23rd July 1601*

John White of Waterford, Merchant Ind	4	C	*Irish* Frieze *Cloth*	8	0	0	0
	23	piece	Coverlet	11	10	0	0
	8	C	Skins, Morkin	2	13	4	0
	6	C	Skins, Sheep Broken	2	0	0	0
	2	C	Coney Staggers	0	5	0	0

The Good Luck aforesaid, *23rd July 1601*

Richard Woodlocke of Clonmel, Merchant Ind	2	C	*Irish* Frieze *Cloth*	4	0	0	0

The Good Luck aforesaid, *23rd July 1601*

Richard Woodlocke of Clonmel, Merchant Ind	16	piece	Coverlet	8	0	0	0
	8	C	Skins, Sheep Broken	2	13	4	0
	5	C	Coney Staggers	0	12	4	0
Nicholas Harforde of Clonmel, Merchant Ind	2	C	*Irish* Frieze *Cloth*	4	0	0	0
	30	piece	Coverlet	15	0	0	0
	10	C	Skins, Morkins & Sheep Skins Broken	3	6	8	0
John Howlett of Bristol, Glover Ind	8	C	Skins, Morkins & Sheep Skins Broken	2	13	4	0

The Waspe of Bristol, burden 15 tons, John Grenewell master, from Waterford, *23rd July 1601*

Henry Wize of Waterford, Merchant Ind	40	piece	Coverlet	20	0	0	0
	10	C	Skins, Morkins & Sheep Skins Broken	3	6	8	0
	3	C	*Irish* Frieze *Cloth*	6	0	0	0
	4	C	*Irish* Check *Cloth*	8	0	0	0
	1+1	Hogshead barrel	Aquavitae	6	0	0	0

---

15 Either this date or the above date is possibly a recording error.

Merchant name	Qty	Unit	Commodity	£	s.	d.	f.

The Truelove of New Ross, burden 12 tons, Mathew Howlen master, from New Ross, *23rd July 1601*

Merchant name	Qty	Unit	Commodity	£	s.	d.	f.
Mark Dormer of New Ross, Merchant Ind	21	piece	Coverlet	10	10	0	0
	2	C	*Irish* Frieze and Check *Cloth*	4	0	0	0
	12	C	Skins, Morkins & Sheep Skins Broken	4	0	0	0
James Hore of New Ross, Merchant Ind	15	C	Skins, Morkins & Sheep Skins Broken	5	0	0	0
	2	C	*Irish* Frieze *Cloth*	4	0	0	0
	5	C	Skins, Coney	0	12	6	0
	30	piece	Coverlet	15	0	0	0
John Butler of New Ross, Merchant Ind	6	C	Skins, Morkins & Sheep Skins Broken	2	0	0	0
	3	C	*Irish* Frieze *Cloth*	6	0	0	0
	12	piece	Coverlet	6	0	0	0
	8	stone	Wool, Flocks	0	13	4	0

The Mathew of Waterford, burden 18 tons, Laurence Talbote master, from Waterford, *23rd July 1601*

Merchant name	Qty	Unit	Commodity	£	s.	d.	f.
John Browne of Waterford, Merchant Ind	20	piece	Coverlet	10	0	0	0
	1.5	C	*Irish* Frieze *Cloth*	3	0	0	0
	8	piece	Mantles	2	0	0	0
	4	C	Skins, Morkin	1	6	8	0

The Mathew aforesaid, *23rd July 1601*

Merchant name	Qty	Unit	Commodity	£	s.	d.	f.
James Lea of Waterford, Merchant Ind	32	C	Coverlet	16	0	0	0
	3.5	C	*Irish* Frieze *Cloth*	7	0	0	0
	4	piece	Mantles	1	0	0	0
	2.5	C	Skins, Morkin	0	16	8	0

The Mathew of Waterford aforesaid, 23rd July 1601

Merchant name	Qty	Unit	Commodity	£	s.	d.	f.
Philip Lynch of Waterford, Merchant Ind	16	piece	Coverlet	8	0	0	0
	3.5	C	*Irish* Frieze and Check *Cloth*	7	0	0	0
	3	C	Skins, Morkin	1	0	0	0
	6	hogshead	Oil, Seville	12	0	0	0
James Lumbart of Waterford, Merchant Ind	4	C	*Irish* Frieze *Cloth*	8	0	0	f.
	4	C	*Irish* Check *Cloth*	8	0	0	0
	24	piece	Caddows	12	0	0	0
	3	C	Skins, Sheep Broken	1	0	0	0
	6	piece	Mantles	1	10	0	0
Nicholas Sharpe of Waterford, Merchant Ind	15	piece	Coverlet	7	10	0	0
	1.5	C	*Irish* Frieze and Check *Cloth*	3	0	0	0
	2	C	Skins, Morkin	0	13	4	0
	8	piece	Mantles	2	0	0	0

864

Merchant name	Qty	Unit	Commodity	£	s.	d.	f.

The John of Waterford, burden 18 tons, Patrick Flaghey master, from Waterford, *23rd July 1601*

Merchant name	Qty	Unit	Commodity	£	s.	d.	f.
John White of Waterford, Merchant Ind	6.5	C	*Irish* Frieze and Check *Cloth*	13	0	0	0
	30	piece	Caddows	15	0	0	0
Edmund Comen of Waterford, Merchant Ind	14	C	Skins, Morkins & Sheep Skins Broken	4	13	4	0
	1	C	*Irish* Frieze *Cloth*	2	0	0	0
Edmund Meaghe of Waterford, Merchant Ind	3	C	*Irish* Frieze *Cloth*	6	0	0	0
	10	piece	Coverlet	5	0	0	0
	18	C	Skins, Morkins & Sheep Skins Broken	6	0	0	0

The Grace of Bristol, burden 30 tons, Thomas Latimer master, from Waterford, *23rd July 1601*

Merchant name	Qty	Unit	Commodity	£	s.	d.	f.
John Sutton of Waterford, Merchant Ind	2	C	*Irish* Frieze *Cloth*	4	0	0	0
	4	piece	Mantles	1	0	0	0
	6	piece	Coverlet	3	0	0	0
	4	C	Skins, Morkin	1	6	8	0
John Rothe of Kilkenny, Merchant Ind	34	piece	Caddows	17	0	0	0
	8	C	*Irish* Frieze and Check *Cloth*	16	0	0	0
	3	piece	Mantles	0	15	0	0
	18	C	Skins, Sheep Broken	6	0	0	0

The Mathew aforesaid, *23rd July 1601*

Merchant name	Qty	Unit	Commodity	£	s.	d.	f.
Robert Tewe of Waterford, Merchant Ind	2	C	*Irish* Frieze and Check *Cloth*	4	0	0	0
	20	piece	Caddows	10	0	0	0

The Grace aforesaid, *23rd July 1601*

Merchant name	Qty	Unit	Commodity	£	s.	d.	f.
John Hackett of Clonmel, Merchant Ind	6	C	Skins, Morkin	2	0	0	0
	6	C	Coney Staggers	0	15	0	0
	2	C	*Irish* Frieze *Cloth*	4	0	0	0
	24	piece	Coverlet	12	0	0	0

The Grace aforesaid, 23rd July 1601

Merchant name	Qty	Unit	Commodity	£	s.	d.	f.
John Butler of New Ross, Merchant Ind	10	C	Skins, Morkins & Sheep Skins Broken	3	6	8	0
	1	C	*Irish* Frieze *Cloth*	2	0	0	0
	12	piece	Coverlet	6	0	0	0
Pierce Braye of Clonmel, Merchant Ind	2	C	*Irish* Frieze *Cloth*	4	0	0	0
	4	C	Skins, Morkins & Sheep Skins Broken	1	6	8	0
	16	piece	Coverlet	8	0	0	0
	5	C	Coney Staggers	0	12	6	0
Thomas Fowlowe of Cashel, Merchant Ind	12	C	Skins, Morkins & Sheep Skins Broken	4	0	0	0
	3	C	Coney Staggers	0	7	6	0

Merchant name	Qty	Unit	Commodity	£	s.	d.	f.

The Peter of Milford Haven, burden 12 tons, John Devorex master, from Waterford, *23rd July 1601*

Merchant name	Qty	Unit	Commodity	£	s.	d.	f.
Nicholas White of Waterford, Merchant Ind	2	C	*Irish* Frieze *Cloth*	4	0	0	0
	12	piece	Coverlet	6	0	0	0
	12	C	Skins, Morkins & Sheep Skins Broken	4	0	0	0
Nicholas Lynster of Clonmel, Merchant Ind	8	C	Skins, Morkins & Sheep Skins Broken	2	13	4	0
Peter Hanrican of Clonmel, Merchant Ind	3	C	*Irish* Frieze *Cloth*	6	0	0	0
	13	C	Skins, Morkins & Sheep Skins Broken	4	6	8	0
	18	piece	Coverlet	9	0	0	0
Richard Neale of Waterford, Merchant Ind	13	C	Skins, Morkins & Sheep Skins Broken	4	6	8	0
	1	C	*Irish* Frieze *Cloth*	2	0	0	0
	15	piece	Coverlet	7	10	0	0

The Marie of Waterford, burden 16 tons, James Baron master, from Waterford, *23rd July 1601*

Merchant name	Qty	Unit	Commodity	£	s.	d.	f.
John Butler of Waterford, Merchant Ind	1	C	*Irish* Frieze *Cloth*	2	0	0	0
	6	piece	Coverlet	3	0	0	0
	6	C	Skins, Morkins & Sheep Skins Broken	2	0	0	0
	3	C	Coney Staggers	0	7	6	0
Edmund Hackett of Waterford, Merchant Ind	6.5	C	Skins, Morkins & Sheep Skins Broken	2	3	4	0
	3	C	*Irish* Frieze and Check *Cloth*	6	0	0	0
	14	piece	Coverlet	7	0	0	0
Robert Cransburrowe of Waterford, Merchant Ind	8	C	Coverlet	4	0	0	0
	1	C	*Irish* Check *Cloth*	2	0	0	0
	4	C	Skins, Sheep Broken	1	6	8	0

The Marie of Wexford, burden 10 tons, Thomas Busher master, from Wexford, 24th July 1601

Merchant name	Qty	Unit	Commodity	£	s.	d.	f.
Stephen Cod of Wexford, Merchant Ind	1	M	Barrel Staves	1	0	0	0
	2	*small* C	Wood, Clapholt	0	10	0	0
	2	dozen	Oar Ends	0	15	10	0
	0.5	C	Skins, Morkin	0	3	4	0

The Gabriell of Bristol, burden 60 tons, Lewes Weaver master, from La Rochelle, 25th July 1601

Merchant name	Qty	Unit	Commodity	£	s.	d.	f.
Thomas Aldworth of Bristol, Merchant Ind	25	ton	Salt	25	0	0	0
John Barker of Bristol, Merchant Ind	21	C	Wool, Spanish Hat	87	10	0	0
	2	tun	Vinegar	4	13	4	0
	18	barrel	Pitch and Tar	3	0	0	0
	10	dozen	Skins, Goat	10	0	0	0
Richard Tagg of Bristol, Merchant Ind	91	cakes	Rosin	15	3	4	0
	2	tun	Vinegar	4	13	4	0

Merchant name	Qty	Unit	Commodity	£	s.	d.	f.

The Marie of Jersey, burden 18 tons, Nicholas Rowse master, from Cork, 14th August 1601

Thomas Mandline of Cork, Merchant Ind	14	animal	Horses, Garones	9	6	8	0

The Recoverie of Bristol, burden 18 tons, John Markes master, from Cork, 17th August 1601

Andrew Roche of Cork, Merchant Ind	20	C	Skins, Morkins & Sheep Skins Broken	6	13	4	0
	5	C	Coney Staggers	0	12	6	0
	4	stone	Wool, Flocks	0	6	8	0
	0.5	dozen	Skins, Deer	1	10	0	0

The Providence of Bristol, burden 27 tons, Edmund Jones master, from La Rochelle, 17th August 1601

William Challin of Bristol, Merchant Ind	16	ton	Salt	16	0	0	0

The Roase of Bristol, burden 18 tons, Christopher Tailor master, from Cork, 18th August 1601

William Slade of Bristol, Grocer Ind	10	C	Skins, Morkins & Sheep Skins Broken	3	6	8	0
	5	animal	Horses, Garones	3	0	0	0
Henry Stone, *domicile & origin unknown,*	4	animal	Horses, Garones	2	13	4	0

The Lion of Barnstaple, burden 16 tons, John Woolsone master, from Saõ Miguel, 18th August 1601

Robert Aldworth & Walter Sherman of Bristol, Merchant Ind	14	ton	Woad, Green	130	0	0	0

The Desier of Bristol, burden 30 tons, William Fletcher master, from Newfoundland, 18th August 1601

John Angell & Barnes of Bristol, Merchants & Company Ind	15	hogshead	Oil, Train	18	10	0	0

The Christopher of Bristol, burden 60 tons, Richard Pendrie master, from Lafoile, 21st August 1601

William Greines, Daniel Addams, Christopher Birkeheade, Richard Wynter & Antony Skinner of Bristol & London, Merchants Ind	10	ton	Fish, Salmon	120	0	0	0
	20	ton	Fish, Salmon Girles	120	0	0	0
	3	ton	Fish, Salmon[16]	0	0	0	0
	10	ton	Fish, Salmon Girles[17]	0	0	0	0

16 Allowed (custom exempt) 'by reason of their pains in catching them'. 17 As above.

Merchant name	Qty	Unit	Commodity	£ s. d. f.
The Maieflower of Bristol, burden 80 tons, Thomas Bennett master, from Newfoundland, 26th August 1601				
Thomas James of Bristol, Merchant Ind	5	tun	Oil, Train	25 0 0 0
The White Swan of Bristol, burden 50 tons, Richard Lux master, from Newfoundland, 1st September 1601				
John Roberts & George White of Bristol, Merchant Ind	2	tun	Oil, Train	10 0 0 0
The Desier of Bristol, burden 60 tons, Mathew Rice master, from Newfoundland, 2nd September 1601				
Walter Oldfeild, William Greines & Francis Dowtie of Bristol, Merchant Ind	3.5	tun	Oil, Train	17 10 0 0
The George of Le Croisic, burden 20 tons, Peter Lestubecke master, from Le Croisic, 7th September 1601				
William Ellis (the younger) of Bristol, Merchant Ind	15	ton	Salt	15 0 0 0
The Antloppe of Crail, burden 50 tons, Thomas Devonson master, from St Gilles Croix-de-Vie, 18th September 1601				
Thomas Devonson, of St Giles in France, Merchant Alien	35	ton	Salt	35 0 0 0
The Dove of Bristol, burden 40 tons, William Hedge master, from Newfoundland, 22nd September 1601				
William Coale of Bristol, Merchant Ind	2.5	tun	Oil, Train	12 10 0 0
The Consent of Bristol, burden 100 tons, Henry Bussell master, from Newfoundland, 22nd September 1601				
John Barnes, John Angell & Thomas Drap of Bristol, Merchants & Company Ind	6	tun	Oil, Train	30 0 0 0
The William of Bristol, burden 50 tons, John Addams master, from Newfoundland, 22nd September 1601				
James Bushe & Richard More of Bristol, Merchant & Company Ind	3	tun	Oil, Train	15 0 0 0
The Amitie of Bristol, burden 120 tons, William Woorgan master, from Newfoundland, 22nd September 1601				
William Hopkins of Bristol, Merchant Ind	6	tun	Oil, Train	30 0 0 0

Merchant name	Qty	Unit	Commodity	£	s.	d.	f.

The Royal Defence of Bristol, burden 70 tons, Thomas Rice master, from Newfoundland, 23rd September 1601

John Whitsonne, Mathew Haviland & John Foens of Bristol, Merchant Ind	5	tun	Oil, Train	25	0	0	0

WINE IMPORTS

The Peter of Westbury-on-Severn, burden 18 tons, Robert Northe master, from Waterford, 29th October 1600

Christopher Whitsonne of Bristol, Merchant Ind	6	butt	Wine, Seck	0	0	0	0

The Salomon of Barnstaple, burden 20 tons, Richard Elliott master, from La Rochelle, 31st October 1600

John Barker of Bristol, Merchant Ind	17	tun	Wine, French	0	0	0	0

The Boneadventure of Ile d' Oleron, burden 50 tons, John Fevora master, from Málaga, *31st October 1600*

Andrew Pearde, *domicile unknown*, Merchant Alien	24	pipe	Wine, *Peresomena*	0	0	0	0

The Mathew of Berkeley, burden 18 tons, Richard Daniell master, from Waterford, 3rd November 1600

John Baron of Waterford, Merchant Ind	11	butt	Wine, Seck	0	0	0	0

The Elizabeth of Jersey, burden 60 tons, John Balharhe master, from Cadiz, 6th November 1600

Laurence Pory of St Malo, Merchant Stranger	54	pipes	Wine, Bastard	0	0	0	0
	5	pipes	Wine, Corrupt	0	0	0	0
	2	butt	Wine, Seck	0	0	0	0
	1	butt	Wine, Seck[18]	0	0	0	0

The Charitie of Bristol, burden 18 tons, John Watte master, from Waterford, 7th November 1600

Patrick Mayler of Waterford, Merchant Ind	6	butt	Wine, Seck	0	0	0	0

The Roase of Bristol, burden 18 tons, William Brooke master, from Waterford, 29th November 1600

Pierce Baron & Michael Quirke of Waterford, Merchants Ind	6	butt	Wine, Seck	0	0	0	0

18 Custom exempt.

Merchant name	Qty	Unit	Commodity	£	s.	d.	f.

The Beniamyne of London, burden 135 tons, William Rixe master, from Bordeaux, 2nd December 1600

Merchant name	Qty	Unit	Commodity	£	s.	d.	f.
John Bowlton, Robert Aldworth & John Roberts of Bristol, Merchant & Company Ind	136.08	tun	Wine, French	o	o	o	o

The Falcon of Millbrook, burden 23 tons, Thomas Serell master, from Bordeaux, 15th December 1600

Merchant name	Qty	Unit	Commodity	£	s.	d.	f.
John Trevill of Milbrook, Merchant Ind	23.5	tun	Wine, French	o	o	o	o

The Spedewell of Millbrook, burden 42 tons, Henry Warwicke master, from Bordeaux, 16th December 1600

Merchant name	Qty	Unit	Commodity	£	s.	d.	f.
Nicholas Bogans & John Larye of Bristol & Totnes, Merchant Ind	40	tun	Wine, French	o	o	o	o

The Spedewell of Millbrook, burden 42 tons, Henry Warwicke master, from Bordeaux, 16th December 1600

Merchant name	Qty	Unit	Commodity	£	s.	d.	f.
Henry Warwicke, domicile unknown, Master Ind	1	tun	Wine, French	o	o	o	o

The Marie of Roscoff, burden 35 tons, Alan Bezien master, from Málaga, *16th December 1600*

Merchant name	Qty	Unit	Commodity	£	s.	d.	f.
Nicholas Bogans & Richard Powle of Bristol, Merchant Ind	15	tun	Wine, *Peresomena*	o	o	o	o
	1	tun	Wine, *Peresomena*[19]	o	o	o	o
Alan Bezian of Roscoff, Master Alien	3	pipe	Wine, *Peresomena*	o	o	o	o

The Esperance of *Olderne*,[20] burden 35 tons, Daniel Angeball master, from unknown destination, 17th December 1600

Merchant name	Qty	Unit	Commodity	£	s.	d.	f.
Daniel Angeball, *domicile unknown*, Merchant & Company Alien	36	tun	Wine, French	o	o	o	o

The Flower of St Malo, burden 60 tons, William Hamlyn master, from Cadiz, 18th December 1600

Merchant name	Qty	Unit	Commodity	£	s.	d.	f.
Michael Quirke of Bristol, Merchant Ind	56.5	tun	Wine, Seck	o	o	o	o
	2	tun	Wine, Seck[21]	o	o	o	o
	1	butt	Wine, Seck[22]	o	o	o	o
William Hamlyn, *domicile unknown*, Merchant Alien	0.75	tun	Wine, Seck	o	o	o	o
	0.5	tun	Wine, Seck[23]	o	o	o	o

19 Allowed for prisage. 20 Possibly Ile d' Oleron, France. 21 Custom exempt. 22 Custom exempt. 23 Custom exempt.

Merchant name	Qty	Unit	Commodity	£	s.	d.	f.

The Royall Defence of Bristol, burden 100 tons, Christopher Tailor master, from Bordeaux, 22nd December 1600

| John Whitsone, John Barker & Mathew Haviland of Bristol, Merchant & Company Ind | 90.5 | tun | Wine, French | o | o | o | o |

The White Swane of Bristol, burden 50 tons, William Browne master, from La Rochelle, 23rd December 1600

| John Roberts & Serge White of Bristol, Merchant Ind | 6 | tun | Wine, French | o | o | o | o |

The Jennett of St-Jean-de-Luz, burden 70 tons, Peter Repaxo master, from Bordeaux, 23rd December 1600

John Barker of Bristol, Merchant Ind	24.58	tun	Wine, French	o	o	o	o
Thomas Anthoney of Bristol, Merchant Ind	10	tun	Wine, French	o	o	o	o
Martin Soriendo, *domicile unknown*, Merchant Alien	20	tun	Wine, French	o	o	o	o
Peter Repaxo, *domicile unknown*, Master Alien	1	tun	Wine, French	o	o	o	o

The Christopher of Plymouth, burden 40 tons, Richard Lorye master, from Bordeaux, 29th December 1600

| William Ellis, John Whitesonne & Mathew Haviland of Bristol, Merchant & Company Ind | 39.75 | tun | Wine, French | o | o | o | o |

The Pleasure of Millbrook, burden 28 tons, Francis Hamlyn master, from Bordeaux, *29th December 1600*

| William Ellis, John Whitesonne & Mathew Haviland of Bristol, Merchant & Company Ind | 27.25 | tun | Wine, French | o | o | o | o |

The John of St Malo, burden 45 tons, Phillipp Lesever master, from Sanlúcar de Barrameda, *29th December 1600*

Robert Aldworth of Bristol, Merchant Ind	41	tun	Wine, Seck	o	o	o	o
	1	butt	Wine, Seck[24]	o	o	o	o
	2	tun	Wine, Seck[25]	o	o	o	o
Philippe Lesever, *domicile unknown*, Master Alien	1	butt	Wine, Seck	o	o	o	o
	2	barrel	Wine, Seck	o	o	o	o

24 Custom exempt.   25 Allowed for prisage.

Merchant name	Qty	Unit	Commodity	£	s.	d.	f.

The Primerose of Sandwich, burden 65 tons, Thomas Page master, from Bordeaux, *29th December 1600*

Merchant name	Qty	Unit	Commodity	£	s.	d.	f.
William Bristoll, *domicile unknown,* Merchant Alien	59.375	tun	Wine, French	o	o	o	o
Thomas Page, *domicile unknown,* Merchant Ind	5	tun	Wine, French	o	o	o	o

The Dennis of Granville, burden 40 tons, Peter Bennice master, from Sanlúcar de Barrameda, *29th December 1600*

Merchant name	Qty	Unit	Commodity	£	s.	d.	f.
John Devarra, *domicile unknown,* Merchant Alien	79	butt	Wine, Seck	o	o	o	o
	1	butt	Wine, Seck[26]	o	o	o	o

The Longe Barcke of Hoorn, burden 120 tons, Cornell Anthoney master, from Aveiro, *30th December 1600*

Merchant name	Qty	Unit	Commodity	£	s.	d.	f.
Cornell Anthoney, domicile unknown, Merchant Alien	6	butt	Wine, Seck	o	o	o	o

The William of Bristol, burden 40 tons, William Meager master, from La Rochelle, *30th December 1600*

Merchant name	Qty	Unit	Commodity	£	s.	d.	f.
John Roberts of Bristol, Merchant Ind	5	tun	Wine, French	o	o	o	o
Richard James of Bristol, Merchant Ind	2.5	tun	Wine, French	o	o	o	o
	1	pipe	Wine, Bevoredge	o	o	o	o

The Daniell of Newcastle, burden 94 tons, John Johnson master, from Bordeaux, *31st December 1600*

Merchant name	Qty	Unit	Commodity	£	s.	d.	f.
John Angell, Richard Teaghe, John Roberowe & John Fowens of Bristol, *Merchants & Company* Ind	86.25	tun	Wine, French	o	o	o	o

The Grene Crosse of St Malo, burden 60 tons, John Bezen master, from Cadiz, *2nd January 1601*

Merchant name	Qty	Unit	Commodity	£	s.	d.	f.
Mathew Haviland of Bristol, Merchant Ind	50	tun	Wine, Seck	o	o	o	o
	1	tun	Wine, Seck[27]	o	o	o	o
	2	tun	Wine, Seck[28]	o	o	o	o

The Blessing of God of Leith, burden 115 tons, David Jamison master, from Bordeaux, *2nd January 1601*

Merchant name	Qty	Unit	Commodity	£	s.	d.	f.
William Ellis, John Whitesonne & Thomas James of Bristol, *Merchants & Company* Ind	113.91	tun	Wine, French	o	o	o	o

26 Custom exempt. **27** Custom exempt. **28** Allowed for prisage.

Merchant name	Qty	Unit	Commodity	£	s.	d.	f.

The John of Glasgow, burden 40 tons, John Hopkyns master, from Málaga, 7th January 1601

Merchant name	Qty	Unit	Commodity	£	s.	d.	f.
Richard Joye, James Coble & Thomas Lamberte of Plymouth, Merchants Ind	22	tun	Wine, Malaga	o	o	o	o
	1	pipe	Wine, Malaga[29]	o	o	o	o
	2	tun	Wine, Malaga[30]	o	o	o	o
Mark Guygan, *domicile unknown*, Merchant Alien	2.25	tun	Wine, Malaga	o	o	o	o

The Greyhownd, *Port Unknown*, burden 100 tons, Cornell Jhonsonne master, from Bordeaux, 12th January 1601

Merchant name	Qty	Unit	Commodity	£	s.	d.	f.
Alexander Bolasander, *domicile unknown*, Merchant Alien	57	tun	Wine, French	o	o	o	o
Cornell Johnson, *domicile unknown*, *Master* Ind	38	tun	Wine, French	o	o	o	o

The Elizabeth of Tenby, burden 6 tons, Thomas Bedforde master, from Tenby, 20th January 1601

Merchant name	Qty	Unit	Commodity	£	s.	d.	f.
Howell Philpen of Tenby, Merchant Ind	4	tun	Wine, French	o	o	o	o

The Fortune of Bayonne, burden 40 tons, Francis Durand master, from Nantes, 22nd January 1601

Merchant name	Qty	Unit	Commodity	£	s.	d.	f.
Philberia Gregoria of Chard, Merchant Ind	34	tun	Wine, French	o	o	o	o

The Mathew of Carmarthen, burden 20 tons, Henry Butler master, from Carmarthen, 26th January 1601

Merchant name	Qty	Unit	Commodity	£	s.	d.	f.
John Morris of Carmarthen, Merchant Ind	6	tun	Wine, French	o	o	o	o

The Trinitie of Tenby, burden 10 tons, Nicholas Stafforde master, from Tenby, 26th January 1601

Merchant name	Qty	Unit	Commodity	£	s.	d.	f.
John Phillpen of Tenby, Merchant Ind	1	tun	Wine, French	o	o	o	o

The Marie of Jersey, burden 38 tons, John Roose master, from Cadiz, 11th February 1601

Merchant name	Qty	Unit	Commodity	£	s.	d.	f.
John Minger of St Malo, Merchant Alien	72	butt	Wine, Seck	o	o	o	o
	1	butt	Wine, Seck[31]	o	o	o	o

The Sanmalena of Brest, burden 70 tons, Asker le Meyer master, from Cadiz, 12th February 1601

Merchant name	Qty	Unit	Commodity	£	s.	d.	f.
William Ellis, John Aldworth & Nicholas Bogans of Bristol, Merchants Ind	72	butt	Wine, Seck	o	o	o	o
	1	butt	Wine, Seck[32]	o	o	o	o
	47	pipe	Wine, Bastard	o	o	o	o
	1	pipe	Wine, Bastard[33]	o	o	o	o
	2	tun	Wine, Bastard[34]	o	o	o	o

---

29 Custom exempt. 30 Allowed for prisage. 31 Custom exempt. 32 Custom exempt. 33 Custom exempt. 34 Allowed for prisage.

Merchant name	Qty	Unit	Commodity	£ s. d. f.

The Pearle of Le Conquet, burden 50 tons, John Bardicke master, from Bordeaux, 16th February 1601

William Ellis & Mathew Haviland of Bristol, Merchant Ind	48.5	tun	Wine, French	o o o o

The Bonaventure of *Olone*,[35] burden 55 tons, John Febra master, from Málaga, 16th February 1601

Nicholas Bogans, John Goninge & Christopher Webb of Bristol, Merchants Ind	34.5	tun	Wine, Malaga	o o o o
	1	pipe	Wine, Malaga[36]	o o o o
	2	tun	Wine, Malaga[37]	o o o o

The Cruelone of Barnstaple, burden 40 tons, James Wynteredge from *Tenereth*[38], 28th February 1601

John Downes & George Stanburie of Barnstaple, Merchant Ind	37	tun	Wine, Canaries	o o o o
	1	pipe	Wine, Canaries[39]	o o o o
	2	tun	Wine, Canaries[40]	o o o o

The Daizie of Bristol, burden 34 tons, Andrew Batten master, from Madeira, 4th April 1601

John Barker, John Fowins, John Roberowe & Robert Johnsone of Bristol, Merchant & Company Ind	9.5	tun	Wine, Madeira	o o o o

The Marie of Brest, burden 50 tons, Gowldhen Lemere master, from Cadiz, 7th April 1601

Nicholas Bogans of Bristol, Merchant Ind	30.25	tun	Wine, Seck	o o o o
	1	hogshead	Wine, Seck[41]	o o o o
	2	tun	Wine, Seck[42]	o o o o
	3	pipes	Wine, Bastard	o o o o
Gowldhen Le Meyre, *domicile unknown*, Master Alien	9.75	tun	Wine, Seck	o o o o
	1	hogshead	Wine, Seck[43]	o o o o

The Jane of Plymouth, burden 40 tons, John Pyke master, from *Candie*, 15th April 1601

John Newman & *Digori* Holman of London & Plymouth, Merchant Ind	35.5	tun	Wine, Muscadell	o o o o

The Falcon of Millbrook, burden 18 tons, Thomas Serell master, from Bayonne, *15th April 1601*

William Ellis of Bristol, Merchant Ind	6	tun	Wine, French	o o o o

---

35 Probably Ile d' Oleron, France. **36** Custom exempt. **37** Allowed for prisage. **38** Probably Tenerife. **39** Custom exempt. **40** Allowed for prisage. **41** Custom exempt. **42** Allowed for prisage. **43** Custom exempt.

Merchant name	*Qty*	*Unit*	*Commodity*	*£ s. d. f.*

The Mynykyne of Bristol, burden 17 tons, Richard Mogridge master, from Bordeaux, 20th April 1601

Merchant name	Qty	Unit	Commodity	£	s.	d.	f.
John Goninge & Roger Grenehill of Bristol, Merchant Ind	9.5	tun	Wine, French	o	o	o	o

The Sonne of Bristol, burden 25 tons, Thomas Latymer, from Galicia, 21st April 1601

Merchant name	Qty	Unit	Commodity	£	s.	d.	f.
Thomas & James Rice of Bristol, Merchants Ind	8	ton	Wine, Spanish called Rob David	24	o	o	o

The Daniell of Bristol, burden 96 tons, John Johnsonne master, from Bordeaux, 2nd May 1601

Merchant name	Qty	Unit	Commodity	£	s.	d.	f.
John Barker, John Roberowe & John Fowens of Bristol, Merchants & Company Ind	96.33	tun	Wine, French	o	o	o	o

The Marie of Roscoff, burden 37 tons, Alan Bezian master, from Málaga, 5th May 1601

Merchant name	Qty	Unit	Commodity	£	s.	d.	f.
Nicholas Bogans & John Roberowe of Bristol, Merchants Ind	34	tun	Wine, Malaga	o	o	o	o
Alien Bezien, *domicile unknown*, Master Alien	0.5	tun	Wine, Malaga	o	o	o	o
	1	pipe	Wine, Malaga	o	o	o	o

The Pellican of Barnstaple, burden 80 tons, William Wynteredge master, from the Canary Islands, 7th May 1601

Merchant name	Qty	Unit	Commodity	£	s.	d.	f.
George Stanburie of Barnstaple & John Roberts, Thomas Pitt & Thomas Willitt of Bristol, Merchants & Company Ind	68.5	tun	Wine, Canaries	o	o	o	o
	1	pipe	Wine, Canaries[44]	o	o	o	o
	1	pipe	Wine, Canaries[45]	o	o	o	o

The Peter of Le Conquet, burden 60 tons, Nowell Tradicke master, from Cadiz, 8th May 1601

Merchant name	Qty	Unit	Commodity	£	s.	d.	f.
Daniel Dorrett, *domicile unknown*, Merchant Alien	105	butt	Wine, Seck	o	o	o	o
	2	butt	Wine, Seck[46]	o	o	o	o
Noel Tradicke, *domicile unknown*, Master Alien	3	butt	Wine, Seck	o	o	o	o

The Jarus of Granville, burden 25 tons, Charles Brittanie master, from Cadiz, 11th May 1601

Merchant name	Qty	Unit	Commodity	£	s.	d.	f.
Masci Arthur, *domicile unknown*, Merchant Alien	45	butt	Wine, Seck	o	o	o	o
	1	butt	Wine, Seck[47]	o	o	o	o

---

44 Allowed to the merchants.   45 Allowed to the master.   46 Allowed to the master & merchants.   47 Custom exempt.

Merchant name	Qty	Unit	Commodity	£	s.	d.	f.

The Antelopp of Crail, burden 70 tons, Thomas Devonson, from Puerto de Santa Maria, 21st May 1601

John Symple, *domicile unknown*,							
Merchant Alien	116	butt	Wine, Seck	o	o	o	o
	1	butt	Wine, Seck[48]	o	o	o	o

The Guifte of Barnstaple, burden 60 tons, John Wize master, from Toulon, 6th June 1601

William Chapple of Barnstaple,							
Merchant Ind	2.5	tun	Wine, Langadoge	o	o	o	o

The Speedwell of Millbrook, burden 40 tons, Henry Warren master, from Le Croisic, 6th July 1601

Nicholas Wilkins of Plymouth,							
Merchant Ind	8	tun	Wine, French	o	o	o	o

The Gabriell of Bristol, burden 70 tons, Lewis Weaver master, from La Rochelle, 25th July 1601

John Barker of Bristol, Merchant Ind	4	tun	Wine, French	o	o	o	o

EXPORTS

The Daisie of Bristol, burden 30 tons, Andrew Batten master, to La Rochelle, 1st October 1600 £ s. d. f.

William Coorie of Bristol, Merchant Ind	4	piece	Cloth of Assize	o	o	o	o
			Cloth of Assize, Overlengths	o	o	o	o
	2	C goad	Cottons (Woollen Cloth)	6	13	4	o

The White Swan of Bristol, burden 50 tons, William Browne master, to *Burniffe*, 1st October 1600

John Roberts of Bristol, Merchant Ind	5	ton	Lead[49]	40	o	o	o

The Daisie aforesaid, 1st October 1600

John Angell of Bristol, Merchant Ind	5	piece	Cloth of Assize, Bridgwaters	o	o	o	o
	1	piece	Cloth of Assize	o	o	o	o
			Cloth of Assize, Overlengths	o	o	o	o

48 Custom exempt.   49 Most entries for lead in this account specify that lead is 'in sowes' and that there are 18 pieces to the ton. Where this is not the case it is specified by the transcriber.

Merchant name	Qty	Unit	Commodity	£	s.	d.	f.

The Daisie aforesaid, 1st October 1600

Merchant name	Qty	Unit	Commodity	£	s.	d.	f.
William Colstone of Bristol, Merchant Ind	3	piece	Cloth of Assize	o	o	o	o
			Cloth of Assize, Overlengths	o	o	o	o

The Daisie aforesaid, 3rd October 1600

Merchant name	Qty	Unit	Commodity	£	s.	d.	f.
John Aldworth of Bristol, Merchant Ind	15	C	Fish, Dry Newfoundland	7	10	o	o
	2	C	Rice	1	13	4	o

The Daisie aforesaid, 3rd October 1600

Merchant name	Qty	Unit	Commodity	£	s.	d.	f.
Andrew Batten of Bristol, Merchant Ind	30	dozen	Flax	4	o	o	o

The Dolphine of Bristol, burden 40 tons, James Partridge master, to Livorno, 4th October 1600

Merchant name	Qty	Unit	Commodity	£	s.	d.	f.
Robert Aldworth of Bristol, Merchant Ind	27	piece	Cloth of Assize	o	o	o	o
	3	piece	Cloth of Assize[50]	o	o	o	o
			Cloth of Assize, Overlengths	o	o	o	o
	18	piece	Bristol Frieze *Cloth*[51]	18	o	o	o
	2	piece	Bristol Frieze *Cloth*[52]	o	o	o	o
	6	M	Fish, Dry Newfoundland	30	o	o	o

The Royall Defence of Bristol, burden 80 tons, Mathew Honywell master, to *Burniffe*, 7th October 1600

Merchant name	Qty	Unit	Commodity	£	s.	d.	f.
John Barker of Bristol, Merchant Ind	4	C goad	Cottons (Woollen Cloth)	13	6	8	o

The Daisie aforesaid, 7th October 1600

Merchant name	Qty	Unit	Commodity	£	s.	d.	f.
Robert Aldworth of Bristol, Merchant Ind	6	piece	Cloth of Assize	o	o	o	o
	6	piece	Bristol Frieze *Cloth*	6	o	o	o

The Dolphine aforesaid, 10th October 1600

Merchant name	Qty	Unit	Commodity	£	s.	d.	f.
Robert Aldworth of Bristol, Merchant Ind	4	ton	Lead	32	o	o	o

The Desier of La Rochelle, burden 20 tons, Nicholas Joanye master, to Dublin, 15th October 1600

Merchant name	Qty	Unit	Commodity	£	s.	d.	f.
Sebastian Fleminge, domicile unknown, Merchant Ind	10	M	Fish, Newfoundland	50	o	o	o

---

50 Custom exempt. **51** Although a value is not given for frieze cloth here, it does pay poundage, and therefore a value has been imputted. **52** Custom exempt.

Merchant name	Qty	Unit	Commodity	£	s.	d.	f.

The Amitie of Bristol, burden 60 tons, William Worgan master, to Le Croisic, 16th October 1600

| William Hoopkins of Bristol, Merchant Ind | 10 | wey | Coal | 3 | 6 | 8 | 0 |
| | 12 | wey | Coal | 4 | 0 | 0 | 0 |

The Roose of Bristol, burden 18 tons, John Marks master, to Cork, 22nd October 1600

Nicholas Holanbriggs of Bristol, Pewterer Ind	16	C	Hops	8	0	0	0
	2	C	Pewter	3	6	8	0
	0.5	C	Soap, Black	0	5	0	0

The Pellicann of Barnstaple, burden 80 tons, William Dawsone master, to Marseille, 31st October 1600

William Carie of Bristol, Merchant Ind	6	piece	Cloth of Assize	0	0	0	0
			Cloth of Assize, Overlengths	0	0	0	0
	4	piece	Bristol Frieze *Cloth*	4	0	0	0

The Pellicann abovesaid, 31st October 1600

| Ronald Barneslie of Bristol, Merchant Ind | 5 | half pieces | Bay *Cloth* | 10 | 0 | 0 | 0 |
| | 5 | C | Fish, Dry Newfoundland | 2 | 10 | 0 | 0 |

The Pellicann aforesaid, 31st October 1600

William Pitt of Bristol, Merchant Ind	9	piece	Cloth of Assize, Half	0	0	0	0
	2	piece	Cloth of Assize, Bridgwaters	0	0	0	0
	6	piece	Bay *Cloth*	12	0	0	0
	2	piece	Cardinal *Cloth*, White	0	0	0	0

The Pellicann aforesaid, 31st October 1600

William Barines of Bristol, Merchant Ind	1	piece	Cloth of Assize	0	0	0	0
	3	piece	Cloth of Assize, Streit	0	0	0	0
	3	piece	Cloth of Assize, Kersey	0	0	0	0
			Cloth of Assize, Overlengths	0	0	0	0

The Salomon of Barnstaple, burden 20 tons, Richard Elliott master, to Barnstaple, 4th November 1600

| Robert Aldworth of Bristol, Merchant Ind | 3 | C | Wax | 9 | 0 | 0 | 0 |

The Barbara of Brest, burden 25 tons, Lucas Corrorell master, to Brest, 7th November 1600

| Lucas Corrorell of Brest, Merchant Stranger | 6 | wey | Coal | 2 | 0 | 0 | 0 |

Merchant name	Qty	Unit	Commodity	£	s.	d.	f.

The Jesus of Westbury-on-Severn, burden 18 tons, Robert North master, to Dublin, 18th November 1600

John Arthur of Dublin, Merchant Ind	10	pair	Milstones, *small* called dogstones	5	0	0	0

The Roe Bucke of Gatcombe, burden 18 tons, William Swanley master, to Cork, 22nd November 1600

John King of Youghal, Merchant Ind	3	C	Hops	1	10	0	0
	3	gross	Trenchers	0	2	6	0
	2	dozen	Cups, Wooden	0	0	20	0
	1	dozen	Wool Cards	0	10	0	0
	6	lb	Seed, Cumin	0	0	20	0
	1	gross	Points, Thread	0	0	10	0
	1	C	Orchil	1	0	0	0
	5	dozen	Glasses, Drinking	0	0	20	0

The Barbara aforesaid, 24th November 1600

Lucas Corrorell of Brest, Merchant Stranger	2	C goad	Cottons (Woollen Cloth)	6	13	4	0
Thomas Howell of Bristol, Merchant Ind	13	C goad	Cottons (Woollen Cloth)	43	6	8	0
	28	piece	Wadmal *Cloth*	28	0	0	0
	3	piece	Wadmal *Cloth*	0	0	0	0

The Mathew of Hinton, burden 18 tons, Richard Daniell master, to Waterford, 28th November 1600

John Barron of Waterford, Merchant Ind	1	burden	Steel	0	5	0	0
	2	M	Nails, Lath	0	0	20	0
	2	clout	Needles	0	0	20	0
	2	ream	Paper, Brown	0	0	20	0
	0.5	gross	Knives (1*d.*)	0	5	0	0
	0.5	gross	Knives (2*d.*)	0	10	0	0
	2	dozen	Flax	0	6	8	0
	4	gross	Trenchers	0	3	4	0
	6	C	Towe	2	0	0	0
	0.5	C	Soap, Black	0	5	0	0
	10	gallon	Oil, Train	0	3	4	0
	11	C	Hops	5	10	0	0
	1	C	Rice	0	15	0	0
	3	dozen	Urinals	0	2	6	0
	2	dozen	Cruses	0	3	4	0
	0.25	C	Soap, Black	0	2	6	0
	10	lb	Seed, Onion	0	3	4	0

The Mathew aforesaid, 28th November 1600

Bennett Sawle of Waterford, Merchant Ind	1	gross	Girdles, Peny	0	10	0	0
	0.5	gross	Knives (1*d.*)	0	5	0	0

Merchant name	Qty	Unit	Commodity	£	s.	d.	f.
	12	lb	Seed, Leek & Onion	0	6	8	0
	0.5	dozen	Hats	0	15	0	0
	0.5	dozen	Caps, Monmouth	0	3	4	0
	3	lb	Cross Bow Thread	0	0	15	0
	2	lb	Girdles, Nob	0	0	20	0
	1	gross	Lace, Statute	0	6	8	0
	3	gross	Trenchers	0	2	6	0
	2	dozen	Cups, Wooden	0	0	20	0
	2	C	Taps and Cannells	0	0	20	0
	1	flacket	Honey	0	6	8	0
	1.5	C	Orchil	1	10	0	0
	3	dozen	Wool Cards	1	10	0	0
	30	ell	Coarse Linen *Cloth*	2	0	0	0
	0.5	dozen	Scythes	0	5	0	0
	0.5	gross	Points, Inkle	0	0	10	0
	2	M	Pins	0	0	10	0
	0.25	C	Alum	0	8	4	0
	2	lb	Fringe, Crewel	0	3	4	0
	0.5	dozen	Lanterns	0	3	4	0
	0.5	piece	Bristol Frieze *Cloth*	0	10	0	0
	0.5	C	Camphor Wood	0	16	8	0
	2	clout	Needles	0	0	20	0
	3	C	Hops	1	10	0	0
	15	C	Towe	5	0	0	0
	2	dozen	Urinals	0	0	20	0

The Bonaventure of *Olone*,[53] burden 50 tons, John Febraa master, to Toulon, 1st December 1600

John Febraa, *domicile unknown*, Merchant Stranger	10	M	Fish, Dry Newfoundland	50	0	0	0
	3	ton	Iron	24	0	0	0

The Roose of Lübeck, burden 60 tons, Henry Roosecke master, to Lübeck, 4th December 1600

Henry Roosecke, *domicile unknown*, Merchant Stranger	20	wey	Coal	6	13	4	0

The Jesus of Bristol, burden 14 ton, John Watts master, to Cork, 5th December 1600

Clement Tirrie & Edmund Pontche of Cork, Merchant Ind	1.5	dozen	Hats	2	0	0	0
	1.5	gross	Knives, Pocket	1	10	0	0
	1	gross	Knives (1*d.*)	0	10	0	0
	3	dozen	Knives, Prage	0	0	20	0
	6	pair	Stockings, Woollen	0	10	0	0
	1	piece	Jean Fustian *Cloth*	0	13	4	0
	6	gross	Points, Single Thread	0	0	10	0
	6	*unknown*	*Yellow Leather*[54]	0	5	0	0
	6	*dozen*	*Unknown, Peny*[55]	0	2	6	0

53 Possibly Ile d' Oleron, France.   54 TNA E190/1132/12 fo3r.   55 As above.

Merchant name	Qty	Unit	Commodity	£	s.	d.	f.
	3	lb	Girdles, Nob	0	2	6	0
	2	gross	Buttons, Silk	0	0	10	0
	12	gross	Buttons, Thread	0	0	10	0
	6	lb	Thread, Brown	0	5	0	0
	2	butt	Thread	0	7	6	0
	4	ream	Paper	0	13	4	0
	2	dozen	Wool Cards	1	0	0	0
	2	dozen	Padlocks	0	0	20	0
	6	gross	Points, Single Thread	0	0	10	0
	1	burden	Steel	0	5	0	0
	8	dozen	Tobacco Pipes	0	0	20	0
	8	piece	Inkle, Coarse	0	3	4	0
	12	lb	Thread, Packet	0	0	10	0
	8	lb	Glue	0	0	10	0
	6	lb	Candles, *Searing*	0	0	20	0
	2	lb	Fringe	0	3	4	0
	2	dozen	Glasses, Looking	0	0	20	0
	2	ream	Paper, Brown	0	3	4	0
	4	gross	Trenchers	0	3	4	0
	3	M	Tressels	1	0	0	0
	2	piece	Grey Frieze *Cloth*	2	0	0	0
	3	piece	Cotton Cloth	1	10	0	0
	20	yard	Cotton *Cloth*	0	8	4	0
	1	C	Argol	1	0	0	0
	2	piece	Raisins, *Great*	0	10	0	0
	6	yard	Cloth of Assize	0	0	0	0
	6	yard	Cloth of Assize, Kersey	0	0	0	0

The Dove of Bristol, burden 40 tons, Richard Parsons master, to Le Croisic, 6th December 1600

William Coole of Bristol, Merchant Ind	10	wey	Coal	3	6	8	0
	3	ton	Lead	24	0	0	0
	5	C	Fish, Newfoundland	2	10	0	0

The Bonaventure aforesaid, burden 50 tons, John Febraa master, to Toulon, 9th December 1600

Adrian Pierra of *Olen*, Merchant Stranger	10	M	Fish, Newfoundland	50	0	0	0
	7	C	Wax	21	0	0	0
	8	piece	Bay *Cloth*	16	0	0	0

The Sampson of Emden, burden 200 tons, James Boye master, to La Rochelle, 10th December 1600

Jasper Venzenden, *domicile unknown*, Merchant Stranger	40	wey	Coal	13	6	8	0

The Tobias of Lübeck, burden 60 tons, George Snore master, to La Rochelle, 10th December 1600

George Snore of Lübeck, Merchant Stranger	14	wey	Coal	4	13	4	0

Merchant name	Qty	Unit	Commodity	£	s.	d.	f.

The Beniamyne of London, burden 136 tons, William Rickes master, to La Rochelle, 18th December 1600

| William Ricks of London, Merchant Ind | 6 | ton | Lead | 48 | 0 | 0 | 0 |

The Beniamyne aforesaid, 20th December 1600

| Henry Adams of Bristol, Merchant Ind | 10 | ton | Lead | 80 | 0 | 0 | 0 |

The Marie of Roscoff, burden 30 tons, *Alien* Beizen master, to Roscoff, 20th December 1600

| Alan Beizen, *domicile unknown*, Merchant Stranger | 10 | M | Fish, Dry Newfoundland | 50 | 0 | 0 | 0 |
| | 3 | ton | Lead | 24 | 0 | 0 | 0 |

The Fawlcon of Millbrook, burden 23 tons, Thomas Searle master, to Bayonne, 22nd December 1600

| William Ellis of Bristol, Merchant Ind | 27 | C | Wax | 81 | 0 | 0 | 0 |
| | 2 | ton | Lead | 16 | 0 | 0 | 0 |

The Fawlcon aforesaid,

| John Trevile, *domicile unknown*, Merchant Ind | 4 | M | Fish, Dry Newfoundland | 20 | 0 | 0 | 0 |

The Marie abovesaid, 23rd December 1600

| Martin Scoriendo, *domicile unknown*, Merchant Stranger | 10 | M | Fish, Dry Newfoundland | 50 | 0 | 0 | 0 |
| | 3 | ton | Iron | 24 | 0 | 0 | 0 |

The Esperance of Ile d' Oleron, burden 37 tons, Daniel Angaball master, to Bordeaux, 23rd December 1600

| Daniel Angaball, *domicile unknown*, Merchant & Master Stranger | 6 | wey | Coal | 2 | 0 | 0 | 0 |

The Spedwell of Millbrook, burden 40 tons, Henry Warwiecke master, to Bayonne, 30th December 1600

John Barker of Bristol, Merchant Ind	6	ton	Lead	48	0	0	0
	8	M	Fish, Dry Newfoundland	40	0	0	0
	2	piece	Cloth of Assize	0	0	0	0
			Cloth of Assize, Overlengths	0	0	0	0

Merchant name	Qty	Unit	Commodity	£	s.	d.	f.

The Flower of St Malo, burden 60 tons, William Hamlyne master, to St-Malo, 3rd January 1601

William Hamline of St Malo, Merchant							
Stranger	20	ton	Lead	160	0	0	0

The John of St Malo, burden 45 tons, Phillippe Leasever master, to St-Malo, 3rd January 1601

Philip Leaffever of St Malo, Merchant Stranger	18	wey	Coal	6	0	0	0

The Spedwell of Millbrook abovesaid, 3rd January 1601

Hugh Pearde of Bristol, Merchant Ind	5	C	Wax	15	0	0	0

The Spedwell of Millbrook aforesaid, 5th January 1601

Thomas Anthony of Bristol, Merchant Ind	30	dicker	Skins, Calf[56]	150	0	0	0

The Greene Crosse of St Malo, burden 60 tons, John Byson master, to St-Malo, 7th January 1601

James Beaver of Guernesey, Merchant Ind	20	ton	Lead	160	0	0	0

The Spedwell abovesaid, 7th January 1601

William Coale of Bristol, Merchant Ind	3	ton	Lead	24	0	0	0
	3	M	Fish, Dry Newfoundland	15	0	0	0

The Dennis of Granville, burden 40 tons, Peter Dennis master, to Granville, 7th January 1601

John Devara, *domicile unknown*, Merchant							
Stranger	12	wey	Coal	8	0	0	0
	7	ton	Iron	56	0	0	0
	67	barrel	Fish, Herring White	33	10	0	0

The Huntsman of Amsterdam, burden 100 tons, Leonard Pettersonne master, to Vlissingen, 8th January 1601

Leonard Pettersonne, *domicile unknown*,							
Merchant Stranger	10	wey	Coal	3	6	8	0

The Recompence of St Malo, burden 50 tons, Brian le Dean master, to St-Malo, 9th January 1601

James Brian of St Malo, Merchant Stranger	10	ton	Lead	80	0	0	0

56 By virtue of a license grated to Arthur Andrea & Hieronimo Bassano, dated 15th September, in the 40th year of her majesties reign.

Merchant name	Qty	Unit	Commodity	£	s.	d.	f.

The Esperance of _Olderne_,[57] burden 27 tons, Daniel Augebawle master, to Bordeaux, 13th January 1601

Daniel Augebawle, _domicile unknown_,

Merchant Stranger	6	ton	Lead	48	0	0	0
	2	wey	Coal	0	13	4	0
	4	M	Fish, Dry Newfoundland	20	0	0	0
	2	kilderkin	Butter[58]	0	0	0	0

The Marie of Roscoff aforesaid, 13th January 1601

James Bevoyre of Guernesey, Merchant Ind	3	ton	Iron	24	0	0	0

The Recompence abovesaid, 14th January 1601

James Brian of St Malo, Merchant Stranger	2	ton	Lead	_16_	_0_	_0_	_0_

The Spedwell of Millbrook abovesaid, 15th January 1601

John Barker of Bristol, Merchant Ind	5	C	Wax	_15_	_0_	_0_	_0_

The Mathewe of Berkeley, burden 18 tons, John Smith master, to Cork, 16th January 1601

Stephen Skiddie of Cork, Merchant Ind	3	C	Hops	_1_	_10_	_0_	_0_
	3	gross	Trenchers	_0_	_2_	_6_	_0_
	2	dozen	Hemp	_0_	_4_	_2_	_0_
	6	lb	Thread, Packet	_0_	_0_	_10_	_0_
	2	dozen	Spurs	_0_	_6_	_8_	_0_
	1	dozen	Horse Combs	_0_	_0_	_25_	_0_
	0.5	gross	Combs, Wooden	_0_	_2_	_6_	_0_
	2	C	Taps and Cannells	_0_	_0_	_10_	_0_
	3	clout	Needles	_0_	_2_	_6_	_0_
	6	C	Awl Blades	_0_	_4_	_2_	_0_
	6	lb	Mail	_0_	_3_	_4_	_0_
	2	dozen	Stock Locks	_0_	_6_	_8_	_0_
	1	dozen	Crab Locks	_0_	_0_	_10_	_0_
	4	dozen	Brushes	_0_	_0_	_20_	_0_
	6	dozen	Tobacco Pipes	_0_	_0_	_10_	_0_
	1	nest	Boxes, Painted	_0_	_0_	_5_	_0_
	2	dozen	Girdles, Peny	_0_	_0_	_20_	_0_
	1	dozen	Girths	_0_	_3_	_4_	_0_
	6	M	Pins	_0_	_2_	_6_	_0_
	1	piece	Welsh Frieze _Cloth_	_1_	_0_	_0_	_0_
	2	M	Nails, Board	_0_	_6_	_8_	_0_
	2	M	Nails, Lath	_0_	_0_	_20_	_0_
	0.5	C	Orchil	_0_	_10_	_0_	_0_
	1	ream	Paper	_0_	_3_	_4_	_0_
	1	burden	Steel	_0_	_5_	_0_	_0_
	6	yard	Taffata _Cloth_	_0_	_10_	_0_	_0_
	6	yard	Cloth of Assize[59]	_0_	_0_	_0_	_0_

57 Possibly Ile d' Oleron, France. 58 Allowed for his provision. 59 This is an example of where the surveyor

Merchant name	*Qty*	Unit	Commodity	£	s.	d.	f.
	10	yard	Cloth of Assize, Penistone	0	0	0	0
	10	yard	Cotton *Cloth*	0	6	8	0

The Jennett of St-Jean-de-Luz, burden 70 tons, Peter Re Peraxa master, to St-Jean-de-Luz, 16th January 1601

Peter Repaxe & John Prestone, Merchants Stranger	8	C	Wax	24	0	0	0

The Longe Barcke of Hoorn, burden 100 tons, Cornell Anthonie master, to La Rochelle, 23rd January 1601

Cornell Anthonie, *domicile unknown*, Merchant Stranger	3	M	Fish, Newfoundland	15	0	0	0

The Reioyce in God of Bristol, burden 20 tons, John Hamptonn master, to Dublin, 29th January 1601

William Kitchinge of *Bigg Weare*, Co. Glouc., Gentleman Ind	12	pair	Milstones, small called dogstones	6	0	0	0

The Blessinge of God of Leith, burden 130 tons, David James master, to La Rochelle, 6th February 1601

James Dollinge, *domicile unknown*, Merchant Alien	6	ton	Lead	48	0	0	0

The Daniell of Bristol, burden 90 tons, John Johnsonne master, to Bordeaux, 12th February 1601

Robert Rogers of Bristol, Merchant Ind	4	ton	Lead	32	0	0	0

The Sanmalena of Brest, burden 70 tons, Asker Le Mayer master, to Brest, 16th February 1601

Asker Le Mayer, *domicile unknown*, Merchant Alien	5	wey	Coal	1	13	4	0

The Jelian of Bayonne, burden 30 tons, Francis Durand master, to Bayonne, 17th February 1601

Francis Durand of Bayonne, Merchant Alien	13	wey	Coal	4	6	8	0

The Marie of Jersey, burden 38 tons, John Roosecke master, to Jersey, 20th February 1601

James Beauvoyre of Guernesey, Merchant	4	ton	Lead[60]	32	0	0	0

includes goods paying other duties in his final values with goods paying poundage. **60** In bars.

Merchant name	Qty	Unit	Commodity	£	s.	d.	f.

The *Sanmalena* aforesaid, 20th February 1601

Asker Le Mayer, *domicile unknown*,							
Merchant Stranger	5	ton	Iron	40	0	0	0
	3	ton	Lead	24	0	0	0

The Jelian abovesaid, 21st February 1601

John Potter of Gloucester, Merchant Ind	5	C goad	Cottons (Woollen Cloth)	16	13	4	0
	8	piece	Cloth of Assize, Devonshire Dozen	0	0	0	0
	5	piece	Cloth of Assize Cloth of Assize, Overlengths	0	0	0	0

The Reioyce in God abovesaid, 21st February 1601

John Burkeberie of Bristol, Yeoman Ind	5.5	C	Hops	2	5	0	0
	3	C	Raisins, of the Sun	2	10	0	0
	2	C	Raisins, Malaga	0	13	4	0
	2	lb	Wormseed	0	4	6	0

The Mathewe of Berkeley aforesaid, 24th February 1601

John Smithe of Berkeley, Merchant Ind	0.5	C	Sugar	1	13	4	0
	1	barrel	Figs	0	10	0	0
	1	piece	Raisins, *Great*	0	5	0	0

The James of Bristol, burden 18 tons, William Moore master, to Waterford, 26th February 1601

Jasper Buttler of Waterford, Merchant Ind	8	C	Oakum	2	0	0	0
	2	C	Hops	1	0	0	0
	4	gross	Knives (1d.)	2	0	0	0
	6	small	Skillets, Small	0	3	4	0
	5	M	Nails, Fourpenny	0	12	6	0
	2	dozen	Stock Locks	0	6	8	0
	1	dozen	Drinking Cans	0	0	10	0
	5	C	Taps and Cannells	0	0	20	0
	3	dozen	Cups, Wooden	0	0	20	0
	6	lb	Soap, Black	0	0	5	0
	2	lb	Starch	0	0	5	0
	2.5	C	Raisins, *Rotta*	0	16	8	0
	0.5	C goad	Cottons (Woollen Cloth)	1	13	4	0

The James aforesaid, 26th February 1601

Martin Archer of Kilkenny, Merchant Ind	2	C	Hops	1	0	0	0
	4	C	Oakum	1	0	0	0
	4	C	Raisins, *Rotta*	1	6	8	0

Merchant name	Qty	Unit	Commodity	£	s.	d.	f.

The Sanmalena aforesaid, 26th February 1601

Merchant name	Qty	Unit	Commodity	£	s.	d.	f.
Nicholas Melior of Brest, Merchant Alien	4	ton	Lead	32	0	0	0
	2	hogshead	Lime	0	12	6	0

The Sanmalena aforesaid, 27th February 1601

Merchant name	Qty	Unit	Commodity	£	s.	d.	f.
Asker Lemayre of Brest, Merchant Alien	5	ton	Lead	40	0	0	0

The Mathewe of Berkeley aforesaid, burden 18 tons, 27th[61] February 1601

Merchant name	Qty	Unit	Commodity	£	s.	d.	f.
William Coopienger of Waterford, Merchant Ind	4	C	Hops	2	0	0	0
	2.5	gross	Trenchers	0	0	25	0
	1	piece	Raisins, *Great*	0	5	0	0
	5	C	Taps and Cannells	0	0	20	0
	0.5	C	Sugar	1	13	4	0

The Sanmalena abovesaid, 28th February 1601

Merchant name	Qty	Unit	Commodity	£	s.	d.	f.
John Stinchcombe of Bristol, Merchant Ind	12	C goad	Cottons (Woollen Cloth)	40	0	0	0
	6	piece	Bay *Cloth*	12	0	0	0
John Meson of Brest, Merchant Alien	3	C	Soap	2	5	0	0

The Daniell aforesaid, 28th February 1601

Merchant name	Qty	Unit	Commodity	£	s.	d.	f.
John Barnes, *domicile unknown*, Merchant Ind	5	ton	Lead[62]	0	0	0	0

The Pearle of Le Conquet, burden 50 tons, John Bardicke master, to Le Conquet, 3rd March 1601

Merchant name	Qty	Unit	Commodity	£	s.	d.	f.
John Bardicke, *domicile unknown*, Merchant Alien	18	yard	Cloth of Assize	0	0	0	0
	2	piece	Cloth of Assize, Penistone Friezed	0	0	0	0
	3	piece	Cotton *Cloth*	3	0	0	0
	1.5	piece	Bristol Frieze *Cloth*	1	10	0	0
	4	piece	Wadmal *Cloth*	4	0	0	0

The Bonaventure of *Olone*, burden 50 tons, John Fevora master, to *Oldron*,[63] 4th March 1601

Merchant name	Qty	Unit	Commodity	£	s.	d.	f.
John Fevora, *domicile unknown*, Merchant Alien	5	ton	Lead	40	0	0	0
	5	ton	Iron	40	0	0	0

The Bonaventure aforesaid, 9th March 1601

Merchant name	Qty	Unit	Commodity	£	s.	d.	f.
Nicholas Buggens of Bristol, Merchant Ind	2	ton	Wood, Brazil[64]	0	0	0	0

61 The surveyor erronously records the date as the 17th February. It is recorded as the 27th in the controller account (T.N.A. E190/1132/12) 62 Custom & subsidy paid in the Consent on 26th September, and not transported. 63 Probably Ile d' Oleron, France. 64 Custom paid in the Marie of Brest, in from Cadiz, on the 7th of March last.

Merchant name	Qty	Unit	Commodity	£	s.	d.	f.

The Lyon of Barnstaple, burden 20 tons, Anthony Fishelee master, to Waterford, 12th March 1601

Merchant name	Qty	Unit	Commodity	£	s.	d.	f.
Peter Heden of Waterford, Merchant Ind	2	burden	Steel	0	10	0	0
	4	lb	Mail	0	0	20	0
	4	lb	Girdles, Nob	0	3	4	0
	4.5	dozen	Wool Cards, Old	1	10	0	0
	0.5	gross	Knives (1d.)	0	5	0	0
	0.5	C	Soap, Black	0	5	0	0
	0.5	C	Orchil	0	10	0	0
	0.5	gross	Trenchers, Common	0	0	5	0
	3	dozen	Playing Cards	0	5	0	0
	3	lb	Thread, Packet	0	0	10	0
	10	C	Oakum	2	10	0	0

The Lion abovesaid, 12th March 1601

Merchant name	Qty	Unit	Commodity	£	s.	d.	f.
John Sutton of Waterford, Merchant Ind	14	C	Oakum	3	10	0	0
	2.5	C	Orchil	2	10	0	0
	14	dozen	Wool Cards, Old	4	13	4	0
	7	C	Hops	3	10	0	0
	1	dozen	Serches	0	10	0	0
	2	ton	Iron	16	0	0	0

The Lion abovesaid, 12th March 1601

Merchant name	Qty	Unit	Commodity	£	s.	d.	f.
Patrick Sherlocke of Waterford, Merchant Ind	10	C	Oakum	2	10	0	0
	6	dozen	Wool Cards, Old	2	0	0	0
	2	gross	Knives (1d.)	1	0	0	0
	2	gross	Points, Single Leather	0	0	10	0
	2	gross	Lace, Statute	0	13	4	0
	3	lb	Girdles, Nob	0	2	6	0
	3	lb	Mail	0	0	10	0
	4	lb	Inkle, Coarse	0	0	20	0
	4	dozen	Girdles, Peny	0	3	4	0
	4	lb	Thread, Black & Brown	0	4	2	0
	0.5	gross	Gartering	0	3	4	0
	3	gross	Buttons, Glass	0	0	20	0
	2	C	Awl Blades	0	0	10	0
	3	dozen	Awl Hafts	0	0	10	0
	1	gross	Trenchers, Common	0	0	10	0
	10	M	Nails, Lath	0	8	4	0
	4	M	Nails, Fourpenny	0	10	0	0
	1	burden	Steel	0	5	0	0
	3	dozen	Playing Cards	0	5	0	0
	4	C	Taps and Cannells	0	0	20	0
	1	dozen	Serches	0	10	0	0
	0.5	C	Soap, Black	0	5	0	0
	0.5	C	Argol	0	10	0	0

Merchant name	Qty	Unit	Commodity	£	s.	d.	f.

The Nicholas of Milford Haven, burden 14 ton, William Kinn[ ] master, to Waterford, 12th March 1601

Merchant name	Qty	Unit	Commodity	£	s.	d.	f.
Thomas Fowler of Cashel, Merchant Ind	1	piece	Bristol Frieze *Cloth*	1	0	0	0
	1	piece	Cotton *Cloth*	1	0	0	0
	12	yard	Bay *Cloth*	0	10	0	0
	24	ell	Ozenbridge *Cloth*	0	6	8	0
	12	lb	Sugar	0	8	4	0
	3.5	dozen	Glasses, Drinking	0	0	20	0
	0.5	dozen	Brushes	0	3	4	0
	1	gross	Knives (1*d*.)	0	10	0	0
	2	ream	Paper, White	0	6	8	0
	2	dozen	Playing Cards	0	3	4	0
	2	dozen	Wool Cards, Old	0	13	4	0
	1	dozen	Hats, Childrens	1	0	0	0
	2	lb	Girdles, Nob	0	0	20	0
	2	gross	Trenchers, Common	0	0	20	0
	1	dozen	Cups, Wooden	0	0	10	0
	2	lb	Mail	0	0	20	0
	2	clout	Needles	0	0	20	0
	2	dozen	Taps and Cannells	0	0	10	0
	1	C	Awl Blades	0	0	10	0
	7	C	Oakum	1	15	0	0
	4	C	Hops	2	0	0	0
	1	gross	Points, Single Thread	0	0	10	0
	6	piece	Inkle	0	0	20	0

The Nicholas aforesaid, 12th March 1601

Merchant name	Qty	Unit	Commodity	£	s.	d.	f.
Simon Sawle of Cashel, Merchant Ind	2	piece	Frieze and Cotton *Cloth*	2	0	0	0
	1	gross	Lace, Statute	0	6	8	0
	3	lb	Mail	0	0	20	0
	2	gross	Trenchers, Common	0	0	20	0
	1	lb	Girdles, Nob	0	0	10	0
	6	dozen	Glasses, Drinking	0	2	6	0
	6	C	Oakum	1	10	0	0
	3	C	Hops	1	10	0	0
	1	dozen	Hats, Childrens	1	0	0	0
	1	gross	Knives (1*d*.)	0	10	0	0
	1	ream	Paper, White	0	3	4	0
	0.5	C	Soap, Black	0	5	0	0
	2	C	Taps and Cannells	0	0	10	0
	4	dozen	Cups, Wooden	0	3	4	0
	2	dozen	Wool Cards, Old	0	13	4	0
	1	C	Awl Blades	0	0	10	0
	1	butt	Thread, Black	0	0	25	0
	2	clout	Needles	0	0	20	0
	1	dozen	Spurs	0	3	4	0
	3	M	Pins	0	0	5	0
	16	lb	Sugar	0	10	0	0
	4	yard	Ozenbridge *Cloth*, Brown	0	0	20	0

Merchant name	Qty	Unit	Commodity	£	s.	d.	f.

The Nicholas abovesaid, 12th March 1601

Thomas Creighe of Cashel, Merchant Ind	2	piece	Frieze and Cotton Cloth	2	0	0	0
	10	yard	Cloth of Assize, Penistone	0	0	0	0
	10	yard	Bay Cloth	0	8	4	0
	6	piece	Hats, Childrens	0	10	0	0
	5	C	Oakum	1	5	0	0
	1	C	Hops	0	10	0	0
	1	dozen	Wool Cards	0	10	0	0
	0.5	dozen	Stock Cards	0	6	8	0
	2	dozen	Bibs	0	0	5	0
	0.5	gross	Knives (1d.)	0	5	0	0
	1	gross	Trenchers, Common	0	0	10	0
	2	lb	Mail	0	0	10	0
	4	pair	Spurs	0	0	15	0

The Nicholas abovesaid, 12th March 1601

Patrick Sawle of Cashel, Merchant Ind	3	piece	Frieze and Cotton Cloth	3	0	0	0
	1	piece	Cloth of Assize, Northern Dozen	0	0	0	0
	24	ell	Ozenbridge Cloth	0	6	8	0
	1	dozen	Candlesticks, Small	0	6	8	0
	1	butt	Thread, Black	0	0	25	0
	1	C	Orchil	1	0	0	0
	1	gross	Knives (1d.)	0	10	0	0
	1	lb	Thread, Brown	0	0	10	0
	4	dozen	Wool Cards, Old	1	6	8	0
	1	ream	Paper	0	3	4	0
	2	lb	Girdles, Nob	0	0	20	0
	2	C	Taps and Cannells	0	0	10	0
	3	dozen	Playing Cards	0	5	0	0
	2	gross	Trenchers, Common	0	0	20	0
	1	gross	Lace, Statute	0	6	8	0
	0.5	dozen	Stock Cards	0	6	8	0
	6	piece	Brushes	0	3	4	0
	2	dozen	Cups, Wooden	0	0	20	0
	12	C	Towe	4	0	0	0
	5	C	Hops	2	10	0	0

The Lion of Barnstaple, aforesaid, 13th March 1601

Richard Bircheley of London, Girdler Ind	6	C	Seed, Onion	10	0	0	0
	3	dozen	Thread, Fine Brown	1	10	0	0
	6	M	Needles, Yellow Band	1	0	0	0
	1	M	Needles, Spanish	1	13	4	0
	22	M	Needles, Jhus	3	10	0	0
	1	M	Needles, great Pack	0	16	8	0
	9.5	gross	Lace, Statute	3	3	4	0

Merchant name	Qty	Unit	Commodity	£	s.	d.	f.
	5.5	gross	Lace, Statute (fff?)	3	13	4	0
	1	gross	Cards	6	0	0	0
	2	piece	Coarse Fustian *Cloth*	1	13	4	0
	6	piece	Milan Fustian *Cloth* (ff?)	6	0	0	0
	3	gross	Gartering	1	0	0	0
	12	pair	Stockings, Cloth	1	0	0	0

The Marie of Brest, burden 50 tons, Gooldenhen Le Meyre master, to Brest, 18th March 1601

Gooldenhen Le Meyre, *domicile unknown,*							
Merchant Alien	14	wey	Coal	4	13	4	0
	4	ton	lead	32	0	0	0
	3	ton	Iron	24	0	0	0

The Marie aforesaid, 18th March 1601

Gooldenhen Le Meyre, *domicile unknown,*							
Merchant Alien	8	butt	Wine, Seck	0	0	0	0

The Good Lucke of Bristol, burden 18 tons, Robert Deniam master, to Cork, 19th March 1601

Nicholas Hellin of Cork, Merchant Ind	0.5	C goad	Cottons (Woollen Cloth)	1	13	4	0
	1	piece	Welsh Frieze *Cloth*	1	0	0	0
	1	gross	Trenchers, Common	0	0	10	0
	1	ream	Paper, Brown	0	0	10	0
	2	lb	Mail	0	0	10	0
	3	dozen	Combs, Wooden	0	0	10	0
	2	dozen	Girdles, Peny	0	0	10	0
	0.5	gross	Gartering	0	3	4	0
	2	butt	Thread	0	4	2	0
	1	dozen	Horse Combs	0	0	25	0
	6	C	Teazles	0	3	4	0
	1	barrel	Apples	0	3	4	0
	2	dozen	Tobacco Pipes	0	0	10	0
	1	gross	Knives (1*d.*)	0	10	0	0
	1	dozen	Penners and Inkhorns	0	0	20	0
	2	dozen	Taps and Cannells	0	0	5	0
	1	dozen	Hemp	0	3	4	0
	1	dozen	Glasses, Looking	0	0	5	0
	0.5	C	Soap, Black	0	5	0	0

The Lyon aforesaid, 19th March 1601

Josiah Kinge of London, Merchant Ind	2	piece	Coarse Grograine *Cloth*	4	13	4	0
	4.5	piece	Velvet *Cloth*	6	0	0	0
	22	pair	Hose, Worsted	5	10	0	0

Merchant name	Qty	Unit	Commodity	£	s.	d.	f.

The Good Lucke of Bristol, burden 18 tons, Robert Deniam master, to Cork, 19th March 1601

Merchant name	Qty	Unit	Commodity	£	s.	d.	f.
William Creighe of Cork, Merchant Ind	0.5	C goad	Cottons (Woollen Cloth)	1	13	4	0
	2	piece	Bristol Frieze *Cloth*	2	0	0	0
	3	gross	Trenchers	0	2	6	0
	3	ream	Paper, Brown	0	2	6	0
	2	lb	Mail	0	0	10	0
	5	dozen	Combs, Wooden	0	0	20	0
	1	burden	Steel	0	5	0	0
	2	dozen	Girdles, Peny	0	0	10	0
	0.5	gross	Gartering	0	3	4	0
	2	butt	Thread	0	4	2	0
	1	dozen	Horse Combs	0	0	25	0
	6	dozen	Tobacco Pipes	0	0	20	0
	1	dozen	Knives, Shoemaker	0	0	20	0
	1	gross	Knives (1*d.*)	0	10	0	0
	12	C	Teazles	0	6	8	0
	1	barrel	Apples	0	3	4	0
	2	dozen	Wool Cards, Old	0	13	4	0
	3	dozen	Penners and Inkhorns	0	2	6	0
	4	dozen	Taps and Cannells	0	0	10	0
	3	dozen	Hemp	0	10	0	0
	1	piece	Raisins, *Great*	0	5	0	0
	1	dozen	Glasses	0	0	10	0
	1	C	Soap, Black	0	10	0	0
	0.5	C	Orchil	0	10	0	0

The Good Lucke aforesaid, 27th March 1601

Merchant name	Qty	Unit	Commodity	£	s.	d.	f.
Nicholas Roche of Cork, Merchant Ind	1	piece	Bristol Frieze *Cloth*	1	0	0	0

The Good Lucke aforesaid, 27th March 1601

Merchant name	Qty	Unit	Commodity	£	s.	d.	f.
Nicholas Roche of Cork, Merchant Ind	12	yard	Cotton *Cloth*	0	6	8	0
	2	dozen	Hemp	0	6	8	0
	2	gross	Trenchers	0	0	20	0
	2	M	Nails, Board	0	13	4	0
	0.5	dozen	Saws, Hand	0	3	4	0
	5	lb	Mail	0	4	2	0
	2	lb	Wire	0	0	20	0
	8	M	Nails, Lath	0	6	8	0
	2	lb	Counters	0	0	20	0
	3	clout	Needles	0	2	6	0
	1	lb	Pile Weights	0	0	10	0
	1	C	Awl Blades	0	0	5	0
	2	dozen	Files, Small	0	0	10	0
	6	burden	Steel	1	10	0	0
	1	barrel	Apples	0	3	4	0
	8	C	Teazles	0	5	0	0
	0.5	C	Orchil	0	10	0	0
	1	barrel	Figs	0	10	0	0

Merchant name	Qty	Unit	Commodity	£	s.	d.	f.
	0.5	C	Raisins, *Great*	0	3	4	0
	1	C	Hops	0	10	0	0

The George Tasker of Milford Haven, burden 18 tons, George Tasker master, to Waterford, 27th March 1601

Richard Comberford, *domicile unknown*,

Merchant Ind	10	C	Towe	3	6	8	0
	4	C	Hops	2	0	0	0
	100	yard	Ozenbridge *Cloth*	1	0	0	0
	6	gross	Trenchers	0	5	0	0
	3	C	Taps and Cannells	0	0	15	0
	2	dozen	Cups, Wooden	0	0	10	0

The George *Tasker* abovesaid, 28th March 1601

Martin Archer of Kilkenny, Merchant Ind	4	C	Towe	1	6	8	0
	6.5	C	Hops	3	5	0	0

The Marie Gould of Gatcombe, burden 20 tons, Christopher Raie master, to Cork, 28th April 1601

Christopher Coomyn of Limerick, Merchant

Ind	5	C	Hops	2	10	0	0
	0.5	dozen	Stock Cards	0	6	8	0
	3	piece	Bristol Frieze *Cloth*	3	0	0	0
	1	dozen	Hats	1	0	0	0
	10	lb	Mail	0	4	2	0
	3	nest	Boxes	0	0	10	0
	6	clout	Needles	0	5	0	0
	6	gross	Trenchers	0	5	0	0
	6	lb	Girdles, Nob	0	5	0	0
	4	C	Taps and Cannells	0	0	20	0
	3	dozen	Stock Locks	0	10	0	0
	2	dozen	Plate Locks	0	5	0	0
	2	piece	Cotton *Cloth*	2	0	0	0
	5	ream	Paper	0	16	8	0

The Beniamyne of London, burden 130 tons, William Rixe master, to Cork, 6th May 1601

George Ketchemaye of *Bigg Weare*, Co.

Glouc., Gent*leman* Ind	14	piece	Milstones, small called dogstones	7	0	0	0

The Marie of Roscoff, burden 40 tons, Alan Bezian master, to Roscoff, 6th May 1601

Alan Bezian, *domicile unknown*, Merchant Alien	11	wey	Coal	3	13	4	0
	1	wey	Coal[65]	0	0	0	0
	4	ton	Lime	0	10	0	0

---

65 Custom exempt.

Merchant name	Qty	Unit	Commodity	£	s.	d.	f.

The Marie of Wexford, burden 9 tons, Thomas Busher master, to Wexford, 6th May 1601

Merchant name	Qty	Unit	Commodity	£	s.	d.	f.
Melcher Stafforde of Wexford, Merchant Ind	1.5	last	Lime	0	7	6	0
	8	C	Hops	4	0	0	0
	4	piece	Bristol Frieze *Cloth*	4	0	0	0
	3	dozen	Hats, Childrens	3	0	0	0
	2.5	C	Soap, Black	1	5	0	0
	3	dozen	Wool Cards, Old	1	0	0	0
	3	ream	Paper, White	0	10	0	0
	1	gross	Combs, Wooden	0	5	0	0
	4	lb	Girdles, Nob	0	3	4	0
	1	C	Wood, Brazil	1	13	4	0
	1	gross	Trenchers, Common	0	0	10	0
	1	gross	Knives, Pocket	0	10	0	0
	4	gross	Lace, Statute	1	6	8	0
	5	gross	Points, Thread	0	4	2	0

The Beniamyne aforesaid, 6th May 1601

Merchant name	Qty	Unit	Commodity	£	s.	d.	f.
John Fowens of Bristol, Merchant Ind	1	ton	Prunes[66]	0	0	0	0

The Peter of Dartmouth, burden 40 tons, Nicholas Malery master, to Rouen, 11th May 1601

Merchant name	Qty	Unit	Commodity	£	s.	d.	f.
Nicholas Buggens of Bristol, Merchant Ind	10	ton	Lead	80	0	0	0
	4	M	Hornes[67] and Glover Shredds	4	0	0	0

The Beniamyne aforesaid, 11th May 1601

Merchant name	Qty	Unit	Commodity	£	s.	d.	f.
George Skiddie of Cork, Merchant Ind	2	piece	Cotton *Cloth*	2	0	0	0
	6	dozen	Wool Cards	3	0	0	0
	0.75	C	Hemp	0	15	0	0
	4	ream	Paper	0	13	4	0
	2	ream	Paper, Brown	0	0	20	0
	2	gross	Trenchers	0	0	20	0
	1	gross	Knives	0	10	0	0
	6	dozen	Girdles, Peny	0	5	0	0
	4	dozen	Locks, Small Hanging	0	6	8	0
	3	dozen	Stock Locks	0	10	0	0
	2	dozen	Penners and Inkhorns	0	3	4	0
	6	piece	Inkle	0	6	8	0
	4	lb	Thread, Brown	0	3	4	0
	4	butt	Thread, Black	0	8	4	0
	12	lb	Glue	0	0	20	0
	6	lb	Fringe, Crewel	0	10	0	0
	12	M	Pins	0	5	0	0
	1	dozen	Hats, Childrens	1	0	0	0

---

66 Custom & subsidy paid in the Royal Defence, inwards, 22nd December, and now allowed. 67 Possibly shoe horns. The other item may be glovers clippings, or similar, which are found in the 1558 rates book at 30s per maund or fat.

Merchant name	Qty	Unit	Commodity	£	s.	d.	f.

The Guye of Le Croisic, burden 40 tons, John Foaker master, to Le Croisic, 12th May 1601

Merchant name	Qty	Unit	Commodity	£	s.	d.	f.
John Fowens of Bristol, Merchant Ind	4	ton	Lead	32	0	0	0

The Beniamyne abovesaid, 12th May 1601

Merchant name	Qty	Unit	Commodity	£	s.	d.	f.
David Lewis of Cork, Merchant Ind	12	yard	Coarse Cotton *Cloth*	0	10	0	0
	6	yard	Bristol Frieze *Cloth*	0	5	0	0
	1	ream	Paper	0	3	4	0
	3	ream	Paper, Brown	0	2	6	0
	1.5	dozen	Wool Cards, Old	0	10	0	0
	2	dozen	Stock Locks	0	6	8	0
	1	dozen	Girdles	0	0	10	0
	3	gross	Trenchers	0	2	6	0
	2	C	Hops	1	0	0	0
	12	dozen	Glasses, Drinking	0	6	8	0

The Elizabeth of Bristol, burden 18 tons, Thomas Boone master, to Cork, 22nd May 1601

Merchant name	Qty	Unit	Commodity	£	s.	d.	f.
John Arthur of Cork, Merchant Ind	70	yard	Coarse Penistone *Cloth*	0	0	0	0
	1	ream	Paper	0	3	4	0
	1	gross	Trenchers	0	0	10	0
	1	gross	Knives (1d.)	0	10	0	0
	1.5	M	Nails, Board	0	5	0	0
	1	M	Nails, Lath	0	0	10	0
	2	dozen	Girdles, Leather	0	0	20	0
	1	dozen	Cups, Wooden	0	0	10	0
	2	dozen	Hemp	0	5	0	0
	1	gross	Points, Leather	0	0	10	0

The Elizabeth aforesaid, 22nd May 1601

Merchant name	Qty	Unit	Commodity	£	s.	d.	f.
Edmund Gould of Cork, Merchant Ind	23	yard	Cotton *Cloth*	0	19	2	0
	0.5	piece	Bristol Frieze *Cloth*	0	10	0	0
	0.5	piece	Cloth of Assize, Kersey	0	0	0	0
	12	ell	Coarse Canvas *Cloth*	0	6	8	0
	6	lb	Thread, Brown	0	5	0	0
	6	lb	Thread, Coarse Coloured	0	5	0	0
	1	butt	Thread, Black	0	0	25	0
	1.5	gross	Combs, Wooden	0	7	6	0
	1	nest	Boxes, Painted	0	0	10	0
	6	piece	Hats, Childrens	0	10	0	0
	6	piece	Hats	0	15	0	0
	3	dozen	Books, Horne	0	0	20	0
	6	lb	Mail	0	3	4	0
	6	gross	Trenchers	0	5	0	0
	2	dozen	Stock Locks	0	10	0	0
	3	dozen	Bibs, Sucking	0	2	6	0
	0.5	dozen	Gartering, Coarse	0	0	20	0

Merchant name	Qty	Unit	Commodity	£	s.	d.	f.
	1.5	M	Nails, Board	0	5	0	0
	2	C	Hops	1	0	0	0
	0.5	C	Soap, Black	0	5	0	0

The Elizabeth abovesaid, 22nd May 1601

Merchant name	Qty	Unit	Commodity	£	s.	d.	f.
Edmund Mowrough of Cork, Merchant Ind	9.75	yard	Cloth of Assize	0	0	0	0
	0.5	piece	Welsh Frieze *Cloth*	0	10	0	0
	12	yard	Coarse Canvas *Cloth*	0	6	8	0
	4	yard	Levant Taffata *Cloth*	0	6	8	0
	0.5	piece	Osborne Fustian *Cloth*	0	6	8	0
	1	paper	Silk, Paris	0	10	0	0
	1	lb	Silk, Black Spanish	1	0	0	0
	1	gross	Inkle	0	6	8	0
	2	dozen	Spurs	0	6	8	0
	4	lb	Thread, Brown	0	3	4	0
	2	dozen	Hemp	0	5	0	0
	1	dozen	Parchment Skins	0	3	4	0
	2	dozen	Boxes, Painted	0	0	20	0
	6	dozen	Combs, Wooden	0	2	6	0
	2	butt	Thread, Black	0	4	2	0
	2	dozen	Books, School of Virtue	0	3	4	0
	6	pair	Hose, Woollen	0	10	0	0
	6	dozen	Tobacco Pipes	0	5	0	0
	4	lb	Girdles, Nob	0	3	4	0
	2	gross	Points, Thread	0	0	20	0
	1	dozen	Penners and Inkhorns	0	2	6	0
	1	dozen	Glasses, Looking (1*d.*)	0	0	10	0
	10	lb	Sugar	0	6	8	0
	2	lb	Starch	0	0	10	0
	2	lb	Thread, Packet	0	0	10	0
	1	gross	Lace, Statute	0	6	8	0
	2	C	Hops	1	0	0	0
	1	M	Nails, Lath	0	0	10	0
	2	dozen	Wool Cards	1	0	0	0
	0.5	gross	Knives (1*d.*)	0	5	0	0

The Pawne of Le Croisic, burden 16 tons, Peter Lucett master, to Le Croisic, 23rd May 1601

Merchant name	Qty	Unit	Commodity	£	s.	d.	f.
Peter Lucett, *domicile unknown, Master* Alien	5	wey	Coal	1	13	4	0
	4	piece	Bristol Frieze *Cloth*	4	0	0	0
	2	piece	Wadmal *Cloth*	2	0	0	0
William Coale of Bristol, Merchant Ind	3	ton	Lead	24	0	0	0
	10	piece	Bristol Frieze *Cloth*	10	0	0	0
	1	piece	Bristol Frieze *Cloth*[68]	0	0	0	0
	1	piece	Cloth of Assize, Kersey	0	0	0	0

68 Custom exempt.

Merchant name	Qty	Unit	Commodity	£	s.	d.	f.

The Guye aforesaid, 27th May 1601

Merchant name	Qty	Unit	Commodity	£	s.	d.	f.
John Foaker, *domicile unknown*, Merchant Alien	4	wey	Coal	1	6	8	0
George Lane of Bristol, Merchant Ind	8	C goad	Cottons (Woollen Cloth)	26	13	4	0

The Esperance of Roscoff, burden 60 tons, Alan Bezian master, to Roscoff, 28th May 1601

Merchant name	Qty	Unit	Commodity	£	s.	d.	f.
John Stinchecombe of Bristol, Merchant Ind	5	C goad	Cottons (Woollen Cloth)	16	13	4	0
Thomas Jewell of Bristol, Merchant Ind	5	C goad	Cottons (Woollen Cloth)	16	13	4	0
Alan Besian, *domicile unknown*, Merchant Alien	16	wey	Coal	5	0	0	0

The Peter of Le Conquet, burden 60 tons, Noel Tradicke master, to Le Conquet, 28th May 1601

Merchant name	Qty	Unit	Commodity	£	s.	d.	f.
Noel Tradicke, *domicile unknown*, Merchant Alien	10	wey	Coal	3	6	8	0
	1	wey	Coal[69]	0	0	0	0
	1	ton	Lead	8	0	0	0

The Clement of Bristol, burden 18 tons, John Smithe master, to Dublin, 29th May 1601[70]

Merchant name	Qty	Unit	Commodity	£	s.	d.	f.
George Catchemye of Bygge Weare, Co. Glouc. Gentleman Ind	15	pair	Milstones, small called dogstones	7	10	0	0

The Antlopp of Crail, burden 60 tons, Thomas Devonson master, to La Rochelle, 29th May 1601

Merchant name	Qty	Unit	Commodity	£	s.	d.	f.
Thomas Devonson, *domicile unknown*, Merchant Stranger	11	wey	Coal	3	13	4	0
	1	wey	Coal[71]	0	0	0	0

The Roebucke of Bristol, burden 16 tons, William Swanley master, to Waterford, 4th June 1601[72]

Merchant name	Qty	Unit	Commodity	£	s.	d.	f.
John White of Waterford, Merchant Ind	16	C	Towe	5	6	8	0
	1	paper	Silk, Paris	0	10	0	0
	2	butt	Thread, Black	0	4	2	0
	3	lb	Thread, Piecing	0	6	8	0
	1	piece	Fustian *Cloth*	0	15	0	0
	12	M	Beads, Bugle	0	3	4	0
	1.5	piece	Jean Fustian *Cloth*	1	0	0	0
	0.5	piece	Tufte Canvas *Cloth*	0	6	8	0
	30	ell	Packing Canvas *Cloth*	0	6	8	0
	1	lb	Combs, Bone	0	6	8	0
	2	dozen	Locks, *Small* Hanging	0	3	4	0

69 Custom exempt. 70 Interestingly, this ship and the following are omitted entirely in corresponding controller's account (TNA E190/1132/12) 71 Custom exempt. 72 In the controllers account (TNA E190/1132/12) this entry is dated 29th May.

Merchant name	Qty	Unit	Commodity	£	s.	d.	f.
	1	dozen	Books, Horne	0	0	10	0
	12	M	Pins	0	3	4	0
	3	dozen	Wool Cards	1	10	0	0
	3	dozen	Wool Cards, Old	1	0	0	0
	8	gross	Buttons, Small Thread	0	0	10	0
	2	dozen	Necklaces, Bugle	0	5	0	0
	4	dozen	*Sheres called forcepts?*	0	0	10	0
	20	ell	Holland *Cloth*	1	5	0	0
	6	piece	Inkle	0	5	0	0
	6	pair	Hose	0	4	2	0
	24	yard	Levant Taffata *Cloth*	2	0	0	0
	3.25	ell	Broad Taffeta *Cloth*	1	12	6	0
	1	gross	Gartering	0	6	8	0
	5	dozen	Thread, Packet	1	0	0	0
	0.5	C	Wood, Brazil	0	16	8	0
	1	dozen	Penners	0	0	20	0
	6	unknown	*Epedences*	0	0	20	0
	3	dozen	Books, Small for Children	0	5	0	0
	3	ream	Paper	0	10	0	0
	1	dozen	Gloves	0	5	0	0
	2	gross	Lace, Statute	0	13	4	0
	1	dozen	Serches	0	10	0	0
	4	dozen	Bibs, Sucking	0	0	20	0
	1	dozen	Hats, Black for men	1	10	0	0
	1	dozen	Hats, Childrens	1	0	0	0
	4	piece	Hats, Womens	0	13	4	0
	2	dozen	Starch	0	5	0	0
	4	gross	Trenchers	0	3	4	0
	1	C	Orchil	1	0	0	0
	8	dozen	Girdles	0	6	8	0
	0.5	C	Prunes	0	5	0	0
	17	dozen	Knives (1d.)	0	15	0	0
	2	lb	Thread, Brown	0	0	20	0
	2	nest	Boxes	0	0	10	0
	1	dozen	Hemp	0	2	6	0
	2	lb	Girdles, Nob	0	0	20	0
	4	dozen	Thimbles	0	0	20	0
	4	clout	Needles	0	3	4	0
	1	bale	Dice and Sannders?	0	0	20	0
	1	dozen	Parchment Skins	0	3	4	0
	1	piece	Bristol Frieze *Cloth*	1	0	0	0
	4	piece	Cotton *Cloth*, Dozen	2	0	0	0
	2	dozen	Combs, Wooden	0	0	20	0
	0.5	dozen	Stock Cards	0	6	8	0

The Gabriell of Bristol, burden 70 tons, Lewis Weaver master, to La Rochelle, 13th June 1601

Merchant name	Qty	Unit	Commodity	£	s.	d.	f.
John Barker of Bristol, Merchant Ind	6	ton	Lead	48	0	0	0
	5	dicker	Skins, Calf	25	0	0	0

Merchant name	Qty	Unit	Commodity	£	s.	d.	f.

The Marie of Marennes, burden 25 tons, John Harvey master, to La Rochelle, 13th June 1601

Merchant name	Qty	Unit	Commodity	£	s.	d.	f.
John Peroll, *domicile unknown*, Merchant Ind	4	wey	Coal	1	6	8	0
	5	ton	Lead	40	0	0	0

The Goodlucke of Bristol, burden 18 tons, Simon Bowman master, to Cork, 16th June 1601

Merchant name	Qty	Unit	Commodity	£	s.	d.	f.
John White of Limerick, Merchant Ind	1	piece	Grey Frieze *Cloth*	1	0	0	0
	1	dozen	Hats	1	10	0	0
	15	yard	Cotton *Cloth*	0	12	6	0
	1	C	Hops	0	10	0	0
	1	burden	Steel	0	5	0	0
	1	butt	Thread, Black	0	0	25	0
	1	lb	Thread, Piecing	0	0	25	0
	0.5	gross	Knives (1*d.*)	0	5	0	0
	2	lb	Mail	0	0	20	0
	10	lb	Sugar	0	6	8	0
	2	lb	Thread, Packet	0	0	10	0
	2	lb	Girdles, Nob	0	0	20	0
	2	gross	Trenchers, Common	0	0	20	0
	2	dozen	Glasses, Looking	0	0	10	0
	2	clout	Needles	0	0	20	0
	2	gross	Points, Thread	0	0	20	0
	2	C	Awl Blades	0	0	20	0
	2	dozen	Wool Cards	1	0	0	0
	1	dozen	Padlocks	0	3	4	0
	2	piece	Inkle	0	0	20	0
	4	gross	Buttons, Thread	0	0	10	0
Nicholas Everett of Limerick Merchant Ind	8	yard	Cloth of Assize	0	0	0	0
	1.5	dozen	Hats	1	10	0	0
	1	piece	Bristol Frieze *Cloth*	1	0	0	0
	20	yard	Cotton *Cloth*	0	16	8	0
	1	piece	Fustian *Cloth*	0	13	4	0
	4	pair	Stockings, Short Woollen	0	3	4	0
	1	butt	Silk, Paris	0	16	8	0
	2	butt	Thread, Black	0	4	2	0
	2	ream	Paper	0	6	8	0
	1.5	C	Hops	0	15	0	0
	10	lb	Steel	0	3	4	0
	1	gross	Points, Thread	0	3	4	0
	1	great gross	Buttons, Thread	0	2	6	0
	2	gross	Points, Thread	0	2	6	0
	10	lb	Hires/Hices?	0	2	6	0
	10	lb	Ginger	0	16	8	0
	0.5	gross	Knives (1*d.*)	0	5	0	0
	2	dozen	Locks	0	10	0	0
	2	lb	Girdles, Nob	0	0	20	0
	1	lb	Thread, Piecing	0	0	20	0
	4	oz	Thread, Sisters	0	3	4	0
	0.25	C	Currants	0	7	6	0
	0.25	C	Prunes	0	2	6	0

899

Merchant name	Qty	Unit	Commodity	£	s.	d.	f.
	10	lb	Sugar	0	6	8	0
	4	piece	Inkle	0	3	4	0
	4	lb	Thread, Packet	0	0	20	0
	1	gross	Buttons, Silk	0	0	20	0
	2	dozen	Glasses, Looking (ob.)	0	0	10	0
	1	dozen	Spurs	0	3	4	0
	4	dozen	Combs, Wooden	0	0	20	0
	1	gross	Lace, Statute	0	6	8	0
	0.5	dozen	Candlesticks, Small	0	0	20	0
	0.5	lb	Points, Silk Peny bredth?	0	5	0	0
	4	gross	Trenchers	0	3	4	0
Thomas Moolroney of Limerick, Merchant Ind	8	yard	Cloth of Assize	0	0	0	0
	1	dozen	Hats, Coarse	1	0	0	0
	24	yard	Cotton *Cloth*	1	0	0	0
	1	piece	Bristol Frieze *Cloth*	1	0	0	0
	0.5	piece	Cloth of Assize, Kersey	0	0	0	0
	1	butt	Thread, Black	0	0	25	0
	2	ream	Paper, White	0	6	8	0
	3	lb	Girdles, Nob	0	2	6	0
	2	lb	Thread, brown	0	0	20	0
	8	gross	Buttons, Thread	0	0	10	0
	4	gross	Buttons, Silk	0	0	20	0
	2	dozen	Crab Locks	0	3	4	0
	3	lb	Mail	0	2	6	0
	2	C	Hops	1	0	0	0
	1	C	Orchil	1	0	0	0
	4	gross	Trenchers	0	3	4	0
	2	dozen	Wool Cards	1	0	0	0
	1	lb	Combs, Bone	0	6	8	0
	2	lb	Thread, Piecing	0	4	2	0
	0.5	gross	Knives (1*d*.)	0	5	0	0
	2	oz	Thread, Sisters	0	2	6	0
	2	piece	Inkle	0	0	20	0
	3	dozen	Glasses (1*d*.)	0	0	20	0
	20	lb	Sugar	0	12	6	0
	0.5	piece	Fustian *Cloth*	0	6	8	0
	2	clout	Needles	0	0	20	0
	0.5	C	Soap, Black	0	5	0	0
	1	burden	Steel	0	5	0	0
	1	C	Awl Blades	0	0	10	0
	1	dozen	Penners	0	2	6	0
	3	lb	Thread, Packet	0	0	20	0
	2	gross	Points, Thread	0	0	20	0
			Various Small Triffles	1	0	0	0
Nicholas Reece of Limerick, Merchant Ind	6	yard	Cloth of Assize	0	0	0	0
	1.5	dozen	Hats	1	10	0	0
	20	yard	Cotton *Cloth*	0	16	8	0
	2	C	Hops	1	0	0	0
	1	piece	Bristol Frieze *Cloth*	1	0	0	0

Merchant name	Qty	Unit	Commodity	£	s.	d.	f.
	0.5	piece	Cloth of Assize, Kersey	0	0	0	0
	1	burden	Steel	0	5	0	0
	1	butt	Thread, Black	0	0	25	0
	4	lb	Girdles, Nob	0	3	4	0
	3	lb	Thread, Brown	0	2	6	0
	6	gross	Buttons, Thread	0	0	10	0
	1	gross	Knives (1d.)	0	10	0	0
	2	lb	Mail	0	0	20	0
	1	C	Orchil	1	0	0	0
	3	gross	Trenchers	0	2	6	0
	2	dozen	Wool Cards	1	0	0	0
	2	lb	Thread, Piecing	0	4	2	0
	0.5	lb	Combs, Bone	0	3	4	0
	4	oz	Thread, Sisters	0	3	4	0
	3	piece	Inkle	0	0	20	0
	2	dozen	Glasses, Looking	0	0	10	0
	25	lb	Sugar	0	16	8	0
	1	piece	Coarse Fustian *Cloth*	0	13	4	0
	2	clout	Needles	0	0	20	0
	2	C	Awl Blades	0	0	20	0
	3	gross	Points, Thread	0	2	6	0
	1	dozen	Crab Locks, *Small*	0	0	20	0
	4	gross	Buttons, Silk	0	0	20	0
	6	dozen	Towe	0	5	0	0

The Jonas of Bristol, burden 40 tons, Harry Ellis master, to La Rochelle, 18th June 1601

Merchant name	Qty	Unit	Commodity	£	s.	d.	f.
William Ellis of Bristol, Merchant Ind	2	ton	Lead	16	0	0	0
	2	dicker	Skins, Calf	10	0	0	0

The Mynikine of Bristol, burden 16 tons, William Browne master, to *Lafoyle*, 19th June 1601

Merchant name	Qty	Unit	Commodity	£	s.	d.	f.
Thomas Pitt of Bristol, Merchant Ind	2	tun	Wine, Canaries[73]	0	0	0	0
	2	tun	Wine, Gascoyne Broken	10	0	0	0

The Marie of Marennes aforesaid, 19th June 1601

Merchant name	Qty	Unit	Commodity	£	s.	d.	f.
Richard Teage of Bristol, Merchant Ind	3	ton	Lead	24	0	0	0

The Providence of Bristol, burden 40 tons, Edmund Johnes master, to La Rochelle, 20th June 1601

Merchant name	Qty	Unit	Commodity	£	s.	d.	f.
William Challender of Bristol, Merchant Ind	3	ton	Lead	24	0	0	0

The Lyon of Amsterdam, burden 100 tons, Isbrane Tizen master, to La Rochelle, 23rd June 1601

Merchant name	Qty	Unit	Commodity	£	s.	d.	f.
John Fowens of Bristol, Merchant Ind	10	ton	Lead	80	0	0	0
William Bigge of Bristol, Merchant Ind	2	ton	Lead	16	0	0	0

73 Custom and subsidy paid by Thomas Pitt in a ship called the Pelican of Barnstaple, 7th of May last and now allowed.

Merchant name	Qty	Unit	Commodity	£	s.	d.	f.

The Samuell of Northam, burden 12 tons, William Morcombe master, to Barnstaple, 25th June 1601[74]

Robert Aldworth of Bristol, Merchant Ind	2	piece	Cloth of Assize	0	0	0	0
			Cloth of Assize, Overlengths	0	0	0	0
	20	piece	Saye *Cloth*	20	0	0	0
	1	ton	Iron	8	0	0	0
	30	C	Soap, Black	15	0	0	0

The Elizabeth of Bristol, burden 40 tons, William Hill master, to Cork, 26th June 1601

Edward Everett of Limerick, Merchant Ind	2	C	Hops	1	0	0	0
	1	piece	Bristol Frieze *Cloth*	1	0	0	0
	10	dozen	Candle-Wicks	0	14	2	0
	4	gross	Buttons, Glass	0	0	20	0
	40	lb	Glue	0	5	0	0
	8	lb	Mail	0	3	4	0
	20	lb	Thread, Packet	0	8	4	0
	10	gross	Buttons, Thread	0	0	20	0
	4	dozen	Glasses (1*d.*)	0	0	20	0
	2	dozen	Snuffers	0	3	4	0
	6	dozen	Combs, Wooden	0	2	6	0
	8	piece	Horse Combs	0	2	6	0
	1	gross	Trenchers, Common	0	0	10	0

The Jesus of Bristol, burden 18 tons, John Flyn master, to *Knocknargus*, 27th June 1601

Thomas Pitt of Bristol, Merchant Ind	1.75	tun	Wine, Canaries[75]	0	0	0	0

The Grace of Bristol, burden 30 tons, Thomas Latymer master, to Waterford, 1st July 1601

Michael Archer of Kilkenny, Merchant Ind	22	C	Oakum	5	10	0	0

The Waspe of Bristol, burden 16 tons, John Grene master, to Waterford, 1st July 1601

John Simple, *domicile unknown*, Merchant Alien	22	butt	Wine, Seck[76]	0	0	0	0

The Grace of Bristol, burden 30 tons, Thomas Latymer master, to Waterford, 1st July 1601

John Symple, *domicile unknown*, Merchant Alien	5	butt	Wine, Seck[77]	0	0	0	0

The Elizabeth of London, burden 40 tons, William Hill master, to Cork, 2nd July 1601

Edmund Pontche of Cork, Merchant Ind	2	dozen	Wool Cards	1	0	0	0
	1	ream	Paper, Brown	0	0	10	0
	2	gross	Knives (1*d.*)	1	0	0	0
	2	gross	Trenchers	0	0	20	0

74 From there to be transported in any other ship or ships. 75 Custom, subsidy and impost paid in the Pelican of Barnstaple. 76 All duties were paid on the Antelope of Crail, 22nd of May, and now allowed. 77 As above.

Merchant name	Qty	Unit	Commodity	£	s.	d.	f.
	1	M	Teazles	0	6	8	0
	2	lb	Mail	0	0	10	0
	2	dozen	Graters, Small	0	0	10	0
	2	dozen	Flax	0	5	0	0
	2	dozen	Hemp	0	5	0	0
	2	dozen	Cups, Wooden	0	0	10	0
	4	dozen	Girdles, Peny	0	3	4	0
	4	M	Nails, Lath	0	0	1	0
	2	M	Nails, Board	0	6	8	0
	2	burden	Steel	0	10	0	0
	4	dozen	Glasses, Drinking	0	3	4	0
	1	butt	Thread, Black	0	0	25	0
	2	lb	Thread, Brown	0	0	20	0
	12	lb	Soap, White	0	0	20	0
	0.5	C	Hops	0	5	0	0
	2	dozen	Combs, Wooden	0	0	10	0
	0.25	C	Orchil	0	5	0	0
	0.25	C	Soap, Black	0	2	6	0
	4	dozen	Tobacco Pipes	0	0	20	0
	1	lb	Tobacco	0	3	4	0
	4	dozen	Knives, Pocket	0	6	8	0
	4	gross	Points, Thread	0	3	4	0
	2	lb	Girdles, Nob	0	0	20	0
	1	ream	Paper	0	3	4	0
	2	dozen	Girths	0	3	4	0
	1	gross	Girth Web	0	6	8	0
	2	gross	Buckles	0	0	20	0

The Sune of Bristol, burden 40 tons, Christopher Birckehead master, to Limerick, 3rd July 1601

Philip Roname & William White of Limerick, Merchant Ind	50	lb	Glue	0	5	0	0
	4	ream	Paper, White	0	13	4	0
	6	M	Pins	0	0	20	0
	4	M	Nails, Board	0	13	4	0
	4	gross	Taps and Cannells	0	0	20	0
	3	dozen	Spurs	0	10	0	0
	4	dozen	Bibs, Childrens	0	0	10	0
	6	dozen	Locks	1	0	0	0
	4	gross	Cutts	2	0	0	0
	1.5	gross	Trenchers, Common	0	0	15	0
	12	dozen	Glasses (1d.)	0	3	4	0
	4	ream	Paper, Brown	0	3	4	0
	0.5	C	Orchil	0	10	0	0
	0.25	C	Soap, White	0	3	9	0
	3	gross	Points, Single Thread	0	2	6	0
	20	lb	Soap, Black	0	0	25	0
	1.5	C	Hops	0	15	0	0
	1	C goad	Grey Cotton *Cloth*	3	6	8	0
	2	piece	Bristol Frieze *Cloth*	2	0	0	0
	4	pair	Tables	0	8	4	0

Merchant name	Qty	Unit	Commodity	£	s.	d.	f.
	4	dozen	Cups, Wooden	0	0	20	0
	0.5	ton	Iron	4	0	0	0

The Elizabeth of London, burden 40 tons, William Hill master, to Cork, 3rd July 1601

Merchant name	Qty	Unit	Commodity	£	s.	d.	f.
William Hill of Bristol, Merchant Ind	1	ton	Iron	8	0	0	0

The Speedewell of Millbrook, burden 40 tons, Henry Warren master, to Lantringuier in Brittany, 8th July 1601

Merchant name	Qty	Unit	Commodity	£	s.	d.	f.
Nicholas Wilkins of Plymouth, Merchant Ind	12	wey	Coal	4	0	0	0
	4[78]	ton	Iron	32	0	0	0

The Marie of Northam, burden 10 tons, William Westicoate master, to Barnstaple, 8th July 1601

Merchant name	Qty	Unit	Commodity	£	s.	d.	f.
Robert Aldworthe of Bristol, Merchant Ind	3	piece	Cloth of Assize[79]	0	0	0	0
			Cloth of Assize, Overlengths	0	0	0	0

The Trynitie of Kinsale, burden 20 tons, Jordan Rooche master, to Cork, 8th July 1601

Merchant name	Qty	Unit	Commodity	£	s.	d.	f.
Dominic Rooche of Kinsale, Merchant Ind	4	dozen	Wool Cards	2	0	0	0
	5	C	Hops	2	10	0	0
	1	dozen	Hats, Childrens	1	0	0	0
	1	dozen	Hats	1	10	0	0
	10	yard	Cloth of Assize	0	0	0	0
	2	piece	Bristol Frieze *Cloth*	2	0	0	0
	12	yard	Cloth of Assize, Penistone	0	0	0	0
	20	yard	Cotton *Cloth*	0	15	0	0
	40	yard	Bay *Cloth*	1	13	4	0
	5	gross	Trenchers	0	4	2	0
	4	dozen	Hemp	0	10	0	0
	6	ream	Paper, Brown	0	5	0	0
	6	lb	Thread, Packet	0	3	4	0
	3	dozen	Spurs	0	10	0	0
	1	dozen	Horse Combs	0	0	25	0
	1	gross	Combs, Wooden	0	5	0	0
	2	C	Taps and Cannells	0	0	20	0
	4	dozen	Bibs	0	0	20	0
	12	M	Pins	0	5	0	0
	6	dozen	Glasses (1d.)	0	2	6	0
	3	burden	Steel	0	15	0	0
	1	paper	Silk, Paris	0	10	0	0
	3	clout	Needles	0	2	6	0
	6	C	Awl Blades	0	3	4	0
	6	pair	Stockings, Woollen	0	6	8	0
	10	lb	Mail	0	5	0	0
	4	lb	Coarse Sadlers Fringe	0	6	8	0

78 The account lists 3 tons of lead but gives custom payment for 4 ton. The controller account confirms the error listing it at 4 tons of lead valued at £32.   79 From there to be carried in any ship or ships wharsoever.

Merchant name	Qty	Unit	Commodity	£	s.	d.	f.
	1	gross	Lace, Statute	0	6	8	0
	12	lb	Copperas	0	0	15	0
	4	dozen	Shoe Horns	0	0	20	0
	3	lb	Candles, *Searing*	0	0	15	0
	1	piece	Jean Fustian *Cloth*	0	13	4	0
	1	piece	Osborne Fustian *Cloth*	0	15	0	0
	1	dozen	Stock Locks	0	5	0	0
	1	dozen	Crab Locks	0	2	6	0
	4	piece	Brushes	0	0	20	0
	20	dozen	Tobacco Pipes	0	10	0	0
	1	nest	Boxes, Painted	0	0	10	0
	6	dozen	Knives, Pocket	0	10	0	0
	4	dozen	Girdles, Peny	0	3	4	0
	2	dozen	Girdles, Yellow	0	0	20	0
	2	lb	Wax, Red	0	0	20	0
	2	gross	Points, Thread	0	0	10	0
	2	gross	Buttons, Thread	0	0	20	0
	4	dozen	Thimbles	0	0	10	0
	2	dozen	Cups, Wooden	0	0	10	0
	1	lb	Thread, Coloured	0	0	20	0
	6	bale	Dice	0	0	20	0
	1.5	C	Orchil	1	10	0	0
	6	gross	Buttons, Hair	0	0	20	0
	2	lb	Thread, Brown	0	0	20	0
	2	butt	Thread, Black	0	4	2	0
	3	ream	Paper, White	0	10	0	0
	2	dozen	Books, School of Virtue	0	3	4	0
	6	piece	Inkle, Narrow	0	0	20	0
	12	piece	Parchment Skins	0	2	6	0
	1	dozen	Ink Horns	0	0	10	0
	1	dozen	Knives, Paring	0	0	20	0
	4	M	Nails, Board	0	13	4	0
	2	M	Nails, Lath	0	0	20	0
	6	piece	Girth Web	0	3	4	0
	0.5	dozen	Buckles, for Girths	0	0	10	0
	0.5	C	Alum	0	16	8	0
	0.5	C	Liquorice	0	5	0	0
	0.5	C	Currants	0	15	0	0
	0.5	C	Glue	0	5	0	0

The Trynitie aforesaid, 8th July 1601

Christopher Tirrie of Kinsale, Merchant Ind	2	piece	Bristol Frieze *Cloth*	2	0	0	0
	20	yard	Coarse Cotton *Cloth*	0	13	4	0
	1	piece	Coarse Canvas *Cloth*	0	10	0	0
	2	lb	Girdles, Nob	0	0	20	0
	4	gross	Points, Small Thread	0	3	4	0
	1	butt	Thread, Black	0	0	25	0
	1	lb	Thread, Brown	0	0	10	0
	3	gross	Buttons, Thread	0	0	15	0
	3	boxes	Combs, Wooden	0	10	0	0

Merchant name	Qty	Unit	Commodity	£	s.	d.	f.
	2	lb	Mail	0	0	25	0
	2	dozen	Padlocks	0	5	0	0
	1	dozen	Headstalls	0	10	0	0
	1	dozen	Spurs	0	3	4	0
	2	dozen	Horse Combs	0	4	2	0
	1	C	Awl Blades	0	0	10	0
	2	C	Needles, Spanish	0	0	20	0
	6	dozen	Hemp	0	15	0	0
	2	ream	Paper, White	0	6	8	0
	3	dozen	Wool Cards, Old	1	0	0	0
	6	gross	Trenchers, Common	0	5	0	0
	2	ream	Paper, Brown	0	0	10	0
	1	gross	Points, White Leather	0	0	10	0
	2	C	Hops	1	0	0	0
	3	dozen	Cups, Wooden	0	2	6	0
	3	dozen	Bibs	0	0	15	0
	1	dozen	Knives	0	0	10	0
	1	nest	Boxes, Painted	0	0	5	0
	1	dozen	Ink Horns	0	0	10	0

The James of Bristol, burden 18 tons, Walter Daniell master, to Cork, 14th July 1601

Merchant name	Qty	Unit	Commodity	£	s.	d.	f.
Francis Knighte of Bristol, Merchant Ind	1	ton	Iron	8	0	0	0

The Katherine of Youghal, burden 18 tons, James Griffith master, to Cork, 22nd July 1601

Merchant name	Qty	Unit	Commodity	£	s.	d.	f.
William Cheshill of Kilmallock, Gent*leman* Ind	1	ton	Iron	8	0	0	0

The James of Bristol, burden 18 tons, Walter Daniell master, to Cork, 22nd July 1601

Merchant name	Qty	Unit	Commodity	£	s.	d.	f.
Andrew Browne of Cork, Merchant Ind	1	C	Hops	0	10	0	0
	3	ream	Paper	0	10	0	0
	2	dozen	Hemp, Coarse	0	5	0	0
	1	lb	Senna	0	0	20	0
	6	dozen	Knives	0	5	0	0
	5	dozen	Knives (ob.)	0	4	2	0
	2	dozen	Girdles, Leather Peny	0	0	20	0
	1	dozen	Spurs	0	3	4	0
	1	M	Pins	0	0	5	0
	1	clout	Needles	0	0	10	0
	3	ell	Coarse Holland *Cloth*	0	5	0	0
	1	M	Nails, Board	0	3	4	0
	2	gross	Trenchers, Common	0	0	20	0
	2	dozen	Cups, Wooden	0	0	20	0
	2	lb	Seed, Fennel	0	0	10	0
	2	gross	Points, Single Thread	0	0	20	0
	2	gross	Buttons, Thread	0	0	10	0
	4	lb	Thread, Brown	0	3	4	0
	1	dozen	Ink Horns	0	0	20	0
	2	nest	Boxes	0	0	10	0

Merchant name	Qty	Unit	Commodity	£	s.	d.	f.

The Elizabeth of Tenby, burden 6 tons, Thomas Waters master, to Dublin, 31st July 1601

Thomas Colman of Dublin, Merchant Ind	3.5	ton	Iron	28	0	0	0
	18	cake	Pitch, Hearth	3	0	0	0
	6	C	Soap, Black	3	0	0	0

The Antlop of Crail, burden 60 tons, Thomas Devonson master, to La Rochelle, 1st August 1601

Thomas Devonson, *domicile unknown, Master*
Alien							
	6	piece	Bristol Frieze *Cloth*	6	0	0	0
	12	wey	Coal	4	0	0	0

The Peter of Milford Haven, burden 12 tons, John Devorex master, to Waterford, 3rd August 1601

Peter Heden of Waterford, Merchant Ind	8.5	C	Hops	4	5	0	0
	3.5	gross	Trenchers, Common	0	0	35	0
	5	dozen	Bibs	0	0	20	0
	1	C	Liquorice	0	10	0	0
	4	lb	Girdles, Nob	0	3	4	0
	2	dozen	Wool Cards, Old	0	13	4	0
	5	gross	Knives (1d.)	2	10	0	0
	5	ream	Paper	0	16	8	0
	1	M	Taps and Cannells	0	3	4	0
	2	gross	Girdles, Peny	1	0	0	0
	6	dozen	Shoe Horns	0	0	20	0
	1	gross	Girth Web	0	6	8	0
	2	gross	Girth Buckles	0	3	4	0
	4	dozen	Books, Horne	0	0	20	0
	6	piece	Mouce Snatches[80]	0	0	10	0
	6	lb	Thread, Packet	0	0'	20	0
	1	dozen	Playing Cards	0	0	20	0
	1	dozen	Penners and Inkhorns	0	0	20	0

The Mathew of Waterford, burden 18 tons, Laurence Talbote master, to Waterford, 3rd August 1601

James Lea of Waterford, Merchant Ind	7.75	C	Hops	3	17	6	0
	2	gross	Trenchers	0	0	20	0
	3	piece	Hats, Womens	0	10	0	0
	10	lb	Mail	0	4	2	0
	1	gross	Knives (1d.)	0	10	0	0

The Mathew aforesaid, 3rd August 1601

John Hackett of Waterford, Merchant Ind	2	C	Hops	1	0	0	0
	1	C	Liquorice	0	10	0	0
	1	gross	Knives, Single Pocket	0	10	0	0
	2	ream	Paper	0	6	8	0
	2	gross	Trenchers	0	0	20	0

80 Perhaps mouse traps.

Merchant name	Qty	Unit	Commodity	£	s.	d.	f.
	2	dozen	Penners	0	3	4	0
	1	burden	Steel	0	5	0	0
	1	nest	Boxes, Painted	0	0	10	0
	2	lb	Fringe, Coarse Crewel	0	3	4	0
	1	gross	Lace, Statute	0	6	8	0
	1	lb	Thread	0	0	10	0
	2	clout	Needles	0	0	20	0
	2	dozen	Cups, Wooden	0	0	20	0
	2	dozen	Wool Cards, Old	0	13	4	0
	2	C	Taps and Cannells	0	0	10	0

The Mathew aforesaid, 3rd August 1601

Robert Teewe of Waterford, Merchant Ind	3	C	Hops	1	10	0	0
	3	C	Combs (old?)	0	15	0	0
	2	dozen	Wool Cards	1	0	0	0

The Mathew aforesaid, 3rd August 1601

James Neale of Waterford, Merchant Ind	3.5	C	Hops	1	15	0	0
	2	gross	Trenchers	0	0	20	0
	4	lb	Mail	0	0	20	0
	4	piece	Hats, Coarse	0	6	8	0

The Peter aforesaid, 4th August 1601

David Neale of Waterford, Merchant Ind	10	C	Iron	4	0	0	0
	4	C	Hops	2	0	0	0
	4	ream	Paper	0	13	4	0
	2	dozen	Wool Cards	1	0	0	0
	4	gross	Points, Inkle	0	3	4	0
	3	dozen	Gartering, Manchester	0	5	0	0
	0.5	C	Soap, Black	0	5	0	0
	0.25	C	Alum	0	8	4	0
	2	dozen	Thimbles	0	0	20	0
	2	lb	Wax, Red	0	0	10	0
	1	dozen M	Pins	0	3	4	0
	1	burden	Steel	0	5	0	0

The Mathew aforesaid, 4th August 1601

John Sharpe of Waterford, Merchant Ind	7	C	Hops	3	10	0	0
	12	yard	Cotton *Cloth*	0	8	4	0
	8	pair	Hose, Short Childrens	0	6	8	0
	1	ream	Paper	0	3	4	0
	2	dozen	Knives (1d.)	0	0	20	0
	30	lb	Soap, Black	0	2	6	0
	6	piece	Hats, Childrens	0	10	0	0
	0.75	C	Lead, White	0	7	6	0
	6	*lb*	Serches	0	3	4	0
	0.5	dozen	Stock Cards	0	6	8	0

Merchant name	Qty	Unit	Commodity	£	s.	d.	f.

The True Love of New Ross, burden 12 tons, Mathew Howlinge master, to New Ross, 4th August 1601

Darby Keogh & Patrick Dowle of New Ross, Merchants Ind							
	6	C	Hops	3	0	0	0
	2	dozen	Wool Cards, Old	0	13	4	0
	0.5	dozen	Stock Cards	0	6	8	0
	2	gross	Trenchers	0	0	20	0
	2	C	Taps and Cannells	0	0	10	0
	1	gross	Knives (1d.)	0	10	0	0
	0.5	piece	Cotton Cloth	0	10	0	0
	3	dozen	Cups, Wooden	0	2	6	0
	2	lb	Thread, Black	0	0	20	0
	4	C	Camphor Wood	6	13	4	0
	0.5	C	Soap, Black	0	5	0	0

The Mathew aforesaid, 4th August 1601

James Hackett of Waterford, Merchant Ind							
	12	lb	Mail	0	6	8	0
	7.5	yard	Tufte Mockado Cloth	0	13	4	0
	1	dozen	Hats, Coarse	1	0	0	0
	2	lb	Seed, Fennel and Cumin	0	0	10	0
	12	piece	Stockings, Short	0	10	0	0
	2.5	gross	Knives (1d.)	1	5	0	0
	10	dozen	Girdles, Peny	0	8	4	0
	1	ream	Paper	0	3	4	0
	2	gross	Gartering, Norwich	0	13	4	0
	2	lb	Girdles, Nob	0	0	20	0
	1	lb	Thread, Raw	0	0	10	0
	40	yard	Sack Cloth	0	6	8	0
	2	C	Taps and Cannells	0	0	10	0
	1	gross	Inkle, Coarse	0	0	20	0
	2	butt	Thread, Black	0	4	2	0
	1	gross	Trenchers	0	0	10	0
	1	dozen	Lanterns	0	5	0	0
	1	dozen	Playing Cards	0	0	20	0

The Grace of Bristol, burden 30 tons, Thomas Latymer master, to Rouen, 7th August 1601

Nicholas Bogans of Bristol, Merchant Ind	10	ton	Lead, White	80	0	0	0

The John of Waterford, burden 16 tons, John Keren master, to Waterford, 7th August 1601

Nicholas Brennocke of Waterford, Merchant Ind	7	C	Hops	3	10	0	0

The Unicorn of Bristol, burden 130 tons, James Powell master, to La Rochelle, 10th August 1601

John Barker of Bristol, Merchant Ind	10	ton	Lead	80	0	0	0
	3	C goad	Cottons (Woollen Cloth)	10	0	0	0

Merchant name	Qty	Unit	Commodity	£	s.	d.	f.
The Unicorn aforesaid, 13th August 1601							
John Fowins of Bristol, Merchant Ind	6	ton	Lead	48	0	0	0
The Unicorn aforesaid, 14th August 1601							
Richard Tagg of Bristol, Merchant Ind	6	ton	Lead	48	0	0	0
John Aldworth of Bristol, Merchant Ind	1	ton	Lead	8	0	0	0
	3	piece	Cloth of Assize	0	0	0	0
			Cloth of Assize, Overlengths	0	0	0	0

The Marie Fortune of Bristol, burden 80 tons, William Browne master, to Cork, 14th August 1601

Merchant name	Qty	Unit	Commodity	£	s.	d.	f.
John Hopkins of Bristol, Merchant Ind	3	ton	Lead	24	0	0	0

The Daizey of Bristol, burden 30 tons, John Heughes master, to Cork, 14th August 1601

Merchant name	Qty	Unit	Commodity	£	s.	d.	f.
John Hopkins of Bristol, Merchant Ind	3	ton	Lead	24	0	0	0

The Unicorn aforesaid, 14th August 1601

Merchant name	Qty	Unit	Commodity	£	s.	d.	f.
Christopher Carie of Bristol, Merchant Ind	4	ton	Lead	32	0	0	0

The John of Waterford, burden 18 tons, Patrick Flaghey master, to Waterford, 20th August 1601

Merchant name	Qty	Unit	Commodity	£	s.	d.	f.
John Sutton of Waterford, Merchant Ind	2	piece	Bristol Frieze *Cloth*	2	0	0	0
	2	piece	Bay *Cloth*	4	0	0	0
	6	dozen	Wick Yarn	0	10	0	0
	9	C	Oakum	2	5	0	0
	3	C	Hops	1	10	0	0
	8	dozen	Wool Cards	4	0	0	0
	4	gross	Knives (1*d.*)	2	0	0	0
	8	dozen	Glasses	0	10	0	0
	1.5	C	Orchil	1	10	0	0

The Unicorn aforesaid, *20th August 1601*

Merchant name	Qty	Unit	Commodity	£	s.	d.	f.
John Whitesonne of Bristol, Merchant Ind	2	ton	Lead	16	0	0	0
John Barker of Bristol, Merchant Ind	5	ton	Lead	40	0	0	0

The Marie Busher of Waterford, burden 16 tons, James Baron master, to Waterford, 22nd August 1601

Merchant name	Qty	Unit	Commodity	£	s.	d.	f.
Robert Cramsburrowe of Waterford, Merchant Ind	4	C	Hops	2	0	0	0
	2	C	Orchil	2	0	0	0
	1	C	Soap, Black	0	10	0	0
	30	lb	Ginger	2	5	0	0
	0.5	C	Raisins, *Great*	0	3	4	0

Merchant name	Qty	Unit	Commodity	£	s.	d.	f.
	0.5	C	Wood, Brazil	0	16	8	0
	5	dozen	Wool Cards	2	10	0	0
	2	piece	Bed Tick	1	0	0	0
	0.5	dozen	Stock Cards	0	6	8	0
	1	gross	Knives	0	10	0	0
	1	gross	Lace, Statute	0	6	8	0
	30	ell	Canvas *Cloth*	0	10	0	0
	8	ream	Paper, White	1	6	8	0
	1	gross	Trenchers	0	0	10	0
	4	lb	Thread, Black and Brown	0	3	4	0
	7	lb	Mail	0	3	4	0
	6	lb	Thread, Packet	0	0	25	0
	2	gross	Points, Thread	0	0	20	0
	2	gross	Buttons, Thread	0	0	10	0
	6	piece	Hats, Childrens	0	10	0	0
	1	piece	Jean Fustian *Cloth*	0	13	4	0
	0.5	piece	Milan Fustian *Cloth*	0	5	0	0
	2	dozen	Books, Horne	0	0	10	0
	1	C	Awl Blades	0	0	5	0
	1	clout	Needles	0	0	10	0
	6	yard	Cloth of Assize	0	0	0	0
	4	ell	Towers Taffeta *Cloth*	0	16	8	0

The Marie *Busher* aforesaid, *22nd August 1601*

Merchant name	Qty	Unit	Commodity	£	s.	d.	f.
Robert Wealshe of Waterford, Merchant Ind	12	yard	Cloth of Assize	0	0	0	0
	3	dozen	Wool Cards	1	10	0	0
	24	lb	Thread, Packet	0	8	4	0
	1	C goad	Cottons (Woollen Cloth)	3	6	8	0
	4	gross	Trenchers	0	3	4	0
	6	gross	Points, Single Thread	0	5	0	0
	1	dozen	Stock Cards	0	13	4	0
	6	pair	Bellows	0	5	0	0
	1	ream	Paper	0	3	4	0
	0.5	C	Soap, Black	0	5	0	0
	1	dozen	Serches	0	6	8	0
	5	dozen	Glasses	0	4	2	0
	10	dozen	Pots, Stone Uncovered	0	6	8	0
	4	C	Towe	1	6	8	0
	5	C	Hops	2	10	0	0

The Marie *Busher* aforesaid, 22nd August 1601

Merchant name	Qty	Unit	Commodity	£	s.	d.	f.
Walter Rian of Kilkenny, Merchant Ind	2	C	Hops	1	0	0	0
	1	gross	Knives (1*d.*)	0	10	0	0
	3	dozen	Knives, Paring	0	7	6	0
	3	dozen	Cutts (*ob.*)	0	0	20	0
	3	dozen	Wool Cards, Old	1	0	0	0
	6	pair	Stock Cards	0	6	8	0
	2	gross	Trenchers	0	0	20	0

Merchant name	Qty	Unit	Commodity	£	s.	d.	f.
	6	pair	Bellows	0	5	0	0
	12	lb	Mail	0	6	8	0
	6	lb	Girdles, Nob	0	5	0	0
	2	clout	Needles	0	0	20	0
	12	knot	Wire, Virginal	0	0	20	0
	2	C	Chalk	0	0	20	0
	12	lb	Frying Pans	0	3	4	0
	1	dozen	Locks, Hanging	0	3	4	0
	6	piece	Horse Combs	0	0	20	0
	5	piece	Stock Locks	0	3	4	0
	3	piece	Locks, Small Spring	0	0	20	0
	9	piece	Handle Rings/Bolts/ Hinges	0	3	4	0
	1	ream	Paper, Brown	0	0	10	0
	0.5	C	Soap, Black	0	5	0	0
	0.25	C	Aniseed	0	6	8	0
	0.5	C	Prunes	0	5	0	0
	0.5	C	Raisins, *Great*	0	3	4	0
	0.25	C	Currants	0	7	6	0
	2	C	Wood, Brazil	3	6	8	0
	2	lb	Comfits	0	0	25	0
	12	yard	Coarse *Bailter* Cloth?	0	2	6	0
	6	dozen	Playing Cards	0	10	0	0
	1	dozen	Hats, Childrens	0	13	4	0
	1	gross	Gartering, Norwich	0	6	8	0
	1	dozen M	Pins	0	3	4	0
	1	lb	Fringe, Crewel	0	0	20	0
	3	lb	Wax, Red	0	0	20	0
	1.5	lb	Silk, Paris	0	10	0	0
	1	lb	Inkle, Coloured	0	0	20	0
	0.5	piece	Holmes Fustian *Cloth*	0	6	8	0
	1	gross	Lace, Statute	0	6	8	0
	1	ream	Paper	0	3	4	0
	1	butt	Thread, Black	0	0	25	0
	2	lb	Thread, Brown	0	0	20	0
	3	piece	Brushes	0	0	10	0
	2	dozen	Bibs	0	0	10	0
	2	C	Orchil	2	0	0	0
	0.5	piece	Holland *Cloth*	0	10	10	0
	0.5	piece	Jean Fustian *Cloth*	0	6	8	0
	40	yard	Cotton *Cloth*	1	13	4	0
	6	yard	Bay *Cloth*	0	5	0	0
	12	yard	Cloth of Assize, Hampshire Kersey	0	0	0	0
	20	yard	Grey Welsh Frieze *Cloth*	0	13	4	0
	8	yard	Cloth of Assize	0	0	0	0
	1	gross	Points, Single Thread	0	0	10	0
	2	dozen	Urinals	0	0	20	0

Merchant name	Qty	Unit	Commodity	£	s.	d.	f.

The Marie *Busher* aforesaid, *22nd August 1601*

Merchant name	Qty	Unit	Commodity	£	s.	d.	f.
Pierce Vyne of Waterford, Merchant Ind	0.5	C	Hops	0	5	0	0
	2	piece	Cotton *Cloth*	2	0	0	0
	2	gross	Knives (1d.)	1	0	0	0
	3	dozen	Girdles, Leather	0	2	6	0
	3	dozen	Padlocks	0	5	0	0
	4	dozen	Glasses, Looking (*ob.*)	0	0	20	0
	2	clout	Needles	0	0	20	0
	2	lb	Thread, Black	0	0	20	0
	2	ream	Paper, White	0	6	8	0
	4	lb	Thread, Packet	0	0	20	0
	2	burden	Steel	0	10	0	0
	2	dozen	Spurs	0	3	4	0
	1.5	lb	Silk, Paris	0	10	0	0
	3	gross	Points, Single Thread	0	2	6	0
	1	dozen	Hats, Coarse	0	13	4	0
	4	ounce	Saffron	0	3	4	0
	2	lb	Mail	0	0	10	0
	2	lb	Girdles, Nob	0	0	20	0
	6	dozen	Glasses, Drinking	0	3	4	0
	0.5	dozen	Stock Cards	0	6	8	0
	0.25	C	Soap, Black	0	2	6	0
	6	lb	Rice	0	0	20	0
	2	dozen	Penners and Inkhorns	0	3	4	0
	2	gross	Points, Thread	0	0	20	0
	2	gross	Gartering, Manchester	0	3	4	0

The Marie *Busher* aforesaid, *22nd August 1601*

Merchant name	Qty	Unit	Commodity	£	s.	d.	f.
Charles Strannge of Waterford, Merchant Ind	3	dozen	Bottles, Glass	0	5	0	0
	3	dozen	Wool Cards, Old	1	0	0	0
	6	gross	Trenchers	0	5	0	0
	2	dozen	Penners and Inkhorns	0	3	4	0
	3	ream	Paper, White	0	10	0	0
	6	piece	Horse Combs	0	0	25	0
	12	lb	Thread, Packet	0	4	2	0
	1	dozen	Books, Grammar	0	3	4	0
	1	dozen	Books, Cato and Pueriles	0	3	4	0
	1	dozen	Hats, Coarse	0	13	4	0
	1.5	C	Hops	0	15	0	0
	1	C	Orchil	1	0	0	0
	0.5	C goad	Cottons (Woollen Cloth)	1	13	4	0
	1	gross	Playing Cards	1	0	0	0
	1	dozen	Lanterns	0	5	0	0
	1	case	Glass	1	0	0	0
	0.5	C	Soap, Black	0	5	0	0

Merchant name	Qty	Unit	Commodity	£	s.	d.	f.

The Joseph of Bristol, burden 80 tons, Mathew Honywell master, to Livorno &Toulon, 25th August 1601

John Whitsone of Bristol, Merchant Ind	5	ton	Lead	40	0	0	0

The Joseph aforesaid, 25th August 1601

William Ellis, John Barker & Mathew Haviland of Bristol, *Merchants* and Company Ind	24	ton	Lead	192	0	0	0

The Lion of Barnstaple, burden 18 tons, John Woolsonne master, to Barnstaple, 25th August 1601[81]

George Standburie of Barnstaple, Merchant Ind	7	ton	Lead[82]	56	0	0	0
	10	C	Wax	30	0	0	0

The John of Waterford *aforesaid*, 25th August 1601

Robert Rooche of Limerick, Merchant Ind	6	C	Hops	3	0	0	0
	3	C	Orchil	3	0	0	0
	1	dozen	Hats, Childrens	0	13	4	0
	2	gross	Combs	0	10	0	0
	8	dozen	Glasses, Looking	0	5	0	0
	1	gross	Points, Thread	0	0	10	0
	2	gross	Lace, Statute	0	6	8	0
	2	dozen	Penners and Inkhorns	0	0	20	0
	2	dozen	Spurs	0	3	4	0
	2	lb	Girdles, Nob	0	0	20	0
	2	dozen	Girdles, Leather	0	0	20	0
	6	clout	Needles	0	5	0	0
	3	nest	Boxes, Painted	0	0	20	0
	3	piece	Chests, Small Painted	0	0	20	0
	3	dozen	Graters	0	0	10	0
	3	piece	Bristol Frieze *Cloth*	3	0	0	0
	1	piece	Tufte Canvas *Cloth*	0	5	0	0
	1	piece	Sack *Cloth*	0	6	8	0
	4	ream	Paper	0	13	4	0
	8	piece	Mailing Cord	0	3	4	0
	0.5	gross	Knives. Prage	0	8	4	0
	8	lb	Thread, Packet	0	3	4	0
	3	dozen	Crossbow Twyne	0	13	4	0
	40	yard	Cotton *Cloth*	1	13	4	0
	2	burden	Steel	0	10	0	0
	1	C	Soap, *Black*	0	10	0	0
	4	gross	Unknown	0	3	4	0
	4	C	Taps and Cannells	0	0	20	0
	3	dozen	Cups, Wooden	0	0	20	0
	1	dozen	Crab Locks	0	2	6	0
	6	piece	Lanterns	0	3	4	0
	2	dozen	Wool Cards	1	0	0	0

81 From there to be transported in any other vessel to St-Jean-de-Luz. 82 In sowes and bars.

Merchant name	Qty	Unit	Commodity	£	s.	d.	f.
	5	M	Nails, Lath	0	4	2	0
	3	lb	Mail	0	0	20	0
	1	dozen	Serches	0	6	8	0
	0.5	gross	Knives (1d.)	0	5	0	0
	3	piece	Brushes	0	2	6	0
	4	dozen	Bibs	0	0	20	0

The Daisie of Bristol aforesaid, 25th August 1601

John Hopkins of Bristol, Merchant Ind	9.5	dicker	Skins, Calf[83]	47	10	0	0

The Marie Busher aforesaid, 26th August 1601

Henry Ellis of Bristol, Merchant Ind	1	ton	Iron	8	0	0	0

The John of Waterford aforesaid, *26th August 1601*

Patrick Motheley of Waterford, Merchant Ind	2	C	Hops	1	0	0	0
	3	rande	Thread, Packet	0	0	20	0
	3	gross	Knives (1d.)	1	10	0	0
	1	M	Nails, Board	0	3	4	0
	5	M	Nails, Lath	0	4	2	0
	2	gross	Buttons, Thread	0	0	5	0
	1	lb	Silk Bredth, Peny ?	0	10	0	0
	1	lb	Thread, Piecing	0	0	20	0
	3	C	Taps and Cannells	0	0	10	0
	1	dozen	Locks, Small *Hanging*	0	0	20	0
	1	C	Liquorice	0	10	0	0
	1	lb	Mail	0	0	5	0
	1	C	Wood, Brazil	1	13	4	0
	1	gross	Points	0	0	10	0

The Joseph aforesaid, *26th August 1601*

Thomas Davis of Bristol, Merchant Ind	5	ton	Lead	40	0	0	0

The Unicorn aforesaid, 27th August 1601

Thomas White & Christopher Carie of Bristol, Merchant Ind	15	dicker	Skins, Calf[84]	75	0	0	0

The Gabriell of Bristol, burden 60 tons, Lewis Weaver master, to St-Jean-de-Luz, *27th August 1601*

Thomas Aldworth of Bristol, Merchant Ind	11	ton	Lead	88	0	0	0

The Daisie aforesaid, *27th August 1601*

John Hopkins of Bristol, Merchant Ind	3	ton	Lead	24	0	0	0
	1	ton	Sulphur	6	13	4	0

83 By virtue of a license granted to Arthur Andrean and Jeronymo Bazan, dated 27th August 1600. 84 By Bazans license aforesaid.

Merchant name	Qty	Unit	Commodity	£	s.	d.	f.

The Marie Fortune aforesaid, 27th August 1601

John Hopkins of Bristol, Merchant Ind	4	dicker	Skins, Calf[85]	20	0	0	0
	3	ton	Lead	24	0	0	0

The Grace of Bristol, burden 30 tons, Thomas Latymer master, to Cork, *27th August 1601*

Edward Didmister of Bristol, Merchant Ind	2	dozen	Bed Cords	0	10	0	0
	5	dozen	Wool Cards	2	10	0	0
	6	pair	Stockings, Woollen	1	0	0	0
	1	C	Currants	1	10	0	0
	1	C	Raisins, *Great*	0	6	8	0
	0.5	C	Soap, Black	0	5	0	0
	0.5	C	Hops	0	5	0	0

The Marie Busher aforesaid, *27th August 1601*

Philip Linche of Waterford, Merchant Ind	6	C	Hops	3	0	0	0
	1	C	Prunes	0	10	0	0
	4	C	Raisins, *Great*	1	6	8	0
	1.5	C	Soap, Black	0	15	0	0
	1	gross	Knives (1*d.*)	0	10	0	0
	12	lb	Girdles, Nob	0	10	0	0
	1	dozen	Spurs	0	3	4	0
	2	ream	Paper	0	6	8	0
	3	dozen	Wool Cards	1	10	0	0
	4	yard	Cloth of Assize	0	0	0	0
	3	piece	Bristol Frieze *Cloth*	3	0	0	0
	1	piece	Dornick *Cloth*	0	6	8	0
	80	goad	Cottons (Woollen Cloth)	2	13	4	0
	10	dozen	Glasses, Drinking	0	6	8	0
	1	C	Pots, Stone Uncovered	0	5	0	0
	1	C	Towe	0	6	8	0
	0.5	C	Hemp	0	10	0	0
	2.5	piece	Fustian *Cloth*	1	5	0	0
	1	great gross	Buttons, Silk	0	10	0	0
	1	great gross	Buttons, Thread	0	2	6	0
	1	role	Buckram *Cloth*	0	2	6	0
	36	piece	Crewel, Cadiz	0	15	0	0
	0.25	C	Wick Yarn	0	3	4	0
	6	lb	Thread, Bottom Packet	0	2	6	0
	2	butt	Thread, Black	0	4	2	0
	1	lb	Isinglass	0	0	10	0
	1	lb	Sandalwood	0	0	10	0
	1	lb	Turnsole	0	0	10	0
	1	C	Soap, White	0	15	0	0
	20	lb	Sugar	0	11	8	0
	2.5	C	Orchil	2	10	0	0
	12	pair	Stockings, Kersey	1	0	0	0
	1	lb	Silk Bredth, Peny ?	0	10	0	0

85 As above.

Merchant name	Qty	Unit	Commodity	£	s.	d.	f.
	2.5	dozen	Hats	2	10	0	0
	1	lb	Silk, Ferrett	0	6	8	0
	14	lb	Glue	0	0	20	0
	0.5	lb	Thread, Sisters	0	0	20	0
	6	lb	Sulphur	0	0	10	0
	6	lb	Seed, Cumin	0	0	10	0
	3	lb	Graines	0	0	10	0
	1	piece	Cloth of Assize	0	0	0	0
			Cloth of Assize, Overlengths	0	0	0	0

The Maie flower of Bristol, burden 100 tons, Edward Williams master, to La Rochelle, 28th August 1601

Thomas James of Bristol, Merchant Ind	10	ton	Lead	80	0	0	0

The Marie Fortune aforesaid, *28th August 1601*

Edmund Gaynforde of Bristol, Merchant Ind	1.5	dicker	Skins, Calf	7	10	0	0

The Elizabeth of Bristol, burden 40 tons, Andrew Davis master, to Waterford, 29th August 1601

Edmund Archer of Kilkenny, Merchant Ind	2	C	Prunes	1	0	0	0
	1	C	Rice	0	16	8	0
	1	C	Currants	1	10	0	0
	2	C	Raisins, *Great*	0	13	4	0
	2	C	Hops	1	0	0	0
	0.5	C	Soap, Black	0	5	0	0
	2	piece	Cotton *Cloth*	2	0	0	0
	6	dozen	Knives (1d.)	0	5	0	0
	1	gross	Points, Thread	0	0	20	0
	0.5	C	Aniseed	0	13	4	0
	0.5	piece	Jean Fustian *Cloth*	0	6	8	0
	1	ream	Paper, White	0	3	4	0
	1	butt	Thread	0	0	25	0
	0.5	piece	Osborne Fustian *Cloth*	0	5	0	0
	1	dozen	Gloves, Coarse	0	3	4	0
	0.5	lb	Saffron	0	6	8	0
	4	dozen	Wool Cards	2	0	0	0
	3	C	Awl Blades	0	0	25	0
	1	gross	Trenchers	0	0	10	0
	4	C	Taps and Cannells	0	0	20	0
	1	gross	Points, Leather	0	0	10	0
	1	gross	Buttons, Thread	0	0	5	0
	2	gross	Glasses (1d.)	0	8	4	0

The Unicorn of Bristol, burden 130 tons, James Powell master, to La Rochelle, *29th August 1601*

John Webb of Bristol, Merchant Ind	2	ton	Lead	16	0	0	0

Merchant name	Qty	Unit	Commodity	£	s.	d.	f.
The Providence aforesaid, 29th August 1601[86]							
David Rice of Limerick, Merchant Ind	4	C	Hops	2	0	0	0
	6	dozen	Wool Cards	3	0	0	0
	1	piece	Bristol Frieze *Cloth*	1	0	0	0
	20	yard	Cotton *Cloth*	0	16	8	0
	6	yard	Bay *Cloth*	0	6	8	0
	4	yard	Cloth of Assize	0	0	0	0
	6	piece	Hats	0	10	0	0
	4	piece	Hats, Childrens	0	6	8	0
	2	pair	Stock Cards	0	2	6	0
	6	dozen	Knives	0	5	0	0
	1	gross	Points, Thread	0	0	20	0
	2	gross	Points, Thread	0	0	20	0
	8	dozen	Glasses, Drinking	0	5	0	0
	5	dozen	Urinals	0	4	2	0
	3	pair	Stockings, Woollen	0	5	0	0
	2	lb	Mail	0	0	10	0
	1	M	Nails, Board	0	3	4	0
	6	lb	Thread, Packet	0	0	25	0
	1	dozen	Penners and Inkhorns	0	0	20	0
	14	lb	Currants	0	3	9	0
	12	lb	Glue	0	0	20	0
	1	ream	Paper, White	0	3	4	0
	1	ream	Paper, Brown	0	0	10	0
	6	piece	Horse Combs	0	0	15	0
	1	barrel	Apples	0	3	4	0
	0.25	C	Prunes	0	4	2	0
	1	butt	Thread, Black	0	0	25	0
	6	lb	Rice	0	0	10	0
	4	lb	Copperas	0	0	5	0
	2	lb	Galls	0	0	10	0
	0.5	burden	Steel	0	2	6	0
	1	lb	Ginger	0	0	20	0
	0.5	lb	Combs, Bone	0	3	4	0
	4	gross	Buttons, Thread	0	0	10	0
	2	gross	Buttons, Silk	0	0	10	0
	3	piece	Brushes	0	0	10	0
	0.5	dozen	Spurs	0	0	20	0
	3	gross	Trenchers	0	2	6	0
	1	dozen	Cups, Wooden	0	0	10	0
	1	nest	Boxes, Painted	0	0	5	0
	6	piece	Lanterns	0	3	4	0
	4	dozen	Combs, Halfpeny	0	0	20	0
	1	clout	Needles	0	0	10	0
	1	dozen	Shoe Horns	0	0	5	0
	4	pair	Bellows	0	0	20	0
	4	unknown	Sleek Stones	0	0	5	0
	1	dozen	Bibs, Sucking	0	0	5	0
	6	piece	Mantles, Dyed	1	10	0	0

86 The only other Providence recorded in this account is going to La Rochell and appears in June. The cargo and the merchants recorded here imply that this ship is definitely bound for Ireland. Therefore, either both the surveyor and controller accounts are missing an entry, or this ship is going to Ireland as well as Rochell.

Merchant name	Qty	Unit	Commodity	£	s.	d.	f.
The Marie Fortune aforesaid, 29th August 1601							
John Hopkins of Bristol, Merchant Ind	7	C	Currants[87]	0	0	0	0
The Elizabeth aforesaid, 29th August 1601							
Robert Lewis of Limerick, Merchant Ind	12	yard	Cotton *Cloth*	0	10	0	0
	10	yard	Bay *Cloth*	0	13	4	0
	0.5	piece	Fustian *Cloth*	0	6	8	0
	0.25	C	Prunes	0	2	6	0
	14	lb	Currants	0	3	9	0
	4	dozen	Wool Cards	2	0	0	0
	0.5	gross	Knives (1*d*.)	0	5	0	0
	1	dozen	Knives	0	0	20	0
	2	gross	Buttons, Silk	0	0	10	0
	0.5	piece	Cloth of Assize, Kersey	0	0	0	0
	2	C	Hops	1	0	0	0
	1	barrel	Onions	0	5	0	0
	2	butt	Thread, Black	0	4	2	0
	2	lb	Thread, Piecing	0	3	4	0
	2	gross	Trenchers	0	0	20	0
	2	dozen	Cups, Wooden	0	0	20	0
	6	lb	Thread, Packet	0	0	25	0
	8	lb	Glue	0	0	10	0
	1	dozen	Bibs	0	0	5	0
	0.5	C	Soap, Black	0	5	0	0
	1	dozen	Shoe Horns	0	0	5	0
	3	pair	Bellows	0	2	6	0
	2	piece	Brushes	0	0	10	0
	4	piece	Mantles, Dyed Frieze	1	0	0	0
	1	ream	Paper, Brown	0	0	10	0
	1	ream	Paper, White	0	3	4	0
	1	burden	Steel	0	5	0	0
	1	C	Taps and Cannells	0	0	5	0
	6	M	Pins	0	0	20	0
	2	clout	Needles	0	0	20	0
	2	C	Needles, Spanish	0	0	20	0
	1	dozen	Glasses, Drinking	0	0	10	0
	1	dozen	Spurs	0	3	4	0
	1	lb	Mail	0	0	5	0
	1	dozen	Girdles, Leather	0	0	20	0
	24	piece	Inkle	0	0	20	0
	2	gross	Points, Thread	0	0	20	0
	1	gross	Points, Leather	0	0	5	0
	6	lb	Copperas	0	0	5	0
	2	lb	Galls	0	0	5	0
	2	dozen	Combs, Wooden	0	0	10	0
	6	piece	Hats	0	10	0	0
	1	gross	Lace, Statute	0	6	8	0

87 Custom & subsidy paid inward on the Marie Fortune, 27th April 1601, and now allowed.

Merchant name	Qty	Unit	Commodity	£	s.	d.	f.
The Elizabeth aforesaid, 29th August 1601							
William Hallie of Limerick, Merchant Ind	3	dozen	Wool Cards	1	10	0	0
	3	dozen	Wool Cards, Old	1	0	0	0
	2	piece	Bristol Frieze *Cloth*	2	0	0	0
	16	yard	Coarse Cotton *Cloth*	0	6	8	0
	8	yard	Bay *Cloth*	0	10	0	0
	2	C	Hops	1	0	0	0
	4	piece	Hats	0	6	8	0
	7	piece	Hats, Childrens	0	10	0	0
	6	yard	Cloth of Assize	0	0	0	0
	2	burden	Steel	0	10	0	0
	2	nest	Boxes, Painted	0	0	10	0
	6	lb	Girdles, Nob	0	5	0	0
	7	dozen	Combs	0	3	4	0
	2	ream	Paper, White	0	6	8	0
	2	ream	Paper, Brown	0	0	20	0
	1	dozen	Spurs	0	3	4	0
	12	dozen	Knives	0	10	0	0
	2	lb	Coarse Fringe	0	3	4	0
	2	dozen	Penners and Inkhorns	0	3	4	0
	2	gross	Points, Thread	0	3	4	0
	8	lb	Thread, Packet	0	3	4	0
	4	piece	Inkle, Small	0	0	10	0
	0.5	piece	Fustian *Cloth*	0	6	8	0
	1	gross	Points, Thread	0	0	10	0
	18	bar	Steel	0	2	6	0
	2	dozen	Books, Horne	0	0	10	0
	8	M	Pins	0	0	20	0
	3	lb	Mail	0	0	20	0
	8	dozen	Glasses, Drinking	0	5	0	0
	12	lb	Soap, White	0	3	4	0
	0.5	C	Soap, Black	0	5	0	0
	0.5	C	Prunes	0	5	0	0
	4	lb	Serches	0	0	20	0
	6	lb	Sugar	0	3	4	0
	3	lb	Comfits	0	3	4	0
	2	dozen	Thimbles	0	0	10	0
	1	butt	Thread, Black	0	0	25	0
	1	C	Awl Blades	0	0	5	0
	0.5	M	Nails, Board	0	0	20	0
	1	M	Nails, Lath	0	0	10	0
	3	gross	Trenchers	0	2	6	0
	2	dozen	Cups, Wooden	0	0	20	0
	3	piece	Lanterns	0	0	20	0
	2	pair	Bellows	0	0	20	0
	1	dozen	Bibs	0	0	5	0
	8	lb	Glue	0	0	20	0
			Apothecary wares and other small triffles	0	20	0	0

Merchant name	Qty	Unit	Commodity	£	s.	d.	f.
The Providence aforesaid, 31st August 1601							
Nicholas Langton of Kilkenny, Merchant Ind	48	yard	Cloth of Assize	0	0	0	0
	3	piece	Cloth of Assize, Devonshire Dozen	0	0	0	0
	2	piece	Bristol Frieze *Cloth*	2	0	0	0
	48	yard	Cotton *Cloth*	2	0	0	0
	30	yard	Bay *Cloth*	2	0	0	0
	1	piece	Holland *Cloth*	1	4	2	0
	3	piece	Fustian *Cloth*	2	0	0	0
	2	piece	Buffin *Cloth*	2	0	0	0
	2	lb	Silk Bredth, Peny ?	1	0	0	0
	1	lb	Silk, Slewed	0	6	8	0
	6	gross	Buttons, Silk	0	2	6	0
	3	dozen	Hats	3	0	0	0
	56	lb	Sugar	1	13	4	0
	0.5	C	Rice	0	8	4	0
	1	C	Prunes	0	10	0	0
	0.5	C	Currants	0	15	0	0
	6	lb	Isinglass	0	0	20	0
	4	lb	Turnsole	0	0	20	0
	6	lb	Candy, White	0	5	0	0
	6	lb	Seed, Cumin	0	0	20	0
	3	lb	Senna	0	5	0	0
	4	ream	Paper, White	0	13	4	0
	1	gross	Knives (1d.)	0	10	0	0
	1	gross	Gartering, Norwich	0	6	8	0
	1	piece	Buckram *Cloth*	0	0	20	0
	2	gross	Lace, Statute	0	13	4	0
	4	butt	Thread, Black	0	8	4	0
	6	lb	Thread, Brown	0	5	0	0
	1	gross	Buttons, Thread	0	0	5	0
	1	dozen M	Pins	0	3	4	0
	3	lb	Inkle	0	3	4	0
	1	dozen	Caps, Monmouth	0	10	0	0
	3	lb	Combs, Bone	0	15	0	0
	2	lb	Fringe, Crewel	0	5	0	0
	12	dozen	Glasses (1d.)	0	4	2	0
	12	lb	Mail	0	6	8	0
	6	lb	Girdles, Nob	0	5	0	0
	1	M	Hooks and Eyes	0	0	20	0
	2	dozen	Spurs	0	6	8	0
	3	dozen	Wool Cards	1	10	0	0
	1	dozen	Stock Cards	0	13	4	0
	1	C	Towe	0	6	8	0
	4	C	Hops	2	0	0	0
	6	hogshead	Vinegar	3	10	0	0

Merchant name	Qty	Unit	Commodity	£	s.	d.	f.
The Providence aforesaid, 31st August 1601							
John Roothe of Kilkenny, Merchant Ind	1	bag	Feathers[88]	0	0	0	0
	9	ende?	Hops[89]	0	0	0	0
	80	yard	Cloth of Assize	0	0	0	0
	1	C goad	Cottons (Woollen Cloth)	3	6	8	0
	4	piece	Cloth of Assize, Devonshire Dozen	0	0	0	0
	6	dozen	Hats	6	0	0	0
	30	yard	Bay *Cloth*	2	0	0	0
	2	piece	Holland *Cloth*	2	8	4	0
	1	piece	Cambric *Cloth*	2	0	0	0
	1	piece	Lawn *Cloth*	2	0	0	0
	4	piece	Fustian *Cloth*	2	13	4	0
	1	paper	Silk, Spanish	2	0	0	0
	1	paper	Silk, Paris	0	13	4	0
	2	lb	Silk Bredth, Peny ?	1	0	0	0
	2	gross	Lace, Statute	0	13	4	0
	2	lb	Combs, Bone	0	10	0	0
	1	piece	Boultel Bewpers	0	4	2	0
	0.5	C	Sugar	1	13	4	0
	1	lb	Saffron	0	13	4	0
	12	lb	Comfits	0	12	4	0
	1	lb	Isinglass	0	0	10	0
	2	lb	Turnsole	0	0	10	0
	2	lb	Sandalwood	0	0	20	0
	2	lb	Candy, White	0	0	20	0
	2	lb	Brown Candy	0	0	20	0
	6	lb	Ginger	0	10	0	0
	2	lb	Pepper	0	3	4	0
	0.5	C	Raisins, of the Sun	0	8	4	0
	1	C	Prunes	0	10	0	0
	1	lb	Benedicts Laxative	0	2	6	0
	1	lb	*Electua* & Sugar of Roses	0	2	6	0
	9	C	Hops	4	10	0	0
	1	C	Steel	0	13	4	0
	24	dozen	Glasses	1	0	0	0
	0.5	C	Currants	0	15	0	0
	1	C	Wood, Brazil	1	13	4	0
	6	lb	Thread, Piecing	0	10	0	0
	6	ream	Paper	1	0	0	0
	6	butt	Thread, Black	0	12	4	0
	72	bale	Dice	0	10	0	0
	12	lb	Girdles, Nob	0	10	0	0
	12	gross	Buttons, Silk	0	10	0	0
	3	lb	Crewel	0	5	0	0
	1	lb	Thread, Coventry	0	0	20	0
	1	lb	Thread, Sisters	0	5	0	0
	6	lb	Thread, Outnal	0	6	8	0

88 No value or customs duty recorded.   89 As above.

Merchant name	Qty	Unit	Commodity	£	s.	d.	f.
	2	dozen	Gloves	0	6	8	0
	2	gross	Knives (1d.)	1	0	0	0
	4	dozen	Wool Cards	2	0	0	0
	1	dozen	Stock Cards	0	13	4	0
	1	C	Soap, Black	0	10	0	0
John Daniell of Kilkenny, Merchant Ind	72	yard	Cotton *Cloth*	3	0	0	0
	1	piece	Welsh Cotton *Cloth*	1	0	0	0
	12	goad	Cottons (Woollen Cloth)	0	15	0	0
	1	piece	Holland *Cloth*	1	4	2	0
	1	dozen	Hats, Childrens	0	15	0	0
	6	lb	Girdles, Nob	0	5	0	0
	2	gross	Lace, Statute	0	13	4	0
	0.5	lb	Silk, Black	0	10	0	0
	1	lb	Silk Bredth, Peny ?	0	10	0	0
	1	lb	Fringe, Crewel	0	3	4	0
	2	dozen	Gloves	0	6	8	0
	2	butt	Thread, Black	0	4	2	0
	4	ream	Paper, White	0	13	4	0
	1	gross	Gartering	0	6	8	0
	2	lb	Thread, Coloured	0	3	4	0
	6	lb	Thread, Brown	0	5	0	0
	3	lb	Thread, Crossbow	0	0	15	0
	1	great gross	Buttons, Silk	0	10	0	0
	2	great gross	Buttons, Thread	0	3	4	0
	1	dozen	Crab Locks, Small	0	0	20	0
	12	lb	Thread, Packet	0	4	2	0
	1	dozen	Horse Combs	0	0	25	0
	1	gross	Knives (1d.)	0	10	0	0
	2	gross	Points, Thread	0	0	20	0
	8	dozen	Glasses, Drinking	0	6	8	0
	2	lb	Inkle, Coarse	0	0	20	0
	4	C	Needles, Spanish	0	0	20	0
	1	C	Hooks, Fish	0	0	10	0
	1	piece	Coarse Sack *Cloth*	0	6	8	0
	3	dozen	Bibs	0	0	10	0
	6	C	Taps and Cannells	0	0	20	0
	4	lb	Thread, Shoemakers	0	3	4	0
	0.5	C	Soap, Black	0	5	0	0
	2	dozen	Needle Cases	0	0	5	0
	4	dozen	Wool Cards	2	0	0	0
	4	gross	Trenchers	0	3	4	0
	1.5	C	Hops	0	15	0	0
	4	pair	Bellows	0	0	20	0

The Providence aforesaid, *31st August 1601*

James Bryne of Kilkenny, Merchant Ind	4	C	Hops	2	0	0	0
	1	gross	Knives (1d.)	0	10	0	0
	6	lb	Girdles, Nob	0	5	0	0
	2	gross	Lace, Statute	0	13	4	0
	1	gross	Girdles, Leather Peny	0	10	0	0

923

Merchant name	Qty	Unit	Commodity	£	s.	d.	f.
	3	dozen	Ribbon, Check	0	0	20	0
	1	piece	Holland *Cloth*	1	4	2	0
	50	yard	Welsh Cotton *Cloth*	1	13	4	0
	12	yard	Cloth of Assize, Northern	0	0	0	0
	6	ream	Paper, White	1	0	0	0
	1.5	C	Raisins, *Great*	0	10	0	0
	2	dozen	Wool Cards	1	0	0	0
	2	gross	Trenchers, Common	0	0	20	0
	12	dozen	Glasses, Drinking	0	10	0	0
	1	C	Soap, Black	0	10	0	0
	6	gross	Points, Thread	0	5	0	0

The Providence aforesaid, *31st August 1601*

	Qty	Unit	Commodity	£	s.	d.	f.
Garrett Wale of Kilkenny, Merchant Ind	8.5	C	Hops	4	5	0	0
	3	dozen	Wool Cards	1	10	0	0
	2	ream	Paper, White	0	6	8	0
	4	ream	Paper, Brown	0	3	4	0
	6	dozen	Knives	0	5	0	0
	1	burden	Steel	0	5	0	0
	12	lb	Thread, Packet	0	4	2	0
	2	clout	Needles	0	0	10	0
	6	dozen	Bibs	0	0	20	0
	6	gross	Trenchers, Common	0	5	0	0

The Roase of Bristol, burden 20 tons, Christopher Tailor master, to New Ross, 31st August 1601

	Qty	Unit	Commodity	£	s.	d.	f.
Thomas Fowlowe of Waterford, Merchant Ind	2	lb	Girdles, Nob	0	0	20	0
	1	gross	Gartering	0	6	8	0
	1	gross	Knives (1*d.*)	0	10	0	0
	4	ream	Paper, White	0	13	4	0
	2	lb	Thread, Coloured	0	3	4	0
	2	piece	Dishes, Iron chafing	0	0	20	0
	6	dozen	Girdles, Peny	0	5	0	0
	6	piece	Hats	0	10	0	0
	20	lb	Sugar	0	12	4	0
	10	lb	Seed, Cumin	0	2	6	0
	1	gross	Points, Thread	0	0	10	0
	3	dozen	Cups, Wooden	0	2	6	0
	4	lb	Mail	0	3	4	0
	2	clout	Needles	0	0	20	0
	1	dozen	Spurs	0	3	4	0
	6	piece	Horse Combs	0	0	15	0
	2	gross	Trenchers, Common	0	0	20	0
	4	dozen	Wool Cards	2	0	0	0
	4	C	Taps and Cannells	0	0	20	0
	4	dozen	Cups, Earthen	0	0	20	0
	2	burden	Steel	0	10	0	0
	4	dicker	Bracelets	0	0	20	0
	0.5	gross	Lace, Statute	0	3	4	0

Merchant name	Qty	Unit	Commodity	£	s.	d.	f.
	1	dozen	Crab Locks, *Small*	0	0	20	0
	6	lb	Thread, Packet	0	0	25	0
	3	dozen	Glasses, Drinking	0	2	6	0
	2	C	Towe	0	13	4	0
	1.5	C	Orchil	1	10	0	0
	1	C	Wood, Brazil	1	13	4	0
	1	dozen	Serches	0	6	8	0
	1	pipe	Iron	4	0	0	0
	2	piece	Grey Frieze *Cloth*	2	0	0	0
	24	yard	Grey Cotton *Cloth*	0	16	8	0
	12	yard	Bay *Cloth*	0	16	8	0
	12	yard	Cloth of Assize, Kersey	0	0	0	0
	0.5	C	Liquorice	0	5	0	0
Simon Sawle of Cashel, Merchant Ind	2	C	Hops	1	0	0	0
	3	dozen	Wool Cards	1	10	0	0
	1	gross	Lace, Statute	0	6	8	0
	6	*lb*	Serches	0	3	4	0
	6	piece	Hats, Childrens	0	6	8	0
	6	dozen	Knives (1*d.*)	0	5	0	0
	12	piece	Candlesticks, Small Brass	0	10	0	0
	2	dozen	Horse Combs	0	4	2	0
	1	dozen	Spurs	0	3	4	0
	1	piece	Grey Frieze *Cloth*	1	0	0	0
	1	piece	Cotton *Cloth*	1	0	0	0
	1	gross	Trenchers, Common	0	0	10	0
	10	yard	Bay *Cloth*	0	13	4	0
	3	dozen	Cups, Wooden	0	3	4	0
	6	dozen	Glasses, Drinking	0	5	0	0
	12	lb	Thread, Packet	0	4	2	0
	10	C	Iron	4	0	0	0
	1	ream	Paper, White	0	3	4	0
	0.25	C	Orchil	0	5	0	0

The Roase aforesaid, 31st August 1601

John Butler of New Ross, Merchant Ind	3	C	Hops	1	10	0	0
	20	yard	Cloth of Assize	0	0	0	0
	14	yard	Cotton *Cloth*	0	10	0	0
	20	yard	Bay *Cloth*	0	13	4	0
	2	piece	Grey Frieze *Cloth*	2	0	0	0
	1	piece	Sack *Cloth*	0	6	8	0
	0.5	piece	Fustian *Cloth*	0	6	8	0
	1	dozen	Hats	1	0	0	0
	8	ream	Paper, White	1	6	8	0
	2	gross	Lace, Statute	0	13	4	0
	2	dozen	Ink Horns	0	0	20	0
	6	pair	Stockings, Short	0	10	0	0
	3	dozen	Thread, Packet	0	12	4	0
	6	lb	Thread, Brown	0	5	0	0
	2	butt	Thread, Black	0	2	6	0
	1	gross	Gartering	0	6	8	0

Merchant name	Qty	Unit	Commodity	£	s.	d.	f.
	2	gross	Points, Thread	0	0	20	0
	2	dozen	Playing Cards	0	3	4	0
	2	dozen	Wool Cards	1	0	0	0
	2	dozen	Manchester Check Cloth	0	3	4	0
	2	lb	Girdles, Nob	0	0	20	0
	6	piece	Inkle	0	3	4	0
	0.5	C	Liquorice	0	5	0	0
	0.5	C	Orchil	0	10	0	0
	0.5	C	Soap, Black	0	5	0	0
	2	M	Nails, Lath	0	0	20	0
	5	C	Taps and Cannells	0	2	6	0
	0.25	C	Rice	0	4	2	0
	14	lb	Currants	0	3	9	0
	0.25	C	Raisins, *Great*	0	2	6	0
	1	C	Prunes	0	10	0	0
	6	dozen	Glasses and Stone Pots	0	10	0	0
	3	gross	Trenchers	0	2	6	0

The Roase aforesaid, 31st August 1601

James Hoare of New Ross, Merchant Ind	3	dozen	Wool Cards, Old	1	0	0	0
	1	dozen	Hemp	0	2	6	0
	9	pair	Stock Cards	0	10	0	0
	1	dozen	Flax	0	2	6	0
	10	dozen	Glasses, Drinking	0	8	4	0
	1	dozen	Brushes	0	0	20	0
	1	burden	Steel	0	5	0	0
	3	dozen	Stock Locks	0	10	0	0
	6	dozen	Knives	0	5	0	0
	9	dozen	Lace, Statute	0	5	0	0

The Roase aforesaid, 31st August 1601

James Rian of New Ross, Merchant Ind	12	yard	Cloth of Assize	0	0	0	0
	40	goad	Cottons (Woollen Cloth)	1	6	8	0
	1	piece	Cloth of Assize, Kersey	0	0	0	0
	2	dozen	Hats	2	0	0	0
	1	piece	Holland *Cloth*	1	4	2	0
	1	piece	Fustian *Cloth*	0	13	4	0
	6	lb	Girdles, Nob	0	5	0	0
	3.25	gross	Laces	0	0	10	0
	4	ream	Paper, White	0	13	4	0
	1	butt	Thread	0	0	25	0
	1	gross	Buttons, Thread	0	0	10	0
	6	lb	Mail	0	3	4	0
	1	gross	Trenchers, Common	0	0	10	0
	1	C	Raisins, *Great*	0	6	8	0
	0.5	C	Prunes	0	5	0	0
	6	dozen	Glasses (1d.)	0	0	25	0

Merchant name	Qty	Unit	Commodity	£	s.	d.	f.
	3	C	Hops	1	10	0	0
	0.25	C	Alum	0	8	4	0
	0.25	C	Rice	0	4	2	0
	3	dozen	Knives	0	2	6	0
Mark Dormar of New Ross, Merchant Ind	1	C	Liquorice	0	10	0	0
	2	C	Hops	1	0	0	0
	0.5	C	Wood, Brazil	0	16	8	0
	0.25	c	Aniseed	0	6	8	0
	1	dozen	Hats	1	0	0	0
	1	dozen	Wool Cards	0	10	0	0
	1	ream	Paper	0	3	4	0
	12	lb	Thread, Packet	0	4	2	0
	6	piece	Brushes	0	0	20	0
	1	gross	Knives (1d.)	0	10	0	0
	2	dozen	Crab Locks	0	3	4	0
	2	lb	Girdles, Nob	0	0	20	0
	6	lb	Mail	0	3	4	0
	2	lb	Senna	0	3	4	0
	2	clout	Needles	0	0	20	0
	1	dozen	Books, Horne	0	0	10	0
	1	great gross	Buttons	0	0	15	0
	0.5	C	Prunes	0	5	0	0
	8	yard	Cloth of Assize	0	0	0	0
	2	piece	Cotton *Cloth*	2	0	0	0
	6	yard	Cloth of Assize, Kersey	0	0	0	0

The Roase aforesaid, 31st August 1601

Merchant name	Qty	Unit	Commodity	£	s.	d.	f.
John Sherelocke of Waterford, Merchant Ind	0.5	c	Hops	0	5	0	0
	2	dozen	Wool Cards	1	0	0	0
	30	lb	Sugar	0	16	8	0
	0.25	C	Seed, Cumin	0	6	8	0
	4	dozen	Thread, Packet	0	16	8	0
	3	dozen	Girdles, Peny	0	0	20	0
	3	lb	Inkle	0	2	6	0
	6	piece	Hats, Coarse Childrens	0	6	8	0
	1	dozen	Horse Combs	0	0	25	0
	6	lb	Mail	0	3	4	0
	6	dozen	Knives (1d.)	0	5	0	0
	3	dozen	Crab Locks	0	5	0	0
	1	gross	Lace, Statute	0	6	8	0
	0.5	dozen	Stock Cards	0	6	8	0
	5	C	Iron	2	0	0	0
	2	ream	Paper	0	6	8	0
	2	gross	Points, Thread	0	0	20	0
	1	gross	Gartering	0	6	8	0
	3	dozen	Glasses, Drinking	0	0	20	0
	4	dozen	Urinals	0	3	4	0
	1	piece	Bristol Frieze *Cloth*	1	0	0	0
	1	piece	Cotton *Cloth*	1	0	0	0
	2	piece	Cloth of Assize, Dozen Kersey?	0	0	0	0

Merchant name	Qty	Unit	Commodity	£	s.	d.	f.

The Charles of Bristol, burden 50 tons, William Browne master, to St-Jean-de-Luz, 2nd September 1601

| Christopher Webb of Bristol, Merchant Ind | 6 | ton | Lead | 48 | 0 | 0 | 0 |
| | 1 | ton | Iron | 8 | 0 | 0 | 0 |

The Peter of Tenby, burden 8 tons, John Lokyer master, to Dublin, *2nd September 1601*

James Duffe of Dublin, Merchant Ind	3	ton	Iron	24	0	0	0
	4	piece	Cotton *Cloth*	4	0	0	0
	2	piece	Cloth of Assize, Penistone Unfriezed	0	0	0	0
	2	piece	Sack *Cloth*, for sacks	0	13	4	0

The Roase aforesaid, 2nd September 1601

William Sherlock of New Ross, Merchant Ind	2	dozen	Stock Cards	1	6	8	0
	4	dozen	Wool Cards	2	0	0	0
	1	gross	Knives (1d.)	0	10	0	0
	12	lb	Thread, Packet	0	4	2	0
	3	dozen	Girdles, Leather Peny	0	0	20	0
	6	lb	Senna	0	10	0	0
	8	lb	Seed, Cumin	0	0	20	0
	6	piece	Candlesticks, Brass	0	3	4	0
	2	dozen	Girths	0	0	20	0
	20	lb	Sugar	0	11	6	0
	2	dozen	Cups, Wooden	0	0	10	0
	4	dozen	Bibs	0	0	10	0
	3	ream	Paper, White	0	10	0	0
	2	butt	Thread, Black	0	4	2	0
	4	lb	Thread, Brown	0	3	4	0
	6	lb	Thread, Coloured	0	5	0	0
	1	gross	Gartering	0	6	8	0
	6	piece	Hats	1	0	0	0
	2	piece	Frieze and Check *Cloth*	2	0	0	0
	12	yard	Bay *Cloth*	0	16	8	0
	2	C	Hops	1	0	0	0

The Roase aforesaid, 2nd September 1601

John Sallenger of New Ross, Merchant Ind	6	yard	Cloth of Assize	0	0	0	0
	24	goad	Cottons (Woollen Cloth)	0	16	8	0
	2	C	Hops	1	0	0	0
	0.25	C	Soap, White	0	3	9	0
	4	ream	Paper, White	0	13	4	0
	4	lb	Girdles, Nob	0	3	4	0
	1	gross	Trenchers	0	0	10	0
	2	dozen	Wool Cards	1	0	0	0
	1	C	Taps and Cannells	0	0	5	0

Merchant name	Qty	Unit	Commodity	£	s.	d.	f.

The Marie of Jersey, burden 18 tons, Nicholas Rowse master, to Cork, *2nd September 1601*

Merchant name	Qty	Unit	Commodity	£	s.	d.	f.
William Smithe of London, Merchant Ind	15	C	Hops	7	10	0	0

The Providence aforesaid, *2nd September 1601*

Merchant name	Qty	Unit	Commodity	£	s.	d.	f.
William Challender of Bristol, Merchant Ind	1	ton	Lead	8	0	0	0
	1	ton	Lead[90]	8	0	0	0
	2	ton	Iron	16	0	0	0

The Gabriell aforesaid, 3rd September 1601

Merchant name	Qty	Unit	Commodity	£	s.	d.	f.
William Ellis of Bristol, Merchant Ind	6	ton	Lead	48	0	0	0

The Elizabeth aforesaid, *3rd September 1601*

Merchant name	Qty	Unit	Commodity	£	s.	d.	f.
John Buckleberrie of Bristol, Merchant Ind	6	C	Prunes	3	0	0	0
	7	C	Hops	3	10	0	0

The Elizabeth aforesaid, *3rd September 1601*

Merchant name	Qty	Unit	Commodity	£	s.	d.	f.
John Browne of Waterford, Merchant Ind	1	ton	Iron	8	0	0	0
	3	dozen	Wool Cards	1	10	0	0
	2	dozen	Stock Cards	1	6	8	0
	6	dozen	Flax	0	16	8	0
	2	piece	Jean Fustian *Cloth*	1	6	8	0
	7	yard	Cloth of Assize	0	0	0	0
	50	goad	Cottons (Woollen Cloth)	1	13	4	0
	6	lb	Girdles, Nob	0	5	0	0
	3	gross	Trenchers, Common	0	2	6	0
	12	lb	Mail	0	5	10	0
	6	clout	Needles	0	5	0	0
	2	dozen	Crab Locks	0	3	4	0
	2	C	Soap, Black	1	0	0	0
	30	lb	Thread, Packet	0	12	4	0
	4	piece	Mailing Cord	0	0	20	0
	0.25	C	Currants	0	7	6	0
	10	piece	Hose, Short	0	8	4	0
	2	dozen	Ink Horns	0	3	4	0
	12	piece	Lanterns	0	5	0	0
	2	ream	Paper	0	6	8	0
	10	lb	Galls	0	2	6	0
	12	piece	Books, Grammar	0	10	0	0
	3	butt	Thread, Black	0	5	15	0
	2	dozen	Wick Yarn	0	3	4	0
	2	gross	Knives	1	0	0	0
	2	gross	Points, Thread	0	0	20	0
	1	gross	Gartering, Norwich	0	6	8	0
	6	dozen	Girdles, Peny	0	5	0	0
	6	dozen	Books, Horne	0	0	20	0

90 In bars, containing 40 ends.

Merchant name	Qty	Unit	Commodity	£	s.	d.	f.
	6	dozen	Bibs	0	0	20	0
	2	C	Taps and Cannells	0	0	10	0

The Providence aforesaid, 3rd September 1601

Arthur Langton of Kilkenny, Merchant Ind	6	piece	Hats	0	10	0	0
	1	piece	Holland *Cloth*	1	4	2	0
	0.5	lb	Lace, Cheyne	0	3	4	0
	2	gross	Lace, Statute	0	13	4	0
	2	lb	Girdles, Nob	0	0	20	0
	3	lb	Thread, Country	0	10	0	0
	3	lb	Mail	0	0	20	0
	3	piece	Dishes, Chafing	0	0	20	0
	1	gross	Knives (1d.)	0	10	0	0
	12	yard	Cotton *Cloth*	0	8	4	0
	1	dozen	Garters	0	3	4	0
	36	yard	Girth Web	0	0	20	0
	1	lb	Inkle, White	0	0	10	0
	2	clout	Needles	0	0	20	0
	1	dozen	Girdles, Peny	0	0	10	0
	0.5	lb	Silk Bredth, Peny ?	0	6	8	0
	1	dozen	Bibs	0	0	10	0
	10	dicker	Bracelets	0	0	20	0
	1	dozen	Crab Locks, *Small*	0	0	20	0

The Joseph aforesaid, 4th September 1601

William Burras of Bristol, Merchant Ind	1.5	ton	Lead	12	0	0	0

The Joseph aforesaid, 4th September 1601

John Mirrecke of Bristol, Merchant Ind	6	ton	Lead	48	0	0	0

The Joseph aforesaid, 4th September 1601

John Stinchecombe of Bristol, Merchant Ind	2	ton	Lead	16	0	0	0

The White Swanne of Bristol, burden 40 tons, William Lux master, to La Rochelle, *4th September 1601*

George White of Bristol, Merchant Ind	7	ton	Lead	56	0	0	0

The Gabriell aforesaid, 5th September 1601

John Fowens of Bristol, Merchant Ind	4	ton	Lead	32	0	0	0
John Whitsonne of Bristol, Merchant Ind	4	ton	Lead	32	0	0	0

The Gabriell aforesaid, 8th September 1601

John Angell of Bristol, Merchant Ind	2	ton	Lead	16	0	0	0

Merchant name	Qty	Unit	Commodity	£	s.	d.	f.

The Desier of Bristol, burden 50 tons, Mathew Rice to Dublin, 8th September 1601

| Walter Olfeild, William Bigge & Christopher Carie of Bristol, Merchant Ind | 9 | ton | Lead | 72 | 0 | 0 | 0 |

The Joseph aforesaid, 8th September 1601

| Thomas James of Bristol, Merchant Ind | 2 | ton | Lead | 16 | 0 | 0 | 0 |
| | 16 | dicker | Skins, Calf[91] | 80 | 0 | 0 | 0 |

The Joseph aforesaid, 8th September 1601

| William Ellis, John Barker, Mathew Haviland, Abel Kitchen, John Bowlton & John Adworth of Bristol, Merchant Ind | 90 | dicker | Skins, Calf[92] | 450 | 0 | 0 | 0 |

The Joseph aforesaid, 9th September 1601

| Richard Tagge of Bristol, Merchant Ind | 4 | dicker | Skins, Calf[93] | 20 | 0 | 0 | 0 |

The Joseph aforesaid, 9th September 1601

| John Hopkins of Bristol, Merchant Ind | 20 | C | Iron, Wrought | 16 | 13 | 4 | 0 |

The Joseph aforesaid, 9th September 1601

| William Puddie of Bristol, Merchant Ind | 2 | ton | Lead | 16 | 0 | 0 | 0 |

The Joseph aforesaid, 9th September 1601

John Barker of Bristol, Merchant Ind	30	dicker	Skins, Calf	150	0	0	0
	160	goad	Cottons (Woollen Cloth)	5	6	8	0
	19	piece	Bristol Frieze Cloth	19	0	0	0
	1	piece	Bristol Frieze Cloth[94]	0	0	0	0

The Joseph aforesaid, 9th September 1601

| John Dorrington of London, Merchant Ind | 14.5 | dicker | Skins, Calf[95] | 72 | 10 | 0 | 0 |

The Joseph aforesaid, 10th September 1601

Robert Smithe of Bristol, Merchant Ind	2	C goad	Cottons (Woollen Cloth)	6	13	4	0
	4	dicker	Skins, Calf	20	0	0	0
	5	piece	Cloth of Assize	0	0	0	0
			Cloth of Assize, Overlengths	0	0	0	0

---

91 Bazans license.   92 Bazans license. The surveyor gives an incorrect total value here of £350. This is confirmed by the fact that the total custom paid is £21 10s.   93 Bazans license.   94 Custom exempt.   95 Bazans license.

Merchant name	Qty	Unit	Commodity	£	s.	d.	f.
The Joseph aforesaid, _10th September 1601_							
William Dawer & John Guy of Bristol, Merchant Ind	7	dicker	Skins, Calf	35	0	0	0
The Joseph aforesaid, 11th September 1601							
Walter Olfeild & John Gunynge of Bristol, Merchant Ind	5.5	dicker	Skins, Calf	27	10	0	0
The Joseph aforesaid, 11th September 1601							
Thomas Davis of Bristol, Merchant Ind	6	dicker	Skins, Calf	30	0	0	0
The Joseph aforesaid, 12th September 1601							
John Whitsonne of Bristol, Merchant Ind	20	dicker	Skins, Calf	100	0	0	0
	5	piece	Cloth of Assize	33	6	8	0
			Cloth of Assize, Overlengths	0	0	0	0
The Joseph aforesaid, _12th September 1601_							
William Burras of Bristol, Merchant Ind	7	dicker	Skins, Calf	35	0	0	0
The Gabriell aforesaid, 15th September 1601							
Mathew Haviland of Bristol, Merchant Ind	3	ton	Lead	24	0	0	0
	6	dicker	Skins, Calf	30	0	0	0
The Gabriell aforesaid, _15th September 1601_							
William Ellis of Bristol, Merchant Ind	14	dicker	Skins, Calf	70	0	0	0
John Whitsonne of Bristol, Merchant Ind	16	dicker	Skins, Calf	80	0	0	0
The Gabriell aforesaid, _15th September 1601_							
John Fowens of Bristol, Merchant Ind	15	dicker	Skins, Calf	75	0	0	0
The Gabriell aforesaid, _15th September 1601_							
George White of Bristol, Merchant Ind	4	dicker	Skins, Calf	20	0	0	0
	1	ton	Lead	8	0	0	0
William Coale of Bristol, Merchant Ind	4	dicker	Skins, Calf	20	0	0	0
The Gabriell aforesaid, _15th September 1601_							
Arthur Hibbins of Bristol, Merchant Ind	4	dicker	Skins, Calf	20	0	0	0
The Gabriell aforesaid, _15th September 1601_							
Able Kitchen of Bristol, Merchant Ind	12	dicker	Skins, Calf	60	0	0	0

Merchant name	Qty	Unit	Commodity	£	s.	d.	f.

The Gabriell aforesaid, 15th September 1601

| John Bowlton of Bristol, Merchant Ind | 6 | dicker | Skins, Calf | 30 | 0 | 0 | 0 |

The Gabriell aforesaid, *15th September 1601*

| John Barker of Bristol, Merchant Ind | | | | | | | |
| | 10 | dicker | Skins, Calf | 50 | 0 | 0 | 0 |

The Joseph aforesaid, *15th September 1601*

| Humphrey Fitzherbert & Morgan Reade of Bristol, Merchant Ind | 16 | dicker | Skins, Calf | 80 | 0 | 0 | 0 |
| | 1 | ton | Lead | 8 | 0 | 0 | 0 |

The Gabriell aforesaid, *15th September 1601*

Robert & Thomas Aldworth of Bristol, Merchant Ind	17	dicker	Skins, Calf	*85*	0	0	0
Daniel Addams of Bristol, Merchant Ind	6	hogshead	Fish, Salmon Girles[96]	0	0	0	0
	2	hogshead	Fish, Salmon	0	0	0	0

The James of Bristol, burden 18 tons, William More master, to Cork, *15th September 1601*

Clement Terrie of Cork, Merchant Ind	1	C	Hops	*0*	*10*	*0*	*0*
	26	yard	Cotton *Cloth*	*1*	*0*	*0*	*0*
	6	yard	Cloth of Assize	*0*	*0*	*0*	*0*
	8	yard	Bay *Cloth*	*0*	*13*	*4*	*0*
	12	yard	Coarse Canvas *Cloth*	*0*	*5*	*0*	*0*
	6	yard	Dornick *Cloth*	*0*	*6*	*8*	*0*
	3	pair	Stockings, Woollen	*0*	*5*	*0*	*0*
	1	ream	Paper	*0*	*3*	*4*	*0*
	12	yard	Bristol Frieze *Cloth*	*0*	*6*	*8*	*0*
	1	lb	Thread, Coloured	*0*	*0*	*20*	*0*
	1	lb	Girdles, Nob	*0*	*0*	*10*	*0*
	1	lb	Mail	*0*	*0*	*10*	*0*
	3	M	Pins	*0*	*0*	*10*	*0*
	3	piece	Inkle	*0*	*0*	*10*	*0*
	1	lb	Sadlers Crewel Fringe	*0*	*0*	*20*	*0*
	2	gross	Points, Thread	*0*	*0*	*10*	*0*
	1	gross	Points, Leather	*0*	*0*	*5*	*0*
	0.5	gross	Knives (1*d.*)	*0*	*5*	*0*	*0*
	9	piece	Hats, Childrens	*0*	*7*	*6*	*0*
	6	pair	Spurs	*0*	*0*	*20*	*0*
	1	burden	Steel	*0*	*5*	*0*	*0*
	1	nest	Boxes, Painted	*0*	*0*	*10*	*0*
	6	lb	Glue	*0*	*0*	*20*	*0*
	1	dozen	Bibs, Childrens	*0*	*0*	*5*	*0*
	1	dozen	Wool Cards, Old	*0*	*6*	*8*	*0*
	3	dozen	Tobacco Pipes	*0*	*0*	*10*	*0*
	1	dozen	Glasses, Looking	*0*	*0*	*5*	*0*

96 Custom and subsidy paid in the Christopher of Bristol on the 21st August last and now allowed.

Merchant name	Qty	Unit	Commodity	£	s.	d.	f.
Edward Rooche of Cork, Merchant Ind	1	piece	Bristol Frieze *Cloth*	1	0	0	0
	2	piece	Cotton *Cloth*	2	0	0	0
	12	yard	Cloth of Assize, Hampshire Kersey	0	0	0	0
	12	yard	Cloth of Assize	0	0	0	0
	12	ell	Canvas *Cloth*	0	5	0	0
	1	dozen	Hemp	0	2	6	0
	1	ream	Paper	0	3	4	0
	6	lb	Soap, White	0	0	20	0
	1	dozen	Hats	1	0	0	0
	1	gross	Girth Web	0	3	4	0
	2	dozen	Girdles, Leather Peny	0	0	20	0
	1	gross	Trenchers, Common	0	0	10	0
	6	yard	Levant Taffata *Cloth*	0	10	0	0
	1	gross	Knives (1*d.*)	0	10	0	0
	6	dozen	Knives, Pocket	0	7	6	0
	8	yard	Bay *Cloth*	0	10	0	0
	0.5	piece	Fustian *Cloth*	0	6	8	0
	1	dozen	Spurs	0	3	4	0
	2	gross	Points, Thread	0	0	10	0
	0.5	gross	Combs, Wooden	0	2	6	0
	6	M	Pins	0	0	20	0
	6	piece	Inkle	0	0	20	0
	1	M	Nails, Board	0	3	4	0
	1	M	Nails, Lath	0	0	10	0
	0.5	burden	Steel	0	2	6	0
	2	lb	Mail	0	0	10	0
	1	lb	Girdles, Nob	0	0	10	0
	1	C	Oakum	0	5	0	0
	3	lb	Galls and Copperas	0	0	10	0
	2	gross	Buttons, Thread	0	0	10	0
	2	gross	Buttons, Silk	0	0	10	0
	1	dozen	Horse Combs	0	0	25	0
	2	dozen	Girdles, Peny	0	0	20	0
	1	dozen	Bands, Falling	0	0	20	0
	6	pair	Stockings, Woollen	0	10	0	0
	1	lb	Mercury	0	0	20	0
	1	lb	Senna	0	0	20	0
	2	lb	Thread, Packet	0	0	10	0
	6	lb	Thread, Black & Brown	0	5	0	0
	4	yard	Carpeting	0	3	4	0
	1	dozen	Girdles, Waist	0	0	20	0
	4	dozen	Tobacco Pipes	0	0	20	0
	1	gross	Points, Silk	0	0	20	0
	6	lb	Sulphur	0	0	5	0
	1	dozen	Penners and Inkhorns	0	0	20	0
	0.5	gross	Buckles for Girths	0	0	20	0
	1	ream	Paper, *Brown*	0	0	10	0
	1	dozen	Knives, Paring	0	0	10	0
	0.5	dozen	Cutts (ob.)	0	0	10	0
	1	C	Awl Blades	0	0	20	0
	1	dozen	Cups, Wooden	0	0	10	0

Merchant name	Qty	Unit	Commodity	£	s.	d.	f.
	1	lb	Ginger	0	0	10	0
	12	lb	Glue	0	0	20	0
	6	piece	Hour Glasses	0	0	10	0
	1	gross	Gartering, Manchester	0	0	20	0
	1	gross	Buttons, Hair	0	0	5	0

The James aforesaid, *15th September 1601*

Andrew Galeway of Cork, Merchant Ind

	Qty	Unit	Commodity	£	s.	d.	f.
	12	yard	Cotton *Cloth*	0	10	0	0
	6	piece	Hats	0	10	0	0
	6	dozen	Hemp	1	10	0	0
	1	ream	Paper, White	0	3	4	0
	1	gross	Combs, Wooden	0	5	0	0
	1	gross	Buttons, Silk	0	0	10	0
	2	dozen	Wool Cards	1	0	0	0
	2	dozen	Cups, Wooden	0	0	20	0
	2	dozen	Urinals	0	0	20	0
	6	M	Pins	0	0	20	0
	1	M	Awl Blades	0	6	8	0
	1	gross	Buttons, Thread	0	0	20	0
	2	dozen	Awl Hafts	0	0	5	0
	3	dozen	Taps and Cannells	0	0	15	0
	1	dozen	Hour Glasses	0	0	20	0
	2	dozen	Glasses, Drinking	0	0	10	0
	12	lb	Thread, Packet	0	4	2	0
	2	nest	Boxes, Painted	0	0	10	0
	3	clout	Needles	0	2	6	0
	1	butt	Thread, Black	0	0	25	0
	2	lb	Thread, Brown	0	0	20	0
	12	dozen	Thimbles	0	3	4	0
	3	dozen	Girdles, Leather	0	2	6	0
	1	burden	Steel	0	5	0	0
	2	M	Nails, Lath	0	0	20	0
	1	gross	Knives (1*d.*)	0	10	0	0
	2	gross	Trenchers	0	0	20	0
	2	ream	Paper, Brown	0	0	20	0
	1	C	Hops	0	10	0	0
	0.5	dozen	Serches	0	5	0	0

The James aforesaid, *15th September 1601*

Pierce Goolde of Cork, Merchant Ind

	Qty	Unit	Commodity	£	s.	d.	f.
	0.5	C	Hops	0	5	0	0
	1	gross	Buttons, Silk	0	0	10	0
	1	butt	Thread, Black	0	0	25	0
	3	piece	Inkle	0	0	10	0
	1	gross	Buttons, Thread	0	0	5	0
	1	gross	Buttons, Glass	0	0	5	0
	1	C	Needles, Spanish	0	0	5	0
	1	clout	Needles	0	0	10	0
	1	lb	Mail	0	0	5	0
	0.5	lb	Currants	0	0	5	0

Merchant name	Qty	Unit	Commodity	£	s.	d.	f.
	1	gross	Points, Thread	0	0	10	0
	0.5	lb	Verdegris	0	0	10	0
	0.5	dozen	Playing Cards	0	0	10	0
	0.5	dozen	Glasses, Looking	0	0	5	0
	5	dozen	Combs, Wooden	0	0	25	0
	1	dozen	Knives (1d.)	0	0	10	0
	1	dozen	Girdles, Peny	0	0	10	0
	1.5	lb	Galls and Copperas	0	0	5	0
	1	dozen	Hemp	0	2	6	0
	1	M	Nails, Board	0	3	4	0
	3	M	Nails, Lath	0	2	11	0
	1	burden	Steel	0	5	0	0
	0.5	dozen	Spurs	0	0	20	0
	1	dozen	Wool Cards, Old	0	6	8	0
	4	gross	Trenchers	0	3	4	0

The George of Le Croisic, burden 25 tons, Peter Lestubecke master, to Le Croisic, 16th September 1601

William Coale of Bristol, Merchant Ind	2	ton	Lead	16	0	0	0
	8	piece	Cloth of Assize, Kersey	0	0	0	0
	6	piece	Wadmal Cloth	6	0	0	0
Peter Lestubeck *domicile unknown*, Merchant Stranger	7	wey	Coal	2	0	0	0
	1	C goad	Cottons (Woollen Cloth)	3	6	8	0

The George aforesaid, *16th September 1601*

George Lane of Bristol, Merchant Ind	2	C goad	Cottons (Woollen Cloth)	6	13	4	0

The Joseph aforesaid, 16th September 1601

Thomas Davis of Bristol, Merchant Ind	5	piece	Cloth of Assize	0	0	0	0
			Cloth of Assize, Overlengths	0	0	0	0
William Bigge of Bristol, Merchant Ind	3	ton	Lead	24	0	0	0
	5	dicker	Skins, Calf	25	0	0	0

The Gabriell aforesaid, *16th September 1601*

Nicholas Bogans of Bristol, Merchant Ind	4	dicker	Skins, Calf	20	0	0	0
John Angell of Bristol, Merchant Ind	4	dicker	Skins, Calf	20	0	0	0

The Elizabeth of Barnstaple, burden 30 tons, John Shereman master, to La Rochelle, 19th September 1601

Robert Johnson of Bristol, Merchant Ind	10	piece	Grind-Stones	1	5	0	0
	8	piece	Cloth of Assize	0	0	0	0
			Cloth of Assize, Overlengths	0	0	0	0

Merchant name	Qty	Unit	Commodity	£	s.	d.	f.

The Jesus of Westbury-on-Severn, burden 18 tons, Robert Northe master, to Waterford, *19th September 1601*

Merchant name	Qty	Unit	Commodity	£	s.	d.	f.
James White of Waterford, Merchant Ind	1	dozen	Skins, Velim for drums head	0	5	0	0
	5	Rowles	Parchment Skins, Small	0	16	8	0
	1	dozen	Candle-Wicks	0	0	20	0
	12	ell	Flannel Cloth	0	5	0	0
	2	dozen	Girth Buckles	0	0	10	0
	2	dozen	Spurs	0	6	8	0
	6	piece	Horse Combs	0	0	15	0
	6	piece	Snaffles and Reins	0	5	0	0
	1	gross	Knives (1*d.*)	0	10	0	0
	1	dozen	Girdles, Peny	0	0	10	0
	8	piece	Caps, Monmouth	0	5	0	0
	2	ream	Paper	0	6	8	0
	3	piece	Portmanteau	0	2	6	0
	2	lb	Thread, Coloured	0	5	0	0
	12	ounce	Points, Copper	0	6	8	0
	30	ell	Inderling/Juderling Cloth?	0	10	0	0
	1	lb	Silk, Bridges	0	15	0	0
	12	ounce	Silk, Stiching	0	10	0	0
	0.5	lb	Thread, Sisters	0	0	20	0
	3	lb	Thread, Brown	0	2	6	0
	1	butt	Thread, Black	0	0	25	0
	4	M	Pins	0	0	20	0
	1	small gross	Buttons, Gold	0	5	0	0
	1	great gross	Buttons, Silk	0	5	0	0
	1	piece	Holland *Cloth*	1	4	2	0
	0.5	piece	Cambric *Cloth*	1	0	0	0
	1	dozen	Coarse Table Napkins	0	3	4	0
	0.5	piece	Tufte Canvas *Cloth*	0	3	4	0
	1	role	Buckram *Cloth*	0	2	6	0
	3	yard	Velvet *Cloth*	2	5	0	0
	0.5	lb	Wax, Hard	0	0	10	0
	5	ell	Towers Taffeta *Cloth*	0	16	8	0
	5	ell	Sarcanet *Cloth*	0	16	8	0
	2	piece	Fustian *Cloth*	1	6	8	0
	2	piece	Jean Fustian *Cloth*	1	6	8	0
	1	lb	Fringe	0	2	6	0
	1	gross	Lace, Statute	0	6	8	0
	1	dozen	Locks, Small Hanging	0	0	20	0
	4	ounce	Saffron	0	3	4	0
	0.5	C	Raisins, *Great*	0	3	4	0
	1	C	Prunes	0	10	0	0
	12	lb	Currants	0	3	4	0
	2	lb	Pepper	0	3	4	0
	0.5	lb	Cloves	0	2	6	0
	1	lb	Nutmeg	0	3	4	0
	1	lb	Cinnamon	0	4	2	0

Merchant name	Qty	Unit	Commodity	£	s.	d.	f.
	16	yard	Cloth of Assize	0	0	0	0
	2	dozen	Hats, Childrens	1	6	8	0
	1	piece	Cloth of Assize, Kersey	0	0	0	0
	10	dozen	Glasses, Drinking	0	8	4	0
	8	yard	Cloth of Assize, Penistone	0	0	0	0
	40	lb	Sugar	1	3	4	0

The Jesus aforesaid

John White of Waterford, Merchant Ind	1	C	Hops	0	10	0	0
	5	dozen	Parchment Skins, Small	0	8	4	0
	12	lb	Candle-Wicks	0	0	20	0
	1	dozen	Spurs	0	3	4	0
	1	dozen	Headstalls for Horses	0	5	0	0
	12	yard	Flannel Cloth	0	3	4	0
	6	piece	Caps, Monmouth	0	5	0	0
	1	dozen	Garters, Manchester	0	0	20	0
	1	C	Wood, Brazil	1	13	4	0
	1	C	Prunes	0	10	0	0
	0.25	C	Raisins, *Great*	0	4	2	0
	6	lb	Pepper	0	10	0	0
	0.25	C	Currants	0	7	6	0
	1	dozen	Hats, Coarse	1	10	0	0
	1	lb	Cinnamon	0	4	2	0
	2	lb	Ginger	0	3	4	0
	4	lb	Comfits	0	3	4	0
	16	lb	Sugar	0	10	0	0
	0.5	piece	Fustian *Cloth*	0	6	8	0
	12	piece	Visors	0	10	0	0
	3	ream	Paper	0	10	0	0
	1	lb	Thread, White	0	0	20	0
	3	lb	Girdles, Nob	0	2	6	0
	0.5	lb	Silk Bredth, Peny ?	0	5	0	0
	4	dozen	Knives (1*d.*)	0	3	4	0
	1	piece	Cloth of Assize, Penistone Unfriezed	0	0	0	0
	10	yard	Cloth of Assize	0	0	0	0
James Gibson of Waterford, Merchant Ind	10	C	Hops	5	0	0	0
	8	C	Orchil	8	0	0	0
	10	piece	Soultwich *Cloth*	3	0	0	0

The Jesus aforesaid, *19th September 1601*

Joseph Kinge of London, Merchant Ind	30	goad	Cottons (Woollen Cloth)	1	1	8	0
	2	piece	Bristol Frieze *Cloth*	2	0	0	0
	10	yard	Cloth of Assize	0	0	0	0
	0.5	piece	Jean Fustian *Cloth*	0	6	8	0

Merchant name	Qty	Unit	Commodity	£	s.	d.	f.
The Joseph aforesaid, 22nd September 1601							
Humphrey Fitzherbett & Benjamin Crockehey							
of Bristol, Merchant Ind	18	piece	Cloth of Assize[97]	120	0	0	0
	2	piece	Cloth of Assize[98]	0	0	0	0
			Cloth of Assize, Overlengths	0	0	0	0
The Gabriell aforesaid, *22nd September 1601*							
William Burres of Bristol, Merchant Ind	3	dicker	Skins, Calf	15	0	0	0
The Gabriell aforesaid, *22nd September 1601*							
John Barker of Bristol, Merchant Ind	3	ton	Lead	24	0	0	0
The Joseph aforesaid, *22nd September 1601*							
John Barker of Bristol, Merchant Ind	5	dicker	Skins, Calf	25	0	0	0
	150	goad	Cottons (Woollen Cloth)	5	0	0	0
The Elizabeth of Barnstaple aforesaid, 23rd September 1601							
Thomas Whithead of Bristol, Merchant Ind	4	piece	Cloth of Assize	0	0	0	0
			Cloth of Assize, Overlengths	0	0	0	0
	5	piece	Bristol Frieze *Cloth*	5	0	0	0
The Elizabeth of Barnstaple aforesaid, 23rd September 1601							
William Carie of Bristol, Merchant Ind	65	yard	Cloth of Assize	0	0	0	0
	1	piece	Bristol Frieze Cloth[99]	0	0	0	0
The Elizabeth of Barnstaple aforesaid, 24th September 1601							
Andrew Batton of Bristol, Merchant Ind	2	piece	Cloth of Assize	0	0	0	0
			Cloth of Assize, Overlengths	0	0	0	0
	8	piece	Bristol Frieze *Cloth*	8	0	0	0
	50	goad	Cottons (Woollen Cloth)	1	13	4	0
	2	C	Soap, Black	1	0	0	0
The Elizabeth of Barnstaple aforesaid, *24th September 1601*							
William Coorie of Bristol, Merchant Ind	14	piece	Cloth of Assize	0	0	0	0
	1	piece	Cloth of Assize[100]	0	0	0	0
			Cloth of Assize, Overlengths	0	0	0	0

[97] The surveyor has entered a value here, based on poundage duties (ie. *1s.* per £) [98] Custom exempt. [99] Allowed for a wrap. [100] Custom exempt.

Merchant name	Qty	Unit	Commodity	£	s.	d.	f.
	4	C goad	Cottons (Woollen Cloth)	13	6	8	0

The Elizabeth of Barnstaple aforesaid, 24th September 1601

Merchant name	Qty	Unit	Commodity	£	s.	d.	f.
Nicholas Boggans of Bristol, Merchant Ind	12	piece	Cloth of Assize	0	0	0	0
	0.5	piece	Cloth of Assize[101]	0	0	0	0
	150	goad	Cottons (Woollen Cloth)	5	0	0	0
	1	ton	Iron	8	0	0	0
			Cloth of Assize, Overlengths	0	0	0	0

The Elizabeth aforesaid, 25th September 1601

Merchant name	Qty	Unit	Commodity	£	s.	d.	f.
Robert Aldworth of Bristol, Merchant Ind	11	piece	Cloth of Assize	0	0	0	0
	1	piece	Cloth of Assize[102]	0	0	0	0
			Cloth of Assize, Overlengths	0	0	0	0
	10	C goad	Cottons (Woollen Cloth)	33	6	8	0
Thomas Aldworth of Bristol, Merchant Ind	4	piece	Cloth of Assize	0	0	0	0
			Cloth of Assize, Overlengths	0	0	0	0
	4	piece	Cloth of Assize[103]	0	0	0	0
	1	C goad	Cottons (Woollen Cloth)[104]	0	0	0	0

The Elizabeth aforesaid, 25th September 1601

Merchant name	Qty	Unit	Commodity	£	s.	d.	f.
Walter Shereman of Barnstaple, Merchant Ind	4	piece	Cloth of Assize	0	0	0	0
			Cloth of Assize, Overlengths	0	0	0	0

The Elizabeth aforesaid, *25th September 1601*

Merchant name	Qty	Unit	Commodity	£	s.	d.	f.
Walter Olfeild of Bristol, Merchant Ind	2.5	piece	Cloth of Assize	0	0	0	0
			Cloth of Assize, Overlengths	0	0	0	0
	2	piece	Cloth of Assize, Streit	0	0	0	0
John Barker of Bristol, Merchant Ind	5	piece	Cotton *Cloth*	5	0	0	0
William Ellis of Bristol, Merchant Ind	6.5	piece	Cloth of Assize	0	0	0	0
			Cloth of Assize, Overlengths	0	0	0	0

The Charles aforesaid, 25th September 1601

Merchant name	Qty	Unit	Commodity	£	s.	d.	f.
William Ellis of Bristol, Merchant Ind	5	dicker	Skins, Calf	25	0	0	0

101 Custom exempt. 102 Custom exempt. 103 Custom paid in the Unicorn on the 18th September 1601 and now allowed. 104 As above.

Merchant name	Qty	Unit	Commodity	£	s.	d.	f.
The Joseph aforesaid, *25th September 1601*							
William Estin of Bristol, Merchant Ind	4	piece	Cloth of Assize	0	0	0	0
	8	piece	Cloth of Assize, Bridgwaters	0	0	0	0
	7	piece	Bristol Frieze *Cloth*	7	0	0	0
	2	C goad	Cottons (Woollen Cloth)	6	13	4	0
			Cloth of Assize, Overlengths	0	0	0	0
The Joseph aforesaid, *25th September 1601*							
John Stinchecombe of Bristol, Merchant Ind	2	piece	Cloth of Assize, Bridgwaters	0	0	0	0
	4	piece	Bristol Frieze *Cloth*	4	0	0	0
The Joseph aforesaid, 25th September 1601							
John Webb of Bristol, Merchant Ind	2	piece	Cloth of Assize	0	0	0	0
			Cloth of Assize, Overlengths	0	0	0	0
	6	piece	Bristol Frieze *Cloth*	6	0	0	0
The James of Bristol aforesaid, 26th September 1601							
William Halie of Waterford, Merchant Ind	3	yard	Cloth of Assize	0	0	0	0
	6	yard	Cloth of Assize, Kersey	0	0	0	0
	10	yard	Bay *Cloth*	0	16	8	0
	9	yard	Cotton *Cloth*	0	6	8	0
	0.5	piece	Bristol Frieze *Cloth*	0	10	0	0
	3	piece	Brushes	0	0	10	0
	6	piece	Hats	0	10	0	0
	3	pair	Stockings	0	5	0	0
	4	yard	Holland *Cloth*	0	5	0	0
	2	dozen	Wool Cards	1	0	0	0
	1	gross	Trenchers, Common	0	0	10	0
	1	dozen	Boxes, Black	0	0	10	0
	2	piece	Portmanteau	0	0	20	0
	2	piece	Gartering, Inkle	0	0	10	0
	4	lb	Thread, Black & Brown	0	3	4	0
	0.5	gross	Lace, Statute	0	3	4	0
	1	gross	Points, Thread	0	0	10	0
	1	dozen	Penners and Inkhorns	0	0	20	0
	1	dozen	Boxes, Painted	0	0	10	0
	0.5	gross	Girth Web	0	3	4	0
	0.5	gross	Buckles	0	0	10	0
	1	lb	Wax, Red	0	0	10	0
	6	lb	Starch	0	0	10	0
	4	dozen	Tobacco Pipes	0	0	20	0

Merchant name	Qty	Unit	Commodity	£	s.	d.	f.
	2	lb	Thread, Packet	0	0	10	0
	1	lb	Tobacco	0	3	4	0
	1	clout	Needles	0	0	10	0
	1	lb	Mail	0	0	5	0
	1	dozen	Spurs	0	3	4	0
	3	dozen	Combs, Wooden	0	0	10	0
	0.5	piece	Fustian *Cloth*	0	6	8	0

The Elizabeth aforesaid, 26th September 1601

John Pawle of Bristol, Merchant Ind	3	piece	Cotton *Cloth*	3	0	0	0
	1	piece	Bristol Frieze *Cloth*	1	0	0	0

The Elizabeth aforesaid, 26th September 1601

William Colston the younger of Bristol, Merchant Ind	6	piece	Cloth of Assize, Half	0	0	0	0
			Cloth of Assize, Overlengths	0	0	0	0

Glossary of commodities, weights and measures

Almonds (Lat.: amigdalum; Text: allmondes, amigdala, amygdala) : The kernel of a drupe or stone-fruit, the produce of the almond tree, of which there are two kinds, sweet and the bitter. (OED)

Alum (Text: alam): A whitish transparent mineral salt, used primarily in cloth dyeing and also for tawing skins, medicine and sizing paper. (OED)

Anchor (Lat.: ancora; Text: anker)

Aniseed (Text: annes, annes sede) : The seed of the anise, used in medicine, confectionary and perfumes.

Apothecary Wares: Sometimes found in the accounts listed as such and without any specification regarding type or content.

Apples (Text: appuls): Found by the barrel, which according to the 1582 rates book, contains three bushels.

Aquavitae (Text: aqua vyta): a generic name for various types of strong distilled alcohol.

Arridence: Unidentified.

Argol (Text: argall, archoll): Bitartrate of potassium, a plant acid formed as a by-product of wine-making, which when purified becomes cream of tartar. There is a difficulty with identifying this for certain as 'Orchil' is often written in a similar fashion and is exactly the same value in the later accounts.

Arrow Heads: The head or pointed part of an arrow.

Arsenic (Text: arsenyck): Name of one of the chemical elements, and of some of its compounds, which are violent poisons'. It was used as a poison for vermin and was also adapted for medicinal use, for example to treat skin diseases.[1]

Artisons: Unidentified. Found by the pair as an export from Bristol to Ireland in 1563.

Ashes, Ore: Possibly ashes from lead ore.

Ashes, Soap: Ashes from burnt wood, which provided the alkaline base for soap.

Awl Blades (Text: alblades): an awl is a small tool with a slender, cylindrical, tapering, sharp-pointed blade, with which holes may be pierced. (OED)

Awl Hafts: Handles for awles.

Bacon: Found by the flitch (see below flitch).

Balances: A device used for weighing goods. Both gold balances and 'unce' balances are found in the 1582 rates book.

Balches: Possibly belts. These are found in the 1575/6 account and are valued at 1s. (12s. per dozen). There is also an entry in this account for 'balches and lins', also unidentified. Medieval Latin balcheus/balteus could be a belt for a crossbow or a military belt.

Bale: A package of woad, alum, almonds etc., capacity varying with the commodity.

Balette: Measurement usually of woad; equalling approximately half a bale.

Bands, Coarse Cyprus: Neck-bands, or collars for shirts. These ones are presumably made from a coarse Cyprus cloth.

Bands, Falling: Unstiffened collars, which were draped over the shoulders of the doublet, or, according to the OED: 'The development of a falling collar into a pair of strips hanging down in front, as part of a conventional dress, clerical, legal, or academical'.

Barley (Lat.: hordeum; Text: ordeum, ordei): usually found by the wey.

---

1 'Arango – Artillery', *Dictionary of traded goods and commodities, 1550/1820* (2007). URL: *http://www.british-history.ac.uk/report.aspx?compid=58689&strquery=arsenic*, accessed 16 October 2008.

Barrel: A cask; a measure of capacity which varies with the commodity. There are twelve barrels of herring to a last and eight barrels of wine and oil to a tun.

Barrels, *Lear*: Unidentified. They occur in the 1545/6 account, valued at 8s. 4d. per last.

Bastard: Sweet Spanish Wine.

Battery (Text: batry): Metal, or articles of metal, especially of brass or copper, wrought by hammering. (OED)

Beads, Amber (Text: beds): Amber is a yellowish translucent fossil resin, found chiefly along the southern shores of the Baltic. These are the most expensive beads found in the accounts.

Beads, Bugle (Text: bugle): Tube shaped, usually black bead, used in ornamental garments. (OED)

Beans (Lat.: fabarum; Text: fabar').

Bed Cord: A cord for stretching the sacking of a bed. (OED)

Bed Tick (Text: tiecke): A large flat quadrangular bag or case, into which feathers, hair, straw, chaff, or other substances are put to form a bed.

Beef: Shipped by the barrel and probably salted.

Beerer: Possibly refers to Beer eger which is sour beer or vinegar, made from beer.

Bellows: An instrument or machine constructed to furnish a strong blast of air. (OED)

Bells (Lat. & Text: campanam): Various types are found including hawk bells, sheep bells and tassel bells, which are probably bells hanging from a cord or fringe. They are usually listed in pairs.

Benedict Laxative: Generic term for various types of mild laxatives. (OED)

Bibs (Text: bibbes): A cloth placed under a child's chin, to keep the front of the dress clean, esp. at meals. A similar article worn over the breast by adults, frequently as the upper part of an apron. (OED)

Biscuit (Text: biskett): A kind of crisp dry bread more or less hard, prepared generally in thin flat cakes.

Bice (Text: bise): A term applied to the pigments, blue bice and green bice, and the shades of blue or green which they yield. Willan describes it as 'a pigment which yields a dull blue colour, prepared from smalt'.[2] According to the *Dictionary of Traded Goods*, the blue pigment was in the nineteenth century prepared from smalt, but in the seventeenth century, it was a product of azurite, then known as lapis Armenius and the term green bice had been applied in the seventeenth century to malachite, but by the nineteenth it was also made from smalt by adding yellow Orpiment [Harley (1970)].[3]

Bit: Metal mouthpiece attached to a horse's bridle.

Blankets (Text: coverige, coverlettes, cadowes) Found in the transcription as they appear in the accounts, i.e. caddows, blankets etc.

Blockwood (Text: logwood): The heartwood of an American tree used in dyeing; so called from being imported in the form of logs. It is used to some extent in medicine as an astringent. (OED)

Bole Armeniac (Text: bolearmeic): An astringent earth used as antidote and styptic.[4]

Bolt: A roll of woven fabric: generally of a definite length; depending on the fabric type.

Bombas: This may be related to bombasine, which is a twilled dress material composed of silk and worsted, cotton and worsted or worsted alone. In the accounts however, it is found by the lb not by the yard. It may therefore be a thread made from the same material.

Books: In the Bristol accounts books, without exception, are found as exports to Ireland. In the first half of the century, the only books found in the accounts are 'primers'. The 1575/6 account contains two entries for books, one for primers and one for 'books for children' (pro pueris). It is not until 1594/5 and 1600/1 that a greater variety is seen, with the appearance of fable books, 'books of the School of Virtue', small books, small books for children, grammar books, horn books and also 'Catoes and Pueriles'.

Books, Catoes and Pueriles: Catoes refers to the classical works of Cato which were used in schools and Pueriles is Evaldus Gallus's *Pueriles confabulatiunculae*, which Gillespie suggests was probably in translation by Leonhard Culmann and was used to teach Latin to those too young for longer *Colloquies*.[5]

Books, for Children: Type unspecified.

Books, Grammar: There is a large variation in values for these, suggesting different types and qualities or sizes of the books.

Books, Horn (Text: horne boks): A leaf of paper containing the alphabet (often with the addition of the

---

2 Willan, *Tudor book of rates*, p. 8.   3 'Bice – Bitter almond', *Dictionary of traded goods*, http://www.british-history.ac.uk/report.aspx?compid=58699, accessed 16 October 2008   4 Willan, *Tudor book of rates*, p. 9.   5 Willan, *Tudor book of rates*, p. 6.

ten digits, some elements of spelling, and the Lord's Prayer) protected by a thin plate of translucent horn, and mounted on a tablet of wood with a projecting piece for a handle.

Books, Primers (Text: primmers): A prayer book or devotional manual for the use of lay people but the books were also used in teaching reading; and there may have been from early times forms of them specially intended for this purpose. Printed books of this sort became common in the sixteenth century. The OED quotes a primer from *c.*1537 that has a section containing the ABC, followed by the Pater Noster, Ave Maria, Creed, Decalogue, forms of Grace before and after meals, and certain prayers and states that smaller works containing the part for children only (probably the 'small books for children' found in the later accounts), began to be officially published in 1545, under the title of *The A.B.C.*

Books, School of Virtue: Francis Seager's *School of Virtue* was first published in England in the 1550s and was a didactic work for children on morals, religion and social behaviour. It was illustrated by wood-cuts.[6]

Borax (Text: boras, borate): A white chemical powder – used as a solder by gold/silver smiths. It probably had other uses also. (OED)

Bornby: Red behen or sea lavender, used in medicine.[7]

Bottles: Various types are found in the accounts, see below.

Bottles, Glass: The 1582 rates book lists glass bottles as being covered, covered with leather and with vices, and uncovered.

Bottles, Leather: A vessel with a narrow neck for holding liquids, now usually made of glass; originally of leather. (OED)

Bottles, Pewter: A grey alloy of tin, originally with about 20 per cent lead (and sometimes other elements) used chiefly for ornaments and utensils. (OED)

Bottles, Sucking: Probably refers to a baby's bottle or perhaps for an animal.

Boultel Bewpers (Text: beaup boulter): Boultel is a kind of cloth used for bolting or sifting flour and bewpers is probably Beaupreau in France.[8]

Bows: Weapon for shooting arrows or similar missiles, consisting of a strip of elastic wood or other material, bent by means of a string stretched between its two ends. (OED)

Bowstaves: Sticks to be made into bows. Found by the bundle, which contains 16 staves.

Bowstrings: Found by the gross, presumably pieces.

Boxes: 'Painted' and 'black' boxes are found in the accounts. They are also found described as a 'nest', which is a box containing similar boxes of graduated sizes packed together.

Box-Staves (Text: bokk staves): Lengths of wood used to make a box. Presumably the price varied according to size as those listed in the accounts are of varying values. Not listed in the 1582 rates book.

Bracelet (Text: braslets): Could refer to an ornamental ring or band worn on the arm or wrist or also a hand-cuff for the wrist. It occurs being shipped by the dicker which probably refers to ten bracelets. There is an example of necklaces being shipped by the dicker in Zupko's dictionary of weights and measures.[9]

Brasers: This could be a type of Brazier, a large flat pan or tray for holding burning charcoal, etc. but the value in 1563, at 15*d.* per dozen seems too low for this.

Brass, Broken: Valued by the lb.

Brushes, Heath (Text: brushes, bruches): Brushes made of something like heather . The term 'heath' according the OED was applied quite vaguely.

Brushes, Rubbing: A hard brush used for rubbing. There are two sorts listed in the 1582 rates book, 'heare' and 'heath'.[10] Found described simply as rubbing brushes in the 1594/5 account.

Brushes, Small: Possibly of a finer quality than the coarse heath brushes as they are more expensive.

Buckles, Unspecified: Varying valuations suggest that different types were sometimes listed in the accounts simply as 'buckles'

Buckles, Boot

---

6 R. Gillespie, 'The book trade in southern Ireland, 1590–1640' in Gerard Long (ed.), *Books beyond the pale: aspects of the provincial book trade in Ireland before 1850* (Dublin: Rare Books Group of the Library Association of Ireland, 1996), p. 5.   7 Willan, *Tudor book of rates*, p. 9.   8 Willan, *Tudor book of rates*, p. 9.   9 R.E. Zupko, *A dictionary of English weights and measures from Anglo-Saxon times to the nineteenth century* (Madison, 1968) p. 107.   10 Willan, *Tudor book of rates*, p. 11.

Buckles, Girth: A belt or band of leather or cloth, placed round the body of a horse or other beast of burden and drawn tight, so as to secure a saddle, pack, etc. upon its back.

Burden: A load, a varying measure of quantity.

Buskin: Knee or calf length boot made of leather or cloth. The accounts also list Spanish Bushkins.

Butt: Measure of wine, fish etc., equal to a pipe.

Butter (Text: buttir): shipped by the barrel.

Buttons: Described as being made of Brass, Glass, Hair, Pewter, Shell, Silk, Steel or Thread. There is also an entry for Scottish buttons. These are usually shipped by the gross.

C (Lat.: centum, centenarium):

(a) a hundredweight; according to Carus-Wilson, when reckoning "great wares" ie. woad, alum etc., C equals 112 lbs and when reckoning "subtle wares", i.e. saffron, it equals 100 lbs.

(b) C can also mean a 'long hundred' of 120 pieces, for example with fish and sheep skins or a hundred of 100 ells when looking at certain cloths.

In practice it is often possible to work out how many pieces or lbs to the C for various commodities, based on a comparative study of values over the course of the century.

Cable & Ropes: Presumably traded in varying thickness and lengths. The 1582 book lists both tarred and un-tarred varieties by the C, containing 112 lb.

Caddow (Text: cade, cadowe, coverlette, coverging): Shipped in bundles and occurring only in the later century from Ireland, these are a type of rough covering or blanket. They are the same or similar to 'coveringes' and 'coverlettes' and are found at the same value.

Cake: Mass or concretion of any solidified or compressed substance in a flattened form, as a cake of soap, wax, etc. (OED). Rosin is found by the cake in the accounts.

Calamine: Zinc ore used in making brass alloy.

Calx (calce): Term of the alchemists and early chemists for a powder or friable substance produced by thoroughly burning or roasting ('calcining') a mineral or metal, so as to consume or drive off all its volatile parts, as lime is burned in a kiln. (OED)

Calx Vive: Quick-lime (OED).

Camphor (Text: camphere): A whitish translucent crystalline volatile substance, belonging chemically to the vegetable oils, and having a bitter aromatic taste and a strong characteristic smell: used in pharmacy, and formerly reputed as an aphrodisiac.

Camphor Wood: 'Camphor is prepared by distillation and sublimation from *Camphora officinarum* (*Laurus Camphora*), a tree indigenous to Java, Sumatra, Japan, etc., and from other lauraceous trees'. (OED) This is most likely to be unprocessed camphor.

Candarn, Bomy: Unidentified. Found in the 1540s by the 'C', possibly lbs.

Candles, *Searing:* Unidentified.

Candles, Wax: Shipped by the dozen.

Candle Wicks: Shipped by the pack which according to the book of rates contains 30C and the C contains 112 lbs. This may be an error as it would mean packs weighing 3360 lb, or a ton and a half, which seems very heavy for a pack of candlewicks.

Candlesticks: Both pewter and brass types occur in the accounts.

Canes: There are a number of possibilities for the meaning of this. It could be actual cane stems. The term 'cane' however was also used for darts or lances made from cane (OED). The 1582 book, lists 'canes of wood' valued at 10s for a 'shock' of sixty pieces, which Willan suggests are wooden drinking vessels. Interestingly, in the 1550 account, there is also a listing for 'Caens' so perhaps they could also be 'caen stones' which were building stones from Caen in Normandy.

Cannells and Tapes: Most likely from *Canel*: 'A pipe or tube; a tap for a cask' (OED). See below 'Tapes and Cannells'.

Canikin (Text: canykine): Small drinking vessels.

Capers: Shrub (*Capparis spinosa*) abundant on walls and rocky places in the South of Europe. The flower-buds are gathered for pickling. (OED)

Caps (Lat.: pilium, pillius; Text: pils', piliors): 'Pils' occur frequently in the accounts. The fact that they occur described as 'pro-noctibus' and 'pro pueris', just as caps do, and at the same value, suggests that they are the same thing.

Cap-Cases: Travelling-case, bag, or wallet.

Cap-Case Locks: Locks for the above.

Cap-Hooks: Unidentified.

Caps, Monmouth: A kind of round knitted woollen cap, which was often worn by soldiers and sailors.

Caps, Velvet

Cards, Hand: These may be playing cards.

Carpeting: Found by the yard. It is probably material for carpets or a carpet-like covering.

Case: Measurement for glass.

Cashe: Same as a chest (of sugar).

Cassia Fistula: A laxative derived from 'a wide variety of trees that produce senna leaves and cassia pods'.[11]

Cast M[ ]lions: Unidentified. An Irish export in 1563/4.

Cathurhisin: Unidentified.

Cauls (Text: cales): A kind of close-fitting cap, worn by women: a net for the hair; a netted cap or head-dress, often richly ornamented. (OED)

Cauls, for Children (Text: cales): A children's version of the caul.

Cauldrons of Brass (Text: cawdrone de bras): Large kettle or boiler.

Ceruse (Text: serry, seurfets): White lead used in medicine and ointment[12]

Chalk: A white soft earthy limestone, burned for lime, and prepared for writing or marking on blackboards or other dark surfaces.

Chappines, for women's slippers of gilt and leather: Unidentified.

Check: The meaning of this is uncertain, as the only other known 'Check' is Irish cloth. This commodity however is always seen as an export to Ireland. It could perhaps be a type of woollen thread or perhaps refers to 'chack' which is the wheat ear and is sometimes recorded as check. (OED)

Cheese (Lat.: caseus; Text: cas', casuor'):[13] Shipped by the pipe, wey or hogshead.

Chest (Text: cist): Found by the nest, which is three pieces and by the piece at varying prices, suggesting differing quality or sizes.

Chest: Variable measurement of sugar. In the pre-1558 accounts a chest equals 120 lbs and later the accounts specify that a chest contains 3C.

Chestone: A species of plum (OED). Found by the 'modul' which is an unknown unit of measurement.

Chisels: Hand tool used to cut or shape wood, metal or stone.

Cider: (Text: sider) Beverage made from the juice of apples expressed and fermented.

Cinnamon (Lat.: cinnamum; Text: cannel or cynamon): The inner bark of an East Indian tree, dried in the sun, in rolls or 'quills', and used as a spice (OED)

Cloth: See below for full cloth glossary.

Clout: A piece of cloth containing a certain number of pins or needles.

Cloves: Dried flower-bud of *Caryophyllus aromaticus*, used as a pungent aromatic spice. Often listed with ginger and mace, as they are spices of the same value.

Coal (Text: carbon', coales): Carbonum can refer to charcoal as well as mineral coal. Since Bristol was a producer of mineral coal in this period, it seems likely that imported carbon refers to charcoal. The 1594/5 and 1600/1 accounts list coal (coales) being exported from Bristol. This is probably the same as the 'Smith Coal' which is listed in the 1563/4 and 1575/6 accounts at the same value.

Coffers: (Text: cofers) A box or chest in which money or valuables are kept. The 1582 rates book lists various types; cofers with iron bars, plain cofers, cofers covered with guilt leather, painted cofers and cofers covered in velvet.

Coifs, Velvet: Close-fitting cap.

Combs (Lat.: pecten; Text: pect'): The accounts record Bone Combs, Halfpenny and Penny Combs, Old Combs, Wooden Combs (most common) and Ivory Combs.

Comb-Cases: Case to keep combs in.

Comfits (confets, comfickes): Sweetmeat made of fruit, root, etc., preserved with sugar.

Conserves: Medicinal or confectionary preparation of some part of a plant (as the flowers, leaves, roots, fruit) preserved with sugar.

---

11 Willan, *Tudor book of rates*, p. 15.   12 Willan, *Tudor book of rates*, p. 52.   13 Probably an error for *caseorum*.

Copperas: Most commonly applied to *green* copperas, the proto-sulphate of iron or ferrous sulphate, also called *green vitriol*, used in dyeing, tanning, and making ink. (OED)

Coral (corall): Relates to *red coral*, an arborescent species, found in the Red Sea and Mediterranean, prized from times of antiquity for ornamental purposes, and often classed among precious stones. (OED) Found by the 'mast' in the rates book.

Cord: A widely applied name which could refer to the ropes of a ship, the string of a bow, etc. It was also applied to strands of wire twisted or woven together.

Cord, Purse: Possibly a purse made from a ribbed fabric.

Coriander (colliand): This presumably refers to coriander seeds.

Cork (corc): *Corc nigri* is presumably black cork. Also recorded in the accounts are red and white *corc*. The OED defines cork as a purple or red dye-stuff obtained from certain lichens growing on rocks in Scotland and the north of England. It notes the 1483 statute of 1 Ric. III cap.8 which refers to the use of orchil or cork called 'Jarecork' for dyeing. Also found in the OED under litmus (a blue colouring matter, obtained from various lichens) is a reference to 'Lytmos otherwise called white Corke' from 1518.[14] The 1525–6 account has an entry of 'cers for botts' which has been transcribed as cork for bottles, but this may be a mistranslation.

Cotton Wool: Cotton in its raw and woolly state, as gathered from the bolls of the plant; raw cotton.

Counters: A 'nest' of counters is presumably 3 counting tables.

Counters, Laten, White and Yellow: Those listed by the lb, are the counters used on a counting table.

Coveringe/Coverlette: See *Caddow* above.

Crab-Locks: A crab can be a 'portable machine for raising weights, etc., consisting of a frame with a horizontal barrel on which a chain or rope is wound by means of handles and gearing. (OED) Therefore a crablock may be a device used to secure the machine etc.

Crewel (Text: cruell): A worsted yarn.

Crewel Fringe (Text: frenge): Fringe is; 'an ornamental bordering, consisting of a narrow band to which are attached threads of silk, cotton, etc., either loose or formed into tassels, twists, etc.'(OED).

Cribb: 'A load of glass is two kribbs; a krib is 100 or 150 foot of cut glass'.

Crossbow Thread (Text: crossbowtird, crossbowthred): thread or twine used on a crossbow.

Cruses, Stone (covered/uncovered): Small earthen vessel for liquids; a pot, jar, or bottle; also a drinking vessel.

Cumin (Text: comyn): See cumin seed below.

Cups, Earthen: Small open vessel for liquids, which is made of clay.

Cups Mead: Mead is an alcoholic liquor made by fermenting a mixture of honey and water. (OED)

Cups, Wooden (Text: cupes): A small open vessel for liquids, made of wood

Currants (Text: currands): Raisin or dried fruit prepared from a dwarf seedless variety of grape, grown in the Levant.

Cushions: Case of cloth, silk, etc. stuffed with soft material, used to give support to the body in sitting, reclining, or kneeling. (OED)

Cute: New wine boiled down to a certain thickness and sweetened. (OED)

Cutts: A common entry in the accounts, particularly in the first half of the sixteenth century. They are almost definitely small knives; *cutts* probably being a latin abbreviation for cultellus. A comparison of the customers and surveyors accounts for 1594 show the same object described as a knife and a *cutt*, which is telling evidence. Furthermore the 1575/6 account, has an entry for 'cutler cutts'.[15]

Cuttlebones: The internal shell of the cuttle-fish, used in medicine as an antacid and absorbent.

Daggers: Various types found in the rates book including; coarse daggers, fine and bone daggers for children and black daggers with velvet sheaths.

Dates (Text: dats,dactyl): Fruit of the date-palm, presumably exported dried.

Dimidium: (Text: Di') Half.

Dials: Type unspecified in the accounts. The 1582 rates book lists 'dialls of wood' at 12d. per dozen and also 'dialls of bone'.

Diaper Cloth: Textile of linen fabric woven with a small and simple pattern, formed by the different

---

14 Many thanks to Wendy Childs for drawing our attention to this definition for cork.   15 TNA E190/1129/12 fo5v.

directions of the thread and consisting of lines crossing diamond-wise, with the spaces variously filled up by parallel lines, a central leaf or dot, etc. (OED)

Diaper Napkin: Napkin made with the above fabric.

Dice: Small cube of ivory, bone, or other material, having its faces marked with spots numbering from one to six, used in games of chance. Listed by the 'bale'.

Dicker (Text: dacra): A measure, particularly of hides. There are ten hides to a dicker.

Dish, Chafing: Vessel to hold burning charcoal or other fuel, for heating anything placed upon it; a portable grate. (OED)

Dish, Iron Chafing: As above.

Doublets, Canvas: An item of clothing used by both sexes. They consisted of a close fitted jacket with an upright collar and short skirt.

Doublet, Sack Cloth: Sack cloth is similar to canvas.

Drinking Can: Vessel for holding liquids; made of various materials, shapes, and sizes.

Drinking Glasses, Coarse: Drinking vessel made of glass.

Drinking Glasses, French: As above.

Drinking Horn: Vessel formed from the horn of a cow or other beast, or shaped after this, for holding liquid.

Electuary: (Text: electuars) 'A medicinal conserve or paste, consisting of a powder or other ingredient mixed with honey, preserve, or syrup of some kind'. (OED)

Elephants Tusks (Text: olipante tethe): Elephant tusks.

Ell: Measurement of cloth, varying in different countries. The Flemish ell equaled 3 quarters of an English yard and five Flemish ells was equal to an English ell.[16]

Falcon (Text: fawcon).

Feathers (fethers): Shipped by the bag. These are probably feathers for beds, as found in the 1507 rates book.

Feathers, Down (Text: plumar'): more expensive than feathers, these are presumably 'down'.

Fell Fomiells: Unidentified. A suggestion is that they may be poultices for wounds etc. as 'fellis' can be translated as poison and 'fomentum' is a poultice or bandage.

Felts, Black: Felt is a textile made from wool or mixed fibres which are compressed, rolled or fulled to bind them together.[17] Felt was used mainly to make felt hats, and by association the term indicated both hats made of felt and, on occasion, hats in general.

Felts, Spanish: Felt hats made from Spanish felt wool.

Ferars: Probably ferret skins, particularly as they are valued by the dicker.

Figs (Lat.: ficus; Text: ficui, fygges): Fruit of the fig-tree or *Ficus*, esp. the fruit of the *Ficus carica* (OED). The accounts also list green figs or *ficni verdi*.

Files, Small: A metal instrument, used for abrading, or smoothing surfaces. (OED)

Fish, Cole (coal): Also known as green cod or black pollock.

Fish, Eels (Lat.: anguilla; Text: anguil'/ eles/conger).

Fish, Gurnard (Text: gurierds): Probably gurnard, a type of large marine fish.

Fish, Haddock

Fish, Hake (Text: hak, haak, hackes): According to Longfield, Hake are only supposed to have been known by that name since the fourteenth or fifteenth century, hence there was no proper latin equivalent and they are found with various spelling of the same word. These are found by the piece as well as by the cwt. There are 120 hake in a C.

Fish, Herring Red (Text: rub' alec): Smoked herring. Found by the meise, according to Longfield contained 5 long hundreds, so 600 fish.[18]

Fish, Herring White (Text: alb' alec): Found by the last and also the *verk*, which appears to be quarter of a barrel. According to Carus-Wilson, a barrel of herring was equal to 30 gallons (0.119 ton).

Fish, Mackerel: Found by the barrel.

---

16 Willan, *Tudor book of rates*, p. 82.   17 'Feather band – Fernambuck', *Dictionary of traded goods*, URL: *http://www.british-history.ac.uk/report.aspx?compid=58762&strquery=felts*, accessed 16 October 2008.   18 Longfield, *Anglo-Irish trade*, p. 48; Carus-Wilson, *Overseas trade of Bristol*, p. 337.

Fish, Newfoundland (Teext: novatera): Salted fish classified in three 'sorts'; big second and third, or as the 1582 book has it, great, middle and small.

Fish, Newfoundland Dry: Valued by the M.

Fish, Salmon: Valued by the pipe/ hogshead/butt/barrel/virkin (firkin).

Fish, Salmon Grilse (Text: girles): The name given to a young salmon on its first return to the river from the sea, and retained during the same year. (OED)

Fish, Salted (Text: pisc' sals'): These unspecified fish probably included the coarser fish, as the value per burden is not very high, and also fish that were known to be exported from Ireland and are not found separately in the accounts, such as cod, whiting, pilchard and bream, as well as hake and pike. [19]

Fish, Sardines: Found by the barrel and hogshead.

Fish, Sprat (Text: sprotts): The term sprat can be applied to many small fish including young herring.

Fish, Sturgeon (Text: sturse): Presumably an abbreviation of stureus, which according to Latham is sturgeon. [20] It is sometimes described as being 'broken'. As sturgeon are a very large fish, broken may refer to cut-up fish as opposed to the whole fish.

Flasket: A small flask. The 1582 rates book lists flaskets for gun powder covered in leather and velvet and also flaskets made of horn.

Flax (Text: flaxe): Flax is the English name of the annual Linum usitatissimum. The term flax or flaxen was used to describe the products of flax such as flax cloth, yarn and seed, or linseed, as well as the stalks from which the textile fibres are obtained.[21] As the term is applied to the plant and the fibres, it is found in the accounts, sometimes described as wrought or unwrought etc.

Fletchers Fryshe: Unidentified. The fact that it is sold by the ell indicates it is something sold by length, perhaps a type of frieze cloth.

Flitch (Text: flege): A salted and cured 'side' of bacon

Flock: Wool refuse or cloth shearings.

Fother: A weight, especially of lead. According to the *Noumbre of Weights*, it equals 19.5 C.[22] In practice, in the 1575 account for example, lead is listed by the 'piece' and fother and the amount of pieces to a fother is variable.

Frankincense (Lat.: tus; Text: thures, frankyncense)

Fringe (Text: frenge): Decorative edging for garments.

Fruit (Lat.: fructus; Text: fruct'): Unspecified types, valued by the piece or the ton.

Fubligar: Unidentified.

Funnels: A cone-shaped vessel usually fitted at the apex with a short tube, by means of which a liquid or powder etc., may be conducted through a small opening. Both tin and unspecified types are found by the dozen.

Furnando Bucke: Unidentified. This is found by the C; listed with brazil in 1594/5.

Gall (Text: gale, galir, gawles): Gall is an 'excrescence produced on trees, especially the oak, by the action of insects. Oak-galls are largely used in the manufacture of ink and tannin, as well as in dyeing and in medicine'. (OED)

Game-birds (Text: forest gylls): It is not clear what type of birds these are.

Garron: A small and inferior kind of horse bred and used chiefly in Ireland and Scotland.

Gartering: Garters are strips of material used to tie around or to stockings just below the knee to hold them in place. They were often made of rich material and could be embellished with goldsmith work or with rich embroidery. Gartering occurs frequently in the later accounts and is found by the roll or dozen, of types including crewel, Norwich and worsted. Possibly 'gartering' relates to rolls of material used to make garters and not the finished product, which turn up in pairs of types including broad, check, coarse and ribbon.

Ginger (Lat.: zingiberi; Text: zinziper, gynis): differing values and names for ginger probably distinguish green from white ginger, the former of which is more highly valued.

---

19 Longfield, *Anglo-Irish trade*, p. 49. 20 Latham, *Revised medieval Latin word list* (OUP, 2004), p. 456. 21 'Flame head – Flaxen yarn', *dictionary of traded goods*, URL: *http://www.british-history.ac.uk/report.aspx?compid=58766*, accessed 16 October 2008 22 H. Hall and F.J. Nicholas (eds) *Select tracts and table books relating to English weights and measures (1100–1742) Camden Miscellany* vol. XV (London, 1929) p. 13.

Girdles (Lat.: zona; Text: sona', zonar'): A belt, fastened at the front and hung about the waist. Described simply as zonar in the earlier accounts, there are a large varity of different types in the later accounts.

Girdle and Penners (Text: sonar' & penners): Leather girdle with a pen-case attached.

Girdle Hangers: Attached to the male girdle and consisted of two straps and a plate to which was buckled the scabbard of the sword.

Girdles, Seal: A belt with an attachment for holding a seal.

Girth: A belt or band of leather or cloth, placed round the body of a horse or other beast of burden and drawn tight, so as to secure a saddle, pack, etc. upon its back. (OED)

Girth Buckles: The buckle used to secure a girth.

Girth Web: Woven material of which girths are made; a strong broad tape used by upholsterers and others; a band made of this material. (OED)

Glass: (Lat.: vitrum; Text: vitri') Valued by the cribb and case. See above.

Glasses, Drinking: These include 'French' drinking glasses, which are the most expensive, along with 'green' glasses and cheaper varieties like 'penny' and 'halfpenny' glasses.

Glasses, Hour: An object for measuring time, consisting of a glass vessel with obconical ends connected by a constricted neck, through which a quantity of sand runs in exactly an hour. (OED)

Glasses, Looking: According to the 1582 rates book, these can be made of crystal or steel.

Gloves: A covering for the whole of the hand, usually one with a separate sheath for each finger. (OED)

Gloves, Venice: Presumably gloves having some connection with Venice.

Glue (Text: glew): 'A hard, brittle, brownish gelatin, obtained by boiling the hides and hoofs of animals to a jelly; when gently heated with water, it is used as a cement for uniting substances'. (OED). Valued by the lb.

Goad: Cloth measure of 1.5 yards.

Goshawks: A large short-winged hawk

Gouge and Formes (Text: gowge and formes): A gouge is a chisel with a concave blade for cutting rounded grooves or holes in wood. Formes is possibly a related object.

Grain: See kermes.

Graters: An instrument with a rough indented surface used for grating or rasping.

Grid-Irons: A cooking utensil formed of parallel bars of iron or other metal in a frame, usually supported on short legs, and used for broiling flesh or fish over a fire. (OED)

Grind-Stones: A disc of stone revolving on an axle, used for grinding, sharpening, or polishing. (OED)

Gross: Twelve dozen. A 'great' gross is twelve gross.

Gunpowder (Text: gounpodor, cornpowder): An explosive mixture of saltpetre, sulphur, and charcoal, chiefly used in discharging projectiles from guns and for blasting. (OED) The 1582 rates book lists 'gunpoulder called corn poulder' and cornpowder is found at the same value as gunpowder in the accounts.

Halbertes, Gilt or Ungilt: A pike fitted with an axe; a battle axe.

Hats: A covering for the head; generally distinguished from other head-gear, such as cap's by having a more or less horizontal brim all round.

Hatchets, Dansk: A smaller or lighter axe with a short handle, adapted for use with one hand. These are presumably from Gdansk, or are made in a similar style.

Hawk Hoods: A covering for a hawk's head and eyes.

Hawser: A large rope or small cable, in size midway between a cable and a tow-line, between 5 and 10 inches in circumference; used in warping and mooring; in large ships now made of steel. (OED)

Headstalls (Text: headstales): The part of a bridle or halter that fits round the head of an animal. Presumably these were not just for horses, since the 1600/1 account has headstalls also headstalls for horses at differing values.

Hedlack: A linen cloth.[23] This is found by the lb in the accounts and so may be a linen thread, rather than cloth.

Hemp (Text: hempe): An annual herbaceous plant, *Cannabis sativa*, cultivated for its valuable fibre or the fibre of this plant, used for making cordage, and woven into stout fabrics. (OED)

---

23 Willan, *Tudor book of rates*, p. 22.

Hides, Ginney[24]: Hides from Guinea, West Africa. The OED has Ginney as a spelling for Guinea. The specific type of hide is unknown.

Hides, India: Type of hide is unknown.

Hides Kip (kip tannat): The hide of a young animal used as leather (OED). It is taxed in the same way as normal tanned hides (see below) but pays half the custom.

Hides Tanned (Lat.: Corium; Text: corrior tannat): Leather. Tanned hides pay the Ancient Custom of 8*d*. per dicker, the Parliamentary subsidy of 40*d*. per dicker, the 'Calais Penny' of 1*d*. per dicker (payable on all leather exported to places other than the Calais Staple). Each consignment also has to pay a sum, usually 2*d*. for the exit cocket (certificate) issued by the customer.

Hilts and Pommells: The hilt is the handle of a sword; the pommel is the counterweight at the top of the handle to provide the desired balance.

Hinges, Portal: Hinges for a door or gate.

Hogshead: Measure of capacity of wine etc., equal to one quarter of a tun.

Holland Sheets: Presumably sheets made from Holland cloth, which was a linen fabric from the province of Holland.

Honey (Lat.: mel; Text: mellis): Valued by the barrel.

Hooks, Fish: Barbed hook used for catching fish.

Hooks and Eyes: Fastenings made of steel wire, sown to the inside of bodices and doublets as invisible fastners. These replaced points in the late 16th century as fasteners of hose to garments, with the points remaining as decoration only.[25]

Hooks, Hake: Fish hooks specific to hake fishing.

Hopes for Serches: See Serches below

Hops (Text: hoppis, hoppys, lupulor): Female flowers of the plant *Humulus Lupulus*, which are used as a flavouring and stabiliser in beer production.

Hoperods: Possibly a rod for removing hops from the poles on which they grew. The National Hop Association of England website has reproduced an image with a quote by Reynolde Scott, dated from 1574; 'Cut them asunder with a sharp hook and with a forked staffe, take them from the poles.'[26] Perhaps these Hop rods are such staffs.

Horse (Lat.: equus; Text: equis): Value was presumably determined by declaration of the merchant. Note, since 1495, the export of horses without a licence had been prohibited, unless it was declared to be for the merchant's own use.[27]

Horse Combs: Values suggest that, like ordinary combs, horse combs came in different types.

Hose: 'An article of clothing for the leg; sometimes reaching down only to the ankle as a legging or gaiter, sometimes also covering the foot like a long stocking'. (OED)

Indigo: Blue dye, obtained from shrubs of the genus *indigofera* in the pea family.

Insense (Text: ensone): An aromatic substance such as wood or gum that is burned to produce a pleasant odour.

Ink Horns: A small portable vessel (originally made of a horn) for holding writing-ink. (OED)

Inkle (Text: yncle): A linen tape of various qualities and widths.

Iron (Lat.: ferrum; Text: ferri): A metal, used for making tools, weapons, implements etc.

Isinglass: A firm whitish semitransparent substance obtained from the sounds or air-bladders of some fresh-water fishes, esp. the sturgeon; used in cookery for making jellies and also for clarifying liquors, in the manufacture of glue, and for other purposes. (OED)

Ivory: A hard, white, substance composing the main part of the tusks of the elephant, hippopotamus etc., very expensive and used ornamentally.

Items misc. (Text: diversus parius rebus): Term used to describe what is probably 'lots' of small manufactured items.

Jerkins, Leather (Text: jurkins): A close-fitting jacket, jersey, or short coat, often made of leather.

---

24 TNA E190/1132/11 fo7r.   **25** URL: *http://www.vertetsable.com/research_vocabulary.htm#h*, accessed 16 October 2008.   **26** National Hops Association of England website, URL: *www.hops.co.uk/sectionone/History.htm*, accessed 18 December 2007,   **27** *Statutes of the Realm*, III, pp 323–5.

Jhumblas: According to Willan 'jumb' is perhaps jujuba a sort of plumb growing mainly in Provence, used as an aperient and expectorant.[28]

Kerchief (Text: kerchers): 'A cloth used to cover the head, formerly a woman's head-dress'. (OED)

Kermes (Text: graynes, graines): 'Graynes' are usually kermes 'the pregnant female of the insect *Coccus ilicis*, formerly supposed to be a berry; gathered in large quantities from a species of evergreen oak in S. Europe and N. Africa, for use in dyeing, and formerly in medicine; the red dye-stuff consisting of the dried bodies of these insects' (OED) There is room for confusion in the accounts however as it seems that 'graynes' can mean kermes or 'graines' which according to Willan are Guinea grains or malagueta pepper.[29]

Kilderkin (Text: kinderkin): A cask for liquids or fish etc. It is usually equal to half a barrel.

Kippe: A measure for skins containing 50 skins.[30]

Knives (Lat.: culter; Text: cult', knyves)

Knives, Almaine: German knives.

Knives, Bumbard/ Bombard: Unidentified.

Knives, Cappe: Unidentified.

Knives, Cullen (Text: collyn, collen): Probably Cologne knives.[31]

Knives, Flanders: From Flanders, or possibly resembling Flanders knives.

Knives, Paring (Text: paringe): It is sometimes difficult to tell if knives in pairs are in fact 'paring knives'. The fact that paring knives do exist in the accounts, despite not being listed in the 1582 rates book, is suggested by the 1575/6 account, which has an entry for *pairs* of 'paringe knyves'at 2d. per pair.[32]

Knives, Prage: Possibly a knife for eating with.

Lace, Chain (Text: cheine): The dictionary of traded commodities suggests that this is similar to 'Chain Boulee', which is described as 'A short rough cord made in macrame lace (made of knotted thread) with two threads'.[33]

Lace, Statute: Likely to be actual lace and not laces/points.

Lacquer (Text: laqor, lacqor): A gold-coloured varnish, consisting chiefly of a solution of pale shellac in alcohol, tinged with saffron, anatta, or other colouring matters; used chiefly as a coating for brass. (OED)

Lanterns (Lat.: lanterna; Text: lanthornes): A transparent case, e.g. of glass, horn, talc, containing and protecting a light.

Last: A measure of hides equal to 20 dickers and of fish, equal to 12 barrels.

Lead (Lat. Plumbum; Text: plumbi'/ plumb' operat): Lead 'in sowes' is a 'large oblong mass of solidified metal as obtained from the blast- or smelting-furnace'. (OED) This is clearly different from the bars of lead also identified in the accounts.

Lead, White: It is possible that white lead was a name used for tin. (OED)

Lemons: Valued by the M (thousand).

Lime (Text: lyme) Alkaline earth obtained by submitting limestone to a red heat, by which the carbonic acid is driven off, leaving a brittle white solid, which is pure lime.

Liquorice (Text: licoric, licor'): The rhizome of the plant *Glycyrrhiza glabra*. Also, a preparation (used medicinally and as a sweetmeat) made from the evaporated juice of this rhizome. (OED)

Loaf: A moulded conical mass of hard sugar made by passing syrup through already refined sugar in a sugar pot. Loaves varied in size.[34] If bought in this form the sugar would have been broken up using sugar nippers. Loaves in the accounts contain anything from 6 to 11lb.

Locks, Hanging: Padlocks.

Locks, Small Spring: A form of lock in which a spring presses the bolt outwards.

M: A thousandweight or ten hundreds or hundred weights. *See* C.

28 Willan, *Tudor book of rates*, p. 76.　29 Willan, *Tudor book of rates*, p. 30.　30 Zupko, *Dictionary of English weights and measures*, p. 213.　31 Willan, *Tudor book of rates*, p. 20.　32 TNA E190/1129/12 f19r.　33 'Chain – Chandelier', *Dictionary of traded goods*, URL: http://www.british-history.ac.uk/report.aspx?compid=58721, accessed 16 October 2008.　34 'Sugar loaf – Surfeit water', *Dictionary of traded goods*, URL: http://www.british-history.ac.uk/report.aspx?compid=58889, accessed 16 October 2008

Mace: Aromatic spice found surrounding the seed in the fruit of the nutmeg tree, dried and used as a spice.

Madder: A reddish-purple dyestuff obtained from the root of the plant *Rubia tinctorum*. Also used medicinally.

Madder,Green: This may be the unprocessed root of the plant.

Madder, Mul: The lowest grade of madder, obtained by grinding the loose fibres and fragments detached from the root during threshing. (OED)

Mail (Text: mayles): Can be a bag or a pack and also the metal rings used in armour. As this is valued by the lb, the latter, also called anlets, is more likely.

Mailing Cord (Text: maylinge corde): Cord for tying round a mail (bag) or for tying a mail to a horse.

Malt (Text: brac' bracy): Barley or other grain prepared for brewing, distilling, or vinegar-making, esp. by steeping, germinating, and kiln-drying.

Mantles (Text: mant'): A kind of blanket worn in rural Ireland and the Scottish Highlands.

Mantles, Small (mant' parvas): Possibly 'waist mantles'.

Marmalade: A preserve, consisting of a sweet, solid jelly.

Masts: Upright pole or spar, fixed in the keel of a sailing ship in order to support the sails. *See also* coral above.

Mastic: Aromatic gum or resin which exudes from the bark of the lentisk or mastic tree, *Pistacia,* used chiefly in making varnishes and in medicine.

Matches: Piece of wick, cord, etc., used to fire a cannon or other firearm.

Match Cords (Text: matye cordes): 'piece of rope prepared as a slow match'. (OED)

Meal: The edible part of a grain or pulse, ground to powder or granules.

Measure: A measure of woad etc., of varying quantity.

Meise: *See* red herring.

Mercury (Text: argent 'vive, quicksilver): According to the OED, quicksilver is 'The metal mercury, so called from its liquid mobile form at ordinary temperatures'.

Merells: The game piece used in nine men's morris.

Millstones: A pair of circular stones which grind corn by the rotation of the upper stone on the lower.

Millstones, Small called Doggstones: A smaller version of the above.

Molasses (Text: malases): Thick, brown, uncrystallized syrup drained from raw sugar.

Morions, Plain (Text: morines): A type of helmet without a visor.

Nail Blades (Text: nalblade): Possibly a blade for cutting nails.

Nails, Board (Text: borde naile, bord naylle, borde nayle): Presumably these were nails used mostly to nail down wooden boards. The OED suggests a brad or a large spike.

Nails, Fourpenny: A type of lath nail, used for 'Pantile Lathing'.[35]

Nails, Lath: Lath is the term 'denoted a thin narrow strip of wood, used to form a groundwork on which to fix slates, tiles or the plaster of a wall or ceiling. A lath nail was a type of headed nail used for fixing lath to battens. There were two types of lath nails. The first were the 'Reparation or Lath Nails, which are used for plain Tile Lathing, and outside and inside Lathing for Plastring'. The other sort were the 'four Penny, and six Penny Nails, used for Pantile Lathing' as above. The former were smaller and seem to have been sometimes described as twopenny or threepenny lath nails.[36]

Nails, Rouze: These are most likely 'rove' nails. A rove, according to the OED is 'A small metal plate or ring on which the point of a nail or rivet is clinched or beaten down in the building of boats or small ships.

Nails, Rouze & Clenth: These are likely to be Rove and Clinch nails as found in the OED above.

Nails, Scopp: Unidentified type of nail.

Neck Bracelets: An ornamental ring or band worn on the neck.

Necklaces: 'An ornamental chain or string of jewels, precious metal, beads, etc., worn round the neck.' Also ' a lace or ribbon for the neck; a necktie'. (OED)

Necklaces, Bugle: *See* bugle bead.

---

35 'Lasch – Lazy back', *Dictionary of traded goods,* URL: *http://www.british-history.ac.uk/report.aspx? compid=58807,* accessed: 16 October 2008.   36 'Lasch – Lazy back', *Dictionary of traded goods,* URL: *http://www.british-history.ac.uk/report.aspx?compid=58807,* accessed: 16 October 2008.

Needles (Text: nelds): Valued by the clout which is a piece of cloth containing a certain number of pins or needles.

Needles, *Jhus*: Unidentified, but presumably specialist needles.

Needles, Spanish: Unidentified type of needle, but presumably of Spanish origin or style. They must also have been quite substantial in size as the OED provides a reference from Markam in 1615, which states that the best substance with which to make Angling hooks, is either old Spanish needles, or else strong wire. [37]

Needles, Yellow Band: Unidentified but presumably specialist needles.

Nickel: 'A hard silvery-white chemical element, which is both malleable and ductile, and which usually occurs in combination with arsenic or sulphur' As nickel was discovered from *kupfernickel* (copper of the devil 'nick') in 1751, this entry possibly relates to the latter, which had some uses for colouring glass green.

Nutmeg (Text: nuttmygge, nutmigg) A spice used for culinary and medicinal purposes. [38]

Oakum (ocam): The fibres of hemp or flax used for caulking the seams of ships and as a wound dressing.

Oclem pro seri: Unidentified.

Oclem Serptorn: Unidentified.

Oars (ores): A long pole, widened and flattened at one end into a blade, used to propel a boat by pressure against the water.

Oar Ends: The blade of the oar, as above.

Oar Staves: Stick of wood used to make oars.

Ochre: A mixture of varying proportions of clay and iron oxide used as a pigment.

Ochre, Yellow: As above, a yellow pigment, when the iron oxide is limonite.

Oil, Olive (Lat.: oleum; Text: olie, olii): This is olive oil which was also sometimes called 'wool oil' because its chief use was in the processing / cleaning of raw wool. *Olium* is sometimes specified as Seville Oil, which according to the OED is olive oil from Seville.

Oil, Bay: Made from bay or laurel berries and used as a perfumed oil.

Oil, for lamps (oleum pro lampadis).

Oil, Petroleum:A viscous liquid, that is formed by the decomposition of organic matter buried in sediments, is present in some rock formations and is extracted and refined to produce fuels. (OED)

Oil, Punice: Unidentified. This commodity only occurs in the 1600/1 account. [39] It is expensive, valued at £20 per tun and is imported to Bristol from France. It is not recorded in the 1582 rates book. One suggestion is that it could be Pomegranate seed oil as *punica* is the latin for pomegranate. There is also an interesting reference cited in the OED from Wornum, 'Punic wax (*cera Punica*) was..the common yellow wax, purified and bleached by being boiled three times in sea-water, with a small quantity of nitre... This wax was the Greek substitute for oil in painters' colours'[40]. It could therefore be an oil used in painting. It seems unusual however that either of these would be found in such large quantities as occur in the account.

Oil, Train (Text: trayn): Train oil comes from boiling the blubber from whales or seals. May also be applied to fish oil – esp. cod liver oil in this period.

Olives (Text: oil berries): Shipped in barrels.

Onions: Found in bunches, ropes and barrels. Onion seed in contrast is found by the C weight.

Orchil (Text: orrchall, archal): a 'red or violet dye prepared from certain lichens'.

Orchement: Unidentified. It does not appear to be Orpiment or Ornament as in the rates book, as its value is much higher.

Organ Pipes (old): Generally made out of metal or wood, these are the sound producing elements of a pipe organ.

---

37 M. Gervase, *Country contentments in two bookes: the first containing the whole art of riding great horses,* etc.: *the second intituled The English huswife* 1615 (1631, 1649, 1668), from OED online. **38** For detail on preparation for trade etc. see 'None so pretty – Nutmeg plums', *Dictionary of traded goods*, URL: *http://www.british-history.ac.uk/report.aspx?compid=58828*, accessed 16 October 2008. **39** TNA E190/1132/11 fo7r., fo7v. **40** R.N. Wornum (ed.) Lectures on painting, by the Royal Academicians Barry, Opie, and Fuseli v.d. (1848) cited in the OED online.

Pane: A bundle of varying from 30 to 100 skins.

Pans: Listed in the accounts by their weight. For example in the 1550/1 account there is '1 pan waying 10lb'.

Pans, Brass: As above.

Pans, Dripping: Pan used to catch the 'dripping' from roasting meat.

Pans, Frying: A shallow pan, usually of iron, with a long handle, in which food is fried.

Paper: Usually either brown or white and valued by the ream, which according to the 1582 rates book is 20 quires.

Paper, Brown: A less expensive type of paper than the white variety.

Paper, Gold: Presumably this is a paper dyed a gold/yellow colour or embossed with gold.

Parchment Skins: Piece of animal skin, esp. from a sheep or goat, dressed and prepared as a surface for writing.

Peas (Lat.: pisum; Text: pisar, pis'): Any of the seeds of the plant *Pisum sativum* which grow in elongated pods and are eaten as a vegetable, or as a pulse when dried.

Pect: In most cases 'pect'' are combs, and are found by the dozen. They also occur however by the bale. In 1516 a bale of 'pect' is valued at 20s. These are possibly reeds from the Latin *pectin*. Reeds are listed in the 1582 rates book, but by the C/M. Nevertheless this seems a possible explanation as a bale is a typical unit for hay etc.

Penners: A metal or leather case for holding pens.

Pepper (Lat. Piper; Text: piperis): Spice derived from the peppercorns of the pepper plant.

Percular: Unidentified. Variable value.

Perfume: Uncertain if this is liquid based or insense.

Petticoat: A women's light loose undergarment in the form of a shirt or dress.

Pewter Salt: As this is found by the dozen, it may relate to a pewter container for salt.

Pile Weights: A series of brass weights, fitting one within another.[41]

Pilus Tinctus: There is uncertainty regarding the exact meaning of this term. Wendy Childs and Elenor Carus-Wilson have both interpreted it as 'dyed hair', possibly a reference to dyed wool. Longfield on the other hand has interpreted it as dyed cloth. Given that it is always found by the lb, the former explanation seems more likely. A further suggestion is that it is a type of coloured thread (phili) which can also be found by the lb. *Pils* have also been found in the accounts and have been translated as caps (see caps above). It is possible that piliors tinct may be a coloured material used in cap making.

Pin-Wheel: A revolving circular box or drum with wooden pins projecting from the inner surface, in which hides are washed, softened in the process of leather making.

Pipe: A cask; hence a measure. A pipe of wine is equal to half a tun. Its varies with other commodities.

Pipe Boards: These are the timber pieces used to make a pipe cask.

Pipe Staves: Similar to the above.

Pipes, Tobacco: Probably made of clay or wood.

Pitch (Text: piche, pytche, pytch, pitche, piche, pich): 'A tenacious resinous substance of a black or black-brown colour, hard when cold, but becoming a thick, semi-viscid liquid when heated. It was used among other things to stop the seams of ships after caulking and to protect wood from moisture. It was also used medicinally to treat coughs, arthritis, and as an ingredient of ointments.'[42]

Pitch, Hearth: May be the same as pitch as it has the same value.

Plate Locks: Probably refers to a lock made from metal plate.

Playing Cards (Text: cardes pro ludendo, cart pict' (picture): Set or pack of cards, used in playing various games.

Playing Tables: Table on which games are played;. one which has a playing board inlaid on its surface.

Pocket: Sack or bag, sometimes used as a measure of quantity, particularly for hops, where it equals 3C.

Points (Lat.: ligula; Text: ligul', laces): 'A tagged lace or cord, of twisted yarn, silk, or leather, for attaching the hose to the doublet, lacing a bodice, and fastening various parts where buttons are now used'. A large variety of types are found.

'Laces' have been entered in the datasets as 'points', since, while the term is not used anymore, it was

---

41 Willan, *Tudor book of rates*, p. 10. 42 'Pine – Pitchfork', *Dictionary of traded goods*, URL: *http://www.british history.ac.uk/report.aspx?compid=58842*, accessed 16 October 2008.

the term used at the time to describe an item of dress-ware that is not used today. A slight difficulty with this however is that it is sometimes difficult to distinguish in the later accounts between laces (points) and lace. For example chain lace and statute lace could be laces or lace, although the dictionary of traded goods suggests that chain lace is a cord.

Porpoise (Text: porpas): Any of various small delphinoid whales of the family Phocoenidae, characterized by a blunt, rounded snout and usually a low, triangular dorsal fin. Presumably porpoise shipped by the barrel is porpoise meat, while those shipped by the piece are intact.

Portmanteau (porteos, portmantial, port manters): A case or bag for carrying clothing and other belongings when travelling.

Potel: A 'pottle' can be a pot or vessel capable of holding a pottle (i.e. half a gallon) of liquid

Pots, Brass: Recorded similarly to pans, so probably 'cxx libr pott brasse' for example means brass pots/pot weighing 120 lbs.

Prunes: Dried plums, but the term was sometimes used for fresh fruit also.[43] They are shipped in 'punchons' and each punchon holds 4 C.

Pullock (Text: pullocke): The OED lists pellock or pullock as 'A dolphin, porpoise, or similar marine animal. This however may also refer to 'Pollack' which the OED defines as any of several edible marine fishes having a protruding lower jaw, now or formerly included in the genus *Pollachius*', which includes such fish as coal-fish, also found in the accounts.

Puncheon: Large wooden vessel, resembling a cask, used for several different commodities.[44]

Purses (Lat.: crumena; Text: purs' / cruminar): Money bag or receptacle for money. Various types exist, defined by the fabric used, or the style/origin/utilisation of the purse, for example 'Venice purses' and 'pin purses'.

Quadraer: Unidentified. A possibility is that this is quartern wire, which the dictionary of traded goods suggests was a fine wire, valued by the lb like virginal wire.[45]

Quarter: The fourth part of some usual measure.

Quern Stones: Stones for grinding grain.

Quintal (Text: kindal): Equal to a hundredweight.[46] Found as a measurement for iron.

Raisins (Text: resyngs, resons, raisinges): Partially dried fruit of some varieties of grape. Listed in the 1582 rates book as 'Great' raisins, a term sometimes used to distinguish between raisins and 'Corinths' or currants.

Raisins, Gallipola: Probably raisins from Gallipoli in Turkey.

Raisins, Malaga: Raisins from Malaga, Spain. The 'dictionary of traded goods' suggests that these were 'Raisins of the Sun', which were probably also produced in other areas.[47] The accounts suggest otherwise however as Malaga raisins are valued at 6s. 8d. per C, the same as 'great' raisins, while raisins of the sun or sundried raisins are valued at 16s. 8d. per C.

Raisins, *Rotta*: Unidentified.

Raisins, *Shoeris* (sheres, shoeris): Unidentified.

Raisins, of the Sun (Text: raysons of the sunne, raisins solis): Sundried raisins.

Ream: *See* paper.

Ribbons (Text: rybbands): Various types found. *See* Caddis, Check, Saye, Crewell.

Rice: Food grain obtained from the seed of the plant *Oryza sativa*.

Rings, Copper: Probably ornamental rings as the 1582 book lists 'copper rings fine with stones the dozen'.

Rope: Usually made of twisted strands of hemp, flax, or other fibrous material, but also of strips of hide, pliant twigs, metal wire. (OED)

Rosin (Text: rozen, rosin, rosen): Obtained as a residue of the distillation of oil of tupentine from crude turpentine and used along with pitch on ships as a sealant / preservative. It was also an ingredient of

---

43 'Precipitate – Prussian blue', *Dictionary of traded goods*, URL: *http://www.british-history.ac.uk/report.aspx?compid=58847*, accessed 16 October 2008.   44 Zupko, *Dictionary of English weights and measures*, p. 329.   45 'Quadrille box – Quoiler', *Dictionary of traded goods*, URL: *http://www.british-history.ac.uk/report.aspx?compid=58849*, accessed 16 October 2008.   46 Zupko, *Dictionary of English weights and measures*, p. 342.   47 'Rabbeting plane – Ranter', *Dictionary of traded goods*, URL: *http://www.british-history.ac.uk/report.aspx?compid=58850*, accessed 16 October 2008.

soap, and was used to treat coughs, arthritis, and as an ingredient of ointments. It was most likely traded in its solid form, as the later accounts mostly contain rosin by the cake.

Rugg: A type of rough woollen blanket from Ireland.

Rye: Food-grain obtained from the plant *Secale cereale.*

Rye Meal: Ground Rye with the bran bolted out.

Saddle (Text: sadles): Seat for a horse rider with side flaps and fitted with girths and stirrups.

Saffron (Lat.: croceus; Text: croc'): An orange-yellow spice, used also as a medicine and a dyestuff, made from the dried stigmas of the crocus.

Sails (sels): Pieces of canvas or other strong textile material fastened to the masts, spars or stays of a vessel, so as to catch the wind and cause it to move through the water. The accounts also contain 'Sail Yardys' which is probably the nautical term for the yards (spars) to which a sail is fixed. (*See* OED.)

Salt (Lat.: sal; Text: sal, sel, sawlte): Listed sometimes as Bay salt, which is from Borgneuf Bay, south of the Loire; made by evaporation, it produces large crystals or white salt, which is prepared and refined mainly for household use.

Sandlewood: A tree of India which has a hard fragrant timber, used as a dyewood and in medicine.

Saws: Sometimes specified as 'hand saws' which were carpenters saws, according to the 1582 rates book.

Saw Files: A file specially adapted for sharpening the teeth of saws.

Scabbard (Text: scaberd): A cover for the blade of a sword or dagger.

Scissors (Text: siseres): Cutting instrument consisting of a pair of handled blades.

Scrofe (Text: scrof): Perhaps refuse wool but as it is valued higher than wool flocks it seems unlikely.

Scythes (Text: sithes): Tool used for cutting crops such as grass or corn with a long curved blade. These could also be 'sithes' which the OED defines as milk strainers.

Sea Horse Teeth: Hippopotamus teeth, traded for their ivory.

Seals (Text: seles, seale fish): In the 16th century seals were sometimes described as a type of fish, along with porpoises.

Seal Pigs: Possibly also seals, although they are half the value of seals in the accounts.

Seeds, Caraway (Text: caraweyes): Small fruits from the plant *Carum Carui* . Used medicinally and as a spice.

Seed, Cumin (Text: commenseed, cummin): Seed of a plant cultivated in the Levant for its fruit, which possesses aromatic and carminative qualities.

Seed Fennel: *Fœniculum vulgare*, cultivated chiefly for its use in cookery.

Seed, Leek (Text: licke, leeke sede): A culinary herb.

Seed, Mustard: Seed of a mustard plant.

Seed, Onion (Text: ynion): Seeds imported to grow onions, a culinary vegetable.

Seed, Porcelic: Perhaps parsnip or parsley seed.

Senna (Text: senys, senie): A large genus of flowering trees, growing in warm climates. The senna in the accounts is probably a laxative prepared from the dried pods of the trees.

Serches: Serches always arrive as a minor part of an iron consignment from the Spanish Basque region and are likely to be sieves. The OED has 'searce' as a sieve or strainer, and it appears to have been often written as serche or sarch. This explanation would also help to explain the presence of 'hopes for serches' in the accounts.

Seron: A bale or package made up in an animal's hide, usually of soap.

Setting Stick: stick used for making holes for 'setting' or planting.

Sheets: these are bed sheets as they are found by the pair. Coarse sheets are possibly hempen and Holland sheets, which are more expensive, are made from Holland linen.

Ship-Boards: Plank of a ship.

Shoe Horns: Tool for assisting the user to put on shoes more easily.

Shovel (Text: showyll): Type not specified.

Silk, Black Spanish: Probably the 'silk of Granado black the pound' (xvi ounces) as listed in the rates book as 'Spanish silk' is more expensive than this.

Silk, *Bredth Peny* (Text: Peny Bredth Silke): Unidentified.

Silk, Bridges: Silk from Bruges.

Silk, Caddis (Text: caedese sylke): 'Floss silk' used as padding etc. (OED)

Silk, Ferrett (Text: floret) : A kind of coarse silke. Also known as floss silk.[48]

Silk, Flanders: From Flanders.

Silk, Nobs: Uncertain. The OED lists 'nob' as a knot (on thread).

Silk, Paris: Found by the 'paper', which is equivalent to two pounds.

Silk Raw (Text: rawe): This can mean silk simply drawn from the cocoons by the process of reeling and also a fabric of spun silk. As this is shipped by the lb, like all other silks, it is likely to be the latter.

Silk, Cyprus (Text: Sipers): A name given to several textile fabrics originally imported from or through Cyprus.

Silk, Slewed: Slew is a filling made of two or more strands worked together.

Silk, Stiching (Text: stitchinge): Silk thread.

Silk, Worked (Lat.: serica operat; Text: seric' op'at): 'Thrown' or 'worked silk' generally refers to silk thread, in particular silk thread consisting of two or more 'singles' twisted together. (OED)

Skillets, Small: Cooking utensil of brass, copper, or other metal, usually having three or four feet and a long handle, used for boiling liquids, stewing meat, etc.

Skins, Beech Marten (Text: pell' foyne): A marten native to southern Europe. Used for the fur or dressed skin.

Skins, Beaver: Amphibious rodent with a coat of soft fur. Valued by the roll, which is a measure of varying length.

Skins, Budge (Text: pell' de boge/bougie): A kind of fur, consisting of lamb's skin with the wool dressed outwards. These originated in North Africa.

Skins, Calf (Lat.: vitula; text: pell' vitul'): A form of leather. The export of calf skins was subject to the same restrictions as the export of tanned hides.

Skins, Civit (Text: pell' de sivett): Wild-cat of central African origin.

Skins, Cony (Text: cunny skyns, coney stagers): a rabbit: formerly the proper and ordinary name, but now superseded in general use by *rabbit*, which was originally a name for the young only. (OED) The grey variety are sometimes called coney 'stagers'.

Skins, Deer (Lat.: cervus; Text: pell' cervor): There were several kinds of deer skins exported from Ireland to Bristol in the sixteenth century and the more expensive type seen here may for example be Hart hides, which, according to Longfield, were more expensive.[49]

Skins, Fawn (Text: pell' fawn): young fallow deer, a buck or doe of the first year.

Skins, Fish (Text: pell' pisc'): Probably had a variety of uses.

Skins, for Fletchers (Text: pro fletchers): The only skin listed in the rates book that is similar to this in spelling is 'fitches' which according to Willan is the skin of a polecat. The entry in the 1503/4 account however clearly states 'pro' fletchers. A fletcher, according to the OED was 'One who makes or deals in arrows; occasionally, one who makes bows and arrows'. It is possible then that fletcher skins were used by fletchers in the regard.

Skins, Fox (Lat.: vulpes; Text: pell' vulpis, fox cases): Used for fur.

Skins, Genet: a civet-cat native to southern Europe and North Africa, that produced a high value pelt.

Skins, Goat (Text: goate skynns): used as a garment but also to make purses and wine bottles etc.

Skins, Golden (Lat.: aureolus; Text: pell' aureor'): presumably some form of dyed and tanned skin.

Skins, Greis: The OED states that 'in grease' was a term used chiefly in hunting and indicates that an animal was in prime and fit to kill. It suggests 'Greis' may be a shortened version denoting a hart or deer killed during this season. These however occur in the 1550/1 account at a value of only 5s. for sixty skins, which seems too little for this quantity of deer skins. In 'greis' may be a general term applied to any animal killed in season. As the value is given per piece it is unlikely that it refers to animal grease of any kind.

Skins, Kid (pell' 'edors, hedorn): mostly used for making gloves and shoes.

Skins, Lamb (Lat.: agnus; Text: pell' agn'): The 1582 book divides between white and black skins, which implies they had wool on them. It is clear though whether the earlier skins had wool on them. Interestingly, while there are a small number of lamb skins imported from Ireland in the 1575/6 account,

---

48 Willan, *Tudor book of rates*, p. 54.   **49** See Longfield, *Anglo-Irish trade*, p. 65, for a detailed discussion.

there are none in the 1594/5 or 1600/1 account and all lamb skins are entered as Morkins, which are, according to the rates book, skins from lambs that died of disease.

Skins, Marten (Text: pell' martron): The fur of martens seems to have been mostly used as edging on fine gowns etc.

Skins, Morkin: The skin of a sheep or lamb that has died of disease or accident.

Skins, Otter (Text: pell' otur): The examples given in the OED suggest that the use of otter skins varied from jerkins to quivers for arrrows.

Skins, Red (pell rub', rubeor): Like 'golden skins' these were probably dyed skins.

Red-Lash (Text: redlesh): A kind of fine red leather. The 1507 book values 'rede lashe for cusshyns' so presumably this is one manner of usage.

Skins, Salted: Salted cow hides.

Skins, Sheep (Lat.: ovis; text: pell' oviu'): Worked or 'tawed' skins are rare in the accounts and it seems likely that these did not have wool.

Skins, Sheep Broken (Text: brok' fell'): short-stapled wool found in certain parts of the fleece, when 'broken' or sorted. A fleece consists of two main kinds of wool distinguished by the length and strength of the fibre; the sorts which are long and suitable for combing being called 'matchings' or 'combing-sorts', the rest 'short wools' or 'brokes'. The spinning of the two sorts is by different processes.

Skins, Spanish: Type of leather.

Skins, Vellim for Drums Head (Text: velum): Fine parchment made from animal skin, used to stretch over a drums head.

Skins, Wolf (Lat.: lupus; Text: pell' lupor): Used for fur.

Sleek Stone: Smooth stone used for smoothing and polishing.

Snaffles: simple form of bridle-bit, having less restraining power than one provided with a curb.

Snatches: A hasp, catch, or fastening.

Snuffers (Text: snoufers): candle snuffers.

Soap, Black (Text: sapon nigri, *smigmates*): The OED states that there were two types of Castile soap, white and mottled, Black soap perhaps relates to the latter. Carus-Wilson suggests 'smigmates' are a kind of soap, based on an entry in the *Account Rolls of Abbey of Durham*,[50] Therefore 'blacksoap' may be the English translation for smigmates. Classical Latin has *smegma* or *smigma* (for which one form of the dative plural is *smigmatis*); the definition in Lewis and Short (under 'smegma') is 'cleansing medicine or detergent', as opposed to 'soap' for *sapo*.[51]

Soap, Castile (Lat.: sapo; Text: sope, sapon): fine hard soap made with olive-oil and soda. There are two kinds, the white and the mottled. (OED)

Sort: *See* figs.

Spectacles: Device for assisting defective eyesight, or for protecting the eyes from dust, light. (OED)

Spectacle Cases, Ungilded: Case for glasses not gilded or in other words overlaid wholly or in parts with a thin coating of gold.

Spermaceti (Text: sparmacete): A fatty substance found in the head of the sperm-whale and used largely in various medicinal preparations, and in the manufacture of candles.

Spert: Possibly refers to hartwort, a herb which, according to Culpepper is ' a warm martial plant, both heating and drying; it provokes urine and the menses, expels the birth and after birth; and is good in disorders of the head and womb'.[52]

Spikenard (Text: spignard): an aromatic substance employed in the preparation of a costly ointment or oil, obtained from an Eastern plant, now identified as the *Nardostachys Jatamansi* of Northern India. (OED)

Spurs: Device for pricking the side of a horse in order to urge it forward. Various types found including 'white' and 'coarse' spurs.

Starch (Text: styrtche, sterche): Substance obtained from flour by removing some of its constituents, various uses including stiffening fabrics and sizing paper.

Stecull: Unidentified.

---

50 Carus-Wilson, *Overseas trade of Bristol*, p. 338.   51 *URL: http://www.perseus.tufts.edu/cgibin/ptext*, accessed 15 October 2008.   52 URL: *http://www.complete-herbal.com/culpepper/sermountain.htm*, accessed 14 October 2008.

Steel: General name for certain artificially produced varieties of iron, distinguished from those known as 'iron' by certain physical properties, esp. greater hardness and elasticity. (OED)

Stock-Card (Text: stockards): Not to be confused with stockings. These are large wool-cards fastened to a stock or support. Probably a quicker and cheaper method than using a wool card.

Stockings: Close-fitting garment covering the foot, the leg, and often the knee. Various types found, defined by length or fabric used.

Stock-Lock: A lock enclosed in a wooden case, usually fitted on an outer door. (OED)

Stone (petra): A weight varying locally and for different commodities; from 8 to 24 lbs.

Strats (stratts): Unidentified but possibly decribes a strait of some commodity such as cloth or ribbon.

Sturse: *See* sturgeon fish.

Stygret: Unidentified; possibly a spice or medicine.

Succade (Text: succado): Fruit preserved in sugar, either candied or in syrup.

Sugar-Candy: Sugar clarified and crystallized by slow evaporation

Sugar, Mucovado: Raw or unrefined sugar obtained from the juice of the sugar cane by evaporating it and draining off the molasses.

Sugar, Panele (Text: panells): Brown unpurified sugar from the Caribbean.

Sugar, Powder (Text: saccari powther de Brasill): Refined sugar, crushed into powder.

Sugar of Roses (Text: succar rosars): Made of red rose buds and double refined sugar reduced to a powder separately and then combined, mixed with a little water, and formed into lozenges before drying.

Sulphur (Text: brymstone): A greenish-yellow non-metallic substance, found in volcanic regions, and occurring free in nature as a brittle crystalline solid, and widely distributed in combination with metals and other substances. (OED)

Sumach: A preparation of the dried and chopped leaves and shoots of plants of the genus *Rhus*, used in tanning, also for dyeing and staining leather black, and medicinally as an astringent. (OED)

Sword Blades: Swords are often traded in their various componants as well as finished.

Sword Hilt: The handle of a sword or dagger.

Taishaill: Unidentified. As this is an export from Ireland in 1503/4, it is unlikely to be a manufactured item.

Tallow, Rough (Lat.: sebum; Text: cepi/cepe rowe): Hard substance made from animal fat, used for making candles and soap. There are two types, rough and rendered or 'molton' which was more expensive.

Tankard: A drinking-vessel, formerly made of wooden staves and hooped. It can also be a tub or basin.

Tapes and Cannelles: 'Tapes', when they occur with 'cannells' are probably Taps, as a cannel according to the OED was a pipe for a cask.

Tar: Dark, thick flammable liquid distilled from wood or coal, used for preserving wood.

Teazle/Teasel (Text: tezell, teasell, tasel): A plant with prickly leaves, used to produce a napped surface on fabrics.

Tennis Ball: used in tha game of tennis.

Terra Sigilla: Perhaps 'Terra Sigillata' as in the 1582 book of rates, an astringent bole used for medicinal purposes. **Testers:** A flat canopy for a bed.

Thimbles: Bell-shaped sheath of metal or leather worn on the end of the finger to push the needle in sewing.

Thread, Bridges (Text: brigges): Bruges thread.

Thread, Inkle (Text: ynkle): A kind of linen tape or the thread or yarn from which it is made.[53]

Thread, Outnall: A kind of linen thread. Willan suggests that it is from Oudenaarde as the 1558 Book of Rates has Owtnarde.[54]

Thread, Packet: Strong cord or twine used for sewing or tying up packs or bundles.

Thread, Paris: Presumably thread from Paris.

Thread, Piecing: Used for repairing cloth.

Thread, Sisters: Bleached thread

Thrummys (Text: thrums): Ends of the warp-threads left unwoven and remaining attached to the loom when the web is cut off. (OED)

---

53 Willan, *Tudor book of rates*, p. 34.　54 Willan, *Tudor book of rates*, p. 61.

Ticks (Text: tikes): The case or cover containing feathers, flocks, or the like, forming a mattress or pillow; also from 16th c., applied to the strong hard linen or cotton material used for making such cases.

Tierce: Measure of capacity equivalent to one third of a pipe, usually of wine but also means a cask or vessel holding this quantity, and can be of various other kinds of provisions such as honey.

Tin (Lat.: stannum; Text: stanum): Well-known metal with many uses including making tin-plate and lining culinary and other iron vessels.

Tobacco: Dried and prepared tobacco plant leaves.

Ton: Measure of capacity for various solid commodities, such as lime, wheat, cheese, etc.

Torch: Hand-carried light, consisting of a stick of resinous wood, or of twisted hemp or similar material soaked with tallow, resin, or other inflammable substance.

Tow (Text: towe): The fibre of flax, hemp, or jute prepared for spinning by some process of scutching.

Treacle (Text: treakle): A medicinal compound, composed of many ingredients, formerly in repute as an antidote to venomous bites, poisons generally, and malignant diseases. (OED)

Treenails (Text: dowels): A cylindrical pin of hard wood used in fastening timbers together, particularly in shipbuilding and other work where the materials are exposed to water.

Trenchers: A plate or platter of wood, metal, or earthenware.

Tressels: Unknown but unlikely to be a 'trestle' as shipped by the 'M'.

Tun: A cask of definite capacity; hence, a measure of capacity for wine and other liquids, usually equivalent to 2 pipes or 4 hogsheads, containing 252 old wine-gallons.

Tunnage: The space occupied by a tun cask of wine which was the unit used in measuring the carrying capacity or burden of a ship.

Turnsole: A violet blue or purple colouring matter.[55]

Turpentine: Resin from coniforous trees. Distilled turpentine is used to create a volatile oil.

Urinals: Glass vessel used to collect urine for medical examination.

Verdigris (Text: vertigris): A chemical with a vivid blue-green colour; used as a pigment and also had medicinal uses.

Vestments: Presumably items of ceremonial clothing from latin *vestimentum*..

Vice, Hand: A mechanical device used to operate another piece of apparatus (OED)

Vinegar (Text: vini egri): This is 'corrupt' wine; produced from the acetous fermentaion of wine and used in food preservation and cooking.

Violes: Possibly small containers for medicine (i.e. vial).

Violes, Square: As above.

Virkin (Text: vyrk, firkin): Measure of salmon; equal to a quarter of a pipe.

Visers (Text: vizars): The front part of a helmet, covering the face but provided with holes or openings to admit of seeing and breathing, and capable of being raised and lowered

Wainscot: Wooden panelling.

Walnut: The nut of the walnut tree. The seed of the mature fruit is eaten like any other nut, and the soft unripe fruit is used entire for pickling. (OED)

Wax (Lat.: cera; Text: wex / cere): Substance produced by bees and when warm it can be moulded to any shape. It could be bleached white or left in its original yello colour. Uses include candle-making, seals and coating writing tables.

Wax, Red (Text: cere rub'): Probably used for seals.

Wey: Measure of salt, coal, wheat etc., varying locally and for different commodities. A wey of wheat for example equals 6 quarters which equals 48 bushels.

Whale Meat (Text: pisc' de whals): Presumably this refers to whale meat since in the sixteenth century, sea mammals such as dolphins and whales were often classed as fish.

Wheat: Grain used to produce flour. Valued by the wey or quarter.

Whittles (Text: whitelles): Coarse shaggy mantles made in Ireland; also blankets.

Wick Yarne (Text: wike): Possibly yarn used to make candle wicks.

Wine: Usually described according to its origin, i.e., Canaries, Bordeaux, Charente, Malaga, Gascon etc.

Wine, *Alegant*: This possibly refers to *alegar*, which is vinegar formed by the acetous fermentation of

---

55 Willan, *Tudor book of rates*, p. 62.

ale ie. malt-vinegar and is to ale what vinegar is to wine. If so, it is not clear why it is recorded as wine. A further possibility is that it refers to Alicante wine.

Wine, Bastard: Sweet Spanish wine.

Wine, Madeira: Fortified dessert wine.

Wine Muscadel: Any of various sweet wines made from muscat or similar grapes.

Wine, Rob Davy: This, according to the OED, is Roberdavy wine, a wine used in the 16th and 17th centuries.

Wine, Seck/Sack: General name for a class of white wines imported from Spain and the Canaries.

Wine *Peresomena*: Unidentified.

Wine, Virginall: Possibly relates to wine used in the virginal, a keyed instrument.

Woad: A yellow flowered plant whose leaves were used to make blue dye. Despite the variety of terms used to describe Woad in the accounts, study of its values and the locations from where it is exported to Bristol over the course of the century suggest that there are actually only two main types, Woad from Toulouse and Azores or Green Woad.

Woad, Azores (Text: wod / gaid de insulis/ gualdi viridi/ pastel de surries): All found in the later accounts coming from Sao Miguel and Terceira in the Azores. Green Woad almost always comes from St Michael's or Sao Miguel which is also known as 'Green Island' and so this name may have been used to identify woad from there.

Woad, Toulouse (Text: wood, ode, gaid de Tholos, Tolos): Toulouse in France.

Wood Ashes: The 1582 book lists 'ashes called wood or sope ashes the last'. Willan suggests that these were 'ashes from burnt wood, which provided the alkaline base for soap.'[56] There is a possibility that the ashes in the accounts are 'woad ashes' as the spelling is always 'wod or wode'. The OED acknowledges that woad ashes can refer to this definition also, but the term more commonly denotes burnt wine lees, which are used to make a dye.

Wood, Block: Logwood. The wood of an American tree used in dyeing and also in medicine as an astringent. The name derives from the fact that it was imported in logs.

Wood, Box, for combs (box pro pecten): Used for making combs.

Wood, Brazil (Text: brazel): A red wood from which dye is obtained.[57] The term can also be used to refer to the dyestuff extracted from the wood.

Wood, Clapholt (Text: clappoll): Clapboard is 'A smaller size of split oak, imported from north Germany, and used by coopers for making barrel-staves' (OED).

Wood, Deal (Text: deale boards): Planks or boards of fir or pine wood.

Wood, Fir (Text: fyreboards): Fir wood imported from Norway.

Wood, Irish (Irish boards): Technically a board is a piece of timber sawn thin, and having considerable extent of surface. The type of timber is not specified.

Wool Cards (Text: wolcards): These were used to disentangle fibres of wool prior to spinning.

Wool, Flock (Text: folic / flox): Refuse wool – tufts of wool suitable for stuffing beds etc.

Wool, Irish (Lat.: lana; Text: lane hibn'): Sheep or lambs wool.

Wool, Spanish (lane hespan'): This is probably Spanish felt wool, used for making hats.

Wormseed (Text: wormsed): Native to Central and South America and the Caribbean. It was used to expel intestinal parasites (especially roundworms and hookworms) in humans and animals. It was also used to make a tea for menstrual cramps, fever, and chills.

Yard (Text: virg): A measurement for cloth. The statute yard is 36 inches.

GLOSSARY OF CLOTH

Cloth of Assize [58]

Cloth of Assize, without Grain (Lat.: pannus sine grano; Text: pann' sine grano): This was the standard woollen broadcloth for customs purposes: 24 yards x 2 yards in size. It is important to note that a

56 Willan, *Tudor book of rates*, p. 6.　　57 Willan, *Tudor book of rates*, p. 10.　　58 Strictly speaking, many

cloth of this size rarely existed in reality, the standard 'broadcloth' type of cloth was assessed for customs purposes in terms of how many cloths it would make up. Without grain meant the cloth was not dyed using the expensive scarlet dyestuff 'grayne' (kermes).

Cloth of Assize, dyed with Grain (Lat.: pannus in grano; Text: pann' in grano): Broadcloth dyed with kermes.

Cloth of Assize, Dozen: A 'dozen' cloth was 12 yards long, rather than the usual 24 yards.

Cloth of Assize, Strait: In the E122 series of accounts, a strait cloth was half the width of standard broadcloth, and paid half custom. In the later accounts however a streit or street is valued as a sixth of a cloth which is confirmed by the 1582 rates book.[59]

Cloth of Assize, Dozen Strait: Half the width and half the length of a standard cloth a quarter of a cloth.

Cloth of Assize, Bridgwater: Equivalent to half a standard cloth.

Cloth Cardinals, White: According to the 1582 rates book, there are 6 cardinals to a standard cloth.

Cloth of Assize, Devonshire Dozen: Usually four to a standard broad cloth.

Cloth of Assize, Devonshire Dozen Double: Two to a standard cloth

Cloth of Assize, Kersey: When paying the ancient custom, there are three of these to one standard cloth.

Cloth of Assize, Northern: Exact size or value unclear.

Cloth of Assize, Northern Dozen: Exact size or value unclear.

Cloth of Assize, Northern Plains and Checks: Four to a standard cloth.

Cloth of Assize, Western Dozen/Western Kersey: Equal to a quarter of a cloth

Cloth of Assize, Penistones:[60] Four unfriezed penistones, or two friezed, to a standard cloth.

Cloth of Assize, Pinwhites: Six to a standard cloth.

Cloth, Other

Cloth, Bay (Text: baie): A napped material, half worsted with a warp of combed wool. Used for stiffening and lining. Range of quality depended on number of threads per inch.[61]

Cloth, Bologna Sarcenet (Text: bollonia): A soft thin silk in plain or twill weaves.

Cloth, Breton (Text: brecnocks): A woollen cloth.

Cloth, Breton Canvas (Text: canvas britan'): Canvas cloth from Brittany.

Cloth, Breton Linen (Text: pan' linen britan'): Linen cloth from Brittany.

Cloth, Bristol White: Probably a white woollen cloth.

Cloth, Buckram: A stiff-finished heavily sized fabric of cotton or linen used for interlinings in garments, for stiffening in millinery, and in bookbinding.

Cloth, Buckram Black: A less expensive variety of buckram.

Cloth, Buffin: A coarse cloth in use for the gowns of the middle classes. (OED)

Cloth, Calico: One of the oldest cottons, originating in Calcutta, India. It is generally plain white, coarse and light-weight.

Cloth, Cambric: A kind of fine white linen, originally made at Cambray in Flanders. (Also applied to an imitation made of hard-spun cotton yarn.)

Cloth, Camlet (Text: chamlet): A fine, lustrous, woollen fabric made of camel hair, angora wool, or silk.

of the cloths in this category had their own customary sizes but the term 'cloth of assize' has been used in this volume to distinguish those cloths of English production which are generally found to be customed pro rata in relation to the standard broadcloth and therefore paid specific rather than 'poundage' duties. These cloths usually do not have nominal values ascribed to them in the accounts. They were taxed in this manner because of the difficulties associated with the many different types, sizes and weights of cloth produced in England. It is clear from the often inconsistent methods of estimating cloth duties used by the customs officers, that a certain amount of rough estimation was used to value such cloths. Due to this and various other methodological issues, any analysis of the relative importance of woollen cloth over the course of the century can only produce very broad trends.   59 Willan, *Tudor book of rates*, p. 73.   60 E. Charlesworth, 'A local example of the factors influencing industrial location', *Geographical Journal*, vol. 91, no. 4. (Apr. 1938), 340–51.   61 URL: *www.vertetsable.com/research_bibliography.htm*, accessed 12 Oct. 2008.

Cloth, Canvas: A strong or coarse unbleached cloth made of hemp or flax, used as the material for sails of ships, for tents, and by painters for oil-paintings, and also for clothing, etc.

Cloth, Changeable Taffeta: A silk taffeta in which the warp threads were of one colour and the weft threads were of another.[62]

Cloth, Check (Text: chek): A rough woollen cloth, imported from Ireland.

Cloth, Check Manchester: A coarse woollen cloth from Manchester

Cloth, Cottons: A woollen cloth found by the goad, which was a measure of 1.5 yards.

Cloth, Damask: Could be a rich silk or a rich linen fabric.[63]

Cloth, Dornick with wool (dornix en Lani): A cloth originally manufactured at Doornick in Flanders.[64]

Cloth, Dowlas or Lockram: A coarse linen, used for cloak bags and cases as well as for neckwear and clothing by the lower classes.[65]

Cloth, Dunster Cotton: Not listed in rates book, presumably a woollen cloth.

Cloth, Flannel (Text: flanen): An open woollen stuff, of various degrees of fineness, usually without a nap. (OED)

Cloth, Frieze: A kind of coarse woollen cloth, with a nap, usually on one side only.

Cloth, Fustian: A cloth made of cotton and flax.

Cloth, Fustian Holmes: A fustian made at Ulm in Germany.

Cloth, Fustian Jeane: A kind of fustian from Genoa, Italy.

Cloth, Fustian Milan: A kind of fustian from Milan, Italy.

Cloth, Fustian, Osborne: Unknown origin.

Cloth, Grosgrain Coarse (Text: grograine): A coarse fabric of silk, of mohair and wool, or of these mixed with silk; often stiffened with gum. (OED)

Cloth, Hamborough & Portingale: Probably Hamburg and Portuguese cloths.

Cloth, Hair (Text: here): 'Cloth or fabric made of hair, used for various purposes such as tents, towels, shirts of penitents and ascetics; also in drying malt, hops, or the like. (OED)

Cloth, Holland: A linen from the province of Holland.

Cloth, *Lemagois*: Unidentified cloth.

Cloth, Mantle Frieze: Presumably the frieze cloth used to make mantles.

Cloth, Mockado: A mixed fabric of wool and silk, in imitation of velvet, from Flanders[66]

Cloth, Molton: OED: A kind of coarse, heavily fulled cloth with the warp of hemp and the weft of poor quality carding wool.

Cloth, Motley: A woollen cloth.

Cloth, Ozenbridge: A linen cloth of Osnabrück.

Cloth, Paris: This may be serge as the account also list 'serge, called Paris cloth' but at a lower value.

Cloth, Poldavis: A coarse canvas cloth from Pouldavid in France.

Cloth, Sack (cloth for sacks): Coarse textile fabric used chiefly in the making of bags or sacks and for the wrapping up of bales.

Cloth, Sarcenet: A fine silk material.[67]

Cloth, Satin: A silk fabric with a glossy surface on one side.

Cloth, Saye: A lightweight cloth usually made from worsted and woollen yarn.

Cloth, Serge: A woollen fabric, which up until the 16th century was chiefly used as material for hangings, bed-covers, etc. After this it is often referred to as worn by the poorer classes (both men and women), probably due to its durability rather than of its price, which was never especially low. (OED)

Cloth, Soultwich: This is a linen cloth, probably from Salzwedel in Germany.[68]

Cloth, *Stolorn:* Unidentified Cloth.

Cloth Taffeta: A name applied at different times to different fabrics, in this case probably a plain-wove glossy silk.

---

62 URL: *www.vertetsable.com/research_bibliography.htm*, accessed 13 Sept. 2008.　63 Willan, *Tudor rook of rates*, p. 21.　64 Willan, *Tudor book of rates*, p. 22.　65 URL: *www.vertetsable.com/research_bibliography.htm*, accessed 11 Aug. 2008.　66 Willan, *Tudor book of rates*, p. 41.　67 Willan, *Tudor book of rates*, p. 51.　68 Willan, *Tudor book of rates*, p. 56.

Cloth, Taffeta Levant: The term 'Levant' signifies that the cloth originated in the eastern part of the Mediterranean.

Cloth, Taffeta Towers: Probably from Tours in France.

Cloth, Tissue: A rich kind of cloth, often interwoven with gold or silver. (OED)

Cloth, Velvet (Text: velure): Textile fabric of silk having a short, dense, and smooth piled surface. (OED)

Cloth, Wadmal (Text: wodnall, wodmal): A coarse woollen material used principally for covering horse-collars, and other rough purposes; for petticoats, mittens, etc. (OED)

Cloth, Worsted: A woollen fabric made from well-twisted yarn spun of long-staple wool combed to lay the fibres parallel. (OED)

Glossary of place-names

Port Modern	Name in Accounts	Country	Co-ordinates
Alderney	Aldern	Channel Islands	49° 42′ 0′ N, 2° 4′ 60 W
Amsterdam	Anster, Anser, Amsam	Netherlands	52° 23′ N, 04° 54′ E
Andalusia	Andolosia, Andolosar	Spain	
Arcuzauries[1]	*Arcuzauries*	Unknown	
Antwerpen	Anwarpe	Belgium	51° 12′ N, 04° 26′ E
Arnemuiden	Armewe	Netherlands	51° 30′ N, 03° 41′ E
Ars-en-Ré[2]	Ile de Ars	France	46° 12′ N, 01° 31′ W
Aveiro	Avero	Portugal	40° 37′ N, 08° 38′ W
Ayamonte	Eymontie, Amounty	Spain	37° 13′ N, 7° 23′ W
Baldeike[3]	Baldeike	Ireland (?)	
Ballyhack	Bellohake	Ireland	52° 15′ N, 6° 58′ W
Barnstaple	Barnestable	England	51°5′ N, 04°03′ W
Barry	Barry	Wales	51° 24′ N, 03° 17′
Bergen-op-Zoom	Barrow	Netherlands	51° 30′ N, 4° 18′ E
Bawnard	Bawdenolle	Ireland	51° 53′ N, 8° 10′ W
Bayonne	Bayon, Bay, Boyne	France	43° 29′ N, 1° 29′ W
Berkeley	Barcklie	England	51° 41′ N, 2 27′ W
Bermeo	Barmew	Spain	43° 25′ N, 2° 43′ W
Bewdley	Bewdeley	England	52° 23′ N, 2° 19′ W
Bideford	Bydford, Byddyforde	England	51° 01′ N, 4° 12′ W
Bigges Weare[4]	Bigges Wear, Bixwier, Co. Gloucestershire	England	
Bilbao	Bilbowe	Spain	43° 15′ N, 02° 54′ W
Blavet	Bluet	France	47° 45′ N, 02° 21′ W
Bloie[5]	Bloie	France (?)	
Bokeslate[6]	Bokeslate	Unknown	
Bordeaux	Burdeux, Burdux	France	44° 51′ N, 0° 34′ W
Boscastle	Bottes Castell, Botescastle	England	50°41′ N, 4°41′W
Bremen	Bremen	Germany	53° 05′ N 08° 51′ E
Brest	Breste. Breeste	France	48° 24′ N, 4° 29′ W
Bridgwater	Briggwatter	England	51°7′ N, 3° 00′ W
Bristol	Bristoll, Bristow	England	51° 27′ N, 2° 35′ W
Bourgneuf (?)	Burniffe	France (?)	
Cabo de San Adrián	Adrian	Spain	43° 21′ 0 N, 8° 49′ 60 W
Cabo de Saõ Vicente	St Vincent	Portugal	37° 01′ N, 8° 59′ W
Cadiz	Cales, Calis, Calix,	Spain	36° 32′ N, 6° 17′ W
Caerleon	Carlyon	Wales	51° 37′ N, 2° 57′ W
Camarinas	Kamyno	Spain	43° 08′ N, 09° 10 W

1 Unidentified. This is the 'home port' of a prize ship, so probably a Spanish port. 2 *Il de Ars* may be Ars-en-Ré, on the island on Il -de-Ré, off the Western Coast of France. 3 Unidentified. Most likely an Irish place-name. 4 Exact location unknown. 5 Possibly Blavet. 6 Unidentified.

Port Modern	Name in Accounts	Country	Co-ordinates
Veere[7]	Camphere	Scotland	
Candelaria[8]	Candalars, Candie, Candalary	Spain/Portugal	
Cardiff	Cardeff	Wales	51° 29′ N, 3° 11′ W
Carigham[9]	Carigham, Kerry	Ireland	
Carmarthen	Carmarthen, Carmthen	Wales	51°51′ N, 04°19′ W
Cashel	Cashel	Ireland	52 °31′ N, 7° 53′ W
Castrow[10]	Castrow	Unknown	
Charente	Sherante	France	
Chepstow	Chepsto′	Wales	51° 38′ N, 2° 40′ W
Cherbourg	Sherbrocke	France	49° 38′ N, 01° 37′ W
Churcham	Churcham	England	51° 51′ N, 02° 20′ W
Clonmel	Clonmell	Ireland	52° 21′ N, 7° 43′ W
Combe Martin	Combe	England	51°12′ N, 4° 01′ W
Combwich	Comewich, Comydge	England	51° 8′ N, 3° 13′ W
Cork	Corke	Ireland	51° 54′ N, 8° 28′ W
Crail	Carell	Scotland	56° 16′ N 2° 38′ W
Crozon	Croyden	France	48° 15′ N, 4° 30′ W
Dartmouth	Dartmouth	England	50° 21′ N, 3° 35′ W
Deusto (Bilbao)[11]	Dews	Spain	43° 15′ N, 2° 55′ W
Dingle	Dengell, Dinglecush	Ireland	52° 8′ N, 10° 16′ W
Drogheda	Dorodats	Ireland	53° 43′ N, 6° 21′ W
Dublin	Devalyg, Devablyn	Ireland	53° 20′ N, 6° 16′ W
Dundalk	Doundawk	Ireland	54° 00′ N, 06° 24′ W
Dungarvan	Dungarvan	Ireland	52° 5′ N, 7° 38′ W
Elmore	Elmor, Elmower	England	51° 50′ N, 02°18′ W
Emden	Emdon, Emdin	Germany	53° 22′ N, 7° 13′ E
Errenteria	Rendrie	Spain	43° 19′ N, 1° 54′ W
Exmouth	Exmoth	England	50° 37′ N, 03° 24′ W
Falmouth	Ffalmothe	England	50° 09′ N, 5° 04′ W
Faro	Farowe	Portugal	37° 01′ N, 07° 56′ W
Fécamp	Feccam, Feckam	France	49° 46′ N, 0° 23′ E
Fethard-on-Sea	Feddar	Ireland	52° 11′ N, 06° 50′ W
Fowey	Foye	England	50° 20′ N, 04° 38′ W
Framilode	Framylade	England	51° 4′ N, 02° 21′ W
Fremington	Fremington	England	51°04′ N 4°07′ W′
Friesland	Freslond	Netherlands	
Fuenterrabia[12]	Fountraby	Spain	43° 22′ N, 1° 28′ W
Galicia	Gallizia	Spain	43° 0′ 0″ N, 8° 0′ 0″ W
Galway	Gallowaye	Ireland	53° 16′ N, 09° 03′ W
Gatcombe	Gatcombe	England	51° 47′ N, 02° 3′ W
Gdańsk	Danncowyck, Dannes, Dansike	Poland	54° 21′ N, 18° 39′ E
Gibraléon	Geburlion	Spain	37° 23′ 0″ N, 6° 58′ 0″ W
Genoa	Jene, Jeynet, Jeyne	Italy	44° 25′ N, 8° 56′ E
Glandore	Glandore	Ireland	51° 34′ N, 09° 07′ W
Glasgow	Glascoe	Scotland	55° 32′ N, 04° 15′ W
Gloucester	Gloc′	England	51° 52′ N, 2° 15′ W
Granville	Grandevilla	France	48°50′ N, 01° 36′ W

7 Campvere, or Veere, is in the Netherlands on the island of Walcheren, near Middelburg. Vere was the location of the Scottish staple in the Low Countries down to the eighteenth century. 8 This could be Saõ Miguel in the Azores, or alternatively Tenerife in the Canary islands. 9 Unidentified town. 10 Unidentified. 11 Deusto or Deustu is a district of the city of *Bilbao*, on the right bank of the *estuary of Bilbao*. 12 Alternate name for Hondarribia.

Port Modern	Name in Accounts	Country	Co-ordinates
Guernsey	Garnesey	Channel Islands	49° 27′ 0′ N, 2° 32′ 0′ W
Guinea	Ginney	Africa	
Haarlem	Harlam	Netherlands	52° 22′ N, 4° 38′ E
Hampton	Hampton	England	50° 45′ N, 3° 3′ W
Hanley Castle	Hanley	England	52° 5′ N, 02° 14′ W
Hasfield	Hasfeld, Haysfeld	England	51° 56′ N, 02° 15′ W
Haverford West	Hereford	England	51° 48′ N, 4° 58′ W
Haydon	Temple Haydon, co. Somerset	England	51.27° N 02.46° W
Holt	Holte	England	52° 16′ N, 02° 15′ W
Hondarribia	Fountraby	Spain	43° 22′ N, 1° 28′ W
Honfleur	Hownflete	France	49 25′ N, 0 14′ E
Hoorn	Hoorne	Netherlands	51° 13′ N, 5° 57′ E
Hull	Hull	England	53° 43′ N, 0° 20′ W
Huntley	Hunteley	England	51° 5′ N, 02° 24′ W
Hutton	Hutton	England	51°19′ N, 2°56′ W
Ile d'Oléron[13]	Olone, Olderone, Olone	France	
Ilfracombe	Ilfercombe	England	51°12′ N, 4° 07′ W
Island of Madeira	Insulas de Mathera	Portugal	
Kenilworth Castle	Kellenworth	England	52° 21′ N, 1° 35′ W
Kingswood	Kingswood, Co. Wilts*hire*	England	
Jersey	Gersey, Gerse	Channel Islands	49° 11′ N, 2° 6′ W
Kenton	Kenton	England	50° 38′ N, 03° 28′ W
Kidwelly	Kydwelly	Wales	51°44′ N, 4°18′ W
Kilkenny	Kilkenny	Ireland	52° 39′ N, 7°15′ W
Kilmallock	Kilmallock	Ireland	52° 39′ N, 7°15′ W
Kingswear	Kingsweye	England	50° 24′ N, 08° 35′ W
Kinsale	Kensale, Kynsale	Ireland	51°42′ N, 8° 31′ W
La Foye[14]	Lafoile, La Foyle	France	
Lantringuier[15]	Lantrea, Lantriger	France	
Larmuster, Larmister[16]	Larmuster, Larmister	France (?)	
La Rochelle	Rochell	France	46° 10′ N, 01° 09′ W
La Tremblade	Tremlado, Trimlavi	France	45° 46′ N, 1° 09′ W
Laugharne	Laugharne	Wales	51° 46′N, 4° 28′ W
Lasa (?)	Lasa	Portugal (?)	
Le Conquet	Conquete	France	48° 22′ N, 4° 47′ W
Le Croisic	Crosewiecke	France	47°18′ N, 2° 30′ W
Leith	Leeth	Scotland	55° 59′ N, 03° 10′ W
Lequeitio	Lettewre[17]	Spain	
Lezo	Lezo	Spain	43° 19′ N, 1° 54′ W
Limerick	Lymbricke	Ireland	52° 40′ N, 08° 37′ W
Lisbon	Luxbon	Portugal	38°44′ N, 9° 08′ W
Liverpool	Lyvorpole	England	53° 25′ N, 2° 59′ W
Livorno	Ligorne	Italy	43° 32′ N, 10° 19′ E
Llansteffan	Lanstaffan	Wales	51° 46′ N, 04° 23′ W
Longney	Langney	England	51° 48′ N, 02° 20′ W
Lübeck	Lubiecke	Germany	53° 52′ N, 10° 42′ E
Lyme Regis	Lyme	England	50° 44′ N, 2° 56′ W

13 Other possibilities include Olonne-sur Mer and Les Sables d'Olonne just north of Rochelle and also the Ile de Ré. 14 Lafoile is possibly La Foye, in the Charente-Maritime Department of France. 15 H. Touchard, *Le commerce maritime Breton a la fin du moyen age* (Paris, 1967) p. 184. 16 A suggestion is Noirmoutier, off Les Sables d'Olonne, France. 17 Lettewre is probably Lettewe, which was often the medieval English form of Lequeitio in Biscay.

Port Modern	Name in Accounts	Country	Co-ordinates
Madeira Islands	Madderooes	Portugal	
Magor	Magor	Wales	51° 34′ N, 2°49′ W
Majorca	Mayorlia	Spain	39° 37′ 0′ N, 2° 59′ 0′ E
Málaga	Malaga	Spain	36° 43′ N, 04° 25′ W
Malahide	Malahyde	Ireland	53° 27′ N, 6° 09′ W
Mallow	Mallow	Ireland	52° 08′ N, 8° 39′ W
Marennes	Maryne	France	45° 49′ N, 1° 06′ W
Marseilles	Marcellus	France	43° 18′ N, 5° 23′ E
Marshfield	Marshfield, Co. Gloucestershire	England	51° 28′ N, 2° 20′ W
Mathern	Mathern	Wales	51° 37′ N, 02° 40′ W
Messes	Messes	France	
Middelburg	Mydleborowe	Netherlands	51° 30′ N, 3° 38′ E
Milford Haven	Milford	Wales	51° 43′ N, 05° 02′ W
Millbrook	Millbrooke	England	50° 20′ 49" N, 04° 12′ 57" W
Minehead	Mynhed	England	51° 12′ N, 03° 29′ W
Minsterworth[18]	Minsterford	England	51° 51′ 10" N, 02° 19′ 30" W
Morales[19]	Morles	Spain	36° 48′ N, 2° 15′ W
Mometes	Mometes	Unknown	
Morbihan	Morbean	France	47° 36′ 0″ N, 2° 48′ 0″ W
Moreton	Morton	England	50° 42′ N, 02° 16′ W
Mortain	Mortania	France	48° 39′ N, 0° 56′ W
Mount's Bay	Mountes Baie	England	50° 07′ N, 05° 32′ W
Mumbles	Mumbull	Wales	
Mundaka	Mundake	Spain	43° 25′ N, 2° 42′ W
Mutriku	Motrico	Spain	43° 18′ N, 2° 23′ W
Nantes	Nantes	France	47° 13′ 1° 33′ W
Newlyn	Newlyn	England	50° 26′ N, 5° 33′ W
Newnham	Newnam	England	51° 48′ N, 02° 27′ W
Newport	Newport	Wales	52° 1′ N, 04° 50′ W
New Ross	Ross	Ireland	52° 23′ N, 6° 57′ W
Nongell[20]	Nongell	Unknown	
Northam	Northam	England	51° 02′ N, 04° 12′ W
Nostradam	Nostradam	Unknown	
Odemira (?)	Odiem	Portugal	37° 35′ 0′ N, 8° 38′ 0′ W (?)
Oldbury-on-Severn	Olebury	England	51° 38′ N, 2° 34′ W
Oloone of Barges[21]	Oloone of Barges	France (?)	
Orio	Orio	Spain	43° 16′ N, 2° 56′ W
Overton	Overton	Wales	52° 58′ N, 2° 34′ W
Padstow	Patstow	England	50° 32′ N, 4° 56′ W
Paimboef	Peimots	France	47° 17′ N, 2° 01′ W
Paimpol	Pympole	France	48° 47′ N, 3° 02′ W
Palma de Mallorca	Palma	Spain	39° 34′ N, 02° 39′ E
Purton[22]	Parton	England	54° 34′ N 03° 35′ W
Pasajes de San Juan	Passage, Pasaia	Spain	43°19′ N, 01°57′ W
Passage East	Passage	Ireland	52° 14′ N, 6° 59′ W

18 Minsterford has not been identified but it is possibly Minsterworth in Gloucestershire. 19 Found in 1516, coming from Seville with a cargo of fruit and wine. Morles may relate to the Morales river in southern Spain. A further possibility, although unlikely in view of the cargo is that Morles is Morlaix in Brittany. 20 Possibly Youghal. 21 Possibly relates to Olonne. See note 76 above. 22 A small pill/loading place on the River Severn. *URL:www.bris.ac.uk/Depts/History/Maritime/Sources/ 1565bristol.htm*, accessed 10 July 2008.

Port Modern	Name in Accounts	Country	Co-ordinates
Pembroke	Penbroke	Wales	51° 40′ N, 04° 55′ W
Penmarch	Penmarch, March (?)	France	47° 49′ N, 04° 20′ W
Piltown	Pilto[ ]n	Ireland	52° 21′ 12″ N, 7° 20′ 25″ W
Plymouth	Plymothe	England	50° 22′ N, 4° 8′ W
Portugal	Portugale	Portugal	
Pouldavid	Poldavy	France	
Puerto de Santa Maria	St Marys Port	Spain	36° 36′ N, 6° 14′ W
Quimper[23]	Kynprollantyne	Unknown	
Quimperlé	Quimperleye	France	47° 52′ N, 3° 32′ W
Renteria[24]	Rendrie	Spain	43° 19′ N, 1° 54′ W
Ribadeo	Ribadew	Spain	43° 33′ , 07° 02′ W
Roosendaal	Rosendale	Netherlands	51° 31′ N 04° 28′ E
Roscoff	Roscoe	France	48° 43′ N, 3° 59′ W
Rothesay	Rothe	Scotland	55° 50′ N, 05° 03′ W
Royan	Roane, Royon	France	48° 38′ N, 1° 01′ W
Saffolania	Saffolania	Unknown	
Salcombe	Saltcome	England	50° 14′ 13″ N, 03° 46′ 08″ W
San Antonio Abad (?)	Sanct Anthonio	Spain	28° 38′ 60″ N, 17° 46′ 0″ W (?)
Sanlúcar de Barremeda	Seint Lucar	Spain	36°46′ N, 06°21′ W
St Pol de Lyon	San Poule de Lyon	France	48°41′ 10′ N 3°59′ 06′ W′
San Sebastián	Sent Sebastyan	Spain	43° 19′ N, 01° 59′ W
Saõ Miguel (Green Island)	St Michaells	Portugal	37° 46′ N, 25° 28′ W
Seville	Seville, Civill	Spain	37° 24′ N, 5° 58′ W
Shirehampton	Sherehampton	England	51° 29′ N, 02° 40′ W
Sines	Synott	Portugal	37° 58′ 08° 52′ W
Sligo	Sligo	Ireland	54° 17′ N, 08° 28′ W
Slimbridge	Slembrigge	England	51° 43′ N, 02° 22′ W
St Bride's	Seynt Brides	Wales	51° 45′ N, 05° 11′ W
St Brieuc	Seint Briak	France	48° 31′ N, 02° 45′ W
St David's	Seynt Davies	Wales	51° 53′ N, 5° 16′ W
St Gilles Croix-de-Vie (?)	St Giles	France	46° 52′ N, 01° 56′ W
St Ives	Seynt Ives	England	50°13′ N, 5° 29′ W
St-Jean-de-Luz	Seynt John de Luce	France	43° 23′ N, 1° 39′ W
St-Malo	St Mallos	France	48° 39′ N, 02° 00′ W
St Surine	St Surine	Unknown	
Stonehouse	Stonehowse	England	51° 45′ 2° 17′ W
Susare	Susare	Unknown	
Swansea	Swaynsey	Wales	51°37′ N, 3° 06′ W
Talmont	Talamounte	France	45° 32′ N 0° 54′ W
Taunton	Taunton	England	51° 01′ N, 04° 42′ W
Teignmouth	Tinmouth	England	50° 33′ N, 03° 30′ W
Tenby	Tinbie, Tynbygh	Wales	51° 40′ N, 04° 42′ W
Terceira	Insulas Tercera	Azores, Portugal	
Tewkesbury	Tewkisbury	England	51° 59′ N, 02° 09′ W
Tidenham	Tidn[ ]	England	51° 39′ N, 02° 38′ W

23 Kynprollantyne may be Quimper, France. Quimper was often known in the middle ages as *Quimpercorentin* after its first bishop, who did miracles and to whom Quimper cathedral is dedicated. We would like to thank Prof. Wendy Childs (Leeds) for this suggestion. 24 Alternate name for Errenteria above.

Port Modern	Name in Accounts	Country	Co-ordinates
Tintern	Tyntorne	Wales	51°41′ N, 02° 41′ W
Tiverton	Tivarton	England	50° 54′ N, 3° 29′ W
Topsham (Exeter)	Opsam	England	50° 41′ N, 3° 27′ W
Totnes	Totnes	England	
Toulon	Tholone	France	43° 08′ N, 5° 56′ E
Uphill	Uphyll	England	51° 19′ N, 02° 59′ W
Ushant	Ussaunt	France	48° 27′ 29″ N. 05° 05′ 44″ W
Vannes	Vanyse, Vanns	France	47°39′ N, 2° 45′ W
Viana do Castelo	Viana	Portugal	41° 42′ N, 8° 49′ W
Vila do Conde	Villacondy	Portugal	41°21′ N, 08° 44′ W
Vlissingen	Flushinge	Netherlands	51° 27′ N, 3° 34′ E
Waterford	Waterford, Watford	Ireland	52° 15′ N, 7° 07′ W
Wexford	Washeford, Waisford	Ireland	52° 20′ N, 6° 28′ W
Weymouth	Waymouth	England	50° 37′ N, 02° 27′ W
Workington	Wirkington	England	54° 39′ N, 03° 33′ W
'Yealm'[25]	Yalme, Yame	England	50° 21′ N 03° 59′ W
Youghal	Yoghall, Youghill	Ireland	51°58′ N, 07°51′ W

---

25 This 'port' probably relates to the mouth of the Yealm. This wasn't a community but it was an anchorage and there are other examples of ships being given as coming from a haven/waterway rather than an actual community – e.g. Mount's Bay.

Glossary of first-names

First names are generally Latinised in the accounts (Jacobus for James, Dionisius for Dennis, Elias for Elliot, Egidius for Giles). For names that have no real Latin form, Latinisation is often achieved by simply adding a 'us' or 'is' ending (e.g. Arthuris, Reginaldus, Gonsalus). If the name appears to be Latinised, it is translated into the vernacular. If there is a common English vernacular equivalent, this is the one that is adopted. It must be remembered, however, that some names, would almost certainly have taken a different form in real life. For example, while all individuals called 'Johannes' are transcribed as John, if the merchant was Spanish, he would probably have been called 'Juan', if French, 'Jean'. If there is no common English equivalent for a Latinised name, the name is translated into the most likely vernacular form (e.g. Affonsus becomes Alfonso, Ffernandus becomes Fernando). Where names have not been Latinised (e.g. Tege, Raphael, Merike, Manuel), the original form is kept. In such cases, the original spelling is maintained (e.g. Dirike is *not* changed to Derick or Derek).

NOTE: Names in (brackets) are the Latinised, or apparently Latinised, versions of the name. In those cases where it has not been possible to identify a vernacular equivalent of the name, the Latin version has been given (e.g. Catuanis). Italics indicate suspensions (e.g. Will*iamus* will appear in the accounts as Willm).

Name in Transcription	Name in Accounts (if different)	Notes
Adam		
Alan	(Alen)	
(Aldrean)		TNA E122/199/9
Alfonso	(Affonsus)	
(Alerno)		
Alexander		
Alvero		
(Amathere)		TNA E122/21/15
Ambrose	(Ambrosius)	
Andrew	(Andreas)	
Anthony	(Antonius)	
Arnold	(Arnaldus)	
Arthur	(Arthuris)	
Asker		Alien (may be variation of Asher)
Auger	(Awger, Auger)	

Name in Transcription	Name in Accounts (if different)	Notes
(Babtaherius)		TNA E190/1131/10
(Balcher)		TNA E190/1131/10
(Baltran)		TNA E122/21/10
Baptist	(Baptiste)	
(Bawdewyn)		
Bennett		
Bernard	(Barnadus)	
Botholl	Bothulph, Botholl	TNA E190/1129/11
(Cataunis)		TNA E122 199/1
Cecilia	(Scisilia)	
Christine	(Christiana)	
Christopher	(Christpoferus, Crisostome)	Written 'Xpoferus'
Claus	(Close)	TNA E122/199/9
Cornell	(Cornelius)	
Daniel		
Darby	(Darbye, Derbie)	
David		
Dennis	(Dionisius)	
Derek	Dirike	
Dominic	(Domingus, Dominick)	
(Domingo)	(Domyngo)	
(Donarte)	(Donarte)	TNA E122/22/4
Edmund	(Edmundus, Edmundus)	
Edward	(Edwardus)	
Emmanuel	(Manuel)	
Elliot	(Elias)	
Englebert	(Anglebart)	
Evan	(Evond)	TNA E122 199/1
Fernado	(Ffernandus)	
Ferdinand	(Fernando)	
(Firsopus)	(Firsopus)	TNA E122/21/15
Florence	(Flowrannce, Florens)	TNA E122/22/4
Fowke?Fulk		TNA E122/199/4, E122/21/15
Francis	(Ffranciscus)	
(Gadelus)		TNA E122 199/1
Gareth	(Garrett, Garrote, Garriett)	
Garrold		
Geoffrey	(Galfrius, Gulfridus)	
George	(Georgius)	
Gerald	(Gerardus)	
Germain	(Germanus, Germyn)	
(Gillam)	(Gillam)	TNA E122/22/4
Gilbert	(Gilbtus)	TNA E122/22/4
(Gillermo)		
Giovanni	(Geovanni)	(form of John)
(Gowldhen)		TNA E190/1132/11
Gonsalo	(Gonsalus)	
(Goveran)		TNA E122/22/4
Gratien	(Gratianus)	
Gravell	(Gravell)	TNA E122/21/2
Griffeth	(Griffeth, Griffith))	
(Gruand)		TNA E122/22/4

Name in Transcription	Name in Accounts (if different)	Notes
(Gwylgo)		TNA E122/22/4
(Hanndridge)		TNA E190/1129/11
(Harinanus)		TNA E122/21/10
Harry	Harrie	
Haus		
Harvy	(Harvye)	
Hector		
Henry	(Henre)	
(Hígon)		TNA E122 199/1
Hugh	(Hugo)	
Humphrey	(Humfrius, Humfridus)	
Isaiah	Esia	TNA E190/1131/10
(Isbrane)	(Isbrane)	Norwegian TNA E190/1132/11
James	(Jacobus, Jacques)	
(Jan)	(Janof)	TNA E122/22/4
Jasper		
Jenkin	(Jenkyn)	
(Jenott)	(Jenott)	TNA E122/22/4
Jeremiah	(Jeronimo, Jeramus)	
Jeremy		
John	(Johanes)	
Johanna		
Jordan	(Jurdanus, Geordannus)	
Josiah	(Josias)	
(Jovands)		
Katherine	(Katerina)	
Laurence	(Laurence)	
Leonard	(Leonardus)	
Lettice	(Leticia)	TNA E122/199/9
Lewis	(Lodwicus/ Lewes)	
(Libard)		TNA E122/21/2
(Lopo)		
Lucas		
Luke	(Lukes)	TNA E122/22/5
Malagur		
Manuel		
(Manus)		TNA E122/22/5
Margaret		
Margery	(Margeria)	
Martin	(Martinius)	
Maurice	(Mauric, Mauricius)	
Matilda		
Matthew	(Matheus)	
Merike		
Michael	(Mighel)	
Morgan		
Nicholas	(Nicholus)	
Noel	(Nowell)	
Ochoa		
Oliver	(Oliverus)	
Owen	(Owen, Owynus)	
Patrick	(Patricius)	

Name in Transcription	Name in Accounts (if different)	Notes
Paul	(Paulus)	
(Peraton)		TNA E122/21/15
Peter	(Petrus, Petro)	
(Pero)		TNA E122/22/4
Philip	(Philipus)	
Pierce	(Peers)	
(Predictus)	(Predictus)	
Ralph	(Radulfus)	
Randal	(Rendell)	TNA E122/24/12
Raphael		
Raymond	(Raimundus)	
(Regerus)		Possibly Reginaldus
Reginald	(Reginaldus)	
Rewe		
Richard	(Ricius)	
Robert	(Robertus)	
Roderigo	Rodrigus	TNA E122/21/15
Roger	(Rogerus)	
Roland	(Rowlond)	
(Ryall)		TNA E122/21/10
Sampson		
Sancho	(Sanchius)	TNA E122 199/1
Sebastian	(Sebastianus, Bastian)	
Silvia	Sivelia	
Simon	(Simon')	
Stephen	(Stephanus)	
Tege		
Tessick	(Tessicke)	TNA E190/1131/11
Thomas		
Tibald	(Tibaldus, Tybalt)	
Tobias	(Tobiott)	
Ultan	(Ulstan)	TNA E122/22/5
(Veronius)		TNA E190/1131/10
Vincent	(Vincens)	
Walter	(Walterus)	
Watkin	Watkyn	
William	(Williamus)	

Index of people

The letter n following a page number denotes that the reference will be found in a note.

Grenewell, John, master 863
Grenwey *see* Greneway
Grevell
John 8
Lewis 243
Greves (Grevis; Grevys)
– 617
John 439, 514
Martin 548, 610, 611, 668
Grey
Humphrey 18, 67
Thomas 66
Greyn *see* Green
Greynfeld, Thomas 36
Griffand, John 134
Griffeth (Griffethe) *see* Griffith
Griffin (Greffyn; Griffan; Griffen; Griffyn;
Gryffyn)
Adam 48
Darby, master 583, 586
Maurice 314
Richard, master (fl 1550/51) 583, 584
Richard, master (fl 1563/64) 626, 651
Walter 48
William 101
Griffith (Greffithe; Griffeth; Griffethe; Griffithe;
Griffiths; Gryffyth; Gryffythe; Gryffyths;
Gryfyth)
– 596, 602, 634
Darby, master 329, 333
David, master (fl 1503/04) 13, 34, 59
David (fl 1545/46) 541
Dennis, master (fl 1516/17) 138, 163, 164
Dennis, master (fl 1525/26) 228, 232
Edmund, master 4, 17, 68, 69, 78, 86
Gerald 162
Germaine, master (fl 1516/17) 104
Germaine, master (fl 1545/46) 505, 507
Hugh 737, 738, 740, 741, 755, 759, 761, 767,
779, 783, 845
James, master 906
John (fl 1516/17) 162, 168
John (fl 1541/42) 363
John (fl 1545/46) 473, 493, 510, 515,
544
John, master (fl 1545/46) 478, 513
John (fl 1550/51) 564, 608
John (fl 1563/64) 624, 652, 657, 662
John (fl 1575/76) 714
John (fl 1594/95) 740
John (fl 1600/01) 857
Philip 279
Richard 59
Thomas, master (fl 1550/51) 599
Thomas (fl 1575/76) 720, 726
Walter, master 600
William, master 747
Griffyn *see* Griffin
Grigge, David, master 67
Gromall, David 432

Gromwell (Gromewell; Grommwell)
– 600, 653
George 627
John 635, 663
Stephen 555, 596
Walter 462
Gromy, David 429
Grossin, Symon 379
Gryen, Thomas, 23; *see also* Green
Gryffyn *see* Griffin
Gryffyth (Gryffythe; Gryffythe; Gryfyth) *see*
Griffith
Grymway, Michael 439
Gryndam (Grynam)
John, master 217, 224, 233, 271, 279
Nicholas, master 544, 597, 606
Richard, master 127
Grynwey *see* Greneway
Gtobo, Gilo, master 189
Guan, Evan de, master 183
Guaras, Anthony 458
Guewe, Richard 313, 362
Guggan, David, master 637
Gully, William, master 343
Gungelet, William, master 539
Gunninge (Gunnynge; Gunynge)
John (fl 1594/95) 754
John (fl 1600/01) 854, 856, 859,
932
Gunsalius *see* Gonsalus
Gunynge *see* Gunninge
Gurdelar *see* Girdelar
Gurney (Gurneye)
John (fl 1525/26) 238, 239, 278
John (fl 1541/42) 300
John (fl 1542/43) 384, 386, 399, 413
John (fl 1545/46) 479
Gurobi, Michael de, master 624
Gurreo, John, master 165, 184, 189
Gurrie, Maurice, master 773
Gusseta (Gussueta), Julian de, master 466, 474,
543, 545
Gutter, John, master 683
Guy, John 860, 932
Guydoll, Anthony 458
Guygan, Mark 873
Gwere, Richard 184
Gwilliam
Hugh, master 673
William, master 615
Gwyn, Owen, master 31
Gybb (Gybbe) *see* Gibb
Gybbonds (Gybbyns) *see* Gibbons
Gybbys *see* Gibbs
Gybeson *see* Gibson
Gylbart, – 537
Gylea, Peter, master 285
Gyles, Simon, master 583
Gylford *see* Gilford
Gyll, Peter 250

Thomas 100
William (fl 1503/04) 35
William, master (fl 1503/04) 41
Vavre, William 755
Vawer, William 752
Veele (Veale; Veell; Vele)
Henry, master 22
Nicholas, master (fl 1516/17) 136, 154
Ncholas, master (fl 1525/26) 234, 235
Thomas (fl 1503/04) 61, 98
Thomas (fl 1525/26) 236, 240, 250
William (fl 1503/04) 22
William (fl 1525/26) 227, 233
Veneam
John, master 516
Thomas, master 479
Venicombe, Robert, master 752
Venyeta, Stephen (Stephende; Steven) de, master
501, 507
Venzenden, Jasper 881
Verdon
–312
Henry (fl 1541/42) 319
Henry (fl 1542/43) 407, 424
Henry (fl 1550/51) 579, 587
John 257
Richard 287, 289, 296
Robert (fl 1516/17) 144
Robert, master (fl 1541/42) 350
Thomas 624, 649
William (fl 1516/17) 168
William (fl 1525/26) 266, 272
Veroys, Michael de 480
Vesero, William de la 541
Veyse, Thomas, master 468
Vicarne, John, master 64
Vincent, John 147
Vine see Vyne
Vinicomb (Vinicombe), Robert, master 813, 816
Vocivita, Julian de, master 511, 512, 513
Vonstonhold, Jaques 775
Vowell, Thomas 483
Vrobie, Arnold de 364
Vuchedon (Vurhedon), James 113, 178
Vusta, John de, master 505
Vusurke, John de 667
Vyne (Vine; Vyen; Vyn; Vynne)
–420, 488
Lawrence (Laurence) (fl 1541/42) 299, 300, 306
Lawrence (Laurence) (fl 1550/51) 603, 604
Pierce 832, 913
Richard 552
Thomas (fl 1545/46) 461, 471
Thomas (fl 1550/51) 552, 562
Vynk (Vynke), Johannes, master 359, 380
Vynyge
Peter 369
Richard 339

Wackelis, Thomas 757

Wadden, David, master 760
Waddyng (Waddinge; Wading; Wadinge; Wadyng)
–315
David (fl 1545/46) 519, 524
David, master (fl 1600/01) 818
Richard (fl 1541/42) 315, 322
Richard (fl 1542/43) 404, 414, 443, 450
Richard (fl 1545/46) 465
Robert 286, 357
Thomas 259, 260
William 437
Wade
John (fl 1503/04) 10
John, master (fl 1541/42) 337, 350, 363
John, master (fl 1542/43) 427, 437
John, master (fl 1563/64) 644
Thomas, master 226
William, master (fl 1503/04) 35, 60
William, master (fl 1516/17) 131, 133–4
William, master (fl 1525/26) 233, 235, 281
Waden, John 138, 154
Wading (Wadyng) see Waddyng
Wakely, Thomas 737
Wale see Whale
Walker
Richard 267
Thomas, master 435
Wall, Redmond 522
Walles, William 737, 756, 759, 795
Walleys, John, master 388
Walron, John 674, 713, 714
Walsall, William 73
Walsh (Walshe)
Cornell 111
David (fl 1503/04) 46, 56, 82, 86
David, master (fl 1503/04) 96
David, master (fl 1516/17) 123, 127
Edmund 770, 842
Edward 75
Henry 80
John (fl 1503/04) 61, 84, 88
John, master (fl 1503/04) 83, 87, 97, 98
John (fl 1516/17) 119, 127, 133, 134, 164, 165,
175
Laurence 15
Maurice 164
Nicholas (fl 1503/04) 81
Nicholas (fl 1516/17) 173, 183
Patrick 173, 182
Peter (fl 1516/17) 176, 184
Peter (fl 1542/43) 444
Philip (fl 1503/04) 44
Philip, master (fl 1516/17) 177, 185
Richard (fl 1503/04) 47, 50
Richard, master (fl 1503/04) 22, 32
Richard (fl 1516/17) 146
Richard (fl 1594/95) 765
Robert, master (fl 1516/17) 117
Robert (fl 1550/51) 606
Tege 2

Index of places

The letter n following a page number denotes that the reference will be found in a note.

1049

Index of Ships

The letter n following a page number denotes that the reference will be found in a note.